FINANCIAL MARKETS and INSTITUTIONS

FINANCIAL MARKETS and INSTITUTIONS

11th Edition

Jeff Madura

Florida Atlantic University

CENGAGE
Learning·

Australia • Brazil • Mexico • Singapore • United Kingdom • United States

Printed in Canada
1 2 3 4 5 6 7 17 16 15 14 13

This text is dedicated to Best Friends Animal Sanctuary in Kanab, Utah, for its commitment to, compassion for, and care of more than 1,500 animals, many of which were previously homeless. Most of the royalties the author receives from this text will be invested in an estate that will ultimately be donated to Best Friends.

In 2012, this fund donated $200,000 to Best Friends as partial support for a new healthcare facility for the animals. During the 2011–2013 period, this fund also donated more than $50,000 to other animal care societies, including Friends of Greyhounds (Fort Lauderdale, FL), Greyhound Pets of America in Central Florida (Melbourne, FL), and Tri-County Humane Society (Boca Raton, FL).

Brief Contents

Contents

11: STOCK VALUATION AND RISK

281

16: FOREIGN EXCHANGE DERIVATIVE MARKETS 439

PART 6: Commercial Banking 473

17: COMMERCIAL BANK OPERATIONS 475

597

609

Preface

Financial markets finance much of the expenditures by corporations, governments, and individuals. Financial institutions are the key intermediaries in financial markets because they transfer funds from savers to the individuals, firms, or government agencies that need funds. *Financial Markets and Institutions,* 11th Edition, describes financial markets and the financial institutions that serve those markets. It provides a conceptual framework that can be used to understand why markets exist. Each type of financial market is described with a focus on the securities that are traded and the participation by financial institutions.

Today, many financial institutions offer all types of financial services, such as banking, securities services, mutual fund services, and insurance services. Each type of financial service is unique, however. Therefore, the discussion of financial services in this book is organized by type of financial service that can be offered by financial institutions.

Since the credit crisis, regulatory actions have been taken to prevent another crisis in the future. Accordingly, this text gives special attention to the impact of financial reform on each type of financial market and financial institution.

INTENDED MARKET

This text is suitable for undergraduate and master's level courses in financial markets, or financial institutions. To maximize students' comprehension, some of the more difficult questions and problems should be assigned in addition to the special applications at the end of each chapter and the Comprehensive Project. A term paper on the credit crisis may also be a valuable exercise, and several possible topics for this paper are provided at the end of the first chapter.

ORGANIZATION OF THE TEXT

Part 1 (Chapters 1 through 3) introduces the key financial markets and financial institutions, explains why interest rates change over time, and explains why yields vary among securities. Part 2 (Chapters 4 and 5) describes the functions of the Federal Reserve System (the Fed) and explains how its monetary policy influences interest rates and other economic conditions. Part 3 (Chapters 6 through 9) covers the major debt security markets, Part 4 (Chapters 10 through 12) describes equity securities markets, and Part 5 (Chapters 13 through 16) covers the derivative security markets. Each chapter in Parts 3 through 5 focuses on a particular market. The integration of each market with other markets is stressed throughout these chapters. Part 6 (Chapters 17 through 20) concentrates on commercial banking, and Part 7 (Chapters 21 through 25) covers all other types of financial services provided by financial institutions.

Courses that emphasize financial markets should focus on the first five parts (Chapters 1 through 16); however, some chapters in the section on commercial banking are also relevant. Courses that emphasize financial institutions and financial services should focus on Parts 1, 2, 6, and 7, although some background on securities markets (Parts 3, 4, and 5) may be helpful.

Professors may wish to focus on certain chapters of this book, and skip others, depending on the other courses available to their students. For example, if a course on derivative securities is commonly offered, Part 5 of this text may be ignored. Alternatively, if an investments course provides a thorough background on types of securities, Parts 3 and 4 can be given less attention.

Chapters can be rearranged without a loss in continuity. Regardless of the order in which chapters are studied, it is highly recommended that some questions and exercises from each chapter be assigned. These exercises may serve as a focal point for class discussion.

The credit crisis receives considerable emphasis in the mortgage markets chapter (Chapter 9) because it was primarily caused by activities in the mortgage market. The crisis has had an impact on every type of financial market and institution, however, so it is covered in each chapter as it applies to the contents of that chapter.

COVERAGE OF MAJOR CONCEPTS AND EVENTS

Numerous concepts relating to recent events and current trends in financial markets are discussed throughout the chapters. These include the following:

- New laws applied to bond rating agencies
- Increased exposure of municipal bonds to default
- Facebook's IPO
- Performance of venture capital and private equity funding
- Government rescues of financial institutions during the credit crisis
- Credit default swaps
- Behavioral finance
- Emergence of private stock exchanges, such as SecondMarket and SharesPost
- Dark pools used to trade stocks
- Recent developments in insider trading
- New restrictions on proprietary trading by banks
- Occupy Wall Street protests
- Backdating of options
- Governance in financial markets
- The Fed's increasing role in financial markets
- Role of analysts
- Value-at-risk applications
- Asymmetric information
- Valuation of financial institutions
- Regulatory reform in financial services

Each chapter is self-contained, so professors can use classroom time to focus on the more complex concepts and rely on the text to cover the other concepts.

FEATURES OF THE TEXT

The features of the text are as follows:

- **Part-Opening Diagram.** A diagram is provided at the beginning of each part to illustrate generally how the key concepts in that part are related.
- **Objectives.** A bulleted list at the beginning of each chapter identifies the key concepts in that chapter.

FINANCIAL REFORM
© Cvijun/ShutterStock.com

GLOBAL ASPECTS
© Marish/ShutterStock.com

- *Examples.* Examples are provided to reinforce key concepts.
- *Financial Reform.* A Financial Reform icon in the margin indicates a discussion of financial reform as it applies to the topics covered in the chapter.
- *Global Aspects.* A Global Aspects icon in the margin indicates international coverage of the topic being discussed.
- *Summary.* A bulleted list at the end of each chapter summarizes the key concepts. This list corresponds to the list of objectives at the beginning of the chapter.
- *Point Counter-Point.* A controversial issue is introduced along with opposing arguments, and students are asked to determine which argument is correct and to explain why.
- *Questions and Applications.* The Questions and Applications section at the end of each chapter tests students' understanding of the key concepts and may serve as homework assignments or study aids in preparation for exams.
- *Interpreting Financial News.* At the end of each chapter, students are challenged to interpret comments made in the media about the chapter's key concepts. This gives students practice in interpreting announcements by the financial media.
- *Managing in Financial Markets.* At the end of each chapter, students are placed in the position of financial managers and must make decisions about specific situations related to the key concepts in that chapter.
- *Flow of Funds Exercise.* A running exercise is provided at the end of each chapter to illustrate how a manufacturing company relies on all types of financial markets and financial services provided by financial institutions.
- *Internet/Excel Exercises.* At the end of each chapter, there are exercises that introduce students to applicable information available on various websites, enable the application of Excel to related topics, or a combination of these. For example, the exercises allow students to assess yield curves, risk premiums, and stock volatility.
- *Problems.* Selected chapters include problems to test students' computational skills.
- *WSJ Exercise.* This exercise appears at the end of selected chapters and gives students an opportunity to apply information provided in the *Wall Street Journal* to specific concepts explained in that chapter.
- *Integrative Problems.* An integrative problem at the end of each part integrates the key concepts of chapters within that part.
- *Term Paper on the Credit Crisis.* Several topics for term papers on the credit crisis are suggested at the end of Chapter 1.
- *Comprehensive Project.* This project, found in Appendix A, requires students to apply real data to several key concepts described throughout the book.
- *Midterm and Final Self-Examinations.* At the end of Chapter 16, a midterm self-exam is offered to test students' knowledge of financial markets. At the end of Chapter 25, a final self-exam is offered to test students' knowledge of financial institutions. An answer key is provided so that students can evaluate their answers after they take the exam.

The concepts in each chapter can be reinforced by using one or more of the features just listed. Professors' use of the features will vary depending on the level of their students and the course focus. A course that focuses mostly on financial markets may emphasize tools such as the WSJ Exercises and Part 1 of the Comprehensive Project (on taking positions in securities and derivative instruments). In contrast, a course that focuses on financial institutions may assign an exercise in which students must review recent annual reports (see Part 2 of the Comprehensive Project) to determine how a particular financial institution's performance is affected by its policies, industry regulations, and economic conditions. In addition, the Internet/Excel Exercises on financial institutions give students practice in assessing the operations and performance of financial institutions.

SUPPLEMENTS TO THE TEXT

To access the instructor resources, go to **www.cengage.com/login**, log in with your faculty account username and password, and use **ISBN 9781133947875** to search for and add instructor resources to your account Bookshelf.

- *Instructor's Manual.* Revised by the author, the instructor's manual contains the chapter outline for each chapter and a summary of key concepts for discussion as well as answers to the end-of-chapter Questions and Problems.

- *Test Bank.* The expanded test bank, which has also been revised by the author, contains a large set of questions in multiple choice or true/false format, including content questions as well as problems.

- *Cognero*™ **Test Bank.** Cengage Learning Testing Powered by Cognero™ is a flexible, online system that allows you to author, edit, and manage test bank content from multiple Cengage Learning solutions; create multiple test versions in an instant; and deliver tests from your LMS, your classroom, or wherever you want. The Cognero™ Test Bank contains the same questions that are in the Microsoft® Word Test Bank. All question content is now tagged according to Tier 1 (Business Program Interdisciplinary Learning Outcomes) and Tier II (Finance-specific) standards topic, Bloom's Taxonomy, and difficulty level.

- *PowerPoint Slides.* The PowerPoint slides clarify content and provide a solid guide for student note-taking. In addition to the regular notes slides, a separate set of exhibit-only PPTs are also available.

ADDITIONAL COURSE TOOLS

Cengage Learning Custom Solutions

Whether you need print, digital, or hybrid course materials, Cengage Learning Custom Solutions can help you create your perfect learning solution. Draw from Cengage Learning's extensive library of texts and collections, add or create your own original work, and create customized media and technology to match your learning and course objectives. Our editorial team will work with you through each step, allowing you to concentrate on the most important thing—your students. Learn more about all our services at **www.cengage.com/custom**.

Cengage Learning's Global Economic Watch

This online portal houses the most current and up-to-date content concerning the economic crisis and is your source for turning today's challenges into tomorrow's solutions. Organized by discipline, the GEW Resource Center offers the solutions instructors and students need in an easy-to-use format. Included are an overview and timeline of the historical events leading up to the crisis, links to the latest news and resources, discussion and testing content, an instructor feedback forum, and a Global Issues Database. Visit **www.cengage.com/thewatch** for more information.

ACKNOWLEDGMENTS

The motivation to write this textbook came primarily from the encouragement of E. Joe Nosari (Florida State University). Several professors helped develop the text outline and offered suggestions on which of the concepts from earlier editions of this book should be covered in this edition. They are acknowledged in alphabetical order:

Ibrihim Affaneh, Indiana University of Pennsylvania

Michael H. Anderson, University of Massachusetts – Dartmouth

Henry C. F. Arnold, Seton Hall University

James C. Baker, Kent State University

Gerald Bierwag, Florida International University

Carol Billingham, Central Michigan University

Randy Billingsley, Virginia Tech University

Rita M. Biswas, SUNY – Albany

Howard W. Bohnen, St. Cloud State University

Paul J. Bolster, Northeastern University

M. E. Bond, University of Memphis

Carol Marie Boyer, Long Island University – C.W. Post Campus

Alka Bramhandkar, Ithaca College

Emile J. Brinkman, University of Houston – University Park

Christopher L. Brown, Western Kentucky University

Bill Brunsen, Eastern New Mexico University

Sarah Bryant, George Washington University

James B. Burnham, Duquesne University

Paul Bursik, St. Norbert College

Deanne Butchey, Florida International University

William Carner, University of Missouri – Columbia

Joseph Cheng, Ithaca College

William T. Chittenden, Northern Illinois University

C. Steven Cole, University of North Texas

M. Cary Collins, University of Tennessee

Mark Correll, University of Colorado

Wayne C. Curtis, Troy State University

Julie Dahlquist, University of Texas – San Antonio

Steven Dobson, California Polytechnic State University

Robert M. Donchez, University of Colorado – Boulder

Lynne Pierson Doti, Chapman University

Richard J. Dowen, Northern Illinois University

Imad Elhaj, University of Louisville

James Felton, Central Michigan University

Donald Flagg, University of Tampa

Stuart Fletcher, Appalachian State University

George C. Fowler, York County Community College

Norman Frost, Loyola University of Maryland

Clifford L. Fry, University of Houston

Ramesh Garg, Eastern Michigan University

Edward K. Gill, California State University – Chico

Claire G. Gilmore, St. Joseph's University

Owen Gregory, University of Illinois – Chicago

Paul Grier, SUNY – Binghamton

Ann Hackert, Idaho State University

John Halloran, University of Notre Dame

Gerald A. Hanweck, George Mason University

Rodney Hardcastle, Pacific Union College

Wei He, Mississippi State University

Hildegard R. Hendrickson, Seattle University

Bradley K. Hobbs, Ph.D., Florida Gulf Coast University

Jerry M. Hood, Loyola University – New Orleans

Ronald M. Horowitz, Oakland University

Paul Hsueh, University of Central Florida

Carl D. Hudson, Auburn University

John S. Jahera, Jr., Auburn University

Rob James, Boston University

Mel Jameson, University of Nevada

Shane Johnson, Louisiana State University

Jody Jones, Oklahoma Christian University

Jan Jusko, College of Staten Island

Richard H. Keehn, University of Wisconsin – Parkside

James B. Kehr, Miami University of Ohio

David F. Kern, Arkansas State University

Elinda F. Kiss, University of Maryland Robert H. Smith School of Business

James W. Kolari, Texas A&M University

Vladimir Kotomin, University of Wisconsin – Eau Claire

Robert A. Kunkel, University of Wisconsin – Oshkosh

George Kutner, Marquette University

Robert Lamy, Wake Forest University

David J. Leahigh, King's College

David N. Leggett, Bentley College

William Lepley, University of Wisconsin – Green Bay

Andrew Light, Liberty University

Morgan Lynge, Jr., University of Illinois

Pawan Madhogarhia, Pennsylvania State University

Judy E. Maese, New Mexico State University

Timothy A. Manuel, University of Montana

L. R. Martindale, Texas A&M University

Joseph S. Mascia, Adelphi University

Robert W. McLeod, University of Alabama

Kathleen S. McNichol, LaSalle University

James McNulty, Florida Atlantic University

Charles Meiburg, University of Virginia

Jose Mercado-Mendez, Central Missouri State University

Edward Miseta, Penn State – Erie

Clay M. Moffett, University of North Carolina – Wilmington

Kenneth Moran, Harding University

J. K. Mullen, Clarkson University

Neil Murphy, Virginia Commonwealth University

Srinivas Nippani, Texas A&M University – Commerce

Hossein Noorain, Boston University & Wentworth Institute of Technology

Dale Osborne, University of Texas – Dallas

Coleen Pantalone, Northeastern University

Thomas H. Payne, University of Tennessee – Chattanooga

Sarah Peck, University of Iowa

Chien-Chih Peng, Morehead State University

Micki Pitcher, Olivet College

D. Anthony Plath, University of North Carolina – Charlotte

Barbara Poole, Roger Williams University

Rose Prasad, Central Michigan University

Xiaoling Pu, Kent State University

David Rayome, Northern Michigan University

Mitchell Ratner, Rider University

Alan Reichert, Cleveland State University

Kenneth L. Rhoda, LaSalle University

Nivine Richie, University of North Carolina – Wilmington

Antonio J. Rodriguez, Texas A&M International University

Lawrence C. Rose, Massey University

Jack Rubens, Bryant College

Atul K. Saxena, Georgia Gwinnett College

Jeff Schultz, Christian Brothers University

Robert Schweitzer, University of Delaware

Mehmet Sencicek, University of New Haven

Kilman Shin, Ferris State University

Ahmad Sorhabian, California State Polytechnic University – Pomona

Andrew Spieler, Hofstra University

K. P. Sridharan, Delta State University

S. R. Stansell, East Carolina University

Richard W. Stolz, University of South Carolina Upstate

Richard S. Swasey, Northeastern University

John Thornton, Kent State University

Olaf J. Thorp, Babson College

James D. Tripp, University of Tennessee – Martin

K. C. Tseng, California State University – Fresno

Harry J. Turtle, University of Manitoba

Emre Unlu, University of Nebraska

Cevdet Uruk, University of Memphis

Geraldo M. Vasconcellos, Lehigh University

John Walker, Kutztown University

Michael C. Walker, University of Cincinnati

Charles Walwyn, SUNY – Maritime

Fang Wang, West Virginia University

Bruce Watson, Wellesley College

Jennifer Westbrook, University of Alabama – Huntsville

David A. Whidbee, Washington State University

Alex H. Wilson, University of Arizona

Colin Young, Bentley College

Stephen Zera, California State University – San Marcos

Mei "Miranda" Zhang, Mercer University

Many of my friends and colleagues offered useful suggestions for this edition, including Kevin Brady (Florida Atlantic University), Kien Cao (Foreign Trade University), Inga Chira (Oregon State University), Jeff Coy (University of Central Florida), Sean Davis (University of North Florida), Ken Johnson (Florida International University), Marek Marciniak (West Chester University), Thanh Ngo (University of Texas – Pan American), Arjan Premti (Florida Atlantic University), Nivine Richie (University of North Carolina – Wilmington), Garrett Smith (Florida Atlantic University), and Nik Volkov (Florida Atlantic University).

I appreciate the help and support from the people at Cengage Learning, including Clara Goosman (Product Manager), Mike Reynolds (Executive Product Manager), Heather Mooney (Marketing Manager), Kendra Brown (Content Developer), Adele Scholtz (Senior Product Assistant), and Chris Walz (Marketing Coordinator). Special thanks are due to Scott Dillon and Tamborah Moore (Senior Content Project Managers) and Nancy Ahr (Copyeditor) for their efforts to ensure a quality final product.

Jeff Madura
Florida Atlantic University

About the Author

Dr. Jeff Madura is presently the SunTrust Bank Professor of Finance at Florida Atlantic University. He has written several successful finance texts, including *International Financial Management*. His research on financial markets and institutions has been published in numerous journals, including *Journal of Financial and Quantitative Analysis*; *Journal of Banking and Finance*; *Journal of Money, Credit and Banking*; *Financial Management*; *Journal of Financial Research*; *Journal of Financial Services Research*; and *Financial Review*. Dr. Madura has received multiple awards for excellence in teaching and research, and he has served as a consultant for international banks, securities firms, and other multinational corporations. He earned his B.S. and M.A. from Northern Illinois University and his D.B.A. from Florida State University. Dr. Madura has served as a director for the Southern Finance Association and Eastern Finance Association, and he is also former president of the Southern Finance Association.

PART 1
Overview of the Financial Environment

Part 1 of this book focuses on the flow of funds across financial markets, interest rates, and security prices. Chapter 1 introduces the key financial markets and the financial institutions that participate in those markets. Chapter 2 explains how various factors influence interest rates and how interest rate movements in turn affect the values of securities purchased by financial institutions. Chapter 3 identifies factors other than interest rates that influence security prices. Participants in financial markets use this information to value securities and make investment decisions within financial markets.

1
Role of Financial Markets and Institutions

CHAPTER OBJECTIVES

The specific objectives of this chapter are to:

■ describe the types of financial markets that facilitate the flow of funds,

■ describe the types of securities traded within financial markets,

■ describe the role of financial institutions within financial markets, and

■ explain how financial institutions were exposed to the credit crisis.

A **financial market** is a market in which financial assets (securities) such as stocks and bonds can be purchased or sold. Funds are transferred in financial markets when one party purchases financial assets previously held by another party. Financial markets facilitate the flow of funds and thereby allow financing and investing by households, firms, and government agencies. This chapter provides some background on financial markets and on the financial institutions that participate in them.

1-1 ROLE OF FINANCIAL MARKETS

Financial markets transfer funds from those who have excess funds to those who need funds. They enable college students to obtain student loans, families to obtain mortgages, businesses to finance their growth, and governments to finance many of their expenditures. Many households and businesses with excess funds are willing to supply funds to financial markets because they earn a return on their investment. If funds were not supplied, the financial markets would not be able to transfer funds to those who need them.

Those participants who receive more money than they spend are referred to as **surplus units** (or investors). They provide their net savings to the financial markets. Those participants who spend more money than they receive are referred to as **deficit units**. They access funds from financial markets so that they can spend more money than they receive. Many individuals provide funds to financial markets in some periods and access funds in other periods.

EXAMPLE

College students are typically deficit units, as they often borrow from financial markets to support their education. After they obtain their degree, they earn more income than they spend and thus become surplus units by investing their excess funds. A few years later, they may become deficit units again by purchasing a home. At this stage, they may provide funds to and access funds from financial markets simultaneously. That is, they may periodically deposit savings in a financial institution while also borrowing a large amount of money from a financial institution to buy a home. ●

Many deficit units such as firms and government agencies access funds from financial markets by issuing **securities**, which represent a claim on the issuer. **Debt securities** represent debt (also called *credit*, or *borrowed funds*) incurred by the issuer. Deficit units that issue the debt securities are borrowers. The surplus units that purchase debt securities are creditors, and they receive interest on a periodic basis (such as every six months). Debt securities have a maturity date, at which time the surplus units can redeem the securities in order to receive the principal (face value) from the deficit units that issued them.

Equity securities (also called *stocks*) represent equity or ownership in the firm. Some large businesses prefer to issue equity securities rather than debt securities when they need funds but might not be financially capable of making the periodic interest payments required for debt securities.

1-1a Accommodating Corporate Finance Needs

A key role of financial markets is to accommodate corporate finance activity. Corporate finance (also called financial management) involves corporate decisions such as how much funding to obtain and what types of securities to issue when financing operations. The financial markets serve as the mechanism whereby corporations (acting as deficit units) can obtain funds from investors (acting as surplus units).

1-1b Accommodating Investment Needs

Another key role of financial markets is accommodating surplus units who want to invest in either debt or equity securities. Investment management involves decisions by investors regarding how to invest their funds. The financial markets offer investors access to a wide variety of investment opportunities, including securities issued by the U.S. Treasury and government agencies as well as securities issued by corporations.

Financial institutions (discussed later in this chapter) serve as intermediaries within the financial markets. They channel funds from surplus units to deficit units. For example, they channel funds received from individuals to corporations. Thus they connect the investment management activity with the corporate finance activity, as shown in Exhibit 1.1. They also commonly serve as investors and channel their own funds to corporations.

1-1c Primary versus Secondary Markets

Primary markets facilitate the issuance of new securities. **Secondary markets** facilitate the trading of existing securities, which allows for a change in the ownership of the securities. Many types of debt securities have a secondary market, so that investors who initially purchased them in the primary market do not have to hold them until maturity. Primary market transactions provide funds to the initial issuer of securities; secondary market transactions do not.

EXAMPLE

Last year, Riverto Co. had excess funds and invested in newly issued Treasury debt securities with a 10-year maturity. This year, it will need $15 million to expand its operations. The company decided to sell its holdings of Treasury debt securities in the secondary market even though those

Exhibit 1.1 How Financial Markets Facilitate Corporate Finance and Investment Management securities will not mature for nine more years. It received $5 million from the sale. In also issued its own debt securities in the primary market today in order to obtain an additional $10 million. Riverto's debt securities have a 10-year maturity, so investors that purchase them can redeem them at maturity (in 10 years) or sell them before that time to other investors in the secondary market. ●

An important characteristic of securities that are traded in secondary markets is **liquidity**, which is the degree to which securities can easily be liquidated (sold) without a loss of value. Some securities have an active secondary market, meaning that there are many willing buyers and sellers of the security at a given moment in time. Investors prefer liquid securities so that they can easily sell the securities whenever they want (without a loss in value). If a security is illiquid, investors may not be able to find a willing buyer for it in the secondary market and may have to sell the security at a large discount just to attract a buyer.

Treasury securities are liquid because they are frequently issued by the Treasury, and there are many investors at any point in time who want to invest in them. Conversely, debt securities issued by a small firm may be illiquid, as there are not many investors who may want to invest in them. Thus investors who purchase these securities in the primary market may not be able to easily sell them in the secondary market.

1-2 Securities Traded in Financial Markets

Securities can be classified as money market securities, capital market securities, or derivative securities.

1-2a Money Market Securities

Money markets facilitate the sale of short-term debt securities by deficit units to surplus units. The securities traded in this market are referred to as **money market securities**, which are debt securities that have a maturity of one year or less. These generally have a relatively high degree of liquidity, not only because of their short-term maturity but also because they are desirable to many investors and therefore commonly have an active secondary market. Money market securities tend to have a low expected return but also a low degree of credit (default) risk. Common types of money market securities include Treasury bills (issued by the U.S. Treasury), commercial paper (issued by corporations), and negotiable certificates of deposit (issued by depository institutions).

1-2b Capital Market Securities

Capital markets facilitate the sale of long-term securities by deficit units to surplus units. The securities traded in this market are referred to as **capital market securities**. Capital market securities are commonly issued to finance the purchase of capital assets, such as buildings, equipment, or machinery. Three common types of capital market securities are bonds, mortgages, and stocks, which are described in turn.

WEB

www.investinginbonds.com
Data and other information about bonds.

Bonds Bonds are long-term debt securities issued by the Treasury, government agencies, and corporations to finance their operations. They provide a return to investors in the form of interest income (coupon payments) every six months. Since bonds represent debt, they specify the amount and timing of interest and principal payments to investors who purchase them. At maturity, investors holding the debt securities are paid the principal. Bonds commonly have maturities of between 10 and 20 years.

Treasury bonds are perceived to be free from default risk because they are issued by the U.S. Treasury. In contrast, bonds issued by corporations are subject to default risk because the issuer could default on its obligation to repay the debt. These bonds must offer a higher expected return than Treasury bonds in order to compensate investors for that default risk.

Bonds can be sold in the secondary market if investors do not want to hold them until maturity. Because the prices of debt securities change over time, they may be worthless when sold in the secondary market than when they were purchased.

Mortgages Mortgages are long-term debt obligations created to finance the purchase of real estate. Residential mortgages are obtained by individuals and families to purchase homes. Financial institutions serve as lenders by providing residential mortgages in their role as a financial intermediary. They can pool deposits received from surplus units, and lend those funds to an individual who wants to purchase a home. Before granting mortgages, they assess the likelihood that the borrower will repay the loan based on certain criteria such as the borrower's income level relative to the value of the home. They offer prime mortgages to borrowers who qualify based on these criteria. The home serves as collateral in the event that the borrower is not able to make the mortgage payments.

Subprime mortgages are offered to some borrowers who do not have sufficient income to qualify for prime mortgages or who are unable to make a down payment. Subprime mortgages exhibit a higher risk of default, thus the lenders providing these mortgages charge a higher interest rate (and additional up-front fees) to compensate. Subprime mortgages received much attention in 2008 because of their high default rates, which led to the credit crisis. Many lenders are no longer willing to provide subprime mortgages, and recent regulations (described later in this chapter) raise the minimum qualifications necessary to obtain a mortgage.

Commercial mortgages are long-term debt obligations created to finance the purchase of commercial property. Real estate developers rely on commercial mortgages so they can build shopping centers, office buildings, or other facilities. Financial institutions serve as lenders by providing commercial mortgages. By channeling funds from surplus units (depositors) to real estate developers, they serve as a financial intermediary and facilitate the development of commercial real estate.

Mortgage-Backed Securities Mortgage-backed securities are debt obligations representing claims on a package of mortgages. There are many forms of mortgage-backed securities. In their simplest form, the investors who purchase these securities receive monthly payments that are made by the homeowners on the mortgages backing the securities.

EXAMPLE

Mountain Savings Bank originates 100 residential mortgages for home buyers and will service the mortgages by processing the monthly payments. However, the bank does not want to use its own funds to finance the mortgages. It issues mortgage-backed securities that represent this package of mortgages to eight financial institutions that are willing to purchase all of these securities. Each month, when Mountain Savings Bank receives interest and principal payments on the mortgages, it passes those payments on to the eight financial institutions that purchased the mortgage-backed securities and thereby provided the financing to the homeowners. If some of the homeowners default on their payments, the payments, and thus the return on investment earned by the financial institutions that purchased the mortgage-backed securities, will be reduced. The securities they purchased are backed (collateralized) by the mortgages.

In many cases, the financial institution that originates the mortgage is not accustomed to the process of issuing mortgage-backed securities. If Mountain Savings Bank is unfamiliar with the process of issuing mortgage-backed securities, another financial institution may participate by bundling Mountain's 100 mortgages with mortgages originated by other institutions. Then the financial institution issues mortgage-backed securities that represent all the mortgages in the bundle. Thus any investor that purchases these mortgage-backed securities is partially financing the 100 mortgages at Mountain Savings Bank and all the other mortgages in the bundle that are backing these securities. ●

As housing prices increased in the 2004–2006 period, many financial institutions used their funds to purchase mortgage-backed securities, some of which represented bundles of subprime mortgages. These financial institutions incorrectly presumed that the homes would serve as sufficient collateral if the mortgages defaulted. In 2008, many subprime mortgages defaulted and home prices plummeted, which meant that the collateral was not adequate to cover the credit provided. Consequently, the values of mortgage-backed securities also plummeted, and the financial institutions holding these securities experienced major losses.

Stocks   Stocks (or equity securities) represent partial ownership in the corporations that issue them. They are classified as capital market securities because they have no maturity and therefore serve as a long-term source of funds. Investors who purchase stocks (referred to as stockholders) issued by a corporation in the primary market can sell the stocks to other investors at any time in the secondary market. However, stocks of some corporations are more liquid than stocks of others. More than a million shares of stocks of large corporations are traded in the secondary market on any given day, as there are many investors who are willing to buy them. Stocks of small corporations are less liquid, because the secondary market is not as active.

Some corporations provide income to their stockholders by distributing a portion of their quarterly earnings in the form of dividends. Other corporations retain and reinvest all of their earnings in their operations, which increase their growth potential.

As corporations grow and increase in value, the value of their stock increases; investors can then earn a capital gain from selling the stock for a higher price than they paid for it. Thus, investors can earn a return from stocks in the form of periodic dividends (if there are any) and in the form a capital gain when they sell the stock. However, stocks are subject to risk because their future prices are uncertain. Their prices commonly decline when the firm performs poorly, resulting in negative returns to investors.

1-2c Derivative Securities

WEB

www.cboe.com
Information about
derivative securities.

In addition to money market and capital market securities, derivative securities are also traded in financial markets. **Derivative securities** are financial contracts whose values are derived from the values of underlying assets (such as debt securities or equity securities). Many derivative securities enable investors to engage in speculation and risk management.

Speculation   Derivative securities allow an investor to speculate on movements in the value of the underlying assets without having to purchase those assets. Some derivative securities allow investors to benefit from an increase in the value of the underlying assets, whereas others allow investors to benefit from a decrease in the assets' value. Investors who speculate in derivative contracts can achieve higher returns than if they had speculated in the underlying assets, but they are also exposed to higher risk.

Risk Management   Derivative securities can be used in a manner that will generate gains if the value of the underlying assets declines. Consequently, financial institutions and other firms can use derivative securities to adjust the risk of their existing investments in securities. If a firm maintains investments in bonds, it can take specific positions in derivative securities that will generate gains if bond values decline. In this way, derivative securities can be used to reduce a firm's risk. The loss on the bonds is offset by the gains on these derivative securities.

1-2d Valuation of Securities

Each type of security generates a unique stream of expected cash flows to investors. The valuation of a security is measured as the present value of its expected cash flows, discounted at a rate that reflects the uncertainty surrounding the cash flows.

Debt securities are easier to value because they promise to investors specific payments (interest and principal) until they mature. The stream of cash flows generated by stocks is more difficult to estimate because some stocks do not pay dividends, and so investors receive cash flow only when they sell the stock. All investors sell the stock at different times. Thus some investors choose to value a stock by valuing the company and then dividing that value by the number of shares of stock.

Impact of Information on Valuation   Investors can attempt to estimate the future cash flows that they will receive by obtaining information that may influence a security's future cash flows. The valuation process is illustrated in Exhibit 1.2.

Some investors rely mostly on economic or industry information to value a security, whereas others rely more on published opinions about the firm's management. When investors receive new information about a security that clearly indicates the likelihood of higher cash flows or less uncertainty surrounding the cash flows, they revise their valuations of that security upward. As a result, investors increase the demand for the security. In addition, investors that previously purchased that security and were planning to sell the security in the secondary market may decide not to sell. This results in a smaller supply of that security for sale (by investors who had previously purchased it) in the secondary market. Thus the market price of the security rises to a new equilibrium level. Conversely, when investors receive unfavorable information, they reduce the expected cash flows or increase the discount rate used in valuation. The valuations of the security

Exhibit 1.2   Use of Information to Make Investment Decisions

are revised downward, which results in a lower demand and an increase in the supply of that security for sale in the secondary market. Consequently, there is a decline in the equilibrium price.

In an **efficient market**, securities are rationally priced. If a security is clearly undervalued based on public information, some investors will capitalize on the discrepancy by purchasing that security. This strong demand for the security will push the security's price higher until the discrepancy no longer exists. The investors who recognized the discrepancy will be rewarded with higher returns on their investment. Their actions to capitalize on valuation discrepancies typically push security prices toward their proper price levels, based on the information that is available.

Impact of the Internet on Valuation

The Internet has improved the valuation of securities in several ways. Prices of securities are quoted online and can be obtained at any given moment by investors. For some securities, investors can track the actual sequence of transactions. Because much more information about the firms that issue securities is available online, securities can be priced more accurately. Furthermore, orders to buy or sell many types of securities can be submitted online, which expedites the adjustment in security prices to new information.

Impact of Behavioral Finance on Valuation

In some cases, a security may be mispriced because of the psychology involved in the decision making. **Behavioral finance** is the application of psychology to make financial decisions. It offers a reason why markets are not always efficient.

EXAMPLE

When Facebook issued stock to the public in May 2012, many critics suggested that the initial high stock price was influenced by market hype rather than fundamentals (such as its expected cash flows). Some of Facebook's customers may invest in Facebook's stock because they commonly use Facebook's services, without really considering whether the stock price was appropriate. Facebook's stock price declined by about 50 percent in a few months as the hype in the stock market wore off. ●

Behavioral finance can sometimes explain the movements of a security's price or even of the entire stock market. In some periods, investors seem to be excessively optimistic, and their stock-buying frenzy can push the prices of the entire stock market higher. This leads to a stock price bubble that bursts once investors consider fundamental characteristics (such as a firm's cash flows) rather than hype when valuing a stock.

Uncertainty Surrounding Valuation of Securities

Even if markets are efficient, the valuation of a firm's security is subject to much uncertainty because investors have limited information available to value that security. Furthermore, the return from investing in a security over a particular period is typically uncertain because the cash flows to be received by investors over that period is uncertain. The higher the degree of uncertainty, the higher is the risk from investing in that security. From the perspective of an investor who purchases a security, risk represents the potential deviation of the security's actual return from what was expected. For any given type of security, risk levels among the issuers of that security can vary.

EXAMPLE

Nike stock provides cash flows to investors in the form of quarterly dividends and when an investor sells the stock. Both the future dividends and the future stock price are uncertain. Thus the cash flows that Nike stock will provide to investors over a future period are uncertain, which means that the return from investing in Nike stock over that period is uncertain.

Yet the cash flow provided by Nike's stock is less uncertain than that provided by a small, young, publicly traded technology company. Because the return on the technology stock over a particular period is more uncertain than the return on Nike stock, the technology stock has more risk. ●

1-2e Securities Regulations

Much of the information that investors use to value securities issued by firms is provided in the form of financial statements by those firms. In particular, investors rely on accounting reports of a firm's revenue and expenses as a basis for estimating its future cash flows. Although firms with publicly traded stock are required to disclose financial information and financial statements, a firm's managers still possess information about its financial condition that is not necessarily available to investors. This situation is referred to as *asymmetric information*. Even when information is disclosed, an asymmetric information problem may still exist if some of the information provided by the firm's managers is intentionally misleading in order to exaggerate the firm's performance.

Required Disclosure Many regulations exist that attempt to ensure that businesses disclose accurate financial information. Similarly, when information is disclosed to only a small set of investors, those investors have a major advantage over other investors. Thus another regulatory goal is to provide all investors with equal access to disclosures by firms. The Securities Act of 1933 was intended to ensure complete disclosure of relevant financial information on publicly offered securities and to prevent fraudulent practices in selling these securities.

The Securities Exchange Act of 1934 extended the disclosure requirements to secondary market issues. It also declared illegal a variety of deceptive practices, such as misleading financial statements and trading strategies designed to manipulate the market price. In addition, it established the Securities and Exchange Commission (SEC) to oversee the securities markets, and the SEC has implemented additional regulations over time. Securities laws do not prevent investors from making poor investment decisions; they seek only to ensure full disclosure of information and thereby protect against fraud.

WEB

www.sec.gov

Background on the Securities and Exchange Commission, and news releases about financial regulations.

Regulatory Response to Financial Reporting Scandals Financial scandals that occurred in the 2001–2002 period proved that the existing regulations were not sufficient to prevent fraud. Several well-known companies such as Enron and WorldCom misled investors by exaggerating their earnings. They also failed to disclose relevant information that would have adversely affected the prices of their stock and debt securities. Firms that have issued stock and debt securities must hire independent auditors to verify that their financial information is accurate. However, in some cases, the auditors who were hired to ensure accuracy were not meeting their responsibility.

In response to the financial scandals, the Sarbanes-Oxley Act (discussed throughout this text) was passed to require that firms provide more complete and accurate financial information. It also imposed restrictions to ensure proper auditing by auditors and proper oversight by the firm's board of directors. These rules were intended to regain the trust of investors who supply the funds to the financial markets. Through these measures, regulators tried to eliminate or at least reduce the asymmetric information problem.

However, the Sarbanes-Oxley Act did not completely eliminate questionable accounting methods. In 2011 and 2012, Groupon Inc. used accounting methods that inflated its reported earnings. As these accounting methods were criticized by the financial media during 2012, the stock price of Groupon declined by about 85 percent.

GLOBAL ASPECTS

© Marish/ShutterStock.com

1-2f International Securities Transactions

Financial markets are continuously being developed throughout the world to improve the transfer of securities between surplus units and deficit units. The financial markets are much more developed in some countries than in others, and they also vary in terms of the volumes of funds transferred from surplus to deficit units. Some countries have more developed financial markets for specific securities, and other countries (in Eastern Europe and Asia, for example) have established financial markets recently.

Under favorable economic conditions, the international integration of securities markets allows governments and corporations easier access to funding from creditors or investors in other countries to support their growth. In addition, investors and creditors in any country can benefit from the investment opportunities in other countries. Yet, under unfavorable economic conditions, the international integration of securities markets allows one country's financial problems to adversely affect other countries. The U.S. financial markets allow foreign investors to pursue investment opportunities in the United States, but during the U.S. financial crisis, many foreign investors who invested in U.S. securities experienced severe losses. Thus the U.S. financial crisis spread beyond the United States.

Many European governments borrow funds from creditors in many different countries, but as the governments of Greece, Portugal, and Spain struggled to repay their loans, they caused financial problems for some creditors in other countries. Economic conditions are more closely connected because of the international integration of securities markets, and this causes each country to be more exposed to the economic conditions of other countries.

Foreign Exchange Market International financial transactions normally require the exchange of currencies. The **foreign exchange market** facilitates this exchange. Many commercial banks and other financial institutions serve as intermediaries in the foreign exchange market by matching up participants who want to exchange one currency for another. Some of these financial institutions also serve as dealers by taking positions in currencies to accommodate foreign exchange requests.

Like securities, most currencies have a market-determined price (exchange rate) that changes in response to supply and demand. If there is a sudden shift in the aggregate demand by corporations, government agencies, and individuals for a given currency, or a shift in the aggregate supply of that currency for sale (to be exchanged for another currency), the price of the currency (exchange rate) will change.

1-2g Government Intervention in Financial Markets

In recent years, the government has increased its role in financial markets. Consider the following examples.

1. During the credit crisis, the Federal Reserve purchased various types of debt securities. The intervention was intended to ensure more liquidity in the debt securities markets, and therefore encourage investors to purchase debt securities.
2. New government regulations changed the manner by which the credit risk of bonds were assessed. The new regulations occurred because of criticisms about the previous process used for rating bonds that did not effectively warn investors about the credit risk of bonds during the credit crisis.
3. The government increased its monitoring of stock trading, and prosecuted cases in which investors traded based on inside information about firms that was not available to other investors. The increased government efforts were intended to ensure that no investor had an unfair advantage when trading in financial markets.

These examples illustrate how the government has increased its efforts to ensure fair and orderly financial markets, which could encourage more investors to participate in the markets, and therefore could increase liquidity.

1-3 ROLE OF FINANCIAL INSTITUTIONS

Because financial markets are **imperfect**, securities buyers and sellers do not have full access to information. Individuals with available funds are not normally capable of identifying credit worthy borrowers to whom they could lend those funds. In addition, they do not have the expertise to assess the creditworthiness of potential borrowers. Financial institutions are needed to resolve the limitations caused by market imperfections. They accept funds from surplus units and channel the funds to deficit units. Without financial institutions, the information and transaction costs of financial market transactions would be excessive. Financial institutions can be classified as depository and nondepository institutions.

1-3a Role of Depository Institutions

Depository institutions accept deposits from surplus units and provide credit to deficit units through loans and purchases of securities. They are popular financial institutions for the following reasons.

- They offer deposit accounts that can accommodate the amount and liquidity characteristics desired by most surplus units.
- They repackage funds received from deposits to provide loans of the size and maturity desired by deficit units.
- They accept the risk on loans provided.
- They have more expertise than individual surplus units in evaluating the creditworthiness of deficit units.
- They diversify their loans among numerous deficit units and therefore can absorb defaulted loans better than individual surplus units could.

To appreciate these advantages, consider the flow of funds from surplus units to deficit units if depository institutions did not exist. Each surplus unit would have to identify a deficit unit desiring to borrow the precise amount of funds available for the precise time period in which funds would be available. Furthermore, each surplus unit would have to perform the credit evaluation and incur the risk of default. Under these conditions, many surplus units would likely hold their funds rather than channel them to deficit units. Hence, the flow of funds from surplus units to deficit units would be disrupted. When a depository institution offers a loan, it is acting as a creditor, just as if it had purchased a debt security. The more personalized loan agreement is less marketable in the secondary market than a debt security, however, because the loan agreement contains detailed provisions that can differ significantly among loans. Potential investors would need to review all provisions before purchasing loans in the secondary market.

A more specific description of each depository institution's role in the financial markets follows.

Commercial Banks In aggregate, commercial banks are the most dominant depository institution. They serve surplus units by offering a wide variety of deposit accounts, and they transfer deposited funds to deficit units by providing direct loans or purchasing debt securities. Commercial bank operations are exposed to risk because their loans and many of their investments in debt securities are subject to the risk of default by the borrowers.

Commercial banks serve both the private and public sectors; their deposit and lending services are utilized by households, businesses, and government agencies. Some commercial banks (including Bank of America, J.P. Morgan Chase, Citigroup, and Sun Trust Banks) have more than $100 billion in assets.

Some commercial banks receive more funds from deposits than they need to make loans or invest in securities. Other commercial banks need more funds to accommodate customer requests than the amount of funds that they receive from deposits. The **federal funds market** facilitates the flow of funds between depository institutions (including banks). A bank that has excess funds can lend to a bank with deficient funds for a short-term period, such as one to five days. In this way, the federal funds market facilitates the flow of funds from banks that have excess funds to banks that are in need of funds.

Commercial banks are subject to regulations that are intended to limit their exposure to the risk of failure. In particular, banks are required to maintain a minimum level of capital, relative to their size, so that they have a cushion to absorb possible losses from defaults on some loans provided to households or businesses. The Federal Reserve ("the Fed") serves as a regulator of banks.

WEB

www.fdic.gov
Information and news about banks and savings institutions.

Savings Institutions   Savings institutions, which are sometimes referred to as thrift institutions, are another type of depository institution. Savings institutions include savings and loan associations (S&Ls) and savings banks. Like commercial banks, savings institutions offer deposit accounts to surplus units and then channel these deposits to deficit units. Savings banks are similar to S&Ls except that they have more diversified uses of funds. Over time, however, this difference has narrowed. Savings institutions can be owned by shareholders, but most are mutual (depositor owned). Like commercial banks, savings institutions rely on the federal funds market to lend their excess funds or to borrow funds on a short-term basis.

Whereas commercial banks concentrate on commercial (business) loans, savings institutions concentrate on residential mortgage loans. Normally, mortgage loans are perceived to exhibit a relatively low level of risk, but many mortgages defaulted in 2008 and 2009. This led to the credit crisis and caused financial problems for many savings institutions.

Credit Unions   Credit unions differ from commercial banks and savings institutions in that they (1) are nonprofit and (2) restrict their business to credit union members, who share a common bond (such as a common employer or union). Like savings institutions, they are sometimes classified as thrift institutions in order to distinguish them from commercial banks. Because of the "common bond" characteristic, credit unions tend to be much smaller than other depository institutions. They use most of their funds to provide loans to their members. Some of the largest credit unions (e.g., the Navy Federal Credit Union, the State Employees Credit Union of North Carolina, the Pentagon Federal Credit Union) have assets of more than $5 billion.

1-3b Role of Nondepository Financial Institutions

Nondepository institutions generate funds from sources other than deposits but also play a major role in financial intermediation. These institutions are briefly described here and are covered in more detail in Part 7.

Finance Companies   Most finance companies obtain funds by issuing securities and then lend the funds to individuals and small businesses. The functions of finance companies and depository institutions overlap, although each type of institution concentrates on a particular segment of the financial markets (explained in the chapters devoted to these institutions).

Mutual Funds

Mutual funds sell shares to surplus units and use the funds received to purchase a portfolio of securities. They are the dominant nondepository financial institution when measured in total assets. Some mutual funds concentrate their investment in capital market securities, such as stocks or bonds. Others, known as **money market mutual funds**, concentrate in money market securities. Typically, mutual funds purchase securities in minimum denominations that are larger than the savings of an individual surplus unit. By purchasing shares of mutual funds and money market mutual funds, small savers are able to invest in a diversified portfolio of securities with a relatively small amount of funds.

WEB

finance.yahoo.com/
funds
Information about
mutual funds.

Securities Firms

Securities firms provide a wide variety of functions in financial markets. Some securities firms act as a **broker**, executing securities transactions between two parties. The broker fee for executing a transaction is reflected in the difference (or **spread**) between the **bid quote** and the **ask quote**. The markup as a percentage of the transaction amount will likely be higher for less common transactions, since more time is needed to match up buyers and sellers. The markup will also likely be higher for transactions involving relatively small amounts so that the broker will be adequately compensated for the time required to execute the transaction.

Furthermore, securities firms often act as **dealers**, making a market in specific securities by maintaining an inventory of securities. Although a broker's income is mostly based on the markup, the dealer's income is influenced by the performance of the security portfolio maintained. Some dealers also provide brokerage services and therefore earn income from both types of activities.

In addition to brokerage and dealer services, securities firms also provide underwriting and advising services. The underwriting and advising services are commonly referred to as *investment banking*, and the securities firms that specialize in these services are sometimes referred to as *investment banks*. Some securities firms place newly issued securities for corporations and government agencies; this task differs from traditional brokerage activities because it involves the primary market. When securities firms **underwrite** newly issued securities, they may sell the securities for a client at a guaranteed price or may simply sell the securities at the best price they can get for their client.

Some securities firms offer advisory services on mergers and other forms of corporate restructuring. In addition to helping a company plan its restructuring, the securities firm also executes the change in the client's capital structure by placing the securities issued by the company.

Insurance Companies

Insurance companies provide individuals and firms with insurance policies that reduce the financial burden associated with death, illness, and damage to property. These companies charge premiums in exchange for the insurance that they provide. They invest the funds received in the form of premiums until the funds are needed to cover insurance claims. Insurance companies commonly invest these funds in stocks or bonds issued by corporations or in bonds issued by the government. In this way, they finance the needs of deficit units and thus serve as important financial intermediaries. Their overall performance is linked to the performance of the stocks and bonds in which they invest. Large insurance companies include State Farm Group, Allstate Insurance, Travelers Group, CNA Insurance, and Liberty Mutual.

Pension Funds

Many corporations and government agencies offer pension plans to their employees. The employees and their employers (or both) periodically contribute funds to the plan. Pension funds provide an efficient way for individuals to save for their retirement. The pension funds manage the money until the individuals with draw the funds from their retirement accounts. The money that is contributed to individual retirement accounts is commonly invested by the pension funds in stocks or bonds issued by corporations or in bonds issued by the government. Thus pension funds are important financial intermediaries that finance the needs of deficit units.

1-3c Comparison of Roles among Financial Institutions

The role of financial institutions in facilitating the flow of funds from individual surplus units (investors) to deficit units is illustrated in Exhibit 1.3. Surplus units are shown on the left side of the exhibit, and deficit units are shown on the right. Three different flows of funds from surplus units to deficit units are shown in the exhibit. One set of flows represents deposits from surplus units that are transformed by depository institutions into loans for deficit units. A second set of flows represents purchases of securities (commercial paper) issued by finance companies that are transformed into finance company loans for deficit units. A third set of flows reflects the purchases of shares issued by mutual funds, which are used by the mutual funds to purchase debt and equity securities of deficit units.

The deficit units also receive funding from insurance companies and pension funds. Because insurance companies and pension funds purchase massive amounts of stocks and bonds, they finance much of the expenditures made by large deficit units, such as corporations and government agencies. Financial institutions such as commercial banks, insurance companies, mutual funds, and pension funds serve the role of investing funds that they have received from surplus units, so they are often referred to as *institutional investors*.

Securities firms are not shown in Exhibit 1.3, but they play an important role in facilitating the flow of funds. Many of the transactions between the financial institutions and

Exhibit 1.3   Comparison of Roles among Financial Institutions

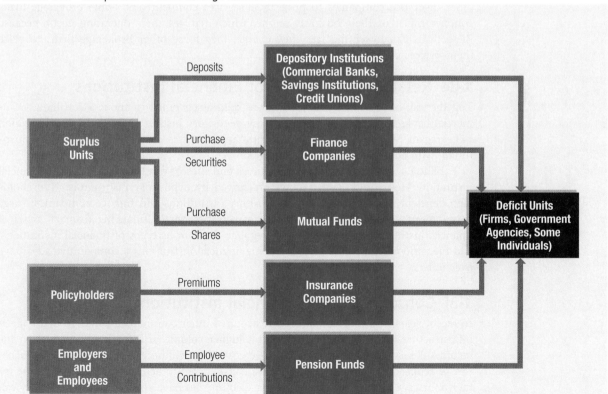

deficit units are executed by securities firms. Furthermore, some funds flow directly from surplus units to deficit units as a result of security transactions, with securities firms serving as brokers.

Institutional Role as a Monitor of Publicly Traded Firms In addition to the roles of financial institutions described in Exhibit 1.3, financial institutions also serve as monitors of publicly traded firms. Because insurance companies, pension funds, and some mutual funds are major investors in stocks, they can influence the management of publicly traded firms. In recent years, many large institutional investors have publicly criticized the management of specific firms, which has resulted in corporate restructuring or even the firing of executives in some cases. Thus institutional investors not only provide financial support to companies but also exercise some degree of corporate control over them. By serving as activist shareholders, they can help ensure that managers of publicly held corporations are making decisions that are in the best interests of the shareholders.

1-3d How the Internet Facilitates Roles of Financial Institutions

The Internet has also enabled financial institutions to perform their roles more efficiently. Some commercial banks have been created solely as online entities. Because they have lower costs, they can offer higher interest rates on deposits and lower rates on loans. Other banks and depository institutions also offer online services, which can reduce costs, increase efficiency, and intensify competition. Many mutual funds allow their shareholders to execute buy or sell transactions online. Some insurance companies conduct much of their business online, which reduces their operating costs and forces other insurance companies to price their services competitively. Some brokerage firms conduct much of their business online, which reduces their operating costs; because these firms can lower the fees they charge, they force other brokerage firms to price their services competitively.

1-3e Relative Importance of Financial Institutions

Together, all of these financial institutions hold assets equal to about $45 trillion. Commercial banks hold the most assets of any depository institution, with about $12 trillion in aggregate. Mutual funds hold the largest amount of assets of any nondepository institution, with about $11 trillion in aggregate.

Exhibit 1.4 summarizes the main sources and uses of funds for each type of financial institution. Households with savings are served by depository institutions. Households with deficient funds are served by depository institutions and finance companies. Large corporations and governments that issue securities obtain financing from all types of financial institutions. Several agencies regulate the various types of financial institutions, and the various regulations may give some financial institutions a comparative advantage over others.

1-3f Consolidation of Financial Institutions

In recent years, commercial banks have acquired other commercial banks so that a given infrastructure can generate and support a higher volume of business. By increasing the volume of services produced, the average cost of providing the services (such as loans) can be reduced. Savings institutions have consolidated to achieve economies of scale for their mortgage lending business. Insurance companies have consolidated so that they can reduce the average cost of providing insurance services.

Exhibit 1.4   Summary of Institutional Sources and Uses of Funds

FINANCIAL INSTITUTIONS	MAIN SOURCES OF FUNDS	MAIN USES OF FUNDS
Commercial banks	Deposits from households, businesses, and government agencies	Purchases of government and corporate securities; loans to businesses and households
Savings institutions	Deposits from households, businesses, and government agencies	Purchases of government and corporate securities; mortgages and other loans to households; some loans to businesses
Credit unions	Deposits from credit union members	Loans to credit union members
Finance companies	Securities sold to households and businesses	Loans to households and businesses
Mutual funds	Shares sold to households, businesses, and government agencies	Purchases of long-term government and corporate securities
Money market funds	Shares sold to households, businesses, and government agencies	Purchases of short-term government and corporate securities
Insurance companies	Insurance premiums and earnings from investments	Purchases of long-term government and corporate securities
Pension funds	Employer/employee contributions	Purchases of long-term government and corporate securities

During the last 10 years, different types of financial institutions were allowed by regulators to expand the types of services they offer and capitalize on economies of scope. Commercial banks merged with savings institutions, securities firms, finance companies, mutual funds, and insurance companies. Although the operations of each type of financial institution are commonly managed separately, a financial conglomerate offers advantages to customers who prefer to obtain all of their financial services from a single financial institution. Because a financial conglomerate is more diversified, it may be less exposed to a possible decline in customer demand for any single financial service.

EXAMPLE   Wells Fargo is a classic example of the evolution in financial services. It originally focused on commercial banking but has expanded its nonbank services to include mortgages, small business loans, consumer loans, real estate, brokerage, investment banking, online financial services, and insurance. In a recent annual report, Wells Fargo stated: "Our diversity in businesses makes us much more than a bank. We're a diversified financial services company. We're competing in a highly fragmented and fast growing industry: Financial Services. This helps us weather downturns that inevitably affect any one segment of our industry." ●

Typical Structure of a Financial Conglomerate   A typical organizational structure of a financial conglomerate is shown in Exhibit 1.5. Historically, each of the financial services (such as banking, mortgages, brokerage, and insurance) had significant barriers to entry, so only a limited number of firms competed in that industry. The barriers prevented most firms from offering a wide variety of these services. In recent years, the barriers to entry have been reduced, allowing firms that had specialized in one service to expand more easily into other financial services. Many firms expanded by acquiring other financial services firms. Thus many financial conglomerates are composed of various financial institutions that were originally independent but are now units (or subsidiaries) of the conglomerate.

Exhibit 1.5 Organizational Structure of a Financial Conglomerate

Holding Company of a Financial Conglomerate

Commercial Bank Operations	Thrift Operations	Consumer Finance Operations	Mutual Fund Operations	Securities Operations	Insurance Operations
• Commercial Loans • Other Corporate Services	• Mortgages	• Consumer Loans • Small Business Loans	• Stock Funds • Bond Funds • Money Market Funds	• Brokerage • Investment Banking	• Insurance for Individuals • Insurance for Firms

Impact of Consolidation on Competition   As financial institutions spread into other financial services, the competition for customers desiring the various types of financial services increased. Prices of financial services declined in response to the competition. In addition, consolidation has provided more convenience. Individual customers can rely on the financial conglomerate for convenient access to life and health insurance, brokerage, mutual funds, investment advice and financial planning, bank deposits, and personal loans. A corporate customer can turn to the financial conglomerate for property and casualty insurance, health insurance plans for employees, business loans, advice on restructuring its businesses, issuing new debt or equity securities, and management of its pension plan.

Global Consolidation of Financial Institutions   Many financial institutions have expanded internationally to capitalize on their expertise. Commercial banks, insurance companies, and securities firms have expanded through international mergers. An international merger between financial institutions enables the merged company to offer the services of both entities to its entire customer base. For example, a U.S. commercial bank may specialize in lending while a European securities firm specializes in services such as underwriting securities. A merger between the two entities allows the U.S. bank to provide its services to the European customer base (clients of the European securities firm) and allows the European securities firm to offer its services to the U.S. customer base. By combining specialized skills and customer bases, the merged institutions can offer more services to clients and have an international customer base.

The adoption of the euro by 17 European countries has increased business between those countries and created a more competitive environment in Europe. European financial institutions, which had primarily competed with other financial institutions based in their own country, recognized that they would now face more competition from financial institutions in other countries.

Many financial institutions have attempted to benefit from opportunities in emerging markets. For example, some large securities firms have expanded into many countries.

to offer underwriting services for firms and government agencies. The need for this service has increased most dramatically in countries where businesses have been privatized. In addition, commercial banks have expanded into emerging markets to provide loans. Although this allows them to capitalize on opportunities in these countries, it also exposes them to financial problems in these countries.

1-4 CREDIT CRISIS FOR FINANCIAL INSTITUTIONS

Following the abrupt increase in home prices in the 2004–2006 period, many financial institutions increased their holdings of mortgages and mortgage-backed securities, whose performance was based on the timely mortgage payments made by homeowners. Some financial institutions (especially commercial banks and savings institutions) aggressively attempted to expand their mortgage business in order to capitalize on the strong housing market. They commonly applied liberal standards when originating new mortgages and often failed to verify the applicant's job status, income level, or credit history. Home prices were expected to continue rising over time, so financial institutions presumed (incorrectly) that the underlying value of the homes would provide adequate collateral to back the mortgage if homeowners could not make their mortgage payments.

In the 2007–2009 period, mortgage defaults increased, and there was an excess of unoccupied homes as homeowners who could not pay the mortgage left their homes. As a result, home prices plummeted, and the value of the property collateral backing many mortgages was less than the outstanding mortgage amount. By January 2009, at least 10 percent of all American homeowners were either behind on their mortgage payments or had defaulted on their mortgage. Many of the financial institutions that originated mortgages suffered major losses.

1-4a Systemic Risk during the Credit Crisis

The credit crisis illustrated how financial problems of some financial institutions spread to others. **Systemic risk** is defined as the spread of financial problems among financial institutions and across financial markets that could cause a collapse in the financial system. It exists because financial institutions invest their funds in similar types of securities and therefore have similar exposure to large declines in the prices of these securities. In this case, mortgage defaults affected financial institutions in several ways. First, many financial institutions that originated mortgages shortly before the crisis sold them to other financial institutions (i.e., commercial banks, savings institutions, mutual funds, insurance companies, securities firms, and pension funds); hence even financial institutions that were not involved in the mortgage origination process experienced large losses because they purchased the mortgages originated by other financial institutions.

Second, many other financial institutions that invested in mortgage-backed securities and promised payments on mortgages were exposed to the crisis. Third, some financial institutions (especially securities firms) relied heavily on short-term debt to finance their operations and used their holdings of mortgage-backed securities as collateral. But when the prices of mortgage-backed securities plummeted, large securities firms such as Bear Stearns and Lehman Brothers could not issue new short-term debt to pay off the principal on maturing debt.

Furthermore, the decline in home building activity caused a decrease in the demand for many related businesses, such as air-conditioning services, roofing, and landscaping. In addition, the loss of income by workers in these industries caused a decline in spending in a wide variety of industries. The weak economy also created more concerns about the potential default on debt securities, causing further declines in bond prices. The financial markets were filled with sellers who wanted to dump debt securities, but there were not many buyers willing to buy securities. Consequently, the prices of debt securities plunged.

Systemic risk was a major concern during the credit crisis because the prices of most equity securities declined substantially, since the operating performance of most firms declined when the economy weakened. Thus most financial institutions experienced large losses on their investments during the credit crisis even if they invested solely inequity securities.

1-4b Government Response to the Credit Crisis

The government intervened in order to correct some of the economic problems caused by the credit crisis.

Emergency Economic Stabilization Act   On October 3, 2008, Congress enacted the Emergency Economic Stabilization Act of 2008 (also referred to as the bailout act), which was intended to resolve the liquidity problems of financial institutions and to restore the confidence of the investors who invest in them. The act directed the Treasury to inject $700 billion into the financial system, primarily by investing money into the banking system by purchasing the preferred stock of financial institutions. In this way, the Treasury provided large commercial banks with capital to cushion their losses, thereby reducing the likelihood that the banks would fail.

Federal Reserve Actions   In 2008, some large securities firms such as Bear Stearns and Lehman Brothers experienced severe financial problems. The Federal Reserve rescued Bear Stearns by financing its acquisition by a commercial bank (J.P. Morgan Chase) in order to calm the financial markets. However, when Lehman Brothers was failing six months later, it was not rescued by the government, and this caused much paranoia in financial markets.

At this time, the Fed also provided emergency loans to many other securities firms that were not subject to its regulation. Some major securities firms (such as Merrill Lynch) were acquired by commercial banks, while others (Goldman Sachs and Morgan Stanley) were converted into commercial banks. These actions resulted in the consolidation of financial institutions and also subjected more financial institutions to Federal Reserve regulations.

Financial Reform Act of 2010   On July 21, 2010, President Obama signed the Financial Reform Act (also referred to as the Wall Street Reform Act or Consumer Financial Reform Act), which was intended to prevent some of the problems that caused the credit crisis. The provisions of the act are frequently discussed in this text when they apply to specific financial markets or financial institutions.

One of the key provisions of the Financial Reform Act of 2010 is that mortgage lenders verify the income, job status, and credit history of mortgage applicants before approving mortgage applications. This provision is intended to prevent applicants from receiving mortgages unless they are creditworthy.

In addition, the Financial Reform Act called for the creation of the Financial Stability Oversight Council, which is responsible for identifying risks to financial stability in the United States and makes regulatory recommendations that could reduce any risks to the financial system. The council consists of 10 members who represent the heads of regulatory agencies that regulate key components of the financial system, including the

FINANCIAL REFORM
© Cvijun/Shutterstock.com

housing industry, securities trading, depository institutions, mutual funds, and insurance companies.

Furthermore, the act established the Consumer Financial Protection Bureau (housed within the Federal Reserve) to regulate specific financial services for consumers, including online banking, checking accounts, credit cards, and student loans. This bureau can set rules to ensure that information regarding endorsements of specific financial products is accurate and to prevent deceptive practices.

1-4c Conclusion about Government Response to the Credit Crisis

In general, the government response to the credit crisis was intended to enhance the safety of financial institutions. Since financial institutions serve as intermediaries for financial markets, the tougher regulations on financial institutions can stabilize the financial markets and encourage more participation by surplus and deficit units in these markets.

SUMMARY

- Financial markets facilitate the transfer of funds from surplus units to deficit units. Because funding needs vary among deficit units, various financial markets have been established. The primary market allows for the issuance of new securities, and the secondary market allows for the sale of existing securities.

- Securities can be classified as money market (short-term) securities or capital market (long-term) securities. Common capital market securities include bonds, mortgages, mortgage-backed securities, and stocks. The valuation of a security represents the present value of future cash flows that it is expected to generate. New information that indicates a change in expected cash flows or degree of uncertainty affects prices of securities in financial markets.

- Depository and nondepository institutions help to finance the needs of deficit units. The main depository institutions are commercial banks, savings institutions, and credit unions. The main nondepository institutions are finance companies, mutual funds,

pension funds, and insurance companies. Many financial institutions have been consolidated (due to mergers) into financial conglomerates, where they serve as subsidiaries of the conglomerate while conducting their specialized services. Thus, some financial conglomerates are able to provide all types of financial services. Consolidation allows for economies of scale and scope, which can enhance cash flows and increase the financial institution's value. In addition, consolidation can diversify the institution's services and increase its value through the reduction in risk.

- The credit crisis in 2008 and 2009 had a profound effect on financial institutions. Those institutions that were heavily involved in originating or investing in mortgages suffered major losses. Many investors were concerned that the institutions might fail and therefore avoided them, which disrupted the ability of financial institutions to facilitate the flow of funds. The credit crisis led to concerns about systemic risk, as financial problems spread among financial institutions that were heavily exposed to mortgages.

POINT COUNTER-POINT

Will Computer Technology Cause Financial Intermediaries to Become Extinct?

Point Yes. Financial intermediaries benefit from access to information. As information becomes more accessible, individuals will have the information they need before investing or borrowing funds. They will not need financial intermediaries to make their decisions.

Counter-Point   No. Individuals rely not only on information but also on expertise. Some financial intermediaries specialize in credit analysis so that they can make loans. Surplus units will continue to provide funds to financial intermediaries, rather than make direct loans, because they are not capable of credit analysis even if more information about prospective borrowers is available. Some financial intermediaries no longer have physical buildings for customer service, but they still require agents who have the expertise to assess the creditworthiness of prospective borrowers.

Who Is Correct?   Use the Internet to learn more about this issue and then formulate your own opinion.

Questions and Applications

1. **Surplus and Deficit Units** Explain the meaning of surplus units and deficit units. Provide an example of each. Which types of financial institutions do you deal with? Explain whether you are acting as a surplus unit or a deficit unit in your relationship with each financial institution.

2. **Types of Markets** Distinguish between primary and secondary markets. Distinguish between money and capital markets.

3. **Imperfect Markets** Distinguish between perfect and imperfect security markets. Explain why the existence of imperfect markets creates a need for financial intermediaries.

4. **Efficient Markets** Explain the meaning of efficient markets. Why might we expect markets to be efficient most of the time? In recent years, several securities firms have been guilty of using inside information when purchasing securities, thereby achieving returns well above the norm (even when accounting for risk). Does this suggest that the security markets are not efficient? Explain.

5. **Securities Laws** What was the purpose of the Securities Act of 1933? What was the purpose of the Securities Exchange Act of 1934? Do these laws prevent investors from making poor investment decisions? Explain.

6. **International Barriers** If barriers to international securities markets are reduced, will a country's interest rate be more or less susceptible to foreign lending and borrowing activities? Explain.

7. **International Flow of Funds** In what way could the international flow of funds cause a decline in interest rates?

8. **Securities Firms** What are the functions of securities firms? Many securities firms employ brokers and dealers. Distinguish between the functions of a broker and those of a dealer, and explain how each is compensated.

9. **Standardized Securities** Why do you think securities are commonly standardized? Explain why some financial flows of funds cannot occur through the sale of standardized securities. If securities were not standardized, how would this affect the volume of financial transactions conducted by brokers?

10. **Marketability** Commercial banks use some funds to purchase securities and other funds to make loans. Why are the securities more marketable than loans in the secondary market?

11. **Depository Institutions** Explain the primary use of funds by commercial banks versus savings institutions.

12. **Credit Unions** With regard to the profit motive, how are credit unions different from other financial institutions?

13. **Nondepository Institutions** Compare the main sources and uses of funds for finance companies, insurance companies, and pension funds.

14. **Mutual Funds** What is the function of a mutual fund? Why are mutual funds popular among investors? How does a money market mutual fund differ from a stock or bond mutual fund?

15. **Impact of Privatization on Financial Markets** Explain how the privatization of companies in Europe can lead to the development of new securities markets.

Advanced Questions

16. **Comparing Financial Institutions** Classify the types of financial institutions mentioned in this chapter

as either depository or nondepository. Explain the general difference between depository and nondepository institution sources of funds. It is often said that all types of financial institutions have begun to offer services that were previously offered only by certain types. Consequently, the operations of many financial institutions are becoming more similar. Nevertheless, performance levels still differ significantly among types of financial institutions. Why?

17. Financial Intermediation Look in a business periodical for news about a recent financial transaction involving two financial institutions. For this transaction, determine the following:

a. How will each institution's balance sheet be affected?

b. Will either institution receive immediate income from the transaction?

c. Who is the ultimate user of funds?

d. Who is the ultimate source of funds?

18. Role of Accounting in Financial Markets Integrate the roles of accounting, regulation, and financial market participation. That is, explain how financial market participants rely on accounting and why regulatory oversight of the accounting process is necessary.

19. Impact of Credit Crisis on Liquidity Explain why the credit crisis caused a lack of liquidity in the secondary markets for many types of debt securities. Explain how such a lack of liquidity would affect the prices of the debt securities in the secondary markets.

20. Impact of Credit Crisis on Institutions Explain why mortgage defaults during the credit crisis adversely affected financial institutions that did not originate the mortgages. What role did these institutions play in financing the mortgages?

21. Regulation of Financial Institutions Financial institutions are subject to regulation to ensure that they do not take excessive risk and can safely facilitate the flow of funds through financial markets. Nevertheless, during the credit crisis, individuals were concerned about using financial institutions to facilitate their financial transactions. Why do you think the existing regulations were ineffective at ensuring a safe financial system?

22. Impact of the Greece Debt Crisis European debt markets have become integrated over time, so that institutional investors (such as commercial banks) commonly purchase debt issued in other European countries. When the government of Greece experienced problems in meeting its debt obligations in 2010, some investors became concerned that the crisis would spread to other European countries. Explain why integrated European financial markets might allow a debt crisis in one European country to spread to other countries in Europe.

23. Global Financial Market Regulations Assume that countries A and B are of similar size, that they have similar economies, and that the government debt levels of both countries are within reasonable limits. Assume that the regulations in country A require complete disclosure of financial reporting by issuers of debt in that country but that regulations in country B do not require much disclosure of financial reporting. Explain why the government of country A is able to issue debt at a lower cost than the government of country B.

24. Influence of Financial Markets Some countries do not have well-established markets for debt securities or equity securities. Why do you think this can limit the development of the country, business expansion, and growth in national income in these countries?

25. Impact of Systemic Risk Different types of financial institutions commonly interact. They provide loans to each other, and take opposite positions on many different types of financial agreements, whereby one will owe the other based on a specific financial outcome. Explain why their relationships cause concerns about systemic risk.

Interpreting Financial News

"Interpreting Financial News" tests your ability to comprehend common statements made by Wall Street analysts and portfolio managers who participate in the financial markets. Interpret the following statements.

a. "The price of IBM stock will not be affected by the announcement that its earnings have increased as expected."

b. "The lending operations at Bank of America should benefit from strong economic growth."

c. "The brokerage and underwriting performance at Goldman Sachs should benefit from strong economic growth."

Managing in Financial Markets

Utilizing Financial Markets As a financial manager of a large firm, you plan to borrow $70 million over the next year.

a. What are the most likely ways in which you can borrow $70 million?

b. Assuming that you decide to issue debt securities, describe the types of financial institutions that may purchase these securities.

c. How do individuals indirectly provide the financing for your firm when they maintain deposits at depository institutions, invest in mutual funds, purchase insurance policies, or invest in pensions?

FLOW OF FUNDS EXERCISE

Roles of Financial Markets and Institutions

This continuing exercise focuses on the interactions of a single manufacturing firm (Carson Company) in the financial markets. It illustrates how financial markets and institutions are integrated and facilitate the flow of funds in the business and financial environment. At the end of every chapter, this exercise provides a list of questions about Carson Company that requires the application of concepts presented in the chapter as they relate to the flow of funds.

Carson Company is a large manufacturing firm in California that was created 20 years ago by the Carson family. It was initially financed with an equity investment by the Carson family and 10 other individuals. Over time, Carson Company obtained substantial loans from finance companies and commercial banks. The interest rate on the loans is tied to market interest rates and is adjusted every six months. Thus Carson's cost of obtaining funds is sensitive to interest rate movements. It has a credit line with a bank in case it suddenly needs additional funds for a temporary period. It has purchased Treasury securities that it could sell if it experiences any liquidity problems.

Carson Company has assets valued at about $50 million and generates sales of about $100 million per year. Some of its growth is attributed to its acquisitions of other firms. Because of its expectations of a strong U.S. economy, Carson plans to grow in the future by expanding its business and by making more acquisitions. It expects that it will need substantial long-term financing and plans to borrow additional funds either through loans or by issuing bonds. It is also considering issuing stock to raise funds in the next year. Carson closely monitors conditions in financial markets that could affect its cash inflows and cash outflows and thereby affect its value.

a. In what way is Carson a surplus unit?

b. In what way is Carson a deficit unit?

c. How might finance companies facilitate Carson's expansion?

d. How might commercial banks facilitate Carson's expansion?

e. Why might Carson have limited access to additional debt financing during its growth phase?

f. How might securities firms facilitate Carson's expansion?

g. How might Carson use the primary market to facilitate its expansion?

h. How might it use the secondary market?

i. If financial markets were perfect, how might this have allowed Carson to avoid financial institutions?

j. The loans that Carson has obtained from commercial banks stipulate that Carson must receive the bank's approval before pursuing any large projects. What is the purpose of this condition? Does this condition benefit the owners of the company?

INTERNET/EXCEL EXERCISES

1. Review the information for the common stock of IBM, using the website finance.yahoo.com. Insert the ticker symbol "IBM" in the box and click on "Get Quotes." The main goal at this point is to become familiar with the information that you can obtain at this website. Review the data that are shown for IBM stock. Compare the price of IBM based on its last trade with the price range for the year. Is the price near its high or low price? What is the total value of IBM stock (market capitalization)? What is the average daily

trading volume (Avg Vol) of IBM stock? Click on "5y" just below the stock price chart to see IBM's stock price movements over the last five years. Describe the trend in IBM's stock over this period. At what points was the stock price the highest and lowest?

2. Repeat the questions in exercise 1 for the Children's Place Retail Stores (symbol PLCE). Explain how the market capitalization and trading volume for PLCE differ from that for IBM.

WSJ Exercise

Differentiating between Primary and Secondary Markets

Review the different tables relating to stock markets and bond markets that appear in Section C of the *Wall Street Journal*. Explain whether each of these tables is focused on the primary or secondary markets.

Online Articles with Real-World Examples

Find a recent practical article available online that describes a real-world example regarding a specific financial institution or financial market that reinforces one or more concepts covered in this chapter.

If your class has an online component, your professor may ask you to post your summary of the article there and provide a link to the article so that other students can access it. If your class is live, your professor may ask you to summarize your application of the article in class. Your professor may assign specific students to complete this assignment or may allow any students to do the assignment on a volunteer basis.

For recent online articles and real-world examples related to this chapter, consider using the following search terms (be sure to include the prevailing year as a search term to ensure that the online articles are recent):

1. secondary market AND liquidity

2. secondary market AND offering

3. money market

4. bond offering

5. stock offering

6. valuation AND stock

7. market efficiency

8. financial AND regulation

9. financial institution AND operations

10. financial institution AND governance

Term Paper on the Credit Crisis

Write a term paper on one of the following topics or on a topic assigned by your professor. Details such as the due date and the length of the paper will be provided by your professor.

Each of the topics listed below can be easily researched because considerable media attention has been devoted to the subject. Although this text offers a brief summary of each topic, much more information is available at online sources that you can find by using a search engine and inserting a few key terms or phrases.

1. **Impact of Lehman Brothers' Bankruptcy on Individual Wealth** Explain how the bankruptcy of Lehman Brothers (the largest bankruptcy ever) affected the wealth and income of many different types of individuals whose money was invested by institutional investors (such as pension funds) in Lehman Brothers' debt.

2. **Impact of the Credit Crisis on Financial Market Liquidity** Explain the link between the credit crisis and the lack of liquidity in the debt markets. Offer some insight as to why the debt markets became inactive. How were interest rates affected? What happened to initial public offering (IPO) activity during the credit crisis? Why?

3. **Transparency of Financial Institutions during the Credit Crisis** Select a financial institution that had serious financial problems as a result of the credit crisis. Review the media stories about this institution during the six months before its financial problems were publicized. Were there any clues that the financial institution was having problems? At what point do you think that the institution recognized that it was having financial difficulties? Did its previous annual report indicate serious problems? Did it announce its problems, or did another media source reveal the problems?

4. **Cause of Problems for Financial Institutions during the Credit Crisis** Select a financial institution that had serious financial problems as a result of the credit crisis. Determine the main underlying causes of the problems experienced by that financial institution. Explain how these problems might have been avoided.

5. **Mortgage-Backed Securities and Risk Taking by Financial Institutions** Do you think that institutional investors that purchased mortgage-backed securities containing subprime mortgages were following reasonable investment guidelines? Address this issue for various types of financial institutions such as pension funds, commercial banks, insurance companies, and mutual funds (your answer might differ with the type

of institutional investor). If financial institutions are taking on too much risk, how should regulations be changed to limit such excessive risk taking?

6.   Pension Fund Investments in Lehman Brothers' Debt At the time that Lehman Brothers filed for bankruptcy, financial institutions serving municipalities in California were holding more than $300 billion in debt issued by Lehman. Do you think that municipal pension funds that purchased commercial paper and other debt securities issued by Lehman Brothers were following reasonable investment guidelines? If a pension fund is taking on too much risk, how should regulations be changed to limit such excessive risk taking?

7.   Future Valuation of Mortgage-Backed Securities Commercial banks must periodically "mark to market" their assets in order to determine the capital they need. Identify some advantages and disadvantages of this method, and propose a solution that would be fair to both commercial banks and regulators.

8.   Future Structure of Fannie Mae Fannie Mae plays an important role in the mortgage market, but it suffered major problems during the credit crisis. Discuss the underlying causes of the problems at Fannie Mae beyond what has been discussed in the text. Should Fannie Mae be owned completely by the government? Should it be privatized? Offer your opinion on a structure for Fannie Mae that would avoid its previous problems and enable it to serve the mortgage market.

9.   Future Structure of Ratings Agencies Rating agencies rated the so-called tranches of mortgage-backed securities that were sold to institutional investors. Explain why the performance of these agencies was criticized, and then defend against this criticism on behalf of the agencies. Was the criticism of the agencies justified? How could rating agencies be structured or regulated in a different manner in order to prevent the problems that occurred during the credit crisis?

10. Future Structure of Credit Default Swaps Explain how credit default swaps maybe partially responsible for the credit crisis. Offer a proposal for how they could be structured in the future to ensure that they are used to enhance the safety of the financial system.

11. Sale of Bear Stearns Review the arguments that have been made for the government-orchestrated sale of Bear Stearns. If Bear Stearns had been allowed to fail, what types of financial institutions would have been adversely affected? In other words, who benefited from the government's action to prevent the failure of Bear Stearns? Do you think Bear Stearns should have been allowed to fail? Explain your opinion.

12. Bailout of AIG Review the arguments that have been made for the bailout of American International Group (AIG). If AIG had been allowed to fail, what types of financial institutions would have been adversely affected? That is, who benefited from the bailout of AIG? Do you think AIG should have been allowed to fail? Explain your opinion.

13. Executive Compensation at Financial Institutions Discuss the compensation received by executives at some financial institutions that experienced financial problems (e.g., AIG, Bear Stearns, Lehman Brothers, Merrill Lynch, Washington Mutual). Should these executives be allowed to retain the bonuses that they received in the 2007–2008 period? Should executive compensation at financial institutions be capped?

14. Impact of the Credit Crisis on Commercial Banks versus Securities Firms Both commercial banks and securities firms were adversely affected by the credit crisis, but for different reasons. Discuss the reasons for the adverse effects on commercial banks and securities firms and explain why the reasons were different.

15. Role of the Fed and the Treasury in the Credit Crisis Summarize the various ways in which the U.S. Treasury and the Federal Reserve intervened to resolve the credit crisis. Discuss the pros and cons of their interventions. Offer your own opinion regarding whether they should have intervened.

2
Determination of Interest Rates

CHAPTER OBJECTIVES

The specific objectives of this chapter are to:

■ apply the loanable funds theory to explain why interest rates change,

■ identify the most relevant factors that affect interest rate movements, and

■ explain how to forecast interest rates.

An interest rate reflects the rate of return that a creditor receives when lending money, or the rate that a borrower pays when borrowing money. Since interest rates change over time, so does the rate earned by creditors who provide loans or the rate paid by borrowers who obtain loans. Interest rate movements have a direct influence on the market values of debt securities, such as money market securities, bonds, and mortgages. They have an indirect influence on equity security values because they can affect the return by investors who invest in equity securities. Thus, participants in financial markets attempt to anticipate interest rate movements when restructuring their investment or loan positions.

Interest rate movements also affect the value of most financial institutions. They influence the cost of funds to depository institutions and the interest received on some loans by financial institutions. Since many financial institutions invest in securities (such as bonds), the market value of their investments is affected by interest rate movements. Thus managers of financial institutions attempt to anticipate interest rate movements and commonly restructure their assets and liabilities to capitalize on their expectations. Individuals attempt to anticipate interest rate movements so that they can monitor the potential cost of borrowing or the potential return from investing in various debt securities.

WEB

www.bloomberg.com
Information on interest rates in recent months.

2-1 LOANABLE FUNDS THEORY

The **loanable funds theory**, commonly used to explain interest rate movements, suggests that the market interest rate is determined by factors controlling the supply of and demand for loanable funds. The theory is especially useful for explaining movements in the general level of interest rates for a particular country. Furthermore, it can be used (along with other concepts) to explain why interest rates among some debt securities of a given country vary, which is the focus of the next chapter. The phrase "demand for loanable funds" is widely used in financial markets to refer to the borrowing activities of households, businesses, and governments. This chapter describes the sectors that commonly affect the demand for loanable funds and then describes the sectors that supply loanable funds to the markets. Finally, the demand and supply concepts are integrated to explain interest rate movements.

2-1a Household Demand for Loanable Funds

Households commonly demand loanable funds to finance housing expenditures. In addition, they finance the purchases of automobiles and household items, which results in installment debt. As the aggregate level of household income rises, so does installment debt. The level of installment debt as a percentage of disposable income has been increasing over time, although it is generally lower in recessionary periods.

If households could be surveyed at any given time to indicate the quantity of loanable funds they would demand at various interest rate levels, the results would reveal an inverse relationship between the interest rate and the quantity of loanable funds demanded. This simply means that, at any moment in time, households would demand a greater quantity of loanable funds at lower rates of interest; in other words, they are willing to borrow more money (in aggregate) at lower rates of interest.

EXAMPLE

Consider the household demand-for-loanable-funds schedule (also called the *demand curve*) in Exhibit 2.1, which shows how the amount of funds that would be demanded is dependent on the interest rate. Various events can cause household borrowing preferences to change and thereby shift the demand curve. For example, if tax rates on household income are expected to decrease significantly in the future, households might believe that they can more easily afford future loan repayments and thus be willing to borrow more funds. For any interest rate, the quantity of loanable funds demanded by households would be greater as a result of the tax rate change. This represents an outward shift (to the right) in the demand curve. ●

2-1b Business Demand for Loanable Funds

Businesses demand loanable funds to invest in long-term (fixed) and short-term assets. The quantity of funds demanded by businesses depends on the number of business projects to be implemented. Businesses evaluate a project by comparing the present value of its cash flows to its initial investment, as follows:

$$NPV = -INV + \sum_{t=1}^{n} \frac{CF_t}{(1+k)^t}$$

Exhibit 2.1   Relationship between Interest Rates and Household Demand (D_h) for Loanable Funds at a Given Point in Time

where

$$NPV = \text{net present value of project}$$
$$INV = \text{initial investment}$$
$$CF_t = \text{cash flow in period } t$$
$$k = \text{required rate of return on project}$$

Projects with a positive net present value (NPV) are accepted because the present value of their benefits outweighs the costs. The required return to implement a given project will be lower if interest rates are lower because the cost of borrowing funds to support the project will be lower. Hence more projects will have positive NPVs, and businesses will need a greater amount of financing. This implies that, all else being equal, businesses will demand a greater quantity of loanable funds when interest rates are lower; this relation is illustrated in Exhibit 2.2.

In addition to long-term assets, businesses also need funds to invest in their short-term assets (such as accounts receivable and inventory) in order to support ongoing operations. Any demand for funds resulting from this type of investment is positively related to the number of projects implemented and thus is inversely related to the interest rate. The opportunity cost of investing in short-term assets is higher when interest rates are higher. Therefore, firms generally attempt to support ongoing operations with fewer funds during periods of high interest rates. This is another reason that a firm's total demand for loanable funds is inversely related to prevailing interest rates. Although the demand for loanable funds by some businesses may be more sensitive to interest rates than others, all businesses are likely to demand more funds when interest rates are lower.

Shifts in the Demand for Loanable Funds

The business demand-for-loanable-funds schedule (as reflected by the demand curve in Exhibit 2.2) can change in reaction to any events that affect business borrowing preferences. If economic conditions become more favorable, the expected cash flows on various proposed projects will increase. More proposed projects will then have expected returns that exceed a particular required rate of return (sometimes called the *hurdle rate*). Additional projects will be acceptable as a result of more favorable economic forecasts, causing an increased demand for loanable funds. The increase in demand will result in an outward shift (to the right) in the demand curve.

WEB

www.treasurydirect.
gov
Information on the U.S.
government's debt.

Exhibit 2.2 Relationship between Interest Rates and Business Demand (D_b) for Loanable Funds at a Given Point in Time

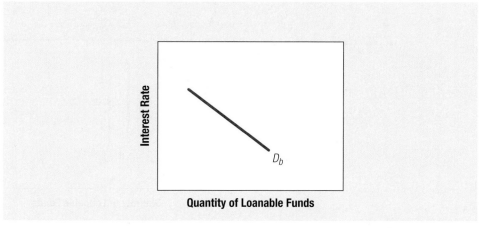

2-1c Government Demand for Loanable Funds

Whenever a government's planned expenditures cannot be completely covered by its incoming revenues from taxes and other sources, it demands loanable funds. Municipal (state and local) governments issue municipal bonds to obtain funds; the federal government and its agencies issue Treasury securities and federal agency securities. These securities constitute government debt.

The federal government's expenditure and tax policies are generally thought to be independent of interest rates. Thus the federal government's demand for funds is referred to as **interest-inelastic**, or insensitive to interest rates. In contrast, municipal governments sometimes postpone proposed expenditures if the cost of financing is too high, implying that their demand for loanable funds is somewhat sensitive to interest rates.

Like household and business demand, government demand for loanable funds can shift in response to various events.

EXAMPLE

The federal government's demand-for-loanable-funds schedule is represented by D_{g1} in Exhibit 2.3. If new bills are passed that cause a net increase of $200 billion in the deficit, the federal government's demand for loanable funds will increase by that amount. In the graph, this new demand schedule is represented by D_{g2}. ●

2-1d Foreign Demand for Loanable Funds

The demand for loanable funds in a given market also includes foreign demand by foreign governments or corporations. For example, the British government may obtain financing by issuing British Treasury securities to U.S. investors; this represents British demand for U.S. funds. Because foreign financial transactions are becoming so common, they can have a significant impact on the demand for loanable funds in any given country. A foreign country's demand for U.S. funds (i.e., preference to borrow U.S. dollars) is influenced by, among other factors, the difference between its own interest rates and U.S. rates. Other things being equal, a larger quantity of U.S. funds will be demanded by foreign governments and corporations if their domestic interest rates are high relative to U.S. rates. As a result, for a given set of foreign interest rates, the quantity of U.S. loanable funds demanded by foreign governments or firms will be inversely related to U.S. interest rates.

WEB

www.bloomberg.com/
markets
Interest rate
information.

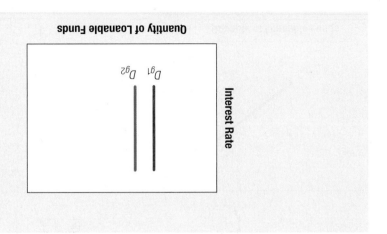

Exhibit 2.3 Impact of Increased Government Deficit on the Government Demand for Loanable Funds

Interest Rate

D_{g1} D_{g2}

Quantity of Loanable Funds

Exhibit 2.4   Impact of Increased Foreign Interest Rates on the Foreign Demand for U.S. Loanable Funds

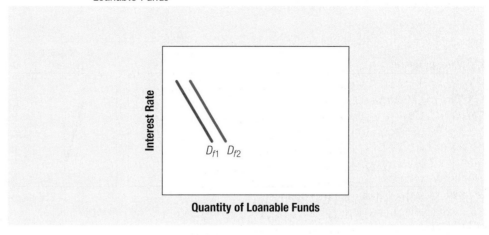

The foreign demand curve can shift in response to economic conditions. For example, assume the original foreign demand schedule is represented by D_{f1} in Exhibit 2.4. If foreign interest rates rise, foreign firms and governments will likely increase their demand for U.S. funds, as represented by the shift from D_{f1} to D_{f2}.

2-1e Aggregate Demand for Loanable Funds

The aggregate demand for loanable funds is the sum of the quantities demanded by the separate sectors at any given interest rate, as shown in Exhibit 2.5. Because most of these sectors are likely to demand a larger quantity of funds at lower interest rates (other things being equal), it follows that the aggregate demand for loanable funds is inversely related to the prevailing interest rate. If the demand schedule of any sector changes, the aggregate demand schedule will also be affected.

2-1f Supply of Loanable Funds

The term "supply of loanable funds" is commonly used to refer to funds provided to financial markets by savers. The household sector is the largest supplier, but loanable funds are also supplied by some government units that temporarily generate more tax revenues than they spend or by some businesses whose cash inflows exceed outflows. Yet households as a group are a net supplier of loanable funds, whereas governments and businesses are net demanders of loanable funds.

Suppliers of loanable funds are willing to supply more funds if the interest rate (reward for supplying funds) is higher, other things being equal. This means that the supply-of-loanable-funds schedule (also called the supply curve) is upward sloping, as shown in Exhibit 2.6. A supply of loanable funds exists at even a very low interest rate because some households choose to postpone consumption until later years, even when the reward (interest rate) for saving is low. Foreign households, governments, and businesses commonly supply funds to their domestic markets by purchasing domestic securities. In addition, they have been a major creditor to the U.S. government by purchasing large amounts of Treasury securities. The large foreign supply of funds to the U.S. market is due in part to the high saving rates of foreign households.

Effects of the Fed   The supply of loanable funds in the United States is also influenced by the monetary policy implemented by the Federal Reserve System. The Fed

Exhibit 2.5   Determination of the Aggregate Demand Curve for Loanable Funds

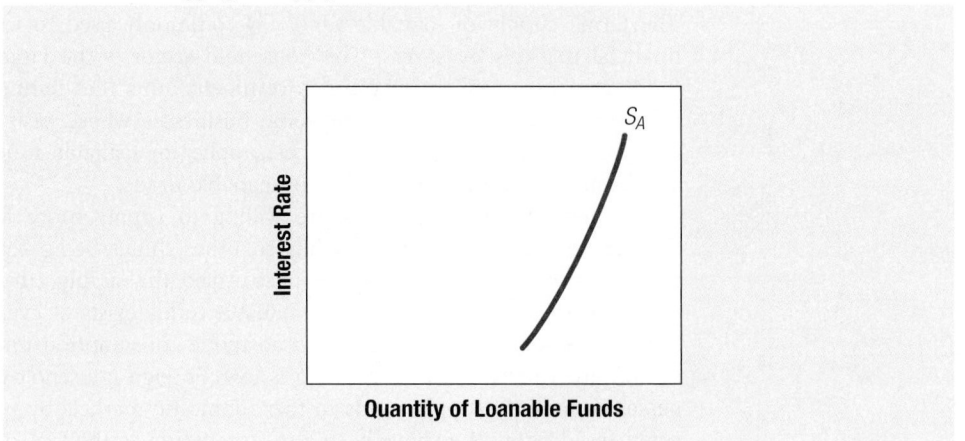

Exhibit 2.6   Aggregate Supply Curve for Loanable Funds

conducts monetary policy in an effort to control U.S. economic conditions. By affecting the supply of loanable funds, the Fed's monetary policy affects interest rates (as will be described shortly). By influencing interest rates, the Fed is able to influence the amount of money that corporations and households are willing to borrow and spend.

Aggregate Supply of Funds   The aggregate supply schedule of loanable funds represents the combination of all sector supply schedules along with the supply of funds provided by the Fed's monetary policy. The steep slope of the aggregate supply curve in Exhibit 2.6 means that it is interest-inelastic. The quantity of loanable funds demanded is normally expected to be more elastic, meaning more sensitive to interest rates, than the quantity of loanable funds supplied.

The supply curve can shift inward or outward in response to various conditions. For example, if the tax rate on interest income is reduced, then the supply curve will shift outward as households save more funds at each possible interest rate level. Conversely, if the tax rate on interest income is increased, then the supply curve will shift inward as households save fewer funds at each possible interest rate level.

In this section, minimal attention has been given to financial institutions. Although financial institutions play a critical intermediary role in channeling funds, they are not the ultimate suppliers of funds. Any change in a financial institution's supply of funds results only from a change in habits of the households, businesses, or governments that supply those funds.

2-1g Equilibrium Interest Rate

An understanding of equilibrium interest rates is necessary to assess how various events can affect interest rates. In reality, there are several different interest rates because some borrowers pay a higher rate than others. At this point, however, the focus is on the forces that cause the general level of interest rates to change, since interest rates across borrowers tend to change in the same direction. The determination of an equilibrium interest rate is presented first from an algebraic perspective and then from a graphical perspective. Following this presentation, several examples are offered to reinforce the concept.

Algebraic Presentation   The equilibrium interest rate is the rate that equates the aggregate demand for funds with the aggregate supply of loanable funds. The aggregate demand for funds (D_A) can be written as

$$D_A = D_h + D_b + D_g + D_m + D_f$$

where

$$D_h = \textbf{household demand for loanable funds}$$
$$D_b = \textbf{business demand for loanable funds}$$
$$D_g = \textbf{federal government demand for loanable funds}$$
$$D_m = \textbf{municipal government demand for loanable funds}$$
$$D_f = \textbf{foreign demand for loanable funds}$$

The aggregate supply of funds (SA) can likewise be written as

$$S_A = S_h + S_b + S_g + S_m + S_f$$

where

$$S_h = \textbf{household supply of loanable funds}$$
$$S_b = \textbf{business supply of loanable funds}$$
$$S_g = \textbf{federal government supply of loanable funds}$$
$$S_m = \textbf{municipal government supply of loanable funds}$$
$$S_f = \textbf{foreign supply of loanable funds}$$

In equilibrium, $D_A = S_A$. If the aggregate demand for loanable funds increases without a corresponding increase in aggregate supply, there will be a shortage of loanable funds. In this case, interest rates will rise until an additional supply of loanable funds is available to accommodate the excess demand. Conversely, an increase in the aggregate supply of loanable funds without a corresponding increase in aggregate demand will result in a surplus of loanable funds. In this case, interest rates will fall until the quantity of funds supplied no longer exceeds the quantity of funds demanded.

In many cases, both supply and demand for loanable funds are changing. Given an initial equilibrium situation, the equilibrium interest rate should rise when $D_A > S_A$ and fall when $D_A S_A$.

Graphical Presentation   By combining the aggregate demand and aggregate supply curves of loanable funds (refer to Exhibits 2.5 and 2.6), it is possible to compare the total amount of funds that would be demanded to the total amount of funds that would be supplied at any particular interest rate. Exhibit 2.7 illustrates the combined demand and supply schedules. At the equilibrium interest rate of i, the supply of loanable funds is equal to the demand for loanable funds.

At any interest rate above i, there is a surplus of loanable funds. Some potential suppliers of funds will be unable to successfully supply their funds at the prevailing interest rate. Once the market interest rate decreases to i, the quantity of funds supplied is sufficiently reduced and the quantity of funds demanded is sufficiently increased such that there is no longer a surplus of funds. When a disequilibrium situation exists, market forces should cause an adjustment in interest rates until equilibrium is achieved.

If the prevailing interest rate is below i, there will be a shortage of loanable funds; borrowers will not be able to obtain all the funds that they desire at that rate. The shortage of funds will cause the interest rate to increase, resulting in two reactions. First, more savers will enter the market to supply loanable funds because the reward (interest rate) is now higher. Second, some potential borrowers will decide not to demand loanable funds at the higher interest rate. Once the interest rate rises to i, the quantity of loanable funds supplied has increased and the quantity of loanable funds demanded has decreased to the extent that a shortage no longer exists. Thus an equilibrium position is achieved once again.

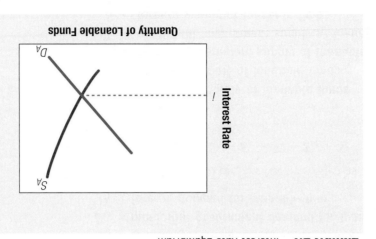

Exhibit 2.7   Interest Rate Equilibrium

2-2 FACTORS THAT AFFECT INTEREST RATES

Although it is useful to identify those who supply or demand loanable funds, it is also necessary to recognize the underlying economic forces that cause a change in either the supply of or the demand for loanable funds. The following economic factors influence this supply and demand and thereby influence interest rates.

2-2a Impact of Economic Growth on Interest Rates

Changes in economic conditions cause a shift in the demand curve for loanable funds, which affects the equilibrium interest rate.

EXAMPLE

When businesses anticipate that economic conditions will improve, they revise upward the cash flows expected for various projects under consideration. Consequently, businesses identify more projects that are worth pursuing, and they are willing to borrow more funds. Their willingness to borrow more funds at any given interest rate reflects an outward shift (to the right) in the demand curve.

The supply-of-loanable-funds schedule may also change in response to economic growth, but it is difficult to know in which direction it will shift. It is possible that the increased expansion by businesses will lead to more income for construction crews and others who service the expansion. In this case, the quantity of savings (loanable funds supplied) could increase regardless of the interest rate, causing an outward shift in the supply schedule. However, there is no assurance that the volume of savings will actually increase. Even if such a shift does occur, it will likely be of smaller magnitude than the shift in the demand schedule.

Overall, the expected impact of the increased expansion by businesses is an outward shift in the demand curve but no obvious change in the supply schedule; see Exhibit 2.8. Note that the shift in the aggregate demand curve to $DA2$ causes an increase in the equilibrium interest rate to i_2. ●

Just as economic growth puts upward pressure on interest rates, an economic slowdown puts downward pressure on the equilibrium interest rate.

EXAMPLE

A slowdown in the economy will cause the demand curve to shift inward (to the left), reflecting less demand for loanable funds at any given interest rate. The supply curve may shift a little, but the direction of its shift is uncertain. One could argue that a slowdown should cause increased saving (regardless of the interest rate) as households prepare for possible layoffs. At the same time, the gradual reduction in labor income that occurs during an economic slowdown could reduce

Exhibit 2.8   Impact of Increased Expansion by Firms

households' ability to save. Historical data support this latter expectation. Once again, any shift that does occur will likely be minor relative to the shift in the demand schedule. The equilibrium interest rate is therefore expected to decrease, as illustrated in Exhibit 2.9. ●

2-2b Impact of Inflation on Interest Rates

Changes in inflationary expectations can affect interest rates by affecting the amount of spending by households or businesses. Decisions to spend affect the amount saved (supply of funds) and the amount borrowed (demand for funds).

EXAMPLE

Assume the U.S. inflation rate is expected to increase. Households that supply funds may reduce their savings at any interest rate level so that they can make more purchases now before prices rise. This shift in behavior is reflected by an inward shift (to the left) in the supply curve of loanable funds. In addition, households and businesses may be willing to borrow more funds at any interest rate level so that they can purchase products now before prices increase. This is reflected by an outward shift (to the right) in the demand curve for loanable funds. These shifts are illustrated in Exhibit 2.10. The new equilibrium interest rate is higher because of these shifts in saving and borrowing behavior. ●

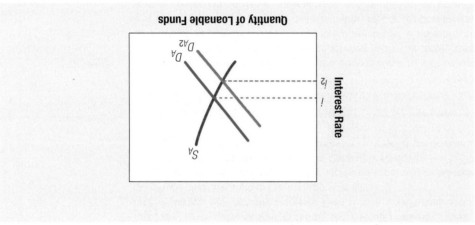

Exhibit 2.9 Impact of an Economic Slowdown

Exhibit 2.10 Impact of an Increase in Inflationary Expectations on Interest Rates

Fisher Effect More than 70 years ago, Irving Fisher proposed a theory of interest rate determination that is still widely used today. It does not contradict the loanable funds theory but simply offers an additional explanation for interest rate movements. Fisher proposed that nominal interest payments compensate savers in two ways. First, they compensate for a saver's reduced purchasing power. Second, they provide an additional premium to savers for forgoing present consumption. Savers are willing to forgo consumption only if they receive a premium on their savings above the anticipated rate of inflation, as shown in the following equation:

$$i = E(\text{INF}) + i_R$$

where

$$i = \text{nominal or quoted rate of interest}$$
$$E(\text{INF}) = \text{expected inflation rate}$$
$$i_R = \text{real interest rate}$$

This relationship between interest rates and expected inflation is often referred to as the Fisher effect. The difference between the nominal interest rate and the expected inflation rate is the real return to a saver after adjusting for the reduced purchasing power over the time period of concern. It is referred to as the **real interest rate** because, unlike the nominal rate of interest, it adjusts for the expected rate of inflation. The preceding equation can be rearranged to express the real interest rate as

$$i_R = i - E(\text{INF})$$

WEB

www.federalreserve. gov/monetarypolicy/ fomc.htm
Information on how the Fed controls the money supply.

When the inflation rate is higher than anticipated, the real interest rate is relatively low. Borrowers benefit because they were able to borrow at a lower nominal interest rate than would have been offered if inflation had been accurately forecasted. When the inflation rate is lower than anticipated, the real interest rate is relatively high and borrowers are adversely affected.

Throughout the text, the term "interest rate" will be used to represent the *nominal*, or *quoted*, rate of interest. Keep in mind, however, that inflation may prevent purchasing power from increasing during periods of rising interest rates.

2-2c Impact of Monetary Policy on Interest Rates

The Federal Reserve can affect the supply of loanable funds by increasing or reducing the total amount of deposits held at commercial banks or other depository institutions. The process by which the Fed adjusts the money supply is described in Chapter 4. When the Fed increases the money supply, it increases the supply of loanable funds and this places downward pressure on interest rates.

EXAMPLE

The credit crisis intensified during the fall of 2008, and economic conditions weakened. The Fed increased the money supply in the banking system as a means of ensuring that funds were available for households or businesses that wanted to borrow funds. Consequently, financial institutions had more funds available that they could lend. The increase in the supply of loanable funds placed downward pressure on interest rates. Because the demand for loanable funds decreased during this period (as explained previously), the downward pressure on interest rates was even more pronounced. Interest rates declined substantially in the fall of 2008 in response to these two forces.

Since the economy remained weak even after the credit crisis, the Fed continued its policy of injecting funds into the banking system during the 2009–2013 period in order to keep interest rates (the cost of borrowing) low. Its policy was intended to encourage corporations and households to borrow and spend money, in order to stimulate the economy. ●

If the Fed reduces the money supply, it reduces the supply of loanable funds. Assuming no change in demand, this action places upward pressure on interest rates.

2-2d Impact of the Budget Deficit on Interest Rates

When the federal government enacts fiscal policies that result in more expenditures than tax revenue, the budget deficit is increased. Because of large budget deficits in recent years, the U.S. government is a major participant in the demand for loanable funds. A higher federal government deficit increases the quantity of loanable funds demanded at any prevailing interest rate, which causes an outward shift in the demand curve. Assuming that all other factors are held constant, interest rates will rise. Given a finite amount of loanable funds supplied to the market (through savings), excessive government demand for these funds tends to "crowd out" the private demand (by consumers and corporations) for funds. The federal government may be willing to pay whatever is necessary to borrow these funds, but the private sector may not. This impact is known as the **crowding-out effect.** Exhibit 2.11 illustrates the flow of funds between the federal government and the private sector.

There is a counterargument that the supply curve might shift outward if the government creates more jobs by spending more funds than it collects from the public (this is what causes the deficit in the first place). If this were to occur, then the deficit might not place upward pressure on interest rates. Much research has investigated this issue and has generally shown that, when holding other factors constant, higher budget deficits place upward pressure on interest rates.

2-2e Impact of Foreign Flows of Funds on Interest Rates

GLOBAL ASPECTS

The interest rate for a specific currency is determined by the demand for funds denominated in that currency and the supply of funds available in that currency.

EXAMPLE

The supply and demand curves for the U.S. dollar and for Brazil's currency, the *real*, are compared for a given point in time in Exhibit 2.12. Although the demand curve for loanable funds should be downward sloping for every currency and the supply schedule should be upward sloping, the actual positions of these curves vary among currencies. First, notice that the demand and supply curves are farther to the right than for the dollar than for the Brazilian real. The amount of U.S. dollar-denominated loanable funds supplied and demanded is much greater than the amount of Brazilian real-denominated loanable funds because the U.S. economy is much larger than Brazil's economy.

Exhibit 2.11   Flow of Funds between the Federal Government and the Private Sector

Exhibit 2.12 Demand and Supply Curves for Loanable Funds Denominated in U.S. Dollars and Brazilian Real

Observe also that the positions of the demand and supply curves for loanable funds are much higher for the Brazilian real than for the dollar. The supply schedule for loanable funds denominated in Brazilian real shows that hardly any amount of savings would be supplied at low interest rate levels because the relatively high inflation in Brazil encourages households to spend more of their disposable income before prices increase. This discourages households from saving unless the interest rate is sufficiently high. In addition, the demand for loanable funds denominated in Brazilian real shows that borrowers are willing to borrow even at relatively high rates of interest because they want to make purchases now before prices increase. Firms are willing to pay 15 percent interest on a loan to purchase machines whose prices may increase 20 percent by the following year.

Because of the different positions of the demand and supply curves for the two currencies shown in Exhibit 2.12, the equilibrium interest rate is much higher for the Brazilian real than for the dollar. As the demand and supply schedules change over time for a specific currency, so will the equilibrium interest rate. For example, if Brazil's government could substantially reduce local inflation, then the supply curve of loanable funds denominated in the Brazilian real would shift out (to the right) while the demand schedule of loanable funds would shift in (to the left). The result would be a lower equilibrium interest rate. ●

In recent years, massive flows of funds have shifted between countries, causing abrupt adjustments in the supply of funds available in each country and thereby affecting interest rates. In general, the shifts are driven by large institutional investors seeking a high return on their investments. These investors commonly attempt to invest funds in debt securities in countries where interest rates are high. However, many countries that typically have relatively high interest rates also tend to have high inflation, which can weaken their local currencies. Since the depreciation (decline in value) of a currency can more than offset a high interest rate in some cases, investors tend to avoid investing in countries with high interest rates if the threat of inflation is very high.

2-2f Summary of Forces That Affect Interest Rates

In general, economic conditions are the primary forces behind a change in the supply of savings provided by households or a change in the demand for funds by households, businesses, or the government. The saving behavior of the households that supply funds in the United States is partially influenced by U.S. fiscal policy, which determines the taxes paid by U.S. households and thus determines the level of disposable income. The Federal Reserve's monetary policy also affects the supply of funds in the United States because it determines the U.S. money supply. The supply of funds provided to the United States by foreign investors is influenced by foreign economic conditions, including foreign interest rates.

The demand for funds in the United States is indirectly affected by U.S. monetary and fiscal policies because these policies influence economic growth and inflation, which in turn affect business demand for funds. Fiscal policy determines the budget deficit and therefore determines the federal government demand for funds.

WEB

http://research.
stlouisfed.org/fred2
Time series of various
interest rates provided
by the Federal Reserve
Economic Databank.

EXAMPLE

Exhibit 2.13 plots U.S. interest rates over recent decades and illustrates how they are affected by the forces of monetary and fiscal policy. From 2000 to the beginning of 2003, the U.S. economy was very weak, which reduced the business and household demand for loanable funds and caused interest rates to decline. During the period 2005-2007, U.S. economic growth increased and interest rates rose.

However, the credit crisis that began in 2008 caused the economy to weaken substantially, and interest rates declined to extremely low levels. During the crisis, the federal government experienced a huge budget deficit as it bailed out some firms and increased its spending in various ways to stimulate the economy. Although the large government demand for funds placed upward pressure on interest rates, this pressure was offset by a weak demand for funds by firms (as businesses canceled their plans to expand). In addition, the Federal Reserve increased the money supply at this time in order to push interest rates lower in an attempt to encourage businesses and households to borrow and spend money. The weak economy and the Fed's monetary policy continued during the next four years, which allowed interest rates to remain at very low levels. The Fed's monetary policy had more influence on U.S. interest rates than any other factor during the 2008-2013 period. In some other periods, the monetary policy is not as pronounced, and other factors have more influence on interest rates. ●

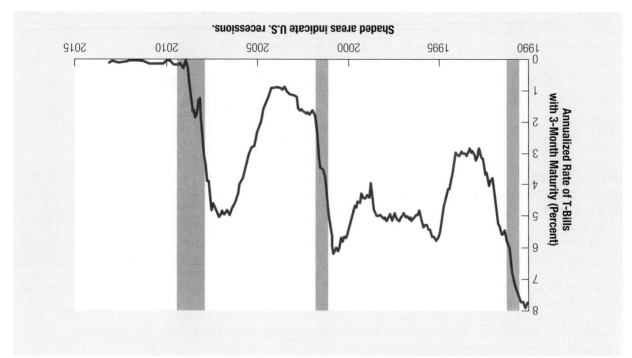

Exhibit 2.13 Interest Rate Movements over Time

Annualized Rate of T-Bills with 3-Month Maturity (Percent)

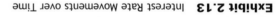

Shaded areas indicate U.S. recessions.

Exhibit 2.14   Framework for Forecasting Interest Rates

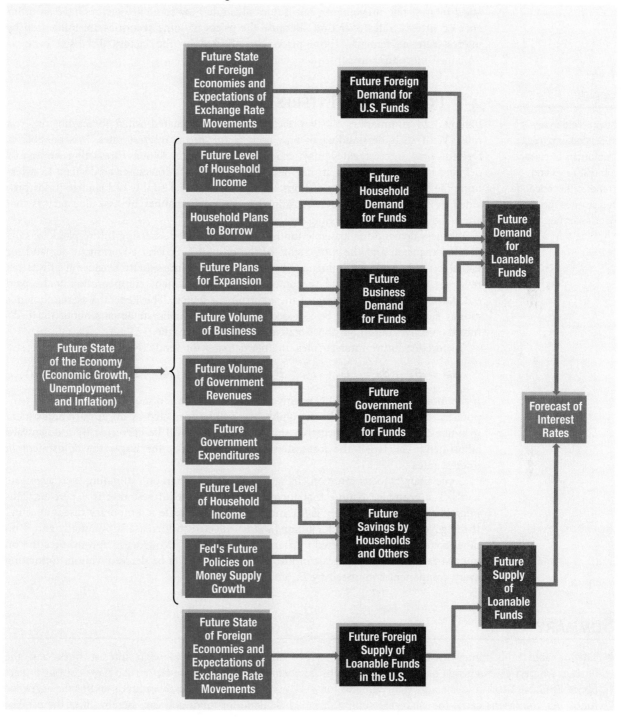

This summary does not cover every possible interaction among the forces that can affect interest rate movements, but it does illustrate how some key factors have an influence on interest rates over time. Because the prices of some securities are influenced by interest rate movements, those prices are affected by the factors discussed here, as explained more fully in subsequent chapters.

2-3 FORECASTING INTEREST RATES

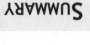

WEB

http://research.
stlouisfed.org/fred2
Quotations of current
interest rates and
trends of historical in-
terest rates for various
debt securities.

Exhibit 2.14 summarizes the key factors that are evaluated when forecasting interest rates. With an understanding of how each factor affects interest rates, it is possible to forecast how interest rates may change in the future. When forecasting household demand for loanable funds, it may be necessary to assess consumer credit data to determine the borrowing capacity of households. The potential supply of loanable funds provided by households may be determined in a similar manner by assessing factors that affect the earning power of households.

Business demand for loanable funds can be forecast by assessing future plans for corporate expansion and the future state of the economy. Federal government demand for loanable funds could be influenced by the economy's future state because it affects tax revenues to be received and the amount of unemployment compensation to be paid out, factors that affect the size of the government deficit. The Federal Reserve System's money supply targets may be assessed by reviewing public statements about the Fed's future objectives, although those statements are rather vague.

To forecast future interest rates, the net demand for funds (ND) should be forecast:

$$ND = D_A - S_A = (D_h + D_b + D_g + D_f) - (S_h + S_b + S_g + S_m + S_f)$$

If the forecasted level of ND is positive or negative, then a disequilibrium will exist temporarily. If ND is positive, the disequilibrium will be corrected by an upward adjustment in interest rates; if ND is negative, the disequilibrium will be corrected by a downward adjustment. The larger the forecasted magnitude of ND, the larger the adjustment in interest rates.

Some analysts focus more on changes in D_A and S_A than on estimating their aggregate levels. For example, assume that today the equilibrium interest rate is 7 percent. This interest rate will change only if D_A and S_A change to create a temporary disequilibrium. If the government demand for funds (D_g) is expected to increase substantially and if no other components are expected to change, D_A will exceed S_A, placing upward pressure on interest rates. Thus the forecast of future interest rates can be derived without estimating every component comprised by D_A and S_A.

SUMMARY

■ The loanable funds framework shows how the equilibrium interest rate depends on the aggregate supply of available funds and the aggregate demand for funds. As conditions cause the aggregate supply or demand schedules to change, interest rates gravitate toward a new equilibrium.

■ The relevant factors that affect interest rate movements include changes in economic growth, inflation, the budget deficit, foreign interest rates, and the money supply. These factors can have a strong impact on the aggregate supply of funds and/or the aggregate demand for funds and can thereby affect the equilibrium interest rate. In particular, economic growth has a strong influence on the demand for loanable funds, and changes in the money supply have a strong impact on the supply of loanable funds.

■ Given that the equilibrium interest rate is determined by supply and demand conditions, changes in the interest rate can be forecasted by forecasting changes in the supply of and the demand for loanable funds. Thus, the factors that influence the supply of funds and the demand for funds must be forecast in order to forecast interest rates.

POINT COUNTER-POINT

Does a Large Fiscal Budget Deficit Result in Higher Interest Rates?

Point   No. In some years (such as 2008), the fiscal budget deficit was large but interest rates were very low.

Counter-Point   Yes. When the federal government borrows large amounts of funds, it can crowd out other potential borrowers, and the interest rates are bid up by the deficit units.

Who Is Correct?   Use the Internet to learn more about this issue and then formulate your own opinion.

QUESTIONS AND APPLICATIONS

1. Interest Rate Movements Explain why interest rates changed as they did over the past year.

2. Interest Elasticity Explain what is meant by interest elasticity. Would you expect the federal government's demand for loanable funds to be more or less interest-elastic than household demand for loanable funds? Why?

3. Impact of Government Spending If the federal government planned to expand the space program, how might this affect interest rates?

4. Impact of a Recession Explain why interest rates tend to decrease during recessionary periods. Review historical interest rates to determine how they reacted to recessionary periods. Explain this reaction.

5. Impact of the Economy Explain how the expected interest rate in one year depends on your expectation of economic growth and inflation.

6. Impact of the Money Supply Should increasing money supply growth place upward or downward pressure on interest rates?

7. Impact of Exchange Rates on Interest Rates Assume that if the U.S. dollar strengthens it can place downward pressure on U.S. inflation. Based on this information, how might expectations of a strong dollar affect the demand for loanable funds in the United States and U.S. interest rates? Is there any reason to think that expectations of a strong dollar could also affect the supply of loanable funds? Explain.

8. Nominal versus Real Interest Rate What is the difference between the nominal interest rate and the real interest rate? What is the logic behind the implied positive relationship between expected inflation and nominal interest rates?

9. Real Interest Rate Estimate the real interest rate over the last year. If financial market participants overestimate inflation in a particular period, will real interest rates be relatively high or low? Explain.

10. Forecasting Interest Rates Why do forecasts of interest rates differ among experts?

Advanced Questions

11. Impact of Stock Market Crises During periods when investors suddenly become fearful that stocks are overvalued, they dump their stocks and the stock market experiences a major decline. During these periods, interest rates also tend to decline. Use the loanable funds framework discussed in this chapter to explain how the massive selling of stocks leads to lower interest rates.

12. Impact of Expected Inflation How might expectations of higher oil prices affect the demand for loanable funds, the supply of loanable funds, and interest rates in the United States? Will the interest rates of other countries be affected in the same way? Explain.

13. Global Interaction of Interest Rates Why might you expect interest rate movements of various industrialized countries to be more highly correlated in recent years than in earlier years?

14. Impact of War War tends to cause significant reactions in financial markets. Why would a war in Iraq place upward pressure on U.S. interest rates? Why might some investors expect a war like this to place downward pressure on U.S. interest rates?

15. Impact of September 11 Offer an argument for why the terrorist attack on the United States on September 11, 2001, could have placed downward pressure on U.S. interest rates. Offer an argument for why that attack could have placed upward pressure on U.S. interest rates.

16. Impact of Government Spending Jayhawk Forecasting Services analyzed several factors that could affect interest rates in the future. Most factors were expected to place downward pressure on interest rates. Jayhawk also expected that, although the annual budget deficit was to be cut by 40 percent from the previous year, it would still be very large. Thus, Jayhawk believed that the deficit's impact would more than offset the effects of other factors, so it forecast interest rates to increase by 2 percentage points. Comment on Jayhawk's logic.

17. Decomposing Interest Rate Movements The interest rate on a one-year loan can be decomposed into a one-year, risk-free (free from default risk) component and a risk premium that reflects the potential for default on the loan in that year. A change in economic conditions can affect the risk-free rate and the risk premium. The risk-free rate is normally affected by changing economic conditions to a greater degree than is the risk premium. Explain how a weaker economy will likely affect the risk-free component, the risk premium, and the overall cost of a one-year loan obtained by (a) the Treasury and (b) a corporation. Will the change in the cost of borrowing be more pronounced for the Treasury or for the corporation? Why?

18. Forecasting Interest Rates Based on Prevailing Conditions Consider the prevailing conditions for inflation (including oil prices), the economy, the budget deficit, and the Fed's monetary policy that could affect interest rates. Based on these conditions, do you think interest rates will likely increase or decrease during this semester? Offer some logic to support your answer. Which factor do you think will have the greatest impact on interest rates?

19. Impact of Economic Crises on Interest Rates When economic crises in countries are due to a weak economy, local interest rates tend to be very low. However, if the crisis was caused by an unusually high rate of inflation, interest rates tend to be very high. Explain why.

20. U.S. Interest Rates during the Credit Crisis During the credit crisis, U.S. interest rates were extremely low, which enabled businesses to borrow at a low cost. Holding other factors constant, this should result in a higher number of feasible projects, which should encourage businesses to borrow more money and expand. Yet many businesses that had access to loanable funds were unwilling to borrow during the credit crisis. What other factor changed during this period that more than offset the potentially favorable effect of the low interest rates on project feasibility, thereby discouraging businesses from expanding?

21. Political Influence on Interest Rates Offer an argument for why a political regime that favors a large government will cause interest rates to be higher. Offer at least one example of why a political regime that favors a large government will cause interest rates to be lower. [Hint: Recognize that the government intervention in the economy can influence other factors that affect interest rates.]

22. Impact of Stock Market Uncertainty Consider a period in which stock prices are very high, such that investors begin to think that stocks are overvalued and their valuations are very uncertain. If investors decide to move their money into much safer investments, how do you think this would affect general interest rate levels? In your answer, use the loanable funds framework by explaining how the supply or demand for loanable funds would be affected by the investor actions, and how this force would affect interest rates.

23. Impact of the European Economy In 2012, some economists suggested that U.S. interest rates are dictated by the weak economic conditions in Europe. Use the loanable funds framework to explain how European economic conditions might affect U.S. interest rates.

Interpreting Financial News

Interpret the following comments made by Wall Street analysts and portfolio managers.

a. "The flight of funds from bank deposits to U.S. stocks will pressure interest rates."

b. "Since Japanese interest rates have recently declined to very low levels, expect a reduction in U.S. interest rates."

c. "The cost of borrowing by U.S. firms is dictated by the degree to which the federal government spends more than it taxes."

Managing in Financial Markets

Forecasting Interest Rates As the treasurer of a manufacturing company, your task is to forecast the direction of interest rates. You plan to borrow funds and may use the forecast of interest rates to determine whether you should obtain a loan with a fixed interest rate or a floating interest rate. The following information can be considered when assessing the future direction of interest rates.

■ Economic growth has been high over the last two years, but you expect that it will be stagnant over the next year.

■ Inflation has been 3 percent over each of the last few years, and you expect that it will be about the same over the next year.

■ The federal government has announced major cuts in its spending, which should have a major impact on the budget deficit.

■ The Federal Reserve is not expected to affect the existing supply of loanable funds over the next year.

■ The overall level of savings by households is not expected to change.

a. Given the preceding information, assess how the demand for and the supply of loanable funds would be affected, if at all, and predict the future direction of interest rates.

b. You can obtain a one-year loan at a fixed rate of 8 percent or a floating-rate loan that is currently at 8 percent but would be revised every month in accordance with general interest rate movements. Which type of loan is more appropriate based on the information provided?

c. Assume that Canadian interest rates have abruptly risen just as you have completed your forecast of future U.S. interest rates. Consequently, Canadian interest rates are now 2 percentage points above U.S. interest rates. How might this specific situation place pressure on U.S. interest rates? Considering this situation along with the other information provided, would you change your forecast of the future direction of U.S. interest rates?

PROBLEMS

1. Nominal Rate of Interest Suppose the real interest rate is 6 percent and the expected inflation rate is 2 percent. What would you expect the nominal rate of interest to be?

2. Real Interest Rate Suppose that Treasury bills are currently paying 9 percent and the expected inflation rate is 3 percent. What is the real interest rate?

FLOW OF FUNDS EXERCISE

How the Flow of Funds Affects Interest Rates

Recall that Carson Company has obtained substantial loans from finance companies and commercial banks. The interest rate on the loans is tied to market interest rates and is adjusted every six months. Thus, Carson's cost of obtaining funds is sensitive to interest rate movements. Given its expectations that the U.S. economy will strengthen, Carson plans to grow in the future by expanding and by making acquisitions. Carson expects that it will need substantial long-term financing to pay for this growth, and it plans to borrow additional funds either through existing loans or by issuing bonds. The company is also considering the possibility of issuing stock to raise funds in the next year.

a. Explain why Carson should be very interested in future interest rate movements.

b. Given Carson's expectations, do you think the company anticipates that interest rates will increase or decrease in the future? Explain.

c. If Carson's expectations of future interest rates are correct, how would this affect its cost of borrowing on its existing loans and on its future loans?

d. Explain why Carson's expectations about future interest rates may affect its decision about when to borrow funds and whether to obtain floating-rate or fixed-rate loans.

INTERNET/EXCEL EXERCISES

1. Go to http://research.stlouisfed.org/fred2. Under "Categories," select "Interest rates" and then select the three-month Treasury-bill series (secondary market). Describe how this rate has changed in recent months. Using the information in this chapter, explain why the interest rate changed as it did.

2. Using the same website, retrieve data at the beginning of the last 20 quarters for interest rates (based on the three-month Treasury-bill rate) and the producer price index for all commodities and place the data in two columns of an Excel spreadsheet. Derive the change in interest rates on a quarterly basis. Then derive the percentage change in the producer price index on a quarterly basis, which serves as a measure of inflation. Apply regression analysis in which the change in interest rates is the dependent variable and inflation is the independent variable (see Appendix B for information about applying regression analysis). Explain the relationship that you find. Does it appear that inflation and interest rate movements are positively related?

WSJ EXERCISE

Forecasting Interest Rates

Review information about the credit markets in a recent issue of the *Wall Street Journal*. Identify the factors that are given attention because they may affect future interest rate movements. Then create your own forecasts as to whether interest rates will increase or decrease from now until the end of the school term, based on your assessment of any factors that affect interest rates. Explain your forecast.

ONLINE ARTICLES WITH REAL-WORLD EXAMPLES

Find a recent practical article available online that describes a real-world example regarding a specific financial institution or financial market that reinforces one or more concepts covered in this chapter.

If your class has an online component, your professor may ask you to post your summary of the article there and provide a link to the article so that other students can access it. If your class is live, your professor may ask you to summarize your application of the article in class. Your professor may assign specific students to do the assignment on a volunteer basis.

For recent online articles and real-world examples related to this chapter, consider using the following search terms (be sure to include the prevailing year as a search term to ensure that the online articles are recent):

1. budget deficit AND interest rate
2. flow of funds AND interest rate
3. Federal Reserve AND interest rate
4. economic growth AND interest rate
5. inflation AND interest rate
6. monetary policy AND interest rate
7. supply of savings AND interest rate
8. business expansion AND interest rate
9. demand for credit AND interest rate
10. interest rate AND forecast

3
Structure of Interest Rates

CHAPTER
OBJECTIVES

The specific
objectives of this
chapter are to:

■ describe how
characteristics of
debt securities
cause their yields
to vary,

■ demonstrate how
to estimate the
appropriate yield
for any particular
debt security, and

■ explain the
theories behind the
term structure of
interest rates
(relationship
between the term
to maturity and the
yield of securities).

The annual interest rate offered by debt securities at any given time varies among debt securities. Individual and institutional investors must understand why quoted yields vary so that they can determine whether the extra yield on a given security outweighs any unfavorable characteristics. Financial managers of corporations or government agencies in need of funds must understand why quoted yields of debt securities vary so that they can estimate the yield they would have to offer in order to sell new debt securities.

3-1 WHY DEBT SECURITY YIELDS VARY

Debt securities offer different yields because they exhibit different characteristics that influence the yield to be offered. In general, securities with unfavorable characteristics will offer higher yields to entice investors. Some debt securities have favorable features; therefore, they can offer relatively low yields and still attract investors. The yields on debt securities are affected by the following characteristics:

■ Credit (default) risk
■ Liquidity
■ Tax status
■ Term to maturity

The yields on bonds may also be affected by special provisions, as described in Chapter 7.

3-1a Credit (Default) Risk

Because most securities are subject to the risk of default, investors must consider the creditworthiness of the security issuer. Although investors always have the option of purchasing risk-free Treasury securities, they may prefer other securities if the yield compensates them for the risk. Thus, if all other characteristics besides credit (default) risk are equal, securities with a higher degree of default risk must offer higher yields before investors will purchase them.

EXAMPLE   Investors can purchase a Treasury bond with a 10-year maturity that presently offers an annualized yield of 7 percent if they hold the bond until maturity. Alternatively, investors can purchase bonds that are being issued by Zanstell Co. Although Zanstell is in good financial condition, there is a small possibility that it could file for bankruptcy during the next 10 years, in which case it would discontinue making payments to investors who purchased the bonds. Thus there is a small possibility that investors could lose most of their investment in these bonds. The only way in which investors would even consider purchasing bonds issued by Zanstell Co. is if the annualized yield offered on these bonds is higher than the Treasury bond yield. Zanstell's bonds presently offer a yield of 8 percent, which is 1 percent higher than the yield offered on Treasury bonds. At this yield, some investors are willing to purchase Zanstell's bonds because they think Zanstell Co. should have sufficient cash flows to repay its debt over the next 10 years. ●

Credit risk is especially relevant for longer-term securities that expose creditors to the possibility of default for a longer time. Credit risk premiums of 1 percent, 2 percent, or more may not seem significant. But for a corporation borrowing $30 million through the issuance of bonds, an extra percentage point as a premium reflects $300,000 in additional interest expenses per year.

Investors can personally assess the creditworthiness of corporations that issue bonds, but they may prefer to rely on bond ratings provided by rating agencies. These ratings are based on a financial assessment of the issuing corporation, with a focus on whether the corporation will receive sufficient cash flows over time to cover its payments to bondholders. The higher the rating on the bond, the lower the perceived credit risk.

As time passes, economic conditions can change, which can influence the ability of a corporation to repay its debt. Thus bonds previously issued by a firm may be rated at one level, whereas a subsequent issue from the same firm is rated at a different level. The ratings can also differ if the collateral provisions differ among the bonds. Rating agencies can also change bond ratings over time in response to changes in the issuing firm's financial condition or to changes in economic conditions.

3-1b Assessing Credit Risk

To assess the credit risk of a corporation that issues bonds, investors can evaluate the corporation's financial statements. Specifically, investors use financial statements to predict the level of cash flows a corporation will generate over future periods, which helps determine if the company will have sufficient cash flows to cover its debt payments. However, financial statements might not indicate how a corporation will perform in the future. Many corporations that were in good financial condition just before they issued debt failed before they repaid their debt.

Rating Agencies Many investors rely heavily on the ratings of debt securities assigned by rating agencies, so that they do not have to assess the financial statements of corporations. The rating agencies charge the issuers of debt securities a fee for assessing the credit risk of those securities. The ratings are then provided through various financial media outlets at no cost to investors. The most popular rating agencies are Moody's Investors Service and Standard & Poor's Corporation. A summary of their rating classification schedules is provided in Exhibit 3.1. The ratings issued by Moody's range from Aaa for the highest quality to C for the lowest quality, and those issued by Standard & Poor's range from AAA to D. Because these rating agencies use different methods to assess the creditworthiness of firms and state governments, a particular bond could be rated at a different quality level by each agency. However, the differences are usually small.

Commercial banks typically invest only in **investment-grade bonds**, which are bonds rated as Baa or better by Moody's and as BBB or better by Standard & Poor's. Other financial institutions, such as pension funds and insurance companies, invest in bonds that are rated lower and offer the potential for higher returns.

WEB
www.moodys.com
Credit rating information.

Exhibit 3.1 Rating Classification by Rating Agencies

DESCRIPTION OF SECURITY	RATINGS ASSIGNED BY:	
	MOODY'S	STANDARD & POOR'S
Highest quality	Aaa	AAA
High quality	Aa	AA
High-medium quality	A	A
Medium quality	Baa	BBB
Medium-low quality	Ba	BB
Low quality (speculative)	B	B
Poor quality	Caa	CCC
Very poor quality	Ca	CC
Lowest quality (in default)	C	DDD, D

Accuracy of Credit Ratings   The ratings issued by the agencies are opinions, not guarantees. Bonds that are assigned a low credit rating experience default more frequently than bonds assigned a high credit rating, which suggests that the rating can be a useful indicator of credit risk. However, credit rating agencies do not always detect firms' financial problems.

Credit rating agencies were criticized for being too liberal in their assignment of ratings on debt issued shortly before the credit crisis, as many highly rated debt issues defaulted over the next few years. The credit rating agencies might counter that they could not have anticipated the credit crisis and that they used all the information available to them when assigning ratings to new securities. Yet because credit rating agencies are paid by the issuers of debt securities and not the investors who purchase those securities, agencies may have a natural incentive to assign a high rating. Doing so facilitates a firm's issuing of debt securities, which in turn should attract more business from other issuers of debt securities.

In response to the criticism, credit rating agencies made some changes to improve their rating process and their transparency. They now disclose more information about how they derived their credit ratings. In addition, employees of each credit rating agency that promote the services of the agency are not allowed to influence the ratings assigned by the rating agency. They are giving more attention to sensitivity analysis in which they assess how creditworthiness might change in response to abrupt changes in the economy.

Oversight of Credit Rating Agencies   The Financial Reform Act of 2010 established an Office of Credit Ratings within the Securities and Exchange Commission in order to regulate credit rating agencies. The act also mandated that credit rating agencies establish internal controls to ensure that their process of assigning ratings is more transparent. The agencies must disclose their rating performance over time, and they are to be held accountable if their ratings prove to be inaccurate. The Financial Reform Act also allows investors to sue an agency for issuing credit ratings that the agency should have known were inaccurate.

FINANCIAL REFORM

3-1c Liquidity

Investors prefer securities that are *liquid*, meaning that they could be easily converted to cash without a loss in value. Thus, if all other characteristics are equal, securities with less liquidity will have to offer a higher yield to attract investors. Debt securities with a short-term maturity or an active secondary market have greater liquidity. Investors that need a high degree of liquidity (because they may need to sell their securities for cash at any moment) prefer liquid securities, even if it means that they will have to accept a lower return on their investment. Investors who will not need their funds until the securities mature are more willing to invest in securities with less liquidity in order to earn a slightly higher return.

3-1d Tax Status

Investors are more concerned with after-tax income than before-tax income earned on securities. If all other characteristics are similar, taxable securities must offer a higher before-tax yield than tax-exempt securities. The extra compensation required on taxable securities depends on the tax rates of individual and institutional investors. Investors in high tax brackets benefit most from tax-exempt securities.

When assessing the expected yields of various securities with similar risk and maturity, it is common to convert them into an after-tax form, as follows:

$$Y_{at} = Y_{bt}(1 - T)$$

where

$$Y_{at} = \textbf{after-tax yield}$$
$$Y_{bt} = \textbf{before-tax yield}$$
$$T = \textbf{investor's marginal tax rate}$$

Investors retain only a percentage $(1 - T)$ of the before-tax yield once taxes are paid.

EXAMPLE

Consider a taxable security that offers a before-tax yield of 8 percent. When converted into after-tax terms, the yield will be reduced by the tax percentage. The precise after-tax yield is dependent on the tax rate T. If the tax rate of the investor is 20 percent, then the after-tax yield will be

$$Y_{at} = Y_{bt}(1 - T)$$
$$= 8\%(1 - 0.2)$$
$$= 6.4\%$$

Exhibit 3.2 presents after-tax yields based on a variety of tax rates and before-tax yields. For example, a taxable security with a before-tax yield of 6 percent will generate an after-tax yield of 5.4 percent to an investor in the 10 percent tax bracket, 5.10 percent to an investor in the

Exhibit 3.2 After-Tax Yields Based on Various Tax Rates and Before-Tax Yields

TAX RATE	BEFORE-TAX YIELD				
	6%	8%	10%	12%	14%
10%	5.40%	7.20%	9.00%	10.80%	12.60%
15	5.10	6.80	8.50	10.20	11.90
25	4.50	6.00	7.50	9.00	10.50
28	4.32	5.76	7.20	8.64	10.08
35	3.90	5.20	6.50	7.80	9.10

15 percent tax bracket, and so on. This exhibit shows why investors in high tax brackets are attracted to tax-exempt securities. ●

Computing the Equivalent Before-Tax Yield   In some cases, investors wish to determine the before-tax yield necessary to match the after-tax yield of a tax-exempt security that has a similar risk and maturity. This can be done by rearranging the terms of the previous equation:

$$Y_{bt} = \frac{Y_{at}}{1 - T}$$

For instance, suppose that a firm in the 20 percent tax bracket is aware of a tax-exempt security that is paying a yield of 8 percent. To match this after-tax yield, taxable securities must offer a before-tax yield of

$$Y_{bt} = \frac{Y_{at}}{1 - T} = \frac{8\%}{1 - 0.2} = 10\%$$

State taxes should be considered along with federal taxes in determining the after-tax yield. Treasury securities are exempt from state income tax, and municipal securities are sometimes exempt as well. Because states impose different income tax rates, a particular security's after-tax yield may vary with the location of the investor.

3-1e Term to Maturity

Maturity differs among debt securities and is another reason that debt security yields differ. The **term structure of interest rates** defines the relationship between the term to maturity and the annualized yield of debt securities at a specific moment in time while holding other factors, such as risk, constant.

WEB

www.treasury.gov
Treasury yields among different maturities.

_____EXAMPLE

Assume that, as of today, the annualized yields for federal government securities (which are free from credit risk) of varied maturities are as shown in Exhibit 3.3. The curve created by connecting

Exhibit 3.3   Example of Relationship between Maturity and Yield of Treasury Securities (as of March 2013)

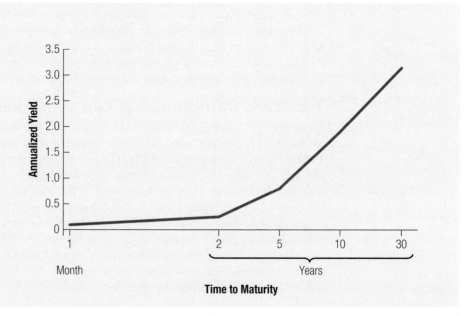

the points plotted in the exhibit is commonly referred to as a *yield curve*. Notice that the yield curve exhibits an upward slope.

The term structure of interest rates in Exhibit 3.3 shows that securities that are similar in all ways except their term to maturity may offer different yields. Because the demand and supply conditions for securities may vary among maturities, so may the price (and therefore the yield) of securities. A comprehensive explanation of the term structure of interest rates is provided later in this chapter. ●

Since the yield curve in Exhibit 3.3 is based on Treasury securities, the curve is not influenced by credit. The yield curve for AA-rated corporate bonds would typically have a slope similar to that of the Treasury yield curve, but the yield of the corporate issue at any particular term to maturity would be higher to reflect the risk premium.

WEB
___
www.bloomberg.com
The section on market interest rates and bonds presents the most recent yield curve.

3-2 EXPLAINING ACTUAL YIELD DIFFERENTIALS

Even small differentials in yield can be relevant to financial institutions that are borrowing or investing millions of dollars. Yield differentials are sometimes measured in basis points; a basis point equals 0.01 percent, so 100 basis points equals 1 percent. If a security offers a yield of 4.3 percent while the a risk-free security offers a yield of 4.0 percent, then the yield differential is 0.30 percent or 30 basis points. Yield differentials are described for money market securities next, followed by differentials for capital market securities.

3-2a Yield Differentials of Money Market Securities

The yields offered on commercial paper (short-term securities offered by creditworthy firms) are typically just slightly higher than Treasury-bill rates, since investors require a slightly higher return (10 to 40 basis points on an annualized basis) to compensate for credit risk and less liquidity. Negotiable certificates of deposit offer slightly higher rates than yields on Treasury bills ("T-bills") with the same maturity because of their lower degree of liquidity and higher degree of credit risk.

Market forces cause the yields of all securities to move in the same direction. To illustrate, assume that the budget deficit increases substantially and that the Treasury issues a large number of T-bills to finance the increased deficit. This action creates a large supply of T-bills in the market, placing downward pressure on the price and upward pressure on the T-bill yield. As the yield begins to rise, it approaches the yield of other short-term securities. Businesses and individual investors are now encouraged to purchase T-bills rather than these risky securities because they can achieve about the same yield while avoiding credit risk. The switch to T-bills lowers the demand for risky securities, thereby placing downward pressure on their price and upward pressure on their yields. Thus the risk premium on risky securities would not disappear completely.

3-2b Yield Differentials of Capital Market Securities

Municipal bonds have the lowest before-tax yield, yet their after-tax yield is typically above that of Treasury bonds from the perspective of investors in high tax brackets. Treasury bonds are expected to offer the lowest yield because they are free from credit risk and can easily be liquidated in the secondary market. Investors prefer municipal or corporate bonds over Treasury bonds only if the after-tax yield is sufficiently higher to compensate for the higher credit risk and lower degree of liquidity.

To illustrate how capital market security yields can vary over time because of credit risk, Exhibit 3.4 shows yields of corporate bonds in two different credit risk classes. The Aaa-rated bonds have very low credit risk, whereas the BAA bonds are perceived to have slightly more risk. Notice that the yield differential between BAA bonds and AAA bonds was relatively large during the recessions (shaded areas), such as in 1991 and in the

Exhibit 3.4   Yield Differentials of Corporate Bonds

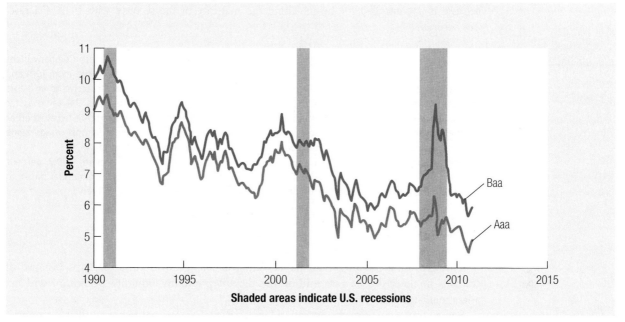

Source: *Federal Reserve.*

2000–2003 period when economic conditions were weak. During these periods, corporations had to pay a relatively high premium if their bonds were rated Baa. The yield differential narrowed during 2004–2007, when economic conditions improved. However, during the credit crisis of 2008–2009, the yield differential increased substantially. At one point during the credit crisis, the yield differential was about 3 percentage points.

Many corporations whose bonds are rated Baa or below were unwilling to issue bonds because of the high credit risk premium they would have to pay to bondholders. This illustrates why the credit crisis restricted access of corporations to credit.

3-3 ESTIMATING THE APPROPRIATE YIELD

The discussion so far suggests that the appropriate yield to be offered on a debt security is based on the risk-free rate for the corresponding maturity, with adjustments to capture various characteristics. A model that captures this estimate may be specified as follows:

$$Y_n = R_{f,n} + DP + LP + TA$$

where

$$Y_n = \textbf{yield of an } \textit{n}\textbf{-day debt security}$$
$$R_{f,n} = \textbf{yield (return) of an } \textit{n}\textbf{-day Treasury (risk-free) security}$$
$$DP = \textbf{default premium to compensate for credit risk}$$
$$LP = \textbf{liquidity premium to compensate for less liquidity}$$
$$TA = \textbf{adjustment due to the difference in tax status}$$

These are the characteristics identified earlier that explain yield differentials among securities (special provisions applicable to bonds also may be included, as described in Chapter 7).

Although maturity is another characteristic that can affect the yield, it is not included here because it is controlled for by matching the maturity of the security with that of a risk-free security.

EXAMPLE

Suppose that the three-month T-bill's annualized rate is 8 percent and that Elizabeth Company plans to issue 90-day commercial paper. Elizabeth Company must determine the default premium (DP) and liquidity premium (LP) to offer on its commercial paper in order to make it as attractive to investors as a three-month (13-week) T-bill. The federal tax status of commercial paper is the same as for T-bills. However, income earned from investing in commercial paper is subject to state taxes whereas income earned from investing in T-bills is not. Investors may require a premium for this reason alone if they reside in a location where state and (and perhaps local) income taxes apply.

Assume Elizabeth Company believes that a 0.7 percent default risk premium, a 0.2 percent liquidity premium, and a 0.3 percent tax adjustment are necessary to sell its commercial paper to investors. The appropriate yield to be offered on the commercial paper, Y_{cp}, is then

$$Y_{cp,n} = R_{f,n} + DP + LP + TA$$
$$= 8\% + 0.7\% + 0.2\% + 0.3\%$$
$$= 9.2\%$$ ●

The appropriate commercial paper rate will change over time, perhaps because of changes in the risk-free rate and/or the default premium, liquidity premium, and tax adjustment factors.

Some corporations may postpone plans to issue commercial paper until the economy improves and the required premium for credit risk is reduced. Even then, however, the market rate of commercial paper may increase if interest rates increase.

EXAMPLE

If the default risk premium decreases from 0.7 percent to 0.5 percent but $R_{f,n}$ increases from 8 percent to 8.7 percent, the appropriate yield to be offered on commercial paper (assuming no change in the previously assumed liquidity and tax adjustment premiums) would be

$$Y_{cp} = R_{f,n} + DP + LP + TA$$
$$= 8.7\% + 0.5\% + 0.2\% + 0.3\%$$
$$= 9.7\%$$

The strategy of postponing the issuance of commercial paper would backfire in this example. Even though the default premium decreased by 0.2 percent, the general level of interest rates rose by 0.7 percent, so the net change in the commercial paper rate is +0.5 percent. ●

As this example shows, the increase in a security's yield over time does not necessarily mean that the default premium has increased. The assessment of yields as described here could also be applied to long-term securities. If, for example, a firm desires to issue a 20-year corporate bond, it will use the yield of a new 20-year Treasury bond as the 20-year risk-free rate and add on the premiums for credit risk, liquidity risk, and so on when determining the yield at which it can sell corporate bonds.

A simpler and more general relationship is that the yield offered on a debt security is positively related to the prevailing risk-free rate and the security's risk premium (RP). This risk premium captures any risk characteristics of the security, including credit and liquidity risk. A more detailed model for the yield of a debt security could be applied by including additional characteristics that can vary among bonds, such as whether the bond is convertible into stock and whether it contains a call premium. The conversion option is favorable for investors, so it could reduce the yield that needs to be offered on a bond. The call premium is unfavorable for investors, so it could increase the yield that needs to be offered on a bond.

3-4 A CLOSER LOOK AT THE TERM STRUCTURE

Of all the factors that affect the yields offered on debt securities, the one that is most difficult to understand is *term to maturity*. For this reason, a more comprehensive explanation of the relationship between term to maturity and annualized yield (referred to as the term structure of interest rates) is necessary.

Various theories have been used to explain the relationship between maturity and annualized yield of securities. These theories include pure expectations theory, liquidity premium theory, and segmented markets theory, and each is explained in this section.

3-4a Pure Expectations Theory

According to pure expectations theory, the term structure of interest rates (as reflected in the shape of the yield curve) is determined solely by expectations of interest rates.

Impact of an Expected Increase in Interest Rates   To understand how interest rate expectations may influence the yield curve, assume that the annualized yields of short-term and long-term risk-free securities are similar; that is, suppose the yield curve is flat. Then assume that investors begin to believe that interest rates will rise. Investors will respond by investing their funds mostly in the short term so that they can soon reinvest their funds at higher yields after interest rates increase. When investors flood the short-term market and avoid the long-term market, they may cause the yield curve to adjust as shown in Panel A of Exhibit 3.5. The large supply of funds in the short-term markets will force annualized yields down. Meanwhile, the reduced supply of long-term funds forces long-term yields up.

Even though the annualized short-term yields become lower than annualized long-term yields, investors in short-term funds are satisfied because they expect interest rates to rise. They will make up for the lower short-term yield when the short-term securities mature, and they reinvest at a higher rate (if interest rates rise) at maturity.

Assuming that the borrowers who plan to issue securities also expect interest rates to increase, they will prefer to lock in the present interest rate over a long period of time. Thus, borrowers will generally prefer to issue long-term securities rather than short-term securities. This results in a relatively small demand for short-term funds. Consequently, there is downward pressure on the yield of short-term funds. There is a corresponding increase in the demand for long-term funds by borrowers, which places upward pressure on long-term funds. Overall, the expectation of higher interest rates changes the demand for funds and the supply of funds in different maturity markets, which forces the original flat yield curve (labeled YC_1 in the two rightmost graphs) to pivot upward (counterclockwise) and become upward sloping (YC_2).

Impact of an Expected Decline in Interest Rates   If investors expect interest rates to decrease in the future, they will prefer to invest in long-term funds rather than short-term funds because they could lock in today's interest rate before interest rates fall. Borrowers will prefer to borrow short-term funds so that they can refinance at a lower interest rate once interest rates decline.

Exhibit 3.5   How Interest Rate Expectations Affect the Yield Curve

Panel A: Impact of a Sudden Expectation of Higher Interest Rates

$E(\uparrow i) \rightarrow$ Supply of funds provided by investors $\uparrow$ in short-term (such as 3-month) markets, and $\downarrow$ in long-term (such as 10-year) markets. Demand for funds by borrowers $\uparrow$ in long-term markets and $\downarrow$ in short-term markets. Therefore, the yield curve becomes upward sloping as shown here.

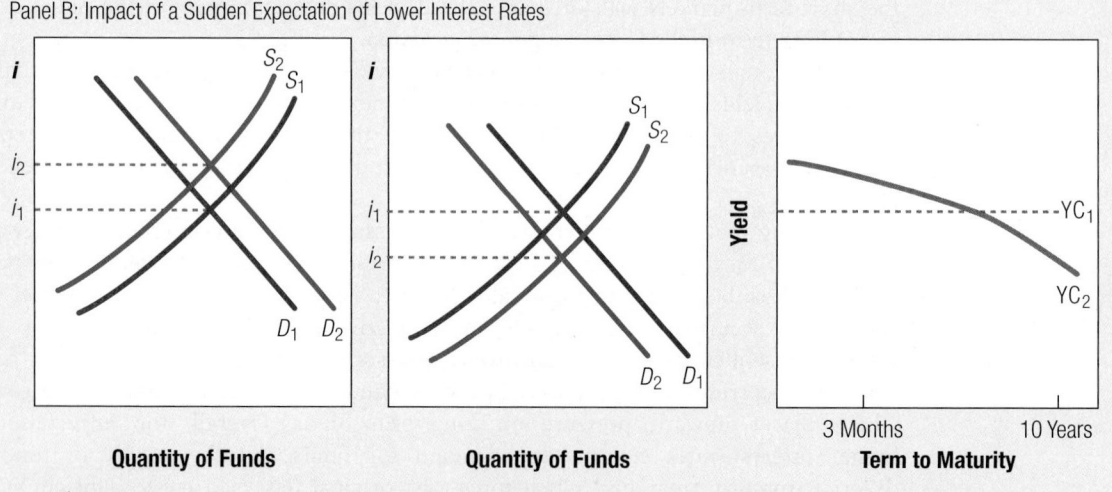

Panel B: Impact of a Sudden Expectation of Lower Interest Rates

$E(\downarrow i) \rightarrow$ Supply of funds provided by investors $\uparrow$ in long-term (such as 10-year) markets, and $\downarrow$ in short-term (such as 3-month) markets. Demand for funds by borrowers $\uparrow$ in short-term markets and $\downarrow$ in long-term markets. Therefore, the yield curve becomes downward sloping as shown here.

Based on the expectation of lower interest rates in the future, the supply of funds provided by investors will be low for short-term funds and high for long-term funds. This will place upward pressure on short-term yields and downward pressure on long-term yields, as shown in Panel B of Exhibit 3.5. Overall, the expectation of lower interest rates causes the shape of the yield curve to pivot downward (clockwise).

Algebraic Presentation   Investors monitor the yield curve to determine the rates that exist for securities with various maturities. They can either purchase a security with a maturity that matches their investment horizon or purchase a security with a shorter term and then reinvest the proceeds at maturity. They may select the strategy that they believe will generate a higher return over the entire investment horizon. This could affect the prices and yields of securities with different maturities, so that the expected return over the investment horizon is similar regardless of the strategy used. If investors were indifferent to maturities, the return of any security should equal the compounded yield of consecutive investments in shorter-term securities. That is, a two-year security should offer a return that is similar to the anticipated return from investing in two consecutive one-year securities. A four-year security should offer a return that is competitive with the expected return from investing in two consecutive two-year securities or four consecutive one-year securities, and so on.

EXAMPLE   To illustrate these equalities, consider the relationship between interest rates on a two-year security and a one-year security as follows:

$$(1 + {_t}i_2)^2 = (1 + {_t}i_1)(1 + {_{t+1}}r_1)$$

where

$${_t}i_2 = \text{known annualized interest rate of a two-year security as of time } t$$
$${_t}i_1 = \text{known annualized interest rate of a one-year security as of time } t$$
$${_{t+1}}r_1 = \text{one-year interest rate that is anticipated as of time } t + 1 \text{ (one year ahead)}$$

The term i represents a quoted rate, which is therefore known, whereas r represents a rate to be quoted at some point in the future, so its value is uncertain. The left side of the equation represents the compounded yield to investors who purchase a two-year security, and the right side represents the anticipated compounded yield from purchasing a one-year security and reinvesting the proceeds in a new one-year security at the end of one year. If time t is today, then ${_{t+1}}r_1$ can be estimated by rearranging terms:

$$1 + {_{t+1}}r_1 = \frac{(1 + {_t}i_2)^2}{1 + {_t}i_1}$$

$${_{t+1}}r_1 = \frac{(1 + {_t}i_2)^2}{1 + {_t}i_1} - 1$$

The term ${_{t+1}}r_1$, referred to as the **forward rate**, is commonly estimated in order to represent the market's forecast of the future interest rate. Here is a numerical example. Assume that, as of today (time t), the annualized two-year interest rate is 10 percent and the one-year interest rate is 8 percent. The forward rate is then estimated as follows:

$${_{t+1}}r_1 = \frac{(1 + 0.10)^2}{1 + 0.08} - 1$$

$$= 0.1203704$$

This result implies that, one year from now, a one-year interest rate must equal about 12.037 percent in order for consecutive investments in two one-year securities to generate a return similar to that of a two-year investment. If the actual one-year rate beginning one year from now (i.e., at time $t + 1$) is above 12.037 percent, the return from two consecutive one-year investments will exceed the return on a two-year investment. ●

The forward rate is sometimes used as an approximation of the market's consensus interest rate forecast. The reason is that, if the market had a different perception, the demand and supply of today's existing two-year and one-year securities would adjust to capitalize on this information. Of course, there is no guarantee that the forward rate will forecast the future interest rate with perfect accuracy.

The greater the difference between the implied one-year forward rate and today's one-year interest rate, the greater the expected change in the one-year interest rate. If the term structure of interest rates is solely influenced by expectations of future interest rates, the following relationships hold:

SCENARIO	STRUCTURE OF YIELD CURVE	EXPECTATIONS ABOUT THE FUTURE INTEREST RATE
1. $_{t+1}r_1 > i_{t_1}$	Upward slope	Higher than today's rate
2. $_{t+1}r_1 = i_{t_1}$	Flat	Same as today's rate
3. $_{t+1}r_1 < i_{t_1}$	Downward slope	Lower than today's rate

Forward rates can be determined for various maturities. The relationships described here can be applied when assessing the change in the interest rate of a security with any particular maturity.

The previous example can be expanded to solve for other forward rates. The equality specified by the pure expectations theory for a three-year horizon is

$$(1 + i_{t_3})^3 = (1 + i_{t_1})(1 + {}_{t+1}r_1)(1 + {}_{t+2}r_1)$$

where

$i_{t_3} =$ **annualized interest rate on a three-year security as of time t**

$_{t+2}r_1 =$ **one-year interest that is anticipated as of time $t + 2$ (two years)**

All other terms were defined previously. By rearranging terms, we can isolate the forward rate of a one-year security beginning two years from now:

$$1 + {}_{t+2}r_1 = \frac{(1 + i_{t_3})^3}{(1 + i_{t_1})(1 + {}_{t+1}r_1)}$$

$${}_{t+2}r_1 = \frac{(1 + i_{t_3})^3}{(1 + i_{t_1})(1 + {}_{t+1}r_1)} - 1$$

If the one-year forward rate beginning one year from now ($_{t+1}r_1$) has already been estimated, then this estimate can be combined with actual one-year and three-year interest rates to estimate the one-year forward rate two years from now. Recall that our previous example assumed $i_{t_1} = 8$ percent and estimated $_{t+1}r_1$ to be about 12.037 percent.

EXAMPLE

Assume that a three-year security has an annualized interest rate of 11 percent (i.e., $i_{t_3} = 11$ percent). Given this information, the one-year forward rate two years from now can be calculated as follows:

$$_{t+2}r_1 = \frac{(1 + i_{t_3})^3}{(1 + i_{t_1})(1 + {}_{t+1}r_1)} - 1$$

$$= \frac{(1 + 0.11)^3}{(1 + 0.08)(1 + 0.12037)} - 1$$

$$= \frac{1.367631}{1.21} - 1$$

$$= \textbf{13.02736\%}$$

Thus, the market anticipates that, two years from now, the one-year interest rate will be 13.02736 percent. ●

The yield curve can also be used to forecast annualized interest rates for periods other than one year. For example, the information provided in the last example could be used to determine the two-year forward rate beginning one year from now.

According to pure expectations theory, a one-year investment followed by a two-year investment should offer the same annualized yield over the three-year horizon as a three-year security that could be purchased today. This relation is expressed as follows:

$$(1 + {}_{t+1}i_3)^3 = (1 + {}_t i_1)(1 + {}_{t+1}r_2)^2$$

where ${}_{t+1}r_2$ is the annual interest rate of a two-year security anticipated as of time $t + 1$. By rearranging terms, ${}_{t+1}r_2$ can be isolated:

$$(1 + {}_{t+1}r_2)^2 = \frac{(1 + {}_t i_3)^3}{1 + {}_t i_1}$$

EXAMPLE Recall that today's annualized yields for one-year and three-year securities are 8 percent and 11 percent, respectively. With this information, ${}_{t+1}r_2$ is estimated as follows:

$$(1 + {}_{t+1}r_2)^2 = \frac{(1 + {}_t i_3)^3}{1 + {}_t i_1}$$
$$= \frac{(1 + 0.11)^3}{1 + 0.08}$$
$$= 1.266325$$
$$1 + {}_{t+1}r_2 = \sqrt{1.266325}$$
$$= 1.1253$$
$${}_{t+1}r_2 = 0.1253$$

Thus, the market anticipates an annualized interest rate of about 12.53 percent for two-year securities beginning one year from now. ●

Pure expectations theory is based on the premise that forward rates are unbiased estimators of future interest rates. If forward rates are biased, investors can attempt to capitalize on the bias.

EXAMPLE In the previous numerical example, the one-year forward rate beginning one year ahead was estimated to be about 12.037 percent. If the forward rate was thought to contain an upward bias, the expected one-year interest rate beginning one year ahead would actually be less than 12.037 percent. Therefore, investors with funds available for two years would earn a higher yield by purchasing two-year securities rather than purchasing one-year securities for two consecutive years. However, their actions would cause an increase in the price of two-year securities and a decrease in that of one-year securities, and the yields of these securities would move inversely with the price movements. Hence any attempt by investors to capitalize on the forward rate bias would essentially eliminate the bias. ●

If forward rates are unbiased estimators of future interest rates, financial market efficiency is supported and the information implied by market rates about the forward rate cannot be used to generate abnormal returns. In response to new information, investor preferences would change, yields would adjust, and the implied forward rate would adjust as well.

If a long-term rate is expected to equal a geometric average of consecutive short-term rates covering the same time horizon (as is suggested by pure expectations theory), long-term rates would likely be more stable than short-term rates. As expectations about consecutive short-term rates change over time, the average of these rates is less volatile than the individual short-term rates. Thus long-term rates are much more stable than short-term rates.

3-4b Liquidity Premium Theory

Some investors may prefer to own short-term rather than long-term securities because a shorter maturity represents greater liquidity. In this case, they may be willing to hold long-term securities only if compensated by a premium for the lower degree of liquidity. Although long-term securities can be liquidated prior to maturity, their prices are more sensitive to interest rate movements. Short-term securities are normally considered to be more liquid because they are more likely to be converted to cash without a loss in value.

The preference for the more liquid short-term securities places upward pressure on the slope of a yield curve. Liquidity may be a more critical factor to investors at some times than at others, and the liquidity premium will accordingly change over time. As it does, the yield curve will change also. This is the liquidity premium theory (sometimes referred to as the liquidity preference theory).

Exhibit 3.6 contains three graphs that reflect the existence of both expectations theory and a liquidity premium. Each graph shows different interest rate expectations by the market. Regardless of the interest rate forecast, the yield curve is affected in a similar manner by the liquidity premium.

Exhibit 3.6 Impact of Liquidity Premium on the Yield Curve under Three Different Scenarios

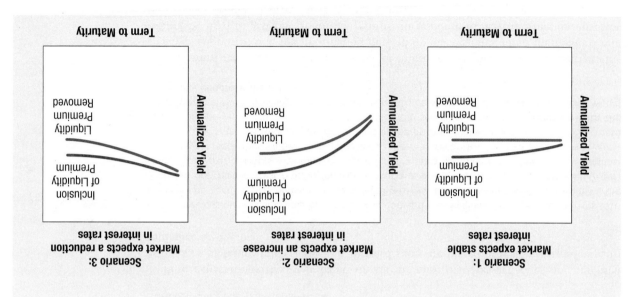

Estimation of the Forward Rate Based on a Liquidity Premium   When expectations theory is combined with liquidity theory, the yield on a security will not necessarily be equal to the yield from consecutive investments in shorter-term securities over the same investment horizon. For example, the yield on a two-year security is now determined as

$$(1 + {}_{t+1}i_2)^2 = (1 + {}_ti_1)(1 + {}_{t+1}r_1) + LP_2$$

where LP_2 denotes the liquidity premium on a two-year security. The yield generated from the two-year security should exceed the yield from consecutive investments in one-year securities by a premium that compensates the investor for less liquidity. The relationship between the liquidity premium and term to maturity can be expressed as follows:

$$0 < LP_1 < LP_2 < LP_3 < \cdots < LP_{20}$$

where the subscripts represent years to maturity. This implies that the liquidity premium would be more influential on the difference between annualized interest rates on one-year and 20-year securities than on the difference between one-year and two-year securities.

If liquidity influences the yield curve, the forward rate overestimates the market's expectation of the future interest rate. A more appropriate formula for the forward rate would account for the liquidity premium. By rearranging terms in the previous equation for forward rates, the one-year forward rate can be derived as follows:

$$_{t+1}r_1 = \frac{(1 + {}_ti_2)^2}{1 + {}_ti_1} - 1 - \frac{LP_2}{1 + {}_ti_1}$$

EXAMPLE

Reconsider the example where $i_1 = 8$ percent and $i_2 = 10$ percent, and assume that the liquidity premium on a two-year security is 0.5 percent. The one-year forward rate can then be derived from this information as follows:

$$_{t+1}r_1 = \frac{(1 + {}_ti_2)^2}{1 + {}_ti_1} - 1 - \frac{LP_2}{1 + {}_ti_1}$$

$$= \frac{(1.10)^2}{1.08} - 1 - \frac{0.005}{1 + 0.08}$$

$$= 0.11574$$

This estimate of the one-year forward rate is lower than the estimate derived in the previous related example in which the liquidity premium was not considered. The previous estimate (12.037 percent) of the forward rate probably overstates the market's expected interest rate because it did not account for a liquidity premium. Thus forecasts of future interest rates implied by a yield curve are reduced slightly when accounting for the liquidity premium. ●

Even with the existence of a liquidity premium, yield curves could still be used to interpret interest rate expectations. A flat yield curve would be interpreted to mean that the market is expecting a slight decrease in interest rates (without the effect of the liquidity premium, the yield curve would have had a slight downward slope). A slight upward slope would be interpreted as no expected change in interest rates: if the liquidity premium were removed, this yield curve would be flat.

3-4c Segmented Markets Theory

According to the segmented markets theory, investors and borrowers choose securities with maturities that satisfy their forecasted cash needs. Pension funds and life insurance companies may generally prefer long-term investments that coincide with their long-term liabilities. Commercial banks may prefer more short-term investments to coincide with their short-term liabilities. If investors and borrowers participate only in the maturity market that satisfies their particular needs, then markets are segmented. That is, investors (or borrowers) will shift from the long-term market to the short-term market, or vice versa, only if the timing of their cash needs changes.

According to segmented markets theory, the choice of long-term versus short-term maturities is determined more by investors' needs than by their expectations of future interest rates.

Assume that most investors have funds available to invest for only a short period of time and therefore desire to invest primarily in short-term securities. Also assume that most borrowers need funds for a long period of time and therefore desire to issue mostly long-term securities. The result will be downward pressure on the yield of short-term securities and upward pressure on the yield of long-term securities. Overall, the scenario described would create an upward-sloping yield curve.

Now consider the opposite scenario in which most investors wish to invest their funds for a long period of time while most borrowers need funds for only a short period of time. According to segmented markets theory, this situation will cause upward pressure on the yield of short-term securities and downward pressure on the yield of long-term securities. If the supply of funds provided by investors and the demand for funds by borrowers were better balanced between the short-term and long-term markets, the yields of short-and long-term securities would be more similar. ●

The preceding example distinguished maturity markets as either short-term or long-term. In reality, several maturity markets may exist. Within the short-term market, some investors may prefer maturities of one month or less whereas others may prefer maturities of one to three months. Regardless of how many maturity markets exist, the yields of securities with various maturities should be influenced in part by the desires of investors and borrowers to participate in the maturity market that best satisfies their needs. A corporation that needs additional funds for 30 days would not consider issuing long-term bonds for such a purpose. Savers with short-term funds would avoid some long-term investments (e.g., 10-year certificates of deposit) that cannot be easily liquidated.

Limitation of the Theory A limitation of segmented markets theory is that some borrowers and savers have the flexibility to choose among various maturity markets. Corporations that need long-term funds may initially obtain short-term financing if they expect interest rates to decline, and investors with long-term funds may make short-term investments if they expect interest rates to rise. Moreover, some investors with short-term funds may be willing to purchase long-term securities that have an active secondary market.

Some financial institutions focus on a particular maturity market, but others are more flexible. Commercial banks obtain most of their funds in short-term markets but spread their investments into short-, medium-, and long-term markets. Savings institutions have historically focused on attracting short-term funds and lending funds for long-term periods. Note that if maturity markets were completely segmented, then an interest rate adjustment in one market would have no impact on other markets. However, there is clear evidence that interest rates among maturity markets move nearly in concert over time. This evidence indicates that there is some interaction among markets, which implies that funds are being transferred across markets. Note also that the theory of segmented markets conflicts with the general presumption of pure expectations theory that maturity markets are perfect substitutes for one another.

Implications Although markets are not completely segmented, the preference for particular maturities can affect the prices and yields of securities with different maturities and thereby affect the yield curve's shape. For this reason, the theory of segmented markets seems to be a partial explanation for the yield curve's shape but not the sole explanation.

A more flexible variant of segmented markets theory, known as preferred habitat theory, offers a compromise explanation for the term structure of interest rates. This theory proposes that, although investors and borrowers may normally concentrate on a particular maturity market, certain events may cause them to wander from their "natural" market. For example, commercial banks that obtain mostly short-term funds may select investments with short-term maturities as a natural habitat. However, if they wish to benefit from an anticipated decline in interest rates, they may select medium- and long-term maturities instead. Preferred habitat theory acknowledges that natural maturity markets may influence the yield curve, but it also recognizes that interest rate expectations could entice market participants to stray from their natural, preferred markets.

3-4d Research on Term Structure Theories

Much research has been conducted on the term structure of interest rates and has offered considerable insight into the various theories. Researchers have found that interest rate expectations have a strong influence on the term structure of interest rates. However, the forward rate derived from a yield curve does not accurately predict future interest rates, and this suggests that other factors may be relevant. The liquidity premium, for example, could cause consistent positive forecasting errors, meaning that forward rates tend to overestimate future interest rates. Studies have documented variation in the yield–maturity relationship that cannot be entirely explained by interest rate expectations or liquidity. The variation could therefore be attributed to different supply and demand conditions for particular maturity segments.

General Research Implications Although the results of research differ, there is some evidence that expectations theory, liquidity premium theory, and segmented markets theory all have some validity. Thus, if term structure is used to assess the market's expectations of future interest rates, then investors should first "net out" the liquidity premium and any unique market conditions for various maturity segments.

3-5 Integrating the Theories of Term Structure

In order to understand how all three theories can simultaneously affect the yield curve, first assume the following conditions.

1. Investors and borrowers who select security maturities based on anticipated interest rate movements currently expect interest rates to rise.

Exhibit 3.7 Effect of Conditions in Example on Yield Curve

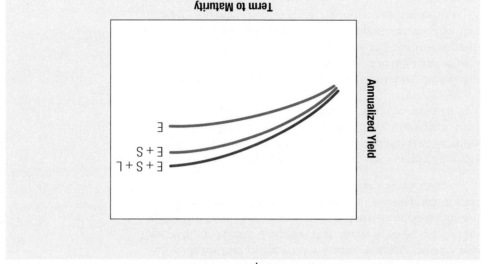

2. Most borrowers are in need of long-term funds, while most investors have only short-term funds to invest.

3. Investors prefer more liquidity to less.

The first condition, which is related to expectations theory, suggests the existence of an upward-sloping yield curve (other things being equal); see curve E in Exhibit 3.7. The segmented markets information (condition 2) also favors the upward-sloping yield curve. When conditions 1 and 2 are considered simultaneously, the appropriate yield curve may look like curve E + S in the graph. The third condition (regarding liquidity) would then place a higher premium on the longer-term securities because of their lower degree of liquidity. When this condition is included with the first two, the yield may be represented by curve E + S + L.

In this example, all conditions placed upward pressure on long-term yields relative to short-term yields. In reality, there will sometimes be offsetting conditions: one condition may put downward pressure on the slope of the yield curve while other conditions cause upward pressure. If condition 1 in the example here were revised so that future interest rates were expected to decline, then this condition (by itself) would result in a downward-sloping yield curve. So when combined with the other conditions, which imply an upward-sloping curve, the result would be a partial offsetting effect. The actual yield curve would exhibit a downward slope if the effect of the interest rate expectations dominated the combined effects of segmented markets and a liquidity premium. In contrast, there would be an upward slope if the liquidity premium and segmented markets effects dominated the effects of interest rate expectations.

3-5a Use of the Term Structure

The term structure of interest rates is used to forecast recessions, and to make investment and financing decisions.

Forecasting Interest Rates At any point in time, the shape of the yield curve can be used to assess the general expectations of investors and borrowers about future interest rates. Recall from expectations theory that an upward-sloping yield curve generally results from the expectation of higher interest rates whereas a downward-sloping yield curve generally results from the expectation of lower interest rates. Expectations about future interest rates must be interpreted cautiously, however, because liquidity and specific maturity preferences could influence the yield curve's shape. Still, it is generally believed that interest rate expectations are a major contributing factor to the yield curve's shape. Thus the curve's shape should provide a reasonable indication (especially once the liquidity premium effect is accounted for) of the market's expectations about future interest rates.

Although they can use the yield curve to interpret the market's consensus expectation of future interest rates, investors may have their own interest rate projections. By comparing their projections with those implied by the yield curve, they can attempt to capitalize on the difference. For example, if an upward-sloping yield curve exists, investors expecting stable interest rates could benefit from investing in long-term securities. From their perspective, long-term securities are undervalued because they reflect the market's (presumed incorrect) expectation of higher interest rates. Strategies such as this are effective only if the investor can consistently forecast better than the market.

Forecasting Recessions   Some analysts believe that flat or inverted yield curves indicate a recession in the near future. The rationale for this belief is that, given a positive liquidity premium, such yield curves reflect the expectation of lower interest rates. This in turn is commonly associated with expectations of a reduced demand for loanable funds, which could be attributed to expectations of a weak economy.

The yield curve became flat or slightly inverted in 2000. At that time, the shape of the curve indicated expectations of a slower economy, which would result in lower interest rates. In 2001, the economy weakened considerably. And in March 2007, the yield curve exhibited a slight negative slope that caused some market participants to forecast a recession. During the credit crisis in 2008 and in the following two years, yields on Treasury securities with various maturities declined. The short-term interest rates experienced the most pronounced decline, which resulted in an upward-sloping yield curve in 2010.

Making Investment Decisions   If the yield curve is upward sloping, some investors may attempt to benefit from the higher yields on longer-term securities even though they have funds to invest for only a short period of time. The secondary market allows investors to implement this strategy, which is known as *riding the yield curve*. Consider an upward-sloping yield curve such that some one-year securities offer an annualized yield of 7 percent while 10-year bonds offer an annualized yield of 10 percent. An investor with funds available for one year may decide to purchase the bonds and sell them in the secondary market after one year. The investor earns 3 percent more than was possible on the one-year securities, but only if the bonds can be sold (after one year) at the price for which they were purchased. The risk of this strategy is the uncertainty in the price for which the security can be sold in the near future. If the upward-sloping yield is interpreted as the market's consensus of higher interest rates in the future, then the price of a security would be expected to decrease in the future.

The yield curve is commonly monitored by financial institutions whose liability maturities are distinctly different from their asset maturities. Consider a bank that obtains much of its funds through short-term deposits and uses the funds to provide long-term loans or purchase long-term securities. An upward-sloping yield curve is favorable to the bank because annualized short-term deposit rates are significantly lower than annualized long-term investment rates. The bank's spread is higher than it would be if the yield curve were flat. However, if it believes that the upward slope of the yield curve indicates higher interest rates in the future (as predicted by expectations theory), then the bank will expect its cost of liabilities to increase over time because future deposits would be obtained at higher interest rates.

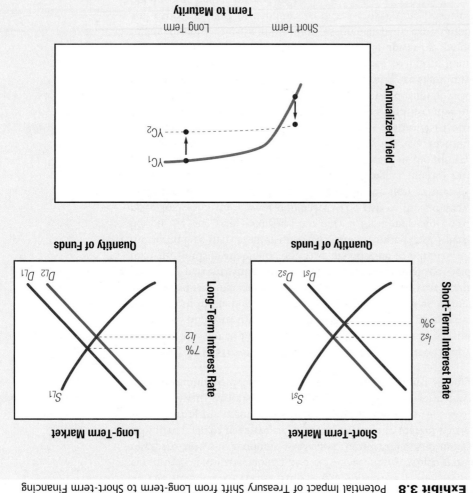

Exhibit 3.8 Potential Impact of Treasury Shift from Long-term to Short-term Financing

Making Decisions about Financing   The yield curve is also useful for firms that plan to issue bonds. By assessing the prevailing rates on securities for various maturities, firms can estimate the rates to be paid on bonds with different maturities. This may enable them to determine the maturity of the bonds they issue. If they need funds for a two-year period, but notice from the yield curve that the annualized yield on one-year debt is much lower than that of two-year debt, they may consider borrowing for a one-year period. After one year when they pay off this debt, they will need to borrow funds for another one-year period.

3-5b Why the Slope of the Yield Curve Changes

If interest rates at all maturities were affected in the same manner by existing conditions, then the slope of the yield curve would remain unchanged. However, conditions may cause short-term yields to change in a manner that differs from the change in long-term yields.

EXAMPLE

Suppose that last July the yield curve had a large upward slope, as shown by yield curve YC1 in Exhibit 3.8. Since then, the Treasury decided to restructure its debt by retiring $300 billion of long-term Treasury securities and increasing its offering of short-term Treasury securities. This caused a large increase in the demand for short-term funds and a large decrease in the demand for long-term funds. The increase in the demand for short-term funds caused an increase in short-term interest rates and thereby increased the yields offered on newly issued short-term securities. Conversely, the decline in demand for long-term funds caused a decrease in long-term interest rates and thereby reduced the yields offered on newly issued long-term securities. Today, the yield curve is YC2 and is much flatter than it was last July. ●

3-5c How the Yield Curve Has Changed over Time

Yield curves at various dates are illustrated in Exhibit 3.9. The yield curve is usually upward sloping, but a slight downward slope has sometimes been evident (see the exhibit's curve for March 21, 2007). Observe that the yield curve for March 18, 2013, is below the other yield curves shown in the exhibit, which means that the yield to maturity was relatively low regardless of the maturity considered. This curve existed during the credit crisis, when economic conditions were extremely weak.

3-5d International Structure of Interest Rates

GLOBAL ASPECTS

Because the factors that affect the shape of the yield curve can vary among countries, the yield curve's shape at any given time also varies among countries. Exhibit 3.10 plots the yield curve for six different countries in July 2013. Each country has a different currency with its own interest rate levels for various maturities, and each country's interest rates are based on conditions of supply and demand.

Interest rate movements across countries tend to be positively correlated as a result of internationally integrated financial markets. Nevertheless, the actual interest rates may vary significantly across countries at a given point in time. This implies that the difference in interest rates is attributable primarily to general supply and demand conditions across countries and less so to differences in default risk premiums, liquidity premiums, or other characteristics of the individual securities.

Exhibit 3.9   Yield Curves at Various Points in Time

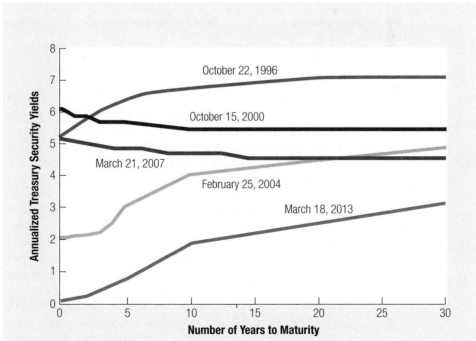

Source: *Federal Reserve.*

Because forward rates (as defined in this chapter) reflect the market's expectations of future interest rates, the term structure of interest rates for various countries should be monitored for the following reasons. First, with the integration of financial markets, movements in one country's interest rate can affect interest rates in other countries. Thus some investors may estimate the forward rate in a foreign country to predict the foreign interest rate, which in turn may affect domestic interest rates. Second, foreign securities and some domestic securities are influenced by foreign interest rates. If the foreign forward rates can be used to forecast foreign interest rates, they can enhance forecasts of foreign economies. Because exchange rates are also influenced by foreign interest rates, exchange rate projections may be more accurate when foreign forward rates are used to forecast foreign interest rates.

If the real interest rate were fixed, inflation rates for future periods could be predicted for any country in which the forward rate could be estimated. Recall from Chapter 2 that the nominal interest rate consists of an expected inflation rate plus a real interest rate. Because the forward rate represents an expected nominal interest rate for a future period, it also represents an expected inflation rate plus a real interest rate in that period. The expected inflation in that period is estimated as the difference between the forward rate and the real interest rate.

Exhibit 3.10 Yield Curves among Foreign Countries (as of July 2013)

SUMMARY

- Quoted yields of debt securities at any given time may vary for the following reasons. First, securities with higher credit (default) risk must offer a higher yield. Second, securities that are less liquid must offer a higher yield. Third, taxable securities must offer a higher before-tax yield than tax-exempt securities. Fourth, securities with longer maturities offer a different yield (not consistently higher or lower) than securities with shorter maturities.

- The appropriate yield for any particular debt security can be estimated by first determining the risk-free yield that is currently offered by a Treasury security with a similar maturity. Then adjustments are made that account for credit risk, liquidity, tax status, and other provisions.

- The term structure of interest rates can be explained by three theories. The pure expectations theory suggests that the shape of the yield curve is dictated by interest rate expectations. The liquidity premium theory suggests that securities with shorter maturities have greater liquidity and therefore should not have to offer as high a yield as securities with longer terms to maturity. The segmented markets theory suggests that investors and borrowers have different needs that cause the demand and supply conditions to vary across different maturities; in other words, there is a segmented market for each term to maturity, which causes yields to vary among these maturity markets. Consolidating the theories suggests that the term structure of interest rates depends on interest rate expectations, investor preferences for liquidity, and the unique needs of investors and borrowers in each maturity market.

POINT COUNTER-POINT

Should a Yield Curve Influence a Borrower's Preferred Maturity of a Loan?

Point   Yes. If there is an upward-sloping yield curve, then a borrower should pursue a short-term loan to capitalize on the lower annualized rate charged for a short-term period. The borrower can obtain a series of short-term loans rather than one loan to match the desired maturity.

Counter-Point   No. The borrower will face uncertainty regarding the interest rate charged on subsequent loans that are needed. An upward-sloping yield curve suggests that interest rates may rise in the future, which will cause the cost of borrowing to increase. Overall, the cost of borrowing may be higher when using a series of loans than when matching the debt maturity to the time period in which funds are needed.

Who Is Correct?   Use the Internet to learn more about this issue and then formulate your own opinion.

QUESTIONS AND APPLICATIONS

1. Characteristics That Affect Security Yields Identify the relevant characteristics of any security that can affect its yield.

2. Impact of Credit Risk on Yield What effect does a high credit risk have on securities?

3. Impact of Liquidity on Yield Discuss the relationship between the yield and liquidity of securities.

4. Tax Effects on Yields Do investors in high tax brackets or those in low tax brackets benefit more from tax-exempt securities? Why? At a given point in time, which offers a higher before-tax yield: municipal bonds or corporate bonds? Why? Which has the higher after-tax yield? If taxes did not exist, would Treasury bonds offer a higher or lower yield than municipal bonds with the same maturity? Why?

5. Pure Expectations Theory Explain how a yield curve would shift in response to a sudden expectation of rising interest rates, according to the pure expectations theory.

6. Forward Rate What is the meaning of the forward rate in the context of the term structure of interest rates? Why might forward rates consistently overestimate future interest rates? How could such a bias be avoided?

7. Pure Expectations Theory Assume there is a sudden expectation of lower interest rates in the future. What would be the effect on the shape of the yield curve? Explain.

8. Liquidity Premium Theory Explain the liquidity premium theory.

9. Impact of Liquidity Premium on Forward Rate Explain how consideration of a liquidity premium affects the estimate of a forward interest rate.

10. Segmented Markets Theory If a downward-sloping yield curve is mainly attributed to segmented markets theory, what does that suggest about the demand for and supply of funds in the short-term and long-term maturity markets?

11. Segmented Markets Theory If the segmented markets theory causes an upward-sloping yield curve, what does this imply? If markets are not completely segmented, should we dismiss the segmented markets theory as even a partial explanation for the term structure of interest rates? Explain.

12. Preferred Habitat Theory Explain the preferred habitat theory.

13. Yield Curve What factors influence the shape of the yield curve? Describe how financial market participants use the yield curve.

Advanced Questions

14. Segmented Markets Theory Suppose that the Treasury decides to finance its deficit with mostly long-term funds. How could this decision affect the term structure of interest rates? If short-term and long-term markets were segmented, would the Treasury's decision have a more or less pronounced impact on the term structure? Explain.

15. Yield Curve Assuming that liquidity and interest rate expectations are both important for explaining the shape of a yield curve, what does a flat yield curve indicate about the market's perception of future interest rates?

16. Global Interaction among Yield Curves Assume that the yield curves in the United States, France, and Japan are flat. If the U.S. yield curve suddenly becomes positively sloped, do you think the yield curves in France and Japan would be affected? If so, how?

17. Multiple Effects on the Yield Curve Assume that (1) investors and borrowers expect that the economy will weaken and that inflation will decline, (2) investors require a small liquidity premium, and (3) markets are partially segmented and the Treasury currently has a preference for borrowing in short-term markets. Explain how each of these forces would affect the term structure, holding other factors constant. Then explain the effect on the term structure overall.

18. Effect of Crises on the Yield Curve During some crises, investors shift their funds out of the stock market and into money market securities for safety, even if they do not fear rising interest rates. Explain how and why these actions by investors affect the yield curve. Is the shift best explained by expectations theory, liquidity premium theory, or segmented markets theory?

19. How the Yield Curve May Respond to Prevailing Conditions Consider how economic conditions affect the default risk premium. Do you think the default risk premium will likely increase or decrease during this semester? How do you think the yield curve will change during this semester? Offer some logic to support your answers.

20. Assessing Interest Rate Differentials among Countries In countries experiencing high inflation, the annual interest rate may exceed 50 percent. In other countries, such as the United States and many European countries, annual interest rates are typically less than 10 percent. Do you think a large difference in interest rates is due primarily to the difference between countries in the risk-free rates or in the credit risk premiums? Explain.

21. Applying the Yield Curve to Risky Debt Securities Assume that the yield curve for Treasury bonds has a slight upward slope, starting at 6 percent for a 10-year maturity and slowly rising to 8 percent for a 30-year maturity. Create a yield curve that you believe would exist for A-rated bonds and a corresponding one for B-rated bonds.

22. Changes to Credit Rating Process Explain how credit raters have changed their process following criticism of their credit ratings during the credit crisis.

Interpreting Financial News

Interpret the following comments made by Wall Street analysts and portfolio managers.

a. "An upward-sloping yield curve persists because many investors stand ready to jump into the stock market."

b. "Low-rated bond yields rose as recession fears caused a flight to quality."

c. "The shift from an upward-sloping yield curve to a downward-sloping yield curve is sending a warning about a possible recession."?

Managing in Financial Markets

Monitoring Yield Curve Adjustments As an analyst of a bond rating agency, you have been asked to interpret the implications of the recent shift in the yield curve. Six months ago, the yield curve exhibited a slight downward slope. Over the last six months, long-term yields declined while short-term yields remained the same. Analysts said that the shift was due to revised expectations of interest rates.

a. Given the shift in the yield curve, does it appear that firms increased or decreased their demand for long-term funds over the last six months?

b. Interpret what the shift in the yield curve suggests about the market's changing expectations of future interest rates.

c. Recently, an analyst argued that the underlying reason for the yield curve shift is that many large U.S. firms anticipate a recession. Explain why an anticipated recession could force the yield curve to shift as it has.

d. What could the specific shift in the yield curve signal about the ratings of existing corporate bonds? What types of corporations would be most likely to experience a change in their bond ratings as a result of this shift in the yield curve?

PROBLEMS

1. Forward Rate

a. Assume that, as of today, the annualized two-year interest rate is 13 percent and the one-year interest rate is 12 percent. Use this information to estimate the one-year forward rate.

b. Assume that the liquidity premium on a two-year security is 0.3 percent. Use this information to estimate the one-year forward rate.

2. Forward Rate Assume that, as of today, the annualized interest rate on a three-year security is 10 percent and the annualized interest rate on a two-year security is 7 percent. Use this information to estimate the one-year forward rate two years from now.

3. Forward Rate If $_ti_1 > {_ti_2}$, what is the market consensus forecast about the one-year forward rate one year from now? Is this rate above or below today's one-year interest rate? Explain.

4. After-Tax Yield You need to choose between investing in a one-year municipal bond with a 7 percent yield and a one-year corporate bond with an 11 percent yield. If your marginal federal income tax rate is 30 percent and no other differences exist between these two securities, which would you invest in?

5. Deriving Current Interest Rates Assume that interest rates for one-year securities are expected to be

2 percent today, 4 percent one year from now, and 6 percent two years from now. Using only pure expectations theory, what are the current interest rates on two-year and three-year securities?

6. Commercial Paper Yield

a. A corporation is planning to sell its 90-day commercial paper to investors by offering an 8.4 percent yield. If the three-month T-bill's annualized rate is 7 percent, the default risk premium is estimated to be 0.6 percent, and there is a 0.4 percent tax adjustment, then what is the appropriate liquidity premium?

b. Suppose that, because of unexpected changes in the economy, the default risk premium increases to 0.8 percent. Assuming that no other changes occur, what is the appropriate yield to be offered on the commercial paper?

7. Forward Rate

a. Determine the forward rate for various one-year interest rate scenarios if the two-year interest rate is 8 percent, assuming no liquidity premium. Explain the relationship between the one-year interest rate and the one-year forward rate while holding the two-year interest rate constant.

b. Determine the one-year forward rate for the same one-year interest rate scenarios described in question

(a) while assuming a liquidity premium of 0.4 percent. Does the relationship between the one-year interest rate and the forward rate change when the liquidity premium is considered?

c. Determine how the one-year forward rate would be affected if the quoted two-year interest rate rises; hold constant the quoted one-year interest rate as well as the liquidity premium. Explain the logic of this relationship.

d. Determine how the one-year forward rate would be affected if the liquidity premium rises and if the quoted one-year interest rate is held constant. What if the quoted two-year interest rate is held constant? Explain the logic of this relationship.

8. After-Tax Yield Determine how the after-tax yield from investing in a corporate bond is affected by higher tax rates, holding the before-tax yield constant. Explain the logic of this relationship.

9. Debt Security Yield

a. Determine how the appropriate yield to be offered on a security is affected by a higher risk-free rate. Explain the logic of this relationship.

b. Determine how the appropriate yield to be offered on a security is affected by a higher default risk premium. Explain the logic of this relationship.

FLOW OF FUNDS EXERCISE

Influence of the Structure of Interest Rates

Recall that Carson Company has obtained substantial loans from finance companies and commercial banks. The interest rate on the loans is tied to the six-month Treasury bill rate (and includes a risk premium) and is adjusted every six months. Therefore, Carson's cost of obtaining funds is sensitive to interest rate movements. The company expects that the U.S. economy will strengthen, so it plans to grow in the future by expanding its business and by making acquisitions. Carson anticipates substantial long-term financing to pay for its growth and plans to borrow additional funds, either through loans or by issuing bonds; it is also considering issuing stock to raise funds in the next year.

a. Assume that the market's expectations for the economy are similar to Carson's expectations. Also assume that the yield curve is primarily influenced by interest rate expectations. Would the yield curve be upward sloping or downward sloping? Why?

b. If Carson could obtain more debt financing for 10-year projects, would it prefer to obtain credit at a long-term fixed interest rate or at a floating rate? Why?

c. If Carson attempts to obtain funds by issuing 10-year bonds, explain what information would help in estimating the yield it would have to pay on 10-year bonds. That is, what are the key factors that would influence the rate Carson would pay on its 10-year bonds?

d. If Carson attempts to obtain funds by issuing loans with floating interest rates every six months, explain what information would help in estimating the yield it would have to pay over the next 10 years. That is, what are the key factors that would influence the rate Carson would pay over the 10-year period?

e. An upward-sloping yield curve suggests that the initial rate that financial institutions could charge on a long-term loan to Carson would be higher than the initial rate they could charge on a loan that floats in accordance with short-term interest rates. Does this imply that creditors should prefer offering Carson a fixed-rate loan to offering them a floating-rate loan? Explain why Carson's expectations of future interest rates are not necessarily the same as those of some financial institutions.

INTERNET/EXCEL EXERCISES

1. Assess the shape of the yield curve by using the website www.bloomberg.com. Click on "Market data" and then on "Rates & bonds." Is the Treasury yield curve upward or downward sloping? What is the yield of a 90-day Treasury bill? What is the yield of a 30-year Treasury bond?

2. Based on the various theories attempting to explain the yield curve's shape, what could explain the difference between the yields of the 90-day Treasury bill and the 30-year Treasury bond? Which theory, in your opinion, is the most reasonable? Why?

WSJ EXERCISE

Interpreting the Structure of Interest Rates

a. Explaining Yield Differentials Using the most recent issue of the *Wall Street Journal*, review the yields for the following securities:

TYPE	MATURITY	YIELD
Treasury	10-year	___
Corporate: high-quality	10-year	___
Corporate: medium-quality	10-year	___
Municipal (tax-exempt)	10-year	___

If credit (default) risk is the only reason for the yield differentials, then what is the default risk premium on the corporate high-quality bonds? On the medium-quality bonds?

During a recent recession, high-quality corporate bonds offered a yield of 0.8 percent above Treasury bonds while medium-quality bonds offered a yield of about 3.1 percent above Treasury bonds. How do these yield differentials compare to the differentials today? Explain the reason for any change.

Using the information in the previous table, complete the following table. In Column 2, indicate the before-tax yield necessary to achieve the existing after-tax yield of tax-exempt bonds. In Column 3, answer this question: If the tax-exempt bonds have the same risk and other features as high-quality corporate bonds, which type of bond is preferable for investors in each tax bracket?

MARGINAL TAX BRACKET OF INVESTORS	EQUIVALENT BEFORE-TAX YIELD	PREFERRED BOND
10%	___	___
15%	___	___
20%	___	___
28%	___	___
34%	___	___

b. Examining Recent Adjustments in Credit Risk Using the most recent issue of the *Wall Street Journal*, review the corporate debt section showing the high-yield issue with the biggest price decrease.

- Why do you think there was such a large decrease in price?
- How does this decrease in price affect the expected yield for any investors who buy bonds now?

c. Determining and Interpreting Today's Term Structure Using the most recent issue of the *Wall Street Journal*, review the yield curve to determine the approximate yields for the following maturities:

TERM TO MATURITY	ANNUALIZED YIELD
1 year	___
2 years	___
3 years	___

Assuming that the differences in these yields are due solely to interest rate expectations, determine the one-year forward rate as of one year from now and the one-year forward rate as of two years from now.

d. The *Wall Street Journal* provides a "Treasury Yield Curve." Use this curve to describe the market's expectations about future interest rates. If a liquidity premium exists, how would this affect your perception of the market's expectations?

ONLINE ARTICLES WITH REAL-WORLD EXAMPLES

Find a recent practical article available online that describes a real-world example regarding a specific financial institution or financial market that reinforces one or more concepts covered in this chapter.

If your class has an online component, your professor may ask you to post your summary of the article there and provide a link to the article so that other students can access it. If your class is live, your professor may ask you to summarize your application of the article in class. Your professor may assign specific students to complete this assignment or may allow any students to do the assignment on a volunteer basis.

For recent online articles and real-world examples related to this chapter, consider using the following search terms (be sure to include the prevailing year as a search term to ensure that the online articles are recent):

1. credit risk
2. credit ratings AND risk
3. risk premium
4. yield curve
5. yield curve AND interest rate
6. interest rate AND liquidity premium
7. interest rate AND credit risk
8. rating agency AND risk
9. term structure AND maturity
10. yield curve AND financing

Interest Rate Forecasts and Investment Decisions

This problem requires an understanding of how economic conditions affect interest rates and bond yields (Chapters 1, 2, and 3).

Your task is to use information about existing economic conditions to forecast U.S. and Canadian interest rates. The following information is available to you.

1. Over the past six months, U.S. interest rates have declined and Canadian interest rates have increased.

2. The U.S. economy has weakened over the past year while the Canadian economy has improved.

3. The U.S. saving rate (proportion of income saved) is expected to decrease slightly over the next year; the Canadian saving rate will remain stable.

4. The U.S. and Canadian central banks are not expected to implement any policy changes that would have a significant impact on interest rates.

5. You expect the U.S. economy to strengthen considerably over the next year but still be weaker than it was two years ago. You expect the Canadian economy to remain stable.

6. You expect the U.S. annual budget deficit to increase slightly from last year but be significantly less than the average annual budget deficit over the past five years. You expect the Canadian budget deficit to be about the same as last year.

7. You expect the U.S. inflation rate to rise slightly but still remain below the relatively high levels of two years ago; you expect the Canadian inflation rate to decline.

8. Based on some events last week, most economists and investors around the world (including yourself) expect the U.S. dollar to weaken against the Canadian dollar and against other foreign currencies over the next year. This expectation was already accounted for in your forecasts of inflation and economic growth.

9. The yield curve in the United States currently exhibits a consistent downward slope. The yield curve in Canada currently exhibits an upward slope. You believe that the liquidity premium on securities is quite small.

Questions

1. Using the information available to you, forecast the direction of U.S. interest rates.

2. Using the information available to you, forecast the direction of Canadian interest rates.

3. Assume that the perceived risk of corporations in the United States is expected to increase. Explain how the yield of newly issued U.S. corporate bonds will change to a different degree than will the yield of newly issued U.S. Treasury bonds.

PART 2
The Fed and Monetary Policy

The chapters in Part 2 explain how the Federal Reserve System (the Fed) affects economic conditions. Because the policies implemented by the Fed can influence securities prices, they are closely monitored by financial market participants. By assessing the Fed's policies, market participants can more accurately value securities and make more effective investment and financing decisions.

4

Functions of the Fed

CHAPTER OBJECTIVES

The specific objectives of this chapter are to:

- describe the organizational structure of the Fed,

- describe how the Fed influences monetary policy,

- explain how the Fed revised its lending role in response to the credit crisis, and

- explain how monetary policy is used in other countries.

WEB

www.clevelandfed.org
Features economic and banking topics.

The **Federal Reserve System** (the Fed) is involved (along with other agencies) in regulating commercial banks. It is responsible for conducting periodic evaluations of state-chartered banks and savings institutions with more than $50 billion in assets. Its role as regulator is discussed in Chapter 18.

4-1 OVERVIEW

As the central bank of the United States, the Fed has the responsibility for conducting national monetary policy in an attempt to achieve full employment and price stability (low or zero inflation) in the United States. With its monetary policy, the Fed can influence the state of the U.S. economy in the following ways. First, since the Fed's monetary policy affects interest rates, it has a strong influence on the cost of borrowing by households and thus affects the amount of monthly payments on mortgages, car loans, and other loans. In this way, monetary policy determines what households can afford and therefore how much consumers spend.

Second, monetary policy also affects the cost of borrowing by businesses and thereby influences how much money businesses are willing to borrow to support or expand their operations. By its effect on the amount of spending by households and businesses, monetary policy influences the aggregate demand for products and services in the United States and therefore influences the national income level and employment level. Since the aggregate demand can affect the price level of products and services, the Fed indirectly influences the price level and hence the rate of inflation in the United States.

Because the Fed's monetary policy affects interest rates, it has a direct effect on the prices of debt securities. It can also indirectly affect the prices of equity securities by affecting economic conditions, which influence the future cash flows generated by publicly traded businesses. Overall, the Fed's monetary policy can have a major impact on households, businesses, and investors. A more detailed explanation of how the Fed's monetary policy affects interest rates is provided in Chapter 5.

4-2 ORGANIZATIONAL STRUCTURE OF THE FED

During the late 1800s and early 1900s, the United States experienced several banking panics that culminated in a major crisis in 1907. This motivated Congress to establish a central bank. In 1913, the Federal Reserve Act was implemented, which established reserve requirements for the commercial banks that chose to become members. It also specified 12 districts across the United States as well as a city in each district where a

Federal Reserve district bank was to be established. Initially, each district bank had the ability to affect the money supply (as will be explained later in this chapter). Each district bank focused on its particular district without much concern for other districts. Over time, the system became more centralized, and money supply decisions were assigned to a particular group of individuals rather than across 12 district banks.

The Fed earns most of its income from the interest on its holdings of U.S. government securities (to be discussed shortly). It also earns some income from providing services to financial institutions. Most of its income is transferred to the Treasury.

The Fed as it exists today has five major components:

- Federal Reserve district banks
- Member banks
- Board of Governors
- Federal Open Market Committee (FOMC)
- Advisory committees

4-2a Federal Reserve District Banks

The 12 Federal Reserve districts are identified in Exhibit 4.1, along with the city where each district bank is located. The New York district bank is considered the most important because many large banks are located in this district. Commercial banks that become members of the Fed are required to purchase stock in their **Federal Reserve district bank**. This stock, which is not traded in a secondary market, pays a maximum dividend of 6 percent annually.

Each Fed district bank has nine directors. There are three Class A directors, who are employees or officers of a bank in that district and are elected by member banks to represent member banks. There are three Class B directors, who are not affiliated with any bank and are elected by member banks to represent the public. There are also three Class C directors, who are not affiliated with any bank and are appointed by the Board of Governors (to be discussed shortly). The president of each Fed district bank is appointed by the three Class B and three Class C directors representing that district.

Fed district banks facilitate operations within the banking system by clearing checks, replacing old currency, and providing loans (through the so-called discount window) to depository institutions in need of funds. They also collect economic data and conduct research projects on commercial banking and economic trends.

4-2b Member Banks

Commercial banks can elect to become member banks if they meet specific requirements of the Board of Governors. All national banks (chartered by the Comptroller of the Currency) are required to be members of the Fed, but other banks (chartered by their respective states) are not. Currently, about 35 percent of all banks are members; these banks account for about 70 percent of all bank deposits.

4-2c Board of Governors

The **Board of Governors** (sometimes called the Federal Reserve Board) is made up of seven individual members with offices in Washington, D.C. Each member is appointed by the President of the United States and serves a nonrenewable 14-year term. This long term is thought to reduce political pressure on the governors and thus encourage the development of policies that will benefit the U.S. economy over the long run. The terms are staggered so that one term expires in every even-numbered year.

WEB

www.federalreserve.
gov

Background on the
Board of Governors,
board meetings, board
members, and the
structure of the Fed.

Exhibit 4.1   Locations of Federal Reserve District Banks

LEGEND

—————— Boundaries of Federal Reserve Districts

—————— Boundaries of Federal Reserve Branch Territories

⊙ Board of Governors of the Federal Reserve System

⊚ Federal Reserve Bank Cities

Source: *Federal Reserve Bulletin.*

One of the seven board members is selected by the president to be the Federal Reserve chairman for a four-year term, which may be renewed. The chairman has no more voting power than any other member but may have more influence. Paul Volcker (chairman from 1979 to 1987), Alan Greenspan (chairman from 1987 to 2006), and Ben Bernanke (whose term began in 2006) were regarded as being highly persuasive.

As a result of the Financial Reform Act of 2010, one of the seven board members is designated by the president to be the Vice Chairman for Supervision; this member is responsible for developing policy recommendations that concern regulating the Board of Governors. The Vice Chairman reports to Congress semiannually. The board participates in setting credit controls, such as margin requirements (percentage of a purchase of securities that must be paid with no borrowed funds). With regard to monetary policy, the board has the power to revise reserve requirements imposed on depository institutions. The board can also control the money supply by participating in the decisions of the Federal Open Market Committee, discussed next.

WEB

www.federalreserve.gov/monetarypolicy/fomc.htm

Find information about the Federal Open Market Committee (FOMC).

4-2d Federal Open Market Committee

The **Federal Open Market Committee (FOMC)** is made up of the seven members of the Board of Governors plus the presidents of five Fed district banks (the New York district bank plus 4 of the other 11 Fed district banks as determined on a rotating basis). Presidents of the seven remaining Fed district banks typically participate in the FOMC meetings but are not allowed to vote on policy decisions. The chairman of the Board of Governors serves as chairman of the FOMC.

The main goals of the FOMC are to achieve stable economic growth and price stability (low inflation). Achievement of these goals would stabilize financial markets and interest rates. The FOMC attempts to achieve its goals by controlling the money supply, as described shortly.

4-2e Advisory Committees

The Federal Advisory Council consists of one member from each Federal Reserve district who represents the banking industry. Each district's member is elected each year by the board of directors of the respective district bank. The council meets with the Board of Governors in Washington, D.C., at least four times a year and makes recommendations about economic and banking issues.

The Consumer Advisory Council is made up of 30 members who represent the financial institutions industry and its consumers. This committee normally meets with the Board of Governors four times a year to discuss consumer issues.

The Thrift Institutions Advisory Council is made up of 12 members who represent savings banks, savings and loan associations, and credit unions. Its purpose is to offer views on issues specifically related to these institutions. It meets with the Board of Governors three times a year.

4-2f Integration of Federal Reserve Components

Exhibit 4.2 shows the relationships among the various components of the Federal Reserve System. The advisory committees advise the board, while the board oversees operations of the district banks. The board and representatives of the district banks make up the FOMC.

4-2g Consumer Financial Protection Bureau

As a result of the Financial Reform Act of 2010, the Consumer Financial Protection Bureau was established. It is housed within the Federal Reserve but is independent of the other Fed committees. The bureau's director is appointed by the president with consent of the Senate. The bureau is responsible for regulating financial products and services, including online banking, certificates of deposit, and mortgages. In theory, the bureau can act quickly to protect consumers from deceptive practices rather than waiting for Congress to pass new laws. Financial services administered by auto dealers are exempt from the bureau's oversight. An Office of Financial Literacy will also be created to educate individuals about financial products and services.

4-3 How the Fed Controls Money Supply

The Fed controls the money supply in order to affect interest rates and thereby affect economic conditions. Financial market participants closely monitor the Fed's actions so that they can anticipate how the money supply will be affected. They then use this information to forecast economic conditions and securities prices. The relationship between

Exhibit 4.2   Integration of Federal Reserve Components

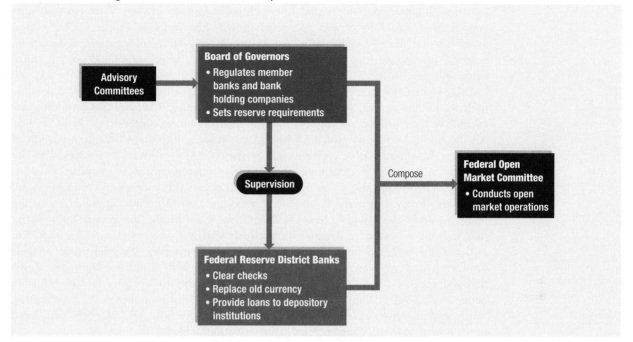

the money supply and economic conditions is discussed in detail in the following chapter. First, it is important to understand *how* the Fed controls the money supply.

4-3a Open Market Operations

The FOMC meets eight times a year. At each meeting, targets for the money supply growth level and the interest rate level are determined, and actions are taken to implement the monetary policy dictated by the FOMC. If the Fed wants to consider changing its targets for money growth or interest rates before its next scheduled meeting it may hold a conference call meeting.

Pre-Meeting Economic Reports   About two weeks before the FOMC meeting, FOMC members are sent the **Beige Book**, which is a consolidated report of regional economic conditions in each of the 12 districts. Each Federal Reserve district bank is responsible for reporting its regional conditions, and all of these reports are consolidated to compose the Beige Book.

About one week before the FOMC meeting, participants receive analyses of the economy and economic forecasts. Thus there is much information for participants to study before the meeting.

Economic Presentations   The FOMC meeting is conducted in the boardroom of the Federal Reserve Building in Washington, D.C. The seven members of the Board of Governors, the 12 presidents of the Fed district banks, and staff members (typically economists) of the Board of Governors are in attendance. The meeting begins with presentations by the staff members about current economic conditions and recent economic trends. Presentations include data and trends for wages, consumer prices, unemployment, gross domestic product, business inventories, foreign exchange rates, interest rates, and financial market conditions.

The staff members also assess production levels, business investment, residential construction, international trade, and international economic growth. This assessment is conducted in order to predict economic growth and inflation in the United States, assuming that the Fed does not adjust its monetary policy. For example, a decline in business inventories may lead to an expectation of stronger economic growth, since firms will need to boost production in order to replenish inventories. Conversely, an increase in inventories may indicate that firms will reduce their production and possibly their workforces as well. An increase in business investment indicates that businesses are expanding their production capacity and are likely to increase production in the future. An increase in economic growth in foreign countries is important because a portion of the rising incomes in those countries will be spent on U.S. products or services. The Fed uses this information to determine whether U.S. economic growth is adequate.

Much attention is also given to any factors that can affect inflation. For example, oil prices are closely monitored because they affect the cost of producing and transporting many products. A decline in business inventories when production is near full capacity may indicate an excessive demand for products that will pull prices up. This condition indicates the potential for higher inflation because firms may raise the prices of their products when they are producing near full capacity and experience shortages. Firms that attempt to expand their capacity under these conditions will have to raise wages to obtain additional qualified employees. The firms will incur higher costs from raising wages and therefore raise the prices of their products. The Fed becomes concerned when several indicators suggest that higher inflation is likely.

The staff members typically base their forecasts for economic conditions on the assumption that the prevailing monetary growth level will continue in the future. When it is highly likely that the monetary growth level will be changed, they provide forecasts for economic conditions under different monetary growth scenarios. Their goal is to provide facts and economic forecasts, not to make judgments about the appropriate monetary policy. The members normally receive some economic information a few days before the meeting so that they are prepared when the staff members make their presentations.

FOMC Decisions Once the presentations are completed, each FOMC member has a chance to offer recommendations as to whether the federal funds target should be changed. The target may be specified as a specific point estimate, such as 2.5 percent, or as a range, such as from 2.5 to 2.75 percent.

In general, evidence that the economy is weakening may result in recommendations that the Fed implement a monetary policy to reduce the federal funds rate and stimulate the economy. For example, Exhibit 4.3 shows how the federal funds rate was reduced near the end of 2007 and in 2008 as the economy weakened. In December 2008, the Fed set the targeted federal funds rate in the form of a range between 0 and 0.25 percent. The goal was to stimulate the economy by reducing interest rates in order to encourage more borrowing and spending by households and businesses. The Fed maintained the federal funds rate within this range over the 2009–2013 period.

When there is evidence of a very strong economy and high inflation, the Fed tends to implement a monetary policy that will increase the federal funds rate and reduce economic growth. This policy would be intended to reduce any inflationary pressure that is attributed to excess demand for products and services. The participants are commonly given three options for monetary policy, which are intended to cover a range of the most reasonable policies and should include at least one policy that is satisfactory to each member.

Exhibit 4.3   Federal Funds Rate over Time

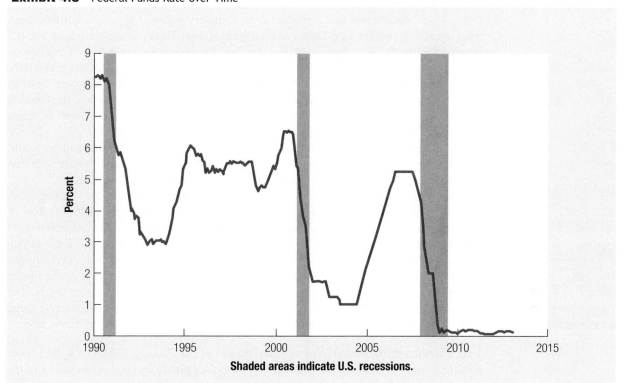

Shaded areas indicate U.S. recessions.

Source: *Board of Governors, Federal Reserve.*

The FOMC meeting allows for participation by voting and nonvoting members. The chairman of the Fed may also offer a recommendation and usually has some influence over the other members. After all members have provided their recommendations, the voting members of the FOMC vote on whether the interest rate target levels should be revised. Most FOMC decisions on monetary policy are unanimous, although it is not unusual for some decisions to have one or two dissenting votes.

FOMC Statement   Following the FOMC meeting, the committee provides a statement that summarizes its conclusion. The FOMC has in recent years begun to recognize the importance of this statement, which is used (along with other information) by many participants in the financial markets to generate forecasts of the economy. Since 2007, voting members vote not only on the proper policy but also on the corresponding communication (statement) of that policy to the public. The statement is clearly written with meaningful details. This is an improvement over previous years, when the statement contained vague phrases that made it difficult for the public to understand the FOMC's plans. The statement provided by the committee following each meeting is widely publicized in the news media and also can be accessed on Federal Reserve websites.

Minutes of FOMC Meeting   Within three weeks of a FOMC meeting, the minutes for that meeting are provided to the public and are also accessible on Federal Reserve websites. The minutes commonly illustrate the different points of view held by various participants at the FOMC meeting.

4-3b Role of the Fed's Trading Desk

If the FOMC determines that a change in its monetary policy is appropriate, its decision is forwarded to the **Trading Desk** (or the **Open Market Desk**) at the New York Federal Reserve District Bank through a statement called the **policy directive**. The FOMC specifies a desired target for the federal funds rate, the rate charged by banks on short-term loans to each other. Even though this rate is determined by the banks that participate in the federal funds market, it is subject to the supply and demand for funds in the banking system. Thus, the Fed influences the federal funds rate by revising the amount of funds in the banking system.

Since all short-term interest rates are affected by the supply of and demand for funds, they tend to move together. Thus the Fed's actions affect all short-term interest rates that are market determined and may even affect long-term interest rates as well.

After receiving a policy directive from the FOMC, the manager of the Trading Desk instructs traders who work at that desk on the amount of Treasury securities to buy or sell in the secondary market based on the directive. The buying and selling of government securities (through the Trading Desk) is referred to as open market operations. Even though the Trading Desk at the Federal Reserve Bank of New York receives a policy directive from the FOMC only eight times a year, it continuously conducts open market operations to control the money supply in response to ongoing changes in bank deposit levels. The FOMC is not limited to issuing new policy directives only on its scheduled meeting dates. It can hold additional meetings at any time to consider changing the federal funds rate.

Fed Purchase of Securities When traders at the Trading Desk at the New York Fed are instructed to *lower* the federal funds rate, they purchase Treasury securities in the secondary market. First, they call government securities dealers to obtain their list of securities for sale, including the denomination and maturity of each security, and the dealer's ask quote (the price at which the dealer is willing to sell the security). From this list, the traders attempt to purchase those Treasury securities that are most attractive (lowest prices for whatever maturities are desired) until they have purchased the amount requested by the manager of the Trading Desk. The accounting department of the New York Fed then notifies the government bond department to receive and pay for those securities.

When the Fed purchases securities through government securities dealers, the bank account balances of the dealers increase and so the total deposits in the banking system increase. This increase in the supply of funds places downward pressure on the federal funds rate. The Fed increases the total amount of funds at the dealers' banks until the federal funds rate declines to the new targeted level. Such activity, which is initiated by the FOMC's policy directive, represents a *loosening* of money supply growth.

The Fed's purchase of government securities has a different impact than a purchase by another investor would have because the Fed's purchase results in additional bank funds and increases the ability of banks to make loans and create new deposits. An increase in funds can allow for a net increase in deposit balances and therefore an increase in the money supply. Conversely, the purchase of government securities by someone other than the Fed (such as an investor) results in offsetting account balance positions at commercial banks. For example, as investors purchase Treasury securities in the secondary market, their bank balances decline while the bank balances of the sellers of the Treasury securities increase.

Fed Sale of Securities If the Trading Desk at the New York Fed is instructed to *increase* the federal funds rate, its traders sell government securities (obtained from previous purchases) to government securities dealers. The securities are sold to the dealers that

WEB

www.treasurydirect.
gov
Treasury note and bond
auction results.

submit the highest bids. As the dealers pay for the securities, their bank account balances are reduced. Thus the total amount of funds in the banking system is reduced by the market value of the securities sold by the Fed. This reduction in the supply of funds in the banking system places upward pressure on the federal funds rate. Such activity, which also is initiated by the FOMC's policy directive, is referred to as a *tightening* of money supply growth.

Fed Trading of Repurchase Agreements   In some cases, the Fed may wish to increase the aggregate level of bank funds for only a few days in order to ensure adequate liquidity in the banking system on those days. Under these conditions, the Trading Desk may trade **repurchase agreements** rather than government securities. It purchases Treasury securities from government securities dealers with an agreement to sell back the securities at a specified date in the near future. Initially, the level of funds rises as the securities are sold; it is then reduced when the dealers repurchase the securities. The Trading Desk uses repurchase agreements during holidays and other such periods to correct temporary imbalances in the level of bank funds. To correct a temporary excess of funds, the Trading Desk sells some of its Treasury securities holdings to securities dealers and agrees to repurchase them at a specified future date.

Control of M1 versus M2   When the Fed conducts open market operations to adjust the money supply, it must also consider the measure of money on which it will focus. For the Fed's purposes, the optimal form of money should (1) be controllable by the Fed and (2) have a predictable impact on economic variables when adjusted by the Fed. The most narrow form of money, known as **M1**, includes currency held by the public and checking deposits (such as demand deposits, NOW accounts, and automatic transfer balances) at depository institutions. The M1 measure does not include all funds that can be used for transactions purposes. For example, checks can be written against a **money market deposit account (MMDA)** offered by depository institutions or against a money market mutual fund. In addition, funds can easily be withdrawn from savings accounts to make transactions. For this reason, a broader measure of money, called **M2**, also deserves consideration. It includes everything in M1 as well as savings accounts and small time deposits, MMDAs, and some other items. Another measure of money, called **M3**, includes everything in M2 in addition to large time deposits and other items. Although there are even a few broader measures of money, it is M1, M2, and M3 that receive the most attention. A comparison of these measures of money is provided in Exhibit 4.4.

The M1 money measure is more volatile than M2 or M3. Since M1 can change owing simply to changes in the types of deposits maintained by households, M2 and M3 are more reliable measures for monitoring and controlling the money supply.

Consideration of Technical Factors   The money supply can shift abruptly as a result of so-called technical factors, such as currency in circulation and Federal Reserve

Exhibit 4.4 Comparison of Money Supply Measures

MONEY SUPPLY MEASURES
M1 = currency + checking deposits
M2 = M1 + savings deposits, MMDAs, overnight repurchase agreements, Eurodollars, no institutional money market mutual funds, and small time deposits
M3 = M2 + institutional money market mutual funds, large time deposits, and repurchase agreements and Eurodollars lasting more than one day

float. When the amount of currency in circulation increases (such as during the holiday season), the corresponding increase in net deposit withdrawals reduces funds; when it decreases, the net addition to deposits increases funds. Federal Reserve float is the amount of checks credited to bank funds that have not yet been collected. A rise in float causes an increase in bank funds, and a decrease in float causes a reduction in bank funds.

The manager of the Trading Desk incorporates the expected impact of technical factors on funds into the instructions to traders. If the policy directive calls for growth in funds but technical factors are expected to increase funds, the instructions will call for a smaller injection of funds than if the technical factors did not exist. Conversely, if technical factors are expected to reduce funds, the instructions will call for a larger injection of funds to offset the impact of the technical factors.

Dynamic versus Defensive Open Market Operations   Depending on the intent, open market operations can be classified as either **dynamic** or **defensive**. Dynamic operations are implemented to increase or decrease the level of funds, whereas defensive operations offset the impact of other conditions that affect the level of funds. For example, if the Fed expected a large inflow of cash into commercial banks then it could offset this inflow by selling some of its Treasury security holdings.

4-3c How Fed Operations Affect All Interest Rates

Even though most interest rates are market determined, the Fed can have a strong influence on these rates by controlling the supply of loanable funds. The use of open market operations to increase bank funds can affect various market-determined interest rates. First, the federal funds rate may decline because some banks have a larger supply of excess funds to lend out in the federal funds market. Second, banks with excess funds may offer new loans at a lower interest rate in order to make use of these funds. Third, these banks may also lower interest rates offered on deposits because they have more than adequate funds to conduct existing operations.

Because open market operations commonly involve the buying or selling of Treasury bills, the yields on Treasury securities are influenced along with the yields (interest rates) offered on bank deposits. For example, when the Fed buys Treasury bills as a means of increasing the money supply, it places upward pressure on their prices. Since these securities offer a fixed value to investors at maturity, a higher price translates into a lower yield for investors who buy them and hold them until maturity. While Treasury yields are affected directly by open market operations, bank rates are also affected because of the change in the money supply that open market operations bring about.

As the yields on Treasury bills and bank deposits decline, investors search for alternative investments such as other debt securities. As more funds are invested in these securities, the yields will decline. Thus open market operations used to increase bank funds influence not only bank deposit and loan rates but also the yields on other debt securities. The reduction in yields on debt securities lowers the cost of borrowing for the issuers of new debt securities. This can encourage potential borrowers (including corporations and individuals) to borrow and make expenditures that they might not have made if interest rates were higher.

If open market operations are used to reduce bank funds, the opposite effects occur. There is upward pressure on the federal funds rate, on the loan rates charged to individuals and firms, and on the rates offered to bank depositors. As bank deposit rates rise, some investors may be encouraged to create bank deposits rather than invest in other debt securities. This activity reduces the amount of funds available for these debt instruments, thereby increasing the yield offered on the instruments.

Open Market Operations in Response to the Economy   During the 2001–2003 period, when economic conditions were weak, the Fed frequently used open market operations to reduce interest rates. During 2004–2007 the economy improved, and the Fed's concern shifted from a weak economy to high inflation. Therefore, it used a policy of raising interest rates in an attempt to keep the economy from overheating and to reduce inflationary pressure.

In 2008, the credit crisis began, and the economy remained weak through 2012. During this period, the Fed used open market operations and reduced interest rates in an attempt to stimulate the economy. Its operations brought short-term T-bill rates down to close to zero percent in an effort to reduce loan rates charged by financial institutions, and thus encourage more borrowing and spending. The impact of monetary policy on economic conditions is given much more attention in the following chapter.

4-3d Adjusting the Reserve Requirement Ratio

Depository institutions are subject to a **reserve requirement ratio**, which is the proportion of their deposit accounts that must be held as required reserves (funds held in reserve). This ratio is set by the Board of Governors. Depository institutions have historically been forced to maintain between 8 and 12 percent of their transactions accounts (such as checking accounts) and a smaller proportion of their other savings accounts as required reserves. The **Depository Institutions Deregulation and Monetary Control Act (DIDMCA)** of 1980 established that all depository institutions are subject to the Fed's reserve requirements. Required reserves were held in a non–interest-bearing form until 2008, when the rule was changed. Now the Fed pays interest on required reserves maintained by depository institutions.

Because the reserve requirement ratio affects the degree to which the money supply can change, it is considered a monetary policy tool. By changing it, the Board of Governors can adjust the money supply. When the board reduces the reserve requirement ratio, it increases the proportion of a bank's deposits that can be lent out by depository institutions. As the funds loaned out are spent, a portion of them will return to the depository institutions in the form of new deposits. The lower the reserve requirement ratio, the greater the lending capacity of depository institutions; for this reason, any initial change in bank required reserves can cause a larger change in the money supply. In 1992, the Fed reduced the reserve requirement ratio on transactions accounts from 12 to 10 percent, where it has remained.

Impact of Reserve Requirements on Money Growth   An adjustment in the reserve requirement ratio changes the proportion of financial institution funds that can be lent out, and this affects the degree to which the money supply can grow.

EXAMPLE

Assume the following conditions in the banking system:

Assumption 1. Banks obtain all their funds from demand deposits and use all funds except required reserves to make loans.

Assumption 2. The public does not store any cash; any funds withdrawn from banks are spent; and any funds received are deposited in banks.

Assumption 3. The reserve requirement ratio on demand deposits is 10 percent.

Based on these assumptions, 10 percent of all bank deposits are maintained as required reserves and the other 90 percent are loaned out (zero excess reserves). Now assume that the Fed initially uses open market operations by purchasing $100 million worth of Treasury securities.

As the Treasury securities dealers sell securities to the Fed, their deposit balances at commercial banks increase by $100 million. Banks maintain 10 percent of the $100 million, or $10 million, as

Exhibit 4.5 Illustration of Multiplier Effect

Increase in deposits at banks	Required reserves held on new deposits	Funds received from new deposits that can be lent out
$100 million	$10 million	$90 million
$90 million	$9.0 million	$81 million
$81 million	$8.1 million	$72.9 million

required reserves and lend out the rest. As the $90 million lent out is spent, it returns to banks as new demand deposit accounts (by whoever received the funds that were spent). Banks maintain 10 percent, or $9 million, of these new deposits as required reserves and lend out the remainder ($81 million). The initial increase in demand deposits (money) multiplies into a much larger amount.

This process, illustrated in Exhibit 4.5, will not continue forever. Every time the funds lent out return to a bank, a portion (10 percent) is retained as required reserves. Thus the amount of new deposits created is less for each round. Under the previous assumptions, the initial money supply injection of $100 million would multiply by 1 divided by the reserve requirement ratio, or 1/0.10, to equal 10; hence the total change in the money supply, once the cycle is complete, is

$100 million × 10 = $1 billion. ●

As this simplified example demonstrates, an initial injection of funds will multiply into a larger amount. The reserve requirement controls the amount of loanable funds that can be created from new deposits. A higher reserve requirement ratio causes an initial injection of funds to multiply by a smaller amount. Conversely, a lower reserve requirement ratio causes it to multiply by a greater amount. In this way, the Fed can adjust money supply growth by changing the reserve requirement ratio.

In reality, households sometimes hold cash and banks sometimes hold excess reserves, contrary to the example's initial assumptions. Hence major leakages occur, and money does not multiply to the extent shown in the example. The money multiplier can change over time because of changes in the excess reserve level and in household preferences for demand deposits versus time deposits, as time deposits are not included in the most narrow definition of money. This complicates the task of forecasting how an initial adjustment in bank-required reserves will ultimately affect the money supply level. Another disadvantage of using the reserve requirement as a monetary policy tool is that an adjustment in its ratio can cause erratic shifts in the money supply. Thus the probability of missing the target money supply level is higher when using the reserve requirement ratio. Because of these limitations, the Fed normally relies on open market operations rather than adjustments in the reserve requirement ratio when controlling the money supply.

4-3e Adjusting the Fed's Loan Rate

The Fed has traditionally provided short-term loans to depository institutions through its discount window. Before 2003, the Fed set its loan rate (then called the "discount rate") at low levels when it wanted to encourage banks to borrow, since this activity increased

Exhibit 4.6   Primary Credit Rate over Time

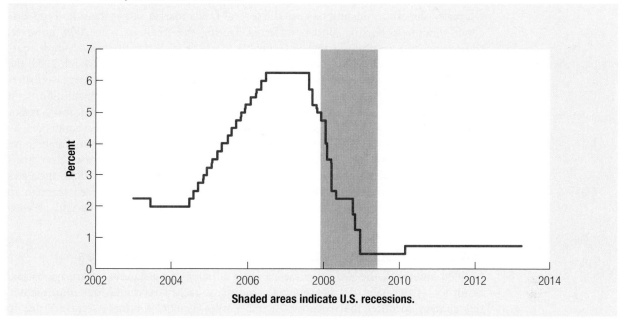

Source: *Board of Governors, Federal Reserve.*

the amount of funds injected into the financial system. The discount rate was viewed as a monetary policy tool because it could have been used to affect the money supply (although it was not an effective tool).

Since 2003, the Fed's rate on short-term loans to depository institutions has been called the *primary credit lending rate,* which is set slightly above the federal funds rate (the rate charged on short-term loans between depository institutions). Depository institutions therefore rely on the Fed only as a backup for loans, since they should be able to obtain short-term loans from other institutions at a lower interest rate.

The primary credit rate is shown in Exhibit 4.6. The Fed periodically increased this rate during the 2003–2007 period when economic conditions were strong. It then periodically reduced this rate during the 2008–2010 period when economic conditions were weak, to keep it in line with the targeted federal funds rate.

In 2003, the Fed began classifying the loans it provides into primary and secondary credit. *Primary credit* may be used for any purpose and is available only to depository institutions that satisfy specific criteria reflecting financial soundness. The loans are typically for a one-day period. *Secondary credit* is provided to depository institutions that do not satisfy those criteria, so they must pay a premium above the loan rate charged on primary credit. The Fed's lending facility can be an important source of liquidity for some depository institutions, but it is no longer used to control the money supply.

4-4 The Fed's Intervention during the Credit Crisis

During and after the credit crisis, the Fed not only engaged in traditional open market operations (purchasing Treasury securities) to reduce interest rates, but also implemented various nontraditional strategies in an effort to improve economic conditions.

4-4a Fed Loans to Facilitate Rescue of Bear Stearns

Normally, depository institutions use the federal funds market rather than the Fed's discount window to borrow short-term funds. During the credit crisis in 2008, however, some depository institutions that were unable to obtain credit in the federal funds market were allowed to obtain funding from the Fed's discount window. In March 2008, the Fed's discount window provided funding that enabled Bear Stearns, a large securities firm, to avoid filing for bankruptcy. Bear Stearns was not a depository institution, so it would not ordinarily be allowed to borrow funds from the Fed. However, it was a major provider of clearing operations for many types of financial transactions conducted by firms and individuals. If it had gone bankrupt those financial transactions might have been delayed, potentially creating liquidity problems for many individuals and firms that were to receive cash as a result of the transactions. On March 16, 2008, the Fed's discount window provided a loan to J.P. Morgan Chase that was passed through to Bear Stearns. This ensured that the clearing operations would continue and avoided liquidity problems.

4-4b Fed Purchases of Mortgage-Backed Securities

In 2008 and 2009, the Fed purchased a large amount of outstanding mortgage-backed securities. It normally did not purchase mortgage-backed securities, but implemented this strategy to offset the reduction in the market demand for these securities due to investor fears. These fears were partially triggered by the failure of Lehman Brothers (a very large financial institution) in 2008, which suffered serious losses in its investments in mortgages and mortgage-backed securities. The market values of these securities had weakened substantially due to the high default rate on mortgages. The Fed's strategy was intended to create a demand for mortgages and securities backed by mortgages in order to stimulate the housing market. The Fed has continued to periodically purchase mortgage-backed securities in recent years.

4-4c Fed's Purchase of Bonds Backed by Loans

In November 2008, the Federal Reserve created a term asset-backed security loan facility (TALF) that provided financing to financial institutions purchasing high-quality bonds backed by consumer loans, credit card loans, or automobile loans. The market for these types of bonds became inactive during the credit crisis, and this discouraged lenders from making consumer loans because they could not easily sell the loans in the secondary market. The facility provided loans to institutional investors that purchased these types of loans. In this way, the Fed encouraged financial institutions to return to this market and thereby increased its liquidity. This was important because it indirectly ensured that more funding would be available to support consumer loans.

4-4d Fed's Purchase of Commercial Paper

During 2008 and 2009, the Fed purchased a large amount of commercial paper. It normally did not purchase commercial paper, but implemented this strategy to offset the reduction in the market demand for commercial paper due to investor fears of defaults on commercial paper. Those fears were partially triggered by the failure of Lehman Brothers, which caused Lehman to default on the commercial paper that it had previously issued. Investors presumed that if Lehman's asset quality was so weak that it could not cover its payments on commercial paper, other financial institutions that issued commercial paper and had large holdings of mortgage-backed securities might have the same outcome.

Furthermore, the issuance of commercial paper and other debt securities in the primary market declined because institutional investors were unwilling to purchase securities that could not be sold in the secondary market. Hence credit was no longer easily accessible, and this made the credit crisis worse. The Fed recognized that some of these debt securities had low risk, yet the financial markets were paralyzed by fear of potential default. The Fed's willingness to purchase commercial paper and other debt securities restored trading and liquidity in some debt markets.

4-4e Fed's Purchase of Long-term Treasury Securities

In 2010, the Fed purchased a large amount of long-term Treasury notes and bonds, which was different from its normal open market operations that focused on purchasing short-term Treasury securities. The emphasis on purchasing long-term securities was intended to reduce long-term Treasury bond yields, which would indirectly result in lower long-term borrowing rates. The Fed was attempting to reduce long-term interest rates to encourage more long-term borrowing by corporations for capital expenditures, or more long-term borrowing by individuals to purchase homes. This strategy is discussed in more detail in the following chapter.

4-4f Perception of Fed Intervention During the Crisis

Most people would agree that the Fed took much initiative to improve economic conditions during the credit crisis. However, opinions vary on exactly what the Fed should have done to improve the economy. Many of the Fed's actions during the credit crisis reflected the purchasing of securities to either lower interest rates (traditional monetary policy) or to restore liquidity in the markets for various types of debt securities. The Fed's focus was on improving conditions in financial markets, which can increase the flow of funds from financial markets to corporations or individuals.

However, some critics argue that the actions taken by the Fed were focused on the financial institutions and not on other sectors in the economy. A portion of the criticism is linked to the very high compensation levels paid by some financial institutions (such as some securities firms) to their employees. Critics contend that if these securities firms can afford to pay such high salaries, they should not need to be bailed out by the government.

The Fed might respond that it did not bail out Lehman Brothers (a securities firm), which is why Lehman failed. In addition, the Fed's actions to restore liquidity in debt markets did not just help financial institutions, but were necessary to ensure that all types of corporations and individuals could obtain funding. That funding is needed for corporations and individuals to increase their spending, which can stimulate the economy and create jobs.

It might seem from the previous discussion that there are primarily two opinions regarding the Fed's intervention. In reality, there are many other opinions not covered here. Consider a classroom exercise in which all students are allowed to express their opinion about what the Fed (or U.S. government in general) should have done to correct the credit crisis. Answers will likely range from "the U.S. government should do nothing and let the market fix itself" to "the U.S. government should completely manage all banks and should control salaries." Many students might suggest that the U.S. government should intervene by directing more of its funds to the automotive, health care, or other industries in which they have a personal interest. Some answers might even suggest that major trade barriers should be imposed to correct the credit crisis, which leads to another set of opposing arguments. The point is that during a severe credit crisis, many critics will believe that intervention taken by the Fed is not serving their own interests because they have diverse special interests. Students would likely agree more on the causes of the credit crisis (which are discussed in detail in Chapter 9) than on how the Fed or U.S. government in general should have resolved the crisis.

4-5 GLOBAL MONETARY POLICY

Each country has its own central bank that conducts monetary policy. The central banks of industrialized countries tend to have somewhat similar goals, which essentially reflect price stability (low inflation) and economic growth (low unemployment). Resources and conditions vary among countries, however, so a given central bank may focus more on a particular economic goal.

Like the Fed, central banks of other industrialized countries use open market opera-tions and reserve requirement adjustments as monetary tools. They also make adjust-ments in the interest rate they charge on loans to banks as a monetary policy tool. The monetary policy tools are generally used as a means of affecting local market interest rates in order to influence economic conditions.

Because country economies are integrated, the Fed must consider economic condi-tions in other major countries when assessing the U.S. economy. The Fed may be most effective when it coordinates its activities with those of central banks of other countries. Central banks commonly work together when they intervene in the foreign exchange market, but conflicts of interest can make it difficult to coordinate monetary policies.

4-5a A Single Eurozone Monetary Policy

One of the goals of the European Union (EU) has been to establish a single currency for its members. In 2002, the following European countries replaced their national currencies with the euro: Austria, Belgium, Finland, France, Germany, Greece, Ireland, Italy, Luxembourg, the Netherlands, Portugal, and Spain. Since that time, five more countries have also adopted the euro: Slovenia in 2007, Cyprus and Malta in 2008, Slovakia in 2009, and Estonia in 2011. When the euro was introduced, three of the EU's members at that time (Denmark, Sweden, and the United Kingdom) decided not to adopt the euro, although they may join later. Since the euro was introduced, 12 emerging countries in Europe have joined the EU (10 countries, including the Czech Republic and Hungary, joined in 2004; Bulgaria and Romania joined in 2007). Five of these new members have already adopted the euro, and others may eventually do so after satisfying the limitations imposed on government deficits.

The European Central Bank (ECB), based in Frankfurt, is responsible for setting mone-tary policy for all European countries that use the euro as their currency. This bank's objective is to control inflation in the participating countries and to stabilize (within rea-sonable boundaries) the value of the euro with respect to other major currencies. Thus the ECB's monetary goals of price and currency stability are similar to those of individual countries around the world; they differ in that they are focused on a group of countries rather than a single country. Because participating countries are subject to the monetary policy imposed by the ECB, a given country no longer has full control over the monetary policy implemented within its borders at any given time. The implementation of a com-mon monetary policy may lead to more political unification among participating countries and encourage them to develop similar national defense and foreign policies.

Impact of the Euro on Monetary Policy   As just described, the use of a com-mon currency forces countries to abide by a common monetary policy. Changes in the money supply affect all European countries that use the euro as their currency. A single currency also means that the risk-free interest rate offered on government securities must

WEB

www.ecb.int
Provides links on the European Central Bank and other foreign central banks.

be similar across the participating European countries. Any discrepancy in risk-free rates would encourage investors within these countries to invest in the country with the highest rate, which would realign the interest rates among the countries.

Although having a single monetary policy may allow for more consistent economic conditions across the euro zone countries, it prevents any participating country from solving local economic problems with its own unique monetary policy. Euro zone governments may disagree on the ideal monetary policy for their local economies, but they must nevertheless agree on a single monetary policy. Yet any given policy used in a particular period may enhance economic conditions in some countries and adversely affect others. Each participating country is still able to apply its own fiscal policy (tax and government expenditure decisions), however.

One concern about the euro is that each of the participating countries has its own agenda, which may prevent unified decisions about the future direction of the euro zone economies. Each country was supposed to show restraint on fiscal policy spending so that it could improve its budget deficit situation. Nevertheless, some countries have ignored restraint in favor of resolving domestic unemployment problems. The euro's initial instability was partially attributed to political maneuvering as individual countries tried to serve their own interests at the expense of the other participating countries. This lack of solidarity is exactly the reason why there was some concern about using a single currency (and therefore monetary policy) among several European countries. Disagreements over policy intensified as the European economies weakened during 2008 and 2009.

4-5b Global Central Bank Coordination

In some cases, the central banks of various countries coordinate their efforts for a common cause. Shortly after the terrorist attack on the United States on September 11, 2001, the central banks of several countries injected money denominated in their respective currencies into the banking system to provide more liquidity. This strategy was intended to ensure that sufficient money would be available in case customers began to withdraw funds from banks or cash machines. On September 17, 2001, the Fed's move to reduce interest rates before the U.S. stock market reopened was immediately followed by similar decisions by the Bank of Canada (Canada's central bank) and the European Central Bank.

Sometimes, however, central banks have conflicting objectives. For example, it is not unusual for two countries to simultaneously experience weak economies. In this situation, each central bank may consider intervening to weaken its home currency, which could increase foreign demand for exports denominated in that currency. But if both central banks attempt this type of intervention simultaneously, the exchange rate between the two currencies will be subject to conflicting forces.

EXAMPLE

Today, the Fed plans to intervene directly in the foreign exchange market by selling dollars for yen in an attempt to weaken the dollar. Meanwhile, the Bank of Japan plans to sell yen for dollars in the foreign exchange market in an attempt to weaken the yen. The effects are offsetting. One central bank can attempt to have a greater impact by selling more of its home currency in the foreign exchange market, but the other central bank may respond to offset that force. ●

Global Monetary Policy during the Credit Crisis   During 2008, the effects of the credit crisis began to spread internationally. During August–October, stock market prices in the United States, Canada, China, France, Germany, Italy, Japan, Mexico, Russia, Spain, and many other countries declined by more than 25 percent. Each central bank has its own local interest rate that it might influence with monetary policy in order to control its local economy. Exhibit 4.7 shows how the targeted interest rate level by various central banks changed over time. Notice how these banks increased their targeted interest rate level during the 2006–2007 period because their economies were strong at that time. However, during the financial crisis in 2008, these economies weakened, and the central banks (like the Fed) reduced their interest rates in an effort to stimulate their respective economies.

Exhibit 4.7 Targeted Interest Rates by Central Banks over Time

Source: *Federal Reserve.*

SUMMARY

- The key components of the Federal Reserve System are the Board of Governors and the Federal Open Market Committee. The Board of Governors determines the reserve requirements on account balances at depository institutions. It is also an important subset of the Federal Open Market Committee (FOMC), which determines U.S. monetary policy. The FOMC's monetary policy has a major influence on interest rates and other economic conditions.

- The Fed uses open market operations (the buying and selling of securities) as a means of adjusting the money supply. The Fed purchases securities to increase the money supply and sells them to reduce the money supply.

- In response to the credit crisis, the Fed provided indirect funding to Bear Stearns (a large securities firm) so that it did not have to file for bankruptcy. It also created various facilities for providing funds to financial institutions and other corporations. One facility allowed primary dealers that serve as financial intermediaries for bonds and other securities to obtain overnight loans. Another facility purchased commercial paper issued by corporations.

- Each country has its own central bank, which is responsible for conducting monetary policy to achieve economic goals such as low inflation and low unemployment. Seventeen countries in Europe have adopted a single currency, which means that all of these countries are subject to the same monetary policy.

POINT COUNTER-POINT

Should There Be a Global Central Bank?

Point   Yes. A global central bank could serve all countries in the manner that the European Central Bank now serves several European countries. With a single central bank, there could be a single monetary policy across all countries.

Counter-Point   No. A global central bank could create a global monetary policy only if a single currency were used throughout the world. Moreover, all countries would not agree on the monetary policy that would be appropriate.

Who Is Correct?   Use the Internet to learn more about this issue and then formulate your own opinion.

QUESTIONS AND APPLICATIONS

1. **The Fed** Briefly describe the origin of the Federal Reserve System. Describe the functions of the Fed district banks.

2. **FOMC** What are the main goals of the Federal Open Market Committee (FOMC)? How does it attempt to achieve these goals?

3. **Open Market Operations** Explain how the Fed increases the money supply through open market operations.

4. **Policy Directive** What is the policy directive, and who carries it out?

5. **Beige Book** What is the Beige Book, and why is it important to the FOMC?

6. **Reserve Requirements** How is money supply growth affected by an increase in the reserve requirement ratio?

7. **Control of Money Supply** Describe the characteristics that a measure of money should have if it is to be manipulated by the Fed.

8. **FOMC Economic Presentations** What is the purpose of economic presentations during an FOMC meeting?

9. **Open Market Operations** Explain how the Fed can use open market operations to reduce the money supply.

10. **Effect on Money Supply** Why do the Fed's open market operations have a different effect on the money supply than do transactions between two depository institutions?

11. **Discount Window Lending during Credit Crisis** Explain how and why the Fed extended its discount window lending to nonbank financial institutions during the credit crisis.

12. **The Fed versus Congress** Should the Fed or Congress decide the fate of large financial institutions that are near bankruptcy?

13. **Bailouts by the Fed** Do you think that the Fed should have bailed out large financial institutions during the credit crisis?

14. **The Fed's Impact on Unemployment** Explain how the Fed's monetary policy affects the unemployment level.

15. **The Fed's Impact on Home Purchases** Explain how the Fed influences the monthly mortgage payments on homes. How might the Fed indirectly influence the total demand for homes by consumers?

16. **The Fed's Impact on Security Prices** Explain how the Fed's monetary policy may indirectly affect the price of equity securities.

17. **Impact of FOMC Statement** How might the FOMC statement (following the committee's meeting) stabilize financial markets more than if no statement were provided?

18. **Fed Facility Programs during the Credit Crisis** Explain how the Fed's facility programs improved liquidity in some debt markets.

19. **Consumer Financial Protection Bureau** As a result of the Financial Reform Act of 2010, the Consumer Financial Protection Bureau was established and housed within the Federal Reserve. Explain the role of this bureau.

20. Euro zone Monetary Policy Explain why participating in the euro zone causes a country to give up its independent monetary policy and control over its domestic interest rates.

21. The Fed's Power What should be the Fed's role? Should it be focused only on monetary policy? Or should it be allowed to engage in the trading of various types of securities in order to stabilize the financial system when securities markets are suffering from investor fears and the potential for high default risk?

22. The Fed and Mortgage-Backed Securities How has the Fed used mortgage-backed securities in recent years, and what has it been trying to accomplish?

23. The Fed and Commercial Paper Why and how did the Fed intervene in the commercial paper market during the credit crisis?

24. The Fed and Long-term Treasury Securities Why did the Fed purchase long-term Treasury securities in 2010, and how did this strategy differ from the Fed's usual operations?

25. The Fed and TALF What was TALF, and why did the Fed create it?

Interpreting Financial News

Interpret the following statements made by Wall Street analysts and portfolio managers.

a. "The Fed's future monetary policy will be dependent on the economic indicators to be reported this week."

b. "The Fed's role is to take the punch bowl away just as the party is coming alive."

c. "Inflation will likely increase because real short-term interest rates currently are negative."

Managing in Financial Markets

Anticipating the Fed's Actions As a manager of a large U.S. firm, one of your assignments is to monitor U.S. economic conditions so that you can forecast the demand for products sold by your firm. You realize that the Federal Reserve implements monetary policy—and that the federal government implements spending and tax policies, or fiscal policy—to affect economic growth and inflation. However, it is difficult to achieve high economic growth without igniting inflation. Although the Federal Reserve is often said to be independent of the administration in office, there is much interaction between monetary and fiscal policies.

Assume that the economy is currently stagnant and that some economists are concerned about the possibility of a recession. Yet some industries are experiencing high growth, and inflation is higher this year than in the previous five years. Assume that the Federal Reserve chairman's term will expire in four months and that the President of the United States will have to appoint a new chairman (or reappoint the existing chairman). It is widely known that the existing chairman would like to be reappointed. Also assume that next year is an election year for the administration.

a. Given the circumstances, do you expect that the administration will be more concerned about increasing economic growth or reducing inflation?

b. Given the circumstances, do you expect that the Fed will be more concerned about increasing economic growth or reducing inflation?

c. Your firm is relying on you for some insight on how the government will influence economic conditions and hence the demand for your firm's products. Given the circumstances, what is your forecast of how the government will affect economic conditions?

FLOW OF FUNDS EXERCISE

Monitoring the Fed

Recall that Carson Company has obtained substantial loans from finance companies and commercial banks. The interest rate on the loans is tied to market interest rates and is adjusted every six months. Expecting a strong U.S. economy, Carson plans to grow by expanding its business and by making acquisitions. The company expects that it will need substantial long-term financing, and it plans to borrow additional funds either through loans or by issuing bonds. The Carson Company is also considering issuing stock to raise funds in the next year.

Given its large exposure to interest rates charged on its debt, Carson closely monitors Fed actions. It subscribes to a special service that attempts to monitor the

Fed's actions in the Treasury security markets. It recently received an alert from the service that suggested the Fed has been selling large holdings of its Treasury securities in the secondary Treasury securities market.

a. How should Carson interpret the actions by the Fed? That is, will these actions place upward or downward pressure on the price of Treasury securities? Explain.

b. Will these actions place upward or downward pressure on Treasury yields? Explain.

c. Will these actions place upward or downward pressure on interest rates? Explain.

INTERNET/EXCEL EXERCISE

Assess the current structure of the Federal Reserve System by using the website www.federalreserve.gov/monetarypolicy/fomc.htm.

Go to the minutes of the most recent meeting. Who is the current chairman? Who is the current vice chairman? How many people attended the meeting? Describe the main issues discussed at the meeting.

WSJ EXERCISE

Reviewing Fed Policies

Review recent issues of the *Wall Street Journal* and search for any comments that relate to the Fed. Does it appear that the Fed may attempt to revise the federal funds rate? If so, how and why?

ONLINE ARTICLES WITH REAL-WORLD EXAMPLES

Find a recent practical article available online that describes a real-world example regarding a specific financial institution or financial market that reinforces one or more concepts covered in this chapter.

If your class has an online component, your professor may ask you to post your summary of the article there and provide a link to the article so that other students can access it. If your class is live, your professor may ask you to summarize your application of the article in class. Your professor may assign specific students to complete this assignment or may allow any students to do the assignment on a volunteer basis.

For recent online articles and real-world examples related to this chapter, consider using the following search terms (be sure to include the prevailing year as a search term to ensure that the online articles are recent):

1. Federal Reserve AND interest rate
2. Federal Reserve AND monetary policy
3. Board of Governors
4. FOMC meeting
5. FOMC AND interest rate
6. Federal Reserve AND policy
7. Federal Reserve AND open market operations
8. money supply AND interest rate
9. open market operations AND interest rate
10. Federal Reserve AND economy

5
Monetary Policy

CHAPTER OBJECTIVES

The specific objectives of this chapter are to:

- describe the mechanics of monetary policy,

- explain the trade-offs involved in monetary policy,

- describe how financial market participants respond to the Fed's policies, and

- explain how monetary policy is affected by the global environment.

The previous chapter discussed the Federal Reserve System and how it controls the money supply, information essential to financial market participants. It is just as important for participants to know how changes in the money supply affect the economy, which is the subject of this chapter.

5-1 MECHANICS OF MONETARY POLICY

Recall from Chapter 4 that the Federal Open Market Committee (FOMC) is responsible for determining the monetary policy. Also recall that the Fed's goals are to achieve a low level of inflation and a low level of unemployment. This goal is consistent with the goals of most central banks, although the stated goals of some central banks are more broadly defined (e.g., "achieving economic stability"). Given the Fed's goals of controlling economic growth and inflation, it must assess the prevailing indicators of these economic variables before determining its monetary policy.

5-1a Monitoring Indicators of Economic Growth

The Fed monitors indicators of economic growth because high economic growth creates a more prosperous economy and can result in lower unemployment. Gross domestic product (GDP), which measures the total value of goods and services produced during a specific period, is measured each month. It serves as the most direct indicator of economic growth in the United States. The level of production adjusts in response to changes in consumers' demand for goods and services. A high production level indicates strong economic growth and can result in an increased demand for labor (lower unemployment).

The Fed also monitors national income, which is the total income earned by firms and individual employees during a specific period. A strong demand for U.S. goods and services results in a large amount of revenue for firms. In order to accommodate demand, firms hire more employees or increase the work hours of their existing employees. Thus the total income earned by employees rises.

The unemployment rate is monitored as well, because one of the Fed's primary goals is to maintain a low rate of unemployment in the United States. However, the unemployment rate does not necessarily indicate the degree of economic growth: it measures only the number and not the types of jobs that are being filled. It is possible to have a substantial reduction in unemployment during a period of weak economic growth if new, low-paying jobs are created during that period.

Several other indexes serve as indicators of growth in specific sectors of the U.S. economy; these include an industrial production index, a retail sales index, and a home sales index. A composite index combines various indexes to indicate economic growth across sectors. In addition to the many indicators reflecting recent conditions, the Fed may also use forward-looking indicators (such as consumer confidence surveys) to forecast future economic growth.

Index of Leading Economic Indicators

Among the economic indicators widely followed by market participants are the indexes of leading, coincident, and lagging economic indicators, which are published by the Conference Board. **Leading economic indicators** are used to predict future economic activity. Usually, three consecutive monthly changes in the same direction in these indicators suggest a turning point in the economy. **Coincident economic indicators** tend to reach their peaks and troughs at the same time as business cycles. **Lagging economic indicators** tend to rise or fall a few months after business-cycle expansions and contractions.

The Conference Board is an independent, not-for-profit, membership organization whose stated goal is to create and disseminate knowledge about management and the marketplace to help businesses strengthen their performance and better serve society. The Conference Board conducts research, convenes conferences, makes forecasts, assesses trends, and publishes information and analyses. A summary of the Conference Board's leading, coincident, and lagging indexes is provided in Exhibit 5.1.

Exhibit 5.1   The Conference Board's Indexes of Leading, Coincident, and Lagging Indicators

Leading Index
1. Average weekly hours, manufacturing
2. Average weekly initial claims for unemployment insurance
3. Manufacturers' new orders, consumer goods and materials
4. Vendor performance, slower deliveries diffusion index
5. Manufacturers' new orders, nondefense capital goods
6. Building permits, new private housing units
7. Stock prices, 500 common stocks
8. Money supply, M2
9. Interest rate spread, 10-year Treasury bonds less federal funds
10. Index of consumer expectations
Coincident Index
1. Employees on nonagricultural payrolls
2. Personal income less transfer payments
3. Industrial production
4. Manufacturing and trade sales
Lagging Index
1. Average duration of unemployment
2. Inventories to sales ratio, manufacturing and trade
3. Labor cost per unit of output, manufacturing
4. Average prime rate
5. Commercial and industrial loans
6. Consumer installment credit to personal income ratio
7. Consumer price index for services

5-1b Monitoring Indicators of Inflation

The Fed closely monitors price indexes and other indicators to assess the U.S. inflation rate.

Producer and Consumer Price Indexes

The producer price index represents prices at the wholesale level, and the consumer price index represents prices paid by consumers (retail level). There is a lag time of about one month after the period being measured due to the time required to compile price information for the indexes. Nevertheless, financial markets closely monitor the price indexes because they may be used to forecast inflation, which affects nominal interest rates and the prices of some securities. Agricultural price indexes reflect recent price movements in grains, fruits, and vegetables. Housing price indexes reflect recent price movements in homes and rental properties.

Other Inflation Indicators

In addition to price indexes, there are several other indicators of inflation. Wage rates are periodically reported in various regions of the United States. Because wages and prices are highly correlated over the long run, wages can indicate price movements. Oil prices can signal future inflation because they affect the costs of some forms of production as well as transportation costs and the prices paid by consumers for gasoline.

The price of gold is closely monitored because gold prices tend to move in tandem with inflation. Some investors buy gold as a hedge against future inflation. Therefore, a rise in gold prices may signal the market's expectation that inflation will increase.

Indicators of economic growth might also be used to indicate inflation. For example, the release of several favorable employment reports may arouse concern that the economy will overheat and lead to **demand-pull inflation**, which occurs when excessive spending pulls up prices. Although these reports offer favorable information about economic growth, their information about inflation is unfavorable. The financial markets can be adversely affected by such reports, because investors anticipate that the Fed will have to increase interest rates in order to reduce the inflationary momentum.

5-2 IMPLEMENTING MONETARY POLICY

The Federal Open Market Committee assesses economic conditions, and identifies its main concerns about the economy to determine the monetary policy that would alleviate its concerns. Its monetary policy changes the money supply in order to influence interest rates, which affect the level of aggregate borrowing and spending by households and firms. The level of aggregate spending affects demand for products and services, and therefore affects both price levels (inflation) and the unemployment level.

5-2a Effects of a Stimulative Monetary Policy

The effects of a stimulative monetary policy can be illustrated using the loanable funds framework described in Chapter 2. Recall that the interaction between the supply of loanable funds and the demand for loanable funds determines the interest rate charged on such funds. Much of the demand for loanable funds is by households, firms, and government agencies that need to borrow money. Recall that the demand curve indicates the quantity of funds that would be demanded (at that time) at various possible interest rates. This curve is downward sloping because many potential borrowers would borrow a larger quantity of funds at lower interest rates.

The supply curve of loanable funds indicates the quantity of funds that would be supplied (at that time) at various possible interest rates. This curve is upward sloping

Exhibit 5.2   Effects of an Increased Money Supply

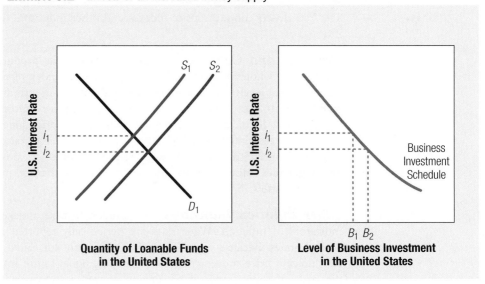

because suppliers of funds tend to supply a larger amount of funds when the interest rate is higher. Assume that, as of today, the demand and supply curves for loanable funds are those labeled D_1 and S_1 (respectively) in the left graph of Exhibit 5.2. This plot reveals that the equilibrium interest rate is i_1. The right graph of Exhibit 5.2 depicts the typical relationship between the interest rate on loanable funds and the current level of business investment. The relation is inverse because firms are more willing to expand when interest rates are relatively low. Given an equilibrium interest rate of i_1, the level of business investment is B_1.

With a stimulative monetary policy, the Fed increases the supply of funds in the banking system, which can increase the level of business investment, and hence aggregate spending in the economy.

The Fed purchases Treasury securities in the secondary market. As the investors who sell their Treasury securities receive payment from the Fed, their account balances at financial institutions increase without any offsetting decrease in the account balances of any other financial institutions. Thus there is a net increase in the total supply of loanable funds in the banking system.

Impact on Interest Rates   If the Fed's action results in an increase of $5 billion in loanable funds, then the quantity of loanable funds supplied will now be $5 billion higher at any possible interest rate level. This means that the supply curve for loanable funds shifts outward to S_2 in Exhibit 5.2. The difference between S_2 and S_1 is that S_2 incorporates the $5 billion of loanable funds added as a result of the Fed's actions.

Given the shift in the supply curve for loanable funds, the quantity of loanable funds supplied exceeds the quantity of loanable funds demanded at the interest rate level i_1. The interest rate will therefore decline to i_2, the level at which the quantities of loanable funds supplied and demanded are equal.

Logic Behind the Impact on Interest Rates   The graphic effects are supplemented here with a logical explanation for why the interest rates decline in response to the monetary policy. When depository institutions experience an increase in supply of funds due to the Fed's stimulative monetary policy, they have more funds than they need at prevailing interest rates. Those depository institutions that commonly obtain very short-term loans (such as one day) in the so-called federal funds may not need to borrow as many funds. Those depository institutions that commonly lend to others in this market may be more willing to accept a lower interest rate (called the federal funds rate) when providing short-term loans in this market. The federal funds rate is directly affected by changes to the supply of money in the banking system. The Fed's monetary policy is commonly intended to alter the supply of funds in the banking system in order to achieve a specific targeted federal funds rate, such as reducing that rate from 3 to 2.75 percent or to a value within the range from 2.75 to 3 percent.

The Fed's monetary policy actions not only have a direct effect on the federal funds rate, but also affect the Treasury yield (or rate). When the Fed purchases a large amount of Treasury securities, it raises the price of Treasury securities, and therefore lowers the yield (or rate) to be earned by any investors who invest in Treasury securities at the higher prevailing price.

Most importantly, the impact of the Fed's stimulative monetary policy indirectly affects other interest rates as well, including loan rates paid by businesses. The lower interest rate level causes an increase in the level of business investment from B_1 to B_2. That is, businesses are willing to pursue additional projects now that their cost of financing is lower. The increase in business investment represents new business spending triggered by lower interest rates, which reduced the corporate cost of financing new projects.

Logic Behind the Effects on Business Cost of Debt   Depository institutions are willing to charge a lower loan rate in response to the stimulative monetary policy, since their cost of funds (based on the rate they pay on deposits) is now lower. The institutions also reduce their rates on loans in order to attract more potential borrowers to make use of the newly available funds.

Another way to understand the effects of a stimulative monetary policy on the business cost of debt is to consider the influence of the risk-free rate on all interest rates. Recall from Chapter 3 that the yield for a security with a particular maturity is primarily based on the risk-free rate (the Treasury rate) for that same maturity plus a credit risk premium. Thus the financing rate on a business loan is based on the risk-free rate plus a premium that reflects the credit risk of the business that is borrowing the money. So if the prevailing Treasury (risk-free) security rate is 5 percent on an annualized basis, a business has a low level of risk that pays a 3 percent credit risk premium when borrowing money would be able to obtain funds at 8 percent (5 percent risk-free rate plus 3 percent credit risk premium). However, if the Fed implements a stimulative monetary policy that reduces the Treasury security rate to 4 percent, the business would be able to borrow funds at 7 percent (4 percent risk-free rate plus 3 percent credit risk premium).

Businesses with other degrees of credit risk will also be affected by the Fed's monetary policy. Consider a business with moderate risk that pays a credit premium of 4 percent above the risk-free rate to obtain funds. When the Treasury (risk-free) rate was 5 percent, this business would be able to borrow funds at 9 percent (5 percent risk-free rate plus 4 percent credit risk premium). However, if the Fed implements a stimulative monetary policy that reduces the Treasury security rate to 4 percent, the business would be able to borrow funds at 8 percent (4 percent risk-free rate plus 4 percent credit risk premium).

The point here is that all businesses (regardless of their risk level) will be able to borrow funds at lower rates as a result of the Fed's stimulative monetary policy. Therefore, when they consider possible projects such as expanding their product line or building a new facility, they may be more willing to implement some projects as a result of the lower cost of funds. As firms implement more projects, they spend more money, and that extra spending results in higher income to individuals or other firms who receive the proceeds. They may also hire more employees in order to expand their businesses. This generates more income for those new employees, who will spend some of their new income, and that spending provides income to the individuals or firms who receive the proceeds.

Effects on Business Cost of Equity   Many businesses also rely on equity as another key source of capital. Monetary policy can also influence the cost of equity. The cost of a firm's equity is based on the risk-free rate, plus a risk premium that reflects the sensitivity of the firm's stock price movements to general stock market movements. This concept is discussed in more detail in Chapter 11, but the main point for now is that the firm's cost of equity is positively related to the risk-free rate. Therefore, if the Fed can reduce the risk-free by 1 percent, it can reduce a firm's cost of equity by 1 percent.

Summary of Effects   In summary, the Fed's ability to stimulate the economy are due to its effects on the Treasury (risk-free) rate, which influences the cost of debt and the cost of equity in Exhibit 5.3. As the Fed reduces the risk-free rate, it reduces the firm's cost of borrowing (debt) and the firm's cost of equity, and therefore reduces the firm's cost of capital. If a firm's cost of capital is reduced, its required return on potential projects is reduced. Thus, more of the possible projects that a firm considers will be judged as feasible and will be implemented. As firms in the U.S. implement more projects that they now believe are feasible, they increase their spending, and this can stimulate the economy and create jobs.

Notice that for the Fed to stimulate the economy and create more jobs, it is not using its money to purchase products. It is not telling firms that they must hire more employees. Instead, its stimulative monetary policy reduces the cost of funds, which encourages firms to spend more money. In a similar manner, the Fed's stimulative monetary policy can reduce the cost of borrowing for households as well. As with firms, their cost of borrowing is based on the prevailing risk-free rate plus a credit risk premium. When the Fed's stimulative monetary policy results in a lower Treasury (risk-free) rate, it lowers the cost of borrowing for households, which encourages households to spend more money. As firms and households increase their spending, they stimulate the economy and create jobs.

Exhibit 5.3   How the Fed Can Stimulate the Economy

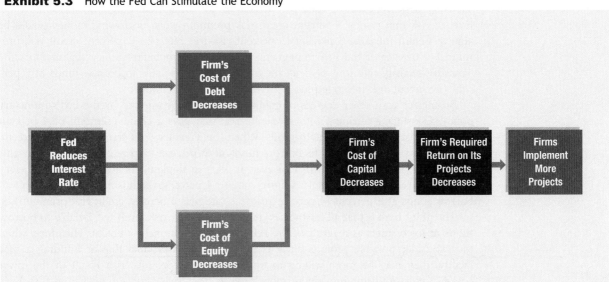

5-2b Fed's Policy Focuses on Long-term Maturities

Yields on Treasury securities can vary among maturities. If the yield curve (discussed in Chapter 3) is upward sloping, this implies that longer-term Treasury securities have higher annualized yields than shorter-term Treasury securities. The Fed had already been able to reduce short-term Treasury rates to near zero with its stimulative monetary policy over the 2010–2012 period. However, this did not have much impact on the firms that borrow at long-term fixed interest rates. These borrowers incur a cost of debt that is highly influenced by the long-term Treasury rates, not the short-term Treasury rates.

To the extent that the Fed wants to encourage businesses to increase their spending on long-term projects, it may need to use a stimulative policy that is focused on reducing the long-term Treasury yields, which would reduce the long-term debt rates. So if the Fed wants to reduce the rate that these potential borrowers would pay for fixed-rate loans with 10-year maturities, it would attempt to use a monetary policy that reduces the yield on Treasury securities with 10-year maturities (which reflects the 10-year risk-free rate).

In some periods, the Fed has directed its monetary policy at the trading of Treasury securities with specific maturities so that it can cause a bigger change for some maturities than others. In 2011 and 2012, the Fed periodically implemented an "operation twist" strategy (which it also implemented in 1961). It sold some holdings of short-term Treasury securities, and used the proceeds to purchase long-term Treasury securities. In theory, the strategy would increase short-term interest rates and reduce long-term interest rates, which would reflect a twist of the yield curve.

The logic behind the strategy is that the Fed should focus on reducing long-term interest rates rather than short-term interest rates in order to encourage firms to borrow and spend more funds. Since firms should be more willing to increase their spending on new projects when long-term interests are reduced, the strategy could help stimulate the economy and create jobs. In addition, potential home buyers might be more willing to purchase homes if long-term interest rates were lower. However, there is not complete agreement on whether this strategy would really have a substantial and sustained effect on long-term interest rates. Money flows between short-term and long-term Treasury markets, which means that it is difficult for the Fed to have one type of impact in the long-term market that is different from that in the short-term market. The operation twist strategy was able to reduce long-term Treasury rates, but its total impact may have been limited for other reasons explained later in this chapter.

5-2c Why a Stimulative Monetary Policy Might Fail

While a stimulative monetary policy is normally desirable when the economy is weak, it is not always effective, for the reasons provided next.

Limited Credit Provided by Banks The ability of the Fed to stimulate the economy is partially influenced by the willingness of depository institutions to lend funds. Even if the Fed increases the level of bank funds during a weak economy, banks may be unwilling to extend credit to some potential borrowers; the result is a *credit crunch*.

Banks provide loans only after confirming that the borrower's future cash flows will be adequate to make loan repayments. In a weak economy, the future cash flows of many potential borrowers are more uncertain, causing a reduction in loan applications (demand for loans) and in the number of loan applicants that meet a bank's qualification standards.

Banks and other lending institutions have a responsibility to their depositors, shareholders, and regulators to avoid loans that are likely to default. Because default risk rises during a weak economy, some potential borrowers will be unable to obtain loans. Others may qualify only if they pay high risk premiums to cover their default risk. Thus the effects of the Fed's monetary policy may be limited if potential borrowers do not qualify or are unwilling to incur the high-risk premiums. If banks do not lend out the additional funds that have been pumped into the banking system by the Fed, the economy will not be stimulated.

EXAMPLE

During the credit crisis that began in 2008, the Fed attempted to stimulate the economy by using monetary policy to reduce interest rates. Initially, however, the effect of the monetary policy was negligible. Firms were unwilling to borrow even at low interest rates because they did not want to expand while economic conditions were so weak. In addition, commercial banks raised the standards necessary to qualify for loans so that they would not repeat any of the mistakes (such as liberal lending standards) that led to the credit crisis. Consequently, the amount of new loans resulting from the Fed's stimulative monetary policy was limited, and therefore the amount of new spending was limited as well. ●

Low Return on Savings

Although the Fed's policy of reducing interest rates allows for lower borrowing rates, it also results in lower returns on savings. The interest rates on bank deposits are close to zero, which limits the potential returns that can be earned by investors who want to save money. This might encourage individuals to borrow (and spend) rather than save, which could allow for a greater stimulative effect on the economy. However, some individuals that are encouraged to borrow because of lower interest rates may not be able to repay their debt. Therefore, the very low interest rates might lead to more personal bankruptcies.

Furthermore, some savers, such as retirees, rely heavily on their interest income to cover their periodic expenses. When interest rates are close to zero, interest income is close to zero, and retirees that rely on interest income have to restrict their spending. This effect can partially offset the expected stimulative effect of lower interest rates. Some retirees may decide to invest their money in alternative ways (such as in stocks) instead of as bank deposits when interest rates are low. However, many alternative investments are risky, and could cause retirees to experience losses on their retirement funds.

Adverse Effects on Inflation

When a stimulative monetary policy is used, the increase in money supply growth may cause an increase in inflationary expectations, which may limit the impact on interest rates.

EXAMPLE

Assume that the U.S. economy is very weak, and suppose the Fed responds by using open market operations (purchasing Treasury securities) to increase the supply of loanable funds. This action is supposed to reduce interest rates and increase the level of borrowing and spending. However, there is some evidence that high money growth may also lead to higher inflation over time. To the extent that businesses and households recognize that an increase in money growth will cause higher inflation, they will revise their inflationary expectations upward as a result. This effect is often referred to as the **theory of rational expectations**. Higher inflationary expectations encourage businesses and households to increase their demand for loanable funds (as explained in Chapter 2) in order to borrow and make planned expenditures before price levels increase. This increase in demand reflects a rush to make planned purchases now.

These effects of the Fed's monetary policy are shown in Exhibit 5.4. The result is an increase in both the supply of loanable funds and the demand for those funds. The effects are offsetting, so the Fed may not be able to reduce interest rates for a sustained period of time. If the Fed cannot force interest rates lower with an active monetary policy, it will be unable to stimulate an increase in the level of business investment. Business investment will increase only if the cost of financing is reduced, making some proposed business projects feasible. If the increase in business investment does not occur, economic conditions will not improve. ●

Exhibit 5.4   Effects of an Increased Money Supply According to Rational Expectations Theory

**Quantity of Loanable Funds
in the United States**

Because the effects of a stimulative policy could be disrupted by expected inflation, an alternative approach is a passive monetary policy that allows the economy to correct itself rather than rely on the Fed's intervention. Interest rates should ultimately decline in a weak economy even without a stimulative monetary policy because the demand for loanable funds should decline as economic growth weakens. In this case, interest rates would decline without a corresponding increase in inflationary expectations, so the interest rates may stay lower for a sustained period of time. Consequently, the level of business investment should ultimately increase, which should lead to a stronger economy and more jobs.

The major criticism of a passive monetary policy is that the weak economy could take years to correct itself. During a slow economy, interest rates might not decrease until a year later if the Fed played a passive role and did not intervene to stimulate the economy. Most people would probably prefer that the Fed take an active role in improving economic conditions—rather than take a passive role and simply hope that the economy will correct itself.

Even if the Fed's stimulative policy does not affect inflation and if banks are willing to lend the funds received, it is possible that firms and businesses will not be willing to borrow more money. Some firms may have already reached their debt capacity, so that they are restricted from borrowing more money, even if loan rates are reduced. They may believe that any additional debt could increase the likelihood of bankruptcy. Thus they may delay their spending until the economy has improved.

Similarly, households that commonly borrow to purchase vehicles, homes, and other products may also prefer to avoid borrowing more money during weak economies, even if interest rates are low. Households who are unemployed are not in a position to borrow more money. And even if employed households can obtain loans from financial institutions, they may believe that they are already at their debt capacity. The economic conditions might make them worry that their job is not stable, and they prefer not to increase their debt until their economic conditions improve and their job is more secure.

So while the Fed hopes that the lower interest rates will encourage more borrowing and spending to stimulate the economy, the potential spenders (firms and households) may delay their borrowing until the economy improves. But the economy may not improve unless firms and households increase their spending. While the Fed can lower interest rates, it cannot necessarily force firms or households to borrow more money. If the firms and households do not borrow more money, they will not be able to spend more money.

One related concern about the Fed's stimulative monetary policy is that if it is successful in encouraging firms and households to borrow funds, it might indirectly cause some of them to borrow beyond what they can afford to borrow. Thus it might ultimately result in more bankruptcies and cause a new phase of economic problems.

5-2d Effects of Restrictive Monetary Policy

If excessive inflation is the Fed's main concern, then the Fed can implement a restrictive (tight-money) policy by using open market operations to reduce money supply growth. A portion of the inflation may be due to demand-pull inflation, which the Fed can reduce by slowing economic growth and thereby the excessive spending that can lead to this type of inflation.

To slow economic growth and reduce inflationary pressures, the Fed can sell some of its holdings of Treasury securities in the secondary market. As investors make payments to purchase these Treasury securities, their account balances decrease without any offsetting increase in the account balances of any other financial institutions. Thus there is a net decrease in deposit accounts (money), which results in a net decrease in the quantity of loanable funds.

Assume that the Fed's action causes a decrease of $5 billion in loanable funds. The quantity of loanable funds supplied will now be $5 billion lower at any possible interest rate level. This reflects an inward shift in the supply curve from S1 to S2, as shown in Exhibit 5.5.

Given the inward shift in the supply curve for loanable funds, the quantity of loanable funds demanded exceeds the quantity of loanable funds supplied at the original interest

Exhibit 5.5   Effects of a Reduced Money Supply

rate level (*i*1). Thus the interest rate will increase to *i*2, the level at which the quantities of loanable funds supplied and demanded are equal.

Depository institutions raise not only the rate charged on loans in the federal funds market but also the interest rates on deposits and on household and business loans. If the Fed's restrictive monetary policy increases the Treasury rate from 5 to 6 percent, a firm that must pay a risk premium of 4 percent must now pay 10 percent (6 percent risk-free rate plus 4 percent credit risk premium) to borrow funds. All firms and households who consider borrowing money incur a higher cost of debt as a result of the Fed's restrictive monetary policy. The effect of the Fed's monetary policy on loans to households and businesses is important, since the Fed's ability to affect the amount of spending in the economy stems from influencing the rates charged on household and business loans.

The higher interest rate level increases the corporate cost of financing new projects and therefore causes a decrease in the level of business investment from B1 to B2. As economic growth is slowed by this reduction in business investment, inflationary pressure may be reduced.

5-2e Summary of Monetary Policy Effects

Exhibit 5.6 summarizes how the Fed can affect economic conditions through its influence on the supply of loanable funds. The top part of the exhibit illustrates a stimulative (loose-money) monetary policy intended to boost economic growth, and the bottom part illustrates a restrictive (tight-money) monetary policy intended to reduce inflation.

Exhibit 5.6   How Monetary Policy Can Affect Economic Conditions

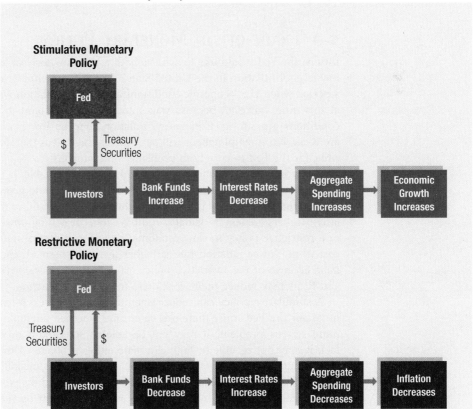

Lagged Effects of Monetary Policy   There are three lags involved in monetary policy that can make the Fed's job more challenging. First, there is a **recognition lag**, or the lag between the time a problem arises and the time it is recognized. Most economic problems are initially revealed by statistics, not actual observation. Because economic statistics are reported only periodically, they will not immediately signal a problem. For example, the unemployment rate is reported monthly. A sudden increase in unemployment may not be detected until the end of the month, when statistics finally reveal the problem. Even if unemployment increases slightly each month for two straight months, the Fed might not act on this information because it may not seem significant. A few more months of steadily increasing unemployment, however, would force the Fed to recognize that a serious problem exists. In such a case, the recognition lag may be four months or longer.

The lag from the time a serious problem is recognized until the time the Fed implements a policy to resolve that problem is known as the **implementation lag**. Then, even after the Fed implements a policy, there will be an **impact lag** until the policy has its full impact on the economy. For example, an adjustment in money supply growth may have an immediate impact on the economy to some degree, but its full impact may not occur until a year or so after the adjustment.

These lags hinder the Fed's control of the economy. Suppose the Fed uses a stimulative policy to stimulate the economy and reduce unemployment. By the time the implemented monetary policy begins to take effect, the unemployment rate may have already reversed itself and may now be trending downward as a result of some other outside factors (such as a weakened dollar that increased foreign demand for U.S. goods and created U.S. jobs). Without monetary policy lags, implemented policies would be more effective.

5-3 TRADE-OFF IN MONETARY POLICY

Ideally, the Fed would like to achieve both a very low level of unemployment and a very low level of inflation in the United States. The U.S. unemployment rate should be low in a period when U.S. economic conditions are strong. Inflation will likely be relatively high at this time, however, because wages and price levels tend to increase when economic conditions are strong. Conversely, inflation may be lower when economic conditions are weak, but unemployment will be relatively high. It is therefore difficult, if not impossible, for the Fed to cure both problems simultaneously.

When inflation is higher than the Fed deems acceptable, it may consider implementing a restrictive (tight-money) policy to reduce economic growth. As economic growth slows, producers cannot as easily raise their prices and still maintain sales volume. Similarly, workers are less in demand and have less bargaining power on wages. Thus the use of a restrictive policy to slow economic growth can reduce the inflation rate. A possible cost of the lower inflation rate is higher unemployment. If the economy becomes stagnant because of the restrictive policy, sales may decrease, inventories may accumulate, and firms may reduce their workforces to reduce production.

A stimulative policy can reduce unemployment whereas a restrictive policy can reduce inflation; the Fed must therefore determine whether unemployment or inflation is the more serious problem. It may not be able to solve both problems simultaneously. In fact, it may not be able to fully eliminate either problem. Although a stimulative policy can stimulate the economy, it does not guarantee that unskilled workers will be hired. Although a restrictive policy can reduce inflation caused by excessive spending, it cannot reduce inflation caused by such factors as an agreement by members of an oil cartel to maintain high oil prices.

Exhibit 5.7 Trade-off between Reducing Inflation and Unemployment

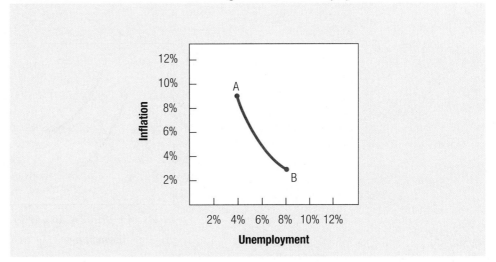

5-3a Impact of Other Forces on the Trade-off

Other forces may also affect the trade-off faced by the Fed. Consider a situation where, because of specific cost factors (e.g., an increase in energy costs), inflation will be at least 3 percent. In other words, this much inflation will exist no matter what type of monetary policy the Fed implements. Assume that, because of the number of unskilled workers and people "between jobs," the unemployment rate will be at least 4 percent. A stimulative policy will stimulate the economy sufficiently to maintain unemployment at that minimum level of 4 percent. However, such a stimulative policy may also cause additional inflation beyond the 3 percent level. Conversely, a restrictive policy could maintain inflation at the 3 percent minimum, but unemployment would likely rise above the 4 percent minimum.

This trade-off is illustrated in Exhibit 5.7. Here the Fed can use a very stimulative (loose-money) policy that is expected to result in point A (9 percent inflation and 4 percent unemployment), or it can use a highly restrictive (tight-money) policy that is expected to result in point B (3 percent inflation and 8 percent unemployment). Alternatively, it can implement a compromise policy that will result in some point along the curve between A and B.

Historical data on annual inflation and unemployment rates show that when one of these problems worsens, the other does not automatically improve. Both variables can rise or fall simultaneously over time. Nevertheless, this does not refute the trade-off faced by the Fed. It simply means that some outside factors have affected inflation or unemployment or both.

EXAMPLE

Recall that the Fed could have achieved point A, point B, or somewhere along the curve connecting these two points during a particular time period. Now assume that oil prices have increased substantially such that the minimum inflation rate will be, say, 6 percent. In addition, assume that various training centers for unskilled workers have been closed, leaving a higher number of unskilled workers. This forces the minimum unemployment rate to 6 percent. Now the Fed's trade-off position has changed. The Fed's new set of possibilities is shown as curve CD in Exhibit 5.8. Note that the points reflected on curve CD are not as desirable as the points along curve AB that were previously attainable. No matter what type of monetary policy the Fed uses, both the inflation rate and the unemployment rate will be higher than in the previous time period. This is not the Fed's fault.

Exhibit 5.8   Adjustment in the Trade-off between Unemployment and Inflation over Time

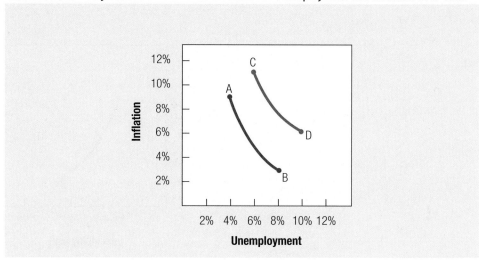

In fact, the Fed is still faced with a trade-off: between point C (11 percent inflation, 6 percent unemployment) and point D (6 percent inflation, 10 percent unemployment), or some other point along curve CD. ●

For example, during the financial crisis of 2008–2009 and during 2010–2013 when the economy was still attempting to recover, the Fed focused more on reducing unemployment than on inflation. While it recognized that a stimulative monetary policy could increase inflation, it viewed inflation as the lesser of two evils. It would rather achieve a reduction in unemployment by stimulating the economy even if that resulted in a higher inflation rate.

When FOMC members are primarily concerned with either inflation or unemployment, they tend to agree on the type of monetary policy that should be implemented. When both inflation and unemployment are relatively high, however, there is more disagreement among the members about the proper monetary policy to implement. Some members would likely argue for a restrictive policy to prevent inflation from rising, while other members would suggest that a stimulative policy should be implemented to reduce unemployment even if it results in higher inflation.

5-3b Shifts in Monetary Policy over Time

WEB

www.federalreserve.
gov/monetarypolicy/
openmarket.htm
Shows recent changes
in the federal funds
target rate.

The trade-offs involved in monetary policy can be understood by considering the Fed's decisions over time. In some periods, the Fed's focus is on stimulating economic growth and reducing the unemployment level, with less concern about inflation. In other periods, the Fed's focus is on reducing inflationary pressure, with less concern about the unemployment level. A brief summary of the following economic cycles illustrates this point.

Focus on Improving Weak Economy in 2001–2003   In 2001, when economic conditions were weak, the Fed reduced the targeted federal funds rate 10 times; this resulted in a cumulative decline of 4.25 percent in the targeted federal funds rate. As the federal funds rate was reduced, other short-term market interest rates declined as well. Despite these interest rate reductions, the economy did not respond. The Fed's effects on the economy might have been stronger had it been able to reduce long-term interest rates. After the economy failed to respond as hoped in 2001, the Fed reduced the federal funds target rate two more times in 2002 and 2003. Finally, in 2004 the economy began to show some signs of improvement.

Focus on Reducing Inflation in 2004–2007   As the economy improved in 2004, the Fed's focus began to shift from concern about the economy to concern about the possibility of higher inflation. It raised the federal funds target rate 17 times over the period from mid-2004 to the summer of 2006. The typical adjustment in the target rate was 0.25 percent. By adjusting in small increments, as it did during this period, the Fed is unlikely to overreact to existing economic conditions. After making each small adjustment in the targeted federal funds rate, it monitors the economic effects and decides at the next meeting whether additional adjustments are needed.

During 2004–2007, there were periodic indications of rising prices, mostly due to high oil prices. Although the Fed's monetary policy could not control oil prices, it wanted to prevent any inflation that could be triggered if the economy became strong and there were either labor shortages or excessive demand for products. Thus the Fed tried to maintain economic growth without letting it become so strong that it could cause higher inflation.

Focus on Improving Weak Economy in 2008–2013   Near the end of 2008, the credit crisis developed and resulted in a severe economic slowdown. The Fed implemented a stimulative monetary policy in this period. Over the 2008–2013 period, it reduced the federal funds rate from 5.25 percent to near 0. However, even with such a major impact on interest rates, the impact on the recovery was slow. Although monetary policy can be effective, it cannot necessarily solve all of the structural problems that occurred in the economy, such as the excess number of homes that were built based on liberal credit standards during the 2004–2007 period. Thus lowering interest rates did not lead to a major increase in the demand for homes, because many homeowners could not afford the homes that they were in. For those households who were in a position to purchase a home, a massive surplus of empty homes was available. Thus there was no need to build new homes, and no need for construction companies to hire additional employees. Furthermore, even with the very low interest rates, many firms were unwilling to expand. During the 2010–2012 period, the aggregate demand for products and services increased slowly. However, the unemployment rate remained high, because businesses remained cautious about hiring new employees.

5-3c How Monetary Policy Responds to Fiscal Policy

The Fed's assessment of the trade-off between improving the unemployment situation versus the inflation situation becomes more complicated when considering the prevailing fiscal policy. Although the Fed has the power to make decisions without the approval of the presidential administration, the Fed's monetary policy is commonly influenced by the administration's fiscal policies. If fiscal policies create large budget deficits, this may place upward pressure on interest rates. Under these conditions, the Fed may be concerned that the higher interest rates caused by fiscal policy could dampen the economy, and it may therefore feel pressured to use a stimulative monetary policy in order to reduce interest rates.

A framework for explaining how monetary policy and fiscal policies affect interest rates is shown in Exhibit 5.9. Although fiscal policy typically shifts the demand for loanable funds, monetary policy normally has a larger impact on the supply of loanable funds. In some situations, the administration has enacted a fiscal policy that causes the Fed to reassess its trade-off between focusing on inflation versus unemployment, as explained below.

Exhibit 5.9   Framework for Explaining How Monetary Policy and Fiscal Policy Affect Interest Rates over Time

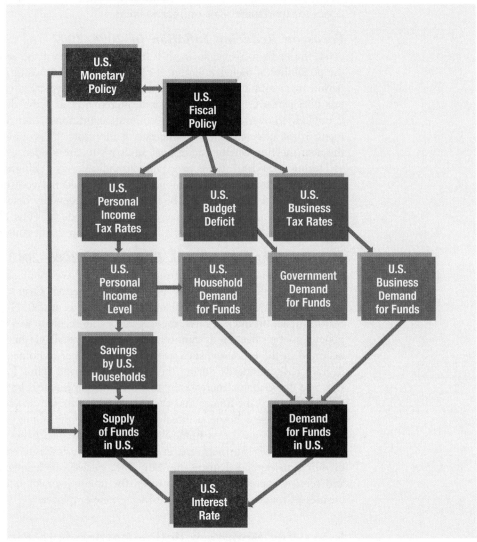

5-3d Proposals to Focus on Inflation

Recently, some have proposed that the Fed should focus more on controlling inflation than unemployment. Ben Bernanke, the current chairman of the Fed, has made some arguments in favor of inflation targeting. If this proposal were adopted in its strictest form, then the Fed would no longer face a trade-off between controlling inflation and controlling unemployment. It would not have to consider responding to any fiscal policy actions such as those shown in Exhibit 5.9. It might be better able to control inflation if it could concentrate on that problem without having to worry about the unemployment rate. In addition, the Fed's role would be more transparent, and there would be less uncertainty in the financial markets about how the Fed would respond to specific economic conditions.

Nevertheless, inflation targeting also has some disadvantages. First, the Fed could lose credibility if the U.S. inflation rate deviated substantially from the Fed's target inflation rate. Factors such as oil prices could cause high inflation regardless of the Fed's targeted inflation rate. Second, focusing only on inflation could result in a much higher unemployment level. Bernanke has argued, however, that inflation targeting could be flexible enough that the employment level would still be given consideration. He believes that inflation targeting may not only satisfy the inflation goal but could also achieve the employment stabilization goal in the long run. For example, if unemployment were slightly higher than normal and inflation were at the peak of the target range, then an inflation targeting approach might be to leave monetary policy unchanged. In this situation, stimulating the economy with lower interest rates might reduce the unemployment rate temporarily but could ultimately lead to excessive inflation. This would require the Fed to use a restrictive policy (higher interest rates) to correct the inflation, which could ultimately lead to a slower economy and an increase in unemployment. In general, the inflation targeting approach would discourage such "quick fix" strategies to stimulate the economy.

Although some Fed members have publicly said that they do not believe in inflation targeting, their opinions are not necessarily much different from those of Bernanke. Flexible inflation targeting would allow changes in monetary policy to increase employment. Fed members disagree on how high unemployment would have to be before monetary policy would be used to stimulate the economy at the risk of raising inflation. In fact, discussion of inflation targeting declined during the credit crisis when the economy weakened and unemployment increased in the United States. This suggests that, though some Fed members might argue for an inflation targeting policy in the long run, they tend to change their focus toward reducing unemployment when the United States is experiencing very weak economic conditions.

5-4 MONITORING THE IMPACT OF MONETARY POLICY

The Fed's monetary policy affects many parts of the economy, as shown in Exhibit 5.10. The effects of monetary policy can vary with the perspective. Households monitor the Fed because their loan rates on cars and mortgages will be affected. Firms monitor the Fed because their cost of borrowing from loans and from issuing new bonds will be affected. Some firms are affected to a greater degree if their businesses are more sensitive to interest rate movements. The Treasury monitors the Fed because its cost of financing the budget deficit will be affected.

5-4a Impact on Financial Markets

Because monetary policy can have a strong influence on interest rates and economic growth, it affects the valuation of most securities traded in financial markets. The changes in values of existing bonds are inversely related to interest rate movements. Therefore, investors who own bonds (Treasury, corporate, or municipal) or fixed-rate mortgages are adversely affected when the Fed raises interest rates, but they are favorably affected when the Fed reduces interest rates (as explained in Chapter 8).

The values of stocks (discussed in Chapter 11) also are commonly affected by interest rate movements, but the effects are not as consistent as they are for bonds.

EXAMPLE

Suppose the Fed lowers interest rates because the economy is weak. If investors anticipate that this action will enhance economic growth, they may expect that firms will generate higher sales and earnings in the future. Thus the values of stocks would increase in response to this favorable information. However, the Fed's decision to reduce interest rates could make investors realize that economic conditions are worse than they thought. In this case, the Fed's actions could signal that corporate sales and earnings may weaken, and the values of stocks would decline because of the negative information. ●

Exhibit 5.10   How Monetary Policy Affects Financial Conditions

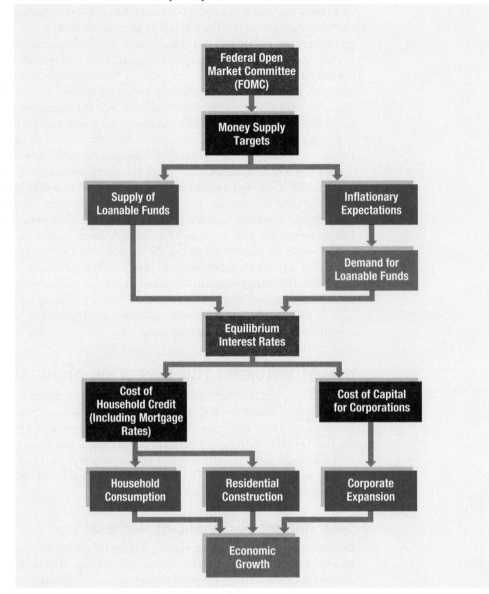

WEB

www.federalreserve.
gov/monetarypolicy/
fomccalendars.htm
Schedule of FOMC
meetings and minutes
of previous FOMC
meetings.

To appreciate the potential impact of the Fed's actions on financial markets, go to any financial news website during the week in which the FOMC holds its meeting. You will see predictions of whether the Fed will change the target federal funds rate, by how much, and how that change will affect the financial markets.

Fed's Communication to Financial Markets

After the Federal Open Market Committee holds a meeting to determine its monetary policy, it announces its conclusion through an *FOMC statement*. The statement is available at www.federalreserve.gov, and it may offer relevant implications about security prices. The following example of an FOMC statement reflects a decision to implement a stimulative monetary policy.

The Federal Open Market Committee decided to reduce its target for the federal funds rate by 0.25% to 2.75%. Economic growth has weakened this year, and indicators suggest more pronounced weakness in the last four months. The Committee expects that the weakness will continue. Inventories at manufacturing firms have risen, which reflects the recent decline in sales by these firms. Inflation is presently low and is expected to remain at very low levels. Thus, there is presently a bias toward correcting the economic growth, without as much concern about inflation. Voting for the FOMC monetary policy action were [list of voting members provided here].

This example could possibly cause the prices of debt securities such as bonds to rise because it suggests that interest rates will decline.

The following example of a typical statement reflects the decision to use a restrictive monetary policy.

The Federal Open Market Committee decided to raise its target for the federal funds rate by 0.25% to 3.25%. Economic growth has been strong so far this year. The Committee expects that growth will continue at a more sustainable pace, partly reflecting a cooling of the housing market. Energy prices have had a modest impact on inflation. Unit labor costs have been stable. Energy prices have the potential to add to inflation. The Committee expects that a more restrictive monetary policy may be needed to address inflation risks, but [it] emphasizes that the extent and timing of any tightening of money supply will depend on future economic conditions. The Committee will respond to changes in economic prospects as needed to support the attainment of its objectives. Voting for the FOMC monetary policy action were [list of voting members provided here].

The type of influence that monetary policy can have on each financial market is summarized in Exhibit 5.11. The financial market participants closely review the FOMC statements to interpret the Fed's future plans and to assess how the monetary policy will affect security prices. Sometimes the markets fully anticipate the Fed's actions. In this case, prices of securities should adjust to the anticipated news before the meeting, and they will not adjust further when the Fed's decision is announced.

Recently, the Fed has been more transparent in its communication to financial markets about its future policy. In the fall of 2012, it emphasized its focus on stimulating the U.S. economy. The Fed also announced that it would continue to purchase Treasury bonds in the financial markets (increase money supply) until unemployment conditions are substantially improved, unless there are strong indications of higher inflation. This statement is unusual because it represents a much stronger commitment to fix one particular problem (unemployment) rather than the other (inflation). The Fed also stated that it planned to keep long-term interest rates low for at least the next three years. This was important because it signaled to potential borrowers who obtain floating-rate loans (such as many firms and some home buyers) that the cost of financing would remain low for at least the next three years.

Perhaps the Fed was comfortable in taking this position because the unemployment problem was clearly causing more difficulties in the economy than inflation. The Fed's strong and clear communication may have been intended to restore confidence in the economy, so that people were more willing to spend money rather than worrying that they need to save money in case they lose their job. The Fed was hoping that heavy spending by households could stimulate the economy and create jobs.

Exhibit 5.11   Impact of Monetary Policy across Financial Markets

TYPE OF FINANCIAL MARKET	RELEVANT FACTORS INFLUENCED BY MONETARY POLICY	KEY INSTITUTIONAL PARTICIPANTS
Money market	• Secondary market values of existing money market securities • Yields on newly issued money market securities	Commercial banks, savings institutions, credit unions, money market funds, insurance companies, finance companies, pension funds
Bond market	• Secondary market values of existing bonds • Yields offered on newly issued bonds	Commercial banks, savings institutions, bond mutual funds, insurance companies, finance companies, pension funds
Mortgage market	• Demand for housing and therefore the demand for mortgages • Secondary market values of existing mortgages • Interest rates on new mortgages • Risk premium on mortgages	Commercial banks, savings institutions, credit unions, insurance companies, pension funds
Stock market	• Required return on stocks and therefore the market values of stocks • Projections for corporate earnings and therefore stock values	Stock mutual funds, insurance companies, pension funds
Foreign exchange	• Demand for currencies and therefore the values of currencies, which in turn affect currency option prices	Institutions that are exposed to exchange rate risk

Impact of the Fed's Response to Oil Shocks   A month rarely goes by without the financial press reporting a potential inflation crisis, such as a hurricane that could affect oil production and refining in Louisiana or Texas, or friction in the Middle East or Russia that could disrupt oil production there. Financial market participants closely monitor oil shocks and the Fed's response to those shocks. Any event that might disrupt the world's production of oil triggers concerns about inflation. Oil prices affect the prices of gasoline and airline fuel, which affect the costs of transporting many products and supplies. In addition, oil is also used in the production of some products. Firms that experience higher costs due to higher oil expenses may raise their prices.

When higher oil prices trigger concerns about inflation, the Fed is pressured to use a restrictive monetary policy. The Fed does not have control over oil prices, but it reasons that it can at least dampen any inflationary pressure on prices if it slows economic growth. In other words, a decline in economic growth may discourage firms from increasing prices of their products because they know that raising prices may cause their sales to drop.

The concerns that an oil price shock will occur and that the Fed will raise interest rates to offset the high oil prices tend to have the following effects. First, bond markets may react negatively because bond prices are inversely related to interest rates. Stock prices are affected by expectations of corporate earnings. If firms incur higher costs of production and transportation due to higher oil prices, then their earnings could decrease. In addition, if the Fed increases interest rates in order to slow economic growth (to reduce inflationary pressure), firms will experience an increase in the cost of financing. This also would reduce their earnings. Consequently, investors who expect a reduction in earnings may sell their holdings of stock, in which case stock prices will decline.

5-4b Impact on Financial Institutions

Many depository institutions obtain most of their funds in the form of short-term loans and then use some of their funds to provide long-term, fixed-rate, mortgage loans. When interest rates rise, their cost of funds rises faster than the return they receive on their loans. Thus they are adversely affected when the Fed increases interest rates.

Financial institutions such as commercial banks, bond mutual funds, insurance companies, and pension funds maintain large portfolios of bonds, so their portfolios are adversely affected when the Fed raises interest rates. Financial institutions such as stock mutual funds, insurance companies, and pension funds maintain large portfolios of stocks, and their stock portfolios are also indirectly affected by changes in interest rates. Thus, all of these financial institutions must closely monitor the Fed's monetary policy so that they can manage their operations based on expectations of future interest rate movements.

GLOBAL
ASPECTS

5-5 GLOBAL MONETARY POLICY

Financial market participants must recognize that the type of monetary policy implemented by the Fed is somewhat dependent on various international factors, as explained next.

5-5a Impact of the Dollar

A weak dollar can stimulate U.S. exports because it reduces the amount of foreign currency needed by foreign companies to obtain dollars in order to purchase U.S. exports. A weak dollar also discourages U.S. imports because it increases the dollars needed to obtain foreign currency in order to purchase imports. Thus a weak dollar can stimulate the U.S. economy. In addition, it tends to exert inflationary pressure in the United States because it reduces foreign competition. The Fed can afford to be less aggressive with a stimulative monetary policy if the dollar is weak, because a weak dollar can itself provide some stimulus to the U.S. economy. Conversely, a strong dollar tends to reduce inflationary pressure but also dampens the U.S. economy. Therefore, if U.S. economic conditions are weak, a strong dollar will not provide the stimulus needed to improve conditions and so the Fed may need to implement a stimulative monetary policy.

5-5b Impact of Global Economic Conditions

The Fed recognizes that economic conditions are integrated across countries, so it considers prevailing global economic conditions when conducting monetary policy. When global economic conditions are strong, foreign countries purchase more U.S. products and can stimulate the U.S. economy. When global economic conditions are weak, the foreign demand for U.S. products weakens.

During the credit crisis that began in 2008, the United States and many other countries experienced very weak economic conditions. The Fed's decision to lower U.S. interest rates and stimulate the U.S. economy was partially driven by these weak global economic conditions. The Fed recognized that the United States would not receive any stimulus (such as a strong demand for U.S. products) from other countries where income and aggregate spending levels were also relatively low.

5-5c Transmission of Interest Rates

Each country has its own currency (except for countries in the euro zone) and its own interest rate, which is based on the supply of and demand for loanable funds in that currency. Investors residing in one country may attempt to capitalize on high interest rates

Exhibit 5.12 Illustration of Global Crowding Out

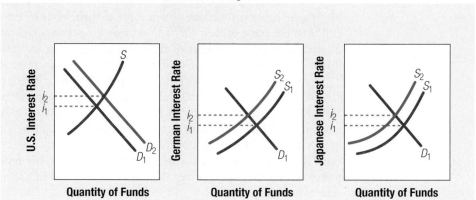

in another country. If there is upward pressure on U.S. interest rates that can be offset by foreign inflows of funds, then the Fed may not feel compelled to use a stimulative policy. However, if foreign investors reduce their investment in U.S. securities, the Fed may be forced to intervene in order to prevent interest rates from rising.

Given the international integration in money and capital markets, a government's budget deficit can affect interest rates of various countries. This concept, referred to as **global crowding out**, is illustrated in Exhibit 5.12. An increase in the U.S. budget deficit causes an outward shift in the federal government's demand for U.S. funds and therefore in the aggregate demand for U.S. funds (from D_1 to D_2). This crowding-out effect forces the U.S. interest rate to increase from i_1 to i_2 if the supply curve (S) is unchanged. As U.S. rates rise, they attract funds from investors in other countries, such as Germany and Japan. As foreign investors use more of their funds to invest in U.S. securities, the supply of available funds in their respective countries declines. Consequently, there is upward pressure on non-U.S. interest rates as well. The impact will be most pronounced in countries whose investors are most likely to find the higher U.S. interest rates attractive. The possibility of global crowding out has caused national governments to criticize one another for large budget deficits.

5-5d Impact of the Crisis in Greece on European Monetary Policy

In the spring of 2010, Greece experienced a weak economy and a large budget deficit. Creditors were less willing to lend the Greece government funds because they feared that the government may be unable to repay the loans. There were even concerns that Greece would abandon the euro, which caused many investors to liquidate their euro-denominated investments and move their money into other currencies. Overall, the lack of demand for euros in the foreign exchange market caused the euro's value to decline by about 20 percent during the spring of 2010.

The debt repayment problems in Greece adversely affected creditors from many other countries in Europe. In addition, Portugal and Spain had large budget deficit problems (because of excessive government spending) and experienced their own financial crises in 2012. The weak economic conditions in these countries caused fear of a financial crisis throughout Europe. The fear discouraged corporations, investors, and creditors outside of Europe from moving funds into Europe, and also encouraged some European investors to move their money out of the euro and out of Europe. Thus, just the fear by itself reduced the amount of capital available within Europe, which resulted in lower growth and lower security prices in Europe.

Since euro zone country governments do not have their own monetary policy, they are restricted from using their own stimulative monetary policy to strengthen economic conditions. They have control of their own fiscal policy, but given that the underlying problems were attributed to heavy government spending, they did not want to attempt stimulating their economy with more deficit spending.

The European Central Bank (ECB) was forced to use a more stimulative monetary policy than desired in order to ease concerns about the Greek crisis, even though this caused other concerns about potential inflation in the euro zone. The Greek crisis illustrated how the ECB's efforts to resolve one country's problems could create more problems in other euro zone countries that are subject to the same monetary policy. The ECB also stood ready to provide credit to help countries in the eurozone experiencing a financial crisis. When the ECB provides credit to a country, it imposes austerity conditions that can correct the government's budget deficit such as reducing government spending and imposing higher tax rates on its citizens.

Like any central bank, the ECB faces a dilemma when trying to resolve a financial crisis. If it provides funding and imposes the austerity conditions that force a country to reduce its budget deficit, it may temporarily weaken the country's economy further. The austerity conditions that reduce a government's budget deficit may also result in a lower level of aggregate spending and higher taxes (less disposable income for households).

SUMMARY

- By using monetary policy, the Fed can affect the interaction between the demand for money and the supply of money, which affects interest rates, aggregate spending, and economic growth. As the Fed increases the money supply, interest rates should decline and result in more aggregate spending (because of cheaper financing rates) and higher economic growth. As the Fed decreases the money supply, interest rates should increase and result in less aggregate spending (because of higher financing rates), lower economic growth, and lower inflation.

- A stimulative monetary policy can increase economic growth, but it could ignite demand-pull inflation. A restrictive monetary policy is likely to reduce inflation but may also reduce economic growth. Thus the Fed faces a trade-off when implementing monetary policy. Given a possible trade-off, the Fed tends to pinpoint its biggest concern (unemployment versus inflation) and assess whether the potential benefits of any proposed monetary policy outweigh the potential adverse effects.

- Because monetary policy can have a strong influence on interest rates and economic growth, it affects the valuation of most securities traded in financial markets. Financial market participants attempt to forecast the Fed's future monetary policies and the effects of these policies on economic conditions. When the Fed implements monetary policy, financial market participants attempt to assess how their security holdings will be affected and adjust their security portfolios accordingly.

- The Fed's monetary policy must take into account the global economic environment. A weak dollar may increase U.S. exports and thereby stimulate the U.S. economy. If economies of other countries are strong, this can also increase U.S. exports and boost the U.S. economy. Thus the Fed may not have to implement a stimulative monetary policy if international conditions can provide some stimulus to the U.S. economy. Conversely, the Fed may consider a more aggressive monetary policy to fix a weak U.S. economy if international conditions are weak, since in that case the Fed cannot rely on other economies to boost the U.S. economy.

POINT COUNTER-POINT

Can the Fed Prevent U.S. Recessions?

Point   Yes. The Fed has the power to reduce market interest rates and can therefore encourage more borrowing and spending. In this way, it stimulates the economy.

Counter-Point   No. When the economy is weak, individuals and firms are unwilling to borrow regardless of the interest rate. Thus the borrowing (by those

who are qualified) and spending will not be influenced by the Fed's actions. The Fed should not intervene but rather allow the economy to work itself out of a recession.

Who Is Correct?   Use the Internet to learn more about this issue and then formulate your own opinion.

QUESTIONS AND APPLICATIONS

1. **Impact of Monetary Policy** How does the Fed's monetary policy affect economic conditions?

2. **Trade-offs of Monetary Policy** Describe the economic trade-off faced by the Fed in achieving its economic goals.

3. **Choice of Monetary Policy** When does the Fed use a stimulative monetary policy, and when does it use a restrictive monetary policy? What is a criticism of a stimulative monetary policy? What is the risk of using a monetary policy that is too restrictive?

4. **Active Monetary Policy** Describe an active monetary policy.

5. **Passive Monetary Policy** Describe a passive monetary policy.

6. **Fed Control** Why may the Fed have difficulty controlling the economy in the manner desired? Be specific.

7. **Lagged Effects of Monetary Policy** Compare the recognition lag and the implementation lag.

8. **Fed's Control of Inflation** Assume that the Fed's primary goal is to reduce inflation. How can it use open market operations to achieve this goal? What is a possible adverse effect of such action by the Fed (even if it achieves the goal)?

9. **Monitoring Money Supply** Why do financial market participants closely monitor money supply movements?

10. **Monetary Policy during the Credit Crisis** Describe the Fed's monetary policy response to the credit crisis.

11. **Impact of Money Supply Growth** Explain why an increase in the money supply can affect interest rates in different ways. Include the potential impact of the money supply on the supply of and the demand for loanable funds when answering this question.

12. **Confounding Effects** What factors might be considered by financial market participants who are assessing whether an increase in money supply growth will affect inflation?

13. **Fed Response to Fiscal Policy** Explain how the Fed's monetary policy could depend on the fiscal policy that is implemented.

Advanced Questions

14. **Interpreting the Fed's Monetary Policy** When the Fed increases the money supply to lower the federal funds rate, will the cost of capital to U.S. companies be reduced? Explain how the segmented markets theory regarding the term structure of interest rates (as explained in Chapter 3) could influence the degree to which the Fed's monetary policy affects long-term interest rates.

15. **Monetary Policy Today** Assess the economic situation today. Is the administration more concerned with reducing unemployment or inflation? Does the Fed have a similar opinion? If not, is the administration publicly criticizing the Fed? Is the Fed publicly criticizing the administration? Explain.

16. **Impact of Foreign Policies** Why might a foreign government's policies be closely monitored by investors in other countries, even if the investors plan no investments in that country? Explain how monetary

policy in one country can affect interest rates in other countries.

17. Monetary Policy during a War Consider a discussion during FOMC meetings in which there is a weak economy and a war, with potential major damage to oil wells. Explain why this possible effect would have received much attention at the FOMC meetings. If this possibility was perceived to be highly likely at the time of the meetings, explain how it may have complicated the decision about monetary policy at that time. Given the conditions stated in this question, would you suggest that the Fed use a restrictive monetary policy, or a stimulative monetary policy? Support your decision logically and acknowledge any adverse effects of your decision.

18. Economic Indicators Stock market conditions serve as a leading economic indicator. If the U.S. economy is in a recession, what are the implications of this indicator? Why might this indicator be inaccurate?

19. How the Fed Should Respond to Prevailing Conditions Consider the current economic conditions, including inflation and economic growth. Do you think the Fed should increase interest rates, reduce interest rates, or leave interest rates at their present levels? Offer some logic to support your answer.

20. Impact of Inflation Targeting by the Fed Assume that the Fed adopts an inflation targeting strategy. Describe how the Fed's monetary policy would be affected by an abrupt 15 percent rise in oil prices in response to an oil shortage. Do you think an inflation targeting strategy would be more or less effective in this situation than a strategy of balancing inflation concerns with unemployment concerns? Explain.

21. Predicting the Fed's Actions Assume the following conditions. The last time the FOMC met, it decided to raise interest rates. At that time, economic growth was very strong and so inflation was relatively high. Since the last meeting, economic growth has weakened, and the unemployment rate will likely rise by 1 percentage point over the quarter. The FOMC's next meeting is tomorrow. Do you think the FOMC will revise its targeted federal funds rate? If so, how?

22. The Fed's Impact on the Housing Market In periods when home prices declined substantially, some homeowners blamed the Fed. In other periods, when home prices increased, homeowners gave credit to the Fed. How can the Fed have such a large impact on home prices? How could news of a substantial increase in the general inflation level affect the Fed's monetary policy and thereby affect home prices?

23. Targeted Federal Funds Rate The Fed uses a targeted federal funds rate when implementing monetary policy. However, the Fed's main purpose in its monetary policy is typically to have an impact on the aggregate demand for products and services. Reconcile the Fed's targeted federal funds rate with its goal of having an impact on the overall economy.

24. Monetary Policy during the Credit Crisis During the credit crisis, the Fed used a stimulative monetary policy. Why do you think the total amount of loans to households and businesses did not increase as much as the Fed had hoped? Are the lending institutions to blame for the relatively small increase in the total amount of loans extended to households and businesses?

25. Stimulative Monetary Policy during a Credit Crunch Explain why a stimulative monetary policy might not be effective during a weak economy in which there is a credit crunch.

26. Response of Firms to a Stimulative Monetary Policy In a weak economy, the Fed commonly implements a stimulative monetary policy to lower interest rates, and presumes that firms will be more willing to borrow. Even if banks are willing to lend, why might such a presumption about the willingness of firms to borrow be wrong? What are the consequences if the presumption is wrong?

27. Fed Policy Focused on Long-term Interest Rates Why might the Fed want to focus its efforts on reducing long-term interest rates rather than short-term interest rates during a weak economy? Explain how it might use a monetary policy focused on influencing long-term interest rates. Why might such a policy also affect short-term interest rates in the same direction?

28. Impact of Monetary Policy on Cost of Capital Explain the effects of a stimulative monetary policy on a firm's cost of capital.

29. Effectiveness of Monetary Policy What circumstances might cause a stimulative monetary policy to be ineffective?

30. Impact of ECB Response to Greece Crisis How did the debt repayment problems in Greece affect creditors from other countries in Europe? How did the ECB's stimulative monetary policy affect the Greek crisis?

Interpreting Financial News

Interpret the following statements made by Wall Street analysts and portfolio managers.

a. "Lately, the Fed's policies are driven by gold prices and other indicators of the future rather than by recent economic data."

b. "The Fed cannot boost money growth at this time because of the weak dollar."

c. "The Fed's fine-tuning may distort the economic picture."

Managing in Financial Markets

Forecasting Monetary Policy As a manager of a firm, you are concerned about a potential increase in interest rates, which would reduce the demand for your firm's products. The Fed is scheduled to meet in one week to assess economic conditions and set monetary policy. Economic growth has been high, but inflation has also increased from 3 to 5 percent (annualized) over the last four months. The level of unemployment is so low that it cannot go much lower.

a. Given the situation, is the Fed likely to adjust monetary policy? If so, how?

b. Recently, the Fed has allowed the money supply to expand beyond its long-term target range. Does this affect your expectation of what the Fed will decide at its upcoming meeting?

c. Suppose the Fed has just learned that the Treasury will need to borrow a larger amount of funds than originally expected. Explain how this information may affect the degree to which the Fed changes the monetary policy.

FLOW OF FUNDS EXERCISE

Anticipating Fed Actions

Recall that Carson Company has obtained substantial loans from finance companies and commercial banks. The interest rate on the loans is tied to market interest rates and is adjusted every six months. Because of its expectations of a strong U.S. economy, Carson plans to grow in the future by expanding the business and by making acquisitions. It expects that it will need substantial long-term financing and plans to borrow additional funds either through loans or by issuing bonds. The company may also issue stock to raise funds in the next year.

An economic report recently highlighted the strong growth in the economy, which has led to nearly full employment. In addition, the report estimated that the annualized inflation rate increased to 5 percent, up from 2 percent last month. The factors that caused the higher inflation (shortages of products and shortages of labor) are expected to continue.

a. How will the Fed's monetary policy change based on the report?

b. How will the likely change in the Fed's monetary policy affect Carson's future performance? Could it affect Carson's plans for future expansion?

c. Explain how a tight monetary policy could affect the amount of funds borrowed at financial institutions by deficit units such as Carson Company. How might it affect the credit risk of these deficit units? How might it affect the performance of financial institutions that provide credit to such deficit units as Carson Company?

INTERNET/EXCEL EXERCISES

1. Go to the website www.federalreserve.gov/monetary policy/fomc.htm to review the activities of the FOMC. Succinctly summarize the minutes of the last FOMC meeting. What did the FOMC discuss at that meeting? Did the FOMC make any changes in the current monetary policy? What is the FOMC's current monetary policy?

2. Is the Fed's present policy focused more on stimulating the economy or on reducing inflation? Or is the present policy evenly balanced? Explain.

3. Using the website http://research.stlouisfed.org/fred2, retrieve interest rate data at the beginning of the last 20 quarters for the federal funds rate and the three-month Treasury bill rate, and place the data in two columns of an Excel spreadsheet. Derive the change in interest rates on a quarterly basis. Apply regression analysis in which the quarterly change in the T-bill rate is the dependent variable (see Appendix B for more information about using regression analysis).

If the Fed's effect on the federal funds rate influences other interest rates (such as the T-bill rate), there should be a positive and significant relationship between the interest rates. Is there such a relationship? Explain.

WSJ Exercise

Market Assessment of Fed Policy

Review a recent issue of the *Wall Street Journal* and then summarize the market's expectations about future interest rates. Are these expectations based primarily on the Fed's monetary policy or on other factors?

Online Articles with Real-World Examples

Find a recent practical article available online that describes a real-world example regarding a specific financial institution or financial market that reinforces one or more concepts covered in this chapter.

If your class has an online component, your professor may ask you to post your summary of the article there and provide a link to the article so that other students can access it. If your class is live, your professor may ask you to summarize your application of the article in class. Your professor may assign specific students to complete this assignment or may allow any students to do the assignment on a volunteer basis.

For recent online articles and real-world examples related to this chapter, consider using the following search terms (be sure to include the prevailing year as a search term to ensure that the online articles are recent):

1. index of leading economic indicators
2. consumer price index AND Federal Reserve
3. inflation AND Federal Reserve
4. inflation AND monetary policy
5. Fed policy AND economy
6. federal funds rate AND economy
7. federal funds rate AND inflation
8. monetary policy AND budget deficit
9. monetary policy AND press release
10. monetary policy AND value of the dollar

Fed Watching

This problem requires an understanding of the Fed (Chapter 4) and monetary policy (Chapter 5). It also requires an understanding of how economic conditions affect interest rates and securities' prices (Chapters 2 and 3).

Like many other investors, you are a "Fed watcher" who constantly monitors any actions taken by the Fed to revise monetary policy. You believe that three key factors affect interest rates. Assume that the most important factor is the Fed's monetary policy. The second most important factor is the state of the economy, which influences the demand for loanable funds. The third factor is the level of inflation, which also influences the demand for loanable funds. Because monetary policy can affect interest rates, it affects economic growth as well. By controlling monetary policy, the Fed influences the prices of all types of securities.

The following information is available to you.

- Economic growth has been consistently strong over the past few years but is beginning to slow down.
- Unemployment is as low as it has been in the past decade, but it has risen slightly over the past two quarters.
- Inflation has been about 5 percent annually for the past few years.
- The dollar has been strong.
- Oil prices have been very low.

Yesterday, an event occurred that you believe will cause much higher oil prices in the United States and a weaker U.S. economy in the near future. You plan to determine whether the Fed will respond to the economic problems that are likely to develop.

You have reviewed previous economic slowdowns caused by a decline in the aggregate demand for goods and services and found that each slowdown precipitated a stimulative policy by the Fed. Inflation was 3 percent or less in each of the previous economic slowdowns. Interest rates generally declined in response to these policies, and the U.S. economy improved.

Assume that the Fed's philosophy regarding monetary policy is to maintain economic growth and low inflation. There does not appear to be any major fiscal policy forthcoming that will have a major effect on the economy. Thus the future economy is up to the Fed. The Fed's present policy is to maintain a 2 percent annual growth rate in the money supply. You believe that the economy is headed toward a recession unless the Fed uses a very stimulative monetary policy, such as a 10 percent annual growth rate in the money supply.

The general consensus of economists is that the Fed will revise its monetary policy to stimulate the economy for three reasons: (1) it recognizes the potential costs of higher unemployment if a recession occurs, (2) it has consistently used a stimulative policy in the past to prevent recessions, and (3) the administration has been pressuring the Fed to use a stimulative monetary policy. Although you will consider the economists' opinions, you plan to make your own assessment of the Fed's future policy. Two quarters ago, GDP declined by 1 percent. Last quarter, GDP declined again by 1 percent. Thus there is clear evidence that the economy has recently slowed down.

Questions

1. Do you think that the Fed will use a stimulative monetary policy at this point? Explain.

2. You maintain a large portfolio of U.S. bonds. You believe that if the Fed does not revise its monetary policy, the U.S. economy will continue to decline. If the Fed stimulates the economy at this point, you believe that you would be better off with stocks than with bonds. Based on this information, do you think you should switch to stocks? Explain.

PART 3
Debt Security Markets

Part 3 focuses on how debt security markets facilitate the flow of funds from surplus units to deficit units. Chapter 6 focuses on money markets for investors and borrowers trading short-term securities. Chapters 7 and 8 focus on the bond markets, and Chapter 9 focuses on the mortgage markets. Because some financial market participants trade securities in all of these markets, there is much interaction among them, as emphasized throughout the chapters.

6
Money Markets

CHAPTER OBJECTIVES

The specific objectives of this chapter are to:

- describe the features of the most popular money market securities,

- explain how money markets are used by institutional investors,

- explain the valuation and risk of money market securities, and

- explain how money markets have become globally integrated.

Money markets are used to facilitate the transfer of short-term funds from individuals, corporations, or governments with excess funds to those with deficient funds. Even investors who focus on long-term securities tend to hold some money market securities. Money markets enable financial market participants to maintain liquidity.

6-1 MONEY MARKET SECURITIES

Money market securities are debt securities with a maturity of one year or less. They are issued in the primary market through a telecommunications network by the Treasury, corporations, and financial intermediaries that wish to obtain short-term financing. The means by which money markets facilitate the flow of funds are illustrated in Exhibit 6.1. The U.S. Treasury issues money market securities (Treasury bills) and uses the proceeds to finance the budget deficit. Corporations issue money market securities and use the proceeds to support their existing operations or to expand their operations. Financial institutions issue money market securities and bundle the proceeds to make loans to households or corporations. Thus, the funds are channeled to support household purchases, such as cars and homes, and to support corporate investment in buildings and machinery. The Treasury and some corporations commonly pay off their debt from maturing money market securities with the proceeds from issuing new money market securities. In this way, they are able to finance expenditures for long periods of time even though money market securities have short-term maturities. Overall, money markets allow households, corporations, and the U.S. government to increase their expenditures; thus the markets finance economic growth.

Money market securities are commonly purchased by households, corporations (including financial institutions), and government agencies that have funds available for a short-term period. Because money market securities have a short-term maturity and can typically be sold in the secondary market, they provide liquidity to investors. Most firms and financial institutions maintain some holdings of money market securities for this reason.

The more popular money market securities are:

- Treasury bills (T-bills)
- Commercial paper
- Negotiable certificates of deposit
- Repurchase agreements
- Federal funds
- Banker's acceptances

Each of these instruments is described in turn.

Exhibit 6.1   How Money Markets Facilitate the Flow of Funds

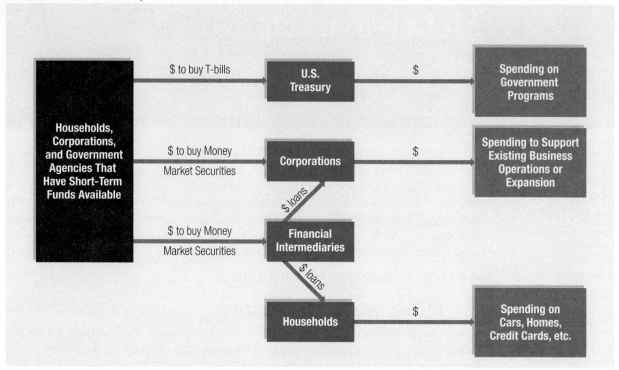

6-1a Treasury Bills

When the U.S. government needs to borrow funds, the U.S. Treasury frequently issues short-term securities known as Treasury bills. The Treasury issues T-bills with 4-week, 13-week, and 26-week maturities on a weekly basis. It periodically issues T-bills with terms shorter than four weeks, which are called *cash management bills*. It also issues T-bills with a one-year maturity on a monthly basis. Treasury bills were formerly issued in paper form but are now maintained electronically.

Investors in Treasury Bills   Depository institutions commonly invest in T-bills so that they can retain a portion of their funds in assets that can easily be liquidated if they suddenly need to accommodate deposit withdrawals. Other financial institutions also invest in T-bills in the event that they need cash because cash outflows exceed cash inflows. Individuals with substantial savings invest in T-bills for liquidity purposes. Many individuals invest in T-bills indirectly by investing in money market funds, which in turn purchase large amounts of T-bills. Corporations invest in T-bills so that they have easy access to funding if they suddenly incur unanticipated expenses.

Credit Risk   Treasury bills are attractive to investors because they are backed by the federal government and are therefore virtually free of credit (default) risk. This is a very desirable feature, because investors do not have to use their time to assess the risk of the issuer, as they do with other issuers of debt securities.

Liquidity   Another attractive feature of T-bills is their liquidity, which is due to their short maturity and strong secondary market. At any given time, many institutional investors are participating in the secondary market by purchasing or selling existing

T-bills. Thus, investors can easily obtain cash by selling their T-bills in the secondary market. Government securities dealers serve as intermediaries in the secondary market by buying existing T-bills from investors who want to sell them, or selling them to investors who want to buy them. These dealers profit by purchasing the bills at a slightly lower price than the price at which they sell them.

Pricing Treasury Bills

The par value (amount received by investors at maturity) of T-bills is $1,000 and multiples of $1,000. Since T-bills do not pay interest, they are sold at a discount from par value, and the gain to the investor holding a T-bill until maturity is the difference between par value and the price paid.

The price that an investor will pay for a T-bill with a particular maturity depends on the investor's required rate of return on that T-bill. That price is determined as the present value of the future cash flows to be received. The value of a T-bill is the present value of the par value. Thus, investors are willing to pay a price for a one-year T-bill that ensures that the amount they receive a year later will generate their desired return.

EXAMPLE   If investors require a 4 percent annualized return on a one-year T-bill with a $10,000 par value, the price that they are willing to pay is

$$P = \$10,000/1.04$$
$$= \$9,615.38$$

If the investors require a higher return, they will discount the $10,000 at that higher rate of return, which will result in a lower price that they are willing to pay today. You can verify this by estimating the price based on a required return of 5 percent and then on a required return of 6 percent. ●

To price a T-bill with a maturity shorter than one year, the annualized return can be reduced by the fraction of the year in which funds will be invested.

EXAMPLE   If investors require a 4 percent annualized return on a six-month T-bill, this reflects a 2 percent unannualized return over six months. The price that they will be willing to pay for a T-bill with a par value of $10,000 is therefore

$$P = \$10,000/1.02$$
$$= \$9,803.92$$ ●

Estimating the Yield

Because T-bills do not offer coupon payments and are sold at a discount from par value, their yield is influenced by the difference between the selling price and the purchase price. If an investor purchases a newly issued T-bill and holdsit until maturity, the return is based on the difference between the par value and the purchase price. If the T-bill is sold prior to maturity, the return is based on the difference between the price for which the bill was sold in the secondary market and the purchase price. The annualized yield from investing in a T-bill (Y_T) can be determined as

$$Y_T = \frac{SP - PP}{PP} \times \frac{365}{n}$$

where

$$SP = \text{selling price}$$
$$PP = \text{purchase price}$$
$$n = \text{number of days of the investment (holding period)}$$

EXAMPLE

An investor purchases a T-bill with a six-month (182-day) maturity and $10,000 par value for $9,800. If this T-bill is held until maturity, its yield is:

$$Y_T = \frac{\$10,000 - \$9,800}{\$9,800} \times \frac{365}{182}$$

$$= 4.09\%$$

WEB

www.federalreserve.
gov/econresdata
Go to the section on
interest rates to review
Treasury bill rates over
time.

Suppose the investor plans to sell the T-bill after 120 days and forecasts a selling price of $9,900 at that time. The expected annualized yield based on this forecast is

$$Y_T = \frac{\$9,950 - \$9,800}{\$9,800} \times \frac{365}{120}$$

$$= 4.65\%$$

The higher the forecasted selling price, the higher the expected annualized yield. ●

Estimating the Treasury Bill Discount Some business periodicals quote the T-bill discount along with the T-bill yield. The T-bill discount represents the percentage discount of the purchase price from par value (Par) for newly issued T-bills, and is computed as follows:

$$\text{T-bill discount} = \frac{\text{Par} - PP}{\text{Par}} \times \frac{360}{n}$$

EXAMPLE

If a newly issued 6-month (182-day) T-bill with a par value of $10,000 is purchased for $9,800, the T-bill discount is

$$Y_T = \frac{\$10,000 - \$9,800}{\$10,000} \times \frac{360}{182}$$

$$= 3.95\%$$ ●

For a newly issued T-bill that is held to maturity, the T-bill yield will always be higher than the discount. The difference occurs because the purchase price is the denominator of the yield equation whereas the par value is the denominator of the T-bill discount equation, and the par value will always exceed the purchase price of a newly issued T-bill. In addition, the yield formula uses a 365-day year versus the 360-day year used for the discount computation.

6-1b Treasury Bill Auction

The primary T-bill market is an auction. Individual investors can submit bids online for newly issued T-bills at www.treasurydirect.gov.

Financial institutions can submit their bids for T-bills (and other Treasury securities) online using the Treasury Automated Auction Processing System (TAAPS). Individuals and financial institutions can set up an account with the Treasury. Then they can select the specific maturity and face value that they desire and submit their bids electronically. Payments to the Treasury are withdrawn electronically from the account, and payments received from the Treasury when the securities mature are deposited electronically into the account.

At the auctions, investors have the option of bidding competitively or noncompetitively. The Treasury has a specified amount of funds that it plans to borrow, which dictates the amount of T-bill bids that it will accept for that maturity. Investors who wish to ensure that their bids will be accepted can use noncompetitive bids. Noncompetitive bidders are limited to purchasing T-bills with a maximum par value of $5 million per auction, however. Consequently, large corporations typically make competitive bids so that they can purchase larger amounts.

After accounting for noncompetitive bids, the Treasury accepts the highest competitive bids first and then works its way down until it has generated the amount of funds from competitive bids that it needs. Any bids below that cutoff point are not accepted. The Treasury applies the lowest accepted bid price to all competitive bids that are accepted and to all noncompetitive bids. Thus, the price paid by competitive and noncompetitive bidders reflects the lowest price of the competitive bids. Competitive bids are still submitted because, as noted before, many bidders want to purchase more T-bills than the maximum that can be purchased on a noncompetitive basis.

At each auction, the prices paid for six-month T-bills are significantly lower than the prices paid for three-month T-bills, because the investment term is longer. The lower price results in a higher unannualized yield that compensates investors for their longer-term investment.

The results of the weekly auction of 13-week and 26-week T-bills are summarized in the financial media each Tuesday and are also provided online at the Treasury Direct website. Some of the more commonly reported statistics are the dollar amount of applications and Treasury securities sold, the average price of the accepted competitive bids, and the coupon equivalent (annualized yield) for investors who paid the average price.

WEB

www.treasurydirect.
gov
Results of recent
Treasury bill auctions.

6-1c Commercial Paper

Commercial paper is a short-term debt instrument issued only by well-known, creditworthy firms that is typically unsecured. It is normally issued to provide liquidity or to finance a firm's investment in inventory and accounts receivable. The issuance of commercial paper is an alternative to short-term bank loans. Some large firms prefer to issue commercial paper rather than borrow from a bank because it is usually a cheaper source of funds. Nevertheless, even the large creditworthy firms that are able to issue commercial paper normally obtain some short-term loans from commercial banks in order to maintain a business relationship with them. Financial institutions such as finance companies and bank holding companies are major issuers of commercial paper.

Denomination The minimum denomination of commercial paper is usually $100,000, and typical denominations are in multiples of $1 million. Maturities are normally between 20 and 45 days but can be as short as 1 day or as long as 270 days. The 270-day maximum is due to a Securities and Exchange Commission ruling that paper with a maturity exceeding 270 days must be registered.

Because of the high minimum denomination, individual investors rarely purchase commercial paper directly, although they may invest in it indirectly by investing in money market funds that have pooled the funds of many individuals. Money market funds are major investors in commercial paper. Although the secondary market for commercial paper is very limited, it is sometimes possible to sell the paper back to the dealer who initially helped to place it. However, in most cases, investors hold commercial paper until maturity.

Credit Risk Because commercial paper is issued by corporations that are susceptible to business failure, commercial paper is subject to credit risk. The risk of default is affected by the issuer's financial condition and cash flow. Investors can attempt to assess the probability that commercial paper will default by monitoring the issuer's financial condition. The focus is on the issuer's ability to repay its debt over the short term because the payments must be completed within a short-term period.

Although issuers of commercial paper are subject to possible default, historically the percentage of issues that have defaulted is very low, as most issuers of commercial paper

Exhibit 6.2   Possible Ratings Assigned to Commercial Paper

	MOODY'S	STANDARD & POOR'S	FITCH
Highest	P1	A1	F1
High	P2	A2	F2
Medium	P3	A3	F3
Low	NP	B or C	F4
Default	NP	D	F5

are very strong financially. In addition, the short time period of the credit reduces the chance that an issuer will suffer financial problems before repaying the funds borrowed. However, during the credit crisis in 2008, Lehman Brothers (a large securities firm) failed. This made investors more cautious before purchasing securities, as discussed later in the chapter.

Credit Risk Ratings   Commercial paper is commonly rated by rating agencies such as Moody's Investors Service, Standard & Poor's Corporation, and Fitch Investor Service. The possible ratings assigned to commercial paper are shown in Exhibit 6.2. The rating serves as an indicator of the potential risk of default. Some investors rely heavily on the rating to assess credit risk, rather than assess the risk of the issuer themselves.

A money market fund can invest only in commercial paper that has a top-tier or second-tier rating, and second-tier paper cannot represent more than 5 percent of the fund's assets. Thus, corporations can more easily place commercial paper that is assigned a top-tier rating. Some commercial paper (called **junk commercial paper**) is rated low or not rated at all.

Placement   Some firms place commercial paper directly with investors. Other firms rely on commercial paper dealers to sell their commercial paper at a transaction cost of about one-eighth of 1 percent of the face value. This transaction cost is generally less than it would cost to establish a department within the firm to place commercial paper directly. However, companies that frequently issue commercial paper may reduce expenses by creating such an in-house department. Most nonfinancial companies use commercial paper dealers rather than in-house resources to place their commercial paper. Their liquidity needs, and therefore their commercial paper issues, are cyclical, so they would use an in-house, direct placement department only a few times during the year. Finance companies typically maintain an in-house department because they frequently borrow in this manner.

Backing Commercial Paper   Some commercial paper is backed by assets of the issuer. Commercial paper that is backed by assets should offer a lower yield than if it were not secured by assets. However, the issuers of asset-backed commercial paper tend to have more risk of default than the well-known firms that can successfully issue unsecured commercial paper, and the value of assets used as collateral may be questionable. Thus yields offered on asset-backed commercial paper are often higher than the yields offered on unsecured commercial paper.

Some issuers of asset-backed commercial paper obtain credit guarantees from a sponsoring institution in the event that they cannot cover their payments on commercial paper. This allows them to more easily sell their commercial paper to investors.

WEB

www.federalreserve.
gov/releases/cp/
about.htm
Provides valuable
information about
commercial paper.

Issuers of commercial paper typically maintain backup lines of credit in case they cannot roll over (reissue) commercial paper at a reasonable rate because, for example, their assigned rating has been lowered. A backup line of credit provided by a commercial bank gives the company the right (but not the obligation) to borrow a specified maximum amount of funds over a specified period of time. The fee for the credit line can either be a direct percentage (e.g., 0.5 percent) of the total accessible credit or be in the form of required compensating balances (e.g., 10 percent of the credit line).

Estimating the Yield   Like T-bills, commercial paper does not pay interest and is priced at a discount from par value. At a given point in time, the yield on commercial paper is slightly higher than the yield on a T-bill with the same maturity because commercial paper carries some credit risk and is less liquid. The nominal return to investors who retain the paper until maturity is the difference between the price paid for the paper and the par value. Thus the yield received by a commercial paper investor can be determined in a manner similar to the T-bill yield, although a 360-day year is usually used.

WEB

www.federalreserve.
gov/releases/cp
Provides information on
current commercial
paper rates as well as a
database of commercial
paper rates over time.

_____ **EXAMPLE**

If an investor purchases 30-day commercial paper with a par value of $1,000,000 for a price of $995,000, and holds the commercial paper until maturity, the yield (Y_{cp}) is

$$Y_{cp} = \frac{\$1,000,000 - \$996,000}{\$996,000} \times \frac{360}{30}$$

$$= 4.82\%$$
●

When a firm plans to issue commercial paper, the price (and hence the yield) to investors is uncertain. Thus the cost of borrowing funds is uncertain until the paper is issued.

When firms sell their commercial paper at a lower (higher) price than projected, their cost of raising funds will be higher (lower) than they initially anticipated.

Ignoring transaction costs, the cost of borrowing with commercial paper is equal to the yield earned by investors holding the paper until maturity. The cost of borrowing can be adjusted for transaction costs (charged by the commercial paper dealers) by subtracting the nominal transaction fees from the price received.

Commercial Paper Yield Curve   The commercial paper yield curve represents the yield offered on commercial paper at various maturities, based on the assumption that the paper is held to maturity. The curve is typically established for a maturity range from 0 to 90 days because most commercial paper has a maturity within that range. This yield curve is important because it may influence the maturity that is used by firms that issue commercial paper and by the institutional investors that purchase commercial paper. The shape of this yield curve could be roughly drawn from the short-term range of the traditional Treasury yield curve. However, that curve is graphed over a long time period, so it is difficult to derive the precise shape of a yield curve over a three-month range from that graph.

The same factors that affect the Treasury yield curve affect the commercial paper yield curve, but they are applied to very short-term horizons. In particular, expectations regarding the interest rate over the next few months can influence the commercial paper yield curve.

Commercial Paper Rate over Time   The rate (or yield) offered on newly issued commercial paper over time is provided in Exhibit 6.3. The movements in the commercial paper rate are highly correlated with the T-bill rate with the same maturity. The annualized commercial paper rate commonly contains a very small premium (such as 0.3 percent or smaller) above the T-bill rate to reflect a slight degree of default risk.

Exhibit 6.3 Commercial Paper Rate over Time

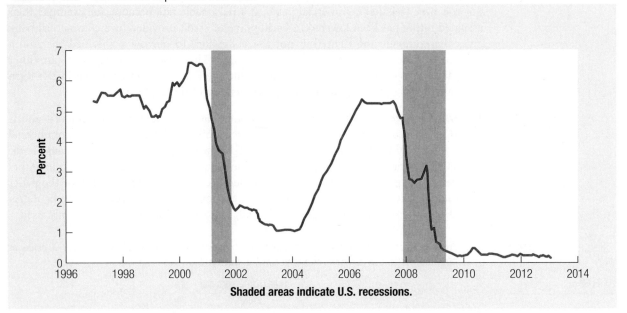

Shaded areas indicate U.S. recessions.

6-1d Negotiable Certificates of Deposit

Negotiable certificates of deposit (NCDs) are certificates issued by large commercial banks and other depository institutions as a short-term source of funds. The minimum denomination is $100,000, although a $1 million denomination is more common. Nonfinancial corporations often purchase NCDs. Although NCD denominations are typically too large for individual investors, they are sometimes purchased by money market funds that have pooled individual investors' funds. Thus, money market funds allow individuals to be indirect investors in NCDs, creating a more active NCD market.

Maturities on NCDs normally range from two weeks to one year. A secondary market for NCDs exists, providing investors with some liquidity. However, institutions prefer not to have their newly issued NCDs compete with their previously issued NCDs being resold in the secondary market. An oversupply of NCDs for sale could force institutions to sell their newly issued NCDs at a lower price.

Placement   Some issuers place their NCDs directly; others use a correspondent institution that specializes in placing NCDs. Another alternative is to sell NCDs to securities dealers who in turn resell them. A portion of unusually large issues is commonly sold to NCD dealers. Normally, however, NCDs can be sold to investors directly at a higher price.

Yield   Negotiable certificates of deposit provide a return in the form of interest along with the difference between the price at which the NCD is redeemed (or sold in the secondary market) and the purchase price. Given that an institution issues an NCD at par value, the annualized yield that it will pay is the annualized interest rate on the NCD. If investors purchase this NCD and hold it until maturity, their annualized yield is the interest rate. However, the annualized yield can differ from the annualized interest rate for investors who either purchase or sell the NCD in the secondary market instead of holding it from inception until maturity.

Negotiable certificates of deposit must offer a slightly higher yield above the T-bill yield with the same maturity in order to compensate for less liquidity and safety. The premiums are generally higher during recessionary periods, and they reflect the market's perception of the financial system's safety.

EXAMPLE

An investor purchased an NCD a year ago in the secondary market for $990,000. He redeems it today upon maturity and receives $1,000,000. He also receives interest of $40,000. His annualized yield (Y_{NCD}) on this investment is

$$Y_{NCD} = \frac{\$1,000,000 - \$990,000 + \$40,000}{\$990,000}$$

$$= 5.05\%$$ ●

6-1e Repurchase Agreements

With a repurchase agreement (or repo), one party sells securities to another with an agreement to repurchase the securities at a specified date and price. In essence, the repo transaction represents a loan backed by the securities. If the borrower defaults on the loan, the lender has claim to the securities. Most repo transactions use government securities, although some involve other securities such as commercial paper or NCDs. A **reverse repo** refers to the purchase of securities by one party from another with an agreement to sell them. Thus, a repo and a reverse repo refer to the same transaction but from different perspectives. These two terms are sometimes used interchangeably, so a transaction described as a repo may actually be a reverse repo.

Financial institutions such as banks, savings and loan associations, and money market funds often participate in repurchase agreements. Many nonfinancial institutions are also active participants. The size of the repo market is about $4.5 trillion, and transaction amounts are usually for $10 million or more. The most common maturities are from 1 to 15 days and for one, three, and six months. A secondary market for repos does not exist. Some firms in need of funds will set the maturity on a repo to be the minimum time period for which they need temporary financing. If they still need funds when the repo is about to mature, they will borrow additional funds through new repos and use these funds to fulfill their obligation on maturing repos.

Placement Repo transactions are negotiated through a telecommunications network. Dealers and repo brokers act as financial intermediaries to create repos for firms with deficient or excess funds, receiving a commission for their services.

When the borrowing firm can find a counterparty to the repo transaction, it avoids the transaction fee involved in having a government securities dealer find the counterparty. Some companies that commonly engage in repo transactions have an in-house department for finding counterparties and executing the transactions. A company that borrows through repos may, from time to time, serve as the lender. That is, it may purchase the government securities and agree to sell them back in the near future. Because the cash flow of any large company changes on a daily basis, it is not unusual for a firm to act as an investor one day (when it has excess funds) and a borrower the next (when it has a cash shortage).

Impact of the Credit Crisis During the credit crisis in 2008, the values of mortgage securities declined and so financial institutions participating in the housing market were exposed to more risk. Consequently, many financial institutions that relied on the repo market for funding were not able to obtain funds. Investors became more

USING THE WALL STREET JOURNAL

Key Interest Rates

The *Wall Street Journal* discloses quoted interest rates for commercial paper, CDs, Treasury bills, and other securities, as shown here. Notice that the rate quoted for commercial paper or CDs is slightly higher than the rate quoted for Treasury securities with the same maturity. Issuers of these securities and investors in these securities closely monitor the prevailing rates.

Source: Republished with permission of Dow Jones & Company, Inc., from the *Wall Street Journal*, January 25, 2011, p. C11.

Key Interest Rates

Data are annualized on a 360-day basis. Treasury yields are per annum, on actively traded noninflation and inflation-indexed issues that are adjusted to constant maturities. Data are from weekly Federal Reserve release H.15.

	WEEK ENDED Jan 21	WEEK ENDED Jan 14	52-WEEK High	52-WEEK Low
Federal funds (effective)	0.17	0.17	0.21	0.12
Commercial paper				
Nonfinancial				
1-month	0.20	0.19	0.22	0.11
2-month	0.23	0.22	0.27	0.12
3-month	0.24	0.24	0.32	0.10
Financial				
1-month	0.21	0.20	0.28	0.11
2-month	0.23	0.23	0.42	0.15
3-month	0.26	0.26	0.51	0.17
CDs (secondary market)				
1-month	0.25	0.25	0.36	0.16
3-month	0.29	0.29	0.54	0.19
6-month	0.39	0.38	0.78	0.29
Discount window primary credit	0.75	0.75	0.75	0.50
Conventional mortgages	4.74	4.71	5.21	4.17
Treasury yields at constant maturities				
1-month	0.15	0.15	0.17	0.02
3-month	0.16	0.15	0.17	0.06
6-month	0.19	0.18	0.25	0.14
1-year	0.27	0.27	0.47	0.22
2-year	0.62	0.60	1.11	0.35
3-year	1.03	1.01	1.71	0.49
5-year	2.01	1.96	2.67	1.11
7-year	2.74	2.67	3.38	1.79
10-year	3.42	3.36	3.94	2.45

	WEEK ENDED Jan 21	WEEK ENDED Jan 14	52-WEEK High	52-WEEK Low
20-year	4.32	4.26	4.63	3.32
Treasury yields (secondary market)				
1-month	0.15	0.15	0.17	0.02
3-month	0.16	0.15	0.17	0.06
6-month	0.19	0.18	0.25	0.14
Treasury inflation-protected securities				
5-year	0.08	0.00	0.76	-0.41
7-year	0.65	0.55	1.27	-0.05
10-year	1.10	0.98	1.64	0.46
20-year	1.72	1.63	2.12	1.22
Long-term avg	1.74	1.67	2.20	1.12
Interest rate swaps				
1-year	0.46	0.47	0.91	0.37
2-year	0.83	0.83	1.26	0.50
3-year	1.30	1.29	1.89	0.73
4-year	1.77	1.75	2.41	1.04
5-year	2.21	2.17	2.84	1.37
7-year	2.88	2.83	3.43	1.97
10-year	3.47	3.41	3.92	2.51
30-year	4.30	4.21	4.61	3.23
Corporate bonds, Moody's seasoned				
Aaa	5.07	5.01	5.44	4.31
Baa	6.12	6.07	6.45	5.51
State and local bonds	5.41	5.39	5.41	3.82
Eurodollars				
1 month	0.32	0.32	0.46	0.28
3 month	0.39	0.39	0.62	0.39
6 month	0.53	0.55	0.76	0.44

Notes on data:
Federal-funds rate is an average for the seven days ended Wednesday, weighted according to rates on broker trades; **Commercial paper rates** are discounted offer rates interpolated from sales by dealers or direct issuers to investors that are settled by the Depository Trust Company; **CD rates** are discounted averages of dealer bid rates on nationally traded certificates of deposit; **Discount window primary credit rate** is charged for discounts made and advances extended under the Federal Reserve's primary credit discount window program; **rate** is average for seven days ended Wednesday; **Inflation-indexed long-term TIPS** average is indexed and is based on the unweighted average bid yields for all TIPS with remaining terms to maturity of 10 years or more; **Swap rates** are International Swaps and Derivatives Association (ISDA(R)) mid-market par rates for a fixed-rate payer, who in return receives three-month Libor, and are based on rates collected at 11:00 a.m. ET by Garban Intercapital PLC; Source is Reuters; **Moody's triple-AAA** rates are averages of industrial bonds only; **Muni rates** are Thursday quotes based on the Bond Buyer Index for general obligation, 20 years to maturity, mixed quality debt; **Mortgage rates** are contract rates on commitments for fixed-rate first mortgages.

Sources: Federal Reserve; for additional information on these rate data and their derivation, please see, www.federalreserve.gov/releases/h15/data.htm.

concerned about the securities that were posted as collateral. Bear Stearns, a large securities firm, relied heavily on repos for funding and used mortgage securities as collateral. But the valuation of these types of securities was subject to much uncertainty because of the credit crisis. Consequently, investors were unwilling to provide funding, and Bear Stearns could not obtain sufficient financing. It avoided bankruptcy only with the aid of the federal government. The lesson of this example is that repo market funding requires collateral that is trusted by investors. When economic conditions are weak, some securities may not serve as adequate collateral to obtain funding.

Estimating the Yield   The repo rate is determined as the difference between the initial selling price of the securities and the agreed-on repurchase price, annualized to a 360-day year.

EXAMPLE

An investor initially purchased securities at a price (*PP*) of $992,000 while agreeing to sell them back at a price (*SP*) of $1,000,000 at the end of a 60-day period. The yield (or repo rate) on this repurchase agreement is

$$\text{Repo rate} = \frac{\$1,000,000 - \$9,992,000}{\$992,000} \times \frac{360}{60}$$

$$= 4.84\%$$

6-1f Federal Funds

The federal funds market enables depository institutions to lend or borrow short-term funds from each other at the so-called **federal funds rate**. This rate is charged on federal funds transactions, and it is influenced by the supply of and demand for funds in the federal funds market. The Federal Reserve adjusts the amount of funds in depository institutions in order to influence the federal funds rate (as explained in Chapter 4) and several other short-term interest rates. All types of firms closely monitor the federal funds rate because the Federal Reserve manipulates it to affect general economic conditions. For this reason, many market participants view changes in the federal funds rate as an indicator of potential changes in other money market rates.

The federal funds rate is normally slightly higher than the T-bill rate at any given time. A lender in the federal funds market is subject to credit risk, since it is possible that the financial institution borrowing the funds could default on the loan. Once a loan transaction is agreed upon, the lending institution can instruct its Federal Reserve district bank to debit its reserve account and to credit the borrowing institution's reserve account by the amount of the loan. If the loan is for just one day, it will likely be based on an oral agreement between the parties, especially if the institutions commonly do business with each other.

Commercial banks are the most active participants in the federal funds market. Federal funds brokers serve as financial intermediaries in the market, matching up institutions that wish to sell (lend) funds with those that wish to purchase (borrow) them. The brokers receive a commission for their service. The transactions are negotiated through a telecommunications network that links federal funds brokers with participating institutions. Most loan transactions are for $5 million or more and usually have a maturity of one to seven days (although the loans may often be extended by the lender if the borrower requests more time).

The volume of interbank loans on commercial bank balance sheets over time is an indication of the importance of lending between depository institutions. The interbank loan volume outstanding now exceeds $200 billion.

6-1g Banker's Acceptances

A **banker's acceptance** indicates that a bank accepts responsibility for a future payment. Banker's acceptances are commonly used for international trade transactions. An exporter that is sending goods to an importer whose credit rating is not known will often prefer that a bank act as a guarantor. The bank therefore facilitates the transaction by stamping ACCEPTED on a draft, which obligates payment at a specified point in time. In turn, the importer will pay the bank what is owed to the exporter along with a fee to the bank for guaranteeing the payment.

Exporters can hold a banker's acceptance until the date at which payment is to be made, but they frequently sell the acceptance before then at a discount to obtain cash immediately. The investor who purchases the acceptance then receives the payment guaranteed by the bank in the future. The investor's return on a banker's acceptance, like that on commercial paper, is derived from the difference between the discounted price paid for the acceptance and the amount to be received in the future. Maturities on banker's acceptances typically range from 30 to 270 days. Because there is a possibility that a bank will default on payment, investors are exposed to a slight degree of credit risk. Thus, they deserve a return above the T-bill yield in compensation.

Because acceptances are often discounted and sold by the exporting firm prior to maturity, an active secondary market exists. Dealers match up companies that wish to sell acceptances with other companies that wish to purchase them. A dealer's bid price is less than its ask price, and this creates the spread (or the dealer's reward for doing business). The spread is normally between one-eighth and seven-eighths of 1 percent.

Steps Involved in Banker's Acceptances

The sequence of steps involved in a banker's acceptance is illustrated in Exhibit 6.4. To understand these steps, consider the example of a U.S. importer of Japanese goods. First, the importer places a purchase order for the goods (Step 1). If the Japanese exporter is unfamiliar with the U.S. importer, it may demand payment before delivery of goods, which the U.S. importer may be unwilling to make. A compromise can be reached by creating a banker's acceptance. The importer asks its bank to issue a **letter of credit (L/C)** on its behalf (Step 2). The L/C represents a commitment by that bank to back the payment owed to the Japanese exporter. Then the L/C is presented to the exporter's bank (Step 3), which informs the exporter that the L/C has been received (Step 4). The exporter then sends the goods to the importer (Step 5) and sends the shipping documents to its bank (Step 6), which passes them along to the importer's bank (Step 7). At this point, the banker's acceptance (B/A) is created, which obligates the importer's bank to make payment to the holder of the banker's acceptance at a specified future date. The banker's acceptance may be sold to a money market investor at a discount. Potential purchasers of acceptances are short-term investors. When the acceptance matures, the importer pays its bank, which in turn pays the money market investor who presents the acceptance.

The creation of a banker's acceptance allows the importer to receive goods from an exporter without sending immediate payment. The selling of the acceptance creates financing for the exporter. Even though banker's acceptances are often created to facilitate international transactions, they are not limited to money market investors with international experience. Investors who purchase acceptances are more concerned with the credit of the bank that guarantees payment than with the credit of the exporter or importer. For this reason, the credit risk on a banker's acceptance is somewhat similar to that of NCDs issued by commercial banks. Yet because it has the backing not only of the bank but also of the importing firm, a banker's acceptance may be perceived as having slightly less credit risk than an NCD.

Exhibit 6.4 Sequence of Steps in the Creation of a Banker's Acceptance

The types of money market securities are summarized in Exhibit 6.5. When money market securities are issued to obtain funds, the type of securities issued depends on whether the issuer is the Treasury, a depository institution, or a corporation. When investors decide which type of money market securities to invest in, their choice depends on the desired return and liquidity characteristics.

6-2 INSTITUTIONAL USE OF MONEY MARKETS

The institutional use of money market securities is summarized in Exhibit 6.6. Financial institutions purchase money market securities in order to earn a return while maintaining adequate liquidity. They issue money market securities when experiencing a temporary shortage of cash. Because money markets serve businesses, the average transaction is very large and is typically executed through a telecommunications network.

Money market securities can be used to enhance liquidity in two ways. First, newly issued securities generate cash. The institutions that issue new securities have created a short-term liability in order to boost their cash balance. Second, institutions that previously purchased money market securities will generate cash upon liquidation of the securities. In this case, one type of asset (the security) is replaced by another (cash).

Most financial institutions maintain sufficient liquidity by holding either securities that have very active secondary markets or securities with short-term maturities. T-bills

Exhibit 6.5   Summary of Commonly Issued Money Market Securities

SECURITIES	ISSUED BY	COMMON INVESTORS	COMMON MATURITIES	SECONDARY MARKET ACTIVITY
Treasury bills	Federal government	Households, firms, and financial institutions	13 weeks, 26 weeks, 1 year	High
Negotiable certificates of deposit (NCDs)	Large banks and savings institutions	Firms	2 weeks to 1 year	Moderate
Commercial paper	Bank holding companies, finance companies, and other companies	Firms	1 day to 270 days	Low
Banker's acceptances	Banks (exporting firms can sell the acceptances at a discount to obtain funds)	Firms	30 days to 270 days	High
Federal funds	Depository institutions	Depository institutions	1 day to 7 days	Nonexistent
Repurchase agreements	Firms and financial institutions	Firms and financial institutions	1 day to 15 days	Nonexistent

Exhibit 6.6   Institutional Use of Money Markets

TYPE OF FINANCIAL INSTITUTION	PARTICIPATION IN THE MONEY MARKETS
Commercial banks and savings institutions	• Bank holding companies issue commercial paper. • Some banks and savings institutions issue NCDs, borrow or lend funds in the federal funds market, engage in repurchase agreements, and purchase T-bills. • Commercial banks create banker's acceptances. • Commercial banks provide backup lines of credit to corporations that issue commercial paper.
Finance companies	• Issue large amounts of commercial paper.
Money market mutual funds	• Use proceeds from shares sold to invest in T-bills, commercial paper, NCDs, repurchase agreements, and banker's acceptances.
Insurance companies	• May maintain a portion of their investment portfolio as money market securities for liquidity.
Pension funds	• May maintain a portion of their investment portfolio as money market securities that may be liquidated when portfolio managers desire to increase their investment in bonds or stocks.

are the most popular money market instrument because of their marketability, safety, and short-term maturity. Although T-bills are purchased through an auction, other money market instruments are commonly purchased through dealers or specialized brokers. For example, commercial paper is purchased through commercial paper dealers or directly from the issuer, NCDs are usually purchased through brokers specializing in NCDs, federal funds are purchased (borrowed) through federal funds brokers, and repurchase agreements are purchased through repo dealers.

Financial institutions whose future cash inflows and outflows are more uncertain will generally maintain additional money market instruments for liquidity. For this reason, depository institutions such as commercial banks allocate a greater portion of their asset portfolio to money market instruments than pension funds usually do.

Financial institutions that purchase money market securities are acting as creditors to the initial issuer of the securities. For example, when they hold T-bills, they are creditors to the Treasury. The T-bill transactions in the secondary market commonly reflect a flow of funds between two nongovernment institutions. Treasury bills represent a source of funds for those financial institutions that liquidate some of their T-bill holdings. In fact, this is the main reason that financial institutions hold T-bills. Liquidity is also the reason financial institutions purchase other money market instruments, including federal funds (purchased by depository institutions) and repurchase agreements (purchased by depository institutions and money market funds) as well as banker's acceptances and NCDs (purchased by money market funds).

Some financial institutions issue their own money market instruments to obtain cash. For example, depository institutions issue NCDs, and bank holding companies and finance companies issue commercial paper. Depository institutions also obtain funds through the use of repurchase agreements or in the federal funds market.

Many money market transactions involve two financial institutions. For example, a federal funds transaction involves two depository institutions. Money market funds commonly purchase NCDs from banks and savings institutions. Repurchase agreements are frequently negotiated between two commercial banks.

6-3 VALUATION OF MONEY MARKET SECURITIES

The market price of money market securities (P_m) should equal the present value of their future cash flows. Since money market securities normally do not make periodic interest payments, their cash flows are in the form of one lump-sum payment of principal. Therefore, the market price of a money market security can be determined as

$$P_m = \frac{Par}{(1 + k)^n}$$

where

Par = par value or principal amount to be provided at maturity
k = required rate of return by investors
n = time to maturity

Since money market securities have maturities of one year or less, n is measured as a fraction of one year.

A change in P_m can be modeled as

$$\Delta P_m = f(\Delta k) \text{ and } \Delta k = f(\Delta R_f, \Delta RP)$$

where

R_f = risk-free interest rate
RP = risk premium

Therefore,

$$\Delta P_m = f(\Delta R_f, \Delta RP)$$

This illustrates how the prices of money market securities would change in response to a change in the required rate of return, which itself is influenced by the risk-free interest rate and the perceived credit risk over time. Exhibit 6.7 identifies the underlying forces that

Exhibit 6.7 Framework for Pricing Money Market Securities

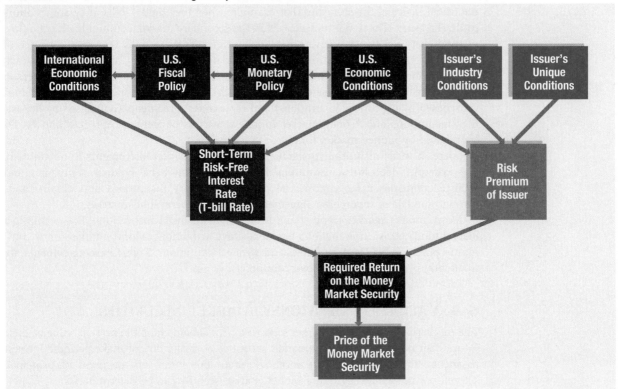

Source: *Board of Governors of the Federal Reserve System.*

can affect the short-term risk-free interest rate (the T-bill rate) and the risk premium and therefore affect the required return and prices of money market securities over time.

In general, the money markets are widely perceived to be efficient in that the prices reflect all available public information. Investors closely monitor economic indicators that may signal future changes in the strength of the economy, which can affect short-term interest rates and hence the required return from investing in money market securities. Some of the more closely monitored indicators of economic growth include employment, gross domestic product, retail sales, industrial production, and consumer confidence. A favorable movement in these indicators tends to create expectations of increased economic growth, which could place upward pressure on market interest rates (including the risk-free rate for short-term maturities) and downward pressure on prices of money market securities.

Investors also closely monitor indicators of inflation, such as the consumer price index and the producer price index. An increase in these indexes may create expectations of higher interest rates and places downward pressure on money market prices.

In addition to the indicators, investors also assess the financial condition of the firms that are issuing commercial paper. Their intent is to ensure that the issuing firm is financially healthy and therefore capable of paying off the debt at maturity.

6-3a Impact of Changes in Credit Risk

If investors want to avoid credit risk, they can purchase T-bills. When investing in other money market securities, they must weigh the higher potential return against the exposure to credit risk. Investors commonly invest in money market securities such as commercial paper and NCDs that offer a slightly higher yield than T-bills and are very unlikely to default. The perception of credit risk can change over time, which affects the required return and therefore the price of money market securities.

Credit Risk Following Lehman's Default

The credit crisis of 2008 had a major impact on the perceived risk of money market securities. Lehman Brothers relied on commercial paper as a permanent source of financing. As its outstanding issues of commercial paper came due, it would issue more and use the proceeds to pay off the paper that was due. It was heavily invested in mortgage-backed securities, and used these securities as collateral when issuing commercial paper to borrow funds. However, as the value of mortgage-backed securities declined, institutional investors were no longer willing to purchase Lehman's commercial paper because they questioned the value of the collateral. Since it could not obtain new funding, it was unable to pay off its existing debt. As Lehman Brothers filed for bankruptcy in September 2008, it defaulted on hundreds of millions of dollars of commercial paper that it had issued. This shocked the commercial paper market. As a result of the Lehman Brothers failure, investors became more concerned that commercial paper issued by other financial institutions might also be backed by assets with questionable quality.

Some issuers of asset-backed commercial paper obtained credit guarantees from a sponsoring institution in the event that they could not cover their payments on commercial paper. Normally, the credit guarantees might calm investors. Yet, during the credit crisis, the financial institutions providing credit guarantees for issuers of commercial paper were highly exposed to mortgages and other risky assets. The credit guarantee is only as good as the credit of the guarantor. Suddenly, institutional investors began to realize their exposure to default risk when investing in asset-backed commercial paper. As these investors cut back on their investments in commercial paper in order to avoid risk, the financial institutions that relied on commercial paper for their financing could no longer obtain the funds that they needed.

In the two months following the bankruptcy of Lehman Brothers, the volume of commercial paper declined by about $370 billion. Those firms that were still able to sell commercial paper had to pay higher risk premiums to compensate for the higher credit risk perceived by investors.

The credit crisis illustrates how problems in one debt security market (e.g., mortgage-backed securities) can be contagious to other debt markets (the commercial paper market). This is one reason why the federal government was concerned about systemic risk, whereby the adverse effects triggered in the market for mortgage-backed securities might spread to affect all types of financial markets and financial institutions. Furthermore, many financial institutions were heavily invested in mortgages and therefore exposed to the same type of risk. The failures of some financial institutions could expose others that provided credit guarantees on commercial paper.

Due to concerns about systemic risk, the U.S. government took action to stabilize the money markets. On October 3, 2008, the Emergency Economic Stabilization Act of 2008 (also referred to as the bailout act) was enacted, whereby the Treasury injected $700 billion into the financial system. This allowed the Treasury to invest in the large commercial banks as a means of providing the banks with capital to cushion their losses and therefore reduce their risk. Since financial institutions are major participants in the money markets, the liquidity of the money markets increased after the Treasury took action.

In November 2008, the Federal Reserve began to purchase commercial paper issued by highly rated firms. The Fed normally does not participate as an investor in the

Exhibit 6.8 Value of Commercial Paper Outstanding over Time

Shaded areas indicate U.S. recessions.

Source: *Federal Reserve.*

commercial paper market, but this new form of participation was intended to restore activity and therefore increase liquidity in the commercial paper market.

However, the commercial paper market has not completely recovered. Exhibit 6.8 shows how the amount of commercial paper outstanding reached a high of about $2.2 trillion in 2007, but has declined to about $1 trillion. Furthermore, investors are requiring that the asset-backed commercial paper be secured with safer securities (such as Treasury securities) rather than mortgage-backed securities.

Risk Premiums Following Lehman's Default During periods of heightened uncertainty about the economy, investors tend to shift from risky money market securities to Treasury securities. This so-called flight to quality creates a greater differential between yields, since risky money market securities must provide a larger risk premium to attract investors. During the credit crisis in 2008, the failure of Lehman Brothers increased the risk premium that some financial institutions had to pay when issuing commercial paper or NCDs, as shown in Exhibit 6.9. In the period shortly after Lehman's collapse, institutional investors were willing to purchase these money market securities only if the yield was sufficiently high to compensate for possible default risk. Months later, the rates on most money market securities declined as the credit risk declined, resulting in a reduction in the credit risk premium. In addition, as the Fed implemented a stimulative monetary policy in 2009 by pumping more money into the banking system, the rates on T-bills declined, and rates on other money market securities declined as well.

Exhibit 6.9 Money Market Yields over Time (Annualized Yields, One-Month Maturity)

Source: *Federal Reserve.*

6-3b Interest Rate Risk

If short-term interest rates increase, the required rate of return on money market securities will increase and the prices of money market securities will decrease. Although money market security values are sensitive to interest rate movements in the same direction as bonds, they are not as sensitive as bond values to interest rate movements. This lower degree of sensitivity is due primarily to the shorter term to maturity. With money market securities, the principal payment will occur in the next year, whereas the principal payment on bonds may be 10 or 20 years away. In other words, an increase in interest rates is not as harmful to a money market security because it will mature soon anyway, and the investor can reinvest the proceeds at the prevailing rate at that time.

Measuring Interest Rate Risk Participants in the money markets can use sensitivity analysis to determine how the value of money market securities may change in response to a change in interest rates.

EXAMPLE

Assume that Long Island Bank has money market securities with a par value of $100 million that will mature in nine months. Since the bank will need a substantial amount of funds in three months, it wants to know how much cash it will receive from selling these securities three months from now. Assume that it expects the unannualized required rate of return on those securities for the remaining six months to be 3 percent, 3.5 percent, or 3.8 percent, with a 33.3 percent (i.e., equal) chance for each of these three scenarios.

Exhibit 6.10 shows the probability distribution of the proceeds that Long Island Bank will receive from selling the money market securities three months later in terms of the possible scenarios for the required rate of return at that time. As this exhibit shows, the bank expects that it will receive at least $96,339,113, but it could receive more if interest rates (and therefore the required rate of return) are relatively low in three months. By deriving a probability distribution of outcomes, the bank can anticipate whether the proceeds to be received will be sufficient to cover the amount of funds that it will need in three months. ●

Exhibit 6.10 Probability Distribution of Proceeds from Selling Money Market Securities

SCENARIO FOR REQUIRED RATE OF RETURN	PROBABILITY	VALUE OF SECURITIES IF SCENARIO OCCURS
3%	33.3%	$97,087,379
3.5%	33.3%	$96,618,357
3.8%	33.3%	$96,339,113

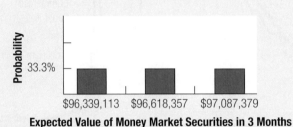

Expected Value of Money Market Securities in 3 Months

GLOBAL ASPECTS

6-4 GLOBALIZATION OF MONEY MARKETS

As international trade and financing have grown, money markets have developed in Europe, Asia, and South America. Corporations commonly accept foreign currencies as revenue if they will need those currencies to pay for imports in the future. Since a corporation may not need to use funds at the time it receives them, it deposits the funds to earn interest until they are needed. Meanwhile, other corporations may need funds denominated in foreign currencies and therefore may wish to borrow those funds from a bank. International banks facilitate the international money markets by accepting deposits and providing loans in a wide variety of currencies.

The flow of funds between countries has increased as a result of tax differences among countries, speculation on exchange rate movements, and a reduction in government barriers that were previously imposed on foreign investment in securities. Consequently, international markets are integrated.

The money market interest rates in each country are influenced by the demand for short-term funds by borrowers, relative to the supply of available short-term funds that are provided by savers. If the demand for short-term funds denominated in a particular currency is high relative to the short-term funds that are available in that currency, the money market interest rates will be relatively high in that country. Conversely, if the demand for short-term funds in that currency is low relative to the supply of short-term funds available, the money market interest rates in that country will be relatively low.

The money market interest rate paid by corporations who borrow short-term funds in a particular country is slightly higher than the rate paid by the federal government in the same country, which reflects the premium to compensate for credit risk of corporate borrowers. There may also be an additional premium to compensate for less liquidity of short-term securities issued by corporations.

Market interest rates vary among countries, as shown in Exhibit 6.11. Notice in the exhibit how money market rates are correlated among countries. Money market rates among several countries increased during the 2005–2006 period, when many economies

Exhibit 6.11   International Money Market Rates over Time

	UK	EUROZONE	CANADA	JAPAN
2009	1.5%	1.0%	1.1%	0.6
2010	1.0	0.9	0.9	0.5
2011	1.0	0.7	0.8	0.4
2012	0.8	0.6	0.7	0.3

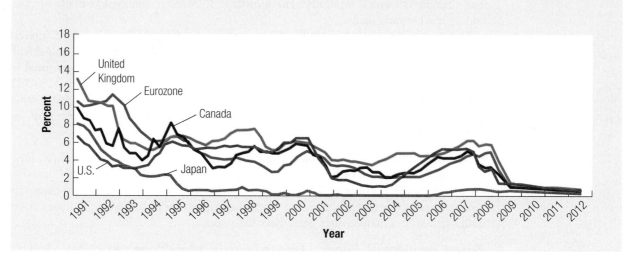

Source: *Federal Reserve.*

were growing. However, money market rates declined during the 2008–2013 period, when most countries experienced weak economies. The interest rates of several European countries are the same as a result of the conversion of their currencies to the euro.

6-4a Eurodollar Securities

As corporations outside the United States (especially in Europe) increasingly engaged in international trade transactions in U.S. dollars, U.S. dollar deposits in non-U.S. banks grew. Furthermore, because interest rate ceilings were historically imposed on dollar deposits in U.S. banks, corporations with large dollar balances often deposited their funds in Europe to receive a higher yield. These dollar deposits in Europe were referred to as **Eurodollars**. Several types of money market securities utilize Eurodollars.

Eurodollar CDs   **Eurodollar certificates of deposit** are large, dollar-denominated deposits (such as $1 million) accepted by banks in Europe. Eurodollar CD volume has grown substantially over time, since the U.S. dollar is used as a medium of exchange in a significant portion of international trade and investment transactions. Some firms overseas receive U.S. dollars as payment for exports and invest in Eurodollar CDs. Because these firms may need dollars to pay for future imports, they retain dollar-denominated deposits rather than convert dollars to their home currency.

In the so-called **Eurodollar market**, banks channel the deposited funds to other firms that need to borrow them in the form of Eurodollar loans. The deposit and loan transactions in Eurodollars are typically $1 million or more per transaction, so only governments and large corporations participate in this market. Because transaction amounts are large, investors in the market avoid some costs associated with the continuous small transactions that occur in retail-oriented markets. In addition, Eurodollar CDs are not subject to reserve requirements, which means that banks can lend out 100 percent of the deposits that arrive. For these reasons, the spread between the rate banks pay on large Eurodollar deposits and what they charge on Eurodollar loans is relatively small. Consequently, interest rates in the Eurodollar market are attractive for both depositors and borrowers. The rates offered on Eurodollar deposits are slightly higher than the rates offered on NCDs.

A secondary market for Eurodollar CDs exists, allowing the initial investors to liquidate their investment if necessary. The growth in Eurodollar volume has made the secondary market more active.

Investors in fixed-rate Eurodollar CDs are adversely affected by rising market interest rates, whereas issuers of these CDs are adversely affected by declining rates. To deal with this interest rate risk, **Eurodollar floating-rate CDs** (called **FRCDs**) have been used in recent years. The rate adjusts periodically to the London Interbank Offer Rate (LIBOR), which is the interest rate charged on international interbank loans. As with other floating-rate instruments, the rate on FRCDs ensures that the borrower's cost and the investor's return reflect prevailing market interest rates.

Euronotes   Short-term **Euronotes** are short-term securities issued in bearer form with common maturities of one, three, and six months. Typical investors in Euronotes often include the Eurobanks (banks that accept large deposits and make large loans in foreign currencies) that are hired to place the paper. These Euronotes are sometimes underwritten in a manner that guarantees the issuer a specific price.

Euro-Commercial Paper   Euro-commercial paper (Euro-CP) is issued without the backing of a banking syndicate. Maturities can be tailored to satisfy investors. Dealers that place commercial paper have created a secondary market by being willing to purchase existing Euro-CP before maturity.

The Euro-CP rate is typically between 50 and 100 basis points above LIBOR. Euro-CP is sold by dealers at a transaction cost ranging from 5 to 10 basis points of the face value. This market is tiny compared to the U.S. commercial paper market. Nevertheless, some European companies that want short-term funding in dollars can more easily place their paper here, where they have a household name.

6-4b International Interbank Market

Some international banks periodically have an excess of funds beyond the amount that other corporations want to borrow. Other international banks may be short of funds because their client corporations want to borrow more funds than the banks have available. An international interbank market facilitates the transfer of funds from banks with excess funds to those with deficient funds. This market is similar to the federal funds market in the United States, but it is worldwide and conducts transactions in a wide variety of currencies. Some of the transactions are direct from one bank to another, while others are channeled through large banks that serve as intermediaries between the lending bank and the borrowing bank. Historically, international banks in London carried out many of these transactions.

The rate charged for a loan from one bank to another in the international interbank market is the LIBOR, which is similar to the federal funds rate in the United States. Several banks report the interest rate that they offer in the interbank market and their rates may vary slightly. The LIBOR is the average of the reported rates at a given point in time. The LIBOR varies among currencies and is usually in line with the prevailing money market rates in the currency. It varies over time in response to changes in money market rates in a particular currency, which are driven by changes in the demand and supply conditions for short-term money in that currency. The term LIBOR is still frequently used, even though many international interbank transactions do not pass through London.

LIBOR Scandal In 2012, some banks that periodically report the interest rate they offer in the interbank market falsely reported their rates. These banks have some investment or loan positions whose performance is dependent on the prevailing LIBOR. For example, some banks provide loans with rates that adjust periodically in accordance with LIBOR, and therefore would benefit from inflating the reported rate they charge on interbank loans in order to push LIBOR higher. Some banks were charged with colluding to manipulate LIBOR in order to boost their trading profits. In particular, many banks have large positions in derivative securities (such as interest rate swaps, described in Chapter 15), and manipulating LIBOR by just 0.1 percent could generate millions of dollars in profits from their positions.

6-4c Performance of Foreign Money Market Securities

The performance of an investment in a foreign money market security is measured by the **effective yield** (yield adjusted for the exchange rate), which is a function of (1) the yield earned on the money market security in the foreign currency and (2) the exchange rate effect. The yield earned on the foreign money market security (Y_f) is

$$Y_f = \frac{SP_f - PP_f}{PP_f}$$

where

$SP_f =$ **selling price of the foreign money market security in the foreign currency**

$PP_f =$ **purchase price of the foreign money market security in the foreign currency**

The exchange rate effect (denoted as %ΔS) measures the percentage change in the spot exchange rate (in dollars) from the time the foreign currency was obtained to invest in the foreign money market security until the time the security was sold and the foreign currency was converted into the investor's home currency. Thus, the effective yield is

$$Y_e = (1 + Y_f) \times (1 + \%\Delta S) - 1$$

EXAMPLE A U.S. investor obtains Mexican pesos when the peso is worth $0.12 and invests in a one-year money market security that provides a yield (in pesos) of 22 percent. At the end of one year, the investor converts the proceeds from the investment back to dollars at the prevailing spot rate of $0.13 per peso. In this example, the peso increased in value by 8.33 percent, or 0.0833. The effective yield earned by the investor is

$$Y_e = (1 + Y_f) \times (1 + \%\Delta S) - 1$$
$$= (1.22) \times (1.0833) - 1$$
$$= 32.16\%$$

●

The effective yield exceeds the yield quoted on the foreign currency whenever the currency denominating the foreign investment increases in value over the investment horizon.

Conversely, it is lower than the yield quoted on the foreign currency whenever the currency denominating the foreign investment decreases in value over the investment horizon. In fact, U.S. investors have sometimes experienced a negative effective yield in periods when the foreign currency denominating their investment depreciated substantially.

SUMMARY

■ The main money market securities are Treasury bills, commercial paper, NCDs, repurchase agreements, federal funds, and banker's acceptances. These securities vary according to the issuer. Consequently, their perceived degree of credit risk can vary. They also have different degrees of liquidity. Therefore, the quoted yields at any given point in time vary among money market securities.

■ Financial institutions manage their liquidity by participating in money markets. They may issue money market securities when they experience cash shortages and need to boost liquidity. They can also sell holdings of money market securities to obtain cash. The value of a money market security represents the present value of the future cash flows generated by that security. Since money market securities represent debt, their expected cash flows are typically known. However, the pricing of money market securities changes in response to a shift in the required rate of return by investors. The required rate of return changes in response to interest rate movements or to a shift in the security's credit risk.

■ Interest rates vary among countries. Some investors are attracted to high interest rates in foreign countries, which cause funds to flow to those countries. Consequently, money markets have become globally integrated. Investments in foreign money market securities are subject to exchange rate risk because the foreign currency denominating the securities could depreciate over time.

POINT COUNTER-POINT

Should Firms Invest in Money Market Securities?

Point   No. Firms are supposed to use money in a manner that generates an adequate return to shareholders. Money market securities provide a return that is less than that required by shareholders. Thus, firms should not be using shareholder funds to invest in money market securities. If firms need liquidity, they can rely on the money markets for short-term borrowing.

Counter-Point   Yes. Firms need money markets for liquidity. If they do not hold any money market securities, they will frequently be forced to borrow to cover unanticipated cash needs. The lenders may charge higher risk premiums when lending so frequently to these firms.

Who Is Correct?   Use the Internet to learn more about this issue and then formulate your own opinion.

QUESTIONS AND APPLICATIONS

1. Primary Market Explain how the Treasury uses the primary market to obtain adequate funding.

2. T-Bill Auction How can investors using the primary T-bill market be assured that their bid will be accepted? Why do large corporations typically make competitive bids rather than noncompetitive bids for T-bills?

3. Secondary Market for T-Bills Describe the activity in the secondary T-bill market. How can this degree of activity benefit investors in T-bills? Why might a financial institution sometimes consider T-bills as a potential source of funds?

4. Commercial Paper Who issues commercial paper? What types of financial institutions issue commercial paper? Why do some firms create a department that can directly place commercial paper? What criteria affect the decision to create such a department?

5. Commercial Paper Ratings Why do ratings agencies assign ratings to commercial paper?

6. Commercial Paper Rates Explain how investors' preferences for commercial paper change during a recession. How should this reaction affect the difference between commercial paper rates and T-bill rates during recessionary periods?

7. Negotiable CDs How can small investors participate in investments in negotiable certificates of deposits (NCDs)?

8. Repurchase Agreements Based on what you know about repurchase agreements, would you expect them to have a lower or higher annualized yield than commercial paper? Why?

9. Banker's Acceptances Explain how each of the following would use banker's acceptances: (a) exporting firms, (b) importing firms, (c) commercial banks, and (d) investors.

10. Foreign Money Market Yield Explain how the yield on a foreign money market security would be affected if the foreign currency denominating that security declined to a greater degree.

11. Motive to Issue Commercial Paper The maximum maturity of commercial paper is 270 days. Why would a firm issue commercial paper instead of longer-term securities, even if it needs funds for a long period of time?

12. Risk and Return of Commercial Paper You have the choice of investing in top-rated commercial paper or commercial paper that has a lower risk rating. How do you think the risk and return performances of the two investments differ?

13. Commercial Paper Yield Curve How do you think the shape of the yield curve for commercial paper and other money market instruments compares to the yield curve for Treasury securities? Explain your logic.

Advanced Questions

14. Influence of Money Market Activity on Working Capital Assume that interest rates for most maturities are unusually high. Also, assume that the net working capital (defined as current assets minus current liabilities) levels of many corporations are relatively low in this period. Explain how the money markets play a role in the relationship between the interest rates and the level of net working capital.

15. Applying Term Structure Theories to Commercial Paper Apply the term structure of interest rate theories that were discussed in Chapter 3 to explain the shape of the existing commercial paper yield curve.

16. How Money Market Rates May Respond to Prevailing Conditions How have money market rates changed since the beginning of the semester? Consider the current economic conditions. Do you think money market rates will increase or decrease during the semester? Offer some logic to support your answer.

17. Impact of Lehman Brothers Failure Explain how the bankruptcy of Lehman Brothers (a large securities firm) reduced the liquidity of the commercial paper market.

18. Bear Stearns and the Repo Market Explain the lesson to be learned about the repo market based on the experience of Bear Stearns.

19. Impact of Credit Crisis on Liquidity Explain why the credit crisis affected the ability of financial institutions to access short-term financing in the money markets.

20. Impact of Credit Crisis on Risk Premiums Explain how the credit crisis affected the credit risk premium in the commercial paper market.

21. Systemic Risk Explain how systemic risk is related to the commercial paper market. That is, why did problems in the market for mortgage-backed securities affect the commercial paper market?

22. Commercial Paper Credit Guarantees Explain why investors that provided guarantees on commercial paper were exposed to much risk during the credit crisis.

Interpreting Financial News

Interpret the following statements made by Wall Street analysts and portfolio managers.

a. "Money markets are not used to get rich, but to avoid being poor."

b. "Until conditions are more favorable, investors are staying on the sidelines."

c. "My portfolio is overinvested in stocks because of the low money market rates."

Managing in Financial Markets

Money Market Portfolio Dilemma As the treasurer of a corporation, one of your jobs is to maintain investments in liquid securities such as Treasury securities and commercial paper. Your goal is to earn as high a return as possible but without taking much of a risk.

a. The yield curve is currently upward sloping, such that 10-year Treasury bonds have an annualized yield 3 percentage points above the annualized yield of three-month T-bills. Should you consider using some of your funds to invest in 10-year Treasury securities?

b. Assume that you have substantially more cash than you would possibly need for any liquidity problems. Your boss suggests that you consider investing the excess funds in some money market securities that have a higher return than short-term Treasury

securities, such as negotiable certificates of deposit (NCDs). Even though NCDs are less liquid, this would not cause a problem if you have more funds than you need. Given the situation, what use of the excess funds would benefit the firm the most?

c. Assume that commercial paper is currently offering an annualized yield of 7.5 percent, while Treasury securities are offering an annualized yield of 7 percent. Economic conditions have been stable, and you expect conditions to be very favorable over the next six months. Given this situation, would you prefer to hold T-bills or a diversified portfolio of commercial paper issued by various corporations?

d. Assume that commercial paper typically offers a premium of 0.5 percent above the T-bill rate. Given that your firm typically maintains about $10 million in liquid funds, how much extra will you generate per year by investing in commercial paper versus T-bills? Is this extra return worth the risk that the commercial paper could default?

PROBLEMS

1. T-Bill Yield Assume an investor purchased a six-month T-bill with a $10,000 par value for $9,000 and sold it 90 days later for $9,100. What is the yield?

2. T-Bill Discount Newly issued three-month T-bills with a par value of $10,000 sold for $9,700. Compute the T-bill discount.

3. Commercial Paper Yield Assume an investor purchased six-month commercial paper with a face value of $1 million for $940,000. What is the yield?

4. Repurchase Agreement Stanford Corporation arranged a repurchase agreement in which it purchased securities for $4.9 million and will sell the securities back for $5 million in 40 days. What is the yield (or repo rate) to Stanford Corporation?

5. T-Bill Yield You paid $98,000 for a $100,000 T-bill maturing in 120 days. If you hold it until maturity, what is the T-bill yield? What is the T-bill discount?

6. T-Bill Yield The Treasury is selling 91-day T-bills with a face value of $10,000 for $9,900. If the investor holds them until maturity, calculate the yield.

7. Required Rate of Return A money market security that has a par value of $10,000 sells for

$8,816.60. Given that the security has a maturity of two years, what is the investor's required rate of return?

8. Effective Yield A U.S. investor obtains British pounds when the pound is worth $1.50 and invests in a one-year money market security that provides a yield of 5 percent (in pounds). At the end of one year, the investor converts the proceeds from the investment back to dollars at the prevailing spot rate of $1.52 per pound. Calculate the effective yield.

9. T-Bill Yield

a. Determine how the annualized yield of a T-bill would be affected if the purchase price were lower. Explain the logic of this relationship.

b. Determine how the annualized yield of a T-bill would be affected if the selling price were lower. Explain the logic of this relationship.

c. Determine how the annualized yield of a T-bill would be affected if the number of days were reduced, holding the purchase price and selling price constant. Explain the logic of this relationship.

10. Return on NCDs Phil purchased an NCD a year ago in the secondary market for $980,000. The NCD matures today at a price of $1million, and Phil received $45,000 in interest. What is Phil's return on the NCD?

11. Return on T-Bills Current T-bill yields are approximately 2 percent. Assume an investor considering the purchase of a newly issued three-month T-bill expects interest rates to increase within the next three months and has a required rate of return of 2.5 percent. Based on this information, how much is this investor willing to pay for a three-month T-bill?

FLOW OF FUNDS EXERCISE

Financing in the Money Markets

Recall that Carson Company has obtained substantial loans from finance companies and commercial banks. The interest rate on the loans is tied to market interest rates and is adjusted every six months. Carson has a credit line with a bank in case it suddenly needs to obtain funds for a temporary period. It previously purchased Treasury securities that it could sell if it experiences any liquidity problems. If the economy continues to be strong, Carson may need to increase its production capacity by about 50 percent over the next few years to satisfy demand. It is concerned about a possible slowing of the economy because of potential Fed actions to reduce inflation. It needs funding to cover payments for supplies. It is also considering issuing stock or bonds to raise funds in the next year.

a. The prevailing commercial paper rate on paper issued by large publicly traded firms is lower than the rate Carson would pay when using a line of credit. Do you think that Carson could issue commercial paper at this prevailing market rate?

b. Should Carson obtain funds to cover payments for supplies by selling its holdings of Treasury securities or by using its credit line? Which alternative has a lower cost? Explain.

INTERNET/EXCEL EXERCISES

1. Go to http://research.stlouisfed.org/fred2. Under "Categories," select "Interest rates." Compare the yield offered on a T-bill with the yield offered by another money market security with a similar maturity. What is the difference in yields? Why do you think the yields differ?

2. How has the risk premium on a specific risky money market security (versus the T-bill) changed since one year ago? Is the change due to a change in economic conditions? Explain.

3. Using the same website, retrieve interest rate data at the beginning of the last 20 quarters for the three-month T-bill and another money market security and place the data in two columns of an Excel spreadsheet. Derive the change in interest rates for both money market securities on a quarterly basis. Apply regression analysis in which the quarterly change in the interest rate of the risky money market security is the dependent variable and the quarterly change in the T-bill rate is the independent variable (see Appendix B for more information about using regression analysis). Is there a positive and significant relationship between the interest rate movements? Explain.

WSJ EXERCISE

Assessing Yield Differentials of Money Market Securities

Use the "Money Rates" section of the *Wall Street Journal* to determine the 30-day yield (annualized) of commercial paper, certificates of deposit, banker's acceptances, and T-bills. Which of these securities has the highest yield? Why? Which of these securities has the lowest yield? Why?

ONLINE ARTICLES WITH REAL-WORLD EXAMPLES

Find a recent practical article available online that describes a real-world example regarding a specific financial institution or financial market that reinforces one or more concepts covered in this chapter. If your class has an online component, your professor may ask you to post your summary of the article there and provide a link to the article so that other students can access it. If your class is live, your professor may ask you to summarize your application of the article in class. Your professor may assign specific students to complete this assignment or may allow any students to do the assignment on a volunteer basis.

For recent online articles and real-world examples related to this chapter, consider using the following search terms (be sure to include the prevailing year as a search term to ensure that the online articles are recent):

1. Treasury bill auction
2. commercial paper AND offering
3. commercial paper AND rating
4. repurchase agreement AND financing
5. money market AND yield
6. commercial paper AND risk
7. institutional investors AND money market
8. banker's acceptance AND yield
9. [name of a specific financial institution] AND repurchase agreement
10. [name of a specific financial institution] AND commercial paper

7

Bond Markets

CHAPTER OBJECTIVES

The specific objectives of this chapter are to:

■ provide a background on bonds,

■ describe the different types of bonds and their characteristics,

■ explain how bond markets have become globally integrated, and

■ describe other types of long-term debt securities.

WEB

finance.yahoo.com/ bonds
Summary of bond market activity and analysis of bond market conditions.

From this chapter through Chapter 12, the focus is on capital market securities. These chapters are distinctly different from the previous chapter on money market securities in that they employ a long-term rather than a short-term perspective. This chapter and the following focus on bond markets, which facilitate the flow of long-term debt from surplus units to deficit units.

7-1 BACKGROUND ON BONDS

Bonds are long-term debt securities that are issued by government agencies or corporations. The issuer of a bond is obligated to pay interest (or coupon) payments periodically (such as annually or semiannually) and the par value (principal) at maturity. An issuer must be able to show that its future cash flows will be sufficient to enable it to make its coupon and principal payments to bondholders. Investors will consider buying bonds for which the repayment is questionable only if the expected return from investing in the bonds is sufficient to compensate for the risk.

Bonds are often classified according to the type of issuer. Treasury bonds are issued by the U.S. Treasury, federal agency bonds are issued by federal agencies, municipal bonds are issued by state and local governments, and corporate bonds are issued by corporations.

Most bonds have maturities of between 10 and 30 years. Bonds are classified by the ownership structure as either bearer bonds or registered bonds. **Bearer bonds** require the owner to clip coupons attached to the bonds and send them to the issuer to receive coupon payments. **Registered bonds** require the issuer to maintain records of who owns the bond and automatically send coupon payments to the owners.

Bonds are issued in the primary market through a telecommunications network. Exhibit 7.1 shows how bond markets facilitate the flow of funds. The U.S. Treasury issues bonds and uses the proceeds to support deficit spending on government programs. Federal agencies issue bonds and use the proceeds to buy mortgages that are originated by financial institutions. Thus, they indirectly finance purchases of homes. Corporations issue bonds and use the proceeds to expand their operations. Overall, by allowing households, corporations, and the U.S. government to increase their expenditures, bond markets finance economic growth.

7-1a Institutional Participation in Bond Markets

All types of financial institutions participate in the bond markets, as summarized in Exhibit 7.2. Commercial banks, savings institutions, and finance companies commonly

Exhibit 7.1 How Bond Markets Facilitate the Flow of Funds

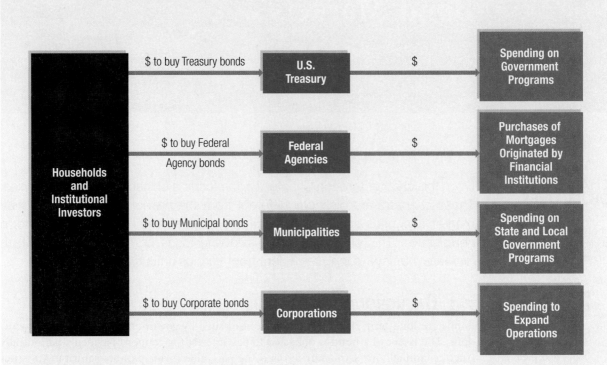

Exhibit 7.2 Participation of Financial Institutions in Bond Markets

FINANCIAL INSTITUTION	PARTICIPATION IN BOND MARKETS
Commercial banks and savings and loan associations (S&Ls)	• Purchase bonds for their asset portfolio. • Sometimes place municipal bonds for municipalities. • Sometimes issue bonds as a source of secondary capital.
Finance companies	• Commonly issue bonds as a source of long-term funds.
Mutual funds	• Use funds received from the sale of shares to purchase bonds. Some bond mutual funds specialize in particular types of bonds, while others invest in all types.
Brokerage firms	• Facilitate bond trading by matching up buyers and sellers of bonds in the secondary market.
Investment banking firms	• Place newly issued bonds for governments and corporations. They may place the bonds and assume the risk of market price uncertainty or place the bonds on a best-efforts basis in which they do not guarantee a price for the issuer.
Insurance companies	• Purchase bonds for their asset portfolio.
Pension funds	• Purchase bonds for their asset portfolio.

issue bonds in order to raise capital to support their operations. Commercial banks, savings institutions, bond mutual funds, insurance companies, and pension funds are investors in the bond market. Financial institutions dominate the bond market in that they purchase a large proportion of bonds issued.

7-1b Bond Yields

The yield on a bond depends on whether it is viewed from the perspective of the issuer of the bond, who is obligated to make payments on the bond until maturity, or from the perspective of the investors who purchase the bond.

Yield from the Issuer's Perspective   The issuer's cost of financing with bonds is commonly measured by the **yield to maturity**, which reflects the annualized yield that is paid by the issuer over the life of the bond. The yield to maturity is the annualized discount rate that equates the future coupon and principal payments to the initial proceeds received from the bond offering. It is based on the assumption that coupon payments received can be reinvested at the same yield.

EXAMPLE

Consider an investor who can purchase bonds with 10 years until maturity, a par value of $1,000, and an 8 percent annualized coupon rate for $936. The yield to maturity on these bonds can be determined by using a financial calculator as follows:

INPUT	10	936	80	1000		
Function Key	N	PV	PMT	FV	CPT	I
Answer						9%

WEB

money.cnn.com/
markets/bondcenter
Yields and information
on all types of bonds for
various maturities.

Notice that the yield paid to investors consists of two components: (1) a set of coupon payments and (2) the difference between the par value that the issuer must pay to investors at maturity and the price it received when selling the bonds. In this example and in most cases, the biggest component of the yield to maturity is the set of coupon payments. The yield to maturity does not include the transaction costs associated with issuing the bonds. When those transaction costs are considered, the issuer's actual cost of borrowing is slightly higher than the yield to maturity. ●

Yield from the Investor's Perspective   An investor who invests in a bond when it is issued and holds it until maturity will earn the yield to maturity. Yet many investors do not hold a bond to maturity and therefore focus on their *holding period return*, or the return from their investment over a particular holding period. If they hold the bond for a very short time period (such as less than one year), they may estimate their holding period return as the sum of the coupon payments plus the difference between the selling price and the purchase price of the bond, as a percentage of the purchase price. For relatively long holding periods, a better approximation of the holding period yield is the annualized discount rate that equates the payments received to the initial investment.

Since the selling price to be received by investors is uncertain if they do not hold the bond to maturity, their holding period yield is uncertain at the time they purchase the bond. Consequently, an investment in bonds is subject to the risk that the holding period return will be less than expected. The valuation and return of bonds from the investor's perspective are discussed more thoroughly in the following chapter.

7-2 TREASURY AND FEDERAL AGENCY BONDS

The U.S. government, like many country governments, commonly wants to use a fiscal policy of spending more money than it receives from taxes. Under these conditions, it needs to borrow funds to cover the difference between what it wants to spend versus what it receives. To facilitate its fiscal policy, the U.S. Treasury issues Treasury notes and Treasury bonds to finance federal government expenditures. The Treasury pays a yield to investors that reflects the risk-free rate, as it is presumed that the Treasury will not default on its payments. Because the Treasury notes and bonds are free from credit (default) risk, they enable the Treasury to borrow funds at a relatively low cost. However, there might be a limit at which any additional borrowing by the U.S. government could cause investors to worry about the Treasury's ability to cover its debt payments. Some other countries (such as Greece, Spain, and Portugal) have already reached that point, and the governments of those countries have to offer a higher yield on their bonds to compensate investors for the credit risk.

The minimum denomination for Treasury notes and bonds is now $100. The key difference between a note and a bond is that note maturities are less than 10 years whereas bond maturities are 10 years or more. Since 2006, the Treasury has commonly issued 10-year Treasury bonds and 30-year Treasury bonds to finance the U.S. budget deficit. An active over-the-counter secondary market allows investors to sell Treasury notes or bonds prior to maturity.

Investors in Treasury notes and bonds receive semiannual interest payments from the Treasury. Although the interest is taxed by the federal government as ordinary income, it is exempt from any state and local taxes. Domestic and foreign firms and individuals are common investors in Treasury notes and bonds.

WEB

www.treasurydirect.
gov
Details about Treasury
bonds.

7-2a Treasury Bond Auctions

The Treasury obtains long-term funding through Treasury bond offerings, which are conducted through periodic auctions. Treasury bond auctions are normally held in the middle of each quarter. The Treasury announces its plans for an auction, including the date, the amount of funding that it needs, and the maturity of the bonds to be issued. At the time of the auction, financial institutions submit bids for their own accounts or for their clients.

As discussed in Chapter 6, bids can be submitted on a competitive or a noncompetitive basis. Competitive bids specify a price that the bidder is willing to pay and a dollar amount of securities to be purchased. Noncompetitive bids specify only a dollar amount of securities to be purchased (subject to a maximum limit). The Treasury ranks the competitive bids in descending order according to the price bid per $100 of par value. All competitive bids are accepted until the point at which the desired amount of funding is achieved. The Treasury uses the lowest accepted bid price as the price applied to all accepted competitive bids and all noncompetitive bids. Competitive bids are commonly used because many bidders want to purchase more Treasury bonds than the maximum that can be purchased on a noncompetitive basis.

7-2b Trading Treasury Bonds

Bond dealers serve as intermediaries in the secondary market by matching up buyers and sellers of Treasury bonds, and they also take positions in these bonds. About 2,000 brokers and dealers are registered to trade Treasury securities, but about 20 so-called primary dealers dominate the trading. These dealers make the secondary market for the Treasury bonds. They quote a bid price for customers who want to sell existing Treasury bonds to the dealers and an ask price for customers who want to buy existing Treasury bonds from them. The dealers profit from the spread between the bid and ask prices. Because of the large volume of secondary market transactions and intense competition among bond dealers, the spread is extremely narrow. When the Federal Reserve engages in open market operations, it normally conducts trading with the primary dealers of government securities. The primary dealers also trade Treasury bonds among themselves.

Treasury bonds are registered at the New York Stock Exchange, but the secondary market trading occurs over the counter (through a telecommunications network). The typical daily transaction volume in government securities (including money market securities) for the primary dealers is about $570 billion. Most of this trading volume occurs in the United States, but Treasury bonds are traded worldwide. They are traded in Tokyo from 7:30 P.M. to 3:00 A.M. New York time. The Tokyo and London markets overlap for part of the time, and the London market remains open until 7:30 A.M., when trading begins in New York.

Investors can contact their broker to buy or sell Treasury bonds. The brokerage firms serve as an intermediary between the investors and the bond dealers. Discount brokers usually charge a fee of between $40 and $70 for Treasury bond transactions valued at $10,000. Institutional investors tend to contact the bond dealers directly.

Online Trading   Investors can also buy bonds through the Treasury Direct program (www.treasurydirect.gov). They can have the Treasury deduct their purchase from their bank account. They can also reinvest proceeds received when Treasury bonds mature into newly issued Treasury bonds.

Online Quotations   Treasury bond prices are accessible online at www.investing inbonds.com. This website provides the spread between the bid and the ask (offer) prices for various maturities. Treasury bond yields are accessible online at www.federalreserve. gov/releases/H15/. The yields are updated daily and are given for several different maturities.

7-2c Stripped Treasury Bonds

The cash flows of Treasury bonds are commonly transformed (stripped) by securities firms into separate securities. A Treasury bond that makes semiannual interest payments can be stripped into several individual securities. One security would represent the payment of principal upon maturity. Each of the other securities would represent payment of interest at the end of a specified period. Consequently, investors could purchase stripped securities that fit their desired investment horizon.

For example, consider a 10-year Treasury bond that pays an interest payment semiannually, for a total of 20 separate interest payments over the life of the bond. If this Treasury bond was stripped, its principal payment would be separated from the interest payments, and therefore would represent a new security that pays only the principal at the end of 10 years. In addition, all 20 interest rate payment portions of the Treasury bond would be separated into individual securities, so that one security would represent payment upon its maturity of 6 months, a second security would represent payment upon its maturity of 12 months, a third security would represent payment upon its maturity of 18 months, and so on. All newly formed securities are zero-coupon securities, because each security has only one payment that occurs upon its maturity.

Stripped Treasury securities are commonly called STRIPS (Separate Trading of Registered Interest and Principal of Securities). STRIPS are not issued by the Treasury but instead are created and sold by various financial institutions. They can be created for any Treasury security. Because they are components of Treasury securities, they are backed by the U.S. government. They do not have to be held until maturity, since there is an active secondary market. STRIPS have become quite popular over time.

7-2d Inflation-Indexed Treasury Bonds

The Treasury periodically issues inflation-indexed bonds that provide returns tied to the inflation rate. These bonds, commonly referred to as TIPS (Treasury Inflation-Protected Securities), are intended for investors who wish to ensure that the returns on their investments keep up with the increase in prices over time. The coupon rate offered on TIPS is lower than the rate on typical Treasury bonds, but the principal value is increased by the amount of the U.S. inflation rate (as measured by the percentage increase in the consumer price index) every six months.

Consider a 10-year, inflation-indexed bond that has a par value of $10,000 and a coupon rate of 4 percent. Assume that, during the first six months since the bond was issued, the inflation rate (as measured by the consumer price index) was 1 percent, in which case the principal of the bond is increased by $100 (0.01 × $10,000). Thus the coupon payment after six months will be 2 percent (half of the yearly coupon rate) of the new par value, or 0.02 × $10,100 = $202. Assume that the inflation rate over the next six months is 3 percent. Then the principal of the bond is increased by $303 (0.03 × $10,100), which results in a new par value of $10,403. The coupon payment at the end of the year is based on the coupon rate and the new par value, or 0.02 × $10,403 = $208.06. This process is applied every six months over the life of the bond. If prices double over the 10-year period in which the bond exists, the par value of the bond will also double and thus will be equal to $20,000 at maturity. ●

Inflation-indexed government bonds have become popular in many countries, including Australia and the United Kingdom. They are especially desirable in countries where inflation tends to be high, such as Brazil and Turkey. Inflation-indexed bonds are also popular in the United States. The Treasury historically focused on TIPS with 10-year maturities but is now offering TIPS with 5-year and 20-year maturities as well.

7-2e Savings Bonds

Savings bonds are issued by the Treasury, but they can be purchased from many financial institutions. They are attractive to small investors because they can be purchased with as little as $25. Larger denominations are also available. The Series EE savings bond provides a market-based rate of interest, and the Series I savings bond provides a rate of interest that is tied to inflation. The interest accumulates monthly and adds value to the amount received at the time of redemption.

Savings bonds have a 30-year maturity and do not have a secondary market. The Treasury does allow savings bonds issued after February 2003 to be redeemed any time after a 12-month period, but there is a penalty equal to the last three months of interest.

Like other Treasury securities, the interest income on savings bonds is not subject to state and local taxes but is subject to federal taxes. For federal tax purposes, investors holding savings bonds can report the accumulated interest either on an annual basis or not until bond redemption or maturity.

7-2f Federal Agency Bonds

Federal agency bonds are issued by federal agencies. The **Federal National Mortgage Association (Fannie Mae)** and the **Federal Home Loan Mortgage Association (Freddie Mac)** issue bonds and use the proceeds to purchase mortgages in the secondary market. Thus they channel funds into the mortgage market, thereby ensuring that there is sufficient financing for homeowners who wish to obtain mortgages. Prior to September 2008, these bonds were not backed by the federal government. During the credit crisis in 2008, however, Fannie Mae and Freddie Mac experienced financial problems because they had purchased risky subprime mortgages that had a high frequency of defaults. Consequently, the agencies were unable to issue bonds because investors feared that they might default. In September 2008, the federal government rescued Fannie Mae and Freddie Mac so that they could resume issuing bonds and continue to channel funds into the mortgage market.

7-3 MUNICIPAL BONDS

Like the federal government, state and local governments frequently spend more than the revenues they receive. To finance the difference, they issue **municipal bonds**, most of which can be classified as either **general obligation bonds** or **revenue bonds**. Payments on general obligation bonds are supported by the municipal government's ability to tax, whereas payments on revenue bonds must be generated by revenues of the project (toll way, toll bridge, state college dormitory, etc.) for which the bonds were issued. Revenue bonds are more common than general obligation bonds. There are more than 44,000 state and local government agencies that issue municipal bonds in order to finance their spending on government projects. The market value of these bonds is almost $4 trillion.

Revenue bonds and general obligation bonds typically promise semiannual interest payments. Common purchasers of these bonds include financial and nonfinancial institutions as well as individuals. The minimum denomination of municipal bonds is usually $5,000. A secondary market exists for them, although it is less active than the one for Treasury bonds.

Most municipal bonds contain a call provision, which allows the issuer to repurchase the bonds at a specified price before the bonds mature. A municipality may exercise its option to repurchase the bonds if interest rates decline substantially because it can then reissue bonds at the lower interest rate and thus reduce its cost of financing.

7-3a Credit Risk of Municipal Bonds

Both types of municipal bonds are subject to some degree of credit (default) risk. If a municipality is unable to increase taxes, it could default on general obligation bonds. If it issues revenue bonds and does not generate sufficient revenue, it could default on these bonds.

Municipal bonds have rarely defaulted, and some investors consider them to be safe because they presume that any government agency in the U.S. can obtain funds to repay its loans. However, some government agencies have serious budget deficits because of excessive spending, and may not be able to repay their loans. Recent economic conditions have reduced the amount of tax revenue that many government agencies have received, and have caused larger deficits for the agencies that have not reduced their spending.

During weak economic conditions, some state and local governments avoid tough decisions about reducing employment or pension obligations. But this results in a larger budget deficit, which requires additional municipal bond offerings to cover the deficits. Consequently, there is a concern that a municipal bond credit crisis could occur if municipalities do not attempt to correct their large budget deficits. As investors recognize the increased credit risk of municipal bonds, they require higher risk premiums as compensation.

Some investors are concerned that municipalities will file for bankruptcy not as a last resort, but as a convenient way to avoid their obligations. That is, they might consider placing the burden on the bondholders rather than correcting the budget deficit with higher taxes or less government spending.

There is very limited disclosure about the financial condition of the state and local governments that issue these bonds. The issuance of municipal securities is regulated by the respective state government, but critics argue that an unbiased regulator would be more appropriate. Better disclosure of financial information by state and local governments could help investors assess the potential default risk of some municipal bonds before they purchase them.

Ratings of Municipal Bonds   Because there is some concern about the risk of default, investors commonly monitor the ratings of municipal bonds. Moody's, Standard & Poor's, and Fitch Investors Service assign ratings to municipal bonds based on the ability of the issuer to repay the debt. The ratings are important to the issuer because a better rating means investors will require a smaller risk premium, in which case the municipal bonds can be issued at a higher price (lower yield). Some critics suggest that the ratings of municipal bonds have not been sufficiently downgraded to reflect the financial condition of municipalities in recent years.

Insurance against Credit Risk of Municipal Bonds   Some municipal bonds are insured to protect against default. The issuer pays for this protection so that it can issue the bond at a higher price, which translates into a higher price paid by the investor. Thus investors indirectly bear the cost of the insurance. Also, there still is the possibility that the insurer will default on its obligation of insuring the bonds. Thus if both the municipal bond and the bond insurer default, the investor will incur the loss. For this reason, investors should know what company is insuring the bonds and should assess its financial condition. During the credit crisis, MBIA (the largest insurer of bonds) experienced major losses because it insured many bonds that ultimately defaulted. Although MBIA issued new bonds to boost its capital level, its credit rating was downgraded by rating agencies.

Whereas about 50 percent of newly issued municipal bonds in 2006 were insured, fewer than 10 percent of newly issued municipal bonds in 2010 were insured. This reduction may be due to fewer insurance companies that are willing to insure bonds as a result of the credit crisis. It may also be attributed to investors recognizing that insured bonds still exhibit the risk that the insurer is unable to meet its obligations if many of the bonds it is insuring default at the same time.

7-3b Variable-Rate Municipal Bonds

Variable-rate municipal bonds have a floating interest rate that is based on a benchmark interest rate: the coupon payment adjusts to movements in the benchmark. Some variable-rate municipal bonds are convertible to a fixed rate until maturity under specified conditions. In general, variable-rate municipal bonds are desirable to investors who expect that interest rates will rise. However, there is the risk that interest rates may decline over time, which would cause the coupon payments to decline as well.

7-3c Tax Advantages of Municipal Bonds

One of the most attractive features of municipal bonds is that the interest income is normally exempt from federal taxes. Second, the interest income earned on bonds that are issued by a municipality within a particular state is normally exempt from the income taxes (if any) of that state. Thus, investors who reside in states that impose income taxes can reduce their taxes further.

7-3d Trading and Quotations of Municipal Bonds

There are hundreds of bond dealers that can accommodate investor requests to buy or sell municipal bonds in the secondary market, although five dealers account for more than half of all the trading volume. Bond dealers can also take positions in municipal bonds.

Investors who expect that they will not hold a municipal bond until maturity should consider only bonds that feature active secondary market trading. Many municipal bonds have an inactive secondary market, so it is difficult to know the prevailing market values of these bonds. Although investors do not pay a direct commission on trades, they incur transaction costs in the form of a bid–ask spread on the bonds. This spread can be large, especially for municipal bonds that are rarely traded in the secondary market.

Electronic trading of municipal bonds has become very popular, in part because it enables investors to circumvent the more expensive route of calling brokers. A popular bond website is www.ebondtrade.com. Such websites provide access to information on municipal bonds and allow online buying and selling of municipal bonds.

7-3e Yields Offered on Municipal Bonds

The yield offered by a municipal bond differs from the yield on a Treasury bond with the same maturity for three reasons. First, the municipal bond must pay a risk premium to compensate for the possibility of default risk. Second, the municipal bond must pay a slight premium to compensate for being less liquid than Treasury bonds with the same maturity. Third, as mentioned previously, the income earned from a municipal bond is exempt from federal taxes. This tax advantage of municipal bonds more than offsets their two disadvantages and allows municipal bonds to offer a lower yield than Treasury bonds. The yield on municipal securities is commonly 20 to 30 percent less than the yield offered on Treasury securities with similar maturities.

Movements in the yield offered on newly issued municipal bonds are highly correlated with movements in the yield offered on newly issued Treasury securities with similar maturities. Notice in Exhibit 7.3 that there has been a general decline in yields offered by municipal bonds since the financial crisis of 2008, which is attributed to the Fed's monetary policy that reduced long-term interest rates (and therefore yields offered on long-term debt). The temporary reversal of municipal bond rates in 2011 was due to an

Exhibit 7.3 Yield Offered on General Obligation Municipal Bonds over Time

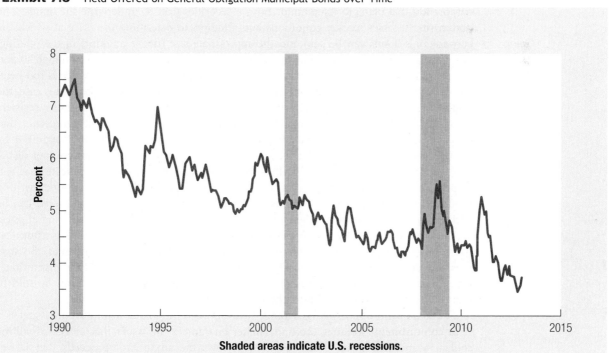

Source: *Board of Governors of the Federal Reserve System.*

increase in credit risk, as investors became more aware that some municipalities had large budget deficits and might not be capable of repaying their debt.

7-4 CORPORATE BONDS

Corporate bonds are long-term debt securities issued by corporations that promise the owner coupon payments (interest) on a semiannual basis. The minimum denomination is $1,000, and their maturity is typically between 10 and 30 years. However, Boeing, Chevron, and other corporations have issued 50-year bonds, and Disney, AT&T, and the Coca-Cola Company have even issued 100-year bonds.

The interest paid by the corporation to investors is tax deductible to the corporation, which reduces the cost of financing with bonds. Equity financing does not offer the same tax advantage because it does not involve interest payments. This is a major reason why many corporations rely heavily on bonds to finance their operations. Nevertheless, the amount of funds a corporation can obtain by issuing bonds is limited by its ability to make the coupon payments.

The interest income earned on corporate bonds represents ordinary income to the bondholders and is therefore subject to federal taxes and to state taxes, if any. For this reason, corporate bonds do not provide the same tax benefits to bondholders as do municipal bonds.

7-4a Corporate Bond Offerings

Corporate bonds can be placed with investors through a public offering or a private placement.

Public Offering Corporations commonly issue bonds through a public offering. A corporation that plans to issue bonds hires a securities firm to underwrite the bonds. The underwriter assesses market conditions and attempts to determine the price at which the corporation's bonds can be sold and the appropriate size (dollar amount) of the offering. The goal is to price the bonds high enough to satisfy the issuer but also low enough so that the entire bond offering can be placed. If the offering is too large or the price is too high, there may not be enough investors who are willing to purchase the bonds. In this case, the underwriter will have to lower the price in order to sell all the bonds. The issuer registers with the Securities and Exchange Commission (SEC) and submits a *prospectus* that explains the planned size of the offering, its updated financial condition (supported by financial statements), and its planned use of the funds. Meanwhile, the underwriter distributes the prospectus to other securities firms that it invites to join a syndicate that will help place the bonds in the market. Once the SEC approves the issue, the underwriting syndicate attempts to place the bonds. A portion of the bonds that are registered can be shelved for up to two years if the issuer wants to defer placing the entire offering at once.

Underwriters typically try to place newly issued corporate bonds with institutional investors (e.g., pension funds, bond mutual funds, and insurance companies) because these investors are more likely to purchase large pieces of the offering. Many institutional investors may plan to hold the bonds for a long-term period, but they can be sold to other investors should their plans change.

For some bond offerings, the arrangement between the underwriter and the issuer is a **firm commitment**, whereby the underwriter guarantees the issuer that all bonds will be sold at a specified price. Thus the issuer knows the amount of proceeds that it will receive. The underwriter is exposed to the risk if it cannot sell the bonds. Normally, the underwriter will only agree to a firm commitment if it has already received strong

USING THE WALL STREET JOURNAL

Bond Yield Quotations

The *Wall Street Journal* provides bond yield quotations for various types of bonds classified by type of bond, rating of issuer, or maturity, as shown here. The yields are quoted under the column "Latest." The range of yields that were offered over the previous 52 weeks for a given type of bond is also disclosed. Investors closely monitor the yields offered on bonds.

Source: Reprinted with permission of the *Wall Street Journal*, Copyright © 2013 Dow Jones & Company, Inc. All Rights Reserved Worldwide.

Bonds | WSJ.com/bonds

Tracking Bond Benchmarks

Return on investment and spreads over Treasurys and/or yields paid to investors compared with 52-week highs and lows for different types of bonds

Total return close	YTD total return (%)	Index	Latest	Low	YIELD (%), 52-WEEK RANGE ○ Latest	High
1740.46	-0.2	**Broad market** Barclays Aggregate	1.860	1.560		2.350
2342.55	-0.1	**U.S. Corporate** Barclays Capital	2.750	2.640		3.510
2291.63	0.3	Intermediate	2.060	1.990		2.900
2985.92	-1.1	Long term	4.560	4.260		5.210
488.94	-0.3	Double-A-rated	1.940	1.760		2.710
582.03	0.02	Triple-B-rated	3.250	3.160		4.120
n.a.	n.a.	**High Yield Constrained** Merrill Lynch	n.a.	n.a.		n.a.
n.a.	n.a.	Triple-C-rated	n.a.	n.a.		n.a.
n.a.	n.a.	High Yield 100	n.a.	n.a.		n.a.
n.a.	n.a.	Global High Yield Constrained	n.a.	n.a.		n.a.
n.a.	n.a.	Europe High Yield Constrained	n.a.	n.a.		n.a.
1528.17	-0.001	**U.S Agency** Barclays	0.900	0.770		1.120
1389.15	0.1	10-20 years	0.700	0.600		0.910
2784.21	-0.9	20-plus years	3.050	2.670		3.620
1784.36	-0.2	**Mortgage-Backed** Barclays	2.570	1.640		2.930
1780.93	-0.4	Ginnie Mae (GNMA)	2.610	1.500		2.930
1038.76	-0.2	Fannie mae (FNMA)	2.520	1.670		2.940
1596.01	-0.1	Freddie Mac (FHLMC)	2.610	1.730		2.930
n.a.	n.a.	**Muni Master** Merrill Lynch	n.a.	n.a.		n.a.
n.a.	n.a.	7-12 year	n.a.	n.a.		n.a.
n.a.	n.a.	12-22 year	n.a.	n.a.		n.a.
n.a.	n.a.	22-plus year	n.a.	n.a.		n.a.
2176.02	-0.6	**Yankee** Barclays	2.110	2.000		2.730
475.75	-0.2	**Global Government** J.P. Morgan	1.880	1.720		2.150
691.49	-0.3	Canada	2.060	1.780		2.350
300.61	-0.7	EMU	2.760	2.582		4.070
601.01	-1.1	France	2.130	1.920		2.930
453.01	-0.7	Germany	1.470	1.170		2.000
258.82	0.9	Japan	1.060	1.010		1.250
487.87	-1.4	Netherlands	1.720	1.420		2.260
736.43	-1.3	U.K.	2.580	2.190		2.850
661.03	-1.6	Emerging Markets **	4.822	4.437		5.873

*Constrained indexes limit individual issuer concentrations to 2%; the High Yield 100 are the 100 largest bonds   In U.S. - dollar terms Euro-zone bonds

** EMBI Global Index   Sources: S&P Dow Jones Indices; Merrill Lynch; Barclays Capital; J.P.Morgan indications of interest from institutional investors. Alternatively, the underwriter may agree to a **best efforts** arrangement, in which it attempts to sell the bonds at a specified price, but makes no guarantee to the issuer.

Private Placement   Some corporate bonds are privately placed rather than sold in a public offering. A private placement does not have to be registered with the SEC. Small firms that borrow relatively small amounts of funds (such as $30 million) may consider private placements rather than public offerings, since they may be able to find an institutional investor that will purchase the entire offering. Although the issuer does not need to register with the SEC, it must still disclose financial data in order to convince any prospective purchasers that the bonds will be repaid in a timely manner. The issuer may hire a securities firm to place the bonds because such firms are normally better able to identify institutional investors interested in purchasing privately placed debt.

The institutional investors that commonly purchase a private placement include insurance companies, pension funds, and bond mutual funds. Because privately placed bonds do not have an active secondary market, they tend to be purchased by institutional investors that are willing to invest for long periods of time. The SEC's Rule 144A creates liquidity for privately placed securities by allowing large institutional investors to trade privately placed bonds (and some other securities) with each other even when the securities need not be registered with the SEC.

Credit Risk of Corporate Bonds   Corporate bonds are subject to the risk of default, and the yield paid by corporations that issue bonds contains a risk premium to reflect the credit risk. The general level of defaults on corporate bonds is a function of economic conditions. When the economy is strong, firms generate higher revenue and are better able to meet their debt payments. When the economy is weak, some firms may not generate sufficient revenue to cover their operating and debt expenses and hence default on their bonds. In the late 1990s, when U.S. economic conditions were strong, the default rate was less than 1 percent. However, this rate exceeded 3 percent in 2002 and during the credit crisis of 2008–2009, when economic conditions were weak. In 2008 when the credit crisis began, the value of bonds that defaulted exceeded $100 billion, versus only $3.5 billion in 2007.

Bond Ratings as a Measure of Credit Risk   When corporations issue bonds, they hire rating agencies to have their bonds rated. Corporate bonds that receive higher ratings can be placed at higher prices (lower yields) because they are perceived to have lower credit risk. For example, Coca-Cola and IBM issued bonds in 2012 at a yield of less than 2 percent. Their cost of borrowing funds was almost as low as that of the U.S. Treasury.

Some corporations obtain bond ratings in order to verify that their bonds qualify for at least investment-grade status (i.e., a rating of medium quality or above). Commercial banks will only consider investing in bonds that have been given an investment-grade rating.

A corporate bond's rating may change over time if the issuer's ability to repay the debt changes. Many investors rely on the rating agencies to detect potential repayment problems on debt. During the credit crisis, however, the rating agencies were slow to downgrade their ratings on some debt securities that ultimately defaulted.

FINANCIAL REFORM

As a result of the Financial Reform Act of 2010, credit rating agencies are subject to oversight by a newly established Office of Credit Ratings, which is housed within the Securities and Exchange Commission. The credit rating agencies are subject to new reporting requirements that mandate disclosure of their methodology for determining ratings. When assigning a rating to an issuer of debt, the agencies must consider credible information from sources other than the issuer. They must also establish new internal controls over their operations. Rating agencies must disclose the performance of their ratings over time and are to be held accountable for poor performance. Their ratings analysts are required to take qualifying exams, and the rating systems should become more transparent overall. Finally, agencies can be sued for issuing credit ratings that they should have known were inaccurate.

However, the act did not change the fee structure, whereby debt issuers pay fees to credit rating agencies in order to have their debt rated. Some critics argue that, as long as the agencies are paid by the issuers whose debt they are rating, the potential exists for agencies to inflate those ratings.

Junk Bonds   Corporate bonds that are perceived to have very high risk are referred to as **junk bonds**. The primary investors in junk bonds are mutual funds, life insurance companies, and pension funds. Some bond mutual funds invest only in bonds with high ratings, but there are more than a hundred *high-yield* mutual funds that commonly invest in junk bonds. High-yield mutual funds allow individual investors to invest in a diversified portfolio of junk bonds with a small investment. Junk bonds offer high yields that contain a risk premium (spread) to compensate investors for the high risk. Typically, the premium is between 3 and 7 percentage points above Treasury bonds with the same maturity.

Although investors always require a higher *yield* on junk bonds than on other bonds, they also require a higher *premium* when the economy is weak because there is a greater likelihood that the issuer will not generate sufficient cash to cover the debt payments. Exhibit 7.4 shows the spread between junk bond yields and Treasury yields over time. During the credit crisis of 2008–2009, risk premiums on newly issued junk bonds exceeded 10 percent. The high premium was required because junk bonds valued at more than $25 billion defaulted during the credit crisis.

Nevertheless, the junk bond market remains popular. Some corporations issued junk bonds in 2012 as a means of financing because interest rates were so low, although they

Exhibit 7.4   Risk Premiums of Junk Bonds versus Other Corporate Bonds over Time

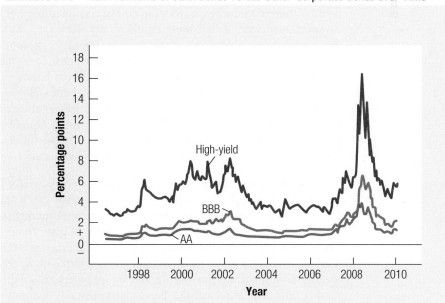

Source: *Federal Reserve.*

still paid a high risk premium. Many of the firms that issued junk bonds recently did so to refinance their operations, by replacing their existing debt that had higher interest rates. Investors may be more willing to purchase junk bonds when it is used for this type of purpose than when it is used to support acquisitions or other types of corporate expansion. In addition, many institutional investors (such as bond mutual funds) have been more willing to invest in junk bonds since the yields on more highly rated bonds are so low.

7-4b Secondary Market for Corporate Bonds

Corporate bonds have a secondary market, so investors who purchase them can sell them to other investors if they prefer not to hold them until maturity. The value of all corporate bonds in the secondary market exceeds $5 trillion. Corporate bonds are listed on an over-the-counter market or on an exchange such as the American Stock Exchange (now part of NYSE Euronext). More than a thousand bonds are listed on the New York Stock Exchange (NYSE). Corporations whose stocks are listed on the exchange can list their bonds for free.

Dealer Role in Secondary Market   The secondary market is served by bond dealers, who can play a broker role by matching up buyers and sellers. Bond dealers also have an inventory of bonds, so they can serve as the counterparty in a bond transaction desired by an investor. For example, if an investor wants to sell bonds that were previously issued by the Coca-Cola Company, bond dealers may execute the deal either by matching the sellers with investors who want to buy the bonds or by purchasing the bonds for their own inventories. Dealers commonly handle large transactions, such as those valued at more than $1 million. Information about the trades in the over-the-counter market is provided by the National Association of Securities Dealers' Trade Reporting and Compliance Engine, which is referred to as TRACE.

Liquidity in Secondary Market   Bonds issued by large, well-known corporations in large volume are liquid because they attract a large number of buyers and sellers in the secondary market. Bonds issued by small corporations in small volume are less liquid because there may be few buyers (or no buyers) for those bonds in some periods. Thus investors who wish to sell these bonds in the secondary market may have to accept a discounted price in order to attract buyers. About 95 percent of the trading volume of corporate bonds in the secondary market is attributed to institutional investors.

Often, a particular company issues many different bonds with variations in maturity, price, and credit rating. Having many different bonds allows investors to find a bond issued by a particular company that fits their desired maturity and other preferences. However, such specialized bonds may exhibit reduced liquidity because they may appeal to only a small group of investors. The trading of these bonds will require higher transaction costs, because brokers require more time to execute transactions for investors.

Electronic Bond Networks   Electronic bond networks have recently been established that can match institutional investors that wish to sell some bond holdings or purchase additional bonds in the over-the-counter bond market at a lower transaction cost. Trading platforms have been created by financial institutions such as J.P. Morgan and Goldman Sachs so that institutional investors can execute bond trades in the secondary market. The institutional investors that wish to purchase bonds can use the platforms to identify bond holdings that are for sale by other institutional investors in the secondary market, and can purchase the bonds electronically, without relying on bond dealers. They pay a small fee (percentage of their transactions) for the use of the trading platforms. However, the participation by investors in electronic bond networks is limited, so that institutional investors interested in purchasing bonds cannot always find the bonds that they wish to purchase.

The NYSE developed an electronic bond trading platform for the bonds sold on its exchange as part of its strategy to increase its presence in the corporate bond market. It allows greater transparency, as investors have access to real-time data and can more easily monitor the prices and trading volume of corporate bonds.

Types of Orders through Brokers   Individual investors buy or sell corporate bonds through brokers, who communicate the orders to bond dealers. Investors who wish to buy or sell bonds can normally place a **market order**; in this case, the desired transaction will occur at the prevailing market price. Alternatively, they can place a **limit order**; in this case, the transaction will occur only if the price reaches the specified limit. When purchasing bonds, investors use a limit order to specify the maximum limit price they are willing to pay for a bond. When selling bonds, investors use a limit order to specify a minimum limit price at which they are willing to sell their bonds.

Trading Online   Orders to buy and sell corporate bonds are increasingly being placed online. For example, popular online bond brokerage websites are www.schwab.com and http://us.etrade.com. The pricing of bonds is more transparent online because investors can easily compare the bid and ask spreads among brokers. This transparency has encouraged some brokers to narrow their spreads so that they do not lose business to competitors.

Some online bond brokerage services, such as Fidelity and Vanguard, now charge a commission instead of posting a bid and ask spread, which ensures that investors can easily understand the fee structure. There is also a standard fee for every trade, whereas bid and ask spreads may vary among bonds. For example, the fee may be $2 per bond with a $25 minimum. Thus an investor who purchases 30 bonds would pay a total fee of $60 (computed as 30 $\times$ $2). Online bond brokerage services can execute transactions in Treasury and municipal bonds as well. Their fees are generally lower for Treasury bond than for corporate bond transactions but higher for municipal bond transactions.

7-4c Characteristics of Corporate Bonds

Corporate bonds can be described in terms of several characteristics. The bond **indenture** is a legal document specifying the rights and obligations of both the issuing firm and the bondholders. It is comprehensive (normally several hundred pages) and is designed to address all matters related to the bond issue (collateral, payment dates, default provisions, call provisions, etc.).

Federal law requires that, for each bond issue of significant size, a trustee be appointed to represent the bondholders in all matters concerning the bond issue. The trustee's duties include monitoring the issuing firm's activities to ensure compliance with the terms of the indenture. If the terms are violated, the trustee initiates legal action against the issuing firm and represents the bondholders in that action. Bank trust departments are frequently hired to perform the duties of trustee.

Bonds are not as standardized as stocks. A single corporation may issue more than 50 different bonds with different maturities and payment terms. Some of the characteristics that differentiate one bond from another are identified here.

Sinking-Fund Provision   Bond indentures frequently include a **sinking-fund provision**, a requirement that the firm retire a certain amount of the bond issue each year. This provision is considered to be an advantage to the remaining bondholders because it reduces the payments necessary at maturity.

WEB

www.investinginbonds.
com
This website contains
much data and other
useful information
about corporate bonds.

Specific sinking-fund provisions can vary significantly among bond issues. For example, a bond with 20 years until maturity could have a provision to retire 5 percent of the bond issue each year. Or it could have a requirement to retire 5 percent each year beginning in the fifth year, with the remaining amount to be retired at maturity. The actual mechanics of bond retirement are carried out by the trustee.

Protective Covenants   Bond indentures normally place restrictions on the issuing firm that are designed to protect bondholders from being exposed to increasing risk during the investment period. These so-called protective covenants frequently limit the amount of dividends and corporate officers' salaries the firm can pay and also restrict the amount of additional debt the firm can issue. Other financial policies may be restricted as well.

Protective covenants are needed because shareholders and bondholders have different expectations of a firm's management. Shareholders may prefer that managers use a relatively large amount of debt because they can benefit directly from risky managerial decisions that will generate higher returns on investment. In contrast, bondholders simply hope to receive their principal back, with interest. Since they do not share in the excess returns generated by a firm, they would prefer that managerial decisions be conservative. Protective covenants can prevent managers from taking excessive risk and therefore cater to the preferences of bondholders. If managers are unwilling to accept some protective covenants, they may not be able to obtain debt financing.

Call Provisions   Most corporate bonds include a provision allowing the firm to call the bonds. A **call provision** normally requires the firm to pay a price above par value when it calls its bonds. The difference between the bond's call price and par value is the **call premium**. Call provisions have two principal uses. First, if market interest rates decline after a bond issue has been sold, the firm might end up paying a higher rate of interest than the prevailing rate for a long period of time. Under these circumstances, the firm may consider selling a new issue of bonds with a lower interest rate and using the proceeds to retire the previous issue by calling the old bonds.

EXAMPLE   Four years ago, Mirossa Company issued 10-year bonds that offered a yield of 11 percent. Since then, interest rates have declined, and Mirossa's credit rating has improved. It could issue 10-year bonds today for a yield of 7 percent. The company is sure that it will need funding for the next 10 years. Therefore, it issues new 10-year bonds at a yield of 7 percent and uses some of the proceeds to call (buy back) the bonds issued four years ago. It reduces its cost of financing as a result of calling these bonds. Ten years from today, Mirossa Company will repay the principal on the newly issued bonds. ●

Second, a call provision may be used to retire bonds as required by a sinking-fund provision. Many bonds have two different call prices: a lower price for calling the bonds to meet sinking-fund requirements and a higher price if the bonds are called for any other reason.

Bondholders normally view a call provision as a disadvantage because it can disrupt their investment plans and reduce their investment returns. As a result, firms must pay slightly higher rates of interest on bonds that are callable, other things being equal.

Bond Collateral   Bonds can be classified according to whether they are secured by collateral and by the nature of that collateral. Usually, the collateral is a mortgage on real property (land and buildings). A **first mortgage bond** has first claim on the specified assets. A **chattel mortgage bond** is secured by personal property.

Bonds unsecured by specific property are called **debentures** (backed only by the general credit of the issuing firm). These bonds are normally issued by large, financially sound firms whose ability to service the debt is not in question. **Subordinated debentures** have claims against the firm's assets that are junior to the claims of both mortgage bonds and regular debentures. Owners of subordinated debentures receive nothing until the claims of mortgage bondholders, regular debenture owners, and secured short-term creditors have been satisfied. The main purchasers of subordinated debt are pension funds and insurance companies.

Low- and Zero-Coupon Bonds   **Low-coupon bonds** and **zero-coupon bonds** are long-term debt securities that are issued at a deep discount from par value. Investors are taxed annually on the amount of interest earned, even though much or all of the interest will not be received until maturity. The amount of interest taxed is the *amortized discount*. (The gain at maturity is prorated over the life of the bond.) Low- and zero-coupon corporate bonds are purchased mainly for tax-exempt investment accounts (such as pension funds and individual retirement accounts).

To the issuing firm, these bonds have the advantage of requiring low or no cash outflow during their life. Additionally, the firm is permitted to deduct the amortized discount as interest expense for federal income tax purposes, even though it does not pay interest.

Variable-Rate Bonds   **Variable-rate bonds** (also called floating-rate bonds) are long-term debt securities with a coupon rate that is periodically adjusted. Most of these bonds tie their coupon rate to the London Interbank Offer Rate (LIBOR), the rate at which banks lend funds to each other on an international basis. The rate is typically adjusted every three months.

Variable-rate bonds became very popular in 2004, when interest rates were at low levels. Because most investors presumed that interest rates were likely to rise, they were more willing to purchase variable-rate than fixed-rate bonds. In fact, the volume of variable-rate bonds exceeded that of fixed-rate bonds during this time.

Convertibility   A **convertible bond** allows investors to exchange the bond for a stated number of shares of the firm's common stock. This conversion feature offers investors the potential for high returns if the price of the firm's common stock rises. Investors are therefore willing to accept a lower rate of interest on these bonds, which allows the firm to obtain financing at a lower cost.

WEB

finance.yahoo.com/
bonds/composite_
bond_rates
Yields on all types of
bonds for various
maturities.

7-4d How Corporate Bonds Finance Restructuring

Firms can issue corporate bonds to finance the restructuring of their assets and to revise their capital structure. Such restructuring can have a major impact on the firm's degree of financial leverage, the potential return to shareholders, the risk to shareholders, and the risk to bondholders.

Using Bonds to Finance a Leveraged Buyout   A leveraged buyout (LBO) involves the use of debt to purchase shares and take a company private. The proceeds from debt are used to buy the outstanding shares of stock, so that the firm is owned by a small number of owners. In order to be able to cover the large debt payments, the owners might sell some of the assets of the firm for cash.

Many firms that engaged in an LBO go public once they have improved their operating performance. They typically use some of the proceeds from the stock issuance to retire a portion of their outstanding debt, thus reducing periodic interest payments on the debt. This process is more feasible for firms that can issue shares of stock for high prices because the proceeds will retire a larger amount of outstanding debt. Firms commonly go public during a period when stock prices are generally high because, under these conditions, they will be able to sell their stock at a higher price.

Using Bonds to Revise the Capital Structure   Corporations commonly issue bonds in order to revise their capital structure. If they believe that they will have sufficient cash flows to cover their debt payments, they may consider using more debt and less equity, which implies a higher degree of financial leverage. Debt is normally perceived to be a cheaper source of capital than equity as long as the corporation can meet its debt payments. Furthermore, a high degree of financial leverage allows the firm's earnings to be distributed to a smaller group of shareholders. In some cases, corporations issue bonds and then use the proceeds to repurchase some of their existing stock. This strategy is referred to as a **debt-for-equity swap**.

When corporations use an excessive amount of debt, they may be unable to make their debt payments. Hence they may seek to revise their capital structure by reducing their level of debt. In an equity-for-debt swap, corporations issue stock and use the proceeds to retire existing debt.

GLOBAL ASPECTS

7-5 GLOBALIZATION OF BOND MARKETS

In recent years, financial institutions such as pension funds, insurance companies, and commercial banks have often purchased foreign bonds. For example, the pension funds of General Electric, United Technologies Corporation, and IBM frequently invest in foreign bonds with the intention of achieving higher returns for their employees. Many public pension funds also invest in foreign bonds for the same reason. Because of the frequent cross-border investments in bonds, bond markets have become increasingly integrated among countries. In addition, mutual funds containing U.S. securities are accessible to foreign investors.

7-5a Global Government Debt Markets

One of the most important global markets is the market for government debt. In general, bonds issued by foreign governments (referred to as *sovereign* bonds) are attractive to investors because of the government's ability to meet debt obligations. Even so, some country governments have defaulted on their bonds. These countries include Argentina (1982, 1989, 1990, 2001), Brazil (1986, 1989, 1991), Costa Rica (1989), Russia and other former Soviet republics (1993, 1998), and the former Yugoslavia (1992). Given that sovereign bonds are exposed to credit risk, credit ratings are assigned to them by Moody's and Standard & Poor's.

Greek Debt Crisis   In the spring of 2010, Greece experienced a credit crisis brought on by weak economic conditions and a large government budget deficit. As Greece's deficit grew and its economy weakened, investors were concerned that the Greek government would not be able to repay its debt. Moreover, credit rating agencies reduced the ratings on the Greek debt several times. The concern about Greece also spread to Spain and Portugal. Exhibit 7.5 shows the risk premiums for various governments in the eurozone relative to the German bond yield. The risk premium offered by Greece was similar to that offered by the other countries shown in Exhibit 7.5 during 2009. In 2010, however, the risk premium on Greek government debt reached 7 percentage points while risk premiums for the other countries ranged between only 1 and 3 percent above the yield offered on German government debt.

Exhibit 7.5   Risk Premiums on Debt Issued by Governments of Eurozone Countries

Source: *Federal Reserve.*

In May 2010, the eurozone countries and the International Monetary Fund (IMF) agreed to provide loans to the Greek government totaling $110 billion euros over a three-year period. The agreement called for the eurozone countries to extend loans of $80 billion and for the IMF to extend loans of $30 billion. As a condition of receiving the loans, the government of Greece was required to reduce its budget deficit over time. The government plans to reduce its spending and to increase taxes in order to reduce its budget deficit.

The weak economy in Greece caused a decline in the Greek demand for products in other European countries, which weakened some European economies. It also caused financial losses for banks in Greece and other European countries. In 2011 and 2012, the governments of Portugal and Spain also experienced debt repayment problems. Consequently, these governments had only limited access to debt in bond markets.

WEB

www.bloomberg.com
Yield curves of major
countries' government
securities.

7-5b Eurobond Market

Non-U.S. investors who desire dollar-denominated bonds may use the Eurobond market if they prefer bearer bonds to the registered corporate bonds issued in the United States. They may also use the Eurobond market simply because they are more familiar with bond placements within their own country.

An underwriting syndicate of securities firms participates in the Eurobond market by placing the bonds issued. It normally underwrites the bonds, guaranteeing a particular value to be received by the issuer. Thus, the syndicate is exposed to underwriting risk: the risk that it will be unable to sell the bonds above the price that it guaranteed the issuer.

The issuer of Eurobonds can choose the currency in which the bonds are denominated. The financing cost of issuing bonds depends on the currency chosen. In some cases, a firm may denominate the bonds in a currency with a low interest rate and use earnings generated by one of its subsidiaries to cover the payments. For example, if the coupon rate on a Eurobond denominated in Swiss francs is 5 percentage points lower than the rate on a dollar-denominated bond, a U.S. firm may consider issuing Swiss franc–denominated bonds and converting the francs to dollars for use in the United

States. Then it could instruct a subsidiary in Switzerland to cover the periodic coupon payments with earnings that the subsidiary generates. In this way, a lower financing rate would be achieved without exposure to exchange rate risk.

7-6 OTHER TYPES OF LONG-TERM DEBT SECURITIES

In recent years, other types of long-term debt securities have been created. Some of the more popular types are discussed here.

7-6a Structured Notes

Firms may borrow funds by issuing structured notes. For these notes, the amount of interest and principal to be paid is based on specified market conditions. The amount of the repayment may be tied to a Treasury bond price index or even to a stock index or a particular currency. Sometimes issuers use structured notes to reduce their risk. For example, a structured product may specify that the principal payment will decline if bond prices decline. A bond portfolio manager that needs to borrow funds could partially insulate the portfolio risk by using structured notes, because the required repayments on the notes would decline if the bond market (and therefore the manager's bond portfolio) performed poorly.

Structured notes became popular in the 1990s, when many participants took positions in the notes in their quest for a high return. One of the reasons for the popularity of structured notes is that some investors may be able to use them to bet indirectly on (or against) a specific market that some restrictions prevent them from betting on directly.

EXAMPLE

The pension fund manager at Cicero Company wants to invest in Brazilian bonds, but the fund has specific restrictions against investing in emerging markets. The restrictions are intended to prevent the manager from taking excessive risk, because she is investing the money that will provide pensions for Cicero's employees when they retire. However, the manager's annual bonus is directly tied to how well the portfolio performs, so she wants to pursue strategies that might generate large returns. She can invest in a structured note issued by a highly rated securities firm that provides large payments when Brazilian bonds perform well. The pension fund's investment holdings will show that it owns a structured product issued by a highly rated securities firm. In this way, the manager circumvents the restrictions and her portfolio has a chance to generate a higher return, but it is also exposed to substantial risk. ●

Risk of Structured Notes   In the early 1990s, the portfolio manager responsible for managing more than $7 billion on behalf of Orange County, California, invested in structured notes that would earn high returns if interest rates declined. The portfolio manager guessed wrong and interest rates increased, which caused the values of the notes to decline substantially. The portfolio manager attempted to make up for the losses by borrowing funds and investing more money in structured notes, but these investments also performed poorly. In 1994, Orange County filed for bankruptcy.

Many other state and local governments also suffered losses because their portfolio managers had invested in structured notes. The portfolio managers took excessive risks with the state and local government money. These managers benefited directly by receiving substantial bonuses or raises when their investments generated high returns. Their investments were questioned only after they suffered losses.

Given the difficulty in assessing the risk of structured notes, some investors rely on credit ratings for such risk assessment. However, credit ratings of structured notes have not always served as accurate indicators of risk. The structured notes purchased by Orange County were, in fact, rated AAA. Apparently, neither the portfolio manager nor the rating agencies understood the risk of those structured notes. The credit ratings of structured notes have been revised frequently over time, and most of the revisions have been downward.

7-6b Exchange-Traded Notes

Exchange-traded notes (ETNs) are debt instruments in which the issuer promises to pay a return based on the performance of a specific debt index after deducting specified fees. The debt typically has a maturity of 10 to 30 years and is not secured by assets, which means that investors are subject to default risk. Common issuers of ETNs are securities firms such as Goldman Sachs and Morgan Stanley. Exchange-traded notes can contain commodities and foreign currencies. They are not legally defined as mutual funds and so are not subject to mutual fund regulations. Therefore, ETNs have more flexibility to use leverage, which means that the funding for the portfolio of debt instruments is enhanced by borrowed funds. The leverage creates higher potential return for investors in ETNs, but it also results in higher risk. Leverage magnifies any gain that investors receive but it magnifies any loss.

7-6c Auction-Rate Securities

Auction-rate securities have been used since the 1980s as a way for specific borrowers (e.g., municipalities and student loan organizations) to borrow for long-term periods while relying on a series of short-term investments by investors. Every 7 to 35 days, the securities can be auctioned off to other investors, and the issuer pays interest based on the new *reset rate* to the winning bidders. The market for auction-rate securities reached $330 billion in 2008. Corporations and individuals with available cash are typical investors in auction-rate securities. Investors can invest for a long-term period or can liquidate their securities to fit their preferred investment horizon. When investors want to sell, the financial institutions that served as intermediaries either repurchase the securities or find other willing buyers.

The auction-rate market suffered in 2008 because some financial institutions were unable to find other buyers and no longer wanted to repurchase the securities. Consequently, when investors wanted to sell their securities at an auction, the financial institutions told them that their investments were frozen and could not be sold for lack of sufficient demand. The values of some of these securities declined substantially, and investors claimed that they had not been informed of the limited liquidity and the risks involved. In response to pressure from the SEC and state regulators, some financial institutions agreed to buy back the securities at face value from individuals who had previously purchased them. These problems occurred after the credit crisis began, when many financial institutions already were holding other types of securities (such as securities backed by subprime mortgages) whose values and liquidity had declined substantially.

SUMMARY

- Bonds are issued to finance government expenditures, housing, and corporate expenditures. Many financial institutions, such as commercial banks, issue bonds to finance their operations. In addition, most types of financial institutions are major investors in bonds.

- Bonds can be classified in four categories according to the type of issuer: Treasury bonds, federal agency bonds, municipal bonds, and corporate bonds. The issuers are perceived to have different levels of credit risk. In addition, the bonds have different degrees of liquidity and different provisions. Thus, quoted yields at a given point in time vary across bonds.

- Bond yields vary among countries. Investors are attracted to high bond yields in foreign countries, causing funds to flow to those countries. Consequently, bond markets have become globally integrated.

■ Structured notes are long-term debt instruments that allow investors to bet indirectly on or against a specific market that they cannot bet on directly because of restrictions. Exchange-traded notes (ETNs) are debt instruments in which the issuer promises to pay a return based on the performance of a specific debt index after deducting specified fees. They are not legally defined as mutual funds and therefore are not subject to mutual fund regulations. They also have more flexibility to use leverage, which can achieve higher returns for investors but also results in higher risk.

Point Counter-Point

Should Financial Institutions Invest in Junk Bonds?

Point   Yes. Financial institutions have managers who are capable of weighing the risk against the potential return. They can earn a significantly higher return when investing in junk bonds than the return on Treasury bonds. Their shareholders benefit when they increase the return on the portfolio.

Counter-Point   No. The financial system is based on trust in financial institutions and confidence that the financial institutions will survive. If financial institutions take excessive risk, the entire financial system is at risk.

Who Is Correct?   Use the Internet to learn more about this issue and then formulate your own opinion.

Questions and Applications

1.   Bond Indenture What is a bond indenture? What is the function of a trustee with respect to the bond indenture?

2.   Sinking-Fund Provision Explain the use of a sinking-fund provision. How can it reduce the investor's risk?

3.   Protective Covenants What are protective covenants? Why are they needed?

4.   Call Provisions Explain the use of call provisions on bonds. How can a call provision affect the price of a bond?

5.   Bond Collateral Explain the use of bond collateral, and identify the common types of collateral for bonds.

6.   Debentures What are debentures? How do they differ from subordinated debentures?

7.   Zero-Coupon Bonds What are the advantages and disadvantages to a firm that issues low- or zero-coupon bonds?

8.   Variable-Rate Bonds Are variable-rate bonds attractive to investors who expect interest rates to decrease? Explain. Would a firm that needs to borrow funds consider issuing variable-rate bonds if it expects that interest rates will decrease? Explain.

9.   Convertible Bonds Why can convertible bonds be issued by firms at a higher price than other bonds?

10. Global Interaction of Bond Yields If bond yields in Japan rise, how might U.S. bond yields be affected? Why?

11. Impact of Credit Crisis on Junk Bonds Explain how the credit crisis affected the default rates of junk bonds and the risk premiums offered on newly issued junk bonds.

12. New Guidelines for Credit Rating Agencies Explain the new guidelines for credit rating agencies resulting from the Financial Reform Act of 2010.

13. Impact of Greek Debt Crisis Explain the conditions that led to the debt crisis in Greece.

14. Bond Downgrade Explain how the downgrading of bonds for a particular corporation affects the prices of those bonds, the return to investors that currently hold these bonds, and the potential return to other investors who may invest in the bonds in the near future.

Advanced Questions

15. Junk Bonds Merrito, Inc., is a large U.S. firm that issued bonds several years ago. Its bond ratings declined over time and, about a year ago, the bonds were rated in the junk bond classification. Nevertheless, investors were buying the bonds in the secondary market because of the attractive yield they offered. Last week, Merrito defaulted on its bonds, and the prices of most other junk bonds declined abruptly on the same day. Explain why news of Merrito's financial problems could cause the prices of junk bonds issued by other firms to decrease, even when those firms had no business relationships with Merrito. Explain why the prices of those junk bonds with less liquidity declined more than those with a high degree of liquidity.

16. Event Risk An insurance company purchased bonds issued by Hartnett Company two years ago. Today, Hartnett Company has begun to issue junk bonds and is using the funds to repurchase most of its existing stock. Why might the market value of those bonds held by the insurance company be affected by this action?

17. Exchange-Traded Notes Explain what exchange-traded notes are and how they are used. Why are they risky?

18. Auction-Rate Securities Explain why the market for auction-rate securities suffered in 2008.

19. Role of Bond Market Explain how the bond market facilitates a government's fiscal policy. How do you think the bond market could discipline a government and discourage the government from borrowing (and spending) excessively?

Interpreting Financial News

Interpret the following statements made by Wall Street analysts and portfolio managers.

a. "The values of some stocks are dependent on the bond market. When investors are not interested in junk bonds, the values of stocks ripe for leveraged buyouts decline."

b. "The recent trend in which many firms are using debt to repurchase some of their stock is a good strategy as long as they can withstand the stagnant economy."

c. "Although yields among bonds are related, today's rumors of a tax cut caused an increase in the yield on municipal bonds, while the yield on corporate bonds declined."

Managing in Financial Markets

Forecasting Bond Returns As a portfolio manager for an insurance company, you are about to invest funds in one of three possible investments: (1) 10-year coupon bonds issued by the U.S. Treasury, (2) 20-year zero-coupon bonds issued by the Treasury, or (3) one-year Treasury securities. Each possible investment is perceived to have no risk of default. You plan to maintain this investment for a one-year period. The return of each investment over a one-year horizon will be about the same if interest rates do not change over the next year. However, you anticipate that the U.S. inflation rate will decline substantially over the next year, while most of the other portfolio managers in the United States expect inflation to increase slightly.

a. If your expectations are correct, how will the return of each investment be affected over the one-year horizon?

b. If your expectations are correct, which of the three investments should have the highest return over the one-year horizon? Why?

c. Offer one reason why you might not select the investment that would have the highest expected return over the one-year investment horizon.

PROBLEMS

1. Inflation-Indexed Treasury Bond An inflation-indexed Treasury bond has a par value of $1,000 and a coupon rate of 6 percent. An investor purchases this bond and holds it for one year. During the year, the consumer price index increases by 1 percent every six months. What are the total interest payments the investor will receive during the year?

2. Inflation-Indexed Treasury Bond Assume that the U.S. economy experienced deflation during the year and that the consumer price index decreased by 1 percent in the first six months of the year and by 2 percent during the second six months of the year. If an investor had purchased inflation-indexed Treasury bonds with a par value of $10,000 and a coupon rate of 5 percent, how much would she have received in interest during the year?

FLOW OF FUNDS EXERCISE

Financing in the Bond Markets

If the economy continues to be strong, Carson Company may need to increase its production capacity by about 50 percent over the next few years to satisfy demand. It would need financing to expand and accommodate the increase in production. Recall that the yield curve is currently upward sloping. Also recall that Carson is concerned about a possible slowing of the economy because of potential Fed actions to reduce inflation. It needs funding to cover payments for supplies. It is also considering issuing stock or bonds to raise funds in the next year.

a. Assume that Carson has two choices to satisfy the increased demand for its products. It could increase production by 10 percent with its existing facilities by obtaining short-term financing to cover the extra production expense and then using a portion of the revenue received to finance this level of production in the future. Alternatively, it could issue bonds and use the proceeds to buy a larger facility that would allow for 50 percent more capacity. Which alternative should Carson select?

b. Carson currently has a large amount of debt, and its assets have already been pledged to back up its existing debt. It does not have additional collateral. At this time, the credit risk premium it would pay is similar in the short-term and long-term debt markets. Does this imply that the cost of financing is the same in both markets?

c. Should Carson consider using a call provision if it issues bonds? Why? Why might Carson decide not to include a call provision on the bonds?

d. If Carson issues bonds, it would be a relatively small bond offering. Should Carson consider a private placement of bonds? What type of investor might be interested in participating in a private placement? Do you think Carson could offer the same yield on a private placement as it could on a public placement? Explain.

e. Financial institutions such as insurance companies and pension funds commonly purchase bonds. Explain the flow of funds that runs through these financial institutions and ultimately reaches corporations that issue bonds such as Carson Company.

INTERNET/EXCEL EXERCISE

Go to finance.yahoo.com/bonds and click on "Composite Bond Rates." Compare the rate of a 10-year Treasury bond to a 10-year municipal bond. Which type of bond would offer you a higher annual yield based on your tax bracket, given that the municipal bond is not subject to federal income taxes? Determine the premium contained in the yield of a 10-year corporate A-rated bond as compared with the 10-year Treasury bonds. Compare that premium to the premium that existed one month ago. Did the premium increase or decrease? Offer an explanation for the change. Is the change attributed to economic conditions?

WSJ EXERCISE

Impact of Treasury Financing on Bond Prices

The Treasury periodically issues new bonds to finance the deficit. Review recent issues of the *Wall Street Journal* or check related online news to find a recent article on such financing. Does the article suggest that financial markets are expecting upward pressure on interest rates as a result of the Treasury financing? What happened to prices of existing bonds when the Treasury announced its intentions to issue new bonds?

ONLINE ARTICLES WITH REAL-WORLD EXAMPLES

Find a recent practical article available online that describes a real-world example regarding a specific financial institution or financial market that reinforces one or more concepts covered in this chapter.

If your class has an online component, your professor may ask you to post your summary of the article there and provide a link to the article so that other students can access it. If your class is live, your professor may ask you to summarize your application of the article in class. Your professor may assign specific students to complete this assignment or may allow any students to do the assignment on a volunteer basis.

For recent online articles and real-world examples related to this chapter, consider using the following search terms (be sure to include the prevailing year as a search term to ensure that the online articles are recent):

1. Treasury bond AND yield
2. Treasury bond AND return
3. bond AND federal agency
4. stripped Treasury bond
5. inflation-indexed Treasury bond
6. municipal bond AND risk
7. [name of a specific financial institution] AND bond
8. bond AND private placement
9. junk bond AND financing
10. structured notes

8
Bond Valuation and Risk

The values of bonds can change substantially over time. Hence, financial institutions that consider buying or selling bonds closely monitor their values.

The specific
objectives of this
chapter are to:

■ explain how bonds
are priced,

■ identify the factors
that affect bond
prices,

■ explain how the
sensitivity of bond
prices to interest
rates depends on
particular bond
characteristics,

■ describe common
strategies used to
invest in bonds,
and

■ explain the
valuation and risk
of international
bonds.

8-1 BOND VALUATION PROCESS

Bonds are debt obligations with long-term maturities that are commonly issued by governments or corporations to obtain long-term funds. They are also purchased by financial institutions that wish to invest funds for long-term periods.

Bond valuation is conceptually similar to the valuation of capital budgeting projects, businesses, or even real estate. The appropriate price reflects the present value of the cash flows to be generated by the bond in the form of periodic interest (or coupon) payments and the principal payment to be provided at maturity. The coupon payment is based on the coupon rate multiplied by the par value of the bond. Thus a bond with a 9 percent coupon rate and $1,000 par value pays $90 in coupon payments per year. Because these expected cash flows are known, the valuation of bonds is generally perceived to be easier than the valuation of equity securities.

The current price of a bond should be the present value (PV) of its remaining cash flows:

$$PV \text{ of bond} = \frac{C}{(1+k)^1} + \frac{C}{(1+k)^2} + \cdots + \frac{C + Par}{(1+k)^n}$$

where

C = coupon payment provided in each period

Par = par value

k = required rate of return per period used to discount the bond

n = number of periods to maturity

EXAMPLE

Consider a bond that has a par value of $1,000, pays $100 at the end of each year in coupon payments, and has three years remaining until maturity. Assume that the prevailing annualized yield on other bonds with similar characteristics is 12 percent. In this case, the appropriate price of the bond can be determined as follows. The future cash flows to investors who would purchase this bond are $100 in Year 1, $100 in Year 2, and $1,100 (computed as $100 in coupon payments plus $1,000 par value) in Year 3. The appropriate market price of the bond is its present value:

$$PV \text{ of bond} = \frac{\$100}{(1+0.12)^1} + \frac{\$100}{(1+0.12)^2} + \frac{\$1,100}{(1+0.12)^3}$$
$$= \$89.29 + \$79.72 + \$782.96$$
$$= \$951.97$$

Exhibit 8.1 Valuation of a Three-Year Bond

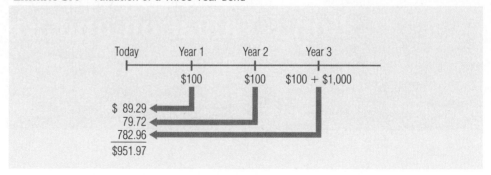

WEB

www.finpipe.com/
valuebnd.htm
More information on
the process of valuing
bonds.

This valuation procedure is illustrated in Exhibit 8.1. Because this example assumes that investors require a 12 percent return, k is set equal to 0.12. At the price of $951.97, the bondholders purchasing this bond will receive a 12 percent annualized return. ●

When using a financial calculator, the present value of the bond in the previous example can be determined as follows:

INPUT	3	12	100	1000		
Function Key	N	I	PMT	FV	CPT	PV
Answer						951.97

8-1a Impact of the Discount Rate on Bond Valuation

The discount rate selected to compute the present value is critical to accurate valuation. Exhibit 8.2 shows the wide range of present value resulting at different discount rates for a $10,000 payment in 10 years. The appropriate discount rate for valuing any asset is the yield that could be earned on alternative investments with similar risk and maturity.

Exhibit 8.2 Relationship between Discount Rate and Present Value of $10,000 Payment to Be Received in 10 Years

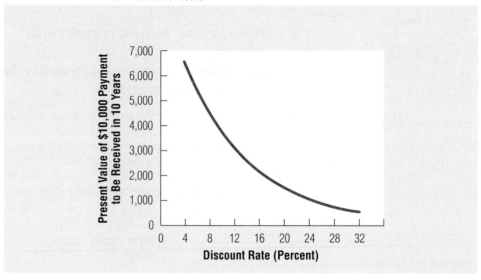

Since investors require higher returns on riskier securities, they use higher discount rates to discount the future cash flows of these securities. Consequently, a high-risk security will have a lower value than a low-risk security even though both securities have the same expected cash flows.

8-1b Impact of the Timing of Payments on Bond Valuation

The market price of a bond is also affected by the timing of the payments made to bondholders. Funds received sooner can be reinvested to earn additional returns. Thus, a dollar to be received soon has a higher present value than one to be received later. The impact of maturity on the present value of a $10,000 payment is shown in Exhibit 8.3 (assuming that a return of 10 percent could be earned on available funds). The $10,000 payment has a present value of $8,264 if it is to be paid in two years. This implies that if $8,264 were invested today and earned 10 percent annually, it would be worth $10,000 in two years. Exhibit 8.3 also shows that a $10,000 payment made 20 years from now has a present value of only $1,486 and that a $10,000 payment made 50 years from now has a present value of only $85 (based on the 10 percent discount rate).

8-1c Valuation of Bonds with Semiannual Payments

In reality, most bonds have semiannual payments. The present value of such bonds can be computed as follows. First, the annualized coupon should be split in half because two payments are made per year. Second, the annual discount rate should be divided by 2 to reflect two six-month periods per year. Third, the number of periods should be doubled to reflect 2 times the number of annual periods. After these adjustments are incorporated, the present value is determined as follows:

$$\textbf{PV of bond with semiannual payments} = \frac{C/2}{[1+(k/2)]^1} + \frac{C/2}{[1+(k/2)]^2} + \cdots + \frac{C/2+\textbf{Par}}{[1+(k/2)]^{2n}}$$

Here $C/2$ is the semiannual coupon payment (half of what the annual coupon payment would have been), and $k/2$ is the periodic discount rate used to discount the bond. The last part of the equation has $2n$ in the denominator's exponent to reflect the doubling of periods.

Exhibit 8.3   Relationship between Time of Payment and Present Value of Payment

EXAMPLE

As an example of the valuation of a bond with semiannual payments, consider a bond with $1,000 par value, a 10 percent coupon rate paid semiannually, and three years to maturity. Assuming a 12 percent required return, the present value is computed as follows:

$$PV \text{ of bond} = \frac{\$50}{(1.06)^1} + \frac{\$50}{(1.06)^2} + \frac{\$50}{(1.06)^3} + \frac{\$50}{(1.06)^4} + \frac{\$50}{(1.06)^5} + \frac{\$50 + \$1,000}{(1.06)^6}$$

$$= \$47.17 + \$44.50 + \$41.98 + \$39.60 + \$37.36 + \$740.21$$

$$= \$950.82$$ ●

When using a financial calculator, the present value of the bond in the previous example can be determined as follows:[1]

INPUT	6	6	50	1000		
Function Key	N	I	PMT	FV	CPT	PV
Answer						950.82

The remaining examples assume annual coupon payments so that we can focus on the concepts presented without concern about adjusting annual payments.

8-1d Relationships between Coupon Rate, Required Return, and Bond Price

Bonds that sell at a price below their par value are called *discount* bonds. The larger the investor's required rate of return relative to the coupon rate, the larger the discount of a bond with a particular par value.

EXAMPLE

Consider a zero-coupon bond (which has no coupon payments) with three years remaining to maturity and $1,000 par value. Assume the investor's required rate of return on the bond is 13 percent. The appropriate price of this bond can be determined by the present value of its future cash flows:

$$PV \text{ of bond} = \frac{\$0}{(1 + 0.13)^1} + \frac{\$0}{(1 + 0.13)^2} + \frac{\$1,000}{(1 + 0.13)^3}$$

$$= \$0 + \$0 + \$693.05$$

$$= \$693.05$$

The very low price of this bond is necessary to generate a 13 percent annualized return to investors. If the bond offered coupon payments, the price would have been higher because those coupon payments would provide part of the return required by investors.

Now consider another bond with a similar par value and maturity that offers a 13 percent coupon rate. The appropriate price of this bond would be

$$PV \text{ of bond} = \frac{\$130}{(1 + 0.13)^1} + \frac{\$130}{(1 + 0.13)^2} + \frac{\$1,130}{(1 + 0.13)^3}$$

$$= \$115.04 + \$101.81 + \$783.15$$

$$= \$1,000$$

Observe that the price of this bond is exactly equal to its par value. This is because the entire compensation required by investors is provided by the coupon payments.

---

[1]Technically, the semiannual rate of 6 percent is overstated. For a required rate of 12 percent per year, the precise six-month rate would be 5.83 percent. With the compounding effect, which would generate interest on interest, this semiannual rate over two periods would achieve a 12 percent return. Because the approximate semiannual rate of 6 percent is higher than the precise rate, the present value of the bonds is slightly understated.

Exhibit 8.4   Relationship between Required Return and Present Value for a 10 Percent Coupon Bond with Various Maturities

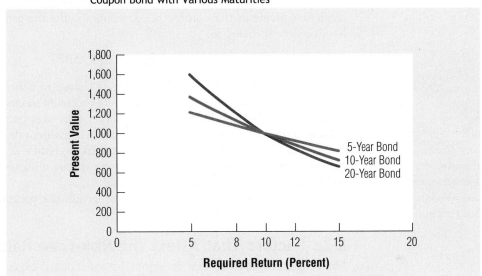

Finally, consider a bond with a similar par value and term to maturity and coupon rate that offers a coupon rate of 15 percent, which is above the investor's required rate of return. The appropriate price of this bond, as determined by its present value, is

WEB

finance.yahoo.com/
bonds
Calculates bond returns
and yields.

$$PV \text{ of bond} = \frac{\$150}{(1+0.13)^1} + \frac{\$150}{(1+0.13)^2} + \frac{\$1,150}{(1+0.13)^3}$$

$$= \$132.74 + \$117.47 + \$797.01$$

$$= \$1,047.22$$

The price of this bond exceeds its par value because the coupon payments are large enough to offset the high price paid for the bond and still provide a 13 percent annualized return. ●

From the examples provided, the following relationships should now be clear. First, if the coupon rate of a bond is below the investor's required rate of return, the present value of the bond (and therefore the price of the bond) should be below the par value. Second, if the coupon rate equals the investor's required rate of return, the price of the bond should be the same as the par value. Finally, if the coupon rate of a bond is above the investor's required rate of return, the price of the bond should be above the par value. These relationships are shown in Exhibit 8.4 for a bond with a 10 percent coupon and a par value of $1,000. If investors require a return of 5 percent and desire a 10-year maturity, they will be willing to pay $1,390 for this bond. If they require a return of 10 percent on this same bond, they will be willing to pay $1,000. If they require a 15 percent return, they will be willing to pay only $745. The relationships described here hold for any bond, regardless of its maturity.

8-2 EXPLAINING BOND PRICE MOVEMENTS

As explained earlier, the price of a bond should reflect the present value of future cash flows (coupon payments and the par value), based on a required rate of return (k), so that

$$\Delta P_b = f(\Delta k)$$

Since the required rate of return on a bond is primarily determined by the prevailing risk-free rate (Rf), which is the yield on a Treasury bond with the same maturity, and the credit risk premium (RP) on the bond, it follows that the general price movements of bonds can be modeled as

$$\Delta P_b = f(\Delta Rf, \Delta RP)$$

Notice how the bond price is affected by a change in either the risk-free rate or the risk premium. An increase in the risk-free rate on bonds results in a higher required rate of return on bonds and therefore causes bond prices to decrease. Thus bond prices are exposed to **interest rate risk**, or the risk that their market value will decline in response to a rise in interest rates. Bonds are also exposed to credit risk: an increase in the credit (default) risk premium also causes investors to require a higher rate of return on bonds and therefore causes bond prices to decrease.

The factors that affect the risk-free rate or default risk premiums, and therefore affect bond prices, are identified next.

8-2a Factors That Affect the Risk-Free Rate

The long-term risk-free rate is driven by inflationary expectations (INF), economic growth (ECON), the money supply (MS), and the budget deficit (DEF):

$$\Delta R_f = f(\underset{+}{\Delta INF}, \underset{+}{\Delta ECON}, \underset{?}{\Delta MS}, \underset{+}{\Delta DEF})$$

The general relationships are summarized next.

Impact of Inflationary Expectations   If the level of inflation is expected to increase, there will be upward pressure on interest rates (as explained in Chapter 2) and hence on the required rate of return on bonds. Conversely, a reduction in the expected level of inflation results in downward pressure on interest rates and thus on the required rate of return on bonds. Bond market participants closely monitor indicators of inflation, such as the consumer price index and the producer price index.

Inflationary expectations are partially dependent on oil prices, which affect the cost of energy and transportation. This is why bond portfolio managers must forecast oil prices and their potential impact on inflation in order to forecast interest rates. A forecast of lower oil prices results in expectations of lower interest rates, causing bond portfolio managers to purchase more bonds. A forecast of higher oil prices results in expectations of higher interest rates, causing bond portfolio managers to sell some of their holdings. The actions of bond portfolio managers change the supply of bonds for sale as well as the demand for bonds in the secondary market, which results in a new equilibrium price for the bonds.

Inflationary expectations are also partially dependent on exchange rate movements. Holding other things equal, inflationary expectations are likely to rise when a weaker dollar is expected because it will increase the prices of imported supplies. A weaker dollar also prices foreign competitors out of the market, allowing U.S. firms to increase their prices. Thus, U.S. interest rates are expected to rise and bond prices are expected to decrease when the dollar is expected to weaken. Foreign investors anticipating dollar depreciation are less willing to hold U.S. bonds because in that case the coupon payments will convert to less of their home currency. This could cause an immediate net sale of bonds, placing further downward pressure on bond prices.

Expectations of a strong dollar should have the opposite results. A stronger dollar reduces the prices paid for foreign supplies, thus lowering retail prices. In addition, because a stronger dollar makes the prices of foreign products more attractive, domestic firms must maintain low prices in order to compete. Consequently, expectations of a stronger dollar may encourage bond portfolio managers to purchase more bonds, which places upward pressure on bond prices.

Impact of Economic Growth

Strong economic growth tends to generate upward pressure on interest rates (as explained in Chapter 2), while weak economic conditions put downward pressure on rates. Any signals about future economic conditions will affect expectations about future interest rate movements and cause bond markets to react immediately. For example, any economic announcements (such as measurements of economic growth or unemployment) that signal stronger than expected economic growth tend to reduce bond prices. Investors anticipate that interest rates will rise, causing a decline in bond prices. Therefore, they sell bonds, which places immediate downward pressure on bond prices.

Conversely, any economic announcements that signal a weaker than expected economy tend to increase bond prices because investors anticipate that interest rates will decrease and thereby cause bond prices to rise. Hence investors buy bonds, which places immediate upward pressure on bond prices. This explains why sudden news of a possible economic recession can cause the bond market to rally. When the credit crisis began in 2008, long-term interest rates declined, which resulted in higher Treasury bond prices.

Bond market participants closely monitor economic indicators that may signal future changes in the strength of the economy, which signal changes in the risk-free interest rate and in the required return from investing in bonds. Some of the more closely monitored indicators of economic growth include employment, gross domestic product, retail sales, industrial production, and consumer confidence.

Impact of Money Supply Growth

When the Federal Reserve increases money supply growth, two reactions are possible (as explained in Chapter 5). First, the increased money supply may result in an increased supply of loanable funds. If the demand schedule (demand curve) for loanable funds is not affected, the increased money supply should place downward pressure on interest rates, causing bond portfolio managers to expect an increase in bond prices and thus to purchase bonds based on such expectations.

In a high-inflation environment, however, bond portfolio managers may expect that the inflationary expectations will cause individuals and firms to borrow more now and spend more now before inflation occurs. In this case, the change in borrowing behavior can increase the demand for loanable funds (as a result of inflationary expectations), which would cause an increase in interest rates and lower bond prices. Such forecasts would encourage immediate sales of long-term bonds.

In response to the credit crisis, the Fed repeatedly increased money supply growth in order to reduce interest rates. At this time, economic growth was weak and inflation was low, and therefore did not counteract the Fed's actions. The Fed's goal was to reduce the cost of borrowing, and therefore encourage individuals and corporations to borrow and spend money. This resulted in a risk-free rate that was close to zero in 2012.

Impact of Budget Deficit

As the annual budget deficit changes, so does the federal government's demand for loanable funds (as explained in Chapter 2). Increased borrowing by the Treasury can result in a higher required return on Treasury bonds. That is, the long-term risk-free rate rises, which results in lower prices on existing bonds with long terms remaining until maturity.

WEB

biz.yahoo.com/c/e .html

Calendar of upcoming announcements of economic conditions that may affect bond prices.

The higher budget deficit leads to the same expected outcome (when other factors are held constant) as higher inflationary expectations. In both cases, there is an increase in the amount of funds borrowed, which leads to higher interest rates. However, inflationary expectations result in more borrowing by individuals and firms, whereas an increased budget deficit results in more borrowing by the federal government.

8-2b Factors That Affect the Credit (Default) Risk Premium

The general level of credit risk on corporate or municipal bonds can change in response to a change in economic growth (ECON):

$$\Delta RP = f(\Delta ECON)$$

Strong economic growth tends to improve a firm's cash flows and reduce the probability that the firm will default on its debt payments. Conversely, weak economic conditions tend to reduce a firm's cash flows and increase the probability that it will default on its bonds. The credit risk premium is relatively low when economic growth is strong. When the economy is weak, however, the credit risk premium is higher: investors will provide credit in such periods only if they are compensated for the high degree of credit risk.

EXAMPLE

After the credit crisis began in 2008, the U.S. economy weakened and numerous U.S. companies defaulted on their bonds. In the most notable case, Lehman Brothers (a large securities firm) filed for bankruptcy and subsequently defaulted on bonds and other debt securities. As a result of the defaults of Lehman Brothers and other firms, investors became more concerned about the credit risk of bonds that corporations issued. Many investors shifted their investments from corporate bonds to Treasury bonds because they wanted to avoid credit risk. Consequently, corporations that needed to borrow long-term funds at this time could issue new bonds only if they were willing to offer a relatively high credit risk premium to compensate investors. ●

Changes in the Credit Risk Premium over Time   As economic conditions change over time, the probability of default on bonds changes, along with credit (default) risk premiums. Exhibit 8.5 compares yields on Baa-rated corporate bonds and Treasury bonds over time. The yields among securities are highly correlated. Notice that the difference between the corporate and Treasury bond yields (which can be used to measure the credit risk premium) widened during periods when the economy was weak, such as during the 2008–2009 credit crisis when investors required a higher credit risk premium. When the credit crisis intensified, the Federal Reserve used a stimulative monetary policy to reduce the risk-free interest rate across maturities. Thus the Treasury bond yield declined. However, the Baa-rated corporate bond yield increased during the crisis, because the increase in the risk premium on the prices of Baa-rated corporate bonds more than offset the impact of the reduction in the risk-free rate.

Impact of Debt Maturity on the Credit Risk Premium   The credit risk premium tends to be larger for bonds that have longer terms to maturity. Consider an extreme example in which an existing bond issued by a corporation has only one month until maturity. If this corporation is in decent financial condition, it should be capable of completely repaying this debt, because conditions should not change drastically over the next month. However, other bonds issued by this same corporation with 15 years until maturity have a higher risk of default, because the corporation's ability to repay this debt is dependent on its performance over the next 15 years. Because economic conditions over the next 15 years are very uncertain, so is the corporation's performance and its ability to repay long-term debt.

Exhibit 8.5 Bond Risk Premium over Time

Source: *Federal Reserve.*

Impact of Issuer Characteristics on the Credit Risk Premium   A bond's price can also be affected by factors specific to the issuer of the bond, such as a change in its capital structure. If a firm that issues bonds subsequently obtains additional loans, it may be less capable of making its coupon payments, thus its credit risk increases. Consequently, investors would now require a higher rate of return if they were to purchase those bonds in the secondary market, which would cause the market value (price) of the bonds to decrease.

8-2c Summary of Factors Affecting Bond Prices

When considering the factors that affect the risk-free rate and the risk premium, the general price movements in bonds can be modeled as follows:

WEB

www.treasurydirect.
gov
Treasury note and bond
auction results.

$$\Delta P_b = f(\Delta R_f, \Delta RP)$$
$$= f(\underset{-}{\underline{\Delta INF}}, \underset{?}{\underline{\Delta ECON}}, \underset{+}{\underline{\Delta MS}}, \underset{-}{\underline{\Delta DEF}})$$

The relationships suggested here assume that other factors are held constant. Yet other factors are actually changing, too, which makes it difficult to disentangle the precise impact of each factor on bond prices. The effect of economic growth is uncertain: a high level of economic growth can adversely affect bond prices by raising the risk-free rate, but it can favorably affect bond prices by lowering the default risk premium. To the extent that international conditions affect each of the factors, they also influence bond prices.

Exhibit 8.6 summarizes the underlying forces that can affect the long-term, risk-free interest rate and the default risk premium and thereby cause the general level of bond

Exhibit 8.6 Framework for Explaining Changes in Bond Prices over Time

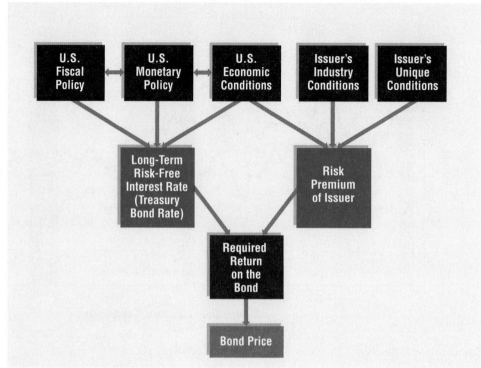

Source: *Federal Reserve*

prices to change over time. When pricing Treasury bonds, investors focus on the factors that affect the long-term, risk-free interest rate because the credit risk premium is not applicable. Thus, for a given maturity, the primary difference in the required return of a risky bond (such as a corporate bond) and a Treasury bond is the credit risk premium, which is influenced by economic and industry conditions.

If the bond market is efficient, then bond prices should fully reflect all available public information. Thus any new information about a firm that changes its perceived ability to repay its bonds could have an immediate effect on the price of the bonds.

8-2d Implications for Financial Institutions

Many financial institutions such as insurance companies, pension funds, and bond mutual funds maintain large holdings of bonds. The values of their bond portfolios are susceptible to changes in the factors, described in this section, that affect bond prices. Any factors that lead to higher interest rates tend to reduce the market values of financial institution assets and therefore reduce their valuations. Conversely, any factors that lead to lower interest rates tend to increase the market values of financial institution assets and therefore increase their valuations. Many financial institutions attempt to adjust the size of their bond portfolio according to their expectations about future interest rates. When they expect interest rates to rise, they sell bonds and use the proceeds to purchase short-term securities that are less sensitive to interest rate movements. If they anticipate that the risk premiums of risky bonds will increase, they shift toward relatively safe bonds that exhibit less credit risk.

Systemic Risk   Financial institutions that participate in bond markets could be exposed to **systemic risk**, which refers to the potential collapse of the entire market or financial system (systemic risk should not be confused with "systematic risk," discussed in Chapter 11). When specific conditions cause a higher risk-free rate and a very high risk premium, they adversely affect the prices of most bonds. Thus all financial institutions that heavily invest in bonds will experience poor performance under these conditions. Many financial institutions rely heavily on debt to fund their operations, and they are interconnected by virtue of financing each other's debt positions. If a financial institution cannot repay its debt, then this may create cash flow problems for the financial institutions from which it borrowed funds.

Some financial institutions use their investments in debt securities as collateral when borrowing funds (such as when using repurchase agreements, discussed in Chapter 6). But this collateral may no longer be acceptable during a credit crisis, because potential lenders may question whether the collateral is subject to default. Thus financial institutions that need new financing to repay other financial institutions may no longer be able to obtain new debt financing because the perceived value of their collateral has deteriorated.

There are various derivative securities (such as credit default swaps, described in Chapter 15) that can insure a creditor against the default of debt securities that they are holding. However, the counterparty in each of those positions serves as the insurer and may itself incur large losses (and potential bankruptcy) if the debt securities that it insures default. Thus, although these securities could protect some participants during a credit crisis, they can result in major losses for the counterparties. This may prevent those counterparty financial institutions from making timely debt payments to other financial institutions from whom they borrowed funds in the past.

In general, most financial institutions are connected by the relationships just described, and the credit crisis illustrated how adverse effects can spread among them. The Financial Reform Act of 2010 was intended to recognize and protect against systemic risk. It resulted in the creation of the Financial Stability Oversight Council, which consists of heads of agencies that oversee key participants in the debt markets and in the debt derivatives (insuring against debt default), including the housing industry, securities trading, depository institutions, mutual funds, and insurance companies. This council is responsible for identifying risks in the U.S. financial system and for making regulatory recommendations that could reduce such risks.

FINANCIAL REFORM

8-3 SENSITIVITY OF BOND PRICES TO INTEREST RATE MOVEMENTS

The sensitivity of a bond's price to interest rate movements is a function of the bond's characteristics. Investors can measure the sensitivity of their bonds' prices to interest rate movements, which will indicate the potential damage to their bond holdings in response to an increase in interest rates (and therefore in the required rate of return on bonds). Two common methods for assessing the sensitivity of bonds to a change in the required rate of return on bonds are (1) bond price elasticity and (2) duration. Each method is described in turn.

8-3a   Bond Price Elasticity

The sensitivity of bond prices (P_b) to changes in the required rate of return (k) is commonly measured by the **bond price elasticity** (P_b^e), which is estimated as

$$P_b^e = \frac{\text{percentage change in } P_b}{\text{percentage change in } k}$$

Exhibit 8.7 Sensitivity of 10-Year Bonds with Different Coupon Rates to Interest Rate Changes

EFFECTS OF A DECLINE IN THE REQUIRED RATE OF RETURN					
(1) BONDS WITH A COUPON RATE OF:	(2) INITIAL PRICE OF BONDS WHEN $k = 10\%$	(3) PRICE OF BONDS WHEN $k = 8\%$	(4) $= [(3) - (2)]/(2)$ PERCENTAGE CHANGE IN BOND PRICE	(5) PERCENTAGE CHANGE IN k	(6) $= (4)/(5)$ BOND PRICE ELASTICITY (P_b^e)
0%	$ 386	$ 463	+19.9%	−20.0%	−.995
5	693	799	+15.3	−20.0	−.765
10	1,000	1,134	+13.4	−20.0	−.670
15	1,307	1,470	+12.5	−20.0	−.625
EFFECTS OF A DECLINE IN THE REQUIRED RATE OF RETURN					
(1) BONDS WITH A COUPON RATE OF:	(2) INITIAL PRICE OF BONDS WHEN $k = 10\%$	(3) PRICE OF BONDS WHEN $k = 12\%$	(4) $= [(3) - (2)]/(2)$ PERCENTAGE CHANGE IN BOND PRICE	(5) PERCENTAGE CHANGE IN k	(6) $= (4)/(5)$ BOND PRICE ELASTICITY (P_b^e)
0%	$ 386	$ 322	−16.6%	+20.0%	−.830
5	693	605	−12.7	+20.0	−.635
10	1,000	887	−11.3	+20.0	−.565
15	1,307	1,170	−10.5	+20.0	−.525

Exhibit 8.7 compares the price sensitivity of 10-year bonds with $1,000 par value and four different coupon rates: 0 percent, 5 percent, 10 percent, and 15 percent. Initially, the required rate of return (k) on the bonds is assumed to be 10 percent. The price of each bond is therefore the present value of its future cash flows, discounted at 10 percent. The initial price of each bond is shown in Column 2. The top panel shows the effect of a decline in interest rates that reduces the investor's required return to 8 percent. The prices of the bonds based on an 8 percent required return are shown in Column 3. The percentage change in the price of each bond resulting from the interest rate movements is shown in Column 4. The bottom panel shows the effect of an increase in interest rates that increases the investor's required return to 12 percent.

The price elasticity for each bond is estimated in Exhibit 8.7 according to the assumed change in the required rate of return. Notice in the exhibit that the price sensitivity of any particular bond is greater for declining interest rates than for rising interest rates. The bond price elasticity is negative in all cases, reflecting the inverse relationship between interest rate movements and bond price movements.

Influence of Coupon Rate on Bond Price Sensitivity

A zero-coupon bond, which pays all of its proceeds to the investor at maturity, is most sensitive to changes in the required rate of return because the adjusted discount rate is applied to one lump sum in the distant future. Conversely, the price of a bond that pays all its yield in the form of coupon payments is less sensitive to changes in the required rate of return because the adjusted discount rate is applied to some payments that occur in the near future. The adjustment in the present value of such payments in the near future due to a change in the required rate of return is not as pronounced as an adjustment in the present value of payments in the distant future.

Exhibit 8.7 confirms that the prices of zero- or low-coupon bonds are more sensitive to changes in the required rate of return than prices of bonds with relatively high coupon rates. The exhibit shows that, when the required rate of return declines from 10 percent to 8 percent, the price of the zero-coupon bonds rises from $386 to $463. Thus the bond price elasticity is

$$
\begin{aligned}
P_b^e &= \frac{(\$463 - \$386)/\$386}{(8\% - 10\%)/10\%} \\
&= \frac{+19.9\%}{-20\%} \\
&= -0.995
\end{aligned}
$$

This implies that, for each 1 percent change in interest rates, zero-coupon bonds change by 0.995 percent in the opposite direction. Column 6 in Exhibit 8.7 shows that the price elasticities of the higher-coupon bonds are considerably lower than the price elasticity of the zero-coupon bond.

Financial institutions commonly restructure their bond portfolios to contain higher-coupon bonds when they are more concerned about a possible increase in interest rates (and therefore an increase in the required rate of return). Conversely, they restructure their portfolios to contain low- or zero-coupon bonds when they expect a decline in interest rates and wish to capitalize on their expectations by holding bonds that are price-sensitive.

Influence of Maturity on Bond Price Sensitivity As interest rates (and therefore required rates of return) decrease, long-term bond prices (as measured by their present value) increase by a greater degree than short-term bond prices because the long-term bonds will continue to offer the same coupon rate over a longer period of time than the short-term bonds. Of course, if interest rates increase, prices of the long-term bonds will decline by a greater degree.

8-3b Duration

An alternative measure of bond price sensitivity is the bond's duration, which is a measurement of the life of the bond on a present value basis. The longer a bond's duration, the greater its sensitivity to interest rate changes. A commonly used measure of a bond's duration (DUR) is

$$
DUR = \frac{\displaystyle\sum_{t=1}^{n} \frac{C_t(t)}{(1+k)^t}}{\displaystyle\sum_{t=1}^{n} \frac{C_t}{(1+k)^t}}
$$

where

C_t = **coupon or principal payment generated by the bond**
t = **time at which the payments are provided**
k = **bond's yield to maturity (reflects investors' required rate of return)**

The numerator of the duration formula represents the present value of future payments weighted by the time interval until the payments occur. The longer the intervals until payments are made, the larger the numerator and the larger the duration. The denominator of the duration formula represents the discounted future cash flows resulting from the bond, which is the present value of the bond.

The duration of a bond with $1,000 par value and a 7 percent coupon rate, three years remaining to maturity, and a 9 percent yield to maturity is calculated as

$$DUR = \frac{\dfrac{\$70}{(1.09)^1} + \dfrac{\$70}{(1.09)^2} + \dfrac{\$1,070(3)}{(1.09)^3}}{\dfrac{\$70}{(1.09)^1} + \dfrac{\$70}{(1.09)^2} + \dfrac{\$1,070}{(1.09)^3}}$$

$$= 2.8 \text{ years}$$

By comparison, the duration of a zero-coupon bond with a similar par value and yield to maturity is

$$DUR = \frac{\dfrac{\$1,000(3)}{(1.09)^3}}{\dfrac{\$1,000}{(1.09)^3}}$$

$$= 3 \text{ years}$$

The duration of a zero-coupon bond is always equal to the bond's term to maturity. The duration of any coupon bond is always less than the bond's term to maturity because some of the payments occur at intervals prior to maturity. ●

Duration of a Portfolio   Bond portfolio managers commonly attempt to *immunize* their portfolio—that is, to insulate it from the effects of interest rate movements. A first step in this process is to determine the sensitivity of their portfolio to such movements. Once the duration of each individual bond is measured, the bond portfolio's duration (DUR_p) can be estimated as

$$DUR_P = \sum_{j=1}^{m} w_j DUR_j$$

where

> m = number of bonds in the portfolio
> w_j = bond j's market value as a percentage of the portfolio market value
> DUR_j = bond j's duration

In other words, the duration of a bond portfolio is the weighted average of bond durations weighted according to relative market value. Financial institutions concerned with interest rate risk may compare their asset duration to their liability duration. A positive difference means that the market value of the institution's assets is more rate-sensitive than the market value of its liabilities. Thus, during a period of rising interest rates, the market value of the assets would be reduced by a greater degree than that of the liabilities. The institution's real net worth (market value of net worth) would therefore decrease.

Modified Duration   The duration measurement of a bond or a bond portfolio can be modified to estimate the impact of a change in the prevailing bond yields on bond prices. The modified duration (denoted as DUR^*) is estimated as

$$DUR^* = \frac{DUR}{(1 + k)}$$

where k denotes the prevailing yield on bonds.

The modified duration can be used to estimate the percentage change in the bond's price in response to a 1 percentage point change in bond yields. For example, assume that Bond X has a duration of 8 years and Bond Y has a duration of 12 years. Assuming that the prevailing bond yield is 10 percent, the modified duration is estimated for each bond as follows:

Bond X **Bond Y**

$$\text{DUR}^* = \frac{8}{(1 + 0.10)} \quad \text{DUR}^* = \frac{12}{(1 + 0.10)}$$

$$= 7.27 \text{ years} \qquad\quad = 10.9 \text{ years}$$

Given the inverse relationship between the change in bond yields and the response in bond prices, the estimate of modified duration should be applied such that the bond price moves in the opposite direction from the change in bond yields. According to the modified duration estimates, a 1 percentage point increase in bond yields (from 10 percent to 11 percent) would lead to a 7.27 percent decline in the price of Bond X and to a 10.9 percent decline in the price of Bond Y. A 0.5 percentage point increase in yields (from 10 percent to 10.5 percent) would lead to a 3.635 percent decline in the price of Bond X (computed as 7.27×0.5) and a 5.45 percent decline in the price of Bond Y (10.9×0.5). The percentage increase in bond prices in response to a decrease in bond yields is estimated in the same manner.

The percentage change in a bond's price in response to a change in yield can be expressed more directly with a simple equation:

$$\%\Delta P_b = -\text{DUR}^* \times \Delta y$$

where

$$\%\Delta P_b = \textbf{percentage change in the bond's price}$$
$$\Delta y = \textbf{change in yield}$$

This equation is simply a mathematical expression of the relationship discussed in the preceding paragraphs. For example, the percentage change in price for Bond X for an increase in yield of 0.2 percentage point would be

$$\%\Delta P_b = -7.27 \times 0.002$$
$$= 1.45\%$$

Thus, according to the modified duration estimate, if interest rates rise by 0.2 percentage point then the price of Bond X will drop 1.45 percent. Similarly, if interest rates decrease by 0.2 percentage point, the price of Bond X will increase by 1.45 percent.

Estimation Errors from Using Modified Duration
If investors rely strictly on modified duration to estimate the percentage change in the price of a bond, they will tend to overestimate the price decline associated with an increase in rates and to underestimate the price increase associated with a decrease in rates.

EXAMPLE

Consider a bond with a 10 percent coupon that pays interest annually and has 20 years to maturity. If the required rate of return is 10 percent (the same as the coupon rate), the value of the bond is $1,000. Based on the formula provided earlier, this bond's modified duration is 8.514 years.

If investors anticipate that bond yields will increase by 1 percentage point (to 11 percent), then they can estimate the percentage change in the bond's price to be

$$\%\Delta P_b = -8.514 \times 0.01$$
$$= -0.08514 \text{ or } -8.514\%$$

If bond yields rise by 1 percentage point as expected, the price (present value) of the bond would now be $920.37. (Verify this new price by using the time value function on your financial calculator.) The new price reflects a decline of 7.96 percent [calculated as ($920.37 − $1,000) ÷ $1,000]. The decline in price is less pronounced than was estimated in the previous equation. The difference between the estimated percentage change in price (8.514 percent) and the actual percentage change in price (7.96 percent) is due to convexity. ●

Bond Convexity   A more complete formula to estimate the percentage change in price in response to a change in yield will incorporate the property of convexity as well as modified duration.

The estimated modified duration suggests a linear relationship in the response of the bond price to a change in bond yields. This is shown by the straight line in Exhibit 8.8. For a given 1 percentage point change in bond yields from our initially assumed bond yield of 10 percent, the modified duration predicts a specific change in bond price. However, the actual response of the bond's price to a change in bond yields is convex and is represented by the red curve in Exhibit 8.8. Notice that if the bond yield (horizontal axis) changes slightly from the initial level of 10 percent, the difference between the expected bond price adjustment according to the modified duration estimate (the straight line in Exhibit 8.8) and the bond's actual price adjustment (the convex curve in Exhibit 8.8) is small. For relatively large changes in the bond yield, however, the bond price adjustment as estimated by modified duration is less accurate. The larger the change in the bond yield, the larger the error from estimating the change in bond price in response to the change in yield.

Exhibit 8.8   Relationship between Bond Yields and Prices

Since a bond's price change in response to a change in yields is positively related to the maturity of the bond, convexity is also more pronounced for bonds with a long maturity. The prices of low- or zero-coupon bonds are more sensitive to changes in yields. Similarly, bond convexity is more pronounced for bonds with low (or no) coupon rates.

8-4 BOND INVESTMENT STRATEGIES

Many investors value bonds and assess their risk when managing investments. Some investors such as bond portfolio managers of financial institutions commonly follow a specific strategy for investing in bonds. A few of the more common strategies are described here.

8-4a Matching Strategy

Some investors create a bond portfolio that will generate periodic income to match their expected periodic expenses. For example, an individual investor may invest in a bond portfolio that will provide sufficient income to cover periodic expenses after retirement. Alternatively, a pension fund may invest in a bond portfolio that will provide employees with a fixed periodic income after retirement. The matching strategy involves estimating future cash outflows and then developing a bond portfolio that can generate sufficient coupon or principal payments to cover those outflows.

8-4b Laddered Strategy

With a laddered strategy, funds are evenly allocated to bonds in each of several different maturity classes. For example, an institutional investor might create a bond portfolio with one-fourth of the funds invested in bonds with five years until maturity, one-fourth invested in 10-year bonds, one-fourth in 15-year bonds, and one-fourth in 20-year bonds. In five years, when the bonds that had five years until maturity are redeemed, the proceeds can be used to buy 20-year bonds. Since all the other bonds in the portfolio will have five years less until maturity than they had when the portfolio was created, a new investment in 20-year bonds achieves the same maturity structure that existed when the portfolio was created.

The laddered strategy has many variations, but in general this strategy achieves diversified maturities and therefore different sensitivities to interest rate risk. Nevertheless, because most bonds are adversely affected by rising interest rates, diversification of maturities in the bond portfolio does not eliminate interest rate risk.

WEB

http://research.
stlouisfed.org
Assess the yield of
30-year Treasury bonds
over the last 24 months.

8-4c Barbell Strategy

With the barbell strategy, funds are allocated to bonds with a short term to maturity as well as to bonds with a long term to maturity. The bonds with the short term to maturity provide liquidity if the investor needs to sell bonds in order to obtain cash. The bonds with the long term to maturity tend to have a higher yield to maturity than the bonds with shorter terms to maturity. Thus this strategy allocates some funds to achieving a relatively high return and other funds to covering liquidity needs.

8-4d Interest Rate Strategy

With the interest rate strategy, funds are allocated in a manner that capitalizes on interest rate forecasts. This strategy requires frequent adjustments in the bond portfolio to reflect the prevailing interest rate forecast.

EXAMPLE   Consider a bond portfolio with funds initially allocated equally across various bond maturities. If recent economic events result in an expectation of higher interest rates, the bond portfolio will be revised to concentrate on bonds with short terms to maturity. Because these bonds are the least sensitive to interest rate movements, they will limit the potential adverse effects on the bond portfolio's value. The sales of all the intermediate-term and long-term bonds will result in significant commissions paid to brokers.

Now assume that after a few weeks, new economic conditions result in an expectation that interest rates will decline in the future. Again the bond portfolio will be restructured, but now it will concentrate on long-term bonds. If interest rates decline as expected, this type of bond portfolio will be most sensitive to that interest rate movement and will experience the largest increase in value. ●

Although this type of strategy is rational for investors who believe that they can accurately forecast interest rate movements, it is difficult for even the most sophisticated investors to consistently forecast future interest rate movements. If investors guess wrong, their portfolio will likely perform worse than if they had used a passive strategy of investing in bonds with a wide variety of maturities.

8-5 VALUATION AND RISK OF INTERNATIONAL BONDS

GLOBAL ASPECTS

The value of an international bond represents the present value of future cash flows to be received by the bond's local investors. Exhibit 8.9 shows the yields offered on newly issued bonds by various governments. Notice that yields vary among countries, since each yield represents the long-term, risk-free rate for the local country (assuming that the government is perceived to be free from default risk). Although the yields on newly issued government bonds vary among countries, the exhibit shows that they tend to move in the same direction. During the 2007–2012 period, interest rates declined in

Exhibit 8.9   Government Bond Yields over Time

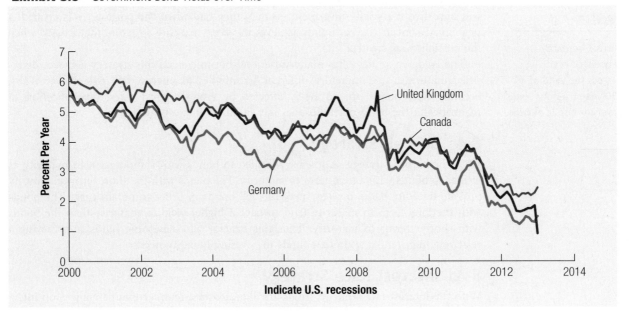

Source: *Federal Reserve.*

most countries and thus the yields offered on newly issued government bonds declined as well. The decline in yields was especially pronounced in response to the financial crisis in 2008, which prompted most central banks to lower their interest rates. As a result, the yields of newly issued bonds declined as well.

The value of government bonds changes over time in response to changes in the risk-free interest rate of the currency denominating the bond and in response to changes in the perceived credit risk of the bond. Since these two factors affect the market price of the bond, they also affect the return on the bond to investors over a particular holding period. An additional factor that affects the return to investors from another country is exchange rate risk. The influence of each of these factors is described next.

8-5a Influence of Foreign Interest Rate Movements

As the risk-free interest rate of a currency changes, the required rate of return by investors in that country changes as well. Thus the present value of a bond denominated in that currency changes. A reduction in the risk-free interest rate of the foreign currency will result in a lower required rate of return by investors who use that currency to invest, which results in a higher value for bonds denominated in that currency. Conversely, an increase in the risk-free rate of that currency results in a lower value for bonds denominated in that currency. In general, the return on a bond denominated in a specific currency over a particular holding period is enhanced if the corresponding interest rate declines over that period; the return is reduced if the corresponding interest rate increases over that period. U.S. bond prices may be rising (owing to a reduction in U.S. interest rates) while the prices of bonds denominated in other currencies are decreasing (owing to an increase in the interest rates of these currencies).

WEB

www.bloomberg.com/ markets
Yields of government securities from major countries.

8-5b Influence of Credit Risk

As the perceived credit (default) risk of an international bond changes, the risk premium within the required rate of return by investors is affected. Consequently, the present value of the bond changes. An increase in risk causes a higher required rate of return on the bond and therefore lowers its present value, whereas a reduction in risk causes a lower required rate of return on the bond and increases its present value. Thus investors who are concerned about a possible increase in the credit risk of an international bond will monitor economic and political conditions in the relevant country that could affect that risk.

8-5c Influence of Exchange Rate Fluctuations

Changes in the value of the foreign currency denominating a bond affect the U.S. dollar cash flows generated from the bond and thereby affect the return to U.S. investors who invested in it. Consider a U.S. financial institution's purchase of bonds with a par value of £2 million, a 10 percent coupon rate (payable at the end of each year), currently priced at par value, and with six years remaining until maturity. Exhibit 8.10 shows how the dollar cash flows to be generated from this investment will differ under three scenarios. The cash flows in the last year also account for the principal payment. The sensitivity of dollar cash flows to the pound's value is obvious.

From the perspective of the investing institution, the most attractive foreign bonds offer a high coupon rate and are denominated in a currency that strengthens over the investment horizon. Although the coupon rates of some bonds are fixed, the future value of any foreign currency is uncertain. Thus there is a risk that the currency will depreciate and more than offset any coupon rate advantage.

Exhibit 8.10 Dollar Cash Flows Generated from a Foreign Bond under Three Scenarios

SCENARIO I (STABLE POUND)	YEAR 1	YEAR 2	YEAR 3	YEAR 4	YEAR 5	YEAR 6
Forecasted value of pound	$1.50	$1.50	$1.50	$1.50	$1.50	$1.50
Forecasted dollar cash flows	$300,000	$300,000	$300,000	$300,000	$300,000	$3,300,000
SCENARIO II (WEAK POUND)						
Forecasted value of pound	$1.48	$1.46	$1.44	$1.40	$1.36	$1.30
Forecasted dollar cash flows	$296,000	$292,000	$288,000	$280,000	$272,000	$2,860,000
SCENARIO III (STRONG POUND)						
Forecasted value of pound	$1.53	$1.56	$1.60	$1.63	$1.66	$1.70
Forecasted dollar cash flows	$306,000	$312,000	$320,000	$326,000	$332,000	$3,740,000

8-5d International Bond Diversification

When investors attempt to capitalize on investments in foreign bonds that have higher interest rates than they can obtain locally, they may diversify their foreign bond holdings among countries to reduce their exposure to different types of risk, as explained next.

Reduction of Interest Rate Risk   Institutional investors diversify their bond portfolios internationally to reduce exposure to interest rate risk. If all bonds in a portfolio are from a single country, their values will all be systematically affected by interest rate movements in that country. International diversification of bonds reduces the sensitivity of the overall bond portfolio to any single country's interest rate movements.

Reduction of Credit Risk   Another key reason for international diversification is the reduction of credit (default) risk. Investment in bonds issued by corporations from a single country can expose investors to a relatively high degree of credit risk. The credit risk of corporations is strongly affected by economic conditions. Shifts in credit risk will likely be systematically related to the country's economic conditions. Because economic cycles differ across countries, there is less chance of a systematic increase in the credit risk of internationally diversified bonds. During the credit crisis of 2008–2009, however, there was a perception of higher credit risk (and therefore lower value) for most corporate bonds regardless of the issuer's country.

Reduction of Exchange Rate Risk   Financial institutions may attempt to reduce their exchange rate risk by diversifying among foreign securities denominated in various foreign currencies. In this way, a smaller proportion of their foreign security holdings will be exposed to the depreciation of any particular foreign currency. Because the movements of many foreign currency values within one continent are highly correlated, a U.S. investor would reduce exchange rate risk only slightly when diversifying among securities. For this reason, U.S. financial institutions commonly attempt to purchase securities across continents rather than within a single continent. This fact is evident from a review of the foreign securities purchased by pension funds, life insurance companies, or most international mutual funds.

The conversion of many European countries to a single currency (the euro) in recent years has resulted in more bond offerings in Europe by European-based firms. Before the introduction of the euro, a European firm needed a different currency for every European country in which it conducted business and therefore borrowed currency from local banks in each country. Now, a firm can use the euro to finance its operations across several European countries and may be able to obtain all the financing it needs with a single, euro-denominated bond offering. The firm can then use a portion of the revenue (in euros) for making coupon payments to bondholders who have purchased the bonds. In addition, European investors based in countries where the euro serves as the local currency can now invest in euro-denominated bonds in other European countries without being exposed to exchange rate risk.

International Integration of Credit Risk   The general credit risk levels of loans among countries is correlated, because country economies are correlated. When one country experiences weak economic conditions, its consumers tend to reduce their demand not only for local products but foreign products as well. The credit risk of the local firms increases, because the weak economy reduces their revenue and their earnings, and could make it difficult for them to repay their loans. Furthermore, as the country's consumers reduce their demand for foreign products, the producers of those products in foreign countries experience lower revenue and earnings, and may not be able to repay their loans to creditors within their own country. Thus, the higher credit risk in one country is transmitted to another country. This process is sometimes referred to as credit contagion, meaning that higher credit risk in one country becomes contagious to other countries whose economies are integrated with it.

8-5e European Debt Crisis

In the 2010–2012 period, the governments of Greece, Portugal, and Spain experienced debt crises because of large budget deficits and their inability to cover their debt payments. As their credit ratings declined, some investors were no longer willing to invest in their bonds, and the prices of outstanding bonds declined. Because these countries commonly obtained debt financing from financial institutions in other European countries, their financial problems have spread to these other countries, resulting in a European debt crisis. As the financial institutions that provided loans to the governments experience loan defaults, their own credit risk increases.

European countries that rely on the euro as their currency cannot use monetary policy to stimulate their economies, because they do not have control of their own money supply. They are part of the eurozone, and therefore subject to the monetary policy conducted by the European Central Bank that is applied to all countries that participate in the euro. Thus, they may want to use their fiscal policy to stimulate their economy. The typical fiscal policy that stimulates the economy is substantial government spending and lower taxes, but these actions would result in a larger budget deficit. This is not a desirable solution for countries that are presently unable to cover their existing debt. They cannot easily issue more bonds to cover a larger deficit when they are unable to repay their existing debt. Bondholders recognize the credit risk, and are only willing to provide credit if they are compensated for accepting the risk that the bonds might default.

The European Central Bank has been willing to provide credit to countries that are unable to cover their debt payments. However, when it provides credit, it commonly imposes austerity conditions that may enable the government to correct its budget deficit over time. These conditions are not necessarily desired by the government, because they might require the government to reduce its spending and increase taxes. The conditions can reduce budget deficits, but do not provide a quick cure to the weak economic conditions in Europe.

Some critics have argued that a country's government should abandon the euro rather than accept funding from the ECB, because the austerity conditions are too harsh. If a country abandons the eurozone, there are possible political implications. The country might be removed from the European Union, and its international trade with some European countries could be reduced. Also, if the country decides to default on its debt, other restrictions might be imposed by the governments of countries where the major creditors are based, such as restrictions on any new credit provided to the government that defaulted. At the very least, some creditors would cut off future funding to the government that defaulted on its debt.

The European debt crisis also raised concerns about credit risk in the United States and Asia. News of European debt repayment problems signaled potential economic weakness in Europe, which caused stock prices in Europe to decline. Moreover, the negative signal spread to other continents, due to the economic integration between continents through international trade. During the 2011–2012 period, the investor sentiment as the U.S. stock market opened each morning was often dependent on the latest news about government debt repayment issues in Europe.

SUMMARY

- The value of a debt security (such as bonds) is the present value of future cash flows generated by that security, using a discount rate that reflects the investor's required rate of return. As market interest rates rise, the investor's required rate of return increases. The discounted value of bond payments declines when the higher discount rate is applied. Thus the present value of a bond declines, which forces the bond price to decline.

- Bond prices are affected by the factors that influence interest rate movements, including economic growth, the money supply, oil prices, and the dollar. Bond prices are also affected by a change in credit risk.

- Investors commonly measure the sensitivity of their bond holdings to potential changes in the required rate of return. Two methods used for this purpose are bond price elasticity and duration. Other things being equal, the longer a bond's time to maturity, the more sensitive its price is to interest rate movements. Prices of bonds with relatively low coupon payments are also more sensitive to interest rate movements.

- Common investment strategies used to invest in bonds are the matching strategy, laddered strategy, barbell strategy, and interest rate strategy. The matching strategy focuses on generating income from the bond portfolio that can cover anticipated expenses. The laddered strategy and barbell strategy are designed to cover liquidity needs while also trying to achieve decent returns. The interest rate strategy is useful for investors who believe that they can predict interest rate movements and therefore shift into long-term bonds when they believe interest rates will decline.

- Foreign bonds may offer higher returns, but they are exposed to exchange rate risk and may also be subject to credit risk. International financial markets are highly integrated, so adverse conditions that cause high credit risk in one country may be contagious to other countries.

POINT COUNTER-POINT

Does Governance of Firms Affect the Prices of Their Bonds?

Point   No. Bond prices are primarily determined by interest rate movements and therefore are not affected by the governance of firms that issued the bonds.

Counter-Point   Yes. Bond prices reflect the risk of default. Firms with more effective governance may be able to reduce their default risk and thereby increase the price of their bonds.

Who Is Correct?   Use the Internet to learn more about this issue and then formulate your own opinion.

QUESTIONS AND APPLICATIONS

1. Bond Investment Decision Based on your forecast of interest rates, would you recommend that investors purchase bonds today? Explain.

2. How Interest Rates Affect Bond Prices Explain the impact of a decline in interest rates on:

a. An investor's required rate of return.

b. The present value of existing bonds.

c. The prices of existing bonds.

3. Relevance of Bond Price Movements Why is the relationship between interest rates and bond prices important to financial institutions?

4. Source of Bond Price Movements Determine the direction of bond prices over the last year and explain the reason for it.

5. Exposure to Bond Price Movements How would a financial institution with a large bond portfolio be affected by falling interest rates? Would it be affected more than a financial institution with a greater concentration of bonds (and fewer short-term securities)? Explain.

6. Comparison of Bonds to Mortgages Since fixed-rate mortgages and bonds have similar payment flows, how is a financial institution with a large portfolio of fixed-rate mortgages affected by rising interest rates? Explain.

7. Coupon Rates If a bond's coupon rate were above its required rate of return, would its price be above or below its par value? Explain.

8. Bond Price Sensitivity Is the price of a long-term bond more or less sensitive to a change in interest rates than to the price of a short-term security? Why?

9. Required Return on Bonds Why does the required rate of return for a particular bond change over time?

10. Inflation Effects Assume that inflation is expected to decline in the near future. How could this affect future bond prices? Would you recommend that financial institutions increase or decrease their concentration in long-term bonds based on this expectation? Explain.

11. Bond Price Elasticity Explain the concept of bond price elasticity. Would bond price elasticity suggest a higher price sensitivity for zero-coupon bonds or high-coupon bonds that are offering the same yield to maturity? Why? What does this suggest about the market value volatility of mutual funds containing zero-coupon Treasury bonds versus high-coupon Treasury bonds?

12. Economic Effects on Bond Prices An analyst recently suggested that there will be a major economic expansion that will favorably affect the prices of high-rated, fixed-rate bonds because the credit risk of bonds will decline as corporations improve their performance. Assuming that the economic expansion occurs, do you agree with the analyst's conclusion? Explain.

13. Impact of War When tensions rise or a war erupts in the Middle East, bond prices in many countries tend to decline. What is the link between problems in the Middle East and bond prices? Would you expect bond prices to decline more in Japan or in the United Kingdom as a result of the crisis? (The answer is tied to how interest rates may change in those countries.) Explain.

14. Bond Price Sensitivity Explain how bond prices may be affected by money supply growth, oil prices, and economic growth.

15. Impact of Oil Prices Assume that oil-producing countries have agreed to reduce their oil production by 30 percent. How would bond prices be affected by this announcement? Explain.

16. Impact of Economic Conditions Assume that breaking news causes bond portfolio managers to suddenly expect much higher economic growth. How might bond prices be affected by this expectation? Explain. Now assume that breaking news causes bond portfolio managers to suddenly anticipate a recession. How might bond prices be affected? Explain.

Advanced Questions

17. Impact of the Fed Assume that bond market participants suddenly expect the Fed to substantially increase the money supply.

a. Assuming no threat of inflation, how would bond prices be affected by this expectation?

b. Assuming that inflation may result, how would bond prices be affected?

c. Given your answers to (a) and (b), explain why expectations of the Fed's increase in the money supply may sometimes cause bond market participants to disagree about how bond prices will be affected.

18. Impact of the Trade Deficit Bond portfolio managers closely monitor the trade deficit figures, because the trade deficit can affect exchange rates, which can affect inflationary expectations and therefore interest rates.

a. When the trade deficit figure is higher than anticipated, bond prices typically decline. Explain why this reaction may occur.

b. On some occasions, the trade deficit figure has been very large but the bond markets did not respond to the announcement. Assuming that no other information offsets the impact, explain why the bond markets may not have responded to the announcement.

19. International Bonds A U.S. insurance company purchased British 20-year Treasury bonds instead of U.S. 20-year Treasury bonds because the coupon rate was 2 percent higher on the British bonds. Assume that the insurance company sold the bonds after five years. Its yield over the five-year period was substantially less than the yield it would have received on the U.S. bonds over the same five-year period. Assume that the U.S. insurance company had hedged its exchange rate exposure. Given that the lower yield was not because of default risk or exchange rate risk, explain how the British bonds could have generated a lower yield than the U.S. bonds. (Assume that either type of bond could have been purchased at the par value.)

20. International Bonds The pension fund manager of Utterback (a U.S. firm) purchased German 20-year Treasury bonds instead of U.S. 20-year Treasury bonds. The coupon rate was 2 percent lower on the German bonds. Assume that the manager sold the bonds after five years. The yield over the five-year period was substantially more than the yield the manager would have received on the U.S. bonds over the same five-year period. Explain how the German bonds could have generated a higher yield than the U.S. bonds for the manager, even if the exchange rate was stable over this five-year period. (Assume that the price of either bond was initially equal to its respective par value.) Be specific.

21. Implications of a Shift in the Yield Curve Assume that there is a sudden shift in the yield curve such that the new yield curve is higher and more steeply sloped today than it was yesterday. If a firm issues new bonds today, would its bonds sell for higher or lower prices than if it had issued the bonds yesterday? Explain.

22. How Bond Prices May Respond to Prevailing Conditions Consider the prevailing conditions for inflation (including oil prices), the economy, the budget deficit, and the Fed's monetary policy that could affect interest rates. Based on prevailing conditions, do you think bond prices will increase or decrease during this semester? Offer some logic to support your answer. Which factor do you think will have the biggest impact on bond prices?

23. Interaction between Bond and Money Markets Assume that you maintain bonds and money market securities in your portfolio, and you suddenly believe that long-term interest rates will rise substantially tomorrow (even though the market does not share your view) while short-term interest rates will remain the same.

a. How would you rebalance your portfolio between bonds and money market securities?

b. If other market participants suddenly recognize that long-term interest rates will rise tomorrow and they respond in the same manner as you do, explain how the demand for these securities (bonds and money market securities), supply of these securities for sale, and prices and yields of these securities will be affected.

c. Assume that the yield curve is flat today. Explain how the slope of the yield curve will change tomorrow in response to the market activity.

24. Impact of the Credit Crisis on Risk Premiums Explain how the prices of bonds were affected by a change in the risk-free rate during the credit crisis. Explain how bond prices were affected by a change in the credit risk premium during this period.

25. Systemic Risk Explain why there are concerns about systemic risk in the bond and other debt markets. Also explain how the Financial Reform Act of 2010 was intended to reduce systemic risk.

26. Link Between Market Uncertainty and Bond Yields When stock market volatility is high, corporate bond yields tend to increase. What market forces cause the increase in corporate bond yields under these conditions?

27. Fed's Impact on Credit Risk This chapter explains how the Fed can change money supply, which can affect the risk-free rate offered on bonds. Why might the Fed's policy also affect the risk premium on corporate bonds?

28. Spread of European Debt Crisis Explain why debt crises in some European countries can cause financial problems in other European countries.

29. European Debt Repayment and Monetary Policy Explain why monetary policy is not normally effective in stimulating the economy of a European country that is experiencing debt repayment problems.

30. European Debt Repayment and Fiscal Policy Explain why fiscal policy is not normally effective in stimulating the economy of a European country that is experiencing debt repayment problems.

31. Conditions Imposed on ECB Loans to Governments with Debt Problems Describe the conditions imposed by the European Central Bank (ECB) when it provides credit to European country governments with debt repayment problems.

Interpreting Financial News

Interpret the following statements made by Wall Street analysts and portfolio managers.

a. "Given the recent uncertainty about future interest rates, investors are fleeing from zero-coupon bonds."

b. "Catrell Insurance Company invests heavily in bonds, and its stock price increased substantially today in response to the Fed's signal that it plans to reduce interest rates."

c. "Bond markets declined when the Treasury flooded the market with its new bond offering."

Managing in Financial Markets

Bond Investment Dilemma As an investor, you plan to invest your funds in long-term bonds. You have $100,000 to invest. You may purchase highly rated municipal bonds at par with a coupon rate of 6 percent; you have a choice of a maturity of 10 years or 20 years. Alternatively, you could purchase highly rated corporate bonds at par with a coupon rate of 8 percent; these bonds also are offered with maturities of 10 years or 20 years. You do not expect to need the funds for five years. At the end of the fifth year, you will definitely sell the bonds because you will need to make a large purchase at that time.

a. What is the annual interest you would earn (before taxes) on the municipal bond? On the corporate bond?

b. Assume that you are in the 20 percent tax bracket. If the level of credit risk and the liquidity for the municipal and corporate bonds are the same, would you invest in the municipal bonds or the corporate bonds? Why?

c. Assume that you expect all yields paid on newly issued notes and bonds (regardless of maturity) to decrease by a total of 4 percentage points over the next two years and to increase by a total of 2 percentage points over the following three years. Would you select the 10-year maturity or the 20-year maturity for the type of bond you plan to purchase? Why?

PROBLEMS

1. Bond Valuation Assume the following information for an existing bond that provides annual coupon payments:

> Par value = $1,000
> Coupon rate = 11%
> Maturity = 4 years
> Required rate of return by investors = 11%

a. What is the present value of the bond?

b. If the required rate of return by investors were 14 percent instead of 11 percent, what would be the present value of the bond?

c. If the required rate of return by investors were 9 percent, what would be the present value of the bond?

2. Valuing a Zero-Coupon Bond Assume the following information for existing zero-coupon bonds:

> Par value = $100,000
> Maturity = 3 years
> Required rate of return by investors = 12%

How much should investors be willing to pay for these bonds?

3. Valuing a Zero-Coupon Bond Assume that you require a 14 percent return on a zero-coupon bond with a par value of $1,000 and six years to maturity. What is the price you should be willing to pay for this bond?

4. Bond Value Sensitivity to Exchange Rates and Interest Rates Cardinal Company, a U.S.-based insurance company, considers purchasing bonds denominated in Canadian dollars, with a maturity of six years, a par value of C$50 million, and a coupon rate of 12 percent. Cardinal can purchase the bonds at par. The current exchange rate of the Canadian dollar is $0.80. Cardinal expects that the required return by Canadian investors on these bonds four years from now will be 9 percent. If Cardinal purchases the bonds, it will sell them in the Canadian secondary market four years from now. It forecasts the exchange rates as follows:

YEAR	EXCHANGE RATE OF C$	YEAR	EXCHANGE RATE OF C$
1	$0.80	4	$0.72
2	0.77	5	0.68
3	0.74	6	0.66

a. Refer to earlier examples in this chapter to determine the expected U.S. dollar cash flows to Cardinal over the next four years. Determine the present value of a bond.

b. Does Cardinal expect to be favorably or adversely affected by the interest rate risk? Explain.

c. Does Cardinal expect to be favorably or adversely affected by exchange rate risk? Explain.

5. Predicting Bond Values (Use the chapter appendix to answer this problem.) Bulldog Bank has just purchased bonds for $106 million that have a par value of $100 million, three years remaining to maturity, and an annual coupon rate of 14 percent. It expects the required rate of return on these bonds to be 12 percent one year from now.

a. At what price could Bulldog Bank sell these bonds one year from now?

b. What is the expected annualized yield on the bonds over the next year, assuming they are to be sold in one year?

6. Predicting Bond Values (Use the chapter appendix to answer this problem.) Sun Devil Savings has just purchased bonds for $38 million that have a par value of $40 million, five years remaining to maturity, and a coupon rate of 12 percent. It expects the required rate of return on these bonds to be 10 percent two years from now.

a. At what price could Sun Devil Savings sell these bonds two years from now?

b. What is the expected annualized yield on the bonds over the next two years, assuming they are to be sold in two years?

c. If the anticipated required rate of return of 10 percent in two years is overestimated, how would the actual selling price differ from the forecasted price? How would the actual annualized yield over the next two years differ from the forecasted yield?

7. Predicting Bond Values (Use the chapter appendix to answer this problem.) Spartan Insurance Company plans to purchase bonds today that have four years remaining to maturity, a par value of $60 million, and a coupon rate of 10 percent. Spartan expects that in three years, the required rate of return on these bonds by investors in the market will be 9 percent. It plans to sell the bonds at that time. What is the expected price it will sell the bonds for in three years?

8. Bond Yields (Use the chapter appendix to answer this problem.) Hankla Company plans to purchase either (1) zero-coupon bonds that have 10 years to maturity, a par value of $100 million, and a purchase price of $40 million; or (2) bonds with similar default risk that have five years to maturity, a 9 percent coupon rate, a par value of $40 million, and a purchase price of $40 million.

Hankla can invest $40 million for five years. Assume that the market's required return in five years is forecasted to be 11 percent. Which alternative would offer Hankla a higher expected return (or yield) over the five-year investment horizon?

9. Predicting Bond Values (Use the chapter appendix to answer this problem.) The portfolio manager of Ludwig Company has excess cash that is to be invested for four years. He can purchase four-year Treasury notes that offer a 9 percent yield. Alternatively, he can purchase new 20-year Treasury bonds for $2.9 million that offer a par value of $3 million and an 11 percent coupon rate with annual payments. The manager expects that the required return on these same 20-year bonds will be 12 percent four years from now.

a. What is the forecasted market value of the 20-year bonds in four years?

b. Which investment is expected to provide a higher yield over the four-year period?

10. Predicting Bond Portfolio Value (Use the chapter appendix to answer this problem.) Ash Investment Company manages a broad portfolio with this composition:

	PAR VALUE	PRESENT MARKET VALUE	YEARS REMAINING TO MATURITY
Zero-coupon bonds	$200,000,000	$ 63,720,000	12
8% Treasury bonds	300,000,000	290,000,000	8
11% corporate bonds	400,000,000	<u>380,000,000</u>	10
		$733,720,000	

Ash expects that in four years, investors in the market will require an 8 percent return on the zero-coupon bonds, a 7 percent return on the Treasury bonds, and a 9 percent return on corporate bonds. Estimate the market value of the bond portfolio four years from now.

11. Valuing a Zero-Coupon Bond

a. A zero-coupon bond with a par value of $1,000 matures in 10 years. At what price would this bond provide a yield to maturity that matches the current market rate of 8 percent?

b. What happens to the price of this bond if interest rates fall to 6 percent?

c. Given the above changes in the price of the bond and the interest rate, calculate the bond price elasticity.

12. Bond Valuation You are interested in buying a $1,000 par value bond with 10 years to maturity and an 8 percent coupon rate that is paid semiannually. How much should you be willing to pay for the bond if the investor's required rate of return is 10 percent?

13. Predicting Bond Values A bond you are interested in pays an annual coupon of 4 percent, has a yield to maturity of 6 percent, and has 13 years to maturity. If interest rates remain unchanged, at what price would you expect this bond to be selling eight years from now? Ten years from now?

14. Sensitivity of Bond Values

a. How would the present value (and therefore the market value) of a bond be affected if the coupon payments are smaller and other factors remain constant?

b. How would the present value (and therefore the market value) of a bond be affected if the required rate of return is smaller and other factors remain constant?

15. Bond Elasticity Determine how the bond elasticity would be affected if the bond price changed by a larger amount, holding the change in the required rate of return constant.

16. Bond Duration Determine how the duration of a bond would be affected if the coupons were extended over additional time periods.

17. Bond Duration A bond has a duration of five years and a yield to maturity of 9 percent. If the yield to maturity changes to 10 percent, what should be the percentage price change of the bond?

18. Bond Convexity Describe how bond convexity affects the theoretical linear price–yield relationship of bonds. What are the implications of bond convexity for estimating changes in bond prices?

FLOW OF FUNDS EXERCISE

Interest Rate Expectations, Economic Growth, and Bond Financing

Recall that if the economy continues to be strong, Carson Company may need to increase its production capacity by about 50 percent over the next few years to satisfy demand. It would need financing to expand and accommodate the increase in production. Recall that the yield curve is currently upward sloping. Also recall that Carson is concerned about a possible slowing of the economy because of potential Fed actions to reduce inflation. It needs funding to cover payments for supplies. It is also considering issuing stock or bonds to raise funds in the next year.

a. At a recent meeting, the chief executive officer (CEO) stated his view that the economy will remain strong, as the Fed's monetary policy is not likely to have a major impact on interest rates. So he wants to expand the business to benefit from the expected increase in demand for Carson's products. The next step would be to determine how to finance the expansion. The chief financial officer (CFO) stated that if Carson Company needs to obtain long-term funds, the issuance of fixed-rate bonds would be ideal at this point in time because she expects that the Fed's monetary policy to reduce inflation will cause long-term interest rates to rise. If the CFO is correct about future interest rates, what does this suggest about future economic growth, the future demand for Carson's products, and the need to issue bonds?

b. If you were involved in the meeting described here, what do you think needs to be resolved before deciding to expand the business?

c. At the meeting described here, the CEO stated: "The decision to expand should not be dictated by whether interest rates are going to increase or not. Bonds should be issued only if the potential increase in interest rates is attributed to a strong demand for loanable funds rather than the Fed's reduction in the supply of loanable funds." What does this statement mean?

INTERNET/EXCEL EXERCISES

Go to www.giddy.org/db/corpspreads.htm. The spreads are listed in the form of basis points (100 basis points = 1 percent) above the Treasury security with the same maturity.

1. First determine the difference between the AAA and CCC spreads. This indicates how much more of a yield is required on CCC-rated bonds versus AAA-rated bonds. Next, determine the difference between AAA and BBB spreads. Then determine the difference between BBB and CCC spreads. Is the difference larger between the AAA and BBB or the BBB and CCC spreads? What does this tell you about the perceived risk of the bonds in these rating categories?

2. Compare the AAA spread for a short-term maturity (such as two years) versus a long-term maturity (such as 10 years). Is the spread larger for the short-term or the long-term maturity? Offer an explanation for this.

3. Next, compare the CCC spread for a short-term maturity (such as two years) versus a long-term maturity (such as 10 years). Is the spread larger for the short-term or the long-term maturity? Offer an explanation for this. Notice that the difference in spreads for a given rating level among maturities varies with the rating level that you assess. Offer an explanation for this.

ONLINE ARTICLES WITH REAL-WORLD EXAMPLES

Find a recent practical article available online that describes a real-world example regarding a specific financial institution or financial market that reinforces one or more concepts covered in this chapter.

If your class has an online component, your professor may ask you to post your summary of the article there and provide a link to the article so that other students can access it. If your class is live, your professor may ask you to summarize your application of the article in class. Your professor may assign specific students to complete this assignment or may allow any students to do the assignment on a volunteer basis.

For recent online articles and real-world examples related to this chapter, consider using the following search terms (be sure to include the prevailing year as

a search term to ensure that the online articles are recent):

1. bond AND valuation

2. bond prices AND economic growth

3. bond prices AND inflation

4. bond prices AND money supply

5. bond prices AND budget deficit

6. bond AND duration

7. bond AND performance

8. bond AND strategy

9. international bonds AND exchange rate

10. international bonds AND credit risk

APPENDIX 8

Forecasting Bond Prices and Yields

FORECASTING BOND PRICES

To illustrate how a financial institution can assess the potential impact of interest rate movements on its bond holdings, assume that Longhorn Savings and Loan recently purchased Treasury bonds in the secondary market with a total par value of $40 million. The bonds will mature in five years and have an annual coupon rate of 10 percent. Longhorn is attempting to forecast the market value of these bonds two years from now because it may sell the bonds at that time. Therefore, it must forecast the investor's required rate of return and use that as the discount rate to determine the present value of the bonds' cash flows over the final three years of their life. The computed present value will represent the forecasted price two years from now.

To continue with our example, assume the investor's required rate of return two years from now is expected to be 12 percent. This rate will be used to discount the periodic cash flows over the remaining three years. Given coupon payments of $4 million per year (10% × $40 million) and a par value of $40 million, the predicted present value is determined as follows:

$$
\textbf{\textit{PV}} \textbf{ of bonds two years from now} = \frac{\$4,000,000}{(1.12)^1} + \frac{\$4,000,000}{(1.12)^2} + \frac{\$44,000,000}{(1.12)^3}
$$

$$
= \$3,571,429 + \$3,188,775 + \$31,318,331
$$

$$
= \$38,078,535
$$

An illustration of this exercise is provided in Exhibit 8A.1, using a time line. The market value of the bonds two years ahead is forecasted to be slightly more than $38 million. This is the amount Longhorn expects to receive if it sells the bonds then.

As a second example, assume that Aggie Insurance Company recently purchased corporate bonds in the secondary market with a par value of $20 million, a coupon rate of 14 percent (with annual coupon payments), and three years until maturity. The firm desires to forecast the market value of these bonds in one year because it may sell the bonds at that time. It expects the investor's required rate of return on similar investments to be 11 percent in one year. Using this information, it discounts the bonds' cash flows ($2.8 million in annual coupon payments and a par value of $20 million)

Exhibit 8A.1 Forecasting the Market Value of Bonds

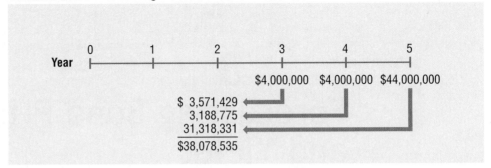

over the final two years at 11 percent to determine their present value (and therefore market value) one year from now:

$$\textit{PV} \text{ of bonds one year from now} = \frac{\$2,800,000}{(1.11)^1} + \frac{\$22,800,000}{(1.11)^2}$$

$$= \$2,522,522 + \$18,504,991$$

$$= \$21,027,513$$

Thus the market value of the bonds is expected to be slightly more than $21 million one year from now.

FORECASTING BOND YIELDS

The yield to maturity can be determined by solving for the discount rate at which the present value of future payments (coupon payments and par value) to the bondholder would equal the bond's current price. The trial-and-error method can be used by applying a discount rate and computing the present value of the payments stream. If the computed present value is higher than the current bond price, the computation should be repeated using a higher discount rate. Conversely, if the computed present value is lower than the current bond price, try a lower discount rate. Calculators and bond tables are also available to determine the yield to maturity.

If bonds are held to maturity, the yield is known. However, if they are sold prior to maturity, the yield is not known until the time of sale. Investors can, however, attempt to forecast the yield with the methods just demonstrated, in which the forecasted required rate of return is used to forecast the market value (and therefore selling price) of the bonds. This selling price can then be incorporated into the cash flow estimates to determine the discount rate at which the present value of cash flows equals the investor's initial purchase price. Suppose that Wildcat Bank purchases bonds with the following characteristics:

- Par value = $30 million
- Coupon rate = 15 percent (annual payments)
- Remaining time to maturity = 5 years
- Purchase price of bonds = $29 million

The bank plans to sell the bonds in four years. The investor's required rate of return on similar securities is expected to be 13 percent at that time. Given this information, Wildcat forecasts its annualized bond yield over the four-year period in the following manner.

The first step is to forecast the present value (or market price) of the bonds four years from now. To do this, the remaining cash flows (one final coupon payment of $4.5 million plus the par value of $30 million) over the fifth and final year should be discounted (at the forecasted required rate of return of 13 percent) back to the fourth year when the bonds are to be sold:

$$PV \text{ of bond four years from now} = \frac{\$34,500,000}{(1.13)^1}$$

$$= \$30,530,973$$

This predicted present value as of four years from now serves as the predicted selling price in four years.

The next step is to incorporate the forecasted selling price at the end of the bond portfolio's cash flow stream. Then the discount rate that equates the present value of the cash flow stream to the price at which the bonds were purchased will represent the annualized yield. In our example, Wildcat Bank's cash flows are coupon payments of $4.5 million over each of the four years it holds the bonds; the fourth year's cash flows should also include the forecasted selling price of $30,530,973 and therefore sum to $35,030,973. Recall that Wildcat Bank purchased the bonds for $29 million. Given this information, the equation to solve for the discount rate (k) is

$$\$29 \text{ million} = \frac{\$4,500,000}{(1+k)^1} + \frac{\$4,500,000}{(1+k)^2} + \frac{\$4,500,000}{(1+k)^3} + \frac{\$35,030,973}{(1+k)^4}$$

The trial-and-error method can be used to determine the discount rate if a calculator is not available. With a discount rate of 17 percent, the present value would be

$$\begin{aligned} PV \text{ of bonds using} \\ \text{a 17\% discount rate} \end{aligned} = \frac{\$4,500,000}{(1.17)^1} + \frac{\$4,500,000}{(1.17)^2} + \frac{\$4,500,000}{(1.17)^3} + \frac{\$35,030,973}{(1.17)^4}$$

$$= \$3,846,154 + \$3,287,311 + \$2,809,667 + \$18,694,280$$

$$= \$28,637,412$$

This present value is slightly less than the initial purchase price. Thus the discount rate at which the present value of expected cash flows equals the purchase price is just slightly less than 17 percent. Consequently, Wildcat Bank's expected return on the bonds is just short of 17 percent.

It should be recognized that the process for determining the yield to maturity assumes that any payments received prior to the end of the holding period can be reinvested at the yield to maturity. If, for example, the payments could be reinvested only at a lower rate, the yield to maturity would overstate the actual return to the investor over the entire holding period.

With a computer program, the financial institution could easily create a distribution of forecasted yields based on various forecasts for the required rate of return four years from now. Without a computer, the process illustrated here must be completed for each forecast of the required rate of return. The computer actually follows the same steps but is much faster.

Financial institutions that forecast bond yields must first forecast interest rates for the point in time when they plan to sell their bonds. These forecasted rates can be used along with information about the securities to predict the required rate of return that will exist for the securities of concern. The predicted required rate of return is applied to cash flows beyond the time of sale to forecast the present value (or selling price) of the bonds at the time of sale. The forecasted selling price is then incorporated when estimating cash flows over the investment horizon. Finally, the yield to maturity on the bonds is determined by solving for the discount rate that equates these cash flows to the initial purchase price. The accuracy of the forecasted yield depends on the accuracy of the forecasted selling price of the bonds, which in turn depends on the accuracy of the forecasted required rate of return for the time of the sale.

FORECASTING BOND PORTFOLIO VALUES

Financial institutions can quantitatively measure the impact of possible interest rate movements on the market value of their bond portfolio by separately assessing the impact on each type of bond and then consolidating the individual impacts. Assume that Seminole Financial, Inc., has a portfolio of bonds with the required return (k) on each type of bond as shown in the upper portion of Exhibit 8A.2. Interest rates are expected to increase, causing an anticipated increase of 1 percent in the required return of each type of bond. Assuming no adjustment in the portfolio, Seminole's anticipated bond portfolio position is displayed in the lower portion of Exhibit 8A.2.

The anticipated market value of each type of bond in the exhibit was determined by discounting the remaining year's cash flows beyond one year by the anticipated required return. The market value of the portfolio is expected to decline by more than $12 million as a result of the anticipated increase in interest rates.

This simplified example assumed a portfolio of only three types of bonds. In reality, a financial institution may have several types of bonds, with several maturities for each type. Computer programs are widely available for assessing the market value of portfolios. The

Exhibit 8A.2 Forecasts of Bond Portfolio Market Value

PRESENT BOND PORTFOLIO POSITION OF SEMINOLE FINANCIAL, INC.				
TYPE OF BONDS	PRESENT k	PAR VALUE	YEARS TO MATURITY	PRESENT MARKET VALUE OF BONDS
9% coupon Treasury bonds	9%	$ 40,000,000	4	$ 40,000,000
14% coupon corporate bonds	12%	100,000,000	5	107,209,552
10% coupon gov't agency bonds	10%	150,000,000	8	150,000,000
		$290,000,000		$297,207,200

FORECASTED BOND PORTFOLIO POSITION OF SEMINOLE FINANCIAL, INC.				
TYPE OF BONDS	FORECASTED k	PAR VALUE	YEARS TO MATURITY AS OF ONE YEAR FROM NOW	FORECASTED MARKET VALUE OF BONDS IN ONE YEAR
9% coupon Treasury bonds	10%	$ 40,000,000	3	$ 39,005,259
14% coupon corporate bonds	13%	100,000,000	4	102,974,471
10% coupon gov't agency bonds	11%	150,000,000	7	142,931,706
		$290,000,000		$284,915,840

financial institution inputs the cash flow trends of all bond holdings and the anticipated required rates of return for each bond at the future time of concern. The computer uses the anticipated rates to estimate the present value of cash flows at that future time. These present values are then consolidated to determine the forecasted value of the bond portfolio.

The key variable in forecasting the bond portfolio's market value is the anticipated required return for each type of bond. The prevailing interest rates on short-term securities are commonly more volatile than rates on longer-term securities, so the required returns on bonds with three or four years to maturity may change to a greater degree than on the longer-term bonds. In addition, as economic conditions change, the required returns of some risky securities could change even if the general level of interest rates remains stable.

FORECASTING BOND PORTFOLIO RETURNS

Financial institutions measure their overall bond portfolio returns in various ways. One way is to account not only for coupon payments but also for the change in market value over the holding period of concern. The market value at the beginning of the holding period is perceived as the initial investment. The market value at the end of that period is perceived as the price at which the bonds would have been sold. Even if the bonds are retained, the measurement of return requires an estimated market value at the end of the period. Finally, the coupon payments must be accounted for as well. A bond portfolio's return is measured the same way as an individual bond's return. Mathematically, the bond portfolio return can be determined by solving for k in the following equation:

$$MVP = \sum_{t=1}^{n} \frac{C_t}{(1+k)^t} + \frac{MVP_n}{(1+k)^n}$$

where

MVP = today's market value of the bond portfolio
C_t = coupon payments received at the end of period t
MVP_n = market value of the bond portfolio at the end of the investment period of concern
k = discount rate that equates the present value of coupon payments and the future portfolio market value to today's portfolio market value

To illustrate, recall that Seminole Financial, Inc., forecasted its bond portfolio value for one year ahead. Its annual coupon payments (C) sum to $32,600,000 (computed by multiplying the coupon rate of each type of bond by the respective par value). Using this information along with today's MVP and the forecasted MVP (called MVP_n), its annual return is determined by solving for k as follows:

$$MVP = \frac{C_1 + MVP_n}{(1+k)^1}$$

$$\$297{,}207{,}200 = \frac{\$32{,}600{,}000 + \$284{,}915{,}840}{(1+k)^1}$$

$$\$297{,}207{,}200 = \frac{\$317{,}515{,}840}{(1+k)^1}$$

The discount rate k is estimated to be about 7 percent. (Work this yourself for verification.) Therefore, the bond portfolio is expected to generate an annual return of about 7 percent over the one-year investment horizon. The computations to determine the bond portfolio return can be tedious, but financial institutions use computer programs. If this type of program is linked with another program to forecast future bond prices, a financial institution can input forecasted required returns for each type of bond and let the computer determine projections of the bond portfolio's future market value and its return over a specified investment horizon.

9

Mortgage Markets

CHAPTER OBJECTIVES

The specific objectives of this chapter are to:

■ provide a background on mortgages,

■ describe the common types of residential mortgages,

■ explain the valuation and risk of mortgages,

■ explain mortgage-backend securities, and

■ explain how mortgage problems led to the 2008-2009 credit crisis.

WEB

www.mbaa.org
News regarding the mortgage markets.

Mortgages are securities used to finance real estate purchases; they are originated by various financial institutions, such as savings institutions and mortgage companies. A secondary mortgage market accommodates originators of mortgages that desire to sell their mortgages prior to maturity. The mortgage markets serve individuals or firms that need long-term funds to purchase real estate. They also serve financial institutions that wish to serve as creditors by lending long-term funds for real estate purchases.

9-1 BACKGROUND ON MORTGAGES

A mortgage is a form of debt created to finance investment in real estate. The debt is secured by the property, so if the property owner does not meet the payment obligations, the creditor can seize the property. Financial institutions such as savings institutions and mortgage companies serve as intermediaries by originating mortgages. They consider mortgage applications and assess the creditworthiness of the applicants.

The mortgage represents the difference between the down payment and the value to be paid for the property. The mortgage contract specifies the mortgage rate, the maturity, and the collateral that is backing the loan. The originator charges an origination fee when providing a mortgage. In addition, if it uses its own funds to finance the property, it will earn profit from the difference between the mortgage rate that it charges and the rate that it paid to obtain the funds. Most mortgages have a maturity of 30 years, but 15-year maturities are also available.

9-1a How Mortgage Markets Facilitate the Flow of Funds

The means by which mortgage markets facilitate the flow of funds are illustrated in Exhibit 9.1. Financial intermediaries originate mortgages and finance purchases of homes. The financial intermediaries that originate mortgages obtain their funding from household deposits. They also obtain funds by selling some of the mortgages that they originate directly to institutional investors in the secondary market. These funds are then used to finance more purchases of homes, condominiums, and commercial property. Overall, mortgage markets allow households and corporations to increase their purchases of homes, condominiums, and commercial property and thereby finance economic growth.

Institutional Use of Mortgage Markets Mortgage companies, savings institutions, and commercial banks originate mortgages. Mortgage companies tend to sell their mortgages in the secondary market, although they may continue to process payments for

Exhibit 9.1   How Mortgage Markets Facilitate the Flow of Funds

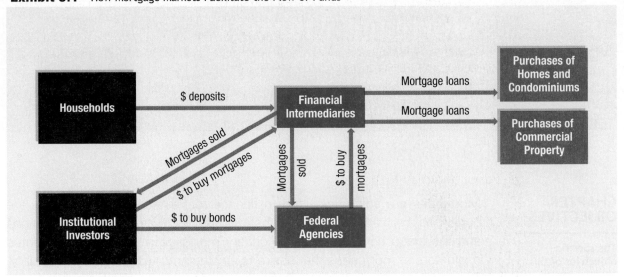

the mortgages that they originated. Thus their income is generated from origination and processing fees, and not from financing the mortgages over a long-term period. Savings institutions and commercial banks commonly originate residential mortgages. Commercial banks also originate mortgages for corporations that purchase commercial property. Savings institutions and commercial banks typically use funds received from household deposits to provide mortgage financing. However, they also sell some of their mortgages in the secondary market.

The common purchasers of mortgages in the secondary market are savings institutions, commercial banks, insurance companies, pension funds, and some types of mutual funds. The participation by financial institutions in the mortgage market is summarized in Exhibit 9.2.

Exhibit 9.2   Institutional Use of Mortgage Markets

TYPE OF FINANCIAL INSTITUTION	INSTITUTION PARTICIPATION IN MORTGAGE MARKETS
Commercial banks and savings institutions	• Originate and service commercial and residential mortgages and maintain mortgages within their investment portfolios. • Bundle packages of mortgages and sell mortgage-backed securities representing the packages of mortgages. • Purchase mortgage-based securities.
Credit unions and finance companies	• Originate mortgages and maintain mortgages within their investment portfolios.
Mortgage companies	• Originate mortgages and sell them in the secondary market.
Mutual funds	• May sell shares and use the proceeds to construct portfolios of mortgage-backed securities.
Securities firms	• Bundle packages of mortgages and sell mortgage-backed securities representing the packages of mortgages. • Offer instruments to help institutional investors in mortgages hedge against interest rate risk.
Insurance companies	• Commonly purchase mortgages or mortgage-backed securities in the secondary market.

9-1b Criteria Used to Measure Creditworthiness

When financial institutions consider mortgage applications, they review information that reflects the prospective borrower's ability to repay the loan. The following are three important criteria that are used to measure a borrower's repayment ability:

- *Level of equity invested by the borrower.* The down payment represents the equity invested by the borrower. The lower the level of equity invested, the higher the probability that the borrower will default. One proxy for this factor is the loan-to-value ratio, which indicates the proportion of the property's value that is financed with debt. When borrowers make relatively small down payments, the loan-to-value ratio is higher and borrowers have less to lose in the event that they stop making their mortgage payments.

- *Borrower's income level.* Borrowers who have a lower level of income relative to the periodic loan payments are more likely to default on their mortgages. Income determines the amount of funds that borrowers have available per month to make mortgage payments. Income levels change over time, however, so it is difficult for mortgage lenders to anticipate whether prospective borrowers will continue to earn their monthly income over the life of the mortgage, especially given the high frequency of layoffs.

- *Borrower's credit history.* Other conditions being similar, borrowers with a history of credit problems are more likely to default on their loans than those without credit problems.

9-1c Classifications of Mortgages

Mortgages can be classified in various ways, but two important classifications are prime versus subprime mortgages and insured versus conventional mortgages.

Prime versus Subprime Mortgages Mortgages can be classified according to whether the borrower meets the traditional lending standards. Borrowers who obtain "prime" mortgages satisfy the traditional lending standards. "Subprime" mortgages are offered to borrowers who do not qualify for prime loans because they have relatively lower income or high existing debt, or can make only a small down payment. In recent years, especially between 2003 and 2005, many financial institutions such as mortgage companies increased their offerings of subprime loans as a way of expanding their business. In addition, they could charge higher fees (such as appraisal fees) and higher interest rates on the mortgages to compensate for the risk of default. Subprime mortgage rates were commonly 1.5 to 2.5 percentage points above the rates of prime mortgages. Although subprime mortgages enabled some people to purchase homes who otherwise could not have, these mortgages were very susceptible to default. The large number of defaults of subprime mortgages led to the credit crisis that began in 2008, as explained later in this chapter.

Mortgages referred to as Alt-A typically satisfy some but not all of the criteria for prime mortgages. Thus Alt-A mortgages are generally perceived to have more risk of default than prime loans but less risk of default than subprime loans.

Insured versus Conventional Mortgages Mortgages are also often classified as federally insured or conventional. Federally insured mortgages guarantee loan repayment to the lending financial institution, thereby protecting it against the possibility of default by the borrower. An insurance fee of 0.5 percent of the loan amount is applied to cover the cost of insuring the mortgage. The guarantor can be either the Federal Housing

Administration (FHA) or the Veterans Administration (VA). To qualify for FHA and VA mortgage loans from a financial institution, borrowers must meet various requirements specified by those government agencies. In addition, the maximum mortgage amount is limited by law (although the limit varies among states to account for differences in the cost of housing). The volume of FHA loans has consistently exceeded that of VA loans since 1960. Both types of mortgages have become increasingly popular over the past 30 years.

Financial institutions also provide conventional mortgages. Although not federally insured, they can be privately insured so that the lending financial institutions can still avoid exposure to credit risk. The insurance premium paid for such private insurance will likely be passed on to the borrowers. Lenders can choose to incur the credit risk themselves and avoid the insurance fee. Some participants in the secondary mortgage market purchase only those conventional mortgages that are privately insured (unless the mortgage's loan-to-value ratio is less than 80 percent).

9-2 Types of Residential Mortgages

Various types of residential mortgages are available to homeowners, including the following:

WEB

www.bloomberg.com/
markets/rates/
keyrates.html
Provides quotes on
mortgage rates.

- Fixed-rate mortgages
- Adjustable-rate mortgages
- Graduated-payment mortgages
- Growing-equity mortgages
- Second mortgages
- Shared-appreciation mortgages
- Balloon-payment mortgages

9-2a Fixed-Rate Mortgages

WEB

www.bloomberg.com/
invest/calculators/
index.html
Calculates monthly
mortgage payments
based on the type of
mortgage, the loan
amount, the maturity,
and the interest rate.

One of the most important provisions in the mortgage contract is the interest rate. It can be specified as a fixed rate or can allow for periodic rate adjustments over time. A **fixed-rate mortgage** locks in the borrower's interest rate over the life of the mortgage. Thus the periodic interest payment received by the lending financial institution is constant, regardless of how market interest rates change over time. A financial institution that holds fixed-rate mortgages in its asset portfolio is exposed to interest rate risk because it commonly uses funds obtained from short-term customer deposits to make long-term mortgage loans. If interest rates increase over time, the financial institution's cost of obtaining funds (from deposits) will increase. The return on its fixed-rate mortgage loans will be unaffected, however, causing its profit margin to decrease.

Borrowers with fixed-rate mortgages do not suffer from the effects of rising interest rates, but they also fail to benefit from declining rates. Although they can attempt to refinance (obtain a new mortgage to replace the existing mortgage) at the lower prevailing market interest rate, they will incur transaction costs such as closing costs and an origination fee.

Amortizing Fixed-Rate Mortgages Given the maturity and interest rate on a fixed-rate mortgage, an **amortization schedule** can be developed to show the monthly payments broken down into principal and interest. During the early years of a mortgage, most of the payment reflects interest. Over time, as some of the principal is paid off, the interest proportion decreases.

Exhibit 9.3   Example of Amortization Schedule for Selected Years (Based on a 30-Year, $100,000 Mortgage at 8 Percent)

PAYMENT NUMBER	PAYMENT OF INTEREST	PAYMENT OF PRINCIPAL	TOTAL PAYMENT	REMAINING LOAN BALANCE
1	$666.66	$ 67.10	$733.76	$99,932.90
2	666.21	67.55	733.76	99,865.35
100	604.22	129.54	733.76	90,504.68
101	603.36	130.40	733.76	90,374.28
200	482.01	251.75	733.76	72,051.18
201	480.34	253.42	733.76	71,797.76
300	244.52	489.24	733.76	36,188.12
301	241.25	492.51	733.76	35,695.61
359	9.68	724.08	733.76	728.91
360	4.85	728.91	733.76	0

The lending institution that holds a fixed-rate mortgage will receive equal periodic payments over a specified period of time. The amount depends on the principal amount of the mortgage, the interest rate, and the maturity. If insurance and taxes are included in the mortgage payment then they, too, influence the amount.

Consider a 30-year (360-month) $100,000 mortgage at an annual interest rate of 8 percent. To focus on the mortgage principal and interest payments, insurance and taxes are not included in this example. A breakdown of the monthly payments into principal versus interest is shown in Exhibit 9.3. In the first month, the interest payment is $666.66 while the principal payment is only $67.10. Observe that a larger proportion of interest is paid in the earlier years and a larger portion of principal in the later years. Website calculators are widely available to determine the amortization schedule for any type of mortgage.

An amortization schedule can also be used to compare monthly payments required on a 30-year mortgage versus a 15-year mortgage.

EXAMPLE   A 30-year, $100,000 mortgage at 8 percent requires monthly payments (excluding taxes and insurance) of approximately $734. The same mortgage for 15 years would require monthly payments of $956. Total payments for the 30-year loan would be $264,155, versus $172,017 for the 15-year mortgage. Total payments are lower on mortgages with shorter lives because of the more rapid amortization and lower cumulative interest. ●

For the financial institutions that provide mortgages, 15-year mortgages are subject to less interest rate risk than 30-year mortgages because of the shorter term to maturity.

9-2b Adjustable-Rate Mortgages

An **adjustable-rate mortgage (ARM)** allows the mortgage interest rate to adjust to market conditions. Its contract will specify a precise formula for this adjustment. The formula and the frequency of adjustment can vary among mortgage contracts. A common ARM uses a one-year adjustment with the interest rate tied to the average Treasury bill rate over the previous year (for example, the average T-bill rate plus 2 percent may be specified).

Some ARMs now contain an option clause that allows mortgage holders to switch to a fixed rate within a specified period, such as one to five years after the mortgage is originated (the specific provisions vary).

Exhibit 9.4 shows the rate charged on newly originated fixed-rate and adjustable-rate mortgages over time. Notice that the fixed rate is typically higher than the adjustable rate at any given time when a mortgage is originated. Home buyers attempt to assess future interest rate movements at the time a mortgage is originated. If they expect that interest rates will remain somewhat stable or decline during the period they will own the property, they will choose an ARM. Conversely, if they expect that interest rates will increase substantially over time, they will prefer a fixed-rate mortgage.

ARMs from the Financial Institution's Perspective   Because the interest rate of an ARM moves with prevailing interest rates, financial institutions can stabilize their profit margin. If their cost of funds rises, so does their return on mortgage loans. For this reason, ARMs have become very popular over time.

Most ARMs specify a maximum allowable fluctuation in the mortgage rate per year and over the mortgage life, regardless of what happens to market interest rates. These caps are commonly 2 percent per year and 5 percent for the mortgage's lifetime. To the extent that market interest rates move outside these boundaries, the financial institution's profit margin on ARMs could be affected by interest rate fluctuations. Nevertheless, this interest rate risk is significantly less than that of fixed-rate mortgages.

Exhibit 9.4   Comparison of Rates on Newly Originated Fixed-Rate and Adjustable-Rate Mortgages over Time

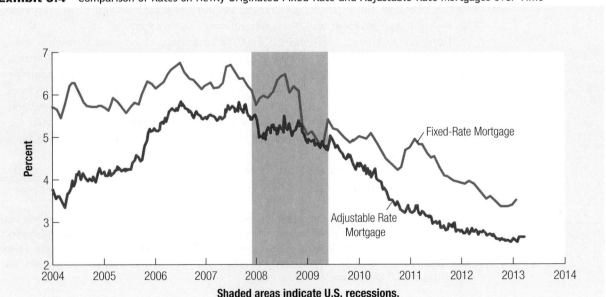

Source: *Federal Reserve.*

9-2c Graduated-Payment Mortgages

A **graduated-payment mortgage (GPM)** allows the borrower to make small payments initially on the mortgage; the payments increase on a graduated basis over the first 5 to 10 years and then level off. This type of mortgage is tailored for families who anticipate higher income (and thus the ability to make larger monthly mortgage payments) as time passes. In a sense, they are delaying part of their mortgage payment.

9-2d Growing-Equity Mortgages

A **growing-equity mortgage** is similar to a GPM in that the monthly payments are initially low and increase over time. Unlike the GPM, however, the payments never level off but continue to increase (typically by about 4 percent per year) throughout the life of the loan. With such an accelerated payment schedule, the entire mortgage may be paid off in 15 years or less.

9-2e Second Mortgages

A **second mortgage** can be used in conjunction with the primary or first mortgage. Some financial institutions may limit the amount of the first mortgage based on the borrower's income. Other financial institutions may then offer a second mortgage with a maturity shorter than that of the first mortgage. In addition, the interest rate on the second mortgage is higher because its priority claim against the property (in the event of default) is behind that of the first mortgage. The higher interest rate reflects greater compensation as a result of the higher risk incurred by the provider of the second mortgage.

Sellers of homes sometimes offer buyers a second mortgage. This practice is especially common when the old mortgage is assumable and the selling price of the home is much higher than the remaining balance on the first mortgage. By offering a second mortgage, the seller can make the house more affordable and therefore more marketable. The seller and the buyer negotiate specific interest rate and maturity terms.

9-2f Shared-Appreciation Mortgages

A **shared-appreciation mortgage** allows a home purchaser to obtain a mortgage at a below-market interest rate. In return, the lender providing the attractive loan rate will share in the price appreciation of the home. The precise percentage of appreciation allocated to the lender is negotiated at the origination of the mortgage.

9-2g Balloon-Payment Mortgages

A **balloon-payment mortgage** requires only interest payments for a three-to five-year period. At the end of this period, the borrower must pay the full amount of the principal (the balloon payment). Because no principal payments are made until maturity, the monthly payments are lower. Realistically, though, most borrowers have not saved enough funds to pay off the mortgage in three to five years, so the balloon payment in effect forces them to request a new mortgage. Therefore, they are subject to the risk that mortgage rates will be higher at the time they refinance the mortgage.

9-3 VALUATION AND RISK OF MORTGAGES

Since mortgages are commonly sold in the secondary market, they are continually valued by institutional investors. The market price (P_M) of a mortgage should equal the present value of its future cash flows:

$$P_M = \sum_{t=1}^{n} \frac{C + \text{Prin}}{(1+k)^t}$$

where C denotes the interest payment (similar to a coupon payment on bonds), Prin the principal payment made each period, and k the required rate of return by investors. As with bonds, the market value of a mortgage is the present value of the future cash flows to be received by the investor. Unlike bonds, however, the periodic cash flows commonly include a payment of principal along with an interest payment.

The required rate of return on a mortgage is primarily determined by the existing risk-free rate for the same maturity. However, other factors such as credit risk and lack of liquidity will cause the required return on many mortgages to exceed the risk-free rate. The difference between the 30-year mortgage rate and the 30-year Treasury bond rate, for example, is due mainly to credit risk and therefore tends to increase during periods when the economy is weak (e.g., during the credit crisis in 2008).

Since the required rate of return on a fixed-rate mortgage is primarily driven by the prevailing risk-free rate (Rf) and the risk premium (RP), the change in the value (and hence in the market price P_M) of a mortgage can be modeled as

$$\Delta P_M = f(\underset{}{\Delta R_f}, \underset{}{\Delta RP})$$

An increase in either the risk-free rate or the risk premium on a fixed-rate mortgage results in a higher required rate of return when investing in the mortgage, which causes the mortgage price to decrease.

9-3a Risk from Investing in Mortgages

Given the uncertainty of the factors that influence mortgage prices, future mortgage prices (and therefore returns) are uncertain. The uncertainty that financial institutions face when investing in mortgages is due to credit risk, interest rate risk, and prepayment risk, as explained next.

Credit Risk   Credit (default) risk represents the size and likelihood of a loss that investors will experience if borrowers make late payments or even default. Whether investors sell their mortgages prior to maturity or hold them until maturity, they are subject to credit risk. Consequently, investors must weigh the higher potential return from investing in mortgages against the exposure to risk (that the actual return could be lower than the expected return). The probability that a borrower will default is influenced both by economic conditions and by the borrower characteristics that lenders consider when assessing a borrower's creditworthiness (level of equity invested by the borrower, the borrower's income level, and the borrower's credit history).

Interest Rate Risk   Financial institutions that hold mortgages are subject to interest rate risk because the values of mortgages tend to decline in response to an increase in interest rates. Mortgages are long term but are commonly financed by some financial institutions with short-term deposits, so the investment in mortgages may create high exposure to interest rate risk. Such mortgages can also generate high returns when interest rates fall, but the potential gains are limited because borrowers tend to refinance (obtain new mortgages at the lower interest rate and prepay their mortgages) when interest rates decline.

When investors hold fixed-rate mortgages until maturity, they do not experience a loss due to a change in interest rates. However, holding fixed-rate mortgages to maturity can create a so-called opportunity cost of what the investors might have earned if they had invested in other securities. For example, if interest rates rise consistently from the time fixed-rate mortgages are purchased until they mature, investors who hold the mortgages to maturity gave up the potential higher return that they would have earned if they had simply invested in money market securities over the same period.

Financial institutions can limit their exposure to interest rate risk by selling mortgages shortly after originating them. However, even institutions that use this strategy are partially exposed to interest rate risk. As a financial institution originates a pool of mortgages, it may commit to a specific fixed rate on some of the mortgages. The mortgages are stored in what is referred to as a *mortgage pipeline* until there is a sufficient pool of mortgages to sell. By the time the complete pool of mortgages is originated and sold, interest rates may have risen. In this case, the value of the mortgages in the pool may have declined by the time the pool is sold.

Another way financial institutions can limit interest rate risk is by offering adjustable-rate residential mortgages. Alternatively, they could invest in fixed-rate mortgages that have a short time remaining until maturity. However, this conservative strategy may reduce the potential gains that could have been earned.

Prepayment Risk **Prepayment risk** is the risk that a borrower may prepay the mortgage in response to a decline in interest rates. This type of risk is distinguished from interest rate risk to emphasize that even if investors in mortgages do not need to liquidate the mortgages, they are still susceptible to the risk that the mortgages they hold will be paid off. In this case, the investor receives a payment to retire the mortgage and must then reinvest at the prevailing (lower) interest rates. Thus the interest rate on the new investment will be lower than the rate that would have been received on the retired mortgages.

Because of prepayments, financial institutions that invest in fixed-rate mortgages may experience only limited benefits in periods when interest rates decline. Although these mortgages offer attractive yields compared to the prevailing low interest rates, they are commonly retired as a result of refinancing. Financial institutions can insulate against prepayment risk in the same manner that they limit exposure to interest rate risk: they can sell loans shortly after originating them or invest in adjustable-rate mortgages.

9-4 MORTGAGE-BACKED SECURITIES

As an alternative to selling their mortgages outright, financial institutions can engage in **securitization**, or the pooling and repackaging of loans into securities called **mortgage-backed securities (MBS)** or **pass-through securities**. These securities are then sold to investors, who become the owners of the loans represented by those securities.

9-4a The Securitization Process

When mortgages are securitized, a financial institution such as a securities firm or commercial bank combine individual mortgages together into packages. Securitization allows the institution to sell mortgage loans in large batches. When several small mortgage loans are packaged together, they become more attractive to the large institutional investors (such as commercial banks, savings institutions, and insurance companies) that focus on large transactions. The issuer of the MBS assigns a trustee to hold the mortgages as collateral for the investors who purchase the securities. After the securities are sold, the financial institution that issued the MBS receives interest and principal payments on the mortgages and then transfers (passes through) the payments to investors that purchased the securities. The financial institution deducts a fee for servicing these mortgages.

9-4b Types of Mortgage-Backed Securities

Five of the more common types of mortgage-backed securities are the following:

- GNMA (Ginnie Mae) mortgage-backed securities
- Private-label pass-through securities

■ FNMA (Fannie Mae) mortgage-backed securities
■ FHLMC participation certificates
■ Collateralized mortgage obligations (CMOs)

Each type is described in turn.

GNMA Mortgage-Backed Securities   The Government National Mortgage Association (called GNMA, or Ginnie Mae) was created in 1968 as a corporation that is wholly owned by the federal government. When mortgages are backed by FHA and VA mortgages, Ginnie Mae guarantees timely payment of principal and interest to investors who purchase these securities. The mortgages must satisfy specific guidelines. They are restricted to a maximum dollar amount (that changes over time), since they are intended to serve low- and moderate-income homeowners. The financial institutions that originate mortgages with the Ginnie Mae guarantee can more easily sell the mortgages in the secondary market, because the institutional investors do not have to worry about credit risk. Thus institutional investors are more willing to invest in MBS that incorporate Ginnie Mae's guarantee, which results in a more active secondary market for mortgages.

Private Label Pass-Through Securities   Private label pass-through securities are similar to Ginnie Mae mortgage-backed securities except that they are backed by conventional rather than FHA or VA mortgages. The mortgages backing the securities are insured through private insurance companies.

FNMA Mortgage-Backed Securities   The Federal National Mortgage Association (called FNMA, or Fannie Mae) was created by the government in 1938 to develop a more liquid secondary market for mortgages. It issues long-term debt securities to institutional investors and uses the funds to purchase mortgages in the secondary market. In essence, Fannie Mae channels funds from institutional investors to financial institutions that desire to sell their mortgages. These financial institutions may continue to service the mortgages and earn a fee for this service. The mortgage payments on mortgages backing these securities are sent to the financial institutions that service the mortgages. The payments are channeled through to the purchasers of MBS, which may be collateralized by conventional or federally insured mortgages.

WEB

http://mtgprofessor.
com/secondary_
markets.htm
Detailed information on
the secondary mort-
gage markets.

FHLMA Participation Certificates   The Federal Home Loan Mortgage Association (called FHLMA or Freddie Mac) was chartered as a corporation by the federal government in 1970 to ensure that sufficient funds flow into the mortgage market. It went public in 1989. It sells **participation certificates (PCs)** and uses the proceeds to finance the origination of conventional mortgages from financial institutions. This provides another outlet for financial institutions that desire to sell their conventional mortgages in the secondary market.

Fannie Mae and Freddie Mac enhance liquidity in the mortgage market, as illustrated in Exhibit 9.5. The proceeds received from selling securities are channeled to purchase mortgages in the secondary market from mortgage originators. As a result of Fannie Mae and Freddie Mac, the secondary mortgage market is more liquid than it otherwise would be. In addition, originators of the mortgages can originate more mortgages because they are not forced to finance the mortgages on their own. Because the mortgage market is more liquid, mortgage rates are more competitive and housing is more affordable for some homeowners.

Collateralized Mortgage Obligations   **Collateralized mortgage obligations (CMOs)** represent a type of MBS in which the underlying mortgages are segmented

Exhibit 9.5 How Fannie Mae and Freddie Mac Enhance Liquidity in the Mortgage Market

into tranches (classes), according to their maturity, and the cash flows provided by each tranche are typically structured in a sequential manner. In this way, the timing of the cash flows generated by a particular tranche are more predictable. The first tranche has the quickest payback. Any repaid principal is initially sent to owners of the first-tranche CMOs until the total principal amount representing that tranche is fully repaid. Then any further principal payments are sent to owners of the second-tranche CMOs until the total principal amount representing that tranche is fully repaid. This process continues until principal payments are made to owners of the last-tranche CMOs. Issues of CMOs typically have from three to ten tranches.

The CMOs are sometimes segmented into *interest-only* (IO) and *principal-only* (PO) tranches. Investors in interest-only CMOs receive only interest payments that are paid on the underlying mortgages. When mortgages are prepaid, the interest payments on the underlying mortgages are terminated, and so are payments to investors in interest-only CMOs. For example, mortgage prepayments may cut off the interest rate payments on the CMO after a few years, even though these payments were initially expected to last five years or more. Consequently, investors in these CMOs could lose 50 percent or more of their initial investment. The relatively high yields offered on interest-only CMOs are attributable to their high degree of risk.

Because investors in the principal-only CMO receive principal payments only, they generally receive payments further into the future. Even though the payments to these investors represent principal, the maturity is uncertain owing to possible prepayment of the underlying mortgages.

Some mortgages are also sold through a **collateralized debt obligation (CDO)**, which is a package of debt securities backed by collateral that is sold to investors. A CDO differs from a CMO in that it also contains some other, nonmortgage types of debt securities (e.g., automobile loans and credit card loans). Collateralized debt obligations became popular in the late 1990s and, by 2007, the value of CDOs issued was about $500 billion.

Like CMOs, CDOs can be separated into tranches based on risk. On average, MBS represent about 45 percent of a CDO, but the percentage may be as low as zero or as high as about 90 percent. The mortgages that are included in CDOs are commonly subprime mortgages. When economic conditions weaken, there are more mortgage defaults and so the riskiest tranches of a CDO may suffer major losses. Even highly rated tranches are subject to losses in such periods. Tranches assigned a AAA rating by rating agencies had a risk premium (above the risk-free Treasury bond rate) of close to zero in 2005 as compared with a risk premium of 5 percent in 2008. This significant increase in the premium reflected the additional compensation that investors required when the housing market collapsed in 2008.

When CMO and CDO values deteriorate, financial institutions have more difficulty selling mortgages that they originate. Thus the activity in the CMO and CDO market influences the volume of funds available to finance new mortgages.

9-4c Valuation of Mortgage-Backed Securities

The valuation of MBS is difficult because of the limited transparency. Although there is a secondary market for mortgage-backed securities, it is not very active in some periods. There is no centralized reporting system that reports the trading of MBS in the secondary market, as there is for other securities such as stocks and Treasury bonds. The only participants who know the price of the securities that were traded are the buyer and the seller. Given the lack of a centralized reporting system, it is quite possible that a financial institution may overpay when buying MBS.

Reliance on Ratings to Assess Value   When deciding whether to purchase MBS, institutional investors may rely on rating agencies (Moody's, Standard & Poor's, or Fitch) rather than attempt to conduct their own valuation. An agency is hired by the issuer of the securities to assign ratings to the MBS that it plans to sell. The financial institutions that create MBS pay a fee to rating agencies to assign a rating to their MBS. Many institutional investors will not purchase MBS unless they are rated high. However, many of the MBS that were highly rated still suffered major losses during the credit crisis.

Fair Value of Mortgage-Backed Securities   When financial institutions believe that they will incur a loss on MBS (or any other long-term assets), they are expected to "write down" the value to reflect its true market value (also called its "fair value"). In doing so, they may attempt to rely on prices of MBS that are traded in the secondary market in order to determine the market value of the MBS they are holding. However, MBS can vary substantially in terms of risk, so that mortgage-backed securities at a particular financial institution may warrant a much higher (or lower) valuation than those recently traded in the secondary market. Furthermore, when the secondary market for MBS is not active (such as during the credit crisis, when investors were no longer willing to buy them), there is insufficient market information to derive a market value.

9-5 MORTGAGE CREDIT CRISIS

In the 2003–2006 period, low interest rates and favorable economic conditions stimulated the demand for new homes. The market values of homes increased substantially, and many institutional investors used funds to invest in mortgages or mortgage-backed securities. Home builders responded to the favorable housing conditions by building more homes. Furthermore, many lenders were so confident that home prices would continue to rise that they reduced the down payment (equity investment) that they required from home buyers. The lenders assumed that, even if the home buyers defaulted on the loan, the home's value would serve as sufficient collateral.

In 2006, however, some prospective buyers were less willing to purchase homes because of the abrupt increase in home prices during 2005. Suddenly, the demand for new homes was less than the supply of new and existing homes for sale, and housing prices declined. Along with these conditions, interest rates increased in 2006, which made it more difficult for existing homeowners with adjustable-rate mortgages to make their mortgage payments. In addition, mortgage companies had previously offered mortgages with low initial rates for the first few years. Now these "teaser rates" were expiring on homes that were recently purchased, and these homeowners also faced higher mortgage payments. Consequently, mortgage defaults increased. Because the market values of homes had declined substantially in some areas, in many cases the collateral backing the mortgage was not sufficient to recapture the entire mortgage amount. Even some mortgages that were insured against default by private insurers defaulted because some insurance companies that insured mortgages did not have adequate funds to cover their obligations.

As economic conditions weakened further, mortgage defaults continued to increase. By June 2008, 9 percent of all American homeowners were either behind on their mortgage payments or were in foreclosure. The defaults were much higher on subprime mortgages than on prime mortgages. In 2008, about 25 percent of all outstanding subprime mortgages had late payments of at least 30 days, versus fewer than 5 percent for prime mortgages. In addition, about 10 percent of outstanding subprime mortgages were subject to foreclosure in 2008, versus fewer than 3 percent for prime mortgages. Some mortgages that were supposed to be backed by insurance were not. Furthermore, while many mortgages were backed by insurance, some private insurers went bankrupt—exposing the institutional investors holding the mortgages to major losses.

9-5a Impact of the Credit Crisis on Fannie Mae and Freddie Mac

As of 2007, Fannie Mae held about $47 billion in subprime mortgages and/or securities backed by these mortgages, while Freddie Mac held about $124 billion in such securities. Although these companies were chartered by the federal government to provide liquidity to the mortgage market, the compensation of their executives was tied to the companies' performance, which led to risk taking. They had reduced their standards in order to attempt to maintain their market share when investing in mortgages. This is an example of a *moral hazard* problem, which occurs when a person or institution does not have to bear the full consequences of its behavior and therefore assumes more risk than it otherwise would. In this case, the executives could take risks knowing that they would benefit if their gambles paid off and that the government would likely bail them out if the gambles failed.

Fannie Mae and Freddie Mac invested heavily in subprime mortgages that required homeowners to pay higher rates of interest. By 2008, many subprime mortgages defaulted, so Fannie Mae and Freddie Mac were left with properties (the collateral) that had a market value substantially below the amount owed on the mortgages that they held. Fannie Mae and Freddie Mac attempted "workouts" in some cases, whereby they renegotiated the terms of mortgage contracts or arranged additional financing for homeowners in order to help them avoid foreclosures. Some of the mortgages that Fannie Mae and Freddie Mac purchased from commercial banks and other mortgage originators misrepresented the qualifications of the homeowners.

By the summer of 2008, Fannie Mae and Freddie Mac owned or guaranteed more than $5 trillion of U.S. home mortgages, or about half the value of all outstanding mortgages in the United States. In August 2008, Fannie Mae and Freddie Mac reported losses of more than $14 billion over the previous year. At that time, they held about $84 billion in capital, which represented less than 2 percent of all the mortgages that they held. This was a very small cushion to cover possible losses on their mortgages.

Funding Problems   Because of their poor financial performance, Fannie Mae and Freddie Mac were incapable of raising capital to improve their financial position or to continue their role of supporting the housing market. Their stock values had declined by more than 90 percent from the previous year, so issuing new equity to obtain funds was not a feasible solution. The yield offered on Fannie Mae and Freddie Mac debt securities was 2.5 percent higher than that of Treasury securities with a similar maturity, which reflected the large risk premium that investors were requiring in order to invest in these securities. Thus the cost of debt to Fannie Mae and Freddie Mac was extremely high because investors feared that these agencies might not be able to repay their debt. Their cost of debt would have been even higher if investors had not presumed that the government would bail out the two companies if necessary.

Rescue of Fannie Mae and Freddie Mac   In September 2008, the U.S. government took over the management of Fannie Mae and Freddie Mac. Their regulator, the Federal Housing Finance Agency, became responsible for managing them until they are determined to be financially healthy. The CEOs of both companies were removed from their positions, but they left with compensation packages that many critics would say were very forgiving. In the previous year, Fannie Mae's CEO received income of $11.6 million and Freddie Mac's CEO received $19.8 million.

The Treasury agreed to provide whatever funding would be necessary to cushion losses from the mortgage defaults. In return, the Treasury received $1 billion of preferred stock in each of the two companies. This arrangement gave Congress time to determine whether and how these companies should be structured in the future. Congress could also establish guidelines that would restrict them from investing in risky mortgages that do not meet specific standards.

The U.S. government rescue of Fannie Mae and Freddie Mac removed the risk of their debt securities defaulting and therefore increased the values of these debt securities. It allowed Fannie Mae and Freddie Mac to obtain funds by issuing debt securities so that they could resume purchasing mortgages and thereby ensure a more liquid secondary market for them.

9-5b Systemic Risk Due to the Credit Crisis

The impact of the credit crisis extends far beyond the homeowners who lost their homes and the financial institutions that lost money on their mortgage investments. Mortgage insurers that provided insurance to homeowners incurred large expenses from many foreclosures because the property collateral was worth less than the amount owed on the mortgage. In this way, the problems of the mortgage sector affected the insurance industry. In addition, some insurance companies that sold credit default swaps on mortgages suffered heavy losses.

As mortgages defaulted, the valuations of mortgage-backed securities (MBS) weakened. Consequently, financial institutions were no longer able to use MBS as collateral when borrowing funds from lenders. The lenders could not trust that the MBS would constitute adequate collateral if the financial institutions that borrowed funds were unable to repay their loans. As a result, some financial institutions (such as Bear Stearns) with large investments in MBS were no longer able to access sufficient funds to support their operations during the credit crisis. Moreover, they could not sell their MBS in the secondary market to obtain cash because by this time there were few investors willing to purchase MBS in the secondary market.

Individual investors whose investments were pooled (by mutual funds, hedge funds, and pension funds) and then used to purchase MBS experienced losses, as did investors who purchased stocks of financial institutions. Several financial institutions went bankrupt, and many employees of financial institutions lost their jobs. Home builders also went bankrupt, and many employees in the home building industry lost their jobs, too. The losses on investments and layoffs contributed to a weaker economy, which made the crisis worse.

The concerns about MBS also spread to other types of debt securities, including corporate bonds. When investors fully recognized the risk associated with MBS during 2008, they no longer considered MBS as adequate collateral to back commercial paper. Consequently, some financial institutions were no longer able to issue commercial paper unless they had better forms of collateral. This paralyzed the commercial paper market, and forced financial institutions to seek alternative markets to obtain short-term funding.

GLOBAL
ASPECTS

International Systemic Risk Although much of the credit crisis was focused on the United States, the problems were contagious to international financial markets as well. Financial institutions in other countries (e.g., the United Kingdom) had offered subprime loans, and they also experienced high delinquency and default rates. In addition, some financial institutions based in foreign countries were common purchasers of subprime mortgages that originated in the United States. Many institutional investors in Asia and Europe had purchased MBS and CDOs that contained subprime mortgages originated in the United States. For example, UBS (a large Swiss bank) incurred a loss of $35 billion from its positions in MBS. Such problems contributed to weaker economies around the world.

9-5c Who Is to Blame?

The credit crisis illustrated some important problems in the mortgage markets. Various participants in the process of mortgage financing were subjected to criticism, as explained next.

Mortgage Originators The mortgage companies and other financial institutions that originate mortgages are supposed to assess the creditworthiness of prospective homeowners. During the housing boom in the 2003–2005 period, however, some mortgage originators were aggressively seeking new business without exercising adequate control over quality. In some cases, they approved loans without even verifying the prospective buyer's income. As described earlier, they also reduced the required down payment because they incorrectly presumed that home prices would not decrease and that the property would therefore be sufficient collateral in the event of default.

Credit Rating Agencies As described earlier, the mortgage-backed securities that are issued by securities firms and financial institutions are assigned credit ratings by credit rating agencies. The rating agencies, which are paid by the issuers that want their MBS rated, were criticized for being too lenient in their ratings shortly before the credit crisis. Mortgage-backed securities were commonly rated AAA even though they represented risky mortgages. Some mortgage-backed securities were rated based on an assessment of the *mean* (average) of the underlying mortgages, which ignores information about the *distribution* of mortgages. Thus an MBS could be rated high as long as some of its constituent mortgages were rated high enough to offset those that were rated low. A large proportion of the mortgage-backed securities that were issued in 2006 and backed by subprime mortgages were either in default or rated at the lowest level by 2010.

According to the Securities and Exchange Commission, many MBS and CDO tranches were overrated for the following reasons. First, credit rating agencies were understaffed and did not perform thorough analyses. Second, credit rating agencies did not monitor the performance of the tranches over time and so did not detect deterioration in existing tranches. Third, some analysts at rating agencies were motivated to assign a high rating because the issuing firms could more easily sell highly rated tranches and would therefore be more likely to hire the same agencies to rate future tranches. A credit rating agency typically receives a fee of between $300,000 and $500,000 from the issuer for rating a package of mortgages. By assigning high ratings to mortgage-backed securities, a credit rating agency attracts future business from financial institutions that want to issue MBS and need to have the securities certified with a high rating.

Publicized results of investigations of credit rating agencies documented that some analysts at credit rating agencies apparently understood that there were problems with their ratings. For example, a manager at one agency sent an e-mail to his co-workers saying that assigning high ratings to tranches of MBS was like building a house of cards that would inevitably fall. As another example, an e-mail message from a rating agency's analyst stated that the rating model used by the agency to assess risk did not capture even half of the risk involved.

The credit ratings come with a disclaimer in small print that says investors should not rely on the credit rating to make investment decisions. Nevertheless, investors who suffered major losses on their MBS investments might well ask why credit rating agencies are hired to assign ratings if it is not to determine the risk of the MBS.

Financial Institutions That Packaged the MBS

Securities firms, commercial banks, and other financial institutions that packaged the mortgage-backed securities could have verified the credit ratings assigned by the credit rating agencies by making their own assessment of the risks involved. After all, such financial institutions have considerable experience in assessing credit quality. Yet they relied on the high ratings assigned by the rating agencies, or presumed that households would continue to make their mortgage payments, or simply assumed that the real estate would serve as adequate collateral if households could not make payments.

Institutional Investors That Purchased MBS

Many financial institutions pooled money that they received from individual investors and used the proceeds to invest in MBS. These institutions could have conducted their own assessment of the credit quality of the MBS, since they also have experience in assessing credit quality. Once again, however, it appears that they relied heavily on the ratings assigned to MBS by credit rating agencies without the due diligence of performing their own independent assessment.

Financial Institutions That Insured MBS

Insurance companies also insured mortgages that backed securities sold in securitizations. MBS that contained insured mortgages provided a slightly lower return to investors (to reflect the fee paid to insurers) but would be viewed as safe and would be easier to sell to investors. Yet, as many MBS defaults occurred, some insurance companies found that the mortgages they insured were fraudulent because of inaccurate information that hid the potential default risk. Thus the financial institution that originated the mortgage was at fault because the mortgage contracts were fraudulent.

Speculators of Credit Default Swaps

A credit default swap (CDS) is a privately negotiated contract that protects investors against the risk of default on particular debt securities such as MBS. The buyer of the CDS provides periodic (usually quarterly) payments to the other party, and the seller of the CDS is obligated to provide a payment in the case of default of the securities specified in the swap agreement.

Although the CDS contracts could be purchased by financial institutions to protect (or hedge) against a possible decline in valuations of mortgages held, they were commonly purchased in 2006 by institutions that were betting on the potential demise of specific mortgages. For example, some financial institutions believed that the MBS containing subprime mortgages were much riskier than perceived by credit rating agencies and other institutional investors. They were able to purchase CDS contracts from other financial institutions (sellers of CDS contracts) at a low price because those sellers presumed, incorrectly, that the MBS would not default. Thus, many of the buyers of CDS contracts on MBS were not holding any mortgages of MBS that they needed to hedge and instead were simply betting that subprime mortgages within the MBS would default. By purchasing CDS contracts, they were "insured" against the defaults on specific pools of mortgages even though they did hold the mortgages that defaulted.

Speculators of credit default swaps were criticized for capitalizing on the collapse of the mortgage market. Yet those speculators may counter that if the sellers of CDS contracts were not so greedy to do business in this market and more properly assessed the risk that they assumed when selling the contracts, the speculators would not have been so willing to take the other side of the CDS contracts.

Conclusion about Blame   The question of who is to blame is still being argued in courtrooms. Participants in the MBS market have filed hundreds of lawsuits claiming that there was a lack of disclosure about the risk of the MBS. Some mortgage companies that originated the mortgages are being sued by securities firms that packaged the mortgages because the mortgages did not fully disclose information to reflect the risk of the home buyers. Mortgage insurers sued mortgage originators for the same reason. In particular, there was a large court battle between MBIA (a large mortgage insurance company) and Countrywide Financial (a large mortgage company) in 2012. The securities firms that sold MBS are being sued by the financial institutions that purchased the MBS. Finally, the individuals whose money was used to purchase the MBS are suing the financial institutions that made investments in the MBS because the investments were not suitable because of their excessive risk.

9-5d Government Programs Implemented in Response to the Crisis

In an effort to stimulate the market for homes and mortgages and reduce the number of foreclosures, the U.S. government implemented various programs. The Housing and Economic Recovery Act of 2008 was passed in July 2008. The act enabled some homeowners to keep their existing homes and therefore reduced the excess supply of homes for sale in the market. The financial institutions must be willing to create a new mortgage that is no more than 90 percent of the present appraised home value. Since the mortgage value exceeds the home value for many of the qualified homeowners, financial institutions that volunteer for the program essentially forgive a portion of the previous mortgage loan when creating a new mortgage.

Other programs promoted "short sale" transactions in which the lender allows homeowners to sell the home for less than what is owed on the existing mortgage. The lender appraises the home and informs the homeowner of the price it is willing to accept on the home. Lenders involved in this program do not recover the full amount owed on the mortgage. However, they may minimize their losses because they do not have to go through the foreclosure process, and the homeowners reduce the potential damage to their credit report.

9-5e Government Bailout of Financial Institutions

As the credit crisis intensified, many investors were unwilling to invest in mortgage-backed securities because of the risk of continued defaults. Thus financial institutions that had large holdings of MBS could not easily sell them in the secondary market. On October 3, 2008, the Emergency Economic Stabilization Act of 2008 (also referred to as the bailout act) enabled the Treasury to inject $700 billion into the financial system and improve the liquidity of these financial institutions. A key part of the act was the Troubled Asset Relief Program (TARP), which allows the Treasury to purchase MBS from financial institutions and thereby provide them with more cash. A key challenge of this activity has been to determine the proper price at which the securities should be purchased, since the secondary market for the securities is not sufficiently active to determine appropriate market prices. The act also allowed the Treasury to invest in the large commercial banks as a means of providing the banks with capital to cushion their losses.

The original proposal for the act was contained in three pages, but by the time the act was passed, it was 451 pages long. Although the initial intent was to resolve the credit crisis, the final act contained many other provisions unrelated to the crisis: tax breaks for producers of rum in the Virgin Islands, racetrack owners, film producers, and alternative energy producers. These additional provisions were included to satisfy special interests of various House and Senate members and win their approval for the act.

9-5f Financial Reform Act

FINANCIAL REFORM

In July 2010 the Dodd-Frank Wall Street Reform and Consumer Protection Act (also called Financial Reform Act) was implemented; one of its main goals was to ensure stability in the financial system. This act mandated that financial institutions granting mortgages verify the income, job status, and credit history of mortgage applicants before approving mortgage applications. The goal was to prevent the looser standards that were instrumental in the credit crisis of 2008.

The Financial Reform Act called for the creation of the Financial Stability Oversight Council to identify risks of the financial system and to make regulatory recommendations that could reduce those risks. The council consists of 10 members representing the heads of agencies that regulate key components of the financial system, including the housing industry, securities trading, depository institutions, mutual funds, and insurance companies.

The act also required that financial institutions that sell mortgage-backed securities retain 5 percent of the portfolio unless the portfolio meets specific standards that reflect low risk. This provision forces financial institutions to maintain a stake in the mortgage portfolios that they sell. The act requires more disclosure regarding the quality of the underlying assets when mortgage-backed securities are sold.

It also requires new rules intended to ensure that credit rating agencies provide unbiased assessments when rating mortgage-backed securities. Specifically, the credit rating agencies are required to publicly disclose data on assumptions used to derive each credit rating. The agencies are also required to provide an annual report about their internal controls used to ensure an unbiased process of rating securities. The act also prevents the SEC from relying on ratings within its regulations, so that it has to use its own assessment of risk.

Summary

- Residential mortgages can be characterized by whether they are prime or subprime, whether they are federally insured, the type of interest rate used (fixed or floating), and the maturity. Quoted interest rates on mortgages vary at a given point in time, depending on these characteristics.

- Various types of residential mortgages are available, including fixed-rate mortgages, adjustable-rate mortgages, graduated-payment mortgages, growing-equity mortgages, second mortgages, and shared-appreciation mortgages.

- The valuation of a mortgage is the present value of its expected future cash flows, discounted at a discount rate that reflects the uncertainty surrounding the cash flows. A mortgage is subject to credit risk, interest rate risk, and prepayment risk.

- Mortgage-backed securities (MBS) represent packages of mortgages; the payments on those mortgages are passed through to investors. Ginnie Mae provides a guarantee of payments on mortgages that meet specific criteria, and these mortgages can be easily packaged and sold. Fannie Mae and Freddie Mac issue debt securities and purchase mortgages in the secondary market.

- Mortgages were provided without adequate qualification standards (including allowing very low down payments) in the 2003–2006 period. Then a glut in the housing market caused a drastic decline in home prices, with the result that the market values of many homes were lower than the mortgages. Many homeowners defaulted on their mortgages, which led to a credit crisis in the 2008–2009 period. The U.S. government used various strategies to revive the U.S. mortgage market, including an emergency housing recovery act, the rescue of Fannie Mae and Freddie Mac, and a bailout of financial institutions that had heavy investments in mortgages and mortgage-backed securities.

POINT COUNTER-POINT

Is the Trading of Mortgages Similar to the Trading of Corporate Bonds?

Point Yes. In both cases, the issuer's ability to repay the debt is based on income. Both types of debt securities are highly influenced by interest rate movements.

Counter-Point No. The assessment of corporate bonds requires an analysis of the financial statements of the firms that issued the bonds. The assessment of mortgages requires an understanding of the structure of the mortgage market (MBS, CMOs, etc.).

Who Is Correct? Use the Internet to learn more about this issue and then formulate your own opinion.

QUESTIONS AND APPLICATIONS

1. **FHA Mortgages** Distinguish between FHA and conventional mortgages.

2. **Mortgage Rates and Risk** What is the general relationship between mortgage rates and long-term government security rates? Explain how mortgage lenders can be affected by interest rate movements. Also explain how they can insulate against interest rate movements.

3. **ARMs** How does the initial rate on adjustable-rate mortgages (ARMs) differ from the rate on fixed-rate mortgages? Why? Explain how caps on ARMs can affect a financial institution's exposure to interest rate risk.

4. **Mortgage Maturities** Why is the 15-year mortgage attractive to homeowners? Is the interest rate risk to the financial institution higher for a 15-year or a 30-year mortgage? Why?

5. **Balloon-Payment Mortgage** Explain the use of a balloon-payment mortgage. Why might a financial institution prefer to offer this type of mortgage?

6. **Graduated-Payment Mortgage** Describe the graduated-payment mortgage. What type of homeowners would prefer this type of mortgage?

7. **Growing-Equity Mortgage** Describe the growing-equity mortgage. How does it differ from a graduated-payment mortgage?

8. **Second Mortgages** Why are second mortgages offered by some home sellers?

9. **Shared-Appreciation Mortgage** Describe the shared-appreciation mortgage.

10. **Exposure to Interest Rate Movements** Mortgage lenders with fixed-rate mortgages should benefit when interest rates decline, yet research has shown that this favorable impact is dampened. By what?

11. **Mortgage Valuation** Describe the factors that affect mortgage prices.

12. **Selling Mortgages** Explain why some financial institutions prefer to sell the mortgages they originate.

13. **Secondary Market** Compare the secondary market activity for mortgages to the activity for other capital market instruments (such as stocks and bonds). Provide a general explanation for the difference in the activity level.

14. **Financing Mortgages** What types of financial institution finance residential mortgages? What type of

financial institution finances the majority of commercial mortgages?

15. Mortgage Companies Explain how a mortgage company's degree of exposure to interest rate risk differs from that of other financial institutions.

Advanced Questions

16. Mortgage-Backed Securities Describe how mortgage-backed securities (MBS) are used.

17. CMOs Describe how collateralized mortgage obligations (CMOs) are used and why they have been popular.

18. Maturities of MBS Explain how the maturity on mortgage-backed securities can be affected by interest rate movements.

19. How Secondary Mortgage Prices May Respond to Prevailing Conditions Consider current conditions that could affect interest rates, including inflation (including oil prices), the economy, the budget deficit, and the Fed's monetary policy. Based on prevailing conditions, do you think the values of mortgages that are sold in the secondary market will increase or decrease during this semester? Offer some logic to support your answer. Which factor do you think will have the biggest impact on the values of existing mortgages?

20. CDOs Explain collateralized debt obligations (CDOs).

21. Motives for Offering Subprime Mortgages Explain subprime mortgages. Why were mortgage companies aggressively offering subprime mortgages?

22. Subprime versus Prime Mortgages How did the repayment of subprime mortgages compare to that of prime mortgages during the credit crisis?

23. MBS Transparency Explain the problems in valuing mortgage-backed securities.

24. Contagion Effects of Credit Crisis Explain how the credit crisis adversely affected many other people beyond homeowners and mortgage companies.

25. Blame for Credit Crisis Many investors that purchased mortgage-backed securities just before the credit crisis believed that they were misled because these securities were riskier than they thought. Who is at fault?

26. Avoiding Another Credit Crisis Do you think that the U.S. financial system will be able to avoid another credit crisis like this in the future?

27. Role of Credit Ratings in Mortgage Market Explain the role of credit rating agencies in facilitating the flow of funds from investors to the mortgage market (through mortgage-backed securities).

28. Fannie and Freddie Problems Explain why Fannie Mae and Freddie Mac experienced mortgage problems.

29. Rescue of Fannie and Freddie Explain why the rescue of Fannie Mae and Freddie Mac improves the ability of mortgage companies to originate mortgages.

30. U.S. Treasury Bailout Plan The U.S. Treasury attempted to resolve the credit crisis by establishing a plan to buy mortgage-backed securities held by financial institutions. Explain how the plan could improve the situation for MBS.

31. Assessing the Risk of MBS Why do you think it is difficult for investors to assess the financial condition of a financial institution that has purchased a large amount of mortgage-backed securities?

32. Mortgage Information during the Credit Crisis Explain why mortgage originators have been criticized for their behavior during the credit crisis. Should other participants in the mortgage securitization process have recognized that lack of complete disclosure in mortgages?

33. Short Sales Explain short sales in the mortgage markets. Are short sales fair to homeowners? Are they fair to mortgage lenders?

34. Government Intervention in Mortgage Markets The government intervened in order to resolve problems in the mortgage markets during the credit crisis. Summarize the advantages and disadvantages of the government intervention during the credit crisis. Should the government intervene when mortgage market conditions are very weak?

35. Dodd-Frank Act and Credit Ratings of MBS Explain how the Dodd-Frank Act of 2010 attempted to prevent biased ratings of mortgage-backed securities by credit rating agencies.

Interpreting Financial News

Interpret the following comments made by Wall Street analysts and portfolio managers.

a. "If interest rates continue to decline, the interest-only CMOs will take a hit."

b. "Estimating the proper value of CMOs is like estimating the proper value of a baseball player; the proper value is much easier to assess five years later."

c. "When purchasing principal-only CMOs, be ready for a bumpy ride."

Managing in Financial Markets

CMO Investment Dilemma As a manager of a savings institution, you must decide whether to invest in collateralized mortgage obligations (CMOs). You can purchase interest-only (IO) or principal-only (PO) classes. You anticipate that economic conditions will weaken in the future and that government spending (and therefore government demand for funds) will decrease.

a. Given your expectations, would IOs or POs be a better investment?

b. Given the situation, is there any reason why you might not purchase the class of CMOs that you selected in the previous question?

c. Your boss suggests that the value of CMOs at any point in time should be the present value of their future payments. He says that since a CMO represents mortgages, its valuation should be simple. Why is your boss wrong?

PROBLEM

Amortization Use an amortization table (such as www. bloomberg.com/invest/calculators/index.html) that determines the monthly mortgage payment based on a specific interest rate and principal with a 15-year maturity and then for a 30-year maturity. Is the monthly payment for the 15-year maturity twice the amount for the 30-year maturity or less than twice the amount? Explain.

FLOW OF FUNDS EXERCISE

Mortgage Financing

Carson Company currently has a mortgage on its office building through a savings institution. It is attempting to determine whether it should convert its mortgage from a floating rate to a fixed rate. Recall that the yield curve is currently upward sloping. Also recall that Carson is concerned about a possible slowing of the economy because of potential Fed actions to reduce inflation. The fixed rate that it would pay if it refinances is higher than the prevailing short-term rate but lower than the rate it would pay from issuing bonds.

a. What macroeconomic factors could affect interest rates and therefore affect the mortgage refinancing decision?

b. If Carson refinances its mortgage, it also must decide on the size of a down payment. If it uses more funds for a larger down payment, it will need to borrow more funds to finance its expansion. Should Carson make a minimum down payment or a larger down payment if it refinances the mortgage? Why?

c. Who is indirectly providing the money that is used by companies such as Carson to purchase office buildings? That is, where does the money that the savings institutions channel into mortgages come from?

INTERNET/EXCEL EXERCISE

Assess a mortgage payment schedule such as http://realestate.yahoo.com/calculators/amortization.html. Assume a loan amount of $120,000, an interest rate of 7.4 percent, and a 30-year maturity. Given this information, what is the monthly payment? In the first month, how much of the monthly payment is interest and how much is principal? What is the outstanding balance after the first year? In the last month of payment, how much of the monthly payment is interest and how much is principal? Why is there such a difference in the composition of the principal versus interest payment over time?

WSJ Exercise

Explaining Mortgage Rate Premiums

Review the "Corporate Borrowing Rates and Yields" table in a recent issue of the *Wall Street Journal* to determine the Treasury bond yield. How do these rates compare to the Fannie Mae yield quoted in the *Journal*'s "Borrowing Benchmarks" section? Why do you think there is a difference between the Fannie Mae rate and Treasury bond yields?

Online Articles with Real-World Examples

Find a recent practical article available online that describes a real-world example regarding a specific financial institution or financial market that reinforces one or more concepts covered in this chapter.

If your class has an online component, your professor may ask you to post your summary of the article there and provide a link to the article so that other students can access it. If your class is live, your professor may ask you to summarize your application of the article in class. Your professor may assign specific students to complete this assignment or may allow any students to do the assignment on a volunteer basis.

For recent online articles and real-world examples related to this chapter, consider using the following search terms (be sure to include the prevailing year as a search term to ensure that the online articles are recent):

1. subprime mortgages AND risk
2. adjustable-rate mortgage AND risk
3. balloon-payment mortgage AND risk
4. mortgage AND credit risk
5. mortgage AND prepayment risk
6. [name of a specific financial institution] AND mortgage
7. credit crisis AND mortgage
8. mortgage-backed securities AND default
9. credit crisis AND Fannie Mae
10. credit crisis AND Freddie Mac

Asset Allocation

This problem requires an understanding of how economic conditions influence interest rates and security prices (Chapters 6, 7, 8, and 9).

As a personal financial planner, one of your tasks is to prescribe the allocation of available funds across money market securities, bonds, and mortgages. Your philosophy is to take positions in securities that will benefit most from your forecasted changes in economic conditions. As a result of a recent event in Singapore, you expect that in the next month investors in Singapore will reduce their investment in U.S. Treasury securities and shift most of their funds into Singapore securities. You expect that this shift in funds will persist for at least a few years. You believe this single event will have a major effect on economic factors in the United States, such as interest rates, exchange rates, and economic growth in the next month. Because the prices of securities in the United States are affected by these economic factors, you must determine how to revise your prescribed allocation of funds across securities.

Questions

1. How will U.S. interest rates be directly affected by the event (holding other factors equal)?

2. How will economic growth in the United States be affected by the event? How might this influence the values of securities?

3. Assume that day-to-day exchange rate movements are dictated primarily by the flow of funds between countries, especially international bond and money market transactions. How will exchange rates be affected by possible changes in the international flow of funds that are caused by the event?

4. Using your answer to (1) only, explain how prices of U.S. money market securities, bonds, and mortgages will be affected.

5. Now use your answer to (2) along with your answer to (1) to assess the impact on security prices. Would prices of risky securities be affected more or less than those of risk-free securities with a similar maturity? Why?

6. Assume that, for diversification purposes, you prescribe that at least 20 percent of an investor's funds should be allocated to money market securities, to bonds, and

to mortgages. This allows you to allocate freely the remaining 40 percent across those same securities. Based on all the information you have about the event, prescribe the proper allocation of funds across the three types of U.S. securities. (Assume that the entire investment will be concentrated in U.S. securities.) Defend your prescription.

7. Would you recommend high-risk or low-risk money market securities? Would you recommend high-risk or low-risk bonds? Why?

8. Assume that you would consider recommending that as much as 20 percent of the funds be invested in foreign debt securities. Revise your prescription to include foreign securities if you desire (identify the type of security and the country).

9. Suppose that, instead of reducing the supply of loanable funds in the United States, the event increased demand for them. Would the assessment of future interest rates be different? What about the general assessment of economic conditions? What about the general assessment of bond prices?

PART 4
Equity Markets

Equity markets facilitate the flow of funds from individual or institutional investors to corporations. Thus, they enable corporations to finance their investments in new or expanded business ventures. They also facilitate the flow of funds between investors. Chapter 10 describes stock offerings and explains how participants in the stock market monitor firms that have publicly traded stock. Chapter 11 explains the valuation of stocks, describes investment strategies involving stocks, and indicates how a stock's performance is measured. Chapter 12 describes the stock market microstructure and explains how orders are placed and executed on stock exchanges.

10

Stock Offerings and Investor Monitoring

Stock markets facilitate equity investment into firms and the transfer of equity investments between investors.

10-1 PRIVATE EQUITY

When a firm is created, its founders typically invest their own money in the business. The founders may also invite some family or friends to invest equity in the business. This is referred to as private equity because the business is privately held and the owners cannot sell their shares to the public. Young businesses use debt financing from financial institutions and are better able to obtain loans if they have substantial equity invested. Over time, businesses commonly retain a large portion of their earnings and reinvest it to support expansion. This serves as another means of building equity in the firm.

The founders of many firms dream of going public someday so that they can obtain a large amount of financing to support the firm's growth. They may also hope to "cash out" by selling their original equity investment to others. Normally, however, a firm's owners do not consider going public until they want to sell at least $50 million in stock. A public offering of stock may be feasible only if the firm will have a large enough shareholder base to support an active secondary market. With an inactive secondary market, the shares would be illiquid. Investors who own shares and want to sell them would be forced to sell at a discount from the fundamental value, almost as if the firm were not publicly traded. This defeats the purpose of being public. In addition, there are many fixed costs associated with going public, and these costs would be prohibitive for a firm that seeks to raise only a small amount of funds.

10-1a Financing by Venture Capital Funds

Even if a firm wants to sell at least $50 million of stock to the public, it may not have a long enough history of stable business performance that it can raise money from a large number of investors. Private firms that need a large equity investment but are not yet in a position to go public may attempt to obtain funding from a venture capital (VC) fund. Such funds receive money from wealthy investors and from pension funds that are willing to maintain the investment for a long-term period, such as 5 or 10 years. These investors are not allowed to withdraw their money before a specified deadline. Venture capital funds have participated in a number of businesses that ultimately went public and became very successful, including Apple, Microsoft, and Oracle Corporation.

Venture Capital Market The venture capital market brings together the private businesses that need equity funding and the VC funds that can provide funding. One way of doing this is through venture capital conferences, where each business briefly makes its pitch as to why it will be successful (and generate high returns to the VC fund) if it receives equity funding. Alternatively, businesses may submit proposals directly to VC funds. If a VC fund identifies a proposal that it believes has much potential, it may arrange a meeting with the business's owners and request more detailed information. Most proposals are rejected, however, since VC funds recognize that the majority of new businesses ultimately fail.

Terms of a Venture Capital Deal   When a VC fund decides to invest in a business, it will negotiate the terms of its investment, including the amount of funds it is willing to invest. It will also set out clear requirements that the firm must meet, such as providing detailed periodic progress reports. When a VC fund invests in a firm, the fund's managers have an incentive to ensure that the business performs well. Thus, the VC fund managers may serve as advisers to the business. They may also insist on having a seat on the board of directors so that they can influence the firm's future progress. The VC fund often provides its funding in stages based on various conditions that the firm must satisfy. In this way, the VC fund's total investment is aligned with the firm's ability to meet specified financial goals.

Exit Strategy of VC Funds   A VC fund typically plans to exit from its original investment within about four to seven years. One common exit strategy is to sell its equity stake to the public after the business engages in a public stock offering. Many VC funds sell their shares of the businesses in which they invest during the first 6 to 24 months after the business goes public. Alternatively, the VC fund may cash out if the company is acquired by another firm, since the acquirer will purchase the shares owned by the VC fund. Thus, the VC fund commonly serves as a bridge for financing the business until it either goes public or is acquired.

Performance of VC Funds   The performance of VC funds tends to vary over time. In periods when stock prices are low, VC funds can invest their money more wisely in companies, and therefore have a better chance of earning decent returns. However, when stock prices are high, VC funds may pay too much when investing in companies.

The performance of VC funds is also influenced by the amount of investment received from investors. In some periods, they might receive more funds from investors than they can feasibly invest, especially if prevailing valuations of companies are high. Under these conditions, they are more likely to compete with each other to buy companies, and the bidding will cause them to pay a higher premium for the company. Conversely, when VC funds receive more limited funds, they can focus only on the most desirable investments, and are less likely to pay too much when investing in companies.

10-1b Financing by Private Equity Funds

Private equity funds pool equity funding provided by institutional investors (such as pension funds and insurance companies) and invest in businesses. They also rely heavily on borrowing to finance their investments. Unlike VC funds, private equity funds commonly take over businesses and manage them. Their managers typically take a percentage of the profits they earn from their investments in return for managing the fund. They pursue companies that are overvalued and mismanaged (in their opinion), because they can more easily achieve a high return on their investment when buying weak firms that they can improve. They also charge an annual fee for managing the fund. Because they commonly purchase a majority stake or all of a business, they have control to restructure the business as they wish. They sell their stake in the business after several years.

If they were able to improve the business substantially while they managed it, they should be able to sell their stake to another firm for a much higher price than what they paid for it. Alternatively, they may be able to take the business public through an initial public offering (IPO) and cash out at that time.

Some critics (including some unions) suggest that private equity firms destroy firms by laying off employees. Yet private equity firms might counter that the firms they target are overstaffed and inefficient, and that they need to restructure these firms to help them survive.

Performance of Private Equity Funds   The performance of private equity firms tends to vary over time. Like VC funds, private equity funds invest their funds more wisely in companies when stock prices are generally low. However, if they invest in companies while stock prices are very high, private equity funds may be subject to large losses (if stock market conditions deteriorate) even if they can improve operations.

Private equity funds may be especially prone to making bad investments when they receive large amounts of funds from investors, and pursue more investments than are feasible. Conversely, when they receive more limited funds, they can more carefully screen their potential targets, and are more likely to make feasible investments.

10-2 PUBLIC EQUITY

When a firm goes public, it issues stock in the primary market in exchange for cash. This changes the firm's ownership structure by increasing the number of owners. It changes the firm's capital structure by increasing the equity investment in the firm, which allows the firm to pay off some of its debt. It also enables corporations to finance their growth.

A stock is a certificate representing partial ownership in the firm. Like debt securities, common stock is issued by firms in the primary market to obtain long-term funds. Yet the purchaser of stock becomes a part owner of the firm, rather than a creditor. This ownership feature attracts many investors who want to have an equity interest in a firm but do not necessarily want to manage their own firm. Owners of stock can benefit from the growth in the value of the firm and therefore have more to gain than creditors. However, they are also susceptible to large losses, as the values of even the most respected corporations have declined substantially in some periods.

The means by which stock markets facilitate the flow of funds are illustrated in Exhibit 10.1. The stock markets are like other financial markets in that they link the surplus units (that have excess funds) with deficit units (that need funds). Stock issued by corporations may be purchased directly by households. Alternatively, households may invest in shares of stock mutual funds; the managers of these funds use the proceeds to invest in stocks. Other institutional investors such as pension funds and insurance companies also purchase stocks. The massive growth in the stock market has enabled many corporations to expand to a much greater degree and has allowed investors to share in the profitability of corporations.

In addition to the primary market, which facilitates new financing for corporations, there is also a secondary market that allows investors to sell the stock they previously purchased to other investors who want to buy it. Thus the secondary market creates liquidity for investors who invest in stocks. In addition to realizing potential gains when they sell their stock, investors may also receive dividends on a quarterly basis from the corporations in which they invest. Some corporations distribute a portion of their earnings to shareholders in the form of dividends, but others reinvest all of their earnings so that they can achieve greater growth.

Exhibit 10.1   How Stock Markets Facilitate the Flow of Funds

10-2a Ownership and Voting Rights

The owners of small companies also tend to be the managers. In publicly traded firms, however, most of the shareholders are not managers. Thus they must rely on the firm's managers to serve as agents and to make decisions in the shareholders' best interests.

The ownership of **common stock** entitles shareholders to a number of rights not available to other individuals. Normally only the owners of common stock are permitted to vote on certain key matters concerning the firm, such as the election of the board of directors, authorization to issue new shares of common stock, approval of amendments to the corporate charter, and adoption of bylaws. Many investors assign their vote to management through the use of a *proxy*, and many other shareholders do not bother to vote. As a result, management normally receives the majority of the votes and can elect its own candidates as directors.

10-2b Preferred Stock

Preferred stock represents an equity interest in a firm that usually does not allow for significant voting rights. Preferred shareholders technically share the ownership of the firm with common shareholders and are therefore compensated only when earnings have been generated. Thus, if the firm does not have sufficient earnings from which to pay the preferred stock dividends, it may omit the dividend without fear of being forced into bankruptcy. A cumulative provision on most preferred stock prevents dividends from being paid on common stock until all preferred stock dividends (both current and those previously omitted) have been paid. The owners of preferred stock normally do not participate in the profits of the firm beyond the stated fixed annual dividend. All profits above those needed to pay dividends on preferred stock belong to the owners of common stock.

Because the dividends on preferred stock can be omitted, a firm assumes less risk when issuing it than when issuing bonds. However, a firm that omits preferred stock dividends may be unable to raise new capital until the omitted dividends have been paid, because investors will be reluctant to make new investments in a firm that is unable to compensate its existing sources of capital.

From a cost perspective, preferred stock is a less desirable source of capital for a firm than bonds. Because a firm is not legally required to pay preferred stock dividends, it must entice investors to assume the risk involved by offering higher dividends. In addition, preferred stock dividends are technically compensation to owners of the firm. Therefore, the dividends paid are not a tax-deductible expense to the firm, whereas interest paid on bonds is tax deductible. Because preferred stock normally has no maturity, it represents a permanent source of financing.

10-2c Participation in Stock Markets

Investors can be classified as individual or institutional. The investment by individuals in a large corporation commonly exceeds 50 percent of the total equity. Each individual's investment is typically small, however, which means that ownership is scattered among numerous individual shareholders.

The various types of institutional investors that participate in the stock markets are summarized in Exhibit 10.2. Because some financial institutions hold large amounts of stock, their collective sales or purchases of stocks can significantly affect stock market prices.

In addition to participating in stock markets by investing funds, financial institutions sometimes issue their own stock as a means of raising funds. Many stock market transactions involve two financial institutions. For example, an insurance company may purchase the newly issued stock of a commercial bank. If the insurance company someday sells this stock in the secondary market, the purchaser may be a mutual fund or pension fund.

Exhibit 10.2   Institutional Use of Stock Markets

TYPE OF FINANCIAL INSTITUTION	PARTICIPATION IN STOCK MARKETS
Commercial banks	• Issue stock to boost their capital base. • Manage trust funds that usually contain stocks.
Stock-owned savings institutions	• Issue stock to boost their capital base.
Savings banks	• Invest in stocks for their investment portfolios.
Finance companies	• Issue stock to boost their capital base.
Stock mutual funds	• Use the proceeds from selling shares to individual investors to invest in stocks.
Securities firms	• Issue stock to boost their capital base. • Place new issues of stock. • Offer advice to corporations that consider acquiring the stock of other companies. • Execute buy and sell stock transactions of investors.
Insurance companies	• Issue stock to boost their capital base. • Invest a large proportion of their premiums in the stock market.
Pension funds	• Invest a large proportion of pension fund contributions in the stock market.

10-2d How Investor Decisions Affect Stock Prices

Investors make decisions to buy a stock when its market price is below their valuation, which means they believe the stock is undervalued. They may sell their holdings of a stock when the market price is above their valuation, which means they believe the stock is overvalued. Thus, stock valuation drives their investment decisions. Investors commonly disagree on how to value a stock (as explained in Chapter 11). Thus some investors may believe a stock is undervalued while others believe it is overvalued. This difference in opinions allows for market trading, because it means that there will be buyers and sellers of the same stock at a given moment in time.

When there is a shift in the demand for shares or the supply of shares for sale, the equilibrium price changes. When investors revise their expectations of a firm's performance upward, they revise their valuations upward. If the consensus among investors is a favorable revision of expected performance, there are more buy orders for the stock. Then the demand for shares exceeds the supply of shares for sale, placing upward pressure on the market price. Conversely, if the consensus among investors is lowered expectations of the firm's future performance, there are more sell orders for the stock. In this case, the supply of shares for sale exceeds the demand for shares, placing downward pressure on the market price. Overall, the prevailing market price is determined by the participation of investors in aggregate. Stock transactions between investors in the secondary market do not affect the capital structure of the issuer; they merely transfer shares from one investor to another.

10-2e Investor Reliance on Information

Investors respond to the release of new information, which affects their opinions about a firm's future performance. In general, favorable news about a firm's performance will make investors believe that the firm's stock is undervalued at its prevailing price. The demand for shares of that stock will increase, placing upward pressure on the stock's price. Unfavorable news about a firm's performance will make investors believe that the firm's stock is overvalued at its prevailing price. Some investors will sell their holdings of that stock, placing downward pressure on the stock's price. Thus, information is incorporated into stock prices through its impact on investors' demand for shares and the supply of shares for sale by investors.

Each stock has its own demand and supply conditions and therefore has a unique market price. Nevertheless, new information about macroeconomic conditions commonly causes expectations for many firms to be revised in the same direction and therefore causes stock prices to move in the same direction.

Investors continually respond to new information in their attempt to purchase stocks that are undervalued or sell their stock holdings that are overvalued. When investors properly determine which stocks are undervalued, they can achieve abnormally high returns from investing in those stocks. Thus, the valuation process used by an investor can have a strong influence on the investor's investment performance.

10-3 Initial Public Offerings

A corporation first decides to issue stock to the public in order to raise funds. It engages in an initial public offering (IPO), which is a first-time offering of shares by a specific firm to the public. An IPO is commonly used not only to obtain new funding but also to offer some founders and VC funds a way to cash out their investment. A typical IPO is for at least $50 million, since this would be the minimum size needed to ensure adequate liquidity in the secondary market if investors wish to sell their shares.

10-3a Process of Going Public

Because firms that engage in an IPO are not well known to investors, they must provide detailed information about their operations and their financial condition. A firm planning on going public normally hires a securities firm that serves as the lead underwriter for the IPO. The lead underwriter is involved in the development of the prospectus and the pricing and placement of the shares.

Developing a Prospectus   A few months before the IPO, the issuing firm (with the help of the lead underwriter) develops a prospectus and files it with the Securities and Exchange Commission (SEC). The prospectus contains detailed information about the firm and includes financial statements and a discussion of the risks involved. It is intended to provide potential investors with the information they need to decide whether to invest in the firm. Within about 30 days, the SEC will assess the prospectus and determine whether it contains all the necessary information. In many cases the SEC, before approving the prospectus, recommends some changes in order to provide more information about the firm's financial condition.

Once the SEC approves the prospectus, it is sent to institutional investors who may want to invest in the IPO. In addition, the firm's management and the underwriters of the IPO meet with institutional investors. Often these meetings occur in the form of a *road show*: the firm's managers travel to various cities and put on a presentation for large institutional investors in each city. The institutional investors are informed of the road show in advance so that they can attend if they have any interest in purchasing shares of the IPO. Some institutional investors may even receive separate individual presentations. Institutional investors are targeted because they may be willing to buy large blocks of shares at the time of the IPO. For this reason, they typically have priority over individual investors in purchasing shares during an IPO.

A law in 2012 loosened the reporting restrictions for smaller firms about to go public. However, most of the firms that could have qualified did not capitalize on the looser requirements, because they wanted to provide investors with as much financial information as possible. They may have attracted more interest from institutional investors by providing more complete information.

Pricing   Before a firm goes public, it attempts to gauge the price that will be paid for its shares. It may rely on the lead underwriter to determine the so-called offer price. The valuation of a firm should equal the present value of the firm's future cash flows. Although the future cash flows are uncertain, the lead underwriter may forecast future cash flows based on the firm's recent earnings.

The offer price also may be influenced by prevailing market and industry conditions. If other publicly traded firms in the same industry are priced high relative to their earnings or sales, then the offer price assigned to shares in the IPO will be relatively high.

During the road show, the lead underwriter solicits indications of interest in the IPO by institutional investors as to the number of shares that they may demand at various possible offer prices. This process is referred to as *bookbuilding*.

EXAMPLE   Saint Louis Company has hired Bucknell Investment Company as lead underwriter for its IPO. Bucknell organizes a road show for a large set of institutional investors that commonly invest in IPO shares. During the road show, managers from St. Louis Company explain the firm's business and how it will use the IPO proceeds. Then Bucknell contacts the investors to request indications of interest. A summary of its findings is provided in Exhibit 10.3. Based on the feedback received, Bucknell decides that an initial offer price of $11 would be appropriate. This price is low enough that it will almost surely result in sufficient demand for 4 million shares, which would provide

Exhibit 10.3   Summary of Bookbuilding Process Just before the IPO

POSSIBLE OFFER PRICE	TOTAL SHARES DEMANDED	TOTAL PROCEEDS TO ISSUER
$13	3,000,000	$39,000,000
$12	3,500,000	$42,000,000
$11	4,000,000	$44,000,000
$10	4,300,000	$43,000,000

$44 million to St. Louis Company. Bucknell is concerned that if it sets the price higher, it might not be able to place all of the shares in the IPO. ●

As a result of the bookbuilding process for setting an offer price, many institutional investors pay a lower price than they would have been willing to pay for the shares. In the preceding example, some institutional investors would have paid $13, but the underwriter used an offer price of $11 for all investors to ensure that at least 4 million shares would be sold. Should the issuing firm be satisfied as long as all the shares are placed? What if St. Louis Company firmly believes that all 4 million shares could have been sold at an offer price of $13 per share? In this case the firm would have received $52 million (4 million shares × $13 per share), but instead received only $44 million. It gave up $8 million because the underwriter sold the shares for a lower price. In finance terminology, this is known as "leaving money on the table." Some issuing firms may be especially concerned that they left money on the table when the market price rises substantially on the day of the IPO, because the price increase may suggest that the demand for shares exceeded the supply of shares for sale on that day. The underwriter might counter that the lower offer price was appropriate because it ensured that all the shares would be sold at the offering. If the stock price rises over time (which means that the IPO investors benefit from their investment), the issuing firm may more easily engage in another stock offering in the future because it has gained investors' trust.

Some critics suggest that setting a lower offer price provides institutional investors with special favors and may be a way for the securities firm that is underwriting the IPO to attract other business from institutional investors. To the extent that the shares were essentially discounted from their appropriate price, the proceeds that the issuing firm receives from the IPO are less than it deserves.

In some other countries, an auction process is used for IPOs and investors pay whatever they bid for the shares. The top bidder's order is accommodated first, followed by the next highest bidder, and so on, until all shares are issued. The issuer can set a minimum price at which the bidding must occur for shares to be issued. This process prevents the underwriter from setting the offer price at a level that is intended to please specific institutional investors.

Allocation of IPO Shares   The lead underwriter may rely on a group (called a *syndicate*) of other securities firms to participate in the underwriting process and share the fees to be received for the underwriting. Each underwriter in the syndicate contacts institutional investors and informs them of the offering. Most of the shares are sold to institutional investors, as it is more convenient for the underwriting syndicate to sell shares in large chunks. Brokerage firms may receive a very small portion (such as 2 percent) of the IPO shares, which they can sell to their individual investors. They normally give priority to their biggest customers.

Transaction Costs   The transaction cost to the issuing firm is usually 7 percent of the funds raised. For example, an IPO of $50 million would result in a transaction cost of $3.5 million (0.07 × $50 million). In addition, the issuer incurs other costs, such as the cost of assessing whether to go public, compiling data for the prospectus, and ensuring that the prospectus is properly written. It also incurs fees from hiring legal or financial advisers during this process. Thus the total cost of engaging in an IPO may be close to 10 percent of the total offering.

10-3b Underwriter Efforts to Ensure Price Stability

The lead underwriter's performance can be partially measured by the movement in the IPO firm's share price following the IPO. If investors quickly sell the stock that they purchased during the IPO in the secondary market, there will be downward pressure on the stock's price. Underwriters may attempt to stabilize the stock's price by purchasing shares that are for sale in the secondary market shortly after the IPO. If most stocks placed by a particular underwriter perform poorly after the IPO, institutional investors may no longer want to purchase shares sold by that underwriter.

Lockup   The lead underwriter attempts to ensure stability in the stock's price after the offering by requiring a lockup provision, which prevents the original owners of the firm and the VC firms from selling their shares for a specified period (usually six months from the date of the IPO). The purpose of the lockup provision is to prevent downward pressure that could occur if the original owners or VC firms immediately sold their shares in the secondary market.

In reality, the provision simply defers the possible excess supply of shares sold in the secondary market. When the lockup period expires, the number of shares for sale in the secondary market may increase abruptly, in which case the share price typically declines significantly. In fact, some investors who are allowed to sell their shares before the lockup expiration date now recognize this effect and sell their IPO shares just before that date. Consequently, the stock price begins to decline shortly before the expiration date.

10-3c Timing of IPOs

Initial public offerings tend to occur more frequently during bullish stock markets, when potential investors are more interested in purchasing new stocks. Prices of stocks tend to be higher in these periods, and issuing firms attempt to capitalize on such prices.

EXAMPLE

WEB

www.nasdaq.com/ markets/ipos/ Information about IPOs, including a schedule of planned IPOs.

In the 2004-2007 period, stocks of most firms were priced high relative to their respective earnings or revenues. Investor demand for new stocks was strong. Firms were more willing to engage in IPOs because they were confident that they could sell all of their shares at relatively high prices.

After the credit crisis began in 2008, the stock market weakened and thus reduced the valuation of stocks relative to earnings or revenues. For this reason, some firms that had planned to go public withdrew their plans. They recognized that their shares would have to be sold for a lower price than they desired. In addition, as economic conditions weakened, some firms cut back on their expansion plans and therefore had less need for additional funds. These firms recognized that they should defer their offering until economic conditions were more favorable and stock prices were higher. ●

10-3d Initial Returns of IPOs

The initial (first-day) return of IPOs in the United States has averaged about 20 percent over the last 30 years. Such a return is unusual for a single day and exceeds the typical return earned on stocks over an entire year. The initial return on IPOs was especially high for Internet firms during the 1996–1999 period. During 1998, for example, the mean increase in price on the first trading day following the IPO was 84 percent for Internet stocks. Thus a $1 million investment in each of the Internet IPOs in 1998 would have resulted in a one-day gain of $840,000.

The successful IPOs of some Internet firms turned small investors into millionaires, and the resulting media attention attracted many other investors who had never invested in the stock market before. Some investors were investing money that they could not afford to lose, not recognizing the risk associated with investing in Internet stocks. Many of the Internet firms wasted the proceeds of their IPOs, and their stock prices fell below their initial IPO prices within a year. Many Internet firms ultimately went bankrupt, and the investors who invested in those IPOs and held on to the shares lost their entire investments.

10-3e Flipping Shares

Some investors who know about the unusually high initial returns on IPOs attempt to purchase the stock at its offer price and sell the stock shortly afterward. This strategy is referred to as *flipping*. Investors who engage in flipping have no intention of investing in the firm over the long run and are simply interested in capitalizing on the initial return that occurs for many IPOs. If many institutional investors flip their shares, the market price of the stock may decline shortly after the IPO. Thus underwriters are concerned that flipping might place excessive downward pressure on the stock's price. To discourage flipping, some securities firms make more shares of future IPOs available to institutional investors that retain shares for a relatively long period of time. The securities firms may also prevent institutional investors that engage in flipping from participating in any subsequent IPOs that they underwrite.

10-3f Google's IPO

On August 18, 2004, Google engaged in an IPO that attracted massive media attention because of the firm's name recognition. Google generated $1.6 billion from the offering, more than four times the combined value of the IPOs by Amazon.com, America Online, Microsoft, Netscape, and Priceline.com. Google's two co-founders, Larry Page and Sergey Brin, sold a portion of their shares within the IPO for about $40 million each but retained shares valued at $3 billion each. The Google IPO offers interesting insight into the process by which firms obtain equity funding from investors.

Estimating the Stock's Value Investors attempt to determine the value of the stock that is to be issued so that they can decide whether to invest in the IPO. In the case of Google, some investors used Yahoo! as a benchmark because Yahoo! stock had been publicly traded since 1996. To determine the appropriate price of Google's stock, investors multiplied Google's earnings per share by Yahoo!'s price-earnings ratio. This method had some major limitations, however. First, Google and Yahoo! are not exactly the same type of business. Some investors might argue that Microsoft would have been a better benchmark than Yahoo! for Google. If Google has more growth potential than Yahoo!, it might deserve a higher multiple. In addition, Yahoo! and Google use different accounting methods, so estimating a value by comparing the earnings of the two firms was subject to further error. These limitations of valuation are discussed in more detail in Chapter 11, but the main point here is that stock valuations are error prone, especially for IPOs, where the firms have no stock market history.

The Auction Process Google's IPO was unique in that it used a Dutch auction process instead of relying almost exclusively on institutional investors. Specifically, it allowed all investors to submit a bid for its stock by a specific deadline. It then ranked the bid prices and determined the minimum price at which it would be able to sell all of the shares that it wished to issue. All bids that were equal to or above that minimum price were accepted, and all bids below the minimum price were rejected.

From Google's perspective, the benefit of the auction process was lower costs (as a percentage of proceeds) than with a traditional IPO. The auction may have saved Google about $20 million in fees. In addition, the auction allowed Google to attract a diversified investor base, including many individual investors. However, such an auction process is unlikely to be as successful for firms that are less well known to individual investors as Google.

Results of Google's Dutch Auction   Google's auction resulted in a price of $85 per share, meaning that all investors whose bids were accepted paid $85 per share. Google was able to sell all of its 19.6 million shares at this price, which generated proceeds of $1.67 billion. Some investors who obtained shares at the time of the IPO sold (flipped) their shares in the secondary market shortly after the auction was completed. The share price increased by 18 percent to $100.34 by the end of the first day, so investors who obtained shares through the auction and sold them at the end of the first day earned an 18 percent return.

In retrospect, Google was undervalued at the time of the IPO, since its price increased more than 700 percent by 2013.

10-3g Facebook's IPO

On May 18, 2012, Facebook engaged in an IPO, and raised about $16 billion with its offering. Because of its popularity, Facebook's IPO attracted much attention. There were 33 securities that served as underwriters by selling the shares to investors. These underwriters earned fees of about $176 million for their services. This fee is actually lower than the norm for underwriters engaged in an IPO, but many securities firms were willing to accept a lower fee in order to participate in this major event. The opening stock price of Facebook was $38 on the IPO date. The stock price initially increased but then declined later in the day. Based on the open price, the market value of Facebook was about $104 billion at that time, larger than almost all other firms in the United States.

On the day of Facebook's IPO, about 571 million shares were traded, and the stock price of Facebook ended at $38.23, just 23 cents above the open price. Yet some traders experienced substantial profits or losses because of wild gyrations in the stock price on the first day. Some institutional traders reportedly lost more than $100 million on this single day of trading.

As the price declined from its high of about $43 and approached the opening price of $38, some of the securities firms that served as underwriters for the offering purchased shares in order to provide price support. They essentially offset the excess supply of shares for sale at that time in order to prevent the market price from declining below the open price on that day.

One month after the IPO, Facebook's stock price was $31.40. Three months after the IPO, Facebook's stock price was about $20 per share, or about 48 percent below the IPO open price. In other words, its market valuation declined by about $50 billion in three months. A $10,000 investment in the IPO at the opening price would have been worth about $5,200 three months later.

One obvious lesson of the Facebook IPO is that a company can be very valuable, yet overpriced. Many investors were willing to invest in Facebook at any price at the time of the IPO, without considering whether the stock price was justified based on fundamental characteristics that influence Facebook's expected cash flows and true valuation. The financial media documented how some investors recognized that the price might be too high at the time of the IPO, but just hoped for a quick "pop" in price, so that they could sell their shares at a quick profit. In other words, some investors did not mind paying an excessive price for an overvalued stock as long as they could quickly sell their shares to other investors who were willing to pay even more than they did.

The opening price of $38 per share reflected a multiple of about 100 times Facebook's annual earnings per share at the time. As a basis of comparison, Apple's price-earnings ratio at that time was about 14. In August 2013, Facebook's stock price surged to about $37 per share. The only way that Facebook's extremely high stock price could be justified was if its growth in earnings would be much higher than that of Apple and other companies. For Facebook's earnings to grow at this rate, its customer base would have to grow substantially across the world. However, some countries already had local firms that provided a similar service. Some of the more conservative valuations based on less aggressive growth assumptions estimated the value of Facebook to be about $20 per share, consistent with the price three months after the IPO.

10-3h Abuses in the IPO Market

Initial public offerings have received negative publicity because of several abuses. In 2003, regulators issued new guidelines in an effort to prevent such abuses in the future. Some of the more common abuses are described here.

Spinning   Spinning occurs when the underwriter allocates shares from an IPO to corporate executives who may be considering an IPO or to another business requiring the help of a securities firm. The underwriter hopes that the executives will remember the favor and hire the securities firm in the future.

Laddering   When there is substantial demand for an IPO, some brokers engage in *laddering*. In other words, these brokers encourage investors to place first-day bids for the shares that are above the offer price. This helps to build upward price momentum. Some investors may be willing to participate to ensure that the broker will reserve some shares of the next hot IPO for them.

Excessive Commission   Some brokers have charged excessive commissions when demand was high for an IPO. Investors were willing to pay the price because they could normally recover the cost from the return on the first day. Because the underwriter set an offer price significantly below the market price that would occur by the end of the first day of trading, investors were willing to accommodate the brokers. The gain to the brokers was a loss to the issuing firm, however, because its proceeds were less than they would have been if the offer price had been set higher.

Distorted Financial Statements   Prior to an IPO, a firm must disclose financial statements to summarize its revenue, expenses, and financial condition. Many investors use this information to derive a valuation of the firm, which can be used to determine a value per share based on the firm's number of shares. With this information, investors can decide whether the offer price of shares at the time of the IPO is below or above their own valuation, which will dictate whether they purchase shares. To the extent that financial statements are distorted, so may be the valuations.

EXAMPLE   On November 4, 2011, Groupon went public. Its stock price quickly jumped from $20 to about $31 (a 55 percent return) on the first day of the IPO, before declining. Critics voiced their concerns that Groupon was understating its expenses, and therefore exaggerating its earnings. In its first year as a public company, Groupon frequently made amendments to its financial statements to correct them. It then acknowledged that its internal controls were weak. By November 2012, its stock price had declined to about $3 per share, which represented an 85 percent loss from its offer price at the time of the IPO. Thus, an employee who owned shares before the IPO was able to sell 1,000 shares for $20,000 at the time of the IPO. But an investor who purchased those 1,000 shares for $20,000 at the time of the IPO would have received about $3,000 from selling those shares one year later. In retrospect, it appears that owners of Groupon before the IPO benefitted from the exaggerated earnings, because the investors who trusted the financial statements paid too much for shares during the IPO. ●

The lesson of this example is that even with all the existing regulations for reporting financial statements, accountants still have much flexibility in their reporting process, and therefore can still exaggerate earnings. Consequently, those investors who rely on earnings to value IPO shares might pay too much if the earnings are later determined to be exaggerated.

10-3i Long-Term Performance Following IPOs

WEB

www.hoovers.com/
ipo-central/ipo-
performance/
100004163-1.html
Information on the
performance of stocks
following the IPO.

There is strong evidence that, on average, IPOs of firms perform poorly over a period of a year or longer. Thus, from a long-term perspective, many IPOs are overpriced at the time of the issue. Investors may be overly optimistic about firms that go public. To the extent that investors base their expectations on the firm's performance before the IPO, they should be aware that firms do not perform as well after going public as they did before. There are several reasons for this. First, this weak performance may be partially attributed to irrational valuations at the time of the IPO, which are corrected over time. Second, the poor performance following an IPO may be caused by the firm's managers, who may spend excessively and waste some of the funds received from the IPO by making bad investments. Third, some firms might have exaggerated their earnings at the time of the IPO in order to maximize the price at which the shares can be sold. The price is corrected downward over time once it becomes obvious that the firm cannot sustain such a high earnings level.

10-4 STOCK OFFERINGS AND REPURCHASES

Even after a firm has gone public, it may issue more stock or repurchase some of the stock that it previously issued. These actions are explained next.

10-4a Secondary Stock Offerings

A firm may need to raise additional equity to support its growth or to expand its operations. A **secondary stock offering** is a new stock offering by a specific firm whose stock is already publicly traded. Some firms have engaged in several secondary offerings to support their expansion. A firm that wants to engage in a secondary stock offering must file the offering with the SEC. It will likely hire a securities firm to advise on the number of shares it can sell, to help develop the prospectus submitted to the SEC, and to place the new shares with investors.

Because there is already a market price for the stock of a firm that engages in a secondary offering, the firm hopes that it can issue shares at the existing market price. But given that a secondary offering may involve millions of shares, there may not be sufficient demand by investors at the prevailing market price. In this case, the underwriter will have to reduce the price so that it can sell all the new shares. Many secondary offerings cause the market price to decline by 1 to 4 percent on the day of the offering, which reflects the new price at which the increased supply of shares in the market is equal to the demand for those shares. Because of the potential for a decline in the equilibrium price of all of its shares, a firm considering a secondary stock offering commonly monitors stock market movements. It prefers to issue new stock when the market price of its outstanding shares is relatively high and when the general outlook for the firm is favorable. Under these conditions, it can issue new shares at a relatively high price, which will generate more funds for a given amount of shares issued.

Corporations sometimes direct their sales of stock toward a particular group, such as their existing shareholders, by giving them preemptive rights (first priority) to purchase the new stock. By placing newly issued stock with existing shareholders, the firm avoids diluting ownership. Preemptive rights are exercised by purchasing new shares during the subscription period (which normally lasts a month or less) at the price specified by the rights. Alternatively, the rights can be sold to someone else.

Shelf Registration   Corporations can publicly place securities without the time lag often caused by registering with the SEC. With this so-called shelf registration, a corporation can fulfill SEC requirements as many as two years before issuing new securities. The registration statement contains financing plans over the upcoming two years. The securities are, in a sense, shelved until the firm needs to issue them. Shelf registrations allow firms quick access to funds without repeatedly being slowed by the registration process. Thus, corporations anticipating unfavorable conditions can quickly lock in their financing costs. Although this is beneficial to the issuing corporation, potential purchasers must realize that the information disclosed in the registration is not continually updated and therefore may not accurately reflect the firm's status over the shelf-registration period.

10-4b Stock Repurchases

Corporate managers have information about the firm's future prospects that is not known by the firm's investors, knowledge that is often referred to as *asymmetric information*. When corporate managers believe that their firm's stock is undervalued, they can use the firm's excess cash to purchase a portion of its shares in the market at a relatively low price based on their valuation of what the shares are really worth. Firms tend to repurchase some of their shares when share prices are at very low levels.

In general, studies have found that stock prices respond favorably to stock repurchase announcements, which implies that investors interpret the announcement as signaling management's perception that the shares are undervalued. Investors respond favorably to this signal.

Although many stock repurchase plans are viewed as a favorable signal, some investors may ask why the firm does not use its funds to expand its business instead of buying back its stock. Thus, investors' response to a stock repurchase plan varies with the firm's characteristics.

10-5 STOCK EXCHANGES

Any shares of stock that have been issued as a result of an IPO or a secondary offering can be traded by investors in the secondary market. In the United States, stock trading between investors occurs on the organized stock exchanges and the over-the-counter (OTC) market.

10-5a Organized Exchanges

Each **organized exchange** has a trading floor where floor traders execute transactions in the secondary market for their clients. Although there are several organized stock exchanges in the United States, the New York Stock Exchange (NYSE) is by far the largest.

The NYSE was merged with stock exchanges in Paris, Brussels, and Amsterdam in 2007, resulting in NYSE Euronext. In December 2012, NYSE Euronext was purchased by Intercontinental Exchange (ICE) Inc., (subject to regulatory approval) although it would still use the NYSE Euronext name. The ICE, based in Atlanta, emerged in 2000 to facilitate electronic trades of futures contracts on commodities such as cotton and oil. It is known for its efficiency in electronic trading of derivative contracts and went public in 2005. The combination of the ICE and NYSE Euronext exchanges creates a massive network that can trade stocks, bonds, commodities, and derivative securities across the world. The firms listed on the NYSE are typically much larger than those listed on the other exchanges. For some firms, more than 100 million shares are traded on a daily basis.

The NYSE has a trading floor where trades can be executed. It has two broad types of members: floor brokers and specialists. **Floor brokers** are either commission brokers or independent brokers. **Commission brokers** are employed by brokerage firms and execute orders for clients on the floor of the NYSE. **Independent brokers** trade for their own account and are not employed by any particular brokerage firm. However, they sometimes handle the overflow for brokerage firms and handle orders for brokerage firms that do not employ full-time brokers. The fee that independent brokers receive depends on the size and liquidity of the order they trade.

Specialists can match orders of buyers and sellers. In addition, they can buy or sell stock for their own account and thereby create more liquidity for the stock.

While the NYSE was always known for its trading floor, much of the trading has been executed by the NYSE Super Display Book System (SDBK), which is an electronic system for matching trades. At the time NYSE Euronext was purchased by Intercontinental Exchange, only about 20 percent of the NYSE trades were executed on the trading floor, versus about 40 percent in 2007. The other trades are executed electronically. The proportion of trades executed electronically will likely increase to the point in which the trading floor is no longer needed.

Listing Requirements   The NYSE charges an initial fee to firms that wish to have their stock listed. The fee depends on the size of the firm. Corporations must meet specific requirements to have their stock listed on the NYSE, such as a minimum number of shares outstanding and a minimum level of earnings, cash flow, and revenue over a recent period. Once a stock is listed, the exchange also requires that the share price of the stock be at least $1 per share. As time passes, new listings are added and some firms are delisted when they no longer meet the requirements.

The requirement of a minimum number of shares outstanding is intended to ensure adequate liquidity. For a stock to be liquid, there should be many willing buyers and sellers at any time so that an investor can easily buy or sell the stock at the prevailing market price. In a liquid market, the bid price that brokers are willing to pay for a stock should be just slightly less than the ask price at which they would sell the stock.

10-5b Over-the-Counter Market

Stocks not listed on the organized exchanges are traded in the over-the-counter (OTC) market. Like the organized exchanges, the OTC market also facilitates secondary market transactions. Unlike the organized exchanges, the OTC market does not have a trading floor. Instead, the buy and sell orders are completed through a telecommunications network. Because there is no trading floor, it is not necessary to buy a seat to trade on this exchange; however, it is necessary to register with the SEC.

Nasdaq   Many stocks in the OTC market are served by the **National Association of Securities Dealers Automatic Quotations (Nasdaq)**, which is an electronic quotation system that provides immediate price quotations. Firms that wish to have their prices quoted by the Nasdaq must meet specific requirements on minimum assets, capital, and number of shareholders. More than 3,000 stocks trade on the Nasdaq. Although most stocks listed in this market are issued by relatively small firms, stocks of some very large firms (e.g., Apple and Intel) are also traded there.

OTC Bulletin Board   The OTC Bulletin Board lists stocks that have a price below $1 per share, which are sometimes referred to as *penny stocks*. More than 3,500 stocks are listed here. Many of these stocks were once traded in the Nasdaq market but no longer meet that exchange's requirements. Penny stocks are less liquid than those traded on exchanges because there is an extremely limited amount of trading. They are typically traded only by individual investors. Institutional investors tend to focus on more liquid stocks that can be easily sold in the secondary market at any time.

Pink Sheets   The OTC market has another segment, known as the "pink sheets," where even smaller stocks are traded. Like those on the OTC Bulletin Board, these stocks typically do not satisfy the Nasdaq's listing requirements. Financial data on them are very limited, if available at all. Companies whose stocks are traded on the pink sheets market do not have to register with the SEC. Some of the stocks have very little trading volume and may not be traded at all for several weeks.

10-5c Extended Trading Sessions

The NYSE and Nasdaq market offer extended trading sessions beyond normal trading hours. A late trading session enables investors to buy or sell stocks after the market closes, and an early morning session (sometimes referred to as a *pre-market* session) enables them to buy or sell stocks just before the market opens on the following day. Beyond the sessions offered by the exchanges, some electronic communication networks (ECNs) allow for trading at any time. Since many announcements about firms are made after normal trading hours, investors can attempt to take advantage of this information before the market opens the next day.

However, market liquidity during the extended trading sessions is limited. For example, the total trading volume of a widely traded stock at night may be only 5 percent (or less) of its trading volume during the day. Some stocks are rarely traded at all during the night. Thus, a large trade is more likely to jolt the stock price during an extended trading session because a large price adjustment may be necessary to entice other investors to take the opposite position. Some investors attempt to take advantage of unusual stock price movements during extended trading sessions, but they are exposed to the risk that the market price will not adjust in the anticipated manner.

10-5d Stock Quotations Provided by Exchanges

The trading of stocks between investors in the secondary market can cause any stock's price to change. Investors can monitor stock price quotations at financial websites and in newspapers. Although the format varies among sources, most quotations provide similar information. Stock prices are always quoted on a per share basis, as in the example of Zikard Company in Exhibit 10.4. Use the exhibit to supplement the following discussion of other information in stock quotations.

52-Week Price Range   The stock's highest price and lowest price over the previous 52 weeks are commonly listed just to the left of the stock's name. The high and low prices indicate the range for the stock's price over the last year. Some investors use this range as an indicator of how much the stock price fluctuates.

Exhibit 10.4 Example of Stock Price Quotations

YTD % CHANGE	HI	LO	STOCK	SYM	DIV	YLD%	PE	VOL 100S	LAST	NET CHG
+10.3	121.88	80.06	ZIKARD CO.	ZIK	.56	.6	20	71979	93.77	+1.06
Year to-date percentage change in stock price	Highest price of the stock in this year	Lowest price of the stock in this year	Name of stock	Stock symbol	Annual dividend paid per year	Dividend yield, which represents the annual dividend as a percentage of the prevailing stock price	Price–earnings ratio based on the prevailing stock price	Trading volume during the previous trading day	Closing stock price	Change in the stock price from the close on the day before

Notice that Zikard's 52-week high price was $121.88 and its low price was $80.06 per share. The low price is about 34 percent below the high price, which indicates a wide range of values over the last year.

Symbol   Each stock has a specific symbol that is used to identify the firm. This symbol may be used to communicate trade orders to brokers. Ticker tapes at brokerage firms or on financial news television shows use the symbol to identify each firm. If included in the stock quotations, the symbol normally appears just to the right of the firm's name. Each symbol is usually composed of two to four letters. Zikard's ticker symbol is ZIK. Nike's symbol is NKE, the symbol for Home Depot is HD, and the symbol for Motorola is MOT.

Dividend   The annual dividend (Div) is commonly listed to the right of the firm's name and symbol. It shows the dividends distributed to stockholders over the last year on a per share basis. Zikard's dividend is $0.56 per share, which indicates an average of $0.14 per share for each quarter. The annual dollar amount of dividends paid can be determined by multiplying the dividends per share by the number of shares outstanding.

Dividend Yield   Next to the annual dividend, some stock quotation tables also show the dividend yield (Yld), which is the annual dividend per share as a percentage of the stock's prevailing price. Since Zikard's annual dividend is $0.56 per share and its prevailing stock price is $93.77, its stock's dividend yield is

$$\text{Dividend yield} = \frac{\text{Dividends paid per share}}{\text{Prevailing stock price}}$$

$$= \frac{\$0.56}{\$93.77}$$

$$= 0.60\%$$

Some firms attempt to provide a fairly stable dividend yield over time, but other firms do not.

Price-Earnings Ratio   Most stock quotations include the stock's price–earnings (PE) ratio, which represents its prevailing stock price per share divided by the firm's earnings per share (earnings divided by number of existing shares of stock) generated over the last year. Zikard's PE ratio of 20 in Exhibit 10.4 is derived by dividing its stock price

USING THE WALL STREET JOURNAL

Late Trading

The *Wall Street Journal* provides information on stocks that were heavily traded after normal trading hours, as shown here. It describes the trading volume and the percentage change in the stock price for specific stocks that were heavily traded.

Late Trading

Most-active and biggest movers among NYSE, NYSE Arca, NYSE MKT and Nasdaq issues from 4 p.m. to 6:30 p.m. ET as reported by electronic trading services, securities dealers and regional exchanges. Minimum share price of $2 and minimum after-hours volume of 5,000 shares.

Most-active issues in late trading

Company	Symbol	Volume (000)	Last	Net chg	AFTER HOURS % chg	High	Low
SPDR S&P 500	SPY	26,284.7	151.97	0.06	0.04	153.29	148.61
Ford Motor	F	13,303.4	12.75	-0.01	-0.08	12.80	12.68
Groupon Inc	GRPN	12,360.4	4.46	-1.52	-25.45	6.17	4.25
Johnson Controls	JCI	4,589.3	31.21	-0.20	-0.65	31.41	31.19
JC Penney	JCP	4,192.2	18.21	-2.95	-13.94	21.35	17.94
PwrShrs QQQ Tr Series 1	QQQ	3,100.4	67.21	-0.03	-0.04	67.56	66.55
Abbott Labs	ABT	2,094.1	34.43	0.17	0.50	34.43	34.22
AbbVie Inc.	ABBV	2,082.9	36.70	-0.03	-0.08	36.73	36.69

Percentage gainers...

Company	Symbol	Volume (000)	Last	Net chg	AFTER HOURS % chg	High	Low
Babcock Wilcox	BWC	5.9	28.75	2.32	8.78	28.75	26.29
Unilife	UNIS	11.8	2.66	0.10	3.91	2.66	2.55
Accuray	ARAY	29.0	4.44	0.16	3.85	4.67	4.28
Universal Display	PANL	40.3	28.89	0.99	3.55	29.10	27.30
Idenix Pharmaceuticals	IDIX	53.4	4.27	0.15	3.53	4.75	4.12

...And losers

Company	Symbol	Volume (000)	Last	Net chg	AFTER HOURS % chg	High	Low
Groupon Inc	GRPN	12,360.4	4.46	-1.52	-25.45	6.17	4.25
BroadSoft	BSFT	819.3	23.92	-6.99	-22.61	43.95	23.92
AegeanMrnPete	ANW	11.5	5.80	-1.19	-17.02	6.21	5.80
JC Penney	JCP	4,192.2	18.21	-2.95	-13.94	21.35	17.94
Vocera Communications	VCRA	7.3	25.90	-3.17	-10.90	29.07	25.00

Online>>

Real-time U.S. stock quotes are available on WSJ.com. Track most-active stocks, new highs/lows, mutual funds and ETFs. Plus, get deeper money-flows data and email delivery of key stock-market data. All are available free at **WSJMarkets.com.**

of $93.77 by the previous year's earnings. Price–earnings ratios are closely monitored by some investors who believe that a low PE ratio (relative to other firms in the same industry) signals that the stock is undervalued in terms of the company's earnings.

Volume Stock quotations also usually include the volume (referred to as "Vol" or "Sales") of shares traded on the previous day. The volume is normally quoted in hundreds of shares. It is not unusual for several million shares of a large firm's stock to be traded on a single day. Exhibit 10.4 shows that more than 7 million shares of ZIK stock were traded. Some financial media also show the percentage change in the volume of trading from the previous day.

Closing Price Quotations Stock quotations show the closing price ("Last") on the day (on the previous day if the quotations are in a newspaper). In addition, the change

WEB

finance.yahoo.com/
indices
Quotations on various
U.S. stock market
indexes.

in the price ("Net Chg") is typically provided and indicates the increase or decrease in the stock price from the closing price on the day before.

10-5e Stock Index Quotations

Stock indexes serve as performance indicators of specific stock exchanges or of particular subsets of the market. The indexes allow investors to compare the performance of individual stocks with more general market indicators. Some of the more closely monitored indexes are identified next.

Dow Jones Industrial Average   The Dow Jones Industrial Average (DJIA) is a value-weighted average of stock prices of 30 large U.S. firms. ExxonMobil, IBM, and the Coca-Cola Company are among the stocks included in the index. Since the DJIA is based on only 30 large stocks, it is not always an accurate indicator of the overall market or (especially) of smaller stocks.

Standard & Poor's 500   The Standard & Poor's (S&P) 500 index is a value-weighted index of stock prices of 500 large U.S. firms. Because this index contains such a large number of stocks, it is more representative of the U.S. stock market than the DJIA. However, because the S&P 500 index focuses on large stocks, it does not serve as a useful indicator for stock prices of smaller firms.

Wilshire 5000 Total Market Index   The Wilshire 5000 Total Market Index was created in 1974 to reflect the values of 5,000 U.S. stocks. Because stocks have been added over time, the index now contains more than 5,000 stocks. The Wilshire 5000 is the broadest index of the U.S. stock market. It is widely quoted in financial media and closely monitored by the Federal Reserve and many financial institutions.

New York Stock Exchange Indexes   The NYSE provides quotations on indexes that it has created. The *Composite Index* is the average of all stocks traded on the NYSE. This is an excellent indicator of the general performance of stocks traded on the NYSE. However, because these stocks represent mostly large firms, the Composite Index is not an appropriate measure of small stock performance. In addition to the Composite Index, the NYSE also provides indexes for four sectors:

1. Industrial
2. Transportation
3. Utility
4. Financial

These indexes are commonly used as benchmarks for comparison to an individual firm or portfolio in that respective sector. Although the indexes are positively correlated, there are substantial differences in their movements during some periods.

Nasdaq Stock Indexes   The National Association of Securities Dealers (NASD) provides quotations on indexes of stocks traded on the Nasdaq. These indexes are useful indicators of small stock performance because many small stocks are traded on that exchange.

10-5f Private Stock Exchanges

Prior to an IPO, some private firms list their private shares on a private stock exchange. Thus, employees or owners who own shares of these firms can sell their shares to other investors. Second Market and Shares Post are examples of private stock exchanges that facilitate the sale of private firm shares. The main advantage of a private stock exchange is that it allows owners of a private firm to obtain cash. The owners can sell some of their shares to investors in exchange for cash. In addition, the private stock exchange allows investors to become part owners of privately held firms. Many of these firms may ultimately engage in IPOs, which would allow investors to purchase shares. However, if investors can invest in private firms, they may be able to obtain shares at a lower price. In addition, they may not have access to purchasing shares at the time of the IPO, because most IPOs give priority to the large institutional investors. When investors purchase shares of a private firm, they might be able to pay a lower price than if they wait until the private firm goes public.

There are some possible disadvantages of a private stock market that should also be considered. First, investors need to register with the private stock exchange, and prove that they have sufficient income (such as about $200,000 per year) and sufficient net worth (such as at least $1 million). Therefore, the private stock exchanges are not for all investors. Second, the required disclosure of information by private firms listed on private stock exchanges may be less than what is required when firms go public. Firms are required to have their financial statements audited when their shares are publicly traded. The limited information could cause some investors to make bad investment decisions. Third, investors should consider why the existing owners of a private firm are willing to sell their shares for a specific price. Is it because the owners need cash, or because they know that the firm is worth less than the price at which they can sell the shares? Investors are at a disadvantage because they do not have all the information that the owners have in order to estimate the proper value of shares. Fourth, the trading volume in a private stock market is very limited. With such limited participation by investors, it is difficult to determine the appropriate market price. The price at which the shares are trading could possibly be much higher than what they would sell at if the shares were publicly traded, which suggests that the investors are paying too much for private shares. Alternatively, the shares might be trading at lower prices than if the shares were publicly traded, which suggests that the existing owners are not receiving a sufficient price for their shares. Even the existing owners can make mistakes when attempting to determine the proper valuation of shares, because the true market valuation (when the firm goes public in the future) is partially influenced by market sentiment, which is difficult to forecast.

10-6 MONITORING PUBLICLY TRADED COMPANIES

Since a firm's stock price is normally related to its performance, the return to investors depends on how well the firm is managed. A publicly traded firm's managers serve as agents for shareholders by making decisions that are supposed to maximize the stock's price. The separation of ownership (by shareholders) and control (by managers) can result in agency problems because of conflicting interests. Managers may be tempted to serve their own interests rather than those of the investors who own the firm's stock.

Many institutional investors own millions of shares of a single firm and therefore have an incentive to ensure that managers serve the shareholders' interests. The easiest way for shareholders to monitor the firm is to monitor changes in its value (as measured by its share price) over time. Since the share price is continuously available, shareholders can quickly detect any abrupt changes in the value of the firm. If the stock price is lower than expected, shareholders may attempt to take action to improve the management of the firm. In addition, publicly traded firms are required to provide financial statements that disclose their financial condition to the public, so investors can monitor these statements as well.

Investors also rely on the board of directors of each firm to ensure that its managers make decisions that enhance the firm's performance and maximize the stock price.

A firm's board of directors is responsible for supervising its business and affairs. The board attempts to ensure that the business is managed in a way that serves the shareholders. Directors are also responsible for monitoring operations and making sure that the firm complies with the laws. They cannot oversee every workplace decision, but they can ensure that the firm has a process that can guide some decisions about moral and ethical conduct. They can also ensure that the firm has a system for internal control and reporting.

10-6a Role of Analysts

WEB

finance.yahoo.com/
marketupdate/
upgrades?
List of stocks that were
upgraded or down-
graded by analysts.

Analysts are often employed by securities firms and assigned to monitor a small set of publicly traded firms. They communicate with the high-level managers of the firms that they cover. Because they have expertise in analyzing the financial condition of these firms and in valuing stocks, analysts may detect financial problems within a firm that would not be recognized by most investors. Analysts publicize their opinion of the companies that they monitor for investors by assigning a rating (or recommendation) to the firm's stock such as Strong Buy, Buy, Hold, or Sell.

Although analysts can provide useful information for investors, they have historically been very generous when rating stocks. Thus, their effectiveness in monitoring publicly traded companies has been limited. In fact, the bonuses paid to analysts were sometimes based on how much business they generated for their employer and not on the accuracy of their stock ratings.

Stock Exchange Rules   In the 2002–2004 period, U.S. stock exchanges imposed new rules to prevent some obvious conflicts of interest faced by analysts. First, analysts cannot be supervised by the division that provides advisory services, and their compensation cannot be based on the amount of advisory business they generate. This rule is intended to encourage analysts to provide more unbiased ratings of stocks. Second, securities firms must disclose summaries of their analysts' ratings for all the firms that they rate so that investors can determine whether the ratings are excessively optimistic.

10-6b Accounting Irregularities

To the extent that managers can manipulate the financial statements, they may be able to hide information from investors. In recent years, many firms (including Enron, Tyco, and WorldCom) used unusual accounting methods to create their financial statements. As a result, it was difficult for investors to ascertain the true financial condition of these firms and therefore to monitor them. The problem was compounded because the auditors hired to audit the financial statements of some firms allowed them to use these irregular accounting methods. A subset of a firm's board members serve on an audit committee, which is supposed to ensure that the audit is performed properly. In some firms, however, the committee failed to monitor the auditors. Overall, investors' monitoring of some firms was limited because the accountants distorted the financial statements, the auditors did not properly audit, and the audit committees of those firms did not properly oversee the audit.

10-6c Sarbanes-Oxley Act

The Sarbanes-Oxley Act was enacted in 2002 to ensure more accurate disclosure of financial information to investors, and therefore allows investors to more effectively monitor the financial condition of firms. It requires firms to establish an internal control process to improve their reporting. It also attempts to prevent potential conflicts of interest that could occur when firms have their financial statements audited by a public accounting firm. For example, it prevents a public accounting firm from auditing a client firm whose chief executive officer (CEO) or other executives were employed by the accounting firm within one year prior to the audit. The act also prevents the members of a firm's audit committee from receiving consulting or advising fees or other compensation from the firm beyond that earned from serving on the board. This provision prevents a firm from providing excessive compensation to the members of an audit committee as a means of paying them off so that they do not closely oversee the audit. In addition, the act requires that the CEO and CFO of firms certify that the audited financial statements are accurate, which forces the CFO and CEO to be accountable. The act specifies major fines or imprisonment for employees who mislead investors or hide evidence.

Although the Sarbanes-Oxley Act has improved transparency, investors still have limited financial information about publicly traded firms, which can cause errors in valuations.

EXAMPLE

Lehman Brothers was ranked the highest in the *Barron's* annual survey of corporate performance for large companies. In 2007, *Fortune* magazine put Lehman Brothers at the top of its list of "Most Admired Securities Firms." In March 2007, the value of Lehman's stock was about $40 billion. Yet in September 2008, Lehman filed for bankruptcy and its stock was worthless. How does a company lose $40 billion in value in 18 months? Some critics would argue that its value should never have been as high as $40 billion because the reported market value of its assets was exaggerated. ●

Cost of Being Public   Establishing a process that satisfies the Sarbanes-Oxley provisions can be very costly. For many firms, the cost of adhering to the guidelines of the act exceeds $1 million per year. Hence many small, publicly traded firms decided to revert back to private ownership as a result of the act. These firms perceived that they would have a higher value if they were private, rather than publicly held, because they could eliminate the substantial reporting costs required of publicly traded firms.

10-6d Shareholder Activism

If shareholders are displeased with the way managers are managing a firm, they have three general choices. The first is to do nothing and retain their shares in the hope that management's actions will ultimately lead to strong stock price performance. A second choice is to sell the stock. This choice is common among shareholders who do not believe that they can change the firm's management or do not wish to spend the time and money needed to bring about change. A third choice is to engage in shareholder activism. Some of the more common types of shareholder activism are examined here.

Communication with the Firm   Shareholders can communicate their concerns to other investors in an effort to place more pressure on the firm's managers or its board members. Institutional investors commonly communicate with high-level corporate managers and have opportunities to offer their concerns about the firm's operations. The managers may be willing to consider changes suggested by a large institutional investor because they do not want such investors to sell their holdings of the firm's stock.

EXAMPLE

The California Public Employees' Retirement System (CALPERS) manages the pensions for employees of the state of California. It manages more than $80 billion of securities and commonly maintains large stock positions in some firms. When CALPERS believes that these firms are not being managed properly, it communicates its concerns and often proposes solutions. It might even request a seat on the board of directors, or that the corporation replace one of the board members with an outside investor. In response, some of the firms adjust their management to accommodate CALPERS.

CALPERS periodically announces a list of firms that it believes have serious agency problems. These firms may have been unwilling to respond to CALPERS's concerns about their management style. ●

Firms are especially responsive when institutional investors communicate as a team. Institutional Shareholder Services (ISS), which is part of Risk Metrics Group, organizes institutional shareholders to push for a common cause. After receiving feedback from institutional investors about a particular firm, ISS organizes a conference call with high-ranking executives so that it can obtain information from the firm. It then announces the time of the conference call to investors and allows them to listen in on the call. The questions focus on institutional shareholders' concerns about the firm's management. Unlike earnings conference calls, which are controlled by firms, ISS runs the conference call. Common questions asked by ISS include:

- Why is your CEO also the chair of the board?
- Why is your executive compensation much higher than the industry norm?
- What is your process for nominating new board members?

Transcripts of the conference calls are available shortly after they conclude.

Proxy Contest   Shareholders may also engage in proxy contests in an attempt to change the composition of the board. This is a more formal effort than communicating with the firm and is normally considered only if an informal request for a change in the board (through communication with the board) is ignored. If the dissident shareholders gain enough votes, they can elect one or more directors who share their views. In this case, shareholders are truly exercising their control.

Institutional Shareholder Services may recommend that shareholders vote a certain way on specific proxy issues. As a result of these more organized efforts, institutional shareholders are having more influence on management decisions. At some firms, they have succeeded in implementing changes that can enhance shareholder value, such as:

- Limiting severance pay for executives who are fired.
- Revising the voting guidelines on the firm's executive compensation policy.
- Requiring more transparent reporting of financial information.
- Imposing ceilings on the CEO's salary and bonus.
- Removing bylaws that prevent takeovers by other firms.
- Allowing for an annual election of all directors so that ineffective directors can be quickly removed from the board.

Shareholder Lawsuits   Investors may sue the board if they believe that the directors are not fulfilling their responsibilities to shareholders. This action is intended to force the board to make decisions that are aligned with the shareholders' interests. Lawsuits are often filed when corporations prevent takeovers, pursue acquisitions, or make other restructuring decisions that some shareholders believe will reduce the stock's value.

At some firms, the boards have been negligent in representing the shareholders. Nevertheless, since business performance is subject to uncertainty, directors cannot be held responsible every time a key business decision has an unsatisfactory outcome. When directors are sued, the court typically focuses on whether the directors' decisions were reasonable, not on whether they increased the firm's profitability. Thus, from the court's perspective, the directors' decision-making process is more relevant than the actual outcome.

10-6e Limited Power of Governance

Although much attention has been given in financial markets to how managers are subject to increased governance, there is some evidence that the governance is not very effective. There are numerous examples of executives who continue to receive extremely high compensation even when the performance of their firm is quite weak. In spite of the Sarbanes-Oxley Act, shareholder activism, proxy contests, and shareholder lawsuits, the agency problems of some firms remain severe.

10-7 MARKET FOR CORPORATE CONTROL

When corporate managers notice that another firm in the same industry has a low stock price as a result of poor management, they may attempt to acquire that firm. They hope to purchase the business at a low price and improve its management so that they can increase the value of the business. In addition, the combination of the two firms may reduce redundancy in some operations and allow for synergistic benefits. In this way, the managers of the acquiring firm may earn a higher return than if they used their funds for some other type of expansion. In essence, weak businesses are subject to a takeover by more efficient corporations and are thus subject to the "market for corporate control." Therefore, if a firm's stock price is relatively low because of poor performance, it may become an attractive target for other corporations.

A firm may especially benefit from acquisitions when its own stock price has risen. It can use its stock as currency to acquire the shares of a target by exchanging some of its own shares for the target's shares. Some critics claim that acquisitions of inefficient firms typically lead to layoffs and are unfair to employees. The counter to this argument is that, without the market for corporate control, firms would be allowed to be inefficient, and this is unfair to the shareholders who invested in them. Managers recognize that if their poorly performing business is taken over, they may lose their jobs. Thus, the market for corporate control can encourage managers to make decisions that maximize the stock's value so that they can better avoid takeovers.

In general, studies have found that the share prices of target firms react positively but that the share prices of acquiring firms are not favorably affected. Investors may not expect the acquiring firm to achieve its objectives. There is some evidence that firms engaging in acquisitions do not eliminate inefficient operations after the acquisitions, perhaps because of the low morale that would result from layoffs. In addition, an acquiring firm commonly has to pay a very large premium, such as 20 to 40 percent above the publicly traded target firm's prevailing stock price, in order to gain control of the target firm. It is difficult to achieve sufficient benefits from the acquisition to offset the very large cost of the acquisition.

10-7a Use of LBOs to Achieve Corporate Control

The market for corporate control is enhanced by the use of leveraged buyouts (LBOs), which are acquisitions that require substantial amounts of borrowed funds. That is, the acquisition requires a substantial amount of financial leverage. Some so-called buyout firms identify poorly managed firms, acquire them (mostly with the use of borrowed funds), improve their management, and then sell them at a higher price than they paid. Alternatively, a group of managers who work for the firm may believe that they can restructure the firm's operations to improve cash flows. These managers may attempt an LBO in the hope that they can improve the firm's performance.

The use of debt to retire a company's stock creates a highly leveraged capital structure. One favorable aspect of such a revised capital structure is that the ownership of the firm is normally reduced to a small group of people, who may be managers of the firm. Agency costs should be reduced when managers' interests are thus aligned with those of the firm. A major concern about LBOs, however, is that the firm will experience cash flow problems over time because of the high periodic debt payments that result from the high degree of financial leverage. A firm financed in this way has a high potential return but is also risky.

Some firms that engage in LBOs issue new stock after improving the firm's performance. This process is referred to as a reverse leveraged buyout (reverse LBO). Whereas an LBO may be used to purchase all the stock of a firm that has not achieved its potential performance (causing its stock to be priced low), a reverse LBO is normally desirable when the stock can be sold at a high price. In essence, the owners hope to issue new stock at a much higher price than they paid when enacting the LBO.

10-7b Barriers to the Market for Corporate Control

The power of corporate control to eliminate agency problems is limited by barriers that can make it more costly for a potential acquiring firm to acquire another firm whose managers are not serving the firm's shareholders. Some of the more common barriers to corporate control are identified next.

Antitakeover Amendments Some firms have added antitakeover amendments to their corporate charter. For example, an amendment may require that at least two-thirds of the shareholder votes approve a takeover before the firm can be acquired. Antitakeover amendments are supposed to be enacted to protect shareholders against an acquisition that will ultimately reduce the value of their investment in the firm. However, it could be argued that shareholders are adversely affected by antitakeover amendments.

Poison Pills Poison pills are special rights awarded to shareholders or specific managers on the occurrence of specified events. They can be enacted by a firm's board of directors without the approval of shareholders. Sometimes a target enacts a poison pill to defend against takeover attempts. For example, a poison pill might give all shareholders the right to be allocated an additional 30 percent of shares (based on their existing share holdings) without cost whenever a potential acquirer attempts to acquire the firm. The poison pill makes it more expensive and more difficult for a potential acquiring firm to acquire the target.

Golden Parachutes A golden parachute specifies compensation to managers in the event that they lose their jobs or there is a change in control of the firm. For example, all managers might have the right to receive 100,000 shares of the firm's stock whenever the firm is acquired. It can be argued that a golden parachute protects managers so that they may be more willing to make decisions that enhance shareholder wealth over the long run, even though the decisions adversely affect the stock price in the short run.

Golden parachutes can discourage takeover attempts by increasing the cost of the acquisition. To the extent that this (or any) defense against takeovers is effective, it disrupts the market for corporate control by allowing managers of some firms to be protected while serving their own interests rather than shareholder interests.

10-8 Globalization of Stock Markets

GLOBAL ASPECTS

Stock markets are becoming globalized in the sense that barriers between countries have been removed or reduced. Thus, firms in need of funds can tap foreign markets, and investors can purchase foreign stocks. In recent years, many firms have obtained funds from foreign markets through international stock offerings. This strategy may represent an effort by a firm to enhance its global image. Another motive is that, because the issuing firm is tapping a larger pool of potential investors, it can more easily place the entire issue of new stock.

10-8a Privatization

In recent years, the governments of many countries have allowed privatization, or the sale of government-owned firms to individuals. Some of these businesses are so large that the local stock markets cannot digest the stock offerings. Consequently, investors from various countries have invested in the privatized businesses.

10-8b Emerging Stock Markets

Emerging markets enable foreign firms to raise large amounts of capital by issuing stock. These markets also provide a means for investors from the United States and other countries to invest their funds. Some emerging stock markets are relatively new and small, and they may not be as efficient as the U.S. stock market. Hence some stocks could be undervalued, which may attract investors to these markets.

However, stock markets in some developing countries are still subject to certain limitations. First, non-U.S. regulatory agencies provide little enforcement to ensure that the financial information offered by issuers is correct. Second, businesses that do not repay investors are rarely prosecuted. Third, courts in many countries do not provide an efficient system that investors can use to obtain the funds they believe they are owed.

Fourth, the smaller markets might be especially susceptible to manipulation by large traders. Furthermore, insider trading is more prevalent in many foreign markets because rules against it are not enforced. In general, large institutional investors and insiders based in the foreign markets may have some advantages.

Although international stocks can generate high returns, they may also exhibit high risk. Some of the emerging stock markets are often referred to as "casinos" because of the wide variation in prices that sometimes occur. Large price swings are common because of two characteristics of emerging markets. For stocks with very limited trading activity, large trades can jolt the equilibrium price. In addition, valid financial information about firms is sometimes lacking, causing investors to trade according to rumors. Trading patterns based on continual rumors are more volatile than trading patterns based on factual data.

10-8c Variation in Characteristics across Stock Markets

The volume of trading activity in each stock market is influenced by legal and other characteristics of the country. Shareholder rights vary among countries, and shareholders in some countries have more voting power and can have a stronger influence on corporate management.

The legal protection of shareholders also varies substantially among countries. Shareholders in some countries can more effectively sue publicly traded firms if their executives or directors commit financial fraud. In general, common law countries such as the United States, Canada, and the United Kingdom allow for more legal protection than civil law countries such as France and Italy.

The government's enforcement of securities laws also varies among countries. If a country has laws to protect shareholders but does not enforce the laws, shareholders are not protected. Some countries tend to have less corporate corruption than others; in these countries, shareholders are less exposed to major losses due to corruption.

In addition, the degree of financial information that must be provided by public companies varies among countries. The variation may be due to the accounting laws set by the government for public companies or to reporting rules enforced by local stock exchanges. Shareholders are less susceptible to losses due to a lack of information if public companies are required to be more transparent in their financial reporting.

In general, more investors are attracted to stock markets in countries that provide voting rights and legal protection for shareholders, strictly enforce the laws, do not tolerate corruption, and impose stringent accounting requirements. These conditions enable investors to have more confidence in the stock market and allow for greater pricing efficiency. In addition, companies are attracted to the stock market when there are many investors because then the companies can easily raise funds in the market. Conversely, if a stock market does not attract investors then it will not attract companies needing to raise funds. Those companies will have to rely on stock markets in other countries or on credit markets to raise funds.

10-8d Methods Used to Invest in Foreign Stocks

Investors can obtain foreign stocks by purchasing shares directly, purchasing American depository receipts (ADRs), investing in international mutual funds, and purchasing exchange-traded funds (ETFs). Each of these methods is explained in turn.

Direct Purchases   Investors can easily invest in stocks of foreign companies that are listed on the local stock exchanges. Foreign stocks not listed on local stock exchanges can be purchased through some brokerage firms.

American Depository Receipts   An alternative means of investing in foreign stocks is by purchasing American depository receipts (ADRs), which are certificates representing shares of non-U.S. stock. Many non-U.S. companies establish ADRs in order to develop name recognition in the United States. In addition, some companies wish to raise funds in the United States.

American depository receipts are attractive to U.S. investors for several reasons. First, they are closely followed by U.S. investment analysts. Second, companies represented by ADRs are required by the SEC to file financial statements that are consistent with generally accepted accounting principles in the United States. These statements may not be available for other non-U.S. companies. Third, reliable quotes on ADR prices are consistently available, with existing currency values factored in to translate the price into dollars. A disadvantage, however, is that the selection of ADRs is limited. Also, the ADR market is less active than other stock markets, so ADRs are less liquid than most listed U.S. stocks.

International Mutual Funds   Another way to invest in foreign stocks is to purchase shares of international mutual funds (IMFs), which are portfolios of international stocks created and managed by various financial institutions. In this way, individuals can diversify across international stocks by investing in a single IMF. Some IMFs focus on a specific foreign country, whereas others contain stocks across several countries or even several continents.

WEB

finance.yahoo.com/
indices
Click on "World" for
quotations on various
stock market indexes
around the world.

International Exchange-Traded Funds   Exchange-traded funds are passive funds that track a specific index. International ETFs represent international stock indexes, and they have become popular in the last few years. By investing in an international ETF, investors can invest in a specific index representing a foreign country's stock market. An ETF trades like a stock: it is listed on an exchange, and its value changes in response to trading activity. Although ETFs are denominated in dollars, the net asset value of an international ETF is determined by translating the foreign currency value of the foreign securities into dollars.

A major difference between ETFs and IMFs is that IMFs are managed whereas ETFs simply represent an index. If investors prefer that the portfolio be rebalanced by portfolio managers over time, they may prefer an IMF. However, ETFs have lower expenses because they avoid the cost of active portfolio management. The difference in expense ratios between an IMF and an ETF may be 2 percent annually or more.

The price of a share of each international ETF is denominated in dollars, but the underlying securities that make up the index are denominated in non-U.S. currencies.

For this reason, the return on the ETF will be influenced by any movement of the foreign country's currency against the dollar. This is true also for IMFs. If the foreign currency appreciates (increases in value), that will boost the value of the index as measured in dollars. Conversely, if the foreign currency depreciates (decreases in value), that will reduce the value of the index as measured in dollars.

SUMMARY

- When businesses are created, they normally rely on private equity along with borrowed funds. Some private businesses that expand attempt to obtain additional private equity funding from venture capital firms. When venture capital firms provide financing, they commonly attempt to pull their cash out in four to seven years. Going public changes the firm's ownership structure by increasing the number of owners, and it changes the firm's capital structure by increasing the equity investment in the firm. Stock market participants include individual investors as well as institutional investors such as stock mutual funds, pension funds, and insurance companies. Upon the release of new information about a firm, some investors respond by either selling their stock holdings or buying more stock. Their actions affect the supply and demand conditions for the stock and thus influence the equilibrium stock price.

- An initial public offering (IPO) is a first-time offering of shares by a specific firm to the public. Many firms engage in an IPO to obtain funding for additional expansion and to give the founders and venture capital funds a way to cash out their investments. A firm that engages in an IPO must develop a prospectus that is filed with the SEC, and it typically uses a road show to promote its offering. The firm hires an underwriter to help with the prospectus and road show and to place the shares with investors.

- A secondary stock offering is an offering of shares by a firm that already has publicly traded stock. Firms engage in secondary offerings when they need more equity funding to support additional expansion.

- There are various ways in which publicly traded firms are monitored. Analysts monitor firms so that they can assign a rating to their stock. Investors that purchase stock of firms monitor performance and may use shareholder activism to ensure that managers make decisions that are beneficial to the firm's shareholders. The market for corporate control allows firms to acquire the control of businesses that they can improve by replacing managers or revising operations.

- Many U.S. firms issue shares in foreign countries, as well as in the United States, so that they can spread their shares among a larger set of investors and possibly enhance the firm's global name recognition. Global stock exchanges exist to facilitate the trading of stocks around the world. U.S. investors can invest in foreign stocks by making direct purchases on foreign stock exchanges, purchasing ADRs, investing in international mutual funds, and investing in international exchange-traded funds.

POINT COUNTER-POINT

Should a Stock Exchange Enforce Some Governance Standards on the Firms Listed on the Exchange?

Point   No. Governance is the responsibility of the firms, not the stock exchange. The stock exchange should simply ensure that the trading rules of the exchange are enforced and should not intervene in the firms' governance issues.

Counter-Point   Yes. By enforcing governance standards such as requiring a listed firm to have a majority of outside members on its board of directors, a stock exchange can enhance its own credibility.

Who Is Correct?   Use the Internet to learn more about this issue and then formulate your own opinion.

QUESTIONS AND APPLICATIONS

1. Shareholder Rights Explain the rights of common stockholders that are not available to other individuals.

2. Stock Offerings What is the danger of issuing too much stock? What is the role of the securities firm that serves as the underwriter, and how can it ensure that the firm does not issue too much stock?

3. IPOs Why do firms engage in IPOs? What is the amount of the fees that the lead underwriter and its syndicate charge a firm that is going public? Why are there many IPOs in some periods and few IPOs in other periods?

4. Venture Capital Explain the difference between obtaining funds from a venture capital firm and engaging in an IPO. Explain how the IPO may serve as a means by which the venture capital firm can cash out.

5. Prospectus and Road Show Explain the use of a prospectus developed before an IPO. Why does a firm do a road show before its IPO? What factors influence the offer price of stock at the time of the IPO?

6. Bookbuilding Describe the process of bookbuilding. Why is bookbuilding sometimes criticized as a means of setting the offer price?

7. Lockups Describe a lockup provision and explain why it might be required by the lead underwriter.

8. Initial Return What is the meaning of an initial return for an IPO? Were initial returns of Internet IPOs in the late 1990s higher or lower than normal? Why?

9. Flipping What does it mean to "flip" shares? Why would investors want to flip shares?

10. Performance of IPOs How do IPOs perform over the long run?

11. Asymmetric Information Discuss the concept of asymmetric information. Explain why it may motivate firms to repurchase some of their stock.

12. Stock Repurchases Explain why the stock price of a firm may rise when the firm announces that it is repurchasing its shares.

13. Corporate Control Describe how the interaction between buyers and sellers affects the market value of a firm, and explain how that value can subject a firm to the market for corporate control.

14. ADRs Explain how ADRs enable U.S. investors to become part owners of foreign companies.

15. NYSE Explain why stocks traded on the New York Stock Exchange generally exhibit less risk than stocks that are traded on other exchanges.

16. Role of Organized Exchanges Are organized stock exchanges used to place newly issued stock? Explain.

Advanced Questions

17. Role of IMFs How have international mutual funds (IMFs) increased the international integration of capital markets among countries?

18. Spinning and Laddering Describe spinning and laddering in the IPO market. How do you think these actions influence the price of a newly issued stock? Who is adversely affected as a result of these actions?

19. Impact of Accounting Irregularities How do you think accounting irregularities affect the pricing of corporate stock in general? From an investor's viewpoint, how do you think the information used to price stocks changes in response to accounting irregularities?

20. Impact of Sarbanes-Oxley Act Briefly describe the provisions of the Sarbanes-Oxley Act. Discuss how this act affects the monitoring by shareholders.

21. IPO Dilemma Denton Company plans to engage in an IPO and will issue 4 million shares of stock. It is hoping to sell the shares for an offer price of $14. It hires a securities firm, which suggests that the offer price for the stock should be $12 per share to ensure that all the shares can easily be sold. Explain the dilemma for Denton Company. What is the advantage of following the advice of the securities firm? What is the disadvantage? Is the securities firm's incentive to place the shares aligned with that of Denton Company?

22. Variation in Investor Protection among Countries Explain how shareholder protection varies among countries. Explain how enforcement of securities laws varies among countries. Why do these characteristics affect the valuations of stocks?

23. International ETFs Describe international ETFs, and explain how ETFs are exposed to exchange rate risk. How do you think an investor decides whether to purchase an ETF representing Japan, Spain, or some other country?

24. VC Fund Participation and Exit Strategy
Explain how venture capital (VC) funds finance private businesses as well as how they exit from the participation.

25. Dilemma of Stock Analysts
Explain the dilemma of stock analysts that work for securities firms and assign ratings to large corporations. Why might they prefer not to assign low ratings to weak but large corporations?

26. 26. Limitations of an IPO
Businesses valued at less than $50 million or so rarely go public. Explain the limitations to such businesses if they did go public.

27. Private Equity Funds
Explain the incentive for private equity funds to invest in a firm and improve its operations.

28. VCs and Lockup Expiration Following IPOs
Venture capital firms commonly attempt to cash out as soon as is possible following IPOs. Describe the likely effect that would have on the stock price at the time of lockup expiration. Would the effect be different for a firm that relied more heavily on VC firms than other investors for its funds?

29. Impact of SOX on Going Private
Explain why some public firms decided to go private in response to the passage of the Sarbanes-Oxley (SOX) Act.

30. Pricing Facebook's IPO Stock Price
Describe the dilemma of securities firms that serve as underwriters for Facebook's IPOs, when attempting to satisfy Facebook and the institutional investors that invest in Facebook's stock. Do you think that the securities firms that served as underwriters for Facebook's IPO satisfied Facebook or its investors in the IPO? Explain.

31. Private Stock Market
What are some possible disadvantages to investors who invest in stocks listed on a private stock market?

Interpreting Financial News

Interpret the following statements made by Wall Street analysts and portfolio managers.

a. "The recent wave of IPOs is an attempt by many small firms to capitalize on the recent runup in stock prices."

b. "IPOs transfer wealth from unsophisticated investors to large institutional investors who get in at the offer price and get out quickly."

c. "Firms must be more accountable to the market when making decisions because they are subject to indirect control by institutional investors."

Managing in Financial Markets

Investing in an IPO As a portfolio manager of a financial institution, you are invited to numerous road shows at which firms that are going public promote themselves and the lead underwriter invites you to invest in the IPO. Beyond any specific information about the firm, what other information would you need to decide whether to invest in the upcoming IPO?

PROBLEM

Dividend Yield Over the last year, Calzone Corporation paid a quarterly dividend of $0.10 in each of the four quarters. The current stock price of Calzone Corporation is $39.78. What is the dividend yield for Calzone stock?

FLOW OF FUNDS EXERCISE

Contemplating an Initial Public Offering

Recall that if the economy continues to be strong, Carson Company may need to increase its production capacity by about 50 percent over the next few years to satisfy demand. It would need financing to expand and accommodate the increase in production. Recall that the yield curve is currently upward sloping. Also recall that Carson is concerned about a possible slowing of the economy because of potential Fed actions to reduce inflation. It is also considering issuing stock or bonds to raise funds in the next year.

a. If Carson issued stock now, it would have the flexibility to obtain more debt and would also be able to reduce its cost of financing with debt. Why?

b. Why would an IPO result in heightened concerns in financial markets about Carson Company's potential agency problems?

c. Explain why institutional investors, such as mutual funds and pension funds, that invest in stock for long-term periods (at least a year or two) might prefer to invest in IPOs rather than to purchase other stocks that have been publicly traded for several years.

d. Given that institutional investors such as insurance companies, pension funds, and mutual funds are the major investors in IPOs, explain the flow of funds that results from an IPO. That is, what is the original source of the money that is channeled through the institutional investors and provided to the firm going public?

INTERNET/EXCEL EXERCISES

Go to http://ipoportal.edgar-online.com/ipo/home.asp and review an IPO that is scheduled for the near future. Review the deal information about this IPO.

1. What is the offer amount? How much are total expenses? How much are total expenses as a percentage of the deal amount? How many shares are issued? How long is the lockup period?

2. Review some additional IPOs that are scheduled. What is the range for the offer amount? What is the range for the lockup period length?

WSJ EXERCISE

Assessing Stock Market Movements

Review a recent issue of the *Wall Street Journal*. Indicate whether the market prices increased or decreased, and explain what caused the market's movement.

ONLINE ARTICLES WITH REAL-WORLD EXAMPLES

Find a recent practical article available online that describes a real-world example regarding a specific financial institution or financial market that reinforces one or more concepts covered in this chapter.

If your class has an online component, your professor may ask you to post your summary of the article there and provide a link to the article so that other students can access it. If your class is live, your professor may ask you to summarize your application of the article in class. Your professor may assign specific students to complete this assignment or may allow any students to do the assignment on a volunteer basis.

For recent online articles and real-world examples related to this chapter, consider using the following search terms (be sure to include the prevailing year as a search term to ensure that the online articles are recent):

1. private equity AND investment
2. venture capital AND investment
3. initial public offering
4. plans to go public
5. stock repurchase
6. stock offering
7. stock listing AND exchange
8. extended trading session AND stock
9. stock AND analyst
10. stock AND shareholder activism

11
Stock Valuation and Risk

CHAPTER OBJECTIVES

The specific objectives of this chapter are to:

■ explain methods of valuing stocks,

■ explain how to determine the required rate of return on stocks,

■ identify the factors that affect stock prices,

■ explain how to measure the risk of stocks, and

■ explain the concept of stock market efficiency.

EXAMPLE

WEB

finance.yahoo.com
Insert ticker symbol to obtain financial data, including earnings forecasts, for a stock.

Since the values of stocks change continuously, so do stock prices. Institutional and individual investors constantly value stocks so that they can capitalize on expected changes in stock prices.

11-1 STOCK VALUATION METHODS

Investors conduct valuations of stocks when making their investment decisions. They consider investing in undervalued stocks and selling their holdings of stocks that they consider to be overvalued. There are many different methods of valuing stocks. **Fundamental analysis** relies on fundamental financial characteristics (such as earnings) of the firm and its corresponding industry that are expected to influence stock values. **Technical analysis** relies on stock price trends to determine stock values. Our focus is on fundamental analysis. Investors who rely on fundamental analysis commonly use the price–earnings method, the dividend discount model, or the free cash flow model to value stocks. Each of these methods is described in turn.

11-1a Price-Earnings Method

A relatively simple method of valuing a stock is to apply the mean price–earnings (PE) ratio (based on expected rather than recent earnings) of all publicly traded competitors in the respective industry to the firm's expected earnings for the next year.

Consider a firm that is expected to generate earnings of $3 per share next year. If the mean ratio of share price to expected earnings of competitors in the same industry is 15, then the valuation of the firm's shares is

$$\text{Valuation per share} = \text{Expected earnings of firm per share} \times \text{Mean industry PE ratio}$$
$$= \$3 \times 15$$
$$= \$45$$

●

The logic of this method is that future earnings are an important determinant of a firm's value. Although earnings beyond the next year are also relevant, this method implicitly assumes that the growth in earnings in future years will be similar to that of the industry.

Reasons for Different Valuations This method has several variations, which can result in different valuations. For example, investors may use different forecasts for the firm's earnings or the mean industry earnings over the next year. The previous year's earnings are often used as a base for forecasting future earnings, but recent earnings do not always yield an accurate forecast. In fact, some firms use creative accounting methods to exaggerate earnings in a particular period and are unable to sustain that earnings level in the future.

A second reason for different valuations when using the PE method is that investors disagree on the proper measure of earnings. Some investors prefer to use operating earnings or exclude some unusually high expenses that result from onetime events. A third reason is that investors may disagree on which firms represent the industry norm. Some investors use a narrow industry composite composed of firms that are similar (in terms of size, lines of business, etc.) to the firm being valued; other investors prefer a broader industry composite. Consequently, even if investors agree on a firm's forecasted earnings, they may still derive different values for that firm as a result of applying different PE ratios. Furthermore, even if investors agree on the firms to include in the industry composite, they may disagree on how to weight each firm.

Limitations of the PE Method   The PE method may result in an inaccurate valuation of a firm if errors are made in forecasting the firm's future earnings or in choosing the industry composite used to derive the PE ratio. The PE ratio varies substantially over time, which suggests that even if investors could properly estimate next year's earnings, it is difficult to know how those earnings should convert into a stock valuation.

11-1b Dividend Discount Model

One of the first models used for pricing stocks was developed by John B. Williams in 1931. This model is still applicable today. Williams stated that the price of a stock should reflect the present value of the stock's future dividends, or

$$\text{Price} = \sum_{t=1}^{\infty} \frac{D_t}{(1+k)^t}$$

where

$$t = \text{period}$$
$$D_t = \text{dividend in period } t$$
$$k = \text{discount rate}$$

The model can account for uncertainty by allowing D_t to be revised in response to revised expectations about a firm's cash flows or by allowing k to be revised in response to changes in the required rate of return by investors.

EXAMPLE   To illustrate how the dividend discount model can be used to value a stock, consider a stock that is expected to pay a dividend of $7 per share annually forever. This constant dividend represents a perpetuity, or an annuity that lasts forever. Hence the present value of the cash flows (dividend payments) to investors in this example is the present value of a perpetuity. Assuming that the required rate of return (k) on the stock of concern is 14 percent, the present value (PV) of the future dividends is

$$
\begin{aligned}
\text{PV of stock} &= D/k \\
&= \$7/0.14 \\
&= \$50 \text{ per share}
\end{aligned}
$$ ●

WEB

www.investingator.com/PEND-stock-investing.html
Information on how practitioners value stock.

Unfortunately, the valuation of most stocks is not this simple because their dividends are not expected to remain constant forever. If the dividend is expected to grow at a constant rate, however, the stock can be valued by applying the constant-growth dividend discount model:

$$\text{PV of stock} = D_1/(k-g)$$

where D_1 is the expected dividend per share to be paid over the next year, k is the required rate of return by investors, and g is the rate at which the dividend is expected to grow. For example, if a stock is expected to provide a dividend of $7 per share next year, the dividend is expected to increase by 4 percent per year, and the required rate of return is 14 percent, the stock can be valued as

$$\text{PV of stock} = \$7/(0.14 - 0.04)$$
$$= \$70 \text{ per share}$$

Relationship with PE Ratio for Valuing Firms   The dividend discount model and the PE ratio may seem to be unrelated, given that the dividend discount model is highly dependent on the required rate of return and the growth rate whereas the PE ratio is driven by the mean multiple of competitors' stock prices relative to their earnings expectations and by the earnings expectations of the firm being valued. Yet the PE multiple is influenced by the required rate of return on stocks of competitors and the expected growth rate of competitor firms. When using the PE ratio for valuation, the investor implicitly assumes that the required rate of return and the growth rate for the firm being valued are similar to those of its competitors. When the required rate of return on competitor firms is relatively high, the PE multiple will be relatively low, which results in a relatively low valuation of the firm for its level of expected earnings. When the competitors' growth rate is relatively high, the PE multiple will be relatively high, which results in a relatively high valuation of the firm for its level of expected earnings. Thus, the inverse relationship between required rate of return and value exists when applying either the PE method or the dividend discount model. In addition, there is a positive relationship between a firm's growth rate and its value when applying either method.

Limitations of the Dividend Discount Model   The dividend discount model may result in an inaccurate valuation of a firm if errors are made in estimating the dividend to be paid over the next year or in estimating the growth rate or the required rate of return by investors. The limitations of this model are more pronounced when valuing firms that retain most of their earnings, rather than distributing them as dividends, because the model relies on the dividend as the base for applying the growth rate. For example, many smaller publicly traded firms that are attempting to grow retain all earnings to support growth and thus are not expected to pay any dividends.

11-1c Adjusted Dividend Discount Model

The dividend discount model can be adapted to assess the value of any firm, even those that retain most or all of their earnings. From the investor's perspective, the value of the stock is equal to (1) the present value of the future dividends to be received over the investment horizon *plus* (2) the present value of the forecasted price at which the stock will be sold at the end of the investment horizon. To forecast this sales price, investors must estimate the firm's earnings per share (after removing any nonrecurring effects) in the year that they plan to sell the stock. This estimate is derived by applying an annual growth rate to the prevailing annual earnings per share. Then, the estimate can be used to derive the expected price per share at which the stock can be sold.

EXAMPLE   Assume that a firm currently has earnings of $12 per share. Future earnings can be forecast by applying the expected annual growth rate to the firm's existing earnings (E):

$$\text{Forecasted earnings in } n \text{ years} = E(1 + G)^n$$

where G is the expected growth rate of earnings and n is the number of years until the stock is to be sold.

If investors expect that the earnings per share will grow by 2 percent annually and expect to sell the firm's stock in three years, the earnings per share in three years are forecast to be

$$\text{Earnings in three years} = \$12 \times (1 + 0.02)^3$$
$$= \$12 \times 1.0612$$
$$= \$12.73$$

The forecasted earnings per share can be multiplied by the PE ratio of the firm's industry to forecast the future stock price. If the mean PE ratio of all other firms in the same industry is 6, the stock price in three years can be forecast as follows:

$$\text{Stock price in three years} = \text{Earnings in three years} \times \text{PE ratio of industry}$$
$$= \$12.73 \times 6$$
$$= \$76.38$$

This forecasted stock price can be used along with expected dividends and the investor's required rate of return to value the stock today. If the firm is expected to pay a dividend of $4 per share over the next three years and if the investor's required rate of return is 14 percent, then the present value of expected cash flows to be received by the investor is

$$PV = \$4/(1.14)^1 + \$4/(1.14)^2 + \$4/(1.14)^3 + \$76.38/(1.14)^3$$
$$= \$3.51 + \$3.08 + \$2.70 + \$51.55$$
$$= \$60.84$$

In this example, the present value of the cash flows is based on (1) the present value of dividends to be received over the three-year investment horizon, which is $9.29 per share ($3.51 + $3.08 + $2.70), and (2) the present value of the forecasted price at which the stock can be sold at the end of the three-year investment horizon, which is $51.55 per share.

Limitations of the Adjusted Dividend Discount Model   This model may result in an inaccurate valuation if errors are made in deriving the present value of dividends over the investment horizon or the present value of the forecasted price at which the stock can be sold at the end of the investment horizon. Since the required rate of return affects both of these factors, using an improper required rate of return will lead to inaccurate valuations. Methods for determining the required rate of return are discussed later in the chapter.

11-1d Free Cash Flow Model

For firms that do not pay dividends, a more suitable valuation may be the free cash flow model, which is based on the present value of future cash flows. The first step is to estimate the free cash flows that will result from operations. Second, subtract existing liabilities to determine the value of the firm. Third, divide the value of the firm by the number of shares to derive a value per share.

Limitations   The limitation of this model is the difficulty of obtaining an accurate estimate of free cash flow per period. One possibility is to start with forecasted earnings and then add a forecast of the firm's noncash expenses and capital investment and working capital investment required to support the growth in the forecasted earnings. Obtaining accurate earnings forecasts can be difficult, however. Even if earnings can be forecast accurately, the flexibility of accounting rules can cause major errors in estimating free cash flow based on earnings.

11-2 Required Rate of Return on Stocks

When investors attempt to value a firm based on discounted cash flows, they must determine the required rate of return by investors who invest in that stock. Investors require a return that reflects the risk-free interest rate plus a risk premium. Although investors generally require a higher return on firms that exhibit more risk, there is not complete agreement on the ideal measure of risk or the way risk should be used to derive the required rate of return.

11-2a Capital Asset Pricing Model

The capital asset pricing model (CAPM) is sometimes used to estimate the required rate of return for any firm with publicly traded stock. The CAPM is based on the premise that the only important risk of a firm is **systematic risk**, or the risk that results from exposure to general stock market movements. The CAPM is not concerned with so-called unsystematic risk, which is specific to an individual firm, because investors can avoid that type of risk by holding diversified portfolios. That is, any particular adverse condition (such as a labor strike) affecting one particular firm in an investor's stock portfolio should be offset in a given period by some favorable condition affecting another firm in the portfolio. In contrast, the systematic impact of general stock market movements on stocks in the portfolio cannot be diversified away because most of the stocks would be adversely affected by a general market decline.

The CAPM suggests that the return of a stock (R_j) is influenced by the prevailing risk-free rate (R_f), the market return (R_m), and the beta (B_j), as follows:

$$R_j = R_f + B_j(R_m - R_f)$$

where B_j is measured as the covariance between R_j and R_m, which reflects the asset's sensitivity to general stock market movements. The CAPM implies that, given a specific R_f and R_m, investors will require a higher return on a stock that has a higher beta. A higher beta implies a higher covariance between the stock's returns and market returns, which reflects a greater sensitivity of the stock's return to general market movements.

Estimating the Market Risk Premium   The yield on newly issued Treasury bonds is commonly used as a proxy for the risk-free rate. The term within parentheses in the previous equation is the market risk premium: the return of the market in excess of the risk-free rate. Historical data for 30 or more years can be used to determine the average market risk premium over time. This serves as an estimate of the market risk premium that will exist in the future. However, in some periods, the market risk premium may be higher than in other periods.

EXAMPLE

During the financial crisis, there was much uncertainty surrounding the valuations of stocks in general. Some investors were only willing to maintain investments in the stock market if the market risk premium was sufficiently high to compensate them for the risk of investing in the stock market. That is, prices of all stocks in the market had to be sufficiently discounted in order to offer sufficient upside potential to attract investors.

In some other periods when stock market conditions are very favorable, investors may not be as concerned about the risk of the stock market in general. In these periods, investors do not require such a large market risk premium, as theydo not fear that the market is susceptible to a major decline. ●

Estimating the Firm's Beta   A stock's beta is typically measured by applying regression analysis to determine the sensitivity of the asset's return to the market return based on monthly or quarterly data over the last four years or so. The stock's return is the dependent variable, and the market's return (as measured by the S&P 500 index or some other suitable proxy) is the independent variable over those same periods. A computer spreadsheet package such as Excel can be used to run the regression analysis. This analysis focuses specifically on estimating the slope coefficient, which represents the estimate of each stock's beta (see Appendix B for more information on using regression analysis). If the slope coefficient of an individual stock is estimated to be 1.2, this means that, for a given return in the market, the stock's expected return is 1.2 times that amount.

The estimated betas for many stocks are reported on many financial websites and in investment services such as *Value Line*, and betas can be computed by the individual investor who understands how to apply regression analysis. Since a stock's sensitivity to market conditions may change over time in response to changes in the firm's operating characteristics, the stock's beta may also change over time.

Application of the CAPM   Given the risk-free rate as well as estimates of the firm's beta and the market risk premium, it is possible to estimate the required rate of return from investing in the firm's stock.

EXAMPLE

The beta of the stock for Vaxon, Inc., is estimated as 1.2 according to the regression analysis just explained. The prevailing risk-free rate is 6 percent, and the market risk premium is estimated to be 7 percent based on historical data. A stock's risk premium is computed as the market risk premium multiplied by the stock's beta, so Vaxon stock's risk premium (above the risk-free rate) is $0.07 \times 1.2 = 8.4$ percent. Therefore, the required rate of return on Vaxon stock is

$$R_j = 6\% + 1.2(7\%)$$
$$= 14.4\%$$

Because the required rate of return on this stock is 14.4 percent, Vaxon's estimated future cash flows can be discounted at that rate when deriving the firm's present value. ●

At any given time, the required rates of return estimated by the CAPM will vary across stocks because of differences in their risk premiums, which are due to differences in their systematic risk (as measured by beta).

11-3 Factors That Affect Stock Prices

Stock prices are driven by three types of factors: (1) economic factors, (2) market-related factors, and (3) firm-specific factors.

11-3a Economic Factors

WEB

biz.yahoo.com/ne.
html
Announcements of
economic conditions
and other news that
may affect stock prices.

A firm's value should reflect the present value of its future cash flows. Investors therefore consider various economic factors that affect a firm's cash flows when valuing a firm to determine whether its stock is over- or undervalued.

Impact of Economic Growth   An increase in economic growth is expected to increase the demand for products and services produced by firms and thereby increase a firm's cash flows and valuation. Participants in the stock markets monitor economic indicators such as employment, gross domestic product, retail sales, and personal income because these indicators may signal information about economic growth and therefore affect cash flows. In general, unexpected favorable information about the economy tends to cause a favorable revision of a firm's expected cash flows and hence places upward pressure on the firm's value. Because the government's fiscal and monetary policies affect economic growth, they are also continually monitored by investors.

WEB

http://research.
stlouisfed.org
Economic information
that can be used to
value securities, in-
cluding money supply
information, gross do-
mestic product, inter-
est rates, and exchange
rates.

Exhibit 11.1 shows U.S. stock market performance based on the S&P 500, an index of 500 large U.S. stocks. The stock market's weak performance in 2008 was partially due to weak economic conditions, while the strong performance in the 2010–2013 period was due to an improvement in economic conditions.

However, there were many short intervals in the 2010–2013 period in which U.S. stock market prices declined. The financial media typically blamed the weakness on con-cerns about the federal budget deficit. The general argument is that the federal budget deficit is out of control, and that if the U.S. government continues its large level of spending, it will encounter problems similar to the governments of Greece, Spain, and Portugal. That is, at some point, creditors will no longer trust that the U.S. government is capable of repaying its debt, and this will lead to a lack of confidence in U.S. financial markets. Consequently, it could encourage investors to withdraw investments from these markets, causing a decline in prices of various securities.

Impact of Interest Rates

One of the most prominent economic forces driving stock market prices is the risk-free interest rate. Investors should consider purchasing a risky asset only if they expect to be compensated with a risk premium for the risk incurred. Given a choice of risk-free Treasury securities or stocks, investors should pur-chase stocks only if they are appropriately priced to reflect a sufficiently high expected return *above* the risk-free rate.

The relationship between interest rates and stock prices can vary over time. In theory, a high interest rate should raise the required rate of return by investors and therefore reduce the present value of future cash flows generated by a stock. However, interest rates

Exhibit 11.1   Stock Market Trend Based on the S&P 500 Index

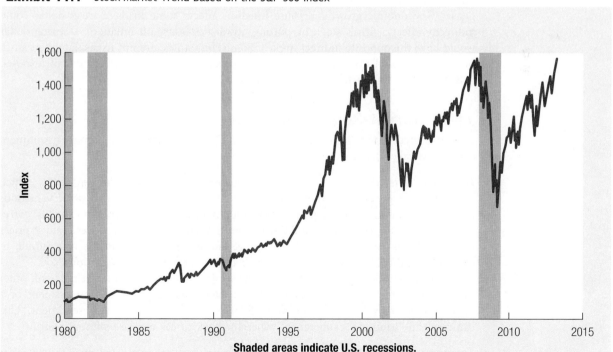

Shaded areas indicate U.S. recessions.

Source: *Federal Reserve.*

commonly rise in response to an increase in economic growth, so stock prices may rise in response to an increase in expected cash flows even if investors' required rate of return rises.

Conversely, a lower interest rate should boost the present value of cash flows and therefore boost stock prices. However, lower interest rates commonly occur in response to weak economic conditions, which tend to reduce expected cash flows of firms. Overall, the effect of interest rates should be considered along with economic growth and other factors when seeking a more complete explanation of stock price movements.

Impact of the Dollar's Exchange Rate Value   The value of the dollar can affect U.S. stock prices for a variety of reasons. First, foreign investors prefer to purchase U.S. stocks when the dollar is weak and to sell them when the dollar is near its peak. Thus, the foreign demand for any given U.S. stock may be higher when the dollar is expected to strengthen, other things being equal. Stock prices are also affected by the impact of the dollar's changing value on cash flows. The stock prices of U.S. firms primarily involved in exporting could be favorably affected by a weak dollar and adversely affected by a strong dollar, whereas U.S. importing firms could be affected in the opposite manner.

Stock prices of U.S. companies may also be affected by exchange rates if stock market participants measure performance by reported earnings. A multinational corporation's consolidated reported earnings will be affected by exchange rate fluctuations even if the company's cash flows are not affected. A weaker dollar tends to inflate the reported earnings of a U.S. based company's foreign subsidiaries. Some analysts argue that any effect of exchange rate movements on financial statements is irrelevant unless cash flows are also affected.

The changing value of the dollar can also affect stock prices by affecting expectations of economic factors that influence the firm's performance. For example, if a weak dollar stimulates the U.S. economy, it may enhance the value of a U.S. firm whose sales depend on the U.S. economy. A strong dollar, however, could adversely affect this firm if it dampens U.S. economic growth. Because inflation affects some firms, a weak dollar could indirectly affect a firm's stock by putting upward pressure on inflation. A strong dollar would have the opposite indirect impact. Some companies attempt to insulate their stock price from the dollar's changing value, but other companies purposely remain exposed with the intent to benefit from any changes.

11-3b Market-Related Factors

Market-related factors also drive stock prices. These factors include investor sentiment and the so-called January effect.

Investor Sentiment   A key market-related factor is investor sentiment, which represents the general mood of investors in the stock market. Since stock valuations reflect expectations, in some periods the stock market performance is not highly correlated with existing economic conditions. Even though the economy is weak, stock prices may rise if most investors expect that the economy will improve in the near future. In other words, there is a positive sentiment because of optimistic expectations.

Movements in stock prices may be partially attributed to investors' reliance on other investors for stock market valuation. Rather than making their own assessment of a firm's value, many investors appear to focus on the general investor sentiment. This can result in "irrational exuberance," whereby stock prices increase without reason.

January Effect   Because many portfolio managers are evaluated over the calendar year, they prefer investing in riskier, small stocks at the beginning of the year and then shifting to larger, more stable companies near the end of the year in order to lock in their gains. This tendency places upward pressure on small stocks in January each year, resulting in the January effect. Some studies have found that most of the annual stock market gains occur in January. Once investors discovered the January effect, they attempted to take more positions in stocks in the prior month. This has placed upward pressure on stocks in mid-December, causing the January effect to begin in December.

11-3c Firm-Specific Factors

A firm's stock price is affected not only by macroeconomic and market conditions but also by firm-specific conditions. Some firms are more exposed to conditions within their own industry than to general economic conditions, so participants monitor industry sales forecasts, entry into the industry by new competitors, and price movements of the industry's products. Stock market participants may focus on announcements by specific firms that signal information about a firm's sales growth, earnings, or other characteristics that may cause a revision in the expected cash flows to be generated by that firm.

Change in Dividend Policy   An increase in dividends may reflect the firm's expectation that it can more easily afford to pay dividends. In contrast, a decrease in dividends may reflect the firm's expectation that it will not have sufficient cash flow.

Earnings Surprises   Recent earnings are used to forecast future earnings and thus to forecast a firm's future cash flows. When a firm's announced earnings are higher than expected, some investors raise their estimates of the firm's future cash flows and hence revalue its stock upward. However, an announcement of lower-than-expected earnings can cause investors to reduce their valuation of a firm's future cash flows and its stock.

Acquisitions and Divestitures   The expected acquisition of a firm typically results in an increased demand for the target's stock, which raises its price. Investors recognize that the target's stock price will be bid up once the acquiring firm attempts to acquire the target's stock. The effect on the acquiring firm's stock is less clear, as it depends on the perceived synergies that could result from the acquisition. Divestitures tend to be regarded as a favorable signal about a firm if the divested assets are unrelated to the firm's core business. The typical interpretation by the market in this case is that the firm intends to focus on its core business.

Expectations   Investors do not necessarily wait for a firm to announce a new policy before they revalue the firm's stock. Instead, they attempt to anticipate new policies so that they can make their move in the market before other investors. In this way, they may be able to pay a lower price for a specific stock or sell the stock at a higher price. For example, they may use the firm's financial reports or recent statements by the firm's executives to speculate on whether the firm will adjust its dividend policy. The disadvantage of trading based on incomplete information is that an investor may not correctly anticipate the firm's future policies.

WEB

http://screen.yahoo.com/stocks.html
Screens stocks based on various possible valuation indicators.

11-3d Tax Effects

The difference between the price at which a stock is sold versus the price at which it was purchased is referred to as the **capital gain**. When investors hold a stock position less than one year, the gain is referred to as a **short-term capital gain**, whereas the gain on a stock position held for one year or longer is referred to as a **long-term capital gain**. Tax laws affect the after-tax cash flows that investors receive from selling stocks, and

USING THE WALL STREET JOURNAL

Biggest Stock Gains and Losses

The *Wall Street Journal* identifies the stocks that experienced the largest percentage gains and losses since the previous day, as shown here. It also discloses the percentage change in those stocks over the last 52 weeks and the range of the stock price over that period.

Percentage Gainers...

Company	Symbol	Volume (in 000s)	Close	Net chg	% chg	High	Low	% chg
Old Second Bancorp	OSBC	114	3.75	0.76	**25.41**	3.75	1.10	**212.5**
Uni-Pixel	UNXL	2,748	22.80	4.00	**21.28**	24.93	4.83	**321.4**
Meru Networks	MERU	2,837	4.91	0.81	**19.76**	5.43	1.42	**4.0**
Innotrac	INOC	3	3.18	0.48	**17.78**	3.60	1.16	**171.8**
Emclaire Financial Corp	EMCF	3	27.50	3.92	**16.62**	30.14	16.75	**63.7**
Guidewire Software	GWRE	4,057	36.75	5.22	**16.56**	38.43	20.04	**62.5**
Spherix	SPEX	123	11.67	1.60	**15.89**	28.20	5.51	**-28.8**
IMPAC Mortgage Holdings	IMH	260	15.17	1.78	**13.29**	18.00	1.93	**451.6**
Optimer Pharm	OPTR	4,173	12.13	1.41	**13.15**	16.49	8.64	**-5.2**
Vicon Indus	VII	23	2.95	0.34	**13.03**	3.70	2.33	**-16.7**
BlueLinx Holdings	BXC	440	3.14	0.35	**12.54**	3.48	1.83	**34.2**
Xinyuan Real Estate	XIN	2,107	5.02	0.55	**12.30**	5.12	2.31	**104.9**
Sinopec Shanghai Petro	SHI	61	44.37	4.63	**11.65**	44.44	24.64	**17.7**
Endeavour Intl	END	1,721	2.72	0.28	**11.48**	13.48	2.38	**-76.5**
U.S. Silica Holdings	SLCA	1,529	23.97	2.35	**10.87**	24.63	9.02	**41.7**
iGo	IGOI	15	3.45	0.34	**10.80**	15.00	2.76	**-58.9**
Research Frontiers	REFR	94	3.42	0.33	**10.68**	5.17	2.79	**-2.3**
Dollar Tree	DLTR	10,535	45.39	4.31	**10.49**	56.82	37.12	**2.6**

Percentage Losers

Company	Symbol	Volume (in 000s)	Close	Net chg	% chg	High	Low	% chg
CombiMatrix	CBMX	1,174	3.56	-1.34	**-27.35**	17.50	1.40	**-76.9**
Cincinnati Bell	CBB	60,307	3.23	-0.92	**-22.17**	5.89	3.15	**-13.9**
Accretive Health	AH	13,171	9.57	-2.54	**-20.97**	27.88	7.75	**-63.2**
ProPhase Labs	PRPH	76	1.80	-0.45	**-20.00**	2.25	0.53	**78.2**
Orbital Corp ADS	OBT	6	4.61	-1.04	**-18.41**	7.00	2.59	**-4.8**
Wireless Ronin Techs	RNIN	45	2.05	-0.35	**-14.58**	5.65	1.70	**-54.4**
ProSharesUltVIXST	UVXY	31,770	10.31	-1.68	**-14.01**	373.80	8.71	**-96.9**
World Energy Sols	XWES	95	4.00	-0.65	**-13.98**	5.49	2.55	**-18.0**
First Solar	FSLR	22,082	27.04	-4.32	**-13.78**	36.98	11.43	**-16.3**
China Mobile Games ADS	CMGE	451	8.30	-1.29	**-13.45**	16.50	3.00	**...**
VS 2x VIX Short Term	TVIX	13,473	4.69	-0.70	**-12.99**	176.40	4.00	**-97.2**
Globus Maritime	GLBS	18	1.80	-0.25	**-12.20**	6.00	1.41	**-63.7**
China Digital TV Hldg ADS	STV	434	1.93	-0.26	**-11.87**	4.38	1.67	**-51.5**
Novogen ADS	NVGN	269	6.68	-0.86	**-11.41**	10.49	0.48	**778.8**
C-TRACKS ETN on CVOL	CVOL	3	16.78	-2.06	**-10.93**	200.00	15.02	**-90.8**
GrafTech Intl	GTI	7,172	7.15	-0.77	**-9.72**	13.00	6.90	**-43.7**
Kadant Inc	KAI	69	24.37	-2.62	**-9.71**	28.74	20.50	**11.6**
IFM Investments ADS	CTC	33	2.42	-0.25	**-9.36**	4.35	0.88	**13.6**

therefore can affect the demand for stocks. Holding other factors constant, stocks should be valued higher when capital gains tax rates are relatively low.

Tax laws can also cause some stocks to be more desirable than others. Some stocks have more potential for large capital gains, and therefore may be more sensitive to the tax laws on capital gains. Conversely, other stocks that pay steady dividends typically have smaller capital gains and therefore may not be affected as much by tax laws on capital gains. However, stocks that pay dividends are affected by dividend tax laws. A low tax rate imposed on dividends will cause dividend-paying stocks to be more desirable, and will increase the valuation of these stocks. A high tax rate imposed on dividends will cause these stocks to be less desirable, and will reduce the valuation of these stocks.

In 2013, tax rates on dividends increased from 15% to 20% for investors in high personal income tax brackets. Some politicians were recommending that dividends should be taxed at the personal income tax rate, which is almost 40% in the highest personal income tax bracket. If such a change in tax rates had occurred, it might have caused a major decline in the demand for stocks that pay dividends.

11-3e Integration of Factors Affecting Stock Prices

Exhibit 11.2 illustrates the underlying forces that cause a stock's price to change over time. As with the pricing of debt securities, the required rate of return is relevant, as are the economic factors that affect the risk-free interest rate. Stock market

Exhibit 11.2 Framework for Explaining Changes in a Firm's Stock Price over Time

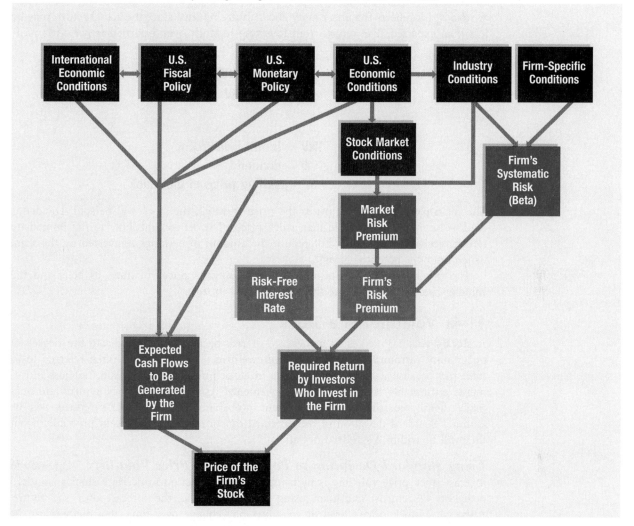

participants also monitor indicators that can affect the risk-free interest rate, which in turn affects the required return by investors who invest in stocks. Indicators of inflation (such as the consumer price index and producer price index) and of government borrowing (such as the budget deficit and the volume of funds borrowed at upcoming Treasury bond auctions) also affect the risk-free rate and thereby the required return of investors. In general, whenever these indicators signal the expectation of higher interest rates, there is upward pressure on the required rate of return by investors and downward pressure on a firm's value.

In addition, it is common to estimate expected future cash flows when deriving a firm's value, and these cash flows are influenced by economic conditions, industry conditions, and firm-specific conditions. Exhibit 11.2 provides an overview of what stock market participants monitor when attempting to anticipate future stock price movements.

11-4 STOCK RISK

A stock's risk reflects the uncertainty about future returns, since the actual return may be less than expected. The return from investing in stock over a particular period is measured as

$$R = \frac{(SP - INV) + D}{INV}$$

where

$$INV = \text{initial investment}$$
$$D = \text{dividend}$$
$$SP = \text{selling price of the stock}$$

The main source of uncertainty is the price at which the stock will be sold. Dividends tend to be much more stable than stock prices. Dividends contribute to the immediate return received by investors but reduce the amount of earnings reinvested by the firm, which limits its potential growth.

The risk of a stock can be measured by using its price volatility, its beta, and the value-at-risk method. Each of these is discussed in turn.

11-4a Volatility of a Stock

A stock's volatility serves as a measure of risk because it may indicate the degree of uncertainty surrounding the stock's future returns. The volatility is often referred to as *total risk* because it reflects movements in stock prices for any reason, not just movements attributable to stock market movements. Assuming that stock returns are normally distributed, there is a 68 percent probability that the stock's returns will be within 1 standard deviation of the expected outcome and a 95 percent probability that they will be within 2 standard deviations.

Using Standard Deviation to Forecast Stock Price Volatility   One way to forecast stock price volatility is by using a historical period to derive a stock's standard deviation of returns, and then using that estimate as the forecast over the future. Although a stock price's level of volatility may change over time, this method can be useful when there is no obvious trend in volatility.

Using Volatility Patterns to Forecast Stock Price Volatility   A second method for forecasting stock price volatility is to use volatility patterns in previous periods.

EXAMPLE

The standard deviation of daily stock returns is determined for each of the last three months. Then, a time-series trend of these standard deviation levels is used to form an estimate for the standard deviation of daily stock returns over the next month. This method differs from the historical method in that it uses information beyond that contained in the previous month. For example, the forecast for September might be based on the following weighting scheme: 50 percent of the standard deviation in the most recent month (August) plus 30 percent of the standard deviation in the month before that (July) plus 20 percent of the standard deviation in the month before that (June). ●

Normally the weights and the number of previous periods (lags) that were most accurate (i.e., had the lowest forecast error) in previous periods are used. However, various economic and political factors can cause stock price volatility to change abruptly, so even a sophisticated time-series model does not necessarily generate accurate forecasts of stock price volatility.

Using Implied Volatility to Forecast Stock Price Volatility A third method for forecasting stock price volatility is to derive the stock's implied standard deviation (ISD) from the stock option pricing model (options are discussed in detail in Chapter 14). The premium on a call option for a stock depends on various factors, including the stock's volatility as anticipated by investors. By considering the actual option premium paid by investors for a specific stock along with the values of all other factors that affect the premium, it is possible to derive the anticipated volatility of that stock.

Forecasting Stock Price Volatility of the Stock Market Market participants who want to forecast volatility of the stock market in general can monitor the volatility index (VIX) derived from stock options on the S&P 500 stock index. At a given point in time, this index measures investors' expectation of the stock market volatility over the next 30 days. Some investors refer to VIX as an indicator of stock market fear. If conditions occur that cause investors to expect more uncertainty surrounding stock prices over the next 30 days, this means that investors would require a higher premium in order to sell call options (as explained in Chapter 14). As the option premium on options representing the S&P 500 index increase, the VIX index will increase.

Conversely, if conditions in the stock market are expected to be more stable over the next 30 days, the premium on call options would decline and the VIX index would decline. While it would be impossible to survey all market participants to obtain their view of stock market volatility, the movements in the premium of options on the stock market index are commonly used to derive an estimate of expected stock market volatility.

Since the VIX index simply measures the expectations of investors in general, it will not necessarily provide a perfectly accurate forecast of the stock market volatility over the next 30 days. Nevertheless, many investors believe that it is a useful indicator of expected stock market volatility.

Exhibit 11.3 shows movements in the VIX level over time. Notice how it increased during the credit crisis in 2008, when there was much uncertainty about the U.S. economy and about stock valuations in general. During the2009–2013 period, economic conditions stabilized, stock market conditions stabilized, and the VIX level declined substantially.

When there is a sharp rise in VIX, stock prices tend to decline, as the conditions that cause more stock market fear also cause investors to sell their stocks, which results in lower stock prices. Conversely, when there is a sharp decline in VIX, stock prices tend to rise, as the conditions that make investors believe that stock prices will be more stable also encourage investors to purchase stocks, which results in higher stock prices.

Volatility of a Stock Portfolio Participants in the stock market tend to invest in a portfolio of stocks rather than a single stock, so they are more concerned with the risk of a portfolio than with the risk of an individual stock. A portfolio's volatility depends on the volatility of the individual stocks in the portfolio, on the correlations between returns of the stocks in the portfolio, and on the proportion of total funds invested in each stock. The portfolio's volatility can be measured by the standard deviation:

$$\sigma_p = \sqrt{w_i^2 \sigma_i^2 + w_j^2 \sigma_j^2 + \sum_{i=1}^{n} \sum_{j=1}^{n} w_i w_j \sigma_i \sigma_j \text{CORR}_{ij}}$$

where

Exhibit 11.3 Implied Volatility Index for U.S. Stocks over Time

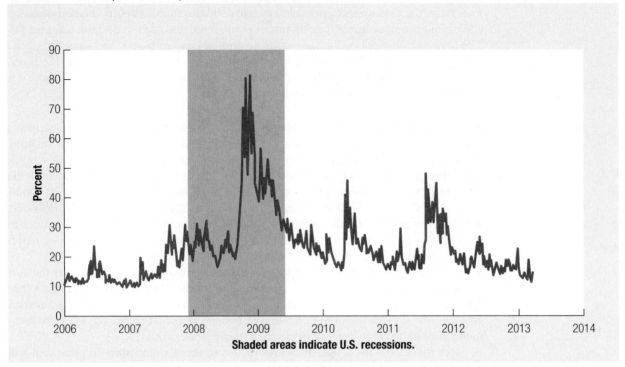

Shaded areas indicate U.S. recessions.

Source: *Federal Reserve and Chicago Board Options Exchange.*

σ_i = **standard deviation of returns of the *i*th stock**
σ_j = **standard deviation of returns of the *j*th stock**
$CORR_{ij}$ = **correlation coefficient between the *i*th and *j*th stocks**
w_i = **proportion of funds invested in the *i*th stock**
w_j = **proportion of funds invested in the *j*th stock**

For portfolios containing more securities, the formula for the standard deviation contains the standard deviation of each stock and the correlation coefficients between all pairs of stocks in the portfolio, weighted by the proportion of funds invested in each stock. The equation for a two-stock portfolio is sufficient to demonstrate that, when other factors are held constant, a stock portfolio has more volatility when its individual stock volatilities are high and when its individual stock returns are highly correlated. As an extreme example, if the returns of the stocks are all perfectly positively correlated (correlation coefficients = 1.0), the portfolio will have a relatively high degree of volatility because all stocks will experience peaks or troughs simultaneously. Conversely, a stock portfolio containing some stocks with low or negative correlation will have less volatility because the stocks will not experience peaks and troughs at the same time. Some offsetting effects will occur, smoothing the returns of the portfolio over time.

Because the volatilities and correlations of a portfolio's individual stocks can change over time, so too can the volatility of the portfolio. One method of forecasting portfolio volatility starts with deriving forecasts of individual volatility levels (as described previously); then the correlation coefficient for each pair of stocks in the portfolio is forecast by estimating the correlation in recent periods. Finally, the forecasted volatilities of individual correlation coefficients are used to estimate the portfolio's future volatility.

11-4b Beta of a Stock

As explained earlier, a stock's beta measures the sensitivity of its returns to market returns. This measure of risk is used by many investors who have a diversified portfolio of stocks and believe that the unsystematic risk of the portfolio is therefore diversified away (because favorable firm-specific characteristics will offset unfavorable firm-specific characteristics).

EXAMPLE

Exhibit 11.4 shows how the probability distribution of a stock's returns depends on its beta. At one extreme, Stock A (with a very low beta) is less responsive to market movements in either direction, so its possible returns range only from −4.8 percent under poor market conditions to 6 percent under the most favorable market conditions. At the other extreme, Stock D (with a very high beta) has possible returns that range from −11.2 percent under poor market conditions to 14 percent under the most favorable market conditions. This stock is perceived to be risky because it experiences large losses when stock market conditions decline. ●

Beta of a Stock Portfolio   Portfolio risk is commonly measured by beta or volatility (standard deviation), just as the risk of individual stocks is.

The beta of a stock portfolio can be measured as

$$\beta_p = \sum w_i \beta_i$$

That is, the portfolio beta is a weighted average of the betas of stocks that make up the portfolio, where the weights reflect the proportion of funds invested in each stock. The equation is intuitive because it simply suggests that a portfolio consisting of high-beta stocks will have a relatively high beta. This type of portfolio normally performs poorly relative to other stock portfolios in a period when the market return is negative.

The beta of each individual stock may be forecast in a subjective manner; for example, a portfolio manager may forecast that a stock's beta will increase from its existing level of 0.8 to 0.9 because the firm has initiated a more aggressive growth strategy. Alternatively, the manager can assess a set of historical periods to determine whether there is a trend in the beta over those periods and then apply the trend.

The beta of a stock and its volatility are typically related. High-beta stocks are expected to be relatively volatile because they are more sensitive to market returns over time. Likewise, low-beta stocks are expected to be less volatile because they are less responsive to market returns.

11-4c Value at Risk

Value at risk is a measurement that estimates the largest expected loss to a particular investment position for a specified confidence level. It is intended to warn investors about the potential maximum loss that could occur. If the investors are uncomfortable with the potential loss that could occur in a day or a week, they can revise their investment portfolio to make it less risky.

The value-at-risk measurement focuses on the pessimistic portion of the probability distribution of returns from the investment of concern. For example, a portfolio manager might use a confidence level of 90 percent, which estimates the maximum daily expected loss for a stock in 90 percent of the trading days over an upcoming period. The higher the level of confidence desired, the larger the maximum expected loss that could occur

Exhibit 11.4   How Beta Influences Probability Distributions

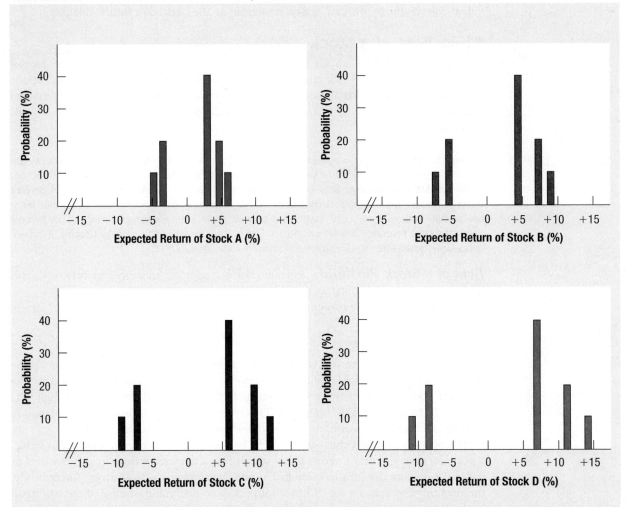

PROBABILITY	R_m	STOCK A'S EXPECTED RETURNS, $E(R)$, if $B_i = 0.6$	STOCK B'S EXPECTED RETURNS, $E(R)$, if $B_i = 0.9$	STOCK C'S EXPECTED RETURNS, $E(R)$, if $B_i = 1.2$	STOCK D'S EXPECTED RETURNS, $E(R)$, if $B_i = 1.4$
10%	−8%	−4.8%	−7.2%	−9.6%	−11.2%
20	−6	−3.6	−5.4	−7.2	−8.4
40	5	3	4.5	6	7
20	8	4.8	7.2	9.6	11.2
10	10	6	9	12	14

for a given type of investment. That is, one may expect that the daily loss from holding a particular stock will be no worse than −5 percent when using a 90 percent confidence level but as much as −8 percent when using a 99 percent confidence level. In essence, the more confidence investors have that the actual loss will be no greater than the expected maximum loss, the further they move into the left tail of the probability distribution.

Application Using Historical Returns   An obvious way of using value at risk is to assess historical data. For example, an investor may determine that, out of the last 100 trading days, a stock experienced a decline of greater than 7 percent on 5 different days, or 5 percent of the days assessed. This information could be used to infer a maximum daily loss of no more than 7 percent for that stock based on a 95 percent confidence level for an upcoming period.

Application Using the Standard Deviation   An alternative approach is to measure the standard deviation of daily returns over the previous period and then apply it to derive boundaries for a specific confidence level.

EXAMPLE

Assume that the standard deviation of daily returns for a particular stock in a recent historical period is 2 percent. Also assume that the 95 percent confidence level is desired for the maximum loss. If the daily returns are normally distributed, the lower boundary (the left tail of the probability distribution) is about 1.65 standard deviations away from the expected outcome. For an expected daily return of 0.1 percent, the lower boundary is

$$0.1\% - [1.65 \times (2\%)] = -3.2\%$$

The expected daily return of 0.1 percent may reflect subjective information, or it could be the average daily return during the recent historical period assessed. The lower boundary for a given confidence level can easily be derived for any expected daily return. For example, if the expected daily return is 0.14 percent, the lower boundary is

$$0.14\% - [1.65 \times (2\%)] = -3.16\%$$ ●

Application Using Beta   A third method of estimating the maximum expected loss for a given confidence level is to apply the stock's beta.

EXAMPLE

Assume that a stock's beta over the last 100 days is 1.2. Also assume that the stock market is expected to perform no worse than −2.5 percent on a daily basis based on a 95 percent confidence level. Given the stock's beta of 1.2 and a maximum market loss of −2.5 percent, the maximum loss to the stock over a given day is estimated to be

$$1.2 \times (-2.5\%) = -3\%$$

The maximum expected market loss for the 95 percent confidence level can be derived subjectively or by assessing the last 100 days or so (in the same manner described for the two previous methods that can be used to derive the maximum expected loss for an individual stock). ●

Deriving the Maximum Dollar Loss   Once the maximum percentage loss for a given confidence level is determined, it can be applied to derive the maximum dollar loss of a particular investment.

EXAMPLE

Assume that an investor has a $20 million investment in a stock. The maximum dollar loss is determined by applying the maximum percentage loss to the value of the investment. If the investor used beta to measure the maximum expected loss as explained previously, the maximum percentage loss over one day would be −3 percent. Hence the maximum daily loss in dollars is

$$(-3\%) \times \$20,000,000 = \$600,000$$ ●

Application to a Stock Portfolio Value at risk is also commonly used to measure the risk of a stock portfolio. The same three methods used to derive the maximum expected loss of one stock can be applied to derive the maximum expected loss of a stock portfolio for a given confidence level. For instance, the returns of a stock portfolio over the past 100 days or so can be assessed to derive the maximum expected loss. Alternatively, the standard deviation of the portfolio's returns can be estimated over the past 100 days to derive a lower boundary at a specified confidence level. Still another alternative is to estimate the beta of the portfolio's returns over the past 100 days and then apply that beta to a maximum expected daily loss in the stock market to derive a maximum expected loss in the stock portfolio over a given day.

Adjusting the Investment Horizon Desired An investor who wants to assess the maximum loss over a week or a month can apply the same methods. However, it is important in this case to use a historical series that matches the investment horizon. In order to assess the maximum loss over a given week in the near future, a historical series of weekly returns of that stock (or stock portfolio) can be used.

Adjusting the Length of the Historical Period The previous examples used a historical series of 100 trading days, but if conditions have changed such that only the most recent 70 days reflect the general state of market conditions, then those 70 days should be used. However, a sub period of weak market performance should not be discarded because a similar one could occur again.

Limitations of the Value-at-Risk Method A common criticism of using historical periods to measure value at risk is that portfolio managers may be using a relatively calm historical period when assessing possible future risk. If, for example, the distribution of returns has been narrow because the economy was unusually stable in the previous period, the maximum loss expected in a future period (when the economy is not as stable) may be underestimated. In the language of portfolio managers, the distribution of possible returns used to estimate value at risk may have short tails (edge of the distribution) whereas the distribution of returns over the future period may have long tails. This implies that the actual loss of a portfolio may be more pronounced than the expected maximum loss. For instance, estimating the maximum loss during the stable period just prior to the credit crisis would have underestimated the risk of a stock portfolio during the credit crisis, when stocks actually experienced major losses.

11-5 RISK-ADJUSTED STOCK PERFORMANCE

The performance of a stock or a stock portfolio over a particular period can be measured by its excess return (return above the risk-free rate) for that period divided by its risk. Two common methods of measuring performance are the Sharpe index and the Treynor index.

11-5a Sharpe Index

If total variability is thought to be the appropriate measure of risk, a stock's risk-adjusted returns can be determined by the reward-to-variability ratio (also called the **Sharpe index**):

$$\text{Sharpe index} = \frac{\overline{R} - \overline{R}_f}{\sigma}$$

where

$$\overline{R} = \text{average return on the stock}$$
$$\overline{R}_f = \text{average risk-free rate}$$
$$\sigma = \text{standard deviation of the stock's return}$$

The higher the stock's mean return relative to the mean risk-free rate and the lower the standard deviation, the higher the Sharpe index. This index measures the excess return above the risk-free rate per unit of risk.

Assume the following information for two stocks:

- Average return for Sooner stock = 16%
- Average return for Longhorn stock = 14%
- Average risk-free rate = 10%
- Standard deviation of Sooner stock returns = 15%
- Standard deviation of Longhorn stock returns = 8%

Then

$$\text{Sharpe index for Sooner stock} = \frac{16\% - 10\%}{15\%}$$
$$= 0.40$$
$$\text{Sharpe index for Longhorn stock} = \frac{14\% - 10\%}{8\%}$$
$$= 0.50$$

Even though Sooner stock had a higher average percentage return, Longhorn stock had a higher performance because of its lower risk. If a stock's average return is less than the average risk-free rate, the Sharpe index for that stock will be negative. ●

11-5b Treynor Index

If beta is thought to be the most appropriate type of risk, a stock's risk-adjusted returns can be determined by the Treynor index, computed as

$$\text{Treynor index} = \frac{\overline{R} - \overline{R}_f}{B}$$

where B is the stock's beta. The Treynor index differs from the Sharpe index only in that it uses beta rather than the standard deviation to measure the stock's risk. The higher the Treynor index, the higher the return (per unit of risk) relative to the risk-free rate.

Using the information provided earlier on Sooner and Longhorn stock and assuming that Sooner's stock beta is 1.2 and Longhorn's beta is 1.0, the Treynor index is computed for each stock as follows:

$$\text{Treynor index for Sooner stock} = \frac{16\% - 10\%}{1.2}$$
$$= 0.05$$
$$\text{Treynor index for Longhorn stock} = \frac{14\% - 10\%}{1.0}$$
$$= 0.04$$

Based on the Treynor index, Sooner stock experienced higher performance. ●

A comparison of this example and the previous one shows that which stock performs better depends on the measure of risk and thus on the index used. In some cases, different indexes will lead to the same conclusions. Like the Sharpe index, the Treynor index is negative for a stock whose average return is less than the average risk-free rate.

11-6 STOCK MARKET EFFICIENCY

If stock markets are efficient, the prices of stocks at any point in time should fully reflect all available information. As investors attempt to capitalize on new information that is not already accounted for, stock prices should adjust immediately. Investors commonly over- or underreact to information. This does not mean that markets are inefficient unless the reaction is biased (i.e., consistently over- or underreacting). Investors who can recognize such bias will be able to earn abnormally high risk-adjusted returns.

11-6a Forms of Efficiency

Efficient markets can be classified into three forms: weak, semistrong, and strong.

Weak-Form Efficiency   **Weak-form efficiency** suggests that security prices reflect all market-related information, such as historical security price movements and volume of securities trades. Thus investors will not be able to earn abnormal returns on a trading strategy that is based solely on past price movements.

Semistrong-Form Efficiency   **Semistrong-form efficiency** suggests that security prices fully reflect all public information. The difference between public information and market-related information is that public information also includes announcements by firms, economic news or events, and political news or events. Market-related information is a subset of public information. Therefore, if semistrong-form efficiency holds, weak-form efficiency must also hold. It is possible, however, for weak-form efficiency to hold even though semistrong-form efficiency does not. In this case, investors could earn abnormal returns by using the relevant information that was not immediately accounted for by the market.

Strong-Form Efficiency   **Strong-form efficiency** suggests that security prices fully reflect all information, including private or insider information. If strong-form efficiency holds, semistrong-form efficiency must hold as well. If insider information leads to abnormal returns, however, semistrong-form efficiency could hold even though strong-form efficiency does not.

Inside information gives insiders (such as some employees or board members) an unfair advantage over other investors. For example, if employees of a firm are aware of favorable news about the firm that has not yet been disclosed to the public, they may consider purchasing shares or advising their friends to purchase the firm's shares. Although such actions are illegal, they do occur and can create market inefficiencies.

11-6b Tests of the Efficient Market Hypothesis

Tests of market efficiency are segmented into three categories, as discussed next.

Test of Weak-Form Efficiency   Weak-form efficiency has been tested by searching for a nonrandom pattern in security prices. If the future change in price is related to recent changes, historical price movements could be used to earn abnormal returns. In general, studies have found that historical price changes are independent over time. This means that historical information is already reflected by today's price and cannot be used to earn abnormal profits. Even when some dependence was detected, the transaction costs offset any excess return earned.

There is some evidence that stocks have performed better in certain time periods. For example, as mentioned earlier, small stocks have performed unusually well in the month of January (the "January effect"). Second, stocks have historically performed better on Fridays than on Mondays (the "weekend effect"). Third, stocks have historically performed well on the trading days just before holidays (the "holiday effect"). To the extent that a given pattern continues and can be used by investors to earn abnormal returns, market inefficiencies exist. In most cases, there is no clear evidence that such patterns persist once they are recognized by the investment community.

One could use the number of market corrections to evaluate stock market inefficiency. During the twentieth century, there were more than 100 days on which the market (as measured by the Dow Jones Industrial Average) declined by 10 percent or more. On more than 300 days, the market declined by more than 5 percent. These abrupt declines frequently followed a market runup, which suggests that the runup might have been excessive. In other words, a market correction was necessary to counteract the excessive runup.

Test of Semistrong-Form Efficiency Semistrong-form efficiency has been tested by assessing how security returns adjust to particular announcements. Some announcements are specific to a firm, such as an announced dividend increase, an acquisition, or a stock split. Other announcements are related to the economy, such as an announced decline in the federal funds rate. In general, it was found that security prices immediately reflected the information from the announcements. Hence the securities were not consistently over- or undervalued, so abnormal returns could not consistently be achieved. This is especially true when transaction costs are accounted for.

There is evidence of unusual profits from investing in initial public offerings (IPOs). In particular, the return over the first day following the IPO tends to be abnormally high. One reason for this underpricing is that the securities firms underwriting an IPO intentionally underprice to ensure that the entire issue can be placed. Underwriters also are required to exercise due diligence in ensuring the accuracy of the information they provide to investors about the corporation. For this reason, underwriters tend to err on the low side when setting a price for IPOs.

Some analysts contend that, given the imperfect information associated with IPOs, investors would not participate unless prices are low. In other words, the potential return must be high enough to compensate not only for the risk incurred but also for the lack of information about these corporations. From this perspective, IPO underpricing does not imply market inefficiencies but rather reflects the high degree of uncertainty involved.

Test of Strong-Form Efficiency Tests of strong-form efficiency are difficult because the inside information used is not publicly available and cannot be properly tested. Nevertheless, many forms of insider trading could easily result in abnormally high returns. For example, there is clear evidence that share prices of target firms rise substantially when the acquisition is announced. If insiders purchased stock of targets prior to other investors, they would normally achieve abnormally high returns. Insiders are discouraged from using this information because it is illegal, not because markets are strong-form efficient.

GLOBAL ASPECTS

11-7 Foreign Stock Valuation and Performance

Some of the key concepts in this chapter can be adjusted so that they apply on a global basis, as explained next.

11-7a Valuation of Foreign Stocks

Foreign stocks can be valued by using the price–earnings method or the dividend discount model with an adjustment to reflect international conditions.

Price–Earnings Method   The expected earnings per share of the foreign firm are multiplied by the appropriate PE ratio (based on the firm's risk and local industry) to determine the appropriate price of the firm's stock. Though easy to use, this method is subject to some limitations when valuing foreign stocks. The PE ratio for a given industry may change continuously in some foreign markets, especially when the industry consists of just a few firms. It is therefore difficult to determine what ratio should be applied to a specific foreign firm. In addition, the PE ratio for any particular industry may need to be adjusted for the firm's country because reported earnings can be influenced by national accounting guidelines and tax laws.

Furthermore, even if U.S. investors are comfortable with their estimate of the proper PE ratio, the value derived by this method is denominated in the local foreign currency (since the estimated earnings are denominated in that currency). Therefore, U.S. investors must also consider exchange rate effects. Even if the stock is undervalued in the foreign country, it may not generate a reasonable return for U.S. investors if the foreign currency depreciates against the dollar.

Dividend Discount Model   The dividend discount model can be applied to the valuation of foreign stocks by discounting the stream of expected dividends while adjusting to account for expected exchange rate movements. Foreign stocks pay dividends in the currency of their denomination. Thus the cash flow per period to U.S. investors is the dividend (denominated in the foreign currency) multiplied by the value of that foreign currency in dollars. An expected appreciation of the currency denominating the foreign stocks will result in higher expected dollar cash flows and a higher present value. The dividend can normally be forecast with more accuracy than can the value of the foreign currency. Because of exchange rate uncertainty, the value of foreign stock from a U.S. investor's perspective is subject to more uncertainty than the value of that stock from a local investor's perspective.

11-7b International Market Efficiency

Some foreign markets are likely to be inefficient because of the relatively small number of analysts and portfolio managers who monitor stocks in those markets. It is easier to find undervalued stocks when a smaller number of market participants monitor the market. Research has documented that some foreign markets are inefficient, basing these conclusions on slow price responses to new information (e.g., earnings announcements) about specific firms. Such inefficiencies are more common in smaller foreign stock markets. Some emerging stock markets are relatively new and small, so they are unlikely to be as efficient as the U.S. stock market. Hence some stocks may be undervalued, a possibility that has attracted investors to these markets. Yet precisely because some of these markets are small, they may be susceptible to manipulation by large traders. Furthermore, insider trading is more prevalent in many foreign markets because rules against it are not enforced. In general, large institutional investors and insiders based in the foreign markets may have some advantages.

11-7c Measuring Performance from Investing in Foreign Stocks

The returns from investing in foreign stocks is most properly measured in terms of the investor's objectives. For example, if portfolio managers are assigned to select stocks in Europe, their performance should be compared to that of a European index measured in U.S. dollars. In this way, the performance measurement controls for general market movements and exchange rate movements in the region where the portfolio manager has been assigned to invest funds. Thus, if the entire European market experiences poor performance over a particular quarter, or if the main European currency (the euro) depreciates against the dollar over the period, the portfolio managers assigned to Europe are not automatically penalized. Conversely, if the entire European market experiences strong performance over a particular quarter or the euro appreciates against the dollar, managers are not automatically rewarded. Instead, the performance of portfolio managers is measured relative to the general market conditions of the region to which they are assigned.

11-7d Performance from Global Diversification

A substantial amount of research has demonstrated that investors in stocks can benefit by diversifying internationally. Most stocks are strongly influenced by the country in which their firms are located (although some firms are more vulnerable to local economic conditions than others).

Since a stock market partially reflects the current and/or forecasted state of its country's economy and since economies do not generally move in tandem, particular stocks of the various markets are not highly correlated. This contrasts with the case of a purely domestic portfolio (e.g., one consisting entirely of U.S. stocks), in which most stocks often move in the same direction and by a similar magnitude.

Nevertheless, stock price movements among international stock markets are correlated to some degree because some underlying economic factors reflecting the world's general financial condition may systematically affect all markets. One country's economy can influence the economies of other countries, so expectations about economies across countries may be similar. Thus stock markets across countries may respond to some of the same expectations. *Integration* is an important concept because of what it implies about the potential benefits of international diversification. A high degree of international economic integration implies that stock returns of different countries are affected by common factors. In that case, the returns of stocks from various countries would move in concert and therefore allow only modest benefits from international diversification.

In general, correlations between stock indexes have been higher in recent years than they were several years ago. One reason for the increased correlations is the increased integration of business between countries. This results in more inter country trade flows and capital flows, which causes each country to have more influence on other countries. In particular, many European countries have become more integrated because of the movement to standardize regulations throughout Europe and the use of a single currency (the euro) to facilitate trade between countries.

Diversification among Emerging Stock Markets   Emerging markets provide an alternative outlet for investors from the United States and other countries to invest their funds. The potential economic growth rate is relatively high. In addition, investors may achieve extra diversification benefits from investing in emerging markets because their respective economies may not move in tandem with those of the more developed countries. Hence the correlation between these stocks and those of other countries is low, so investors can reduce risk by including some stocks from these markets in their portfolios.

However, emerging market stocks tend to exhibit a high degree of volatility, which partially offsets the advantage of their low correlations with stocks of other countries. Stocks in emerging markets are more exposed to major government turnovers and other forms of political risk. They also expose U.S. investors to a high degree of exchange rate risk because the local currencies involved are typically volatile.

SUMMARY

- Stocks are commonly valued using the price–earnings (PE) method, the dividend discount model, or the free cash flow model. The PE method applies the industry PE ratio to the firm's earnings to derive its value. The dividend discount model estimates the value as the present value of expected future dividends. The free cash flow model is based on the present value of future cash flows.

- When applying the free cash flow model to value a stock, a required rate of return must be estimated. One method of estimating the required rate of return is to apply the capital asset pricing model, in which the required return depends on the risk-free interest rate and the firm's beta.

- Stock prices are affected by those factors that affect future cash flows or the required rate of return by investors. Economic conditions, market conditions, and firm-specific conditions can affect a firm's cash flows or the required rate of return.

- The risk of a stock is measured by its volatility, its beta, or its value-at-risk estimate. Investors are giving more attention to risk measurement in light of abrupt downturns in the prices of some stocks in recent years.

- Stock market efficiency implies that stock prices reflect all available information. Weak-form efficiency suggests that security prices reflect all trade-related information, such as historical security price movements and the volume of securities trades. Semistrong-form efficiency suggests that security prices fully reflect all public information. Strong-form efficiency suggests that security prices fully reflect all information, including private or insider information. Evidence supports weak-form efficiency to a degree, but there is less support for semistrong- or strong-form efficiency.

POINT COUNTER-POINT

Is the Stock Market Efficient?

Point   Yes. Investors fully incorporate all available information when trading stocks. Thus, the prices of stocks fully reflect all information.

Counter-Point   No. The high degree of stock price volatility offers evidence of how much disagreement there is among stock prices. The fact that many stocks declined by more than 40 percent during the end of 2008 and beginning of 2009 suggests that stock prices are not always properly valued to reflect available information.

Who Is Correct?   Use the Internet to learn more about this issue and then formulate your own opinion.

QUESTIONS AND APPLICATIONS

1. Price-Earnings Model Explain the use of the price–earnings ratio for valuing a stock. Why might investors derive different valuations for a stock when using the PE method? Why might investors derive an inaccurate valuation of a firm when using the PE method?

2. Dividend Discount Model Describe the dividend discount valuation model. What are some limitations of the dividend discount model?

3. Impact of Economic Growth Explain how economic growth affects the valuation of a stock.

4. Impact of Interest Rates How are the interest rate, the required rate of return on a stock, and the valuation of a stock related?

5. Impact of Inflation Assume that the expected inflation rate has just been revised upward by the market. Would the required return by investors who invest in stocks be affected? Explain.

6. Impact of Exchange Rates Explain how the value of the dollar affects stock valuations.

7. Investor Sentiment Explain why investor sentiment can affect stock prices.

8. January Effect Describe the January effect.

9. Earnings Surprises How do earnings surprises affect valuations of stocks?

10. Impact of Takeover Rumors Why can expectations of an acquisition affect the value of the target's stock?

11. Emerging Markets What are the risks of investing in stocks in emerging markets?

12. Stock Volatility during the Credit Crisis Explain how stock volatility changed during the credit crisis.

13. Stock Portfolio Volatility Identify the factors that affect a stock portfolio's volatility and explain their effects.

14. Beta Explain how to estimate the beta of a stock. Explain why beta serves as a measure of the stock's risk.

15. Wall Street In the movie *Wall Street*, Bud Fox is a broker who conducts trades for Gordon Gekko's firm. Gekko purchases shares of firms he believes are undervalued. Various scenes in the movie offer excellent examples of concepts discussed in this chapter.

a. Bud Fox comments to Gordon Gekko that a firm's breakup value is twice its market price. What is Bud suggesting in this statement? How would employees of the firm respond to Bud's statement?

b. When Bud informs Gekko that another investor, Mr. Wildman, is secretly planning to acquire a target firm in Pennsylvania, Gekko tells Bud to buy a large amount of this stock. Why?

c. Gekko says, "Wonder why fund managers can't beat the S&P 500? Because they are sheep." What is Gekko's point? How does it relate to market efficiency?

16. Market Efficiency Explain the difference between weak-form, semistrong-form, and strong-form efficiency. Which of these forms of efficiency is most difficult to test? Which is most likely to be refuted? Explain how to test weak-form efficiency in the stock market.

17. Market Efficiency A consulting firm was hired to determine whether a particular trading strategy could generate abnormal returns. The strategy involved taking positions based on recent historical movements in stock prices. The strategy did not achieve abnormal returns. Consequently, the consulting firm concluded that the stock market is weak-form efficient. Do you agree? Explain.

Advanced Questions

18. Value at Risk Describe the value-at-risk method for measuring risk.

19. Implied Volatility Explain the meaning and use of implied volatility.

20. Leveraged Buyout At the time a management group of RJR Nabisco initially considered engaging in a leveraged buyout, RJR's stock price was less than $70 per share. Ultimately, RJR was acquired by the firm Kohlberg Kravis Roberts (KKR) for about $108 per share. Does the large discrepancy between the stock price before an acquisition was considered and after the acquisition mean that RJR's price was initially undervalued? If so, does this imply that the market was inefficient?

21. How Stock Prices May Respond to Prevailing Conditions Consider the prevailing conditions that could affect the demand for stocks, including inflation, the economy, the budget deficit, the Fed's monetary policy, political conditions, and the general mood of investors. Based on these conditions, do you think stock prices will increase or decrease during this semester? Offer some logic to support your answer. Which factor do you think will have the biggest impact on stock prices?

22. Application of CAPM to Stock Pricing Explain (using intuition instead of math) why stock prices may decrease in response to a higher risk-free rate according to the CAPM. Explain (using intuition instead of math) why stock prices may increase in this situation even though the risk-free rate increases.

23. Impact of SOX on Stock Valuations Use a stock valuation framework to explain why the Sarbanes-Oxley Act (SOX) could improve the valuation of a stock. Why might SOX cause a reduction in the valuation of a stock? (See the Appendix.)

24. Interpretation of the VIX Index Explain why participants in the stock market monitor the VIX index. What does a decline in the VIX index imply about a change in expected volatility by market participants?

Interpreting Financial News

Interpret the following statements made by Wall Street analysts and portfolio managers.

a. "The stock market's recent climb has been driven by falling interest rates."

b. "Future stock prices are dependent on the Fed's policy meeting next week."

c. "Given the recent climb in stocks that cannot be explained by fundamentals, a correction is inevitable."

Managing in Financial Markets

Stock Portfolio Dilemma As an investment manager, you frequently make decisions about investing in stocks versus other types of investments and about types of stocks to purchase.

a. You have noticed that investors tend to invest more heavily in stocks after interest rates have declined. You are considering this strategy as well. Is it rational to invest more heavily in stocks once interest rates have declined?

b. Assume that you are about to select a specific stock that will perform well in response to an expected runup in the stock market. You are very confident that the stock market will perform well in the near future. Recently, a friend recommended that you consider purchasing stock of a specific firm because it had decent earnings over the last few years, it has a low beta (reflecting a low degree of systematic risk), and its beta is expected to remain low. You normally rely on beta as a measurement of a firm's systematic risk. Should you seriously consider buying that stock? Explain.

c. You are considering an investment in an initial public offering by Marx Company, which has performed very well recently, according to its financial statements. The firm will use some of the proceeds from selling stock to pay off some of its bank loans. How can you apply stock valuation models to estimate this firm's value when its stock is not yet publicly traded? Once you estimate the value of the firm, how can you use this information to determine whether to invest in it? What are some limitations in estimating the value of this firm?

d. In the past, your boss assessed your performance based on the actual return on the portfolio of U.S. stocks that you manage. For each quarter in which your portfolio generated an annualized return of at least 20 percent, you received a bonus. Now your boss wants you to develop a method for measuring your performance from managing the portfolio. Offer a method that accurately measures your performance.

e. Assume that you were also asked to manage a portfolio of European stocks. How would your method for measuring your performance in managing this portfolio differ from the method you devised for the U.S. stock portfolio in the previous question?

PROBLEMS

1. Risk-Adjusted Return Measurements Assume the following information over a five-year period:

- Average risk-free rate = 6%
- Average return for Crane stock = 11%
- Average return for Load stock = 14%
- Standard deviation of Crane stock returns = 2%
- Standard deviation of Load stock returns = 4%
- Beta of Crane stock = 0.8
- Beta of Load stock = 1.1

Determine which stock has higher risk-adjusted returns according to the Sharpe index. Which stock has higher risk-adjusted returns according to the Treynor index? Show your work.

2. Measuring Expected Return Assume Mess stock has a beta of 1.2. If the risk-free rate is 7 percent and the market return is 10 percent, what is the expected return of Mess stock?

3. Using the PE Method You found that Verto stock is expected to generate earnings of $4.38 per share this year and that the mean PE ratio for its industry is 27.195. Use the PE valuation method to determine the value of Verto shares.

4. Using the Dividend Discount Model Suppose that you are interested in buying the stock of a company that has a policy of paying a $6 per share dividend every year. Assuming no changes in the firm's policies, what is the value of a share of stock if the required rate of return is 11 percent?

5. Using the Dividend Discount Model Micro, Inc., will pay a dividend of $2.30 per share next year. If the company plans to increase its dividend by 9 percent per year indefinitely, and you require a 12 percent return on your investment, what should you pay for the company's stock?

6. Using the Dividend Discount Model Suppose you know that a company *just paid* an annual dividend of $1.75 per share on its stock and that the dividend will continue to grow at a rate of 8 percent per year. If the required return on this stock is 10 percent, what is the current share price?

7. Deriving the Required Rate of Return The next expected annual dividend for Sun, Inc., will be $1.20 per share, and analysts expect the dividend to grow at an annual rate of 7 percent indefinitely. If Sun stock currently sells for $22 per share, what is the required rate of return?

8. Deriving the Required Rate of Return A share of common stock currently sells for $110. Current dividends are $8 per share annually and are expected to grow at 6 percent per year indefinitely. What is the rate of return required by investors in the stock?

9. Deriving the Required Rate of Return A stock has a beta of 2.2, the risk-free rate is 6 percent, and the expected return on the market is 12 percent. Using the CAPM, what would you expect the required rate of return on this stock to be? What is the market risk premium?

10. Deriving a Stock's Beta You are considering investing in a stock that has an expected return of 13 percent. If the risk-free rate is 5 percent and the market risk premium is 7 percent, what must the beta of this stock be?

11. Measuring Stock Returns Suppose you bought a stock at the beginning of the year for $76.50. During the year, the stock paid a dividend of $0.70 per share and had an ending share price of $99.25. What is the total percentage return from investing in that stock over the year?

12. Measuring the Portfolio Beta Assume the following information:

- Beta of IBM = 1.31
- Beta of LUV = 0.85
- Beta of ODP = 0.94

If you invest 40 percent of your money in IBM, 30 percent in LUV, and 30 percent in ODP, what is your portfolio's beta?

13. Measuring the Portfolio Beta Using the information from Problem 12, suppose that you instead decide to invest $20,000 in IBM, $30,000 in LUV, and $50,000 in ODP. What is the beta of your portfolio now?

14. Value at Risk Assume that Quitar Co. has a beta of 1.31.

a. If you assume that the stock market has a maximum expected loss of −3.2 percent on a daily basis (based on a 95 percent confidence level), what is the maximum daily loss for the Quitar Co. stock?

b. If you have $19,000 invested in Quitar Co. stock, what is your maximum daily dollar loss?

15. Value at Risk If your portfolio beta is 0.89 and the stock market has a maximum expected loss of −2.5 percent on a daily basis, what is the maximum daily loss to your portfolio?

16. Dividend Model Relationships

a. When computing the price of a stock with the dividend discount model, how would the price be affected if the required rate of return is increased? Explain the logic of this relationship.

b. When computing the price of a stock using the constant-growth dividend discount model, how would the price be affected if the growth rate is reduced? Explain the logic of this relationship.

17. CAPM Relationships

a. When using the CAPM, how would the required rate of return on a stock be affected if the risk-free rate were lower?

b. When using the CAPM, how would the required rate of return on a stock be affected if the market return were lower?

c. When using the CAPM, how would the required rate of return on a stock be affected if the beta were higher?

18. Value at Risk

a. How is the maximum expected loss on a stock affected by an increase in the volatility (standard deviation), based on a 95 percent confidence interval?

b. Determine how the maximum expected loss on a stock would be affected by an increase in the expected return of the stock, based on a 95 percent confidence interval.

Flow of Funds Exercise

Valuing Stocks

Recall that if the economy continues to be strong, Carson Company may need to increase its production capacity by about 50 percent over the next few years to satisfy demand. It would need financing to expand and accommodate the increase in production. Recall that the yield curve is currently upward sloping. Also recall that Carson is concerned about a possible slowing of the economy because of potential Fed actions to reduce inflation. It is also considering issuing stock or bonds to raise funds in the next year. If Carson goes public, it might even consider using its stock as a means of acquiring some target firms. It would also consider engaging in a secondary offering at a future point in time if the IPO is successful and if its growth continues over time. It would also change its compensation system so that most of its managers would receive about 30 percent of their compensation in shares of Carson stock and the remainder as salary.

a. At the present time, the price–earnings ratio (stock price per share divided by earnings per share) of other firms in Carson's industry is relatively low but should rise in the future. Why might this information affect the time at which Carson issues its stock?

b. Assume that Carson Company believes that issuing stock is an efficient means of circumventing the potential for high interest rates. Even if long-term interest rates have increased by the time it issues stock, Carson thinks that it would be insulated by issuing stock instead of bonds. Is this view correct?

c. Carson Company recognizes the importance of a high stock price at the time it engages in an IPO (if it goes public). But why would its stock price be important to Carson Company even after the IPO?

d. If Carson Company goes public, it may be able to motivate its managers by granting them stock as part of their compensation. Explain why the stock may motivate them to perform well. Then explain why the use of stock as compensation may motivate them to focus on short-term goals even though they are supposed to focus on maximizing shareholder wealth over the long run. How can a firm provide stock as motivation but prevent its managers from using a short-term focus?

Internet/Excel Exercises

1. Go to finance.yahoo.com/indices?. Compare the performance of the Dow, Nasdaq, and S&P 500 indexes. Click on each of these indexes and describe the trend for that index since January. Which index has had the best performance?

2. Go to finance.yahoo.com, type in the symbol DELL (for Dell, Inc.), and click on "Get Quotes." Then go to the bottom of the stock price chart and retrieve the end-of-month stock price of Dell over the last 12 months. Record this information on an Excel spreadsheet and estimate the standard deviation of the stock's price movements. (See Appendix B for guidance on how to estimate the standard deviation of a stock's price movements.) Repeat the process for Oracle Corporation (its symbol is ORCL). Which stock does your analysis show to be riskier?

3. Assume that the expected return on Dell stock and Oracle stock is 0 percent for the next month. Use the value-at-risk method to determine the maximum expected loss of Dell and Oracle for the next month, based on a 95 percent confidence level.

WSJ Exercise

Reviewing Abrupt Shifts in Stock Valuation

Review Section C of a recent issue of the *Wall Street Journal*. Notice that the stocks with the largest one-day gains and losses are shown. Do an Internet search for news about the stock with the biggest gain. What is the reason for the gain? Repeat the exercise for the stock with the biggest loss.

ONLINE ARTICLES WITH REAL-WORLD EXAMPLES

Find a recent practical article available online that describes a real-world example regarding a specific financial institution or financial market that reinforces one or more concepts covered in this chapter.

If your class has an online component, your professor may ask you to post your summary of the article there and provide a link to the article so that other students can access it. If your class is live, your professor may ask you to summarize your application of the article in class. Your professor may assign specific students to complete this assignment or may allow any students to do the assignment on a volunteer basis.

For recent online articles and real-world examples related to this chapter, consider using the following search terms (be sure to include the prevailing year as a search term to ensure that the online articles are recent):

1. stock AND valuation
2. price-earnings AND valuation
3. free cash flow AND valuation
4. stock AND investor sentiment
5. stock AND risk
6. stock valuation AND uncertainty
7. stock valuation AND beta
8. stock AND value at risk
9. stock AND volatility
10. stock market AND efficient

The Link Between Accounting and Stock Valuation

In a publicly traded firm, the managers who run the firm are separate from the investors who own it. Managers are hired to serve as agents of the corporation and are expected to serve the interests of the firm's shareholders by making decisions that maximize the value of the firm. The firm's management is required to provide substantial information about the firm's financial condition and performance. Shareholders and other investors use this information to monitor management and to value the firm. For example, if investors use the price–earnings method to derive a valuation, they rely on the reported earnings. If they use the dividend discount model, they may derive an expected growth rate from recently reported earnings or revenue figures. If they use the adjusted dividend discount model, they may rely on financial statements to estimate future cash flows.

If firms provide inaccurate financial information, investors will derive inaccurate valuations and money will flow to the wrong sources in the stock markets. In addition, inaccurate financial information creates more risk for stocks because investors must worry about the uncertainty surrounding the reported financial statement numbers. If financial statement data are questionable, stock values may decline whenever investors recognize that the earnings or some other proxy used to estimate cash flows is overstated. Investors will require a higher rate of return to hold stocks subject to downside risk because of distorted accounting. Thus, deceptive accounting practices disrupt the stock market and increase the cost of capital raised by issuing stock.

To ensure that managers serve shareholder interests, firms commonly tie managerial compensation to the stock price. For example, managers may be granted stock options that allow them to buy the firm's stock at a specified price over a specified time period (such as the next five years). In this way, the managers benefit directly from a high stock price just like other shareholders and thus should make decisions that result in a high stock price.

Unfortunately, some managers recognize that it may be easier to increase their stock's price by manipulating the financial statements than by improving the firm's operations. When the firm's reported earnings are inflated, investors will likely overestimate the value of its stock, regardless of the method they use to value stocks.

Managers may be tempted to temporarily inflate reported earnings because doing so may temporarily inflate the stock's price. If no limits are imposed on the stock options granted, managers may be able to exercise their options (buying the stock at the price specified in the option contracts) during this period of a temporarily inflated price and immediately sell the stock in the secondary market. Thus they can capitalize on the inflated stock price before other investors realize that the earnings and stock price are inflated.

PROBLEMS WITH CREATIVE ACCOUNTING

Managers would not be able to manipulate a firm's financial information if accounting rules did not allow them to be creative. The accounting for a firm's financial statement items is guided by generally accepted accounting principles (GAAP) set by the Financial Accounting Standards Board (FASB). However, these guidelines allow for substantial flexibility in accounting, which means that there is no standard formula for converting accounting numbers into cash flows. The accounting confusion is compounded by the desire of some managers to inflate their firm's earnings in particular periods when they wish to sell their holdings of the firm's stock. Specifically, the accounting can inflate revenue in a particular period without inflating expenses or defer the reporting of some expenses until a future quarter. Investors who do not recognize that some of the accounting numbers are distorted may overestimate the value of the firm.

Creative accounting can also be used to distort expenses. When a firm discontinues one of its business projects, it commonly records this as a write-off, or a onetime charge against earnings. Investors tend to ignore write-offs when estimating future expenses because they do not expect them to occur again. Some firms, however, shift a portion of their normal operating expenses into the write-off even though those expenses will occur again in the future. Investors who do not recognize this accounting gimmick will underestimate the future expenses.

As a classic example of shifting expenses, WorldCom attempted to write off more than $7 billion following its acquisition of MCI in 1998. When the Securities and Exchange Commission (SEC) questioned this accounting, WorldCom changed the amount to about $3 billion. If it had succeeded in including the extra $4 billion in the write-off, WorldCom could have reduced its reported operating expenses by $4 billion. Thus investors who trusted WorldCom's income statement would have underestimated its future expenses by about $4 billion per year and therefore would have grossly overestimated the value of the stock.

When firms go beyond the loose accounting guidelines, the SEC may require them to restate their earnings and provide a corrected set of financial statements. The SEC has forced hundreds of firms to restate their earnings in recent years, but the investors who lost money because they trusted a firm's distorted accounting were not reimbursed.

GOVERNANCE OF ACCOUNTING

Several types of governance can be used to attempt to prevent firms from using distorted accounting, as explained next.

Auditing

Firms are required to hire auditors to audit their financial statements and verify that the statements are within the accounting guidelines. The auditors, however, rely on these firms for their future business. Many large firms pay auditors more than $1 million per year for their auditing services and also for nonauditing services. Thus auditors may be tempted to sign off on distorted accounting so that they will be rehired by their clients in the future. If the auditors uphold proper standards that force their clients to revise their reported earnings, they may not be hired again. The temptation to sign off on creative accounting used by client firms is especially strong given the subjectivity allowed by the accounting rules. Auditors may be more willing to sign off on financial statements that are somewhat confusing but do not directly violate accounting rules.

Board of Directors

A firm's board of directors is expected to represent the firm's shareholders. The directors oversee the firm's financial reporting process and should attempt to ensure that the financial information provided by the firm is accurate. However, some boards have not forced managers to accurately disclose the firm's financial condition. A board can be ineffective if it is run by insiders who are the same managers that the board is supposed to monitor. Board members who are managers of the firm (insiders) are less likely to scrutinize the firm's management. In recent years, many firms have increased the proportion of independent board members (outsiders), who are not subject to pressure from the firm's executives. Even some independent board members, however, have strong ties to the firm's executives or receive substantial consulting income beyond their compensation for serving on the board. Thus they may be willing to overlook distorted accounting or other unethical behavior in order to maintain their existing income stream from the firm.

Several proposals have been made to try to increase the independence of board members. For example, the Commission on Public Trust and Private Enterprise has recommended that corporations consider separating the offices of chair of the board and CEO and that the board chair should be an independent director.

Compensation of Board Members Some boards are ineffective because of the way the board members are compensated. If board members receive stock options from the firm as compensation, the options' value is tied to the firm's stock price. Consequently, some board members may be tempted to ignore their oversight duties because they may benefit from selling their shares of the stock (received as compensation) while the price is temporarily inflated. Meanwhile, shareholders who hold their stock for a longer time period will be adversely affected once the market recognizes that the financial statements are distorted.

Board members are more likely to serve the long-term interests of shareholders if they are compensated in a manner that encourages them to maximize the long-term value of the firm. If they are provided stock that they cannot sell for a long time, they are more likely to focus on maximizing the long-term value of the firm.

Several regulations have been issued to address the potential abuses resulting from granting stock options to managers and board members. In 2003, the SEC ruled that corporations listed on the New York Stock Exchange (NYSE) or the Nasdaq market must have shareholder approval before giving executives company stock or options. The rules were drafted and approved by the NYSE and Nasdaq. In addition, FASB recently required that corporations expense their executive stock options on their income statements. This increases transparency in financial reporting and might improve corporate governance.

Board's Independent Audit Committee Some board members may serve on an independent audit committee, which is responsible for monitoring the firm's auditor. The committee is expected to ensure that the audit is completed without conflicts of interest so that the auditors will provide an unbiased audit. Some boards have not prevented distorted audits, however, either because they did not recognize the conflicts of interest or because they were unwilling to acknowledge them.

Role of Credit Rating Agencies

Investors may also rely on credit rating agencies such as Standard & Poor's and Moody's to assess a firm's risk level. However, these agencies do not always detect a firm's financial problems in advance. They normally focus on assessing a firm's risk level based on the financial statements provided and not on determining whether the financial statements are accurate. The agencies may simply assume that the financial statements are accurate because they were verified by an auditor.

Role of the Market for Corporate Control

In the market for corporate control, firms that perform poorly should be acquired and reorganized by other more efficient firms (called raiders). The raiders have an incentive to seek out inefficient firms because they can buy them at a low price (reflecting their poor performance) and remove their inefficient management. Nevertheless, the market for corporate control does not necessarily prevent faulty accounting. First, raiders may not be able to identify firms that inflated their earnings. Second, firms that have inflated their earnings are probably overvalued, and raiders will not want to acquire them at their inflated price. Third, an acquisition involves substantial costs of integrating businesses, and there is the risk that these costs will offset any potential benefits.

THE ENRON SCANDAL

The most famous recent example of the use of creative accounting occurred at Enron Corporation. Enron was formed in 1985 from the merger of two natural gas pipeline companies. It grew relatively slowly until the 1990s, when the deregulation of the utilities industry presented new opportunities. Enron began to expand in several directions. It acquired power plants in the United States and also expanded internationally, acquiring a power distributor in Brazil, a power plant in India, and a water company in the United Kingdom, among others. Perhaps most importantly, it took advantage of the new deregulated environment to pioneer the trading of natural gas and electricity. Soon it had branched out beyond simple energy trading to trade such instruments as weather derivatives. In 1999 it introduced Enron Online, an Internet-based trading platform that gave the company the appeal of an "Internet stock" at a time when such stocks were highly desired. The company introduced online trading of metals, wood products, and even broadband capacity as well as energy. By 2000, Enron was the seventh largest firm (in terms of gross revenues) in the United States.

Most investors were caught by surprise when Enron began to experience financial problems in October 2001 and then filed for bankruptcy on December 2, 2001. At the time, it was the largest U.S. firm to go bankrupt. In retrospect, Enron's stock may have been overvalued for many years, but some investors and creditors were fooled by its financial statements. The Enron fiasco received much publicity because it demonstrated how a firm could manipulate its financial statements, and therefore manipulate its valuation, in spite of various controls designed to prevent that type of behavior. This section offers some insight into why investor valuations and risk assessments of Enron were so poor.

Enron's Letter to Its Shareholders

If investors trusted the claims made by Enron in its annual report, it is understandable that they would value the stock highly. The letter to shareholders in Enron's 2000 annual report included the following statements.

- "Enron's performance in 2000 was a success by any measure, as we continued to outdistance the competition and solidify our leadership in each of our businesses.
- Enron has built unique and strong businesses that have limitless opportunities for growth.
- At a minimum, we see our market opportunities company-wide tripling over the next five years.
- Enron is laser-focused on earnings per share, and we expect to continue strong performance.
- Enron is increasing earnings per share and continuing our strong return to shareholders.
- The company's total return to shareholders was 89% in 2000, compared with a −9% return by the S&P 500.
- The 10-year return to Enron shareholders was 1,415%, compared with 383% for the S&P 500.
- We plan to...create significant shareholder value for our shareholders."

Enron's Stock Valuation

Normally, the valuation of a firm is obtained by using the firm's financial statements to derive cash flows and to derive a required rate of return that is used to discount those cash flows. Enron's valuation was excessive because of various irregularities in its financial statements.

Estimating Cash Flows Since Enron's earnings were distorted, the estimates of its cash flows derived from those earnings were also distorted. Moreover, Enron's earnings were manipulated to create the perception of consistent earnings growth, which tempted investors to apply a high growth rate when estimating future cash flows.

Estimating the Required Rate of Return Investors can derive a required rate of return as the prevailing long-term, risk-free interest rate plus the firm's risk premium. The risk premium can be measured by the firm's existing degree of financial leverage, its ability to cover interest payments with operating earnings, and its sensitivity to market movements.

Until the accounting distortions were publicized, Enron's risk was underestimated. The company concealed much of its debt by keeping it off its consolidated financial statements, as will be explained shortly. Consequently, investors who estimated Enron's sensitivity to market movements using historical data were unable to detect Enron's potential for failure. As a result, they used a lower risk premium than was appropriate. The financial statements therefore caused investors both to overestimate Enron's future cash flows and to underestimate its risk. Both effects led to a superficially high stock price.

Applying Market Multiples Given the difficulty of estimating cash flows and the required rate of return, some investors may have tried to value Enron's stock by using market multiples. Determining the appropriate PE multiple for Enron was also difficult, however, because its reported earnings did not represent its real earnings.

Another problem with applying the industry PE method to Enron was the difficulty of identifying the proper industry. One of the company's main businesses was trading various types of energy derivative contracts. Yet Enron did not want to be known as a trading company because the valuations of companies (e.g., securities firms) that engage in trading are generally lower for a given level of earnings per share.

Motives of Enron's Management

One of the main reasons for Enron's problems was its management. Managers are expected to maximize the value of the firm's stock. Like many firms, Enron granted stock options to some of its managers as a means of motivating them to make decisions that would maximize the value of its stock. However, Enron's management seemed to focus more on creating the perception of strong business performance than on improving the firm's actual performance. By manipulating the financial statements, Enron consistently met its earnings forecasts and increased its earnings over 20 consecutive quarters leading up to 2001. In this way, it created a false sense of security about its performance, thereby increasing the demand for its stock. This resulted in a superficially high stock price over a period in which some managers sold their stock holdings. Twenty-nine Enron executives or board members sold their holdings of Enron stock for more than $1 billion in total before the stock price plummeted.

Internal Monitoring Some firms use internal monitoring to ensure some degree of control over managers and encourage them to make decisions that benefit shareholders. Unfortunately, Enron's internal monitoring was also susceptible to manipulation. For example, managers were periodically required to measure the market value of various energy contracts that the company held. Since there was not an active market for some of these contracts, the prevailing valuations of the contracts were arbitrary. Managers used estimates that resulted in favorable valuations, which in turn led to a higher level of reported performance and higher managerial compensation.

Monitoring by the Board of Directors Board members serve as representatives of the firm's shareholders and are responsible for ensuring that the managers serve shareholder interests. In fact, board members are commonly compensated with stock so that they have an incentive to ensure that the stock price is maximized. In the case of Enron, some board members followed executives in selling their shares while the stock price was superficially high.

Enron's Financial Statement Manipulation

Some of the methods Enron used to report its financial conditions were inconsistent with accounting guidelines. Other methods were within the rules but were misleading. Consequently, many investors invested in Enron without recognizing the financial problems that were hidden from the financial statements. Some of these investors lost most or all of their investment.

Accounting for Partnerships One of the most common methods used by Enron to manipulate its financial statements involved the transfer of assets to partnerships it owned called special-purpose entities (SPEs). It found outside investors to invest at least 3 percent of each partnership's capital. Under accounting guidelines, a partnership with this minimum level of investment from an outside investor does not have to be classified as a subsidiary. Since Enron thus did not classify its SPEs as subsidiaries, it was not required to include any financial information about them in its consolidated financial statements. For this reason, none of the debt incurred by the SPEs appeared on Enron's consolidated financial statements. Since most investors focused on the consolidated financial statements, they did not detect Enron's financial problems.

In addition, whenever Enron created a partnership that would buy one of its business segments, it would book a gain on its consolidated financial statements from the sale of the asset to the partnership. Yet losses from a partnership were booked on the partnership's financial statements. Thus Enron was booking gains from its partnerships on its consolidated financial statements while hiding its losses. On November 8, 2001, Enron announced that it was restating its earnings for the previous five years because three of its partnerships should have been included in the consolidated financial statements. This announcement confirmed the suspicion of some investors that previous earnings figures were exaggerated. Enron's previously reported earnings were reduced by about $600 million over the preceding five years, but the correction came too late for many investors who had purchased Enron stock when the reported earnings (and share price) were much higher.

Financing of Partnerships Enron's partnerships were financed by various creditors, such as banks. The loans were to be paid off either from the cash flow generated by the assets transferred to the partnership or from the ultimate sale of the assets. When the partnerships performed poorly, they could not cover their debt payments. In some cases, Enron backed the debt with its stock. But as its stock price plummeted, this collateral no longer covered the debt, setting in motion the downward spiral that ultimately led to the company's bankruptcy.

Arthur Andersen's Audit

Investors and creditors commonly presume that financial statements used to value a firm are accurate when they have been audited by an independent accounting firm. In reality, however, the auditor and the firm do not always have an arm's-length relationship. The accounting firm that conducts an audit is paid for the audit and recognizes the potential annuity from repeating this audit every year. In addition, accounting firms that provide auditing services also provide consulting services. Enron hired Arthur Andersen both to serve as its auditor and to provide substantial consulting services. In 2000, Arthur Andersen received $25 million in auditing fees from Enron and an additional $27 million in consulting fees.

Although Arthur Andersen was supposed to be completely independent, the auditing firm recognized that if it did not sign off on the audit it would lose this lucrative audit and consulting business. Furthermore, the annual bonus an accounting firm pays to its employees assigned to audit a client may be partially based on their billable hours, which would have been reduced if the firm's relationship with such a large client were severed.

Oversight by Investment Analysts

Even if financial statements are contrived, some investors may presume that investment analysts will detect discrepancies. Yet if analysts simply accept a financial statement without questioning its accuracy, they will fail to serve as a control mechanism. The difficulties analysts faced in interpreting Enron's financial statements are highlighted by a humorous list created by some Enron employees of why the company restructured its operations so frequently. Reason number 7 was "Because the basic business model is to keep the outside investment analysts so confused that they will not be able to figure out that we do not know what we are doing." The humor now escapes some analysts, as well as most creditors and investors.

Another problem is that, like the supposedly independent auditors who hope to generate more business for their accounting firm, investment analysts may encounter a conflict of interest when they attempt to rate firms. As explained in Chapter 10, analysts employed by securities firms have been criticized for assigning high ratings to firms they cover so that their employer may later receive some consulting business from those firms.

As an example of what can happen to analysts who are "too critical," consider the experience of an analyst at BNP Paribus who downgraded Enron in August 2001, a few months before the company's financial problems became public. At the time, BNP Paribus was providing some consulting services for Enron. Shortly after his downgrade of Enron, the analyst was demoted and then fired. To the extent that many other analysts were subjected to a similar conflict of interest, it may explain why they did not downgrade Enron until after its financial problems were publicized. Even if analysts had detected financial problems at Enron, they might have been reluctant to lower their rating.

Market for Corporate Control

As explained earlier, if a firm's managers are running a firm into the ground, a raider has an incentive to purchase that firm at a low price and improve it so that someday it can be sold for a much higher price. Yet this theory presumes that a firm's stock price properly reflects its actual business performance. If the firm's financial statements reflect strong performance, a raider may not realize that the firm is experiencing financial problems. Moreover, even if the raider is able to detect the problems, it will not be willing to pursue a firm whose value is overpriced by the market because of its contrived financial statements.

When Enron's stock price was high, few raiders could have afforded to acquire it. Once the stock price plummeted, Dynegy considered acquiring Enron. Dynegy quickly backed off, however, even though the stock price had fallen 90 percent from its high. Dynegy was concerned about problems it found when trying to reconcile Enron's financial statements.

Monitoring by Creditors

Enron relied heavily on creditors for its financing. Because Enron's consolidated financial statements showed a superficially high level of earnings and a low level of debt, it had easy access to credit from a wide variety of creditors. Enron maintained a low cost of capital by using contrived statements that concealed its risk. Its balance sheet showed debt of $13 billion, but by some accounts the true amount was closer to $20 billion. The hidden debt concealed Enron's actual degree of financial leverage.

Bank of America and J.P. Morgan Chase each had exposure estimated at $500 million. Many other banks had exposure estimated at more than $100 million. They would not have provided so much credit if they had fully understood Enron's financial situation.

Even the debt rating agencies had difficulty understanding Enron's financial situation. On October 16, 2001, Enron announced $2 billion in write-offs that would reduce its earnings. At this time, Standard & Poor's affirmed Enron's rating of BBB+ and stated that Enron's balance sheet should improve in the future. Over the next 45 days, S&P became more aware of Enron's financial condition and lowered its rating to junk status.

Many of Enron's creditors attempted to sue Enron once it became clear that the financial statements were misrepresented. By that time, however, Enron's value was depleted because its price had already fallen to less than $1 per share.

PREVENTION OF ACCOUNTING FRAUD

In response to the accounting fraud at Enron and other firms, regulators attempted to ensure more accurate financial disclosure by firms. Stock exchanges have instituted new regulations for listed firms. The SEC has been given more resources and power to monitor financial reporting. Perhaps the most important regulatory changes occurred as a result of the Sarbanes-Oxley Act of 2002. Some of the act's more important provisions were summarized in Chapter 10.

Alleged Accounting Fraud at Lehman Brothers

Despite the Sarbanes-Oxley Act, there remain some cases of accounting irregularities. For example, the financial statements of Lehman Brothers did not fully disclose its level of debt prior to filing for bankruptcy in September 2008. An external bankruptcy report on Lehman in March 2010 concluded that Lehman manipulated its accounting to reduce its degree of reported financial leverage so that it would receive higher credit ratings. During the 2001–2008 period, Lehman employed an accounting procedure called "Repo 105" whereby it engaged in repurchase transactions that would temporarily delete up to $50 billion of its debt just before the time to report its financial position. The report also suggested that Lehman inflated the value of its real estate investments and did not properly adjust its controls to deal with its increased exposure to risk.

DISCUSSION QUESTIONS

The following discussion questions focus on the use of financial statements in the valuation of firms. They should generate much discussion, especially when accounting and finance students are present. These questions can be used in several ways. They may serve as an assignment on a day that the professor is unable to attend class. They are also useful for small group exercises. For each issue, one group could be randomly selected and asked to present its solution. Then, other students not in that group may suggest alternative answers if they feel that the solution can be improved. Each issue does not necessarily have a perfect solution, so students should be able to present different points of view.

1. Should an accounting firm be prohibited from providing both auditing and consulting services to the same client? Explain your answer. If an accounting firm is allowed to offer only one service, could there still be conflicts of interest due to referrals (and finder's fees)?

2. Should members of Congress be allowed to set regulations on accounting and financial matters while receiving donations from related lobbying groups?

3. What alternative sources of information about a firm should investors rely on if they cannot rely on financial statements?

4. Should investors have confidence in ratings by analysts who are affiliated with securities firms that provide consulting services to firms? Explain.

5. Does an analyst employed by a securities firm to rate firms face a conflict of interest? If so, can the conflict be resolved?

6. How might a firm's board of directors discourage its managers from attempting to manipulate financial statements to create a temporarily high stock price?

7. How can the compensation of a firm's board of directors be structured so that board members will not be tempted to allow accounting or other managerial decisions that could cause a superficially high price over a short period?

12

Market Microstructure and Strategies

CHAPTER OBJECTIVES

The specific objectives of this chapter are to:

- describe the common types of stock transactions,

- explain how stock transactions are executed,

- describe the regulation of stock transactions, and

- explain how barriers to international stock transactions have been reduced.

WEB

finance.yahoo.com/ marketupdate/ overview?u

Overview of stock market performance.

Recently, much attention has been given to **market microstructure**, which is the process by which securities such as stocks are traded. For a stock market to function properly, a structure is needed to facilitate the placing of orders, speed the execution of the trades ordered, and provide equal access to information for all investors.

12-1 STOCK MARKET TRANSACTIONS

Some of the more common stock market transactions desired by investors are market and limit orders, margin trades, and short sales. Each of these types of transactions is discussed next.

12-1a Placing an Order

To place an order to buy or sell a specific stock, an investor contacts a brokerage firm. Brokerage firms serve as financial intermediaries between buyers and sellers of stock in the secondary market. They receive orders from customers and pass the orders on to the exchange through a telecommunications network. The orders are frequently executed a few seconds later. Full-service brokers offer advice to customers on stocks to buy or sell; discount brokers only execute the transactions desired by customers. The larger the transaction amount, the lower the percentage charged by many brokers. Some discount brokers charge a fixed price per trade, such as $10 to $30 for any trade that is less than 500 shares.

Investors can contact their brokers to determine the prevailing price of a stock. The broker may provide a *bid* quote if the investor wants to sell a stock or an *ask* quote if the investor wants to buy a stock. The investor communicates the order to the broker by specifying (1) the name of the stock, (2) whether to buy or sell that stock, (3) the number of shares to be bought or sold, and (4) whether the order is a market or a limit order. A **market order** to buy or sell a stock means to execute the transaction at the best possible price. A **limit order** differs from a market order in that a limit is placed on the price at which a stock can be purchased or sold.

EXAMPLE

Creo stock is currently selling for $55 per share. If an investor places a market order to purchase (or sell) the stock, the transaction will be executed at the prevailing price at the time the transaction takes place. For example, the price may have risen to $55.25 per share or declined to $54.75 by the time the transaction occurs.

Alternatively, the investor could place a limit order to purchase Creo stock only at a price of $54.50 or less. The limit order can be placed either for the day only or for a longer period. Other investors who wish to sell Creo stock may place limit orders to sell the stock only if it can be sold for $55.25 or more. The advantage of a limit order is that it may enable an investor to obtain the stock at a lower price. The disadvantage is that there is no guarantee the market price will ever reach the limit price established by the investor. ●

Stop-Loss Order   A stop-loss order is a particular type of limit order. The investor specifies a selling price that is below the current market price of the stock. When the stock price drops to the specified level, the stop-loss order becomes a market order. If the stock price does not reach the specified minimum, the stop-loss order will not be executed. Investors generally place stop-loss orders either to protect gains or to limit losses.

EXAMPLE   Paul bought 100 shares of Bostner Corporation one year ago at a price of $50 per share. Today, Bostner stock trades for $60 per share. Paul believes that Bostner stock has additional upside potential and does not want to liquidate his position. Nonetheless, he would like to make sure that he realizes at least a 10 percent gain from the stock transaction. He therefore places a stop-loss order with a price of $55. If the stock price drops to $55, the stop-loss order will convert to a market order and Paul will receive the prevailing market price at that time, which will be about $55. If Paul receives exactly $55, his gain from the transaction would be 100 shares × ($55 − $50) = $500. If the price of Bostner stock continues to increase, the stop-loss order will never be executed. ●

Stop-Buy Order   A **stop-buy order** is another type of limit order. In this case, the investor specifies a purchase price that is above the current market price. When the stock price rises to the specified level, the stop-buy order becomes a market order. If the stock price does not reach the specified maximum, the stop-buy order will not be executed.

EXAMPLE   Karen would like to invest in the stock of Quan Company, but only if there is some evidence that stock market participants are demanding that stock. The stock is currently priced at $12. She places a stop-buy order at $14 per share, so if demand for Quan stock is sufficient to push the price to $14, she will purchase the stock. If the price remains below $14, her order will not be executed. ●

Placing an Order Online   Many Internet brokers accept orders online, provide real-time quotes, and provide access to information about stocks. Some of the more popular online brokerage firms include TD Ameritrade (www.tdameritrade.com), Charles Schwab (www.schwab.com), and E*Trade (www.etrade.com).

Some online brokerage services offer zero-commission trades. However, investors must maintain a certain amount of funds in their brokerage accounts. Brokerage firms can still profit from these no-commission trades because they can use the funds in the accounts to earn a higher return than they pay the investors as interest.

12-1b Margin Trading

When investors place an order, they may consider purchasing the stock on margin; in that case, they use cash along with funds borrowed from their broker to make the purchase. The Federal Reserve imposes **margin requirements**, which represent the minimum proportion of funds that must be covered with cash. This limits the proportion of funds that may be borrowed from the brokerage firm to make the investment. Margin requirements were first imposed in 1934, following a period of volatile market swings, to discourage excessive speculation and ensure greater stability. Currently, at least 50 percent of an investor's invested funds must be paid in cash. Margin requirements are intended to ensure that investors can cover their position if the value of their investment declines over time. Thus, with margin requirements, a major decline in stock prices is less likely to cause defaults on loans from brokers and therefore will be less damaging to the financial system.

To purchase stock on margin, investors must establish an account (called a **margin account**) with their broker. Their initial deposit of cash is referred to as the **initial margin**. To meet the requirements imposed by the Federal Reserve, the initial margin must be at least 50 percent of the total investment (although some brokerage firms impose a higher minimum). The brokerage firm can provide financing for the remainder of the stock investment, and the stock serves as collateral. Over time, the market value of the stock will change. Investors are subject to **a maintenance margin**, which is the minimum proportion of equity that an investor must maintain in the account as a proportion of the market value of the stock. The investor's equity position represents what the stock is worth to the investor after paying off the loan from the broker. The New York Stock Exchange (NYSE, which is now part of the company NYSE Euronext following its merger with the European electronic stock exchange, Euronext) and Nasdaq have set the minimum maintenance margin at 25 percent, but some brokerage firms require a higher minimum. If the investor's equity position falls below the maintenance margin, the investor will receive a **margin call** from the brokerage firm and will have to deposit cash to the account in order to boost the equity.

EXAMPLE

Five days ago, Trish purchased 100 shares of Rimax stock at $60 per share through Ohio Brokerage Firm, thus the shares were valued at $6,000. Ohio Brokerage required an initial margin of 50 percent. Trish used $3,000 cash as her equity investment and borrowed the remaining $3,000 from Ohio Brokerage to purchase the stock. Ohio Brokerage requires a maintenance margin of 30 percent. Two days later, the price of Rimax stock declined to $50 per share, so the total value of her shares was $5,000. Since Trish still owed the brokerage firm $3,000, her equity position was equal to $2,000 (computed as the market value of the stock minus the $3,000 that is still owed to the broker). The equity position represented 40 percent of the market value of the stock (computed as $2,000/$5,000), which was still above the maintenance margin of 30 percent. Today, the stock price declined to $40 per share, so the market value of the stock is $4,000. Now Trish's equity position is $1,000 (computed as $4,000 minus $3,000). This position represents 25 percent of the market value of the stock (computed as $l,000/$4,000). Now this position is below the 30 percent maintenance margin required by Ohio Brokerage. Consequently, Trish receives a margin call from Ohio Brokerage, in which she is informed that she must deposit sufficient cash to her account to raise her equity position to at least 30 percent of the market value of the stock. ●

Margin Calls Because of the potential for margin calls, a large volume of margin lending exposes the stock markets to a potential crisis. A major downturn in the market could result in many margin calls, some of which may force investors to sell their stock holdings if they do not have the cash to build their maintenance margin. Such a response results in more sales of stocks, additional downward pressure on stock prices, and additional margin calls. When the stock market plummeted during the credit crisis in 2008, investors who did not have cash available to respond to margin calls sold their stock, putting additional downward pressure on stock prices.

WEB

www.bloomberg.com
Discloses today's return
for stocks contained in
major stock indexes.

Impact on Returns The return on a stock is affected by the proportion of the investment that is from borrowed funds. Over short-term periods, the return (R) on stocks purchased on margin can be estimated as follows:

$$R = \frac{SP - INV - LOAN + D}{INV}$$

where

SP = selling price of stock

INV = initial investment by investor, not including borrowed funds

$LOAN$ = loan payments on borrowed funds, including principal and interest

D = dividend payments

EXAMPLE

Consider a stock priced at $40 that pays an annual dividend of $1 per share. An investor purchases the stock on margin, paying $20 per share and borrowing the remainder from the brokerage firm at 10 percent annual interest. If, after one year, the stock is sold at a price of $60 per share, the return on the stock is

$$R = \frac{\$60 - \$20 - \$22 + \$1}{\$20}$$

$$= \frac{\$19}{\$20}$$

$$= 95\%$$

In this example, the stock return (including the dividend) would have been 52.5 percent if the investor had used only personal funds rather than borrowing funds. This illustrates how the use of borrowed funds can magnify the returns on an investment.

Any losses are also magnified, however, when borrowed funds are used to invest in stocks. Reconsider the previous example and assume that the stock is sold at a price of $30 per share (instead of $60) at the end of the year. If the investor did not use any borrowed funds when purchasing the stock for $40 per share at the beginning of the year, the return on this investment would be

$$R = \frac{\$30 - \$40 - \$0 + \$1}{\$40}$$

$$= -22.5\%$$

However, if the investor had purchased the stock on margin at the beginning of the year, paying $20 per share and borrowing the remainder from the brokerage firm at 10 percent annual interest, the return over the year would be

$$R = \frac{\$30 - \$20 - \$22 + \$1}{\$20}$$

$$= -55\%$$

As these examples illustrate, purchasing stock on margin not only increases the potential return from investing in stock but also magnifies the potential losses.

12-1c Short Selling

In a **short sale**, investors place an order to sell a stock that they do not own. They sell a stock short (or "short the stock") when they anticipate that its price will decline. When they sell short, they are essentially borrowing the stock from another investor and will ultimately have to return that stock to the investor from whom they borrowed it. The short-sellers borrow the stock through a brokerage firm, which facilitates the process. The investors who own the stock are not affected when their shares are borrowed and, in fact, are not even aware of it.

If the price of the stock declines by the time the short-sellers purchase it in the market (to return to the investor from whom they borrowed), the short-sellers earn the difference between the price at which they initially sold the stock and the price they paid to obtain the stock. Short-sellers must make payments to the investor from whom the stock was borrowed to cover the dividend payments that the investor would have received if the stock had not been borrowed. After subtracting any dividend payments made, the short-seller's profit is the difference between the original selling price and the price paid for the stock. The risk of a short sale is that the stock price may increase over time, forcing the short-seller to pay a higher price for the stock than the price at which it was initially sold.

EXAMPLE

On May 5, the market value of Vizer Company stock was $70 per share. Ed conducted an analysis of Vizer stock and concluded that the price should be much lower. He called his broker and placed an order to sell 100 shares of Vizer stock. Since he did not have shares of Vizer to sell, this transaction was a short sale. Vizer stock does not pay dividends, so Ed did not have to cover dividend payments for the stock that his brokerage firm borrowed and sold for him. The sale of the stock resulted in proceeds of $7,000, which he placed in his account at the brokerage firm. During the next two months, the price of Vizer stock declined. On July 18, Ed placed an order through his brokerage firm to purchase 100 shares of Vizer stock and offset his short position. The market value at the time was $60, so he paid $6,000 for the shares. Thus Ed earned $1,000 from his short position. This example ignores transaction costs associated with the short sale.

The risk from taking a short position is that the stock's price may rise instead of decline as expected. If the price had increased after Ed created the short position, his purchase price would have been higher than his selling price. In this case, Ed would have incurred a loss on the short position. ●

Measuring the Short Position of a Stock

One measure of the degree of short positions is the ratio of the number of shares that are currently sold short divided by the total number of shares outstanding. For many stocks, this measure is between 0.5 and 2 percent. A higher percentage (such as 3 percent) suggests a large amount of short positions in the market, which implies that a relatively large number of investors expect the stock's price to decline.

Some financial publications disclose the level of short sales for stocks with the short interest ratio, which is the number of shares that are currently sold short divided by the average daily trading volume over a recent period. The higher the ratio, the higher the level of short sales. A short interest ratio of 2 for a particular stock indicates that the number of shares currently sold short is two times the number of shares traded per day, on average. A short interest ratio of 20 or more reflects an unusually high level of short sales, indicating that many investors believe that the stock price is currently overvalued. Some stocks have had short interest ratios exceeding 100 at certain times.

The short interest ratio is also measured for the market to determine the level of short sales for the market overall. A high short interest ratio for the market indicates a high level of short-selling activity in the market. The largest short positions are periodically disclosed in The Wall Street Journal. For each firm with a large short position, the number of shares sold short is disclosed and compared to the corresponding number a month earlier. The change in the overall short position by investors from the previous month is also shown.

Using a Stop-Buy Order to Offset Short Selling

Investors who have established a short position commonly use a stop-buy order to limit their losses.

EXAMPLE

A year ago, Mary sold short 200 shares of Patronum Corporation stock for $70 per share. Patronum's stock currently trades for $80 a share. Consequently, Mary currently has an unrealized loss on the short sale, but she believes that Patronum stock will drop below $70 in the near future. She is unwilling to accept a loss of more than $15 per share on the transaction. Consequently, she places a stop-buy order for 200 shares with a specified purchase price of $85 per share. If Patronum stock increases to $85 per share, the stop-buy order becomes a market order and Mary will pay approximately $85 per share. If Patronum stock does not increase to $85 per share, the stop-buy order will never be executed. ●

USING THE WALL STREET JOURNAL

Short Selling

The *Wall Street Journal* provides information on short selling, as shown here. Specifically, it discloses the stocks that have the biggest short positions. For these stocks, it discloses the market valuation, final closing (close) price over the previous trading day, and 52-week range (high and low).

Source: Reprinted with permission of the *Wall Street Journal*, Copyright © 2013 Dow Jones & Company, Inc. All Rights Reserved Worldwide.

Biggest short positions
Companies with the biggest number of shares that are shorted

Shares shorted (000s)	% float	Days to cover	Avg daily volume (000s)	Name	Symbol	Close	Market value, in millions ($)	52-WEEK RANGE ($) Low	Close(●)	High
406,288.2	21.3	7	58,658	Sirius XM Radio	SIRI	3.08	20,108.80	1.78		3.25
330,970.7	8.8	8	39,559	Nokia	NOK	3.77	13,326.30	1.63		5.57
221,337.2	n.a.	2	120,554	SPDR S&P 500	SPY	151.91	n.a.	127.14		153.28
211,680.6	21.3	15	14,271	Frontier Communications	FTR	4.12	4,063.67	3.06		5.15
208,197.8	4.2	7	30,642	Intel	INTC	20.93	101,789.00	19.23		29.27
166,002.6	1.5	1	164,707	Bank Of America	BAC	11.30	119,964.00	6.72		12.42
151,176.5	n.a.	6	25,182	iShrs Russell 2000	IWM	90.31	n.a.	72.94		92.68
136,511.7	27.6	2	81,221	Research in Motion	BBRY	13.25	7,055.19	6.22		18.32
116,663.4	n.a.	3	45,430	Select Sector SPDR-Finl	XLF	17.62	n.a.	13.30		17.94
102,096.1	3.7	11	9,183	Johnson & Johnson	JNJ	76.32	213,143.00	61.71		77.02

Two Measures

One way to evaluate the significance of a short position is to measure the number of shares shorted as a percentage of freely trading shares outstanding, or float. A second is to count how many days of trading at the average daily volume it would take to cover or equal the number of shares shorted.

Shorts as a percentage of float
Selected companies where shares shorted represent large percentages of float

Shares shorted (000s)	% float	Days to cover	Avg daily volume (000s)	Name	Symbol	Close	Market value, in millions ($)	52-WEEK RANGE ($) Low	Close(●)	High
5,128.7	97.5	4	1,259	Yelp Inc	YELP	21.86	1,484.38	14.10		31.96
6,486.8	65.6	19	351	Blyth	BTH	14.65	253.82	12.66		46.15
4,189.0	57.4	11	377	USANA Health Sciences	USNA	43.86	633.01	30.51		50.23
8,308.3	56.3	13	659	ITT Educational Svcs	ESI	14.44	339.73	11.69		71.76
10,586.0	52.7	33	319	Vera Bradley	VRA	25.92	1,048.53	18.91		39.48
4,791.2	49.4	18	273	magicJack VocalTec	CALL	11.19	220.24	11.19		28.22
6,391.6	48.1	14	471	HHGregg Inc	HGG	9.31	304.96	5.84		12.87
14,255.6	47.9	9	1,654	Coinstar	CSTR	52.60	1,396.21	40.50		71.82
27,230.3	47.7	47	585	Spectrum Pharmaceuticals	SPPI	11.39	669.86	9.31		17.48
26,533.8	46.0	18	1,468	Questcor Pharma	QCOR	33.00	1,909.01	17.25		58.91

More days to cover

It would take these firms the most days, trading at their average daily volume, to "cover" the shorts, based on minimum average daily volume of 100,000 shares.

Shares shorted (000s)	% float	Days to cover	Avg daily volume (000s)	Name	Symbol	Close	Market value, in millions ($)	52-WEEK RANGE ($) Low	Close(●)	High
11,254.3	44.0	98	115	Amer Greetings A	AM	16.50	545.84	12.53		17.49
10,108.4	2.4	78	130	Lake Shore Gold	LSG	0.56	241.08	0.56		1.71
6,699.8	33.7	61	109	Quad/Graphics	QUAD	21.48	1,002.86	11.83		22.31
19,251.1	21.3	61	315	Ritchie Bros	RBA	22.54	2,414.28	17.81		24.79
9,232.4	12.6	61	151	Stewart Enterprs Cl A	STEI	8.44	714.56	4.92		8.65
10,089.5	33.6	55	182	Miller Energy Resources	MILL	4.00	183.46	3.34		5.59
10,081.7	22.4	55	182	Dex One	DEXO	1.85	92.36	0.66		2.17
18,570.6	35.8	53	352	Sealy Corp	ZZ	2.19	228.97	1.52		2.45
26,478.2	18.2	50	524	Logitech Intl SA	LOGI	6.93	1,191.21	6.59		11.47
4,979.5	n.a.	49	102	Grupo Galicia	GGAL	5.75	1,094.32	4.14		7.40

Sources: FactSet Research Systems; WSJ Market Data Group

Concerns about Short Selling   When the credit crisis intensified in 2008, hedge funds and other investors took large short positions on many stocks, especially those of financial institutions. Some critics argued that the large short sales placed additional downward pressure on prices and created paranoia in the stock market. Such fear could make stock prices decline to a greater degree, which would be beneficial to the short-sellers.

EXAMPLE

Just after the failure of the securities firm Lehman Brothers in September 2008, there were rumors that Morgan Stanley (another securities firm) was unable to obtain financing and was about to fail. During the three-day period from September 15 to 17, 2008, the number of Morgan Stanley shares sold short increased from fewer than 5 million shares to about 39 million shares. Many of these short sales may be attributable to this unfounded rumor. During this three-day period, the stock price of Morgan Stanley declined by a third. Arguably, much of the decline in the stock price was due to the massive short selling, which was likely triggered by the rumor. ●

Restrictions on Short Selling   Following the massive short sales of Morgan Stanley, the Securities and Exchange Commission (SEC) temporarily protected more than 800 firms from short sales. For the most part, the protected firms were financial institutions and other companies that were exposed to the credit crisis; the SEC was attempting to limit the adverse effect that short sales might have on the stock prices of these firms. The SEC also mandated that traders had to borrow the stock before they could execute a short sale. In some cases, traders were using loopholes in the short sale rules to short stock without borrowing it. The SEC delegated authority to the stock exchanges to identify other firms that should be protected from short sales. Some other countries including Australia, Taiwan, and the Netherlands subsequently instituted their own short-selling regulations.

Many critics argued that these restrictions did not affect the general behavior of the speculators who were engaging in short sales. Some short-sellers were focused on financial institutions that had very little equity and used mostly borrowed funds (financial leverage) to generate large returns on their equity. These short-sellers might argue that the stock prices of the target financial institutions were declining not because of the short selling but rather because regulators failed to ensure that these institutions would have sufficient capital backing their business. Furthermore, even though short sales were banned, speculators have other methods (e.g., put options) of betting against a stock that might place downward pressure on a stock's price. In October 2008, the ban on short selling was eliminated in the United States because regulators determined that the ban was not stabilizing stock values.

However, in 2008 and 2009, the Securities and Exchange Commission imposed new restrictions on short selling. In October 2008, it required that short-sellers borrow and deliver the shares to the buyers within three days. This rule is important because there were many cases in which brokerage firms were allowing speculators to engage in naked shorting, in which they sell a stock short without first borrowing the stock. Therefore, speculators were able to take larger short positions than would have been possible if they were required to first borrow the shares that they were selling, which resulted in more downward pressure on the stock's prices. This new rule by the SEC was a stronger version of an SEC rule implemented to prevent naked short selling in 2005 (called Regulation SHO), which applied only to specific stocks and was not strictly enforced.

In 2009, the SEC also reinstated the uptick rule (previously eliminated in 2007), which prohibits speculators from taking a short position in stocks that experienced a decline of at least 10 percent for the day, except when the most recent trade resulted in an increase in the stock price. This rule is intended to prevent short selling in response to a stock's continuous downward price momentum.

WEB

www.nyse.com
Information about how trading is conducted on the NYSE.

12-2 How Stock Transactions Are Executed

Transactions on the stock exchanges and the Nasdaq are facilitated by floor brokers and market-makers.

12-2a Floor Brokers

Floor brokers are situated on the floor of a stock exchange. There are hundreds of computer booths along the perimeter of the trading floor, where floor brokers receive orders from brokerage firms. The floor brokers then fulfill and execute those orders.

EXAMPLE

Bryan Adams calls his broker at Zepellin Securities, where he has a brokerage account, and requests the purchase of 1,000 shares of stock in Clapton, Inc., which is traded on the NYSE. The broker at Zepellin communicates this information to the NYSE trading floor. A floor broker (who may be an employee of Zepellin or of some other brokerage firm) receives the order at a booth and goes to a specific trading post where Clapton stock is traded. There are 20 trading posts on the NYSE, and a different set of stocks is traded at each trading post. The floor broker communicates the desire to purchase 1,000 shares of Clapton stock at a specific price. Other floor brokers who have orders to sell Clapton stock either communicate their willingness to accept the bid or signal the "ask" price at which they would be willing to sell the shares. If the floor brokers can agree on a price, a transaction is executed. The transaction is recorded and transmitted to the tape display. Bryan will likely receive a message from the broker indicating that the trade was executed, and he will receive confirmation in the mail within three days. Bryan provides payment to his brokerage firm within three days. ●

12-2b Market-Makers

Market-makers (previously referred to as "specialists" on the NYSE) can serve a broker function by matching up buy and sell orders on the New York Stock Exchange. They gain from accommodating these orders because their bid and ask prices differ. In addition, they also take positions in specific stocks. Market-makers facilitate trading on the NYSE. The role of the market maker has been subject to much controversy. In the past, this role was described as "making a market" in particular stocks. Making a market implies that they stand ready to buy or sell certain stocks even if no other investors are willing to participate. However, it does not mean that such specialists are offsetting all orders by taking the opposite side of every transaction. In fact, many transactions on the NYSE are executed electronically and do not require participation by market-makers.

Transactions in the Nasdaq market are also facilitated by market-makers. They benefit from the difference (spread) between the bid and ask prices and can also take positions in stocks. Some market-makers make a market in a few stocks, while others make a market for many stocks. However, stocks that are more actively traded tend to have a larger number of market-makers.

Market-makers take positions to capitalize on the discrepancy between the prevailing stock price and their own valuation of the stock. When many uninformed investors take buy or sell positions that push a stock's price away from its fundamental value, the stock price is distorted as a result of the "noise" caused by the uninformed investors (called "**noise traders**"). Market-makers may take the opposite position of the uninformed investors and therefore stand to benefit if their expectations are correct.

Brokers choose the route by which an order is executed, which means that they determine whether the order will be filled by a specific market-maker. The spread quoted for a given stock may vary among market-makers. Therefore, the manner by which the trade is routed by the broker can affect the size of the spread. Some market-makers compensate brokers for orders routed to them. So, while a brokerage firm may charge a customer only $10 for a trade, it may also receive a payment from the market-maker. The market-maker may use a wider spread so that it can offer such a payment to the broker. The point is that some customers may pay only $10 for a buy order to be executed, but the order is executed at a price that is relatively high because the market-maker charged a large spread. Customers should attempt to compare not only the fee brokers charge for a trade, but also the spread quoted by the market-maker selected by the brokerage firm. Investors do not have direct control over the routing process, but they can at least select a broker that uses their preferred type of process. The market is not sufficiently transparent for the routing process to be monitored, but technology may soon allow customers to more easily monitor the routing and the quoted spreads.

12-2c The Spread on Stock Transactions

When investors place an order, they are quoted an ask price, or the price that the broker is asking for that stock. There is also a bid price, or the price at which the broker would purchase the stock. The *spread* is the difference between the ask price and the bid price, and it is commonly measured as a percentage of the ask price.

EXAMPLE

Boletto Company stock is quoted by a broker as bid $39.80, ask $40.00. The bid-ask spread is

$$\text{Spread} = \frac{\$40.00 - \$39.80}{\$40.00}$$
$$= 0.5\%$$

This spread of 0.5 percent implies that if investors purchased the stock and then immediately sold it back before market prices changed, they would incur a cost of 0.5 percent of their investment for the round-trip transaction. ●

The transaction cost due to the spread is separate from the commission charged by the broker. The spread has declined substantially over time in response to more efficient methods of executing orders and increased competition from electronic communications networks. The spread is influenced by the following factors:

$$\text{Spread} = f(\underbrace{\text{Order costs}}_{+}, \underbrace{\text{Inventory costs}}_{+}, \underbrace{\text{Competition}}_{-}, \underbrace{\text{Volume}}_{-}, \underbrace{\text{Risk}}_{+})$$

Order Costs   Order costs are the costs of processing orders, including clearing costs and the costs of recording transactions.

Inventory Costs   Inventory costs include the cost of maintaining an inventory of a particular stock. There is an opportunity cost because the funds could have been used for some other purpose. If interest rates are relatively high, the opportunity cost of holding an inventory should be relatively high. The higher the inventory costs, the larger the spread that will be established to cover these costs.

Competition   For stocks traded on the NYSE or the Nasdaq market, having multiple market-makers promotes competition. When more market-makers are competing to sell a particular stock, the spread is likely to be smaller.

Volume   Stocks that are more liquid have less chance of experiencing an abrupt change in price, and stocks that have a large trading volume are more liquid because there is a sufficient number of buyers and sellers at any time. This liquidity makes it easier to sell a stock at any point in time and therefore reduces the risk of a sudden decline in the stock's price.

Risk   If the firm represented by a stock has relatively risky operations, its stock price is normally more volatile. Thus a market-maker is subject to more risk when holding inventory in this type of stock and will therefore set a higher spread.

At any particular moment, the spread can vary among stocks. Those who make a market for a particular stock are exposed to the risk that the stock's price could change abruptly in the secondary market and reduce the value of their position in that stock. Thus any factors that affect this type of risk to a stock's market-maker can affect the spread of that stock.

12-2d Electronic Communication Networks

Electronic communication networks (ECNs) are automated systems for disclosing and sometimes executing stock trades. The SEC requires that any quote provided by a market-maker be made available to all market participants. This requirement eliminated the practice of providing more favorable quotes exclusively to proprietary clients. It also resulted in significantly lower spreads between quoted bid and ask prices. Electronic communication networks are appealing to investors because they may allow for more efficient execution of trades.

Some ECNs focus on market orders. They receive orders and route them through various networks searching for the best price. Other ECNs receive limit orders and electronically match them up with other orders that are still not fulfilled. Exhibit 12.1 shows an example of an ECN book at a given moment in time. The book lists the limit buy orders and limit sell orders that are currently not fulfilled. When a new limit order matches an existing order, the transaction is immediately executed and the matching order is removed from the book. If the new limit order cannot immediately be matched to an existing order on the ECN book, it is added to the book.

EXAMPLE Assume that the ECN book shown in Exhibit 12.1 is the book for a particular stock and that a new limit order is placed to sell 300 shares of that stock at a price of no less than $32.68. This order

Exhibit 12.1   Example of an ECN Book at a Given Point in Time

BID OR ASK?	SHARES	PRICE
Bid	500	$32.50
Bid	300	$32.50
Bid	400	$32.56
Bid	1,000	$32.60
Bid	400	$32.64
Bid	1,200	$32.64
Bid	300	$32.68
Ask	400	$32.78
Ask	1,000	$32.80
Ask	300	$32.84
Ask	500	$32.84
Ask	600	$32.88

can be matched by the order to buy 300 shares at a bid price of $32.68. Upon the execution of this trade, the order on the ECN book to buy 300 shares at a bid price of $32.68 is removed. Assume now that a new limit order is placed to purchase 1,400 shares at a price of no more than $32.80. This order is matched up with the order to sell 400 shares at an ask price of $32.78 and the order to sell 1,000 shares at $32.80. Then those orders are removed from the ECN book because they have been fulfilled. ●

In order to improve execution of orders, both the NYSE and Nasdaq have acquired companies that developed ECNs.

Interaction between Direct Access Brokers and ECNs   A direct access broker is a trading platform on a computer website that allows investors to trade stocks without the use of a broker. The website itself serves as the broker and interacts with ECNs that can execute the trade. Some of the more popular direct access brokers include a division of Charles Schwab (www.schwab.com), Interactive Brokers (www.interactivebrokers.com), and NobleTrading (www.nobletrading.com). Each of these websites offers a variety of trading platforms, which range from those that are easier to use and offer less information to those that are more complex but provide more information. A monthly fee is usually charged for access to a trading platform; the fee is higher for platforms that offer more information.

The advantage of a direct access broker is that investors interested in trading a particular stock can monitor the supply and prices of shares for sale and the demand for shares at various prices on different ECNs. Thus the market becomes more transparent because investors can visualize the overall supply and demand conditions at various possible prices. Investors can use this information to determine how stock prices may change in the near future.

The use of direct access brokers and ECNs allows computers to match buyers and sellers without relying on the floor brokers or traders on stock exchanges. The trend is toward a "floorless" exchange in which all trades are executed in cyberspace and orders are submitted and confirmed through automated systems. As this technology is implemented across countries, it may ultimately create a single global floorless exchange where investors can easily trade any security in any country by submitting requests from a personal computer.

Dark Pools   Dark pools are platforms that use software to connect buyers and sellers of stocks. They represent private stock markets that can be used by institutional investors, and were established since electronic trading became popular. The trades executed in dark pools are not immediately disclosed to the public. Some investors prefer to trade in dark pools so they may more easily accumulate a large amount of shares of a particular stock without the public's knowledge of these trades. Thus an investor may be more able to accumulate all the shares without placing excessive upward pressure on the stock price. Conversely, if the investor executed these trades to accumulate the shares on a public stock exchange, other investors who see the trades might attempt to buy shares of that stock as well, thereby hoping to free ride while the accumulation of shares pushes the stock price up. In this case, the cost to the original investor of accumulating shares might be higher.

Dark pools also attract other types of traders, such as high-frequency traders who use computer algorithms to catch price discrepancies in stocks. Dark pools also offer bid or ask prices that are slightly more favorable for specific institutional traders than what is available in the public stock markets.

Dark pools are increasing in popularity. Some estimates suggest that dark pools might account for 40 percent of all trading of stocks. There are about 30 popular dark pools, including Cross-Finder (operated by Credit Suisse), Liquidnet, Posit, Pipeline, and Sigma

X (operated by Goldman Sachs). Public stock exchanges are losing business as a result of the popularity of dark pools.

One concern about dark pools is that they could reduce the transparency in the stock market because the supply and demand for each given stock is fragmented across several markets. The public stock markets such as the NYSE and Nasdaq have criticized dark pools for reducing transparency, thereby making it more difficult for investors to asses existing demand and supply conditions for a particular stock.

In August 2012, the NYSE initiated a trading program called Retail Liquidity Program. It is similar to a dark pool and allows its members to offer stock price improvements (better prices than the prevailing quotes) for retail customers. The trades are not visible to the public. This program enables the NYSE to be more competitive with the dark pools offered by private stock markets. The Nasdaq market followed with a similar type of program.

12-2e Program Trading

A common form of computerized trading is program trading, which the NYSE defines as the simultaneous buying and selling of a portfolio comprising at least 15 different stocks with a combined value of more than $1 million. This is a narrow definition, and the term is often used in other contexts. More generally, program trading represents a computerized response by institutional investors to either buy or sell a large basket of stocks in response to movements in a particular stock index.

For example, in one form of program trading, numerous stocks that have become "overpriced" (based on a particular model used to value those stocks) are sold. In other words, program trading may reflect the sale of a large basket of stocks because a stock index just reached an unusually high level, indicating a likely decline in stock prices in the near future. Likewise, the program might call for the purchase of a large basket of stocks because a stock index just reached an unusually low level, indicating a likely increase in stock prices in the near future.

Institutional investors establish their own unique program trading strategies. In fact, the trigger that leads one institutional investor to buy a large basket of stocks might lead another to sell a large basket of stocks. The most common program traders are large securities firms. They conduct the trades for their own accounts or for other institutional investors such as pension funds, mutual funds, and insurance companies.

Program trading can be combined with the trading of stock index futures to create **portfolio insurance**. With this strategy, the investor uses futures or options contracts on a stock index. Thus, a decline in the market would result in a gain on the futures or options position, which can offset the reduced market value of the stock portfolio.

Impact of Program Trading on Stock Volatility Program trading is often cited as the cause of a decline or rise in the stock market. The underlying reason for a large amount of program trading, however, is that institutional investors believe that numerous stocks are over- or undervalued. Although program trading can cause share prices to reach a new equilibrium more rapidly, this does not imply that it causes more volatility in the stock market.

Yet on May 6, 2010, stock prices declined abruptly in what is now referred to as the "flash crash." Overall, stocks declined by more than 9 percent on average before reversing and recovering most of those losses on that same day, when more than 19 billion shares were traded. It appears that the flash crash was triggered by computerized trading. Computers were programmed to trade based on specific trigger points, for example, automatically selling shares if a stock index declined by a certain percentage. These automated sales of shares pushed the stock levels lower, which triggered additional sales by computers. Finally, the stock index levels reached such low levels that the computer programs were triggered to start purchasing shares. Most of this activity occurred in a 30-minute period, the most volatile half hour in the history of the New York Stock Exchange.

12-3 Regulation of Stock Trading

WEB

www.nyse.com
Describes regulations imposed on firms that are listed on the NYSE.

Regulation of stock markets is necessary to ensure that investors are treated fairly. Without regulation, there would be more trading abuses that would discourage many investors from participating in the market. Stock trading is regulated by the individual exchanges and by the SEC. The **Securities Act of 1933** and the **Securities Exchange Act of 1934** were enacted to prevent unfair or unethical trading practices on the security exchanges. As a result of the 1934 act, stock exchanges were empowered and expected to discipline individuals or firms that violate regulations imposed by the exchange. The NYSE states that every transaction made at the exchange is under surveillance. The NYSE uses a computerized system to detect unusual trading of any particular stock that is traded on the exchange. It also employs personnel who investigate any abnormal price or trading volume of a particular stock or unusual trading practices of individuals.

In 2002, the NYSE issued a regulation requiring its listed firms to have a majority of independent directors (not employees of the firm) on their respective boards of directors. This requirement was intended to reduce directors' potential conflicts of interests so that they will concentrate on ensuring that the firm's management is focused on maximizing the stock's value for shareholders.

12-3a Circuit Breakers

Stock exchanges can impose circuit breakers, which are restrictions on trading when stock prices or a stock index reaches a specified threshold level. In general, circuit breakers are intended to temporarily stop the trading of stocks in response to a large decline in stock prices within a single day. They may prevent an initial pronounced stock market decline from causing panic selling in the market. See www.nyse.com/press/circuit_breakers.html for more information on circuit breakers.

12-3b Trading Halts

Stock exchanges may impose trading halts on particular stocks when they believe market participants need more time to receive and absorb material information that could affect the stock's value. They have imposed trading halts on stocks that are associated with mergers, earnings reports, lawsuits, and other news. A trading halt does not prevent a stock from experiencing a loss in response to news. Instead, the purpose of the halt is to ensure that the market has complete information before trading on the news. A trading halt may last for just a few minutes or for several hours or even for several days. Once the stock exchange believes that the market has complete information, it will allow trading to resume.

WEB

www.sec.gov
Information about the SEC's role and its regulatory actions.

Trading halts are intended to reduce stock price volatility, as the market price is adjusted by market forces in response to news. Thus the halts can prevent excessive optimism or pessimism about a stock by restricting trading until the news about the firm is completely and widely disseminated to the market. However, some critics believe that the trading halts slow the inevitable adjustment in the stock's price to the news. In general, research has found that stock volatility is relatively high after a halt is lifted but that the volatility subsides over the next few days.

12-3c Taxes Imposed on Stock Transactions

In 2012, long-term capital gains were taxed at 15 percent. Conversely, short-term capital gains were taxed at the investor's marginal tax rate on ordinary income. Investors subject to high marginal tax brackets on ordinary income commonly attempt to reduce their taxes by holding their stocks for at least one year. The tax rate on dividend income from stocks was increased from 15 percent to 20 percent in 2013 for investors in high tax brackets.

12-3d Securities and Exchange Commission

The Securities Act of 1933 and the Securities Exchange Act of 1934 gave the Securities and Exchange Commission authority to monitor the exchanges and required listed companies to file a registration statement and financial reports with the SEC and the exchanges. In general, the SEC attempts to protect investors by ensuring full disclosure of pertinent information that could affect the values of securities. In particular, some of the more relevant SEC regulations involve the following requirements.

- Firms must publicly disclose all information about themselves that could affect the value of their securities.
- Employees of firms may take positions in their own firm's securities only during periods when they do not know of inside information that will affect the value of the firm once the information becomes public.
- Participants in security markets who facilitate trades must work in a fair and orderly manner.

These regulations are meant to prevent abuses that would give someone an unfair advantage over other investors, reducing the willingness of investors to participate in security markets. The SEC regulations allow all investors to have the same access to public information. Note that the SEC's focus is on sufficient disclosure, not on accuracy; it relies on auditors to certify that the financial statements are accurate.

Structure of the SEC The SEC consists of five commissioners appointed by the President of the United States and confirmed by the Senate. Each commissioner serves a five-year term. The terms are staggered so that, each year, one commissioner's term ends and a new appointee is added. The president also selects one of the five commissioners to chair the commission.

The commissioners meet to assess whether existing regulations are successfully preventing abuses and to revise the regulations as needed. Specific staff members of the SEC may be assigned to develop a proposal for a new regulation to prevent a particular abuse that is occurring. When the commission adopts new regulations, they are distributed to the public for feedback before final approval. Some of the more important proposals are subject to congressional review before final approval.

Key Divisions of the SEC The SEC has several important divisions that attempt to ensure a fair and orderly stock market. The Division of Corporate Finance reviews the registration statement filed when a firm goes public, corporate filings for annual and quarterly reports, and proxy statements that involve voting for board members or other corporate issues. The Division of Market Regulation requires the orderly disclosure of securities trades by various organizations that facilitate the trading of securities. The Division of Enforcement assesses possible violations of the SEC's regulations and can take action against individuals or firms. An investigation can involve the examination of securities data or transactions, and the SEC has subpoena power to obtain information from specific individuals. When the SEC finds that action is warranted, it may negotiate a settlement with the individuals or firms that are cited for violations, file a case against them in federal court, or even work with law enforcement agencies if the violations involve criminal activity. Such actions are normally intended to prevent the violations from continuing and to discourage other individuals or firms from engaging in illegal securities activities.

SEC Oversight of Corporate Disclosure

In October 2000, the SEC issued Regulation Fair Disclosure (FD), which requires firms to disclose relevant information broadly to investors at the same time. One of the most important results of Regulation FD is that a firm may no longer provide analysts with information that they could use before the market was aware of the information. Before Regulation FD, some firms would commonly hint to analysts that their earnings would be higher than initially anticipated. Thus, analysts could advise their preferred clients to purchase the stocks before the price was pushed up by the increased demand for shares by other investors who received the information later.

Since the implementation of Regulation FD, a firm must announce a change in expected earnings to all investors and other interested parties (such as analysts) at the same time. The firm may disclose the information on its website, through a filing of a document (8-K form) with the SEC, and through a news release. The firm may hold a conference call with analysts after the news is announced, but is expected to include all material information in the announcement. Thus the conference call will not give analysts an unfair advantage because the key information has already been disclosed. In addition, most firms have now opened up their conference calls to investors, who can listen in by phone or online through a website. Analysts who always relied on their own analytical abilities to develop their recommendations are continuing business as usual, but analysts who relied on what might be considered inside information from firms have had to modify their methods of forming opinions about the firms they cover.

Some analysts suggest that the regulation has caused firms to disclose less information to them and to the public than before. To ensure that they do not violate Regulation FD, some firms may offer less information so that no parties have an unfair advantage. In particular, smaller firms find it expensive to issue a press release every time they have relevant information. The SEC is reviewing Regulation FD, which may be altered to continue allowing for a flow of information from firms while ensuring that investors receive this information at the same time as analysts.

SEC Oversight of Insider Trading

Insiders of a publicly traded company (such as managers or board members) sometimes have inside information about the company that has not yet been publicized. For example, they might know that a company has just invented a patent that will be very valuable. It is illegal for insiders to take positions in the stock based on their inside information, because this would give them an unfair advantage over other investors. It is also illegal for insiders to pass the information on to other investors, or for those investors to take positions in the stock based on that information.

However, there is evidence to suggest that insider trading commonly occurs. Numerous studies have shown that a public company's stock price commonly increases a few weeks before an announcement that the company will be acquired. Bidders often pay a large premium to buy targets, such as 30 percent or more above the prevailing stock price. Thus investors who can obtain the stock before the bid is announced can sometimes earn a return of 30 percent or more in just a few weeks. In many cases, the stock price of a public company that is targeted for an acquisition experiences an abnormal increase in stock price a few weeks before the acquisition announcement. Such an abnormal increase in price for many targeted companies suggests that some traders have inside information that the company will be acquired. Such insider trading is not restricted to mergers but can occur in advance of many different events that will likely push up the stock price once the information is publicized.

A recent concern is that so-called expert networks leak information to institutional investors. Some managers or executives of publicly traded companies are hired as consultants ("experts") by a hedge fund, whereby they provide the hedge fund with insight about their company. Such a relationship can be completely legitimate if the consultants divulge only information about the company that is already public. Yet some of these consultants are paid more than $100,000 to have phone conversations with the hedge fund. Some regulators have suggested that a hedge fund would only be willing to incur such a high expense for information if it expects to receive inside information from the consultants.

The SEC attempts to prevent investors from trading based on inside information. In October 2009, it (along with other government agencies such as the Justice Department and FBI) charged many defendants connected with the Galleon Fund (a hedge fund) with trading based on inside information. Over the next three years, more than 60 defendants charged with insider trading (or related charges) either pled guilty or were convicted within the court system.

The Galleon case received special attention because the government effectively used wiretap evidence to prosecute insider trading cases. In addition, the government exposed the illegal activities of some insiders that were hired on the side as consultants or experts by hedge funds. Furthermore, the penalties to defendants who were found guilty of insider trading (or related charges) were much more severe than in previous years.

GLOBAL ASPECTS

12-4 TRADING INTERNATIONAL STOCKS

Although the international trading of stocks has grown over time, until recently it was limited by three barriers: transaction costs, information costs, and exchange rate risk. Now, however, these barriers have been reduced, as explained next.

12-4a Reduction in Transaction Costs

Most countries have their own stock exchanges where the stocks of local, publicly held companies are traded. In recent years, countries have consolidated their exchanges, increasing efficiency and reducing transaction costs. Some European stock exchanges use an extensive cross-listing system (called Eurolist) so that investors in a given European country can easily purchase stocks of companies based in other European countries.

Many international stock exchanges (such as that used in Switzerland and in Belgium) are now fully computerized, so a trading floor is not needed to execute orders. The details of the orders (including the stock's name, the number of shares to be bought or sold, and the price at which the investor is willing to buy or sell) are fed into a computer system. The system matches buyers and sellers and then sends information confirming the transaction to the financial institution, which informs the investor that the transaction has been completed.

When there are many more buy orders than sell orders for a given stock, the computer will not be able to accommodate all orders. Some buyers will then increase the price they are willing to pay for the stock. Thus the price adjusts in response to the demand (buy orders) for the stock and the supply (sell orders) of the stock for sale, as recorded by the computer system. Furthermore, the Internet allows investors to use their computers to place orders (through the website of a member of the stock exchange) that will then be executed and confirmed by the computer system back through the Internet to the investor. Thus all parts of the trading process, from the placement of orders to the confirmations that transactions have been executed, will be conducted by computers. The ease of placing such orders regardless of the investor's location and that of the stock exchange will likely increase the volume of international stock transactions in the future.

12-4b Reduction in Information Costs

Information about foreign stocks is now available on the Internet, enabling investors to make more informed decisions without having to purchase information about these stocks. Consequently, investors should be more comfortable assessing foreign stocks. Differences in accounting rules may still limit the degree to which financial data about foreign companies can be interpreted or compared to data about firms in other countries, but there has been some progress in making accounting standards uniform across countries.

12-4c Reduction in Exchange Rate Risk

When investing in a foreign stock denominated in a foreign currency, investors are subject to the possibility that the currency denominating the stock will depreciate against the investor's currency over time. The potential for a major decline in a stock's value simply because of a large degree of depreciation is greater in emerging markets, such as Indonesia or Russia, where the local currency can change by 10 percent or more on a single day.

The ongoing conversion of European countries to a single currency (the euro) should lead to more stock offerings in Europe by U.S.- and European-based firms. Previously, a European firm needed a different currency in every European country in which it conducted business, so the firm would borrow currency from local banks in each country. Now that firm can use the euro to finance its operations across several European countries and may be able to obtain all the financing it needs with one stock offering denominated in euros. The firm can then use a portion of the revenue (in euros) to pay dividends to shareholders who have purchased the stock. In addition, European investors based in countries where the euro serves as the local currency can now invest in euro-denominated stocks in other European countries without being exposed to exchange rate risk.

SUMMARY

- Investors engage in various types of stock transactions. They can place an order by phone or online. They can request that a transaction be executed at the prevailing price or only if the stock price reaches a specified level. They can finance a portion of their stock purchase with borrowed funds as a means of increasing the potential return on their investment. They can also sell stocks short.

- Organized stock exchanges such as the NYSE and the Nasdaq market facilitate secondary stock market transactions. Members of the exchanges trade stock for their

own accounts or for their clients. The exchanges are served by floor brokers and market-makers, who execute transactions. An over-the-counter exchange also exists, where stock transactions are executed through a telecommunications network. Electronic communication networks (ECNs) facilitate the execution of orders. ECNs can interact with a trading platform on a website that allows investors to trade stocks without the use of a broker.

- Stock markets are regulated to ensure that investors are treated fairly. Stock trading is regulated by the individual exchanges and by the SEC. Many of the regulations are intended to prevent unfair or unethical trading practices on the security exchanges. The stock exchanges and the SEC attempt to prevent the use of inside information by investors.

■ As various stock markets have removed their barriers to foreign investors, they have become more globally integrated. Transaction costs, information costs, and exchange rate risk have all been reduced, making it easier for investors to engage in international stock trading.

POINT COUNTER-POINT

Is a Market-Maker Needed?

Point   Yes. A market-maker can make a market by serving as the counterparty on a transaction. Without market-makers, stock orders might be heavily weighted toward buys or sells, and price movements would be more volatile.

Counter-Point   No. Market-makers do not prevent stock prices from declining. A stock that has more selling pressure than buying pressure will experience a decline in price, as it should. The electronic communication networks can serve as the intermediary between buyer and seller.

Who Is Correct?   Use the Internet to learn more about this issue and then formulate your own opinion.

QUESTIONS AND APPLICATIONS

1.   Orders Explain the difference between a market order and a limit order.

2.   Margins Explain how margin requirements can affect the potential return and risk from investing in a stock. What is the maintenance margin?

3.   Short Selling Under what conditions might investors consider short selling a specific stock?

4.   Short Selling Describe the short-selling process. Explain the short interest ratio.

5.   Market-Makers Describe the roles of market-makers.

6.   ECNs What are electronic communication networks (ECNs)?

7.   SEC Structure and Role Briefly describe the structure and role of the Securities and Exchange Commission (SEC).

8.   SEC Enforcement Explain how the Securities and Exchange Commission attempts to prevent violations of SEC regulations.

9.   Circuit Breakers Explain how circuit breakers are used to reduce the likelihood of a large stock market crash.

10. Trading Halts Why are trading halts sometimes imposed on particular stocks?

Advanced Questions

11. Regulation FD What are the implications of Regulation FD?

12. Stock Exchange Transaction Costs Explain how foreign stock exchanges such as the Swiss stock exchange have reduced transaction costs.

13. Bid-Ask Spread of Penny Stocks Your friend just told you about a penny stock he purchased, which increased in price from $0.10 to $0.50 per share. You start investigating penny stocks and, after conducting a large amount of research, you find a stock with a quoted price of $0.05. Upon further investigation, you notice that the ask price for the stock is $0.08 and that the bid price is $0.01. Discuss the possible reasons for this wide bid–ask spread.

14. Ban on Short Selling Why did the SEC impose a temporary ban on short sales of specific stocks in 2008? Do you think a ban on short selling is effective?

15. Dark Pools What are dark pools? How can they help investors accumulate shares without other investors knowing about the trades? Why are dark pools criticized by public stock exchanges? Explain the strategy used by public stock exchanges to compete with dark pools.

16. Inside Information Describe inside information as applied to the trading of stocks. Why is it illegal to trade based on inside information? Describe the evidence that suggests some investors use inside information.

17. Expert Networks Explain expert networks. How can expert networks affect the trading of specific stocks?

18. Galleon Insider Trading Case Explain how the Galleon case led to stronger enforcement against insider trading.

Interpreting Financial News

Interpret the following statements made by Wall Street analysts and portfolio managers.

a. "Individual investors who purchase stock on margin might as well go to Vegas."

b. "During a major stock market downturn, market-makers suddenly are not available."

c. "The trading floor may become extinct due to ECNs."

Managing in Financial Markets

Focus on Heavily Shorted Stocks As a portfolio manager, you commonly take short positions in stocks that have a high short interest ratio. What is the advantage of focusing on these types of firms? What is a possible disadvantage?

PROBLEMS

1. Buying on Margin Assume that Vogl stock is priced at $50 per share and pays a dividend of $1 per share. An investor purchases the stock on margin, paying $30 per share and borrowing the remainder from the brokerage firm at 10 percent annualized interest. If, after one year, the stock is sold at a price of $60 per share, what is the return to the investor?

2. Buying on Margin Assume that Duever stock is priced at $80 per share and pays a dividend of $2 per share. An investor purchases the stock on margin, paying $50 per share and borrowing the remainder from the brokerage firm at 12 percent annualized interest. If, after one year, the stock is sold at a price of $90 per share, what is the return to the investor?

3. Buying on Margin Suppose that you buy a stock for $48 by paying $25 and borrowing the remaining $23 from a brokerage firm at 8 percent annualized interest. The stock pays an annual dividend of $0.80 per share, and after one year you are able to sell it for $65. Calculate your return on the stock. Then, calculate the return on the stock if you had used only personal funds to make the purchase. Repeat the problem assuming that only personal funds are used and that you are able to sell the stock at $40 at the end of one year.

4. Buying on Margin How would the return on a stock be affected by a lower initial investment (and higher loan amount)? Explain the relationship between the proportion of funds borrowed and the return.

FLOW OF FUNDS EXERCISE

Shorting Stocks

Recall that if the economy continues to be strong, Carson Company may need to increase its production capacity by about 50 percent over the next few years to satisfy demand. It would need financing to expand and accommodate the increase in production. Recall that the yield curve is currently upward sloping. Also recall that Carson is concerned about a possible slowing of the economy because of potential Fed actions to reduce inflation. It is also considering issuing stock or bonds to raise funds in the next year.

a. In some cases, a stock's price is too high or too low because of asymmetric information (information known by the firm but not by investors). How can Carson attempt to minimize asymmetric information?

b. Carson Company is concerned that if it issues stock, its stock price over time could be adversely affected by certain institutional investors that take large short positions in a stock. When this happens, the stock's price may be undervalued because of the pressure on the price caused by the large short positions.

What can Carson do to counter major short positions taken by institutional investors if it really believes that its stock price should be higher? What is the potential risk involved in this strategy?

INTERNET/EXCEL EXERCISES

1. Go to finance.yahoo.com and insert the ticker symbol of the firm of your choice in the "Get Quotes" section. Review the statistics provided. What is the average daily trading volume (Avg Vol)? What is the market capitalization of the firm? What is its price–earnings ratio (P/E)? What is the amount of dividends paid, if any, and what is the dividend yield (Div & Yield)?

2. For the same firm, click on "Key Statistics." What is the firm's beta? What are its return on assets (ROA) and return on equity (ROE)? What is its short ratio?

ONLINE ARTICLES WITH REAL-WORLD EXAMPLES

Find a recent practical article available online that describes a real-world example regarding a specific financial institution or financial market that reinforces one or more concepts covered in this chapter.

If your class has an online component, your professor may ask you to post your summary of the article there and provide a link to the article so that other students can access it. If your class is live, your professor may ask you to summarize your application of the article in class. Your professor may assign specific students to complete this assignment or may allow any students to do the assignment on a volunteer basis.

For recent online articles and real-world examples related to this chapter, consider using the following search terms (be sure to include the prevailing year as a search term to ensure that the online articles are recent):

1. stock AND transaction cost
2. stock loss AND margin requirement
3. buying on margin AND risk
4. short selling AND gains
5. short selling AND risk
6. stock AND bid/ask spread
7. stock AND market-makers
8. stock AND ECNs
9. stock regulations AND conflict
10. international stock AND transaction cost

Stock Market Analysis

This problem requires an understanding of the different methods for valuing stocks.

As a stock portfolio manager, you spend most of your day searching for stocks that appear to be undervalued. In the last few days, you have received information about two stocks that you are assessing, Olympic stock and Kenner stock. Many stock analysts believe that these stocks are undervalued because their price–earnings ratios are lower than the industry average. Olympic, Inc., has a PE ratio of 6 versus an industry PE ratio of 8. Its stock price declined recently in response to an announcement that its quarterly earnings would be lower than expected because of expenses from recent restructuring. The restructuring is expected to improve Olympic's future performance, but its earnings will take a large onetime hit this quarter.

Kenner Company has a PE ratio of 9 versus a PE ratio of 11 in its industry. Its earnings have been decent in recent years, but it has not kept up with new technology and may lose market share to competitors in the future.

Questions

1. Should you still consider purchasing Olympic stock in light of the analysts' arguments about why it may be undervalued?

2. Should you still consider purchasing Kenner stock in light of the analysts' arguments about why it may be undervalued?

3. Some stock analysts have just predicted that the prices of most stocks will fall because interest rates are expected to rise, which would cause investors to use higher required rates of return when valuing stocks. The analysts used this logic to suggest that the present value of future cash flows would decline if interest rates rise. The expected increase in interest rates is due to expectations of a stronger economy, which will result in an increased demand for loanable funds by corporations and individuals. Do you believe that stock prices will decline if the economy strengthens and interest rates rise?

PART 5
Derivative Security Markets

Derivatives are financial contracts whose values are derived from the values of underlying assets. They are widely used to speculate on future expectations or to reduce a
security portfolio's risk. The chapters in Part 5 focus on derivative security markets,
and each explains how institutional portfolio managers and speculators use them.
Many financial market participants simultaneously use all these markets, as is
emphasized throughout the chapters.

13
Financial Futures Markets

CHAPTER OBJECTIVES

The specific objectives of this chapter are to:

■ provide a background on financial futures contracts,

■ explain how interest rate futures contracts are used to speculate or hedge based on anticipated interest rate movements,

■ explain how stock index futures contracts are used to speculate or hedge based on anticipated stock price movements,

■ explain how single stock futures are used to speculate on anticipated stock price movements, and

■ describe the different types of risk to which traders in financial futures contracts are exposed.

In recent years, financial futures markets have received much attention because they have the potential to generate large returns to speculators and because they entail a high degree of risk. However, these markets can also be used to reduce the risk of financial institutions and other corporations. Financial futures markets facilitate the trading of financial futures contracts.

13-1 BACKGROUND ON FINANCIAL FUTURES

A **financial futures contract** is a standardized agreement to deliver or receive a specified amount of a specified financial instrument at a specified price and date. The buyer of a financial futures contract buys the financial instrument, and the seller of a financial futures contract delivers the instrument for the specified price.

13-1a Popular Futures Contracts

Futures contracts are traded on a wide variety of securities and indexes.

Interest Rate Futures   Many of the popular financial futures contracts are on debt securities such as Treasury bills, Treasury notes, Treasury bonds, and Eurodollar CDs. These contracts are referred to as **interest rate futures**. For each type of contract, the settlement dates at which delivery would occur are in March, June, September, and December.

Stock Index Futures   There are also financial futures contracts on stock indexes, which are referred to as **stock index futures**. A stock index futures contract allows for the buying and selling of a stock index for a specified price at a specified date. Various stock index futures contracts are described in Exhibit 13.1.

13-1b Markets for Financial Futures

Markets have been established to facilitate the trading of futures contracts.

Futures Exchanges   Futures exchanges provide an organized marketplace where standardized futures contracts can be traded. The exchanges clear, settle, and guarantee all transactions. They can ensure that each party's position is sufficiently backed by collateral as the market value of the position changes over time. In this way, any losses that occur are covered, so that counterparties are not adversely affected. Consequently, participants are more willing to trade financial futures contracts on an exchange.

Exhibit 13.1   Stock Index Futures Contracts

TYPE OF STOCK INDEX FUTURES CONTRACT	CONTRACT IS VALUED AS
S&P 500 index	$250 times index
Mini S&P 500 index	$50 times index
S&P Midcap 400 index	$500 times index
S&P Small Cap index	$200 times index
Nasdaq 100 index	$100 times index
Mini Nasdaq 100 index	$20 times index
Mini Nasdaq Composite index	$20 times index
Russell 2000 index	$500 times index

Most financial futures contracts in the United States are traded through the CME Group, which was formed in July 2007 by the merger of the Chicago Board of Trade (CBOT) and the Chicago Mercantile Exchange (CME). The CBOT specialized in futures contracts on Treasury bonds and agricultural products, and also traded stock options (described in the next chapter). The CME specialized in futures contracts on money market securities, stock indexes, and currencies.

The CME went public in 2002, and the CBOT went public in 2005. Their merger to form the CME Group created the world's largest and most diverse derivatives exchange, which serves international markets for derivative products. As part of the restructuring to increase efficiency, the CME and CBOT trading floors were consolidated into a single trading floor (at the CBOT) and their products were consolidated on a single electronic platform, which has reduced operating and maintenance expenses.

The operations of financial futures exchanges are regulated by the Commodity Futures Trading Commission (CFTC). The CFTC approves futures contracts before they can be listed by futures exchanges and imposes regulations to prevent unfair trading practices.

Over-the-Counter Market   Some specialized futures contracts are sold "over the counter" rather than on an exchange, whereby a financial intermediary (such as a commercial bank or an investment bank) finds a counterparty or serves as the counterparty. These over-the-counter arrangements are more personalized and can be tailored to the specific preferences of the parties involved. Such tailoring is not possible for the more standardized futures contracts sold on the exchanges.

13-1c Purpose of Trading Financial Futures

Financial futures are traded either to speculate on prices of securities or to hedge existing exposure to security price movements. **Speculators** in financial futures markets take positions to profit from expected changes in the price of futures contracts over time. They can be classified according to their methods. **Day traders** attempt to capitalize on price movements during a single day; normally, they close out their futures positions on the same day the positions were initiated. **Position traders** maintain their futures positions for longer periods of time (for weeks or months) and thus attempt to capitalize on expected price movements over a more extended time horizon.

WEB

www.cftc.gov
Detailed information
on the CFTC.

WEB

www.nfa.futures.org
Information for inves-
tors who wish to trade
futures contracts.

Hedgers take positions in financial futures to reduce their exposure to future movements in interest rates or stock prices. Many hedgers who maintain large portfolios of stocks or bonds take a futures position to hedge their risk. Speculators commonly take the opposite position and therefore serve as the counterparty on many futures transactions. Thus, speculators provide liquidity to the futures market.

WEB

www.cmegroup.com
Offers details about the products offered by the CME Group and also provides price quotations of the various futures contracts.

13-1d Institutional Trading of Futures Contracts

Exhibit 13.2 summarizes how various types of financial institutions participate in futures markets. Financial institutions generally use futures contracts to reduce risk. Some commercial banks, savings institutions, bond mutual funds, pension funds, and insurance companies trade interest rate futures contracts to protect against a possible increase in interest rates, thereby insulating their long-term debt securities from interest rate risk. Some stock mutual funds, pension funds, and insurance companies trade stock index futures to partially insulate their respective stock portfolios from adverse movements in the stock market.

WEB

www.bloomberg.com
Today's prices of U.S. bond futures contracts and prices of currency futures contracts.

13-1e Trading Process

When the futures exchanges were created, they relied on **commission brokers** (also called floor brokers) to execute orders for their customers, which generally were brokerage firms. In addition, **floor traders** (also called **locals**) traded futures contracts for their own account. The commission brokers and floor traders went to a specific location on the trading floor where the futures contract was traded to execute the order. Market-makers can also execute futures contract transactions for customers. They may facilitate a buy order for one customer and a sell order for a different customer. The market-maker earns the difference between the bid price and the ask price for such a trade, although the spread has declined significantly in recent years. Market-makers also earn profits when they use their own funds to take positions in futures contracts. Like any investors, they are subject to the risk of losses on their positions.

Electronic Trading   Most futures contracts are now traded electronically. The CME Group has an electronic trading platform called Globex that complements its floor

Exhibit 13.2   Institutional Use of Futures Markets

TYPE OF FINANCIAL INSTITUTION	PARTICIPATION IN FUTURES MARKETS
Commercial banks	• Take positions in futures contracts to hedge against interest rate risk.
Savings institutions	• Take positions in futures contracts to hedge against interest rate risk.
Securities firms	• Execute futures transactions for individuals and firms. • Take positions in futures contracts to hedge their own portfolios against stock market or interest rate movements.
Mutual funds	• Take positions in futures contracts to speculate on future stock market or interest rate movements. • Take positions in futures contracts to hedge their portfolios against stock market or interest rate movements.
Pension funds	• Take positions in futures contracts to hedge their portfolios against stock market or interest rate movements.
Insurance companies	• Take positions in futures contracts to hedge their portfolios against stock market or interest rate movements.

trading. Some futures contracts are traded both on the trading floor and on Globex, whereas others are traded only on Globex. Transactions can occur on Globex virtually around the clock (the platform is closed about one hour per day for maintenance) and on weekends. In 2004, the Chicago Board Options Exchange (CBOE) opened a fully electronic futures exchange.

13-1f Trading Requirements

Customers who desire to buy or sell futures contracts open accounts at brokerage firms that execute futures transactions. Under exchange requirements, a customer must establish a margin deposit with the broker before a transaction can be executed. This initial margin is typically between 5 and 18 percent of a futures contract's full value. Brokers commonly require margin deposits above those required by the exchanges. As the futures contract price changes on a daily basis, its value is "marked to market," or revised to reflect the prevailing conditions. A customer whose contract values moves in an unfavorable direction may receive a margin call from the broker, requiring that additional funds be deposited in the margin account. The margin requirements reduce the risk that customers will later default on their obligations.

Type of Orders   Customers can place a market order or a limit order. With a market order, the trade will automatically be executed at the prevailing price of the futures contract; with a limit order, the trade will be executed only if the price is within the limit specified by the customer. For example, a customer may place a limit order to buy a particular futures contract if it is priced no higher than a specified price. Similarly, a customer may place an order to sell a futures contract if it is priced no lower than a specified minimum price.

How Orders Are Executed   Although most trading now takes place electronically, some trades are still conducted on the trading floor. In that case, the brokerage firm

USING THE WALL STREET JOURNAL

Interest Rate Futures

The *Wall Street Journal* provides information on interest rate futures, as shown here. Specifically, it discloses the recent open price, range (high and low), and final closing (settle) price over the previous trading day. It also discloses the number of existing contracts (open interest). Financial institutions closely monitor interest rate futures prices when considering whether to hedge their interest rate risk.

Source: Reprinted with permission of the *Wall Street Journal*, Copyright © 2013 Dow Jones & Company, Inc. All Rights Reserved Worldwide.

Interest Rate Futures

Treasury Bonds (CBT)-$100,000; pts 32nds of 100%

March	145-170	146-110	145-000	**145-050**	−15.0	298,397

Treasury Notes (CBT)-$100,000; pts 32nds of 100%

| March | 132-200 | 132-315 | 132-170 | **132-185** | −3.0 | 725,004 |
| June | 131-155 | 131-270 | 131-120 | **131-140** | −3.0 | 1,450,878 |

5 Yr. Treasury Notes (CBT); pts 32nds of 100%

| March | 124-102 | 124-145 | 124-095 | **124-102** | −.2 | 580,267 |
| June | 123-292 | 124-017 | 123-287 | **123-295** | ... | 1,276,366 |

2 Yr. Treasury Notes (CBT)-$200,000; pts 32nds of 100%

| March | 110-085 | 110-090 | 110-077 | **110-080** | −.5 | 438,873 |
| June | 110-072 | 110-077 | 110-070 | **110-072** | ... | 708,150 |

30 Day Federal Funds (CBT)-$5,000,000; 100 - daily avg.

| Feb | 99.855 | 99.855 | 99.853 | **99.855** | ... | 43,817 |
| March | 99.855 | 99.860 | 99.850 | **99.855** | ... | 40,419 |

10 Yr. Int. Rate Swaps (CBT)-$100,000; pts 32nds of 100%

| March | 118.422 | 118.516 | 118.000 | **117.984** | −.203 | 12,308 |

1 Month Libor (CME)-$3,000,000; pts of 100%

| March | ... | ... | ... | **99.7950** | −.0025 | 446 |

Eurodollar (CME)-$1,000,000; pts of 100%

March	99.7050	99.7075	99.7025	**99.7050**	−.0025	895,003
June	99.6800	99.6800	99.6750	**99.6800**	...	789,912
Sept	99.6550	99.6600	99.6500	**99.6600**	...	737,645
Dec	99.6350	99.6350	99.6250	**99.6350**	...	808,956

communicates its customers' orders to telephone stations located near the trading floor of the futures exchange. The floor brokers accommodate these orders. Each type of financial futures contract is traded in a particular location on the trading floor. The floor brokers make their offers to trade by open outcry, specifying the quantity of contracts they wish to buy or sell. Other floor brokers and traders interested in trading the particular type of futures contract can respond to the open outcry. When two traders on the trading floor reach an agreement, each trader documents the specifics of the agreement (including the price), and the information is transmitted to the customers.

Floor brokers receive transaction fees in the form of a bid–ask spread. That is, they purchase a given futures contract for one party at a slightly lower price than the price at which they sell the contract to another party. For every buyer of a futures contract, there must be a corresponding seller.

The futures exchange facilitates the trading process but does not itself take buy or sell positions on the futures contract. Instead, the exchange acts as a clearinghouse. A clearinghouse facilitates the trading process by recording all transactions and guaranteeing timely payments. This precludes the need for a purchaser of a futures contract to check the creditworthiness of the contract seller. In fact, purchasers of contracts do not even know who the sellers are, and vice versa. The clearinghouse also supervises the delivery specified by contracts as of the settlement date.

Futures contracts representing debt securities such as bonds result in the delivery of those securities at the settlement date. Futures contracts that represent an index (such as a bond index or stock index) are settled in cash.

WEB

www.cmegroup.com
Quotations for futures contracts.

13-2 INTEREST RATE FUTURES CONTRACTS

Interest rate futures contracts specify a face value of the underlying securities (such as $1,000,000 for T-bill futures and $100,000 for Treasury bond futures), a maturity of the underlying securities, and the settlement date when delivery would occur. There is a minimum price fluctuation for each contract, such as $1/_{32}$ of a point ($1,000), or $31.25 per contract.

There are also futures contracts on bond indexes, which allow for the buying and selling of a particular bond index for a specified price at a specified date. For financial institutions that trade in municipal bonds, there are **Municipal Bond Index (MBI) futures**. The index is based on the **Bond Buyer Index** of 40 actively traded general obligation and revenue bonds. The specific characteristics of MBI futures are shown in Exhibit 13.3.

Exhibit 13.3   Characteristics of Municipal Bond Index Futures

CHARACTERISTICS OF FUTURES CONTRACT	MUNICIPAL BOND INDEX FUTURES
Trading unit	1,000 times the Bond Buyer Municipal Bond Index. A price of 90–00 represents a contract size of $90,000.
Price quotation	In points and thirty-seconds of a point.
Minimum price fluctuation	One thirty-second ($1/_{32}$) of a point, or $31.25 per contract.
Daily trading limits	Three points ($3,000) per contract above or below the previous day's settlement price.
Settlement months	March, June, September, December.
Settlement procedure	Municipal Bond Index futures settle in cash on the last day of trading.

13-2a Valuing Interest Rate Futures

The price of an interest rate futures contract generally reflects the expected price of the underlying security on the settlement date. Thus any factors that influence that expected price should influence the current prices of the interest futures contracts. Participants in the Treasury bond futures market closely monitor the economic indicators that affect Treasury bond prices, as shown in Exhibit 13.4. Some of the more closely monitored indicators of economic growth include employment, gross domestic product, retail sales, industrial production, and consumer confidence. When indicators signal an increase in economic growth, participants anticipate an increase in interest rates, which places downward pressure on bond prices and therefore also on Treasury bond futures prices. Conversely, when indicators signal a decrease in economic growth, participants

Exhibit 13.4 Framework for Explaining Changes over Time in the Futures Prices of Treasury Bonds and Treasury Bills

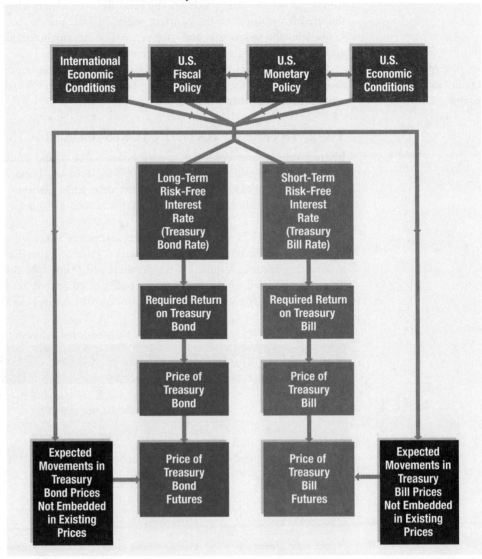

anticipate lower interest rates, which places upward pressure on bond prices and therefore also on Treasury bond futures.

Participants in the Treasury bond futures market also closely monitor indicators of inflation, such as the consumer price index and the producer price index. In general, an unexpected increase in these indexes tends to create expectations of higher interest rates and places downward pressure on bond prices and hence also on Treasury bond futures prices.

Indicators that reflect the amount of long-term financing are also monitored. For example, announcements about the government deficit or the amount of money that the Treasury hopes to borrow in a Treasury bond auction are closely monitored. Any information that implies more government borrowing than expected tends to signal upward pressure on the long-term risk-free interest rate (the Treasury bond rate), downward pressure on bond prices, and therefore downward pressure on Treasury bond futures prices.

13-2b Speculating in Interest Rate Futures

Speculators who anticipate future movements in interest rates can likewise anticipate the future direction of Treasury security values and therefore how valuations of interest rate futures will change. Speculators take positions in interest rate futures that will benefit them if their expectations prove to be correct.

EXAMPLE

In February, Jim Sanders forecasts that interest rates will decrease over the next month. If his expectation is correct, the market value of T-bills should increase. Sanders calls a broker and purchases a T-bill futures contract. Assume that the price of the contract was 94.00 (a 6 percent discount) and that the price of T-bills on the March settlement date is 94.90 (a 5.1 percent discount). Sanders can accept delivery of these T-bills and sell them for more than he paid for them. Because the T-bill futures represent $1 million of par value, the nominal profit from this speculative strategy is

Selling price	$949,000	(94.90% of $1,000,000)
− Purchase price	−940,000	(94.00% of $1,000,000)
= Profit	$9,000	(0.90% of $1,000,000)

●

In this example, Sanders benefited from his speculative strategy because interest rates declined from the time he took the futures position until the settlement date. If interest rates had risen over this period, the price of T-bills on the settlement date would have been below 94.00 (reflecting a discount above 6 percent), and Sanders would have incurred a loss.

EXAMPLE

Assume that the price of T-bills as of the March settlement date is 92.50 (representing a discount of 7.5 percent). In this case, the nominal profit from Sanders's speculative strategy is

Selling price	$925,000	(92.50% of $1,000,000)
− Purchase price	−940,000	(94.00% of $1,000,000)
= Profit	−$15,000	(−1.50% of $1,000,000)

Now suppose instead that, in February, Sanders had anticipated that interest rates would rise by March. He therefore sold a T-bill futures contract with a March settlement date, obligating him to provide T-bills to the purchaser on that delivery date. When T-bill prices declined in March, Sanders was able to obtain T-bills at a market price lower than the price at which he was obligated to sell those bills. Again, there is always the risk that interest rates (and therefore T-bill prices) will move contrary to expectations. In that case, Sanders would have paid a higher market price for the T-bills than the price at which he could sell them. ●

Payoffs from Speculating in Interest Rate Futures The potential payoffs from speculating in futures contracts are illustrated in Exhibit 13.5. The left graph

Exhibit 13.5   Potential Payoffs from Speculating in Financial Futures

represents a purchaser of futures, and the right graph represents a seller of futures. The S on each graph indicates the initial price at which a futures position is created. The horizontal axis represents the market value of the securities in terms of a futures contract as of the delivery date. The maximum possible loss when purchasing futures is the amount to be paid for the securities, but this loss will occur only if the market value of the securities falls to zero. The amount of gain (or loss) to a speculator who initially purchased futures will equal the loss (or gain) to a speculator who initially sold futures on the same date, assuming zero transaction costs.

Impact of Leverage   Because investors commonly use a margin account to take futures positions, the return from speculating in interest rate futures should reflect the degree of financial leverage involved. This return is magnified substantially when considering the relatively small margin maintained by many investors.

EXAMPLE

In the example where Jim Sanders earned a profit of $9,000 on a futures contract, this profit represents 0.90 percent of the value of the underlying contract par value. Consider that Sanders could have taken the interest rate futures position with an initial margin of perhaps $10,000. Under these conditions, the $9,000 profit represents a return of 90 percent over the period of less than two months in which he maintained the futures position.

Just as financial leverage magnifies positive returns, it also magnifies losses. In the example where Sanders lost $15,000 on a futures contract, he would have lost 100 percent of his initial margin, and thus would have been required to add more funds to his margin account, when the value of the futures position began to decline. ●

Closing Out the Futures Position   Most buyers or sellers of financial futures contracts do not actually make or accept delivery of the financial instrument; instead, they offset their positions by the settlement date. In the previous example, if Jim Sanders did not want to accept delivery of the T-bills at settlement date, he could have sold a T-bill futures contract with a March settlement date at any time before that date. Since his second transaction requires that he deliver T-bills at the March settlement date but his initial transaction allows him to receive T-bills at the March settlement date, his obligations net out.

When closing out a futures position, a speculator's gain (or loss) is based on the difference between the price at which a futures contract is sold and the price at which that same type of contract is purchased.

EXAMPLE

Suppose Kim Bennett purchased a futures contract on Treasury bonds at a price of 90-00 on October 2. One month later, she sells the same futures contract in order to close out the position. At this time, the futures contract specifies the price as 92-10, or $92^{10}/_{32}$ percent of the par value. Given that the futures contract on Treasury bonds specifies a par value of $100,000, the nominal profit is

Selling price	**$92,312**	($92^{10}/_{32}\%$ of $100,000)
− **Purchase price**	**−90,000**	(90.00% of $100,000)
= **Profit**	**$2,312**	($2^{10}/_{32}\%$ of $100,000)

When the initial position is a sale of the futures contract, a purchase of that same type of contract will close out the position. For example, assume that Chris Harper sold Treasury bond futures on October 2 at a price of 90−00 and then took an offsetting position one month later to close out his position. Using the same numbers as before, a loss of $2,312 (ignoring transaction costs) will result from closing out his position one month later. Speculators are willing to close out a position at a loss when they expect that a larger loss will occur if the position is not closed out. ●

13-2c Hedging with Interest Rate Futures

Financial institutions can classify their assets and liabilities in terms of the sensitivity of their market value to interest rate movements. The difference between a financial institution's volume of rate-sensitive assets and rate sensitive liabilities represents its exposure to interest rate risk. Over the long run, an institution may attempt to restructure its assets or liabilities in order to balance its degree of rate sensitivity. However, restructuring the balance sheet takes time. In the short run, the institution may consider using financial futures to hedge its exposure to interest rate movements. A variety of financial institutions use financial futures to hedge their interest rate risk, including mortgage companies, securities dealers, commercial banks, savings institutions, pension funds, and insurance companies.

Using Interest Rate Futures to Create a Short Hedge   Financial institutions commonly take a position in interest rate futures to create a short hedge, which represents the sale of a futures contract on debt securities or an index that is similar to its assets. The "short" position from the futures contract is taken to hedge the institution's "long" position (in its own assets).

Consider a commercial bank that currently holds a large amount of corporate bonds. Its primary source of funds is short-term deposits. The bank will be adversely affected if interest rates rise in the near future because its liabilities are more rate-sensitive than its assets. Although the bank believes that its bonds are a reasonable long-term investment, it anticipates that interest rates will rise temporarily. Therefore, it hedges against the interest rate risk by selling futures on securities that have characteristics similar to the securities it is holding, so that the futures prices will change in tandem with these securities. One strategy is to sell Treasury bond futures, since the price movements of Treasury bonds are highly correlated with movements in corporate bond prices.

If interest rates rise as expected, the market value of existing corporate bonds held by the bank will decline. Yet this decline could be offset by the favorable impact of the futures position. The bank locked in the price at which it could sell Treasury bonds. It can purchase Treasury bonds at a lower price just prior to settlement of the futures contract (because the value of bonds will have decreased) and profit after fulfilling its futures contract obligation. Alternatively, it could offset its short position by purchasing futures contracts similar to the type that it sold earlier.

EXAMPLE

Assume that Charlotte Insurance Company plans to satisfy cash needs in six months by selling its Treasury bond holdings for $5 million at that time. It is concerned that interest rates might increase over the next three months, which would reduce the market value of the bonds by the time they are sold. To hedge against this possibility, Charlotte plans to sell Treasury bond futures. It sells 50 Treasury bond futures contracts with a par value of $5 million ($100,000 per contract) for 98-16 (i.e., 98^{16}/$_{32}$ percent of par value).

Suppose that the actual price of the futures contract declines to 94-16 because of an increase in interest rates. Charlotte can close out its short futures position by purchasing contracts identical to those it has sold. If it purchases 50 Treasury bond futures contracts at the prevailing price of 94-16, its profit per futures contract will be

Selling price	$98,500	(98.50% of $100,000)
− Purchase price	−94,500	(94.50% of $100,000)
= Profit	$4,000	(4.00% of $100,000)

Charlotte had a position in 50 futures contracts, so its total profit from that position will be $200,000 ($4,000 per contract × 50 contracts). This gain on the futures contract position will help offset the reduced market value of Charlotte's bond holdings. Charlotte could also have earned a gain on its position by purchasing an identical futures contract just before the settlement date.

If interest rates rise by a greater degree over the six-month period, the market value of Charlotte's Treasury bond holdings will decrease further. However, the price of Treasury bond futures contracts will also decrease by a greater degree, creating a larger gain from the short position in Treasury bond futures. If interest rates decrease, the futures prices will rise, causing a loss on Charlotte's futures position. But that will be offset by a gain in the market value of Charlotte's bond holdings. In this case, the firm would have experienced better overall performance without the hedge. Firms cannot know whether a hedge of interest rate risk will be beneficial in a future period because they cannot always predict the direction of future interest rates. ●

Cross-Hedging   The preceding example presumes that the basis, or the difference between the price of a security and the price of a futures contract, remains the same. In reality, the price of the security may fluctuate more or less than the futures contract used to hedge it. If so, a perfect offset will not result when a given face value amount of securities is hedged with the same face value amount of futures contracts.

The use of a futures contract on one financial instrument to hedge a position in a different financial instrument is known as cross-hedging. The effectiveness of a cross-hedge depends on the degree of correlation between the market values of the two financial instruments. If the price of the underlying security of the futures contract moves nearly in tandem with the security being hedged, the futures contract can provide an effective hedge.

Even when the futures contract is highly correlated with the portfolio being hedged, the value of the futures contract may change by a higher or lower percentage than the portfolio's market value. If the futures contract value is less volatile than the portfolio value, hedging will require a greater amount of principal represented by the futures contracts. For example, assume that the value of the portfolio moves by 1.25 percent for every percentage point movement in the price of the futures contract. In this case, the value of futures contracts needed to fully hedge the portfolio would be 1.25 times the principal of the portfolio.

Trade-off from Using a Short Hedge   When considering the rising and the declining interest rate scenarios, the advantages and disadvantages of interest rate futures are obvious. Interest rate futures can hedge against both adverse and favorable events. Exhibit 13.6 compares two probability distributions of returns generated by a financial institution whose liabilities are more rate-sensitive than its assets. If the institution hedges its exposure to interest rate risk, its probability distribution of returns is narrower than if it does not hedge. The return when hedging would have been higher than the return without hedging if interest rates increased (left side of the graph) but lower if interest rates decreased (right side).

Exhibit 13.6 Comparison of Probability Distributions of Returns; Hedged versus Unhedged Positions

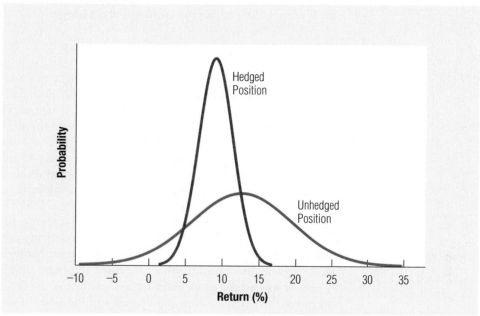

WEB

www.cmegroup.com
Go to the section on
Market Data where
quotes are provided in
order to review quotes
on interest rate
futures.

A financial institution that hedges with interest rate futures is less sensitive to economic events. Thus, financial institutions that frequently use interest rate futures may be able to reduce the variability of their earnings over time, which reflects a lower degree of risk. However, it is virtually impossible to perfectly hedge the sensitivity of all cash flows to interest rate movements.

Using Interest Rate Futures to Create a Long Hedge Some financial institutions use a **long hedge** to reduce exposure to the possibility of declining interest rates. Consider government securities dealers who plan to purchase long-term bonds in a few months. If the dealers are concerned that prices of these securities will rise before the time of their purchases, they may purchase Treasury bond futures contracts. These contracts lock in the price at which Treasury bonds can be purchased, regardless of what happens to market rates prior to actual purchase of the bonds.

As another example, consider a bank that has obtained a significant portion of its funds from large CDs with a maturity of five years. Also assume that most of its assets represent loans with rates that adjust every six months. This bank would be adversely affected by a decline in interest rates because interest earned on assets would be more sensitive than interest paid on liabilities. To hedge against the possibility of lower interest rates, the bank could purchase T-bill futures to lock in the price on T-bills at a specified future date. If interest rates decline, the gain on the futures position could partially offset any reduction in the bank's earnings due to the reduction in interest rates.

Hedging Net Exposure Because interest rate futures contracts entail transaction costs, they should be used only to hedge **net exposure**, which is the difference between asset and liability positions. Consider a bank that has $300 million in long-term assets and $220 million worth of long-term, fixed-rate liabilities. If interest rates rise, the market value of the long-term assets will decline but the bank will benefit from the fixed rate on the $220 million in long-term liabilities. Thus, the bank's net exposure is only $80 million (assuming that the long-term assets and liabilities are similarly affected by rising interest rates). This financial institution should therefore focus on hedging its net exposure of $80 million by creating a short hedge.

13-3 STOCK INDEX FUTURES

A futures contract on a stock index is an agreement to purchase or sell an index at a specified price and date. For example, the purchase of an S&P 500 (which represents a composite of 500 large corporations) futures contract obligates the purchaser to purchase the S&P 500 index at a specified settlement date for a specified amount.

The S&P 500 index futures contract is valued as the index times $250 (see Exhibit 13.1), so if the index is valued at 1600, the contract is valued at 1600 × $250 = $400,000. Mini S&P 500 index futures contracts are available for small investors. These contracts are valued at $50 times the index, so if the index is valued at 1600, the contract is valued at 1600 × $50 = $80,000.

Stock index futures contracts have settlement dates on the third Friday in March, June, September, and December. The securities underlying the stock index futures contracts are not actually deliverable, so settlement occurs through a cash payment. On the settlement date, the futures contract is valued according to the quoted stock index. The net gain or loss on the stock index futures contract is the difference between the futures price when the initial position was created and the value of the contract as of the settlement date.

Like other financial futures contracts, stock index futures can be closed out before the settlement date by taking an offsetting position. For example, if an S&P 500 futures contract with a December settlement date is purchased in September, this position can be closed out in November by selling an S&P 500 futures contract with the same December settlement date. When a position is closed out prior to the settlement date, the net gain or loss on the stock index futures contract is the difference between the futures price when the position was created and the futures price when the position is closed out.

Recently, sector index futures have also been created so that investors can buy or sell an index that reflects a particular sector. These contracts are distinguished from stock index futures because they represent a component of a stock index. Investors who are optimistic about the stock market in general might be more interested in stock index futures, while investors who are especially optimistic about one particular sector may be more interested in sector index futures. Sector index futures contracts are available for many different sectors, including consumer goods, energy, financial services, health care, industrial, materials, technology, and utilities.

13-3a Valuing Stock Index Futures

The value of a stock index futures contract is highly correlated with the value of the underlying stock index. However, the value of the stock index futures contract commonly differs from the price of the underlying asset because of some unique features of the stock index futures contract.

EXAMPLE   Consider that an investor can buy either a stock index or a futures contract on the stock index with a settlement date of six months from now. On the one hand, the buyer of the index receives dividends whereas the buyer of the index futures does not. On the other hand, the buyer of the index must use funds to buy the index whereas the buyer of index futures can engage in the futures contract simply by establishing a margin deposit with a relatively small amount of assets (such as Treasury securities), which may generate interest while being used to satisfy margin requirements.

Assume that the index will pay dividends equal to 3 percent over the next six months. Also assume that the purchaser of the index will borrow funds to purchase the index at an interest rate of 2 percent over the six-month period. In this example, the advantage of holding the index (a 3 percent dividend yield) relative to holding a futures contract on the index more than offsets the 2 percent cost of financing the purchase of the index. The *net financing cost* (also called "cost of carry") to the purchaser of the underlying assets (the index) is the 2 percent cost of financing minus the 3 percent yield earned on the assets, or −1 percent. A negative cost of carry indicates that the cost of financing is less than the yield earned from dividends. Therefore, the stock index futures contract should be valued about 1 percent above the underlying stock index so that it is no less desirable to investors than is the stock index itself. ●

In general, the underlying security (or index) tends to change by a much greater degree than the cost of carry, so changes in financial futures prices are primarily attributed to changes in the values of the underlying securities (or indexes).

In some cases, numerous institutional investors may buy or sell index futures instead of selling stocks to prepare for a change in market conditions, and their actions can cause the movement in the index futures price to deviate from the underlying value of the actual stocks that make up the index. The futures can be purchased immediately with a small, up-front payment. Purchasing actual stocks may take longer because of the time needed to select specific stocks, and a larger up-front investment is necessary. Thus, stock index futures may be more responsive to investor expectations about the market than are values of the underlying stock prices.

Indicators of Stock Index Futures Prices Because stock index futures prices are primarily driven by movements in the corresponding stock indexes, participants in stock index futures monitor indicators that may signal movements in the stock indexes. The economic indicators that signal changes in bond futures prices can also affect stock futures prices, but not necessarily in the same manner. Whereas economic conditions that cause expectations of higher interest rates adversely affect prices of Treasury bonds (and therefore Treasury bond futures), the impact of such expectations on a stock index (and therefore on stock index futures) is not as clear.

13-3b Speculating in Stock Index Futures

Stock index futures can be traded to capitalize on expectations about general stock market movements. Speculators who expect the stock market to perform well before the settlement date may consider purchasing S&P 500 index futures. Conversely, participants who expect the stock market to perform poorly before the settlement date may consider selling S&P 500 index futures.

EXAMPLE   Boulder Insurance Company plans to purchase a variety of stocks for its stock portfolio in December, once cash inflows are received. Although the company does not have cash to purchase the stocks immediately, it is anticipating a large jump in stock market prices before December. Given this situation, it decides to purchase S&P 500 index futures. The futures price on the S&P 500 index with a December settlement date is 1500. The value of an S&P 500 futures contract is $250 times the index. Because the S&P 500 futures price should move with the stock market, it will rise over time if the company's expectations are correct. Assume that the S&P 500 index rises to 1600 on the settlement date.

In this example, the nominal profit on the S&P 500 index futures is

Selling price	$400,000	(Index value of 1600 × $250)
− **Purchase price**	−375,500	(Index value of 1500 × $250)
= **Profit**	$25,000	

USING THE WALL STREET JOURNAL

Index Futures

The *Wall Street Journal* provides information on stock index futures, as shown here. Specifically, it discloses the recent open price, range (high and low), and final closing (settle) price over the previous trading day. In addition, it discloses the number of existing contracts (open interest). Financial institutions closely monitor interest rate futures prices when considering whether to hedge their market risk.

Source: Reprinted with permission of the *Wall Street Journal*, Copyright © 2013 Dow Jones & Company, Inc. All Rights Reserved Worldwide.

Index Futures

	Open	High	Low	Settle	Chg	Open Int
DJ Industrial Average (CBT)-$10 x index						
March	13876	14086 ▲	13848	**14060**	201	15,656
Mini DJ Industrial Average (CBT)-$5 x index						
March	13870	14091 ▲	13846	**14060**	201	119,082
June	13807	14018 ▲	13780	**13991**	200	5,173
S&P 500 Index (CME)-$250 x index						
March	1493.30	1519.00	1490.20	**1515.80**	23.40	217,537
June	1492.50	1510.50	1500.70	**1509.80**	23.30	7,911
Mini S&P 500 (CME)-$50 x index						
March	1493.25	1519.25	1490.00	**1515.75**	23.25	3,129,679
June	1487.50	1513.00	1484.25	**1509.75**	23.25	101,889
Mini S&P Midcap 400 (CME)-$100 x index						
March	1084.60	1106.20	1082.60	**1102.80**	18.50	122,060
June	1084.00	1103.20	1081.10	**1100.00**	18.40	766
Nasdaq 100 (CME)-$100 x index						
March	2710.50	2759.00	▼ 2704.75	**2740.50**	32.75	15,205
June	2710.00	2749.00	2733.00	**2734.25**	33.00	130
Mini Nasdaq 100 (CME)-$20 x index						
March	2711.0	2757.8	▼ 2703.3	**2740.5**	32.8	325,434
June	2705.0	2751.8	▼ 2697.5	**2734.3**	33.0	6,277
Mini Russell 2000 (ICE-US)-$100 x index						
March	895.90	913.60	894.90	**909.10**	12.50	369,541
June	893.90	909.90	893.20	**905.30**	12.40	567
Mini Russell 1000 (ICE-US)-$100 x index						
March	829.60	843.90	829.60	**842.40**	12.60	11,613
U.S. Dollar Index (ICE-US)-$1,000 x index						
March	81.94	81.99 ▲	81.56	**81.67**	-.27	67,947
June	82.15	82.20 ▲	81.75	**81.87**	-.28	1,633

Source: SIX Financial Information

Thus Boulder was able to capitalize on its expectations even though it did not have sufficient cash to purchase stock. If stock prices had declined over the period of concern, the S&P 500 futures price would have decreased and Boulder would have incurred a loss on its futures position. ●

13-3c Hedging with Stock Index Futures

Stock index futures are also commonly used to hedge the market risk of an existing stock portfolio.

EXAMPLE Glacier Stock Mutual Fund expects the stock market to decline temporarily, causing a temporary decline in its stock portfolio. The fund could sell its stocks with the intent to repurchase them in the near future, but this would incur excessive transaction costs. A more efficient solution is to sell stock index futures. If the fund's stock portfolio is similar to the S&P 500 index, Glacier can sell futures contracts on that index. If the stock market declines as expected, Glacier will generate a gain when closing out the stock index futures position, which will somewhat offset the loss on its stock portfolio. ●

This hedge is more effective when the investor's portfolio, like the S&P 500 index, is diversified. The value of a less diversified stock portfolio will correlate less with the S&P 500 index, in which case a gain from selling index futures may not completely offset the loss in the portfolio during a market downturn.

Assuming that the stock portfolio moves in tandem with the S&P 500, a full hedge would involve the sale of the amount of futures contracts whose combined underlying value is equal to the market value of the stock portfolio being hedged.

Suppose that a portfolio manager has a stock portfolio valued at $400,000. In addition, assume the S&P 500 index futures contracts are available for a settlement date one month from now at a level of 1600, which is about equal to today's index value. The manager could sell S&P 500 futures contracts to hedge the stock portfolio. Since the futures contract is valued at $250 times the index level, the contract will result in a payment of $400,000 at settlement date. One index futures contract can be used to match the existing value of the stock portfolio. Assuming that the stock index moves in tandem with the manager's stock portfolio, any loss on the portfolio should be offset by a corresponding gain on the futures contract. For example, if the stock portfolio declines by about 5 percent over one month, this reflects a loss of $20,000 (0.05 × $400,000 = $20,000). Yet the S&P 500 index should also have declined by 5 percent (to a level of 1520). Therefore, the S&P 500 index futures contract that was sold by the manager should result in a gain of $20,000 [(1600 − 1520) × $250], which offsets the loss on the stock portfolio. ●

If the stock market experiences higher prices over the month, the S&P 500 index will rise and create a loss on the futures contract. However, the value of the manager's stock portfolio will have increased to offset the loss.

Most investors who had hedged their stock portfolios with index futures benefited from the hedge when the credit crisis began in 2008. In particular, hedging during the second half of the year was especially beneficial because many stocks declined by more than 30 percent during that period.

Test of Suitability of Stock Index Futures

The suitability of using stock index futures to hedge can be assessed by measuring the sensitivity of the portfolio's performance to market movements over a period prior to taking a hedge position. The sensitivity of a hypothetical position in futures to those same market movements in that period could also be assessed. A general test of suitability is to determine whether the hypothetical derivative position would have offset adverse market effects on the portfolio's performance. Although it may be extremely difficult to perfectly hedge all of a portfolio's exposure to market risk, for a hedge to be suitable there should be some evidence that such a hypothetical hedge would have been moderately effective for that firm. That is, if the position in financial derivatives would not have provided an effective hedge of market risk over a recent period, a firm should not expect that it will provide an effective hedge in the future. This test of suitability uses only data that were available at the time the hedge was to be enacted.

Determining the Proportion of the Portfolio to Hedge

Portfolio managers do not necessarily hedge their entire stock portfolio, because they may wish to be partially exposed in the event that stock prices rise. For instance, if the portfolio in the preceding example were valued at $1.2 million, the portfolio manager could have hedged one-third of the stock portfolio by selling one stock index futures contract. The short position in one index futures contract would reflect one-third of the stock portfolio's value. Alternatively, the manager could have hedged two-thirds of the stock portfolio by selling two stock index futures contracts. The higher the proportion of the portfolio that is hedged, the more insulated the manager's performance is from market conditions, whether those conditions are favorable or unfavorable.

Exhibit 13.7 illustrates the net gain (including the gain on the futures and the gain on the stock portfolio) to the portfolio manager under five possible scenarios for the market return (shown in the first column). If the stock market declines, any degree of hedging is beneficial, but the benefits are greater if a higher proportion of the portfolio is hedged. If the stock market performs well, any degree of hedging reduces the net gain, but the reduction is greater if a higher proportion of the portfolio is hedged. In essence, hedging with stock index futures reduces the sensitivity to both unfavorable and favorable market conditions.

Exhibit 13.7   Net Gain (on Stock Portfolio and Short Position in Stock Index Futures) for Different Degrees of Hedging

	PROPORTION OF STOCK PORTFOLIO HEDGED			
SCENARIO FOR MARKET RETURN	0%	33%	67%	100%
−20%	−20%	−13.4%	−6.7%	0%
−10	−10	−6.7	−3.3	0

Note: Numbers are based on the assumption that the stock portfolio moves in perfect tandem with the market.

13-3d Dynamic Asset Allocation with Stock Index Futures

Institutional investors are increasingly using dynamic asset allocation, in which they switch between risky and low-risk investment positions over time in response to changing expectations. This strategy allows managers to increase the exposure of their portfolios when they expect favorable market conditions and to reduce their exposure when they expect unfavorable conditions. When they anticipate favorable market movements, stock portfolio managers can purchase stock index futures, which intensify the effects of market conditions. Conversely, when they anticipate unfavorable market movements, they can sell stock index futures to reduce the effects that market conditions will have on their stock portfolios. Because expectations change frequently, it is not uncommon for portfolio managers to alter their degree of exposure. Stock index futures allow portfolio managers to alter their risk–return position without restructuring their existing stock portfolios. Using dynamic asset allocation in this way avoids the substantial transaction costs that would be associated with restructuring the stock portfolios.

13-3e Arbitrage with Stock Index Futures

The New York Stock Exchange narrowly defines program trading as the simultaneous buying and selling of at least 15 different stocks that, in aggregate, are valued at more than $1 million. Program trading is commonly used in conjunction with the trading of stock index futures contracts in a strategy known as **index arbitrage**. Securities firms act as **arbitrageurs** by capitalizing on discrepancies between prices of index futures and stocks. Index arbitrage involves the buying or selling of stock index futures with a simultaneous opposite position in the stocks that the index comprises. The index arbitrage is instigated when prices of stock index futures differ significantly from the stocks represented by the index. For example, if the index futures contract is priced high relative to the stocks representing the index, an arbitrageur may consider purchasing the stocks and simultaneously selling stock index futures. Conversely, if the index futures are priced low relative to the stocks representing the index, an arbitrageur may purchase index futures and simultaneously sell stocks. An arbitrage profit is attainable if the price differential exceeds the costs incurred from trading in both markets.

Index arbitrage does not cause the price discrepancy between the two markets but instead responds to it. The arbitrageur's ability to detect price discrepancies between the stock and futures markets is enhanced by computers. Roughly half of all program trading activity is for the purpose of index arbitrage.

Some critics suggest that the index arbitrage activity of purchasing index futures while selling stocks adversely affects stock prices. However, if index futures did not exist, institutional investors could not use portfolio insurance. In this case, a general expectation of a temporary market decline would be more likely to encourage sales of stocks to prepare for the decline, which would actually accelerate the drop in prices.

13-3f Circuit Breakers on Stock Index Futures

As mentioned in Chapter 12, *circuit breakers* are trading restrictions imposed on specific stocks or stock indexes. The CME Group imposes circuit breakers on several stock index futures, including the S&P 500 futures contract.

By prohibiting trading for short time periods when prices decline to specific threshold levels, circuit breakers may allow investors to determine whether circulating rumors are true and to work out credit arrangements if they have received a margin call. If prices are still perceived to be too high when the markets reopen, the prices will decline further. Thus circuit breakers do not guarantee that prices will turn upward. Nevertheless, they may be able to prevent large declines in prices that would be due to panic selling rather than to fundamental forces.

13-4 SINGLE STOCK FUTURES

A *single* stock futures contract is an agreement to buy or sell a specified number of shares of a specified stock on a specified future date. Such contracts have been traded on futures exchanges in Australia and Europe since the 1990s. The Chicago Board Options Exchange and the CME Group recently engaged in a joint venture called OneChicago, where single stock futures contracts of U.S. stocks are traded. The size of a contract is 100 shares. Investors can buy or sell singles stock futures contracts through their broker, and they can be purchased on margin. The orders to buy and sell a specific single stock futures contract are matched electronically. Single stock futures have become increasingly popular, and today are available on more than 2,200 stocks. They are regulated by the Commodity Futures Trading Commission and the Securities and Exchange Commission.

Settlement dates are on the third Friday of the delivery month on a quarterly basis (March, June, September, and December) for the next five quarters as well as for the nearest two months. For example, on January 3, an investor could purchase a stock futures contract for the third Friday in the next two months (January or February) or over the next five quarters (March, June, September, December, and March of the following year).

Investors who expect a particular stock's price to rise over time may consider buying futures on that stock. To obtain a contract to buy March futures on 100 shares of Zyco stock for $5,000 ($50 per share), an investor must submit the $5,000 payment to the clearinghouse on the third Friday in March and will receive shares of Zyco stock on the settlement date. If Zyco stock is valued at $53 at the time of settlement, the investor can sell the stock in the stock market for a gain of $3 per share or $300 for the contract (ignoring commissions). This gain would likely reflect a substantial return on the investment, since the investor had to invest only a small margin (perhaps 20 percent of the contract price) to take a position in futures. If Zyco stock is valued at $46 at the time of settlement, the investor would incur a loss of $4 share, which would reflect a substantial percentage loss on the investment. Thus, single stock futures offer potential high returns but also high risk.

Investors who expect a particular stock's price to decline over time can sell futures contracts on that stock. This activity is similar to selling a stock short, except that single stock futures can be sold without borrowing the underlying stock from a broker (as short-sellers must do). To obtain a contract to sell March futures of Zyco stock, an investor must deliver Zyco stock to the clearinghouse on the third Friday in March and will receive the payment specified in the futures contract.

Investors can close out their position at any time by taking the opposite position. Suppose that, shortly after the investor purchased futures on Zyco stock with a March delivery at $50 per share, the stock price declines. Rather than incur the risk that the price could continue to decline, the investor could sell a Zyco futures contract with a March delivery. If this contract specifies a price of $48 per share, the investor's gain will be the difference between the selling price and the buying price, which is −$2 per share or −$200 for the contract.

Recently, futures contracts for exchange-traded funds (ETFs) have also been introduced. These allow an investor to buy or sell a particular ETF at a specified price. More information about ETFs is provided in Chapter 23.

13-5 RISK OF TRADING FUTURES CONTRACTS

Users of futures contracts must recognize the various types of risk exhibited by such contracts and other derivative instruments.

13-5a Market Risk

Market risk refers to fluctuations in the value of the instrument as a result of market conditions. Firms that use futures contracts to speculate should be concerned about market risk. If their expectations about future market conditions are wrong, they may suffer losses on their futures contracts. Firms that use futures contracts to hedge are less concerned about market risk because if market conditions cause a loss on their derivative instruments, they should have a partial offsetting gain on the positions that they were hedging.

13-5b Basis Risk

A second type of risk is basis risk, or the risk that the position being hedged by the futures contracts is not affected in the same manner as the instrument underlying the futures contract. This type of risk applies only to those firms or individuals who are using futures contracts to hedge. The change in the value of the futures contract position may not move in perfect tandem with the change in value of the portfolio that is being hedged, so the hedge might not perfectly hedge the risk of the portfolio.

13-5c Liquidity Risk

A third type of risk is liquidity risk, which refers to potential price distortions due to a lack of liquidity. For example, a firm may purchase a particular bond futures contract to speculate on expectations of rising bond prices. However, when it attempts to close out its position by selling an identical futures contract, it may find that there are no willing buyers for this type of futures contract at that time. In this case, the firm will have to sell the futures contract at a lower price. Users of futures contracts may reduce liquidity risk by using only those futures contracts that are widely traded.

13-5d Credit Risk

A fourth type of risk is **credit risk**, which is the risk that a loss will occur because a counterparty defaults on the contract. This type of risk exists for over-the-counter transactions, in which a firm or individual relies on the creditworthiness of a counterparty.

The credit risk of counterparties is not a concern when trading futures and other derivatives on exchanges, because the exchanges normally guarantee that the provisions of the contract will be honored. The financial intermediaries that make the arrangements in the over-the-counter market can also take some steps to reduce this type of risk. First, the financial intermediary can require that each party provide some form of collateral to back up its position. Second, the financial intermediary can serve (for a fee) as a guarantor in the event that the counterparty does not fulfill its obligation.

13-5e Prepayment Risk

Prepayment risk refers to the possibility that the assets to be hedged may be prepaid earlier than their designated maturity. Suppose that a commercial bank sells Treasury bond futures in order to hedge its holdings of corporate bonds and that, just after the futures position is created, the bonds are called by the corporation that initially issued them. If interest rates subsequently decline, the bank will incur a loss from its futures position without a corresponding gain from its bond position (because the bonds were called earlier).

As a second example, consider a savings and loan association with large holdings of long-term, fixed-rate mortgages that are mostly financed by short-term funds. It sells Treasury bond futures to hedge against the possibility of rising interest rates; then, after the futures position is established, interest rates decline and many of the existing mortgages are prepaid by homeowners. The savings and loan association will incur a loss from its futures position without a corresponding gain from its fixed-rate mortgage position (because the mortgages were prepaid).

13-5f Operational Risk

A sixth type of risk is operational risk, which is the risk of losses as a result of inadequate management or controls. For example, firms that use futures contracts to hedge are exposed to the possibility that the employees responsible for their futures positions do not fully understand how values of specific futures contracts will respond to market conditions. Furthermore, those employees may take more speculative positions than the firms desire if the firms do not have adequate controls to monitor them.

EXAMPLE

The case of MF Global Holdings serves as a good example of operational risk. During 2011, it experienced major losses from its speculative positions, and it pulled funds from its customer accounts to cover its losses. It ultimately experienced liquidity problems and went bankrupt in October 2011. The funds that it pulled from customer accounts were not repaid. A few months later, another brokerage firm for futures traders (Peregine Financial Group) also experienced liquidity problems, as its actual bank cash balance was more than $100 million less than what it had reported. It ultimately filed for bankruptcy in July 2012. These events triggered concerns about the exposure of traders to financial fraud in the futures markets. ●

13-5g Exposure of Futures Market to Systemic Risk

To the extent that traders of financial futures contracts or other derivative securities are unable to cover their derivative contract obligations in over-the-counter transactions, they could cause financial problems for their respective counterparties. This could expose the futures market to systemic risk whereby the intertwined relationships among firms may cause one trader's financial problems to be passed on to other traders (if there is not enough collateral backing the contracts).

EXAMPLE

Nexus, Inc., requests several transactions in derivative securities that involve buying futures on Treasury bonds in an over-the-counter market. Bangor Bank accommodates Nexus by taking the opposite side of the transactions. The bank's positions in these contracts also serve as a hedge against its existing exposure to interest rate risk. As time passes, Nexus experiences financial problems. As interest rates rise and the value of a Treasury bond futures contract declines, Nexus will take a major loss on the futures transactions. It files for bankruptcy, since it is unable to fulfill its obligation to buy the Treasury bonds from Bangor Bank at the settlement date. Bangor Bank was relying on this payment to hedge its exposure to interest rate risk. Consequently, Bangor Bank experiences financial problems and cannot make the payments on other over-the-counter derivatives contracts that it has with three other financial institutions. These financial institutions were relying on those funds to cover their own obligations on derivative contracts with several other firms. These firms may then be unable to honor their payment obligations resulting from the derivative contract agreements, causing the adverse effects to spread further. ●

FINANCIAL REFORM

The credit crisis in 2008 and 2009 demonstrated that some financial institutions had high exposure to risk because their derivative security positions were intended to enhance profits rather than to hedge portfolio risk. Since then, regulators have become more aware of the potential systemic risk.

The Financial Reform Act in 2010 resulted in the creation of the Financial Stability Oversight Council, which is responsible for identifying risks to financial stability in the United States and making regulatory recommendations that could reduce any risks to the financial system. The council consists of ten members who head regulatory agencies overseeing key components of the financial system (including the CFTC, which regulates financial futures trading).

GLOBAL ASPECTS

13-6 GLOBALIZATION OF FUTURES MARKETS

The trading of financial futures also requires the assessment of international financial market conditions. The flow of foreign funds into and out of the United States can affect interest rates and therefore the market value of Treasury bonds, corporate bonds, mortgages, and other long-term debt securities. Portfolio managers assess international flows of funds to forecast changes in interest rate movements, which in turn affect the value of their respective portfolios. Even speculators assess international flows of funds to forecast interest rates so that they can determine whether to take short or long futures positions.

13-6a Non-U.S. Participation in U.S. Futures Contracts

Financial futures contracts on U.S. securities are commonly traded by non-U.S. financial institutions that maintain holdings of U.S. securities. These institutions use financial futures to reduce their exposure to movements in the U.S. stock market or interest rates.

13-6b Foreign Stock Index Futures

Foreign stock index futures have been created both for speculating on and hedging against potential movements in foreign stock markets. Expectations of a strong foreign stock market encourage the purchase of futures contracts on the representative index. Conversely, if firms expect a decline in the foreign market, they will consider selling futures on the representative index. Financial institutions with substantial investments in a particular foreign stock market can hedge against a temporary decline in that market by selling foreign stock index futures.

Some of the more popular foreign stock index futures contracts are identified in Exhibit 13.8. Numerous other foreign stock index futures contracts have been created. In fact, futures exchanges have been established in Ireland, France, Spain, and Italy. Financial institutions around the world can use futures contracts to hedge against temporary declines in their asset portfolios. Speculators can take long or short positions to speculate on a particular market with a relatively small initial investment. Financial futures on debt instruments (such as futures on German government bonds) are also offered by numerous exchanges in non-U.S. markets, including the London International Financial Futures Exchange (LIFFE), Singapore International Monetary Exchange (SIMEX), and Sydney Futures Exchange (SFE). In 2001, the LIFFE was acquired by Euronext, an alliance of European stock exchanges.

Exhibit 13.8 Popular Foreign Stock Index Futures Contracts

NAME OF STOCK FUTURES INDEX	DESCRIPTION
Nikkei 225	225 Japanese stocks
Toronto 35	35 stocks on Toronto stock exchange
Financial Times Stock Exchange 100	100 stocks on London stock exchange
Barclays share price	40 stocks on New Zealand stock exchange
Hang Seng	33 stocks on Hong Kong stock exchange
Osaka	50 Japanese stocks
All Ordinaries share price	307 Australian stocks

Electronic trading of futures contracts is creating an internationally integrated futures market. As mentioned previously, the CME Group has instituted Globex, a round-the-world electronic trading network. It allows financial futures contracts to be traded even when the trading floor is closed.

13-6c Currency Futures Contracts

A **currency futures contract** is a standardized agreement to deliver or receive a specified amount of a specified foreign currency at a specified price (exchange rate) and date. The settlement months are March, June, September, and December. Some companies act as hedgers in the currency futures market by purchasing futures on currencies that they will need in the future to cover payables or by selling futures on currencies that they will receive in the future. Speculators in the currency futures market may purchase futures on a foreign currency that they expect to strengthen against the U.S. dollar or sell futures on currencies that they expect to weaken against the U.S. dollar.

Purchasers of currency futures contracts can hold the contract until the settlement date and accept delivery of the foreign currency at that time, or they can close out their long position prior to the settlement date by selling the identical type and number of contracts before then. If they close out their long position, their gain or loss is determined by the difference between the futures price when they created the position and the futures price at the time the position was closed out. Sellers of currency futures contracts either deliver the foreign currency at the settlement date or close out their position by purchasing an identical type and number of contracts prior to the settlement date.

Summary

- A financial futures contract is a standardized agreement to deliver or receive a specified amount of a specified financial instrument at a specified price and date. Financial institutions such as commercial banks, savings institutions, bond mutual funds, pension funds, and insurance companies trade interest rate futures contracts to hedge their exposure to interest rate risk. Some stock mutual funds, pension funds, and insurance companies trade stock index futures to hedge their exposure to adverse stock market movements.

- An interest rate futures contract locks in the price to be paid for a specified debt instrument. Speculators who expect interest rates to decline can purchase interest rate futures contracts, because the market value of the underlying debt instrument should rise. Speculators who expect interest rates to rise can sell interest rate futures contracts, because the market value of the underlying debt instrument should decrease.

- Financial institutions (or other firms) that desire to hedge against rising interest rates can sell interest rate futures contracts. Financial institutions that desire to hedge against declining interest rates can purchase these contracts. If interest rates move in the anticipated direction, the financial institutions will gain from their futures position, which can partially offset any adverse effects of the interest rate movements on their normal operations.

- Speculators who expect stock prices to increase can purchase stock index futures contracts; speculators who expect stock prices to decrease can sell these contracts. Stock index futures can be sold by financial institutions that expect a temporary decline in stock prices and wish to hedge their stock portfolios.

- A single stock futures contract is an agreement to buy or sell a specified number of shares of a specified stock on a specified future date. The trading of single stock futures is regulated by the Commodity Futures Trading Commission (CFTC) and the Securities and Exchange Commission (SEC).

- Investors who expect a particular stock's price to rise over time may consider buying futures on that stock. Investors who expect a particular stock's price to decline over time can sell futures contracts on that stock. This activity is similar to selling a stock short, but single stock futures can be sold without borrowing the underlying stock from a broker. Investors can close out their position at any time by taking the opposite position.

- Traders in the futures market may be exposed to market risk, basis risk, liquidity risk, credit risk, prepayment risk, and operational risk. The over-the-counter trading of futures contracts and other derivative securities can expose the entire financial system to systemic risk, in which the trading losses of one firm could spread to others if collateral is not sufficient to cover losses. The Financial Reform Act in 2010 resulted in the creation of the Financial Stability Oversight Council, which is responsible for making recommendations that could reduce any risks to the financial system. The council includes the head of the Commodity Futures Trading Commission, which regulates financial futures trading.

POINT COUNTER-POINT

Has the Futures Market Created More Uncertainty for Stocks?

Point   Yes. Futures contracts encourage speculation on indexes. Thus, an entire market can be influenced by the trading of speculators.

Counter-Point   No. Futures contracts are commonly used to hedge portfolios and therefore can

reduce the effects of weak market conditions. Moreover, investing in stocks is just as speculative as taking a position in futures markets.

Who Is Correct?   Use the Internet to learn more about this issue and then formulate your own opinion.

QUESTIONS AND APPLICATIONS

1. Futures Contracts Describe the general characteristics of a futures contract. How does a clearinghouse facilitate the trading of financial futures contracts?

2. Futures Pricing How does the price of a financial futures contract change as the market price of the security it represents changes? Why?

3. Hedging with Futures Explain why some futures contracts may be more suitable than others for hedging exposure to interest rate risk.

4. Treasury Bond Futures Will speculators buy or sell Treasury bond futures contracts if they expect interest rates to increase? Explain.

5. Gains from Purchasing Futures Explain how purchasers of financial futures contracts can offset their position. How is their gain or loss determined? What is the maximum loss to a purchaser of a futures contract?

6. Gains from Selling Futures Explain how sellers of financial futures contracts can offset their position. How is their gain or loss determined?

7. Hedging with Futures Assume a financial institution has more rate-sensitive assets than rate-sensitive liabilities. Would it be more likely to be adversely affected by an increase or a decrease in interest rates? Should it purchase or sell interest rate futures contracts in order to hedge its exposure?

8. Hedging with Futures Assume a financial institution has more rate-sensitive liabilities than rate-sensitive assets. Would it be more likely to be adversely affected by an increase or a decrease in interest rates? Should it purchase or sell interest rate futures contracts in order to hedge its exposure?

9. Hedging Decision Why do some financial institutions remain exposed to interest rate risk, even when they believe that the use of interest rate futures could reduce their exposure?

10. Long versus Short Hedge Explain the difference between a long hedge and a short hedge used by financial institutions. When is a long hedge more appropriate than a short hedge?

11. Impact of Futures Hedge Explain how the probability distribution of a financial institution's returns is affected when it uses interest rate futures to hedge. What does this imply about its risk?

12. Cross-Hedging Describe the act of cross-hedging. What determines the effectiveness of a cross-hedge?

13. Hedging with Bond Futures How might a savings and loan association use Treasury bond futures to hedge its fixed-rate mortgage portfolio (assuming that its main source of funds is short-term deposits)? Explain how prepayments on mortgages can limit the effectiveness of the hedge.

14. Stock Index Futures Describe stock index futures. How could they be used by a financial institution that is anticipating a jump in stock prices but does not yet have sufficient funds to purchase large amounts of stock? Explain why stock index futures may reflect investor expectations about the market more quickly than stock prices.

15. Selling Stock Index Futures Why would a pension fund or insurance company consider selling stock index futures?

16. Systemic Risk Explain systemic risk as it relates to the futures market. Explain how the Financial Reform Act of 2010 attempts to monitor systemic risk in the futures market and other markets.

17. Circuit Breakers Explain the use of circuit breakers.

Advanced Questions

18. Hedging with Futures Elon Savings and Loan Association has a large number of 30-year mortgages with floating interest rates that adjust on an annual basis and obtains most of its funds by issuing five-year certificates of deposit. It uses the yield curve to assess the market's anticipation of future interest rates. It believes that expectations of future interest rates are the major force affecting the yield curve. Assume that a downward-sloping yield curve with a steep slope exists. Based on this information, should Elon consider using financial futures as a hedging technique? Explain.

19. Hedging Decision Blue Devil Savings and Loan Association has a large number of 10-year fixed-rate mortgages and obtains most of its funds from short-term deposits. It uses the yield curve to assess the market's anticipation of future interest rates. It believes that expectations of future interest rates are the major force affecting the yield curve. Assume that an upward-sloping yield curve with a steep slope exists. Based on this information, should Blue Devil consider using financial futures as a hedging technique? Explain.

20. How Futures Prices May Respond to Prevailing Conditions Consider the prevailing conditions for inflation (including oil prices), the economy, the budget deficit, and other conditions that could affect the values of futures contracts. Based on these conditions, would you prefer to buy or sell Treasury bond futures at this time? Would you prefer to buy or sell stock index futures at this time? Assume that you would close out your position at the end of this semester. Offer some logic to support your answers. Which factor is most influential on your decision regarding Treasury bond futures and on your decision regarding stock index futures?

21. Use of Interest Rate Futures When Interest Rates Are Low Short-term and long-term interest rates are presently very low. You believe that the Fed will use a monetary policy to maintain interest rates at a very low level. Do you think financial institutions that could be adversely affected by a decline in interest rates would benefit from hedging their exposure with interest rate futures? Explain.

Interpreting Financial News

Interpret the following statements made by Wall Street analysts and portfolio managers.

a. "The existence of financial futures contracts allows our firm to hedge against temporary market declines without liquidating our portfolios."

b. "Given my confidence in the market, I plan to use stock index futures to increase my exposure to market movements."

c. "We used currency futures to hedge the exchange rate exposure of our international mutual fund focused on German stocks."

Managing in Financial Markets

Managing Portfolios with Futures Contracts As a portfolio manager, you are monitoring previous investments that you made in stocks and bonds of U.S. firms and in stocks and bonds of Japanese firms. Though you plan to keep all of these investments over the long run, you are willing to hedge against adverse effects on your investments that result from economic conditions. You expect that, over the next year, U.S. and Japanese interest rates will decline, the U.S. stock market will perform poorly, the Japanese stock market will perform well, and the Japanese yen (the currency) will depreciate against the dollar.

a. Should you consider taking a position in U.S. bond index futures to hedge your investment in U.S. bonds? Explain.

b. Should you consider taking a position in Japanese bond index futures to hedge your investment in Japanese bonds? Explain.

c. Should you consider taking a position in U.S. stock index futures to hedge your investment in U.S. stocks? Explain.

d. Should you consider taking a position in Japanese stock index futures to hedge your investment in Japanese stocks? (Note: The Japanese stock index is denominated in yen and therefore is used to hedge stock movements, not currency movements.)

e. Should you consider taking a position in Japanese yen futures to hedge the exchange rate risk of your investment in Japanese stocks and bonds?

PROBLEMS

1. Profit from T-Bill Futures Spratt Company purchased T-bill futures contracts when the quoted price was 93.50. When this position was closed out, the quoted price was 94.75. Determine the profit or loss per contract, ignoring transaction costs.

2. Profit from T-Bill Futures Suerth Investments, Inc., purchased T-bill futures contracts when the quoted price was 95.00. When this position was closed out, the quoted price was 93.60. Determine the profit or loss per contract, ignoring transaction costs.

3. Profit from T-Bill Futures Toland Company sold T-bill futures contracts when the quoted price was 94.00. When this position was closed out, the quoted price was 93.20. Determine the profit or loss per contract, ignoring transaction costs.

4. Profit from T-Bill Futures Rude Dynamics, Inc., sold T-bill futures contracts when the quoted price was 93.26. When this position was closed out, the quoted price was 93.90. Determine the profit or loss per contract, ignoring transaction costs.

5. Profit from T-Bond Futures Egan Company purchased a futures contract on Treasury bonds that specified a price of 91-00. When the position was closed out, the price of the Treasury bond futures contract was 90-10. Determine the profit or loss, ignoring transaction costs.

6. Profit from T-Bond Futures R. C. Clark sold a futures contract on Treasury bonds that specified a price of 92-10. When the position was closed out, the price of the Treasury bond futures contract was 93-00. Determine the profit or loss, ignoring transaction costs.

7. Profit from Stock Index Futures Marks Insurance Company sold S&P 500 stock index futures that specified an index of 1690. When the position was closed out, the index specified by the futures contract was 1720. Determine the profit or loss, ignoring transaction costs.

FLOW OF FUNDS EXERCISE

Hedging with Futures Contracts

Recall that if the economy continues to be strong, Carson Company may need to increase its production capacity by about 50 percent over the next few years to satisfy demand. It would need financing to expand and accommodate the increase in production. Recall that the yield curve is currently upward sloping. Also recall that Carson is concerned about a possible slowing of the economy because of potential Fed actions to reduce inflation. Carson currently relies mostly on commercial loans with floating interest rates for its debt financing.

a. How could Carson use futures contracts to reduce the exposure of its cost of debt to interest rate movements? Be specific about whether it would use a short hedge or a long hedge.

b. Will the hedge that you described in the previous question perfectly offset the increase in debt costs if interest rates increase? Explain what drives the profit from the short hedge, versus what drives the higher cost of debt to Carson, if interest rates increase.

INTERNET/EXCEL EXERCISES

1. Go to http://futuresource.quote.com and review the charts for an equity index product such as the S&P 500. Explain how the price pattern moved recently.

2. Now compare that pattern to the actual trend of the S&P 500, which is provided at the Yahoo! Finance website (finance.yahoo.com). Describe the relationship between the movements in S&P 500 futures and movements in the S&P 500 index.

ONLINE ARTICLES WITH REAL-WORLD EXAMPLES

Find a recent practical article available online that describes a real-world example regarding a specific financial institution or financial market that reinforces one or more concepts covered in this chapter.

If your class has an online component, your professor may ask you to post your summary of the article there and provide a link to the article so that other students can access it. If your class is live, your professor may ask you to summarize your application of the article in class. Your professor may assign specific students to complete this assignment or may allow any students to do the assignment on a volunteer basis.

For recent online articles and real-world examples related to this chapter, consider using the following search terms (be sure to include the prevailing year as a search term to ensure that the online articles are recent):

1. interest rate futures AND investment
2. interest rate futures AND gains
3. interest rate futures AND losses
4. interest rate futures AND speculators
5. interest rate futures AND hedge
6. stock index futures AND gains
7. stock index futures AND losses
8. stock index futures AND speculators
9. stock index futures AND hedge
10. futures AND risk

14

Option Markets

The specific objectives of this chapter are to:

- provide a background on options,

- explain why stock option premiums vary,

- explain how stock options are used to speculate,

- explain how stock options are used to hedge,

- explain the use of stock index options, and

- explain the use of options on futures.

WEB

www.cboe.com

The volume of calls versus the volume of puts are used to assess their respective popularity.

Stock options can be used by speculators to benefit from their expectations and by financial institutions to reduce their risk. Options markets facilitate the trading of stock options.

14-1 BACKGROUND ON OPTIONS

Options are classified as *calls* or *puts*. A **call option** grants the owner the right to purchase a specified financial instrument (such as a stock) for a specified price (called the **exercise price** or **strike price**) within a specified period of time.

A call option is said to be **in the money** when the market price of the underlying security exceeds the exercise price, **at the money** when the market price is equal to the exercise price, and **out of the money** when it is below the exercise price.

The second type of option is known as a **put option**. It grants the owner the right to sell a specified financial instrument for a specified price within a specified period of time. As with call options, owners pay a premium to obtain put options. They can exercise the options at any time up to the expiration date but are not obligated to do so.

A put option is said to be "in the money" when the market price of the underlying security is below the exercise price, "at the money" when the market price is equal to the exercise price, and "out of the money" when it exceeds the exercise price.

Call and put options specify 100 shares for the stocks to which they are assigned. Premiums paid for call and put options are determined by the participants engaged in trading. The premium for a particular option changes over time as it becomes more or less desirable to traders.

Participants can close out their option positions by making an offsetting transaction. For example, purchasers of an option can offset their positions at any time by selling an identical option. The gain or loss is determined by the premium paid when purchasing the option versus the premium received when selling an identical option. Sellers of options can close out their positions at any time by purchasing an identical option.

The stock options just described are known as *American-style* stock options. They can be exercised at any time until the expiration date. In contrast, *European-style* stock options can be exercised only just before expiration.

In addition to options on stocks there are options on stock indexes, which allow investors the right to buy (with a call option) or sell (with a put option) a specified stock index for a specified price up to a specified expiration date. There are also options on interest rate futures contracts, which allow investors the right to buy or sell a specified interest rate futures contract for a specified price up to a specified expiration date. Options on stock indexes and on interest rate futures are covered later in this chapter.

14-1a Comparison of Options and Futures

There are two major differences between purchasing an option and purchasing a futures contract. First, to obtain an option, a premium must be paid in addition to the price of the financial instrument. Second, the owner of an option can choose to let the option expire on the expiration date without exercising it. Call options grant a right, but not an obligation, to purchase a specified financial instrument. In contrast, buyers of futures contracts are obligated to purchase the financial instrument at a specified date. If the owner does exercise the call option, the seller (sometimes called the **writer**) of the option is obligated to provide the specified financial instrument at the price specified by the option contract if the owner exercises the option. Sellers of call options receive an up-front fee (the premium) from the purchaser as compensation.

WEB

biz.yahoo.com/opt
Daily coverage of options market activity.

14-1b Markets Used to Trade Options

The Chicago Board Options Exchange (CBOE), which was created in 1973, is the most important exchange for trading options. It serves as a market for options on more than 2,000 different stocks. The options listed on the CBOE have a standardized format, as will be explained shortly. The standardization of the contracts on the CBOE proved to be a major advantage because it allowed for easy trading of existing contracts (a secondary market). With standardization, the popularity of options increased and the options became more liquid. Since there were numerous buyers and sellers of the standardized contracts, buyers and sellers of a particular option contract could be matched.

Options are also traded at the CME Group, which was formed in July 2007 by the merger of the Chicago Board of Trade (CBOT) and the Chicago Mercantile Exchange (CME). As discussed in Chapter 13, the CME Group serves international markets for derivative products. To increase efficiency and reduce operating and maintenance expenses after the merger, the CME Group consolidated the CME and CBOT trading floors into a single trading floor at the CBOT and consolidated the products of the CME and CBOT on a single electronic platform. Transactions of new derivative products typically are executed by the CME Group's electronic platform.

As the popularity of stock options increased, various stock exchanges began to list options. In particular, the American Stock Exchange (acquired by NYSE Euronext in 2008), the Nasdaq, and the Philadelphia Stock Exchange (acquired by Nasdaq in 2008) list options on many different stocks. So does the International Securities Exchange, which was the first fully electronic U.S. options exchange. Today, any particular options contract may be traded on various exchanges, and competition among the exchanges may result in more favorable prices for customers.

Some specialized option contracts are sold "over the counter," rather than on an exchange, whereby a financial intermediary (such as a commercial bank or an investment bank) finds a counterparty or serves as the counterparty. These over-the-counter arrangements are more personalized and can be tailored to the specific preferences of the parties involved. Such tailoring is not possible for the more standardized option contracts sold on the exchanges.

Listing Requirements   Each exchange has its own requirements concerning the stocks for which it creates options. One key requirement is a minimum trading volume of the underlying stock, since the volume of options traded on a particular stock will normally be higher if the stock trading volume is high. The decision to list an option is made by each exchange, not by the firms represented by the options contracts.

Role of the Options Clearing Corporation   Like a stock transaction, the trading of an option involves a buyer and a seller. The sale of an option imposes specific obligations on the seller under specific conditions. The exchange itself does not take positions in option contracts, but provides a market where the options can be bought or sold. The Options Clearing Corporation (OCC) serves as a guarantor on option contracts traded in the United States, which means that the buyer of an option contract does not have to be concerned that the seller will back out of the obligation.

Regulation of Options Trading   Options trading is regulated by the Securities and Exchange Commission and by the various option exchanges. The regulation is intended to ensure fair and orderly trading. For example, it attempts to prevent insider trading (trading based on information that insiders have about their firms and that is not yet disclosed to the public). It also attempts to prevent price fixing among floor brokers that could cause wider bid–ask spreads that would impose higher costs on customers.

14-1c How Option Trades Are Executed

When options exchanges were created, floor brokers of exchanges were available to execute orders for brokerage firms. They went to a specific location on the trading floor where the option was traded to execute the order. Today, computer technology allows investors to have trades executed electronically. Most small, standardized transactions are executed electronically, whereas complex transactions are executed by competitive open outcry among exchange members. Many electronic communication networks (ECNs) are programmed to consider all possible trades and execute the order at the best possible price.

Market-makers can also execute stock option transactions for customers. They earn the difference between the bid price and the ask price for this trade, although the spread has declined significantly in recent years. Market-makers also generate profits or losses when they invest their own funds in options.

14-1d Types of Orders

As with stocks, an investor can use either a market order or a limit order for an option transaction. A market order will result in the immediate purchase or sale of an option at its prevailing market price. With a limit order, the transaction will occur only if the market price is no higher or lower than a specified price limit. For example, an investor may request the purchase of a specific option only if it can be purchased at or below some specified price. Conversely, an investor may request to sell an option only if it can be sold for some specified limit or more.

Online Trading   Option contracts can also be purchased or sold online. Many online brokerage firms, including E*Trade and TD Ameritrade, facilitate options orders. Online option contract orders are commonly routed to computerized networks on options exchanges, where they are executed. For these orders, computers handle the order from the time it is placed until it is executed.

14-1e Stock Option Quotations

Financial newspapers and other financial media publish quotations for stock options. Exhibit 14.1 provides an example of stock options for Viperon Company stock as of

Exhibit 14.1   Viperon Company Stock Option Quotations

	STRIKE	EXP.	VOLUME	CALL	VOLUME	PUT
Option 1	45	Jun	180	4½	60	2¾
Option 2	45	Oct	70	5¾	120	3¾
Option 3	50	Jun	360	1⅛	40	5⅛
Option 4	50	Oct	90	3½	40	6½

WEB

biz.yahoo.com/opt
Summary of the most
actively traded stock
options.

May 1, when the stock was priced at about $45.62 per share. There are normally more options on each stock than what is disclosed in financial newspapers, with additional exercise prices and expiration dates. Each row represents a specific option on Viperon stock. The first data column lists the exercise (strike) price, and the second column lists the expiration date. (The expiration date for stock options traded on the CBOE is the Saturday following the third Friday of the specified month.) The third and fourth columns show the volume and the most recently quoted premium of the call option with that exercise price and expiration date. The fifth and sixth columns show the volume and the most recently quoted premium of the put option with that exercise price and expiration date.

A comparison of the premiums among the four options illustrates how specific factors affect option premiums. First, comparing Options 1 and 3 (to control for the same expiration date) reveals that an option with a higher exercise price has a lower call option premium and a higher put option premium. A comparison of Options 2 and 4 confirms this relationship. Second, comparing Options 1 and 2 (to control for the same exercise price) reveals that an option with a longer term to maturity has a higher call option premium and a higher put option premium. A comparison of Options 3 and 4 confirms this relationship.

14-1f Institutional Use of Options

Exhibit 14.2 summarizes the use of options by various types of financial institutions. Although options positions are sometimes taken by financial institutions for speculative purposes, they are more commonly used for hedging. Savings institutions and bond mutual funds use options to hedge interest rate risk. Stock mutual funds, insurance companies, and pension funds use stock index options and options on stock index futures to hedge their stock portfolios. Some of the large commercial banks often serve as an intermediary between two parties that take derivative positions in an over-the-counter market.

14-2 DETERMINANTS OF STOCK OPTION PREMIUMS

Stock option premiums are determined by market forces. Any characteristic of an option that results in many willing buyers but few willing sellers will place upward pressure on the option premium. Thus the option premium must be sufficiently high to equalize the demand by buyers and the supply that sellers are willing to sell. This generalization applies to both call options and put options. The specific characteristics that affect the demand and supply conditions, and therefore affect the stock option premiums, are described in what follows.

Exhibit 14.2 Institutional Use of Options Markets

TYPE OF FINANCIAL INSTITUTION	PARTICIPATION IN OPTIONS MARKETS
Commercial banks	• Sometimes offer options to businesses.
Savings institutions	• Sometimes take positions in options on futures contracts to hedge interest rate risk.
Mutual funds	• Stock mutual funds take positions in stock index options to hedge against a possible decline in prices of stocks in their portfolios. • Stock mutual funds sometimes take speculative positions in stock index options in an attempt to increase their returns. • Bond mutual funds sometimes take positions in options on futures to hedge interest rate risk.
Securities firms	• Serve as brokers by executing stock option transactions for individuals and businesses.
Pension funds	• Take positions in stock index options to hedge against a possible decline in prices of stocks in their portfolio. • Take positions in options on futures contracts to hedge their bond portfolios against interest rate movements.
Insurance companies	• Take positions in stock index options to hedge against a possible decline in prices of stocks in their portfolio. • Take positions in options on futures contracts to hedge their bond portfolios against interest rate movements.

14-2a Determinants of Call Option Premiums

Call option premiums are affected primarily by the following factors:

- Market price of the underlying instrument (relative to the option's exercise price)
- Volatility of the underlying instrument
- Time to maturity of the call option

Influence of the Market Price　The higher the existing market price of the underlying financial instrument relative to the exercise price, the higher the call option premium, other things being equal. A stock's value has a higher probability of increasing well above the exercise price if it is already close to or above the exercise price. Thus a purchaser would be willing to pay a higher premium for a call option on such a stock.

The influence of the market price of a stock (relative to the exercise price) on the call option premium can also be understood by comparing stock options with different exercise prices on the same instrument at a given time.

EXAMPLE　Consider the data shown in Exhibit 14.3 for KSR call options quoted on February 25, with a similar expiration date. The stock price of KSR was about $140 at that time. The premium for the call option with the $130 exercise price was almost $10 higher than the premium for the option with the $150 exercise price. This example confirms that a higher premium is required to lock in a lower exercise price on call options. ●

Influence of the Stock's Volatility　The greater the volatility of the underlying stock, the higher the call option premium, other things being equal. If a stock is volatile, there is a higher probability that its price will increase well above the exercise price. Thus a purchaser would be willing to pay a higher premium for a call option on that stock. For instance, call options on small stocks normally have higher premiums than call options on large stocks because small stocks are typically more volatile.

Exhibit 14.3 Relationship between Exercise Price and Call Option Premium on KSR Stock

EXERCISE PRICE	PREMIUM FOR APRIL EXPIRATION DATE
$130	11⅝
135	7½
140	5¼
145	3¼
150	1⅞

Influence of the Call Option's Time to Maturity The longer the call option's time to maturity, the higher the call option premium, other things being equal. A longer time period until expiration allows the owner of the option more time to exercise the option. Thus there is a higher probability that the stock's price will move well above the exercise price before the option expires.

The relationship between the time to maturity and the call option premium is illustrated in Exhibit 14.4 for KSR call options quoted on February 25, with a similar exercise price of $135. The premium was $4.50 per share for the call option with a March expiration month versus $7.50 per share for the call option with an April expiration month. The difference reflects the additional time in which the April call option can be exercised.

14-2b Determinants of Put Option Premiums

The premium paid on a put option depends on the same factors that affect the premium paid on a call option. However, the direction of influence varies for one of the factors, as explained next.

Influence of the Market Price The higher the existing market price of the underlying stock relative to the exercise price, the lower the put option premium, all other things being equal. A stock's value has a higher probability of decreasing well below the exercise price if it is already close to or below the exercise price. Thus a purchaser would be willing to pay a higher premium for a put option on that stock. This influence on the put option premium differs from the influence on the call option premium because, from the perspective of put option purchasers, a *lower* market price is preferable.

The influence of the market price of a stock (relative to the exercise price) on the put option premium can also be understood by comparing options with different exercise prices on the same instrument at a given moment in time. For example, consider the data shown in Exhibit 14.5 for KSR put options with a similar expiration date quoted

Exhibit 14.4 Relationship between Time to Maturity and Call Option Premium on KSR Stock

EXPIRATION DATE	PREMIUM FOR OPTION WITH A $135 EXERCISE PRICE
March	4½
April	7½
July	13¼

Exhibit 14.5 Relationship between Exercise Price and Put Option Premium on KSR Stock

EXERCISE PRICE	PREMIUM FOR JUNE EXPIRATION DATE
$130	$1\frac{7}{8}$
135	$3\frac{1}{8}$
140	$5\frac{3}{8}$
145	$8\frac{1}{2}$
150	$12\frac{1}{4}$

on February 25, 2010. The premium for the put option with the $150 exercise price was more than $9 per share higher than the premium for the option with the $135 exercise price. The difference reflects the more favorable price at which the stock can be sold when holding the put option with the higher exercise price.

Influence of the Stock's Volatility   The greater the volatility of the underlying stock, the higher the put option premium, all other things being equal. This relationship also held for call option premiums. If a stock is volatile, there is a higher probability of its price deviating far from the exercise price. Thus a purchaser would be willing to pay a higher premium for a put option on that stock because its market price is more likely to decline well below the option's exercise price.

Influence of the Put Option's Time to Maturity   The longer the time to maturity, the higher the put option premium, all other things being equal. This relationship also held for call option premiums. A longer time period until expiration allows the owner of the option more time to exercise the option. Thus there is a higher probability that the stock's price will move well below the exercise price before the option expires.

The relationship between the time to maturity and the put option premium is shown in Exhibit 14.6 for KSR put options with a similar exercise price of $135 quoted on February 25, 2010. The premium was $7.25 per share for the put option with a July expiration month versus $0.50 per share for the put option with a March expiration month. This difference reflects the additional time during which the put option with the July expiration date can be exercised.

14-2c How Option Pricing Can Be Used to Derive a Stock's Volatility

The general relationships between the determinants described previously and the option premium are explained in the text of this chapter, but see the Appendix for discussion of a well-known formula used to price stock options. Since the anticipated volatility of a

Exhibit 14.6 Relationship between Time to Maturity and Put Option Premium on KSR Stock

EXPIRATION DATE	PREMIUM FOR OPTION WITH A $135 EXERCISE PRICE
March	$\frac{1}{2}$
April	$3\frac{1}{8}$
July	$7\frac{1}{4}$

stock is not observable, investors can input their own estimate of it when calculating the premium that should be paid for a particular option.

Some investors who are assessing a specific stock's risk adapt the option-pricing formula to derive an estimate of that stock's anticipated volatility. By plugging in values for the other factors that affect the particular stock option's premium and for the prevailing premium quoted in the market, it is possible to derive the stock's anticipated volatility, which is referred to as the *implied standard deviation* (or *implied volatility*). The implied standard deviation is derived by determining what its value must be, given the quoted option premium and the values of other factors that affect the stock option's premium. Various software packages and calculators are available that can estimate a stock's implied volatility. Such an estimate is of interest to investors because it indicates the market's view of the stock's potential volatility. Some investors may use this estimate as a measure of a stock's risk when they consider what stocks to purchase.

14-2d Explaining Changes in Option Premiums

Exhibit 14.7 identifies the underlying forces that cause option prices to change over time. Economic conditions and market conditions can cause abrupt changes in the stock price or in the anticipated volatility of the stock price over the time remaining until option expiration. Such changes would have a major impact on the stock option's premium.

Indicators Monitored by Participants in the Options Market   Since the premiums paid on stock options are highly influenced by the price movements of the underlying stocks, participants in the stock option market closely monitor the same indicators that are monitored when trading the underlying stocks. Traders of options tend to monitor economic indicators because economic conditions affect cash flows of firms and thus can affect expected stock valuations and stock option premiums. Economic conditions can also affect the premiums by influencing expected stock volatility.

EXAMPLE

During the fall of 2008, the credit crisis intensified and stock volatility increased substantially. Consequently, premiums for options increased as well. Under these conditions, more portfolio managers wanted to hedge their stock positions, but they had to pay a higher premium for put options. The sellers of put options recognized that their risk had increased because of the higher volatility and priced the put options accordingly.

In the years after the financial crisis, stock volatility declined. Consequently, the sellers of put options were exposed to a lower level of risk, and were more willing to accept a lower premium. ●

14-3 SPECULATING WITH STOCK OPTIONS

Stock options are frequently traded by investors who are attempting to capitalize on their expectations. When investors purchase an option that does not cover (hedge) their existing investments, the option can be referred to as "naked" (uncovered). Since speculators trade options to gamble on price movements rather than to hedge existing investments, their positions in options are naked. Whether speculators purchase call options or put options depends on their expectations.

In some cases, speculators borrow a portion of the funds that they use to invest in stock options. The use of borrowed funds can magnify their gains, but it can also magnify their losses. The gains and losses described in this chapter would be more

Exhibit 14.7   Framework for Explaining Why a Stock Option's Premium Changes over Time

pronounced if the speculators cited in the examples used borrowed funds for a portion of their investment.

14-3a Speculating with Call Options

Call options can be used to speculate on the expectation of an increase in the price of the underlying stock.

EXAMPLE   Pat Jackson expects Steelco stock to increase from its current price of $113 per share but does not want to tie up her available funds by investing in stocks. She purchases a call option on Steelco with an exercise price of $115 for a premium of $4 per share. Before the option's expiration date, Steelco's price rises to $121. At that time, Jackson exercises her option, purchasing shares at $115 per share. She then immediately sells those shares at the market price of $121 per share. Her net gain on this transaction is measured as follows:

Amount received when selling shares	**$121 per share**
− **Amount paid for shares**	− **$115 per share**
− **Amount paid for the call option**	− **$ 4 per share**
= **Net gain**	**$ 2 per share**
	or **$200 for one contract**

Pat's net gain of $2 per share reflects a return of 50 percent (not annualized). ●

If the price of Steelco stock had not risen above $115 before the option's expiration date, Pat would have let the option expire. Her net loss would have been the $4 per share she initially paid for the option, or $400 for one option contract. This example reflects a 100 percent loss, since the entire amount of the investment is lost.

The potential gains or losses from this call option are shown in the left portion of Exhibit 14.8, based on the assumptions that (1) the call option is exercised on the expiration date, if at all, and (2) if the call option is exercised, the shares received are immediately sold. Exhibit 14.8 shows that the maximum loss when purchasing this option is the premium of $4 per share. For stock prices between $115 and $119, the option is exercised and the purchaser of a call option incurs a net loss of less than $4 per share. The stock price of $119 is the break-even point, because the gain from exercising the option exactly offsets the premium paid for it. At stock prices above $119, a net gain is realized.

The right portion of Exhibit 14.8 shows the net gain or loss to a writer of the same call option, assuming that the writer obtains the stock only when the option is exercised. Under this condition, the call option writer's net gain (loss) is the call option purchaser's net loss (gain), assuming zero transaction costs. The maximum gain to the writer of a call option is the premium received.

Exhibit 14.8   Potential Gains or Losses on a Call Option: Exercise Price = $115, Premium = $4

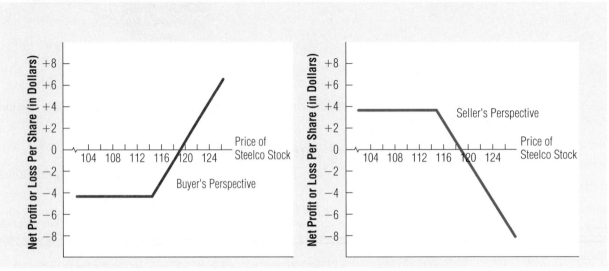

Exhibit 14.9   Potential Gains or Losses for Three Call Options (Buyer's Perspective)

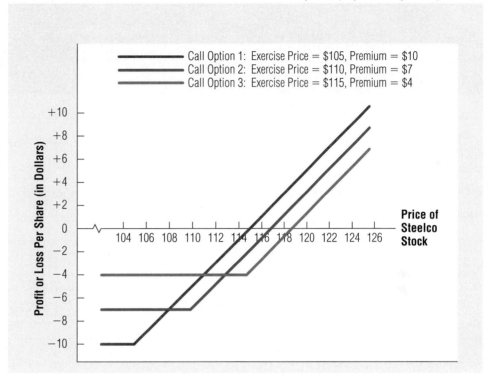

Several call options are available for a given stock, and the risk–return potential will vary among them. Assume that three types of call options were available on Steelco stock with a similar expiration date, as described in Exhibit 14.9. The potential gains or losses per unit for each option are also shown in the exhibit, assuming that the option is exercised (if at all) on the expiration date. It is also assumed that if the speculators exercise the call option, they immediately sell the stock. This comparison of different options for a given stock illustrates the various risk–return trade-offs from which speculators can choose.

Purchasers of call options are normally most interested in returns (profit as a percentage of the initial investment) under various scenarios. For this purpose, the contingency graph can be revised to reflect returns for each possible price per share of the underlying stock. The first step is to convert the profit per unit into a return for each possible price, as shown in Exhibit 14.10. For example, for the stock price of $116, Call Option 1 generates a return of 10 percent ($1 per share profit as a percentage of the $10 premium paid), Call Option 2 generates a loss of about 14 percent ($1 per share loss as a percentage of the $7 premium paid), and Call Option 3 generates a loss of 75 percent ($3 per share loss as a percentage of the $4 premium paid).

The data can be transformed into a contingency graph as shown in Exhibit 14.11. This graph illustrates that, for Call Option 1, both the potential losses and the potential returns in the event of a high stock price are relatively low. Conversely, the potential losses for Call Option 3 are relatively high but so are the potential returns in the event of a high stock price.

Exhibit 14.10 Potential Returns on Three Different Call Options

PRICE OF STEELCO	OPTION 1: EXERCISE PRICE = $105 PREMIUM = $10		OPTION 2: EXERCISE PRICE = $110 PREMIUM = $7		OPTION 3: EXERCISE PRICE = $115 PREMIUM = $4	
	PROFIT PER UNIT	PERCENTAGE RETURN	PROFIT PER UNIT	PERCENTAGE RETURN	PROFIT PER UNIT	PERCENTAGE RETURN
$104	−$10	−100%	−$7	−100%	−$4	−100%
106	−9	−90	−7	−100	−4	−100
108	−7	−70	−7	−100	−4	−100
110	−5	−50	−7	−100	−4	−100
112	−3	−30	−5	−71	−4	−100
114	−1	−10	−3	−43	−4	−100
116	1	10	−1	−14	−3	−75
118	3	30	1	14	−1	−25
120	5	50	3	43	1	25
122	7	70	5	71	3	75
124	9	90	7	100	5	125
126	11	110	9	129	7	175

14-3b Speculating with Put Options

Put options can be used to speculate on the expectation of a decrease in the price of the underlying stock.

EXAMPLE

A put option on Steelco is available with an exercise price of $110 and a premium of $2. If the price of Steelco stock falls below $110, speculators could purchase the stock and then exercise their put options to benefit from the transaction. However, they would need to make at least $2 per share on this transaction to fully recover the premium paid for the option. If the speculators exercise the option when the market price is $104, their net gain is measured as follows:

Amount received when selling shares	**$110 per share**
− Amount paid for shares	**− $104 per share**
− Amount paid for the put option	**− $ 2 per share**
= Net gain	**$ 4 per share**

The net gain here is 200 percent, or twice as much as the amount paid for the put options. ●

The potential gains or losses from the put option described here are shown in the left portion of Exhibit 14.12, based on the assumptions that (1) the put option is exercised on the expiration date, if at all, and (2) the shares would be purchased just before the put option is exercised. The exhibit shows that the maximum loss when purchasing this option is $2 per share. For stock prices between $108 and $110, the purchaser of a put option incurs a net loss of less than $2 per share. The stock price of $108 is the break-even point, because the gain from exercising the put option would exactly offset the $2 per share premium.

Exhibit 14.11   Potential Returns for Three Call Options (Buyer's Perspective)

The right portion of Exhibit 14.12 shows the net gain or loss to a writer of the same put option, assuming that the writer sells the stock received as the put option is exercised. Under this condition, the put option writer's net gain (loss) is the put option purchaser's net loss (gain), assuming zero transaction costs. The maximum gain to the writer of a put option is the premium received. As with call options, several put options are typically available for a given stock, and the potential gains or losses will vary among them.

14-3c Excessive Risk from Speculation

Speculating in options can be very risky. Financial institutions or other corporations that speculate in options normally have methods to closely monitor their risk and to measure their exposure to possible option market conditions. In several cases, however, a financial institution or a corporation incurred a major loss on options positions because of a lack of oversight over its options trading.

EXAMPLE   One of the most famous cases in which a financial institution took excessive risk with stock options is Barings PLC, an investment bank in the United Kingdom. In 1992, a clerk in Barings's

Exhibit 14.12 Potential Gains or Losses on a Put Option: Exercise Price = $110, Premium = $2

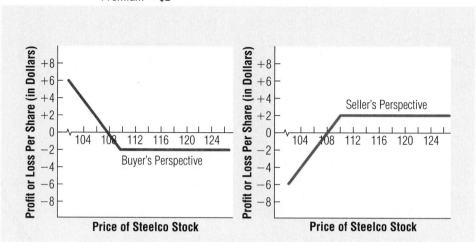

London office named Nicholas Leeson was sent to manage the accounting at a Singapore subsidiary called Barings Futures. Shortly after he began his new position in Singapore, Leeson took and passed the examinations required to trade on the floor of the Singapore International Monetary Exchange (SIMEX). Barings Futures served as a broker on this exchange for some of its customers. Within a year of arriving in Singapore, Leeson was trading derivative contracts on the SIMEX as a broker for Barings Futures. He then began to trade for the firm's own account rather than just as a broker, trading options on the Nikkei (Japanese) stock index. At the same time, he also continued to serve as the accounting manager for Barings Futures. In this role Leeson was able to conceal losses on any derivative positions, so the financial reports to Barings PLC showed massive profits.

By January 1995, Leeson's losses had accumulated to exceed the equivalent of $300 million. Leeson had periodically required funds to cover margin calls as his positions declined in value. Barings PLC met these funding requests, covering the equivalent of millions of dollars to satisfy the margin calls, yet did not recognize that the margin calls signaled a major problem.

In late February 1995, an accounting clerk at Barings who noticed some discrepancies met with Leeson to reconcile the records. When Leeson was asked to explain specific accounting entries, he excused himself from the meeting and never returned. He left Singapore that night and faxed his resignation to Barings PLC from Kuala Lumpur, Malaysia. Barings PLC investigated and found that Leeson had accumulated losses totaling more than the equivalent of $1 billion, which caused Barings PLC to become insolvent. Leeson pleaded guilty to charges of fraud, and he was sentenced to prison for six and one-half years. ●

Any firms that use futures or other derivative instruments can draw a few obvious lessons from the Barings collapse. First, firms should closely monitor the trading of derivative contracts by their employees to ensure that derivatives are being used within the firm's guidelines. Second, firms should separate the reporting function from the trading function so that traders cannot conceal trading losses. Third, when firms receive margin calls on derivative positions, they should recognize that there may be potential losses on their derivative instruments and should closely evaluate those positions. The Barings case was a wake-up call to many firms, which recognized the need to establish guidelines for their employees who take derivative positions and to monitor more closely the actions of these employees.

14-4 HEDGING WITH STOCK OPTIONS

Call and put options on selected stocks and stock indexes are commonly used for hedging against possible stock price movements. Financial institutions such as mutual funds, insurance companies, and pension funds manage large stock portfolios and are the most common users of options for hedging.

14-4a Hedging with Covered Call Options

Call options on a stock can be used to hedge a position in that stock.

EXAMPLE

Portland Pension Fund owns a substantial amount of Steelco stock. It expects that the stock will perform well in the long run, but it is concerned that the stock may perform poorly over the next few months because of temporary problems Steelco is experiencing. The sale of a call option on Steelco stock can hedge against such a potential loss. This is known as a covered call because the option is covered, or backed, by stocks already owned.

If the market price of Steelco stock rises, the call option will likely be exercised and Portland will fulfill its obligation by selling its Steelco stock to the purchaser of the call option at the exercise price. But if the market price of Steelco stock declines, the option will not be exercised. Hence Portland would not have to sell its Steelco stock, and the premium received from selling the call option would represent a gain that could partially offset the decline in the price of the stock. In this case, although the market value of the institution's stock portfolio is adversely affected, the decline is at least partially offset by the premium received from selling the call option.

Assume that Portland Pension Fund purchased Steelco stock at the market price of $112 per share. To hedge against a temporary decline in Steelco's stock price, Portland sells call options on Steelco stock with an exercise price of $110 per share for a premium of $5 per share. The net profit to Portland when using covered call writing is shown in Exhibit 14.13 for various possible scenarios. For comparison purposes, the profit that Portland would earn if it did not use covered call writing but instead sold the stock on the option's expiration date is also shown (see the diagonal line) for various possible scenarios. The results show how covered call writing can partially offset losses when the stock performs poorly but can also partially offset gains when the stock performs well. ●

The table in Exhibit 14.13 explains the profit or loss per share from covered call writing. At any price above $110 per share as of the expiration date, the call option would be exercised and so Portland would have to sell its holdings of Steelco stock at the exercise price of $110 per share to the purchaser of the call option. The net gain to Portland would be $3 per share, determined as the premium of $5 per share (received when writing the option) minus the $2 per share difference between the price paid for the Steelco stock and the price at which the stock is sold. Comparing the profit or loss per scenarios with and without covered call writing, it is clear that covered call writing limits the upside potential return on stocks but also reduces the risk.

14-4b Hedging with Put Options

Put options on stock are also used to hedge stock positions.

EXAMPLE

Reconsider the example in which Portland Pension Fund was concerned about a possible temporary decline in the price of Steelco stock. Portland could hedge against a temporary decline in Steelco's stock price by purchasing put options on that stock. In the event that Steelco's stock price declines, Portland would likely generate a gain on its option position, which would help offset the reduction in the stock's price. If Steelco's stock price does not decline, Portland would not exercise its put option. ●

Put options are typically used to hedge when portfolio managers are mainly concerned about a temporary decline in a stock's value. When portfolio managers are

Exhibit 14.13 Risk-Return Trade-off from Covered Call Writing

EXPLANATION OF PROFIT PER SHARE FROM COVERED CALL WRITING								
MARKET PRICE OF STEELCO AS OF THE EXPIRATION DATE	PRICE AT WHICH PORTLAND PENSION FUND SELLS STEELCO STOCK		PREMIUM RECEIVED FROM WRITING THE CALL OPTION		PRICE PAID FOR STEELCO STOCK		PROFIT OR LOSS PER SHARE
$104	$104	+	$5	−	$112	=	−$3
105	105	+	5	−	112	=	−2
106	106	+	5	−	112	=	−1
107	107	+	5	−	112	=	0
108	108	+	5	−	112	=	1
109	109	+	5	−	112	=	2
110	110	+	5	−	112	=	3
111	110	+	5	−	112	=	3
112	110	+	5	−	112	=	3
113	110	+	5	−	112	=	3
114	110	+	5	−	112	=	3
115	110	+	5	−	112	=	3
116	110	+	5	−	112	=	3
117	110	+	5	−	112	=	3
118	110	+	5	−	112	=	3
119	110	+	5	−	112	=	3
120	110	+	5	−	112	=	3

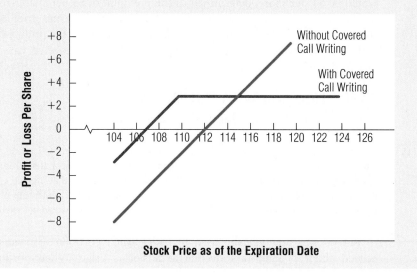

mainly concerned about the long-term performance of a stock, they are likely to sell the stock itself rather than hedge the position.

Hedging with LEAPs **Long-term equity anticipations (LEAPs)** are options that have longer terms to expiration, usually between two and three years from the initial listing date. These options are available for some large capitalization stocks, and they may be a more effective hedge over a longer term period than using options with shorter terms to expiration. The transaction costs for hedging over a long period are lower than the costs of continually repurchasing short-term put options each time the options expire or are exercised. Furthermore, the costs of continually repurchasing put options are uncertain, whereas the costs of purchasing a put option on a long-term index option are known immediately.

14-5 OPTIONS ON ETFS AND STOCK INDEXES

Options are also traded on exchange-traded funds (ETFs) and stock indexes. Exchange-traded funds are funds that are designed to mimic particular indexes and are traded on an exchange. Thus, an ETF option provides the right to trade a specified ETF at a specified price by a specified expiration date. Since ETFs are traded like stocks, options on ETFs are traded like options on stocks. Investors who exercise a call option on an ETF will receive delivery of the ETF in their account. Investors who exercise a put option on an ETF will have the ETF transferred from their account to the counterparty on the put option.

A **stock index option** provides the right to trade a specified stock index at a specified price by a specified expiration date. Call options on stock indexes allow the right to purchase the index, and put options on stock indexes allow the right to sell the index. If and when the index option is exercised, the cash payment is equal to a specified dollar amount multiplied by the difference between the index level and the exercise price.

Options on stock indexes are similar to options on ETFs. However, the values of stock indexes change only at the end of each trading day, whereas ETF values can change throughout the day. Therefore, an investor who wants to capitalize on the expected movement of an index within a particular day will trade options on ETFs. An investor who wants to capitalize on the expected movement of an index over a longer period of time (such as a week or several months) can trade options on either ETFs or indexes.

Options on indexes have become popular for speculating on general movements in the stock market. Speculators who anticipate a sharp increase in stock market prices overall may consider purchasing call options on one of the market indexes. Likewise, speculators who anticipate a stock market decline may consider purchasing put options on these indexes. A sampling of options that are traded on ETFs and on stock indexes is provided in Exhibit 14.14, where SPDR stands for Standard & Poor's Depositary Receipts.

Options on sector indexes also exist, allowing investors the option to buy or sell an index that reflects a particular sector. These contracts are distinguished from stock index options because they represent a component of a stock index. Investors who are optimistic about the stock market in general might be more interested in stock index options, while investors who are especially optimistic about one particular sector may be more interested in options on a sector index. There are options available for many different sectors, including banking, energy, housing, oil exploration, semiconductors, and utilities.

14-5a Hedging with Stock Index Options

Financial institutions and other firms commonly take positions in options on ETFs or indexes to hedge against market or sector conditions that would adversely affect their

Exhibit 14.14 Sampling of ETFs and Indexes on Which Options Are Traded

SAMPLING OF ETFs ON WHICH OPTIONS ARE TRADED	
iShares Nasdaq Biotechnology	iShares Russell 1000 Growth Index Fund
iShares Goldman Sachs Technology Index	Energy Select Sector SPDR
iShares Goldman Sachs Software Index	Financial Select Sector SPDR
iShares Russell 1000 Index Fund	Utilities Select Sector SPDR
iShares Russell 1000 Value Index Fund	Health Care Select Sector SPDR
SAMPLING OF INDEXES ON WHICH OPTIONS ARE TRADED	
Asia 25 Index	S&P SmallCap 600 Index
Euro 25 Index	Nasdaq 100 Index
Mexico Index	Russell 1000 Index
Dow Jones Industrial Average	Russell 1000 Value Index
Dow Jones Transportation Average	Russell 1000 Growth Index
Dow Jones Utilities Average	Russell Midcap Index
S&P 100 Index	Goldman Sachs Internet Index
S&P 500 Index	Goldman Sachs Software Index
Morgan Stanley Biotechnology Index	

asset portfolio or cash flows. The following discussion is based on the use of options on stock indexes, but options on ETFs could be used in the same manner.

Financial institutions such as insurance companies and pension funds maintain large stock portfolios whose values are driven by general market movements. If the stock portfolio is broad enough, any changes in its value will likely be highly correlated with market movements. For this reason, portfolio managers consider purchasing put options on a stock index to protect against stock market declines. The put options should be purchased on the stock index that most closely mirrors the portfolio to be hedged. If the stock market experiences a severe downturn, the market value of the portfolio declines. However, the put options on the stock index will generate a gain because the value of the index will be less than the exercise price. The greater the market downturn, the greater the decline in the market value of the portfolio but also the greater the gain from holding put options on a stock index. Thus, this offsetting effect minimizes the overall impact on the firm.

If the stock market rises, the put options on the stock index will not be exercised. In this case, the firm will not recover the cost of purchasing the options. This situation is similar to purchasing other forms of insurance and then not using them. Some portfolio managers may still believe the options were worthwhile for temporary protection against downside risk.

Hedging with Long-Term Stock Index Options   Long-term equity anticipations are used by option market participants who want options with longer terms until

expiration. For example, LEAPs on the S&P 100 and S&P 500 indexes are available, with expiration dates extending at least two years ahead from the initial listing date. Each of these indexes is revised to one-tenth its normal size when applying LEAPs. The result is smaller premiums, which makes the LEAPs more affordable to smaller investors.

Dynamic Asset Allocation with Stock Index Options Dynamic asset allocation involves switching between risky and low-risk investment positions over time in response to changing expectations. Some portfolio managers use stock index options as a tool for dynamic asset allocation. For example, when portfolio managers anticipate favorable market conditions, they purchase call options on a stock index, which intensify the effects of the market conditions. Essentially, the managers are using stock index options to increase their exposure to stock market conditions. Conversely, when they anticipate unfavorable market movements, they can purchase put options on a stock index in order to reduce the effects that market conditions will have on their stock portfolios.

Because stock options are available with various exercise prices, portfolio managers can select an exercise price that provides the degree of protection desired. For example, assume an existing stock index is quite similar to a manager's stock portfolio and that he wants to protect against any loss exceeding 5 percent. If the prevailing level of the index is 400, the manager should purchase put options with an exercise price of 380 because that level is 5 percent lower than 400. If the index declines to a level below 380, the manager will exercise the options and the gain from doing so will partially offset the reduction in the stock portfolio's market value.

This strategy is essentially a form of insurance, where the premium paid for the put option is similar to an insurance premium. Because the index must decline by 5 percent before there is any possibility that the option will be exercised, this is similar to the "deductible" that is typical of insurance policies. If portfolio managers desire to protect against even smaller losses, they can purchase a put option that specifies a higher exercise price on the index, such as 390. To obtain the extra protection, however, they would have to pay a higher premium for the option. In other words, the cost of the portfolio insurance would be higher because of the smaller "deductible" desired.

In another form of dynamic asset allocation, portfolio managers sell (write) call options on stock indexes in periods when they expect the stock market to be stable. This strategy does not create a perfect hedge, but it can enhance the portfolio's performance in periods when stock prices are stagnant or declining.

Portfolio managers can adjust the risk–return profile of their investment position by using stock index options rather than restructuring their existing stock portfolios. This form of dynamic asset allocation avoids the substantial transaction costs associated with restructuring the stock portfolios.

14-5b Using Index Options to Measure the Market's Risk

Just as a stock's implied volatility can be derived from information about options on that stock, a stock index's implied volatility can be derived from information about options on that stock index. The same factors that affect the option premium on a stock affect the option premium on an index. Thus, the premium on an index option is positively related to the expected volatility of the underlying stock index. If investors want to estimate the expected volatility of the stock index, they can use software packages to insert values for the prevailing option premium and all the other factors (except volatility) that affect an option premium.

The CBOE volatility index (VIX) represents the implied volatility derived from options on the S&P 500 index (an index of 500 large stocks). This index is closely monitored by many investors because it indicates the market's anticipated volatility for the market (with the S&P 500 serving as proxy for the market). The VIX is sometimes referred to as the "fear index" because high values are perceived to reflect a high degree of fear that stock prices could decline.

14-6 Options on Futures Contracts

In recent years, the concept of options has been applied to futures contracts to create options on futures contracts (sometimes referred to as "futures options"). An option on a particular futures contract gives its owner the right (but not an obligation) to purchase or sell that futures contract for a specified price within a specified period of time. Thus, options on futures grant the power to take the futures position if favorable conditions occur but the flexibility to avoid the futures position (by letting the option expire) if unfavorable conditions occur. As with other options, the purchaser of options on futures pays a premium.

Similarly, options are available on stock index futures. They are used for speculating on expected stock market movements or hedging against adverse market conditions. Individuals and financial institutions use them in a manner similar to the way stock index options are used.

Options are also available on interest rate futures, such as Treasury note futures or Treasury bond futures. The settlement dates of the underlying futures contracts are usually a few weeks after the expiration date of the corresponding options contracts.

A call option on interest rate futures grants the right to purchase a futures contract at a specified price within a specified period of time. A put option on financial futures grants the right (again, not an obligation) to sell a particular financial futures contract at a specified price within a specified period of time. Because interest rate futures contracts can hedge interest rate risk, options on interest rate futures might be considered by any financial institution that is exposed to that risk, including savings institutions, commercial banks, life insurance companies, and pension funds.

14-6a Speculating with Options on Futures

Speculators who anticipate a change in interest rates should also expect a change in bond prices. They could take a position in options on Treasury bond futures to capitalize on their expectations.

Speculation Based on an Expected Decline in Interest Rates If speculators expect a decline in interest rates, they may consider purchasing a call option on Treasury bond futures. If their expectations are correct, the market value of Treasury bonds will rise and the price of a Treasury bond futures contract will rise as well. The speculators can exercise their option to purchase futures at the exercise price, which will be lower than the value of the futures contract.

EXAMPLE Kelly Warden expects interest rates to decline and purchases a call option on Treasury bond futures. The exercise price on Treasury bond futures is 94-32 (9432/64 percent of $100,000, or $94,500). The call option is purchased at a premium of 2-00 (i.e., 2 percent of $100,000), which equals $2,000. Assume that interest rates do decline and, as a result, the price of the Treasury bond futures contract rises over time to a value of 99-00 ($99,000) shortly before the option's expiration date. At this time, Kelly decides to exercise the option and closes out the position by selling an identical futures contract (to create an offsetting position) at a higher price than the price at which she purchased the futures. Kelly's net gain from this speculative strategy is

Selling price of T-bond futures	$99,000	(99.00% of $100,000)
− Purchase price of T-bond futures	− $94,500	(94.50% of $100,000)
− Call option premium paid	− $ 2,000	(2.00% of $100,000)
= Net gain to purchaser of call option of futures	$ 2,500	(2.50% of $100,000)

This net gain of $2,500 represents a return on investment of 125 percent. ●

The seller of the call option will have the opposite position to the buyer. Thus the gain (or loss) to the buyer will equal the loss (or gain) to the seller of the call option.

EXAMPLE Ellen Rose sold the call option purchased by Kelly Warden in the previous example. Ellen is obligated to purchase and provide the futures contract at the time the option is exercised. Her net gain from this speculative strategy is

Selling price of T-bond futures	$94,500	(94.50% of $100,000)
− Purchase price of T-bond futures	− $99,000	(99.00% of $100,000)
− Call option premium received	+ $ 2,000	(2.00% of $100,000)
= Net gain to Seller of call option of futures	− $ 2,500	(−2.50% of $100,000)

In the absence of transaction costs, Ellen's loss is equal to Kelly's gain. If the Treasury bond futures price had remained below the exercise price of 94-32 ($94,500) until the expiration date, the option would not have been exercised. In that case, the net gain from purchasing the call option on Treasury bond futures would have been −$2,000 (the premium paid for the option) and the net gain from selling the call option would have been $2,000. ●

When interest rates decline, the buyers of call options on Treasury bonds may simply sell their previously purchased options just before expiration. If interest rates rise, the options will not be desirable. Then buyers of call options on Treasury bond futures will let their options expire, and their loss will be the premium paid for the call options on futures. Thus the loss from purchasing options on futures is more limited than the loss from simply purchasing futures contracts.

Some speculators who expect interest rates to remain stable or decline may be willing to sell a put option on Treasury bond futures. If their expectations are correct, the price of a futures contract will likely rise and so the put option will not be exercised. Therefore, sellers of the put option would earn the premium that was paid to them when they sold the option.

Speculation Based on an Expected Increase in Interest Rates

If speculators expect interest rates to increase, they can benefit from purchasing a put option on Treasury bond futures. If their expectations are correct, the market value of Treasury bonds will decline and so the price of a Treasury bond futures contract will also decline. The speculators can exercise their option to sell futures at the exercise price, which will be higher than the value of the futures contract. They can then purchase futures (to create an offsetting position) at a lower price than the price at which they sold futures. If interest rates decline, the speculators will likely let the options expire and their loss will be the premium paid for the put options on futures.

EXAMPLE John Drummer expects interest rates to increase and purchases a put option on Treasury bond futures. Assume the exercise price on Treasury bond futures is 97-00 ($97,000) and the premium paid for the put option is 3-00 ($3,000). Assume that interest rates do increase and, as a result, the price of the Treasury bond futures contract declines over time to a value of 89-00 ($89,000) shortly before the option's expiration date. At this time, John decides to exercise the option and closes out the position by purchasing an identical futures contract. John's net gain from this speculative strategy is

Selling price of T-bond futures	**$97,000**	(97.00% of $100,000)
− Purchase price of T-bond futures	**− $89,000**	(89.00% of $100,000)
− Put option premium received	**− $ 3,000**	(3.00% of $100,000)
= Net gain to purchaser of put option of futures	**$ 5,000**	(5.00% of $100,000)

The net gain of $5,000 represents a return on investment of about 167 percent. ●

The person who sold the put option on Treasury bond futures to John in this example incurred a loss of $5,000, assuming that the position was closed out (by selling an identical futures contract) on the same date that John's position was closed out. If the Treasury bond futures price had remained above the exercise price of 97–00 until the expiration date, then the option would not have been exercised and John would have lost $3,000 (the premium paid for the put option).

Some speculators who anticipate an increase in interest rates may be willing to sell a call option on Treasury bond futures. If their expectations are correct, the price of the futures contract will likely decline and hence the call option will not be exercised.

14-6b Hedging with Options on Interest Rate Futures

Options on futures contracts are also used to hedge against risk. Financial institutions commonly hedge their bond or mortgage portfolios with options on interest rate futures contracts. The position they take on the options contract is designed to create a gain that can offset a loss on their bond or mortgage portfolio while still allowing some upside potential.

EXAMPLE

Emory Savings and Loan Association has a large number of long-term, fixed-rate mortgages that are mainly supported by short-term funds and would therefore be adversely affected by rising interest rates. As shown in the previous chapter, sales of Treasury bond futures can partially offset the adverse effect of rising interest rates in such a situation. Recall that if interest rates decline instead, the potential increase in Emory's interest rate spread (difference between interest revenues and expenses) would be partially offset by the loss on the futures contract.

One potential limitation of selling interest rate futures to hedge mortgages is that households may prepay their mortgages. If interest rates decline and most fixed-rate mortgages are prepaid, Emory will incur a loss on the futures position without an offsetting gain on its spread. To protect against this risk, Emory can purchase put options on Treasury bond futures. Suppose that Emory purchases put options on Treasury bond futures with an exercise price of 98-00 ($98,000) for a premium of 2-00 ($2,000) per contract. The initial Treasury bond futures price is 99-00 at the time. First, assume that interest rates rise, causing a decline in the Treasury bond futures price to 91-00. In this scenario, Emory will exercise its right to sell Treasury bond futures and offset its position by purchasing identical futures contracts and thereby generate a net gain of $5,000 per contract, as shown in Exhibit 14.15. The gain on the futures position helps to offset the reduction in Emory's spread that occurs because of the higher interest rates.

Now consider a second scenario in which interest rates decline, causing the Treasury bond futures price to rise to 104-00. In this scenario, Emory does not exercise the put options on Treasury bond futures because the futures position would result in a loss. ●

This example shows how a put option on futures offers more flexibility than simply selling futures. However, a premium must be paid for the put option. Financial institutions

Exhibit 14.15 Results from Hedging with Put Options on Treasury Bond Futures

	SCENARIO 1: • INTEREST RATES RISE • T-BOND FUTURES PRICE DECLINES TO 91–00	SCENARIO 2: • INTEREST RATES DECLINE • T-BOND FUTURES PRICE INCREASES TO 104–00
Effect on Emory's spread	Spread is reduced.	Spread is increased, but mortgage prepayments may occur.
Effect on T-bond futures price	Futures price decreases.	Futures price increases.
Decision on exercising the put option	Exercise put option.	Do not exercise put option.
Selling price of T-bond futures	$98,000	Not sold
− Purchase price of T-bond futures	− $91,000	Not purchased
− Price paid for put option	− $2,000	− $2,000
= Net gain per option	$5,000	− $2,000

that wish to hedge against rising interest rate risk should compare the possible outcomes from selling interest rate futures contracts versus purchasing put options on interest rate futures in order to hedge interest rate risk.

14-6c Hedging with Options on Stock Index Futures

Financial institutions and other investors commonly hedge their stock portfolios with options on stock index futures contracts. The position they take on the options contract is designed to create a gain that can offset a loss on their stock portfolio while still allowing some upside potential.

EXAMPLE   You currently manage a stock portfolio that is valued at $400,000, and you plan to hold these stocks over a long-term period. However, you are concerned that the stock market may experience a temporary decline over the next three months and that your stock portfolio will probably decline by about the same degree as the market. You want to create a hedge so that your portfolio will decline no more than 3 percent from its present value, but you would like to maintain any upside potential. You can purchase a put option on index futures to hedge your stock portfolio. Put options on S&P 500 index futures are available with an expiration date about three months from now.

Assume that the S&P 500 index level is currently 1600 and that one particular put option on index futures has a strike price of 1552 (3 percent less than the prevailing index level) and a premium of 10. Since the options on S&P 500 index futures are priced at $250 times the quoted premium, the dollar amount to be paid for this option is 10 × $250 = $2,500. If the index level declines below 1552 (reflecting a decline of more than 3 percent), then you may exercise the put option on index futures, which gives you the right to sell the index for a price of 1552. At the settlement date of the futures contract, you will receive $250 times the difference between the futures price of 1552 and the prevailing index level. If the market declines by 5 percent, for example, the index will decline from 1600 to 1520. There will be a gain on the index futures contract of (1552 − 1520) × $250 = $8,000. Meanwhile, a 5 percent decline in the value of the portfolio reflects a loss of $20,000 (0.05 × $400,000 = $20,000). The $8,000 gain (excluding the premium paid) from the options contract reduces the overall loss to $12,000, or 3 percent of the portfolio. ●

Determining the Degree of the Hedge with Options on Stock Index Futures   In the previous example, losses of less than 3 percent are not hedged. When using put options to hedge, various strike prices exist for an option on a specific stock index and for a specific expiration date. For example, put options on the S&P 500 index may be available with strike prices of 1760, 1800, 1840, and so on. The higher the strike price relative to the prevailing index value, the higher the price at which the investor can lock in the sale of the index. However, a higher premium must be paid to purchase put options with a higher strike price. From a hedging perspective, this simply illustrates that a higher price must be paid to "insure" (hedge) against losses resulting from stock market downturns. This concept is analogous to automobile insurance, where a person must pay a higher premium for a policy that features a lower deductible.

Selling Call Options to Cover the Cost of Put Options In the previous example, the cost of hedging with a put option on index futures is $2,500. Given your expectations of a weak stock market over the next three months, you could generate some fees by selling call options on S&P 500 index futures to help cover the cost of purchasing put options.

EXAMPLE Assume that there is a call option on S&P 500 index futures with a strike price of 1648 (3 percent above the existing index level) and a premium of 10. You can sell a call option on index futures for $2,500 (10 × $250) and use the proceeds to pay the premium on the put option. The obvious disadvantage of selling a call option to finance the purchase of the put option is that it limits your upside potential. For example, if the market rises by 5 percent over the three-month period, the S&P 500 index level will rise to 1680. The difference between this level and the strike price of 1648 on the call option forces you to make a payment of (1680 − 1648) × $250 = $8,000 to the owner of the call option. This partially offsets the gain to your portfolio that resulted from the favorable market conditions. ●

When attempting to hedge larger portfolios than the one in the previous example, additional put options would be purchased to hedge the entire portfolio against a possible decline in the market. For example, if your stock portfolio were $1.2 million, you would need to purchase three put options on S&P 500 index futures contracts. Since each index futures contract would have a value of $400,000, you would need a short position in three index futures contracts to hedge the entire stock portfolio (assuming that the index and the stock portfolio move in tandem).

14-7 OPTIONS AS EXECUTIVE COMPENSATION

Many firms distribute stock options to executives and other managers as a reward for good performance. For example, a manager may receive a salary along with call options on 10,000 shares of stock that have an exercise price above the prevailing price and an expiration date of five years from today. The purpose of awarding options as compensation is to increase the executive's incentive to make decisions that increase the value of the firm's stock, as their compensation from options is tied to the stock price.

14-7a Limitations of Option Compensation

Many option compensation programs do not account for general market conditions. Thus executives who owned stock options when general stock market conditions were more favorable may have earned high compensation because their firms' stock prices increased substantially during that period, even for firms that performed poorly relative to others in the same industry. Because compensation from holding options is driven more by general stock market conditions than by the firm's relative performance, stock options are not always effective at aligning executives' incentives with actual firm performance.

Another concern with using options as compensation is that executives with substantial options may be tempted to manipulate the stock's price upward in the short term, even though doing so adversely affects the stock price in the long term. For example, they might use accounting methods that defer the reporting of some expenses until next year and accelerate the reporting of some revenue. In this way, short-term earnings will appear favorable but earnings in the following period will be reduced. When these executives believe that the stock price has peaked in the short term, they can exercise their options by selling their shares in the secondary market. Firms can prevent the wrongful use of options by requiring that executives hold them for several years before exercising them.

Until 2006, firms did not have to report their options as an expense but could claim them as a tax deduction. If Enron Corporation had reported its option compensation as expenses on its income statements over the five-year period preceding its 2001 bankruptcy, its net income would have been reduced by $600 million. Because options did not have to be reported as an expense on the income statements, some firms were overly generous in awarding options. Global Crossing's CEO earned $730 million from options before the firm filed for bankruptcy. Largely as a result of options, U.S. CEO compensation is more than 500 times the average compensation of a firm's employees.

Backdating Options   In the late 1990s and early 2000s, some firms allowed their CEOs to backdate options they had already been granted to an earlier period when the stock price was lower. This enabled the CEOs to use a lower exercise price on their call options, generating larger gains for them when they exercised their options. Thus option compensation to some CEOs was mostly influenced by the backdating process and not by how well the stock performed. When the practice of backdating options was publicized in 2006, firms that allowed backdating terminated the practice.

GLOBAL ASPECTS

14-8 GLOBALIZATION OF OPTIONS MARKETS

The globalization of stock markets has resulted in the need for a globalized market in stock options. Options on stock indexes representing various countries are now available. Options exchanges have been established in numerous countries, including Australia, Austria, Belgium, France, Germany, and Singapore. U.S. portfolio managers who maintain large holdings of stocks from specific countries are heavily exposed to the conditions of those markets. Rather than liquidate the portfolio of foreign stocks to protect against a possible temporary decline, the managers can purchase put options on the foreign stock index of concern. Portfolio managers residing in these countries can also use this strategy to hedge their stock portfolios.

Portfolio managers desiring to capitalize on the expectation of temporary favorable movements in foreign markets can purchase call options on the corresponding stock indexes. Thus the existence of options on foreign stock indexes allows portfolio managers to hedge or speculate based on forecasts of foreign market conditions. The trading of options on foreign stock indexes avoids the transaction costs associated with buying and selling large portfolios of foreign stocks.

14-8a Currency Options Contracts

A **currency call option** provides the right to purchase a specified currency for a specified price within a specified period of time. Corporations involved in international business transactions use currency call options to hedge future payables. If the exchange rate at the time payables are due exceeds the exercise price, corporations can exercise their options and purchase the currency at the exercise price. If the prevailing exchange rate is lower than the exercise price, corporations can purchase the currency at the prevailing exchange rate and let the options expire.

Speculators purchase call options on currencies that they expect to strengthen against the dollar. If the foreign currency strengthens as expected, they can exercise their call options to purchase the currency at the exercise price and then sell the currency at the prevailing exchange rate.

A **currency put option** provides the right to sell a specified currency for a specified price within a specified period of time. Corporations involved in international business transactions may purchase put options to hedge future receivables. If the exchange rate at the time they receive payment in a foreign currency is less than the strike price, they can exercise their option by selling the currency at that price. But if the prevailing exchange rate is higher than the exercise price, they can sell the currency at the prevailing exchange rate and let the options expire.

Speculators purchase put options on currencies they expect to weaken against the dollar. If the foreign currency weakens as expected, the speculators can purchase the currency at the prevailing spot rate and exercise their put options to sell the currency at the exercise price.

For every buyer of a currency call or put option, there must be a seller (or writer). A writer of a call option is obligated to sell the specified currency at the specified strike price if the option is exercised. A writer of a put option is obligated to purchase the specified currency at the specified strike price if the option is exercised. Speculators are inclined to write call options on foreign currencies that they expect to weaken against the dollar or to write put options on those they expect to strengthen against the dollar. If a currency option expires without being exercised, the writer earns the up-front premium received.

SUMMARY

- Stock options are traded on exchanges, just as many stocks are. Orders submitted by a brokerage firm are transmitted to a trading floor, where floor brokers execute the trades. Many trades are executed electronically.
- The premium of a call option is influenced by the characteristics of the option and of the underlying stock that can affect the potential gains. In particular, the premium is higher when the market price of the stock is high relative to the exercise price, when the stock's volatility is greater, and when the term until expiration is longer. For put options, the higher the market price of the stock relative to the exercise price, the lower the premium. The volatility of the underlying stock and the term to expiration are related to the put option premium in the same manner as they are to the call option premium.
- Speculators purchase call options on stocks whose prices are expected to rise and purchase put options on those expected to decrease.
- Financial institutions can hedge against adverse movements in a stock by selling call options on that stock. Alternatively, they can purchase put options on that stock.

- Financial institutions commonly hedge their stock portfolios by purchasing put options on stock indexes. They may also use stock index options as a tool for dynamic asset allocation, increasing their exposure when they have optimistic views about the stock market and reducing their exposure (buying put options on stock indexes) when they have pessimistic views.
- Speculators purchase call options on interest rate futures contracts when they expect interest rates to decrease. Financial institutions with large holdings of long-term debt securities hedge against interest rate risk by purchasing put options on interest rate futures. Index options can be used to speculate on movements in stock indexes and require only a small investment. Put options on stock indexes can be purchased to hedge a stock portfolio whose movements are similar to that of the stock index. Options on stock index futures can be used to speculate on movements in the value of the stock index futures contract. Put options on stock index futures can be purchased to hedge portfolios of stocks that move in tandem with the stock index.

POINT COUNTER-POINT

If You Were a Major Shareholder of a Publicly Traded Firm, Would You Prefer That Stock Options Be Traded on That Stock?

Point   No. Options can be used by investors to speculate, and excessive trading of the options may push the stock price away from its fundamental price.

Counter-Point   Yes. Options can be used by investors to temporarily hedge against adverse move-

ments in the stock, so they may reduce the selling pressure on the stock in some periods.

Who Is Correct?   Use the Internet to learn more about this issue and then formulate your own opinion.

QUESTIONS AND APPLICATIONS

1.   Options versus Futures Describe the general differences between a call option and a futures contract.

2.   Speculating with Call Options How are call options used by speculators? Describe the conditions under which their strategy would backfire. What is the maximum loss that could occur for a purchaser of a call option?

3.   Speculating with Put Options How are put options used by speculators? Describe the conditions under which their strategy would backfire. What is the maximum loss that could occur for a purchaser of a put option?

4.   Selling Options Under what conditions would speculators sell a call option? What is the risk to speculators who sell put options?

5.   Factors Affecting Call Option Premiums Identify the factors affecting the premium paid on a call option. Describe how each factor affects the size of the premium.

6.   Factors Affecting Put Option Premiums Identify the factors affecting the premium paid on a put option. Describe how each factor affects the size of the premium.

7.   Leverage of Options How can financial institutions with stock portfolios use stock options when they expect stock prices to rise substantially but do not yet have sufficient funds to purchase more stock?

8.   Hedging with Put Options Why would a financial institution holding the stock of Hinton Co. consider buying a put option on that stock rather than simply selling it?

9.   Call Options on Futures Describe a call option on interest rate futures. How does it differ from purchasing a futures contract?

10. Put Options on Futures Describe a put option on interest rate futures. How does it differ from selling a futures contract?

Advanced Questions

11. Hedging Interest Rate Risk Assume a savings institution has a large amount of fixed-rate mortgages and obtains most of its funds from short-term deposits. How could it use options on financial futures to hedge its exposure to interest rate movements? Would futures or options on futures be more appropriate if the institution is concerned that interest rates will decline, causing a large number of mortgage prepayments?

12. Hedging Effectiveness Three savings and loan institutions (S&Ls) have identical balance sheet compositions: a high concentration of short-term deposits that are used to provide long-term, fixed-rate mortgages. The S&Ls took the following positions one year ago.

NAME OF S&L	POSITION
LaCrosse	Sold financial futures
Stevens Point	Purchased put options on interest rate futures
Whitewater	Did not take any position in futures

Assume that interest rates declined consistently over the last year. Which of the three S&Ls would have achieved the best performance based on this information? Explain.

13. Change in Stock Option Premiums Explain how and why the option premiums may change in response to a surprise announcement that the Fed will increase interest rates, even if stock prices are not affected.

14. Speculating with Stock Options The price of Garner stock is $40. There is a call option on Garner stock that is at the money with a premium of $2.00. There is a put option on Garner stock that is at the money with a premium of $1.80. Why would investors consider writing this call option and this put option? Why would some investors consider buying this call option and this put option?

15. How Stock Index Option Prices May Respond to Prevailing Conditions Consider the prevailing conditions that could affect the demand for stocks, including inflation, the economy, the budget deficit, the Fed's monetary policy, political conditions, and the general mood of investors. Based on these conditions, would you consider purchasing stock index options at this time? Offer some logic to support your answer. Which factor do you think will have the biggest impact on stock index option prices?

16. Backdating Stock Options Explain what backdating stock options entails. Is backdating consistent with rewarding executives who help to maximize shareholder wealth?

17. CBOE Volatility Index How would you interpret a large increase in the CBOE volatility index (VIX)? Explain why the VIX increased substantially during the credit crisis.

Interpreting Financial News

Interpret the following comments made by Wall Street analysts and portfolio managers.

a. "Our firm took a hit because we wrote put options on stocks just before the stock market crash."

b. "Before hedging our stock portfolio with options on index futures, we search for the index that is most appropriate."

c. "We prefer to use covered call writing to hedge our stock portfolios."

Managing in Financial Markets

Hedging with Stock Options As a stock portfolio manager, you have investments in many U.S. stocks and plan to hold these stocks over a long-term period. However, you are concerned that the stock market may experience a temporary decline over the next three months and that your stock portfolio will probably decline by about the same degree as the market. You are aware that options on S&P 500 index futures are available. The following options on S&P 500 index futures are available and have an expiration date about three months from now:

STRIKE PRICE	CALL PREMIUM	PUT PREMIUM
1372	40	24
1428	24	40

The options on S&P 500 index futures are priced at $250 times the quoted premium. Currently, the S&P 500 index level is 1400. The strike price of 1372 represents a 2 percent decline from the prevailing index level, and the strike price of 1428 represents an increase of 2 percent above the prevailing index level.

a. Assume that you want to take an options position to hedge your entire portfolio, which is currently valued at about $700,000. How many index option contracts should you take a position in to hedge your entire portfolio?

b. Assume that you want to create a hedge so that your portfolio will lose no more than 2 percent from its present value. How can you take a position in options on index futures to achieve this goal? What is the cost to you as a result of creating this hedge?

c. Given your expectations of a weak stock market over the next three months, how can you generate some fees from the sale of options on S&P 500 index futures to help cover the cost of purchasing options?

PROBLEMS

1. Writing Call Options A call option on Illinois stock specifies an exercise price of $38. Today, the stock's price is $40. The premium on the call option is $5. Assume the option will not be exercised until maturity, if at all. Complete the following table:

ASSUMED STOCK PRICE AT THE TIME THE CALL OPTION IS ABOUT TO EXPIRE	NET PROFIT OR LOSS PER SHARE TO BE EARNED BY THE WRITER (SELLER) OF THE CALL OPTION
$37	
39	
41	
43	
45	
48	

2. Purchasing Call Options A call option on Michigan stock specifies an exercise price of $55. Today, the stock's price is $54 per share. The premium on the call option is $3. Assume the option will not be exercised until maturity, if at all. Complete the following table for a speculator who purchases the call option:

ASSUMED STOCK PRICE AT THE TIME THE CALL OPTION IS ABOUT TO EXPIRE	NET PROFIT OR LOSS PER SHARE TO BE EARNED BY THE SPECULATOR
$50	
52	
54	
56	
58	
60	
62	

3. Purchasing Put Options A put option on Iowa stock specifies an exercise price of $71. Today, the stock's price is $68. The premium on the put option is

$8. Assume the option will not be exercised until maturity, if at all. Complete the following table for a speculator who purchases the put option (and currently does not own the stock):

ASSUMED STOCK PRICE AT THE TIME THE PUT OPTION IS ABOUT TO EXPIRE	NET PROFIT OR LOSS PER SHARE TO BE EARNED BY THE SPECULATOR
$60	
64	
68	
70	
72	
74	
76	

4. Writing Put Options A put option on Indiana stock specifies an exercise price of $23. Today, the stock's price is $24. The premium on the put option is $3. Assume the option will not be exercised until maturity, if at all. Complete the following table:

ASSUMED STOCK PRICE AT THE TIME THE PUT OPTION IS ABOUT TO EXPIRE	NET PROFIT OR LOSS PER SHARE TO BE EARNED BY THE WRITER (OR SELLER) OF THE PUT OPTION
$20	
21	
22	
23	
24	
25	
26	

5. Covered Call Strategy

a. Evanston Insurance, Inc., has purchased shares of Stock E at $50 per share. It will sell the stock in six months. It considers using a strategy of covered call writing to partially hedge its position in this stock. The exercise price is $53, the expiration date is six months, and the premium on the call option is $2. Complete the following table:

POSSIBLE PRICE OF STOCK E IN SIX MONTHS	PROFIT OR LOSS PER SHARE IF A COVERED CALL STRATEGY IS USED	PROFIT OR LOSS PER SHARE IF A COVERED CALL STRATEGY IS NOT USED
$47		
50		
52		
55		
57		
60		

b. Assume that each of the six stock prices in the table's first column has an equal probability of occurring. Compare the probability distribution of the profits (or losses) per share when using covered call writing versus not using it. Would you recommend covered call writing in this situation? Explain.

6. Put Options on Futures Purdue Savings and Loan Association purchased a put option on Treasury bond futures with a September delivery date and an exercise price of 91–16. The put option has a premium of 1–32. Assume that the price of the Treasury bond futures decreases to 88–16. Should Purdue exercise the option or let it expire? What is Purdue's net gain or loss after accounting for the premium paid on the option?

7. Call Options on Futures Wisconsin, Inc., purchased a call option on Treasury bond futures at a premium of 2–00. The exercise price is 92–08. If the price of the Treasury bond futures rises to 93–08, should Wisconsin exercise the call option or let it expire? What is Wisconsin's net gain or loss after accounting for the premium paid on the option?

8. Call Options on Futures DePaul Insurance Company purchased a call option on an S&P 500 futures contract. The option premium is quoted as $6. The exercise price is 1430. Assume the index on the futures contract becomes 1440. Should DePaul exercise the call option or let it expire? What is the net gain or loss to DePaul after accounting for the premium paid for the option?

9. Covered Call Strategy Coral, Inc., has purchased shares of Stock M at $28 per share. Coral will sell the stock in six months. It considers using a strategy of covered call writing to partially hedge its position in this stock. The exercise price is $32, the expiration date is six months, and the premium on the call option is $2.50. Complete the following table:

POSSIBLE PRICE OF STOCK M IN SIX MONTHS	PROFIT OR LOSS PER SHARE IF COVERED CALL STRATEGY IS USED
$25	
28	
33	
36	

10. Hedging with Bond Futures Smart Savings Bank desired to hedge its interest rate risk. It considered two possibilities: (1) sell Treasury bond futures at a price of 94–00, or (2) purchase a put option on Treasury bond futures. At the time, the price of Treasury bond futures was 95–00. The face value of Treasury bond futures was $100,000. The put option premium was 2–00, and the exercise price was 94–00. Just before the option expired, the Treasury bond futures price was 91–00, and Smart Savings Bank would have exercised the put option at that time, if at all. This is also the time when it would have offset its futures position, if it had sold futures. Determine the net gain to Smart Savings Bank if it had sold Treasury bond futures versus if it had purchased a put option on Treasury bond futures. Which alternative would have been more favorable, based on the situation that occurred?

FLOW OF FUNDS EXERCISE

Hedging with Options Contracts

Carson Company would like to acquire Vinnet, Inc., a publicly traded firm in the same industry. Vinnet's stock price is currently much lower than the prices of other firms in the industry because it is inefficiently managed. Carson believes that it could restructure Vinnet's operations and improve its performance. It is about to contact Vinnet to determine whether Vinnet will agree to an acquisition. Carson is somewhat concerned that investors may learn of its plans and buy Vinnet stock in anticipation that Carson will need to pay a high premium (perhaps a 30 percent premium above the prevailing stock price) in order to complete the acquisition. Carson decides to call a bank about its

risk, as the bank has a brokerage subsidiary that can help it hedge with stock options.

a. How can Carson use stock options to reduce its exposure to this risk? Are there any limitations to this strategy, given that Carson will ultimately have to buy most or all of the Vinnet stock?

b. Describe the maximum possible loss that may be directly incurred by Carson as a result of engaging in this strategy.

c. Explain the results of the strategy you offered in the previous question if Vinnet plans to avoid the acquisition attempt by Carson.

INTERNET/EXCEL EXERCISES

1. Go to www.cboe.com and, under "Quotes & Data," select "Delayed Quotes Classic." Insert the ticker symbol for a stock option in which you are interested. Assess the results. Did the premium ("Net") on the call options increase or decrease today? Did the premium on the put options increase or decrease today?

2. Based on the changes in the premium, do you think the underlying stock price increased or decreased? Explain.

ONLINE ARTICLES WITH REAL-WORLD EXAMPLES

Find a recent practical article available online that describes a real-world example regarding a specific financial institution or financial market that reinforces one or more concepts covered in this chapter.

If your class has an online component, your professor may ask you to post your summary of the article there and provide a link to the article so that other students can access it. If your class is live, your professor may ask you to summarize your application of the article in class. Your professor may assign specific students to complete this assignment or may allow any students to do the assignment on a volunteer basis.

For recent online articles and real-world examples related to this chapter, consider using the following search terms (be sure to include the prevailing year as

a search term to ensure that the online articles are recent):

1. stock options AND profits
2. stock options AND losses
3. stock options AND speculators
4. stock options AND hedge
5. stock option premium AND volatility
6. stock option AND ETFs
7. stock index option
8. LEAPs AND speculate
9. selling stock options AND cover
10. stock options AND compensation

Option Valuation

THE BINOMIAL PRICING MODEL

The binomial option-pricing model was originally developed by William F. Sharpe. An advantage of the model is that it can be used to price both European-style and American-style options with or without dividends. European options are put or call options that can be exercised only at maturity; American options can be exercised at any time prior to maturity.

Assumptions of the Binomial Pricing Model

The following are the main assumptions of the binomial pricing model:

1. The continuous random walk underlying the Black-Scholes model can be modeled by a discrete random walk with the following properties:

   ■ The asset price changes only at discrete (noninfinitesimal) time steps.
   ■ At each time step, the asset price may move either up or down; thus there are only two returns, and these two returns are the same for all time steps.
   ■ The probabilities of moving up and down are known.

2. The world is risk-neutral. This allows the assumption that investors' risk preferences are irrelevant and that investors are risk-neutral. Furthermore, the return from the underlying asset is the risk-free interest rate.

Using the Binomial Pricing Model to Price Call Options

The following is an example of how the binomial pricing model can be employed to price a call option (i.e., to determine a call option premium). To use the model, we need information for three securities: the underlying stock, a risk-free security, and the stock option.

Assume that the price of Gem Corporation stock today is $100. Furthermore, it is estimated that Gem stock will be selling for either $150 or $70 in one year. That is, the stock is expected either to rise by 50 percent or to fall by 30 percent. Also assume that the annual risk-free interest rate on a one-year Treasury bill is 10 percent, compounded continuously. Assume that a T-bill currently sells for $100. Since interest is continuously compounded, the T-bill will pay interest of $100 \times (e^{10} - 1)$, or $10.52.

Currently, a call option on Gem stock is available with an exercise price of $100 and an expiration date one year from now. Since the call option is an option to buy Gem stock, the option will have a value of $50 if the stock price is $150 in one year. If the stock price in one year is $70, the call option will have a value of $0. Our objective is to value this call option using the binomial pricing model.

The first step in applying the model to this call option is to recognize that three investments are involved: the stock, a risk-free security, and the call option. Using the information already given, we have the following payoff matrix in one year:

SECURITY	PRICE IF STOCK IS WORTH $150 IN ONE YEAR	PRICE IF STOCK IS WORTH $70 IN ONE YEAR	CURRENT PRICE
Gem stock	$150.00	$70.00	$100.00
Treasury bill	110.52	110.52	100.00
Call option	50.00	0.00	?

The objective of the binomial pricing model is to determine the current price of the call option. The key to understanding the valuation of the call option using the binomial pricing model is that the option's value must be based on a combination of the value of the stock and the T-bill. If this were not the case, arbitrage opportunities would result. Consequently, in either the up or the down state, the payoff of a portfolio consisting of N_s shares of Gem stock and N_b T-bills must be equal to the value of the call option in that state. Using the payoff matrix just given, we derive the following system of two equations:

$$150N_s + 110.52N_b = 50$$
$$70N_s + 110.52N_b = 0$$

Since we are dealing with two linear equations with two unknowns, we can easily solve for the two variables by substitution. Doing so gives the following values for the number of shares and the number of T-bills in the investor's so-called replicating portfolio:

$$N_s = 0.625$$
$$N_b = -0.3959$$

In other words, the payoffs of the call option on Gem stock can be replicated by borrowing $39.59 at the risk-free rate and buying 0.625 shares of Gem stock for $62.50 (since one share currently sells for $100). Since the payoff of this replicating portfolio is the same as that for the call, the cost to the investor must be the value of the call. In this case, since $39.59 of the outlay of $62.50 is financed by borrowing, the outlay to the investor is $62.50 − $39.59 = $22.91. Thus the call option premium must be $22.91.

In equation form, the value of the call option (V_c) can therefore be written as

$$V_c = N_s P_s + N_b P_b$$

Computation of the N_s can be simplified somewhat. More specifically,

$$N_s = h = \frac{P_{ou} - P_{od}}{P_{su} - P_{sd}}$$

where

$$P_{ou} = \text{value of the option in the up state}$$
$$P_{od} = \text{value of the option in the down state}$$
$$P_{su} = \text{price of Gem stock in the up state}$$
$$P_{sd} = \text{price of Gem stock in the down state}$$

This is also referred to as the *hedge ratio (h).*

In this example, the amount borrowed (BOR) is equal to the product of the number of risk-free securities in the replicating portfolio and the price of the risk-free security:

$$N_b P_b = \text{BOR} = PV(h P_{sd} - P_{od})$$

where

$$PV = \text{present value of a continuously compounded sum}$$
$$h = \text{hedge ratio}$$

Thus the value of the call option can be expressed more simply as

$$V_c = h P_s + \text{BOR}$$

To illustrate why the relationships discussed so far should hold, we assume for the moment that a call option on Gem stock is selling for a premium of $25 (i.e., the call option is overpriced). In this case, investors are presented with an arbitrage opportunity to make an instantaneous, riskless profit. In particular, investors could write a call, buy the stock, and borrow at the risk-free rate. Now assume that the call option on Gem stock is selling for a premium of only $20 (i.e., the call option is underpriced). Using arbitrage, investors would buy a call, sell the stock short, and invest at the risk-free rate.

Using the Binomial Pricing Model to Price Put Options

Continuing with the example of Gem Corporation, the only item that changes in the payoff matrix when the option is a put option (i.e., an option to sell Gem stock) is the value of the option at expiration in the up and down states. If Gem stock is worth $150 in one year, the put option will be worthless; if Gem stock is worth only $70 in one year, the put option will be worth $30. Since the value of the risk-free security is contingent only on the T-bill interest rate, it will be unaffected by the fact that we are now dealing with a put option.

The hedge ratio and the amount borrowed can be easily determined using the formulas introduced previously. The hedge ratio is

$$h = \frac{0 - 30}{150 - 70} = -0.375$$

The amount borrowed is

$$\text{BOR} = PV[-0.375(70) - 30] = \frac{-56.25}{e^{RT}} = -50.90$$

Therefore, to replicate the put option, the investor would sell short 0.375 Gem shares and lend $50.90 at the risk-free rate. Thus the net amount the investor must put up is $50.90 − $37.50 = $13.40. Accordingly, this is the fair value of the put.

Put-Call Parity

With some mathematical manipulation, the following relationship can be derived between the prices of puts and calls (that have the same exercise price and time to expiration):

$$P_p = P_c + \frac{E}{e^{RT}} - P_s$$

where

P_p = price of a put option
P_c = price of a call option
E = exercise price of the option
e^{RT} = present value operator for a continuously compounded sum, discounted at interest rate R for T years
P_s = price of the stock

Using the example of Gem Corporation,

$$P_p = \$22.91 + \frac{\$100}{e^{0.10}} - \$100 = \$13.39$$

THE BLACK-SCHOLES OPTION-PRICING MODEL FOR CALL OPTIONS

In 1973, Black and Scholes devised an option-pricing model that motivated further research on option valuation that continues to this day.

Assumptions of the Black-Scholes Option-Pricing Model

The following are some of the key assumptions underlying the Black-Scholes option-pricing model:

1. The risk-free rate is known and constant over the life of the option.

2. The probability distribution of stock prices is lognormal.

3. The variability of a stock's return is constant.

4. The option is to be exercised only at maturity, if at all.

5. There are no transaction costs involved in trading options.

6. Tax rates are similar for all participants who trade options.

7. The stock of concern does not pay cash dividends.

The Black-Scholes Partial Differential Equation

The Black-Scholes option-pricing model was one of the first to introduce the concept *of a riskless hedge*. Assume that an amount π is invested in a risk-free asset. Thus the investor would earn a return of $r\pi dt$ over a time interval dt. If an appropriately selected portfolio—with a current value of π consisting of a company's stock and an offsetting position in an option on that stock—returns more than $r\pi dt$ over a time interval dt, an investor could conduct arbitrage by borrowing at the risk-free rate and investing in the portfolio. Conversely, if the portfolio returns less than $r\pi dt$, the investor would short the portfolio and invest in the risk-free asset. In either case, the arbitrageur would make a riskless, no-cost, instantaneous profit. Thus the return on the portfolio and on the risk-less asset must be roughly equal.

Using this argument, Black and Scholes developed what has become known as the *Black-Scholes partial differential equation:*

$$\frac{\partial V}{\partial t} + \frac{1}{2}\sigma^2 S^2 \frac{\partial^2 V}{\partial S^2} + rS\frac{\partial V}{\partial S} - rV = 0$$

where

V = value of an option
S = price of the underlying stock
r = risk-free rate of return
t = a measure of time
σ^2 = variance of the underlying stock's price
∂ and ∂^2 = first- and second-order partial derivatives

The Black-Scholes Option-Pricing Model for European Call Options

In order to price an option, the partial differential equation must be solved for V, the value of the option. Assuming that the risk-free interest rate and stock price volatility are constant, solving the Black-Scholes partial differential equation results in the Black-Scholes formula for European call options:

$$V = SN(d_1) - Ee^{-rT}N(d_2)$$

where

V = value of the call option
S = stock price
$N(\cdot)$ = cumulative distribution function for a standardized normal random variable
E = exercise price of the call option
e = base e antilog or 2.7183
r = risk-free rate of return for one year assuming continuous compounding
T = time remaining to maturity of the call option, expressed as a fraction of a year

The terms $N(d_1)$ and $N(d_2)$ deserve further elaboration. The term N represents a cumulative probability for a unit normal variable, where

$$d_1 = \frac{\ln(S/E) + \left(r + \frac{1}{2}\sigma^2\right)(T)}{\sigma\sqrt{T}}$$

and

$$d_2 = \frac{\ln(S/E) + \left(r - \frac{1}{2}\sigma^2\right)(T)}{\sigma\sqrt{T}}$$

$$= d_1 - \sigma\sqrt{T}$$

Here $\ln(S/E)$ is the natural logarithm and σ denotes the standard deviation of the continuously compounded rate of return on the underlying stock.

Using the Black-Scholes Option-Pricing Model to Price a European Call Option

To illustrate how the Black-Scholes equation can be used to price a call option, assume you observe a call option on MPB Corporation stock expiring in six months with an exercise price of $70. Thus $T = 0.50$ and $E = \$70$. Furthermore, the current price of MPB stock is $72 and the stock has a standard deviation of 0.10. The annual risk-free rate is 7 percent. Solving for d_1 and d_2, we obtain

$$d_1 = \frac{\ln(72/70) + [0.07 + 0.5(0.10)^2](0.5)}{0.10\sqrt{0.5}} = 0.9287$$

$$d_2 = 0.9287 - 0.10\sqrt{0.50} = 0.8580$$

A table that identifies the area under the standard normal distribution function (see Exhibit 14A.1) can now be used to determine the cumulative probability. Because d_1 is 0.9287, the cumulative probability from zero to 0.9287 is about 0.3235 (from Exhibit 14A.1, using linear interpolation). Because the cumulative probability for a unit normal variable from negative infinity to zero is 0.50, the cumulative probability from negative infinity to 0.9287 is $0.50 + 0.3235 = 0.8235$. For d_2, the cumulative probability from zero to 0.8580 is 0.3045. Therefore, the cumulative probability from negative infinity to 0.8580 is $0.50 + 0.3042 = 0.8042$.

Now that $N(d_1)$ and $N(d_2)$ have been calculated, the call option value can be estimated as follows:

$$V_c = (\$72 \times 0.8235) - \left(\frac{\$70}{e^{0.07 \times 0.50}} \times 0.8045 \right) = \$4.91$$

Thus a call option on MPB stock should sell for a premium of $4.91.

Put-Call Parity

Using the Black-Scholes option-pricing model, the same relationship exists between the price of a call and that of a put as in the binomial option-pricing model. Thus we have

$$P_p = P_c + \frac{E}{e^{RT}} - P_s$$

Deriving the Implied Volatility

In the example of deriving the value of a call option, an estimate of the stock's standard deviation was used. In some cases, investors want to derive the market's implied volatility rather than a valuation of the call option. The volatility is referred to as "implied" under these circumstances because it is not directly observable in the market. The implied volatility can be derived with some software packages by inputting values for the other variables (prevailing stock price, exercise price, option's time to expiration, and interest rate) in the call option-pricing model and also inputting the market premium of the call option. Instead of deriving a value for the call option premium, the prevailing market premium of the call option is used along with these other variables to derive the implied volatility. The software package will also show how the stock's implied volatility is affected for different values of the call option premium. An increase in the market premium of the call option, when other variables have not changed, reflects an increase in the implied volatility. This relationship can be verified by entering a slightly

Exhibit 14A.1 Institutional Use of Options Markets

d	0.00	0.01	0.02	0.03	0.04	0.05	0.06	0.07	0.08	0.09
0.0	0.0000	0.0040	0.0080	0.0120	0.0160	0.0199	0.0239	0.0279	0.0319	0.0359
0.1	0.0398	0.0438	0.0478	0.0517	0.0557	0.0596	0.0636	0.0675	0.0714	0.0753
0.2	0.0793	0.0832	0.0871	0.0910	0.0948	0.0987	0.1026	0.1064	0.1103	0.1141
0.3	0.1179	0.1217	0.1255	0.1293	0.1331	0.1368	0.1406	0.1443	0.1480	0.1517
0.4	0.1554	0.1591	0.1628	0.1664	0.1700	0.1736	0.1772	0.1808	0.1844	0.1879
0.5	0.1915	0.1950	0.1985	0.2019	0.2054	0.2088	0.2123	0.2157	0.2190	0.2224
0.6	0.2257	0.2291	0.2324	0.2357	0.2389	0.2422	0.2454	0.2486	0.2517	0.2549
0.7	0.2580	0.2611	0.2642	0.2673	0.2704	0.2734	0.2764	0.2794	0.2823	0.2852
0.8	0.2881	0.2910	0.2939	0.2967	0.2995	0.3023	0.3051	0.3078	0.3106	0.3133
0.9	0.3159	0.3186	0.3213	0.3238	0.3264	0.3289	0.3315	0.3340	0.3365	0.3389
1.0	0.3413	0.3438	0.3461	0.3485	0.3508	0.3531	0.3554	0.3577	0.3599	0.3621
1.1	0.3643	0.3665	0.3686	0.3708	0.3729	0.3749	0.3770	0.3790	0.3810	0.3830
1.2	0.3849	0.3869	0.3888	0.3907	0.3925	0.3944	0.3962	0.3980	0.3997	0.4015
1.3	0.4032	0.4049	0.4066	0.4082	0.4099	0.4115	0.4131	0.4147	0.4162	0.4177
1.4	0.4192	0.4207	0.4222	0.4236	0.4251	0.4265	0.4279	0.4292	0.4306	0.4319
1.5	0.4332	0.4345	0.4357	0.4370	0.4382	0.4394	0.4406	0.4418	0.4429	0.4441
1.6	0.4452	0.4463	0.4474	0.4484	0.4495	0.4505	0.4515	0.4525	0.4535	0.4545
1.7	0.4554	0.4564	0.4573	0.4582	0.4591	0.4599	0.4608	0.4616	0.4625	0.4633
1.8	0.4641	0.4649	0.4656	0.4664	0.4671	0.4678	0.4686	0.4693	0.4699	0.4706
1.9	0.4713	0.4719	0.4726	0.4732	0.4738	0.4744	0.4750	0.4756	0.4761	0.4767
2.0	0.4773	0.4778	0.4783	0.4788	0.4793	0.4798	0.4803	0.4808	0.4812	0.4817
2.1	0.4821	0.4826	0.4830	0.4834	0.4838	0.4842	0.4846	0.4850	0.4854	0.4857
2.2	0.4861	0.4866	0.4868	0.4871	0.4875	0.4878	0.4881	0.4884	0.4887	0.4890
2.3	0.4893	0.4896	0.4898	0.4901	0.4904	0.4906	0.4909	0.4911	0.4913	0.4916
2.4	0.4918	0.4920	0.4922	0.4925	0.4927	0.4929	0.4931	0.4932	0.4934	0.4936
2.5	0.4938	0.4940	0.4941	0.4943	0.4945	0.4946	0.4948	0.4949	0.4951	0.4952
2.6	0.4953	0.4955	0.4956	0.4957	0.4959	0.4960	0.4961	0.4962	0.4963	0.4964
2.7	0.4965	0.4966	0.4967	0.4968	0.4969	0.4970	0.4971	0.4972	0.4973	0.4974
2.8	0.4974	0.4975	0.4976	0.4977	0.4977	0.4978	0.4979	0.4979	0.4980	0.4981
2.9	0.4981	0.4982	0.4982	0.4982	0.4984	0.4984	0.4985	0.4985	0.4986	0.4986
3.0	0.4987	0.4987	0.4987	0.4988	0.4988	0.4989	0.4989	0.4989	0.4990	0.4990

higher market premium into the software program and checking how the implied volatility changes in response to that increase. The point is that investors can detect changes in the implied volatility of a stock by monitoring how the stock's call option premium changes over short intervals of time.

American versus European Options

American Call Options

An American call option is an option to purchase stock that can be exercised at any time prior to maturity. However, the original Black-Scholes model was developed to price European call options, which are options to purchase stock that can be exercised only at maturity. Naturally, European puts could be directly derived using the put–call parity relationship. Consequently, the question is whether the Black-Scholes equation can be used to price American call options.

In general, early exercise of a call may be justified only if the asset makes a cash payment such as a dividend on a stock. If there are no dividends during the life of the option, early exercise would be equivalent to buying something earlier than you need it and then giving up the right to decide later whether you really wanted it. However, if it is possible to save a little money in doing so, early purchase/exercise can sometimes be justified. Early exercise is not appropriate every time there is a dividend, but if early exercise is justified then it should occur just before the stock's ex-dividend date. This minimizes the amount of time value given up without sacrificing the dividend. If there are no dividends on the underlying stock, the Black-Scholes model can be used to price American call options. If the underlying stock pays dividends, however, the Black-Scholes model may not be directly applicable. The binomial option-pricing model can be used to price American call options that pay dividends.

American Put Options

Suppose you purchase a European put option. If the value of the underlying asset goes to zero, then the option has reached its maximum value. It allows you to sell a worthless asset for the exercise price. Yet because the option is European, it cannot be exercised prior to maturity. Its value will simply be the present value of the exercise price, and this value will gradually rise as a function of the time value of money until expiration, when the option will be exercised. This is clearly a situation where you would want an American option, so you could exercise it as soon as the asset value goes to zero.

The previous example indicates that there would be a demand for an option that allowed early exercise. It is not necessary, however, for the asset price to go to zero. The European put price must be at least the present value of the exercise price minus the asset price. Clearly, the present value of the exercise price minus the asset price is less than the exercise price minus the asset price, which is the amount that could be claimed if the put could be exercised early. Thus an American put will sell for more than the European put and so the Black-Scholes option-pricing model cannot be used to price an American put option. There is a point where the right to exercise early is at its maximum value, and at that point the American put would be exercised. Finding that point is difficult, but to do so is to unlock the mystery of pricing the American put.

The only surefire way to price the American put correctly is to use a numerical procedure such as the binomial model. The procedure is similar to partitioning a two-dimensional space of time and the asset price into finer points and then solving either a difference or a differential equation at each time point. The process starts at expiration and successively works its way back to the present by using the solution at the preceding step. Thus a closed-form solution does not exist. American puts can be viewed as an infinite series of compound options (that is, an option on an option). At each point in time, the holder of the put has the right to decide whether to exercise it or not. A decision not to exercise the put is tantamount to exercising the compound option and obtaining a position in a new compound option, which can be exercised an instant later. The sequence reiterates until the expiration day. This logic can lead to an intuitive but complex mathematical formula that contains an infinite number of terms. Thus, the holders of American puts face an infinite series of early exercise decisions. Only at an instant before the asset goes ex-dividend do the holders know that they should wait to exercise. This is because they know the asset will fall in value an instant later, so they might as well wait an instant and benefit from the decline in value.

15

Swap Markets

Many firms have inflow and outflow payments that are not equally sensitive to interest rate patterns. Consequently, they are exposed to interest rate risk. Interest rate swap contracts have been established to reduce these risks. In addition, credit default swap contracts have been established to reduce credit risk.

15-1 BACKGROUND

An **interest rate swap** is an arrangement whereby one party exchanges one set of interest payments for another. In the most common arrangement, fixed-rate interest payments are exchanged for floating-rate interest payments over time. The provisions of an interest rate swap include the following:

■ The **notional principal** value to which the interest rates are applied to determine the interest payments involved
■ The fixed interest rate
■ The formula and type of index used to determine the floating rate
■ The frequency of payments, such as every six months or every year
■ The lifetime of the swap

For example, a swap arrangement may involve an exchange of 11 percent fixed-rate payments for floating payments at the prevailing one-year Treasury bill rate plus 1 percent, based on $30 million of notional principal, at the end of each of the next seven years. Other money market rates are sometimes used instead of the T-bill rate to index the interest rate.

Although each participant in the swap agreement owes the other participant at each payment date, the amounts owed are typically netted out so that only the net payment is made. If a firm owes 11 percent of $30 million (the notional principal) but is supposed to receive 10 percent of $30 million on a given payment date, it will send a net payment of 1 percent of the $30 million, or $300,000.

The market for swaps is facilitated by over-the-counter trading rather than trading on an organized exchange. Given the uniqueness of the provisions in each swap arrangement, swaps are less standardized than other derivative instruments such as futures or options. Thus, a telecommunications network is more appropriate than an exchange to work out specific provisions of swaps.

Interest rate swaps became more popular in the early 1980s when corporations were experiencing the effects of large fluctuations in interest rates. Although some manufacturing companies were exposed to interest rate movements, financial institutions were exposed to a greater degree and became the primary users of interest rate swaps. Initially, only those institutions wishing to swap payments on amounts of $10 million or more engaged in interest rate swaps. In recent years, however, swaps have been conducted on smaller amounts as well.

15-1a Use of Swaps for Hedging

Financial institutions such as savings institutions and commercial banks in the United States traditionally had more interest rate–sensitive liabilities than assets and therefore were adversely affected by *increasing* interest rates. Conversely, some financial institutions in other countries (such as some commercial banks in Europe) had access to long-term fixed-rate funding but used funds primarily for floating-rate loans. These institutions were adversely affected by *declining* interest rates.

By engaging in an interest rate swap, both types of financial institutions could reduce their exposure to interest rate risk. Specifically, a U.S. financial institution could send fixed-rate interest payments to a European financial institution in exchange for floating-rate payments. This type of arrangement is illustrated in Exhibit 15.1. In the event of rising interest rates, the U.S. financial institution receives higher interest payments from the floating-rate portion of the swap agreement, which helps to offset the rising cost of obtaining deposits. In the event of declining interest rates, the European financial institution provides lower interest payments in the swap arrangement, which helps to offset the lower interest payments received on its floating-rate loans.

In our example, the U.S. financial institution forgoes the potential benefits from a decline in interest rates while the European financial institution forgoes the potential benefits from an increase in interest rates. The interest rate swap enables each institution to offset any gains or losses that result specifically from interest rate movements. Consequently, as

Exhibit 15.1   Illustration of an Interest Rate Swap

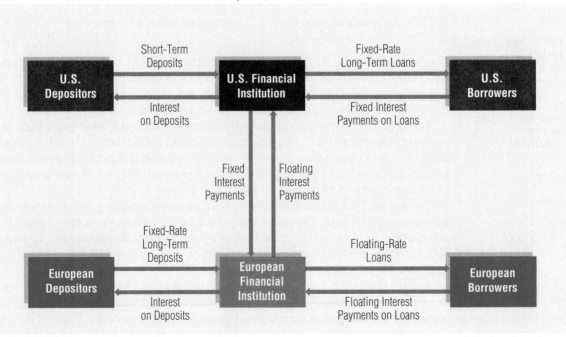

interest rate swaps reduce interest rate risk, they can also reduce potential returns. Most financial institutions that anticipate that interest rates will move in a favorable direction do not hedge their positions. Interest rate swaps are primarily used by financial institutions that would be adversely affected by the expected movement in interest rates.

A primary reason for the popularity of interest rate swaps is the existence of market imperfections. If the parties involved in a swap could easily access funds from various markets without having to pay a premium, they would not need to engage in swaps. Using our previous example, a U.S. financial institution could access long-term funds directly from the European market while the European institution could access short-term funds directly from the U.S. depositors. However, a lack of information about foreign institutions and convenience encourages individual depositors to place deposits locally. Consequently, swaps are necessary for some financial institutions to obtain the maturities or rate sensitivities on funds that they desire.

15-1b Use of Swaps for Speculating

Interest rate swaps are sometimes used by financial institutions and other firms for speculative purposes. For example, a firm may engage in a swap to benefit from its expectations that interest rates will rise even if not all of its operations are exposed to interest rate movements. When the swap is used for speculating rather than for hedging, any loss on the swap positions will not be offset by gains from other operations.

EXAMPLE

Gibson Greetings, Inc., incurred a loss of almost $17 million in 1994 as a result of its positions in interest rate swaps. In the same year, Procter & Gamble incurred a loss of about $157 million as a result of its positions in interest rate swaps. Procter & Gamble then claimed that Bankers Trust (a commercial bank that served as an intermediary and an adviser on interest rate swaps) did not properly advise it about the risk of its swap positions.

Also in 1994, Orange County, California, lost more than $2 billion as a result of its positions in interest rate swaps and other derivative securities. It was positioned to generate large gains if interest rates declined. But instead interest rates increased, and the treasurer of the county took more positions to make up for the resulting losses. He continued to take positions in anticipation that interest rates would decline, but the rates kept on rising throughout 1994. In December 1994, the treasurer resigned and Orange County announced that it would be filing for bankruptcy.

The substantial losses incurred in these cases encouraged firms to more closely monitor the actions of their managers who take derivative positions in order to ensure that those positions are aligned with the firm's goals. ●

15-1c Participation by Financial Institutions

Financial institutions participate in the swap markets in various ways, as summarized in Exhibit 15.2. Financial institutions such as commercial banks, savings institutions, insurance companies, and pension funds that are exposed to interest rate movements commonly engage in swaps to reduce interest rate risk.

A second way to participate in the swap market is by acting as an intermediary. Some commercial banks and securities firms serve in this capacity by matching up firms and facilitating the swap arrangement. Financial institutions that serve as intermediaries for swaps charge fees for their services. They may even provide credit guarantees (for a fee) to each party in the event that the counterparty does not fulfill its obligation. Under these circumstances, the parties engaged in swap agreements assess the creditworthiness of the intermediary that is backing the swap obligations. For this reason, participants in the swap market prefer intermediaries that have a high credit rating.

Exhibit 15.2 Participation of Financial Institutions in Swap Markets

FINANCIAL INSTITUTION	PARTICIPATION IN SWAP MARKETS
Commercial banks	• Engage in swaps to reduce interest rate risk. • Serve as an intermediary by matching up two parties in a swap. • Serve as a dealer by taking the counterparty position to accommodate a party that desires to engage in a swap.
Savings and loan associations and savings banks	• Engage in swaps to reduce interest rate risk.
Finance companies	• Engage in swaps to reduce interest rate risk.
Securities firms	• Serve as an intermediary by matching up two parties in a swap. • Serve as a dealer by taking the counterparty position to accommodate a party that desires to engage in a swap.
Insurance companies	• Engage in swaps to reduce interest rate risk.
Pension funds	• Engage in swaps to reduce interest rate risk.

A third way to participate is by acting as a dealer in swaps. The financial institution takes the counterparty position in order to serve a client. In such a case, the financial institution may be exposing itself to interest rate risk unless it has recently taken the opposite position as a counterparty to another swap agreement.

15-2 TYPES OF INTEREST RATE SWAPS

In response to firms' diverse needs, a variety of interest rate swaps have been created. The following are some of the more commonly used swaps:

- Plain vanilla swaps
- Forward swaps
- Callable swaps
- Putable swaps
- Extendable swaps
- Zero-coupon-for-floating swaps
- Rate-capped swaps
- Equity swaps

Some types of interest rate swaps are more effective than others at offsetting any unfavorable effects of interest rate movements on the U.S. institution. However, those swaps also offset any favorable effects to a greater degree. Other types of interest rate swaps do not provide as effective a hedge but do allow the institution more flexibility to benefit from favorable interest rate movements.

15-2a Plain Vanilla Swaps

In a **plain vanilla swap**, sometimes referred to as a fixed-for-floating swap, fixed-rate payments are periodically exchanged for floating-rate payments. The earlier example of the U.S. and European institutions involved this type of swap.

Consider the exchange of payments under different interest rate scenarios in Exhibit 15.3 when using a plain vanilla swap. Although infinite possible interest rate scenarios exist, only two scenarios are considered: (1) a consistent rise in market interest rates and (2) a consistent decline in market interest rates.

Exhibit 15.3 Illustration of a Plain Vanilla (Fixed-for-Floating) Swap

EXAMPLE

The Bank of Orlando has negotiated a plain vanilla swap in which it will exchange fixed payments of 9 percent for floating payments equal to LIBOR plus 1 percent at the end of each of the next five years. LIBOR is the **London Interbank Offer Rate**, or the interest rate charged on loans between European banks. The LIBOR varies among currencies; for swap examples involving U.S. firms, the LIBOR on U.S. dollars would normally be used. Assume the notional principal is $100 million.

Two scenarios for LIBOR are shown in Exhibit 15.4. The first scenario (in the upper panel of the exhibit) reflects rising U.S. interest rates, which cause LIBOR to increase. The second scenario (in the lower panel) reflects declining U.S. interest rates, which cause LIBOR to decrease. The swap

Exhibit 15.4 Possible Effects of a Plain Vanilla Swap Agreement (Fixed Rate of 9 Percent in Exchange for Floating Rate of LIBOR + 1 Percent)

SCENARIO I	YEAR				
	1	2	3	4	5
LIBOR	7.0%	7.5%	8.5%	9.5%	10.0%
Floating rate received	8.0%	8.5%	9.5%	10.5%	11.0%
Fixed rate paid	9.0%	9.0%	9.0%	9.0%	9.0%
Swap differential	−1.0%	−0.5%	+0.5%	+1.5%	+2.0%
Net dollar amount received based on notional value of $100 million	−$1,000,000	−$500,000	+$500,000	+$1,500,000	+$2,000,000

SCENARIO II	YEAR				
	1	2	3	4	5
LIBOR	6.5%	6.0%	5.0%	4.5%	4.0%
Floating rate received	7.5%	7.0%	6.0%	5.5%	5.0%
Fixed rate paid	9.0%	9.0%	9.0%	9.0%	9.0%
Swap differential	−1.5%	−2.0%	−3.0%	−3.5%	−4.0%
Net dollar amount received based on notional value of $100 million	−$1,500,000	−$2,000,000	−$3,000,000	−$3,500,000	−$4,000,000

differential derived for each scenario represents the floating interest rate received minus the fixed interest rate paid. The net dollar amount to be transferred as a result of the swap is determined by multiplying the swap differential by the notional principal. ●

15-2b Forward Swaps

A **forward swap** involves an exchange of interest payments that does not begin until a specified future time. It is useful for financial institutions or other firms that expect to be exposed to interest rate risk at some time in the future.

EXAMPLE

Detroit Bank is currently insulated against interest rate risk. Three years from now, it plans to increase its proportion of fixed-rate loans (in response to consumer demand for these loans) and reduce its proportion of floating-rate loans. In order to prevent the adverse effects of rising interest rates after these changes go into effect, Detroit Bank may want to engage in interest rate swaps. It can immediately arrange for a forward swap that will begin three years from now. The forward swap allows Detroit Bank to lock in the terms of the arrangement today even though the swap period is delayed (see Exhibit 15.5).

Although Detroit Bank could have waited before arranging for a swap, it may prefer a forward swap to lock in the terms of the swap arrangement at the prevailing interest rates. If it expects interest rates to be higher three years from now than they are today, and waits until then to negotiate a swap arrangement, the fixed interest rate specified in the arrangement will likely be higher. A forward interest rate swap may allow Detroit Bank to negotiate a fixed rate today that is less than the expected fixed rate on a swap negotiated in the future. Because Detroit Bank will be exchanging fixed payments for floating-rate payments, it wants to minimize the fixed rate used for the swap agreement. ●

The fixed rate negotiated on a forward swap will not necessarily be the same as the fixed rate negotiated on a swap that begins immediately. The pricing conditions on any swap are based on expected interest rates over the swap's lifetime.

Like any interest rate swap, forward swaps involve two parties. Our example of a forward swap involves a U.S. institution that expects interest rates to rise and wants to immediately lock in the fixed rate that it will pay when the swap period begins. The party that takes the opposite position in the forward swap will likely be a firm that will be adversely affected by declining interest rates and expects interest rates to decline. This firm would prefer to lock in the prevailing fixed rate because that rate is expected to be higher than the applicable fixed rate when the swap period begins. This institution will

Exhibit 15.5 Illustration of a Forward Swap

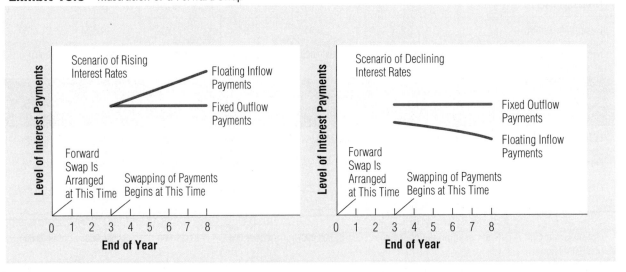

Exhibit 15.6 Illustration of a Callable Swap

Note that the fixed outflow payments in a callable swap are slightly higher than those in a plain vanilla swap because the payer of the fixed outflow payments incurs the cost for the option to terminate the swap before it matures.

be receiving the fixed interest payments, so it wishes to maximize the fixed rate specified in the swap arrangement.

15-2c Callable Swaps

Another use of interest rate swaps is through **swap options** (or **swaptions**). A **callable swap** gives the party making the fixed payments the right to terminate the swap prior to its maturity. It allows the fixed-rate payer to avoid exchanging future interest payments if it desires.

EXAMPLE

Reconsider the U.S. institution that wanted to swap fixed interest payments for floating interest payments to reduce any adverse effects of rising interest rates. If interest rates decline, the interest rate swap arrangement offsets the potential favorable effects on this institution. A callable swap allows the institution to terminate the swap in the event that interest rates decline (see Exhibit 15.6). ●

The disadvantage of a callable swap is that the party given the right to terminate the swap pays a premium that is reflected in a higher fixed interest rate than that party would pay without the call feature. The party may also incur a termination fee in the event that it exercises its right to terminate the swap arrangement.

15-2d Putable Swaps

A **putable swap** gives the party making the floating-rate payments the right to terminate the swap. To illustrate, reconsider the European institution that wanted to exchange floating-rate payments for fixed-rate payments to reduce the adverse effects of declining interest rates. If interest rates rise, the interest rate swap arrangement offsets the potential favorable effects on the financial institution. A putable swap allows the institution to terminate the swap in the event that interest rates rise (see Exhibit 15.7). As with callable swaps, the party given the right to terminate the swap pays a premium. For putable swaps, the premium is reflected in a higher floating rate than would be paid without the put feature. The party may also incur a termination fee in the event that it exercises its right to terminate the swap arrangement.

Exhibit 15.7 Illustration of a Putable Swap

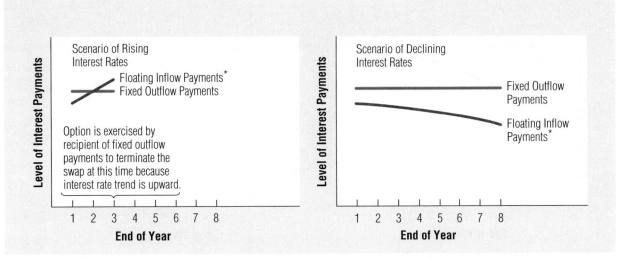

Note that the floating inflow payments in a putable swap are slightly higher than those in a plain vanilla swap because the payer of the floating inflow payments incurs the cost for the option to terminate the swap before it matures.

15-2e Extendable Swaps

An **extendable swap** contains a feature that allows the fixed-for-floating party to extend the swap period.

EXAMPLE Cleveland Bank negotiates a fixed-for-floating swap for eight years. Assume that interest rates increase over this time period as expected. If Cleveland Bank believes interest rates will continue to rise, it may prefer to extend the swap period (see Exhibit 15.8). Although it could create a new swap, the terms would reflect the current economic conditions. A new swap would typically involve an exchange of fixed payments at the prevailing higher interest rate for floating payments.

Exhibit 15.8 Illustration of an Extendable Swap

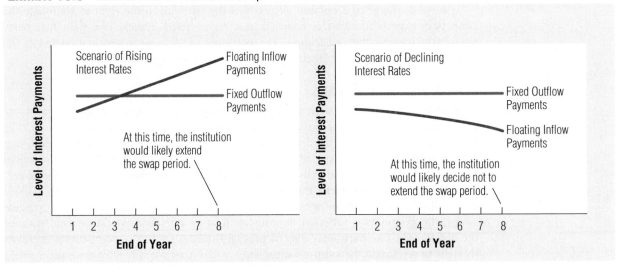

Cleveland Bank would prefer to extend the previous swap agreement that calls for fixed payments at the lower interest rate that existed at the time the swap was created. It has additional flexibility because of the extendable feature. ●

The terms of an extendable swap reflect a price paid for the extendability feature. That is, the interest rates specified in a swap agreement allowing an extension are not as favorable for Cleveland Bank as they would have been without the feature. In addition, if Cleveland Bank does extend the swap period, it may have to pay an extra fee.

15-2f Zero-Coupon-for-Floating Swaps

Another special type of interest rate swap is the **zero-coupon-for-floating swap**. The fixed-rate payer makes a single payment at the maturity date of the swap agreement, and the floating-rate payer makes periodic payments throughout the swap period. For example, consider a financial institution that primarily attracts short-term deposits and currently has large holdings of zero-coupon bonds that it purchased several years ago. At the time it purchased the bonds, it expected interest rates to decline. Now it has become concerned that interest rates will rise over time, which will not only increase its cost of funds but also reduce the market value of the bonds. This financial institution can request a swap period that matches the maturity of its bond holdings. If interest rates rise over the period of concern, the institution will benefit from the swap arrangement, thereby offsetting any adverse effects on the institution's cost of funds. The other party in this type of transaction might be a firm that expects interest rates to decline (see Exhibit 15.9). Such a firm would be willing to provide floating-rate payments based on this expectation because the payments will decline over time even though the single payment to be received at the end of the swap period is fixed.

15-2g Rate-Capped Swaps

A **rate-capped swap** involves the exchange of fixed-rate payments for floating-rate payments that are capped.

Exhibit 15.9   Illustration of a Zero-Coupon-for-Floating Swap

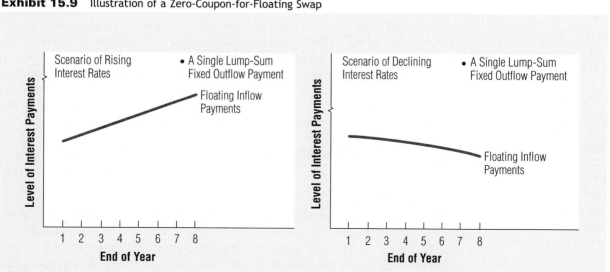

Exhibit 15.10   Illustration of a Rate-Capped Swap Equity Swaps

EXAMPLE

Reconsider the example in which the Bank of Orlando arranges to swap fixed payments for floating payments. The counterparty may want to limit its possible payments by setting a cap or ceiling on the interest rate it must pay. The floating-rate payer pays an up-front fee to the fixed-rate payer for this feature.

In this case, the size of the potential floating payments to be received by the Bank of Orlando would now be limited by the cap, which may reduce the effectiveness of the swap in hedging its interest rate risk. If interest rates rise above the cap, the floating payments received will not move in tandem with the interest the Bank of Orlando will pay depositors for funds (see Exhibit 15.10). Yet the Bank of Orlando might believe that interest rates will not exceed a specified level and would therefore be willing to allow a cap. Moreover, the Bank of Orlando would receive an up-front fee from the counterparty for allowing this cap. ●

An **equity swap** involves the exchange of interest payments for payments linked to the degree of change in a stock index. For example, using an equity swap arrangement, a company could swap a fixed interest rate of 7 percent in exchange for the rate of appreciation on the S&P 500 index each year over a four-year period. If the stock index appreciates by 9 percent over the year, the differential is 2 percent (9 percent received minus 7 percent paid), which will be multiplied by the notional principal to determine the dollar amount received. If the stock index appreciates by less than 7 percent, the company will have to make a net payment. This type of swap arrangement may be appropriate for portfolio managers of insurance companies or pension funds that are managing stocks and bonds. The swap would enhance their investment performance in bullish stock market periods without requiring the managers to change their existing allocation of stocks and bonds.

15-2h Other Types of Swaps

WEB

www.cmegroup.com
Review this website for information on various types of interest rate contracts that are available.

A variety of other swaps are also available, and additional types will be created to accommodate firms' future needs.

Use of Swaps to Accommodate Financing Preferences   Some interest rate swaps are combined with other financial transactions such as the issuance of bonds. Corporate borrowers may be able to borrow at a more attractive interest rate when using floating-rate debt than when using fixed-rate debt. Even so, if they want to make fixed payments on their debt, they can swap fixed-rate payments for floating-rate payments and use the floating-rate payments received to cover their coupon payments. Alternatively, some corporations may prefer to borrow at a floating rate but find it advantageous to borrow at a fixed rate. These corporations can issue fixed-rate bonds and then swap floating-rate payments in exchange for fixed-rate payments.

EXAMPLE

Quality Company is a highly rated firm that prefers to borrow at a variable rate. Risky Company is a low-rated firm that prefers to borrow at a fixed rate. These companies would pay the following rates when issuing either variable-rate or fixed-rate Eurobonds:

	FIXED-RATE BOND	VARIABLE-RATE BOND
Quality Company	9%	LIBOR + ½%
Risky Company	10½%	LIBOR + 1%

Based on the information given, Quality Company has an advantage when issuing either fixed-rate or variable-rate bonds, but its advantage is greater when issuing fixed-rate bonds. Quality Company could issue fixed-rate bonds while Risky Company issues variable-rate bonds. Quality could then provide variable-rate payments to Risky in exchange for fixed-rate payments.

Assume that Quality negotiated with Risky to provide variable-rate payments at LIBOR plus ½ percent in exchange for fixed-rate payments of 9½ percent. This interest rate swap is shown in Exhibit 15.11. Quality Company benefits because its fixed-rate payments received on the swap exceed the payments owed to bondholders by ½ percent. Its variable-rate payments to Risky Company are the same as what it would have paid if it had issued variable-rate bonds. Risky is receiving LIBOR plus ½ percent on the swap, which is ½ percent less than what it must pay on its variable-rate bonds. However, it is making fixed payments of 9½ percent, which is 1 percent less than it would have paid if it had issued fixed-rate bonds. Overall, it saves ½ percent per year on financing costs. ●

Two limitations of the swap just described are worth mentioning. First, the process of searching for a suitable swap candidate and negotiating the swap terms entails a cost in time and resources. Second, each swap participant faces the risk that the counterparty could default on payments. For this reason, financial intermediaries may match up participants and sometimes assume the credit (default) risk involved (for a fee).

Exhibit 15.11 Illustration of an Interest Rate Swap to Reconfigure Bond Payments

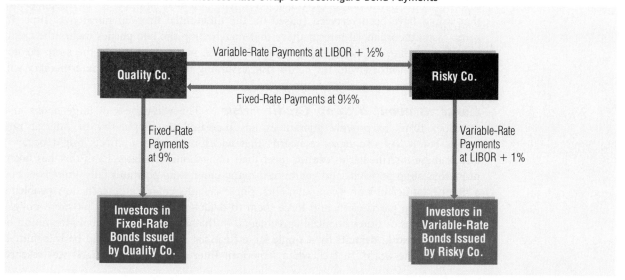

Tax Advantage Swaps   Some swaps have recently been used by firms for tax purposes.

EXAMPLE

Columbus, Inc., has expiring tax loss carry forwards from previous years. To utilize the carryforwards before they expire, it may engage in a swap that calls for receipt of a large up-front payment with somewhat less favorable terms over time. However, Columbus may realize an immediate gain on the swap with possible losses in future years. The tax loss carryforwards from previous years can be applied to offset any taxes on the immediate gain from the swap. Any future losses realized from future payments due to the swap agreement may be used to offset future gains from other operations.

Meanwhile, Ann Arbor Co. expects future losses but will realize large gains from operations in this year. It can take a position opposite to that of Columbus. That is, Ann Arbor will arrange for a swap in which it makes an immediate large payment and receives somewhat favorable terms on future payments. This year the firm will incur a tax loss on the swap, which can be used to offset some of its gains from other operations and thereby reduce its tax liability. ●

15-3 RISKS OF INTEREST RATE SWAPS

Several types of risk must be considered when engaging in interest rate swaps. Three of the more common types of risks are basis risk, credit risk, and sovereign risk.

15-3a Basis Risk

The interest rate of the index used for an interest rate swap will not necessarily move perfectly in tandem with the floating-rate instruments of the parties involved in the swap. For example, the index used on a swap may rise by 0.7 percent over a particular period while the cost of deposits to a U.S. financial institution rises by 1.0 percent over the same period. The net effect is that the higher interest rate payments received from the swap agreement do not fully offset the increase in the cost of funds. This so-called **basis risk** prevents the interest rate swap from completely eliminating the financial institution's exposure to interest rate risk.

15-3b Credit Risk

There is risk that a firm involved in an interest rate swap will not meet its payment obligations. This credit risk is not a deal breaker, however, for the following reasons. As soon as the firm recognizes that it has not received the interest payments it is owed, it will discontinue its payments to the other party. The potential loss is a set of net payments that would have been received (based on the differential in swap rates) over time. In some cases, the financial intermediary that matched up the two parties incurs the credit risk by providing a guarantee (for a fee). If so, the parties engaged in the swap do not need to be concerned with the credit risk, assuming that the financial intermediary will be able to cover any guarantees promised.

Concerns about a Swap Credit Crisis   The willingness of large banks and securities firms to provide guarantees has increased the popularity of interest rate swaps, but it has also raised concerns that widespread adverse effects might occur if any of these intermediaries cannot meet their obligations. If a large bank that has taken numerous swap positions and guaranteed many other swap positions fails, there could be a number of defaults on swap payments. These defaults could cause cash flow problems for other swap participants and force them to default on some of their payment obligations on swaps or other financial agreements. In this way, given the global integration of the swap network, defaults by a single large financial intermediary could be transmitted throughout the world. In fact, when American International Group (AIG) was rescued by the federal government during the credit crisis (as discussed later in this chapter), the potential damage throughout the swap network was cited as a reason for the rescue.

Because of the potential damage that a single shock could cause throughout the swap network, various regulators have considered methods of reducing credit risk in the market. For example, bank regulators have considered forcing banks to maintain more capital if they provide numerous guarantees on swap payments. Other proposals include creating a regulatory agency that would oversee the swap market and minimize credit risk and requiring more complete disclosure of swap positions and guarantees created by financial intermediaries. Given the large growth in swaps, the concerns about credit risk in the market should continue to receive much attention.

15-3c Sovereign Risk

Sovereign risk reflects potential adverse effects resulting from a country's political conditions. Various political conditions could prevent the counterparty from meeting its obligation in the swap agreement. For example, the local government might take over the counterparty and then decide not to meet its payment obligations. Alternatively, the government might impose foreign exchange controls that prohibit the counterparty from making its payments.

Sovereign risk differs from credit risk because it depends on the financial status of the government rather than on the counterparty itself. A counterparty could have very low credit risk but conceivably be perceived as having high sovereign risk because of its government. The counterparty does not have control over some restrictions that may be imposed by its government.

15-4 Pricing Interest Rate Swaps

The setting of specific interest rates for an interest rate swap is referred to as *pricing* the swap. This pricing is influenced by several factors, including prevailing market interest rates, availability of counterparties, and credit and sovereign risk.

15-4a Prevailing Market Interest Rates

The fixed interest rate specified in a swap is influenced by supply and demand conditions for funds having the appropriate maturity. For example, a plain vanilla (fixed-for-floating) interest rate swap structured when interest rates are very high would have a much higher fixed interest rate than one structured when interest rates were low. In general, the interest rates specified in a swap agreement reflect the prevailing interest rates at the time of the agreement.

15-4b Availability of Counterparties

Swap pricing is also determined by the availability of counterparties. When numerous counterparties are available for a particular desired swap, a party may be able to negotiate a more attractive deal. For example, consider a U.S. financial institution that wants a fixed-for-floating swap. If several European institutions are willing to serve as the counterparty, the U.S. institution may be able to negotiate a slightly lower fixed rate.

The availability of counterparties can change in response to economic conditions. For example, in a period when interest rates are expected to rise, many institutions will want a fixed-for-floating swap but few institutions will be willing to serve as the counterparty. The fixed rate specified on interest rate swaps will be higher under these conditions than in a period when many financial institutions expect interest rates to decline.

15-4c Credit and Sovereign Risk

A party involved in an interest rate swap must assess the probability of default by the counterparty. For example, a firm that desires a fixed-for-floating swap will likely require a lower fixed rate applied to its outflow payments if the credit risk or sovereign risk of the counterparty is high. If a well-respected financial intermediary guarantees payments by the counterparty, however, the fixed rate will be higher.

15-5 PERFORMANCE OF INTEREST RATE SWAPS

Exhibit 15.12 shows how the performance of an interest rate swap is influenced by several underlying forces that affect interest rate movements. The impact of the underlying forces on the performance of an interest rate swap depends on the party's swap position. For example, to the extent that strong economic growth can increase interest rates, it will be beneficial for a party that is swapping fixed-rate payments for floating-rate payments but detrimental to a party that is swapping floating-rate payments for fixed-rate payments.

Exhibit 15.12 Framework for Explaining Net Payments Resulting from an Interest Rate Swap

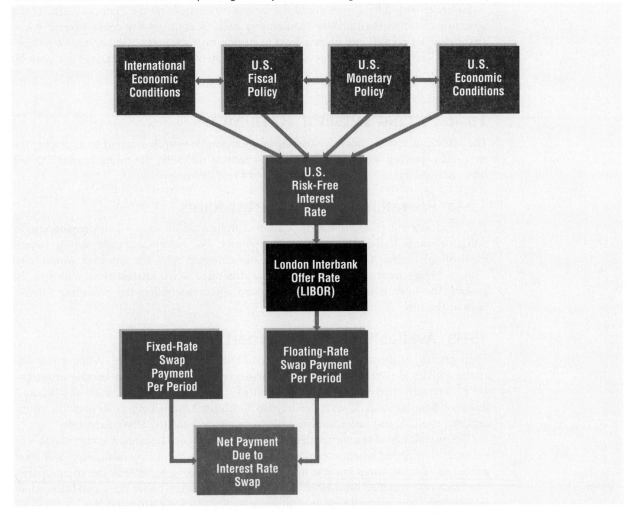

The diagram in Exhibit 15.12 can be adjusted to fit any currency. For an interest rate swap involving an interest rate benchmark denominated in a foreign currency, the economic conditions of that country are the primary forces that determine interest rate movements in that currency and thereby the performance of the interest rate swap.

Because the performance of a particular interest rate swap position is normally influenced by future interest rate movements, participants in the interest rate swap market closely monitor indicators that may affect these movements. Among the more closely watched indicators are indicators of economic growth (employment, gross domestic product), indicators of inflation (consumer price index, producer price index), and indicators of government borrowing (budget deficit, expected volume of funds borrowed at upcoming Treasury bond auctions).

15-6 Interest Rate Caps, Floors, and Collars

In addition to the more traditional forms of interest rate swaps, three other interest rate derivative instruments are commonly used:

- Interest rate caps
- Interest rate floors
- Interest rate collars

These instruments are normally classified separately from interest rate swaps, but they do result in interest payments between participants. Each of these instruments can be used by financial institutions to capitalize on expected interest rate movements or to hedge their interest rate risk.

15-6a Interest Rate Caps

An **interest rate cap** offers payments in periods when a specified interest rate index exceeds a specified ceiling (cap) interest rate. The payments are based on the amount by which the interest rate exceeds the ceiling, multiplied as usual by the notional principal specified in the agreement. A fee is paid upfront to purchase an interest rate cap, and the lifetime of a cap commonly ranges between three and eight years.

The typical purchaser of an interest rate cap is a financial institution that is adversely affected by rising interest rates. If interest rates rise, the payments received from the interest rate cap agreement will help offset any adverse effects.

The seller of an interest rate cap receives the fee paid upfront and is obligated to provide periodic payments when the prevailing interest rates exceed the ceiling rate specified in the agreement. The typical seller of an interest rate cap is a financial institution that expects interest rates to remain stable or to decline.

Large commercial banks and securities firms serve as dealers for interest rate caps in which they act as the counterparty to the transaction. They also serve as brokers, matching up participants that wish to purchase or sell interest rate caps. They may even guarantee (for a fee) the interest payments that are to be paid to the purchaser of the interest rate cap over time.

EXAMPLE

Assume that Buffalo Savings Bank purchases a five-year cap for a fee of 4 percent of notional principal valued at $60 million (so the fee is $2.4 million) with an interest rate ceiling of 10 percent. The agreement specifies LIBOR as the index used to represent the prevailing market interest rate.

Assume that LIBOR moved over the next five years as shown in Exhibit 15.13. Based on these movements in LIBOR, Buffalo Savings Bank received payments in three of the five years. The amount received by Buffalo in any year is based on the percentage points above the 10 percent ceiling multiplied by the notional principal. For example, in Year 1 the payment is zero because LIBOR was below

Exhibit 15.13 Illustration of an Interest Rate Cap

		END OF YEAR:				
	0	1	2	3	4	5
LIBOR		6%	11%	13%	12%	7%
Interest rate ceiling		10%	10%	10%	10%	10%
LIBOR's percent above the ceiling		0%	1%	3%	2%	0%
Payments received (based on $60 million of notional principal)		$0	$600,000	$1,800,000	$1,200,000	$0
Fee paid	$2,400,000					

the ceiling rate. In Year 2, however, LIBOR exceeded the ceiling by 1 percentage point and so Buffalo received a payment of $600,000 (0.01 × $60 million). To the extent that Buffalo's performance is adversely affected by high interest rates, the interest rate cap creates a partial hedge by providing payments to Buffalo that are proportionately related to the interest rate level. The seller of the interest rate cap in this example had the opposite payments of those shown for Buffalo in Exhibit 15.13. ●

Interest rate caps can be devised to meet various risk-return profiles. For example, Buffalo Savings Bank could have purchased an interest rate cap with a ceiling rate of 9 percent to generate payments whenever interest rates exceeded that ceiling. The bank would have had to pay a higher up-front fee for this interest rate cap, however.

15-6b Interest Rate Floors

An **interest rate floor** offers payments in periods when a specified interest rate index falls below a specified floor rate. The payments are based on the amount by which the interest rate falls below the floor rate, which is multiplied by the notional principal specified in the agreement. A fee is paid upfront to purchase an interest rate floor, and the lifetime of the floor commonly ranges between three and eight years. The interest rate floor can be used to hedge against lower interest rates in the same manner that the interest rate cap hedges against higher interest rates. Any financial institution that purchases an interest rate floor will receive payments if interest rates decline below the floor, and these payments will help offset any adverse interest rate effects.

The seller of an interest rate floor receives the fee paid upfront and is obligated to provide periodic payments when the interest rate on a specified money market instrument falls below the floor rate specified in the agreement. The typical seller of an interest rate floor is a financial institution that expects interest rates to remain stable or to rise. Large commercial banks or securities firms serve as dealers and/or brokers of interest rate floors, just as they do for interest rate swaps or caps.

EXAMPLE

Assume that Toland Finance Company purchases a five-year interest rate floor for a fee of 4 percent of notional principal valued at $60 million (so the fee is $2.4 million) with an interest rate floor of 8 percent. The agreement specifies LIBOR as the index used to represent the prevailing interest rate.

Assume that LIBOR moved over the next five years as shown in Exhibit 15.14. Based on these movements in LIBOR, Toland received payments in two of the five years. The dollar amount received by Toland in any year is based on the percentage points below the 8 percent floor multiplied by the notional principal. In Year 1, for example, LIBOR was 2 percentage points below the interest rate floor and so Toland received a payment of $1.2 million (0.02 × $60 million). The seller of the interest rate floor in this example had the opposite payments of those shown for Toland in Exhibit 15.14. ●

Exhibit 15.14 Illustration of an Interest Rate Floor

		END OF YEAR:				
	0	1	2	3	4	5
LIBOR		6%	11%	13%	12%	7%
Interest rate floor		8%	8%	8%	8%	8%
LIBOR's percent below the floor		2%	0%	0%	0%	1%
Payments received (based on $60 million of notional principal)		$1,200,000	$0	$0	$0	$600,000
Fee paid	$2,400,000					

15-6c Interest Rate Collars

An **interest rate collar** involves the purchase of an interest rate cap and the simultaneous sale of an interest rate floor. In its simplest form, the up-front fee received from selling the interest rate floor to one party can be used to pay the fee for purchasing the interest rate cap from another party. Any financial institution that desires to hedge against the possibility of rising interest rates can purchase an interest rate collar. The hedge results from the interest rate cap, which will generate payments to the institution if interest rates rise above the interest rate ceiling.

Because the collar also involves the sale of an interest rate floor, the financial institution is obligated to make payments if interest rates decline below the floor. However, if interest rates rise as expected then the rates will remain above the floor, so the financial institution will not have to make payments.

EXAMPLE

Assume that Pittsburgh Bank's performance is inversely related to interest rates. It anticipates that interest rates will rise over the next several years and decides to hedge its interest rate risk by purchasing a five-year interest rate collar, with LIBOR as the index used to represent the prevailing interest rate. The interest rate cap specifies a fee of 4 percent of notional principal valued at $60 million (so the fee is $2.4 million) with an interest rate ceiling of 10 percent. The interest rate floor specifies a fee of 4 percent of notional principal valued at $60 million and an interest rate floor of 8 percent.

Assume that LIBOR moved over the next five years as shown in Exhibit 15.15. Based on these movements in LIBOR, the payments received from purchasing the interest rate cap and the payments made from selling the interest rate floor are derived separately over each of the five years.

Because the fee received from selling the interest rate floor was equal to the fee paid for the interest rate cap, the initial fees offset. The net payments received by Pittsburgh Bank as a result of purchasing the collar are equal to the payments received from the interest rate cap minus the payments made as a result of the interest rate floor. In the years when interest rates were relatively high, the net payments received by Pittsburgh Bank were positive.

As this example illustrates, when interest rates are high, the collar can generate payments that may offset the adverse effects of the high interest rates on the bank's normal operations. Although the net payments were negative in those years when interest rates were low, the performance of the bank's normal operations should have been strong. Like many other hedging strategies, the interest rate collar reduces the sensitivity of the financial institution's performance to interest rate movements. ●

Exhibit 15.15 Illustration of an Interest Rate Collar (Combined Purchase of Interest Rate Cap and Sale of Interest Rate Floor)

		END OF YEAR:				
	0	1	2	3	4	5
Purchase of interest rate cap:						
LIBOR		6%	11%	13%	12%	7%
Interest rate ceiling		10%	10%	10%	10%	10%
LIBOR's percent above the ceiling		0%	1%	3%	2%	0%
Payments received		$0	$600,000	$1,800,000	$1,200,000	$0
Fee paid	$2,400,000					
Sale of interest rate floor:						
Interest rate floor		8%	8%	8%	8%	8%
LIBOR's percent below the floor		2%	0%	0%	0%	1%
Payments made		$1,200,000	$0	$0	$0	$600,000
Fee received	$2,400,000					
Fee received minus fee paid	$0					
Payments received minus payments made		−$1,200,000	+$600,000	+$1,800,000	+$1,200,000	−$600,000

15-7 CREDIT DEFAULT SWAPS

A **credit default swap** (CDS) is a privately negotiated contract that protects investors against the risk of default on particular debt securities. The main participants in the CDS market are commercial banks, insurance companies, hedge funds, and securities firms. The swap involves two parties that have different needs or expectations about the future performance of particular debt securities. One party is the buyer, who is willing to provide periodic (usually quarterly) payments to the other party, the seller. Thus, the seller receives the payments from the buyer but is obligated to reimburse the buyer if the securities specified in the swap agreement default. In this case, the seller pays the par value of the securities in exchange for the securities. Alternatively, the securities may be auctioned off by the buyer, in which case the seller must pay the buyer of the CDS the difference between the par value of the securities and the price at which those securities were sold.

The buyer of a CDS is protected if the securities specified in the CDS contract default. Financial institutions purchase CDS contracts to protect their own investments in debt securities against default risk. The seller of a CDS expects that the CDS is unlikely to default. If its expectations come true, it will not have to make a payment and therefore benefits from the quarterly payments it receives over the life of the CDS contract.

EXAMPLE

Last year, Inve Co. purchased bonds (issued by Zykmo Co.) with a par value of $30 million. Since then, Inve has become concerned that the bonds it purchased could default over the next five years. Inve Co. therefore purchases a CDS on these bonds. The CDS refers to Zykmo Co. as the reference entity, since that is the company for which credit protection is purchased. The maximum amount to be paid (notional principal) of this CDS is $30 million. A financial institution is willing to sell the CDS contract for these bonds over the five years for a premium of 2 percent of the value per year, or 0.02 × $30 million = $600,000. Inve Co. needs to make a quarterly premium of $150,000 to cover the $600,00 payment over one year. If at any time over the next five years Zykmo Co. files for bankruptcy and the bonds become worthless, Inve would not make any additional payments and the seller of the CDS contract would be obligated to pay Inve Co. $30 million. If, however, the bonds do not default over the next five years (i.e., while the CDS contract exists), Inve Co. would make quarterly payments until maturity. In this case, the seller of the CDS contract is not obligated to pay any funds to Inve Co., and it received $600,000 annually for five years because it was willing to insure the bonds. ●

This example is simplified in that it focuses on insuring against default of one particular type of bond issued by one firm. Many CDS contracts insure against default of mortgage-backed securities that represent bundles of mortgages.

The maturity of a CDS is typically between 1 and 10 years, but the most common maturity is 5 years. The notional value of the securities represented by a CDS contract is typically between $10 million and $20 million. The CDS contracts are traded over the counter and are not backed by an organized exchange.

15-7a Secondary Market for CDS Contracts

There is a secondary market for CDS contracts in which CDS dealers serve as intermediaries. Some of the major dealers that facilitate secondary market transactions include Goldman Sachs, Citigroup, Bank of America, and Morgan Stanley. The secondary market allows financial institutions participating in a CDS contract to pass on their obligations to other willing parties.

When the securities protected by a CDS contract decline in price because of conditions that increase the likelihood of their default, the seller of the CDS must post a higher level of collateral to back its position. This requirement is intended to ensure that the seller of the CDS does not default on its position.

15-7b Collateral on CDS Contracts

The value of a CDS contract is known only by the dealer serving as intermediary between buyer and seller, and transaction prices are not publicized. Without transparency, dealers may not acknowledge that the market price of a specific CDS contract has changed, especially if their position would force them to post more collateral in response to a change in price. Furthermore, if there is not much activity in the secondary market then today's valuation of the CDS may be based on the price of the last transaction for that type of CDS that occurred several weeks ago. If the prevailing valuation is inaccurate, the amount of collateral posted might not be sufficient to cover potential losses to a participant. The lack of transparency in CDS pricing has caused conflicts regarding the levels of collateral to be held and has resulted in lawsuits.

15-7c Payments on a Credit Default Swap

Holding maturity and notional value constant, the payments required on a new CDS are positively related to the default risk. For example, a CDS on $10 million of debt securities that have a relatively low likelihood of default may require an annual payment of 1 percent or $100,000 per year (divided into quarterly payments). A CDS on $10 million of riskier debt securities might require an annual payment of 3 percent, or $300,000 per year. A seller of a CDS requires more compensation to provide protection against default if the likelihood of default is higher.

In periods when economic growth is strong, the payments required on a CDS contract on most securities should be relatively low because the default risk is usually low under these conditions. When economic conditions are weak, the payments required on a CDS contract on most securities should be relatively high because the default risk is high.

15-7d How CDS Contracts Affect Debtor-Creditor Negotiations

When a firm encounters financial problems, its creditors attempt to work with the firm to prevent it from going bankrupt. They may be willing to help the debtor firm avoid bankruptcy by accepting a fraction of what they are owed, since they may receive even less if the firm files for bankruptcy. Yet if the creditors have purchased a CDS contract, they may benefit more if the debtor firm goes bankrupt because then they will receive payment from the seller of the CDS. Thus, creditors who hold CDS contracts have less incentive to help a debtor firm avoid bankruptcy.

15-7e Development of the CDS Market

Credit default swaps were created in the 1990s as a way to protect bond-purchasing investors against default risk. Over time, CDS contracts were adapted to protect investors that purchased mortgage-backed securities. The CDS market grew rapidly and represented $2 trillion of notional principal in 2003, $13 trillion in 2006, and $35 trillion in 2009. (These values count each contract only once, even though there are two parties involved, in order to avoid double-counting.)

One reason for this rapid growth was that many financial institutions that invested in mortgage-backed securities wanted to purchase CDS contracts in order to protect against default. Other financial institutions that believed the mortgage-backed securities were safe served as the counterparties in order to generate periodic income. The CDS market is estimated to be more than five times the size of the mortgage market, more than seven times the market for U.S. Treasury securities, and more than twice the size of the U.S. stock market.

15-7f Impact of the Credit Crisis on the CDS Market

Many financial institutions accumulated large holdings of mortgage-backed securities during the housing boom in the 2003–2005 period. They may have believed that the return was favorable and that the risk was negligible because home prices were rising consistently. As the housing market began to weaken in 2006, they purchased CDS contracts as protection against the default of these mortgage-backed securities.

Using CDS Contracts to Bet on Mortgage Defaults   During the 2003–2006 housing boom, the economy was strong, mortgage companies applied loose standards when granting mortgages, and rating agencies rated mortgage-backed securities (MBS) highly even when they contained subprime mortgages. Some institutional investors were willing to purchase mortgages and MBS because they presumed that households would continue to make their mortgage payments or that home values would remain high enough to provide sufficient collateral to cover against defaults. Housing prices continued to rise during this period, but households were able to obtain home mortgages anyway because of a general perception that home prices would continue to rise. These conditions signaled the likelihood of a housing price bubble that was about to burst.

Some financial institutions that anticipated a major decline in housing prices purchased CDS contracts on MBS even when they had no exposure to MBS. That is, they were not hedging an existing position but instead were simply taking a speculative position based on their expectations that many mortgages would default. The cost of their bet was the periodic premium they paid to sellers of the CDS contracts; their potential benefit was the money that they would be owed if the MBS specified by their CDS contracts defaulted before the contract matured.

EXAMPLE

In 2006, Spec Co. purchased a CDS contract that protected against the default on specific mortgage-backed securities, with a notional principal of $20 million, that stipulated Spec Co. would make quarterly payments of $200,000. Spec Co. was not hedging a position, since it had not invested in any mortgage-backed securities, but rather believed that the specific mortgage-backed security in the CDS contract would default. In 2009, the mortgage-backed security defaulted and so Spec Co. received $20 million from the seller of the CDS. ●

During the credit crisis, many MBS defaulted; this generated large profits for the buyers of CDS contracts and major losses for the sellers. Not all MBS were the same, and some had a much higher probability of failure. Some speculators targeted MBS that contained subprime mortgages because these mortgages were more likely to default. Many of these MBS were rated highly even though they contained subprime mortgages. Speculators could easily find sellers of the CDS contracts they wanted to buy, because many sellers of CDS contracts (wrongly) presumed that any MBS rated highly by the agencies had a low risk of default.

Insufficient Margins on CDS Contracts During the credit crisis, many credit default swaps did not have a sufficient margin backing the agreement. The assets (such as mortgage-backed securities) referenced by these swaps were not standardized and therefore were not traded on a frequent basis. Thus the market prices of the assets were uncertain. Even when an asset was likely to fail, there was no documented market value that could force the seller of the credit default swap to post a larger margin. By the time the asset officially failed, the margin covered only a small portion of the payment that the seller of the credit default swap owed the buyer of that swap. Although it was typical for the underlying assets referenced in a credit default swap to be rated, this rating was not always adjusted to reflect conditions that increased the probability of the asset defaulting.

Impact of Lehman Brothers' Failure The securities firm Lehman Brothers was a major participant in the CDS market. When it went bankrupt in September 2008, it did not cover all of its CDS obligations. Thus many financial institutions that had purchased CDS contracts from Lehman to protect against the default of mortgage-backed securities were not protected once the firm went bankrupt. Since the CDS market was over-the-counter at the time, there was little information about the exposure of financial institutions to CDS contracts. The credit crisis illustrated how protection provided to buyers of a CDS is only as good as the creditworthiness of the CDS seller.

Another impact of the Lehman Brothers failure was that participants recognized that the government will not automatically rescue all large financial institutions. Thus the annual payments necessary to buy new CDS contracts on large financial institutions increased substantially shortly after the Lehman Brothers failure. Sellers of new CDS contracts required higher payments because the risk premium on the CDS contracts increased. The sellers were willing to sell CDS contracts only if they received higher payments that would compensate for the higher risk.

Impact of AIG's Financial Problems American International Group, the world's largest insurance company, frequently sold CDS contracts as a means of generating periodic revenue. By 2008, it was on the sale side of CDS contracts representing about $440 billion in debt securities. Many of its CDS contracts obligated AIG to cover risky, mortgage-backed securities that represented subprime mortgages. As housing conditions weakened further, rumors circulated that AIG might not be able to cover all the future claims on its CDS contracts due to defaults. The federal government was concerned that if AIG could not satisfy its obligations, all the financial institutions that had purchased CDS contracts from AIG would lose their protection and might fail. In September 2008, the Federal Reserve injected billions of dollars into AIG because it feared the company's failure would cause major damage to the financial sector. In the following months, the bailout continued. By early 2009, AIG had received $150 billion in government funds.

15-7g Reform of CDS Contracts

FINANCIAL REFORM

As a result of the Financial Reform Act of 2010, derivative securities such as swaps are to be traded on an exchange or clearinghouse. The Commodity Futures Trading Commission and the Securities and Exchange Commission are expected to play an important role in developing specific rules that apply to the trading of swap contracts in the future. One obvious result of having derivatives traded on an exchange or clearinghouse instead of over the counter is that the derivative contracts should become more standardized. Second, the pricing of these contracts should become more transparent, as the exchange should post prices paid for the standardized derivative contracts that are traded on the exchange.

Third, the use of standardized contracts should increase the trading volume, which in turn should reduce the uncertainty surrounding the price of a standardized derivative contract. That is, one may have more confidence in the valuation of a swap contract that is based on many transactions as opposed to a single, over-the-counter transaction. Fourth, market participants and regulators should be more informed about the use of particular swap contracts if they are traded on an exchange, because the exchange should publicize the trading volume per contract.

Given that an exchange should result in more accurate pricing of the swap contracts, the amount of collateral backing any participant's contract should be more accurate as well. Thus, even if a participant defaults on its obligation to pay on a particular contract, the exchange should have access to sufficient collateral to cover the payment. In this manner, a possible default in any contract should not cause possible contagion effects for other counterparties of swap contracts.

The Chicago Mercantile Exchange (CME) offers futures contracts on interest rate swaps. These contracts allow participants to engage in interest rate swaps, but with the efficiency and transparency of a futures contract.

15-8 GLOBALIZATION OF SWAP MARKETS

GLOBAL ASPECTS

The market for interest rate swaps is not restricted to the United States. As mentioned earlier, European financial institutions commonly have the opposite exposure to interest rate risk and therefore take swap positions counter to the positions desired by U.S. financial institutions. Manufacturing corporations from various countries that are exposed to interest rate risk also engage in interest rate swaps.

Interest rate swaps are executed in various countries and are denominated in many different currencies. Dollar-denominated interest rate swaps account for about half the value of all interest rate swaps outstanding.

Given that swap participants are from various countries, the banks and securities firms that serve as intermediaries have a globalized network of subsidiaries. In this way, they can link participants from various countries. One obvious barrier to the global swap market is the lack of information about participants based in other countries. Thus, concerns about credit risk may discourage some participants from engaging in swaps. This barrier is reduced when international banks and securities firms that serve as intermediaries are willing to back the payments that are supposed to occur under the provisions of the swap agreement.

Financial institutions from numerous countries also participated in the credit default swap market. Some of them were attempting to protect against default risk of their investments in bonds issued by governments around the world. In fact, some of the most popular CDS contracts were written on bonds issued by governments of emerging markets such as Brazil, Russia, and Turkey. Because CDS contracts were traded internationally, the credit crisis spread globally as participants began to realize that their counterparties might not be able to fulfill their obligations.

15-8a Currency Swaps

A **currency swap** is an arrangement whereby currencies are exchanged at specified exchange rates and at specified intervals. It is essentially a combination of currency futures contracts, although most futures contracts are not available for periods in the distant future. Currency swaps are commonly used by firms to hedge their exposure to exchange rate fluctuations.

EXAMPLE   Springfield Company is a U.S. firm that expects to receive 2 million British pounds (£) in each of the next four years. It may therefore want to lock in the exchange rate at which it can sell British pounds over the next four years. A currency swap will specify the exchange rate at which the £2 million can be exchanged in each year. Assume the exchange rate specified by a swap is $1.70 (the spot exchange rate at the time of the swap arrangement), so Springfield will receive $3.4 million (£2 million × $1.70 per £) in each of the four years. If the firm does not engage in a currency swap, the dollar amount received will depend on the spot exchange rate at the time the pounds are converted to dollars.

The impact of the currency swap is illustrated in Exhibit 15.16. This exhibit also shows the payments that would have been received under two alternative scenarios if the currency swap had not been arranged. Note that the payments received from the swap would have been less favorable than the unhedged strategy if the pound appreciated against the dollar over that period. However, the payments received from the swap would have been more favorable than the unhedged strategy

Exhibit 15.16   Impact of Currency Swaps

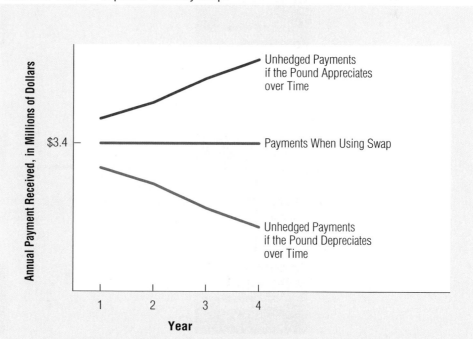

if the pound depreciated against the dollar over that period. The currency swap arrangement reduces the firm's exposure to changes in the pound's value. ●

The large commercial banks that serve as financial intermediaries sometimes take positions. That is, they may agree to swap currencies with a firm rather than simply search for a suitable swap candidate.

Like interest rate swaps, currency swaps are available in several variations. Some currency swap arrangements allow one of the parties an option to terminate the contract. That party incurs a premium for the option, which is either charged upfront or reflected in the exchange rates specified in the swap arrangement.

Using Currency Swaps to Hedge Bond Payments

Although currency swaps are commonly used to hedge payments on international trade, they may also be used in conjunction with bond issues to hedge foreign cash flows.

EXAMPLE

Philly Company, a U.S. firm, wants to issue a bond denominated in euros (the currency now used in several European countries) because it could make payments with euro inflows to be generated from ongoing operations. Philly, however, is not well known to investors who would consider purchasing euro-denominated bonds. Another firm, Windy Company, wants to issue dollar-denominated bonds because its inflow payments are mostly in dollars, but Windy is not well known to the investors who would purchase these bonds. If Philly is known in the dollar-denominated market and Windy is known in the euro-denominated market, the following transactions are appropriate. Philly can issue dollar-denominated bonds while Windy issues euro-denominated bonds. Philly can exchange euros for dollars to make its bond payments, and Windy will receive euros in exchange for dollars to make its bond payments. This currency swap is illustrated in Exhibit 15.17. ●

Exhibit 15.17 Illustration of a Currency Swap

Risk of Currency Swaps   The same types of risk that apply to interest rate swaps may also apply to currency swaps. First, there may be basis risk if the firm cannot obtain a currency swap on the currency to which it is exposed and instead uses a related currency. For example, consider a U.S. firm with cash inflows in British pounds that cannot find a counterparty to enact a swap in pounds. The firm may enact a swap in euros because movements (against the dollar) in the euro and the pound are highly correlated. Specifically, the firm will enact a currency swap to exchange euros for dollars. As it receives pounds, it will convert them to euros and then exchange the euros for dollars as specified by the swap arrangement. The exchange rate between pounds and euros is not constant, however, so basis risk exists.

Currency swaps can also be subject to credit risk, which reflects the possibility that the counterparty may default on its obligation. However, the potential loss is somewhat limited because one party can stop exchanging its currency if it no longer receives currency from the counterparty.

A third type of risk is sovereign risk, which reflects the possibility that a country may restrict the convertibility of a particular currency. In this case, a party involved in a swap arrangement may not be able to fulfill its obligation because its government prohibits local currency from being converted to another currency. This scenario is less likely in countries that encourage free trade of goods and securities across borders.

SUMMARY

- Various types of interest rate swaps are used to reduce interest rate risk. Some of the more popular types of interest rate swaps are plain vanilla swaps, forward swaps, callable swaps, putable swaps, extendable swaps, rate-capped swaps, and equity swaps. Each type of swap accommodates a particular need of financial institutions or other firms that are exposed to interest rate risk.

- When engaging in interest rate swaps, the participants can be exposed to basis risk, credit risk, and sovereign risk. Basis risk prevents the interest rate swap from completely eliminating the swap user's exposure to interest rate risk. Credit risk reflects the possibility that the counterparty on a swap agreement may not meet its payment obligations. Sovereign risk reflects the possibility that political conditions could prevent the counterparty in a swap agreement from meeting its payment obligations.

- In addition to the traditional forms of interest rate swaps, three other interest rate derivative instruments are commonly used to hedge interest rate risk: interest rate caps, interest rate floors, and interest rate collars. Interest rate caps offer payments when a specified interest rate index exceeds the interest rate ceiling (cap) and therefore can hedge against rising interest rates. Interest rate floors offer payments when a specified interest rate index falls below a specified interest rate floor; they can be used to hedge against declining interest rates. An interest rate collar involves the purchase of an interest rate cap and the simultaneous sale of an interest rate floor; it is used to hedge against rising interest rates.

- Credit default swaps are commonly purchased by financial institutions to protect against default on specific debt securities that they previously purchased. These swaps are sold by financial institutions that are willing to insure against the securities' default. Some financial institutions with major positions in CDS contracts experienced financial problems during the credit crisis in 2008 and were unable to cover their obligations. The credit crisis was intensified by the uncertainty surrounding potential losses of financial institutions that had positions in credit default swaps.

- The interest rate swap market has become globalized in the sense that financial institutions from various countries participate. Interest rate swaps are available in a variety of currencies.

POINT COUNTER-POINT

Should Financial Institutions Engage in Interest Rate Swaps for Speculative Purposes?

Point Yes. They have expertise in forecasting future interest rate movements and can generate gains for their shareholders by taking speculative positions.

Counter-Point No. They should use their main business to generate gains for their shareholders. They should serve as intermediaries for swap transactions only in order to generate transaction fees or should take a position only if it is to hedge their exposure to interest rate risk.

Who Is Correct? Use the Internet to learn more about this issue and then formulate your own opinion.

QUESTIONS AND APPLICATIONS

1. **Hedging with Interest Rate Swaps** Bowling Green Savings & Loan uses short-term deposits to fund fixed-rate mortgages. Explain how Bowling Green can use interest rate swaps to hedge its interest rate risk.

2. **Decision to Hedge with Interest Rate Swaps** Explain the types of cash flow characteristics that would cause a firm to hedge interest rate risk by swapping floating-rate payments for fixed payments. Why would some firms avoid the use of interest rate swaps even when they are highly exposed to interest rate risk?

3. **Role of Securities Firms in Swap Market** Describe the possible roles of securities firms in the swap market.

4. **Hedging with Swaps** Chelsea Finance Company receives floating inflow payments from its provision of floating-rate loans. Its outflow payments are fixed because of its recent issuance of long-term bonds. Chelsea is concerned that interest rates will decline in the future. Yet, it does not want to hedge its interest rate risk because it believes interest rates may increase. Recommend a solution to Chelsea's dilemma.

5. **Basis Risk** Comiskey Savings provides fixed-rate mortgages of various maturities, depending on what customers want. It obtains most of its funds from issuing certificates of deposit with maturities ranging from one month to five years. Comiskey has decided to engage in a fixed-for-floating swap to hedge its interest rate risk. Is Comiskey exposed to basis risk?

6. **Fixed-for-Floating Swaps** Shea Savings negotiates a fixed-for-floating swap with a reputable firm in South America that has an exceptional credit rating. Shea is very confident that there will not be a default on inflow payments because of the very low credit risk of the South American firm. Do you agree? Explain.

7. **Fixed-for-Floating Swaps** North Pier Company entered into a two-year swap agreement, which would provide fixed-rate payments for floating-rate payments. Over the next two years, interest rates declined. Based on these conditions, did North Pier Company benefit from the swap?

8. **Equity Swap** Explain how an equity swap could allow Marathon Insurance Company to capitalize on expectations of a strong stock market performance over the next year without altering its existing portfolio mix of stocks and bonds.

9. **Swap Network** Explain how the failure of a large commercial bank could cause a worldwide swap credit crisis.

10. **Currency Swaps** Markus Company purchases supplies from France once a year. Would Markus be favorably affected if it establishes a currency swap arrangement and the dollar strengthens? What if it establishes a currency swap arrangement and the dollar weakens?

11. **Basis Risk** Explain basis risk as it relates to a currency swap.

12. **Sovereign Risk** Give an example of how sovereign risk is related to currency swaps.

13. **Use of Interest Rate Swaps** Explain why some companies that issue bonds engage in interest rate swaps in financial markets. Why do they not simply issue bonds that require the type of payments (fixed or variable) that they prefer to make?

14. Use of Currency Swaps Explain why some companies that issue bonds engage in currency swaps. Why do they not simply issue bonds in the currency that they would prefer to use for making payments?

Advanced Questions

15. Rate-Capped Swaps Bull and Finch Company wants a fixed-for-floating swap. It expects interest rates to rise far above the fixed rate that it would pay and to remain very high until the swap maturity date. Should it consider negotiating for a rate-capped swap with the cap set at 2 percentage points above the fixed rate? Explain.

16. Forward Swaps Rider Company negotiates a forward swap, to begin two years from now, in which it will swap fixed payments for floating-rate payments. What will be the effect on Rider if interest rates rise substantially over the next two years? That is, would Rider be better off using this forward swap than if it had simply waited two years before negotiating the swap? Explain.

17. Swap Options Explain the advantage of a swap option to a financial institution that wants to swap fixed payments for floating payments.

18. Callable Swaps Back Bay Insurance Company negotiated a callable swap involving fixed payments in exchange for floating payments. Assume that interest rates decline consistently up until the swap maturity date. Do you think Back Bay might terminate the swap prior to maturity? Explain.

19. Credit Default Swaps Credit default swaps were once viewed as a great innovation for making mortgage markets more stable. Recently, however, the swaps have been criticized for making the credit crisis worse. Why?

20. Credit Default Swap Prices Explain why the failure of Lehman Brothers caused prices on credit default swap contracts to increase.

21. Reform of CDS Contracts Explain how the Financial Reform Act of 2010 attempted to reduce the risk in the financial system resulting from the use of credit default swaps.

Interpreting Financial News

Interpret the following comments made by Wall Street analysts and portfolio managers.

a. "The swaps market is another Wall Street–developed house of cards."

b. "As a dealer in interest rate swaps, our bank takes various steps to limit our exposure."

c. "The regulation of commercial banks, securities firms, and other financial institutions that participate in the swaps market could create a regulatory war."

Managing in Financial Markets

Assessing the Effects of an Interest Rate Collar
As a manager of a commercial bank, you just purchased a three-year interest rate collar with LIBOR as the interest rate index. The interest rate cap specifies a fee of 2 percent of notional principal (valued at $100 million) and an interest rate ceiling of 9 percent. The interest rate floor specifies a fee of 3 percent of the $100 million notional principal and an interest rate floor of 7 percent. Assume that LIBOR is expected to be 6 percent, 10 percent, and 11 percent (respectively) at the end of each of the next three years.

a. Determine the net fees paid, and also determine the expected net payments to be received as a result of purchasing the interest rate collar.

b. Assuming you are very confident that interest rates will rise, should you consider purchasing a callable swap instead of the collar? Explain.

c. Explain the conditions under which your purchase of an interest rate collar could backfire.

PROBLEMS

1. Vanilla Swaps Cleveland Insurance Company has just negotiated a three-year plain vanilla swap in which it will exchange fixed payments of 8 percent for floating payments of LIBOR plus 1 percent. The notional principal is $50 million. LIBOR is expected to be 7 percent, 9 percent, and 10 percent (respectively) at the end of each of the next three years.

a. Determine the net dollar amount to be received (or paid) by Cleveland each year.

b. Determine the dollar amount to be received (or paid) by the counterparty on this interest rate swap each year based on the assumed forecasts of LIBOR.

2. Interest Rate Caps Northbrook Bank purchases a four-year cap for a fee of 3 percent of notional principal valued at $100 million, with an interest rate ceiling of 9 percent and LIBOR as the index representing the market interest rate. Assume that LIBOR is expected to be 8 percent, 10 percent, 12 percent, and 13 percent (respectively) at the end of each of the next four years.

a. Determine the initial fee paid, and also determine the expected payments to be received by Northbrook if LIBOR moves as forecasted.

b. Determine the dollar amount to be received (or paid) by the seller of the interest rate cap based on the assumed forecasts of LIBOR.

3. Interest Rate Floors Iowa City Bank purchases a three-year interest rate floor for a fee of 2 percent of notional principal valued at $80 million, with an interest rate floor of 6 percent and LIBOR representing the interest rate index. The bank expects LIBOR to be 6 percent, 5 percent, and 4 percent (respectively) at the end of each of the next three years.

a. Determine the initial fee paid, and also determine the expected payments to be received by Iowa City if LIBOR moves as forecasted.

b. Determine the dollar amounts to be received (or paid) by the seller of the interest rate floor based on the assumed forecasts of LIBOR.

FLOW OF FUNDS EXERCISE

Hedging with Interest Rate Derivatives

Recall that if the economy continues to be strong, Carson Company may need to increase its production capacity by about 50 percent over the next few years to satisfy demand. It would need financing to expand and accommodate the increase in production. Recall that the yield curve is currently upward sloping. Also recall that Carson is concerned about a possible slowing of the economy because of potential Fed actions to reduce inflation. Carson currently relies mostly on commercial loans with floating interest rates for its debt financing. It has contacted Blazo Bank about the use of interest rate derivatives to hedge the risk.

a. How could Carson use interest rate swaps to reduce the exposure of its cost of debt to interest rate movements?

b. What is a possible disadvantage of Carson using the interest rate swap hedge as opposed to no hedge?

c. How could Carson use an interest rate cap to reduce the exposure of its cost of debt to interest rate movements?

d. What is a possible disadvantage of Carson using the interest cap hedge as opposed to no hedge? Explain the trade-off between using an interest rate swap versus an interest rate cap.

INTERNET/EXCEL EXERCISES

1. Go to www.economagic.com/fedbog.htm and review the recent annualized rate for a short-term security (such as the 1-year Treasury rate) versus a long-term security (such as the 10-year Treasury rate). Based on this information, do you think that the market expects interest rates to rise over time? Explain.

2. Assume that you need long-term funds and can borrow at the short-term Treasury rate. Based on the existing interest rates, would you consider engaging in a swap of a floating rate in exchange for a fixed rate? Explain.

WSJ EXERCISE

Impact of Interest Rates on a Swap Arrangement

Use a recent issue of the *Wall Street Journal* to determine how short-term interest rates have changed over the last year (assess the Treasury yield for a three-month maturity based on the yield curve shown for today versus the yield curve shown for a year ago). The three-month Treasury bill rate at the present time and one year ago are quoted in the Money & Investing section of the *Journal*. Explain whether the interest rate movement would have had a favorable impact on a firm that initiated a fixed-for-floating swap agreement one year ago.

ONLINE ARTICLES WITH REAL-WORLD EXAMPLES

Find a recent practical article available online that describes a real-world example regarding a specific financial institution or financial market that reinforces one or more concepts covered in this chapter.

If your class has an online component, your professor may ask you to post your summary of the article there and provide a link to the article so that other students can access it. If your class is live, your professor may ask you to summarize your application of the article in class. Your professor may assign specific students to complete this assignment or may allow any students to do the assignment on a volunteer basis.

For recent online articles and real-world examples related to this chapter, consider using the following search terms (be sure to include the prevailing year as a search term to ensure that the online articles are recent):

1. interest rate swap AND hedge
2. interest rate swap AND losses
3. interest rate swap AND financial institutions
4. interest rate swap AND pricing
5. interest rate swap AND risk
6. credit default swap AND losses
7. credit default swap AND crisis
8. credit default swap AND risk
9. credit default swap AND failure
10. credit default swap AND hedge

16

Foreign Exchange Derivative Markets

CHAPTER OBJECTIVES

The specific objectives of this chapter are to:

- provide a background on foreign exchange markets,

- explain how various factors affect exchange rates,

- explain how to forecast exchange rates,

- describe the use of foreign exchange rate derivatives, and

- explain international arbitrage.

In recent years, various derivative instruments have been created to manage or capitalize on exchange rate movements. These so-called **foreign exchange derivatives** (or "forex" derivatives) include forward contracts, currency futures contracts, currency swaps, and currency options. Foreign exchange derivatives account for about half of the daily foreign exchange transaction volume.

The potential benefits from using foreign exchange derivatives are dependent on the expected exchange rate movements. Thus, it is necessary to understand why exchange rates change over time before exploring the use of foreign exchange derivatives.

16-1 FOREIGN EXCHANGE MARKETS

As international trade and investing have increased over time, so has the need to exchange currencies. Foreign exchange markets consist of a global telecommunications network among the large commercial banks that serve as financial intermediaries for such exchange. These banks are located in New York, Tokyo, Hong Kong, Singapore, Frankfurt, Zurich, and London. Foreign exchange transactions at these banks have been increasing over time.

At any given time, the price at which banks will buy a currency (bid price) is slightly lower than the price at which they will sell it (ask price). Like markets for other commodities and securities, the market for foreign currencies is more efficient because of financial intermediaries (commercial banks). Otherwise, individual buyers and sellers of currency would be unable to identify counterparties to accommodate their needs.

16-1a Institutional Use of Foreign Exchange Markets

Exhibit 16.1 summarizes how financial institutions utilize the foreign exchange markets and foreign exchange derivatives. The degree of international investment by financial institutions is influenced by potential return, risk, and government regulations. Commercial banks use international lending as their primary form of international investing. Mutual funds, pension funds, and insurance companies purchase foreign securities. In recent years, technology has reduced information costs and other transaction costs associated with purchasing foreign securities, prompting an increase in institutional purchases of foreign securities. Consequently, financial institutions are increasing their use of the foreign exchange markets to exchange currencies. They are also increasing their use of foreign exchange derivatives to hedge their investments in foreign securities.

Exhibit 16.1 Institutional Use of Foreign Exchange Markets

TYPE OF FINANCIAL INSTITUTION	USES OF FOREIGN EXCHANGE MARKETS
Commercial banks	• Serve as financial intermediaries in the foreign exchange market by buying or selling currencies to accommodate customers. • Speculate on foreign currency movements by taking long positions in some currencies and short positions in others. • Provide forward contracts to customers. • Some commercial banks offer currency options to customers; unlike the standardized currency options traded on an exchange, these options can be tailored to a customer's specific needs.
International mutual funds	• Use foreign exchange markets to exchange currencies when reconstructing their portfolios. • Use foreign exchange derivatives to hedge a portion of their exposure.
Brokerage firms and securities firms	• Some brokerage firms and securities firms engage in foreign security transactions for their customers or for their own accounts.
Insurance companies	• Use foreign exchange markets when exchanging currencies for their international operations. • Use foreign exchange markets when purchasing foreign securities for their investment portfolios or when selling foreign securities. • Use foreign exchange derivatives to hedge a portion of their exposure.
Pension funds	• Require foreign exchange of currencies when investing in foreign securities for their stock or bond portfolios. • Use foreign exchange derivatives to hedge a portion of their exposure.

WEB

www.bloomberg.com
Spot rates of currencies and cross-exchange rates among currencies.

16-1b Exchange Rate Quotations

The **direct exchange rate** specifies the value of a currency in U.S. dollars. For example, the Mexican peso may have a value such as $0.10 while the British pound is valued at $2.00. The **indirect exchange rate** specifies the number of units of a currency equal to a U.S. dollar. For the example values given here, the indirect exchange rates are 10 pesos per dollar and 0.50 pounds per dollar. The indirect exchange rate is the reciprocal of the direct exchange rate.

Forward Rate   For widely used currencies, **forward rates** are available and are commonly quoted next to the respective spot rates. The forward rates indicate the rate at which a currency can be exchanged in the future. If the forward rate is above the spot rate, it contains a premium. If the forward rate is below the spot rate, it contains a negative premium (also called a discount).

Cross-Exchange Rates   Most exchange rate quotation tables express currencies relative to the dollar. In some instances, however, the exchange rate between two nondollar currencies is needed.

EXAMPLE   If a Canadian firm needs Mexican pesos to buy Mexican goods, it is concerned about the value of the Mexican peso relative to the Canadian dollar. This type of rate is known as a cross-exchange rate because it reflects the amount of one foreign currency per unit of another foreign currency. Cross-exchange rates can be easily determined with the use of foreign exchange quotations. The general formula follows:

$$\frac{\text{Value of 1 unit of Currency A}}{\text{in units of Currency B}} = \frac{\text{Value of Currency A in \$}}{\text{Value of Currency B in \$}}$$

If the peso is worth $0.07 and the Canadian dollar (C$) is worth $0.70, the value of the peso in Canadian dollars is calculated as follows:

$$\text{Value of peso in C\$} = \frac{\text{Value of peso in \$}}{\text{Value of C\$ in \$}} = \frac{\$0.07}{\$0.70} = 0.10$$

Thus a Mexican peso is worth C$0.10. The exchange rate can also be expressed as the number of pesos equal to one Canadian dollar. This figure can be computed by taking the reciprocal, $0.70/0.07 = 10$, which indicates that a Canadian dollar is worth 10 pesos according to the information provided. ●

16-1c Types of Exchange Rate Systems

From 1944 to 1971, the exchange rate at which one currency could be exchanged for another was maintained by governments within 1 percent of a specified rate. This period was known as the **Bretton Woods era** because the agreement establishing the system was negotiated at the Bretton Woods Conference in Bretton Woods, New Hampshire. The manner by which governments were able to control exchange rates is discussed later in the chapter.

By 1971, the U.S. dollar was clearly overvalued. That is, its value was maintained only by central bank intervention. In 1971, an agreement among all major countries (known as the **Smithsonian Agreement**) allowed for devaluation of the dollar. In addition, the Smithsonian Agreement called for a widening of the boundaries from 1 percent to 2¼ percent around each currency's set value. Governments intervened in the foreign exchange markets whenever exchange rates threatened to wander outside the boundaries.

In 1973, the boundaries were eliminated. Since then, the exchange rates of major currencies have been floating without any government-imposed boundaries. A government may still intervene in the foreign exchange markets to influence the market value of its currency, however. A system with no boundaries and in which exchange rates are market determined but still subject to government intervention is called a **dirty float**. This is to be distinguished from a **freely floating system**, in which the foreign exchange market is totally free from government intervention. Most countries allow their local currency to float but periodically intervene in the foreign exchange market to influence the value of that currency, as will be explained shortly.

Pegged Exchange Rate System Some countries today use a pegged exchange rate system. For example, Hong Kong has tied the value of its currency (the Hong Kong dollar) to the U.S. dollar (HK$78 = $1) since 1983. Thus, its currency's value is fixed relative to the U.S. dollar, which means that its value moves in tandem with the U.S. dollar against other currencies, including other Asian currencies. Thus if the Japanese yen depreciates against the U.S. dollar, it will also depreciate against the Hong Kong dollar.

A country that pegs its currency cannot control its local interest rate because its interest rate must be aligned with the interest rate of the currency to which its currency is tied.

EXAMPLE

If Hong Kong lowered its interest rates to stimulate its economy, investors based in Hong Kong would then be enticed to exchange Hong Kong dollars for U.S. dollars and invest in the United States, where interest rates are higher. Since the Hong Kong dollar is tied to the U.S. dollar, the investors would be able to exchange their investment proceeds back to Hong Kong dollars at the end of the investment period without concern for exchange rate risk, which does not exist because the exchange rate is fixed. Therefore, Hong Kong does not attempt to control its own interest rate, which is typically equal to the U.S. interest rate plus a slight premium for risk. As the U.S. interest rate changes, Hong Kong's interest rate changes by about the same degree and in the same direction. ●

The government of Venezuela has historically pegged its currency (the bolivar) to the dollar, although there have been periodic devaluations. The most recent devaluation was on January 9, 2010, when Venezuela devalued the bolivar by 50 percent to 1 bolivar = $0.232.

The new pegged exchange rate reduced the value of the bolivar by 50 percent not only against the dollar but also against all other currencies. For any nondollar currencies that appreciate against the dollar, they appreciate against the bolivar to the same extent.

Because the devaluation of the bolivar makes foreign products expensive for consumers in Venezuela, it encourages more consumption of locally produced products at the expense of foreign products. Furthermore, since the devaluation cut the bolivar's value in half, it increases foreign demand for Venezuela's products. Thus the devaluation is intended to improve Venezuela's economy and reduce its unemployment. However, one possible adverse effect of the devaluation is that the new exchange rate could eliminate foreign competition as foreign products become too expensive. This would allow local producers in Venezuela to increase their prices without much concern about losing customers to foreign firms, which could lead to higher inflation in Venezuela.

China's currency (the yuan) was pegged to the U.S. dollar until 2005. Many U.S. politicians argued that China was maintaining its currency at a level that was too low, which caused an annual U.S. balance of trade deficit of about $200 billion with that country. In July 2005, China implemented a new system that allowed the yuan to float within narrow boundaries based on a set of major currencies. Yet this had only a limited effect on the relative pricing of Chinese and U.S. products, and the balance of trade between the two countries remained large.

16-1d Eurozone Arrangement

In January 1999, the euro replaced the national currencies of eleven European countries; since then, five more countries have converted their home currency to the euro. The countries that now use the euro as their home currency are Austria, Belgium, Cyprus, Estonia, Finland, France, Germany, Greece, Ireland, Italy, Luxembourg, Malta, Netherlands, Portugal, Slovakia, Slovenia, and Spain. The countries that participate in the euro make up a region that is referred to as the eurozone. Since all of these countries use the same currency, transactions between them do not require any exchange of currencies. Together, the participating countries produce more than 20 percent of the world's gross domestic product, which exceeds the total production of the United States. In Europe, the countries of Denmark, Norway, Sweden, Switzerland, and the United Kingdom continue to use their own home currency.

The ten countries in Eastern Europe that joined the European Union in 2004 are eligible to participate in the euro if they meet specific economic goals, including a maximum limit on their budget deficit. Some of these countries peg their currency's value to the euro, which allows them to assess how their economy is affected while that value moves in tandem with the euro against other currencies. Under this arrangement, they still have the flexibility to adjust their exchange rate system. If these countries ultimately adopt the euro as their currency, it will be more difficult for them to reverse such decisions.

Eurozone Monetary Policy   The European Central Bank (ECB) is responsible for setting monetary policy for all countries in the eurozone. The bank's objective is to maintain price stability (control inflation) in these countries, as it believes that price stability is necessary to achieve economic growth. Since the interest rate on the euro is based on the eurozone monetary policy, all participating countries have the same risk-free interest rate. Thus, eurozone monetary policy simultaneously affects the interest rate in all countries that have adopted the euro as their currency. Although a single monetary policy may allow for more consistent economic conditions across countries, it prevents any individual country from solving local economic problems via its own, unique monetary policy. However, the member countries can still apply their own fiscal policies (i.e., decisions on taxing and government expenditures).

Eurozone Crisis   In the 2010–2012 period, Greece suffered from a weak economy and a large increase in its government budget deficit. Its debt rating was lowered substantially by debt rating agencies, which increased the cost of funds borrowed by the governments. Portugal and Spain also experienced severe financial problems, and the economies of Italy and Ireland weakened as well. Just as integration among economies within the eurozone can allow one country's stimulus to benefit others, a given country's weakness can adversely affect others. Institutional investors moved their investments out of the eurozone and into other regions, which placed downward pressure on the euro's exchange rate.

16-1e Abandoning the Euro

When a government in the eurozone is unable to obtain sufficient credit to cover its budget deficit, it may need to rely on the European Central Bank (ECB) for funds. However, when the ECB provides credit to a country, it imposes austerity conditions that are intended to help the government resolve its budget deficit problems over time. These conditions may include a reduction in government spending and higher tax rates on citizens. Although these conditions may be necessary to correct the budget deficit, they may weaken an economy.

Some critics have argued that a country's government should abandon the euro rather than accept funding from the ECB, because the austerity conditions are too harsh. If a country had its own currency, it may be able to weaken it to a degree that would increase the demand for its exports, and therefore stimulate its economy. However, a weak home currency is not a perfect cure for a country, because it can cause higher inflation. In addition, if the country still planned to repay its debt, it would now have to pay with a new weak home currency, which would require larger payments to cover the existing debt.

Impact of Abandoning the Euro on Eurozone Conditions   If a country abandoned use of the euro, it might signal the possible abandonment by other countries that presently participate in the euro. If multinational corporations (MNCs) and large institutional investors outside of the eurozone feared other countries would follow, they may not be willing to invest any more funds in the eurozone, because they might fear the collapse of the euro. This might encourage them to sell their assets in the eurozone now so that they could move their money into their home currency or another currency before the euro weakens.

16-2 FACTORS AFFECTING EXCHANGE RATES

As the value of a currency adjusts to changes in demand and supply conditions, it moves toward equilibrium. In equilibrium, there is no excess or deficiency of that currency.

EXAMPLE

A large increase in the U.S. demand for European goods and securities will result in an increased demand for euros. Because the demand for euros will then exceed the supply of euros for sale, the foreign exchange dealers (commercial banks) will experience a shortage of euros and will respond by increasing the quoted price of euros. Hence the euro will appreciate, or increase in value.

Conversely, if European corporations begin to purchase more U.S. goods and European investors purchase more U.S. securities, the opposite forces will occur. There will be an increased sale of euros in exchange for dollars, causing a surplus of euros in the market. The value of the euro will therefore decline until it once again achieves equilibrium. ●

In reality, both the demand for euros and the supply of euros for sale can change simultaneously. The adjustment in the exchange rate will depend on the direction and magnitude of these changes.

A currency's supply and demand are influenced by a variety of factors, including (1) differential inflation rates, (2) differential interest rates, and (3) government (central bank) intervention. These factors will be discussed next.

16-2a Differential Inflation Rates

WEB

http://biz.yahoo.com/
topic/currency
Updated news of interest to speculators about specific currencies that are frequently traded in the foreign exchange market.

Begin with an equilibrium situation and consider what will happen to the U.S. demand for euros, and to the supply of euros for sale, if U.S. inflation suddenly becomes much higher than European inflation. The U.S. demand for European goods will increase, reflecting an increased U.S. demand for euros. In addition, the supply of euros to be sold for dollars will decline as the European desire for U.S. goods decreases. Both forces will place upward pressure on the value of the euro.

Under the reverse situation, where European inflation suddenly becomes much higher than U.S. inflation, the U.S. demand for euros will decrease while the supply of euros for sale increases, placing downward pressure on the value of the euro.

A well-known theory about the relationship between inflation and exchange rates, **purchasing power parity (PPP)** suggests that the exchange rate will, on average, change by a percentage that reflects the inflation differential between the two countries of concern.

EXAMPLE   Assume an initial equilibrium situation where the British pound's spot rate is $1.60, U.S. inflation is 3 percent, and British inflation is also 3 percent. If U.S. inflation suddenly increases to 5 percent then, according to PPP, the British pound will appreciate against the dollar by approximately 2 percent. The rationale is that, as a result of the higher U.S. prices, U.S. demand for British goods will increase and thereby place upward pressure on the pound's value. Once the pound appreciates by 2 percent, the purchasing power of U.S. consumers will be the same whether they purchase U.S. goods or British goods. Although the prices of the U.S. goods will have risen by a higher percentage, the British goods will then be just as expensive to U.S. consumers because of the pound's appreciation. Thus a new equilibrium exchange rate results from the change in U.S. inflation. ●

In reality, exchange rates do not always change as suggested by the PPP theory. Other factors that influence exchange rates (discussed next) can distort the PPP relationship. All these factors must be considered when assessing why an exchange rate has changed. Furthermore, forecasts of future exchange rates must account for the potential direction and magnitude of changes in all factors that affect exchange rates.

16-2b Differential Interest Rates

Interest rate movements affect exchange rates by influencing the capital flows between countries. An increase in interest rates may attract foreign investors, especially if the higher interest rates do not reflect an increase in inflationary expectations.

EXAMPLE   Assume U.S. interest rates suddenly become much higher than European interest rates. The demand by U.S. investors for European interest-bearing securities decreases as these securities become less attractive. In addition, the supply of euros to be sold in exchange for dollars expands as European investors increase their purchases of U.S. interest-bearing securities. Both forces put downward pressure on the euro's value.

Conversely, opposite forces play out in the case of higher European than U.S. interest rates, resulting in upward pressure on the euro's value. In general, the currency of the country with a higher increase (or smaller decrease) in interest rates is expected to appreciate, other factors held constant. ●

16-2c Central Bank Intervention

Central banks commonly consider adjusting a currency's value to influence economic conditions. For example, the U.S. central bank may wish to weaken the dollar to increase demand for U.S. exports, which can stimulate the economy. However, a weaker dollar can also cause U.S. inflation by reducing foreign competition (because it raises the price of foreign goods to U.S. consumers). Alternatively, the U.S. central bank may prefer to strengthen the dollar to intensify foreign competition, which can reduce U.S. inflation.

Direct Intervention   A country's government can intervene in the foreign exchange market to affect a currency's value. Direct intervention occurs when a country's central bank (such as the Federal Reserve Bank for the United States or the European Central Bank for the eurozone countries) sells some of its currency reserves for a different currency.

EXAMPLE

Assume that the Federal Reserve and the European Central Bank desire to strengthen the value of the euro against the dollar. They use dollar reserves to purchase euros in the foreign exchange market. In essence, they dump dollars in the foreign exchange market and thereby increase the demand for euros. ●

However, central bank intervention can be overwhelmed by market forces and so may not always succeed in reversing exchange rate movements. In fact, the efforts of the Fed and the ECB to boost the value of the euro in 2000 were not successful. Nevertheless, central bank intervention may significantly affect the foreign exchange markets in two ways. First, it may slow the momentum of adverse exchange rate movements. Second, commercial banks and other corporations may reassess their foreign exchange strategies if they believe the central banks will continue to intervene.

Indirect Intervention   The Fed can affect the dollar's value indirectly by influencing the factors that determine its value. For example, the Fed can attempt to lower interest rates by increasing the U.S. money supply (assuming that inflationary expectations are not affected). Lower U.S. interest rates tend to discourage foreign investors from investing in U.S. securities, thereby putting downward pressure on the value of the dollar. Or, to boost the dollar's value, the Fed can attempt to increase interest rates by reducing the U.S. money supply. Indirect intervention can be an effective means of influencing a currency's value.

When countries experience substantial net outflows of funds (which put severe downward pressure on their currency), they commonly use indirect intervention by raising interest rates to discourage excessive outflows and thus limit the downward pressure on their currency's value. However, this action adversely affects local borrowers (government agencies, corporations, and consumers) and may weaken the economy.

Indirect Intervention during the Peso Crisis   In 1994, Mexico experienced a large balance of trade deficit, perhaps because the peso was stronger than it should have been, which encouraged Mexican firms and consumers to buy an excessive amount of imports. By December 1994, there was substantial downward pressure on the peso. On December 20, 1994, Mexico's central bank devalued the peso by about 13 percent. Mexico's stock prices plummeted, as many foreign investors sold their shares and withdrew their funds from Mexico in anticipation of further devaluation in the peso. On December 22, the central bank allowed the peso to float freely; it declined by another 15 percent. This was the beginning of the so-called Mexican peso crisis. The central bank increased interest rates as a form of indirect intervention to discourage foreign investors from withdrawing their investments in Mexico's debt securities. The higher interest rates increased the cost of borrowing for Mexican firms and consumers, thereby slowing economic growth.

Indirect Intervention during the Asian Crisis   In the fall of 1997, many Asian countries experienced weak economies and their banks suffered from substantial defaults on loans. Concerned about their investments, investors began to withdraw their funds. Some countries (e.g., Thailand and Malaysia) increased their interest rates as a form of indirect intervention aimed at encouraging investors to leave their funds in Asia. However, the higher interest rates increased the cost to firms that had borrowed funds there, making it more difficult for them to repay their loans. In addition, the high interest rates discouraged new borrowing by firms and weakened the region's economies.

During the Asian crisis, investors also withdrew funds from Brazil and reinvested them in other countries, causing major capital outflows and putting extreme downward pressure on Brazil's currency (the real). At the end of October, the central bank of Brazil responded by doubling its interest rates from about 20 percent to about 40 percent. This action discouraged investors from pulling funds out of Brazil because they could now earn twice the interest from investing in some securities there. Although the bank's action was successful in defending the real, it reduced economic growth because the cost of borrowing funds was too high for many firms.

Indirect Intervention during the Russian Crisis   A similar situation occurred in Russia in May 1998. Over the previous four months, the Russian currency (the ruble) had consistently declined and stock market prices had declined by more than 50 percent. Because the lack of confidence in Russia's currency and stocks could cause massive outflows of funds, the Russian central bank attempted to minimize such outflows by tripling interest rates (from about 50 to 150 percent). The ruble was temporarily stabilized, but stock prices continued to decline because investors were concerned that the high interest rates would reduce economic growth.

Indirect Intervention during the Greek Crisis   Greece is one of the European countries that uses the euro as its local currency. In the spring of 2010, it experienced weak economic conditions and a large increase in its government budget deficit. Its debt rating was lowered substantially by debt rating agencies to the point where it was paying about 11 percent on its debt, versus 4 percent for other countries in the eurozone. As the government of Greece attempted to cut its spending to correct the budget deficit, the economy weakened. There were even rumors that Greece would abandon the euro as its currency, which could have caused still more uncertainty about the euro and about the future of eurozone country economies. Thus the Greek crisis led to concerns about the eurozone and encouraged speculators to dump euros in favor of dollars or other currencies. In spring 2010, the euro declined by 20 percent.

The ECB responded with a stimulative monetary policy that was intended to keep interest rates low. Although the ECB might well have preferred a more restrictive monetary policy in order to keep inflation low, its policy evidently considered the potential weakening of the eurozone economy due to the Greek crisis. An important lesson from the crisis is how the conditions in one eurozone country can affect every country that uses the same currency.

16-3 FORECASTING EXCHANGE RATES

Market participants who use foreign exchange derivatives tend to take positions based on their expectations of future exchange rates. For example, multinational corporations take positions in foreign exchange derivatives to hedge their future cash flows denominated in foreign currencies, especially when they expect that they will be adversely affected by that exposure. Portfolio managers of financial institutions may take positions in foreign exchange derivatives to hedge their exposure if they anticipate a decline in the value of the currency denominating their stocks. Speculators may take positions in foreign exchange derivatives to benefit from the expectation that specific currencies will strengthen. Thus, the initial task is to develop a forecast of specific exchange rates. There are various techniques for forecasting, but no specific technique stands out because most have had limited success in forecasting future exchange rates. Most forecasting techniques can be classified as one of the following types:

- Technical forecasting
- Fundamental forecasting
- Market-based forecasting
- Mixed forecasting

WEB

www.oanda.com
Historical exchange rates.

16-3a Technical Forecasting

Technical forecasting involves the use of historical exchange rate data to predict future values. For example, the fact that a given currency has increased in value over four consecutive days may provide an indication of how the currency will move tomorrow. Sometimes a more complex statistical analysis is applied. For example, a computer program can be developed to detect particular historical trends.

There are also several **time-series models** that examine moving averages and thus allow a forecaster to identify patterns, such as currency tending to decline in value after a rise in moving average over three consecutive periods. Normally, consultants who use such a method will not disclose their particular rule for forecasting. If they did, potential clients might apply the rules themselves rather than pay for the consultant's advice.

Technical forecasting of exchange rates is similar to technical forecasting of stock prices. If the pattern of currency values over time appears to be random, then technical forecasting is not appropriate. Unless historical trends in exchange rate movements can be identified, examination of past movements will not be useful for indicating future movements.

16-3b Fundamental Forecasting

Fundamental forecasting is based on fundamental relationships between economic variables and exchange rates. Given current values of these variables along with their historical impact on a currency's value, corporations can develop exchange rate projections. For example, high inflation in a given country can lead to depreciation in its currency. Of course, all other factors that may influence exchange rates should also be considered.

A forecast may arise simply from a subjective assessment of the degree to which general movements in economic variables in one country are expected to affect exchange rates. From a statistical perspective, a forecast would be based on quantitatively measured impacts of factors on exchange rates.

16-3c Market-Based Forecasting

Market-based forecasting, or the process of developing forecasts from market indicators, is usually based on either the spot rate or the forward rate.

Use of the Spot Rate To clarify why the spot rate can serve as a market-based forecast, assume the British pound is expected to appreciate against the dollar in the very near future. This will encourage speculators to buy the pound with U.S. dollars today in anticipation of its appreciation, and these purchases could immediately force the pound's value upward. Conversely, if the pound is expected to depreciate against the dollar, speculators will sell off pounds now and hope to purchase them back at a lower price after they decline in value. Such action could force the pound to depreciate immediately. Thus, the current value of the pound should reflect the expectation of that currency's value in the very near future. In other words, corporations can use the spot rate to forecast because it represents the market's expectation of the spot rate in the near future.

Use of the Forward Rate   The forward rate can also serve as a forecast of the future spot rate. The reason is that speculators would take positions if there were a large discrepancy between the forward rate and expectations of the future spot rate.

EXAMPLE

The 30-day forward rate of the British pound is $1.40, and the general expectation of speculators is that the future spot rate of the pound will be $1.45 in 30 days. Since speculators expect the future spot rate to be $1.45 and since the prevailing forward rate is $1.40, they might buy pounds 30 days forward at $1.40 and then sell them when received (in 30 days) at the spot rate existing then. If their forecast is correct, they will earn $0.05 ($1.45 − $1.40) per pound. If a large number of speculators implement this strategy, the substantial forward purchases of pounds will cause the forward rate to increase until this speculative demand stops. Perhaps this speculative demand will terminate when the forward rate reaches $1.45, since at this rate no profits could be expected from implementing the strategy. Thus, the forward rate should move toward the market's general expectation of the future spot rate. In this sense, the forward rate serves as a market-based forecast because it reflects the market's expectation of the spot rate at the end of the forward horizon (in this example, 30 days from now). ●

16-3d Mixed Forecasting

Because no single forecasting technique has been found to be consistently superior to the others, some MNCs use a combination of forecasting techniques. This method is referred to as **mixed forecasting**. Various forecasts for a particular currency value are developed using several forecasting techniques. Each of the techniques used is assigned a weight, and the techniques believed to be more reliable are assigned higher weights. Thus the MNC's forecast of the currency will be a weighted average of the various forecasts developed.

16-4 FOREIGN EXCHANGE DERIVATIVES

Foreign exchange derivatives can be used to speculate on future exchange rate movements or to hedge anticipated cash inflows or outflows in a given foreign currency. As foreign securities markets have become more accessible, institutional investors have increased their international investments, which in turn has increased their exposure to exchange rate risk. Some institutional investors use foreign exchange derivatives to hedge their exposure. The most popular foreign exchange derivatives are forward contracts, currency futures contracts, currency swaps, and currency options contracts.

16-4a Forward Contracts

Forward contracts are contracts, typically negotiated with a commercial bank, that allow the purchase or sale of a specified amount of a particular foreign currency at a specified exchange rate (the forward rate) on a specified future date. A **forward market** facilitates the trading of forward contracts. This market is not in one physical place; it is a telecommunications network through which large commercial banks match participants who wish to buy a currency forward with other participants who wish to sell a currency forward.

Many of the commercial banks that offer foreign exchange on a spot basis also offer forward transactions for widely traded currencies. By enabling a firm to lock in the price to be paid for a foreign currency, forward purchases or sales can hedge the firm's risk that the currency's value may change over time.

<dl><dt>EXAMPLE</dt></dl>

St. Louis Insurance Company plans to invest about $20 million in Mexican stocks two months from now. Because the Mexican stocks are denominated in pesos, the amount of stock that can be purchased depends on the peso's value at the time of the purchase. If St. Louis Insurance Company is concerned that the peso will appreciate by the time of the purchase, it can buy pesos forward to lock in the exchange rate. ●

A corporation receiving payments denominated in a particular foreign currency in the future can lock in the price at which the currency can be sold by selling that currency forward.

<dl><dt>EXAMPLE</dt></dl>

The pension fund manager of Gonzaga, Inc., plans to liquidate the fund's holdings of British stocks in six months but anticipates that the British pound will depreciate by that time. The pension fund manager can insulate the future transaction from exchange rate risk by negotiating a forward contract to sell British pounds six months forward. In this way, the British pounds received when the stocks are liquidated can be converted to dollars at the exchange rate specified in the forward contract. ●

Some commercial banks accommodate requests by firms to buy or sell currencies forward. If a bank's forward purchase and sale contracts do not even out for a given date, the bank is exposed to exchange rate risk.

<dl><dt>EXAMPLE</dt></dl>

Nebraska Bank has contracts committed to selling C$100 million and purchasing C$150 million 90 days from now. It will receive C$50 million more than it sells. An increase in the Canadian dollar's value 90 days from now will be advantageous, but if the Canadian dollar depreciates then the bank will be adversely affected by its exposure to the exchange rate risk. ●

Estimating the Forward Premium The forward rate of a currency will sometimes exceed the existing spot rate, thereby exhibiting a premium. At other times, it will be below the spot rate, exhibiting a discount. Forward contracts are sometimes referred to in terms of their percentage premium or discount rather than their actual rate. For example, assume that the spot rate (S) of the Canadian dollar is $0.70 while the 180-day (n = 180) forward rate (FR) is $0.71. The forward rate premium (p) would be

$$
\begin{aligned}
p &= \frac{FR - S}{S} \times \frac{360}{n} \\
&= \frac{\$0.71 - \$0.70}{\$0.70} \times \frac{360}{180} \\
&= 2.86\%
\end{aligned}
$$

This premium simply reflects the percentage by which the forward rate exceeds the spot rate on an annualized basis.

WEB

www.cmegroup.com
Review this website for
information on currency
futures contracts.

16-4b Currency Futures Contracts

An alternative to the forward contract is a currency futures contract, which is a standardized contract that specifies an amount of a particular currency to be exchanged on a specified date and at a specified exchange rate. A firm can purchase a futures contract to hedge payables in a foreign currency by locking in the price at which it could purchase that specific currency at a particular point in time. To hedge receivables denominated in a foreign currency, it could sell futures and thereby lock in the price at which it could sell that currency. A futures contract represents a standard number of units. Currency futures contracts also have specific maturity (or "settlement") dates from which the firm must choose.

Futures contracts are standardized, whereas forward contracts can specify whatever amount and maturity date the firm desires. Forward contracts have this flexibility because they are negotiated with commercial banks rather than on a trading floor.

16-4c Currency Swaps

A currency swap is an agreement that allows one currency to be periodically swapped for another at specified exchange rates. It essentially represents a series of forward contracts. Commercial banks facilitate currency swaps by serving as the intermediary that links two parties with opposite needs. Alternatively, commercial banks may be willing to take the position counter to that desired by a particular party. In such a case, they expose themselves to exchange rate risk unless the position they have assumed will offset existing exposure.

16-4d Currency Options Contracts

Another foreign exchange derivative used for hedging is the currency option. Its primary advantage over forward and futures contracts is in stipulating that the parties have the right but not the *obligation* to purchase or sell a particular currency at a specified price within a given period.

A currency call option provides the right to purchase a particular currency at a specified price (called the *exercise* price) within a specified period. This type of option can be used to hedge future cash payments denominated in a foreign currency. If the spot rate remains below the exercise price, the option will not be exercised because the firm could purchase the foreign currency at a lower cost in the spot market. However, a fee (or a premium) must be paid for options, so there is a cost to hedging with options even if the options are not exercised.

A put option provides the right to sell a particular currency at a specified price (the exercise price) within a specified period. If the spot rate remains above that price, the option will not be exercised because the firm could sell the foreign currency at a higher price in the spot market. But if the spot rate is below the exercise price at the time the foreign currency is received, the firm will exercise its put option.

16-4e Use of Foreign Exchange Derivatives for Hedging

When deciding whether to use forward, futures, or options contracts for hedging, a firm should consider the following characteristics of each contract. First, if the firm requires a tailor-made hedge that cannot be matched by existing futures contracts, a forward contract may be preferred. Otherwise, forward and futures contracts should generate somewhat similar results.

The choice between an obligation type of contract (forward or futures) or an options contract depends on the expected trend of the spot rate. If the currency in which payables are denominated appreciates, the firm will benefit more from a futures or forward contract than from a call option contract. The call option contract requires an up-front fee, but it is a wiser choice when the firm is less certain of a currency's future direction. The call option allows the firm to hedge against possible appreciation and also to ignore the contract, and use the spot market instead, if the currency depreciates. Similarly, put options may be preferred over futures or forward contracts for hedging receivables when future currency movements are especially uncertain, because the firm has the flexibility of letting the options expire if the currencies strengthen.

16-4f Use of Foreign Exchange Derivatives for Speculating

The forward, currency futures, and currency options markets may be used for speculating as well as for hedging. A speculator who expects the Singapore dollar to appreciate could consider any of the following strategies.

1. Purchase Singapore dollars forward; when they are received, sell them in the spot market.
2. Purchase futures contracts on Singapore dollars; when the Singapore dollars are received, sell them in the spot market.
3. Purchase call options on Singapore dollars; at some point before the expiration date, when the spot rate exceeds the exercise price, exercise the call option and then sell the Singapore dollars received in the spot market.

Conversely, a speculator who expects the Singapore dollar to depreciate could consider any of the following strategies.

1. Sell Singapore dollars forward, and then purchase them in the spot market just before fulfilling the forward obligation.
2. Sell futures contracts on Singapore dollars; purchase Singapore dollars in the spot market just before fulfilling the futures obligation.
3. Purchase put options on Singapore dollars; at some point before the expiration date, when the spot rate is less than the exercise price, purchase Singapore dollars in the spot market and then exercise the put option.

Speculating with Currency Futures As an example of speculating with currency futures, consider the following information.

■ Spot rate of the British pound is $1.56 per pound.
■ Price of a futures contract is $1.57 per pound.
■ Expectation of the pound's spot rate on the settlement date of the futures contract is $1.63 per pound.

Given that the future spot rate is expected to be higher than the futures price, you could buy currency futures. You would receive pounds on the settlement date for $1.57. If your expectations are correct, you would then sell the pounds for $0.06 more per unit than you paid for them. The risk of your speculative strategy is that the pound may decline rather than increase in value. If it declines to $1.55 by the settlement date, you would have sold the pounds for $0.02 less per unit than you paid.

To account for uncertainty, speculators may develop a probability distribution for the future spot rate as follows.

FUTURE SPOT RATE OF BRITISH POUND	PROBABILITY
$1.50	10%
1.59	20
1.63	50
1.66	20

This probability distribution suggests that four outcomes are possible. For each possible outcome, the anticipated gain or loss can be determined:

POSSIBLE OUTCOME FOR FUTURE SPOT RATE	PROBABILITY	GAIN OR LOSS PER UNIT
$1.50	10%	−$0.07
1.59	20	0.02
1.63	50	0.06
1.66	20	0.09

This analysis measures the probability and potential magnitude of a loss from the speculative strategy.

Speculating with Currency Options   Consider the information from the previous example and assume that a British call option is available with an exercise price of $1.57 and a premium of $0.03 per unit. Recall that your best guess of the future spot rate was $1.63. If your guess is correct, you will earn $0.06 per unit on the difference between what you paid (the exercise price of $1.57) and the price for which you could sell a pound ($1.63). After the premium paid for the option ($0.03 per unit) is deducted, the net gain is $0.03 per unit.

The risk of purchasing this option is that the pound's value might decline over time. If so, you will be unable to exercise the option, and your loss will be the premium paid for it. To assess the risk involved, a probability distribution can be developed. In Exhibit 16.2, the probability distribution from the previous example is applied here. The distribution of net gains from the strategy is shown in the sixth column.

Speculators should always compare the potential gains from currency options and currency futures contracts to determine which type of contract (if any) to trade. It is possible for two speculators to have similar expectations about potential gains from both types of contracts yet to prefer different types of contracts because they have different degrees of risk aversion.

Exhibit 16.2   Estimating Speculative Gains from Options Using a Probability Distribution

(1) POSSIBLE OUTCOME FOR FUTURE SPOT RATE	(2) PROBABILITY	(3) WILL THE OPTION BE EXERCISED BASED ON THIS OUTCOME?	(4) GAIN PER UNIT FROM EXERCISING OPTION	(5) PREMIUM PAID PER UNIT FOR THE OPTION	(6) NET GAIN OR LOSS PER UNIT
$1.50	10%	No	—	$.03	−$.03
1.59	20	Yes	$.02	.03	−.01
1.63	50	Yes	.06	.03	.03
1.66	20	Yes	.09	.03	.06

16-5 INTERNATIONAL ARBITRAGE

Exchange rates and exchange rate derivatives are market determined. If they become misaligned, various forms of arbitrage can occur, forcing realignment. Common types of international arbitrage are explained next.

16-5a Locational Arbitrage

Locational arbitrage is the act of capitalizing on a discrepancy between the spot exchange rate at two different locations by purchasing the currency where it is priced low and selling it where it is priced high.

EXAMPLE

The exchange rates of the European euro quoted by two banks differ, as shown in Exhibit 16.3. The ask quote is higher than the bid quote to reflect the transaction costs charged by each bank. Because Baltimore Bank is asking $1.046 for euros and Sacramento Bank is willing to pay (bid) $1.050 for euros, an institution could execute locational arbitrage. That is, it could achieve a risk-free return without tying funds up for any length of time by buying euros at one location (Baltimore Bank) and simultaneously selling them at the other location (Sacramento Bank). ●

As locational arbitrage is executed, Baltimore Bank will begin to raise its ask price on euros in response to the strong demand. In addition, Sacramento Bank will begin to lower its bid price in response to the excess supply of euros it has recently received. Once Baltimore's ask price is at least as high as Sacramento's bid price, locational arbitrage will no longer be possible. Because some financial institutions (particularly the foreign exchange departments of commercial banks) watch for locational arbitrage opportunities, any discrepancy in exchange rates among locations is quickly eliminated.

16-5b Triangular Arbitrage

If the quoted cross-exchange rate between two foreign currencies is not aligned with the two corresponding exchange rates, there is a discrepancy in the exchange rate quotations. Under this condition, investors can engage in **triangular arbitrage**, which involves buying or selling the currency that is subject to a mispriced cross-exchange rate.

EXAMPLE

If the spot rate is $0.07 for the Mexican peso and $0.70 for the Canadian dollar, the cross-exchange rate should be C$1 = 10 pesos (computed as $0.70/$0.07). Assume that the Canadian dollar/peso exchange rate is quoted as C$1 = 10.3 pesos. In this case, the quote for the Canadian dollar is higher than it should be. An investor could benefit by using U.S. dollars to buy Canadian dollars, using those Canadian dollars to buy pesos, and then using the pesos to buy U.S. dollars. These three transactions would be executed at about the same time, before the exchange rates change. With $1,000, you could buy C$1,428.57 (computed as 1,000 ÷ 0.70), convert those Canadian dollars into 14,714 pesos (computed as 1,428.57 × 10.3), and then convert the pesos into $1,030 (computed as 14,714 × 0.07). Thus, you would have a gain of $30. Of course, the gain would be larger if you engaged in triangular arbitrage using a larger amount of money. ●

Exhibit 16.3 Bank Quotes Used for Locational Arbitrage Example

	BID RATE ON EUROS	ASK RATE ON EUROS
Sacramento Bank	$1.050	$1.056
Baltimore Bank	$1.042	$1.046

Whenever there is a discrepancy in exchange rates, financial institutions with large amounts of money will engage in triangular arbitrage, causing the quoted exchange rates to quickly adjust. The arbitrage transaction of using U.S. dollars to buy Canadian dollars will cause the Canadian dollar to appreciate with respect to the U.S. dollar. The arbitrage transaction of using Canadian dollars to buy pesos will cause the Canadian dollar to depreciate against the peso, and the transaction of using pesos to buy U.S. dollars will cause the peso to depreciate against the U.S. dollar. Once the cross-exchange rate adjusts to its appropriate level, triangular arbitrage will no longer be feasible. The rates may adjust within a matter of seconds in response to the market forces. Quoted cross-exchange rates normally do not reflect a discrepancy because, if they did, financial institutions would capitalize on the discrepancy until the exchange rates were realigned.

16-5c Covered Interest Arbitrage

The coexistence of international money markets and forward markets forces a special relationship, between a forward rate premium and the interest rate differential of two countries, that is known as **interest rate parity**. This relationship also has implications for currency futures contracts, since they are normally priced like forward contracts.

According the interest rate parity, the premium on the forward rate can be determined as

$$p = \frac{(1 + i_h)}{(1 + i_f)} - 1$$

where

p = **forward premium of foreign currency**
i_h = **home country interest rate**
i_f = **foreign interest rate**

EXAMPLE

The spot rate of the New Zealand dollar is $0.50, the one-year U.S. interest rate is 9 percent, and the one-year New Zealand interest rate is 6 percent. Under conditions of interest rate parity, the forward premium of the New Zealand dollar will be

$$p = \frac{(1 + 9\%)}{(1 + 6\%)} - 1$$
$$\simeq 2.8\%$$

This means that the forward rate of the New Zealand dollar will be about $0.514, reflecting a 2.8 percent premium above the spot rate. ●

Examining the equation for interest rate parity reveals that if the interest rate is lower in the foreign country than in the home country, the forward rate of the foreign currency will exhibit a premium. In the opposite situation, the forward rate will exhibit a discount.

Interest rate parity suggests that the forward rate premium (or discount) should be about equal to the differential in interest rates between the countries of concern. If this relationship does not hold, market forces should occur that will restore it. The act of capitalizing on the discrepancy between the forward rate premium and the interest rate differential is called **covered interest arbitrage**.

EXAMPLE

Both the spot rate and the one-year forward rate of the Canadian dollar are $0.80. The Canadian interest rate is 10 percent and the U.S. interest rate is 8 percent. Hence U.S. investors can take advantage of the higher Canadian interest rate, without being exposed to exchange rate risk, by executing covered interest arbitrage. Specifically, they will exchange U.S. dollars for Canadian dollars and invest at the rate of 10 percent. They will simultaneously sell Canadian dollars one year forward. Because they are able to purchase and sell Canadian dollars for the same price, their return is the 10 percent interest earned on their investment. ●

As the U.S. investors demand Canadian dollars in the spot market while selling Canadian dollars forward, they place upward pressure on the spot rate and downward pressure on the one-year forward rate of the Canadian dollar. Thus, the Canadian dollar's forward rate will exhibit a discount. Once the discount becomes large enough, the interest rate advantage in Canada will be offset. In other words, what U.S. investors gain on the higher Canadian interest rate is offset by having to buy Canadian dollars at a higher (spot) rate than the selling (forward) rate. Then covered interest arbitrage will no longer generate a return that is any higher for U.S. investors than an alternative investment in the United States. Once the forward discount (or premium) offsets the interest rate differential in this manner, interest rate parity exists.

The interest rate parity equation determines the forward discount that the Canadian dollar must exhibit in order to offset the interest rate differential:

$$p = \frac{(1 + i_h)}{(1 + i_f)} - 1$$
$$= \frac{(1 + 8\%)}{(1 + 10\%)} - 1$$
$$\simeq -1.82\%$$

If the forward rate is lower than the spot rate by 1.82 percent, the interest rate is offset and covered interest arbitrage would yield a return to U.S. investors similar to the U.S. interest rate.

The existence of interest rate parity prevents investors from earning higher returns from covered interest arbitrage than can be earned in the United States. Nevertheless, international investing may still be feasible if the investing firm does not simultaneously cover in the forward market. Of course, failure to do so usually exposes the firm to exchange rate risk; if the currency denominating the investment depreciates over the investment horizon, the return on the investment is reduced.

Summary

- Exchange rate systems vary in the degree to which a country's central bank controls its currency's exchange rate. Many countries allow their currency to float yet periodically engage in intervention to control the exchange rate. Some countries use a pegged exchange rate system in which the currency's value is pegged to the U.S. dollar or to another currency. Several European countries have adopted the euro as their currency; a single monetary policy is implemented in those countries.

- Exchange rates are influenced by differential inflation rates, differential interest rates, and central bank intervention. There is upward pressure on a foreign currency's value when its home country has relatively low inflation or relatively high interest rates. Central banks can place upward pressure on a currency by purchasing that currency in the foreign exchange markets (by exchanging other currencies held in reserve for that currency). Alternatively, they can place downward pressure on a currency by selling that currency in the foreign exchange markets in exchange for other currencies.

- Exchange rates can be forecasted using technical, fundamental, and market-based methods. Each method has its own advantages and limitations.

■ Foreign exchange derivatives include forward contracts, currency futures contracts, currency swaps, and currency options contracts. Forward contracts can be purchased to hedge future payables or be sold to hedge future receivables in a foreign currency. Currency futures contracts can be used in a manner similar to forward contracts to hedge payables or receivables in a foreign currency. Currency swaps can be used to lock in the exchange rate of a foreign currency to be received or purchased in the future. Currency call (put) options can be purchased to hedge future payables (receivables) in a foreign currency. Currency options offer more flexibility than the other foreign exchange derivatives, but a premium must be paid for them.

Foreign exchange derivatives can also be used to speculate on expected exchange rate movements. When speculators expect a foreign currency to appreciate, they can lock in the exchange rate at which they may purchase that currency by purchasing forward contracts, futures contracts, or call options on that currency. When speculators expect a currency to depreciate, they can lock in the

exchange rate at which they may sell that currency by selling forward contracts or futures contracts on that currency. They could also purchase put options on that currency.

■ International arbitrage ensures that foreign exchange market prices are set properly. If exchange rates vary among the banks that serve the foreign exchange market, locational arbitrage will be possible. Foreign exchange market participants will purchase a currency at the bank with a low quote and sell it to another bank where the quote is higher. If a quoted cross-exchange rate is misaligned with the corresponding exchange rates, triangular arbitrage will be possible. This involves buying or selling the currency that is subject to the mispriced exchange rate. If the interest rate differential is not offset by the forward rate premium (as suggested by interest rate parity), covered interest arbitrage will be possible. This involves investing in a foreign currency and simultaneously selling the currency forward. Arbitrage will occur until interest rate parity is restored.

POINT COUNTER-POINT

Do Financial Institutions Need to Consider Foreign Exchange Market Conditions When Making Domestic Security Market Decisions?

Point   No. If there is no exchange of currencies, there is no need to monitor the foreign exchange market.

Counter-Point   Yes. Foreign exchange market conditions can affect an economy or an industry and therefore affect the valuation of securities. In addition,

the valuation of a firm can be affected by currency movements because of its international business.

Who Is Correct?   Use the Internet to learn more about this issue and then formulate your own opinion on this issue.

QUESTIONS AND APPLICATIONS

1. Exchange Rate Systems Explain the exchange rate system that existed during the 1950s and 1960s. How did the Smithsonian Agreement in 1971 revise it? How does today's exchange rate system differ?

2. Dirty Float Explain the difference between a freely floating system and a dirty float. Which type is more representative of the U.S. system?

3. Impact of Quotas Assume that European countries impose a quota on goods imported from the

United States and that the United States does not plan to retaliate. How could this affect the value of the euro? Explain.

4. Impact of Capital Flows Assume that stocks in the United Kingdom become very attractive to U.S. investors. How could this affect the value of the British pound? Explain.

5. Impact of Inflation Assume that Mexico suddenly experiences high and unexpected inflation.

How could this affect the value of the Mexican peso according to purchasing power parity (PPP) theory?

6. Impact of Economic Conditions Assume that Switzerland has a very strong economy, putting upward pressure on both inflation and interest rates. Explain how these conditions could put pressure on the value of the Swiss franc, and determine whether the franc's value will rise or fall.

7. Central Bank Intervention The Bank of Japan desires to decrease the value of the Japanese yen against the U.S. dollar. How could it use direct intervention to do this?

8. Conditions for Speculation Explain the conditions under which a speculator would like to invest in a foreign currency today even when it has no use for that currency in the future.

9. Risk from Speculating Seattle Bank just took speculative positions by borrowing Canadian dollars and converting the funds to invest in Australian dollars. Explain a possible future scenario that could adversely affect the bank's performance.

10. Impact of a Weak Dollar How does a weak dollar affect U.S. inflation? Explain.

11. Speculating with Foreign Exchange Derivatives Explain how U.S. speculators could use foreign exchange derivatives to speculate on the expected appreciation of the Japanese yen.

Advanced Questions

12. Interaction of Capital Flows and Yield Curve Assume a horizontal yield curve exists. How do you think the yield curve would be affected if foreign investors in short-term securities and long-term securities suddenly anticipate that the value of the dollar will strengthen? (You may find it helpful to refer back to the discussion of the yield curve in Chapter 3.)

13. How the Euro's Value May Respond to Prevailing Conditions Consider the prevailing conditions for inflation (including oil prices), the economy, interest rates, and any other factors that could affect exchange rates. Based on these conditions, do you think the euro's value will likely appreciate or depreciate against the dollar for the remainder of this semester? Offer some logic to support your answer. Which factor do you think will have the biggest impact on the euro's exchange rate?

14. Obtaining Credit from the European Central Bank What are the consequences to a government in the eurozone when it obtains credit from the ECB?

15. Impact of Abandoning the Euro on Eurozone Conditions. Explain the possible signal that would be transmitted to the market if a country abandoned use of the euro.

Interpreting Financial News

Interpret the following statements made by Wall Street analysts and portfolio managers.

a. "Our use of currency futures has completely changed our risk–return profile."

b. "Our use of currency options resulted in an upgrade in our credit rating."

c. "Our strategy of using forward contracts to hedge backfired on us."

Managing in Financial Markets

Using Forex Derivatives for Hedging You are the manager of a stock portfolio for a financial institution, and about 20 percent of the stock portfolio that you manage is in British stocks. You expect the British stock market to perform well over the next year, and you plan to sell the stocks one year from now (and will convert the British pounds received to dollars at that time). However, you are concerned that the British pound may depreciate against the dollar over the next year.

a. Explain how you could use a forward contract to hedge the exchange rate risk associated with your position in British stocks.

b. If interest rate parity holds, does this limit the effectiveness of a forward contract as a hedge?

c. Explain how you could use an options contract to hedge the exchange rate risk associated with your position in stocks.

d. Assume that, although you are concerned about the potential decline in the pound's value, you also believe that the pound could appreciate against the dollar over the next year. You would like to benefit from the potential appreciation but also wish to hedge against the possible depreciation. Should you use a forward contract or options contracts to hedge your position? Explain.

PROBLEMS

1. Currency Futures Use the following information to determine the probability distribution of per unit gains from selling Mexican peso futures.

- Spot rate of the peso is $0.10.
- Price of peso futures is $0.102 per unit.
- Your expectation of the peso spot rate at maturity of the futures contract is:

POSSIBLE OUTCOME FOR FUTURE SPOT RATE	PROBABILITY
$0.090	10%
0.095	70
0.110	20

2. Currency Call Options Use the following information to determine the probability distribution of net gains per unit from purchasing a call option on British pounds.

- Spot rate of the British pound is $1.45.
- Premium on the British pound option is $0.04 per unit.
- Exercise price of a British pound option is $1.46.
- Your expectation of the British pound spot rate prior to the expiration of the option is:

POSSIBLE OUTCOME FOR FUTURE SPOT RATE	PROBABILITY
$1.48	30%
1.49	40
1.52	30

3. Locational Arbitrage Assume the following exchange rate quotes on British pounds:

	BID	ASK
Orleans Bank	$1.46	$1.47
Kansas Bank	1.48	1.49

Explain how locational arbitrage would occur. Also explain why this arbitrage will realign the exchange rates.

4. Covered Interest Arbitrage Assume the following information:

- British pound spot rate = $1.58
- British pound one-year forward rate = $1.58
- British one-year interest rate = 11 percent
- U.S. one-year interest rate = 9 percent

Explain how U.S. investors could use covered interest arbitrage to lock in a higher yield than 9 percent. What would be their yield? Explain how the spot and forward rates of the pound would change as covered interest arbitrage occurs.

5. Covered Interest Arbitrage Assume the following information:

- Mexican one-year interest rate = 15 percent
- U.S. one-year interest rate = 11 percent

If interest rate parity exists, what would be the forward premium or discount on the Mexican peso's forward rate? Would covered interest arbitrage be more profitable to U.S. investors than investing at home? Explain.

FLOW OF FUNDS EXERCISE

Hedging with Foreign Exchange Derivatives

Carson Company expects that it will receive a large order from the government of Spain. If the order occurs, Carson will be paid about 3 million euros. Since all of its expenses are in dollars, Carson would like to hedge this position. Carson has contacted a bank with brokerage subsidiaries that can help it hedge with foreign exchange derivatives.

a. How could Carson use currency futures to hedge its position?

b. What is the risk of hedging with currency futures?

c. How could Carson use currency options to hedge its position?

d. Explain the advantage and disadvantage to Carson of using currency options instead of currency futures.

INTERNET/EXCEL EXERCISES

Use the website www.oanda.com to assess exchange rates.

1. What is the most recent value of the Australian dollar in terms of U.S. dollars? For large transactions, how many British pounds does a U.S. dollar buy?

2. Review the pound's value over the past year. Offer a possible explanation for the recent movements in the pound's value.

3. What is the most recent value of the Hong Kong dollar in terms of U.S. dollars? Do you notice anything unusual about this value over time? What could explain an exchange rate trend such as this?

WSJ EXERCISE

Assessing Exchange Rate Movements

Use a recent issue of the *Wall Street Journal* to determine how a particular currency's value has changed against the dollar since the beginning of the year. The "Currencies" table lists the percentage change in many currencies since the beginning of the year.

ONLINE ARTICLES WITH REAL-WORLD EXAMPLES

Find a recent practical article available online that describes a real-world example regarding a specific financial institution or financial market that reinforces one or more concepts covered in this chapter. If your class has an online component, your professor may ask you to post your summary of the article there and provide a link to the article so that other students can access it.

If your class is live, your professor may ask you to summarize your application of the article in class. Your professor may assign specific students to complete this assignment or may allow any students to do the assignment on a volunteer basis.

For recent online articles and real-world examples related to this chapter, consider using the following search terms (be sure to include the prevailing year as a search term to ensure that the online articles are recent):

1. foreign exchange AND institutional investors

2. inflation AND exchange rate

3. interest rate AND exchange rate

4. central bank intervention

5. foreign exchange controls

6. currency AND forecasting

7. currency AND forward contract

8. forward contract AND hedge

9. currency futures AND speculate

10. currency options AND hedge

Currency Option Pricing

Understanding what drives the premiums paid for currency options makes it easier to recognize the various factors that must be monitored when anticipating future movements in currency option premiums. Because participants in the currency options market typically take positions based on their expectations of how the premiums will change over time, they can benefit from understanding how options are priced.

BOUNDARY CONDITIONS

The first step in pricing currency options is to recognize boundary conditions that force the option premium to be within lower and upper bounds.

Lower Bounds

The lower bound of a call option premium (C) is either zero or the difference between the underlying spot exchange rate (S) and the exercise price (X), whichever is greater:

$$C \geq \max(0, S - X)$$

This floor is enforced by arbitrage restrictions. For example, assume that the premium on a British pound call option is $0.01 while the spot rate of the pound is $1.62 and the exercise price is $1.60. In this example the spread $(S - X)$ exceeds the call premium, which would allow for arbitrage. One could purchase the call option for $0.01 per unit, immediately exercise the option at $1.60 per pound, and then sell the pounds in the spot market for $1.62 per unit. These actions would generate an immediate profit of $0.01 per unit. Arbitrage would continue until the market forces realigned the spread $(S - X)$ to be less than or equal to the call premium.

The put option premium (P) has a lower bound of either zero or the difference between the exercise price and the underlying spot exchange rate, whichever is greater:

$$P \geq \max(0, X - S)$$

This floor is also enforced by arbitrage restrictions. For example, assume that the premium on a British pound put option is $0.02 while the spot rate of the pound is $1.60 and the exercise price is $1.63. One could purchase the pound put option for $0.02 per unit, purchase pounds in the spot market at $1.60, and immediately exercise the option by selling the pounds at $1.63 per unit to yield a profit of $0.01 per unit. Arbitrage would continue until the market forces realigned the spread $(X - S)$ to be less than or equal to the put premium.

Upper Bounds

The upper bound for a call option premium is the spot exchange rate, S:

$$C \le S$$

If the call option premium ever exceeds the spot exchange rate, one could engage in arbitrage by selling call options for a higher price per unit than the cost of purchasing the underlying currency. Even if those call options were exercised, one could pay them off using the currency purchased earlier. The arbitrage profit in this example would be the difference between the amount received when selling (which is the premium) and the cost of purchasing the currency in the spot market. Arbitrage would occur until the call option's premium was less than or equal to the spot rate.

The upper bound for a put option is equal to the option's exercise price, X:

$$P \le X$$

If the put option premium ever exceeds the exercise price, one could engage in arbitrage by selling put options. Even if the put options were exercised, the proceeds received from selling the put options would exceed the price paid (which is the exercise price) at the time of exercise.

Option premiums lie within these boundaries because the boundaries are enforced by arbitrage.

APPLICATION OF PRICING MODELS

Although boundary conditions can be used to determine the possible range for a currency option's premium, they do not precisely indicate the appropriate premium for the option. However, pricing models have been developed to price currency options. Based on information about an option (e.g., the exercise price and time to maturity) and about the currency (e.g., its spot rate, standard deviation, and interest rate), pricing models can derive the premium on a currency option. The currency option pricing model of Biger and Hull (1983) is

$$C = e^{-R_f^* T} S \cdot N(d_1) - e^{-R_f T} X \cdot N(d_1 - \sigma \sqrt{T})$$

where

$d_1 = \{[\ln(S/X) + (R_f - R_f^* + (\sigma^2/2))T]/\sigma\sqrt{T}\}$
C = price of the currency call option
S = underlying spot exchange rate
X = exercise price
R_f = U.S. riskless rate of interest
R_f^* = foreign riskless rate of interest
σ = instantaneous standard deviation of the return on a holding of foreign currency
T = time to option maturity expressed as a fraction of year
$N(\cdot)$ = standard normal cumulative distribution function

This equation is based on the stock option-pricing model (OPM) when allowing for continuous dividends. Since the interest gained on holding a foreign security (R_f^*) is equivalent to a continuously paid dividend on a stock share, this version of the OPM holds completely. The key transformation in adapting the stock OPM to value currency options is the substitution of exchange rates for stock prices. Thus, the percentage change of exchange rates (like that of stocks) is assumed to follow a diffusion process with constant mean and variance.

The model developed by Biger and Hull is sometimes referred to as the European model because it does not account for early exercise.[*] Unlike American currency options, European currency options do not allow for early exercise (i.e., before the expiration date). The extra flexibility of American currency options should entail a higher premium than on European currency options with similar characteristics. However, there is not a closed-form model for pricing American currency options. Although various techniques are used to price such options, the European model is commonly applied because it can be just as accurate for American as for European currency options.

Given all other parameters, the currency option pricing model can be used to impute the standard deviation σ. This implied parameter represents the option's market assessment of currency volatility over the life of the option.

Pricing Currency Put Options According to Put-Call Parity

Given the premium C of a European call option, the premium P for a European put option on the same currency and with the same exercise price X can be derived from put–call parity as follows:

$$P = C + Xe^{-R_f T} - Se^{-R_f^* T}$$

where R_f is the riskless rate of interest, R_f^* is the foreign rate of interest, and T is the option's time to maturity expressed as a fraction of the year.

If the actual put option premium is *less* than suggested by the put–call parity equation just shown, arbitrage is possible. Specifically, one could (1) buy the put option, (2) sell the call option, and (3) buy the underlying currency. The purchases would be financed with the proceeds from selling the call option and from borrowing at the rate R_f. Meanwhile, the foreign currency that was purchased can be deposited to earn the foreign rate R_f^*. Regardless of the path of the currency's exchange rate movement over the option's lifetime, the arbitrage will result in a profit. First, if the exchange rate is equal to the exercise price so that each option expires worthless, the foreign currency can be converted in the spot market to dollars, and this amount will exceed the amount required to repay the loan. Second, if the foreign currency appreciates and therefore exceeds the exercise price, there will be a loss from the call option being exercised. Although the put option would expire, the foreign currency would be converted in the spot market to dollars, and this amount will exceed the amount required to repay the loan and the amount of the loss on the call option. Third, if the foreign currency depreciates and thus is below the exercise price, the amount received from selling the put option plus the amount received from converting the foreign currency to dollars will exceed the amount required to repay the loan. Since the arbitrage generates a profit under any exchange rate scenario, it will force an adjustment in the option premiums so that put–call parity is no longer violated.

If the actual put option premium is *more* than suggested by put–call parity, arbitrage would again be possible. The arbitrage strategy would be the reverse of that just described for the case when the actual put option premium is less than suggested by put–call parity. Again, the arbitrage would eventually force an adjustment in option

[*]Nahum Biger and John Hull, "The Valuation of Currency Options," *Financial Management* (Spring 1983): 24–28.

premiums so that put–call parity is no longer violated. Note, however, that the arbitrage applicable when there is a violation of put–call parity on American currency options differs slightly from the arbitrage applicable to European currency options. Even so, the concept still holds that the premium of a currency put option is determined by the premium of a call option on the same currency and with the same exercise price.

Choosing among Derivative Securities

This problem requires an understanding of futures contracts (Chapter 13), options markets (Chapter 14), interest rate swap markets (Chapter 15), and foreign exchange derivative markets (Chapter 16). It also requires an understanding of how economic conditions affect interest rates and security prices.

Assume that the United States has just experienced a mild recession. As a result, interest rates have declined to their lowest levels in a decade. The U.S. interest rates appear to be influenced more by changes in the demand for funds than by changes in the supply of U.S. savings, because the savings rate does not change much regardless of economic conditions. The yield curve is currently flat. The federal budget deficit has been reduced lately and is not expected to rise substantially.

The federal government recently decided to reduce personal tax rates significantly for all tax brackets and also to reduce corporate tax rates. The U.S. dollar has just recently weakened. Economies of other countries were somewhat stagnant but have improved in the past quarter. Your assignment is to recommend how various financial institutions should respond to the preceding information.

Questions

1. A savings institution holds 50 percent of its assets as long-term, fixed-rate mortgages. Virtually all of its funds are in the form of short-term deposits. Which of the following strategies would be most appropriate for this institution?

   ■ Use a fixed-for-floating swap.
   ■ Use a swap of floating payments for fixed payments.
   ■ Use a put option on interest rate futures contracts.
   ■ Remain unhedged.

   Defend your recommendation.

2. An insurance company maintains a large portfolio of U.S. stocks. Which of the following would be more appropriate?

   ■ Sell stock index futures contracts.
   ■ Remain unhedged.

   Defend your recommendation.

3. A pension fund maintains a large bond portfolio of U.S. bonds. Which of the following would be most appropriate?

- ■ Sell bond index futures.
- ■ Buy bond index futures.
- ■ Remain unhedged.

Defend your recommendation.

4. An international mutual fund sponsored by a U.S. securities firm consists of bonds evenly allocated across the United States and the United Kingdom. One of the portfolio managers has decided to hedge all the assets by selling futures on a popular U.S. bond index. The manager has stated that, because the fund concentrates only on risk-free Treasury bonds, the only concern is interest rate risk. Assuming that interest rate risk is the only risk of concern, will the manager's hedging strategy be effective? Why or why not? Is there any other risk that deserves to be considered? If so, how would you hedge that risk?

Midterm Self-Exam

MIDTERM REVIEW

You have just completed all of the chapters focused on the financial markets. Here is a brief summary of some of the key points in those chapters.

Chapter 1 provides an overview of the types of financial markets, the securities that are traded within those markets, and the financial institutions that serve those markets. Chapter 2 explains how general interest rate levels are driven by factors that affect the demand for loanable funds (such as inflation and economic growth) and the supply of loanable funds (such as the Fed's monetary policy). Chapter 3 explains how interest rates vary among securities in response to differences in credit risk, liquidity, tax status, and term to maturity. Chapter 4 describes the Fed's monetary policy, and Chapter 5 explains how the Fed's policy adjusts the supply of loanable funds to affect interest rates and economic conditions.

Chapter 6 explains how money market securities serve investors whose primary need is liquidity rather than high returns. Chapters 7 through 12 describe the characteristics, pricing, and risk of capital market securities. In particular, Chapters 7 through 9 focus on long-term debt securities and explain the sensitivity of long-term debt's market values to interest rate movements. Chapter 10 describes how stocks are placed and how institutional investors attempt to ensure that managers of publicly traded companies make decisions that maximize the stock's value. Chapter 11 shows how the value of a stock is influenced by the factors that influence the firm's future cash flows or risk. Chapter 12 describes how stocks are traded and how the trading is regulated. Because money market securities, long-term debt securities, and stocks have different characteristics, they serve different investors. In addition, the sensitivity of their prices to various factors differs among securities. Investors are therefore able to allocate their investments in securities in a way that reflects their specific return and risk preferences.

Chapter 13 explains how interest rate futures contracts can be sold to speculate on expectations of rising rates and also how such contracts can be sold to speculate on expectations of declining interest rates. In addition, this chapter explains how interest rate futures can be sold to hedge the interest rate risk of portfolios containing long-term debt securities and how stock index futures contracts can be used to hedge the market risk of stock portfolios. Chapter 14 explains how call (put) options can be used to speculate on expectations of rising (falling) stock prices. It also explains how put options on stock indexes can be used to hedge stock portfolios and how put options on bond index futures can be used to hedge long-term debt security portfolios. Chapter 15 explains how interest rate swaps can be used to speculate on expectations of rising or declining interest rates, and Chapter 16 explains how foreign exchange markets are used to facilitate the trading of international securities.

This exam does not cover all of the concepts that have been presented up to this point. It is simply intended to allow you to test yourself on a general overview of key concepts. Simulate taking an exam by answering all of the questions *without* using your book and your notes. The answer key is provided just after the exam. If you have any wrong answers, you should reread the related material and then redo any exam questions that you had wrong.

This exam may not match the level of rigor in your course. Your instructor may provide specific information about how this Midterm Self-Exam relates to the coverage and rigor of the midterm exam in your course.

MIDTERM SELF-EXAM

1. Explain the meaning of asymmetric information and how it can have an impact on trading in the stock market.

2. In the last year, the one-year risk-free interest rate increased from 3 to 7 percent.

a. What is a likely reason for the large increase in the risk-free rate?

b. In the last year, the 10-year risk-free rate declined from 7 to 6 percent. How can you reconcile the change in the short-term interest rate with the change in the long-term interest rate? According to expectations theory, what does the shift in the yield curve imply about future interest rates?

3. The prevailing yield on a B-rated corporate bond is 7 percent. Explain how the yield offered on new B-rated bonds could be affected if economic conditions deteriorate. There are two forces that deserve consideration.

4. Consider the components that determine the prevailing yield of a highly rated corporate bond, such as the risk-free rate, the default risk premium, and the liquidity premium. The yield offered on a corporate bond in the secondary market changes over time. Which component do you think is typically the main source of changes over time in the yield offered on a highly rated corporate bond? Explain.

5. Recently, economic conditions have weakened. Although consumer prices have not increased in the last year, oil prices have risen by 20 percent in the last month. The Fed wants to show its dedication to controlling inflation and therefore decides to restrict the money supply and increase the target federal funds rate by 0.5 percent.

a. If you were on the FOMC, would you support the Fed's decision? Explain.

b. Explain how prices of money market securities would change in response to this policy. Why might bond prices be more sensitive than money market securities to this change in the Fed's policy? Why might bond prices be less sensitive than money market securities to changes in the Fed's policy?

6. Assume that the Fed decided to reduce the federal funds rate by 0.5 percent today and that this decision was not anticipated by the financial markets.

a. Why might this change in monetary policy affect the yields paid by corporations when they issue corporate bonds?

b. Why might the change in monetary policy have no effect on the yields paid by corporations when they issue corporate bonds?

7. Why do bond market participants pay close attention to the fiscal policy decisions of the U.S. government?

8. A Treasury bond's coupon and principal payments are guaranteed. Does this mean that the value of the Treasury bond is almost constant over time? Explain.

9. Offer a logical explanation for why higher expected inflation could affect the yield on new, 30-year, fixed-rate mortgages. Why are secondary price movements of fixed-rate mortgages correlated with price movements of corporate bonds?

10. Assume that the Fed uses monetary policy to reduce the target federal funds rate, and assume that the market does not anticipate this reduction. Use the CAPM framework to explain why this policy could enhance the prices of stocks.

11. Assume that the standard deviation of a stock's monthly returns is 4 percent and that the expected return of the stock over the next month is zero. Use the value-at-risk method to estimate the maximum expected loss for a month based on a 95 percent confidence level.

12. Based on what you learned in the chapters on the bond markets and stock markets, are these markets complements or substitutes from an issuer's perspective? From an investor's perspective?

13. Explain why a publicly traded firm's ability to place stock in a secondary offering is dependent on the stock's liquidity in the secondary market.

14. Why would a publicly traded firm go private? Why might the Sarbanes-Oxley Act encourage some publicly traded firms to go private?

15. Why does the market for corporate control affect stock valuations? Offer a reason why the market for corporate control will not always force corporate managers to serve in the best interests of shareholders.

16. Charleston Investment Company just purchased Renfro stock for $50. It engages in a covered call strategy whereby it sells call options on Renfro stock. A call option on Renfro stock is available with an exercise price of $52, a one-year expiration date, and a premium of $2. Assume that the buyers of the call option will exercise the option on the expiration date if it is feasible to do so. Charleston will sell the stock at the end of one year even if the option is not exercised. Determine the net profit per share for Charleston based on the following possible prices for Renfro stock at the end of one year:

    a. $45

    b. $49

    c. $50

    d. $53

    e. $55

17. a. Compare the purchase of stock index futures versus index options. Why might institutional investors use futures to hedge their stock portfolios in some periods and use options for that same purpose in other periods?

    b. For hedging a stock portfolio, explain the trade-off involved when purchasing a put option with an exercise price that is at the money versus deep out of the money.

18. Assume that interest rate parity holds. Assume U.S. investors plan to invest in a government security denominated in a foreign currency.

a. If the security has a higher interest rate than the U.S. interest rate, will the forward rate of the currency exhibit a discount? Explain.

b. If the investors engage in covered interest arbitrage, will they achieve a return that is higher than, lower than, or the same as the foreign interest rate? Explain.

c. If the investors engage in covered interest arbitrage, will they achieve a return that is higher than, lower than, or the same as the U.S. interest rate? Explain.

Answers to Midterm Self-Exam

1. Asymmetric information occurs because managers of publicly traded firms have more information about their firms than do investors, who do not work at the firm. Consequently, the valuation of firms by investors is limited because there may be private information about the firms that they do not have. This can result in improper pricing of stocks and a wide dispersion among investors regarding the proper valuation of stocks.

2. a. Common reasons for higher interest rates include a stronger economy, higher inflation, and a more restrictive monetary policy.

b. The yield curve had a steep upward slope one year ago. Now the yield curve has a slight downward slope. According to expectations theory, the prevailing yield curve indicates that interest rates are expected to decline in the future.

3. If deteriorating economic conditions cause a decline in the demand for loanable funds, the risk-free interest rate will decline. However, the risk premium should increase because the chance of default by the issuer of the bonds will be higher as a result of the weaker economy.

4. Changes in the risk-free rate can have a major impact on the yield offered on a corporate bond. The default risk premium and liquidity premium may change, but normally they have less impact on the yield offered over time.

5. a. No, because the policy will not necessarily have any impact on oil prices. However, the policy will slow economic growth and the economy is already weak.

b. Prices of money market securities will decline in response to the Fed's policy change because the interest rate and hence the required rate of return on short-term securities will increase, so the present value of their cash flows will be reduced. When the Fed reduces the money supply in order to increase the federal funds rate, this shift could also affect long-term interest rates. If so, the required rate of return on bonds will change and, in response, long-term bond prices will decline. If the Fed's policy has no effect on long-term interest rates, the prices of long-term bonds should not change. In this case, bond prices are less sensitive than are money market security prices to the Fed's policy.

6. a. The short-term and long-term markets for debt securities are partially integrated. Therefore, when the Fed increases the money supply in order to reduce the federal funds rate, some of the increased funds in the financial system may be used to invest in bonds. The additional funds supplied to the bond market can reduce the rate that corporations must pay when they borrow by issuing bonds.

b. Sometimes, when the Fed increases the money supply, most of the additional funds are channeled into short-term debt securities rather than long-term debt securities. In this case, there may be no effect on the yields offered on new corporate bonds.

7. The U.S. government's fiscal policy can affect the budget deficit, which can influence interest rates and thereby affect bond prices.

8. No. Movements in the long-term interest rate cause movements in the required rate of return, which can have a major impact on the valuation of Treasury bonds.

9. The higher inflationary expectations may result in a higher demand for and in a smaller supply of loanable funds, which would drive interest rates higher. This results in a higher long-term, risk-free interest rate, which is a key component of the required rate of return when investing in long-term, fixed-rate mortgages.

10. The lower target federal funds rate may result in a lower long-term, risk-free rate, which increases the present value of future cash flows generated by the stock. In addition, the lower interest rate may stimulate borrowing and spending by consumers, which could increase demand for the firm's products and thus increase cash flows.

11. $0 - (1.64 \times 0.04) = -6.56$ percent.

12. Issuers may view the markets as complements because they may use both types of markets to raise funds. In some cases, however, the markets serve as substitutes because a firm may tap only one market or the other. Investors may view the markets as complements because they have used both types of markets to invest funds. Yet in some cases the markets serve as substitutes, as when an investor may tap only one market or the other at a given time when investing funds.

13. Most investors that purchase publicly traded stock want to be able to sell the stock easily in the secondary market in the future. If a stock is illiquid, investors may not be able to sell the stock easily because there may be no interested investors who are willing to purchase it. Thus, investors may have to sell the stock at a discount because of the illiquidity.

14. A publicly traded firm may go private if its managers believe that it is undervalued in the public market. Thus, the managers may suggest that the firm use cash and debt to repurchase all of its outstanding stock. The Sarbanes-Oxley Act increased the reporting requirements for publicly traded firms, which increased the cost of financial reporting by more than $1 million per year for some publicly traded firms. Some firms decided that these costs outweighed the benefits of being public, so they went private to avoid the reporting requirements.

15. The market for corporate control may encourage an efficient firm to acquire an inefficient firm whose stock price is relatively low because of poor performance. Efficient firms may restructure the firms that they purchase and improve their performance. Thus, the market for corporate control allows for a change in control so that more efficient managers replace weak managers.

However, the market for corporate control does not cure every weak firm. There is limited information about firms, which may discourage other firms from trying to acquire them. For example, these weak firms could have many legal problems that might have to be assumed by any firm that acquires them.

16. a. −$3
  b. $1
  c. $2
  d. $4
  e. $4

17. a. Institutional investors may prefer to hedge with stock index futures when they are less confident about stock market conditions, because they forgo the potential gain if market conditions are favorable. Index options may be more desirable when investors want to hedge but also believe there is a reasonable chance that market conditions will be favorable. They must pay a premium for such flexibility.

b. When hedging against market declines, a lower premium is paid when purchasing a stock index option that is deep out of the money. However, the hedge is less effective because the exercise price is low; hence the stock portfolio is hedged against only large losses. Purchasing a stock index put option at the money to hedge against market declines will insulate a stock portfolio even if losses are small, but the premium paid for this type of option is high.

18. a. Yes, based on the interest rate parity formula.

b. Lower, because there is a discount on the forward rate.

c. The same, based on interest rate parity.

PART 6
Commercial Banking

The chapters in Part 6 focus on commercial banking. Chapter 17 identifies the common sources and uses of funds for commercial banks, and Chapter 18 describes the regulations that are imposed on sources and uses of funds and other banking operations. Chapter 19 explains how banks manage their sources and uses of funds to deal with risk. Chapter 20 explains how commercial bank performance can be measured and monitored to assess previous managerial policies.

17

Commercial Bank Operations

Measured by total assets, commercial banks are the most important type of financial intermediary. Like other financial intermediaries, they perform the critical function of facilitating the flow of funds from surplus units to deficit units.

17-1 BACKGROUND ON COMMERCIAL BANKS

Up to this point, the text has focused on the role and functions of financial markets. From this point forward, the emphasis is on the role and functions of financial institutions. Recall from Chapter 1 that financial institutions commonly facilitate the flow of funds between surplus units and deficit units. Commercial banks represent a key financial intermediary because they serve all types of surplus and deficit units. They offer deposit accounts with the size and maturity characteristics desired by surplus units. They repackage the funds received from deposits to provide loans of the size and maturity desired by deficit units. They have the ability to assess the creditworthiness of deficit units that apply for loans, so they can limit their exposure to credit (default) risk on the loans they provide.

17-1a Bank Market Structure

In 1985, more than 14,000 banks were located in the United States. Since then, the market structure has changed dramatically. Banks have been consolidating for several reasons. One reason is that interstate banking regulations were changed in 1994 to allow banks more freedom to acquire other banks across state lines. Consequently, banks in a particular region are now subject to competition not only from other local banks but also from any bank that may penetrate that market. This has prompted banks to become more efficient in order to survive. They have pursued growth also as a means of capitalizing on economies of scale (lower average costs for larger scales of operations) and enhanced efficiency. Acquisitions have been a convenient way to grow quickly.

As a result of this trend, there are less than half as many banks today as there were in 1985, and consolidation is still occurring. Exhibit 17.1 shows how the number of banks has declined over time, thereby increasing concentration in the banking industry. The largest 100 banks now account for about 75 percent of all bank assets versus about 50 percent in 1985. The largest five banks now account for more than 50 percent of bank assets, versus 30 percent in 2001. JPMorgan Chase & Company is the largest bank in the United States with about $2.3 trillion in assets, while Bank of America Corporation has about $2.2 trillion in assets and Citigroup Inc. has about $1.9 trillion in assets.

Large banks have expanded over time by acquiring other banks. They also acquired many other types of financial service firms in recent years.

Exhibit 17.1   Consolidation among Commercial Banks over Time

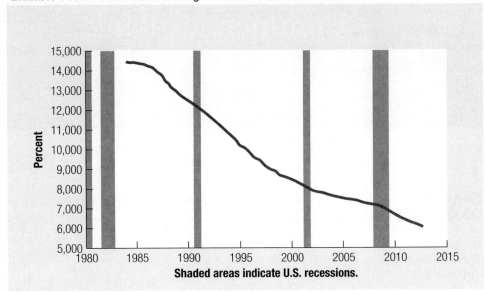

Source: *Federal Reserve.*

Many banks are owned by bank holding companies, which are companies that own at least 10 percent of a bank. The holding company structure allows more flexibility to borrow funds, issue stock, repurchase the company's own stock, and acquire other firms. Bank holding companies may also avoid some state banking regulations.

The operations, management, and regulation of a commercial bank vary with the types of services offered. Therefore, the different types of financial services (such as banking, securities, and insurance) are discussed in separate chapters. This chapter on commercial bank operations applies to independent commercial banks as well as to commercial bank units that are part of a financial conglomerate formed by combining a bank and other financial services firms.

The traditional role of a bank was to serve depositors who want to deposit funds and borrowers who want to borrow funds. Banks charge a higher interest rate on funds loaned out than the interest rate they pay on deposits. The difference in interest between loans and deposits must be sufficient to cover other expenses (such as salaries) and generate a reasonable profit for the bank's owners. Although banks have become much more sophisticated over time, the traditional role still applies.

The primary operations of commercial banks can be most easily identified by reviewing their main sources of funds, their main uses of funds, and the off–balance sheet activities that they provide, as explained in this chapter.

17-2 BANK SOURCES OF FUNDS

WEB

www.fdic.gov
Statistics on bank
sources and uses of
funds.

To understand how any financial institution (or subsidiary of that institution) obtains funds and uses funds, its balance sheet can be reviewed. The institution's reported liabilities and equity indicate its sources of funds, and its reported assets indicate its uses of funds. The major sources of commercial bank funds are summarized as follows.

Deposit Accounts

1. Transaction deposits
2. Savings deposits
3. Time deposits
4. Money market deposit accounts

Borrowed Funds

1. Federal funds purchased (borrowed)
2. Borrowing from the Federal Reserve banks
3. Repurchase agreements
4. Eurodollar borrowings

Long-Term Sources of Funds

1. Bonds issued by the bank
2. Bank capital

Each source of funds is briefly described in the following subsections.

17-2a Transaction Deposits

A **demand deposit account**, or checking account, is offered to customers who desire to write checks against their account. A conventional demand deposit account requires a small minimum balance and pays no interest. From the bank's perspective, demand deposit accounts are classified as transaction accounts that provide a source of funds that can be used until withdrawn by customers (as checks are written).

Another type of transaction deposit is the **negotiable order of withdrawal (NOW) account**, which pays interest as well as providing checking services. Because NOW accounts at most financial institutions require a larger minimum balance than some consumers are willing to maintain in a transaction account, traditional demand deposit accounts are still popular.

Electronic Transactions   Some transactions originating from transaction accounts have become much more efficient as a result of electronic banking. Most employees in the United States have direct deposit accounts, which allow their paychecks to be directly deposited to their transaction account (or other accounts). Social Security recipients have their checks deposited directly to their bank accounts. Computer banking enables bank customers to view their bank accounts online, pay bills, make credit card payments, order more checks, and transfer funds between accounts.

Bank customers use automated teller machines (ATMs) to make withdrawals from their transaction accounts, add deposits, check account balances, and transfer funds. Debit cards allow bank customers to use a card when making purchases and have their bank account debited to reflect the amount spent. Banks also allow preauthorized debits, in which specific periodic payments are automatically transferred from a customer's bank account to a particular recipient. Preauthorized debits are commonly used to cover recurring monthly expenses such as utility bills, car loan payments, and mortgage payments.

17-2b Savings Deposits

The traditional savings account is the passbook savings account, which does not permit check writing. Passbook savings accounts continue to attract savers with a small amount of funds, as such accounts often have no required minimum balance.

17-2c Time Deposits

Time deposits are deposits that cannot be withdrawn until a specified maturity date. The two most common types of time deposits are certificates of deposit (CDs) and negotiable certificates of deposit.

Certificates of Deposit   A common type of time deposit is a retail certificate of deposit (or retail CD), which requires a specified minimum amount of funds to be deposited for a specified period of time. Banks offer a wide variety of CDs to satisfy depositors' needs. Annualized interest rates offered on CDs vary among banks and even among maturity types at a single bank. There is no secondary market for retail CDs. Depositors must leave their funds in the bank until the specified maturity or forgo a portion of their interest as a penalty.

The rates offered by CDs are easily accessible on numerous websites. For example, Bank-Rate (www.bankrate.com) and Bank CD-Rate Scanner (www.bankcd.com) identify banks that are currently paying the highest rates on CDs. Because of easy access to CD rate information online, many depositors invest in CDs at banks far away to earn a higher rate than that offered by local banks. Some banks allow depositors to invest in CDs online by providing a credit card number.

In recent years, some financial institutions have begun to offer CDs with a callable feature (referred to as callable CDs). That is, they can be called by the financial institution, forcing an earlier maturity. For example, a bank could issue a callable CD with a five-year maturity, callable after two years. In two years, the financial institution will likely call the CD if it can obtain funds at a lower rate over the following three years than the rate paid on that CD. Depositors who invest in callable CDs earn a slightly higher interest rate, which compensates them for the risk that the CD may be called.

Negotiable Certificates of Deposit   Another type of time deposit is the **negotiable CD (NCD)**, which is offered by some large banks to corporations. Negotiable CDs are similar to retail CDs in that they have a specified maturity date and require a minimum deposit. Their maturities are typically short term, and their minimum deposit requirement is $100,000. A secondary market for NCDs does exist.

The level of large time deposits is much more volatile than that of small time deposits, because investors with large sums of money frequently shift their funds to wherever they can earn higher rates. Small investors do not have as many options as large investors and are less likely to shift in and out of small time deposits.

17-2d Money Market Deposit Accounts

Money market deposit accounts (MMDAs) differ from conventional time deposits in that they do not specify a maturity. From the depositor's point of view, MMDAs are more liquid than retail CDs but offer a lower interest rate. They differ from NOW accounts in that they provide limited check-writing ability (a limited number of transactions is allowed per month), require a larger minimum balance, and offer a higher yield.

The remaining sources of funds to be described are of a nondepository nature. Such sources are necessary when a bank temporarily needs more funds than are being deposited. Some banks use nondepository funds as a permanent source of funds.

17-2e Federal Funds Purchased

The federal funds market allows depository institutions to accommodate the short-term liquidity needs of other financial institutions. Federal funds purchased (or borrowed) represent a liability to the borrowing bank and an asset to the lending bank that sells them. Loans in the federal funds market are typically for one to seven days. Such loans can be rolled over so that a series of one-day loans can be made. The intent of federal funds transactions is to correct short-term fund imbalances experienced by banks. A bank may act as a lender of federal funds on one day and as a borrower shortly thereafter, since its fund balance changes on a daily basis.

The interest rate charged in the federal funds market is called the **federal funds rate**. Like other market interest rates, it moves in reaction to changes in demand or supply or both. If many banks have excess funds and few banks are short of funds, the federal funds rate will be low. Conversely, a high demand by many banks to borrow in the federal funds market combined with a small supply of excess funds available at other banks will result in a higher federal funds rate. The federal funds rate is typically the same for all banks borrowing in the federal funds market, although a financially troubled bank may have to pay a higher rate. The federal funds rate is quoted on an annualized basis (using a 360-day year) even though the loans are usually for terms of less than one week. This rate is typically close to the yield on a Treasury security with a similar term remaining until maturity. The federal funds market is typically most active on Wednesday, because that is the final day of each particular settlement period for which each bank must maintain a specified volume of reserves required by the Fed. Banks that were short of required reserves on average over the period must compensate with additional required reserves before the settlement period ends. Large banks frequently need temporary funds and therefore are common borrowers in the federal funds market.

17-2f Borrowing from the Federal Reserve Banks

WEB

www.newyorkfed.org/
markets/markets/
omo/dmm/
fedfundsdata.cfm
Information about bank borrowing in the federal funds market.

Another temporary source of funds for banks is the Federal Reserve System, which serves as the U.S. central bank. Along with other bank regulators, the Federal Reserve district banks regulate certain activities of banks. They also provide short-term loans to banks (as well as to some other depository institutions). This form of borrowing by banks is often referred to as borrowing at the discount window. The interest rate charged on these loans is known as the **primary credit lending rate**.

As of January 2003, the primary credit lending rate was to be set at a level that always exceeded the federal funds rate. This was intended to ensure that banks rely on the federal funds market for normal short-term financing and borrow from the Fed only as a last resort.

Loans from the Federal Reserve are short term, commonly from one day to a few weeks. To ensure there is a justifiable need for the funds, banks that wish to borrow at the Federal Reserve must first obtain the Fed's approval. Like the federal funds market, loans from the Fed are mainly used to resolve a temporary shortage of funds. If a bank needs more permanent sources of funds, it will develop a strategy to increase its level of deposits.

The Federal Reserve is intended to be a source of funds for banks that experience unanticipated shortages of reserves. Frequent borrowing to offset reserve shortages implies that the bank has a permanent rather than a temporary need for funds and should therefore satisfy this need with a more permanent source of funds. The Fed may veto continuous borrowing by a bank unless there are extenuating circumstances that prevent the bank from obtaining temporary financing from other financial institutions.

17-2g Repurchase Agreements

A **repurchase agreement (repo)** represents the sale of securities by one party to another with an agreement to repurchase the securities at a specified date and price. Banks often use a repo as a source of funds when they expect to need funds for just a few days. The bank simply sells some of its government securities (such as Treasury bills) to a corporation with a temporary excess of funds and buys those securities back shortly thereafter. The government securities involved in the repo transaction serve as collateral for the corporation providing funds to the bank.

Repurchase agreement transactions occur through a telecommunications network connecting large banks, other corporations, government securities dealers, and federal funds brokers. The federal funds brokers match up firms or dealers that need funds (wish to sell and later repurchase their securities) with those that have excess funds (are willing to purchase securities now and sell them back on a specified date). Transactions are typically in blocks of $1 million. Like the federal funds rate, the yield on repurchase agreements is quoted on an annualized basis (using a 360-day year) even though the loans are for short-term periods. The yield on repurchase agreements is slightly less than the federal funds rate at any given time because the funds loaned out are backed by collateral and are therefore less risky.

17-2h Eurodollar Borrowings

If a U.S. bank is in need of short-term funds, it may borrow dollars from those banks outside the United States (typically in Europe) that accept dollar-denominated deposits, or **Eurodollars**. Some foreign banks (or foreign branches of U.S. banks) accept large short-term deposits and make short-term loans in dollars. Because U.S. dollars are widely used as an international medium of exchange, the Eurodollar market is very active.

17-2i Bonds Issued by the Bank

Like other corporations, banks own some fixed assets such as land, buildings, and equipment. These assets often have an expected life of 20 years or more and are usually financed with such long-term sources as the issuance of bonds. Common purchasers of these bonds are households and various financial institutions, including life insurance companies and pension funds. Banks finance less with bonds than do most other corporations because they have fewer fixed assets than corporations that use industrial equipment and machinery for production. Therefore, banks have less need for long-term funds.

17-2j Bank Capital

Bank capital generally represents funds acquired by the issuance of stock or the retention of earnings. In either case, the bank has no obligation to pay out funds in the future. This distinguishes bank capital from all the other sources of funds, which represent a future obligation by the bank to pay out funds. Bank capital as defined here represents the equity or net worth of the bank. Capital can be classified as primary or secondary. Primary capital results from issuing common or preferred stock or retaining earnings, whereas secondary capital results from issuing subordinated notes and bonds.

A bank's capital must be sufficient to absorb operating losses in the event that expenses or losses exceed revenues, regardless of the reason for the losses. Although long-term bonds are sometimes considered to be secondary capital, they are a liability to the bank and therefore do not appropriately cushion against operating losses.

Although the issuance of new stock increases a bank's capital, it dilutes the bank's ownership because the proportion of the bank owned by existing shareholders decreases. A bank's reported earnings per share are also reduced when additional shares of stock are issued unless earnings increase by a greater proportion than the increase in outstanding shares. For these reasons, banks generally avoid issuing new stock unless absolutely necessary.

Bank regulators are concerned that banks might maintain a lower level of capital than they should and have therefore imposed capital requirements on them. Because capital can absorb losses, a higher level of capital is thought to enhance a bank's safety and may increase the public's confidence in the banking system.

The required level of capital for each bank depends on its risk. Assets with low risk are assigned relatively low weights while assets with high risk are assigned high weights. The capital level is set as a percentage of the risk-weighted assets.

Therefore, riskier banks are subject to higher capital requirements. The same risk-based capital guidelines have been imposed in several other industrialized countries. Additional details are provided in the next chapter.

17-2k Distribution of Bank Sources of Funds

Exhibit 17.2 shows the distribution of bank sources of funds. Transaction and savings deposits make up 38 percent of all bank liabilities. The distribution of bank sources of funds is influenced by bank size. Smaller banks rely more heavily on savings deposits than do larger banks because small banks concentrate on household savings and therefore on small deposits. Much of this differential is made up in large time deposits (such as NCDs) for very large banks. In addition, the larger banks rely more on short-term borrowings than do small banks. The impact of the differences in the composition of fund sources on bank performance is discussed in Chapter 20.

The main sources of funds have been identified, so now the bank uses of funds can be discussed. The more common uses of funds by banks include the following:

- Cash
- Bank loans

Exhibit 17.2 Bank Sources of Funds (as a Proportion of Total Liabilities)

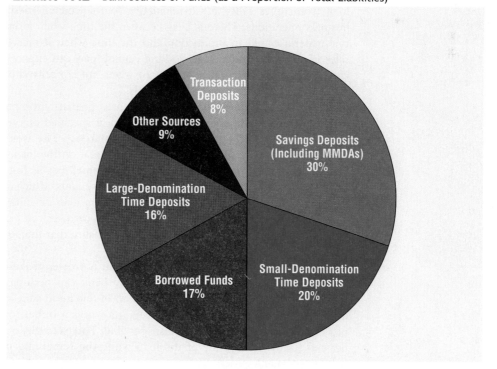

Source: *Federal Reserve.*

- Investment in securities
- Federal funds sold (loaned out)
- Repurchase agreements
- Eurodollar loans
- Fixed assets
- Proprietary trading

17-2l Cash

Banks must hold some cash as reserves to meet the reserve requirements enforced by the Federal Reserve. Banks also hold cash to maintain some liquidity and to accommodate any withdrawal requests by depositors. Because banks do not earn income from cash, they hold only as much cash as is necessary to maintain a sufficient degree of liquidity. They can tap various sources for temporary funds and therefore are not overly concerned with maintaining excess reserves.

Banks hold cash in their vaults and at their Federal Reserve district bank. Vault cash is useful for accommodating withdrawal requests by customers or for qualifying as required reserves, while cash held at the Federal Reserve district banks represents the major portion of required reserves. The Fed mandates that banks maintain required reserves because they provide a means by which the Fed can control the money supply. The required reserves of each bank depend on the composition of its deposits.

17-2m Bank Loans

The main use of bank funds is for loans. The loan amount and maturity can be tailored to the borrower's needs.

Types of Business Loans   A common type of business loan is the **working capital loan** (sometimes called a self-liquidating loan), which is designed to support ongoing business operations. There is a lag between the time when a firm needs cash to purchase raw materials used in production and the time when it receives cash inflows from the sales of finished products. A working capital loan can support the business until sufficient cash inflows are generated. These loans are typically short term, but they may be needed by businesses on a frequent basis.

Banks also offer **term loans**, which are used primarily to finance the purchase of fixed assets such as machinery. With a term loan, a specified amount of funds is loaned out for a specified period of time and a specified purpose. The assets purchased with the borrowed funds may serve as partial or full collateral on the loan. Maturities on term loans commonly range from 2 to 5 years and are sometimes as long as 10 years. Banks that offer term loans typically impose protective covenants, which specify specific conditions for the borrower that may protect the bank from loan default. For example, a bank may specify a maximum level of dividends that the borrower can pay to its shareholders each year. This protective covenant is intended to ensure that the borrower has sufficient cash to repay its loan on time.

Term loans can be amortized so that the borrower makes fixed periodic payments over the life of the loan. Alternatively, the bank can periodically request interest payments, with the loan principal to be paid off in one lump sum (called a **balloon payment**) at a specified date in the future. This is known as a **bullet loan**. Several combinations of these payment methods are also possible. For example, a portion of the loan may be amortized over the life of the loan while the remaining portion is covered with a balloon payment.

As an alternative to providing a term loan, the bank may purchase the assets and lease them to the firm in need. This method, known as a **direct lease loan**, may be especially appropriate when the firm wishes to avoid adding more debt to its balance sheet. Because the bank is the owner of the assets, it can depreciate them over time for tax purposes.

A more flexible financing arrangement is the informal line of credit, which allows the business to borrow up to a specified amount within a specified period of time. This is useful for firms that may experience a sudden need for funds but do not know precisely when. The interest rate charged on any borrowed funds is typically adjustable in accordance with prevailing market rates. Banks are not legally obligated to provide funds to the business, but they usually honor the arrangement to avoid harming their reputation.

An alternative to the informal line of credit is the **revolving credit loan**, which obligates the bank to offer up to some specified maximum amount of funds over a specified period of time (typically less than five years). Because the bank is committed to provide funds when requested, it normally charges businesses a commitment fee (of about one-half of 1 percent) on any unused funds.

The interest rate charged by banks on loans to their most creditworthy customers is known as the **prime rate**. Banks periodically revise the prime rate in response to changes in market interest rates, which reflect changes in the bank's cost of funds. Thus the prime rate moves in tandem with the Treasury bill rate and other market interest rates. The prime rate in recent years is shown in Exhibit 17.3. It increased during the 2004–2006 period when economic conditions were strong. Conversely, it decreased during recessions, such as during the financial crisis in 2008. The prime rate tends to adjust in response to changes in other interest rates that influence the bank's cost of funds. When economic conditions are weak, however, the spread between the prime rate and the bank's cost of funds tends to widen because banks require a higher premium to compensate for credit risk.

Exhibit 17.3   Prime Rate over Time

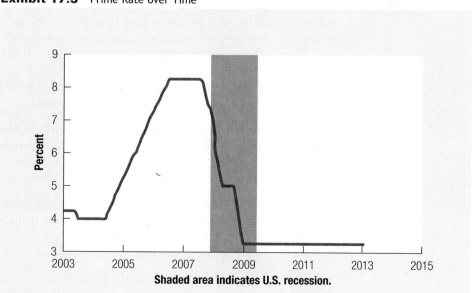

Source: *Federal Reserve.*

Loan Participations   Some large corporations wish to borrow a larger amount of funds than any individual bank is willing to provide. To accommodate a corporation, several banks may be willing to pool their available funds in what is referred to as a **loan participation**. One of the banks serves as the lead bank by arranging for the documentation, disbursement, and payment structure of the loan. The main role of the other banks is to supply funds that are channeled to the borrower by the lead bank. The borrower may not even realize that other banks have provided much of the funds. As interest payments are received, the lead bank passes the payments on to the other participants in proportion to the original loan amounts they provided. The lead bank receives fees for servicing the loan in addition to its share of interest payments.

The lead bank is expected to ensure that the borrower repays the loan. Normally, however, the lead bank is not required to guarantee the interest payments. Thus all participating banks are exposed to credit (default) risk.

Loans Supporting Leveraged Buyouts   Some commercial banks finance leveraged buyouts (LBOs), in which a management group or a business relies mostly on debt to purchase the equity of another business. Firms request LBO financing because they perceive that the market value of certain publicly held shares is too low. Yet because the borrowers are highly leveraged, they may experience cash flow pressure during periods when sales are lower than normal. It is desirable that these firms have access to equity funds because it can serve as a cushion during periods of poor economic conditions. Although such firms prefer not to go public again during such periods, they are at least capable of doing so. Banks financing these firms can, as a condition of any loan, require that the firms reissue stock if they experience cash flow problems.

Some banks originate the loans designed for LBOs and then sell them to other financial institutions, such as insurance companies, pension funds, and foreign banks. In this way, they can generate fee income by servicing the loans while avoiding the credit risk associated with them.

Bank regulators monitor the amount of bank financing provided to corporate borrowers that have a relatively high degree of financial leverage. These loans, known as **highly leveraged transactions (HLTs)**, are defined by the Federal Reserve as credit that results in a debt-to-asset ratio of at least 75 percent. In other words, the level of debt is at least three times the level of equity. About 60 percent of HLT funds are used to finance LBOs, and some of the remaining funds are used to repurchase a portion of the outstanding stock. HLTs are usually originated by a large commercial bank that provides 10 to 20 percent of the financing itself. Other financial institutions participate by providing the remaining 80 to 90 percent of the funds needed.

Collateral Requirements on Business Loans   Commercial banks are increasingly accepting intangible assets (such as patents, brand names, and licenses to franchises and distributorships) as collateral for commercial loans. This change is especially important to service-oriented companies that do not have tangible assets.

Lender Liability on Business Loans   In recent years, businesses that previously obtained loans from banks have filed lawsuits claiming that the banks terminated further financing without sufficient notice. These so-called lender liability suits have been prevalent in the farming, grocery, clothing, and oil industries.

Volume of Business Loans   The volume of business loans provided by commercial banks changes over time in response to economic conditions. When the economy is strong, businesses are more willing to finance expansion. When economic conditions are weak, businesses defer expansion plans and therefore do not need as much financing. Economic growth increased during the 2004–2006 period, resulting in a major increase in business loans provided by banks. During the credit crisis of 2008–2009, however, the volume of business loans decreased.

WEB

www.fdic.com
Information about bank loan and deposit volume.

Types of Consumer Loans   Commercial banks provide individuals with **installment loans** to finance purchases of cars and household products. These loans require the borrowers to make periodic payments over time.

Banks also provide credit cards to consumers who qualify, enabling them to purchase various goods without having to reapply for credit on each purchase. Credit card holders are assigned a maximum limit based on their income and employment record, and a fixed annual fee may be charged. This service often involves an agreement with VISA or MasterCard. If consumers pay off the balance each month, they normally are not charged interest. Bank rates on credit card balances are sometimes about double the rate charged on business loans. State regulators can impose **usury laws** that restrict the maximum rate of interest charged by banks, and these laws may be applied to credit card loans as well. A federal law requires that banks abide by the usury laws of the state where they are located rather than the state where the consumer lives.

Assessing the applicant's creditworthiness is much easier for consumer loans than for corporate loans. An individual's cash flow is typically simpler and more predictable than a firm's cash flow. In addition, the average loan amount to an individual is relatively small, warranting a less detailed credit analysis.

Since the interest rate on credit card loans and personal loans is typically much higher than the cost of funds, many commercial banks have pursued these types of loans as a means of increasing their earnings. The most common method of increasing such loans is to use more lenient guidelines when assessing the creditworthiness of potential customers. However, there is an obvious trade-off between the potential return and exposure to credit risk. When commercial banks experience an increase in defaults on credit card loans and other personal loans, they respond by increasing their standards for extending such loans. This results in a reduced allocation of funds to credit card loans, which also reduces the potential returns of the bank. When the economy weakened during the credit crisis in 2008 and 2009, for example, many banks raised their standards for credit card loans and reduced the amount of credit that they would allow consumers to have. As economic conditions improve, commercial banks tend to increase their allocation of funds toward credit card loans.

Real Estate Loans   Banks also provide real estate loans. For residential real estate loans, the maturity on a mortgage is typically 15 to 30 years, although shorter-term mortgages with a balloon payment are also common. The loan is backed by the residence purchased. During the economic expansion in the 2004–2006 period, many banks offered loans to home buyers of questionable credit standards. These *subprime* mortgages were given to home buyers who had relatively lower income, high existing debt, or only a small down payment for purchasing a home. Many commercial banks expected to benefit from subprime mortgage loans because they could charge up-front fees (such as appraisal fees) and higher interest rates on the mortgages to compensate for the risk of default. Furthermore, they presumed that real estate values would continue to rise and so the residence backing the loan would serve as adequate collateral.

In 2008, however, there were many defaults on subprime mortgages. As of January 2009, about 10 percent of all homeowners with mortgages were either late on their payments or subject to foreclosure. Banks and other financial institutions were forced to take over the ownership of many homes, which led to an excess supply of homes in the housing market. Consequently, the prices of homes declined substantially, which further reduced the collateral value of the homes taken back by the banks. Thus banks that originated mortgages and held them as assets were adversely affected by the credit crisis.

Commercial banks also provide commercial real estate loans, such as loans to build shopping malls. In general, during the early 2000s banks required more stringent standards for borrowers to qualify for commercial real estate loans. For this reason, the default rate on commercial real estate loans provided by commercial banks was low compared to the default rate on residential loans during the credit crisis. In addition, commercial banks commonly retain the commercial real estate loans that they originate as assets. Banks and other financial institutions are likely to use greater diligence in assessing real estate loan applicants when they retain the mortgages that they originate.

17-2n Investment in Securities

Banks purchase various types of securities. One advantage of investing funds in securities rather than loans is that the securities tend to be more liquid. In addition, banks can easily invest in securities whereas more resources are required to assess loan applicants and service loans. However, they normally expect to generate higher rates of return on funds used to provide loans.

Treasury and Agency Securities   Banks purchase Treasury securities as well as securities issued by agencies of the federal government. Government agency securities can be sold in the secondary market, but the market is not as active as it is for Treasury securities. Federal agency securities are commonly issued by federal agencies, such as the Federal National Mortgage Association (Fannie Mae) and the Federal Home Loan Mortgage Corporation (Freddie Mac). Funds received by the agencies issuing these securities are used to purchase mortgages from various financial institutions. Such securities have maturities that can range from one month to 25 years.

The values of the mortgages held by Fannie Mae and Freddie Mac declined in 2008 as a result of the large amount of late payments and mortgage defaults during the credit crisis. Consequently, there were concerns that Fannie Mae and Freddie Mac might not be able to cover their debt security payments. In September 2008, the U.S. government took control of Fannie Mae and Freddie Mac, thereby ensuring the safety of the debt securities issued by these agencies.

Corporate and Municipal Bonds   Banks also purchase corporate and municipal bonds. Although corporate bonds are subject to credit risk, they offer a higher return than Treasury or government agency securities. Municipal bonds exhibit some degree of risk but can also provide an attractive return to banks, especially when their after-tax return is considered. The interest income earned from municipal securities is exempt from federal taxation. Banks purchase only **investment-grade securities**, which are those rated as "medium quality" or higher by rating agencies.

Mortgage-Backed Securities   Banks also commonly purchase mortgage-backed securities (MBS), which represent packages of mortgages. Banks tend to purchase mortgages within a particular "tranche" that is categorized as having relatively low risk. During the credit crisis in 2008 and 2009, however, there were many defaults on mortgages within tranches that had been assigned high ratings by rating agencies. Consequently, banks that had invested in MBS experienced losses during the credit crisis. The market value of MBS at any bank is difficult to measure because the MBS are not standardized and the secondary market transactions between parties are not conducted through an organized exchange. Thus two banks could have an equal proportion of their assets classified as MBS, but one bank's MBS may be much riskier than the other bank's MBS.

17-2o Federal Funds Sold

Some banks often lend funds to other banks in the federal funds market. The funds sold, or lent out, will be returned (with interest) at the time specified in the loan agreement. The loan period is typically very short, such as a day or a few days. Small banks are common providers of funds in the federal funds market. If the transaction is executed by a broker, the borrower's cost on a federal funds loan is slightly higher than the lender's return because the broker matching up the two parties charges a transaction fee.

17-2p Repurchase Agreements

Recall that, from the borrower's perspective, a repurchase agreement transaction involves repurchasing the securities it had previously sold. From a lender's perspective, the repo represents a sale of securities that it had previously purchased. Banks can act as the lender (on a repo) by purchasing a corporation's holdings of Treasury securities and then selling them back at a later date. This provides short-term funds to the corporation, and the bank's loan is backed by these securities.

17-2q Eurodollar Loans

Branches of U.S. banks located outside the United States, as well as some foreign-owned banks, provide dollar-denominated loans to corporations and governments. These so-called Eurodollar loans are common because the dollar is frequently used for international transactions. Eurodollar loans are short term and denominated in large amounts, such as $1 million or more.

17-2r Fixed Assets

Banks must maintain some amount of fixed assets, such as office buildings and land, so that they can conduct their business operations. However, this is not a concern to the bank managers who decide how day-to-day incoming funds will be used. They direct these funds into the other types of assets already identified.

17-2s Proprietary Trading

Banks also engage in proprietary (or "prop") trading, in which they use their own funds to make investments for their own account. For example, banks may have an equity trading desk that takes positions in equity securities as well as a fixed-income desk that takes speculative positions in bonds and other debt securities; they may also have a derivatives trading desk that takes speculative positions in derivative securities. Proprietary trading was a major contributor to the total income generated by commercial banks prior to the credit crisis, when economic conditions were very favorable. The trading desks tend to engage in much more risk than traditional bank lending operations, and some commercial banks experienced large losses on their proprietary trading during the financial crisis.

Banks also manage investment portfolios in which they pool funds provided by clients and make investments with the funds on behalf of the bank's clients. They charge an annual management fee to clients for managing these funds. The hedge fund may generate periodic fees from clients for managing the funds. Banks may own private equity funds, which pool funds provided by wealthy individual and institutional investors, and then invest the funds in businesses. They may charge their investor clients fees for their service and take a portion of the profit from managing the funds before distributing profits to their investor clients.

The Wall Street Reform and Consumer Protection Act (also called the Dodd-Frank Act) of 2010 imposes a limit on the amount of proprietary trading by banks. This provision is referred to as the Volcker rule, because it was recommended by Paul Volcker, a previous member of the Board of Governors of the Fed. However, its implementation was delayed due to many arguments about its interpretation. The arguments were intense because some banks wanted to retain their flexibility to engage in a large amount on proprietary trading.

17-2t Summary of Bank Uses of Funds

The distribution of bank uses of funds is illustrated in Exhibit 17.4. Loans of all types make up about 59 percent of bank assets while securities account for about 27 percent. The distribution of assets for an individual bank varies with the type of bank. For example, smaller banks tend to have a relatively large amount of household loans and government securities; larger banks have a higher level of business loans (including loans to foreign firms).

The distribution of bank uses of funds indicates how commercial banks operate. In recent years, however, banks have begun to provide numerous services that are not indicated on their balance sheet. These services differ markedly from banks' traditional operations, which focused mostly on channeling deposited funds into various types of loans and investments.

Commercial Bank Balance Sheet   A commercial bank's sources of funds represent its liabilities or equity, and its uses of funds represent its assets. Each commercial bank determines its own composition of liabilities and assets, which determines its specific operations.

Exhibit 17.4   Bank Uses of Funds (as a Proportion of Total Assets)

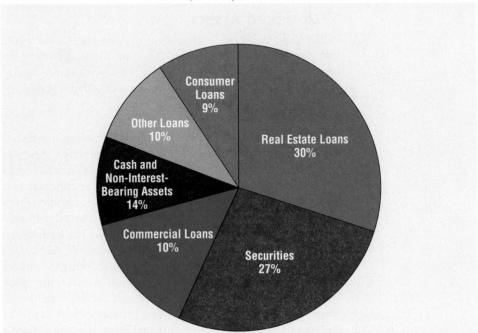

Source: *Federal Reserve.*

Exhibit 17.5 shows the balance sheet of Hornet Bank. The bank's assets are shown on the left side of the balance sheet. The second column indicates the dollar amount of each asset, and the third column shows the size of each asset in proportion to total assets in order to illustrate how Hornet Bank distributes its funds. Hornet's main assets are commercial and consumer loans in addition to securities. The balance sheet shows the bank's holdings at a particular moment in time, but the bank frequently revises the composition of its assets in response to economic conditions. When the economy improves and creditworthy businesses want to expand, Hornet Bank will sell some of its holdings of Treasury securities and use the funds to provide more corporate loans.

Hornet Bank's liabilities and stockholders' equity are shown on the right side of the balance sheet. Hornet obtains funds from various types of deposits, and incurs some expenses from all types of deposits. In particular, it must hire employees to serve depositors. The composition of Hornet's liabilities determines its interest expenses: it does not pay interest on demand deposits, but it does pay a relatively high interest rate on large CDs.

Hornet also incurs expenses from managing its assets. Its main expense is the cost of hiring employees to assess the creditworthiness of businesses and households that request loans. In general, Hornet wants to generate enough income from its assets so that it can cover its expenses and provide a reasonable return to its shareholders. Its primary source of income is the interest received on the business loans that it provides. Its capital is shown on the balance sheet as common stock issued and retained earnings. ●

Exhibit 17.5 Balance Sheet of Hornet Bank as of June 30, 2013

ASSETS	DOLLAR AMOUNT (IN MILLIONS)	PROPORTION OF TOTAL ASSETS	LIABILITIES AND STOCKHOLDERS' EQUITY	DOLLAR AMOUNT (IN MILLIONS)	PROPORTION OF TOTAL LIABILITIES AND STOCK-HOLDERS' EQUITY
Cash (includes required reserves)	$ 50	5%	Demand deposits	$ 250	25%
Commercial loans	400	40%	NOW accounts	60	6%
Consumer loans	250	25%	Money market deposit accounts	200	20%
Treasury securities	80	8%	Short-term CDs	250	25%
Corporate securities	120	12%	CDs with maturities beyond one year	120	12%
Federal funds sold (lent out)	10	1%	Federal funds purchased (borrowed)	0	0%
Repurchase agreements	20	2%	Long-term debt	30	3%
Eurodollar loans	0	0%			
Fixed assets	70	7%	Common stock issued	50	5%
			Retained earnings	40	4%
TOTAL ASSETS	$1,000	100%	TOTAL LIABILITIES AND STOCKHOLDERS' EQUITY	$1,000	100%

Exhibit 17.6   How Commercial Banks Finance Economic Growth

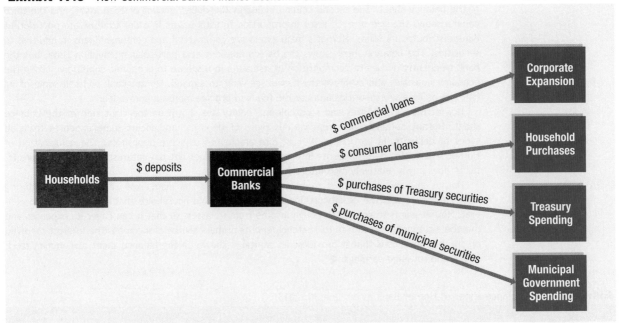

Exhibit 17.6 shows how commercial banks use the key balance sheet items to finance economic growth. They channel funds from their depositors to households and thereby finance household spending. They channel funds from depositors to corporations and thereby finance corporate expansion. They also use some deposits to purchase Treasury and municipal securities and thereby finance spending by the Treasury and municipalities.

17-3 OFF–BALANCE SHEET ACTIVITIES

Banks commonly engage in off–balance sheet activities, which generate fee income without requiring an investment of funds. However, these activities do create a contingent obligation for banks. The following are some of the more popular off–balance sheet activities:

- Loan commitments
- Standby letters of credit
- Forward contracts on currencies
- Interest rate swap contracts
- Credit default swap contracts

17-3a Loan Commitments

A loan commitment is an obligation by a bank to provide a specified loan amount to a particular firm upon the firm's request. The interest rate and purpose of the loan may also be specified. The bank charges a fee for offering the commitment.

One type of loan commitment is a **note issuance facility (NIF)**, in which the bank agrees to purchase the commercial paper of a firm if the firm cannot place its paper in the market at an acceptable interest rate. Although banks earn fees for their commitments, they could experience illiquidity if numerous firms request their loans at the same time.

17-3b Standby Letters of Credit

A **standby letter of credit (SLC)** backs a customer's obligation to a third party. If the customer does not meet its obligation, the bank will. The third party may require that the customer obtain an SLC to complete a business transaction. For example, consider a municipality that wants to issue bonds. To ensure that the bonds are easily placed, a bank could provide an SLC that guarantees payment of interest and principal. In essence, the bank uses its credit rating to enhance the perceived safety of the bonds. In return for the guarantee, the bank charges a fee to the municipality. The bank should be willing to provide SLCs only if the fee received compensates for the possibility that the municipality will default on its obligation.

17-3c Forward Contracts on Currencies

A forward contract on currency is an agreement between a customer and a bank to exchange one currency for another on a particular future date at a specified exchange rate. Banks engage in forward contracts with customers that desire to hedge their exchange rate risk. For example, a U.S. bank may agree to purchase 5 million euros in one year from a firm for $1.10 per euro. The bank may simultaneously find another firm that wishes to exchange 5 million euros for dollars in one year. The bank can serve as an intermediary and accommodate both requests, earning a transaction fee for its services. However, it is exposed to the possibility that one of the parties will default on its obligation.

17-3d Interest Rate Swap Contracts

Banks also serve as intermediaries for interest rate swaps, whereby two parties agree to periodically exchange interest payments on a specified notional amount of principal. Once again, the bank receives a transaction fee for its services. If it guarantees payments to both parties, it is exposed to the possibility that one of the parties will default on its obligation. In that event, the bank must assume the role of that party and fulfill the obligation to the other party.

Some banks facilitate currency swaps (for a fee) by finding parties with opposite future currency needs and executing a swap agreement. Currency swaps are similar to forward contracts, but they are usually for more distant future dates.

17-3e Credit Default Swap Contracts

Credit default swaps are privately negotiated contracts that protect investors against the risk of default on particular debt securities. Some commercial banks and other financial institutions buy them in order to protect their own investments in debt securities against default risk. Other banks and financial institutions sell them. The banks that sell credit default swaps receive periodic coupon payments for the term of the swap agreement. A typical term of a credit default swap is five years. If there are no defaults on the debt securities, the banks that sold the credit default swaps benefit because they have received periodic payments but are not required to make any payments. However, when there are defaults on the debt securities, the sellers of credit default swaps must make payments to the buyers to cover the damages. In essence, the sellers of credit default swaps are providing insurance against default.

These contracts were heavily used to protect against the default risk from investing in mortgage-backed securities. During the credit crisis in 2008, commercial banks that sold credit default swap contracts incurred major expenses because of the high frequency of defaults on mortgage-backed securities. Conversely, commercial banks that purchased credit default swap contracts reduced the adverse impact of defaults on mortgage-backed securities (assuming that the counterparty that sold them the swaps did not default on its obligation).

GLOBAL ASPECTS

17-4 INTERNATIONAL BANKING

Until historical barriers against interstate banking were largely removed in 1994, some U.S. commercial banks were better able to achieve growth by penetrating foreign markets than by expanding at home. Many U.S. banks have expanded internationally to improve their prospects for growth and to diversify so that their business will not be dependent on a single economy.

17-4a International Expansion

The most common way for U.S. commercial banks to expand internationally is by establishing branches, full-service banking offices that can compete directly with other banks located in a particular area. Before establishing foreign branches, a U.S. bank must obtain the approval of the Federal Reserve Board. Among the factors considered by the Fed are the bank's financial condition and experience in international business. Commercial banks may also consider establishing agencies, which can provide loans but cannot accept deposits or provide trust services.

U.S. banks have recently established foreign subsidiaries wherever they expect more foreign expansion by U.S. firms, such as in Southeast Asia and Eastern Europe. Recently, expansion has also been focused on Latin America. The banks offer banker's acceptances, foreign exchange services, credit card services, and other household services.

As an example of the diversity in international banking services, Citigroup offers a number of key services to firms around the world including foreign exchange transactions, forecasting, risk management, cross-border trade finance, acquisition finance, cash management services, and local currency funding. Citigroup serves not only large multinational corporations (e.g., Coca-Cola, Dow Chemical, IBM, Sony) but also small firms that need international banking services. By spreading itself across the world, Citigroup can typically handle the banking needs of all the subsidiaries of a multinational corporation.

17-4b Impact of the Euro on Global Competition

The use of a single currency in a number of European countries simplifies transactions because the majority of a bank's transactions between those countries are now denominated in euros. Use of the euro also reduces exposure to exchange rate risk, as banks can accept deposits in euros and use euros to lend funds or invest in securities. The use of a single currency throughout many European countries may also encourage firms to engage in bond or stock offerings to support their European business, as the euro can be used to support most of that business. Commercial banks can serve as intermediaries by underwriting and placing the debt or the equity issued by firms.

The single currency makes it easier to achieve economies of scale and enables banks' internal reporting systems to be more efficient. As banks expand and capitalize on economies of scale, global competition has become more intense. Furthermore, the euro enables businesses in Europe to more easily compare the prices of services offered by banks based in different European countries. This also forces banks to be more competitive.

17-4c International Exposure

As banks attempt to penetrate international markets in order to capitalize on opportunities, they become exposed to conditions in those markets. In particular, European countries such as Greece, Portugal, and Spain have experienced weak economies and large budget deficits. The governments of these countries have borrowed substantially from banks in order to finance their budget deficits. They have struggled to meet their debt payments. Consequently, banks with large loans to these governments are exposed to the possibility of loan defaults. In addition, banks that penetrated these countries by offering loans to corporations in these countries are subject to possible loan defaults because the economies of these countries have been weak.

SUMMARY

- Commercial banks have consolidated over time in an effort to achieve economies of scale and to become more efficient. Consequently, there are less than half as many banks today as there were in 1985, and consolidation is still occurring. Commercial banks have also acquired many other types of financial service firms in recent years.

- The most common sources of commercial bank funds are deposit accounts, borrowed funds, and long-term sources of funds. The common types of deposit accounts are transaction deposits, savings deposits, time deposits, and money market deposit accounts. These accounts vary in terms of liquidity (for the depositor) and the interest rates offered. Commercial banks can solve temporary deficiencies in funds by borrowing from other banks (federal

funds market), from the Federal Reserve, or from other sources by issuing short-term securities such as repurchase agreements. When banks need long-term funds to support expansion, they may use retained earnings, issue new stock, or issue new bonds.

- The most common uses of funds by commercial banks are bank loans and investment in securities. Banks can use excess funds by providing loans to other banks or by purchasing short-term securities.

- Banks engage in off–balance sheet activities such as loan commitments, standby letters of credit, forward contracts, and swap contracts. These types of activities generate fees for commercial banks. However, they also reflect commitments by the banks, which can expose them to more risk.

POINT COUNTER-POINT

Should Banks Engage in Other Financial Services Besides Banking?

Point   No. Banks should focus on what they do best.

Counter-Point   Yes. Banks should increase their value by engaging in other services. They can appeal to

customers who want to have all their financial services provided by one financial institution.

Who Is Correct?   Use the Internet to learn more about this issue and then formulate your own opinion.

QUESTIONS AND APPLICATIONS

1. Bank Balance Sheet Create a balance sheet for a typical bank, showing its main liabilities (sources of funds) and assets (uses of funds).

2. Bank Sources of Funds What are four major sources of funds for banks? What alternatives does a

bank have if it needs temporary funds? What is the most common reason that banks issue bonds?

3. CDs Compare and contrast a retail CD and a negotiable CD.

4. Money Market Deposit Accounts How does a money market deposit account differ from other bank sources of funds?

5. Federal Funds Define federal funds, federal funds market, and federal funds rate. Who sets the federal funds rate? Why is the federal funds market more active on Wednesday?

6. Federal Funds Market Explain how the federal funds market facilitates bank operations.

7. Borrowing from the Federal Reserve Describe the process of "borrowing at the Federal Reserve." What rate is charged, and who sets it? Why do banks commonly borrow in the federal funds market rather than through the Federal Reserve?

8. Repurchase Agreements How does the yield on a repurchase agreement differ from a loan in the federal funds market? Why?

9. Bullet Loan Explain the advantage of a bullet loan.

10. Bank Use of Funds Why do banks invest in securities even though loans typically generate a higher return? Explain how a bank decides the appropriate percentage of funds that should be allocated to each type of asset.

11. Bank Capital Explain the dilemma faced by banks when determining the optimal amount of capital to hold. A bank's capital is less than 10 percent of its assets. How do you think this percentage would compare to that of manufacturing corporations? How would you explain this difference?

12. HLTs Would you expect a bank to charge a higher rate on a term loan or on a highly leveraged transaction (HLT) loan? Why?

13. Credit Crisis Explain how some mortgage operations by some commercial banks (along with other financial institutions) played a major role in instigating the credit crisis.

14. Bank Use of Credit Default Swaps Explain how banks have used credit default swaps.

Interpreting Financial News

Interpret the following comments made by Wall Street analysts and portfolio managers.

a. "Lower interest rates may reduce the size of banks."

b. "Banks are no longer as limited when competing with other financial institutions for funds targeted for the stock market."

c. "If the demand for loans rises substantially, interest rates will adjust to ensure that commercial banks can accommodate the demand."

Managing in Financial Markets

Managing Sources and Uses of Funds As a consultant, you have been asked to assess a bank's sources and uses of funds and to offer recommendations on how it can restructure its sources and uses of funds to improve its performance. This bank has traditionally focused on attracting funds by offering certificates of deposit. It offers checking accounts and money market deposit accounts, but it has not advertised these accounts because it has obtained an adequate amount of funds from the CDs. It pays about 3 percentage points more on its CDs than on its MMDAs, but the bank prefers to know the precise length of time it can use the deposited funds. (The CDs have a specified maturity whereas the MMDAs do not.) Its cost of funds has historically been higher than that of most banks, but it has not been concerned because its earnings have been relatively high. The bank's use of funds has historically focused on local real estate loans to build shopping malls and apartment complexes. The real estate loans have provided a very high return over the last several years. However, the demand for real estate in the local area has slowed.

a. Should the bank continue to focus on attracting funds by offering CDs, or should it push its other types of deposits?

b. Should the bank continue to focus on real estate loans? If the bank reduces its real estate loans, where should the funds be allocated?

c. How will the potential return on the bank's uses of funds be affected by your restructuring of the asset portfolio? How will the cost of funds be affected by your restructuring of the bank's liabilities?

Flow of Funds Exercise

Services Provided by Financial Conglomerates

Carson Company is attempting to compare the services offered by different banks, as it would like to have all services provided by one bank.

a. Explain the different types of services provided by a financial institution that may allow Carson Company to obtain funds or to hedge its risk.

b. Review the services that you listed in the previous question. What services could provide financing to Carson Company? What services could hedge Carson's exposure to risk?

Internet/Excel Exercise

Go to the website www.chase.com and list the various services offered by Chase that were mentioned in this chapter. For each service, state whether it reflects an asset (use of funds) or a liability (source of funds) for the bank. What interest rates does Chase offer on its CDs?

Online Articles with Real-World Examples

Find a recent practical article available online that describes a real-world example regarding a specific financial institution or financial market that reinforces one or more concepts covered in this chapter.

If your class has an online component, your professor may ask you to post your summary of the article there and provide a link to the article so that other students can access it. If your class is live, your professor may ask you to summarize your application of the article in class. Your professor may assign specific students to complete this assignment or may allow any students to do the assignment on a volunteer basis.

For recent online articles and real-world examples related to this chapter, consider using the following search terms (be sure to include the prevailing year as a search term to ensure that the online articles are recent):

1. bank competition
2. [name of specific bank] AND loans
3. [name of specific bank] AND deposits
4. [name of specific bank] AND capital
5. [name of specific bank] AND balance sheet
6. [name of specific bank] AND assets
7. [name of specific bank] AND liabilities
8. bank AND capital
9. bank AND assets
10. bank AND loans

18

Bank Regulation

Bank regulations are designed to maintain public confidence in the financial system by preventing commercial banks from becoming too risky.

CHAPTER OBJECTIVES

The specific objectives of this chapter are to:

- describe the key regulations imposed on commercial banks,

- explain capital requirements of banks,

- explain how regulators monitor banks,

- explain the issues regarding government rescue of failed banks, and

- describe how the Financial Reform Act of 2010 affects the regulation of commercial bank operations.

18-1 BACKGROUND

Because banks rely on funds from depositors, they have been subject to regulations that are intended to ensure the safety of the financial system. Many of the regulations are intended to prevent banks from taking excessive risk that could cause them to fail. In particular, regulations are imposed on the types of assets in which banks can invest, and the minimum amount of capital that banks must maintain. However, there are trade-offs due to bank regulation. Some critics suggest that the regulation is excessive, and it restricts banks from serving their owners. Banks might be more efficient if they were not subject to regulations. Given these trade-offs, regulations are commonly revised over time in response to bank conditions, as regulators seek the optimal level of regulation that ensures the safety of the banking system, but also allows banks to be efficient.

Many regulations of bank operations were removed or reduced over time, which allowed banks to become more competitive. Because of deregulation, banks have considerable flexibility in the services they offer, the locations where they operate, and the rates they pay depositors for deposits.

Yet some banks and other financial institutions engaged in excessive risk taking in the 2005–2007 period, which is one the reasons for the credit crisis in the 2008–2009 period. Many banks failed as a result of the credit crisis, and government subsidies were extended to many other banks in order to prevent more failures and restore financial stability. This has led to much scrutiny over existing regulations and proposals for new regulations that can still allow for intense competition while preventing bank managers from taking excessive risks. This chapter provides a background on the prevailing regulatory structure, explains how bank regulators attempted to resolve the credit crisis, and describes recent changes in regulations that are intended to prevent another crisis.

18-2 REGULATORY STRUCTURE

The regulatory structure of the banking system in the United States is dramatically different from that of other countries. It is often referred to as a dual banking system because it includes both a federal and a state regulatory system. There are more than 6,000 separately owned commercial banks in the United States, which are supervised by three federal agencies and 50 state agencies. The regulatory structure in other countries is much simpler.

WEB

www.federalreserve.
gov/bankinforeg/
reglisting.htm
Detailed descriptions of
bank regulations from
the Federal Reserve
Board.

WEB

www.federalreserve.
gov
Click on "Banking
Information &
Regulation" to find
key bank regulations
at the website of the
Board of Governors
of the Federal Reserve
System.

A charter from either a state or the federal government is required to open a commercial bank in the United States. A bank that obtains a state charter is referred to as a state bank; a bank that obtains a federal charter is known as a national bank. All national banks are required to be members of the Federal Reserve System (the Fed). The federal charter is issued by the Comptroller of the Currency. An application for a bank charter must be submitted to the proper supervisory agency, should provide evidence of the need for a new bank, and should disclose how the bank will be operated. Regulators determine if the bank satisfies general guidelines to qualify for the charter.

State banks may decide whether they wish to be members of the Federal Reserve System. The Fed provides a variety of services for commercial banks and controls the amount of funds within the banking system. About 35 percent of all banks are members of the Federal Reserve. These banks are generally larger than the norm; their combined deposits make up about 70 percent of all bank deposits. Both member and nonmember banks can borrow from the Fed, and both are subject to the Fed's reserve requirements.

18-2a Regulators

National banks are regulated by the Comptroller of the Currency; state banks are regulated by their respective state agency. Banks that are insured by the **Federal Deposit Insurance Corporation (FDIC)** are also regulated by the FDIC. Because all national banks must be members of the Federal Reserve and all Fed member banks must hold FDIC insurance, national banks are regulated by the Comptroller of the Currency, the Fed, and the FDIC. State banks are regulated by their respective state agency, the Fed (if they are Fed members), and the FDIC. The Comptroller of the Currency is responsible for conducting periodic evaluations of national banks, the FDIC holds the same responsibility for state-chartered banks and savings institutions with less than $50 billion in assets, and the Federal Reserve is responsible for state-chartered banks and savings institutions with more than $50 billion in assets.

18-2b Regulation of Bank Ownership

Commercial banks can be either independently owned or owned by a **bank holding** company (BHC). Although some multibank holding companies (owning more than one bank) exist, one-bank holding companies are more common. More banks are owned by holding companies than are owned independently.

18-3 REGULATION OF BANK OPERATIONS

Banks are regulated according to how they obtain funds, how they use their funds, and the types of financial services they can offer. Some of the most important regulations are discussed here.

18-3a Regulation of Deposit Insurance

Federal deposit insurance has existed since the creation in 1933 of the FDIC in response to the bank runs that occurred in the late 1920s and early 1930s. During the 1930–1932 period of the Great Depression more than 5,000 banks failed, or more than 20 percent of the existing banks. The initial wave of failures caused depositors to withdraw their deposits from other banks, fearing that the failures would spread. These actions actually caused more banks to fail. If deposit insurance had been available, depositors might not have removed their deposits and some bank failures might have been avoided.

The FDIC preserves public confidence in the U.S. financial system by providing deposit insurance to commercial banks and savings institutions. The FDIC is managed by a board of five directors, who are appointed by the President. Its headquarters is in Washington, D.C., but it has eight regional offices and other field offices within each region. Today, the FDIC's insurance funds are responsible for insuring deposits of more than $3 trillion.

Insurance Limits   The specified amount of deposits per person insured by the FDIC was increased from $100,000 to $250,000 as part of the Emergency Economic Stabilization Act of 2008, which was intended to resolve the liquidity problems of financial institutions and to restore confidence in the banking system. The $250,000 limit was made permanent by the Financial Reform Act of 2010. Large deposit accounts beyond the $250,000 limit are insured only up to this limit. Note that deposits in foreign branches of U.S. banks are *not* insured by the FDIC.

In general, deposit insurance has allowed depositors to deposit funds under the insured limits in any insured depository institution without the need to assess the institution's financial condition. In addition, the insurance system minimizes bank runs on deposits because insured depositors believe that their deposits are backed by the U.S. government even if the insured depository institution fails. When a bank fails, insured depositors normally have access to their money within a few days.

Risk-Based Deposit Premiums   Banks insured by the FDIC must pay annual insurance premiums. Until 1991, all banks obtained insurance for their depositors at the same rate. Because the riskiest banks were more likely to fail, they were being indirectly subsidized by safer banks. This system encouraged some banks to assume more risk because they could still attract deposits from depositors who knew they would be covered regardless of the bank's risk. The act of insured banks taking on more risk because their depositors are protected is one example of what is called a **moral hazard problem**. As a result of many banks taking excessive risks, bank failures increased during the 1980s and early 1990s. The balance in the FDIC's insurance fund declined because the FDIC had to reimburse depositors who had deposits at the banks that failed.

This moral hazard problem prompted bank regulators and Congress to search for a way to discourage banks from taking excessive risk and to replenish the FDIC's insurance fund. As a result of the Federal Deposit Insurance Corporation Improvement Act (FDICIA) of 1991, risk-based deposit insurance premiums were phased in. Consequently, bank insurance premiums are now aligned with the risk of banks, thereby reducing the moral hazard problem.

Deposit Insurance Fund   Before 2006, the Bank Insurance Fund was used to collect premiums and provide insurance for banks and the Savings Association Insurance Fund was used to collect premiums and provide insurance for savings institutions. In 2006 the two funds were merged into one insurance fund called the **Deposit Insurance Fund**, which is regulated by the FDIC.

The deposit insurance premiums were increased in 2009 because the FDIC had used substantial reserves during the credit crisis to reimburse depositors of failed banks. The range of premiums is now typically between 13 and 53 cents per $100, with most banks paying between 13 and 18 cents. The FDIC's reserves are currently about $45 billion, or about 1 percent of all insured deposits. The FDIC also has a large credit line against which it can borrow from the Treasury.

Bank Deposit Insurance Reserves   The Wall Street Reform and Consumer Protection Act (also called the Dodd-Frank Act) of 2010 requires that the Deposit Insurance

Fund should maintain reserves of at least 1.35 percent of total insured bank deposits, to ensure that it always has sufficient reserves to cover losses. If the reserves fall below that level, the FDIC is required to develop a restoration plan to boost reserves to that minimum level. The act also requires that if the reserves exceed 1.50 percent of total insured bank deposits, the FDIC should distribute the excess as dividends to banks.

18-3b Regulation of Deposits

Three regulatory acts created more competition for bank deposits over time, as discussed next.

DIDMCA   In 1980, the **Depository Institutions Deregulation and Monetary Control Act (DIDMCA)** was enacted to (1) deregulate the banking (and other depository institutions) industry and (2) improve monetary policy. Because this chapter focuses on regulation and deregulation, only the first goal is discussed here.

The DIDMCA was a major force in deregulating the banking industry and increasing competition among banks. It removed interest rate ceilings on deposits, allowing banks and other depository institutions to make their own decisions on what interest rates to offer for time and savings deposits. In addition, it allowed banks to offer NOW accounts.

The DIDMCA has had a significant impact on the banking industry, most importantly by increasing competition among depository institutions.

Garn-St. Germain Act   Banks and other depository institutions were further deregulated in 1982 as a result of the **Garn-St. Germain Act**. The act came at a time when some depository institutions (especially savings institutions) were experiencing severe financial problems. One of its more important provisions permitted depository institutions to offer money market deposit accounts (MMDAs), which have no minimum maturity and no interest ceiling. These accounts allow a maximum of six transactions per month (three by check). They are similar to the traditional accounts offered by **money market mutual funds** (whose main function is to sell shares and pool the funds to purchase short-term securities that offer market-determined rates). Because MMDAs offer savers similar benefits, they allow depository institutions to compete against money market funds in attracting savers' funds.

A second key deregulatory provision of the Garn-St. Germain Act permitted depository institutions (including banks) to acquire failing institutions across geographic boundaries. The intent was to reduce the number of failures that require liquidation, as the chances of finding a potential acquirer for a failing institution improve when geographic barriers are removed. Also, competition was expected to increase because depository institutions previously barred from entering specific geographic areas could now do so by acquiring failing institutions.

Interstate Banking Act   In September 1994, Congress passed the Reigle-Neal Interstate Banking and Branching Efficiency Act, which removed interstate branching restrictions and thereby further increased the competition among banks for deposits. Nationwide interstate banking enabled banks to grow and achieve **economies of scale**. It also allowed banks in stagnant markets to penetrate other markets where economic conditions were more favorable. Banks in all markets were pressured to become more efficient as a result of the increased competition.

18-3c Regulation of Bank Loans

Since loans represent the key asset of commercial banks, they are regulated to limit a bank's exposure to default risk.

Regulation of Highly Leveraged Transactions   As a result of concern about the popularity of highly leveraged loans (for supporting leveraged buyouts and other activities), bank regulators monitor the amount of highly leveraged transactions (HLTs). HLTs are commonly defined as loan transactions in which the borrower's liabilities are valued at more than 75 percent of total assets.

Regulation of Foreign Loans   Regulators also monitor a bank's exposure to loans to foreign countries. Because regulators require banks to report significant exposure to foreign debt, investors and creditors have access to more detailed information about the composition of bank loan portfolios.

Regulation of Loans to a Single Borrower   Banks are restricted to a maximum loan amount of 15 percent of their capital to any single borrower (up to 25 percent if the loan is adequately collateralized). This forces them to diversify their loans to some degree.

Regulation of Loans to Community   Banks are also regulated to ensure that they attempt to accommodate the credit needs of the communities in which they operate. The Community Reinvestment Act (CRA) of 1977 (revised in 1995) requires banks to meet the credit needs of qualified borrowers in their community, even those with low or moderate incomes. The CRA is not intended to force banks to make high-risk loans but rather to ensure that qualified lower-income borrowers receive the loans that they request. Each bank's performance in this regard is evaluated periodically by its respective regulator.

18-3d Regulation of Bank Investment in Securities

Banks are not allowed to use borrowed or deposited funds to purchase common stock, although they can manage stock portfolios through trust accounts that are owned by individuals. Banks can invest only in bonds that are investment-grade quality. This was measured by a Baa rating or higher by Moody's or a BBB rating or higher by Standard & Poor's. The regulations on bonds are intended to prevent banks from taking excessive risks.

However, during the credit crisis, the ratings agencies were criticized for being too liberal with their ratings. The Wall Street Reform and Consumer Protection Act (also called the Dodd-Frank Act) of 2010 changed the rules to require that banks use not only credit ratings assigned by credit rating agencies, but also other methods to assess the risk of debt securities, including their own assessment of risk. This is intended to ensure that banks do not rely exclusively on credit rating agencies when investing in debt securities. Thus, even if the credit rating agencies apply liberal ratings, the bank should be able to detect when debt securities are too risky when using its own analysis or other methods to assess risk.

18-3e Regulation of Securities Services

The Banking Act of 1933 (better known as the Glass-Steagall Act) separated banking and securities activities. The act was prompted by problems during 1929 when some banks sold some of their poor-quality securities to their trust accounts established for individuals. Some banks also engaged in insider trading: buying or selling corporate securities based on confidential information provided by firms that had requested loans. The **Glass-Steagall** Act prevented any firm that accepted deposits from underwriting stocks and bonds of corporations.

The separation of securities activities from banking activities was intended to prevent potential conflicts of interest. For example, the concern was that if a bank were allowed to underwrite securities, it might advise its corporate customers to purchase these securities and could threaten to cut off future loans if the customers did not oblige.

Financial Services Modernization Act In 1999, Congress passed the **Financial Services Modernization Act** (also called the **Gramm-Leach-Bliley Act**), which essentially repealed the Glass-Steagall Act. The 1999 act allows affiliations between banks, securities firms, and insurance companies. It also allows bank holding companies to engage in any financial activity through their ownership of subsidiaries. Consequently, a single holding company can engage in traditional banking activities, securities trading, underwriting, and insurance. The act also requires that the holding company be well managed and have sufficient capital in order to expand its financial services. The Securities and Exchange Commission regulates any securities products that are created, but the bank subsidiaries that offer the securities products are overseen by bank regulators.

Although many commercial banks had previously pursued securities services, the 1999 act increased the extent to which banks could offer these services. Furthermore, it allowed securities firms and insurance companies to acquire banks. Under the act, commercial banks must have a strong rating in community lending (which indicates that they have actively provided loans in lower-income communities) in order to pursue additional expansion in securities and other nonbank activities.

Since the passage of the Financial Services Modernization Act, there has been much more consolidation of financial institutions. Many of the larger financial institutions are able to offer all types of financial services through their various subsidiaries. Because individuals commonly use financial institutions to deposit funds, obtain mortgage loans and consumer loans (such as an automobile loan), purchase shares of mutual funds, order stock transactions (brokerage), and purchase insurance, they can obtain all their financial services from a single financial conglomerate. And because firms commonly use financial institutions to maintain a business checking account, obtain loans, issue stocks or bonds, have their pension fund managed, and purchase insurance services, they can obtain all of their financial services from a single financial conglomerate.

The Financial Services Modernization Act also offers benefits to financial institutions. By offering more diversified services, financial institutions can reduce their reliance on the demand for any single service that they offer. This diversification may result in less risk for the institution's consolidated business provided the new services are not subject to a much higher degree of risk than its traditional services.

The individual units of a financial conglomerate may generate some new business simply because they are part of the conglomerate and offer convenience to clients who already rely on its other services. Each financial unit's list of existing clients represents a potential source of new clients for the other financial units to pursue.

The consolidation of banks and securities firms continued during the credit crisis in 2008, as some major securities firms (e.g., Bear Stearns and Merrill Lynch) were acquired by commercial banks while others (e.g., Goldman Sachs and Morgan Stanley) applied and were approved to become bank holding companies. This consolidation improved the stability of the financial system because regulations on bank holding companies are generally more stringent than the regulations on independent securities firms.

18-3f Regulation of Insurance Services

As with securities services, banks have been eager to offer insurance services. The arguments for and against bank involvement in insurance are quite similar to those regarding bank involvement in securities. Banks could increase competition in the insurance industry by offering services at a lower cost. In addition, they could offer their customers the convenience of one-stop shopping (especially if the bank could also offer securities services).

In 1998, regulators allowed the merger between Citicorp and Traveler's Insurance Group, which essentially paved the way for the consolidation of bank and insurance services. Passage of the Financial Services Modernization Act in the following year confirmed that banks and insurance companies could merge and consolidate their operations. These events encouraged banks and insurance companies to pursue mergers as a means of offering a full set of financial services.

18-3g Regulation of Off-Balance Sheet Transactions

Banks offer a variety of off–balance sheet commitments. For example, banks provide letters of credit to back commercial paper issued by corporations. They also act as the intermediary on interest rate swaps and usually guarantee payments over the specified period in the event that one of the parties defaults on its payments.

Various off–balance sheet transactions have become popular because they provide fee income. That is, banks charge a fee for guaranteeing against the default of another party and for facilitating transactions between parties. Off–balance sheet transactions do expose a bank to risk, however. If a severe economic downturn causes many corporations to default on their commercial paper or on payments specified by interest rate swap agreements, the banks that provided guarantees would incur large losses.

Bank exposure to off–balance sheet activities has become a major concern of regulators. Banks could be riskier than their balance sheets indicate because of these transactions. Therefore, the risk-based capital requirements are higher for banks that conduct more off–balance sheet activities. In this way, regulators discourage banks from excessive involvement in such activities.

Regulation of Credit Default Swaps Credit default swaps are a type of off–balance sheet transaction that became popular during the 2004–2008 period as a means of protecting against the risk of default on bonds and mortgage–backed securities. A swap allows a commercial bank to make periodic payments to a counterparty in return for protection in the event that its holdings of mortgage-backed securities default. While some commercial banks purchased these swaps as a means of protecting their assets against default, other commercial banks sold them (to provide protection) as a means of generating fee income. By 2008, credit default swaps represented more than $30 trillion of mortgage-backed securities or other types of securities ($60 trillion when counting each contract for both parties).

When commercial banks purchase credit default swaps to protect their assets against possible default, these assets are not subject to capital requirements. But if the sellers of the credit default swaps are overexposed, they may not be able to provide the protection they promised. Thus the banks that purchased credit default swaps might not be protected if the sellers default. As the credit crisis intensified in 2008 and 2009, regulators became concerned about credit default swaps because of the lack of transparency regarding the exposure of each commercial bank and the credibility of the counterparties on the swaps. They increased their oversight of this market and asked commercial banks to provide more information about their credit default swap positions.

18-3h Regulation of the Accounting Process

Publicly traded banks, like other publicly traded companies, are required to provide financial statements that indicate their recent financial position and performance. The Sarbanes-Oxley (SOX) Act was enacted in 2002 to ensure a more transparent process for reporting on a firm's productivity and financial condition. It was created following news about how some publicly traded firms (such as Enron) inflated their earnings, which caused many investors to pay a much higher stock price than was appropriate. The act requires all firms (including banks) to implement an internal reporting process that can be easily monitored by executives and makes it impossible for executives to pretend that they were unaware of accounting fraud.

Some of the key provisions of the act require banks to improve their internal control processes and establish a centralized database of information. In addition, executives are now more accountable for a bank's financial statements because they must personally verify the accuracy of the statements. Investors may have more confidence in the financial statements now that there is greater accountability that could discourage accounting fraud.

Nevertheless, questionable accounting practices may still occur at banks. Some types of assets do not have a market in which they are actively traded. Thus banks have some flexibility on valuing these assets. During the credit crisis, many banks assigned values to some types of securities they held that clearly exceeded their proper market values. Consequently, they were able to hide a portion of their losses.

One negative effect of the SOX Act is that publicly traded banks have incurred expenses of more than $1 million per year to comply with its provisions. Such a high expense may encourage smaller publicly traded banks to go private.

18-4 REGULATION OF CAPITAL

Banks are subject to capital requirements, which force them to maintain a minimum amount of capital (or equity) as a percentage of total assets. They rely on their capital as a cushion against possible losses. If a bank has insufficient capital to cover losses, it will not be able to cover its expenses and will fail. Therefore, regulators closely monitor bank capital levels.

Some bank managers and shareholders would prefer that banks hold a lower level of capital, because a given dollar level of profits would represent a higher return on equity if the bank holds less capital. This might allow for larger bonuses to managers and higher stock prices for shareholders during strong economic conditions. However, regulators are more interested in the safety of the banking system than managerial bonuses, and have increased bank capital requirements in recent years as a means of stabilizing the banking system.

18-4a How Banks Satisfy Regulatory Requirements

When a bank's capital declines below the amount required by regulators, it can increase its capital ratio in the following ways.

Retaining Earnings   As a bank generates new earnings, and retains them rather than distributing them as dividends to shareholders, it boosts its capital. However, it cannot retain earnings if it does not generate earnings. If it incurs losses, it needs to use some of its existing capital to cover some of its expenses, because its revenue was not sufficient to cover its expenses. Thus losses (negative earnings) result in a lower level of capital. Poorly performing banks cannot rely on retained earnings to boost capital levels because they may not have any new earnings to retain.

Issuing Stock   Banks can boost their capital by issuing stock to the public. However, a bank's capital level becomes deficient when its performance is weak; under these conditions, the bank's stock price is probably depressed. If the bank has to sell stock when its stock price is very low it might not receive a sufficient amount of funds from its stock offering. Furthermore, investors may not have much interest in purchasing new shares in a bank that is weak and desperate to build capital because they might reasonably expect the bank to fail.

Reducing Dividends   Banks can increase their capital by reducing their dividends, which enables them to retain a larger amount of any earnings. However, shareholders might interpret a cut in dividends as a signal that the bank is desperate for capital, which could cause its stock price to decline further. This type of effect could make it more difficult for the bank to issue stock in the future.

Selling Assets   When banks sell assets, they can improve on their capital position. Assuming the assets were perceived to be risky, banks would have been required to maintain some capital to back those assets. By selling the assets, they are no longer required to back those assets with capital.

18-4b Basel I Accord

When bank regulators of various countries develop their set of guidelines for capital requirements, they are commonly guided by the recommendations in the Basel guidelines. These guidelines are intended to guide the banks in setting their own capital requirements.

In the first Basel Accord (1988, often called Basel I), the central banks of 12 major countries agreed to establish a framework for determining uniform capital requirements. A key provision in the Basel Accord bases the capital requirements on a bank's risk level. Banks with greater risk are required to maintain a higher level of capital, which discourages banks from excessive exposure to credit risk.

Assets are weighted according to risk. Very safe assets such as cash are assigned a zero weight, while very risky assets are assigned a 100 percent weight. Because the required capital is set as a percentage of risk-weighted assets, riskier banks are subject to more stringent capital requirements.

WEB

www.federalreserve.
gov/bankinforeg/
basel/USImplemen
tation.htm
Information about the
Basel framework.

18-4c Basel II Framework

A committee of central bank and regulatory authorities of numerous countries (called the Basel Committee on Banking Supervision) created a framework in 2004 called Basel II, which was added to the Basel Accord. It has two major parts: revising the measurement of credit risk and explicitly accounting for operational risk.

Revising the Measurement of Credit Risk   When banks categorize their assets and assign risk weights to the categories, they account for possible differences in risk levels of loans within a category. Risk levels could differ if some banks required better collateral to back their loans. In addition, some banks may take positions in derivative securities that can reduce their credit risk, while other banks may have positions in derivative securities that increase their credit risk.

A bank's loans that are past due are assigned a higher weight. This adjustment inflates the size of these assets for the purpose of determining minimum capital requirements. Thus, banks with more loans that are past due are forced to maintain a higher level of capital (other things being equal).

An alternative method of calculating credit risk, called the internal ratings-based (IRB) approach, allows banks to use their own processes for estimating the probability of default on their loans.

Explicitly Accounting for Operational Risk   The Basel Committee defines operational risk as the risk of losses resulting from inadequate or failed internal processes or systems. Banks are encouraged to improve their techniques for controlling operational risk because doing so could reduce failures in the banking system. By imposing higher capital requirements on banks with higher levels of operational risk, Basel II provided an incentive for banks to reduce their operational risk.

The United States, Canada, and countries in the European Union created regulations for their banks that conform to some parts of Basel II. When applying the Basel II guidelines, many banks underestimated the probability of loan default during the credit crisis. This motivated the creation of the Basel III framework, described next.

18-4d Basel III Framework

In response to the credit crisis, the Basel Committee on Banking Supervision began to develop a Basel III framework in 2011, which attempts to correct deficiencies of Basel II. This framework recommends that banks maintain Tier 1 capital (retained earnings and common stock) of at least 6 percent of total risk-weighted asset. It also recommended a more rigorous process for determining risk-weighted assets. Prior to Basel III, some assets were assigned low risk based on liberal ratings by ratings agencies. Basel III proposed that banks apply scenario analysis to determine how the values of their assets would be affected based on possible adverse economic scenarios.

Basel III also recommended that banks maintain an extra layer of Tier 1 capital (called a capital conservation buffer) of at least 2.5 percent of risk-weighted assets by 2016. Banks that do not maintain this extra layer could be restricted from making dividend payments, repurchasing stock, or granting bonuses to executives.

In addition to the increased capital requirements, Basel III also called for liquidity requirements. Some banks that specialize in low-risk loans and have adequate capital might not have adequate liquidity to survive an economic crisis. Basel III proposes that banks maintain sufficient liquidity so that they can easily cover their cash needs under adverse conditions.

18-4e Use of the VaR Method to Determine Capital Levels

To comply with the Basel Accord, banks commonly apply a value-at-risk (VaR) model to assess the risk of their assets, and determine how much capital they should hold. The VaR model can be applied in various ways to determine capital requirements. In general, a bank defines the VaR as the estimated potential loss from its trading businesses that could result from adverse movements in market prices. Banks typically use a 99 percent confidence level, meaning that there is a 99 percent chance that the loss on a given day will be more favorable than the VaR estimate. When applied to a daily time horizon, the actual loss from a bank's trading businesses should not exceed the estimated loss by VaR on more than 1 out of every 100 days. Banks estimate the VaR by assessing the probability of specific adverse market events (such as an abrupt change in interest rates) and the sensitivity of responses to those events. Banks with a higher maximum loss (based on a 99 percent confidence interval) are subject to higher capital requirements.

This focus on daily price movements forces banks to monitor their trading positions continuously so that they are immediately aware of any losses. Many banks now have access to the market values of their trading businesses at the end of every day. If banks used a longer-term horizon (such as a month), larger losses might build up before being recognized.

Limitations of the VaR Model   The VaR model was generally ineffective at detecting the risk of banks during the credit crisis. The VaR model failed to recognize the degree to which the value of bank assets (such as mortgages or mortgage-backed securities) could decline under adverse conditions. The use of historical data from before 2007 did not capture the risk of mortgages because investments in mortgages during that period normally resulted in low defaults. Thus, the VaR model was not adequate for predicting the possible estimated losses.

18-4f Stress Tests Imposed to Determine Capital Levels

Some banks supplement the VaR estimate with their own stress tests.

EXAMPLE

Kenosha Bank wants to estimate the loss that would occur in response to an extreme adverse market event. First, it identifies an extreme scenario that could occur, such as an increase in interest rates on one day that is at least three standard deviations from the mean daily change in interest rates. (The mean and standard deviation of daily interest rate movements may be based on a recent historical period, such as the last 300 days.) Kenosha Bank then uses this scenario, along with the typical sensitivity of its trading businesses to such a scenario, to estimate the resulting loss on its trading businesses. It may then repeat this exercise based on a scenario of a decline in the market value of stocks that is at least three standard deviations from the mean daily change in stock prices. It may even estimate the possible losses in its trading businesses from an adverse scenario in which interest rates increase and stock prices decline substantially on a given day. ●

Regulatory Stress Tests during the Credit Crisis   In 2009, regulators applied stress tests to the largest bank holding companies to determine if the banks had enough capital. These banks account for about half of all loans provided by U.S. banks.

One of the stress tests applied to banks in April 2009 involved forecasting the likely effect on the banks' capital levels if the recession existing at that time lasted longer than expected. This adverse scenario would cause banks to incur larger losses farther into the future. As a result, the banks would periodically be forced to use a portion of their capital to cover their losses, resulting in a reduction of their capital over time.

The potential impact of an adverse scenario such as a deeper recession varies among banks. During the credit crisis, banks that had a larger proportion of real estate assets were expected to suffer larger losses if economic conditions worsened because real estate values were extremely sensitive to economic conditions. Thus banks with considerable exposure to real estate values were more likely to experience capital deficiencies if the recession lasted longer than expected. Regulators focused on banks that were graded poorly on the stress tests in order to ensure that these banks would have sufficient capital even if the recession lasted for a longer period of time. Regulators now impose stress tests on an annual basis for banks with asset levels of $50 billion or larger, but will apply the tests in the future to smaller banks with at least $10 billion in assets.

18-4g Government Infusion of Capital during the Credit Crisis

During the 2008–2010 period, the Troubled Asset Relief Program (TARP) was implemented to boost the capital levels of banks and other financial institutions with excessive exposure to mortgages or mortgage-backed securities. The Treasury injected more than $300 billion into banks and financial institutions, primarily by purchasing preferred stock.

The injection of funds allowed banks to cushion their loan losses. It was also intended to encourage additional lending by banks and other financial institutions so that qualified firms or individuals could borrow funds. The Treasury also purchased some "toxic" assets that had declined in value, and it even guaranteed against losses of other assets at banks and financial institutions. The financial institutions that received these capital injections were required to make dividend payments to the Treasury, but they could repurchase the preferred stock that they had issued to the Treasury (in essence, repaying the funds injected by the Treasury) once their financial position improved.

As a result of this program, the government became a large investor in banks and other financial institutions. For example, by February 2009, the Treasury had a 36 percent ownership stake in Citicorp. By June 2010, more than half of the TARP funds that were extended by the federal government were repaid, and the program generated more than $20 billion in revenue that was due primarily to dividends received on preferred stock that was purchased.

In October 2010, the TARP program stopped extending new funds to banks and other financial institutions. Although the government was subject to some criticism for its intervention in the banking system, it was also complimented for restoring the confidence of depositors and investors in the system.

WEB

www.fdic.gov
Information about specific bank regulations.

18-5 How Regulators Monitor Banks

Bank regulators typically conduct an on-site examination of each commercial bank at least once a year. During the examination, regulators assess the bank's compliance with existing regulations and its financial condition. In addition to on-site examinations, regulators periodically monitor commercial banks with computerized monitoring systems that analyze data provided by the banks on a quarterly basis.

18-5a CAMELS Ratings

Regulators monitor banks to detect any serious deficiencies that might develop so that they can correct the deficiencies before the bank fails. The more failures they can prevent, the more confidence the public will have in the banking industry. The evaluation approach described here is used by the FDIC, the Federal Reserve, and the Comptroller of the Currency.

The single most common cause of bank failure is poor management. Unfortunately, no reliable measure of poor management exists. Therefore, the regulators rate banks on the basis of six characteristics that constitute the **CAMELS ratings**, so named for the acronym that identifies the six characteristics:

- Capital adequacy
- Asset quality
- Management
- Earnings
- Liquidity
- Sensitivity

Each of the CAMELS characteristics is rated on a 1-to-5 scale, with 1 indicating outstanding and 5 very poor. A composite rating is determined as the mean rating of the six characteristics. Banks with a composite rating of 4.0 or higher are considered to be problem banks. They are closely monitored because their risk level is perceived to be very high.

Capital Adequacy   Because adequate bank capital is thought to reduce a bank's risk, regulators determine the **capital ratio** (typically defined as capital divided by assets). Regulators have become increasingly concerned that some banks do not hold enough capital, so they have increased capital requirements. If banks hold more capital, they can more easily absorb potential losses and are more likely to survive. Banks with higher capital ratios are therefore assigned a higher capital adequacy rating. Even a bank with a relatively high level of capital could fail, however, if the other components of its balance sheet have not been properly managed. Thus, regulators must evaluate other characteristics of banks in addition to capital adequacy.

Because a bank's capital requirements depend on the value of its assets, they are subject to the accounting method that is used in the valuation process. *Fair value accounting* is used to measure the value of bank assets. That is, a bank is required to periodically mark its assets to market so that it can revise the amount of needed capital based on the reduced market value of the assets. During the credit crisis, the secondary market for mortgage-backed securities and mortgage loans was so illiquid that banks would have had to sell these assets at very low prices (large discounts). Consequently, the fair value accounting method forced the banks to "write down" the value of their assets.

Given a decline in a bank's book value of assets and no associated change in its book value of liabilities, a bank's balance sheet is balanced by reducing its capital. Thus many banks were required to replenish their capital in order to meet the capital requirements, and some banks came under extra scrutiny by regulators. Some banks satisfied the capital requirements by selling some of their assets, but they would have preferred not to sell assets during this period because there were not many buyers and the market price of these assets was low. An alternative method of meeting capital requirements is to issue new stock, but since bank stock values were so low during the credit crisis, this was not a viable option at that time.

Banks complained that their capital was reduced because of the fair value accounting rules. They argued that their assets should have been valued higher if the banks intended to hold them until the credit crisis ended and the secondary market for these assets became more liquid. If the banks' assets had been valued in this manner, their write-downs of assets would have been much smaller, and the banks could have more easily met the capital requirements. As a result of the banks' complaints, the fair value accounting rules were modified somewhat in 2009.

Asset Quality Each bank makes its own decisions as to how deposited funds should be allocated, and these decisions determine its level of credit (default) risk. Regulators therefore evaluate the quality of the bank's assets, including its loans and its securities.

EXAMPLE

The Fed considers "the 5 Cs" to assess the quality of the loans extended by Skyler Bank, which it is examining:

- Capacity—the borrower's ability to pay
- Collateral—the quality of the assets that back the loan
- Condition—the circumstances that led to the need for funds
- Capital—the difference between the value of the borrower's assets and its liabilities
- Character—the borrower's willingness to repay loans as measured by its payment history on the loan and credit report

From an assessment of a sample of Skyler Bank's loans, the Fed determines that the borrowers have excessive debt, minimal collateral, and low capital levels. Thus, the Fed concludes that Skyler Bank's asset quality is weak. ●

Rating an asset portfolio can be difficult, as the following example illustrates.

EXAMPLE

A bank currently has 1,000 loans outstanding to firms in a variety of industries. Each loan has specific provisions as to how it is secured (if at all) by the borrower's assets; some of the loans have short-term maturities, while others are for longer terms. Imagine the task of assigning a rating to this bank's asset quality. Even if all the bank's loan recipients are current on their loan repayment schedules, this does not guarantee that the bank's asset quality deserves a high rating. The economic conditions existing during the period of prompt loan repayment may not persist in the future. Thus, an appropriate examination of the bank's asset portfolio should incorporate the portfolio's exposure to potential events (such as a recession). The reason for the regulatory examination is not to grade past performance but rather to detect any problem that could cause the bank to fail in the future. ●

Because of the difficulty in assigning a rating to a bank's asset portfolio, it is possible that some banks will be rated lower or higher than they deserve.

Management   Each of the characteristics examined relates to the bank's management. In addition, regulators specifically rate the bank's management according to administrative skills, ability to comply with existing regulations, and ability to cope with a changing environment. They also assess the bank's internal control systems, which may indicate how easily the bank's management could detect its own financial problems. This evaluation is clearly subjective.

Earnings   Although the CAMELS ratings are mostly concerned with risk, earnings are very important. Banks fail when their earnings become consistently negative. A profitability ratio commonly used to evaluate banks is **return on assets (ROA)**, defined as after-tax earnings divided by assets. In addition to assessing a bank's earnings over time, it is also useful to compare the bank's earnings with industry earnings. This allows for an evaluation of the bank relative to its competitors. In addition, regulators are concerned about how a bank's earnings would change if economic conditions change.

Liquidity   Some banks commonly obtain funds from outside sources (such as the Federal Reserve or the federal funds market), but regulators would prefer that banks not consistently rely on these sources. Such banks are more likely to experience a liquidity crisis whereby they are forced to borrow excessive amounts of funds from outside sources. If existing depositors sense that the bank is experiencing a liquidity problem, they may withdraw their funds, compounding the problem.

Sensitivity   Regulators also assess the degree to which a bank might be exposed to adverse financial market conditions. Two banks could be rated similarly in terms of recent earnings, liquidity, and other characteristics, yet one of them may be much more sensitive than the other to financial market conditions. Regulators began to explicitly consider banks' sensitivity to financial market conditions in 1996 and added this characteristic to what was previously referred to as the CAMEL ratings. In particular, regulators place much emphasis on a bank's sensitivity to interest rate movements. Many banks have liabilities that are repriced more frequently than their assets and are therefore adversely affected by rising interest rates. Banks that are more sensitive to rising interest rates are more likely to experience financial problems.

Limitations of the CAMELS Rating System   The CAMELS rating system is essentially a screening device. Because there are so many banks, regulators do not have the resources to closely monitor each bank on a frequent basis. The rating system identifies what are believed to be problem banks. Over time, other banks are added to the "problem list," some problem banks improve and are removed from the list, and others may deteriorate further and ultimately fail.

Although examinations by regulators may help detect problems experienced by some banks in time to save them, many problems still go unnoticed; by the time they are detected, it may be too late to find a remedy. Because financial ratios measure current or past performance rather than future performance, they do not always detect problems in time to correct them. Thus, although an analysis of financial ratios can be useful, the task of assessing a bank is as much an art as it is a science. Subjective opinion must complement objective measurements to provide the best possible evaluation of a bank.

Any system used to detect financial problems may err in one of two ways. It may classify a bank as safe when in fact it is failing or it may classify a bank as risky when in fact it is safe. The first type of mistake is more costly, because some failing banks are not identified in time to help them. To avoid this mistake, bank regulators could lower their benchmark composite rating. If they did, however, many more banks would be on the problem list and require close supervision, so regulators' limited resources would be spread too thin.

WEB

www.occ.treas.gov/
interp/monthly.htm
Information on the latest bank regulations and their interpretation from the Office of the Comptroller.

18-5b Corrective Action by Regulators

When a bank is classified as a problem bank, regulators thoroughly investigate the cause of its deterioration. Corrective action is often necessary. Regulators may examine such banks frequently and thoroughly and will discuss with bank management possible remedies to cure the key problems. For example, regulators may request that a bank boost its capital level or delay its plans to expand. They can require that additional financial information be periodically updated to allow continued monitoring. They have the authority to remove particular officers and directors of a problem bank if doing so would enhance the bank's performance. They even have the authority to take legal action against a problem bank if the bank does not comply with their suggested remedies. Such a drastic measure is rare, however, and would not solve the existing problems of the bank.

18-5c Funding the Closure of Failing Banks

If a failing bank cannot be saved, it will be closed. The FDIC is responsible for the closure of failing banks. It must decide whether to liquidate the failed bank's assets or to facilitate the acquisition of that bank by another bank. When liquidating a failed bank, the FDIC draws from its Deposit Insurance Fund to reimburse insured depositors. After reimbursing depositors, the FDIC attempts to sell any marketable assets (such as securities and some loans) of the failed bank. The cost to the FDIC of closing a failed bank is the difference between the reimbursement to depositors and the proceeds received from selling the failed bank's assets.

18-6 GOVERNMENT RESCUE OF FAILING BANKS

The U.S. government periodically rescues failed banks in various ways. The FDIC provides some financial support to facilitate another bank's acquisition of the failed bank. The financial support is necessary because the acquiring bank recognizes that the market value of the failed bank's assets is less than its liabilities. The FDIC may be willing to provide funding if doing so would be less costly than liquidating the failed bank. Whether a failing bank is liquidated or acquired by another bank, it loses its identity.

In some cases, the government has given preferential treatment to certain large troubled banks. For example, the government has occasionally provided short-term loans to a distressed bank or insured all its deposits, even those above the insurance limit, in an effort to encourage depositors to leave their funds in the troubled bank. Or the government might orchestrate a takeover of the troubled bank in a manner that enables the shareholders to receive at least some payment for their shares (when a failed bank is acquired, shareholders ordinarily lose their investment). However, such intervention by the government is controversial.

18-6a Argument for Government Rescue

If all financial institutions that were weak during the credit crisis had been allowed to fail without any intervention, the FDIC might have had to use all of its reserves to reimburse depositors. To the extent that FDIC intervention can reduce the extent of losses at depository institutions, it may reduce the cost to the government (and therefore the taxpayers).

How a Rescue Might Reduce Systemic Risk The financial problems of a large bank failure can be contagious to other banks. This so-called systemic risk occurs because of the interconnected transactions between banks. The rescue of large banks might be necessary to reduce systemic risk in the financial system, as illustrated next.

EXAMPLE   Consider a financial system with only four large banks, all of which make many mortgage loans and invest in mortgage-backed securities. Assume that Bank A sold credit default swaps to Banks B, C, and D and so receives periodic payments from those banks. It will have to make a large payment to these banks if a particular set of mortgages default.

Now assume that the economy weakens and many mortgages default, including the mortgages referenced by the credit default swap agreements. This means that Bank A now owes a large payment to Banks B, C, and D. But since Bank A incurred losses from its own mortgage portfolio, it cannot follow through on its payment obligation to the other banks. Meanwhile, Banks B, C, and D may have used the credit default swap position to hedge their existing mortgage holdings; however, if they do not receive the large payment from Bank A, they incur losses without any offsetting gains.

If bank regulators do not rescue Bank A, then all four banks may fail because of Bank A's connections with the other three banks. However, if bank regulators rescue Bank A then Bank A can make its payments to Banks B, C, and D, and all banks should survive. Thus, a rescue may be necessary to stabilize the financial system. ●

In reality, the financial system is supported not only by a few large banks, but by many different types of financial institutions. The previous example is not restricted to banks, but extends to all types of financial institutions that can engage in those types of transactions. Furthermore, a government rescue of a bank benefits not only bank executives, but bank employees at all levels. To the extent that a government rescue can stabilize the banking system, it can indirectly stimulate all the sectors that rely on funding from the banking system. This potential benefit was especially relevant during the credit crisis.

18-6b Argument against Government Rescue

Those who oppose government rescues say that, when the federal government rescues a large bank, it sends a message to the banking industry that large banks will not be allowed to fail. Consequently, large banks may take excessive risks without concern about failure. If a large bank's risky ventures (such as loans to risky borrowers) pay off, the return will be high. If they do not pay off, the federal government will bail the bank out. If large banks can be sure that they will be rescued, their shareholders will benefit because they face limited downside risk.

Some critics recommend a policy of letting the market work, meaning that no financial institution would ever be bailed out. In this case, managers of a troubled bank would be held accountable for their bad management because their jobs would be terminated in response to the bank's failure. In addition, shareholders would more closely monitor the bank managers to make sure that they do not take excessive risk.

18-6c Government Rescue of Bear Stearns

The credit crisis led to new arguments about government rescues of failing financial institutions. In March 2008, Bear Stearns (a large securities firm) was about to go bankrupt. Bear Stearns had facilitated many transactions in financial markets, and its failure would have delayed them and so caused liquidity problems for many individuals and firms that were to receive cash as a result of those transactions. The Federal Reserve provided short-term loans to Bear Stearns to ensure that it had adequate liquidity. The Fed then backed the acquisition of Bear Stearns by JPMorgan Chase by providing a loan so that JPMorgan Chase could afford the acquisition.

At this point, the question was whether the Federal Reserve (a regulator of commercial banks) should be assisting a securities firm such as Bear Stearns that it did not regulate. Some critics (including Paul Volcker, a previous chair of the Fed) suggested that the rescue of a firm other than a commercial bank should be the responsibility of Congress and not the Fed. The Fed's counter was that it recognized that many financial transactions would potentially be frozen if it did not intervene. Thus, it was acting in an attempt to stabilize the financial system rather than in its role as a regulator of commercial banks.

18-6d Failure of Lehman and Rescue of AIG

In September 2008, Lehman Brothers (another large securities firm) was allowed to go bankrupt without any assistance from the Fed even though American International Group (AIG, a large insurance company) was rescued by the Fed. Some critics asked why some large financial institutions were bailed out but others were not. At what point does a financial institution become sufficiently large or important that it deserves to be rescued? This question will continue to trigger heated arguments.

Lehman Brothers was a large financial institution with more than $600 billion in assets. However, it might have been difficult to find another financial institution willing to acquire Lehman Brothers without an enormous subsidy from the federal government. Many of the assets held by Lehman Brothers (such as the mortgage-backed securities) were worth substantially less in the market than the book value assigned to them by Lehman.

American International Group had more than $1 trillion in assets when it was rescued and, like Lehman, had many obligations to other financial institutions because of its credit default swap arrangements. However, one important difference between AIG and Lehman Brothers was that AIG had various subsidiaries that were financially sound at the time, and the assets in these subsidiaries served as collateral for the loans extended by the federal government to rescue AIG. From the federal government's perspective, the risk of taxpayer loss due to the AIG rescue was low. In contrast, Lehman Brothers did not have adequate collateral available and so a large loan from the government could have been costly to U.S. taxpayers.

18-6e Protests of Bank Bailouts

The bailouts during the credit crisis led to the organization of various groups. In 2009, the Tea Party organized and staged protests throughout the United States. Its main theme was that the government was spending excessively, which led to larger budget deficits that arguably could weaken economic conditions. Their proposed solution is to eliminate the bailouts as one form of reducing the excessive government spending.

In 2011, Occupy Wall Street organized and also staged protests. While this movement also protested government funding decisions, its underlying theme is not as clear. Some protestors within this movement believe that bank bailouts are appropriate, whereas others do not. In addition, many protestors wanted the government to direct more funding to their own specials interests, such as health care, education, or programs to reduce unemployment. This led to the common sign or phrase associated with Occupy Wall Street protests: "Where's my bailout?" Although the Occupy Wall Street movement gained much support for protesting against the government, there does not appear to be a clear consensus solution among protestors regarding bailouts or the proper use of government funding.

18-7 Financial Reform Act of 2010

In July, 2010, the Financial Reform Act (also referred to as the Dodd-Frank Act, or the Wall Street Reform and Consumer Protection Act) was implemented. This act contained numerous provisions regarding financial services. The provisions that concern bank regulation are summarized here.

18-7a Mortgage Origination

The Financial Reform Act requires that banks and other financial institutions granting mortgages verify the income, job status, and credit history of mortgage applicants before approving mortgage applications. This provision is intended to prevent applicants from receiving mortgages unless they are creditworthy, which should minimize the possibility of a future credit crisis. It may seem that this provision would naturally be followed even if there was no law. Yet there were many blatant violations shortly before and during the credit crisis in which mortgages were approved for applicants who were clearly not creditworthy.

18-7b Sales of Mortgage-Backed Securities

The act requires that banks and other financial institutions that sell mortgage-backed securities retain 5 percent of the portfolio unless it meets specific standards that reflect low risk. This provision forces financial institutions to maintain a stake in the mortgage portfolios that they sell. The act also requires more disclosure regarding the quality of the underlying assets when mortgage-backed securities are sold.

18-7c Financial Stability Oversight Council

The Financial Reform Act created the Financial Stability Oversight Council, which is responsible for identifying risks to financial stability in the United States and makes recommendations that regulators can follow to reduce risks to the financial system. The council can recommend methods to ensure that banks do not rely on regulatory bailouts, which may prevent situations where a large financial institution is viewed as too big to fail. Furthermore, it can recommend rules such as higher capital requirements for banks that are perceived to be too big and complex, which may prevent these banks from becoming too risky.

The council consists of 10 members, including the Treasury Secretary (who chairs the council) and the heads of three regulatory agencies that monitor banks: the Federal Reserve, the Comptroller of the Currency, and the Federal Deposit Insurance Corporation. Because systemic risk in the financial system may be caused by financial security transactions that connect banks with other types of financial institutions, the council also includes the head of the Securities and Exchange Commission and of the U.S. Commodities Futures Trading Commission. The remaining members are the heads of the National Credit Union Association, the Federal Housing Finance Agency, and the

Consumer Financial Protection Bureau (described shortly) as well as an independent member with insurance experience who is appointed by the President.

18-7d Orderly Liquidation

The act assigned specific regulators with the authority to determine whether any particular financial institution should be liquidated. This expedites the liquidation process and can limit the losses incurred by a failing financial institution. The act calls for the creation of an orderly liquidation fund that can be used to finance the liquidation of any financial institution that is not covered by the Federal Deposit Insurance Corporation. Shareholders and unsecured creditors are expected to bear most of the losses of failing financial institutions, so they are not covered by this fund. If losses are beyond what can be absorbed by shareholders and unsecured creditors, other financial institutions in the corresponding industry are expected to bear the cost of the liquidation. The liquidations are not to be financed by taxpayers.

18-7e Consumer Financial Protection Bureau

The act established the Consumer Financial Protection Bureau, which is responsible for regulating consumer finance products and services offered by commercial banks and other financial institutions, such as online banking, checking accounts, and credit cards. The bureau can set rules to ensure that bank disclosure about financial products is accurate and to prevent deceptive financial practices.

18-7f Limits on Bank Proprietary Trading

The act mandates that commercial banks must limit their proprietary trading, in which they pool money received from customers and use it to make investments for the bank's clients. A commercial bank can use no more than 3 percent of its capital to invest in hedge fund institutions, private equity funds, or real estate funds (combined). This requirement has also been referred to as the Volcker rule, and it has led to much controversy.

The implementation of the limits on proprietary trading has been deferred to July 2014. This gives banks time to sell divisions if they exceed the limit. This provision had a larger impact on securities firms (such as Goldman Sachs and Morgan Stanley) that had converted to bank holding companies shortly before the act, because those firms had previously engaged in heavy proprietary trading.

The general argument for this rule is that commercial banks should not be making investments in extremely risky projects. If they want to pursue very high returns (and therefore be exposed to very high risk), they should not be part of the banking system, and should not have access to depositor funds, or be able to obtain deposit insurance. That is, if they want to invest like hedge funds, they should apply to be hedge funds and not commercial banks.

However, some critics believe that the Volcker rule could prevent U.S. banks from competing against other banks on a global basis. In addition, there is much disagreement regarding the degree to which banks should be allowed to take risks. Some critics argue that the Volcker rule would not have prevented some banks from making the risky investments that caused them to go bankrupt during the credit crisis. Furthermore, although JPMorgan Chase posted a trading loss of $2 billion in May 2012 while the Volcker rules were still being developed, it has been argued that the trades that caused that loss would not have been prohibited by the Volcker rule. There are also concerns that the provisions of the Volcker rule are not sufficiently clear, which will allow some banks to circumvent the rule when making investments by using their own interpretations of the rule.

18-7g Trading of Derivative Securities

The act requires that derivative securities be traded through a clearinghouse or exchange, rather than over the counter. This provision should enable a more standardized structure regarding margins and collateral as well as more transparency of prices in the market. Consequently, banks that trade these derivatives should be less susceptible to risk that the counterparty posted insufficient collateral.

GLOBAL ASPECTS

18-8 GLOBAL BANK REGULATIONS

Although the division of regulatory power between the central bank and other regulators varies among countries, each country has a system for monitoring and regulating commercial banks. Most countries also maintain different guidelines for deposit insurance. Differences in regulatory restrictions give some banks a competitive advantage in a global banking environment.

Historically, Canadian banks were not as restricted in offering securities services as U.S. banks and therefore control much of the Canadian securities industry. Recently, Canadian banks have begun to enter the insurance industry. European banks have had much more freedom than U.S. banks in offering securities services such as underwriting corporate securities. Many European banks are allowed to invest in stocks.

Japanese commercial banks have some flexibility to provide investment banking services, but not as much as European banks. Perhaps the most obvious difference between Japanese and U.S. bank regulations is that Japanese banks are allowed to use depositor funds to invest in stocks of corporations. Thus, Japanese banks are not only the creditors of firms but also their shareholders.

SUMMARY

- Banks must observe regulations on the deposit insurance they must maintain, their loan composition, the bonds they are allowed to purchase, and the financial services they can offer. In general, regulations on deposits and financial services have been loosened in recent decades in order to allow for more competition among banks.
- Capital requirements are intended to ensure that banks have a cushion against any losses. The requirements have become more stringent and are risk adjusted so that banks with more risk are required to maintain a higher level of capital.
- Bank regulators monitor banks by focusing on six criteria: capital, asset quality, management, earnings, liquidity, and sensitivity to financial market conditions. Regulators assign ratings to these criteria in order to determine whether corrective action is necessary.

When a bank is failing, the FDIC or other government agencies consider whether it can be saved. During the credit crisis, many banks failed and also Lehman Brothers failed, but the government rescued American International Group (AIG). Unlike Lehman brothers, AIG had various subsidiaries that were financially sound at the time, and the assets in these subsidiaries served as collateral for the loans extended by the government to rescue AIG.

- In July 2010, the Financial Reform Act was implemented. It set more stringent standards for mortgage applicants, required banks to maintain a stake in the mortgage portfolios that they sell, and established a Consumer Financial Protection Bureau to regulate consumer finance products and services offered by commercial banks and other financial institutions.

POINT COUNTER-POINT

Should Regulators Intervene to Take Over Weak Banks?

Point   Yes. Intervention could turn a bank around before weak management results in failure. Bank failures require funding from the FDIC to reimburse depositors up to the deposit insurance limit. This cost could be avoided if the bank's problems are corrected before it fails.

Counter-Point   No. Regulators will not necessarily manage banks any better. Also, this would lead to

excessive government intervention each time a bank experienced problems. Banks would use a very conservative management approach to avoid intervention, but this approach would not necessarily appeal to their shareholders who want high returns on their investment.

Who Is Correct?   Use the Internet to learn more about this issue and then formulate your own opinion.

QUESTIONS AND APPLICATIONS

1.   Regulation of Bank Sources and Uses of Funds How are a bank's balance sheet decisions regulated?

2.   Off-Balance Sheet Activities Provide examples of off–balance sheet activities. Why are regulators concerned about them?

3.   Moral Hazard and the Credit Crisis Explain why the moral hazard problem received so much attention during the credit crisis.

4.   FDIC Insurance What led to the establishment of FDIC insurance?

5.   Glass-Steagall Act Briefly describe the Glass-Steagall Act. Then explain how the related regulations have changed.

6.   DIDMCA Describe the main provisions of the DIDMCA that relate to deregulation.

7.   CAMELS Ratings Explain how the CAMELS ratings are used.

8.   Uniform Capital Requirements Explain how the uniform capital requirements established by the Basel Accord can discourage banks from taking excessive risk.

9.   Value at Risk Explain how the value at risk (VaR) method can be used to determine whether a bank has adequate capital.

10. HLTs Describe highly leveraged transactions (HLTs), and explain why a bank's exposure to HLTs is closely monitored by regulators.

11. Bank Underwriting Given the higher capital requirements now imposed on them, why might banks be even more interested in underwriting corporate debt issues?

12. Moral Hazard Explain the moral hazard problem as it relates to deposit insurance.

13. Economies of Scale How do economies of scale in banking relate to the issue of interstate banking?

14. Contagion Effects How can the financial problems of one large bank affect the market's risk evaluation of other large banks?

15. Regulating Bank Failures Why are bank regulators more concerned about a large bank failure than a small bank failure?

16. Financial Services Modernization Act Describe the Financial Services Modernization Act of 1999. Explain how it affected commercial bank operations and changed the competitive landscape among financial institutions.

17. Impact of SOX on Banks Explain how the Sarbanes-Oxley Act improved the transparency of banks. Why might the act have a negative impact on some banks?

18. Conversion of Securities Firms to BHCs Explain how the conversion of a securities firm to a bank holding company (BHC) structure might reduce its risk.

19. Capital Requirements during the Credit Crisis Explain how the accounting method applied to mortgage-backed securities made it more difficult for banks to satisfy capital requirements during the credit crisis.

20. Fed Assistance to Bear Stearns Explain why regulators might argue that the assistance they provided to Bear Stearns was necessary.

21. Fed Aid to Nonbanks Should the Fed have the power to provide assistance to firms, such as Bear Stearns, that are not commercial banks?

22. Regulation of Credit Default Swaps Why were bank regulators concerned about credit default swaps during the credit crisis?

23. Impact of Bank Consolidation on Regulation Explain how bank regulation can be more effective when there is consolidation of banks and securities firms.

24. Concerns about Systemic Risk during the Credit Crisis Explain why the credit crisis caused concerns about systemic risk.

25. Troubled Asset Relief Program (TARP) Explain how the Troubled Asset Relief Program was expected to help resolve problems during the credit crisis.

26. Financial Reform Act Explain how the Financial Reform Act resolved some problems during the credit crisis.

27. Bank Deposit Insurance Reserves What changes to reserve requirements were added by The Wall Street Reform and Consumer Protection Act (also called the Dodd-Frank Act) of 2010?

28. Basel III Changes to Capital and Liquidity Requirements How did Basel III change capital and liquidity requirements for banks?

Interpreting Financial News

Interpret the following comments made by Wall Street analysts and portfolio managers.

a. "The FDIC recently subsidized a buyer for a failing bank, which had different effects on FDIC costs than if the FDIC had closed the bank."

b. "Bank of America has pursued the acquisition of many failed banks because it sees potential benefits."

c. "By allowing a failing bank time to resolve its financial problems, the FDIC imposes an additional tax on taxpayers."

Managing in Financial Markets

Effect of Bank Strategies on Bank Ratings A bank has asked you to assess various strategies it is considering and explain how they could affect its regulatory review. Regulatory reviews include an assessment of capital, asset quality, management, earnings, liquidity, and sensitivity to financial market conditions. Many types of strategies can result in more favorable regulatory reviews based on some criteria but less favorable reviews based on other criteria. The bank is planning to issue more stock, retain more of its earnings, increase its holdings of Treasury securities, and reduce its business loans. The bank has historically been rated favorably by regulators yet believes that these strategies will result in an even more favorable regulatory assessment.

a. Which regulatory criteria will be affected by the bank's strategies? How?

b. Do you believe that the strategies planned by the bank will satisfy its shareholders? Is it possible for the bank to use strategies that would satisfy both regulators and shareholders? Explain.

c. Do you believe that the strategies planned by the bank will satisfy the bank's managers? Explain.

FLOW OF FUNDS EXERCISE

Impact of Regulation and Deregulation on Financial Services

Carson Company relies heavily on commercial banks for funding and for some other services.

a. Explain how the services provided by a commercial bank (just the banking, not the nonbank, services) to Carson may be limited because of bank regulation.

b. Explain the types of nonbank services that Carson Company can receive from the subsidiaries of a commercial bank as a result of deregulation. How might Carson Company be affected by the deregulation that allows subsidiaries of a commercial bank to offer nonbank services?

INTERNET/EXCEL EXERCISE

Browse the most recent Quarterly Banking Profile at www.fdic.gov/bank/analytical/index.html. Review the information provided about failed banks, and describe how regulators responded to one recent bank failure listed here.

WSJ EXERCISE

Impact of Bank Regulations

Using a recent issue of the *Wall Street Journal,* summarize an article that discusses a particular commercial bank regulation that has recently been passed or is currently being considered by regulators. (You may wish to use the *Wall Street Journal Index* to identify a specific article on a commercial banking regulation or bill.) Would this regulation have a favorable or unfavorable impact on commercial banks? Explain.

ONLINE ARTICLES WITH REAL-WORLD EXAMPLES

Find a recent practical article available online that describes a real-world example regarding a specific financial institution or financial market that reinforces one or more concepts covered in this chapter.

If your class has an online component, your professor may ask you to post your summary of the article there and provide a link to the article so that other students can access it. If your class is live, your professor may ask you to summarize your application of the article in class. Your professor may assign specific students to complete this assignment or may allow any students to do the assignment on a volunteer basis.

For recent online articles and real-world examples related to this chapter, consider using the following search terms (be sure to include the prevailing year as a search term to ensure that the online articles are recent):

1. bank AND deposit insurance

2. bank AND moral hazard

3. bank loans AND regulation

4. bank investments AND regulation

5. bank capital AND regulation

6. bank regulator AND rating banks

7. bank regulator AND stress test

8. too big to fail AND conflict

9. bank regulation AND conflict

10. government rescue AND bank

19

Bank Management

CHAPTER OBJECTIVES

The specific objectives of this chapter are to:

- describe the underlying goal, strategy, and governance of banks,

- explain how banks manage liquidity,

- explain how banks manage interest rate risk,

- explain how banks manage credit risk, and

- explain integrated bank management.

The performance of any commercial bank depends on the management of the bank's assets, liabilities, and capital. Increased competition has made efficient management essential for survival.

19-1 BANK GOALS, STRATEGY, AND GOVERNANCE

The underlying goal behind the managerial policies of a bank is to maximize the wealth of the bank's shareholders. Thus, bank managers should make decisions that maximize the price of the bank's stock. However, bank managers may make decisions that serve their own goals rather than the preferences of shareholders. For example, if they receive a fixed salary without a bonus, they may prefer to make very conservative decisions that avoid the risk of failure. In this way, they may secure their existing job position for a long-term period. Bank shareholders might prefer that bank managers take some risk in order to strive for higher returns, and this may justify why bank manager compensation is typically tied to a measure of performance such as earnings.

19-1a Aligning Managerial Compensation with Bank Goals

In order to ensure that managers serve shareholder interests, banks commonly implement compensation programs that provide bonuses to high-level managers that satisfy bank goals. For example, managerial compensation may include stock options, which encourage managers to serve shareholders because they become shareholders. However, this might encourage bank managers to forgo the development of some long-term projects in order to focus more exclusively on increasing the current stock price in order to achieve a high bonus. Compensation programs that provide stock options are thus more effective (in terms of realizing the bank's goals) when managers are required to hold their stock for several years before selling it.

Banks have been criticized for implementing compensation programs that are overly generous and that do not necessarily align compensation with long-term performance. Many compensation programs of banks are based on existing compensation programs used by other banks. It is difficult to correct for deficiencies in compensation programs when they are fairly standard across the industry.

Some compensation programs could cause bank managers to take excessive risk, especially if the bonus would be very high when the bank's earnings are very high. They may be more willing to take excessive risk if they believe that the government will rescue them under conditions in which their risky strategies result in large losses. In this case, they earn large bonuses if their risky strategies are successful and expect to be rescued if their strategies are not successful, so they have little to lose by taking risks.

19-1b Bank Strategy

A bank's strategy involves the management of its sources of funds (liabilities) and its uses of funds (assets). Its managerial decisions will affect its performance, as measured by its income statement, in the following ways. First, a bank's decisions on sources of funds will heavily influence its interest expenses on the income statement. Second, its asset structure will strongly influence its interest revenue on the income statement. The bank's asset structure also affects its expenses; for example, an emphasis on commercial loans will result in a high labor cost for assessing loan applicants.

A bank must also manage the operating risk that results from its general business operations. Specifically, banks face risk related to information (sorting, processing, transmitting through technology), execution of transactions, damaged relationships with clients, legal issues (lawsuits by employees and customers), and regulatory issues (increased costs due to new compliance requirements or penalties due to lack of compliance).

How Financial Markets Facilitate the Bank's Strategy   To implement their strategy, commercial banks rely heavily on financial markets, as explained in Exhibit 19.1. They rely on the money markets to obtain funds, on the mortgage and bond markets to use some of their funds, and on the futures, options, and swaps markets to hedge their risk (as explained in this chapter).

19-1c Bank Governance by the Board of Directors

A bank's board of directors oversees the operations of the bank and attempts to ensure that managerial decisions are in the best interests of the shareholders. Bank boards tend to have more directors and a higher percentage of outside directors than do boards of other types of firms. Some of the more important functions of bank directors are to:

- Determine a compensation system for the bank's executives
- Ensure proper disclosure of the bank's financial condition and performance to investors
- Oversee growth strategies such as acquisitions

Exhibit 19.1   Participation of Commercial Banks in Financial Markets

FINANCIAL MARKET	PARTICIPATION BY COMMERCIAL BANKS
Money markets	As banks offer deposits, they must compete with other financial institutions in the money market along with the Treasury to obtain short-term funds. They serve households that wish to invest funds for short-term periods.
Mortgage markets	Some banks offer mortgage loans on homes and commercial property and therefore provide financing in the mortgage market.
Bond markets	Commercial banks purchase bonds issued by corporations, the Treasury, and municipalities.
Futures markets	Commercial banks take positions in futures to hedge interest rate risk.
Options markets	Commercial banks take positions in options on futures to hedge interest rate risk.
Swaps markets	Commercial banks engage in interest rate swaps to hedge interest rate risk.

- Oversee policies for changing the capital structure, including decisions to raise capital or to engage in stock repurchases
- Assess the bank's performance and ensure that corrective action is taken if the performance is weak because of poor management

Bank directors are liable if they do not fulfill their duties. The Sarbanes-Oxley (SOX) Act, described in the previous chapter, has had a major effect on the monitoring conducted by board members of commercial banks. Recall that this act requires publicly traded firms to implement a more thorough internal control process to ensure more accurate financial reporting to shareholders. As a result of SOX, directors are now held more accountable for their oversight because the internal process requires them to document their assessment and opinion of key decisions made by the bank's executives. Furthermore, directors more frequently hire outside legal and financial advisers to aid in assessing key decisions (such as acquisitions) by bank executives to determine whether the decisions are justified.

Inside versus Outside Directors   Board members who are also managers of the bank (called inside directors) may sometimes face a conflict of interests because their decisions as board members may affect their jobs as managers. Outside directors (directors who are not managers) are generally expected to be more effective at overseeing a bank: they do not face a conflict of interests in serving shareholders.

19-1d Other Forms of Bank Governance

In addition to the board of directors, publicly traded banks are subject to potential shareholder activism. In particular, institutional investors holding a relatively large amount of shares can attempt to influence the approach taken by the bank's managers. Shareholders may also pursue proxy contests if they want to change the composition of the board, and they can pursue lawsuits if they believe that the board is not serving shareholder interests.

The market for corporate control serves as an additional form of governance over publicly traded banks, since a bank that performs poorly may be subject to a takeover. To the extent that a bank's management serves its own rather than shareholder interests, the bank's prevailing stock valuation may be low, which could encourage another bank to acquire it. The market for corporate control serves as a form of governance because bank managers recognize that they could lose their jobs if their bank is acquired.

19-2 MANAGING LIQUIDITY

Healthy banks tend to have easy access to liquidity. However, banks can experience illiquidity when cash outflows (due to deposit withdrawals, loans, etc.) exceed cash inflows (new deposits, loan repayments, etc.). Bank liquidity problems are typically preceded by other financial problems such as major defaults on their loans. A bank that is performing poorly has less ability to obtain short-term funds because it may not be able to repay the credit that it desires.Banks can resolve liquidity problems with proper management of their liabilities or their assets.

19-2a Management of Liabilities

Banks have access to various forms of borrowing, such as the federal funds market. The decision regarding how to obtain funds depends on the situation. If the need for funds is temporary, an increase in short-term liabilities (from the federal funds market) may be appropriate. If the need is permanent, however, then a policy for increasing deposits or selling liquid assets may be appropriate.

Some banks may borrow frequently by issuing short-term securities such as commercial paper, especially when short-term interest rates are low. They may use this strategy as a form of long-term financing, as the proceeds received from each new issuance of commercial paper is used to repay the principal owed as a result of the previous issuance. However, this strategy is dangerous because if economic conditions deteriorate, causing bank loan defaults to increase, banks may no longer be able to obtain funds by issuing commercial paper. Some banks have experienced liquidity problems because they were cut off from their short-term funding sources once weak economic conditions caused their assets to appear risky.

19-2b Management of Money Market Securities

Because some assets are more marketable than others, the bank's asset composition can affect its degree of liquidity. At an extreme, banks can ensure sufficient liquidity by using most of their funds to purchase short-term Treasury securities or other money market securities. Banks could easily sell their holdings of these securities at any time in order to obtain cash. However, banks must also be concerned with achieving a reasonable return on their assets, which often conflicts with the liquidity objective. Although short-term Treasury securities are liquid, their yield is low relative to bank loans or investments in other securities. In fact, the return that banks earn on short-term Treasury securities might be lower than the interest rate they pay on deposits. Banks should maintain the level of liquid assets (such as money market securities) that will satisfy their liquidity needs but use their remaining assets to earn a higher return.

19-2c Management of Loans

Since the secondary market for loans has become active, banks can attempt to satisfy their liquidity needs with a higher proportion of loans while striving for higher profitability. However, loans are not as liquid as money market securities. Banks may be unable to sell their loans when economic conditions weaken, because many other banks may be attempting to sell loans as well, and very few financial institutions will be willing to purchase loans under those conditions.

19-2d Use of Securitization to Boost Liquidity

The ability to securitize assets such as automobile and mortgage loans can enhance a bank's liquidity position. The process of securitization commonly involves the sale of assets by the bank to a trustee, who issues securities that are collateralized by the assets. The bank may still service the loans, but the interest and principal payments it receives are passed on to the investors who purchased the securities. Banks are more liquid as a result of securitization because they effectively convert future cash flows into immediate cash. In most cases, the process includes a guarantor who, for a fee, guarantees future payments to the investors who purchased the securities. The loans that collateralize the securities normally either exceed the amount of the securities issued or are backed by an additional guarantee from the bank that sells the loans.

Collateralized Loan Obligations As one form of securitization, commercial banks can obtain funds by packaging their commercial loans with those of other financial institutions as collateralized loan obligations (CLOs) and then selling securities that represent ownership of these loans. The banks earn a fee for selling these loans. The pool of loans might be perceived to be less risky than a typical individual loan within the pool because the loans were provided to a diversified set of borrowers. The securities that are issued to investors who invest in the loan pool represent various classes.

For example, one class of notes issued to investors may be BB-rated notes, which offer an interest rate of LIBOR (London Interbank Offer Rate) plus 3.5 percent. If there are loan defaults by the corporate borrowers whose loans are in the pool, this group of investors will be the first to suffer losses. Another class may consist of BBB-rated notes that offer a slightly lower interest rate. Investors in these notes are slightly less exposed to defaults on the loans. The AAA-rated notes offer investors the most protection against loan defaults but provide the lowest interest rate, such as LIBOR plus 0.25 percent. Insurance companies and pension funds are common investors in CLOs.

Banks learned during the credit crisis that not all AAA-rated CLOs are risk free. Their CLOs experienced substantial defaults in 2008. The AAA rating was apparently based on the assumption of much better economic conditions than the crisis conditions that occurred in the second half of 2008.

19-3 Managing Interest Rate Risk

The performance of a bank is highly influenced by the interest payments earned on its assets relative to the interest paid on its liabilities (deposits). The difference between interest payments received and interest paid is measured by the net interest margin (also known as the *spread*):

$$\text{Net interest margin} = \frac{\text{Interest revenues} - \text{Interest expenses}}{\text{Assets}}$$

In some cases, net interest margin is defined to include only the earning assets so as to exclude any assets (such as required reserves) that do not generate a return to the bank. Because the rate sensitivity of a bank's liabilities normally does not perfectly match that of the assets, the net interest margin changes over time. The change depends on whether bank assets are more or less rate sensitive than bank liabilities, the degree of difference in rate sensitivity, and the direction of interest rate movements.

During a period of rising interest rates, a bank's net interest margin will likely decrease if its liabilities are more rate sensitive than its assets, as illustrated in Exhibit 19.2. Under the opposite scenario, when market interest rates are declining over time, rates offered on new bank deposits (as well as those earned on new bank loans) will be affected by the decline in interest rates. The deposit rates will typically be more sensitive if their turnover is quicker, as illustrated in Exhibit 19.3.

To manage interest rate risk, a bank measures the risk and then uses its assessment of future interest rates to decide whether and how to hedge the risk. Methods of assessing the risk are described next, followed by a discussion of the hedging decision and methods of reducing interest rate risk.

19-3a Methods Used to Assess Interest Rate Risk

No method of measuring interest rate risk is perfect, so commercial banks use a variety of methods to assess their exposure to interest rate movements. The following are the most common methods of measuring interest rate risk:

- Gap analysis
- Duration analysis
- Regression analysis

Exhibit 19.2 Impact of Increasing Interest Rates on a Bank's Net Interest Margin (If the Bank's Liabilities Are More Rate Sensitive Than Its Assets)

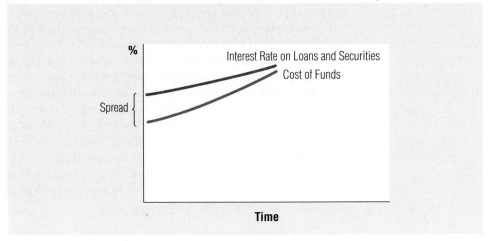

Exhibit 19.3 Impact of Decreasing Interest Rates on a Bank's Net Interest Margin (If the Bank's Liabilities Are More Rate Sensitive Than Its Assets)

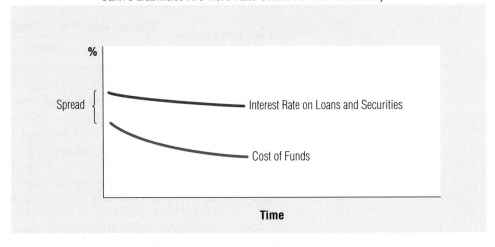

Gap Analysis   Banks can attempt to determine their interest rate risk by monitoring their **gap** over time, where

Gap = Rate-sensitive assets − Rate-sensitive liabilities

An alternative formula is the gap ratio, which is measured as the volume of rate-sensitive assets divided by rate-sensitive liabilities. A gap of zero (or gap ratio of 1.00) indicates that rate-sensitive assets equal rate-sensitive liabilities, so the net interest margin should not be significantly influenced by interest rate fluctuations. A negative gap (or gap ratio of less than 1.00) indicates that rate-sensitive liabilities exceed rate-sensitive assets. Banks with a negative gap are typically concerned about a potential increase in interest rates, which could reduce their net interest margin.

Chapter 19: Bank Management

Kansas City (K.C.) Bank had interest revenues of $80 million last year and interest expenses of $35 million. About $400 million of its $1 billion in assets are rate sensitive, and $700 million of its liabilities are rate sensitive. K.C. Bank's net interest margin is

$$\text{Net interest margin} = (\$80{,}000{,}000 - \$35{,}000{,}000) \div \$1{,}000{,}000{,}000$$
$$= 0.045, \text{ or } 4.5\%$$

K.C. Bank's gap is

$$\text{Gap} = \$400{,}000{,}000 - \$700{,}000{,}000$$
$$= -\$300{,}000{,}000$$

and its gap ratio is

$$\text{Gap} = \$400{,}000{,}000 \div \$700{,}000{,}000$$
$$= 0.5714, \text{ or } 57.14\%$$

Based on the gap analysis of K.C. Bank, an increase in market interest rates would cause its net interest margin to decline from its recent level of 4.5 percent. Conversely, a decrease in interest rates would cause its net interest margin to increase above 4.5 percent. ●

Many banks classify interest-sensitive assets and liabilities into various categories based on the timing in which interest rates are reset. Then the bank can determine the gap in each category so that its exposure to interest rate risk can be more accurately assessed.

Deacon Bank compares the interest rate sensitivity of its assets versus its liabilities as shown in Exhibit 19.4. It has a negative gap in the less-than-1-month maturity range, in the 3–6-month range, and in the 6–12-month range. Hence, the bank may hedge this gap if it believes that interest rates are rising. ●

Although the gap as described here is an easy method for measuring a bank's interest rate risk, it has limitations. Banks must determine which of their liabilities and assets are rate sensitive. For example, should a Treasury security with a year to maturity be classified as rate sensitive or rate insensitive? How short must a maturity be to qualify for the rate-sensitive classification?

Each bank may have its own classification system. Whatever system is used, there is a possibility that the measurement will be misinterpreted.

Spencer Bank obtains much of its funds by issuing CDs with seven-day and one-month maturities as well as money market deposit accounts (MMDAs). Assume that it typically uses these funds to provide loans with a floating rate that is adjusted once per year. These sources and uses of funds will likely be classified as rate sensitive. Thus the gap will be close to zero, implying that the bank is not exposed to interest rate risk. However, there is a difference in rate sensitivity between the bank's sources and uses of funds: the rates paid by the bank on its sources of funds will change more frequently than the rates earned on its uses of funds. Thus, Spencer Bank's net interest margin will likely decline during periods of rising interest rates. This exposure would not be detected by the gap measurement. ●

Duration Measurement An alternative approach to assessing interest rate risk is to measure duration. Some assets or liabilities are more rate sensitive than others, even if the frequency of adjustment and the maturity are the same. A 10-year, zero-coupon bond is more sensitive to interest rate fluctuations than is a 10-year bond that generates coupon payments. Thus the market value of assets in a bank that has invested heavily in zero-coupon bonds will be susceptible to interest rate movements. The duration measurement can capture these different degrees of sensitivity. In recent years, banks and

Exhibit 19.4 Interest-Sensitive Assets and Liabilities: Illustration of the Gap Measured for Various Maturity Ranges for Deacon Bank

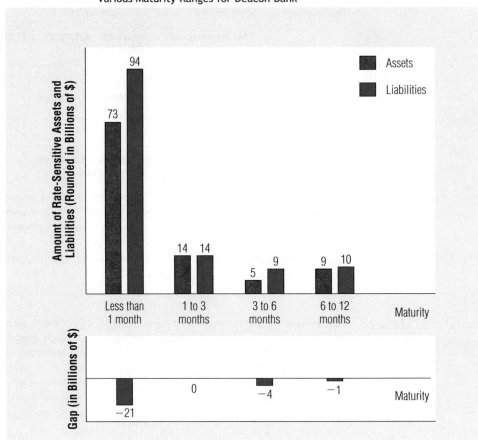

other financial institutions have used the concept of duration to measure the sensitivity of their assets to interest rate movements. There are various measurements for an asset's duration; one of the more common is

$$DUR = \frac{\sum\limits_{t=1}^{n} \frac{C_t(t)}{(1+k)^t}}{\sum\limits_{t=1}^{n} \frac{C_t}{(1+k)^t}}$$

Here C_t represents the interest or principal payments of the asset; t is the time at which the payments are provided; and k is the required rate of return on the asset, which reflects the asset's yield to maturity. The duration of each type of bank asset can be determined, and the duration of the asset portfolio is the weighted average (based on the relative proportion invested in each asset) of the durations of the individual assets.

The duration of each type of bank liability can also be estimated, and the duration of the liability portfolio is likewise estimated as the weighted average of the durations of the liabilities. The bank can then estimate its **duration gap**, which is commonly measured as the difference between the weighted duration of the bank's assets and the weighted duration of its liabilities, adjusted for the firm's asset size:

$$\textbf{DURGAP} = \frac{\textbf{(DURAS} \times \textbf{AS)}}{\textbf{AS}} - \frac{\textbf{(DURLIAB} \times \textbf{LIAB)}}{\textbf{AS}}$$

$$= \textbf{DURAS} - \left[\textbf{DURLIAB} \left(\frac{\textbf{LIAB}}{\textbf{AS}} \right) \right]$$

Here DURAS is the weighted average duration of the bank's assets, DURLIAB is the weighted average duration of the bank's liabilities, and AS and LIAB represent the market value of the bank's assets and liabilities, respectively. A duration gap of zero suggests that the bank's value should be insensitive to interest rate movements, meaning that the bank is not exposed to interest rate risk. For most banks, the average duration of assets exceeds the average duration of liabilities, so the duration gap is positive. This implies that the market value of the bank's assets is more sensitive to interest rate movements than the value of its liabilities. So if interest rates rise, banks with positive duration gaps will be adversely affected. Conversely, if interest rates decline, then banks with positive duration gaps will benefit. The larger the duration gap, the more sensitive the bank should be to interest rate movements.

Other things being equal, assets with shorter maturities have shorter durations; also, assets that generate more frequent coupon payments have shorter durations than those that generate less frequent payments. Banks and other financial institutions concerned with interest rate risk use duration to compare the rate sensitivity of their entire asset and liability portfolios. Because duration is especially critical for a savings institution's operations, Chapter 21 gives a numerical example showing the measurement of the duration of a savings institution's entire asset and liability portfolio.

Although duration is a valuable technique for comparing the rate sensitivity of various securities, its capabilities are limited when applied to assets that can be terminated on a moment's notice. For example, consider a bank that offers a fixed-rate, five-year loan that can be paid off early without penalty. If the loan is not paid off early, it is perceived as rate insensitive. Yet the loan could be terminated at any time over the five-year period. If it is paid off, the bank would reinvest the funds at the prevailing market rate. Thus the funds used to provide the loan *can* be sensitive to interest rate movements, but the degree of sensitivity depends on when the loan is paid off. In general, loan prepayments are more common when market rates decline because borrowers refinance by obtaining lower-rate loans to pay off existing loans. The point here is that the possibility of prepayment makes it impossible to perfectly match the rate sensitivity of assets and liabilities.

Regression Analysis Gap analysis and duration analysis are based on the bank's balance sheet composition. Alternatively, a bank can assess interest rate risk simply by determining how performance has historically been influenced by interest rate movements. This approach requires that proxies be identified for bank performance and for prevailing interest rates and that a model be chosen that can estimate the relationship between the proxies. Common proxies for performance include return on assets, return on equity, and the percentage change in stock price. To determine how performance is affected by interest rates, regression analysis can be applied to historical data. For example, using an interest rate proxy called i, the S&P 500 stock index as the market, and the bank's stock return (R) as the performance proxy, the following regression model could be used:

$$R = B_0 + B_1 R_m + B_2 i + \mu$$

where R_m is the return on the market; B_0, B_1, and B_2 are regression coefficients; and μ is an error term. The regression coefficient B_2 in this model can also be called the interest rate coefficient because it measures the sensitivity of the bank's performance to interest rate movements. A positive (negative) coefficient suggests that performance is favorably (adversely) affected by rising interest rates. If the interest rate coefficient is not significantly different from zero, this suggests that the bank's stock returns are insulated from interest rate movements.

Models similar to the one just described have been tested on the portfolio of all publicly traded banks to determine whether bank stock levels are affected by interest rate movements. The vast majority of this research has found that bank stock levels are inversely related to interest rate movements (i.e., the B_2 coefficient is negative and significant). These results can be attributed to the common imbalance between a bank's rate-sensitive liabilities and its assets. Because banks tend to have a negative gap (their liabilities are more rate sensitive than their assets), rising interest rates reduce bank performance. These results are generalized for the banking industry and do not apply to every bank.

Because a bank's assets and liabilities are replaced over time, exposure to interest rate risk must be continually reassessed. As exposure changes, the reaction of bank performance to a particular interest rate pattern will change.

When a bank uses regression analysis to determine its sensitivity to interest rate movements, it may combine this analysis with the value-at-risk (VaR) method to determine how its market value would change in response to specific interest rate movements. The VaR method can be applied by combining a probability distribution of interest rate movements with the interest rate coefficient (measured from the regression analysis) to determine a maximum expected loss due to adverse interest rate movements.

EXAMPLE

After applying the regression model to monthly data, Dixon Bank determines that its interest rate regression coefficient is −2.4. This implies that, for a 1 percentage point increase in interest rates, the value of the bank would decline by 2.4 percent. The model also indicates (at the 99 percent confidence level) that the change in the interest rate should not exceed +2.0 percent. For a 2 percentage point increase, the value of Dixon Bank is expected to decline by 4.8 percent (computed as 2.0 percent multiplied by the regression coefficient of −2.4). Thus the maximum expected loss due to interest rate movements (based on a 99 percent confidence level) is a 4.8 percent loss in market value. ●

19-3b Whether to Hedge Interest Rate Risk

A bank can consider the measurement of its interest rate risk along with its forecast of interest rate movements to determine whether it should consider hedging that risk. The general conclusions resulting from a bank's analysis of its interest rate risk are presented in Exhibit 19.5. This exhibit shows the three methods commonly used by banks to measure their interest rate risk. Since none of these measures is perfect for all situations, some banks measure interest rate risk using all three methods. Other banks prefer just one of the methods. Using any method along with an interest rate forecast can help a bank determine whether it should consider hedging its interest rate risk. However, since interest rate movements cannot always be accurately forecasted, banks should not be overly aggressive in attempting to capitalize on interest rate forecasts. They should assess the sensitivity of their future performance to each possible interest rate scenario that could occur to ensure that they can survive any possible scenario.

In general, the three methods of measuring interest rate risk should lead to a similar conclusion. If a bank has a negative gap, its average asset duration is probably larger than its liability duration (positive duration gap) and its past performance level is probably inversely related to interest rate movements. If a bank recently revised the composition of

Exhibit 19.5 Framework for Managing Interest Rate Risk

its assets or liabilities, it may wish to focus on the gap or the duration gap because regression analysis is based on a historical relationship that may no longer exist. Banks can use their analysis of gap along with their forecast of interest rates to make their hedging decision. If a bank decides to reduce its interest rate risk then it must consider the methods of hedging, which are described next.

19-3c Methods Used to Reduce Interest Rate Risk

Interest rate risk can be reduced by

- Maturity matching
- Using floating-rate loans
- Using interest rate futures contracts
- Using interest rate swaps
- Using interest rate caps

Maturity Matching   One obvious method of reducing interest rate risk is to match each deposit's maturity with an asset of the same maturity. For example, if the bank receives funds for a one-year CD, it could provide a one-year loan or invest in a security with a one-year maturity. Although this strategy would avoid interest rate risk, it cannot be implemented effectively. Banks receive a large volume of short-term deposits and would not be able to match up maturities on deposits with the longer loan maturities. Borrowers rarely request funds for a period as short as one month or even six months. In addition, the deposit amounts are typically small relative to the loan amounts. A bank would have difficulty combining deposits with a particular maturity to accommodate a loan request with the same maturity.

Using Floating-Rate Loans   An alternative solution is to use floating-rate loans, which allow banks to support long-term assets with short term deposits without overly exposing themselves to interest rate risk. However, floating-rate loans cannot completely eliminate the risk. If the cost of funds is changing more frequently than the rate on assets, the bank's net interest margin is still affected by interest rate fluctuations.

When banks reduce their exposure to interest rate risk by replacing long-term securities with more floating-rate commercial loans, they increase their exposure to credit risk because the commercial loans provided by banks typically have a higher frequency of default than the securities they hold. In addition, bank liquidity risk would increase because loans are less marketable than securities.

Using Interest Rate Futures Contracts   Large banks frequently use interest rate futures and other types of derivative instruments to hedge interest rate risk. A common method of reducing interest rate risk is to use interest rate futures contracts, which lock in the price at which specified financial instruments can be purchased or sold on a specified future settlement date. Recall that the sale of a futures contract on Treasury bonds prior to an increase in interest rates will result in a gain, because an identical futures contract can be purchased later at a lower price once interest rates rise. Thus a gain on the Treasury bond futures contracts can offset the adverse effects of higher interest rates on a bank's performance. The size of the bank's position in Treasury bond futures should depend on the size of its asset portfolio, the degree of its exposure to interest rate movements, and its forecasts of future interest rate movements.

Exhibit 19.6 illustrates how the use of financial futures contracts can reduce the uncertainty about a bank's net interest margin. The sale of interest rate futures, for example, reduces the potential adverse effect of rising interest rates on the bank's interest expenses, yet it also reduces the potential favorable effect of declining interest rates on the bank's interest expenses. Assuming that the bank initially had more rate-sensitive liabilities, its use of futures would reduce the impact of interest rates on its net interest margin.

Using Interest Rate Swaps   Commercial banks can hedge interest rate risk by engaging in an interest rate swap, which is an arrangement to exchange periodic cash flows based on specified interest rates. A fixed-for-floating swap allows one party to periodically exchange fixed cash flows for cash flows that are based on prevailing market interest rates.

Exhibit 19.6   Effect of Financial Futures on the Net Interest Margin of Banks That Have More Rate-Sensitive Liabilities Than Assets

A bank whose liabilities are more rate sensitive than its assets can swap payments with a fixed interest rate in exchange for payments with a variable interest rate over a specified period of time. If interest rates rise, the bank benefits because the payments to be received from the swap will increase while its outflow payments are fixed. This can offset the adverse impact of rising interest rates on the bank's net interest margin. An interest rate swap requires another party that is willing to provide variable-rate payments in exchange for fixed-rate payments. Financial institutions that have more rate-sensitive assets than liabilities may be willing to assume such a position because they could reduce their exposure to interest rate movements in this manner. A financial intermediary is typically needed to match up the two parties that desire an interest rate swap. Some securities firms and large commercial banks serve in this role.

EXAMPLE   Assume that Denver Bank (DB) has large holdings of 11 percent, fixed-rate loans. Because most of its sources of funds are sensitive to interest rates, DB desires to swap fixed-rate payments in exchange for variable-rate payments. It informs Colorado Bank of its situation because it knows that this bank commonly engages in swap transactions. Colorado Bank searches for a client and finds that Brit Eurobank desires to swap variable-rate dollar payments in exchange for fixed dollar payments. Colorado Bank then develops the swap arrangement illustrated in Exhibit 19.7. Denver Bank will swap fixed-rate payments in exchange for variable-rate payments *based on* LIBOR (the rate charged on loans between Eurobanks). Because the variable-rate payments will fluctuate with market conditions, DB's payments received will vary over time. The length of the swap period and the notional amount (the amount to which the interest rates are applied in order to determine the payments) can be structured to meet the participants' needs. Colorado Bank, the financial intermediary conducting the swap, charges a fee amounting to 0.1 percent of the notional amount per year. Some financial intermediaries for swaps may serve as the counterparty and exchange the payments desired rather than matching up two parties.

Now assume that the fixed payments are based on a fixed rate of 9 percent. Also assume that LIBOR is initially 7 percent and that DB's cost of funds is 6 percent. Exhibit 19.8 shows how DB's spread is affected by various possible interest rates when unhedged versus when hedged with an

Exhibit 19.7 Illustration of an Interest Rate Swap

interest rate swap. If LIBOR remains at 7 percent, DB's spread would be 5 percent if unhedged and only 3 percent when using a swap. However, if LIBOR increases beyond 9 percent, the spread when using the swap exceeds the unhedged spread because the higher cost of funds causes a lower unhedged spread. The swap arrangement would provide DB with increased payments that offset the higher cost of funds. The advantage of a swap is that it can lock in the spread to be earned on existing assets or at least reduce the possible variability of the spread. ●

When interest rates decrease, a bank's outflow payments would exceed inflow payments on a swap. However, the spread between the interest rates received on existing fixed-rate loans and those paid on deposits should increase, offsetting the net outflow from the swap. During periods of declining interest rates, fixed-rate loans are often prepaid, which could result in a net outflow from the swap without any offsetting effect.

Using Interest Rate Caps   An alternative method of hedging interest rate risk is an interest rate cap, an agreement (for a fee) to receive payments when the interest rate

Exhibit 19.8 Comparison of Denver Bank's Spread: Unhedged versus Hedged

	POSSIBLE FUTURE LIBOR RATES					
UNHEDGED STRATEGY	7%	8%	9%	10%	11%	12%
Average rate on existing mortgages	11%	11%	11%	11%	11%	11%
Average cost of deposits	6	7	8	9	10	11
Spread	5	4	3	2	1	0
HEDGING WITH AN INTEREST RATE SWAP						
Fixed interest rate earned on fixed-rate mortgages	11	11	11	11	11	11
Fixed interest rate owed on swap arrangement	9	9	9	9	9	9
Spread on fixed-rate payments	2	2	2	2	2	2
Variable interest rate earned on swap arrangement	7	8	9	10	11	12
Variable interest rate owed on deposits	6	7	8	9	10	11
Spread on variable-rate payments	1	1	1	1	1	1
Combined total spread when using the swap	3	3	3	3	3	3

of a particular security or index rises above a specified level during a specified time period. Various financial intermediaries (such as commercial banks and brokerage firms) offer interest rate caps. During periods of rising interest rates, the cap provides compensation that can offset the reduction in spread during such periods.

19-3d International Interest Rate Risk

When a bank has foreign currency balances, the strategy of matching the overall interest rate sensitivity of assets to that of liabilities will not automatically achieve a low degree of interest rate risk.

EXAMPLE   California Bank has deposits denominated mostly in euros, whereas its floating-rate loans are denominated mostly in dollars. It matches its average deposit maturity with its average loan maturity. However, the difference in currency denominations creates interest rate risk. The deposit and loan rates depend on the interest rate movements of the respective currencies. The performance of California Bank will be adversely affected if the interest rate on the euro increases and the U.S. interest rate decreases. ●

Even though a bank matches the mix of currencies in its assets and its liabilities, it can still be exposed to interest rate risk if the rate sensitivities differ between assets and liabilities for each currency.

EXAMPLE   Oklahoma Bank uses its dollar deposits to make dollar loans and its euro deposits to make euro loans. It has short-term dollar deposits and uses the funds to make long-term dollar loans. It also has medium-and long-term fixed-rate deposits in euros and uses those funds to make euro loans with adjustable rates. An increase in U.S. rates will reduce the spread on Oklahoma Bank's dollar loans versus deposits, because the dollar liabilities are more rate sensitive than the dollar assets. In addition, a decline in interest rates on the euro will decrease the spread on the euro loans versus deposits, because the euro assets are more rate sensitive than the euro liabilities. Thus exposure to interest rate risk can be minimized only if the rate sensitivities of assets and liabilities are matched for each currency. ●

WEB

www.fdic.gov
Information about bank loan and deposit volume.

19-4 Managing Credit Risk

Most of a bank's funds are used either to make loans or to purchase debt securities. For either use of funds, the bank is acting as a creditor and is subject to credit (default) risk, or the possibility that credit provided by the bank will not be repaid. The types of loans provided and the securities purchased will determine the overall credit risk of the asset portfolio. A bank also can be exposed to credit risk if it serves as a guarantor on interest rate swaps and other derivative contracts in which it is the intermediary.

19-4a Measuring Credit Risk

An important part of managing credit risk is to assess the creditworthiness of prospective borrowers before extending credit. Banks employ credit analysts who review the financial information of corporations applying for loans and evaluate their creditworthiness. The evaluation should indicate the probability of the firm meeting its loan payments so that the bank can decide whether to grant the loan.

Determining the Collateral   When a bank assesses a request for credit, it must decide whether to require collateral that can back the loan in case the borrower is unable to make the payments. For example, if a firm applies for a loan to purchase machinery, the loan agreement may specify that the machinery will serve as collateral. When a bank serves as an intermediary and a guarantor on derivative contracts, it commonly attempts to require collateral such as securities owned by the client.

Determining the Loan Rate   If the bank decides to grant the loan, it can use its evaluation of the firm to determine the appropriate interest rate. Loan applicants deserving of a loan may be rated on a scale of 1 to 5 (with 1 as the highest quality) in terms of their degree of credit risk. The rating dictates the premium to be added to the base rate. For example, a rating of 5 may dictate a 2 percentage point premium above the prime rate (the rate a bank offers to its most creditworthy customers), while a rating of 3 may dictate a 1 percentage point premium. Given the current prime rate along with the rating of the potential borrower, the loan rate can be determined.

Some loans to high-quality (low-risk) customers are commonly offered at rates below the prime rate. This does not necessarily mean that the bank has reduced its spread. It may instead imply that the bank has redefined the prime rate to represent the appropriate loan rate for borrowers with a moderate risk rating. Thus a discount would be attached to the prime rate when determining the loan rate for borrowers with a superior rating.

Measuring Credit Risk of a Bank Portfolio   The exposure of a bank's loan portfolio to credit risk is dependent on the types of loans that it provides. When it uses a larger proportion of loans for financing credit cards, it increases its exposure to credit risk. A bank's exposure also changes over time in response to economic conditions. As economic conditions weaken, the expected cash flows to be earned by businesses are reduced because their sales will likely decline. Consequently, they are more likely to default on loans. In addition, individuals are more likely to lose their jobs when the economy weakens, which could increase their likelihood of defaulting on loans.

19-4b Trade-off between Credit Risk and Return

If a bank wants to minimize credit risk, it can use most of its funds to purchase Treasury securities, which are virtually free of credit risk. However, these securities may not generate a much higher yield than the average overall cost of obtaining funds. In fact, some bank sources of funds can be more costly to banks than the yield earned on Treasury securities.

At the other extreme, a bank concerned with maximizing its return could use most of its funds to provide credit card and consumer loans. While this strategy may allow a bank to achieve a high return, these types of loans experience more defaults than other types of loans. Thus the bank may experience high loan losses, which could offset the high interest payments it received from those loans that were repaid. A bank that pursues the high potential returns associated with credit card loans or other loans that generate relatively high interest payments must accept a high degree of credit risk. Because riskier assets offer higher potential returns, a bank's strategy to increase its return on assets will typically entail an increase in the overall credit risk of its asset portfolio. Thus a bank's decision to create a very safe versus a moderate or high-risk asset portfolio is a function of its risk–return preferences.

Expected Return and Risk of Subprime Mortgage Loans   Many commercial banks aggressively funded subprime mortgage loans in the 2004–2006 period by originating the mortgages or purchasing mortgage-backed securities that represented subprime mortgages. The banks pursuing this strategy expected that they would earn a relatively high interest rate compared to prime mortgages and that the subprime mortgages would have low default risk because the home serves as collateral. They provided many mortgages without requiring much collateral, as they presumed that market values of homes would continue to increase over time. Even after home prices increased substantially, many banks continued to aggressively offer subprime mortgages, as they were blinded by the expected return to be earned on this strategy without concern about risk. Perhaps many banks justified their strategy by trying to keep up with all other banks that were using an aggressive strategy for achieving high returns. Furthermore, since bank managerial compensation is commonly tied to the bank's earnings, they could benefit directly from pursuing aggressive strategies.

Bank managers did not anticipate the credit crisis in the 2008–2009 period, in which the value of many homes declined far below the amount owed on the mortgages. As the economy weakened, many homeowners were not able to continue their payments. The banks were forced to initiate mortgage foreclosures and sell some homes at a large discount in the weak housing market. Alternatively, some banks worked out arrangements with homeowners who were behind in their mortgage payments, but the banks had to provide more favorable terms so that the homeowners could afford the mortgage. Banks incurred major expenses from these arrangements.

19-4c Reducing Credit Risk

Although all consumer and commercial loans exhibit some credit risk, banks can use several methods to reduce this risk.

Industry Diversification of Loans Banks should diversify their loans to ensure that their customers are not dependent on a common source of income. For example, a bank in a small farming town that provides consumer loans to farmers and commercial loans to farm equipment manufacturers is highly susceptible to credit risk. If the farmers experience a bad growing season because of poor weather conditions, they may be unable to repay their consumer loans. Furthermore, the farm equipment manufacturers would simultaneously experience a drop in sales and may be unable to repay their commercial loans.

When a bank's loans are too heavily concentrated in a specific industry, it should attempt to expand its loans into other industries. In this way, if one particular industry experiences weakness (which will lead to loan defaults by firms in that industry), loans provided to other industries will be insulated from that industry's conditions. However, a bank's loan portfolio may still be subject to high credit risk even though its loans are diversified across industries.

International Diversification of Loans Many banks reduce their exposure to U.S. economic conditions by diversifying their loan portfolio internationally. They use a country risk assessment system to assess country characteristics that may influence the ability of a government or corporation to repay its debt. In particular, the country risk assessment focuses on a country's financial and political conditions. Banks are more likely to invest in countries to which they have assigned a high rating.

Diversifying loans across countries can often reduce the loan portfolio's exposure to any single economy or event. But if diversification across geographic regions means that the bank must accept loan applicants with very high risk, the bank is defeating its purpose. Furthermore, international diversification does not necessarily avoid adverse economic conditions. The credit crisis adversely affected most countries and therefore affected the ability of borrowers around the world to repay their loans.

Selling Loans Banks can eliminate loans that are causing excessive risk to their loan portfolios by selling them in the secondary market. Most loan sales enable the bank originating the loan to continue servicing it by collecting payments and monitoring the borrower's collateral. However, the bank that originated the loan is no longer funding it, so the loan is removed from the bank's assets. Bank loans are commonly purchased by other banks and financial institutions, such as pension funds, insurance companies, and mutual funds.

Revising the Loan Portfolio in Response to Economic Conditions   Banks continuously assess both the overall composition of their loan portfolios and the economic environment. As economic conditions change, so does the risk of a bank's loan portfolio. A bank is typically more willing to extend loans during strong economic conditions because businesses are more likely to meet their loan payments under those conditions. During weak economic conditions, the bank is more cautious and increases its standards, which results in a smaller amount of new loans extended to businesses. Under these conditions, the bank typically increases the credit it extends to the Treasury by purchasing more Treasury securities. Nevertheless, its loan portfolio may still be heavily exposed to economic conditions because some of the businesses that have already borrowed may be unable to repay their loans.

WEB

www.fdic.gov
Analytical assessment of the banking industry, including the recent performance of banks.

19-5 MANAGING MARKET RISK

From a bank management perspective, market risk results from changes in the value of securities due to changes in financial market conditions such as interest rate movements, exchange rate movements, and equity prices. As banks pursue new services related to the trading of securities, they have become much more susceptible to market risk. For example, some banks now provide loans to various types of investment funds, which use the borrowed funds to invest in stocks or derivative securities. Thus these loans may not be repaid if the prices of the stocks or derivative securities held by the investment funds decline substantially.

The increase in banks' exposure to market risk is also attributed to their increased participation in the trading of derivative contracts. Many banks now serve as intermediaries between firms that take positions in derivative securities and will be exchanging payments in the future. For some of these transactions, a bank serves as a guarantor to one of the parties if the counterparty in the transaction does not fulfill its payment obligation. If derivative security prices change abruptly and cause several parties involved in these transactions to default, a bank that served as a guarantor could suffer major losses. Furthermore, banks that purchase debt securities issued in developing countries are subject to abrupt losses resulting from sudden swings in the economic or currency conditions in those countries.

19-5a Measuring Market Risk

Banks commonly measure their exposure to market risk by applying the value-at-risk (VaR) method, which involves determining the largest possible loss that would occur as a result of changes in market prices based on a specified percent confidence level. To estimate this loss, the bank first determines an adverse scenario (e.g., a 20 percent decline in derivative security prices) that has a 1 percent chance of occurring. Then it estimates the impact of that scenario on its investment or loan positions given the sensitivity of investments' values to the scenario. All of the losses that would occur from the bank's existing positions are summed to determine the estimated total loss to the bank under this scenario. This estimate reflects the largest possible loss at the 99 percent confidence level, since there is only a 1-in-100 chance that such an unfavorable scenario would occur. By determining its exposure to market risk, the bank can ensure that it has sufficient capital to cushion against the adverse effects of such an event.

Bank Revisions of Market Risk Measurements Banks continually revise their estimate of market risk in response to changes in their investment and credit positions and to changes in market conditions. When market prices become more volatile, banks recognize that market prices could change to a greater degree and typically increase their estimate of their potential losses due to market conditions.

Relationship between a Bank's Market Risk and Interest Rate Risk A bank's market risk is partially dependent on its exposure to interest rate risk. Banks give special attention to interest rate risk, because it is commonly the most important component of market risk. Moreover, many banks assess interest rate risk by itself when evaluating their positions over a longer time horizon. For example, a bank might assess interest rate risk over the next year using the methods described earlier in the chapter. In this case, the bank might use the assessment to alter the maturities on the deposits it attempts to obtain or on its uses of funds. In contrast, banks' assessment of *market* risk tends to be focused on a shorter-term horizon, such as the next month. Nevertheless, banks may still use their assessment of market risk to alter their operations, as explained next.

19-5b Methods Used to Reduce Market Risk

If a bank determines that its exposure to market risk is excessive, it can reduce its involvement in the activities that cause the high exposure. For example, the bank could reduce the amount of transactions in which it serves as guarantor for its clients or reduce its investment in foreign debt securities that are subject to adverse events in a specific region. Alternatively, it could attempt to take some trading positions to offset some of its exposure to market risk. It could also sell some of its securities that are heavily exposed to market risk.

19-6 INTEGRATED BANK MANAGEMENT

Bank management of assets, liabilities, and capital is integrated. A bank's asset growth can be achieved only if it obtains the necessary funds. Furthermore, growth may require an investment in fixed assets (such as additional offices) that will require an accumulation of bank capital. Integration of asset, liability, and capital management ensures that all policies will be consistent with a cohesive set of economic forecasts. An integrated management approach is necessary to manage liquidity risk, interest rate risk, and credit risk.

19-6a Application

Assume that you are hired as a consultant by Atlanta Bank to evaluate its favorable and unfavorable aspects. Atlanta Bank's balance sheet is shown in Exhibit 19.9. A bank's balance sheet can best be evaluated by converting the actual dollar amounts of balance sheet components to a percentage of assets. This conversion enables the bank to be compared with its competitors. Exhibit 19.10 shows each balance sheet component as a percentage of total assets for Atlanta Bank (derived from Exhibit 19.9). To the right of each bank percentage is the assumed industry average percentage for a sample of banks with a similar amount of assets. For example, the bank's required reserves are 4 percent of assets (the same as the industry average), its floating-rate commercial loans are 30 percent of assets (versus an industry average of 20 percent), and so on. The same type of comparison is

Exhibit 19.9   Balance Sheet of Atlanta Bank (in Millions of Dollars)

ASSETS			LIABILITIES AND CAPITAL		
Required reserves		$400	Demand deposits		$500
Commercial loans			NOW accounts		1,200
Floating-rate	3,000		MMDAs		2,000
Fixed-rate	1,100		CDs		
Total		4,100	Short-term	1,500	
Consumer loans		2,500	From 1 to 5 years.	3,800	
Mortgages			Total		5,300
Floating-rate	500		Long-term bonds		200
Fixed-rate	None		CAPITAL		800
Total		500			
Treasury securities					
Short-term	1,000				
Long-term	None				
Total		1,000			
Corporate securities					
High-rated	None				
Medium-rated	1,000				
Total		1,000			
Municipal securities					
High-rated	None				
Medium-rated	None				
Total		None			
Fixed assets		500			
TOTAL ASSETS		$10,000	TOTAL LIABILITIES AND CAPITAL		$10,000

provided for liabilities and capital on the right side of the exhibit. A comparative analysis relative to the industry can indicate the management style of Atlanta Bank.

It is possible to evaluate the potential level of interest revenues, interest expenses, noninterest revenues, and noninterest expenses for Atlanta Bank relative to the industry. Furthermore, it is possible to assess the bank's exposure to credit risk and interest rate risk as compared to the industry.

A summary of Atlanta Bank based on the information in Exhibit 19.10 is provided in Exhibit 19.11. Although its interest expenses are expected to be above the industry average, so are its interest revenues. Thus it is difficult to determine whether Atlanta Bank's

Exhibit 19.10 Comparative Balance Sheet of Atlanta Bank

ASSETS	PERCENTAGE OF ASSETS FOR ATLANTA BANK	AVERAGE PERCENTAGE FOR INDUSTRY	LIABILITIES AND CAPITAL	PERCENTAGE OF TOTAL FOR ATLANTA BANK	AVERAGE PERCENTAGE FOR INDUSTRY
Required reserves	4%	4%	Demand deposits	5%	17%
Commercial loans			NOW accounts	12	8
Floating-rate	30	20	MMDAs	20	20
Fixed-rate	11	11	CDs		
Total	41	31	Short-term	15	35
Consumer loans	25	20	From 1 to 5 years	38	10
Mortgages			Long-term bonds	2	2
Floating-rate	5	7	CAPITAL	8	8
Fixed-rate	0	3			
Total	5	10			
Treasury securities					
Short-term	10	7			
Long-term	0	8			
Total	10	15			
Corporate securities					
High-rated	0	5			
Medium-rated	10	5			
Total	10	10			
Municipal securities					
High-rated	0	3			
Medium-rated	0	2			
Total	0	5			
Fixed assets	5	5			
TOTAL ASSETS	100%	100%	TOTAL LIABILITIES AND CAPITAL	100%	100%

net interest margin will be above or below the industry average. Because it is more heavily concentrated in risky loans and securities, its credit risk is higher than that of the average bank; however, its interest rate risk is less because of its relatively high concentration of medium-term CDs and floating-rate loans. A gap measurement of Atlanta

Exhibit 19.11 Evaluation of Atlanta Bank Based on Its Balance Sheet

	MAIN INFLUENTIAL COMPONENTS	EVALUATION OF ATLANTA BANK RELATIVE TO INDUSTRY
Interest expenses	All liabilities except demand deposits	Higher than industry average because it concentrates more on high-rate deposits than the norm
Noninterest expenses	Loan volume and checkable deposit volume	Possibly higher than the norm; its checkable deposit volume is less than the norm, but its loan volume is greater than the norm
Interest revenues	Volume and composition of loans and securities	Potentially higher than industry average because its assets are generally riskier than the norm
Exposure to credit risk	Volume and composition of loans and securities	Higher concentration of loans than industry average; it has a greater percentage of risky assets than the norm
Exposure to interest rate risk	Maturities on liabilities and assets; use of floating-rate loans	Lower than the industry average; it has more medium-term liabilities, fewer assets with very long maturities, and more floating-rate loans

Bank can be conducted by first identifying the rate-sensitive liabilities and assets, as follows:

RATE-SENSITIVE ASSETS	AMOUNT (IN MILLIONS)	RATE-SENSITIVE LIABILITIES	AMOUNT (IN MILLIONS)
Floating-rate loans	$3,000	NOW accounts	$1,200
Floating-rate mortgages	500	MMDAs	2,000
Short-term Treasury securities	1,000	Short-term CDs	1,500
Total	$4,500	Total	$4,700

$$\text{Gap} = \$4{,}500 \text{ million} - \$4{,}700 \text{ million}$$
$$= -\$200 \text{ million}$$
$$\text{Gap ratio} = \frac{\$4{,}500 \text{ million}}{\$4{,}700 \text{ million}}$$
$$= 0.957$$

The gap measurements suggest a similar rate sensitivity on both sides of the balance sheet.

The future performance of Atlanta Bank relative to the industry depends on future economic conditions. If interest rates rise then it will be more insulated than other banks; if interest rates fall, other banks will likely benefit to a greater degree. Under conditions of a strong economy, Atlanta Bank would likely benefit more than other banks because of its aggressive lending approach. Conversely, an economic slowdown could cause more loan defaults, and Atlanta Bank would be more susceptible to possible defaults than other banks. This could be confirmed only if more details were provided (such as a more comprehensive breakdown of the balance sheet).

Management of Bank Capital An evaluation of Atlanta Bank should also include an assessment of its capital. As with all banks, the future performance of Atlanta

Bank is influenced by the amount of capital that it holds. It needs to maintain at least the minimum capital ratio required by regulators. However, if Atlanta Bank maintains too much capital, each shareholder will receive a smaller proportion of any distributed earnings. A common measure of the return to the shareholders is the return on equity (ROE), measured as

$$\text{ROE} = \frac{\text{Net profit after taxes}}{\text{Equity}}$$

The term *equity* represents the bank's capital. The return on equity can be broken down as follows:

$$\text{ROE} = \text{Return on assets (ROA)} \times \text{Leverage measure}$$

$$\frac{\text{Net profit after taxes}}{\text{Equity}} = \frac{\text{Net profit after taxes}}{\text{Assets}} \times \frac{\text{Assets}}{\text{Equity}}$$

The ratio (assets/equity) is sometimes called the leverage measure because leverage reflects the volume of assets a firm supports with equity. The greater the leverage measure, the greater the amount of assets per dollar's worth of equity. The preceding breakdown of ROE is useful because it demonstrates how Atlanta Bank's capital can affect its ROE. For a given level of return on assets (ROA), a higher capital level reduces the bank's leverage measure and therefore reduces its ROE.

If Atlanta Bank is holding an excessive amount of capital, it may not need to rely on retained earnings to build its capital and so can distribute a high percentage of its earnings to shareholders (as dividends). Thus its capital management is related to its dividend policy. If Atlanta Bank is expanding, it may need more capital to support construction of new buildings, office equipment, and other expenses. In this case, it would need to retain a larger proportion of its earnings to support its expansion plans.

WEB

www.risknews.net

Links to risk-related information in international banking.

19-7 Managing Risk of International Operations

Banks that are engaged in international banking face additional types of risk, including exchange rate risk and settlement risk.

19-7a Exchange Rate Risk

When a bank providing a loan requires that the borrower repay in the currency denominating the loan, it may be able to avoid exchange rate risk. However, some international loans contain a clause that allows repayment in a foreign currency, thus allowing the borrower to avoid exchange rate risk.

In many cases, banks convert available funds (from recent deposits) to whatever currency corporations want to borrow. Thus, they create an asset denominated in that currency while the liability (deposits) is denominated in a different currency. If the liability currency appreciates against the asset currency, the bank's profit margin is reduced.

All large banks are exposed to exchange rate risk to some degree. They can attempt to hedge this risk in various ways.

EXAMPLE

Cameron Bank, a U.S. bank, converts dollar deposits into a British pound (£) loan for a British corporation, which will pay £50,000 in interest per year. Cameron Bank may attempt to engage in forward contracts to sell £50,000 forward for each date when it will receive those interest payments. That is, it will search for corporations that wish to purchase £50,000 on the dates of concern. ●

In practice, a large bank will not hedge every individual transaction and instead will net out the exposure and be concerned only with net exposure. Large banks enter into several international transactions on any given day. Some reflect future cash inflows in a particular currency while others reflect cash outflows in that currency. The bank's exposure to exchange rate risk is determined by the net cash flow in each currency.

19-7b Settlement Risk

International banks that engage in large currency transactions are exposed not only to exchange rate risk as a result of their different currency positions but also to settlement risk, or the risk of a loss due to settling their transactions. For example, a bank may send its currency to another bank as part of a transaction agreement, yet it may not receive any currency from the other bank if that bank defaults before sending its payment.

The failure of a single large bank could create more losses if other banks were relying on receivables from the failed bank to make future payables of their own. Consequently, there is concern about systemic risk, or the risk that many participants will be unable to meet their obligations because they did not receive payments on obligations due to them.

SUMMARY

- The underlying goal of bank management is to maximize the wealth of the bank's shareholders, which implies maximizing the price of the bank's stock (if the bank is publicly traded). A bank's board of directors needs to monitor bank managers to ensure that managerial decisions are intended to serve shareholders.

- Banks manage liquidity by maintaining some liquid assets such as short-term securities and ensuring easy access to funds (through the federal funds market).

- Banks measure their sensitivity to interest rate movements so that they can assess their exposure to interest rate risk. Common methods of measuring interest rate risk include gap analysis, duration analysis, and measuring the sensitivity of earnings (or stock returns) to interest rate movements.

- Banks can reduce their interest rate risk by matching the maturities of their assets and liabilities or by using floating-rate loans to create more rate sensitivity in their assets. Alternatively, they could sell financial futures contracts or engage in a swap of fixed-rate payments for floating-rate payments.

- Banks manage credit risk by carefully assessing the borrowers who apply for loans and by limiting the amount of funds they allocate toward risky loans (such as credit card loans). They also diversify their loans across borrowers of different regions and industries so that the loan portfolio is not overly susceptible to financial problems in any single region or industry.

- An evaluation of a bank includes assessment of its exposure to interest rate movements and to credit risk. This assessment can be used along with a forecast of interest rates and economic conditions to forecast the bank's future performance.

POINT COUNTER-POINT

Can Bank Failures Be Avoided?

Point   No. Banks are in the business of providing credit. When economic conditions deteriorate, there will be loan defaults and some banks will not be able to survive.

Counter-Point   Yes. If banks focus on providing loans to creditworthy borrowers, most loans will not default even during recessionary periods.

Who Is Correct?   Use the Internet to learn more about this issue and then formulate your own opinion.

QUESTIONS AND APPLICATIONS

1. Integrating Asset and Liability Management What is accomplished when a bank integrates its liability management with its asset management?

2. Liquidity Given the liquidity advantage of holding Treasury bills, why do banks hold only a relatively small portion of their assets as T-bills?

3. Illiquidity How do banks resolve illiquidity problems?

4. Managing Interest Rate Risk If a bank expects interest rates to decrease over time, how might it alter the rate sensitivity of its assets and liabilities?

5. Rate Sensitivity List some rate-sensitive assets and some rate-insensitive assets of banks.

6. Managing Interest Rate Risk If a bank is very uncertain about future interest rates, how might it insulate its future performance from future interest rate movements?

7. Net Interest Margin What is the formula for the net interest margin? Explain why it is closely monitored by banks.

8. Managing Interest Rate Risk Assume that a bank expects to attract most of its funds through short-term CDs and would prefer to use most of its funds to provide long-term loans. How could it follow this strategy and still reduce interest rate risk?

9. Bank Exposure to Interest Rate Movements According to this chapter, have banks been able to insulate themselves against interest rate movements? Explain.

10. Gap Management What is a bank's gap, and what does it attempt to determine? Interpret a negative gap. What are some limitations of measuring a bank's gap?

11. Duration How do banks use duration analysis?

12. Measuring Interest Rate Risk Why do loans that can be prepaid on a moment's notice complicate the bank's assessment of interest rate risk?

13. Bank Management Dilemma Can a bank simultaneously maximize return and minimize default risk? If not, what can it do instead?

14. Bank Exposure to Economic Conditions As economic conditions change, how do banks adjust their asset portfolios?

15. Bank Loan Diversification In what two ways should a bank diversify its loans? Why? Is international diversification of loans a viable strategy for dealing with credit risk? Defend your answer.

16. Commercial Borrowing Do all commercial borrowers receive the same interest rate on loans?

17. Bank Dividend Policy Why might a bank retain some excess earnings rather than distribute them as dividends?

18. Managing Interest Rate Risk If a bank has more rate-sensitive liabilities than rate-sensitive assets, what will happen to its net interest margin during a period of rising interest rates? During a period of declining interest rates?

19. Floating-Rate Loans Does the use of floating-rate loans eliminate interest rate risk? Explain.

20. Managing Exchange Rate Risk Explain how banks become exposed to exchange rate risk.

Advanced Questions

21. Bank Exposure to Interest Rate Risk Oregon Bank has branches overseas that concentrate on short-term deposits in dollars and floating-rate loans in British pounds. Because it maintains rate-sensitive assets and liabilities of equal amounts, it believes it has essentially eliminated its interest rate risk. Do you agree? Explain.

22. Managing Interest Rate Risk Dakota Bank has a branch overseas with the following balance sheet characteristics: 50 percent of the liabilities are rate sensitive and denominated in Swiss francs; the remaining 50 percent of liabilities are rate insensitive and are denominated in dollars. With regard to assets, 50 percent are rate sensitive and are denominated in dollars; the remaining 50 percent of assets are rate insensitive and are denominated in Swiss francs.

a. Is the performance of this branch susceptible to interest rate movements? Explain.

b. Assume that Dakota Bank plans to replace its short-term deposits denominated in U.S. dollars with short-term deposits denominated in Swiss francs because Swiss interest rates are currently lower than U.S. interest rates. The asset composition would not change. This strategy is intended to widen the spread between the rate earned on assets and the rate paid on liabilities. Offer your insight on how this strategy could backfire.

c. One consultant has suggested to Dakota Bank that it could avoid exchange rate risk by making loans in whatever currencies it receives as deposits. In this way, it will not have to exchange one currency for another. Offer your insight on whether there are any disadvantages to this strategy.

Interpreting Financial News

Interpret the following comments made by Wall Street analysts and portfolio managers.

a. "The bank's biggest mistake was that it did not recognize that its forecasts of a strong local real estate market and declining interest rates could be wrong."

b. "Banks still need some degree of interest rate risk to be profitable."

c. "The bank used interest rate swaps so that its spread is no longer exposed to interest rate movements. However, its loan volume and therefore its profits are still exposed to interest rate movements."

Managing in Financial Markets

Hedging with Interest Rate Swaps As a manager of Stetson Bank, you are responsible for hedging Stetson's interest rate risk. Stetson has forecasted its cost of funds as follows:

YEAR	COST OF FUNDS
1	6%
2	5%
3	7%
4	9%
5	7%

It expects to earn an average rate of 11 percent on some assets that charge a fixed interest rate over the next five years. It considers engaging in an interest rate swap in which it would swap fixed payments of 10 percent in exchange for variable-rate payments of LIBOR plus 1 percent. Assume LIBOR is expected to be consistently 1 percent above Stetson's cost of funds.

a. Determine the spread that would be earned each year if Stetson uses an interest rate swap to hedge all of its interest rate risk. Would you recommend that Stetson use an interest rate swap?

b. Although Stetson has forecasted its cost of funds, it recognizes that its forecasts may be inaccurate. Offer a method that Stetson can use to assess the potential results from using an interest rate swap while accounting for the uncertainty surrounding future interest rates.

c. The reason for Stetson's interest rate risk is that it uses some of its funds to make fixed-rate loans, as some borrowers prefer fixed rates. An alternative method of hedging interest rate risk is to use adjustable-rate loans. Would you recommend that Stetson use only adjustable-rate loans to hedge its interest rate risk? Explain.

PROBLEMS

1. Net Interest Margin Suppose a bank earns $201 million in interest revenue but pays $156 million in interest expense. It also has $800 million in earning assets. What is its net interest margin?

2. Calculating Return on Assets If a bank earns $169 million net profit after tax and has $17 billion invested in assets, what is its return on assets?

3. Calculating Return on Equity If a bank earns $75 million net profits after tax and has $7.5 billion invested in assets and $600 million equity investment, what is its return on equity?

4. Managing Risk Use the balance sheet for San Diego Bank in Exhibit A and the industry norms in Exhibit B to answer the following questions.

a. Estimate the gap and the gap ratio and determine how San Diego Bank would be affected by an increase in interest rates over time.

b. Assess San Diego's credit risk. Does it appear high or low relative to the industry? Would San Diego Bank perform better or worse than other banks during a recession?

Exhibit A Balance Sheet for San Diego Bank (in Millions of Dollars)

ASSETS			LIABILITIES AND CAPITAL		
Required reserves		$800	Demand deposits		$800
Commercial loans			NOW accounts		2,500
Floating-rate	None		MMDAs		6,000
Fixed-rate	7,000		CDs		
Total		7,000	Short-term	9,000	
Consumer loans		5,000	From 1 to 5 yrs.	None	
Mortgages			Total		9,000
Floating-rate	None		Federal funds		500
Fixed-rate	2,000		Long-term bonds		400
Total		2,000	CAPITAL		800
Treasury securities					
Short-term	None				
Long-term	1,000				
Total		1,000			
Long-term corporate securities					
High-rated	None				
Moderate-rated	2,000				
Total		2,000			
Long-term municipal securities					
High-rated	None				
Moderate-rated	1,700				
Total		1,700			
Fixed assets		500			
TOTAL ASSETS		$20,000	TOTAL LIABILITIES and CAPITAL		$20,000

Exhibit B Industry Norms in Percentage Terms

ASSETS		LIABILITIES AND CAPITAL	
Required reserves	4%	Demand deposits	17%
Commercial loans		NOW accounts	10
Floating-rate	20	MMDAs	20
Fixed-rate	11	CDs	
Total	31	Short-term	35
Consumer loans	20	From 1 to 5 yrs.	10
Mortgages		Total	45
Floating-rate	7	Long-term bonds	2
Fixed-rate	3	CAPITAL	6
Total	10		
Treasury securities			
Short-term	7		
Long-term	8		
Total	15		
Long-term corporate securities			
High-rated	5		
Moderate-rated	5		
Total	10		
Long-term municipal securities			
High-rated	3		
Moderate-rated	2		
Total	5		
Fixed assets	5		
TOTAL ASSETS	100%	TOTAL LIABILITIES and CAPITAL	100%

c. For any type of bank risk that appears to be higher than the industry, explain how the balance sheet could be restructured to reduce the risk.

5. Measuring Risk Montana Bank wants to determine the sensitivity of its stock returns to interest rate movements, based on the following information:

QUARTER	RETURN ON MONTANA STOCK	RETURN ON MARKET	INTEREST RATE
1	2%	3%	6.0%
2	2	2	7.5
3	−1	−2	9.0
4	0	−1	8.2
5	2	1	7.3
6	−3	−4	8.1
7	1	5	7.4
8	0	1	9.1
9	−2	0	8.2
10	1	−1	7.1
11	3	3	6.4
12	6	4	5.5

Use a regression model in which Montana's stock return is a function of the stock market return and the interest rate. Determine the relationship between the interest rate and Montana's stock return by assessing the regression coefficient applied to the interest rate. Is the sign of the coefficient positive or negative? What does it suggest about the bank's exposure to interest rate risk? Should Montana Bank be concerned about rising or declining interest rate movements in the future?

FLOW OF FUNDS EXERCISE

Managing Credit Risk

Recall that Carson Company relies heavily on commercial banks for loans. When the company was first established with equity funding from its owners, Carson Company could easily obtain debt financing because the financing was backed by some of the firm's assets. However, as Carson expanded, it continually relied on extra debt financing, which increased its ratio of debt to equity. Some banks were unwilling to provide more debt financing because of the risk that Carson would not be able to repay additional loans. A few banks were still willing to provide funding, but they required an extra premium to compensate for the risk.

a. Explain the difference in the willingness of banks to provide loans to Carson Company. Why is there a difference between banks when they are assessing the same information about a firm that wants to borrow funds?

b. Consider the flow of funds for a publicly traded bank that is a key lender to Carson Company. This bank received equity funding from shareholders, which it used to establish its business. It channels bank deposit funds, which are insured by the Federal Deposit Insurance Corporation (FDIC), to provide loans to Carson Company and other firms. The depositors have no idea how the bank uses their funds. Yet, the FDIC does not prevent the bank from making risky loans. So who is monitoring the bank? Do you think the bank is taking more risk than its shareholders desire? How does the FDIC discourage the bank from taking too much risk? Why might the bank ignore the FDIC's efforts to discourage excessive risk taking?

INTERNET/EXCEL EXERCISES

1. Assess the services offered by an Internet bank. Describe the types of online services offered by the bank. Do you think an Internet bank such as this offers higher or lower interest rates than a "regular" commercial bank? Why or why not?

2. Go to finance.yahoo.com/, enter the symbol BK (Bank of New York Mellon Corporation), and click on "Get Quotes." Click on "5y" just below the stock price trend to review the stock price movements over the last five years. Click on "Compare" and then on "S&P 500" in order to compare the trend of Bank of New York Mellon with the movements in the S&P stock index. Has Bank of New York Mellon Corporation performed better or worse than the index? Offer an explanation for its performance.

3. Go to finance.yahoo.com/, enter the symbol WFC (Wells Fargo Bank), and click on "Get Quotes."

Retrieve stock price data at the beginning of the last 20 quarters. Then go to http://research.stlouisfed.org/fred2/ and retrieve interest rate data at the beginning of the last 20 quarters for the three-month Treasury bill. Record the data on an Excel spreadsheet. Derive the quarterly return of Wells Fargo Bank. Derive the quarterly change in the interest rate. Apply regression analysis in which the quarterly return of Wells Fargo Bank is the dependent variable and the quarterly change in the interest rate is the independent variable (see Appendix B for more information about using regression analysis). Is there a positive or negative relationship between the interest rate movement and the return of Wells Fargo Bank stock? Is the relationship significant? Offer an explanation for this relationship.

WSJ EXERCISE

Bank Management Strategies

Summarize an article in the *Wall Street Journal* that discussed a recent change in managerial strategy by a particular commercial bank. (You may wish to do an Internet search in the online version of the *Wall Street Journal* to identify an article on a commercial bank's change in strategy.) Describe the change in managerial strategy. How will the bank's balance sheet be affected by this change? How will the bank's potential return and risk be affected? What reason does the article give for the bank's decision to change its strategy?

ONLINE ARTICLES WITH REAL-WORLD EXAMPLES

Find a recent practical article available online that describes a real-world example regarding a specific financial institution or financial market that reinforces one or more concepts covered in this chapter.

If your class has an online component, your professor may ask you to post your summary of the article there and provide a link to the article so that other students can access it. If your class is live, your professor may ask you to summarize your application of the article in class. Your professor may assign specific students to complete this assignment or may allow any students to do the assignment on a volunteer basis.

For recent online articles and real-world examples related to this chapter, consider using the following search terms (be sure to include the prevailing year as a search term to ensure that the online articles are recent):

1. [name of a specific bank] AND liquidity
2. [name of a specific bank] AND management
3. [name of a specific bank] AND interest rate risk
4. [name of a specific bank] AND credit risk
5. [name of a specific bank] AND strategy
6. bank AND management
7. bank AND strategy
8. bank AND loans
9. bank AND asset management
10. bank AND operations

20

Bank Performance

CHAPTER OBJECTIVES

The specific objectives of this chapter are to:

■ identify the factors that affect the valuation of a commercial bank,

■ compare the performance of banks in different size classifications over recent years, and

■ explain how to evaluate the performance of a particular bank based on financial statement data.

A commercial bank's performance is examined for various reasons. Bank regulators identify banks that are experiencing severe problems so that they can be remedied. Shareholders need to determine whether they should buy or sell the stock of various banks. Investment analysts must be able to advise prospective investors on which banks to select for investment. Commercial banks also evaluate their own performance over time to determine the outcomes of previous management decisions so that changes can be made where appropriate. Without persistent monitoring of performance, existing problems can remain unnoticed and lead to financial failure in the future.

20-1 VALUATION OF A COMMERCIAL BANK

Commercial banks (or commercial bank units that are part of a financial conglomerate) are commonly valued by their managers as part of their efforts to monitor performance over time and to determine the proper mix of services that will maximize the bank's value. Banks may also be valued by other financial institutions that are considering an acquisition. An understanding of commercial bank valuation is useful because it identifies the factors that determine a commercial bank's value, which can be modeled as the present value of its future cash flows:

$$V = \sum_{t=1}^{n} \frac{E(CF_t)}{(1+k)^t}$$

where $E(CF_t)$ represents the expected cash flow to be generated in period t and k represents the required rate of return by investors who invest in the commercial bank. Thus, the value of a commercial bank should change in response to changes in its expected cash flows in the future and to changes in the required rate of return by investors:

$$\Delta V = f[\underbrace{\Delta E(CF)}_{+}, \underbrace{\Delta k}_{-}]$$

20-1a Factors That Affect Cash Flows

The change in a commercial bank's expected cash flows may be modeled as

$$\Delta E(CF) = f(\underbrace{\Delta ECON}_{+}, \underbrace{\Delta R_f}_{-}, \underbrace{\Delta INDUS}_{?}, \underbrace{\Delta MANAB}_{+})$$

where ECON denotes economic growth, R_f the risk-free interest rate, INDUS the prevailing bank industry conditions (including regulations and competition), and MANAB the abilities of the commercial bank's management.

Change in Economic Growth   Economic growth can enhance a commercial bank's cash flows by increasing the household or business demand for loans. During periods of strong economic growth, loan demand tends to be higher, which allows commercial banks to provide more loans. Because loans tend to generate better returns to commercial banks than investment in Treasury securities or other securities, expected cash flows should be higher. Another reason cash flows may be higher is that, normally, fewer loan defaults occur during periods of strong economic growth.

Furthermore, the demand for other financial services provided by commercial banks tends to be higher during periods of strong economic growth. For example, brokerage, insurance, and financial planning services typically receive more business when economic growth is strong because households then have relatively high levels of disposable income.

Change in the Risk-Free Interest Rate   Interest rate movements may be inversely related to a commercial bank's cash flows. If the risk-free interest rate decreases other market rates may also decline, which may result in a stronger demand for the commercial bank's loans. Second, commercial banks rely heavily on short-term deposits as a source of funds, and the rates paid on these deposits are typically revised in accordance with other interest rate movements. Banks' uses of funds (such as loans) also are normally sensitive to interest rate movements, but to a smaller degree. Therefore, when interest rates fall, the depository institution's cost of obtaining funds declines more than the decline in the interest earned on its loans and investments. Conversely, an increase in interest rates could reduce a commercial bank's expected cash flows because the interest paid on deposits may increase to a greater degree than the interest earned on loans and investments.

Change in Industry Conditions   One of the most important industry characteristics that can affect a commercial bank's cash flows is regulation. If regulators reduce the constraints imposed on commercial banks, banks' expected cash flows should increase. For example, when regulators eliminated certain geographic constraints, commercial banks were able to expand across new regions in the United States. As regulators reduced constraints on the types of businesses that commercial banks could pursue, the banks were able to expand by offering other financial services (such as brokerage and insurance services).

Another important industry characteristic that can affect a bank's cash flows is technological innovation, which can improve efficiencies and thereby enhance cash flows. The level of competition is an additional industry characteristic that can affect cash flows, because a high level of competition may reduce the bank's volume of business or reduce the prices it can charge for its services. As regulation has been reduced, competition has intensified. Some commercial banks benefit from this competition, but others may lose some of their market share.

Management Abilities   Of the four characteristics that commonly affect cash flows, the only one over which the bank has control is management abilities. It cannot dictate economic growth, interest rate movements, or regulations, but it can determine its organizational structure, and its sources and uses of funds. The managers can attempt to make internal decisions that will capitalize on the external forces (economic growth, interest rates, regulatory constraints) that the bank cannot control.

As the management skills of a commercial bank improve, so should its expected cash flows. For example, skillful managers will recognize how to revise the composition of the bank's assets and liabilities to capitalize on existing economic or regulatory conditions.

They can capitalize on economies of scale by expanding specific types of businesses and by offering a diversified set of services that accommodate specific customers. They may restructure operations and use technology in a manner that reduces expenses.

20-1b Factors That Affect the Required Rate of Return by Investors

The required rate of return by investors who invest in a commercial bank can be modeled as

$$\Delta k = f(\underset{+}{\underbrace{\Delta R_f}}, \underset{+}{\underbrace{\Delta RP}})$$

where ΔR_f represents a change in the risk-free interest rate and ΔRP a change in the bank's risk premium.

Change in the Risk-Free Rate   When the risk-free rate increases, so does the return required by investors. Recall that the risk-free rate of interest is driven by inflationary expectations (INF), economic growth (ECON), the money supply (MS), and the budget deficit (DEF):

$$\Delta R_f = f(\underset{+}{\underbrace{\Delta INF}}, \underset{+}{\underbrace{\Delta ECON}}, \underset{-}{\underbrace{\Delta MS}}, \underset{+}{\underbrace{\Delta DEF}})$$

High inflation, economic growth, and a high budget deficit place upward pressure on interest rates, whereas money supply growth places downward pressure on interest rates (assuming it does not cause inflation).

Change in the Risk Premium   If the risk premium on a commercial bank rises, so will the required rate of return by investors who invest in the bank. The risk premium can change in response to changes in economic growth, industry conditions, or management abilities:

$$\Delta RP = f(\underset{-}{\underbrace{\Delta ECON}}, \underset{?}{\underbrace{\Delta INDUS}}, \underset{-}{\underbrace{\Delta MANAB}})$$

High economic growth results in less risk for a commercial bank because its loans and investments in debt securities are less likely to default.

Bank industry characteristics such as regulatory constraints, technological innovations, and the level of competition can affect the risk premium on banks. Regulatory constraints may include a minimum level of capital required of banks. Capital requirements have increased recently; this change alone reduces the risk premium of banks.

Regulators have allowed commercial banks to diversify their offerings, which could reduce risk. At the same time, it may allow commercial banks to engage in some services that are riskier than their traditional services and to pursue some services that they cannot provide efficiently. Thus, the reduction in regulatory constraints could actually increase the risk premium required by investors.

An improvement in management skills may reduce the perceived risk of a commercial bank. To the extent that more skillful managers allocate funds to assets that exhibit less risk, they may reduce the risk premium required by investors who invest in the bank.

Exhibit 20.1 provides a framework for valuing commercial banks that is based on the preceding discussion. In general, the valuation is favorably affected by economic growth, lower interest rates, a reduction in regulatory constraints (assuming the bank focuses on

Exhibit 20.1   Framework for Valuing a Commercial Bank

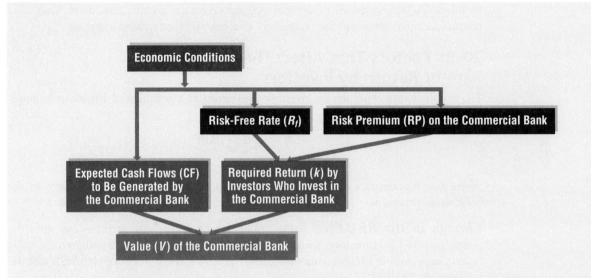

- A stronger economy leads to an increased demand for loans (interest income) and other services provided by the commercial bank (noninterest income), fewer loan defaults, and better cash flows.
- A lower risk-free rate can enhance the valuation of bank assets that do not have an adjustable interest rate, such as some consumer and mortgage loans. It can also increase the valuations of bonds. Commercial banks that have a higher proportion of these types of assets will benefit more from a decline in the risk-free rate and will be adversely affected to a greater degree by an increase in the risk-free rate.
- The valuation is also influenced by industry conditions and the commercial bank's management (not shown in the diagram). These factors affect the risk premium (and therefore the required return by investors) and the expected cash flows to be generated by the commercial bank.

services that it can provide efficiently), and an improvement in the bank's management abilities.

20-1c Impact of the Credit Crisis on Bank Valuations

Exhibit 20.2 shows the movement in a bank equity index over time, which suggests how bank valuations overall were affected during the credit crisis. Notice the steep decline in bank valuations that occurred during the 2008–2009 recession, which is when the credit crisis was most severe. Many publicly traded banks experienced a decline in their valuation of more than 70 percent during the crisis before rebounding. The main reason for this decline was the weak economic conditions that affected bank cash flows. In addition, investors recognized that they were more susceptible to failure during that period and required higher risk premiums. The banks with weaker management abilities that were overly exposed to mortgage problems suffered more severe losses. In the 2003–2007 period just before the crisis, only 11 banks failed. However, 140 banks failed in 2009 and another 157 banks failed in 2010.

20-2 Assessing Bank Performance

Exhibit 20.3 illustrates how the general performance of a bank is commonly summarized based mostly on income statement items. This summary is very basic but still offers much insight about a bank's income, expenses, and its efficiency. Each item in

Exhibit 20.2   Movements in Bank Equity Values Before and After the Financial Crisis

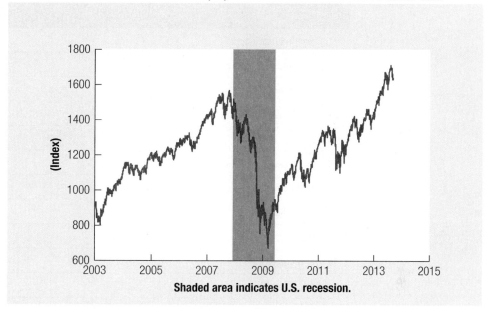

Shaded area indicates U.S. recession.

Source: *Federal Reserve, Standard & Poor's.*

Exhibit 20.3 is measured as a percentage of assets, which allows for easy comparison to other banks or to a set of banks within the same region. Analysts commonly compare a bank's performance with that of other banks of the same size. The Federal Reserve provides bank performance summaries for banks in four size classifications: money center banks (the 10 largest banks that serve money centers such as New York), large banks (ranked 11 to 100 in size), medium banks (ranked 101 to 1,000 in size), and small banks (ranked lower than 1,000 in size).

Measuring each item in Exhibit 20.3 as a percentage of assets also allows for an assessment of the bank's performance over time. The measurement of the dollar amount of income and expenses over time could be misleading without controlling for the change in the size (as measured by total assets) of the bank over time. A complete analysis of a bank would require the use of a bank's income statement and balance sheet. Yet Exhibit 20.3 is sufficient for identifying the key indicators of a bank's performance that deserve much attention.

The following discussion examines the items in Exhibit 20.3 in the order listed.

20-2a Interest Income and Expenses

Gross interest income (Row 1 of Exhibit 20.3) is interest income generated from all assets. It is affected by market rates and the composition of assets held by the bank. Gross interest income tends to increase when interest rates rise and to decrease when interest rates decline.

The gross interest income varies among banks of different sizes because of the rates they may charge on particular types of loans. Small banks tend to make more loans to small local businesses, which may allow them to charge higher interest rates than the money center and large banks charge on loans they provide to larger businesses. The

Exhibit 20.3 Example of Performance Summary of Canyon Bank 2012

ITEM	2013
1. Gross interest income	6.2%
2. Gross interest expenses	3.2
3. Net interest income	3.0
4. Noninterest income	2.0
5. Loan loss provision	.6
6. Noninterest expenses	3.
7. Securities gains (losses)	0.0
8. Income before tax	1.4
9. Taxes	.4
10. Net income	1.0
11. Cash dividends provided	.3
12. Retained earnings	.7

Note: All items in the exhibit are estimated as a proportion of total assets.

rates charged to larger businesses tend to be lower because those businesses generally have more options for obtaining funds than do small local businesses.

Gross interest expenses (Row 2) represent interest paid on deposits and on other borrowed funds (from the federal funds market). These expenses are affected by market rates and the composition of the bank's liabilities. Gross interest expenses will normally be higher when market interest rates are higher. The gross interest expenses will vary among banks depending on how they obtain their deposits. Banks that rely more heavily on NOW accounts, money market deposit accounts, and CDs instead of checking accounts for deposits will incur higher gross interest expenses.

Net interest income (Row 3 of Exhibit 20.3) is the difference between gross interest income and interest expenses and is measured as a percentage of assets. This measure is commonly referred to as net interest margin. It has a major effect on the bank's performance. Banks need to earn more interest income than their interest expenses in order to cover their other expenses. Yet competition prevents them from charging excessive rates (and earning excessive income). In general, the net interest margin of all banks is fairly stable over time.

20-2b Noninterest Income and Expenses

Noninterest income (Row 4 of Exhibit 20.3) results from fees charged on services provided, such as lockbox services, banker's acceptances, cashier's checks, and foreign exchange transactions. During the 1990s, banks increased their noninterest income as they offered more fee-based services. Since 2000, however, noninterest income has stabilized because of more intense competition among financial institutions offering fee-based services. Noninterest income is usually higher for money center, large, and medium banks than for small banks. This difference occurs because the larger banks tend to provide more services for which they can charge fees.

The **loan loss provision** (Row 5 of Exhibit 20.3) is a reserve account established by the bank in anticipation of loan losses in the future. It should increase during periods when loan losses are more likely, such as during a recessionary period. The amount of loan losses as a percentage of assets is higher for banks that provide riskier loans, especially when economic conditions weaken. For example, as a result of the financial crisis, the average loan loss provision was 1.95 percent of total assets in 2009 among banks, whereas it was only 0.27 percent just two years earlier. The increase was primarily due to mortgage and real estate loan defaults. The large loan loss provision in 2009 offset bank profits from all other operations of banks in that year.

The reporting of a bank's earnings requires managerial judgment on the amount of existing loans that will default. This can cause two banks with similar loan portfolios to have different earnings. A bank with conservative management may account for larger loan losses, which reduces the reported earnings now. In contrast, a bank with more aggressive management may understate the likely level of loan losses, which essentially defers the bad news until some future time. This lack of transparency can be beneficial in the short run to the bank with more aggressive management. Because the stock price is partially driven by earnings, the bank may be able to keep its stock price artificially high by understating its loan losses (and therefore overstating its earnings). If managerial compensation is tied to the bank's short-term stock price movements or earnings, managers may be tempted to understate loan losses.

Noninterest expenses (Row 6 of Exhibit 20.3) include salaries, office equipment, and other expenses not related to the payment of interest on deposits. Noninterest expenses depend partially on personnel costs associated with the credit assessment of loan applications, which in turn are affected by the bank's asset composition (proportion of funds allocated to loans). Noninterest expenses also depend on the liability composition because small deposits are more time-consuming to handle than large deposits. Banks offering more nontraditional services will incur higher noninterest expenses, although they expect to offset the higher costs with higher noninterest income.

Securities gains and losses (Row 7 of Exhibit 20.3) result from the bank's sale of securities. They are usually negligible for banks in aggregate, although an individual bank's gains or losses can be significant. During the financial crisis, securities losses were pronounced as banks in general suffered losses on their investments in mortgage-backed securities during the credit crisis.

Income before tax (Row 8 of Exhibit 20.3) is obtained by summing net interest income, noninterest income, and securities gains and then subtracting from this sum the provision for loan losses and noninterest expenses.

The key income statement item, according to many analysts, is net income (Row 10 of Exhibit 20.3), which accounts for any taxes paid. Therefore, the net income is the focus in the following section.

WEB

www.fdic.gov
Financial data provided for individual commercial banks allows their performance to be evaluated. The site also provides a quarterly outlook for the banking industry.

20-3 EVALUATION OF A BANK'S ROA

The net income figure shown in Exhibit 20.3 is measured as a percentage of assets and therefore represents the **return on assets (ROA)**. The ROA is influenced by all previously mentioned income statement items and therefore by all policies and other factors that affect those items.

Exhibit 20.4 identifies some of the key policy decisions that influence a bank's income statement. This exhibit also identifies factors not controlled by the bank that affect the bank's income statement.

Exhibit 20.4 Influence of Bank Policies and Other Factors on a Bank's Income Statement

INCOME STATEMENT ITEM AS A PERCENTAGE OF ASSETS	BANK POLICY DECISIONS AFFECTING THE INCOME STATEMENT ITEM	UNCONTROLLABLE FACTORS AFFECTING THE INCOME STATEMENT ITEM
(1) Gross interest income	• Composition of assets • Quality of assets • Maturity and rate sensitivity of assets • Loan pricing policy	• Economic conditions • Market interest rate movements
(2) Gross interest expenses	• Composition of liabilities • Maturities and rate sensitivity of liabilities	• Market interest rate movements
(3) Net interest income = (1) − (2)		
(4) Noninterest income	• Service charges • Nontraditional activities	• Regulatory provisions
(5) Noninterest expenses	• Composition of assets • Composition of liabilities • Nontraditional activities • Efficiency of personnel • Costs of office space and equipment • Marketing costs • Other costs	• Inflation
(6) Loan losses	• Composition of assets • Quality of assets • Collection department capabilities	• Economic conditions • Market interest rate movements
(7) Pretax return on assets = (3) + (4) − (5) − (6)		
(8) Taxes	• Tax planning	• Tax laws
(9) After-tax return on assets = (7) − (8)		
(10) Financial leverage, measured here as (assets/equity)	• Capital structure policies	• Capital structure regulations
(11) Return on equity = (9) × (10)		

20-3a Reasons for a Low ROA

The ROA will usually reveal when a bank's performance is not up to par, but it does not indicate the reason for the poor performance. Therefore, its components must be evaluated separately. Exhibit 20.5 identifies the factors that affect bank performance as measured by ROA and ROE. If a bank's ROA is less than desired, the bank is possibly incurring excessive interest expenses. Banks typically know what deposit rate is necessary to attract deposits and therefore are not likely to pay excessive interest. Yet if all a bank's sources of funds require a market-determined rate, the bank will face relatively high interest expenses. A relatively low ROA could also be due to low interest received on loans and securities because the bank has been overly conservative with its funds or was locked into fixed rates prior to an increase in market interest rates. High interest expenses and/or low interest revenues (on a relative basis) will reduce the net interest margin and thereby reduce ROA.

Exhibit 20.5 Breakdown of Performance Measures

MEASURES OF BANK PERFORMANCE	FINANCIAL CHARACTERISTICS INFLUENCING PERFORMANCE	BANK DECISIONS AFFECTING FINANCIAL CHARACTERISTICS
(1) Return on assets (ROA)	Net interest margin	Deposit rate decisions
		Loan rate decisions
		Loan losses
	Noninterest revenues	Bank services offered
	Noninterest expenses	Overhead requirements
		Efficiency
		Advertising
	Loan losses	Risk level of loans provided
(2) Return on equity (ROE)	ROA	Same as for ROA
	Leverage measure	Capital structure decision

A relatively low ROA may also result from insufficient noninterest income. Some banks have made a much greater effort than others to offer services that generate fee (noninterest) income. Because a bank's net interest margin is dictated in part by interest rate trends and balance sheet composition, many banks attempt to focus on noninterest income to boost their ROA.

A bank's ROA can also be damaged by heavy loan losses. However, if the bank is too conservative in attempting to avoid loan losses then its net interest margin will be low (because of the low interest rates received from very safe loans and investments). Because of the obvious trade-off here, banks generally attempt to shift their risk–return preferences according to economic conditions. They may increase their concentration of relatively risky loans during periods of prosperity, when they can improve their net interest margin without incurring excessive loan losses. Conversely, they may increase their concentration of relatively low-risk (and low-return) investments when economic conditions are less favorable.

A low ROA may also be attributed to excessive noninterest expenses, such as overhead and advertising expenses. Any waste of resources due to inefficiencies can lead to relatively high noninterest expenses.

20-3b Converting ROA to ROE

An alternative measure of overall bank performance is return on equity (ROE). A bank's ROE is affected by the same income statement items that affect ROA but also by the bank's degree of financial leverage:

$$\text{ROE} = \text{ROA} \times \text{Leverage measure}$$
$$\frac{\text{Net income}}{\text{Equity capital}} = \frac{\text{Net income}}{\text{Total assets}} \times \frac{\text{Total assets}}{\text{Equity capital}}$$

The leverage measure is simply the inverse of the capital ratio (when only equity counts as capital). The higher the capital ratio, the lower the leverage measure and the lower the degree of financial leverage. For a given positive level of ROA, a bank's ROE will be higher if it uses more financial leverage.

Exhibit 20.6   Average ROE among Banks Over Time

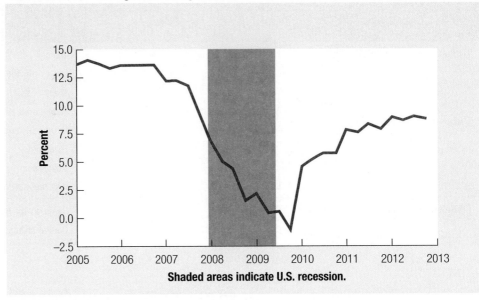

Source: *Federal Reserve and Federal Financial Institutions Examination Council.*

Exhibit 20.6 shows the average annualized return on equity among banks over time. The ROE was relatively high during the 2005–2007 period when the U.S. economy was expanding. However, it declined substantially during the financial crisis, even reaching negative levels in 2009, and gradually increased over time as the effects of the crisis subsided.

20-3c Application

Consider the performance characteristics for Zager Bank and the industry in Exhibit 20.7 over the last five years. The years in the exhibit are labeled Year 1 through Year 5, whereby Year 5 just ended. Because of differences in accounting procedures, the information may not be perfectly comparable. Since Zager Bank is a medium-sized bank, it is compared here to other medium-sized banks.

Zager Bank has used an aggressive management style of providing loans to borrowers that might be viewed as risky given their limited collateral and their cash flow situation. The bank charges high interest rates on these loans because the borrowers do not have alternative lenders. It also charges these borrowers high annual fees after providing its loans. During the strong economic conditions in Years 1 and 2, Zager's strategy was very successful. It achieved a high net interest margin and high noninterest income. The borrowers typically made their loan payments in a timely manner. However, when the economy weakened in Year 3, many of the borrowers who received loans from Zager Bank could not repay them. Furthermore, Zager was not able to extend many new loans because the demand for loans declined.

Although other banks also experienced weak performance when the economy weakened, Zager Bank experienced a more pronounced decline in performance because it had more loans that were susceptible to default. Exhibit 20.7 shows that net income declined for medium-sized banks in general during Year 3, but it actually turned negative for

Exhibit 20.7 Comparison of Zager Bank's Expenses and Income to the Industry

Zager Bank because of its large loan losses. This example illustrates the risk–return trade-off for Zager Bank. It was rewarded for its risky strategy when the economy was strong, but it was severely penalized for that strategy when the economy was weak.

Any particular bank will perform a more thorough evaluation of itself than that shown here, including a comprehensive explanation for its performance in recent years. Investors can evaluate any particular bank's performance by conducting an analysis similar to the one described here.

SUMMARY

- A bank's value depends on its expected future cash flows and the required rate of return by investors who invest in the bank. The bank's expected cash flows are influenced by economic growth, interest rate movements, regulatory constraints, and the abilities of the bank's managers. The required rate of return by investors who invest in the bank is influenced by the prevailing interest rate (which is affected by other economic conditions) and the risk premium (which is affected by economic growth, regulatory constraints, and the management abilities of the bank). In general, the value of commercial banks is favorably affected by strong economic growth, declining interest rates, and strong management abilities.

- A bank's performance can be evaluated by comparing its income statement items (as a percentage of total assets) to a control group of other banks with a similar size classification. The performance of the bank may be compared to the performance of a control group of banks. Any difference in performance between the bank and the control group is typically because of differences in net interest margin, loan loss reserves, noninterest income, or noninterest expenses.

If the bank's net interest margin is relatively low, it either is relying too heavily on deposits with higher interest rates or is not earning adequate interest on its loans. If the bank is forced to boost loan loss reserves, this suggests that its loan portfolio may be too risky. If its noninterest income is relatively low, the bank is not providing enough services that generate fee income. If the bank's noninterest expenses are relatively high, its cost of operations is excessive. There may be other specific details that make the assessment more complex, but the key problems of a bank can usually be detected with the approach described here.

- A common measure of a bank's overall performance is its return on assets (ROA). The ROA of a bank is partially determined by movements in market interest rates, as many banks benefit from lower interest rates. In addition, the ROA is highly dependent on economic conditions, because banks can extend more loans to creditworthy customers and may also experience a higher demand for their services.

- Another useful measure of a bank's overall performance is return on equity (ROE). A bank can increase its ROE by increasing its financial leverage, but its leverage is constrained by capital requirements.

POINT COUNTER-POINT

Does a Bank's Income Statement Clearly Indicate the Bank's Performance?

Point   Yes. The bank's income statement can be partitioned to determine its performance and the underlying reasons for its performance.

Counter-Point   No. The bank's income statement can be manipulated because the bank may not fully

recognize loan losses (will not write off loans that are likely to default) until a future period.

Who Is Correct?   Use the Internet to learn more about this issue and then formulate your own opinion.

QUESTIONS AND APPLICATIONS

1. Interest Income How can gross interest income rise while the net interest margin remains somewhat stable for a particular bank?

2. Impact on Income If a bank shifts its loan policy to pursue more credit card loans, how will its net interest margin be affected?

3. Noninterest Income What has been the trend in noninterest income in recent years? Explain.

4. Net Interest Margin How could a bank generate higher income before tax (as a percentage of assets) when its net interest margin has decreased?

5. Net Interest Income Suppose the net interest income generated by a bank is equal to 1.5 percent of its assets. Based on past experience, would the bank experience a loss or a gain? Explain.

6. Noninterest Income Why have large money center banks' noninterest income levels typically been higher than those of smaller banks?

7. Bank Leverage What does the assets/equity ratio of a bank indicate?

8. Analysis of a Bank's ROA What are some of the more common reasons why a bank may experience a low ROA?

9. Loan Loss Provisions Explain why loan loss provisions of most banks could increase in a particular period.

10. Bank Performance during the Credit Crisis Why do you think some banks suffered larger losses than other banks during the credit crisis?

11. Weak Performance What are likely reasons for weak bank performance?

12. Bank Income Statement Assume that SUNY Bank plans to liquidate Treasury security holdings and use the proceeds for small business loans. Explain how this strategy will affect the different income statement items. Also identify any income statement items for which the effects of this strategy are more difficult to estimate.

Interpreting Financial News

Interpret the following comments made by Wall Street analysts and portfolio managers.

a. "The three most important factors that determine a local bank's bad debt level are the bank's location, location, and location."

b. "The bank's profitability was enhanced by its limited use of capital."

c. "Low risk is not always desirable. Our bank's risk has been too low, given the market conditions. We will restructure operations in a manner to increase risk."

Managing in Financial Markets

Forecasting Bank Performance As a manager of Hawaii Bank, you anticipate the following:

- Loan loss provision at end of year = 1 percent of assets
- Gross interest income over the next year = 9 percent of assets
- Noninterest expenses over the next year = 3 percent of assets
- Noninterest income over the next year = 1 percent of assets
- Gross interest expenses over the next year = 5 percent of assets
- Tax rate on income = 30 percent
- Capital ratio (capital/assets) at end of year = 5 percent

a. Forecast Hawaii Bank's net interest margin.

b. Forecast Hawaii Bank's earnings before taxes as a percentage of assets.

c. Forecast Hawaii Bank's earnings after taxes as a percentage of assets.

d. Forecast Hawaii Bank's return on equity.

e. Hawaii Bank is considering a shift in its asset structure to reduce its concentration of Treasury bonds and increase its volume of loans to small businesses. Identify each income statement item that would be affected by this strategy, and explain whether the forecast for that item would increase or decrease as a result.

PROBLEM

Assessing Bank Performance Select a bank whose income statement data are available. Using recent income statement information about the commercial bank, assess its performance. How does the performance of this bank compare to the performance of other banks? Compared with the other banks assessed in this chapter, is its return on equity higher or lower? What is the main reason why its ROE is different from the norm? (Is it due to its interest expenses? Its noninterest income?)

Flow of Funds Exercise

How the Flow of Funds Affects Bank Performance

In recent years, Carson Company has requested the services listed below from Blazo Financial, a financial conglomerate. These transactions have created a flow of funds between Carson Company and Blazo.

a. Classify each service according to how Blazo benefits from the service.

■ Advising on possible targets that Carson may acquire
■ Futures contract transactions
■ Options contract transactions
■ Interest rate derivative transactions
■ Loans
■ Line of credit
■ Purchase of short-term CDs
■ Checking account

b. Explain why Blazo's performance from providing these services to Carson Company and other firms will decline if economic growth is reduced.

c. Given the potential impact of slow economic growth on a bank's performance, do you think that commercial banks would prefer that the Fed use a restrictive monetary policy or an expansionary monetary policy?

Internet/Excel Exercises

1. Go to www.suntrust.com and retrieve a recent annual report of the SunTrust Bank. Use the income statement to determine SunTrust's performance. Describe SunTrust's performance in recent years.

2. Has SunTrust's ROA increased since the year before? Explain what caused its ROA to change over the last year. Has its net interest margin changed since last year? How has its noninterest income (as a percentage of assets) changed over the last year? How have its noninterest expenses changed over the last year? How have its loan loss reserves changed in the last year? Discuss how SunTrust's recent strategy and economic conditions might explain the changes in these components of its income statement.

WSJ Exercise

Assessing Bank Performance

Using a recent issue of the *Wall Street Journal*, summarize an article that discussed the recent performance of a particular commercial bank. Does the article suggest that the bank's performance was better or worse than the norm? What is the reason given for the performance?

Online Articles with Real-World Examples

Find a recent practical article available online that describes a real-world example regarding a specific financial institution or financial market that reinforces one or more concepts covered in this chapter.

If your class has an online component, your professor may ask you to post your summary of the article there and provide a link to the article so that other students can access it.

If your class is live, your professor may ask you to summarize your application of the article in class. Your professor may assign specific students to complete this assignment or may allow any students to do the assignment on a volunteer basis.

For recent online articles and real-world examples related to this chapter, consider using the following search terms (be sure to include the prevailing year as a search term to ensure that the online articles are recent):

1. [name of a specific bank] AND interest income
2. [name of a specific bank] AND interest expense
3. [name of a specific bank] AND loan loss
4. [name of a specific bank] AND net income
5. [name of a specific bank] AND net interest margin
6. [name of a specific bank] AND earnings
7. [name of a specific bank] AND return on equity
8. bank AND income
9. bank AND return on assets
10. bank AND net interest margin

Forecasting Bank Performance

This problem requires an understanding of banks' sources and uses of funds (Chapter 17), bank management (Chapter 19), and bank performance (Chapter 20). It also requires the use of spreadsheet software such as Microsoft Excel. The data provided can be input onto a spreadsheet so that the necessary computations can be completed more easily. A conceptual understanding of commercial banking is needed to interpret the computations.

As an analyst of a medium-sized commercial bank, you have been asked to forecast next year's performance. In June you were provided with information about the sources and uses of funds for the upcoming year. The bank's sources of funds for the upcoming year are as follows (where NCDs are negotiable certificates of deposit):

SOURCES OF FUNDS	DOLLAR AMOUNT (IN MILLIONS)	INTEREST RATE TO BE OFFERED
Demand deposits	$5,000	0%
Time deposits	2,000	6%
1-year NCDs	3,000	T-bill rate + 1%
5-year NCDs	2,500	1-year NCD rate + 1%

The bank also has $1 billion in capital.

The bank's uses of funds for the upcoming year are as follows:

USES OF FUNDS	DOLLAR AMOUNT (IN MILLIONS)	INTEREST RATE	LOAN LOSS PERCENTAGE
Loans to small businesses	$4,000	T-bill rate + 6%	2%
Loans to large businesses	2,000	T-bill rate + 4%	1
Consumer loans	3,000	T-bill rate + 7%	4
Treasury bills	1,000	T-bill rate	0
Treasury bonds	1,500	T-bill rate + 2%	0
Corporate bonds	1,100	Treasury bond rate + 2%	0

The bank also has $900 million in fixed assets. The interest rates on loans to small and large businesses are tied to the T-bill rate and will change at the beginning of each new year. The forecasted Treasury bond rate is tied to the future T-bill rate because an upward-sloping yield curve is expected at the beginning of next year. The corporate bond rate is tied to the Treasury bond rate, allowing for a risk premium of 2 percent. Consumer loans will be provided at the beginning of next year, and interest rates will be fixed over the lifetime of the loan. The remaining time to maturity on all assets except T-bills exceeds three years. As the one-year T-bills mature, the funds are to be reinvested in new one-year T-bills (all T-bills are to be purchased at the beginning of the year). The bank's loan loss percentage reflects the percentage of bad loans. Assume that no interest will be received on these loans. In addition, assume that this percentage of loans will be accounted for as loan loss reserves (i.e., assume that they should be subtracted when determining before-tax income).

The bank has forecast its noninterest revenues to be $200 million and its noninterest expenses to be $740 million. A tax rate of 34 percent can be applied to the before-tax income in order to estimate after-tax income. The bank has developed the following probability distribution for the one-year T-bill rate at the beginning of next year:

POSSIBLE T-BILL RATE	PROBABILITY
8%	30%
9	50
10	20

Questions

1. Using the information provided, determine the probability distribution of return on assets (ROA) for next year by completing the following table:

INTEREST RATE SCENARIO (POSSIBLE T-BILL RATE)	FORECASTED ROA	PROBABILITY
8%		
9		
10		

2. Will the bank's ROA next year be higher or lower if market interest rates are higher? (Use the T-bill rate as a proxy for market interest rates.) Why? The information provided did not assume any required reserves. Explain how including required reserves would affect forecasted interest revenue, ROA, and ROE.

3. The bank is considering a strategy of attempting to attract an extra $1 billion as one-year negotiable certificates of deposit to replace $1 billion of five-year NCDs. Develop the probability distribution of ROA based on this strategy:

INTEREST RATE SCENARIO	FORECASTED ROA BASED ON THE STRATEGY OF INCREASING ONE-YEAR NCDs	PROBABILITY
8%		
9		
10		

4. Is the bank's ROA likely to be higher next year if it uses this strategy of attracting more one-year NCDs?

5. What would be an obvious concern about a strategy of using more one-year NCDs and fewer five-year NCDs beyond the next year?

6. The bank is considering a strategy of using $1 billion to offer additional loans to small businesses instead of purchasing T-bills. Using all the original assumptions provided, determine the probability distribution of ROA (assume that noninterest expenses would not be affected by this change in strategy).

INTEREST RATE SCENARIO (POSSIBLE T-BILL RATE)	FORECASTED ROA IF AN EXTRA $1 BILLION IS USED FOR LOANS TO SMALL BUSINESSES	PROBABILITY
8%		
9		
10		

7. Would the bank's ROA likely be higher or lower over the next year if it allocates the extra funds to small business loans?

8. What is the obvious risk of such a strategy beyond the next year?

9. The previous strategy of attracting more one-year NCDs could affect noninterest expenses and revenues. How would noninterest expenses be affected by this strategy of offering additional loans to small businesses? How would noninterest revenues be affected by this strategy?

10. Now assume that the bank is considering a strategy of increasing its consumer loans by $1 billion instead of using the funds for loans to small businesses. Using this information along with all the original assumptions provided, determine the probability distribution of ROA.

INTEREST RATE SCENARIO (POSSIBLE T-BILL RATE)	POSSIBLE ROA IF AN EXTRA $1 BILLION IS USED FOR CONSUMER LOANS	PROBABILITY
8%		
9		
10		

11. Other than possible changes in the economy that may affect credit risk, what key factor will determine whether this strategy is beneficial beyond one year?

12. Now assume that the bank wants to determine how its forecasted return on equity (ROE) next year would be affected by boosting its capital from $1 billion to $1.2 billion. (The extra capital would not be used to increase interest or noninterest

revenues.) Using all the original assumptions provided, complete the following table:

INTEREST RATE SCENARIO (POSSIBLE T-BILL RATE)	FORECASTED ROE IF CAPITAL = $1 BILLION	FORECASTED ROE IF CAPITAL = $1.2 BILLION	PROBABILITY
8%			
9			
10			

Briefly state how the ROE will be affected if the capital level is increased.

PART 7
Nonbank Operations

The chapters in Part 7 cover the key nonbank operations. Each chapter is devoted to a particular type of operation, with a focus on sources of funds, uses of funds, regulations, management, and recent performance. Some of the institutions discussed are independent; others are units (subsidiaries) of financial conglomerates. Each financial institution's interactions with other institutions and its participation in financial markets are also emphasized in these chapters.

21
Thrift Operations

The term *thrift institution* (or *savings institution*) is normally used to refer to a depository institution that specializes in mortgage lending. These institutions were created to accept deposits and use much of the funds for mortgage loans, home-equity loans, and mortgage-backed securities. Some thrift operations are independent financial institutions, whereas others are units (subsidiaries) of financial conglomerates. Sometimes credit unions are also considered to be thrift institutions. For this reason, credit unions are also covered in this chapter.

21-1 BACKGROUND ON SAVINGS INSTITUTIONS

Savings institutions include savings banks and savings and loan associations (S&Ls). Savings and loan associations are the dominant type. The two types of thrifts now have very similar sources and uses of funds. Therefore, the remainder of the chapter focuses on savings institutions in general, abbreviated as SIs. Most SIs are small, with assets of less than $1 billion. SIs can be chartered at the state or federal level.

21-1a Ownership of Savings Institutions

Savings institutions are classified as either stock owned or mutual (owned by depositors). Although most SIs are mutual, many SIs have shifted their ownership structure from depositors to shareholders through what is known as a mutual-to-stock conversion. This conversion allows SIs to obtain additional capital by issuing stock.

Beyond having the capability to boost capital, stock-owned institutions also provide their owners with greater potential to benefit from their performance. The dividends and/or stock price of a high-performance institution can grow, thereby providing direct benefits to the shareholders. In contrast, the owners (depositors) of a mutual institution do not benefit directly from high performance. Although they have a pro rata claim to the mutual SI's net worth while they maintain deposits there, their claim is eliminated once they close their account.

Because of the difference in owner control, stock-owned institutions are more susceptible to unfriendly takeovers. It is virtually impossible for another firm to take control of a mutual institution because management generally holds all voting rights. From the owners' perspective, the stock-owned institution may seem more desirable because the owners may have more influence on managerial decisions.

When a mutual SI is involved in an acquisition, it first converts to a stock-owned SI. If it is the acquiring firm, it then arranges to purchase the existing stock of the institution to

WEB

www.occ.gov
Background on laws and
regulations imposed on
savings institutions.

be acquired. Conversely, if it is to be acquired, its stock is purchased by the acquiring institution. This process is often referred to as a **merger-conversion**.

Some SIs have been acquired by commercial banks that wanted to diversify their operations. Even after such an acquisition, the SI may still maintain its operations but under the ownership of the commercial bank. Consolidation and acquisitions have caused the number of mutual and stock SIs to decline consistently over the years. There are less than half as many SIs today as in 1994.

Although consolidation among SIs has resulted in a smaller number of institutions, the total assets of SIs in aggregate have increased. The total assets of stock SIs have more than doubled since 1994 while the total assets of mutual SIs have remained steady.

21-1b Regulation of Savings Institutions

As a result of the Dodd–Frank Act, the regulation of SIs has been revised. The Office of the Controller of the Currency supervises mutual SIs and federal SIs. The Federal Reserve regulates parent holding companies of SIs. The Bureau of Consumer Protection supervises larger SIs (with at least $10 billion in assets) to ensure that they comply with federal consumer protection laws. Thus there is some regulatory overlap among the regulators. State-chartered SIs are regulated by the respective state. SIs may also need to satisfy various guidelines established by the Federal Deposit Insurance Corporation (FDIC) in addition to satisfying their respective regulators.

The Dodd–Frank Act removed some advantages of SIs. Holding companies of SIs will have to satisfy minimum capital standards that are imposed on bank holding companies. Federal SIs have to satisfy the Qualified Thrift Lender Test, which requires that at least 65 percent of the asset portfolio contain qualified thrift investments such as housing loans, home-equity loans, mortgage-backed securities, small business loans, and credit card loans. Yet SIs are subject to limits on commercial loans and consumer loans.

Although regulations are converging among regulators, there are still differences. Consequently, SIs have an incentive to go regulator shopping, in search of a more lenient regulator that allows more freedom in operations, or requires less paperwork for compliance purposes. In fact, some SIs are now attempting to become commercial banks or credit unions because of the recent regulatory changes that have removed some of the previous advantages of being an SI.

Deposit Insurance The insuring agency for SIs is the Deposit Insurance Fund (DIF), which is administered by the FDIC and insures deposits. The insurable limit is presently $250,000. The DIF was formed on March 31, 2006, as a result of the merger of the **Savings Association Insurance Fund (SAIF)**, which had formerly insured S&Ls, and the Bank Insurance Fund (BIF), which had insured savings banks. The FDIC charges the SIs annual insurance premiums, which are placed in the DIF. If an SI fails, the FDIC uses funds from the DIF to reimburse depositors.

Regulatory Assessment of Savings Institutions Regulators conduct periodic on-site examinations of SIs using the CAMELS rating system in a manner similar to commercial banks. CAMELS is an acronym that represents the following characteristics: capital adequacy, asset quality, management, earnings, liquidity, and sensitivity to market conditions. Each SI is assigned a composite CAMELS rating between 1 (best) and 5 (worst). If an SI receives a composite CAMELS rating of 4 or higher, it is classified as a "problem" and receives close attention. It may be subject to corrective action by regulators.

Deregulation of Services In recent years, SIs have been granted more flexibility to diversify the products and services they provide. They have diversified their business by merging with other businesses specializing in real estate, insurance, and brokerage. By offering discount brokerage service and other nontraditional services, an SI can attract customers searching for a one-stop shop.

WEB

http://research.
stlouisfed.org/fred2
Time-series data on
various savings rates
and total savings
breakdown.

21-2 SOURCES AND USES OF FUNDS

Like commercial banks, SIs serve as valuable financial intermediaries. However, their sources and uses of funds are different from those of commercial banks, so their management also differs from that of commercial banks.

21-2a Sources of Funds

The main sources of funds for SIs are described next.

Deposits   Savings institutions obtain most of their funds from a variety of savings and time deposits, including passbook savings, retail certificates of deposit (CDs), and money market deposit accounts (MMDAs).

Borrowed Funds   When SIs are unable to attract sufficient deposits, they can borrow on a short-term basis from three sources. First, they can borrow from other depository institutions that have excess funds in the federal funds market. The interest rate on funds borrowed in this market is referred to as the federal funds rate.

Second, SIs can borrow through a repurchase agreement (repo). With a repo, an institution sells government securities with a commitment to repurchase those securities shortly thereafter. This essentially reflects a short-term loan to the institution that initially sold the securities until the time when it buys the securities back.

Third, SIs can borrow at the Federal Reserve, but this is not as common as the other alternatives.

Capital   The **capital** (or net worth) of an SI is primarily composed of retained earnings and funds obtained from issuing stock. During periods when SIs are performing well, capital is boosted by additional retained earnings. Capital is commonly used to support ongoing or expanding operations. Capital also serves as a cushion for SIs that experience losses, such as during the credit crisis for many SIs.

21-2b Uses of Funds

The main uses of funds for SIs are:

- Cash
- Mortgages
- Mortgage-backed securities
- Other securities
- Consumer and commercial loans
- Other uses

Cash   Savings institutions maintain cash to satisfy reserve requirements enforced by the Federal Reserve System and to accommodate withdrawal requests of depositors. In addition, some SIs hold correspondent cash balances at other financial institutions in return for various services.

Mortgages   Mortgages are the primary asset of SIs. They typically have long-term maturities and can usually be prepaid by borrowers. About 90 percent of the mortgages originated are for homes or multifamily dwellings, while 10 percent are for commercial properties.

Mortgages can be sold in the secondary market, although their market value changes in response to interest rate movements, so they are subject to interest rate risk as well as credit (default) risk. To protect against interest rate risk, SIs use a variety of techniques, discussed later in the chapter.

Mortgage-Backed Securities Some savings institutions purchase mortgage-backed securities. The return on these securities is highly influenced by the default rate on the underlying mortgages. During the credit crisis there were many defaults, and savings institutions that had purchased mortgage-backed securities commonly experienced losses.

Other Securities Savings institutions invest in securities such as Treasury bonds and corporate bonds. These securities provide liquidity, as they can quickly be sold in the secondary market if funds are needed.

Savings institutions sometimes rely on credit ratings when considering an investment in corporate bonds. However, during the financial crisis, the ratings agencies were criticized for being too liberal with their ratings. The Wall Street Reform and Consumer Protection Act (also called the Dodd-Frank Act) of 2010 required that SIs use not only credit ratings assigned by credit rating agencies, but also other methods to assess the risk of debt securities, including their own assessment of risk. By complementing credit ratings with their own analysis, SIs should be less likely to invest in securities with excessive risk.

Consumer and Commercial Loans Many SIs have increased their consumer and commercial loans. This can reduce their heavy exposure to mortgage loans.

Because consumer and corporate loan maturities closely match their liability maturities, SIs that reduce their fixed-rate mortgage loans in favor of consumer loans reduce their exposure to interest rate risk.

Other Uses of Funds Savings institutions can provide temporary financing to other institutions through the use of repurchase agreements. In addition, they can lend funds on a short-term basis through the federal funds market. Both methods allow them to efficiently use funds that they will have available for only a short period of time.

21-2c Balance Sheet of Savings Institutions

The sources of funds represent liabilities or equity of an SI, while the uses of funds represent assets. Each SI determines its own composition of liabilities and assets, which determines its specific operations.

EXAMPLE

Exhibit 21.1 summarizes the main sources and uses of funds of SIs by showing the balance sheet of Ashland Savings. The assets are shown on the left side of the balance sheet. The second column shows the dollar amount, and the third column shows the size of each asset in proportion to the total assets, to illustrate how Ashland Savings distributes its funds. Ashland's main asset is mortgage loans. The allocation of assets by Ashland Savings reflects the average allocation for all SIs. Allocations vary considerably among SIs, however, as some institutions maintain a much larger amount of mortgages than others.

Ashland Savings incurs some expenses from all types of deposits. Specifically, it hires employees to serve depositors. Its composition of liabilities determines its interest expenses, since it must pay a higher interest rate on large CDs than on small savings deposits. Ashland also incurs expenses from managing its assets. In particular, it hires employees to assess the creditworthiness of individuals

Exhibit 21.1 Balance Sheet of Ashland Savings as of June 30, 2011

ASSETS	DOLLAR AMOUNT (IN MILLIONS)	PROPORTION OF TOTAL ASSETS	LIABILITIES AND STOCK HOLDERS' EQUITY	DOLLAR AMOUNT (IN MILLIONS)	PROPORTION OF TOTAL LIABILITIES AND STOCKHOLDERS' EQUITY
Cash (includes required reserves)	$ 60	6%	Savings deposits	$ 100	10%
Single-family mortgages	500	50%	NOW accounts	50	5%
Multifamily mortgages	50	5%	Money market deposit accounts	300	30%
Other mortgages	40	4%	Short-term CDs	360	36%
Mortgage-backed securities	70	7%	CDs with maturities beyond one year	100	10%
Other securities	100	10%			
Consumer loans	70	7%			
Commercial loans	40	4%			
Fixed assets	70	7%	Common stock issued	50	5%
			Retained earnings	40	4%
TOTAL ASSETS	$1,000	100%	TOTAL LIABILITIES AND STOCK HOLDERS' EQUITY	$1,000	100%

and businesses that request loans. In general, Ashland wants to generate enough income from its assets to cover its expenses and provide a reasonable return to its shareholders. Its primary source of income is interest received from the mortgage loans that it provides. Its capital is shown on the balance sheet as common stock issued and retained earnings. ●

Exhibit 21.2 shows how savings institutions use the key balance sheet items to finance economic growth. They channel funds from their depositors with surplus funds to other households that purchase homes. They also channel funds to support investment in commercial property. They serve a major role in the development of the housing and commercial property market. They also use some deposits to purchase Treasury and municipal securities and thereby finance spending by the Treasury and municipalities.

21-2d Interaction with Other Financial Institutions

When SIs obtain and use funds, they commonly interact with other financial institutions, as summarized in Exhibit 21.3. They compete with commercial banks and money market mutual funds to obtain funds, and they compete with commercial banks and finance companies in lending funds. After originating mortgages, they sometimes sell them to insurance companies in the secondary market. Many SIs have other financial institutions as subsidiaries that provide a variety of services, including consumer finance, trust company, mortgage banking, discount brokerage, and insurance.

Exhibit 21.2 How Savings Institutions Finance Economic Growth

Exhibit 21.3 Interactions between Savings Institutions and Other Financial Institutions

TYPE OF FINANCIAL INSTITUTION	INTERACTION WITH SAVINGS INSTITUTIONS
Commercial banks	• Compete with SIs in attracting deposits, providing consumer loans, and providing commercial loans. • Have merged with SIs in recent years.
Finance companies	• Compete with SIs in providing consumer and commercial loans.
Money market mutual funds	• Compete with SIs in attracting short-term investments from investors.
Investment companies and brokerage firms	• Serve SIs that wish to engage in interest rate swaps and interest rate caps. • Have agreements with SIs to offer brokerage services to their customers.
Insurance companies	• Purchase mortgages from SIs in the secondary market.

21-2e Participation in Financial Markets

When SIs perform their various functions, they rely on various financial markets, as summarized in Exhibit 21.4. Mortgage markets provide a source of funds to SIs that desire to issue mortgage-backed securities or sell their mortgages in the secondary market. Bond markets serve as a use of funds for SIs with excess funds and as a source of funds for SIs that issue new bonds in the primary market or sell bond holdings in the secondary market.

21-3 VALUATION OF A SAVINGS INSTITUTION

Savings institutions (or SI operating units that are part of a financial conglomerate) are commonly valued by their managers to monitor progress over time or by other financial institutions that are considering an acquisition. The value of an SI can be modeled as the

Exhibit 21.4 Participation of Savings Institutions in Financial Markets

FINANCIAL MARKET	HOW SAVINGS INSTITUTIONS PARTICIPATE IN THIS MARKET
Money markets	• Compete with other depository institutions for short-term deposits by issuing commercial paper.
Mortgage markets	• Sell mortgages in the secondary market and issue mortgage-backed securities.
Bond markets	• Purchase bonds for their investment portfolios. • Issue bonds to obtain long-term funds.
Futures markets	• Hedge against interest rate movements by taking positions in interest rate futures.
Options markets	• Hedge against interest rate movements by purchasing put options on interest rate futures.
Swap markets	• Hedge against interest rate movements by engaging in interest rate swaps.

present value of its future cash flows. Thus the value of an SI should change in response to changes in its expected cash flows in the future and to changes in the required rate by investors:

$$\Delta V = f[\underset{+}{\underline{\Delta E(CF)}}, \underset{-}{\underline{\Delta k}}]$$

21-3a Factors That Affect Cash Flows

The change in an SI's expected cash flows may be modeled as

$$\Delta E(CF) = f(\underset{+}{\underline{\Delta ECON}}, \underset{-}{\underline{\Delta R_f}}, \underset{?}{\underline{\Delta INDUS}}, \underset{+}{\underline{\Delta MANAB}})$$

where ECON represents economic growth, R_f represents the risk-free interest rate, INDUS represents the industry conditions (such as regulations) to which SIs are exposed, and MANAB represents abilities of the SI's management.

Change in Economic Growth   Economic growth can enhance an SI's cash flows by increasing household demand for consumer or mortgage loans, thereby allowing the SI to provide more loans. In addition, loan defaults are normally reduced in periods of strong economic growth. Furthermore, the demand for other financial services (such as real estate and insurance services) provided by SIs tends to be higher during periods of strong economic growth when households have relatively high levels of disposable income.

Change in the Risk-Free Interest Rate   An SI's cash flows may be inversely related to interest rate movements. First, if the risk-free interest rate decreases, other market rates may also decline, and the result may be a stronger demand for the SI's loans. Second, SIs rely heavily on short-term deposits as a source of funds, and the rates paid on these deposits are typically revised in accordance with other interest rate movements. The assets (such as consumer loans and fixed-rate mortgage loans) of savings institutions commonly have fixed rates, so interest income does not adjust to interest rate movements until those assets reach maturity or are sold. Therefore, when interest rates fall, an SI's cost of obtaining funds declines more than the decline in the interest earned on its loans and investments. An increase in interest rates can reduce the SI's expected cash flows because the interest paid on deposits may increase more than the interest earned on loans and investments.

Change in Industry Conditions   Savings institutions are exposed to industry conditions such as regulatory constraints, technology, and competition. If regulatory constraints are reduced, the expected cash flows of some SIs should increase. For example, when regulators reduced constraints on the services that could be offered, SIs were able to provide more services for their customers. At the same time, however, a reduction in regulations can cause less efficient SIs to lose market share and therefore experience a reduction in cash flows.

Change in Management Abilities   An SI has control over the composition of its managers and its organizational structure. Its managers attempt to make internal decisions that will capitalize on the external forces (economic growth, interest rates, regulatory constraints) that the institution cannot control. Thus the management skills of an SI influence its expected cash flows. For example, skillful managers will recognize whether to increase the funds allocated to fixed-rate mortgages based on expectations of future interest rates. They can capitalize on regulatory changes by offering a diversified set of services that accommodate specific customers. They can use technology in a manner that reduces expenses. They may also use derivative securities to alter the potential return and the exposure of the SI to interest rate movements.

WEB

www.fdic.gov
Information about the
performance of savings
institutions.

21-3b Factors That Affect the Required Rate of Return

The change in required rate of return by investors who invest in an SI can be modeled as

$$\Delta k = f(\underset{+}{\underline{\Delta R_f}} , \underset{+}{\underline{\Delta RP}})$$

where R_f represents the risk-free interest rate and RP represents the risk premium.

An increase in the risk-free rate results in a higher return required by investors. High inflation, economic growth, and a high budget deficit place upward pressure on interest rates, whereas money supply growth places downward pressure on interest rates (assuming it does not cause inflation).

Change in the Risk Premium   If the risk premium on an SI rises, so will the required rate of return by investors who invest in the SI. High economic growth results in less risk for an SI because its consumer loans, mortgage loans, and investments in debt securities are less likely to default. The effect of industry conditions on SIs can be mixed. A reduction in regulatory constraints on services can reduce the risk of SIs as they diversify their offerings, or it can increase their risk if they engage in some services that are riskier than their traditional services. An improvement in management skills may reduce the perceived risk of the SIs and therefore reduce the risk premium.

Exhibit 21.5 provides a framework for valuing an SI based on the preceding discussion. In general, the value of an SI is favorably affected by strong economic growth, a reduction in interest rates, and high-quality management. The sensitivity of an SI's value to these conditions depends on its own characteristics. For example, the value of an SI that emphasizes real estate and insurance services will be more sensitive to regulations that restrict or limit the offering of these services than will the value of an SI that focuses on traditional mortgage lending.

WEB

www.occ.gov
Review of performance
of savings institutions
overall.

21-4 EXPOSURE TO RISK

Like commercial banks, SIs are exposed to liquidity risk, credit risk, and interest rate risk. However, because their sources and uses of funds differ from those of banks, their exposure to risk varies as well.

Exhibit 21.5 Framework for Valuing a Savings Institution

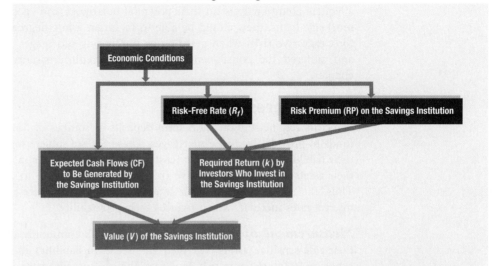

- A stronger economy leads to an increase in the demand for loans (interest income) and other services (noninterest income), fewer loan defaults, and therefore better cash flows for the savings institution.
- A lower risk-free rate leads to a lower cost of deposits obtained and more favorable valuations of the mortgages held by the savings institution.
- The valuation is also influenced by industry conditions and the saving institution's management (not shown in the diagram). These factors affect the risk premium (and therefore the required return by investors) and the expected cash flows to be generated by the savings institution. In particular, regulatory changes can affect the level of competition and therefore affect the savings institution's cash flows and risk premium.

21-4a Liquidity Risk

Because SIs commonly use short-term liabilities to finance long-term assets, they depend on additional deposits to accommodate withdrawal requests. If new deposits are not sufficient to cover withdrawal requests, these institutions can experience liquidity problems. To remedy this situation, they can obtain funds through repurchase agreements or borrow funds in the federal funds market. However, these sources of funds will resolve only a short-term deficiency. They will not be appropriate if a longer-term liquidity problem exists.

An alternative way to remedy a problem of insufficient liquidity is to sell assets in exchange for cash. Savings institutions can sell their Treasury securities or even some of their mortgages in the secondary market. Although the sale of assets can boost liquidity, it also reduces the SI's size and possibly its earnings. Therefore, minor liquidity deficiencies are typically resolved by increasing liabilities rather than selling assets.

21-4b Credit Risk

Because mortgages represent the primary asset, they are the main reason for credit risk at SIs. Although Federal Housing Authority (FHA) and Veterans Administration (VA) mortgages originated by SIs are insured against credit risk, conventional mortgages are not. Private insurance can normally be obtained for conventional mortgages, but

SIs often incur the risk themselves rather than pay for the insurance. If they perform adequate credit analysis on their potential borrowers and geographically diversify their mortgage loans, they should be able to maintain a low degree of credit risk. Many SIs took excessive risks when granting or purchasing mortgages in the 2003–2006 period and suffered the consequences during the credit crisis, as explained later in this chapter.

21-4c Interest Rate Risk

Some SIs rely heavily on short-term deposits as sources of funds and use most of their funds to provide fixed-rate mortgages. These SIs are subject to interest rate risk because their liabilities are rate sensitive (cost is sensitive to changes in market interest rates) but their assets are not rate sensitive (revenue is not sensitive to changes in market rates). Thus, the spread between their interest revenue and interest expenses narrows when interest rates increase, which reduces their profitability.

Measurement of Interest Rate Risk SIs commonly measure the gap between their rate-sensitive assets and their rate-sensitive liabilities in order to determine their exposure to interest rate risk. However, the gap measurement is dependent on the criteria used to classify an asset or liability as rate sensitive.

EXAMPLE | Siesta Savings Institution was recently created. It obtains most of its funds from two-year CDs and offers 30-year fixed-rate mortgages. It defines its assets and liabilities as rate sensitive if they are repriced within a year or less. Most of Siesta's liabilities are initially considered to be rate insensitive because their rate will not be affected within the year. Its assets are also considered to be rate insensitive because their rate will not be affected within the year. Thus, Siesta's gap is close to zero because its rate-sensitive assets and liabilities are close to zero, which implies that the institution is not exposed to interest rate risk. Nevertheless, Siesta will be adversely affected by an increase in interest rates because its interest expenses would rise over time while the rate on its mortgage loans is fixed for a long-term period. Thus, the gap measurement is not an accurate indicator of Siesta's exposure to interest rate risk. ●

Given the limitations of the gap measurement, some SIs measure the duration of their respective assets and liabilities to determine the imbalance in sensitivity of interest revenue versus expenses to interest rate movements. An example follows.

EXAMPLE | Tucson Savings Institution (TSI) desires to measure the duration of its assets and liabilities. It first needs to classify each balance sheet component into various maturity categories, as shown in Exhibit 21.6. The rates on most adjustable-rate mortgages are adjusted every year, which is why the amounts under the longer-term categories show zero. The average duration for each asset category is provided below the dollar amount. Some fixed-rate mortgages are classified in the earlier term categories because they are maturing or will be sold soon. The duration of 0.91 for adjustable-rate mortgages is a weighted average of their durations, computed as $0.30(7,000/27,000) + 0.80(15,000/27,000) + 1.9(4,000/27,000)1.9 + 2.9(1,000/27,000)$.

The durations for fixed-rate mortgages and investment securities were computed in a similar manner. The duration for total assets of 2.76 years was computed as a weighted average of the individual assets: $0.91(27,000/61,000) + 5.32(20,000/61,000) + 2.65(14,000/61,000) = 2.76$.

A similar procedure was used to estimate the duration of liabilities. NOW accounts and passbook savings have no specified maturity, but their rate is adjusted less frequently than the rate on MMDAs, which is why MMDAs have a shorter duration. The total liability duration is about 0.45. Tucson Savings Institution's total asset duration is more than six times its liability duration. Thus its future performance is highly exposed to interest rate movements. Its market value would decrease

Exhibit 21.6 Duration Schedule for Tucson Savings Institution (Dollar Amounts Are in Thousands)

ASSETS	LESS THAN 6 MONTHS	6 MONTHS TO 1 YEAR	1–3 YEARS	3–5 YEARS	5–10 YEARS	10–20 YEARS	OVER 20 YEARS	TOTAL
RATE READJUSTMENT PERIOD								
Adjustable-rate mortgages								
Amount ($)	$ 7,000	$15,000	$4,000	$1,000	$ 0	$ 0	$ 0	$27,000
Average duration (yr)	.30	.80	1.90	2.90	0	0	0	.91
Fixed-rate mortgages								
Amount ($)	500	500	1,000	1,000	2,000	10,000	5,000	20,000
Average duration (yr)	.25	.60	1.80	2.60	4.30	5.50	7.60	5.32
Investment securities								
Amount ($)	2,000	3,000	4,000	2,000	1,000	0	2,000	14,000
Average duration (yr)	.20	.70	1.70	3.20	5.30	0	8.05	2.65
Total amount ($)	$ 9,500	$18,500	$9,000	$4,000	$3,000	$10,000	$7,000	$61,000

Asset duration = 2.76

LIABILITIES	LESS THAN 6 MONTHS	6 MONTHS TO 1 YEAR	1–3 YEARS	3–5 YEARS	5–10 YEARS	10–20 YEARS	OVER 20 YEARS	TOTAL
Fixed-maturity deposits								
Amount ($)	$14,000	$ 9,000	$2,000	$1,000	$0	$0	$0	$26,000
Average duration (yr)	.30	.60	1.80	2.80	0	0	0	.62
NOW accounts								
Amount ($)	4,000	0	0	0	0	0	0	4,000
Average duration (yr)	.40	0	0	0	0	0	0	.40
MMDAs								
Amount ($)	15,000	0	0	0	0	0	0	15,000
Average duration (yr)	.20	0	0	0	0	0	0	.20
Passbook accounts								
Amount ($)	13,000	0	0	0	0		0	13,000
Average duration (yr)	.40	0	0	0	0		0	.40
Total amount ($)	$46,000	$ 9,000	$2,000	$1,000	$0	$0	$0	$58,000

Liability duration = .45

substantially in response to an increase in interest rates. TSI can reduce its exposure to interest rate risk by reducing the proportion of its assets in the long-duration categories. ●

Financial institutions use computer programs to estimate their asset and liability duration and apply sensitivity analysis to proposed balance sheet adjustments. For example, TSI could determine how its asset and liability duration would change if it engaged in a promotional effort to issue five-year deposits and used the funds to offer adjustable-rate mortgages.

21-5 MANAGEMENT OF INTEREST RATE RISK

Savings institutions can use a variety of methods to manage their interest rate risk, including the following:

- Adjustable-rate mortgages
- Interest rate futures contracts
- Interest rate swaps

21-5a Adjustable-Rate Mortgages

The interest rates on adjustable-rate mortgages (ARMs) are tied to market-determined rates such as the one-year Treasury bill rate and are periodically adjusted in accordance with the formula stated in the ARM contract. A variety of formulas are used. Adjustable-rate mortgages enable SIs to maintain a more stable spread between interest revenue and interest expenses.

Although ARMs reduce the adverse impact of rising interest rates, they also reduce the favorable impact of declining interest rates. Suppose an SI that obtains most of its funds from short-term deposits uses the funds to provide fixed-rate mortgages. If interest rates decline and the SI does not hedge its exposure to interest rate risk, the spread will increase. If the SI uses ARMs as a hedging strategy, however, the interest on loans will decrease during a period of declining rates, so the spread will not widen.

While ARMs reduce the risks of SIs, they expose consumers to interest rate risk. Although ARMs typically have a maximum cap limiting the increase in interest rates (such as 2 percent per year and 5 percent over the loan life), the impact on household mortgage payments is still significant. Because some homeowners prefer fixed-rate mortgages, most SIs continue to offer them and therefore incur interest rate risk. Thus, additional strategies besides the use of ARMs are necessary to reduce this risk.

21-5b Interest Rate Futures Contracts

An interest rate futures contract allows for the purchase of a specific amount of a particular debt security for a specified price at a future point in time. Sellers of futures contracts are obligated to sell the securities for the contract price at the stated future point in time.

Some SIs use Treasury bond futures contracts because the cash flow characteristics of Treasury bonds resemble those of fixed-rate mortgages. Like mortgages, Treasury bonds offer fixed periodic payments, so their market value moves inversely to interest rate fluctuations. Savings institutions that sell futures contracts on these securities can effectively hedge their fixed-rate mortgages. If interest rates rise, the market value of the securities represented by the futures contract will decrease. The SIs will benefit from the difference between the market value at which they can purchase these securities in the future and the futures price at which they will sell the securities. This can offset the reduced spread between their interest revenue and interest expenses during the period of rising interest rates.

21-5c Interest Rate Swaps

Another strategy for reducing interest rate risk is the interest rate swap, which allows an SI to swap fixed-rate payments (an outflow) for variable-rate payments (an inflow). The fixed-rate outflow payments can be matched against the fixed-rate mortgages held so that a certain spread can be achieved. In addition, the variable-rate inflows due to the swap can be matched against the variable cost of funds. In a rising rate environment, the institution's fixed-rate outflow payments from the swap agreement remain fixed while the variable-rate inflow payments due to the swap increase. This favorable result can partially offset the normally unfavorable impact of rising interest rates on an SI's spread. However, an interest rate swap also reduces the favorable impact of declining interest rates. Inflow interest payments decrease while the outflow interest payments remain the same during a period of declining rates.

21-5d Conclusions about Managing Interest Rate Risk

WEB

www.fdic.gov
Profiles of individual
savings institutions.

Many SIs have used the strategies just described to reduce their interest rate risk. Although these strategies are useful, it is virtually impossible to eliminate the risk completely. One reason for this is the potential prepayment of mortgages. Homeowners often pay off their mortgages before maturity without much advance notice to the SI. Consequently, SIs do not really know the actual maturity of the mortgages they hold and cannot perfectly match the interest rate sensitivity of their assets and liabilities.

21-6 EXPOSURE OF SAVINGS INSTITUTIONS TO CRISES

Savings institutions were devastated by the savings institution crisis during the late 1980s and by the credit crisis in the 2008–2009 period, as explained next.

21-6a Savings Institution Crisis in the Late 1980s

One reason for the crisis of the late 1980s was an increase in interest rates. Those SIs that had provided long-term mortgages were adversely affected because the interest they earned on assets remained constant while the interest they paid on liabilities increased. Consequently, their net interest income declined.

In addition, many SIs had been making commercial loans without much expertise in assessing the ability of firms to repay their loans. Many loan defaults occurred in the Southwest, where economies were devastated by a decline in oil prices. Layoffs in the oil industry resulted, causing a decline in income. Real estate prices dropped so dramatically that when SIs foreclosed on the bad real estate loans, the property that had served as collateral was worth less than the loans. Although some housing loans defaulted, the major loan losses were in commercial real estate, such as office complexes. Some SIs also experienced losses on their investments in junk bonds.

Many SIs experienced a cash flow deficiency as a result of their loan losses, as the inflows from loan repayments were not sufficient to cover depositor withdrawals. Consequently, they were forced to offer higher interest rates on deposits to attract more funds. As depositors became aware of the crisis, they began to withdraw their savings from SIs, which exacerbated the illiquidity problem.

Fraud In addition, many SIs experienced financial problems because of various fraudulent activities. In one of the most common types of fraud, managers used depositors' funds to purchase personal assets, including yachts, artwork, and automobile dealerships. At many SIs, there had clearly been a lack of oversight by executives and by the board of directors, which allowed some managers to serve their own interests rather than shareholder interests. Many of the problems of the SIs could have been reduced if proper governance had been applied.

Provisions of the FIRREA To prevent further failures and restore confidence, the Financial Institutions Reform, Recovery, and Enforcement Act (FIRREA) was enacted in 1989. Among other things, the FIRREA increased penalties for officers of SIs and other financial institutions convicted of fraud, revised the regulation of SIs, and raised the capital requirements for SIs. It also allowed commercial banks to acquire SIs. In addition,

SIs were required to sell off any holdings of junk bonds and prohibited from investing in them in the future.

The Resolution Trust Corporation (RTC) was formed to deal with insolvent SIs. The RTC liquidated the assets of the insolvent SIs and reimbursed depositors or sold the SIs to other financial institutions. By the time the RTC was closed at the end of 1995, it had either liquidated or found a buyer for 747 insolvent SIs. It had also recovered $394 billion from liquidating assets and another $2.4 billion from legal settlements.

Beyond restoring confidence in the SI industry, the FIRREA significantly improved conditions for SIs over the next 15 years. Savings institutions slowly built their capital and sold off risky assets. Nevertheless, many SIs pursued risky strategies again in the 2004–2006 period, which led to high returns when economic conditions were strong, but caused major problems for them during the credit crisis, as described next.

21-6b Credit Crisis of 2008–2009

During the 2003–2006 period of strong economic growth, some SIs used very liberal standards when offering subprime mortgage loans for borrowers who did not qualify for conventional mortgages. They were commonly charging a premium of 3 percentage points or more on subprime mortgage loans over the rate charged on conventional mortgages, along with additional fees at the time the loans were originated.

The interest rates on subprime mortgage loans were commonly fixed for the first two years and were adjusted in line with market interest rates after that. As market interest rates increased in the 2005–2006 period, some subprime mortgage borrowers could not meet their monthly payments. In addition, the supply of new homes continued to rise while the demand for homes suddenly declined, causing a surplus of homes. Furthermore, the economy weakened in the 2008–2009 period, and home prices plummeted. The values of many homes were substantially less than the respective mortgage balances on the homes. Consequently, there were many mortgage foreclosures. By January 2009, about 10 percent of all mortgages were experiencing late payments or were in foreclosure.

Some SIs originated subprime loans and then immediately sold them to institutional investors in the secondary market. These institutions were less exposed to credit risk because they limited their holdings of subprime mortgages. However, the financial firms that focused entirely on subprime mortgages and maintained the mortgages after originating them experienced poor performance in the 2008–2009 period when many borrowers could not cover their mortgage payments. Several subprime lenders went bankrupt. Even the subprime lenders that sold all the mortgages they created were adversely affected by the credit crisis, because once the economy weakened, the level of mortgage originations declined substantially.

Many SIs invested heavily in mortgage-backed securities without recognizing the potential credit risk of these securities. They incurred losses on these investments because of late payments or defaults on the mortgages represented by these securities. Some SIs sold credit default swap contracts on mortgage-backed securities, which required them to cover damages when some mortgage-backed securities held by other financial institutions defaulted.

In general, the adverse effects of the credit crisis in the 2008–2009 period were very similar to the adverse effects during the savings institution crisis in the late 1980s. For both crises, those SIs that used their funds to engage in loans and investments with very high risk suffered major losses once economic conditions weakened.

Notable Failures during the Credit Crisis   The financial problems of SIs were highlighted by several large failures, including Countrywide Financial (the second largest SI), IndyMac (the eighth largest SI), and Washington Mutual (the largest SI). Countrywide Financial used a very aggressive strategy in which it approved subprime mortgage loans of questionable quality. Many of these loans defaulted in 2007. In January 2008, Countrywide Financial was failing and was acquired by Bank of America.

IndyMac suffered major losses on its $32 billion portfolio of mortgages. In July 2008, as rumors circulated about the possible failure of IndyMac, depositors began to withdraw an average of $100 million per day. This created severe liquidity problems for IndyMac, which caused the FDIC to intervene and take it over.

In September 2008, Washington Mutual became the largest depository institution (with assets of $307 billion) ever to fail in the United States. Like IndyMac, Washington Mutual suffered liquidity problems as its depositors were withdrawing funds because of rumors about its financial problems. The main reason for Washington Mutual's failure was its heavy investment in mortgages and mortgage-backed securities. The FDIC seized the assets of Washington Mutual and then sold most of them to JPMorgan Chase. As a result of this acquisition, JPMorgan Chase became the second largest commercial bank in the United States.

21-6c Reform in Response to the Credit Crisis

FINANCIAL REFORM

Following the credit crisis, the Financial Reform Act was implemented in 2010. This act contained numerous provisions that were intended to stabilize the financial system. Those provisions related to savings institutions are summarized here.

Mortgage Origination   The Financial Reform Act requires that savings institutions and other financial institutions granting mortgages verify the income, job status, and credit history of mortgage applicants before approving mortgage applications. This provision is intended to strengthen the standards to obtain a mortgage in order to prevent another credit crisis in the future.

Sales of Mortgage-Backed Securities   The act requires that savings institutions and other financial institutions that sell mortgage-backed securities retain 5 percent of the portfolio unless the portfolio meets specific standards that reflect low risk. This provision forces financial institutions to maintain a stake in the mortgage portfolios that they sell. The act also requires more disclosure regarding the quality of the underlying assets when mortgage-backed securities are sold.

Financial Stability Oversight Council   The Financial Reform Act created the Financial Stability Oversight Council, which is responsible for identifying risks to financial stability in the United States and makes regulatory recommendations to regulators that could reduce systemic risk, whereby the financial problems of savings institutions or other financial institutions spread. The council can recommend methods to ensure that depository institutions do not rely on regulatory bailouts and can recommend rules such as higher capital requirements for savings institutions that are perceived to be too big and complex.

The council consists of ten members, including the Treasury Secretary (who chairs the council) and the heads of the Federal Reserve, Comptroller of the Currency, Federal Deposit Insurance Corporation, National Credit Union Administration (discussed later in the chapter), Securities and Exchange Commission, and Federal Housing Finance Agency.

Orderly Liquidation   The act assigned specific regulators with the authority to determine whether any particular financial institution should be liquidated. This expedites the liquidation process and can limit the losses due to a failing financial institution. Shareholders and unsecured creditors are expected to bear most of the losses of failing financial institutions.

Consumer Financial Protection Bureau   The act established the Consumer Financial Protection Bureau, which is responsible for regulating various consumer finance products and services that are offered by savings institutions and other financial institutions, such as online accounts and credit cards. The bureau can set rules to ensure that savings institutions disclose accurate information about their financial services and to prevent deceptive financial practices.

Trading of Derivative Securities   The act requires that derivative securities be traded through a clearinghouse or exchange, rather than over the counter. This should allow for a more standardized structure regarding margins and collateral and more transparency of prices in the market. Consequently, savings institutions that trade these derivatives should be less susceptible to risk that the counterparty posted insufficient collateral.

21-7 CREDIT UNIONS

Credit unions (CUs) are nonprofit organizations composed of members with a common bond, such as an affiliation with a particular labor union, church, university, or even residential area. Their objective is to serve as an intermediary for those members. Credit unions offer interest on share deposits to members who invest funds. They channel those funds to members who need loans.

Because of their common bond requirement, CUs tend to be much smaller than other depository institutions. There are about 7,800 CUs in the United States. Although the number of CUs now exceeds the number of commercial banks, the total assets of CUs are less than one-tenth the amount of total assets in commercial banks.

21-7a Ownership of Credit Unions

Because CUs do not issue stock, they are technically owned by the depositors. The deposits are called shares, and interest paid on the deposits is called a dividend. Because CUs are nonprofit organizations, their income is not taxed. If CUs accumulate earnings, they can use the earnings either to offer higher rates on deposits or to reduce rates on loans.

Like savings institutions and commercial banks, CUs can be federally or state chartered. If the state does not offer a charter, a federal charter is necessary. Although a few CUs (such as the Navy Federal CU) have assets of more than $1 billion, most are very small. Federally chartered CUs are growing at a faster rate than state-chartered CUs, and their total assets are now significantly larger than the aggregate assets of state-chartered CUs.

21-7b Advantages and Disadvantages of Credit Unions

As mentioned earlier, CUs are nonprofit and therefore are not taxed. This creates a major advantage for CUs over other types of financial institutions. Credit unions can offer higher deposit rates and lower loan rates than their competitors and still achieve a satisfactory level of performance, because their profits are not taxed and they do not have to achieve a desired return for shareholders. In addition, their noninterest expenses are relatively low because their office and furniture are often donated or provided at a very low cost through the affiliation of their members.

Some characteristics of CUs can be unfavorable. Their employees may not have the incentive to manage operations efficiently. In addition, the common bond requirement for membership restricts a given CU from growing beyond the potential size of that particular affiliation. The common bond also limits the ability of CUs to diversify. This is especially true when all members are employees of a particular institution. If that institution lays off a number of workers, many members may simultaneously experience financial problems and withdraw their share deposits or default on their loans. This could cause the CU to become illiquid at a time when more members need loans to survive the layoff.

Even when the common bond does not represent a particular employer, many CUs are unable to diversify geographically because all members live in the same area. Thus, an economic slowdown in this area would have an adverse impact on most members. Furthermore, CUs cannot diversify among various products the way that commercial banks and savings institutions do. They are created to serve the members and therefore concentrate heavily on providing loans to members. Finally, in the event that CUs do need funds, they are unable to issue stock because they are owned by depositors rather than shareholders.

To try to overcome some of these disadvantages as well as to better diversify their services and take greater advantage of economies of scale, CUs increasingly have been merging. Consequently, some CUs now draw their members from a number of employers, organizations, and other affiliations. CUs are also trying to diversify their products by offering traveler's checks, money orders, and life insurance to their members.

21-7c Deposit Insurance for Credit Unions

About 90 percent of CUs are insured by the National Credit Union Share Insurance Fund (NCUSIF), which is administered by the National Credit Union Administration (NCUA). The NCUSIF was created in 1970 without any contributing start-up capital from the U.S. Treasury and Federal Reserve. All federally chartered CUs are required to obtain insurance from the NCUSIF. State-chartered CUs are eligible for NCUSIF insurance only if they meet various guidelines. The maximum insurance per depositor is $250,000. Some states require their CUs to be federally insured; others allow insurance to be offered by alternative insurance agencies.

The CUs typically pay an annual insurance premium of about one-tenth of 1 percent of share deposits. The NCUSIF sets aside a portion of its funds as reserves to cover expenses resulting from CU failures each year. Given the low number of failures, the reserves are normally adequate to cover these expenses.

However, the fund was depleted during the credit crisis because of some credit union failures. A supplemental premium was charged in 2009 and in 2010 to replenish the fund.

21-7d Regulatory Assessment of Credit Unions

Federal CUs are supervised and regulated by the National Credit Union Administration (NCUA), whereas state-chartered CUs are regulated by their respective states. The NCUA employs a staff of examiners to monitor CUs each year. The examiners conduct assessments of all federally chartered CUs as well as any state-chartered CUs applying for federal insurance. Each CU completes a semiannual financial report. From this information, the NCUA examiners derive financial ratios that measure the financial condition of the CU. The ratios are then compared to an industry norm to detect any significant deviations. Then a summary of the CU, called a Financial Performance Report, is completed to identify any potential problems that deserve special attention in the future.

As part of the assessment, the examiners classify each CU into a specific risk category, ranging from Code 1 (low risk) to Code 5 (high risk). This is intended to serve as an early warning system so that CUs that are experiencing problems or are in potential danger can be closely monitored in the future. The criteria used by the NCUA to assess risk are capital adequacy, asset quality, management, earnings, liquidity, and sensitivity to market conditions, the same characteristics used by the FDIC to assess commercial banks and savings institutions.

21-7e Credit Union Sources of Funds

Credit union sources of funds can be classified as deposits, borrowed funds, and capital, as explained next.

Deposits   Credit unions obtain most of their funds from share deposits by members. The typical deposit is similar to a passbook savings account deposit at commercial banks or savings institutions, as it has no specified maturity and is insured up to $250,000. Credit unions also offer share certificates, which provide higher rates than share deposits but require a minimum amount (such as $500) and a specified maturity. The share certificates offered by CUs compete against the retail CDs offered by commercial banks and SIs.

In addition to share deposits and certificates, most CUs also offer checkable accounts called share drafts. These accounts can pay interest and allow an unlimited amount of checks to be written. They normally require a minimum balance to be maintained. Share drafts offered by CUs compete against the NOW accounts and MMDAs offered by commercial banks and SIs.

Borrowed Funds   If a CU needs funds temporarily, it can borrow from other CUs or from the Central Liquidity Facility (CLF). The CLF acts as a lender for CUs to accommodate seasonal funding and specialized needs or to boost the liquidity of troubled CUs.

Capital   Like other depository institutions, CUs maintain capital. Their primary source of capital is retained earnings. In recent years, CUs have boosted their capital, which helps cushion against any future loan losses. Given that CUs tend to use conservative management, their capital ratio is relatively high compared with other depository institutions.

21-7f Credit Union Uses of Funds

Credit unions use the majority of their funds for loans to members. These loans finance automobiles, home improvements, and other personal expenses. They are typically secured and carry maturities of five years or less. Some CUs offer long-term mortgage loans, but many prefer to avoid loans with long maturities. In addition to providing loans, CUs purchase government and agency securities to maintain adequate liquidity. The degree to which CUs can offer various products and services is influenced by the type of charter and by their location.

21-7g Exposure of Credit Unions to Risk

Like other depository institutions, CUs are exposed to liquidity risk, credit risk, and interest rate risk. Their balance sheet structure differs from that of other institutions, however, so their exposure to each type of risk also differs.

Liquidity Risk of Credit Unions   If a CU experiences an unanticipated wave of withdrawals without an offsetting amount of new deposits, it could become illiquid. It can borrow from the Central Liquidity Facility to resolve temporary liquidity problems, but if the shortage of funds is expected to continue, the CU must search for a more permanent cure. Other depository institutions have greater ability to boost deposit levels because they can tap various markets. Because the market for a CU is restricted to those consumers who qualify as members, CUs have less ability to generate additional deposits quickly.

Credit Risk of Credit Unions   Because CUs concentrate on personal loans to their members, their exposure to credit (default) risk is primarily derived from those loans. Most of their loans are secured, which reduces the loss to CUs in the event of default. Poor economic conditions can have a significant impact on loan defaults. Some CUs will perform much better than others because of more favorable economic conditions in their area. However, even during favorable economic periods, CUs with very lenient loan policies could experience losses. A common concern is that CUs may not conduct a thorough credit analysis of loan applicants; the loans provided by CUs are consumer oriented, however, so an elaborate credit analysis generally is not required.

Although CUs are normally viewed as the most conservative of all depository institutions, they also were exposed to adverse effects of the credit crisis that began in 2008. Some CUs suffered large losses due to late payments or defaults on second mortgages and home equity loans that they provided. They also experienced some losses on mortgage-backed securities in which they had invested. Credit unions are restricted from investing in risky securities, but some of the mortgage-backed securities that they purchased were highly rated at the time of purchase. As housing conditions worsened, the demand for securities backed by mortgages declined and the values of mortgage-backed securities declined as well.

Interest Rate Risk of Credit Unions   Loans by CUs to their members typically have short or intermediate maturities, so their asset portfolios are rate sensitive. Because their sources of funds are also generally rate sensitive, movements in interest revenues and interest expenses of CUs are highly correlated. The spread between interest revenues and interest expenses remains somewhat stable over time, regardless of how interest rates change. Thus, CUs tend to have less exposure to interest rate risk than savings institutions.

SUMMARY

- The main sources of funds for SIs are deposits and borrowed funds. The main uses of funds for SIs are mortgages, mortgage-backed securities, and other securities.

- Savings institutions are exposed to credit risk as a result of their heavy concentration in mortgages, mortgage-backed securities, and other securities. They attempt to diversify their investments to reduce credit risk. Savings institutions are highly susceptible to interest rate risk because their asset portfolios are typically less rate sensitive than their liability portfolios to interest rate movements.

- Savings institutions can reduce their interest rate risk by using adjustable-rate mortgages instead of fixed-rate mortgages so that the rate sensitivity of their assets is more similar to that of their liabilities. Alternatively, they can sell interest rate futures contracts, which would generate gains if interest rates increase. Third, they can engage in interest rate swaps in which they swap fixed rates for floating rates, which would generate gains if interest rates rise.

- The valuation of an SI is a function of its expected cash flows and the required return by its investors. The expected cash flows are influenced by economic growth, interest rate movements, regulatory constraints, and the abilities of the institution's managers. The required rate of return is influenced by the prevailing risk-free rate and the risk premium. The risk premium is lower when economic conditions are strong.

- In the late 1980s, many SIs made very risky loans and investments and experienced heavy losses from loan defaults, adverse interest rate movements, and fraud. In the 2004–2006 period, many SIs pursued aggressive mortgage lending strategies, which led to major problems during the credit crisis of 2008–2009.

- Credit unions obtain most of their funds from share deposits by members. They use the majority of their funds for personal loans to members and therefore are exposed to credit risk.

POINT COUNTER-POINT

Can All Savings Institutions Avoid Failure?

Point   Yes. If SIs use conservative management by focusing on adjustable-rate mortgages with limited default risk, they can limit their risk and avoid failure.

Counter-Point   No. Some SIs will be crowded out of the market for high-quality adjustable-rate mort-

gages and will have to take some risk. There are too many SIs, and some that have weaker management will inevitably fail.

Who Is Correct?   Use the Internet to learn more about this issue and then formulate your own opinion.

QUESTIONS AND APPLICATIONS

1.   SI Sources and Uses of Funds Explain in general terms how savings institutions differ from commercial banks with respect to their sources of funds and uses of funds. Discuss each source of funds for SIs. Identify and discuss the main uses of funds for SIs.

2.   Ownership of SIs What are the alternative forms of ownership of a savings institution?

3.   Regulation of SIs What criteria are used by regulators to examine a thrift institution?

4.   MMDAs How did the creation of money market deposit accounts influence the overall cost of funds for a savings institution?

5.   Offering More Diversified Services Discuss the entrance of savings institutions into consumer and commercial lending. What are the potential risks and rewards of this strategy? Discuss the conflict between diversification and specialization of SIs.

6.   Liquidity and Credit Risk Describe the liquidity and credit risk of savings institutions, and discuss how each is managed.

7.   ARMs What is an adjustable-rate mortgage (ARM)? Discuss potential advantages such mortgages offer a savings institution.

8.   Use of Financial Futures Explain how savings institutions could use interest rate futures to reduce interest rate risk.

9.   Use of Interest Rate Swaps Explain how savings institutions could use interest rate swaps to reduce interest rate risk. Will SIs that use swaps perform better or worse than those that were unhedged during a period of declining interest rates? Explain.

10. Risk Explain why many savings institutions experience financial problems at the same time.

11. Hedging Interest Rate Movements If market interest rates are expected to decline over time, will a savings institution with rate-sensitive liabilities and a large amount of fixed-rate mortgages perform best by (a) using an interest rate swap, (b) selling financial futures, or (c) remaining unhedged? Explain.

12. Exposure to Interest Rate Risk The following table discloses the interest rate sensitivity of two savings institutions (dollar amounts are in millions). Based on this information only, which institution's stock price would likely be affected more by a given change in interest rates? Justify your opinion.

	INTEREST SENSITIVITY PERIOD			
	WITHIN 1 YEAR	FROM 1 TO 5 YEARS	FROM 5 TO 10 YEARS	OVER 10 YEARS
Lawrence S&L				
Interest-earning assets	$8,000	$3,000	$7,000	$3,000
Interest-bearing liabilities	11,000	6,000	2,000	1,000
Manhattan S&L				
Interest-earning assets	1,000	1,000	4,000	3,000
Interest-bearing liabilities	2,000	2,000	1,000	1,000

13. SI Crisis What were some of the more obvious reasons for the savings institution crisis of the late 1980s?

14. FIRREA Explain how the Financial Institutions Reform, Recovery, and Enforcement Act (FIRREA) reduced the perceived risk of savings institutions.

15. Background on CUs Who are the owners of credit unions? Explain the tax status of CUs and the reason for that status. Why are CUs typically smaller than commercial banks or savings institutions?

16. Sources of CU Funds Describe the main source of funds for credit unions. Why might the average cost of funds to CUs be relatively stable even when market interest rates are volatile?

17. Regulation of CUs Who regulates credit unions? What are the regulators' powers? Where do CUs obtain deposit insurance?

18. Risk of CUs Explain how credit union exposure to liquidity risk differs from that of other financial institutions. Explain why CUs are more insulated from interest rate risk than some other financial institutions.

19. Advantages and Disadvantages of CUs Identify some advantages of credit unions. Identify disadvantages of CUs that relate to their common bond requirement.

20. Impact of the Credit Crisis Explain how the credit crisis in the 2008–2009 period affected some savings institutions. Compare the causes of the credit crisis to the causes of the SI crisis in the late 1980s.

21. Impact of Interest Rates on an SI Explain why savings institutions may benefit when interest rates fall.

22. Impact of Economic Growth on an SI How does high economic growth affect an SI?

Interpreting Financial News

Interpret the following comments made by Wall Street analysts and portfolio managers.

a. "Deposit insurance can fuel a crisis because it allows weak SIs to grow."

b. "Thrifts are no longer so sensitive to interest rate movements, even if their asset and liability compositions have not changed."

c. "Many SIs did not understand that higher returns from subprime mortgages must be weighed against risk."

Managing in Financial Markets

Hedging Interest Rate Risk As a consultant to Boca Savings & Loan Association, you notice that a large portion of its 15-year, fixed-rate mortgages are financed with funds from short-term deposits. You believe the yield curve is useful in indicating the market's anticipation of future interest rates and that the yield curve is primarily determined by interest rate expectations. At the present time, Boca has not hedged its interest rate risk. Assume that a steeply upward-sloping yield curve currently exists.

a. Boca asks you to assess its exposure to interest rate risk. Describe how Boca will be affected by rising interest rates and by a decline in interest rates.

b. Given the information about the yield curve, would you advise Boca to hedge its exposure to interest rate risk? Explain.

c. Explain why your advice to Boca may possibly backfire.

Flow of Funds Exercise

Market Participation by Savings Institutions

Rimsa Savings is a savings institution that provided Carson Company with a mortgage for its office building. Rimsa recently offered to refinance the mortgage if Carson Company will change to a fixed-rate loan from an adjustable-rate loan.

a. Explain the interaction between Carson Company and Rimsa Savings.

b. Why is Rimsa willing to allow Carson Company to transfer its interest rate risk to Rimsa? (Assume that there is an upward-sloping yield curve.)

c. If Rimsa maintains the mortgage on the office building purchased by Carson Company, who is the ultimate source of the money that was provided for the office building? If Rimsa sells the mortgage in the secondary market to a pension fund, who is the source that is essentially financing the office building? Why would a pension fund be willing to purchase this mortgage in the secondary market?

INTERNET/EXCEL EXERCISES

1. Assess the recent performance of savings institutions using the website www2.fdic.gov/qbp/index.asp. Click on "Quarterly Banking Profile," then on "Savings Institution Section," and summarize the general performance of SIs in the last two years.

2. Retrieve the annual report of Heritage Financial Corporation (ticker symbol is HFWA) or another savings institution of your choice. To access income statement information, go to finance.yahoo.com, enter the ticker symbol, and click on "Get Quotes." Then click on "SEC Filings" (under "Company") to retrieve recent income statements. Review the SI's recent performance. Has its income as a percentage of assets increased since the year before? Explain what caused this change over the last year. Has the SI's net interest margin changed since last year? How has its noninterest income (as a percentage of assets) changed over the last year? How have its noninterest expenses changed over the last year? How have its loan loss reserves changed in the last year? Discuss how the SI's recent strategy and economic conditions may explain the changes in these components of its income statement.

3. Go to finance.yahoo.com, enter the symbol HFWA (Heritage Financial Corporation), and click on "Get Quotes." Then retrieve stock price data at the beginning of the last 20 quarters. Then go to http://research.stlouisfed.org/fred2 and retrieve interest rate data at the beginning of the last 20 quarters for the three-month Treasury bill. Record the data on an Excel spreadsheet. Derive the quarterly return of Heritage Financial. Derive the quarterly change in the interest rate. Apply regression analysis in which the quarterly return of Heritage Financial is the dependent variable and the quarterly change in the interest rate is the independent variable (see Appendix B for more information about using regression analysis). Is there a positive or negative relationship between the interest rate movement and the stock return of Heritage Financial? Is the relationship significant? Offer an explanation for this relationship.

WSJ EXERCISE

Assessing the Performance of Savings Institutions

Using a recent issue of the *Wall Street Journal*, summarize an article that discusses the recent performance of a particular savings institution. Does the article suggest that the SI's performance was better or worse than the norm? What reason is given for the unusual level of performance?

ONLINE ARTICLES WITH REAL-WORLD EXAMPLES

Find a recent practical article available online that describes a real-world example regarding a specific financial institution or financial market that reinforces one or more concepts covered in this chapter.

If your class has an online component, your professor may ask you to post your summary of the article there and provide a link to the article so that other students can access it. If your class is live, your professor may ask you to summarize your application of the article in class. Your professor may assign specific students to complete this assignment or may allow any students to do the assignment on a volunteer basis.

For recent online articles and real-world examples related to this chapter, consider using the following search terms (be sure to include the prevailing year as a search term to ensure that the online articles are recent):

1. [name of a specific savings institution] AND interest income

2. [name of a specific savings institution] AND interest expense

3. [name of a specific savings institution] AND loan loss

4. [name of a specific savings institution] AND credit risk

5. [name of a specific savings institution] AND interest rate risk

6. [name of a specific savings institution] AND earnings

7. [name of a specific savings institution] AND operations

8. savings institution AND income

9. savings institution AND return on assets

10. savings institution AND risk

22

Finance Company Operations

CHAPTER OBJECTIVES

The specific objectives of this chapter are to:

■ describe the main types of finance companies,

■ identify the main sources and uses of finance company funds,

■ describe how finance companies are exposed to various forms of risk,

■ identify the factors that determine the values of finance companies, and

■ explain how finance companies interact with other financial institutions.

Finance companies provide short- and intermediate-term credit to consumers and small businesses. Although other financial institutions provide this service, only finance companies specialize in it. Many finance companies operate with a single office; others have hundreds of offices across the country and even in foreign countries. Consumer finance operations can be conducted by an independent finance company or a unit (subsidiary) of a financial conglomerate.

22-1 TYPES OF FINANCE COMPANIES

Finance companies have more than $1 trillion in assets. In aggregate, the amount of their business is similar to that of savings institutions. Some finance companies are independently owned; others are subsidiaries of financial institutions or other corporations. For example, some very large finance companies are subsidiaries of General Motors, Ford Motor Company, Citigroup, American Express, Capital One, and General Electric.

Finance companies are commonly classified into the different types described below according to the specific services that they offer. Some finance companies could fit in every category because they offer all types of services.

22-1a Consumer Finance Companies

Consumer finance companies provide financing for customers of retail stores or wholesalers. For example, a consumer finance company can sponsor a credit card for a retailer so that the retailer can offer its own credit card for its customers. The customers can purchase products there on credit, which is provided by the finance company.

Many consumer finance companies also provide personal loans directly to individuals to finance purchases of large household items. Some consumer finance companies also provide mortgage loans.

22-1b Business Finance Companies

Business finance companies offer loans to small businesses. For example, they may provide loans to finance inventory. The business uses the loan to purchase materials that are used in the production process. Once the products are manufactured and sold, the business uses the revenue to pay off the loan. Business finance companies also provide financing in the form of credit cards that are used by a business's employees for travel or for making purchases on behalf of the business.

22-1c Captive Finance Subsidiaries

A captive finance subsidiary (CFS) is a wholly owned subsidiary whose primary purpose is to finance sales of the parent company's products and services, provide wholesale financing to distributors of the parent company's products, and purchase receivables of the parent company. The actual business practices of a CFS typically include various types of financing apart from just the parent company business. When a captive is formed, the captive and the parent company draw up an operating agreement containing specific stipulations, such as the type of receivables that qualify for sale to the captive and specific services to be provided by the parent.

The motive for creating a CFS can be easily understood by considering the automobile industry. Historically, automobile manufacturers were unable to finance dealers' inventories and had to demand cash from each dealer. Many dealers were unable to sell cars on an installment basis because they needed cash immediately. Banks were the primary source of capital to dealers. However, banks viewed automobiles as luxury items not suitable for bank financing and were unwilling to buy the installment plans created from automobile sales. For this reason, the automobile manufacturers became involved in financing.

Advantages of Captive Finance Subsidiaries   There are several advantages to maintaining a CFS. A CFS can be used to finance distributor or dealer inventories until a sale occurs, making production less cyclical for the manufacturer. It can serve as an effective marketing tool by providing retail financing. It can also be used to finance products leased to others.

A CFS allows a corporation to clearly separate its manufacturing and retailing activities from its financing activities. Therefore, analysis of each segment of the parent company is less expensive and easier. Also, when lending to a CFS rather than a division of the parent company, the lender does not have to be so concerned about the claims of others. Unlike commercial banks, a CFS has no reserve requirements and no legal prohibitions on how it obtains or uses funds. Furthermore, a firm with a CFS can gain a competitive advantage because sale items such as automobiles and housing may depend on the financing arrangements available.

Captive finance subsidiaries have diversified their financing activities to include more than just the parent company's product installment plans. General Electric Capital Corporation (GECC) has been the most innovative of all the CFSs. Its financing includes industrial and equipment sales, consumer installment credit, and second mortgage loans on private residences.

22-2 Sources and Uses of Funds

Finance companies are distinctly different from commercial banks and savings institutions in that they do not rely heavily on deposits. Their sources and uses of funds are described next.

22-2a Sources of Funds

The main sources of funds for finance companies are:

- Loans from banks
- Commercial paper
- Deposits
- Bonds
- Capital

Loans from Banks   Finance companies commonly borrow from commercial banks and can consistently renew the loans over time. For this reason, bank loans can provide a continual source of funds, although some finance companies use bank loans mainly to accommodate seasonal swings in their business.

Commercial Paper   Although commercial paper is available only for short-term financing, finance companies can continually roll over their issues to create a permanent source of funds. Only the most well-known finance companies have traditionally been able to issue commercial paper to attract funds, because unsecured commercial paper exposes investors to the risk of default. In the past, small or medium-sized finance companies had difficulty placing unsecured commercial paper. In recent years, as secured commercial paper has become popular, more finance companies have access to funds through this market.

The best-known finance companies can issue commercial paper through direct placement, thereby avoiding a transaction fee and lowering their cost of funds. Most companies, however, utilize the services of a commercial paper dealer.

Deposits   Under certain conditions, some states allow finance companies to attract funds by offering customer deposits similar to those of the depository institutions discussed in previous chapters. Although deposits have not been a major source of funds for finance companies, they may become more widely used where legal.

Bonds   Finance companies in need of long-term funds can issue bonds. The decision to issue bonds versus some alternative short-term financing depends on the company's balance sheet structure and its expectations about future interest rates. When the company's assets are less interest rate sensitive than its liabilities and when interest rates are expected to increase, bonds can provide long-term financing at a rate that is completely insulated from rising market rates. If the finance company is confident that interest rates will rise, it might consider using the funds obtained from bonds to offer loans with variable interest rates. When interest rates decline, finance companies may use more long-term debt to lock in the cost of funds over an extended period of time.

Capital   Finance companies can build their capital base by retaining earnings or by issuing stock. Like other financial institutions, finance companies maintain a low level of capital as a percentage of total assets. Several finance companies have engaged in initial public offerings of stock so that they could expand their businesses.

22-2b Uses of Finance Company Funds

WEB

www.nfcc.org
More detailed information about consumer loans.

Finance companies use funds for:

- Consumer loans
- Business loans and leasing
- Real estate loans

Each use of funds is described in turn.

Consumer Loans   Finance companies extend consumer loans in the form of personal loans. One of the most popular types is the automobile loan offered by a finance company that is owned by a car manufacturer. For example, General Motors Acceptance Corporation (GMAC) finances purchases of automobiles built by General Motors. Ford Motor Company and Chrysler also have their own finance companies. Subsidiaries of automobile manufacturers may offer unusually low rates to increase automobile sales.

In addition to offering automobile loans, finance companies offer personal loans for home improvement, mobile homes, and a variety of other personal expenses. Personal loans are often secured by a co-signer or by real property. The maturities on personal loans are typically less than five years.

Finance company loans are subject to ceiling interest rates on the loans provided and to a maximum length on the loan maturity. These regulations are imposed by states, and they vary among the states. Because ceiling rates are now sufficiently above market rates, they normally do not interfere with the rate-setting decisions of finance companies. Finance companies are also subject to state regulations on intrastate business. If a finance company wishes to set up a new branch, it must convince regulators that the branch would serve the needs of the people in that location.

Some finance companies also offer credit card loans through a particular retailer. For example, a retail store may sell products to customers on credit and then sell the credit contract to a finance company. Customers make payments to the finance company under the terms negotiated with the retail store. The finance company is responsible for the initial credit approval and for processing the credit card payments. The retailer can benefit from the finance company's credit allowance through increased sales; the finance company benefits by obtaining increased business. Finance companies increase their customer base in this way and are accessible for additional financing for those customers who prove to be creditworthy. The specific arrangement between a finance company and retailer can vary.

The main competition to finance companies in the consumer loan market comes from commercial banks and credit unions. Finance companies have consistently provided more credit to consumers than credit unions have, but they are a distant second to commercial banks. Savings institutions have recently entered this market and are now also considered a major competitor.

Business Loans and Leasing   In addition to consumer loans, finance companies also provide business (commercial) loans. Companies commonly obtain these loans from the time they purchase raw materials until cash is generated from sales of the finished goods. Such loans are short term but may be renewed, as many companies permanently need financing to support their cash cycle. Business loans are often backed by inventory or accounts receivable.

Some finance companies provide loans to support leveraged buyouts (LBOs). These loans are generally riskier than other business loans but offer a higher expected return.

Finance companies commonly act as factors for accounts receivable; that is, they purchase a firm's receivables at a discount and are responsible for processing and collecting the balances of these accounts. The finance company incurs any losses due to bad debt. Factoring reduces a business's processing costs and also provides short-term financing, as the business receives cash from the finance company earlier than it would have obtained funds from collecting the receivables.

Another way finance companies provide financing is by leasing. They purchase machinery or equipment and then lease it to businesses that prefer to avoid the additional debt on their balance sheet that purchases would require. Avoiding debt can be important to a business that is already close to its debt capacity and is concerned that additional debt will adversely affect its credit rating.

As the economy remained weak over the 2009–2013 period, business demand for loans declined. Thus finance companies reduced their business loans over this period.

Real Estate Loans   Finance companies offer real estate loans in the form of mortgages on commercial real estate and second mortgages on residential real estate. The offering of second mortgages has become increasingly popular over time. These mortgages are typically secured and historically have had a relatively low default rate. In the

Exhibit 22.1 How Finance Companies Finance Economic Growth

2003–2006 period, however, some finance companies offered subprime (low quality) mortgage loans, which resulted in a higher proportion of loan defaults during the credit crisis in 2008. Consequently, many finance companies substantially reduced their real estate loans over the 2009–2013 period.

Summary of Uses of Funds The particular allocation of a finance company's uses of funds depends on whether the company is focused on business or consumer lending. Some finance companies, such as GE Capital, provide all types of services. Exhibit 22.1 summarizes the sources and uses of funds by illustrating how finance companies finance economic growth. They channel funds from institutional investors who purchase the securities they issue to households and small businesses that need funds.

In 2010, the Financial Reform Act established the Consumer Financial Protection Bureau, which is responsible for regulating various consumer finance products and services that may be offered by finance companies and other financial institutions. Perhaps the most important requirement on finance companies is that they ensure proper disclosure of information about their financial services.

22-2c Interaction with Other Financial Institutions

When finance companies obtain or use funds, they interact with other financial institutions, as summarized in Exhibit 22.2. Because of their concentration in consumer lending, finance companies compete with commercial banks, savings institutions, and credit

Exhibit 22.2 Interaction between Finance Companies and Other Financial Institutions

TYPE OF FINANCIAL INSTITUTION	INTERACTION WITH FINANCE COMPANIES
Commercial banks and savings institutions	• Compete with finance companies for consumer loan business (including credit cards), commercial loans, and leasing.
Credit unions	• Compete with finance companies for consumer loan business.
Securities firms	• Underwrite bonds that are issued by finance companies.
Pension funds	• Compete with insurance subsidiaries of finance companies that manage pension plans.
Insurance companies	• Compete directly with insurance subsidiaries of finance companies.

Exhibit 22.3 Participation of Finance Companies in Financial Markets

TYPE OF FINANCIAL MARKET	PARTICIPATION BY FINANCE COMPANIES
Money markets	• Finance companies obtain funds by issuing commercial paper.
Bond markets	• Finance companies issue bonds as a method of obtaining long-term funds. • Subsidiaries of finance companies commonly purchase corporate and Treasury bonds.
Mortgage markets	• Finance companies purchase real estate and also provide loans to real estate investors. • Subsidiaries of finance companies commonly purchase mortgages.
Stock markets	• Finance companies issue stock to establish a capital base. • Subsidiaries of finance companies commonly purchase stocks.
Futures markets	• Subsidiaries of finance companies that offer insurance-related services sometimes use futures contracts to reduce the sensitivity of their bond portfolio to interest rate movements and may also trade stock index futures to reduce the sensitivity of their stock portfolio to stock market movements.
Options markets	• Subsidiaries of finance companies that offer insurance-related services sometimes use options contracts to protect against temporary declines in particular stock holdings.
Swap markets	• Finance companies may engage in interest rate swaps to hedge their exposure to interest rate risk.

unions. However, those finance companies with subsidiaries that specialize in other financial services compete with insurance companies and pension plans.

Finance companies utilize various financial markets to manage their operations, as summarized in Exhibit 22.3. For their core business, finance companies commonly rely on money markets (commercial paper) and bond markets to obtain funds. Furthermore, the insurance subsidiaries of finance companies often utilize bond and stock markets to invest funds. These subsidiaries may also use futures, options, and swap markets to hedge their risk.

22-3 VALUATION OF A FINANCE COMPANY

Finance companies (or consumer finance units that are part of a financial conglomerate) are commonly valued by their managers to monitor progress over time or by other financial institutions that are considering an acquisition. The value of a finance company can be modeled as the present value of its future cash flows. Thus, the value of a finance company should change in response to changes in its expected cash flows in the future and to changes in the required rate of return by investors:

$$\Delta V = f[\underbrace{\Delta E(CF)}_{+}, \underbrace{\Delta k}_{-}]$$

22-3a Factors That Affect Cash Flows

The change in a finance company's expected cash flows may be modeled as

$$\Delta E(CF) = f(\underbrace{\Delta ECON}_{+}, \underbrace{\Delta R_f}_{-}, \underbrace{\Delta INDUS}_{?}, \underbrace{\Delta MANAB}_{+})$$

where ECON represents economic growth, R_f represents the risk-free interest rate, INDUS represents industry conditions (such as regulatory constraints), and MANAB represents the abilities of the finance company's management.

Economic Growth   Economic growth can enhance a finance company's cash flows by increasing household demand for consumer loans, thereby allowing the finance company to provide more loans. In addition, loan defaults are normally reduced in periods of strong growth. The valuation of finance companies can be very sensitive to economic conditions because they commonly offer relatively risky loans; thus, loan repayments are sensitive to economic conditions.

Change in the Risk-Free Interest Rates   A finance company's cash flows may be inversely related to interest rate movements. If the risk-free interest rate decreases, other market rates may also decline and, as a result, there may be stronger demand for the finance company's loans.

Second, finance companies rely heavily on short-term funds, and the rates paid on these funds are typically revised in accordance with other interest rate movements. Finance companies' assets (such as consumer loans) commonly have fixed rates, so interest income does not adjust to interest rate movements until those assets reach maturity. Therefore, when interest rates fall, the finance company's cost of obtaining funds declines more than the decline in the interest earned on its loans and investments. An increase in interest rates could reduce the finance company's expected cash flows because the interest paid on its sources of funds increases while the interest earned on its existing loans and investments does not.

Change in Industry Conditions   Industry conditions include regulatory constraints, technology, and competition within the industry. Some finance companies may be valued higher if state regulators give them the opportunity to generate economies of scale by expanding throughout the state. However, this would result in more competition, causing some finance companies to gain at the expense of others.

Change in Management Abilities   A finance company has control over the composition of its managers and its organizational structure. Its managers attempt to make internal decisions that will capitalize on the external forces (economic growth, interest rates, regulatory constraints) that the institution cannot control. Thus, the management skills of a finance company can influence its expected cash flows. In particular, finance companies need skilled managers to analyze the creditworthiness of potential borrowers and assess how future economic conditions may affect their ability to repay their loans. Finance company managers may also capitalize on technology by advertising to consumers and accepting loan applications over the Internet.

22-3b Factors That Affect the Required Rate of Return

The required rate of return by investors who invest in a finance company can be modeled as

$$\Delta k = f(\underset{+}{\underbrace{\Delta R_f}}, \underset{+}{\underbrace{\Delta RP}})$$

where R_f represents the risk-free interest rate and RP represents the risk premium.

The risk-free interest rate is normally expected to be positively related to inflation, economic growth, and the budget deficit level but inversely related to money supply growth (assuming it does not cause inflation). The risk premium on a finance company is inversely related to economic growth because there is less uncertainty about loan repayments when economic conditions are strong. The risk premium is also inversely

Exhibit 22.4 Framework for Valuing a Finance Company

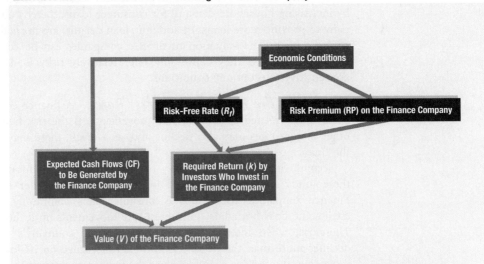

- A stronger economy leads to an increased demand for loans (interest income) and other services provided by the finance company (noninterest income), fewer loan defaults, and better cash flows. The economic conditions are especially important for finance companies because the risk of default on loans tends to be higher for them. A weak economy could result in major loan losses.
- The valuation is also influenced by industry conditions and the finance company's management (not shown in the diagram). These factors affect the risk premium (and therefore the required return by investors) and the expected cash flows to be generated by the finance company.

related to the company's management skills, as more skillful managers may be able to focus on financial services that reduce the finance company's exposure to risk.

Exhibit 22.4 provides a framework for valuing a finance company based on the preceding discussion. In general, the value of a finance company is favorably affected by strong economic growth, a reduction in interest rates, and skilled management. The sensitivity of a finance company's value to these conditions depends on its own characteristics. The higher the risk tolerance reflected in the loans provided by a finance company, the more sensitive its valuation to changes in economic growth (and therefore in the ability of borrowers to repay their loans).

22-4 EXPOSURE OF FINANCE COMPANIES TO RISK

Finance companies, like other financial institutions, are exposed to three types of risk:

- Liquidity risk
- Interest rate risk
- Credit risk

Because finance companies' characteristics differ from those of other financial institutions, their degree of exposure to each type of risk differs as well.

22-4a Liquidity Risk

Finance companies generally do not hold assets that could be easily sold in the secondary market. Thus, if they are in need of funds, they have to borrow. However, their balance sheet structure does not call for much liquidity. Virtually all of their funds are from borrowings rather than deposits. Consequently, they are not susceptible to unexpected deposit withdrawals. Overall, the liquidity risk of finance companies is less than that of other financial institutions.

22-4b Interest Rate Risk

Both liability and asset maturities of finance companies are short or intermediate term. Therefore, they are not as susceptible to increasing interest rates as are savings institutions. Finance companies can still be adversely affected, however, because their assets are typically not as rate sensitive as their liabilities. They can shorten their average asset life or make greater use of adjustable rates if they wish to reduce their interest rate risk.

22-4c Credit Risk

Because the majority of a finance company's funds are allocated as loans to consumers and businesses, credit risk is a major concern. Customers who borrow from finance companies usually exhibit a moderate degree of risk. The loan delinquency rate of finance companies is typically higher than that of other lending financial institutions. However, this higher default level may be more than offset by the higher average rate charged on loans. Because their loans entail both relatively high returns and high risk, the performance of finance companies can be quite sensitive to prevailing economic conditions.

GLOBAL ASPECTS

22-5 MULTINATIONAL FINANCE COMPANIES

Some finance companies are large multinational corporations with subsidiaries in several countries. For example, GE Money provides consumer finance services in 55 countries and serves more than 130 million customers around the world. It provides products and services in local currencies where it does business.

SUMMARY

- Finance companies are classified by type. A consumer finance company provides financing for customers of retail stores or wholesalers, whereas a business finance company offers loans to small businesses. A captive finance subsidiary (CFS) is a wholly owned subsidiary whose primary purpose is to finance sales of the parent company's products and services, provide wholesale financing to distributors of the parent company's products, and purchase receivables of the parent company.

- The main sources of finance company funds are loans from banks, sales of commercial paper, bonds, and capital. The main uses of finance company funds are consumer loans, business loans, leasing, and real estate loans.

- Finance companies are exposed to credit risk as a result of their consumer loans, business loans, and

real estate loans. They are also exposed to liquidity risk because their assets are not very marketable in the secondary market. They may also be exposed to interest rate risk.

- Finance companies are valued at the present value of their expected cash flows. Their valuation is highly dependent on economic conditions because there are more requests for loans by qualified borrowers when economic conditions are favorable. In addition, the amount of loan defaults is normally lower when the economy is strong.

- Finance companies compete with depository institutions (such as commercial banks, savings institutions, and credit unions) that provide loans to consumers and businesses. Many finance companies have insurance subsidiaries that compete directly with other insurance subsidiaries.

POINT COUNTER-POINT

Will Finance Companies Be Replaced by Banks?

Point   Yes. Commercial banks specialize in loans and can provide the services that are provided by finance companies. The two types of financial institutions will eventually merge into one.

Counter-Point   No. Finance companies and commercial banks tend to target different markets for loans. Thus, commercial banks will not replace finance companies because they do not serve the same market.

Who Is Correct?   Use the Internet to learn more about this issue and then formulate your own opinion.

QUESTIONS AND APPLICATIONS

1. Exposure to Interest Rate Risk Is the cost of funds obtained by finance companies very sensitive to market interest rate movements? Explain.

2. Issuance of Commercial Paper How are small and medium-sized finance companies able to issue commercial paper? Why do some well-known finance companies directly place their commercial paper?

3. Finance Company Affiliations Explain why some finance companies are associated with automobile manufacturers. Why do some of these finance companies offer below-market rates on loans?

4. Uses of Funds Describe the major uses of funds by finance companies.

5. Credit Card Services Explain how finance companies benefit from offering consumers a credit card.

6. Leasing Services Explain how finance companies provide financing through leasing.

7. Regulation of Finance Companies Describe the kinds of regulations that are imposed on finance companies.

8. Liquidity Position Explain how the liquidity position of finance companies differs from that of depository institutions such as commercial banks.

9. Exposure to Interest Rate Risk Explain how the interest rate risk of finance companies differs from that of savings institutions.

10. Exposure to Credit Risk Explain how the default risk of finance companies differs from that of other lending financial institutions.

Interpreting Financial News

Interpret the following comments made by Wall Street analysts and portfolio managers.

a. "During a credit crunch, finance companies tend to generate a large amount of business."

b. "Some finance companies took a huge hit as a result of the last recession because they opened their wallets too wide before the recession occurred."

c. "During periods of strong economic growth, finance companies generate unusually high returns without any hint of excessive risk; but their returns are at the mercy of the economy."

Managing in Financial Markets

Managing a Finance Company As a manager of a finance company, you are attempting to increase the spread between the rate earned on your assets and the rate paid on your liabilities.

a. Assume that you expect interest rates to decline over time. Should you issue bonds or commercial paper in order to obtain funds?

b. If you expect interest rates to decline, will you benefit more from providing medium-term, fixed-rate loans to consumers or floating-rate loans to businesses?

c. Why would you still maintain some balance between medium-term, fixed-rate loans and floating-rate loans to businesses even if you anticipate that one type of loan will be more profitable under a cycle of declining interest rates?

FLOW OF FUNDS EXERCISE

How Finance Companies Facilitate the Flow of Funds

Carson Company has sometimes relied on debt financing from Fente Finance Company. Fente has been willing to lend money even when most commercial banks have not. Fente obtains funding from issuing commercial paper and focuses mostly on channeling the funds to borrowers.

a. Explain how finance companies are unique by comparing Fente's net interest income, noninterest income, noninterest expenses, and loan losses to those of commercial banks.

b. Explain why Fente performs better than commercial banks in some periods.

c. Describe the flow of funds channeled through finance companies to firms such as Carson Company. What is the original source of the money that is channeled to firms or households that borrow from finance companies?

INTERNET/EXCEL EXERCISES

1. Go to www.ally.com. Describe the services offered by Ally Commercial Finance.

2. Retrieve the annual report of American International Group (its ticker symbol is AIG), which owns a large consumer finance company, or select your own consumer finance company. To access income statement information, go to finance.yahoo.com, enter the ticker symbol, and click on "Get Quotes." Then click on "SEC Filings."

Review the consumer finance company's recent performance. Has its income as a percentage of assets increased since the year before? Explain what caused this change over the last year. How have its operating expenses changed over the last year? Discuss how the finance company's recent strategy and economic conditions may explain the changes in these components of its income statement.

WSJ EXERCISE

Finance Company Performance

Using a recent issue of the *Wall Street Journal*, summarize an article that discussed the recent performance of a particular finance company. Does the article suggest that the finance company's performance was better or worse than the norm? What was the reason for the unusual level of performance?

ONLINE ARTICLES WITH REAL-WORLD EXAMPLES

Find a recent practical article available online that describes a real-world example regarding a specific financial institution or financial market that reinforces one or more concepts covered in this chapter.

If your class has an online component, your professor may ask you to post your summary of the article there and provide a link to the article so that other students can access it. If your class is live, your professor may ask you to summarize your application of the article in class. Your professor may assign specific students to complete this assignment or may allow any students to do the assignment on a volunteer basis.

For recent online articles and real-world examples related to this chapter, consider using the following search terms (be sure to include the prevailing year as a search term to ensure that the online articles are recent):

1. [name of a specific finance company] AND earnings

2. [name of a specific finance company] AND loans

3. [name of a specific finance company] AND risk

4. [name of a specific finance company] AND net income

5. [name of a specific finance company] AND competition

6. [name of a specific finance company] AND operations

7. [name of a specific finance company] AND return on equity

8. finance company AND income

9. finance company AND return on assets

10. finance company AND risk

23
Mutual Fund Operations

CHAPTER OBJECTIVES

The specific objectives of this chapter are to:

■ provide a background on mutual funds,

■ describe the various types of stock and bond mutual funds,

■ describe the performance of mutual funds,

■ describe key characteristics of money market funds, and

■ describe other types of funds.

WEB

www.bloomberg.com
Information on mutual fund performance.

A **mutual fund** is an investment company that sells shares and uses the proceeds to manage a portfolio of securities. Mutual funds have grown substantially in recent years, and they serve as major suppliers of funds in financial markets.

23-1 BACKGROUND ON MUTUAL FUNDS

Mutual funds serve as a key financial intermediary. They sell shares to individual investors and invest the money they receive in a portfolio of securities for the investors. They accommodate financing needs of corporations by purchasing newly issued stocks and corporate bonds in the primary market. They also accommodate the financing needs of the Treasury and municipal governments by purchasing newly issued Treasury and municipal bonds in the primary market. Their function as an intermediary is shown in Exhibit 23.1. They also frequently purchase securities in the secondary market.

Mutual funds also provide an important service for individual investors who wish to invest funds. Small investors are unable to diversify their investments because of their limited funds. A mutual fund may have holdings of 50 or more securities and yet require a minimum investment of only $250 to $2,500. Thus, small investors can invest in a diversified portfolio with a small investment. Investors who purchase shares of the mutual fund rely on the fund's portfolio managers to make the investment decisions.

Some investment companies such as Fidelity and Vanguard offer a family (collection) of many different mutual funds so that they can accommodate the diverse preferences of investors. Investors can normally transfer money from one mutual fund to another within the same family by making a phone call or requesting the transfer on their online account.

Mutual funds are sometimes referred to as **open-end funds** because they are open to investors, meaning that they will sell shares to investors at any time. In addition, they allow investors to sell (redeem) the shares back to the fund at any time. Thus the number of shares of an open-end fund is always changing. Mutual funds also offer various services, such as 24-hour telephone or Internet access to account information, money transfers between different funds operated by the same firm, consolidated account statements, check-writing privileges on some types of funds, and tax information. The three largest open-end mutual funds are Vanguard, Fidelity, and American Funds. In aggregate, they have more than $1.7 trillion in mutual fund assets.

Mutual funds have grown at a rapid pace over time, as is illustrated in Exhibit 23.2. Today there are more than 7,500 different mutual funds, with total assets of about $12 trillion. The value of mutual fund assets more than doubled between 1993 and 2010.

Exhibit 23.1   How Mutual Funds Finance Economic Growth

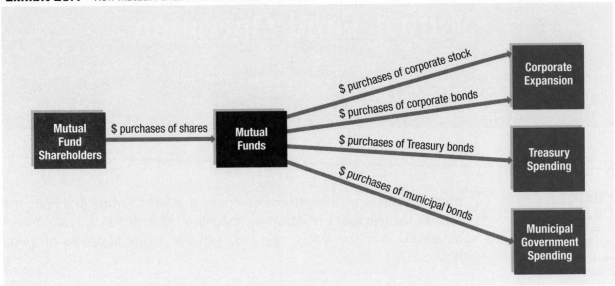

Exhibit 23.2   Growth in Mutual Funds

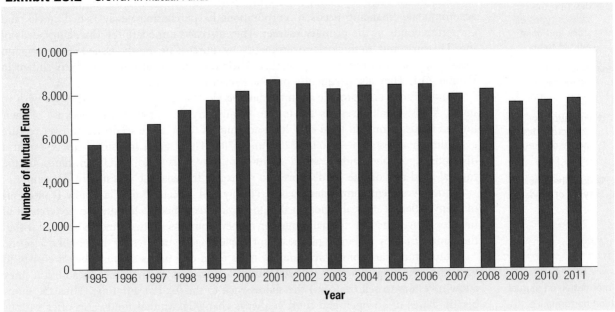

Note: The numbers shown here include money market funds.
Source: *Investment Company Institute.*

23-1a Pricing Shares of the Mutual Fund

The price per share of a mutual fund is equal to the **net asset value (NAV)** per share, which represents the value of the portfolio (per share) after accounting for expenses incurred from managing the fund. Specifically, the net asset value is estimated at the end of each day by first determining the market value of all securities that constitute the mutual fund (any cash is also accounted for). Any interest or dividends accrued in the mutual fund are added to the market value. Then any expenses are subtracted, and the amount is divided by the number of shares of the fund outstanding.

EXAMPLE

Newark Mutual Fund has 20 million shares issued to its investors. It used the proceeds to buy stock of 55 different firms. A partial list of its stock holdings is as follows:

NAME OF STOCK	NUMBER OF SHARES	PREVAILING SHARE PRICE	MARKET VALUE
Aztec Co.	10,000	$40	$ 400,000
Caldero, Inc.	20,000	30	600,000
⋮	⋮	⋮	⋮
Zurkin, Inc.	8,000	70	560,000
Total market value of shares today			$500,020,000
+ Interest and dividends received today			+10,000
− Expenses incurred today			−30,000
= Market value of fund			$500,000,000

Net asset value = Market value of fund ÷ number of shares
= $500,000,000 ÷ 20,000,000
= $25 per share ●

When a mutual fund pays its shareholders dividends, its NAV declines by the per share amount of the dividend payout. The NAV per share of a mutual fund represents the price at which investors can purchase shares or can sell shares back to the mutual fund.

23-1b Mutual Fund Distributions to Shareholders

Mutual funds can generate returns to their shareholders in three ways. First, they can pass on any earned income (from dividends or coupon payments) as dividend payments to the shareholders. Second, they distribute the capital gains resulting from the sale of securities within the fund. A third type of return to shareholders is through mutual fund share price appreciation. As the market value of a fund's security holdings increases, the fund's NAV increases, and the shareholders benefit when they sell their mutual fund shares.

23-1c Regulation of Mutual Funds

Mutual funds must adhere to a variety of federal regulations. They must register with the Securities and Exchange Commission (SEC) and provide interested investors with a prospectus that discloses details about the components of the fund and the risks involved. Mutual funds are also regulated by state laws, many of which attempt to ensure that investors fully understand the risks.

If a mutual fund distributes at least 90 percent of its taxable income to shareholders, it is exempt from taxes on dividends, interest, and capital gains distributed to shareholders. The shareholders are subject to taxation on these forms of income.

USING THE WALL STREET JOURNAL

Mutual Fund Quotations

The *Wall Street Journal* provides price quotations for some open-end mutual funds, as shown here. The fund family is listed, with various funds in the family shown below the family name. For each fund, the net asset value (NAV) is disclosed, along with the return generated by the fund over the year to date (YTD %Ret).

Source: Reprinted with permission of the *Wall Street Journal*, Copyright © 2013 Dow Jones & Company, Inc. All Rights Reserved Worldwide.

Mutual Funds | WSJ.com/fundresearch

Explanatory Notes

Data provided by LIPPER

Top 250 mutual-funds listings for Nasdaq-published share classes with net assets of at least $500 million each. **NAV** is net asset value. Percentage performance figures are total returns, assuming reinvestment of all distributions and after subtracting annual expenses. Figures don't reflect sales charges ("loads") or redemption fees. **NET CHG** is change in NAV from previous trading day. **YTD%RET** is year-to-date return. **3-YR%RET** is trailing three-year return annualized.

e-Ex-distribution. **f**-Previous day's quotation. **g**-Footnotes x and s apply. **J**-Footnotes e and s apply. **k**-Recalculated by Lipper, using updated data. **p**-Distribution costs apply, 12b-1. **r**-Redemption charge may apply. **s**-Stock split or dividend. **t**-Footnotes p and r apply. **v**-Footnotes x and e apply. **x**-Ex-dividend. **z**-Footnote x, e and s apply. **NA**-Not available due to incomplete price, performance or cost data. **NE**-Not released by Lipper; data under review. **NN**-Fund not tracked. **NS**-Fund didn't exist at start of period.

Wednesday, February 27, 2013

Fund	NAV	Net Chg	YTD %Ret
A			
American Funds Cl A			
AmcpA p	23.04	+0.28	6.2
AMutlA p	30.14	+0.36	6.3
BalA p	21.29	+0.22	4.4
BondA p	12.88	-0.01	-0.2
CapIBA p	54.21	+0.37	2.7
CapWA p	20.93	+0.04	-1.3
CapWGrA p	38.60	+0.40	3.8
EupacA p	42.12	+0.38	2.2
FdInvA p	43.03	+0.56	5.5
GwthA p	36.12	+0.45	5.2
HI TrA p	11.44	+0.01	1.7
ICAA p	31.78	+0.37	5.4
IncoA p	18.75	+0.16	3.8
IntBdA p	13.71	...	-0.1
N PerA p	32.61	+0.38	4.3
NwWrldA	55.14	+0.40	1.2
SmCpA p	42.37	+0.44	6.2
TxExA p	13.21	+0.01	0.9
WshA p	33.05	+0.46	5.9
Artisan Funds			
Intl Inv	25.56	+0.35	3.9
MidCapVal inv	22.96	+0.27	10.4
B			
BlackRock Funds A			
EqtyDivd p	20.97	+0.25	5.4
GblAlloc p	20.26	+0.13	2.6
BlackRock Funds C			
GblAlloc t	18.85	+0.13	2.6
BlackRock Funds Inst			
EqtyDivd	21.02	+0.25	5.5
GblAlloc	20.36	+0.13	2.7
C D			
Columbia Class Z			
AcornZ	32.33	+0.41	6.2
Davis Funds A			
NYVen A	37.45	+0.45	7.7
Dimensional Fds			
5GlbFxdInc	11.17	+0.01	0.2
EmgMktVa	29.87	+0.31	0.1
EmMktCorEq	20.45	+0.20	0.2
Fixd	10.33	...	0.1
IntlCoreEq	11.02	+0.12	3.4
IntSmCo	16.64	+0.15	4.5
IntSmVa	16.90	+0.18	5.8
US CoreEq2	13.11	+0.18	7.6
US SmCpVal	28.42	+0.32	8.4
USLgVa	24.85	+0.39	8.5
Dodge & Cox			
Balanced	82.45	+0.80	5.6
Income	13.90	-0.01	0.3
Intl Stk	35.73	+0.45	3.1
Stock	130.85	+1.76	7.3
DoubleLine Funds			
TotRetBdI	NA	...	NA
TotRetBdN	NA	...	NA
F			
Fairholme	32.94	+0.29	4.8
Fidelity Advisor A			
NwInsghtA p	23.92	+0.31	5.1
Fidelity Advisor I			
NwInsghtI	24.22	+0.31	5.2
Fidelity Freedom			
FF2015	12.08	+0.06	2.3
FF2020	14.68	+0.08	2.6
FF2025	12.32	+0.09	3.1
FF2030	14.70	+0.11	3.3
FF2040	8.57	+0.08	3.8
FreedomK2015	13.26	+0.07	2.3
FreedomK2020	13.74	+0.08	2.6
FreedomK2025	14.00	+0.10	3.1
FreedomK2030	14.17	+0.10	3.3
FreedomK2035	14.39	+0.13	3.7
FreedomK2040	14.44	+0.13	3.8
Fidelity Invest			
AMgr50%	16.89	+0.10	2.7
Balanc	20.92	+0.18	3.7
BluCh	51.85	+0.70	5.7
Contra	80.91	+1.04	5.3
ContraK	80.86	+1.04	5.3

Fund	NAV	Net Chg	YTD %Ret
CpInc r	9.61	+0.02	2.0
DivIntl	30.54	+0.28	2.0
DivIntlK r	30.49	+0.28	2.0
GNMA	11.70	...	-0.1
GroCo	97.13	+1.39	4.2
GrowCoK	97.03	+1.38	4.2
IntlDisc	34.01	+0.36	2.8
InvGrBd	11.53	-0.01	-0.2
LowP r	41.60	+0.43	5.3
LowPriStkK r	41.57	+0.43	5.3
MagIn	77.51	+1.18	5.8
MuniInc	13.58	...	0.6
NewMkt r	17.40	+0.01	-0.9
Purltn	20.15	+0.18	3.8
SrsInvGrdF	11.53	-0.01	-0.2
STBF	8.60	...	0.1
StratInc	11.30	+0.01	...
TotalBond	10.91	...	...
Fidelity Spartan			
500IdxInv	53.86	+0.69	6.7
500IndInst	53.87	+0.69	6.7
Fidelity Spartan Adv			
500IdxAd	53.87	+0.69	6.7
TotMktAd r	44.08	+0.57	6.9
First Eagle Funds			
GlbA	49.69	+0.18	2.3
FMI Funds			
LgCap	18.37	+0.22	7.4
FPA Funds			
FPACres	29.52	+0.22	4.9
FrankTemp/Frank Adv			
IncomeAdv	2.27	+0.02	2.8
FrankTemp/Franklin A			
CA TF A p	7.56	...	0.9
Fed TF A p	12.77	...	0.5
HY TF A p	10.97	...	0.9
IncomeA p	2.28	+0.01	2.8
US Gov A p	6.76	...	-0.3
FrankTemp/Franklin C			
Income C t	2.31	+0.02	3.1
FrankTemp/Temp A			
GlBond A p	13.43	+0.04	1.0
Growth A p	20.23	+0.21	4.1
FrankTemp/Temp Adv			
GlBondAdv p	13.38	+0.03	0.9
FrankTemp/Temp B&C			
GlBond C p	13.45	+0.03	0.8
G			
GMO Trust Class III			
Quality	23.80	+0.18	6.5
GMO Trust Class IV			
IntlIntrVal	21.19	+0.28	1.3
H			
Harbor Funds			
Bond	12.51	...	0.2
CapApInst	44.11	+0.65	3.7
IntlInst r	63.42	+0.63	2.1
Hartford HLS Fds IA			
CapApp	46.48	+0.68	7.2
I			
Invesco Funds A			
EqIncA	9.76	+0.10	6.2
Ivy Funds			
AssetStrA p	26.86	+0.35	3.8
AssetStrC t	26.17	+0.34	3.7
AssetStr I r	27.07	+0.36	3.8
J			
John Hancock Class 1			
LSBalncd	13.99	+0.11	3.2
LSGwth	14.04	+0.13	4.2
JPMorgan Select Cls			
CoreBond	12.03	...	...
HighYld	8.23	+0.01	1.6
ShtDurBnd	10.99	...	0.1
L			
Lazard Instl			
EmgMkt	19.73	+0.18	1.0
Longleaf Partners			
Partners	28.59	+0.34	8.3

Fund	NAV	Net Chg	YTD %Ret
Loomis Sayles Fds			
LSBondI	15.18	+0.04	1.1
LSBondR p	15.12	+0.04	1.1
Lord Abbett A			
ShtDurIncmA p	4.64	...	0.4
Lord Abbett C			
ShtDurIncmC t	4.67	...	0.3
Lord Abbett F			
ShtDurIncm	4.64	...	0.6
M			
Manning & Napier Fds			
WldOppA	8.09	+0.08	4.4
Metropolitan West			
TotRetBd	10.91	...	0.5
TotRetBdI	10.90	-0.01	0.6
MFS Funds Class A			
ValueA p	27.35	+0.33	7.9
MFS Funds I			
ValueI	27.48	+0.33	7.9
Mutual Series			
GlbDiscA	29.80	+0.25	5.4
GlbDiscZ	30.21	+0.26	5.5
SharesZ	23.84	+0.23	6.0
N O			
Natixis Funds			
InvGradeBdY	12.63	+0.01	0.4
Oakmark Funds Cl I			
EqtyInc	29.52	+0.30	3.6
Oakmark	51.70	+0.68	6.5
OakmrkInt r	22.00	+0.14	5.1
Old Westbury Fds			
GlbOpp	7.78	+0.03	2.9
Oppenheimer A			
DevMktA	35.66	+0.25	1.0
GlobIA p	68.00	+0.82	5.4
Oppenheimer Y			
DevMktY	35.25	+0.24	1.1
OppenheimerRochester			
RoMu A p	17.27	+0.02	2.5
P			
Perm Port Funds			
Permanent	48.66	+0.05	...
PIMCO Fds Admin			
TotRtAd p	11.22	...	0.1
PIMCO Fds Instl			
AllAsset	12.68	+0.04	0.8
AllAssetAuth r	11.07	-0.01	-0.2
CommodtyRR	6.54	-0.01	-1.5
HiYld	9.67	+0.01	1.3
LowDur	10.49	...	0.1
RealRtnI	12.19	+0.01	-0.5
ShortT	9.89	...	0.3
TotRt	11.22	...	0.2
PIMCO Funds A			
TotRetA	11.22	...	0.1
PIMCO Funds C			
TotRetIncC	11.22	...	...
PIMCO Funds D			
TRtn	11.22	...	0.1
PIMCO Funds P			
TotRtP	11.22	...	0.2
Price Funds			
BlChip	48.08	+0.74	5.4
CapApp	23.35	+0.19	4.9
EmMktS	33.53	+0.28	-1.6
EqInc	28.36	+0.39	7.2
EqIndex	40.96	+0.53	6.7
Growth	39.57	+0.59	4.7
HiYield	7.06	+0.01	2.2
IntlStk	14.72	+0.16	2.2
MCapGro	60.71	+0.96	7.5
MCapVal	25.85	+0.29	7.5
N Horiz	36.17	+0.52	9.0
N Inc	9.80	...	-0.1
R2015	13.28	+0.11	3.1
R2020	18.50	+0.16	3.5
R2025	13.63	+0.14	3.9
R2030	19.71	+0.21	4.2
R2040	19.96	+0.24	4.6
SmCapStk	36.81	+0.54	8.2
SmCapVal	41.79	+0.49	6.7
SpecInc	13.04	+0.03	0.8
Value	28.56	+0.46	8.3
S			
Schwab Funds			
S&P Sel	23.67	+0.30	6.7
Scout Funds			
Intl	33.76	+0.31	1.2
T			
Thornburg Fds			
IntVal I	28.51	+0.12	1.5
V			
VANGUARD ADMIRAL			
500Adml	140.16	+1.79	6.7

Information Contained in a Prospectus Mutual funds are required to provide a prospectus with information about their objectives, management, and risk. Specifically, the prospectus is required to disclose the following information:

1. The minimum amount of investment required
2. The investment objective of the mutual fund
3. The return on the fund over the past year, the past three years, and the past five years, in comparison to a broad market index
4. The exposure of the mutual fund to various types of risk
5. The services (such as check writing, ability to transfer money by telephone, etc.) offered by the mutual fund
6. The fees incurred by the mutual fund (such as management fees) that are passed on to the investors
7. Names of their portfolio managers and the length of time that they have been employed by the fund in that position

23-1d Management of Mutual Funds

Each mutual fund is managed by one or more portfolio managers, who must focus on the stated investment objective of that fund. These managers tend to purchase stocks in large blocks. They prefer liquid securities that can easily be sold in the secondary market at any time. Because open-end mutual funds allow shareholders to buy shares at any time, their managers stand ready to channel any new cash inflows from investors into new investments. They may maintain a small amount of cash for liquidity purposes. If there are more redemptions than sales of shares at a given point in time, the managers can use the cash to cover the redemptions. If the cash is not sufficient to cover the redemptions, they sell some of their holdings of securities to obtain the cash they need.

Interaction of Mutual Funds with Other Financial Institutions The managing of a mutual fund sometimes leads to interaction with other financial institutions, as described in Exhibit 23.3. Mutual funds sometimes purchase newly issued stocks or

Exhibit 23.3 Interaction between Mutual Funds and Other Financial Institutions

TYPE OF FINANCIAL INSTITUTION	INTERACTION WITH MUTUAL FUNDS
Commercial banks and savings institutions (SIs)	• Money market mutual funds invest in certificates of deposit at banks and SIs and in commercial paper issued by bank holding companies. • Some commercial banks (such as Citigroup and JPMorgan Chase) have investment company subsidiaries that offer mutual funds. • Some stock and bond mutual funds invest in securities issued by banks and SIs.
Finance companies	• Some money market mutual funds invest in commercial paper issued by finance companies. • Some stock and bond mutual funds invest in stocks and bonds issued by finance companies.
Securities firms	• Mutual funds hire securities firms to execute security transactions for them. • Some mutual funds own a discount brokerage subsidiary that competes with other securities firms for brokerage services
Insurance companies	• Some stock mutual funds invest in stocks issued by insurance companies. • Some insurance companies (such as Kemper) have investment company subsidiaries that offer mutual funds. • Some insurance companies invest in mutual funds.
Pension funds	• Pension fund portfolio managers invest in mutual funds.

Exhibit 23.4 How Mutual Funds Utilize Financial Markets

TYPE OF MARKET	HOW MUTUAL FUNDS USE THAT MARKET
Money markets	• Money market mutual funds invest in various money market instruments, such as Treasury bills, commercial paper, banker's acceptances, and certificates of deposit.
Bond markets	• Some bond mutual funds invest mostly in bonds issued by the U.S. Treasury or a government agency. Others invest in bonds issued by municipalities or firms. • Foreign bonds are sometimes included in a bond mutual fund portfolio.
Mortgage markets	• Some bond mutual funds invest in bonds issued by the Government National Mortgage Association (GNMA, or "Ginnie Mae"), which uses the proceeds to purchase mortgages that were originated by some financial institutions.
Stock markets	• Numerous stock mutual funds purchase stocks with various degrees of risk and potential return.
Futures markets	• Some bond mutual funds periodically attempt to hedge against interest rate risk by taking positions in interest rate futures contracts.
Options markets	• Some stock mutual funds periodically hedge specific stocks by taking positions in stock options. • Some mutual funds take positions in stock options for speculative purposes.
Swap markets	• Some bond mutual funds engage in interest rate swaps to hedge interest rate risk.

bonds by financial institutions and therefore are partially financing the expansion of those institutions. Some mutual funds are owned by commercial banks, in which case bank customers can periodically switch their savings between bank deposits and mutual funds.

Mutual Fund Use of Financial Markets   Each type of mutual fund uses one or more financial markets to manage its portfolio, as described in Exhibit 23.4. Because mutual funds are focused on investing in securities, they frequently participate in securities markets. They also participate in futures and options markets to hedge against interest rate risk or the risk of adverse stock market conditions. Some mutual funds take speculative positions in futures or options contracts.

23-1e Expenses Incurred by Mutual Fund Shareholders

Mutual funds pass on their expenses to their shareholders. The expenses include compensation to the portfolio managers and other employees, research support, record-keeping and clerical fees, and marketing fees. Some mutual funds have recently increased their focus on marketing, but marketing does not necessarily enable a mutual fund to achieve high performance relative to the market or other mutual funds. In fact, marketing expenses increase the expenses that are passed on to the mutual fund's shareholders.

Expenses can be compared among mutual funds by measuring the expense ratio, which is equal to the annual expenses per share divided by the fund's NAV. An expense ratio of 2 percent in a given year means that shareholders incur annual expenses reflecting 2 percent of the value of the fund. Many mutual funds have an expense ratio between 0.6 and 1.5 percent. The average expense ratio among actively managed open-end mutual funds is about .93 percent. A high expense ratio can have a major impact on the returns generated by a mutual fund for its shareholders over time.

EXAMPLE   Consider two mutual funds, each of which generates a return on its portfolio of 9.2 percent per year, ignoring expenses. One mutual fund has an expense ratio of 3.2 percent, so its actual return to shareholders is 6 percent per year. The other mutual fund has an expense ratio of 0.2 percent per year (some mutual funds have expense ratios at this level), so its actual return to shareholders

Exhibit 23.5 How the Accumulated Value Can Be Affected by Expenses (Assume Initial Investment of $10,000 and a Return before Expenses of 9.2 Percent)

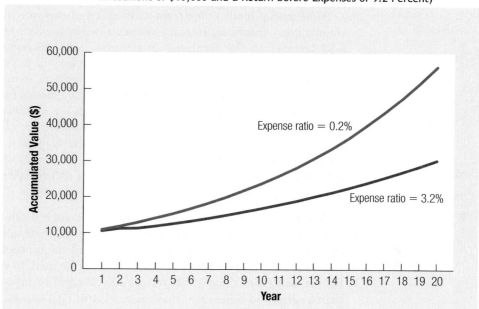

is 9 percent per year. Assume you have $10,000 to invest. Exhibit 23.5 compares the accumulated value of your shares in the two mutual funds over time. After five years, the value of the mutual fund with the low expense ratio is about 20 percent higher than the value of the mutual fund with the high expense ratio. After 10 years, its value is about 40 percent more than the value of the mutual fund with the high expense ratio. After 20 years, its value is about 87 percent more. Even though both mutual funds had the same return on investment when ignoring expenses, the returns to shareholders after expenses are very different because of the difference in expenses charged. ●

Thus, the higher the expense ratio, the lower the return for a given level of portfolio performance. Mutual funds with lower expense ratios tend to outperform others that have a similar investment objective. That is, funds with higher expenses are generally unable to generate higher returns that could offset those expenses. Since expenses can vary substantially among mutual funds, investors should review the annual expenses of any fund before making an investment.

Sales Charge   Mutual funds may be referred to as either as a **load fund** or a **no-load fund**. Load funds are promoted by registered representatives of brokerage firms, who earn a sales charge upon the investment in the fund (commonly referred to as a front-end load) ranging between 3 and 8.5 percent. No-load funds are promoted strictly by the mutual fund of concern, thereby avoiding an intermediary.

EXAMPLE

If you invest $10,000 in a load fund and are charged 6 percent, you incur a sales charge of $600 (0.06 × 10,000), so your actual investment in the load fund is $9,400. In other words, on the day you invest in the fund, the value of your holdings is 6 percent less than the amount of funds you initially had available to invest. In contrast, if you invest $10,000 in a no-load fund, you do not incur a sales charge and so your actual investment in the fund is $10,000. ●

Some investors may feel that a sales charge is worthwhile because the brokerage firm helps determine the type of fund that is appropriate for them. Other investors who feel capable of making their own investment decisions often prefer to invest in no-load funds.

Some mutual funds with a front-end load often may offer the following types of discounts. Break points are basically volume discounts, which means that the percentage load becomes smaller for larger investments. Such discounts often start at $25,000. Many funds waive their loads entirely for investments of more than $1 million. A right of accumulation is a discount based on the total amount of money invested in the fund family (as opposed to just the individual fund). Some mutual funds have a **back-end load** (also known as a rear load or reverse load), which is a withdrawal fee charged when you withdraw money from the mutual fund. Back-end loads are often between 5 and 6 percent for the first year but decline by a certain percentage each subsequent year. Mutual funds with a back-end load may permit investors to withdraw dividends and capital gains at any time without a charge or may allow a specified proportion of the investment to be withdrawn each year without incurring a load.

12b-1 Fees   Some mutual funds charge shareholders a 12b-l fee (in reference to SEC rule 12b-l) as part of the fund's annual expenses to cover administrative or marketing expenses. In some cases, mutual funds have used the proceeds from 12b-l fees to pay commissions to brokers whose clients invested in the fund. In essence, the fee substituted for the load (sales charge) that was directly charged to investors in load funds. Some shareholders who believe that they are not incurring a cost on a no-load fund do pay a commission indirectly through the 12b-l fees. These fees are controversial because many mutual funds do not clarify how they use the money received from the fees.

23-1f Governance of Mutual Funds

A mutual fund is usually run by an investment company whose owners are different from the shareholders in the mutual funds. In fact, some managers employed by mutual funds invest their money in the investment company rather than in the mutual funds that they manage. Thus the investment company may have an incentive to charge high fees to the shareholders of the mutual fund. The expenses charged to the fund represent income generated by the investment company. Although valid expenses are incurred in running a mutual fund, the expenses charged by some investment companies may be excessive. Many mutual funds have grown substantially over time and should be able to capitalize on economies of scale. Yet their expense ratios have generally increased over time. Competition is expected to ensure that mutual funds will charge shareholders only reasonable expenses, but many investors are not aware of the expenses that they are charged.

Mutual funds, like corporations, are subject to some forms of governance that are intended to ensure that the managers are serving the shareholders. Each mutual fund has a board of directors that is supposed to represent the fund's shareholders. The effectiveness of the boards is questionable, however. The SEC requires that a majority of the directors of a mutual fund board be independent (not employed by the fund). However, an employee of the company can retire and qualify as an independent board member just two years later. In addition, the average annual compensation paid to the board members of large mutual funds exceeds $100,000. Thus, some board members may be willing to avoid confrontation with management if doing so enables them to keep their positions. Another problem is that board members of a mutual fund family commonly oversee all funds in the entire family. Consequently, they may concentrate on general issues that are not particular to any one fund and spend a relatively small amount of time on any individual fund within the family.

Mutual funds also have a compliance officer who is supposed to ensure that the fund's operations are in line with its objective and guidelines. Until recently, however, some compliance officers reported to the investment company instead of the mutual fund's board of directors.

Governance of Corporations by Mutual Funds Regardless of whether mutual funds monitor their own management effectively, they have the power to monitor the management of the firms in which they invest. Since mutual funds invest large amounts of money in some stocks, they become major shareholders of firms. A mutual fund is commonly the largest shareholder of many stocks. Portfolio managers of mutual funds that have a large investment in stocks commonly serve on the board of directors of various firms. Even when a fund's managers do not serve on a firm's board, the firm may still attempt to satisfy them so that they do not sell their holdings of the firm's stock.

23-1g Mutual Fund Categories

Mutual funds are commonly classified as stock (or equity) mutual funds, bond mutual funds, or money market funds, depending on the types of securities in which they invest. The distribution of investments in these three classes of mutual funds is shown in Exhibit 23.6. Stock funds are dominant when measured by the market value of total assets among mutual funds. Because investors have various objectives, no single portfolio can satisfy everyone. Consequently, a variety of mutual funds have been created.

Exhibit 23.6   Composition of Mutual Funds

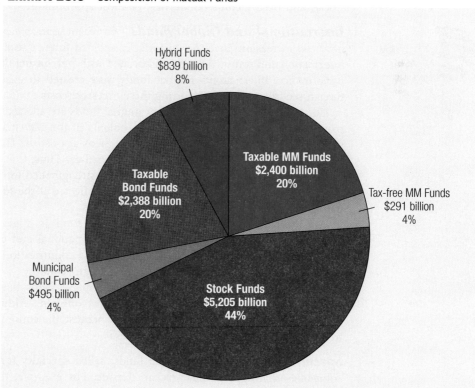

Source: *Investment Company Institute.*

23-1h Stock Mutual Fund Categories

The more popular stock mutual fund categories include:

- Growth funds
- Capital appreciation funds
- Growth and income funds
- International and global funds
- Specialty funds
- Index funds
- Multifund funds

Growth Funds   For investors who desire a high return and are willing to accept a moderate degree of risk, **growth funds** are appropriate. These funds are typically composed of stocks of companies that have not fully matured and are expected to grow at a higher than average rate in the future. The primary objective of a growth fund is to achieve an increase in the value of stocks with less concern about the generation of steady income.

Capital Appreciation Funds   Also known as aggressive growth funds, **capital appreciation funds** are composed of stocks that have potential for very high growth but may also be unproven. These funds are suited to investors who are willing to risk a possible loss in value.

Growth and Income Funds   Some investors are looking for potential for capital appreciation along with some stability in income. For these investors, a **growth and income** fund, which contains a unique combination of growth stocks, high-dividend stocks, and fixed-income bonds, may be most appropriate.

GLOBAL
ASPECTS

International and Global Funds   In recent years, awareness of foreign securities has been increasing. Investors historically avoided foreign securities because of the high information and transaction costs associated with purchasing them and monitoring their performance. International mutual funds were created to enable investors to invest in foreign securities without incurring these excessive costs.

The returns on international stock mutual funds are affected not only by foreign companies' stock prices but also by the movements of the currencies that denominate these stocks. As a foreign currency's value strengthens against the U.S. dollar, the value of the foreign stock as measured in U.S. dollars increases. Thus, U.S. investors can benefit not only from higher stock prices but also from a strengthened foreign currency (against the dollar). Of course, they can also be adversely affected if the foreign currencies denominating the stocks depreciate.

An alternative to an international mutual fund is a global mutual fund, which includes some U.S. stocks in its portfolio. International and global mutual funds have historically included stocks from several different countries to limit the portfolio's exposure to economic conditions in any single foreign economy.

In recent years, some new international mutual funds have been designed to fully benefit from a particular emerging country or continent. Although the potential return from such a strategy is greater, so is the risk because the entire portfolio value is sensitive to a single economy.

Specialty Funds   Some mutual funds, called **specialty funds**, focus on a group of companies sharing a particular characteristic. For example, there are industry-specific funds such as energy, banking, and high-tech funds. Some funds include only stocks of firms that are likely takeover targets. Other mutual funds specialize in options or other commodities, such as precious metals. There are also mutual funds that invest only in socially conscious firms. The risk of specialty funds varies with the particular characteristics of each fund.

Index Funds   Some mutual funds are designed to simply match the performance of an existing stock index. For example, Vanguard offers an **index fund** that is designed to match the S&P 500 index. Index funds are composed of stocks that, in aggregate, are expected to move in line with a specific index. They contain many of the same stocks contained in the corresponding index and tend to have very low expenses because they require little portfolio management and execute a relatively small number of transactions.

Index funds have become very popular over time as investors recognize that most mutual funds do not outperform indexes. Furthermore, investors benefit because the expenses of index funds are much lower than the expenses of actively managed mutual funds. There are also index funds that represent specific non-U.S. countries or regions. These funds may be attractive to investors who wish to invest in a particular foreign market but do not have much knowledge about the specific stocks in that market.

Multifund Funds   In recent years, **multifund mutual funds** have been created. A multifund mutual fund's portfolio managers invest in a portfolio of different mutual funds. A multifund mutual fund achieves even more diversification than a typical mutual fund because it contains several mutual funds. However, investors incur two types of management expenses: (1) the expenses of managing each individual mutual fund and (2) the expenses of managing the multifund mutual fund.

23-1i Bond Mutual Fund Categories

Investors in bonds are primarily concerned about interest rate risk, credit (default) risk, and tax implications. Thus most bond funds are classified according to either their maturities (which affect interest rate risk) or the type of bond issuers (which affects credit risk and taxes incurred).

Income Funds   For investors who are mainly concerned with stability of income rather than capital appreciation, **income funds** are appropriate. These funds are usually composed of bonds that offer periodic coupon payments and vary in exposure to risk. Income funds composed of only corporate bonds are susceptible to credit risk, while those composed of only Treasury bonds are not. A third type of income fund contains bonds backed by government agencies, such as the Government National Mortgage Association (GNMA, or Ginnie Mae). Those income funds exhibiting more credit risk will offer a higher potential return, other things being equal.

The market values of even medium-term income funds are quite volatile over time because of their sensitivity to interest rate movements. Thus income funds are best suited for investors who rely on the fund for periodic income and plan to maintain the fund over a long period of time.

Tax-Free Funds   Investors in high tax brackets have historically purchased municipal bonds as a way to avoid taxes. Because these bonds are susceptible to default, a diversified portfolio is desirable. Mutual funds containing municipal bonds allow investors in high tax brackets with even small amounts of money to avoid taxes while maintaining a low degree of credit risk.

High-Yield (Junk) Bond Funds   Investors desiring high returns and willing to incur high risk may wish to consider bond portfolios with at least two-thirds of the bonds rated below Baa by Moody's or BBB by Standard & Poor's. These portfolios are sometimes referred to as **high-yield** (or **junk bond**) **funds**. Typically, the bonds are issued by highly leveraged firms. The issuing firm's ability to repay junk bonds is very sensitive to economic conditions.

GLOBAL ASPECTS

International and Global Bond Funds   International bond funds contain bonds issued by corporations or governments based in other countries. Global bond funds differ from international bond funds in that they contain U.S. as well as foreign bonds. Global funds may be more appropriate for investors who want a fund that includes U.S. bonds within a diversified portfolio, whereas investors in international bond funds may already have a sufficient investment in U.S. bonds and prefer a fund that focuses entirely on foreign bonds. International and global bond funds provide U.S. investors with an easy way to invest in foreign bonds.

Like bond funds containing U.S. bonds, these funds are subject to credit risk based on the financial position of the corporations or governments that issued the bonds. They are also subject to interest rate risk, as the bond prices are inversely related to the interest rate movements in the currency denominating each bond. These funds are also subject to exchange rate risk, as the NAV of the funds is determined by translating the foreign bond holdings to dollars. Thus, when the foreign currency denominating the bonds weakens, the translated dollar value of those bonds will decrease.

Maturity Classifications   Since the interest rate sensitivity of bonds is dependent on the maturity, bond funds are commonly segmented according to the maturities of the bonds they contain. Intermediate-term bond funds invest in bonds with 5 to 10 years remaining until maturity. Long-term bond funds typically contain bonds with 15 to 30 years until maturity. The bonds in these funds normally have a higher yield to maturity but their values are more sensitive to interest rate movements than the bonds in intermediate-term funds. For a given type of bond fund classification (such as income or tax-free bond funds), various alternatives with different maturity characteristics are available, so investors can select a fund with the desired exposure to interest rate risk.

The variety of bond funds available can satisfy investors who desire combinations of the features described here. For example, investors who are concerned about interest rate risk and credit risk could invest in bond funds that focus on Treasury bonds with intermediate terms to maturity. Investors who expect interest rates to decline but are concerned about credit risk could invest in a long-term Treasury bond fund. Investors who expect interest rates to decline and are not concerned about credit risk may invest in high-yield bond funds. Investors who wish to avoid federal taxes on interest income and are concerned about interest rate risk may consider short-term municipal bond funds.

23-1j Asset Allocation Funds

Asset allocation funds contain a variety of investments (such as stocks, bonds, and money market securities). The portfolio managers adjust the compositions of these funds in response to expectations. For example, a given asset allocation fund will tend to concentrate more heavily on bonds if interest rates are expected to decline; it will focus on stocks if a strong stock market is expected. These funds may even concentrate on international securities if the portfolio managers forecast favorable economic conditions in foreign countries.

23-1k Growth and Size of Mutual Funds

Exhibit 23.7 shows how the number of mutual funds has grown over time. The relative growth of investment in stock mutual funds versus bond mutual funds (in terms of asset size) is illustrated in Exhibit 23.8. In the 1980s, investment in bond funds exceeded that

Exhibit 23.7   Growth in the Number of Stock Funds and Bond Funds

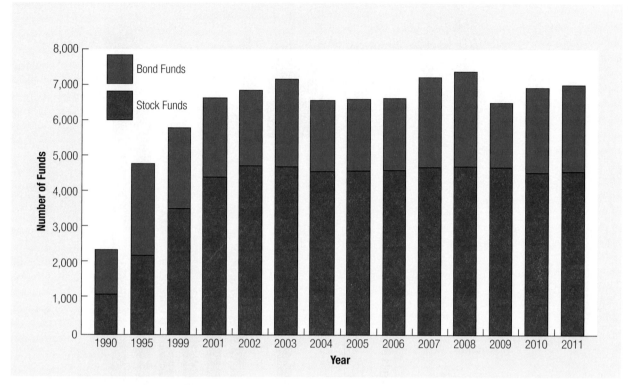

Source: *Investment Company Institute.*

of stock funds, but since the mid-1990s, investment in stock funds has been higher as investors have substantially increased their investment in stock funds in response to the generally higher returns in the stock market.

23-2 PERFORMANCE OF MUTUAL FUNDS

Investors in mutual funds closely monitor the performance of these funds. They also monitor the performance of other mutual funds in which they may invest in the future. In addition, portfolio managers of a mutual fund closely monitor its performance, as their compensation is typically influenced by the performance level.

23-2a Valuation of Stock Mutual Funds

Over a specified period, the change in the valuation of a mutual fund that invests in stocks can be modeled as

$$\Delta V = f(\underset{+}{\underline{\Delta \mathbf{MKT}}}, \underset{-}{\underline{\Delta \mathbf{SECTOR}}}, \underset{+}{\underline{\Delta \mathbf{MANAB}}})$$

where MKT represents general stock market conditions, SECTOR represents conditions of the specific sector (if there is one) in which the mutual fund is focused, and MANAB represents the abilities of the mutual fund's management.

Change in Market Conditions   A change in a stock mutual fund's valuation is usually closely related to a change in stock market conditions. In fact, some mutual funds (index funds) attempt to resemble a particular stock market index.

Exhibit 23.8   Investment in Bond and Stock Mutual Funds

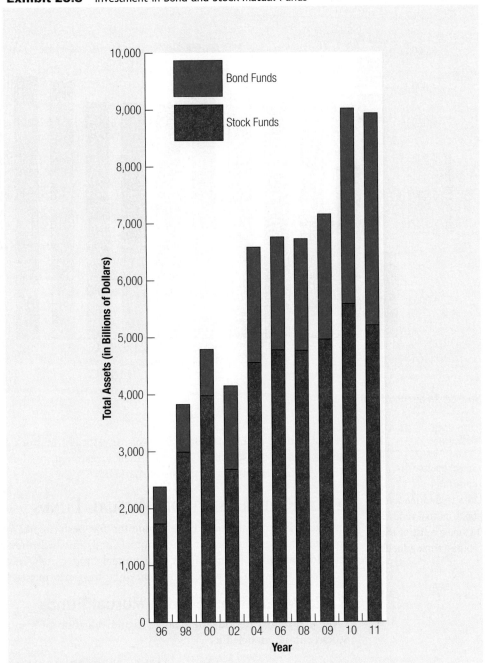

Source: *Investment Company Institute.*

To measure the sensitivity of a mutual fund's exposure to a change in stock market conditions, investors estimate its beta. A mutual fund's beta is estimated in the same manner as a stock's beta. Mutual funds with high betas are more sensitive to market conditions and therefore have more potential to benefit from favorable market conditions.

If unfavorable market conditions occur, they are subject to a more pronounced decline in their NAV and therefore in their price.

When the credit crisis intensified in the third quarter of 2008, the valuations of many stock indexes declined by at least 25 percent. Stock mutual funds also experienced very poor returns, and those stock mutual funds with higher risk experienced more pronounced losses. Even relatively safe stock mutual funds experienced losses in that quarter.

Change in Sector Conditions   The valuation of a stock mutual fund focused on a specific sector is influenced by conditions in that sector. The valuations of mutual funds that focus on U.S. technology stocks tend to rise substantially whenever the technology sector performs well. During the credit crisis, stock mutual funds focused on financial institutions suffered severe losses because that sector was devastated by the credit crisis.

Change in Management Abilities   In addition to market and sector conditions, a mutual fund's performance may also be affected by the abilities of its managers. Mutual funds in the same sector can experience different changes in valuation because of differences in management abilities. If the portfolio managers of one mutual fund have superior abilities for detecting undervalued stocks, that fund should generate higher returns for its investors. In addition, a fund that is managed efficiently so that its expenses are low may be able to achieve higher returns than other stock mutual funds in the same sector.

23-2b Valuation of Bond Mutual Funds

Over a specified period, the change in the valuation of a mutual fund that invests in bonds can be modeled as

$$\Delta V = f(\underbrace{\Delta R_f}_{-}, \underbrace{\Delta RP}_{-}, \underbrace{\Delta \mathbf{MANAB}}_{+})$$

where R_f represents the risk-free rate, RP represents the risk premium, and MANAB represents the abilities of the fund's managers.

Change in the Risk-Free Rate   The prices of bonds tend to be inversely related to changes in the risk-free interest rate. In periods when the risk-free interest rate declines substantially, the required rate of return by bondholders declines, and most bond funds perform well. Those bond funds that are focused on bonds with longer maturities are more exposed to changes in the risk-free rate.

Change in the Risk Premium   The prices of bonds tend to decline in response to an increase in the risk premiums required by investors who purchase bonds. When economic conditions deteriorate, the risk premium required by bondholders usually increases, which results in a higher required rate of return (assuming no change in the risk-free rate) and lower prices on risky bonds. Thus, bond mutual funds focusing on risky bonds perform poorly.

Change in Management Abilities   The performance levels of bond mutual funds in a specific bond classification can vary because of differences in the abilities of the funds' portfolio managers. If the portfolio managers of one bond fund in that classification have superior abilities for selecting undervalued bonds, that bond fund should generate higher returns. In addition, a bond fund that is managed efficiently so that its expenses are low may be able to achieve higher returns than other bond mutual funds in the same classification.

USING THE WALL STREET JOURNAL

Performance of Mutual Funds

The *Wall Street Journal* provides recent performance information on various mutual fund indexes, as shown here. Each index represents a particular type of mutual fund and reflects a specific category and the size of the firms targeted by the fund (small versus large capitalization stocks). Investors can review the information to determine how various types of mutual funds performed over the last week and since the beginning of the year.

Source: Reprinted with permission of the *Wall Street Journal*, Copyright © 2013 Dow Jones & Company, Inc. All Rights Reserved Worldwide.

Lipper Indexes

Stock-Fund Indexes	PRELIM CLOSE	PREV CLOSE	WK AGO	DEC. 31
Large-Cap Growth	4568.33	+1.32	+0.13	+4.81
Large-Cap Core	3384.13	+1.28	+0.19	+6.74
Large-Cap Value	14644.42	+1.42	-0.01	+7.15
Multi-Cap Growth	4340.39	+1.44	+0.29	+6.00
Multi-Cap Core	11446.38	+1.29	+0.10	+6.68
Multi-Cap Value	6221.33	+1.39	+0.11	+7.78
Mid-Cap Growth	1211.83	+1.60	+0.39	+7.62
Mid-Cap Core	1192.59	+1.42	-0.03	+7.73
Mid-Cap Value	1828.51	+1.55	+0.11	+8.87
Small-Cap Growth	870.99	+1.15	-0.58	+6.69
Small-Cap Core	716.29	+1.15	-0.44	+7.08
Small-Cap Value	1147.97	+1.05	-0.32	+7.46
Equity Income Fd	6706.22	+1.16	+0.22	+6.53
Science and Tech Fd	1020.41	+1.05	-0.28	+4.65
International Fund	1332.14	+0.94	-0.79	+2.63
Balanced Fund	7947.57	+0.76	+0.15	+3.37
Bond-Fund Indexes				
Short Inv Grade	333.24	-0.04	+0.08	+0.25
Intmdt Inv Grade	478.32	-0.03	+0.37	+0.06
US Government	599.92	-0.05	+0.45	-0.53
GNMA	673.77	-0.06	+0.25	-0.24
Corp A-Rated Debt	1685.14	-0.07	+0.59	-0.05

Indexes are based on the largest funds within the same investment objective and do not include multiple share classes of similar funds.

Source: Lipper Inc.

23-2c Performance from Diversifying among Funds

The performance of any given mutual fund may be primarily driven by a single economic factor. For example, the performance of growth stock funds may be highly dependent on the stock market's performance (market risk). The performance of any bond mutual fund is highly dependent on interest rate movements (interest rate risk). The performance of any international mutual fund is influenced by the dollar's value (exchange rate risk). When all securities in a given mutual fund are similarly influenced by an underlying economic factor, the fund does not achieve full diversification benefits. For this reason, some investors diversify among different types of mutual funds so that only a portion of their entire investment is susceptible to a particular type of risk. Diversification among types of mutual funds can substantially reduce the volatility of returns on the overall investment.

23-2d Ratings on Mutual Funds

There are many rating services that rate mutual funds. Some ratings are based on past performance over a recent period, such as the last year or three years. Mutual funds with high ratings based on past performance commonly attract large inflows of new investments. In fact, mutual fund families heavily advertise their specific funds that have earned high ratings in order to attract more funds from investors. However, ratings based on recent performance are not necessarily a useful indicator of future performance.

23-2e Research on Mutual Fund Performance

A variety of studies have attempted to assess mutual fund performance over time. Measuring mutual fund performance solely by return is not a valid test because the return will likely be highly dependent on the performance of the stock and bond markets during the period of concern. A more appropriate measure of performance is to compare the mutual fund return to the return of a benchmark market index. Thus, the performance of a stock mutual fund focused on large stocks might be compared to that of an index representing large stocks (such as the S&P 500 index), while the performance of a bond mutual fund focused on high quality corporate bonds might be compared to that of a highly rated corporate bond index.

Most studies that assess mutual fund performance find that mutual funds do not outperform benchmarks, especially when accounting for the type of securities that each fund invests in. Furthermore, mutual funds that have high expense ratios tend to perform worse. Even when returns are adjusted to account for risk, mutual funds have, on average, failed to outperform the market.

Advocates of market efficiency suggest that, beyond insider information, market prices should already reflect any good or bad characteristics of each stock, making it difficult to construct a portfolio whose risk-adjusted returns will consistently outperform the market. Even if mutual funds do not outperform the market, they can still be attractive to investors who wish to diversify and who prefer that a portfolio manager make their investment decisions.

23-3 MONEY MARKET FUNDS

Money market mutual funds, sometimes called money market funds (MMFs), sell shares to individuals and use the proceeds to invest in money market (short-term) instruments for their investors. The main difference between money market funds and the mutual funds discussed earlier is that money market funds focus their investment in money market securities. Because investors can participate in some MMFs with $1,000 or less, they are able to invest in money market instruments that they could not afford on their own. Most MMFs allow check-writing privileges, although there may be restrictions on the number of checks written per month or on the minimum amount of the check. If the fund distributes at least 90 percent of its income to its shareholders, the fund itself is exempt from federal taxation.

Money market funds send periodic account statements to their shareholders to update them on any changes in their balance. They also send shareholders periodic updates on any changes in the asset portfolio composition, providing a breakdown of the names of securities and amounts held in the MMF portfolio.

Because the sponsoring investment company is willing to purchase MMFs back at any time, investors can liquidate their investment whenever they desire. In most years, additional sales of shares exceed redemptions, allowing the companies to build their MMF portfolios by purchasing more securities. When redemptions exceed sales, the company accommodates the amount of excessive redemptions by selling some of the assets contained in the MMF portfolios.

Exhibit 23.9 illustrates the growth in assets of MMFs over time. As investors increase their investment in MMFs, the asset level increases. When economic conditions are weak, investment in MMFs tends to increase as investors become more concerned about the risks of stocks and bonds.

MMFs can be distinguished from one another and from other mutual funds by the composition, maturity, and risk of their assets. Each of these characteristics is described next.

WEB

www.imoneynet.com
Detailed information about money market funds.

Exhibit 23.9   Growth in Money Market Fund Assets

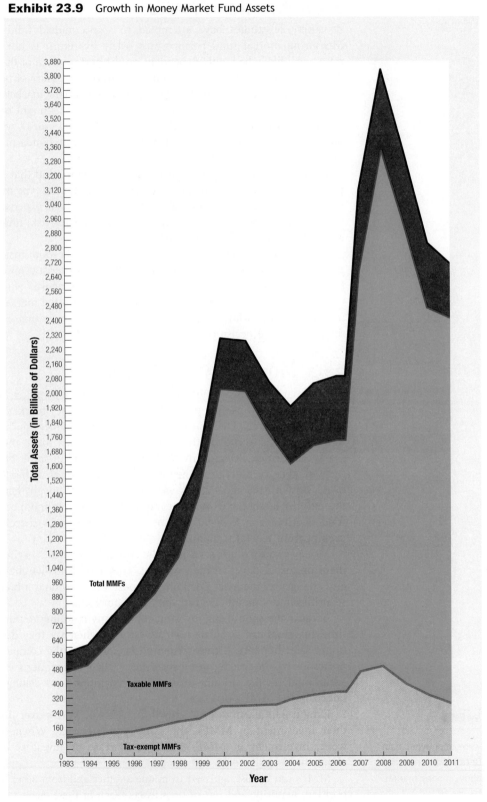

Source: *Investment Company Institute.*

Exhibit 23.10 Composition of Taxable Money Market Fund Assets in Aggregate

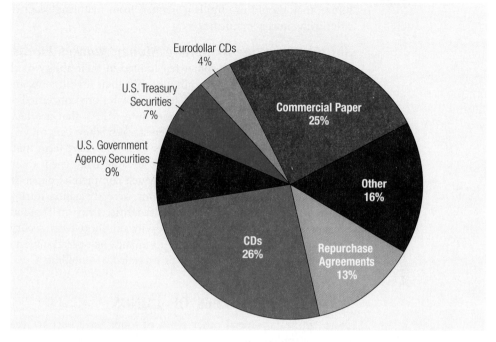

Source: *Investment Company Institute.*

23-3a Asset Composition of Money Market Funds

Exhibit 23.10 shows the composition of money market fund assets in aggregate. Commercial paper, CDs, repurchase agreements, and Treasury securities are the most common components. This composition reflects the importance of each type of asset for MMFs overall and does not represent the typical composition of any particular MMF. Each MMF is usually more concentrated in whatever assets serve its objective.

23-3b Risk of Money Market Funds

MMFs usually have a low level of credit risk because the money market securities they invest in have low credit risk. Because MMFs contain instruments with short-term maturities, their market values are not too sensitive to movements in market interest rates (as are mutual funds containing long-term bonds). Therefore, their exposure to interest rate risk is low. In general, MMFs are normally characterized as having relatively low risk and low expected returns and so are popular among investors who need a conservative investment medium.

23-3c Management of Money Market Funds

The role of MMF portfolio managers is to maintain an asset portfolio that satisfies the underlying objective of a fund. If the managers expect a stronger economy, they may replace maturing risk-free securities (Treasury bills) with more commercial paper or CDs.

Some MMFs have very little flexibility in their composition. For example, some MMFs may as a rule maintain a high percentage of their investment in T-bills to assure investors that they will continue to refrain from risky securities.

Even if managers are unable to change the type of money market securities in the portfolio, they can still influence performance by changing the maturities of the securities in which they invest. For example, if managers expect interest rates to increase in the future, they should use funds generated from maturing securities to purchase new securities with shorter maturities.

Shifting Investments among Money Market Funds Although managers of money market funds are somewhat limited in their ability to change the composition of the fund, investors have the ability to shift their investments among funds in response to changing economic conditions. Investors who are concerned about a potential increase in credit risk can move their money into MMFs that are heavily invested in Treasury bills. If investors expect rising interest rates, they can move their money into MMFs that are heavily invested in securities with very short-term maturities.

During the credit crisis, investors became concerned about the risk of MMFs that were focused on commercial paper. Much commercial paper is issued by financial institutions, and many financial institutions were struggling during the financial crisis. The failure of Lehman Brothers (a large securities firm) in September 2008 scared investors because Lehman Brothers relied heavily on short-term securities (such as commercial paper and repurchase agreements) to finance its operations. In one week during September 2008, withdrawals from MMFs exceeded $140 billion.

23-4 OTHER TYPES OF FUNDS

In recent years, several other types of funds have become very popular. These include exchange-traded funds, venture capital funds, private equity funds, hedge funds, and real estate investment trusts. Each type is described in turn.

23-4a Closed-End Funds

Closed-end funds issue shares and use the proceeds to make investments in stocks or bonds representing a particular sector or country for their investors. Unlike open-end mutual funds, closed-end funds are closed to new investors after the initial offering of shares. In addition, they do not repurchase (redeem) the shares they sold. Investors who purchased shares of closed-end funds can sell the shares on a stock exchange (in the secondary market), and new investors can purchase the shares on the stock exchange.

Some closed-end funds engage in secondary offerings of new shares and use the proceeds to expand their investment portfolios. In addition, some closed-end funds periodically buy back some of their existing shares on the stock exchange where their shares are listed when they believe that the shares are undervalued.

There are about 630 closed-end funds. Approximately 70 percent of these funds invest mainly in bonds or other debt securities, while the other 30 percent focus on stocks. The closed-end stock funds represent particular sectors or countries, which enables investors to invest in a portfolio of stocks that reflects a particular sector or country. The total market value of closed-end funds is less than $300 billion, which is much smaller than the total market value of open-end mutual funds.

Unlike open-end funds, closed-end funds can be sold short by investors. This allows investors to capitalize on their expectations that stock prices of a particular sector or country represented by the closed-end fund will decline.

Market Price of Closed-End Funds The market price of a closed-end fund can deviate from the aggregate value of the underlying stocks (measured by net asset value per share). For some closed-end funds, the shares are priced higher than the aggregate value of the respective portfolio. This often occurs when the shares represent stocks of countries that have investment restrictions. Investors from the United States who want to invest in those stocks are willing to pay a premium beyond the market value of the stocks because they cannot easily obtain the stocks otherwise. For many other closed-end funds, the shares are priced at a discount relative to the underlying stocks. This may occur because some of the stocks held by the closed-end funds are illiquid because they represent small firms.

The premium or discount on a closed-end fund can change over time. Thus, if a fund's premium increases relative to its NAV (or if its discount is reduced), the return to the fund's shareholders is increased. Some investment strategies focus on investing in closed-end funds that are priced at a large discount from their NAV. This is based on the premise that closed-end funds with large discounts in price are undervalued. Applying this strategy will not always generate high risk-adjusted returns, however, because the market price of some closed-end funds with large discounts could continue to decline over time (their discount could become more pronounced).

23-4b Exchange-Traded Funds

Exchange-traded funds (ETFs) are designed to mimic particular stock indexes and are traded on a stock exchange just like stocks. Unlike an open-end fund, an ETF has a fixed number of shares. They are somewhat similar to those open-end mutual funds that invest in a specific stock index. Yet they differ from open-end mutual funds in that their shares are traded on an exchange and their share price changes throughout the day. They can be purchased on margin, just like stocks. They are very appealing to institutional investors and individual investors; more than $1.3 trillion is invested in ETFs. Vanguard, BlackRock, and State Street offer a wide variety of ETFs and dominate the ETF market. Today more than 1,400 different ETFs are offered. However, it is now difficult for investment companies to offer new types of ETFs that are different than those that already exist.

Management of ETFs Because ETFs are intended to mimic a particular index, they differ from most open- and closed-end funds in that they are not actively managed.

This may be viewed by some investors as a disadvantage because they are not trying to outperform an existing index. Yet mutual funds with active management do not necessarily achieve higher returns than benchmarks, and could have lower returns. In addition, some investors prefer the lack of active management because the fees are much lower for ETFs. The annual fee on ETFs is, on average, about .50 percent.

Some investment companies have recently established actively managed ETFs. For example, there may be ETFs in the future that mimic a particular index but that can be revised by a manager to increase the level of investment (with borrowed funds) when the manager expects more favorable returns, and no use of borrowed funds when the manager expects less favorable returns. The annual fees of actively managed ETFs are, on average, about .70 percent. This is higher than the traditional non-managed ETF, but lower than the typical annual fee of open-end mutual funds. Many critics question whether the concept of managed ETFs will appeal to investors.

Capital Gains on ETFs Because ETFs are not actively managed, they normally do not have capital gains and losses that must be distributed to shareholders. Exchange-traded funds have become very popular in recent years because they are an efficient way for investors to invest in a particular stock index.

Liquidity of ETFs ETFs are more liquid than shares of open-end mutual funds because they can be sold at any moment during trading hours. Conversely, mutual fund shares are sold at the end of the day. This difference can be important for investors who trade shares frequently. However, for investors who hold their investments for long-term periods, this difference may not be important.

Brokerage Fees   One disadvantage of ETFs is that each purchase of additional shares must be executed through the exchange where they are traded. Investors incur a brokerage fee from purchasing the shares just as if they had purchased shares of a stock. This cost is especially important to investors who plan on making frequent additions to their investment in a particular ETF.

Short Sales of ETFs   Like closed-end funds, ETFs can be sold short. In fact, investors more commonly short ETFs than closed-end funds because ETFs are more liquid, which makes it easier to execute the short sales. The shares of ETFs sold short represent about 19 percent of all ETF shares. This ratio is about 10 times larger than it is for individual stocks. It is attributed to investors who may more commonly bet on price declines of sectors or countries in aggregate than on individual stocks. In addition, some of the short selling of ETFs is conducted by investors in order to hedge a portion of their existing assets. For example, a financial institution that currently holds a very large portfolio of technology stocks may be concerned about the price movements during the next week even though it has confidence in those stocks over the long run. It could take a short position in a technology stock ETF over the next week to hedge its holdings of individual technology stocks.

Popular ETFs   Exchange-traded funds are commonly classified as broad based, sector, or global, depending on the specific index that they mimic. The broad-based funds are the most popular, but both sector and global ETFs have experienced substantial growth in recent years. A popular ETF is the so-called PowerShares QQQ, or Cube (its trading symbol is QQQQ), which represents the Nasdaq 100 index of technology firms. Thus, Cubes are ideal for investors who believe that technology stocks will perform well but do not want to select individual technology stocks. Another popular ETF is the Standard & Poor's Depository Receipt (SPDR or Spider), which represents the S&P 500 index. Investors who anticipate that the stock market as represented by the S&P 500 will perform well may purchase shares of Spiders, especially when their expectations reflect the composite as a whole rather than any individual stock within the composite. Spiders trade at one-tenth the S&P 500 value, so if the S&P 500 is valued at 1400, a Spider is valued at $140. The percentage change in the price of the shares over time is equivalent to the percentage change in the value of the S&P 500 index.

WEB

http://us.ishares.com/
home.htm
Information on the
trading of iShares.

23-4c Venture Capital Funds

Venture capital (VC) funds use money that they receive from wealthy individuals and some institutional investors to invest in companies. They pool the money that is invested in the fund and use the proceeds to create a diversified equity portfolio. These funds typically require a large minimum investment (such as $100,000 or more) and therefore exclude small investors. A fund charges investors fees for managing the fund, such as 1 to 2 percent of the dollar value of its portfolio per year. Unlike mutual funds, VC funds typically invest in privately held firms rather than publicly traded firms, so their investments are not liquid. They invest in young, growing firms that need equity funding but are not ready or willing to go public. They may invest in businesses that are just being created, that have existed for only a few years, or that are in a later stage of growth. More than half of all VC investing is in businesses that are being created.

USING THE WALL STREET JOURNAL

Exchange-Traded Funds

The *Wall Street Journal* provides price quotations for the largest exchange-traded funds, as shown here. The symbol and closing price are shown, along with the percentage change from the previous day (CHG) and the year-to-date (YTD) percentage change.

Source: Reprinted with permission of the *Wall Street Journal*, Copyright © 2013 Dow Jones & Company, Inc. All Rights Reserved Worldwide.

Exchange-Traded Portfolios | WSJ.com/ETFresearch

Largest 100 exchange-traded funds, latest session

Wednesday, February 27, 2013

ETF	Symbol	Closing Price	Chg (%)	YTD (%)
AlerianMLPETF	AMLP	17.04	0.35	6.8
GuggenheimSP500EqW	RSP	57.41	1.40	7.7
iShrBrclIntCrBd	CIU	111.00	0.03	-0.3
iShrBrclMBS BF	MBB	107.96	-0.02	-0.0
iShrBrcl1-3CrBd	CSJ	105.71	-0.03	0.2
iShrBrclShrtTreas	SHV	110.22	...	-0.0
iShrTIPSBdFd	TIP	120.74	...	-0.6
iShCoreS&P500ETF	IVV	152.63	1.22	6.6
iShCoreS&PMdCp	IJH	110.32	1.43	8.5
iShCoreS&PSmCpETF	IJR	83.62	1.11	7.1
iShCoreTotlUSBdMkt	AGG	110.73	0.03	-0.3
iShrDJSelDiv	DVY	61.08	1.04	6.7
iShrDJUSRE	IYR	68.11	0.77	5.3
iSharesGold	IAU	15.53	-1.08	-4.6
iShriBoxxFd	LQD	120.29	-0.03	-0.6
iShr iBxxHYCorp	HYG	94.08	0.17	0.8
iShrJPMEmMktBd	EMB	119.28	0.06	-2.9
iShrMSCI ACWI	ACWI	49.91	1.20	3.8
iShMSCIBrazilCap	EWZ	55.03	0.68	-1.6
iShrMSCI Can	EWC	28.30	0.89	-0.4
iShrMSEAFE	EFA	58.28	1.27	2.5
iShrMSCIEmrgMkt	EEM	43.41	1.09	-2.1
iShrMSGer	EWG	24.74	1.56	0.2
iShrMSCI HK	EWH	20.01	1.94	3.0
iShrMSCI Jpn	EWJ	10.17	-0.10	4.3
iShrMSCI Pac	EPP	49.66	1.33	5.3
iShMSCISouthKorea	EWY	62.18	1.42	-1.8
iShrRu1000G	IWF	69.11	1.20	5.5
iShrRu1000	IWB	84.51	1.31	6.8
iShrRu1000V	IWD	78.62	1.39	8.0
iShrRu2000G	IWO	102.46	1.13	7.5

ETF	Symbol	Closing Price	Chg (%)	YTD (%)
iShrRu2000	IWM	90.31	1.05	7.1
iShrRu2000V	IWN	80.74	0.97	6.9
iShrRu3000	IWV	90.37	1.28	6.7
iShrRuMid	IWR	122.42	1.47	8.2
iShrRuMidVlu	IWS	54.88	1.42	9.2
iShrSP100	OEF	68.74	1.21	6.3
iShrSP400G	IJK	122.96	1.62	7.5
iShrSP500G	IVW	79.84	1.10	5.4
iShrSP500V	IVE	71.66	1.40	7.9
iShrSPUSPref	PFF	40.25	0.10	1.6
iShsSPNtlAMTMunFd	MUB	111.81	0.18	1.1
iShrSilverTr	SLV	28.01	-1.41	-4.6
iShrBrcl1-3	SHY	84.47	...	0.1
iShrBrcl7-10	IEF	107.01	-0.05	-0.4
iShrBrcl20+	TLT	118.29	-0.30	-2.4
iShrFTSEChina25	FXI	38.47	0.92	-4.9
iShrRuMidGrth	IWP	67.24	1.62	7.1
JPMorgAlerian	AMJ	43.06	1.47	12.0
MktVecAgBusETF	MOO	54.18	1.33	2.7
MktVectorsBkETF	RKH	47.71	1.59	4.3
MktVectorsBiotech	BBH	58.83	1.31	10.0
MktVecGold	GDX	38.26	-2.02	-17.5
MktVectorsOilSvcs	OIH	42.93	1.90	11.1
MktVectorsPharm	PPH	42.76	1.06	7.6
MktVectorsRetail	RTH	46.50	1.29	6.1
MktVectorsSemi	SMH	35.16	1.56	8.8
PIMCOTRETF	BOND	109.55	-0.21	0.5
PwrShsDBComTr	DBC	27.25	-0.62	-1.9
PwrShr DBGoldDblLng	DGP	47.03	-2.24	-9.6
PwrShr DBGoldDblShrt	DZZ	4.91	2.08	9.8
PwrShrs QQQ	QQQ	67.24	1.02	3.2
PS SP500LoVoltlPrt	SPLV	29.69	1.06	7.3
ProShrUltra20	TBT	65.67	0.54	3.5
SPDRBarclaysHiYdBd	JNK	40.96	0.10	0.6
CnsDscrSel SPDR	XLY	50.68	1.52	6.8
ConStplSel SPDR	XLP	38.11	0.74	9.2
HlthcarSel SPDR	XLV	43.49	1.09	9.1
InduSelSctr SPDR	XLI	41.00	1.89	8.2
MatrlsSel SPDR	XLB	38.42	1.77	2.3
TechSelSctr SPDR	XLK	29.69	0.84	2.9
UtilsSelSctr SPDR	XLU	37.30	0.92	6.8
SPDR DJRIEst	RWX	41.81	1.09	1.1
SPDR DJIA Tr	DIA	140.60	1.31	7.7
SPDR EngySelSct	XLE	77.85	1.53	9.0
SPDR FnclSelSct	XLF	17.62	1.56	7.5
SPDR GldTr	GLD	154.57	-1.06	-4.6
SPDR S&PMdCpTr	MDY	201.00	1.45	8.2
SPDR S&P 500	SPY	151.91	1.26	6.7
SPDR S&P Div	SDY	63.32	1.13	8.9
VangdDivApp	VIG	63.96	1.22	7.4
VanguardFTSEEmgMk	VWO	43.72	0.90	-1.8
VangdAllWldxUS	VEU	46.27	1.20	1.1
VangdGrowth	VUG	75.12	1.24	5.5
VangdHiDivYld	VYM	53.33	1.18	8.0
VngdInter-Term	BIV	87.85	-0.02	-0.5
VangIntrCorpBd	VCIT	87.37	0.05	-0.3
VangdLgCap	VV	69.56	1.28	6.8
VanguardMSCIEAFE	VEA	36.18	1.26	2.7
VanguardMSCIEuro	VGK	49.46	1.50	1.3
VangdMdCap	VO	88.92	1.61	7.9
VangdReit	VNQ	69.16	0.73	5.1
VanguardS&P500	VOO	69.55	1.25	6.7
VangdShrtTrm	BSV	81.01	0.01	0.0
VangShrtCorpBd	VCSH	80.51	0.09	0.2
VangdSmCap	VB	87.09	1.28	7.7
VangdTtlBndMkt	BND	83.69	-0.02	-0.4
VangdTtlStock	VTI	78.31	1.23	6.9
VangdValue	VTV	63.54	1.32	8.1
WisdmTrEmrgMktEqty	DEM	55.75	0.74	-2.5

Venture capital funds tend to focus on technology firms, which have the potential for high returns but also exhibit a high level of risk. They receive numerous business proposals from businesses that need funding but invest in less than 1 percent of all the businesses that submit proposals. Sequoia Capital and Menlo Ventures are examples of popular VC funds.

VC fund managers typically have some experience in running a business. When a VC fund provides equity funding, it becomes a partial owner and may expect to have some control (such as a seat on the board of directors) over the business. Thus, VC fund managers may also be advisers to the business. Because VC funds commonly invest in new risky business ventures, a high percentage of their ventures fail. Even with a high failure rate, however, a fund can still perform well because some of its ventures may be major success stories. Many businesses that ultimately became famous, including Apple, Microsoft, and Oracle Corporation, were partially supported with venture capital in their earlier years.

A VC fund typically plans to exit from its original investment in a business within about four to seven years. If the business goes public, the fund commonly can sell its stake (shares) in the secondary market between 6 and 24 months after the initial public offering (IPO). More than half of businesses that go public are partially backed by VC funds before the IPO. Many businesses backed by venture capital never become large enough to go public. They are typically acquired by other firms, and the VC funds receive payment for their stake in the business.

23-4d Private Equity Funds

Private equity funds pool money provided by individual and institutional investors and buy majority (or entire) stakes in businesses. Such a fund is usually created as a limited liability partnership, and the general partners develop a business plan for investing in businesses and managing the businesses that they acquire. They promote their business plan to attract funds from outside investors, who become limited partners of the fund. Private equity funds appeal to institutional investors such as pension funds and insurance companies because they have the potential to earn very high returns. They also appeal to university endowments and individuals who can afford to invest $1 million or more.

A private equity fund is typically closed to outside investors once it has reached its funding goal. The fund may be opened again to obtain more funding if it develops new plans for investing additional money. The fund managers commonly distribute 80 percent of the profits from their investments to their investors and retain 20 percent for themselves.

When a private equity fund purchases a business, it assumes control and is able to restructure the business in a manner that will improve its performance. These funds usually purchase private businesses, but sometimes they acquire public companies. They commonly purchase businesses that are struggling and have potential to improve. Thus, a private equity fund may purchase a business at a low price, restructure its operations to improve it, and sell the business for a much higher price than it paid. Examples of businesses purchased by private equity funds include Dunkin' Donuts, Hertz, La Quinta, and Neiman Marcus.

Among the most popular private equity funds are Blackstone, Permira, Apollo Investment, Providence Equity, Carlyle Group, Kohlberg Kravis Roberts (KKR), and Texas Pacific Group. Each of these private equity funds has more than $10 billion in assets. Some major private equity funds are owned by commercial banks. Examples include Credit Suisse Private Equity and Barclays Private Equity. The United States has the largest market for private equity, followed by the United Kingdom, but private equity investments are increasing rapidly throughout Europe and Asia.

The Market for Private Equity Businesses   The market for private businesses is not as efficient as the market for publicly traded stocks. Information about private businesses is very limited, so private equity fund managers may see opportunities to buy undervalued businesses. The potential to capitalize on inefficiencies in this market has attracted much more investment in private equity and has led to the creation of many new private equity funds.

Although private equity funds in aggregate raise more than $500 billion per year, these funds also commonly restructure the businesses they buy to rely on more debt financing. This enables them to use less equity per deal and to spread their investments across more deals. It also results in a higher degree of financial leverage for the businesses in which they invest. Thus, the funds can generate a higher rate of return on their equity investment from a given level of business profit, but the increased leverage increases the risk that the business will be unable to repay the debt.

A potential problem is that the large inflow of money into private equity funds could result in too much money chasing too few deals. The intense competition could cause some private equity funds to pay too much for some acquisitions in order to outbid competitors. This may result in a winner's curse, meaning that the winning bidders get the target firms but have paid too much money for them. It is more difficult for private equity firms to acquire undervalued firms when there is intense competition with other bidders.

WEB

www.sec.gov/answers/
hedge.htm
Provides information on
hedge funds.

23-4e Hedge Funds

Hedge funds sell shares to wealthy individuals and financial institutions and use the proceeds to invest in securities. They differ from open-end mutual funds in several ways. First, they require a much larger initial investment (such as $1 million), whereas mutual funds typically allow a minimum investment in the range of $250 to $2,500. Second, many hedge funds are not "open" in the sense that they may not always accept additional investments or accommodate redemption requests unless advance notice is provided. Some hedge funds permit investors to withdraw their investments but require advance notice of 30 days or more. Third, hedge funds have been subject to minimal regulation. They provide very limited information to prospective investors. Fourth, hedge funds invest in a wide variety of investments to achieve high returns. Consequently, they tend to take more risk than mutual funds. Although some hedge funds have performed well, many have failed.

Most hedge funds are organized as limited partnerships. There are at least 9,000 hedge funds, with a combined market value of about $2 trillion. The investment strategies used by hedge funds include investing in derivative securities and selling stocks short. In recent years, some hedge funds have purchased businesses that they manage, similar to private equity funds. They either oversee or replace managers to improve the performance of the business with the goal of ultimately selling the business for a much higher price than they paid. Some hedge funds purchase distressed assets of bankrupt firms, similar to a vulture fund.

Use of Financial Leverage   Hedge funds commonly use borrowed funds to complement the equity that they receive and invest. This use of financial leverage allows them to make more investments with a given amount of equity and can magnify the returns.

EXAMPLE   Durham Hedge Fund uses $3 of borrowed funds for every $1 of equity that it invests. It can obtain $4 of assets for each $1 of equity that it invests. If its investment results in a positive 20 percent return on assets (ROA), this represents a return on its equity (ROE) investment of

$$
\begin{aligned}
\textbf{ROE} &= \textbf{ROA} \times (\textbf{Assets}/\textbf{Equity}) \\
&= \textbf{20\%} \times \textbf{4} \\
&= \textbf{80\%}
\end{aligned}
$$

If Durham Hedge Fund used only equity (no borrowed funds) to invest in assets, its return on equity would have been only 20 percent, the same as its return on assets. The financial leverage in this example allowed the hedge fund to magnify its returns to investors by four times the return on assets. ●

Financial leverage can also magnify negative returns (losses) and therefore increases the risk to investors.

EXAMPLE   Consider the previous example in which Durham Hedge Fund used $3 of borrowed funds for every $1 of equity that it invests. But now assume that its investment results in a negative 20 percent return on the assets. This represents a return on its equity investment of

$$
\begin{aligned}
\textbf{ROE} &= \textbf{ROA} \times (\textbf{Assets}/\textbf{Equity}) \\
&= \textbf{-20\%} \times \textbf{4} \\
&= \textbf{-80\%}
\end{aligned}
$$

If this hedge fund used only equity (no borrowed funds) to invest in assets, its loss would have been only 20 percent. ●

Hedge Fund Fees   Hedge funds charge a management fee of between 1 and 2 percent of the investment per year. In addition, they charge an incentive fee that is based on the return of the fund. The typical incentive fee is 20 percent of the return.

EXAMPLE   Consider a hedge fund that charges a management fee of 2 percent and an incentive fee of 20 percent of the annual return. In the most recent year, the fund earned a return of 15 percent. The investors in this fund would have paid an incentive fee of 3 percent (computed as 20 percent of the 15 percent return) along with a 2 percent management fee, or a total fee of 5 percent of their total investment. Considering that some index mutual funds have a very small management fee and no incentive fee, this hedge fund would have been a better investment only if its performance exceeded that of index funds by about 5 percent in that year. ●

Financial Problems Experienced by LTCM   One of the best-known hedge funds was Long-Term Capital Management (LTCM), which was created in 1994 and managed by a group of partners who had a very strong track record.

Long-Term Capital Management relied heavily on financial leverage to boost its returns. By 1998, LTCM had about $5 billion in equity and $125 billion in debt to support its $130 billion portfolio, a ratio of $25 of debt for every dollar of equity. Furthermore, some of its investments were in financial derivative positions that magnify returns beyond the level of the underlying securities. In August 1998, Russia defaulted on some of its bonds, which aroused general concern about bond credit risk throughout the world. At the time, LTCM had investments in relatively risky bonds and lost more than $2 billion, or about 40 percent of its total equity. After accounting for the loss, its existing debt of $125 billion was about 50 times its remaining equity. On September 23, 1998, the Federal Reserve Bank of New York organized a rescue of LTCM by 14 large commercial banks and securities firms. These firms provided a capital infusion of $3.6 billion, which gave them a 90 percent stake in LTCM. The rescue plan was intended to prevent

LTCM from defaulting on all of its derivative contract positions, which could have caused the counterparties of those positions to lose billions of dollars. Nevertheless, some critics suggest that LTCM was given preferential treatment because it was too big to fail.

Performance of Hedge Funds during the Credit Crisis

Some hedge funds failed during the credit crisis in 2008 because they had invested heavily in mortgage-related securities just before subprime mortgage values collapsed. Their losses, which were magnified because of their use of financial leverage, wiped out all of their equity. Some hedge funds that used excessive borrowing received margin calls from their lenders when the values of their investments declined during the credit crisis. They had to sell some investments such as mortgage-backed securities and stocks in order to obtain cash to post more collateral. This caused additional downward pressure on the prices of these securities during the credit crisis.

Short Selling by Hedge Funds

One reason for the success of some hedge funds is that they can take a very large short position (selling stocks that they do not own) on overvalued stocks. In some cases, firms have issued misleading financial statements, causing their stock prices to be higher than their actual earnings justified. Hedge funds thoroughly investigate such firms, because they can earn very large returns by shorting the stocks of these firms before other investors (and various regulators or credit agencies that attempt to detect financial fraud) recognize that the financial statements are misleading. For example, some hedge funds took large short positions in the stocks of Enron, WorldCom, and Krispy Kreme while their stocks were highly valued. Once the media reported that the financial statements of these firms were questionable, the prices of these stocks declined, and the hedge funds closed out their positions.

During the credit crisis in 2008, hedge funds were accused of making market conditions worse by taking short positions in some of the financial institutions that held subprime mortgages or other mortgage-related securities. The SEC imposed temporary restrictions on short sales of stocks of financial institutions that were highly exposed to subprime mortgages. The hedge funds would likely justify their short sale strategies by arguing that the financial institutions with subprime mortgages were overvalued because they had not been fully transparent about their exposure. To the extent that the short selling actions of the hedge funds lower the stock price toward its proper value, these actions make the market more efficient.

Madoff Fund Scandal

Bernard Madoff managed a large and well-respected hedge fund that included various institutions, charities, and wealthy individuals among its investors. The fund reportedly earned favorable returns every year. When some investors wanted to cash out of their investments in December 2008, there was no money available for them. Madoff admitted that he had been periodically using money from new investors to pay off investors who wanted to cash out of the fund. The potential losses to investors were estimated to be as high as $50 billion, making this possibly the biggest financial scandal in U.S. history.

One major lesson from this scandal is that hedge funds deserve closer scrutiny from regulators than they have received in the past. The SEC was alerted several times over the previous nine years to possible irregularities in the Madoff fund, but it failed to detect the fraud.

Hedge Funds of Funds

Since the minimum investment in some hedge funds may be $1 million or more, most small investors are unable to invest in them. However, some "hedge funds of funds" have been created to pool smaller investments by individuals and invest in hedge funds. Thus, investors who invest in a hedge fund of funds are essentially owners of a diversified set of hedge funds. The typical minimum investment to invest in a hedge fund of funds is between $25,000 and $100,000. The sponsor of a fund of funds has a portfolio manager who decides how to allocate the money, and the costs incurred from that management are charged to investors. In addition, the investment in any particular hedge funds is subject to the normal fees charged by those funds. Thus, investors in a hedge fund of funds essentially pay for two layers of fees resulting from the management of their money.

Regulatory Reform of Hedge Funds In July 2010, the Financial Reform Act was implemented; it contained many provisions that were designed to stabilize the financial system. The act mandates that hedge funds managing more than $100 million are required to register with the Securities and Exchange Commission as investment advisors. These hedge funds must also disclose financial data that can be used by the Financial Stability Oversight Council (created by the Financial Reform Act) in order to assess systemic risk in the financial system. The act also prevents commercial banks from investing more than 3 percent of their capital in hedge fund institutions, private equity funds, or real estate funds.

23-4f Real Estate Investment Trusts

A real estate investment trust (REIT) (pronounced "reet") is a closed-end fund that invests in real estate or mortgages. Like other mutual funds, REITs allow small investors to participate with a low minimum investment. The funds are pooled to invest in mortgages and in commercial real estate. REITs generate income for shareholders by passing through rents on real estate or interest payments on mortgages. Most existing REITs can be sold on stock exchanges, so investors can sell them at any time. The composition of a REIT is determined by its portfolio manager, who is presumed to have expertise in real estate investments.

Real estate investment trusts can be classified as equity REITs, which invest directly in properties, or mortgage REITs, which invest in mortgage and construction loans. A third type of REIT, called a hybrid, invests in both properties and mortgages.

Equity REITs are sometimes purchased to hedge against inflation, as rents and property values tend to rise with inflation. Their performance varies according to the perceived future value of the real estate held in each portfolio. Real estate investment trusts that have concentrated in potential high-growth properties are expected to generate a higher return than those with a more nationally diversified portfolio. However, they are also susceptible to more risk if the specific locations experience slow growth.

Because mortgage REITs essentially represent a fixed-income portfolio, their market value will be influenced by interest rate movements. As interest rates rise, the market value of mortgages declines, and therefore the demand for mortgage REITs declines. If interest rates are expected to decrease, mortgage REITs become more attractive. Mortgage REITs are also influenced by credit risk since the mortgages are subject to possible default.

Impact of Credit Crisis on REITs During the credit crisis in the 2008–2009 period, many mortgages experienced late payments or default. Consequently, mortgage REITs experienced losses during that period. In particular, those REITs that invested heavily in subprime mortgages suffered severe losses.

SUMMARY

- Mutual funds accommodate financing needs of corporations, the Treasury, and municipal governments by purchasing newly issued stocks and bonds in the primary market. They also frequently purchase securities in the secondary market. They enable individual investors to diversify their investments with a limited amount of funds. The more common types of mutual funds include capital appreciation funds, growth and income funds, income funds, tax-free funds, high-yield funds, international funds, global funds, asset allocation funds, and specialty funds.

- The performance of stock mutual funds is highly influenced by stock market conditions, the prevailing conditions of the sectors in which the mutual fund invests, and the management abilities of their portfolio managers. The performance of bond mutual funds is relatively strong in periods when interest rates decline and when the credit risk premium on bonds declines.

- Money market funds (MMFs) invest in short-term securities, such as commercial paper, repurchase agreements, CDs, and Treasury bills. The expected returns on MMFs are relatively low, but the risk levels are also low.

- Closed-end funds are similar to mutual funds, except that they are closed to new investors and to redemptions and their shares are traded on a stock exchange. Exchange-traded funds (ETFs) are designed to mimic particular stock indexes and are traded on a stock exchange. Venture capital (VC) funds use money that they receive from wealthy individuals and some institutional investors to invest in young, growing firms that need equity funding but are not ready or willing to go public. Private equity funds pool money provided by individual and institutional investors and buy majority (or entire) stakes in businesses. Hedge funds sell shares to wealthy individuals and financial institutions and use the proceeds to invest in securities. They are subject to minimal regulation and commonly pursue investments that can achieve high returns but are also exposed to a high degree of risk. Real estate investment trusts (REITs) are closed-end funds that invest in real estate or mortgages.

POINT COUNTER-POINT

Should Mutual Funds Be Subject to More Regulation?

Point No. Mutual funds can be monitored by their shareholders (just like many firms), and the shareholders can enforce governance.

Counter-Point Yes. Mutual funds need to be governed by regulators because they are accountable for such a large amount of money. Without regulation, there could be massive withdrawals from mutual funds when unethical behavior by managers of mutual funds is publicized.

Who Is Correct? Use the Internet to learn more about this issue and then formulate your own opinion.

QUESTIONS AND APPLICATIONS

1. Mutual Fund Services Explain why mutual funds are attractive to small investors. How can mutual funds generate returns to their shareholders?

2. Open- versus Closed-End Funds How do open-end mutual funds differ from closed-end funds?

3. Load versus No-Load Mutual Funds Explain the difference between load and no-load mutual funds.

4. Use of Funds Like mutual funds, commercial banks and stock-owned savings institutions sell shares, but the proceeds received by mutual funds are used in a different way. Explain.

5. Risk of Treasury Bond Funds Support or refute the following statement: Investors can avoid all types of risk by purchasing a mutual fund that contains only Treasury bonds.

6. Fund Selection Describe the ideal mutual fund for investors who wish to generate tax-free income and also maintain a low degree of interest rate risk.

7. Exposure to Exchange Rate Movements Explain how changing foreign currency values can affect the performance of international mutual funds.

8. Reform of Hedge Funds Explain how the Financial Reform Act of 2010 applies to hedge funds.

9. Tax Effects on Mutual Funds Explain how the income generated by a mutual fund is taxed when the fund distributes at least 90 percent of its taxable income to shareholders.

10. Performance According to research, have mutual funds outperformed the market? Explain. Would mutual funds be attractive to some investors even if they are not expected to outperform the market? Explain.

11. Money Market Funds How do money market funds differ from other types of mutual funds in terms of how they use the money invested by shareholders? Which security do MMFs invest in most often? How can an MMF accommodate shareholders who wish to sell their shares when the amount of proceeds received from selling new shares is less than the amount needed?

12. Risk of Money Market Funds Explain the relative risk of the various types of securities in which a money market fund may invest.

13. Interest Rate Risk of Funds Is the value of a money market fund or a bond fund more susceptible to rising interest rates? Explain.

14. Diversification among Mutual Funds Explain why diversification across different types of mutual funds is highly recommended.

15. Impact of Credit Crisis on Hedge Funds Explain why some hedge funds failed as a result of the credit crisis.

16. REITs Explain the difference between equity REITs and mortgage REITs. Which type would likely be a better hedge against high inflation? Why?

Advanced Questions

17. Comparing Management of Open- versus Closed-End Funds Compare the management of a closed-end fund with that of an open-end fund. Given the differences in the funds' characteristics, explain why the management of liquidity is different in the open-end

fund as compared with the closed-end fund. Assume that the funds are the same size and have the same goal to invest in stocks and to earn a very high return. Which portfolio manager do you think will achieve a larger increase in the fund's net asset value? Explain.

18. Selecting a Type of Mutual Fund Consider the prevailing conditions that could affect the demand for stocks, including inflation, the economy, the budget deficit, the Fed's monetary policy, political conditions, and the general mood of investors. Based on current conditions, recommend a specific type of stock mutual fund that you think would perform well. Offer some logic to support your recommendation.

19. Comparing Hedge Funds and Mutual Funds Explain why hedge funds may be able to achieve higher returns for their investors than mutual funds. Explain why hedge funds and mutual funds may have different risks. When the market is overvalued, why might hedge funds be better able to capitalize on the excessive market optimism than mutual funds?

20. How Private Equity Funds Can Improve Business Conditions Describe private equity funds. How can they improve business conditions? Money that individual and institutional investors previously invested in stocks is now being invested in private equity funds. Explain why this should result in improved business conditions.

21. Source of Mutual Fund versus Private Equity Fund Returns Equity mutual funds and private equity funds generate returns for their investors in different ways. Explain this difference. Which type of fund do you think would be better able to capitalize on a weak, publicly traded firm that has ignored all forms of shareholder activism?

22. Impact of Private Equity Funds on Market Efficiency In recent years, private equity funds have grown substantially. Will the creation of private equity funds increase the semistrong form of market efficiency in the stock market? Explain.

Interpreting Financial News

Interpret the following comments made by Wall Street analysts and portfolio managers.

a. "Just because a mutual fund earned a 20 percent return in one year, that does not mean that investors should rush into it. The fund's performance must be market adjusted."

b. "An international mutual fund's performance is subject to conditions beyond the fund manager's control."

c. "Small mutual funds will need to merge to compete with the major players in terms of efficiency."

Managing in Financial Markets

Investing in Mutual Funds As an individual investor, you are attempting to invest in a well-diversified portfolio of mutual funds so that you will be somewhat insulated from any type of economic shock that may occur.

a. An investment adviser recommends that you buy four different U.S. growth stock funds. Since these funds contain over 400 different U.S. stocks, the adviser says that you will be well insulated from any economic shocks. Do you agree? Explain.

b. A second investment adviser recommends that you invest in four different mutual funds that are focused on different countries in Europe. The adviser says that you will be completely insulated from U.S. economic conditions and that your portfolio will therefore have low risk. Do you agree? Explain.

c. A third investment adviser recommends that you avoid exposure to the stock markets by investing in four different U.S. bond funds. The adviser says that because bonds make fixed payments, these bond funds have very low risk. Do you agree? Explain.

FLOW OF FUNDS EXERCISE

How Mutual Funds Facilitate the Flow of Funds

Carson Company is considering a private placement of bonds with Venus Mutual Fund.

a. Explain the interaction between Carson and Venus. How would Venus serve Carson's needs, and how would Carson serve the needs of Venus?

b. Why does Carson interact with Venus Mutual Fund instead of trying to obtain the funds directly from individuals who invested in Venus Mutual Fund?

c. Would Venus Mutual Fund serve as a better monitor of Carson Company than the individuals who provided money to the mutual fund? Explain.

INTERNET/EXCEL EXERCISES

1. Assess today's mutual fund performance using the website www.bloomberg.com/markets. Under "Market Data," click on "Mutual Funds." What is the best-performing mutual fund today in terms of the yield-to-date (YTD)? What is the net asset value (NAV) of this fund, and what is its YTD? What is the five-year return on this fund, and what is its YTD this year? Do you think mutual fund rankings change frequently? Why or why not?

2. Go to screen.yahoo.com/funds.html. Describe the constraints that you would impose when selecting funds. Impose those constraints on the category, past performance, ratings, and other characteristics, and then allow the screener to screen the mutual funds for you. List one or more mutual funds that satisfied your criteria.

3. Go to finance.yahoo.com, enter the symbol MVC (for the closed-end fund MVC Capital that invests in U.S. stocks), and click on "Get Quotes." Click on "5y" just below the stock price trend to review the stock price movements over the last five years. Click on "Compare" just above the graph and then select "S&P500" in order to compare the trend of MVC's price with the movements in the S&P stock index. Does it appear that MVC's performance is influenced by general stock market movements?

4. Go to finance.yahoo.com, enter the symbol DNP (for the closed-end fund DNP Select Income Fund that invests in bonds), and click on "Get Quotes." Retrieve stock price data at the beginning of the last 20 quarters. Then go to http://research.stlouisfed.org/fred2 and retrieve interest rate data at the beginning of the last 20 quarters for the three-month T-bill. Record the data on an Excel spreadsheet. Derive the quarterly return of DNP. Derive the quarterly change in the interest rate. Apply regression analysis in which the quarterly return of DNP is the dependent variable and the quarterly change in the interest rate is the independent variable (see Appendix B for more information about using regression analysis). Is there a positive or negative relationship between the interest rate movement and the stock return of DNP? Is the relationship significant? Offer an explanation for this relationship.

WSJ Exercise

Performance of Mutual Funds

Using an issue of the *Wall Street Journal*, summarize an article that discusses the recent performance of a specific mutual fund. Has this mutual fund's performance been better or worse than the norm? What reason is given for the particular level of performance?

Online Articles with Real-World Examples

Find a recent practical article available online that describes a real-world example regarding a specific financial institution or financial market that reinforces one or more concepts covered in this chapter.

If your class has an online component, your professor may ask you to post your summary of the article there and provide a link to the article so that other students can access it. If your class is live, your professor may ask you to summarize your application of the article in class. Your professor may assign specific students to complete this assignment or may allow any students to do the assignment on a volunteer basis.

For recent online articles and real-world examples related to this chapter, consider using the following search terms (be sure to include the prevailing year as a search term to ensure that the online articles are recent):

1. [name of a specific mutual fund] AND objective

2. [name of a specific mutual fund] AND expense ratio

3. [name of a specific mutual fund] AND risk

4. [name of a specific mutual fund] AND classification

5. [name of a specific mutual fund] AND management

6. [name of a specific mutual fund] AND performance

7. [name of a specific closed-end fund] AND performance

8. [name of a specific closed-end fund] AND risk

9. [name of a specific money market fund] AND performance

10. [name of a specific exchange-traded fund] AND performance

24
Securities Operations

CHAPTER OBJECTIVES

The specific objectives of this chapter are to:

■ describe the key functions of securities firms,

■ describe how securities firms are regulated,

■ explain the exposure of securities firms to risk,

■ identify the factors that affect the valuation of securities firms, and

■ explain how the credit crisis affected securities firms.

WEB

finance.yahoo.com
Search engine for information about publicly traded stocks in the United States.

Securities firms serve as important intermediaries by helping governments and firms raise funds. They also facilitate the transactions between investors in the secondary market.

24-1 FUNCTIONS OF SECURITIES FIRMS

Securities firms perform many different functions. They engage in investment banking services such as facilitating security offerings for corporations and government agencies, the securitization of mortgages, and advisory and financing services for corporations that want to restructure their operations. Securities firms that perform the investment banking functions just listed are sometimes referred to as *investment banks*. Some securities firms also provide brokerage services or engage in proprietary trading.

Some securities firms are independent, but many of them are part of a financial conglomerate. Recently, some securities firms have become part of a bank holding company structure. Nevertheless, their securities operations are distinctly different from commercial banking operations, which is why they deserve coverage as a separate chapter. The functions of securities firms are described next.

24-1a Facilitating Stock Offerings

A securities firm acts as an intermediary between a corporation issuing securities and investors by providing the following services:

■ Origination
■ Underwriting
■ Distribution of stock
■ Advising
■ Private placement of stock

Origination When a corporation decides to issue stock publicly, it may contact a securities firm. The securities firm can recommend the appropriate amount of stock to issue because it can anticipate the amount of stock that the market can likely absorb without causing a reduction in the stock price. It evaluates the corporation's financial condition to determine the appropriate price for the newly issued stock. If the corporation has issued stock to the public before, the price should be similar to the market price on its outstanding stock.

In the case of an initial public offering (IPO), there is no prevailing market price for the shares to be sold. Thus the securities firm will compare the corporation's financial characteristics with those of other similar firms in the same industry that have stock outstanding to help determine the proper valuation of the corporation and therefore the price at which the stock should be sold.

The issuing corporation registers with the Securities and Exchange Commission (SEC). All information relevant to the security, as well as the agreement between the issuer and the securities firm, must be provided in the **registration statement**, which is intended to ensure that accurate information is disclosed by the issuing corporation. Included in the required registration information is the **prospectus**, which discloses relevant financial data on the firm and provisions applicable to the security. The prospectus can be issued only after the registration is approved, which typically takes 20 to 40 days. SEC approval does not guarantee the quality or safety of the securities to be issued; it simply acknowledges that a firm is disclosing accurate information about itself.

The securities firm along with the issuing firm may meet with institutional investors who may be interested in the offering. They engage in a road show in which they travel to various cities where they meet with institutional investors to discuss the issuing firm's plans for using the funds that will be obtained from the offering.

WEB

www.sec.gov/edgar.
shtml
Identifies upcoming
IPOs and the securities
firms that are involved
in the underwriting
process.

Underwriting   The original securities firm may form an **underwriting syndicate** by asking other securities firms to underwrite a portion of the stock. Each participating securities firm shares in the underwriting fees charged to the issuer. Some of the more well-known securities firms for underwriting include Bank of America's Merrill Lynch division, Goldman Sachs, and Morgan Stanley.

The term *underwrite* is sometimes wrongly interpreted to mean that the underwriting syndicate guarantees the price at which shares will be sold. However, stock offerings are normally based on a **best-efforts agreement** whereby the securities firm does not guarantee a price to the issuing corporation. In such a case, the issuing corporation bears the risk because it does not receive a guaranteed price from the securities firm on the stock to be issued.

When securities firms facilitate initial public offerings (IPOs), they attempt to price the stock high enough to satisfy the issuing firm. The higher the average price at which the shares are issued, the greater the proceeds received by the issuing firm. If the securities firms price the stock too high, however, they will not be able to place the entire issue. The reputation of the underwriting syndicate is at stake when it attempts to place the stock of the issuing firm. It knows that other corporations that may issue stock in the future will monitor its ability to place the stock.

Securities firms must also attempt to satisfy the institutional investors that may invest in the IPO. The higher the price institutional investors pay for the stock being issued, the lower the return they earn on their investment when they sell the stock. Underwriting syndicates recognize that other institutional investors monitor stock prices after offerings to determine whether the initial offer price charged by the syndicate was appropriate. If the institutional investors do not earn reasonable returns on their investment, they may not invest in future IPOs. Since securities firms rely on institutional investors when placing shares of newly issued stock, they want to maintain a good relationship with them.

Research indicates that securities firms tend to underprice IPOs. That is, institutional investors that invest at the offer price earn high returns on average if they retain the investment for a short-term period, such as three months or less. Much of the return occurs within the first few days after the IPO. Consequently, the returns to investors who purchase the shares shortly after the IPO are generally poor.

Distribution of Stock   Once all agreements between the issuing firm, the originating securities firm, and other participating securities firms are complete and the registration is approved by the SEC, the stock may be sold. The prospectus is distributed to all potential purchasers of the stock, and the issue is advertised to the public. In some cases, the issue sells within hours. If the issue does not sell as expected, the underwriting syndicate will likely have to reduce the price to complete the sale. The demand for the stock is somewhat influenced by the sales force involved in selling the stock. Some securities firms participating in a syndicate have brokerage subsidiaries that can sell stock on a retail level. Others may specialize in underwriting but still utilize a group of brokerage firms to sell the newly issued stock. The brokers earn a commission on the amount they sell but do not guarantee a specific amount of sales.

When a corporation places stock publicly, it incurs two types of **flotation costs**, or costs of placing the securities. First, it must pay fees to the underwriters who place the stock with investors. Second, it incurs **issue costs** including printing, legal, registration, and accounting expenses. Because these issue costs are not significantly affected by the size of the issue, flotation costs as a percentage of the value of securities issued are lower for larger issues.

Advising   The securities firm acts as an adviser throughout the **origination** stage. Even after the stock is issued, the securities firm may continue to provide advice on the timing, amount, and terms of future financing. Included with this advice are recommendations on the appropriate type of financing (bonds, stocks, or long-term commercial loans).

Private Placements of Stock   Securities firms are also hired to facilitate private placements of stock. With a **private placement** (or direct placement), an entire stock offering may be placed with a small set of institutional investors and not offered to the general public. Under the SEC's Rule 144A, firms may engage in private placements of stock without filing the extensive registration statement that is required for public placements. Consequently, the issuing firm's costs of reporting are lower than with a public placement. In addition, the underwriting services are more manageable because an underwriting syndicate may not be necessary.

Institutional investors that are willing to hold the stock for a long period of time are prime candidates for participating in a private placement. Since all the stock is held by a small set of institutional investors, there will not be an established secondary market for the stock. Thus, institutional investors may expect a higher return on the stock to compensate for the lack of liquidity.

24-1b Facilitating Bond Offerings

A securities firm's role in placing bonds is somewhat similar to its role in placing stock. The five main services of a securities firm in placing bonds are explained in turn.

Origination   The securities firm may suggest a maximum amount of bonds that should be issued based on the issuer's characteristics. If the issuer already has a high level of outstanding debt, the bonds may not be well received by the market because the issuer's ability to meet the debt payments will be questionable. Consequently, the bonds will need to offer a relatively high yield, which will increase the cost of borrowing to the issuer.

Next, the coupon rate, the maturity, and other provisions are decided based on the characteristics of the issuing firm. The asking price on the bonds is determined by evaluating market prices of existing bonds that are similar in their degree of risk, term to maturity, and other provisions.

Issuers of bonds must register with the SEC. The registration statement contains information about the bonds to be issued, states the agreement between the securities firm and the issuer, and also includes a prospectus with financial information about the issuer.

Underwriting Bonds   Some issuers of bonds, particularly public utilities, may solicit competitive bids on the price of bonds from various securities firms so that they can select the firm with the highest bid. Securities firms provide several services to the issuer, however, so price is not the only consideration. Corporations typically select a securities firm based on reputation rather than competitive bids.

Bonds can often be sold in large blocks to financial institutions. In contrast, a stock issue must be segmented into smaller pieces and is more difficult to sell. The main concern of institutional investors that purchase bonds is the credit risk of the issuer, which may be easier to assess than the risk of newly issued stock.

As with stocks, the securities firm may organize an underwriting syndicate of securities firms to participate in placing the bonds. Each securities firm assumes a portion of the risk. Of course, the potential income earned by the original securities firm is reduced, too. If the securities firm is uncomfortable guaranteeing a price to the issuer, it may offer only a best-efforts agreement.

Distribution of Bonds   Upon SEC approval of the registration, a prospectus is distributed to all potential purchasers of the bonds and the issue is advertised to the public. The asking price on the bonds is normally set at a level that will ensure a sale of the entire issue. The flotation costs generally range from 0.5 to 3 percent of the value of the bonds issued, which can be significantly lower than the flotation costs of issuing common or preferred stock.

Advising   As with a stock placement, a securities firm that places bonds for issuers may serve as an adviser to the issuer even after the placement is completed. Most issuers of bonds will need to raise long-term funds in the future and will consider the securities firm's advice on the type of securities to issue at that time.

Private Placements of Bonds   If an issuing corporation knows of a potential purchaser for its entire issue, it may be able to sell its securities directly without offering the bonds to the general public (or using the underwriting services of a securities firm). This private placement avoids the underwriting fee. Corporations have been increasingly using private placements. Potential purchasers of securities that are large enough to buy an entire issue include insurance companies, commercial banks, pension funds, and bond mutual funds. Securities can even be privately placed with two or more of these institutions. Private placements of bonds are more common than private placements of stocks.

The price paid for privately placed securities is determined by negotiations between the issuing corporation and the purchaser. Although the securities firm is not needed here for underwriting, it may advise the issuing corporation on the appropriate terms of the securities and identify potential purchasers.

Unlike the standardized provisions of a publicly placed issue, the provisions of a privately placed issue can be tailored to the desires of the purchaser. A possible disadvantage of a private placement is that the demand may not be as strong as for a publicly placed issue because only a fraction of the market is targeted. This could force a lower price for the bonds, resulting in a higher cost of financing for the issuing firm.

By facilitating bond offerings, securities firms serve as important financial intermediaries between corporations (and governments) and institutional investors. Exhibit 24.1 illustrates how they influence the flow of funds and help corporations and governments raise funds, thereby facilitating economic growth.

Exhibit 24.1   How Securities Firms Facilitate Economic Growth

24-1c Securitizing Mortgages

Some securities firms securitize individual mortgages by obtaining them from the financial institutions that originates them, bundling them into packages (in tranches) based on their risk level, hiring a credit rating agency to assign a rating to the packages, and selling the packages to institutional investors. This securitization process is beneficial to the mortgage originators that want to focus on origination or servicing of mortgages and not on financing them. Securitization facilitates the sale of smaller mortgage loans that could not be easily sold in the secondary market on an individual basis. It enables institutional investors such as mutual funds, pension funds, and insurance companies to invest in large bundles of mortgages that have already been assigned a risk rating. Securities firms earn a fee for serving as an intermediary between the mortgage originators and the institutional investors that purchase the packages of mortgages. They also commonly invest in some of the packages that they sold to institutional investors.

Securities firms may also package mortgages with other debt securities (such as automobile loans and credit card loans) when engaged in the securitization process. During the credit crisis, many mortgage loans and other types of loans defaulted, causing major losses to the institutional investors that purchased packages of debt securities. Some securities firms that invested in these packages of debt securities experienced large losses. Many securities firms were criticized for not understating the risk of the packages of securities that they sold. They countered that they relied on the credit rating agencies to assess the risk.

24-1d Advising Corporations

Securities firms often serve as advisers for corporations that wish to restructure their operations. They conduct a valuation of various existing and potential components of a corporation so that they can recommend how a corporation should restructure its operations.

Securities firms commonly suggest that the corporation could benefit from revising its ownership structure. It may recommend a **carve-out**, in which the corporation would sell one of its units to new shareholders through an IPO. The proceeds of the IPO go to the parent firm.

Alternatively, a securities firm may advise the corporation to spin off a unit by creating new shares representing the unit and distributing them to existing shareholders. Or a securities firm might recommend that a corporation engage in a divestiture, in which it sells one or more of its existing divisions that suffered recent losses. In this case, the securities firm may receive a fee for advising and a separate fee for finding buyers of the divisions that are sold.

Securities firms also commonly serve as advisors on mergers. They assess potential synergies that might result from combining two businesses, and they attempt to determine whether the synergies would be worthwhile for the potential acquirer after considering the premium that the acquirer will likely have to pay to obtain controlling interest in the target firm. Securities firms may suggest that some of a target firm's divisions will not be compatible with the acquirer's business. Thus, after a target firm is acquired, some of its individual divisions may be sold. This process is referred to as **asset stripping**.

24-1e Financing for Corporations

When securities firms serve as advisor on mergers, they may also help the acquirer obtain financing. The financing by securities firms may be especially important for acquirers that pursue leveraged buyouts (LBOs). An acquirer may not be able to afford an LBO because of constraints on the amount of funds it can borrow. Securities firms can help the acquirers issue stock or bonds, as explained earlier. They may also provide a **bridge loan** that serves as temporary financing until the acquirer has access to other funds. Some securities firms may even provide equity financing, whereby they become part owner of the acquired firm.

Exhibit 24.2 illustrates how securities firms participate in an acquisition. Note how many different functions the securities firms may perform for the acquiring firms, all of which generate fees or interest.

24-1f Providing Brokerage Services

Securities firms commonly serve as brokers by executing buy or sell orders desired by their customers. They execute large orders placed by institutional investors, such as an order to purchase 100,000 shares of a specific stock. They also execute orders placed by individuals as well as short-sale transactions for their customers.

Full-Service versus Discount Brokerage Services   Brokerage firms can be classified by the services they provide. **Full-service brokerage firms** provide information and personalized advice and execute orders. **Discount brokerage firms** execute orders only upon request and do not provide advice. They are often unable to maintain a long-term relationship with clients because they provide a service difficult to differentiate from competitors. Their required minimum opening balance is typically in the range of $1,000 to $3,000.

Although discount brokers still concentrate on executing stock transactions, they have expanded their services to include precious metals, options, and municipal bonds. Some also offer credit cards, cash management accounts, and website access to research on stocks for their clients.

Online Orders   Many investors now place orders online rather than calling brokers. Brokerage firms have reduced their costs by implementing online order systems because the online format is less expensive than having brokers receive the orders by phone. Online trading has become very competitive, however, with numerous brokerage firms fighting for market share. Consequently, the prices charged for online orders are very low. The fee for an online order to trade 100 shares of stock is typically $20 or less for investors who have an established account with the brokerage firm.

Exhibit 24.2 Participation of Securities Firms in an Acquisition

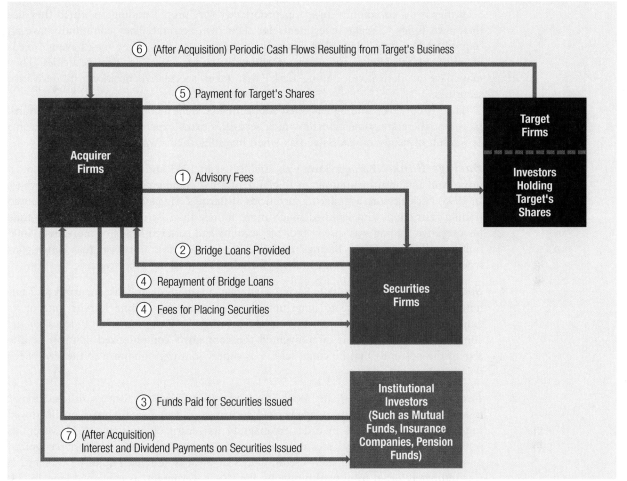

Management of Customer Accounts Some securities firms not only execute transactions for customers but also manage the portfolios of securities owned by the customers. That is, the firm decides when to buy or sell securities owned by the customers. Securities firms commonly provide this type of service to manage the pension funds of companies, but the service may also be offered to individuals. The securities firm charges a management fee for its services, which may be expressed as an annual percentage (such as 1 percent) of the assets that are managed. The firm may also charge fees for any securities transactions that it executes on behalf of the customer.

24-1g Operating Mutual Funds

Some securities firms operate mutual funds. They may offer stock, bond, and money market funds. They may offer a family (collection) of funds, so that investors can move money between different types of funds in response to economic conditions. The securities firms hire portfolio managers to manage the mutual funds. The funds charge investors an annual fee, which covers expenses and provides income to the securities firms that operate the funds.

24-1h Proprietary Trading

Securities firms commonly engage in proprietary (or "prop") trading, in which they use their own funds to make investments for their own account. They commonly have an "equity trading desk" that takes positions in equity securities. They may have a "fixed-income desk" that takes speculative positions in bonds and other debt securities. They may have a "derivatives trading desk" that takes speculative positions in derivative securities.

Their proprietary trading has often supplemented their income from other operations. However, there are some cases in which securities firms experienced financial problems as a result of taking on excessive risk when investing their own funds.

Barings Bank Barings Bank was established in 1763 and became one of the most prominent financial institutions in England, offering commercial and securities services. In 1995, Nick Leeson, a trader of currencies at Barings' Singapore branch, circumvented trading restrictions and invested much more money than Barings realized. By the time his excessive trading was discovered, his account had suffered losses of more than $600 million, which wiped out Barings' capital. The lesson of this story was that better controls were necessary to prevent individual traders from taking excessive risk.

Société Générale In 2008, Société Générale, a large French bank, incurred $7.2 billion in trading losses due to huge unauthorized trades by Jérôme Kerviel, one of its employees. Kerviel's assignment was to take positions in European stock indexes for the company. During 2007, he circumvented the company's computerized controls on the size of the positions that he could take. His supervisors were unaware of the size of his positions.

Bear Stearns In 2008, the Wall Street securities firm Bear Stearns suffered major losses from investing in mortgage-backed securities. It had relied heavily on borrowed funds (financial leverage) in order to magnify its return on investment. However, its return was negative, so its losses were magnified. Furthermore, once creditors recognized its difficulties, they cut off their credit, and Bear Stearns suffered liquidity problems. It was ultimately saved from bankruptcy by the U.S. government, as explained later in this chapter.

Lehman Brothers Lehman Brothers, another Wall Street securities firm, also suffered financial problems due to bad investments in mortgage-backed securities and heavy reliance on borrowed funds. It filed for bankruptcy in September 2008, as explained later in this chapter.

WEB

www2.goldmansachs. com
Information on a securities firm's performance and services provided.

Underlying Cause of Investment Problems The underlying cause of the problems experienced by the four securities firms just described is the huge incentive to take risk. Many employees of securities firms have earned bonuses of more than a million dollars in one year as a result of generating high returns on investment for their securities firms. Thus they have a strong incentive to pursue investments that may offer high returns, even if the risks are high.

24-1i Summary of Services Provided

Exhibit 24.3 summarizes the services that are commonly provided by securities firms. The proportion of income derived from each type of service in any particular year varies among securities firms. Some securities firms emphasize investment banking functions such as underwriting and advising and therefore generate a higher proportion of income

Exhibit 24.3 Sources of Income for a Securities Firm

INVESTMENT BANKING SERVICES	
Underwriting	Fees from underwriting stock offerings by firms or underwriting bond offerings by firms and government agencies
Advising	Fees for providing advice to firms about: • Identifying potential targets • Valuing targets • Identifying potential acquirers • Protecting against takeovers
Restructuring	Fees for facilitating: • Mergers • Divestitures • Carve-outs • Spin-offs
BROKERAGE SERVICES	
Management fees	Fees for managing an individual's or a firm's securities portfolio
Trading commissions	Fees for executing securities trades requested by individuals or firms in the secondary market
Margin interest	Interest charged to investors who buy securities on margin
INVESTING ITS OWN FUNDS	
Investing	Profits from investing in securities

from underwriting and advising fees. Conversely, other securities firms emphasize brokerage services and therefore generate a higher proportion of their income from trading commissions.

Market conditions can also affect the proportion of income earned by a securities firm from particular services. When there are many IPOs, securities firms will generate more income from underwriting activities. When there is a high level of merger activity, securities firms generate more income from advisory services for corporate restructuring.

Some securities firms attempt to diversify their services so that they can capitalize on economies of scope and also possibly reduce their exposure if the demand for any particular service is weak. However, the demand is highly correlated across services. When market conditions are weak, the volume of IPOs, mergers, securitizations, and secondary market trades is usually low. Thus, securities firms will likely perform poorly under these conditions.

24-1j Interaction with Other Financial Institutions

When securities firms provide their financial services, they commonly interact with various types of financial institutions, as summarized in Exhibit 24.4. They offer investment advice and execute security transactions for financial institutions that maintain security portfolios. They also compete against those financial institutions that have brokerage subsidiaries. Furthermore, they compete with some commercial banks that underwrite securities and manage mutual funds. Because securities firms commonly offer some banking and insurance services and because many insurance companies and commercial banks offer securities services, it is sometimes difficult to distinguish among financial institutions.

Exhibit 24.4 Interaction between Securities Firms and Other Financial Institutions

TYPE OF FINANCIAL INSTITUTION	INTERACTION WITH SECURITIES FIRMS
Commercial banks and savings institutions	• Compete with securities firms that provide brokerage services. • Compete directly with securities firms to provide merger advisory services.
Mutual funds	• Rely on securities firms to execute trades. • Are sometimes owned by securities firms. • Purchase newly issued securities that are underwritten by securities firms.
Insurance companies	• Receive advice from securities firms on what securities to buy or sell. • Rely on securities firms to execute securities transactions. • Receive advice from securities firms on how to hedge against interest rate risk and market risk. • Purchase stocks and bonds that are underwritten by securities firms. • May compete directly with securities firms to sell mutual funds to investors. • May provide financing for LBOs to securities firms. • May acquire or merge with a securities firm in order to offer more diversified services.
Pension funds	• Receive advice from securities firms on what securities to buy or sell. • Rely on securities firms to execute securities transactions. • Receive advice from securities firms on how to hedge against interest rate risk and market risk. • Purchase newly issued securities that are underwritten by securities firms.

24-1k Participation in Financial Markets

When securities firms provide financial services, they participate in all types of financial markets, as summarized in Exhibit 24.5. They place newly issued securities and execute trades of existing securities for their clients in money markets, mortgage markets, bond markets, and stock markets. In addition, their proprietary trading activity exposes them to fluctuations in stock markets and bond markets.

24-1l Conflicts of Interest from Participation

When securities firms serve as brokers or as advisors on financial transactions, they are subject to some potential conflicts of interest. In the brokerage business, their fees are likely to be dependent on the amount of shares traded, which means they would benefit more from recommending that investors change their investments often rather than retain their investments over a long-term period. In the merger advisory business, they would benefit more from advising companies to engage in mergers than they would from advising companies to avoid mergers, because many of their fees will only be charged if a merger occurs.

Since securities firms tend to earn larger profits when they execute transactions for their clients, they commonly offer incentives to their employees that are based on (or influenced by) the volume of transactions executed. Consequently, employees have an incentive to generate a large number of transactions even if that does not serve the best interests of the client. There are some cases in which investor accounts managed by securities firms have an unusually large number of transactions. There are also cases in which securities firms have promoted specific securities to their clients while taking the opposite position (the counter-party) of those transactions. Some blatant cases of unethical behavior have been highly publicized, in which a securities firm was promoting a specific security while referring to that security as junk among employees and attempting to dump its holdings of that security.

Exhibit 24.5 Participation of Securities Firms in Financial Markets

TYPE OF FINANCIAL MARKET	PARTICIPATION BY SECURITIES FIRMS
Money markets	• Some securities firms have created money market mutual funds, which invest in money market securities. • Securities firms underwrite commercial paper and purchase short-term securities for their own investment portfolios.
Bond markets	• Securities firms underwrite bonds in the primary market, advise clients on bonds to purchase or sell, and serve as brokers for bond transactions in the secondary market. • Some bond mutual funds have been created by securities firms. • Securities firms facilitate mergers, acquisitions, and LBOs by placing bonds for their clients. • Securities firms purchase bonds for their own investment portfolios.
Mortgage markets	• Securities firms underwrite securities that are backed by mortgages for various financial institutions.
Stock markets	• Securities firms underwrite stocks in the primary market, advise clients on what stocks to purchase or sell, and serve as brokers for stock transactions in the secondary market. • Securities firms purchase stocks for their own investment portfolios.
Futures markets	• Securities firms advise large financial institutions on how to hedge their portfolios with financial futures contracts. • Securities firms serve as brokers for financial futures transactions.
Options markets	• Securities firms advise large financial institutions on how to hedge portfolios with options contracts. • Securities firms serve as brokers for options transactions.
Swap markets	• Some securities firms engage in interest rate swaps to reduce their exposure to interest rate risk. • Many securities firms serve as financial intermediaries in swap markets.

Cases like these are sometimes triggered by a few employees and do not necessarily reflect the culture of the securities firm. However, a securities firm can influence the behavior of its employees by the incentives it uses to set their compensation. Providing employees with a code of principles of ethical behavior is not sufficient for ensuring ethical conduct if the incentives to increase compensation are strictly based on maximizing the number of transactions that are executed. In most publicized cases of unethical behavior, the actions of the employees at securities firms are motivated by the compensation they received due to those actions.

Securities firms that compensate their employees based on criteria such as client assessment of their employee services might ensure that employees serve the client's needs instead of themselves. In the long run, the securities firms that satisfy the vast majority of their clients should be more capable of growing their reputation and their business.

GLOBAL ASPECTS

24-1m Expanding Functions Internationally

Most large securities firms have expanded their functions internationally, which offers several possible advantages. First, their international presence allows them to place securities in international markets for corporations or governments. Second, some corporations that are heavily involved with international mergers and acquisitions prefer advice from securities firms that have subsidiaries in all potential markets. Third, institutional investors that invest in foreign securities prefer securities firms that can easily handle such transactions.

Growth in International Joint Ventures   In recent years, securities firms have expanded their international business by engaging in joint ventures with foreign securities firms. In this way, they penetrate foreign markets but have a limited stake in each project. Many securities firms have also increased their global presence by facilitating privatizations of firms in foreign markets such as Latin America and Eastern Europe.

Growth in International Securities Transactions   The growth in international securities transactions has created more business for the larger securities firms. For example, many stock offerings are now conducted across numerous countries as some corporations attempt to achieve global name recognition. In addition, an international stock offering can avoid the downward pressure on the stock's price that might occur if the entire issue is sold in the domestic country. Large securities firms facilitate international stock offerings by creating an international syndicate to place the securities in various countries. Those securities firms that have established a global presence receive most of the requests for international stock offerings.

WEB

www.seclaw.com/
secrules.htm
Federal rules and
regulations related
to securities firms.

24-2 REGULATION OF SECURITIES FIRMS

Securities firms are subject to a wide variety of regulations. The SEC plays a key role in regulation by enforcing financial disclosure laws that attempt to ensure that investors who buy or sell securities have access to financial information. These laws give the SEC the power to require publicly traded companies to provide sufficient financial information to existing or prospective investors. However, securities firms have generally been subject to very limited regulation in terms of how they use their funds.

24-2a Stock Exchange Regulations

Stock exchanges impose regulations on securities firms to prevent unfair or illegal practices, ensure orderly trading, and address customer complaints. Stock exchanges have regulatory divisions, and the Nasdaq market is regulated by the National Association of Securities Dealers (NASD). Both the exchanges and the NASD have surveillance departments that monitor trading patterns and behavior by market-makers and floor traders. They also have enforcement divisions that investigate possible violations and can take disciplinary action. They can take legal action as well and sometimes work with the SEC to correct cases of market trading abuse.

The SEC tends to establish general guidelines that can affect trading on security exchanges, but the day-to-day regulation of exchange trading is the responsibility of the exchange. Regulation of trading behavior is necessary to ensure that investors who place orders are properly accommodated. This can establish credibility within the systems used to execute securities transactions. In addition to the SEC, NASD, and exchanges, the Federal Reserve Board has some regulatory influence because it determines the credit limits (margin requirements) on securities purchased.

Insurance on Cash and Securities Deposited at Brokerage Firms   The **Securities Investor Protection Corporation (SIPC)** offers insurance on cash and securities deposited at brokerage firms and can liquidate failing brokerage firms. The insurance limit is $500,000, including $100,000 against claims on cash. The SIPC uses premiums assessed on brokers that are registered with the SEC to maintain its insurance fund. In addition to its insurance fund, the SIPC has a $500 million revolving line of credit with a group of banks and can borrow up to $1 billion from the SEC. Because the SIPC boosts investor confidence in the securities industry, economic efficiency is increased, so market concerns are less likely to cause a run on deposits of cash and securities at securities firms.

24-2b Regulatory Events That Affected Securities Firms

Several regulatory events that were mentioned in previous chapters had a direct or indirect effect on securities firms. Here is a summary of recent regulatory events that are related to securities firms.

Financial Services Modernization Act In the 1990s, financial institutions focusing on different types of financial services found numerous loopholes in regulations. To clarify the situation, Congress enacted the Financial Services Modernization Act of 1999, which allowed banking, securities activities, and insurance to be consolidated. As a result, financial institutions no longer need to search for loopholes. Specifically, the act provides for a special holding company structure that enables a financial holding company to own subsidiaries that focus on various financial services. Firms that adopt this structure are regulated by the Federal Reserve. Capital requirements for the bank subsidiaries are imposed by bank regulators. Capital requirements for the insurance subsidiaries are subject to state insurance regulators.

The Financial Services Modernization Act resulted in the creation of more financial conglomerates that include securities firms. One of the key benefits to securities firms in a financial conglomerate is cross-listing. When individuals use brokerage services of a securities firm, that firm may steer them to do their banking with the affiliated commercial bank or to obtain a mortgage with the affiliated savings institution. When firms use investment banking services of a securities firm, that firm may steer them to do their banking with the affiliated commercial bank. The other types of financial institutions that form the conglomerate can reciprocate by steering their customers toward the securities firm. Thus, the bundling of financial services can generate more business for each type of financial institution that is part of the financial conglomerate. However, just as a financial conglomerate can increase market share by pulling business away from other financial institutions, it may lose market share when other financial conglomerates use their bundling of financial services to attract customers.

The Financial Services Modernization Act of 1999 created a more competitive environment for securities firms by allowing commercial banks, securities firms, and insurance companies to merge. It removed limitations on the degree to which banks could offer securities services, which resulted in more intense competition from the banks. Some banks acquired securities firms so that they could provide a wide range of securities services to their existing customer base.

Regulation FD In October 2000, the SEC enacted Regulation Fair Disclosure (FD), which requires firms to disclose any significant information simultaneously to all market participants. This rule was partially intended to prevent firms from leaking information to analysts who work for securities firms. Before Regulation FD, a firm's chief financial officer could have legally leaked information to an analyst about the firm's earnings or other relevant financial details before announcing this information to the public. Some analysts capitalized on the information by disclosing it to their key clients. Small investors were left out of the loop and were at a competitive disadvantage.

As a result of Regulation FD, firms more frequently provide their information in the form of news releases or conference calls rather than leaking it to a few analysts. Those analysts who relied on inside information when providing their insight to clients have lost their competitive advantage, while analysts who relied on their own analysis rather than information leaks have gained a competitive edge.

Regulation of Analyst Ratings In the 2001–2002 period, the process by which analysts rated stocks was widely criticized. Firms recognize that the demand for their stock may be partially dictated by the rating assigned by an analyst. When they need underwriting or advisory services from a securities firm, they are more likely to hire a firm whose analysts rate their stock highly. Securities firms also recognize that they are more likely to attract business from a firm if they give its stock a high rating, regardless of their real opinion of the stock. In fact, some analysts were spending much of their time generating new business, and their compensation was sometimes aligned with the business they brought to the securities firm. Consequently, analysts were tempted to inflate the ratings they assigned to stocks, and the investors who relied on the ratings to make investment decisions were misled.

WEB

www.sec.gov
How the SEC monitors securities trading activity and enforces securities laws.

In 2002, in an attempt to prevent the obvious conflict of interest, the SEC implemented new rules, as summarized here.

- If a securities firm underwrites an IPO, its analysts cannot promote the stock for the first 40 days after the IPO. Thus, the price of the stock should be driven by factors other than hype provided by the underwriter's analysts in the first 40 days.
- An analyst's compensation cannot be directly aligned with the amount of business that the analyst brings to the securities firm. Analysts cannot be supervised by the investment banking department within the securities firm. This rule is intended to prevent investment bankers from pressuring analysts to provide high rankings of firms in order to attract more underwriting business from those firms.
- An analyst's rating must also divulge any recent investment banking business provided by the securities firm that assigned the rating.

Regulation of the IPO Market In the 2001–2003 period, various abuses in the IPO market were highly publicized.

- Some securities firms that served as underwriters on IPOs allocated shares to corporate executives who were considering an IPO for their own firm. Some critics viewed this process, referred to as *spinning,* as an implicit bribe to obtain the future business of the firm.
- Some securities firms that served as underwriters of IPOs encouraged institutional investors to place bids above the offer price on the first day that the shares traded as a condition for being allowed to participate in the next IPO. They also charged excessive commissions to investors in some cases when the demand for the IPO shares was well in excess of the supply.

The SEC investigated cases of abuse and imposed fines on some securities firms. In addition, it enacted rules to prevent such abuses from occurring in the future.

24-3 VALUATION OF A SECURITIES FIRM

Securities firms (or securities operating units that are part of a financial conglomerate) are commonly valued by their managers to monitor progress over time or by other financial institutions that are considering an acquisition. The value of a securities firm can be modeled as the present value of its future cash flows. Thus, the value of a securities firm should change in response to changes in its expected cash flows in the future and to changes in the required rate of return by investors:

$$\Delta V = f[\underbrace{\Delta E(CF)}_{+}, \underbrace{\Delta k}_{-}]$$

24-3a Factors That Affect Cash Flows

The change in a securities firm's expected cash flows may be modeled as

$$\Delta E(CF) = f(\underbrace{\Delta ECON}_{+}, \underbrace{\Delta R_f}_{-}, \underbrace{\Delta INDUS}_{?}, \underbrace{\Delta MANAB}_{+})$$

where ECON represents economic growth, R_f represents the risk-free interest rate, INDUS represents industry conditions, and MANAB represents the abilities of the securities firm's management.

Change in Economic Growth   Economic growth can enhance a securities firm's cash flows because it increases the level of income of firms and households and can increase the demand for the firm's services. Specifically, the volume of brokerage activity tends to increase when households have more income, and corporations are more likely to hire securities firms to help them raise funds for expansion when economic conditions are favorable.

Change in the Risk-Free Interest Rate   A securities firm's holdings of debt securities (such as bonds) are affected by interest rate movements. If interest rates rise, the valuation of the debt holdings declines, which reduces the valuation of the security firm.

Change in Industry Conditions   Securities firms can be affected by industry conditions, including regulations, technology, and competition. For example, regulatory constraints can restrict firms from offering specific banking services or set the margin limits for investors. In general, securities firms tend to prefer limited regulation so that they can pursue ventures that offer the potential for high returns. However, some securities firms such as Lehman Brothers took excessive risks, which led to failure.

Change in Management Abilities   A securities firm has control over the composition of its managers and its organizational structure. Its managers can attempt to make internal decisions that will capitalize on the external forces (economic growth, interest rates, regulatory constraints) that the firm cannot control. It needs skillful management to create new financial services that may complement the brokerage services offered to individuals. Skillful management is also needed to create new products (such as specialized derivative instruments) that will be used by firms.

24-3b Factors That Affect the Required Rate of Return

The required rate of return by investors who invest in a securities firm can be modeled as

$$\Delta k = f(\underbrace{\Delta R_f}_{+}, \underbrace{\Delta RP}_{+})$$

where ΔR_f represents a change in the risk-free interest rate and ΔRP represents a change in the risk premium. The risk-free interest rate is normally expected to be positively related to inflation, economic growth, and the budget deficit level but inversely related to money supply growth (assuming such growth does not cause inflation). The risk premium on a securities firm is inversely related to economic growth and the company's management skills. The management of some securities firms use compensation incentives that are focused on increasing return on investment without much emphasis on controlling risk.

Exhibit 24.6 provides a framework for valuing a securities firm based on the preceding discussion. In general, the value of a securities firm is favorably affected by strong economic growth, a reduction in interest rates, and strong management capabilities.

24-4 Exposure of Securities Firms to Risk

The operations conducted by securities firms create exposure to market risk, interest rate risk, credit risk, and exchange rate risk, as explained next.

24-4a Market Risk

Securities firms offer many services that are linked to stock market conditions. When stock prices are rising, there is normally a greater volume of stock offerings and secondary market transactions. Because securities firms typically are needed to facilitate these transactions, they benefit from a bullish stock market. Those securities firms that manage mutual funds typically benefit from the large investment in mutual funds during a bullish market.

Exhibit 24.6   Framework for Valuing a Securities Firm

- A stronger economy leads to more securities transactions (brokerage fee income), an increase in security offerings and other services provided by the securities firm, and therefore better cash flows.
- A lower risk-free rate enhances the valuations of bonds held by securities firms. It also may encourage some corporations to pursue bond offerings while interest rates are low and therefore may create more business for the securities firm.
- The valuation is also influenced by industry conditions and the securities firm's management (not shown in the diagram). These factors affect the risk premium (and therefore the required return by investors) and the expected cash flows to be generated by the securities firm. In particular, regulations that affect the degree of competition for securities services affect the risk premium and cash flows generated by the securities firm.

When the stock market is depressed, stock transactions tend to decline, causing a reduction in business for securities firms. Although securities firms have diversified into different services, the demand for many of these services is tied to stock market conditions. Thus, the performance of most securities firms is highly sensitive to the stock market cycles.

24-4b Interest Rate Risk

The performance of securities firms can be sensitive to interest rate movements for the following reasons. First, lower interest rates can encourage corporations or government agencies to issue more bonds, which requires more underwriting activity by securities firms. Second, the market values of bonds held as investments by securities firms increase as interest rates decline. Thus the performance of some securities firms is inversely related to interest rate movements.

24-4c Credit Risk

Many securities firms offer bridge loans and other types of credit to corporations. The securities firms are subject to the possibility that these corporations will default on their loans. The probability of default tends to increase during periods when economic conditions deteriorate. Securities firms that invest in mortgages and other types of debt securities may be more exposed to credit risk.

GLOBAL
ASPECTS

24-4d Exchange Rate Risk

Many securities firms have operations in foreign countries. The earnings remitted by foreign subsidiaries are reduced when the foreign currencies weaken against the parent firm's home currency. In addition, the market values of securities maintained as investments and denominated in foreign currencies decline as the currencies weaken against the parent firm's home currency.

24-4e Impact of Financial Leverage on Exposure to Risk

The degree to which a securities firm is exposed to the risks just described is influenced by its financial leverage. While a high degree of financial leverage increases the potential return on investment, it also increases the exposure of the securities firm to major losses.

EXAMPLE

Optima Securities Co. has $1 billion in assets and estimates its net income for next year to be $10 million, which represents a return on assets of $10 million ÷ $1 billion = 1%. It considers supporting its assets with equity (a source of capital) in the range between $80 million (8 percent of its assets) and $40 million (4 percent of its assets), and the remainder of the financing will be with debt or other liabilities. It considers five different equity levels; for each level, the estimated return on equity (ROE) is shown in Exhibit 24.7. It can determine its ROE as

$$ROE = \frac{Income}{Equity} = \frac{Income}{Assets} \times \frac{Assets}{Equity}$$
$$= ROA \times Equity\ Multiplier$$

This equation shows how return on equity (ROE) for next year is influenced by the security firm's return on assets (income/equity) and its degree of financial leverage (as measured by the equity multiplier). Notice that if it maintains a level of equity that represents 8 percent of its assets, its estimated ROE for next year will be 12.5 percent. Yet if it considers lower levels of equity to support its assets (and therefore uses more debt to finance its assets), it will achieve a higher ROE.

To illustrate how financial leverage can affect the risk of Optima Securities Co., consider how its ROA and ROE would be affected if it incurred a loss of $10 million this year instead of positive net income of $10 million. Its ROA in Column 3 of Exhibit 24.7 would now be −1% instead of 1%.

Exhibit 24.7   Illustration of How Level of Equity Affects Return on Equity

POSSIBLE LEVEL OF EQUITY	EQUITY AS % OF ITS $1 BILLION IN ASSETS	ASSUMED ROA	EQUITY MULTIPLIER (INVERSE OF CAPITAL/ ASSET RATIO)	ROE = ROA × EQUITY MULTIPLIER
$80 million	8%	1%	1/8% = 12.5	12.5%
$70 million	7%	1%	1/7% = 14.28	14.28%
$60 million	6%	1%	1/6% = 16.67	16.67%
$50 million	5%	1%	1/5% = 20	20%
$40 million	4%	1%	1/4% = 25	25%

In addition, the ROE levels in Column 5 of the exhibit would now have a negative sign. That is, if the firm used $80 million of equity financing and incurred a loss of $10 million, its loss would represent 12.5 percent of its equity. At the other extreme, if it used only $40 million of equity financing and incurred a loss on $10 million, its loss would represent 25 percent of its equity. Thus, just as a higher degree of financial leverage (lower proportion of equity financing) can enhance return on equity, it also results in more risk. ●

WEB

www.bloomberg.com
Insert the ticker symbol for any securities firm and click on "News" to review news about specific securities firms and the industry overall.

To appreciate the effect on risk, consider a new example in which Optima Securities Co. experienced losses on some of its investments in assets such as mortgage-backed securities and had to write down the value of its assets by $50 million (5 percent of their original value) to reflect their prevailing market value. If it maintained a level of equity of less than $50 million, it would not have sufficient equity to absorb the loss. Therefore, the value of its liabilities would now exceed the value of its assets, and its creditors may force the firm to file for bankruptcy.

24-5 IMPACT OF THE CREDIT CRISIS ON SECURITIES FIRMS

During the credit crisis in 2008, some large securities firms experienced serious financial problems. Various types of debt securities such as mortgages that they had purchased defaulted. As the credit crisis intensified, institutional investors that commonly purchased debt securities were less willing to participate after noticing the higher default rates on credit. Thus some credit markets became inactive, the volume of services provided by securities firms declined, and the fees earned by securities firms declined. Stock prices plummeted, so firms did not want to issue stock at the prevailing stock prices, and the fees earned by securities firms for facilitating stock offerings also declined. Merger volume declined as well, and therefore so did the fees earned by securities firms for facilitating merger transactions. In general, the crisis caused a major reduction in underwriting income, merger fee income, and brokerage income earned by securities firms. In addition, the value of mortgage holdings of some securities firms declined substantially.

24-5a Government Assistance to Bear Stearns

Bear Stearns was a financial intermediary of mortgage-backed securities linked to low-quality (subprime) mortgages, and it also invested in many mortgage-backed securities. As the credit crisis intensified, the value of its mortgage-backed securities declined. In fact, Bear owned two hedge funds that collapsed because of their heavy investment in subprime mortgage securities. From March 2007 until March 2008, it wrote down

$3 billion of its assets so that their valuation would be more closely in line with the true market value.

Bear's Liquidity Problems   By March 2008, Bear Stearns was suffering from liquidity problems. Some of the financial institutions that were providing loans to Bear were no longer willing to provide funding because they were doubtful that Bear would be able to repay the loans. Bear was not in a position to raise funds with an equity offering because its stock price was slipping and would have fallen further if the company had signaled its need for funding with a secondary stock offering.

On Thursday, March 13, Bear Stearns secretly notified the Federal Reserve that it was experiencing liquidity problems and would have to file for bankruptcy the next day if it could not obtain funds.

Fed Intervention   The next morning, the Fed's Board of Governors met to discuss the situation. The Board of Governors recognized that the bankruptcy of Bear Stearns could be contagious and create chaos in the financial markets. Since Bear facilitated various financial transactions for many people and firms, its bankruptcy could cause liquidity problems for all the people and firms that were relying on it to complete financial transactions in its intermediary role.

On Friday, March 14, 2008, it was announced that JPMorgan Chase (a commercial bank) was going to offer a loan to Bear Stearns. Rather than calming the markets, however, the announcement validated the suspicion that Bear Stearns lacked adequate liquidity, and its stock price immediately declined from about $57 to $30.

During the weekend, Fed officials met with executives from Bear Stearns and JPMorgan Chase. Before the financial markets opened on Monday, March 17, 2008, the Fed extended a $30 billion credit line to JPMorgan Chase to help it acquire Bear Stearns. The Fed's role was critical because it would allow JPMorgan Chase to obtain more permanent financing for the acquisition over time. JPMorgan Chase agreed to pay $10 per share, which was about 90 percent less than Bear's stock price one year earlier.

The Fed also allowed JPMorgan Chase an 18-month exemption on the capital requirements that are imposed on commercial banks. This was to allow JPMorgan Chase time to absorb Bear's assets and to sell off high-risk assets that could require a higher capital level.

On Monday, March 17, the Fed also announced that it was willing to provide emergency loans to about 20 primary dealers that serve as key financial intermediaries for the large Treasury securities transactions in the secondary market. It also committed to loans of up to $200 billion of Treasury securities to primary dealers for a term of 28 days (rather than overnight) in exchange for other types of securities. These provisions were also intended to calm the financial markets.

The Fed's assistance to Bear Stearns offered only limited help to its stockholders. Most of the stockholders that had invested in Bear before its liquidity problems surfaced lost most of their investment. Instead, the major beneficiaries of the Fed's intervention were the creditors that had provided credit to Bear Stearns; if Bear had failed and been liquidated, they would probably have received only a small fraction of the credit that they had provided.

Potential Systemic Risk Due to the Bear Stearns Problems   The Fed's assistance to Bear Stearns led to questions about whether there should be a consistent policy for dealing with financial institutions that are deemed too big to fail. In general, the typical strategy would be to allow the equity value of the failing firm to be dictated by market forces, meaning that equity investors would lose their entire investment. Creditors would have rights to the remaining value of the firm, but in liquidation they would receive only a portion of the funds they had loaned to the firm. But the Fed's intervention protected the creditors holding debt securities that were issued by Bear Stearns.

The Fed's justification for its intervention was the high exposure to systemic risk, whereby the failure of Bear Stearns could have spread adverse effects throughout financial markets. Since Bear Stearns was a major provider of clearing operations for many types of financial transactions, its failure might have frozen or delayed many financial transactions, which could have resulted in a liquidity crisis for many individuals and firms that were to receive cash as a result of the transactions. Bear Stearns also served as a counterparty to various types of financial agreements. If Bear had defaulted on all of its counterparty positions, this could have caused problems for the financial institutions on the other side of those agreements, which could have created chaos in financial markets. That is, Bear Stearns may have been viewed as "too entangled" (in financial transactions) to fail.

Criticism of the Fed's Assistance to Bear Stearns Some critics (including Paul Volcker, a previous chair of the Board of Governors of the Fed) have questioned the Fed's role in aiding Bear Stearns, since Bear was a securities firm, not a commercial bank. They suggest that providing assistance to a firm other than a commercial bank should be the responsibility of Congress and not the Fed.

In addition, a rescue can cause a moral hazard problem, meaning that financial institutions may pursue high-risk opportunities in order to achieve high returns with the assumption that they will be bailed out if their strategies fail. Managers who pursue such strategies may be able to keep their jobs if the firm is rescued before it fails. The Fed's actions also raise the question of what other types of firms might be aided by the Fed rather than Congress. Some people, though, might counter that the Fed is in a better position to intervene when a potential bankruptcy could undermine the financial system.

24-5b Failure of Lehman Brothers

Lehman Brothers specialized in the underwriting of fixed-income securities such as bonds and in asset management for companies and wealthy individuals. In 2006, it was ranked number one in the *Barron's* annual survey of corporate performance for large companies. In 2007, it was ranked at the top of *Fortune* magazine's list of "Most Admired Securities Firms." By 2008, it had grown to become the fourth largest securities firm in the United States. However, Lehman had considerable exposure to mortgage-backed securities, which led to financial problems in 2008. It had a relatively low level of cash, and its high degree of financial leverage created more pressure. For every dollar of equity, it had about $30 of debt. Furthermore, some of its debt was short term and therefore could be cut off (not renewed) if creditors sensed that Lehman was experiencing financial problems.

Lehman Brothers was using an accounting method that allowed its capital position to look stronger because capital was measured in proportion to total assets (which were reduced by the accounting treatment). Thus, Lehman's degree of financial leverage was even higher than what was reported on its balance sheet.

Lehman's Liquidity Problems From March 2008 to September 2008, its stock price declined by about 85 percent, and it was unable to raise sufficient funds through a stock offering. In addition, concerns about its creditworthiness prevented it from obtaining credit at a reasonable cost. The growing concerns about Lehman led some clients to cut their business ties, which further reduced its cash inflows. On September 15, 2008, it filed for bankruptcy.

Lehman's financial problems created a very difficult dilemma for the U.S. government, because it had become so large and played a very important role as a financial intermediary. If the U.S. government did not rescue Lehman, it would cause financial problems for many other firms (such as creditors and counterparties on swap agreements) that would not receive payments owed to them if Lehman failed. Lehman was not a commercial bank and therefore was not subject to bank regulations. This allowed it to have some competitive advantages and also allowed it to engage in some risky operations (that potentially offer high returns) that were not allowed for banks. Yet, as Lehman experienced financial problems as a result of its risky operations, it apparently expected that it would be treated like a large commercial bank and be rescued by bank regulators. It may have been able to rescue itself if it was willing to find a suitable financial institution to acquire it several months before its bankruptcy filing.

24-5c Impact of the Crisis on Regulatory Reform

The Federal Reserve's assistance to Bear Stearns and offer of temporary financing to other securities firms provided a rationale for the Fed to require that securities firms meet specified regulations such as capital requirements just like commercial banks. Historically, securities firms were subject to looser regulations than those imposed on commercial banks. In particular, securities firms were not subject to the capital requirements imposed on banks and therefore could use more debt to support their operations. They used a higher degree of financial leverage, which magnified their positive returns, but also magnified their losses. The problems of Bear Stearns and Lehman Brothers illustrated how the high degree of financial leverage used by securities firms could create excessive risk to the firms and to the financial system.

The momentum for regulatory reform of financial services continued when Merrill Lynch was acquired by Bank of America. Like Bear Stearns and Lehman, Merrill Lynch experienced major losses from its mortgage-backed securities. Its stock price had been declining, and its access to new capital was limited because of investor concerns about its financial condition. While the Federal Reserve was the primary regulator of Bank of America's operations, the SEC was the primary regulator of Merrill Lynch's operations. But when Merrill Lynch was acquired by Bank of America, it became subject to oversight by the Federal Reserve.

Conversion of Securities Firms to BHCs   During the credit crisis, some securities firms were unable to access funds by issuing securities. They did not want to issue stock while stock prices were weak. In addition, they were unable to issue debt securities because investors were concerned about their financial condition. The lack of funding deepened the financial problems of Bear Stearns and Merrill Lynch before they were acquired and of Lehman Brothers before it went bankrupt. As a result of the consolidation during the credit crisis, Goldman Sachs and Morgan Stanley were the only two large securities firms remaining. They applied to become bank holding companies (BHCs), and the Fed approved the requests in September 2008. This new structure gave the firms more flexibility to obtain financing. Securities firms were allowed to borrow short-term funds from the Federal Reserve during the credit crisis, but their conversion to a BHC structure would give them permanent access to Federal Reserve funding.

A BHC can have commercial banking and securities subsidiaries. The commercial banking subsidiary can accept deposits and perform the functions of commercial banks, such as lending to businesses. It can create some stability for the company overall because it has steady access to deposits that are insured up to a limit. The securities subsidiary performs the traditional securities functions such as advising and underwriting securities for client firms.

Overall, the BHC structure results in a greater degree of regulatory oversight by the Federal Reserve. The companies will need to satisfy capital requirements established by the Fed. These requirements are higher than the capital normally maintained by securities firms. Consequently, the securities firms may be viewed as safer as a result of their conversion to BHCs.

FINANCIAL REFORM

Financial Reform Act of 2010   The Financial Reform Act of 2010 was implemented to stabilize the financial system. Those provisions that have a direct impact on securities firms are briefly summarized here.

First, the Financial Reform Act mandated that financial institutions granting mortgages verify the income, job status, and credit history of mortgage applicants before approving mortgage applications. Thus, when securities firms serve as intermediaries in the securitization process, the mortgage backing the securities that they sell should be less risky.

Second, the Financial Reform Act requires that securities firms and other financial institutions that sell securities through the securitization process retain 5 percent of the portfolio unless the portfolio meets specific standards that reflect low risk. This provision encourages firms to ensure that the mortgages backing the securities they sell are less risky.

Third, the act created the Financial Stability Oversight Council, which is responsible for identifying risks to financial stability in the United States and makes regulatory recommendations to regulators that could reduce any risks to the financial system. The council can recommend methods to ensure that securities firms and other financial institutions do not rely on regulatory bailouts.

Fourth, the act assigned specific regulators with the authority to determine that any particular securities firm or other financial institution should be liquidated. This expedites the liquidation process and can limit the losses incurred by a failing financial institution.

Fifth, the act requires that derivative securities be traded through a clearinghouse or exchange rather than over the counter. This should allow for a more standardized structure regarding margins and collateral and more transparency of derivative security prices. Consequently, securities firms that trade these derivative securities should be less susceptible to risk that the counterparty posted insufficient collateral.

SUMMARY

- Securities firms facilitate new issues of stock by advising how much stock the firm can issue, determining the appropriate price for the stock, underwriting the stock, and distributing the stock. They facilitate new issues of bonds in a somewhat similar manner. They also provide advice and financing to corporations pursuing mergers, provide brokerage services, operate mutual funds, and engage in proprietary trading.

- Many regulations have been imposed on securities firms that attempt to ensure that transactions in financial markets do not allow any particular investors an unfair advantage. Stock exchanges impose regulations on securities firms to prevent unfair or illegal practices, ensure orderly trading, and address customer complaints. Several regulatory events have allowed more competition between securities firms and other financial institutions. Regulations require that corporations disclose any information to the public, which prevents them from leaking information to analysts of securities firms. Rules have been implemented to prevent or discourage analysts from assigning inflated ratings to stocks and to prevent analysts from being compensated by investment bank divisions that seek business from corporate clients.

■ Securities firms are exposed to market risk because their volume of business is larger when stock market conditions are stronger. They are subject to interest rate risk because their underwriting business is sensitive to interest rate movements. They also hold some long-term financial assets whose values decline in response to higher interest rates. Securities firms are also subject to credit risk, since they commonly purchase debt securities and provide loans to some of their business clients. The potential damage due to these types of risk is more pronounced for securities firms that use a very high degree of financial leverage.

■ As a result of the credit crisis, several major securities firms experienced financial problems, which were partially due to their high exposure to credit risk and their high degree of financial leverage. The acquisitions of securities firms by commercial banks and conversion of other securities firms into bank holding companies led to more oversight of security firm operations by the Federal Reserve.

POINT COUNTER-POINT

Should Analysts Be Separated from Securities Firms to Prevent Conflicts of Interest?

Point No. Securities firms are known for their ability to analyze companies and value them. Investors may be more comfortable when analysts work within a securities firm because they have access to substantial information.

Counter-Point Yes. Analysts have a conflict of interest because they may be unwilling to offer negative views about a company that is a client of their securities firm.

Who Is Correct? Use the Internet to learn more about this issue and then formulate your own opinion.

QUESTIONS AND APPLICATIONS

1. Regulation of Securities Activities Explain the role of the SEC, the NASD, and the stock exchanges in regulating the securities industry.

2. SIPC What is the purpose of the SIPC?

3. Investment Banking Services How do securities firms facilitate leveraged buyouts? Why are securities firms that are better able to raise funds in the capital markets preferred by corporations that need advice on proposed acquisitions?

4. Origination Process Describe the origination process for corporations that are about to issue new stock.

5. Underwriting Function Describe the underwriting function of a securities firm.

6. Best-Efforts Agreement What is a best-efforts agreement?

7. Failure of Lehman Brothers Why did Lehman Brothers experience financial problems during the credit crisis?

8. Direct Placement Describe a direct placement of bonds. What is an advantage of a private placement? What is a disadvantage?

9. International Expansion Explain why securities firms from the United States have expanded into foreign markets.

10. Proprietary Trading Explain the process of proprietary trading by securities firms.

11. Asset Stripping What is asset stripping?

12. Securities Firms' Use of Leverage Explain why securities firms have used a high level of financial leverage in the past. Explain how the leverage affects their expected return and their risk.

13. Systemic Risk Why was the Federal Reserve concerned about systemic risk due to the financial problems of Bear Stearns?

14. Access to Inside Information Why do securities firms typically have some inside information that could affect future stock prices of other firms?

15. Sensitivity to Stock Market Conditions Most securities firms experience poor profit performance during periods in which the stock market performs poorly. Given what you know about securities firms, offer some possible reasons for these reduced profits.

16. Conversion to BHC Structure Explain how the credit crisis encouraged some securities firms to convert to a bank holding company (BHC) structure. Why might the expected return on equity be lower for securities firms that convert to a BHC structure?

17. Financial Services Modernization Act How did the Financial Services Modernization Act affect securities firms?

18. Regulation FD What impact has the SEC's Regulation Fair Disclosure (FD) had on securities firms?

Interpreting Financial News

Interpret the following comments made by Wall Street analysts and portfolio managers.

a. "The stock prices of most securities firms took a hit because of the recent increase in interest rates."

b. "Now that commercial banks are allowed more freedom to offer securities services, there may be a shakeout in the underwriting arena."

c. "Chaos in the securities markets can be good for some securities firms."

Managing in Financial Markets

Assessing the Operations of Securities Firms
As a consultant, you are assessing the operations of a securities firm.

a. The securities firm relies heavily on full-service brokerage commissions. Do you think the firm's heavy reliance on these commissions is risky? Explain.

b. If this firm attempts to enter the underwriting business, would it be an easy transition?

c. In recent years, the stock market volume has increased substantially, and this securities firm has performed very well. In the future, however, many institutional and individual investors may invest in indexes rather than in individual stocks. How would this affect the securities firm?

FLOW OF FUNDS EXERCISE

How Securities Firms Facilitate the Flow of Funds

Recall that Carson Company has periodically borrowed funds but contemplates a stock or bond offering so that it can expand by acquiring some other businesses. It has contacted Kelly Investment Company, a securities firm.

a. Explain how Kelly Investment Company can serve Carson and how it will serve other clients as well when it serves Carson. Also explain how Carson Company can serve Kelly Investment Company.

b. In a securities offering, Kelly Investment Company would like to do a good job for its clients, which include both the issuer and institutional investors. Explain Kelly's dilemma.

c. The issuing firm in an IPO hopes that there will be strong demand for its shares at the offer price, which will ensure that it receives a reasonable amount of proceeds from its offering. In some previous IPOs, the share price by the end of the first day was more than 80 percent above the offer price at the beginning of the day. This reflects a very strong demand relative to the price at the end of the day. In fact, it probably suggests that the IPO was fully subscribed at the offer price and that some institutional investors who purchased the stock at the offer price flipped their shares near the end of the first day to individual investors who were willing to pay the market price. Do you think that the issuing firm would be pleased that its stock price increased by more than 80 percent on the first day? Explain. Who really benefits from the increase in price on the first day?

d. Continuing the previous question, assume that the stock price drifts back down to near the original offer price over the next three weeks (even though the general stock market conditions were stable over this period) and then moves in tandem with the market over the next several years. Based on this information, do you think the offer price was appropriate? If so, how can you explain the unusually high one-day return on the stock? Who benefited from this stock price behavior, and who was adversely affected?

INTERNET/EXCEL EXERCISES

1. Go to www2.goldmansachs.com. Using this website, describe the different types of financial services offered by Goldman Sachs. Summarize its main business. Is Goldman Sachs focused on brokerage, investment banking, or a combination of these? Describe its performance over the last year. Explain why its performance was higher or lower than normal. Was the change in its performance due to the economy, recent interest rate movements, the stock market's performance, or changes in the amount of stock-trading or merger activity?

2. Retrieve information about Morgan Stanley (ticker symbol is MS) or another publicly traded securities firm of your choice. Go to the firm's website and retrieve its most recent annual report or access information from finance.yahoo.com by entering the ticker symbol and clicking on "Get Quotes." Then click on "SEC Filings" to retrieve income statement information. Review the security firm's recent performance. Has its income as a percentage of assets increased since the year before? Explain what caused this change over the last year. How have the firm's operating expenses changed over the last year? Discuss how the firm's recent strategy and economic conditions may explain the changes in these components of its income statement.

3. Go to finance.yahoo.com, enter the symbol MS (Morgan Stanley), and click on "Get Quotes." Click on "5y" just below the stock price trend to review the stock price movements over the last five years. Check the "Compare" box just above the graph and then select "S&P 500" in order to compare the trend of Morgan Stanley's stock price with the movements in the S&P stock index. Has Morgan Stanley performed better or worse than the index? Offer an explanation for its performance.

4. Go to finance.yahoo.com, enter the symbol MS (Morgan Stanley), and retrieve stock price data at the beginning of the last 20 quarters. Then go to http://research.stlouisfed.org/fred2/ and retrieve interest rate data at the beginning of the last 20 quarters for the three-month Treasury bill. Record the data on an Excel spreadsheet. Derive the quarterly return of Morgan Stanley. Derive the quarterly change in the interest rate. Apply regression analysis in which the quarterly return of Morgan Stanley is the dependent variable and the quarterly change in the interest rate is the independent variable (see Appendix B for more information about using regression analysis). Is there a positive or negative relationship between the interest rate movement and the stock return of Morgan Stanley? Is the relationship significant? Offer an explanation for this relationship.

WSJ EXERCISE

Performance of Securities Firms

Using a recent issue of the *Wall Street Journal*, summarize an article that discusses the recent performance of a particular securities firm. Does the article suggest that the securities firm's performance was better or worse than the norm? What reason is given for the particular level of performance?

ONLINE ARTICLES WITH REAL-WORLD EXAMPLES

Find a recent practical article available online that describes a real-world example regarding a specific financial institution or financial market that reinforces one or more concepts covered in this chapter.

If your class has an online component, your professor may ask you to post your summary of the article there and provide a link to the article so that other students can access it. If your class is live, your professor may ask you to summarize your application of the article in class. Your professor may assign specific students to complete this assignment or may allow any students to do the assignment on a volunteer basis.

For recent online articles and real-world examples related to this chapter, consider using the following search terms (be sure to include the prevailing year as a search term to ensure that the online articles are recent):

1. [name of a specific securities firm] AND income
2. [name of a specific securities firm] AND operations
3. [name of a specific securities firm] AND risk
4. [name of a specific securities firm] AND earnings
5. securities firm AND underwriting
6. securities firm AND earnings
7. securities firm AND risk
8. securities firm AND regulation
9. securities firm AND operations
10. securities firm AND credit

25

Insurance and Pension Fund Operations

CHAPTER OBJECTIVES

The specific objectives of this chapter are to:

■ describe the main operations of insurance companies,

■ explain the exposure of insurance companies to various forms of risk,

■ identify the factors that affect the value of insurance companies,

■ describe the common types of private pension plans,

■ explain how pension funds are managed, and

■ explain the key factors that influence the performance of pension portfolios.

WEB

www.insure.com
Information about more than 200 insurance companies.

Insurance companies and pension funds were created to provide insurance and retirement funding for individuals, firms, and government agencies. They serve financial markets by supplying funds to a variety of financial and nonfinancial corporations as well as government agencies. Some insurance and pension operations are independent companies, whereas others are units (or subsidiaries) of financial conglomerates.

25-1 BACKGROUND

Insurance companies provide various forms of insurance and investment services to individuals and charge a fee (called a premium) for this financial service. In general, the insurance provides a payment to the insured (or a named beneficiary) under conditions specified by the insurance policy contract. These conditions typically result in expenses or lost income, so the insurance is a means of financial protection. It reduces the potential financial damage incurred by individuals or firms due to specified conditions.

Common types of insurance offered by insurance companies include life insurance, property and casualty insurance, health insurance, and business insurance. Many insurance companies offer multiple types of insurance.

An individual's decision to purchase insurance may be influenced by the likelihood of the conditions that would result in receiving an insurance payment. Individuals who are more exposed to specific conditions that cause financial damage will purchase insurance against those conditions. Consequently, the insurance industry faces an **adverse selection** problem, meaning that those who are most likely to need insurance are most likely to purchase it. Furthermore, insurance can cause the insured to take more risks because they are protected. This is known as the **moral hazard problem** in the insurance industry.

Insurance companies employ underwriters to calculate the risk of specific insurance policies. The companies decide what types of policies to offer based on the potential level of claims to be paid on those policies and the premiums that they can charge.

25-1a Determinants of Insurance Premiums

The premium charged by an insurance company for each insurance policy is based on the probability of the condition under which the company will have to provide a payment to the insured (or the insured's beneficiary) and the potential size of the payment. The premium may also be influenced by the degree of competition within the industry for the specific type of insurance offered. Insurance companies can estimate the present value of a payment that they will have to make for a specific insurance policy. The premium charged for that insurance is influenced by the present value of the expected payment. The premium will also contain a markup to cover overhead expenses and to provide a profit beyond expenses.

The insurance premium is higher when there is more uncertainty about the size of the payment that may ultimately have to be made. Insurance companies recognize that the timing of the payout of any particular policy may be difficult to predict, but they are more concerned with the total flow of payments in any particular period. That is, if an insurance company has 20,000 policies, it may not know which policies will require payment this month but it may be able to predict the typical amount of payments per month.

Insurance companies tend to charge lower premiums when they provide services to all employees of a corporation through group plans. The lower premium represents a form of quantity discount in return for being selected to provide a particular type of insurance to all employees.

Dilemma When Setting Insurance Premiums

When insurance companies assess the probability of a condition that will result in a payment to the insured (or the insured's beneficiary), they rely on statistics about the general population. Individuals, however, have private information about themselves that is not available to the insurance company. This results in the adverse selection problem mentioned earlier. Those who have private information that makes them more likely to need insurance will buy it, whereas those who have private information that makes them less likely to need insurance will not buy it. For the insurance industry, the adverse selection problem means that people who have insurance are more likely to suffer losses (and therefore to file claims) than people who do not have insurance.

EXAMPLE

An insurance company representative arrives on a college campus and asks all students whether they want to purchase insurance in case any of the property (such as stereo equipment) in their dorm rooms is stolen. Beth declines the offer because she always locks the door when she leaves her dorm room. Conversely, Randy decides to buy the insurance because he never locks his dorm room and realizes that he may need the insurance. Even though Randy is a higher risk to the insurance company, he pays the same premium for the insurance as other students because the insurance company does not have the private information about his behavior.

Assume the insurance company sets the premium based on historical police reports showing that 3 percent of all students on campus have property stolen from their dorm rooms. Now consider that many careless students like Randy buy the insurance while many careful students like Beth do not. Since the students who purchase the insurance often forget to lock their dorm rooms, they are more likely to have property stolen than the norm. Conversely, the students who do not purchase the insurance generally lock their dorm rooms and thus are less likely to have property stolen than the norm. In general, this adverse selection problem means that the insurance company will likely experience more stolen property claims than it anticipated. If the company does not consider the adverse selection problem when setting its premiums, the premiums may be too low. ●

A related problem is the moral hazard problem, which, as mentioned earlier, means that some people take more risks once they are insured. This problem can also cause insurance companies to set their premiums too low if they do not take this tendency into account.

EXAMPLE

Refer back to the previous example in which the insurance company offers insurance to students in case property is stolen from their dorm rooms. Assume that Mina purchases this insurance even though she is normally very careful about locking her dorm room. Once she has insurance, she decides that she does not need to worry about locking her room because she is protected if her property is stolen. At the time Mina purchased the insurance, she was less likely to have property stolen than other students who were more careless than she was. But once she had insurance, she became a high risk because she changed her behavior as a result of having insurance. ●

As a result of the adverse selection and moral hazard problems, insurance companies need to assess the probability of a loss incurred by the people who obtain insurance rather than by the population in general. By doing this, the companies can charge premiums that more closely fit the likelihood that those who have insurance will file claims to cover their losses.

25-1b Investments by Insurance Companies

Insurance companies invest the insurance premiums and fees received from other services until the funds are needed to pay insurance claims. In some cases, the claims occur several years after the premiums are received. Thus, the performance of insurance companies is partially dependent on the return on the invested funds. Their investment decisions balance the goals of return, liquidity, and risk. They want to generate a high rate of return while maintaining risk at a tolerable level. They need to maintain sufficient liquidity so that they can easily access funds to accommodate claims by policyholders. Those insurance companies whose claims are less predictable need to maintain more liquidity.

25-1c Regulation of Insurance Companies

The insurance industry is highly regulated by state agencies (called commissions in some states), although the degree of regulation varies among states. Each state attempts to make sure that insurance companies are providing adequate services, and the state also approves the rates insurers may charge. Insurance company agents must be licensed. In addition, the forms used for policies must be approved by the state to ensure that they do not contain misleading wording.

State regulators also evaluate the asset portfolios of insurance companies to ensure that investments are reasonably safe and that adequate reserves are maintained to protect policyholders. For example, some states have limited an insurance company's investment in junk bonds to no more than 20 percent of total assets.

The **National Association of Insurance Commissioners (NAIC)** facilitates cooperation among the various state agencies whenever an insurance issue is a national concern. It attempts to maintain a degree of uniformity in common reporting issues. It also conducts research on insurance issues and participates in legislative discussions.

The Insurance Regulatory Information System (IRIS) has been developed by a committee of state insurance agencies to assist in each state's regulatory duties. The IRIS compiles financial statements, lists of insurers, and other relevant information pertaining to the insurance industry. In addition, it assesses the companies' respective financial statements by calculating 11 ratios that are then evaluated by NAIC regulators to monitor the financial health of a company. The NAIC provides all state insurance departments with IRIS assessment results that can be used as a basis for comparison when evaluating the financial health of any company. The regulatory duties of state agencies often require a comparison of the financial ratios of a particular insurance company to the industry norm. Use of the industry norm facilitates the evaluation.

Assessment System The regulatory system is designed to detect any problems in time to search for a remedy before the company deteriorates further. The more commonly used financial ratios assess a variety of relevant characteristics, including the following:

- The ability of the company to absorb either losses or a decline in the market value of its investments
- Return on investment
- Relative size of operating expenses
- Liquidity of the asset portfolio

Regulators monitor these characteristics to ensure that insurance companies do not become overly exposed to credit risk, interest rate risk, or liquidity risk.

Regulation of Capital   Insurance companies are required to report a risk-based capital ratio to insurance regulators. The ratio was created by the NAIC and is intended to force those insurance companies with a higher exposure to insurance claims, potential losses on assets, and interest rate risk to hold a higher level of capital. The application of risk-based capital ratios not only discourages insurance companies from excessive exposure to risk, it also forces companies that take high risks to back their business with a large amount of capital. Consequently, there is less likelihood of failures in the insurance industry.

Regulation of Failed Insurance Companies   If an insurance company files for bankruptcy, the insurance commissioner proposes a plan within the court system on how the assets should be distributed to the creditors. If the company is to be liquidated, property insurance policies are canceled and state guaranty funds, which are funded by solvent insurers, are used to cover claims based on limits set by state laws. The limits can vary among states. The state insurance department will typically assume management of the failed insurance company to preserve the remaining assets and ensure that policy-holders' rights are maintained. Owners of life insurance, health insurance, or annuities can have their policies assumed by other insurance companies.

Regulation of Financial Services Offered   Before 1999, insurance operations were mostly separated from other types of financial services. In 1998, Citicorp merged with Traveler's Insurance Company, resulting in the financial conglomerate named Citigroup. This merger forced Congress to deal with the issue of whether insurance operations can be offered along with all other types of financial services. In 1999, Congress passed the Financial Services Modernization Act, which allowed insurance companies to merge with commercial banks and securities firms. Some banks acquired insurance companies, which then marketed their insurance services under the bank's brand name to the bank's existing customer base.

Federal Insurance Office   In July 2010, the Financial Reform Act was implemented. This act contained several provisions intended to enhance the safety of the financial system. Although most provisions were directed at the banking industry, mortgage market, and derivative security markets, one provision called for creation of the Federal Insurance Office to be housed within the Treasury Department. This office is responsible for monitoring the insurance industry and providing recommendations to Congress about insurance regulations.

GLOBAL ASPECTS

International Insurance Regulations   Some life insurance companies based in the United States have expanded their business internationally to areas where insurance services have been very limited. These companies must comply with foreign regulations regarding services offered in the respective countries. The differences in regulations among countries increase the information costs of entering foreign markets.

25-2 LIFE INSURANCE OPERATIONS

Because life insurance companies are a dominant force in the insurance industry, they receive more attention in this chapter. In aggregate, they generate more than $100 billion in premiums each year and serve as key financial intermediaries by investing their funds in financial markets.

Life insurance companies compensate (provide benefits to) the beneficiary of a policy upon the policyholder's death. They charge policyholders a premium that should reflect the probability of making a payment to the beneficiary as well as the size and timing of the payment. Despite the difficulty of forecasting the life expectancy of a given individual, life insurance companies have historically forecast with reasonable accuracy the benefits they will have to provide beneficiaries. Because they hold a large portfolio of policies, these companies use actuarial tables and mortality figures to forecast the percentage of policies that will require compensation over a given period based on characteristics such as the age distribution of policyholders.

Life insurance companies also commonly offer employees of a corporation a **group life policy**. This service has become quite popular and has generated a large volume of business in recent years. Group policies can be provided at a low cost because of the high volume. Group life coverage now makes up about 40 percent of total life insurance coverage, up from only 26 percent in 1974.

25-2a Ownership

WEB

www.insurance.com

Provides quotes on any type of insurance.

There are about 900 life insurance companies classified as having stock ownership, while about 100 companies have mutual ownership. A stock-owned company is owned by its shareholders, whereas a mutual life insurance company is owned by its policyholders. In recent years, some mutual life insurance companies have converted to become stock owned. As in the savings institutions industry, a primary reason for the conversions is to gain access to capital by issuing stock.

25-2b Types of Life Insurance

Some of the more common types of life insurance policies are described here.

Whole Life Insurance   **Whole life insurance** protects policyholders until death or as long as the premiums are promptly paid. In addition, a whole life policy provides a form of savings to the policyholder. It builds a cash value that the policyholder is entitled to even if the policy is canceled.

From the perspective of the life insurance company, whole life policies generate periodic (typically, quarterly or semiannual) premiums that can be invested until the policyholder's death, when benefits are paid to the beneficiary. The amount of benefits is typically fixed.

Term Insurance   **Term insurance** is temporary, providing insurance only over a specified term, and does not build a cash value for policyholders. The premiums paid represent only insurance, not savings. Term insurance, however, is significantly less expensive than whole life insurance. Policyholders must compare the cash value of whole life insurance to the additional costs to determine whether it is preferable to term insurance. Those who prefer to invest their savings themselves will likely opt for term insurance.

People who need more insurance now than later may choose decreasing term insurance, in which the benefits paid to the beneficiary decrease over time. Families with mortgages commonly select this form of insurance. As time passes, the mortgage balance decreases and the family is more capable of surviving without the breadwinner's earnings. Thus, less compensation is needed in later years.

Variable Life Insurance   Under **variable life insurance**, the benefits awarded by the life insurance company to a beneficiary vary with the assets backing the policy. Flexible-premium variable life insurance policies are available, allowing flexibility on the size and timing of payments.

Universal Life Insurance   **Universal life insurance** combines the features of term and whole life insurance. It specifies a period of time over which the policy will exist but also builds a cash value for the policyholder over time. Interest is accumulated from the cash value until the policyholder uses those funds. Universal life insurance allows flexibility regarding the size and timing of the premiums, too. The growth in a policy's cash value is dependent on the pace of the premiums. The premium payment is divided into two portions. The first is used to pay the death benefit identified in the policy and to cover any administrative expenses. The second is used for investments and reflects savings for the policyholder. The Internal Revenue Service prohibits the value of these savings from exceeding the policy's death benefits.

25-2c Sources of Funds

Life insurance companies obtain much of their funds from premiums, as shown in Exhibit 25.1. Total premiums (life plus health insurance) represent about 31 percent of total income. The largest single source of funds, however, is the provision of **annuity plans**, which offer a predetermined amount of retirement income to individuals. Annuity plans have become very popular and now generate proportionately more income to

Exhibit 25.1   Distribution of U.S. Life Insurance Company Income

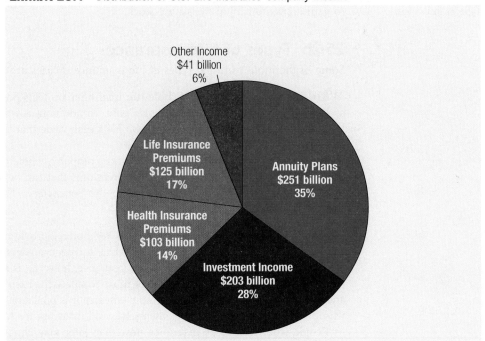

Source: *Life Insurance Fact Book, 2012.*

insurance companies than in previous years. More information about the annuities provided by numerous life insurance companies can be found at www.annuity.com. The third largest source of funds is investment income, which results from the investment of funds received from premium payments.

25-2d Capital

Insurance companies build capital by retaining earnings or issuing new stock. They use capital as a means of financing investment in fixed assets, such as buildings, and as a cushion against operating losses. Since a relatively large amount of capital can enhance safety, insurance companies are required to maintain adequate capital. Insurance companies are required to maintain a larger amount of capital when they are exposed to a higher degree of risk. Their risk can be measured by assessing the risk of their assets (as some assets are more exposed to losses than others) and their exposure stemming from the types of hazards against which they provide insurance.

Insurance companies maintain an adequate capital level not only to cushion potential losses but also to reassure their customers. When customers purchase insurance, the benefits are received at a future point in time. The customers are more comfortable purchasing insurance from an insurance company that has an adequate capital level and is therefore likely to be in existence at the time the benefits are to be provided.

25-2e Uses of Funds

The uses of funds by life insurance companies strongly influence their performance. Life insurance companies are major institutional investors. Exhibit 25.2, which shows the

Exhibit 25.2   Assets of U.S. Life Insurance Companies

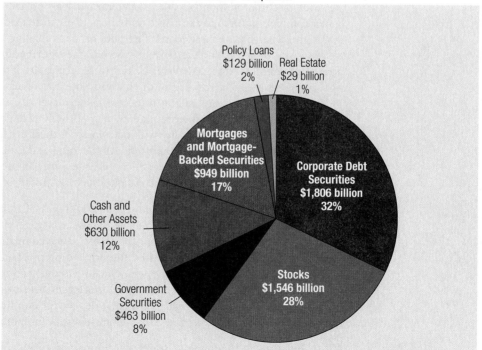

Source: *Life Insurance Fact Book, 2012.*

assets of life insurance companies, indicates how funds have been used. The main assets are described in the following subsections.

Government Securities

Life insurance companies invest in U.S. Treasury securities, state and local government bonds, and foreign bonds. They maintain investments in U.S. Treasury securities because of their safety and liquidity, but they also invest in bonds issued by foreign governments in an attempt to enhance profits.

In recent years, long-term interest rates have been very low. Consequently, returns from investing in U.S. government securities have been low. Under these conditions, insurance companies that desire safe investments must accept very low returns.

Corporate Securities

Corporate bonds are the most popular asset of life insurance companies. Companies usually hold a mix of medium- and long-term bonds for cash management and liquidity needs. Although corporate bonds provide a higher yield than government securities, they have a higher degree of credit (default) risk. Some insurance companies focus on high-grade corporate bonds, while others invest a portion of their funds in junk bonds.

Because life insurance companies expect to maintain a portion of their long-term securities until maturity, this portion can be somewhat illiquid. Thus they have the flexibility to obtain some high-yielding, directly placed securities when they can directly negotiate the provisions. Because such nonstandard securities are less liquid, life insurance companies balance their asset portfolios with other, more liquid securities. A minor portion of corporate securities are foreign. The foreign holdings typically represent industrialized countries and are therefore considered to have low credit risk. Of course, the market values of these foreign bonds are still susceptible to interest rate and currency fluctuations.

In addition to buying individual corporate bonds, insurance companies invest in packages of corporate bonds, called collateralized loan obligations (CLOs). Commercial banks combine numerous existing commercial loans into a pool and sell securities that represent ownership of these loans. The pool of loans making up a CLO is perceived to be less risky than the individual loans within the pool because the loans represent a diversified set of borrowers. Several classes of securities are issued, so insurance companies can select their desired degree of risk and potential return.

An insurance company willing to accept a high level of risk might choose BB-rated notes, which offer a high interest rate such as LIBOR (London Interbank Offer Rate) plus 3.5 percent. But the company will incur losses if there are loan defaults by corporate borrowers whose loans are in the pool. At the other extreme, an insurance company could purchase AAA-rated notes, which provide much more protection against loan defaults but offer a much lower interest rate, such as LIBOR plus 0.25 percent.

Mortgages

Life insurance companies hold all types of mortgages, including family, multifamily, commercial, and farm-related. These mortgages are typically originated by another financial institution and then sold to insurance companies in the secondary market. The mortgages are still serviced by the originating financial institution. Commercial mortgages that finance shopping centers, office buildings, and other commercial property make up more than 90 percent of the total mortgages held by life insurance companies. The return from holding mortgages is highly dependent on interest rates. Because of low interest rates in recent years, the return from investing in mortgages is very limited.

Real Estate

Although life insurance companies finance real estate by purchasing mortgages, their return is limited to the mortgage payments because they are simply acting as a creditor. In an attempt to achieve higher returns, they sometimes purchase real estate and lease it for commercial purposes. The ownership of real estate offers them the opportunity to generate very high returns but also exposes them to greater risk. Real estate values can be volatile over time and can have a significant effect on the market value of a life insurance company's asset portfolio.

Policy Loans   Life insurance companies lend a small portion of their funds to whole life policyholders (called *policy loans*). Whole life policyholders can borrow up to their policy's cash value (or a specified proportion of the cash value). The rate of interest is sometimes guaranteed over a specified period of time, as stated in the policy. Other sources of funds for individuals typically do not guarantee an interest rate at which they can borrow. For this reason, policyholders tend to borrow more from life insurance companies during periods of rising interest rates, when alternative forms of borrowing would be more expensive.

Summary of Uses of Funds   Exhibit 25.3 summarizes the uses of funds by illustrating how insurance companies finance economic growth. They channel funds received from insurance premiums to purchase stocks and bonds issued by corporations. They purchase bonds issued by the Treasury and municipalities and thereby finance government spending. They also use some of their funds to purchase household and commercial real estate.

25-2f Asset Management of Life Insurance Companies

Because life insurance companies tend to receive premiums from policyholders for several years before paying out benefits to a beneficiary, their performance can be significantly affected by their asset portfolio management. Like other financial institutions, they adjust their asset portfolios to counter changes in the factors that affect their risk. If they expect a downturn in the economy, they may reduce their holdings of corporate

Exhibit 25.3   How Insurance Companies Finance Economic Growth

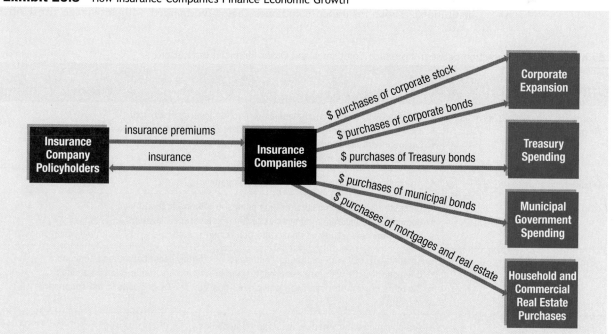

stocks and real estate. If they expect higher interest rates, they may reduce their holdings of fixed-rate bonds and mortgages.

To cope with the existing forms of risk, life insurance companies attempt to balance their portfolios so that any adverse movements in the market value of some assets will be offset by favorable movements in others. For example, assuming that interest rates will move in tandem with inflation, life insurance companies can use real estate holdings to partially offset the potential adverse effect of inflation on bonds. When higher inflation causes higher interest rates, the market value of existing bonds decreases, whereas the market value of real estate holdings tends to increase. Conversely, an environment of low or decreasing inflation may cause real estate values to stagnate but have a favorable impact on the market value of bonds and mortgages (because interest rates would likely decline). Although such a strategy may be useful, it is much easier to implement on paper than in practice. Because real estate values can fluctuate to a great degree, life insurance companies allocate only a limited amount of funds to real estate. In addition, real estate is less liquid than most other assets.

Many insurance companies are diversifying into other businesses by offering a wide variety of financial products. Such a strategy not only provides diversification but also enables these companies to offer packages of products to policyholders who desire to cover all these needs at once.

Overall, life insurance companies want to earn a reasonable return while maintaining their risk at a tolerable level. The degree to which they avoid or accept the various forms of risk depends on their degree of risk aversion. Companies that accept a greater amount of risk in their asset portfolios are likely to generate a higher return. If market conditions move in an unexpected manner, however, they will be more severely damaged than companies that employed a more conservative approach.

25-2g Interaction with Other Financial Institutions

Life insurance companies interact with financial institutions in several ways, as summarized in Exhibit 25.4. They compete in one form or another with all types of financial institutions. Those insurance companies that have merged with brokerage firms offer

Exhibit 25.4 Interaction between Insurance Companies and Other Financial Institutions

TYPE OF FINANCIAL INSTITUTION	INTERACTION WITH INSURANCE COMPANIES
Commercial banks and savings institutions (SIs)	• Compete with insurance companies to finance leveraged buyouts. • Merge with insurance companies in order to offer various insurance-related services. • Compete with insurance companies to provide insurance-related services. • Provide loans to insurance companies.
Finance companies	• Are sometimes acquired by insurance companies.
Securities firms	• Compete directly with insurance companies in offering mutual funds. • Compete with insurance companies to finance leveraged buyouts. • Underwrite new issues of stocks and bonds that are purchased by insurance companies.
Brokerage firms	• Compete directly with insurance companies in offering securities-related services. • Compete directly with insurance companies in offering insurance-related services. • Serve as brokers for insurance companies that buy stocks or bonds in the secondary market.
Pension funds	• Are sometimes managed by insurance companies.

Exhibit 25.5 Participation of Insurance Companies in Financial Markets

FINANCIAL MARKET	HOW INSURANCE COMPANIES PARTICIPATE IN THIS MARKET
Money markets	• Maintain a portion of their funds in money market securities, such as Treasury bills and commercial paper, to maintain adequate liquidity.
Bond markets	• Purchase bonds for their portfolios.
Mortgage markets	• Purchase mortgages and mortgage-backed securities for their portfolios.
Stock markets	• Purchase stocks for their portfolios.
Futures markets	• May sell futures contracts on bonds or a bond market index to hedge their bond and mortgage portfolios against interest rate risk. • May take positions in stock market index futures to hedge their stock portfolios against market risk.
Options markets	• Purchase call options on particular stocks that they plan to purchase in the near future. • Purchase put options or write call options on stocks they own that may experience a temporary decline in price.
Swap markets	• Engage in interest rate swaps to hedge the exposure of their bond and mortgage portfolios to interest rate risk.

a wide variety of securities-related services. Several insurance companies offer mutual funds to investors. Some state insurance regulators have allowed commercial banks to underwrite and sell insurance, which will result in more intense competition in the insurance industry.

Participation in Financial Markets The manner in which life insurance companies use their funds indicates their form of participation in the various financial markets. Insurance companies are common participants in the stock, bond, and mortgage markets because their asset portfolios are concentrated in these securities. They also use the money markets to purchase short-term securities for liquidity purposes. However, their participation in money markets is less than in capital markets. Exhibit 25.5 summarizes the manner in which insurance companies participate in financial markets.

25-3 OTHER TYPES OF INSURANCE OPERATIONS

In addition to life insurance, other common types of insurance operations include property and casualty insurance, health insurance, business insurance, bond insurance, and mortgage insurance. Each of these types of insurance is described in turn.

25-3a Property and Casualty Insurance

Property and casualty (PC) insurance protects against fire, theft, liability, and other events that result in economic or noneconomic damage. Property insurance protects businesses and individuals from the impact of financial risks associated with the ownership of property, such as buildings, automobiles, and other assets. Casualty insurance protects policyholders from potential liabilities for harm to others as a result of product failure or accidents. Property and casualty insurance companies charge policyholders a premium that should reflect the probability of a payout to the insured and the potential magnitude of the payout.

There are about 3,800 individual PC companies. The largest providers of PC insurance are State Farm Insurance Group, Allstate Insurance Group, Farmers Insurance

Group, and Nationwide Insurance Enterprise. No single company controls more than 10 percent of the PC insurance market. Although there are more PC companies than life insurance companies, the PC insurance business in aggregate is only about one-fourth as large as the life insurance business in aggregate (based on assets held). Nevertheless, the PC insurance business generates about the same amount of insurance premiums as the life insurance business. Many insurance companies now diversify their business, offering both life and PC insurance.

Life insurance and PC insurance have very different characteristics. First, PC policies often last one year or less, as opposed to the long-term or even permanent life insurance policies. Second, PC insurance encompasses a wide variety of activities, ranging from auto insurance to business liability insurance. Life insurance is more focused. Third, forecasting the amount of future compensation to be paid is more difficult for PC insurance than for life insurance. Property and casualty compensation depends on a variety of factors, including inflation, hurricanes, trends in terrorism, and the generosity of courts in lawsuits. Because of the greater uncertainty, PC insurance companies need to maintain more liquid asset portfolios. Earnings can be quite volatile over time, as the premiums charged may be based on highly overestimated or underestimated compensation.

Cash Flow Underwriting

A unique aspect of the PC insurance industry is its cyclical nature. As interest rates rise, companies tend to lower their rates so as to write more policies and acquire more premium dollars to invest. They are hoping losses will hold off long enough to make the cheaper premiums profitable through increased investment income. As interest rates decline, the price of insurance rises to offset decreased investment income. This method of adapting prices to interest rates is called **cash flow underwriting**. It can backfire for companies that focus on what they can earn in the short run and ignore what they will pay out later. A company that does not accurately predict the timing of the cycle can experience inadequate reserves and a drain on cash.

Uses of Funds

The primary uses of funds for PC insurance companies are illustrated in Exhibit 25.6. Municipal securities and corporate bonds dominate, followed by common stock. The amount of common stock holdings has been more volatile than that of the other components. The most obvious difference in the asset structure of PC companies relative to life insurance companies is the much higher concentration of government (municipal, Treasury, and government agency) securities.

Property and Casualty Reinsurance

PC companies commonly obtain reinsurance, which effectively allocates a portion of their return and risk to other insurance companies. It is similar to a commercial bank acting as the lending agent by allowing other banks to participate in the loan. A particular PC insurance company may agree to insure a corporation but spread the risk by inviting other insurance companies to participate. Reinsurance allows a company to write larger policies because a portion of the risk involved will be assumed by other companies.

The number of companies willing to offer reinsurance has declined significantly because of generous court awards and the difficulty of assessing the amount of potential claims. Reinsurance policies are often described in the insurance industry as "having long tails," which means that the probability distribution of possible returns on reinsurance is widely dispersed. Although many companies still offer reinsurance, their premiums have increased substantially in recent years. If the desire to offer reinsurance continues to decline, the primary insurers will be less able to "sell off" a portion of the risk they assume when writing policies. Consequently, they will be under pressure to more closely evaluate the risk of the policies they write.

Exhibit 25.6 Assets of Property and Casualty Insurance Companies

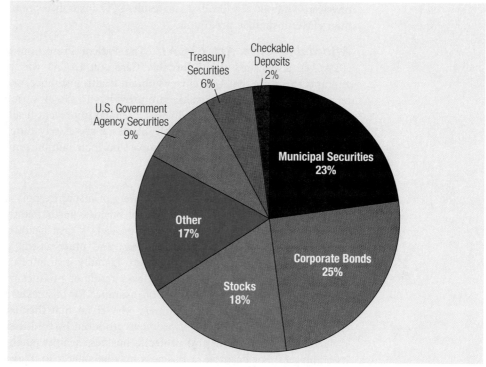

Source: *Federal Reserve.*

25-3b Health Care Insurance

Insurance companies provide various types of health care insurance, including coverage for hospital stays, visits to physicians, and surgical procedures. They serve as intermediaries between health care providers and the recipients of health care. Since the cost of health care is so high, individuals seek health care insurance as a form of protection against conditions that cause them to incur large health care expenses.

Types of Health Care Plans   Insurance companies offer two types of health care plans: managed health care plans and indemnity plans. The primary difference between the two types of plans is that individuals who are insured by a managed care plan may choose only specified health care providers (hospitals and physicians) who participate in the plan. Individuals who are insured under an indemnity plan can usually choose any provider of health care services. The payment systems of the two types of plans are also distinctly different. The premiums for managed health care plans are generally lower, and payment is typically made directly to the provider. In contrast, indemnity plans reimburse insured individuals for the health care expenses they incur.

Managed health care plans can be classified as **health maintenance organizations** (HMOs) or preferred provider organizations (PPOs). Health maintenance organizations usually require individuals to choose a primary care physician (PCP). The PCP is the "gatekeeper" for that individual's health care. Before patients insured under an HMO can see a specialist, they must first see a PCP to obtain a referral for the specialist. This helps to keep costs for the HMO down, since patients will not see high-cost specialists unless their PCP sees them first and determines whether a referral to a specialist is necessary. Preferred provider organizations usually allow insured individuals to see any physician without a referral. As a result, PPO insurance premiums are typically higher than HMO insurance premiums.

Affordable Care Act (ACA) The Patient Protection and Affordable Care Act (PPACA), also called the Affordable Care Act (ACA) was passed in 2010. This act attempts to ensure that U.S. citizens obtain health insurance, and therefore maintain better health. It also requires health care providers to satisfy various conditions before they can bill insurance companies, which is intended to prevent health insurance fraud. Insurance companies that provide health insurance are closely monitoring the effects of this law, because it could have a major impact on their reimbursement expenses.

25-3c Business Insurance

Insurance companies provide a wide variety of insurance policies that protect businesses from many types of risk. Some forms of business insurance overlap with property and casualty insurance. Property insurance protects a firm against the risk associated with ownership of property, such as buildings and other assets. It can provide insurance against property damage by fire or theft. Liability insurance can protect a firm against potential liability for harm to others as a result of product failure or a wide range of other conditions. This is a key type of insurance for businesses because of the increasing number of lawsuits filed by customers who claim that they suffered physical injury or emotional distress as a result of products produced by businesses.

Liability insurance can also protect a business against potential liability for claims by its employees. For example, a business may be subject to a lawsuit by an employee who is hurt on the job. Employment liability insurance also covers claims of wrongful termination and sexual harassment.

Some other forms of business insurance are separate from property and casualty insurance. Key employee insurance provides a financial payout if specified employees of a business become disabled or die. The insurance is intended to enable the business to replace the skills of the key employees so that the business can continue. Business interruption insurance protects against losses due to a temporary closing of the business. Credit line insurance covers debt payments owed to a creditor if a borrower dies. Fidelity bond insurance covers losses due to dishonest employees. Marine insurance covers losses due to damage during transport. Malpractice insurance protects business professionals from losses due to lawsuits by dissatisfied customers. Surety bond insurance covers losses due to a contract not being fulfilled. Umbrella liability insurance provides additional coverage beyond that provided by the other existing insurance policies.

25-3d Bond Insurance

Bond insurance protects the investors that purchase bonds in the event that the bond issuers default on their bonds. Many municipal bonds are backed by insurance. Some municipalities are willing to pay for the insurance because it allows them to more easily sell their bonds at lower prices; thus the insurance reduces their cost of borrowing. The risk of default may be minimized when an insurance company insures the bonds. Many insurance companies, including Ambac Financial Group and MBIA, Inc., provide bond insurance.

The insurance on bonds is only as good as the insurance company's ability to cover claims, however. It is possible that both a bond issuer and the insurer backing the bond issuer might not satisfy their obligations, which could cause major losses to institutional investors holding these bonds. A downgrade in the credit rating of a bond insurer is a signal that there is a greater likelihood that the insurance company could not cover a claim in the event that the bond defaults. Thus, bonds insured by this company will need to offer higher yields in order to compensate for the higher risk. Existing bonds insured by this insurer will experience a decline in price to reflect the higher risk of loss from holding these bonds.

During the credit crisis in 2008, the credit ratings of several large insurance companies were assessed for possible downgrade, and this aroused concerns that many insured bonds might suffer major losses. Consequently, the prices of these insured bonds declined. Some mutual funds that invest heavily in municipal bonds may only be willing to hold bonds that are insured by a company that is assigned the highest credit rating. This situation illustrates the importance of creditworthy insurance companies in facilitating the flow of funds from bond issuers to institutional investors such as mutual funds.

25-3e Mortgage Insurance

Mortgage insurance protects the lender that provides mortgage loans in the event that homeowners cannot cover their payments and default on their mortgages. The insurance is normally intended to cover the lender's losses when the lender is forced to foreclose on the home and sells it for less than the prevailing mortgage amount.

Mortgage lenders commonly require homeowners to obtain mortgage insurance. Sometimes, obtaining the insurance may allow a homeowner to qualify for a lower interest rate on the mortgage. The insurance companies that sell mortgage insurance typically receive periodic insurance premiums for providing this insurance. In the event of a mortgage default, they cover the damages to the creditor.

Credit Default Swaps as a Form of Mortgage Insurance   Some insurance companies provide insurance on mortgages by taking a position in credit default swaps, which are privately negotiated contracts that protect investors against the risk of default on particular debt securities. An institutional investor that previously purchased mortgage securities may become concerned that these securities could perform poorly. Therefore, it may be willing to engage in a credit default swap in which it will make monthly or quarterly payments to the counterparty.

Insurance companies commonly serve as the counterparty and have to make payments only if there is a default on the securities covered by the swap. In this event, the insurance companies have to pay the face value of the securities covered by the swap in exchange for those securities. When there are no defaults on the debt securities, the insurance companies benefit from their swap positions because they are not required to make payments. When there are defaults, however, the insurance companies can incur large expenses to cover the payments.

Insurance companies reduce their exposure to various types of insurance through diversification. They have numerous policyholders, and an adverse event that causes an insurance claim from one policyholder is unlikely to happen to many other policyholders at the same time. However, credit defaults on mortgage-backed securities can occur across financial institutions at the same time if mortgage qualification standards are low and the economy is weak. Consequently, diversification among credit default swaps on mortgage-backed securities does not effectively reduce risk. Insurance companies that sold credit default swaps were highly exposed to mortgage conditions during the credit crisis.

25-4 EXPOSURE OF INSURANCE COMPANIES TO RISK

The major types of risk faced by insurance companies are interest rate risk, credit risk, market risk, and liquidity risk.

25-4a Interest Rate Risk

Because insurance companies carry a large amount of fixed-rate, long-term debt securities, the market value of their asset portfolios can be very sensitive to interest rate fluctuations. Some insurance companies have reduced their average maturity on securities, which reduces their exposure to interest rate risk.

Since long-term interest rates have been very low in recent years, there is much room for long-term interest rates to rise over time. Because insurance companies invest a large proportion of their funds in long-term debt securities, they are highly exposed to interest rate risk.

25-4b Credit Risk

The corporate bonds, mortgages, and state and local government securities in insurance companies' asset portfolios are subject to credit risk. To deal with this risk, some insurance companies typically invest only in securities assigned a high credit rating. They also diversify among securities issuers so that the repayment problems experienced by any single issuer will have only a minor impact on the overall portfolio.

Because long-term interest rates have been so low in recent years, some insurance companies have shifted more funds out of Treasury bonds and into corporate bonds (including junk bonds) that offer higher yields. However, by striving for higher returns, they are exposed to a much higher degree of credit risk.

25-4c Market Risk

Because insurance companies invest in stock, they are exposed to possible losses on their stock portfolios during weak stock market conditions. When stock prices declined substantially during the credit crisis in 2008, those insurance companies with a large proportion of their investments in stock suffered from their high exposure to market risk. However, many insurance companies that heavily invested in stocks during the 2010–2012 period when market conditions improved generated large gains.

25-4d Liquidity Risk

An additional risk to insurance companies is liquidity risk. A high frequency of claims at a single point in time could force a company to liquidate assets at a time when the market value is low, thereby depressing its performance. Claims due to death are not likely to occur simultaneously, however. Life insurance companies can therefore reduce their exposure to this risk by diversifying the age distribution of their customer base. If the customer base becomes unbalanced and is heavily concentrated in the older age group, life insurance companies should increase their proportion of liquid assets to prepare for a higher frequency of claims.

25-4e Exposure to Risk during the Credit Crisis

As the credit crisis intensified in 2008, many insurance companies experienced losses. Many insurance companies that had invested some of their funds in mortgage-backed securities or in junk bonds experienced losses on their investments. Some insurance companies sold private mortgage insurance to offer protection on mortgages and had to cover insurance claims filed by creditors when homeowners defaulted on their mortgage payments. Other insurance companies incurred losses from their credit default swaps. Furthermore, most insurance companies suffered losses on their stock holdings during the credit crisis.

25-4f Government Rescue of AIG

American International Group (AIG) is the largest insurance company in the world, with annual revenue of more than $100 billion and operations in more than 130 countries. The company had sold credit default swaps that were intended to cover against default for about $440 billion in debt securities, many of which represented subprime mortgages. In 2008, AIG experienced severe financial problems because many of these debt securities defaulted.

If AIG failed, all of the financial institutions that had purchased credit default swaps from AIG to protect against default on their mortgage-backed securities might have failed or suffered severe losses. Because the failure of AIG could have a devastating effect on the insurance industry and the rest of the financial sector, the Federal Reserve bailed out AIG in September 2008 with support from the U.S. Treasury. The Fed may have viewed AIG as too big and too entangled with other financial institutions to fail. The bailout allowed AIG to borrow up to $85 billion from the Federal Reserve over a two-year period, and the government received an equity stake of about 80 percent of AIG. As part of the agreement, AIG was required to sell off some of its businesses in order to increase its liquidity.

The Fed's rescue of AIG occurred one day after it allowed Lehman Brothers to fail. Perhaps one reason for rescuing AIG and not rescuing Lehman Brothers was that AIG had various subsidiaries that were financially sound at the time. The assets in these subsidiaries served as collateral for the loans extended by the federal government to rescue AIG. Thus, the risk of a loss to taxpayers due to the AIG rescue was perceived by the federal government to be low. Conversely, Lehman Brothers did not have adequate collateral available, and so a large loan from the U.S. government could have been costly to U.S. taxpayers.

WEB

finance.yahoo.com/
insurance
Information about
individual insurance
companies and updates
on the industry.

25-5 Valuation of an Insurance Company

Insurance companies (or insurance company units that are part of a financial conglomerate) are commonly valued by their managers to monitor progress over time or by other financial institutions that are considering an acquisition. The value of an insurance company can be modeled as the present value of its future cash flows. Thus the value of an insurance company should change in response to changes in its expected cash flows (CF) in the future and to changes in the required rate of return (k) by investors:

$$\Delta V = f[\underbrace{\Delta E(CF)}_{+}, \underbrace{\Delta k}_{-}]$$

25-5a Factors That Affect Cash Flows

The change in an insurance company's expected cash flows may be modeled as

$$\Delta E(CF) = f(\underbrace{\Delta \text{PAYOUT}}_{-}, \underbrace{\Delta \text{ECON}}_{+}, \underbrace{\Delta R_f}_{-}, \underbrace{\Delta \text{INDUS}}_{?}, \underbrace{\Delta \text{MANAB}}_{+})$$

where PAYOUT represents insurance payouts to beneficiaries, ECON represents economic growth, R_f represents the risk-free interest rate, INDUS represents industry conditions, and MANAB represents the abilities of the insurance company's management.

Change in Payouts   The payouts on insurance claims are somewhat stable for most life insurance companies with a diversified set of customers. In contrast, the payouts on property and casualty claims can be volatile for PC companies.

Change in Economic Conditions Economic growth can enhance an insurance company's cash flows because it increases the level of income of firms and households and can increase the demand for the company's services. During periods of strong economic growth, debt securities maintained by insurance companies are less likely to default. In addition, equity securities maintained by insurance companies should perform well because the firms represented by these securities should perform well.

Change in the Risk-Free Interest Rate Some of an insurance company's assets (such as bonds) are adversely affected by rising interest rates. Thus the valuation of an insurance company may be inversely related to interest rate movements.

Change in Industry Conditions Insurance companies are subject to industry conditions, including regulatory constraints, technology, and competition within the industry. For example, they now compete against various financial institutions when offering some services. As regulators have reduced barriers, competition within the insurance industry has become more intense.

Change in Management Abilities An insurance company has control over the composition of its managers and its organizational structure. Its managers can attempt to make internal decisions that will capitalize on the external forces (economic growth, interest rates, regulatory constraints) that the company cannot control. Thus, the management skills of an insurance company can influence its expected cash flows. In particular, skillful management is needed to determine the likelihood of events that could cause massive payouts to policyholders.

25-5b Factors That Affect the Required Rate of Return by Investors

The required rate of return by investors who invest in an insurance company can be modeled as

$$\Delta k = f(\underset{+}{\Delta R_f}, \underset{+}{\Delta RP})$$

where R_f represents the risk-free interest rate and RP represents the risk premium.

The risk-free interest rate is normally expected to be positively related to inflation, economic growth, and the budget deficit level but inversely related to money supply growth (assuming it does not cause inflation). The risk premium on an insurance company is inversely related to economic growth. It can also be affected by industry conditions (such as regulations) and management abilities.

Exhibit 25.7 provides a framework for valuing an insurance company based on the preceding discussion. In general, the value of an insurance company is favorably affected by strong economic growth, a reduction in interest rates, and strong management capabilities.

25-5c Indicators of Value and Performance

Some of the more common indicators of an insurance company's value and performance are available in investment service publications such as *Value Line*. A time-series assessment of the dollar amount of life insurance and/or PC insurance premiums indicates the growth in the company's insurance business. A time-series analysis of investment income can be used to assess the performance of the company's portfolio managers. However, the dollar amount of investment income is affected by several factors that are not under the control of portfolio managers, such as the amount of funds received as

Exhibit 25.7 A Framework for Valuing an Insurance Company

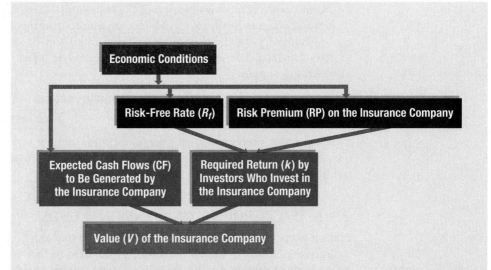

- A stronger economy leads to more services being provided by insurance companies and better cash flows. It may also enhance stock valuations and therefore can enhance the valuations of stocks held by the insurance company.
- A lower risk-free rate results in more favorable valuations of the bonds held by the insurance company.
- The valuation of an insurance company is also influenced by industry conditions and the firm's management (not shown in the diagram). These factors affect the risk premium (and therefore the required return by investors) and the expected cash flows to be generated by the insurance company. In particular, property and casualty companies are exposed to court rulings that result in large damages awards paid by insurance, and health insurance companies are exposed to regulations regarding reimbursement for health care services.

premiums that can be invested in securities and market interest rates. In addition, a relatively low level of investment income may result from a high concentration in stocks that pay low or no dividends rather than from poor performance.

Indicator of Liquidity   Because insurance companies have unique characteristics, the financial ratios of other financial institutions are generally not applicable. An insurance company's liquidity can be measured using the following ratio:

$$\text{Liquidity ratio} = \frac{\text{Invested assets}}{\text{Loss reserves and unearned premium reserves}}$$

The higher the ratio, the more liquid the company. This ratio can be evaluated by comparing it to the industry average.

Indicators of Profitability   The profitability of insurance companies is often assessed using the return on net worth (or policyholders' surplus) as a ratio, as follows:

$$\text{Return on net worth} = \frac{\text{Net profit}}{\text{Policyholders' surplus}}$$

Net profit consists of underwriting profits, investment income, and realized capital gains. Changes in this ratio over time should be compared to changes in the industry norms, as the norm is quite volatile over time. The return on net worth tends to be quite volatile for PC insurance companies because of the volatility in their claims.

Although the net profit reflects all income sources and therefore provides only a general measure of profitability, various financial ratios can be used to focus on a specific source of income. For example, underwriting gains or losses are measured by the net underwriting margin:

$$\textbf{Net underwriting margin} = \frac{\textbf{Premium income} - \textbf{Policy expenses}}{\textbf{Total assets}}$$

When policy expenses exceed premium income, the net underwriting margin is negative. As long as other sources of income can offset such a loss, however, net profit will still be positive.

25-6 BACKGROUND ON PENSION FUNDS

Pension plans provide a savings plan for employees that can be used for retirement. They commonly increase the amount of money in the fund in four ways: (1) new contributions by the employee sponsored by the pension plan, (2) new contributions by the employer sponsored by the pension plan on behalf of the employee, and (3) dividends or interest earned by the fund that is due to its investment in equity or debt securities, and (4) appreciation in the values (capital gains) of the securities in which the fund has invested. In aggregate, most of the contributions come from the employer. Pension funds are major investors in stocks, bonds, and various types of loan packages such as mortgage-backed securities.

25-6a Public versus Private Pension Funds

Pension funds can be categorized as public or private pension funds.

Public Pension Funds   Public pension funds can be either state, local, or federal. The best-known government pension fund is Social Security. In addition to that system, all government employees and almost half of all nongovernment employees participate in other pension funds.

Many public pension plans are funded on a pay-as-you-go basis. Thus, existing employee and employer contributors are essentially supporting previous employees. At some point, this strategy could cause the future benefits owed to outweigh contributions to such an extent that the pension fund would be unable to fulfill its promises or would have to obtain more contributions to do so.

Private Pension Plans   Private pension plans are created by private agencies, including industrial, labor, service, nonprofit, charitable, and educational organizations. Some pension funds are so large that they are major investors in corporate securities.

25-6b Defined-Benefit versus Defined-Contribution Plans

Pension funds are commonly categorized as defined-benefit or defined-contribution plans depending on how contributions are made and on the level of benefits provided.

Defined-Benefit Plans   With a **defined-benefit plan**, contributions are dictated by the benefits that will eventually be provided. The future pension obligations of a defined-benefit plan are uncertain because the obligations are stated in terms of fixed payments to retirees. These payments are dependent on salary levels, retirement ages, and life expectancies. Even if future payment obligations can be accurately predicted, the amount the plan needs today will be uncertain because of the uncertain rate of return on today's investments. The higher the future return on the plan's investments, the lower the level of funds that must be invested today to satisfy future payments.

Many defined-benefit plans used optimistic projections of the rate of return to be earned on their investments, which created the appearance that their existing investments were adequate to cover future payment obligations. This allowed corporations to reduce their contributions (an expense) to the plan and thereby increase their earnings. When projected rates of return on the pension funds were overestimated, however, the pension funds became underfunded, or inadequate to cover future payment obligations.

Some pension funds make risky investments in real estate, junk bonds, and international securities in order to justify their high projected rates of return. Although these investments could generate high returns, they might instead generate large losses. Thus it is possible that some pension plans could be substantially underfunded if these investments perform poorly.

Some state government agencies attempted to resolve their underfunded defined-benefit plans by increasing the retirement age when state employees could start receiving their pensions, or by forcing state employees to increase the proportion of their salary that is contributed to the pension fund. However, many of the actions taken by state governments apply only to future employees who have not yet been hired. Thus, the actions taken by state government agencies will not provide a quick cure to the underfunded pensions. Consequently, some states face a very real risk that their pension fund will run out of money. The concerns are well publicized, but pension reform has generally been lacking because pension plans do not want to take actions that reduce benefits to existing state employees.

The state of California is a prime example of problems associated with pension funding. In 1999, it set high defined benefits for its state employees. It did not raise the required contributions by employees because it presumed that its return on the invested funds would be sufficient to cover future obligations. It substantially overestimated its returns on investment, as it only earned about 75 percent of what it projected. Consequently, the value of its pension fund contributions did not grow over time as much as was necessary to cover the future pension fund obligations. This resulted in a pension fund deficiency of about $2 billion per year over the 2000–2012 period.

The state has to make up the difference between its pension obligations to state employees and the contribution funds received from employees. It has cut expenditures in many ways to offset its excessive pension expenses, such as allocating smaller amounts of funds for state education. In essence, the state education system has been penalized because of unrealistic pension promises made about the expected return to be earned on pensions many years ago.

These types of problems with government pensions are common. The large budget deficits due to large pensions were not anticipated because of overly optimistic projections about the return on pension fund investments. The retirees who were promised large pensions want what they were promised. Some governments are changing their pension plan structure, which reduces the pension benefits for new employees. However, this does not solve the deficiency in the existing budgets to cover pension obligations.

Defined-Contribution Plans

A **defined-contribution plan** provides benefits that are determined by the accumulated contributions and the fund's investment performance. Some firms match a portion of the contribution made by their employees. With this type of plan, a firm knows with certainty the amount of funds to contribute, whereas that amount is undetermined in a defined-benefit plan. With a defined-contribution plan, however, the benefits to the participants are uncertain. Firms commonly hire an investment company to manage the pension portfolios of employees.

Defined-contribution plans outnumber defined-benefit plans, but defined-benefit plans have more participants and a greater aggregate value of assets. New plans allow employees more flexibility to choose what they want. In recent years, defined-benefit plans have commonly been replaced by defined-contribution plans. Employees can often decide the pace of their contributions and how their contributions will be invested. Common investment alternatives include stocks, investment-grade bonds, real estate, and money market securities. Communications from the benefits coordinator to the employees have become much more important because employees now have more influence on their pension plan contributions and the investment approach used to invest the premiums.

25-6c Pension Fund Participation in Financial Markets

To set up a pension fund, a sponsor corporation establishes a trust pension fund through a commercial bank's trust department or an insured pension fund through an insurance company. The financial institution that is delegated the task of managing the pension fund then receives periodic contributions and invests them. Many of the transactions by pension funds in the financial markets finance economic growth, as illustrated in Exhibit 25.8. Pension funds are major participants in stock and bond offerings and thereby finance corporate expansion. They are also major participants in bond offerings by the Treasury and municipalities and thereby finance government spending.

Many of pension funds' investments in the stock, bond, and mortgage markets require the brokerage services of securities firms. Managers of pension funds instruct securities firms on the type and amount of investment instruments to purchase. Exhibit 25.9 summarizes the interaction between pension funds and other financial institutions.

Exhibit 25.10 summarizes how pension fund managers participate in various financial markets. Because pension fund portfolios are normally dominated by stocks and bonds, the participation of pension fund managers in the stock and bond markets is obvious. Pension fund managers also participate in money and mortgage markets to fill out the remainder of their portfolios. They sometimes utilize the futures and options markets as well in order to partially insulate their portfolio performance from interest rate and/ or stock market movements.

WEB

www.eric.org
Information about pension guidelines.

Exhibit 25.8 How Pension Funds Finance Economic Growth

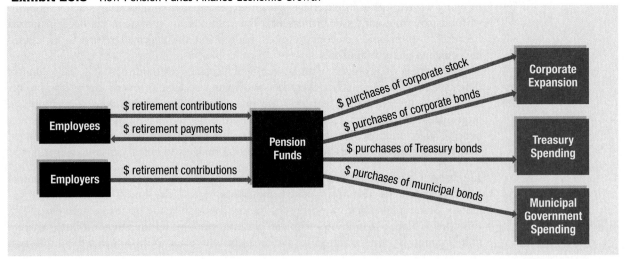

Exhibit 25.9 Interaction between Pension Funds and Other Financial Institutions

TYPE OF FINANCIAL INSTITUTION	INTERACTION WITH PENSION FUNDS
Commercial banks	• Sometimes manage pension funds. • Sell commercial loans to pension funds in the secondary market.
Insurance companies	• Create annuities for pension funds.
Mutual funds	• Serve as investments for some pension funds.
Securities firms	• Execute securities transactions for pension funds. • Offer investment advice to pension portfolio managers. • Underwrite newly issued stocks and bonds that are purchased by pension funds.

Exhibit 25.10 Participation of Pension Funds in Financial Markets

FINANCIAL MARKET	HOW PENSION FUNDS PARTICIPATE IN THIS MARKET
Money markets	• Pension fund managers maintain a small proportion of liquid money market securities that can be liquidated when they wish to increase investment in stocks, bonds, or other alternatives.
Bond markets	• At least 25 percent of a pension fund portfolio is typically allocated to bonds. Portfolios of defined-benefit plans usually have a higher concentration of bonds than defined-contribution plans. Pension fund managers frequently conduct transactions in the bond market.
Mortgage markets	• Pension portfolios frequently contain some mortgages, although the relative proportion is low compared with bonds and stocks.
Stock markets	• At least 30 percent of a pension fund portfolio is typically allocated to stocks. In general, defined-contribution plans usually have a higher concentration of stocks than defined-benefit plans.
Futures markets	• Some pension funds use futures contracts on debt securities and on bond indexes to hedge the exposure of their bond holdings to interest rate risk. In addition, some pension funds use futures on stock indexes to hedge against market risk. Other pension funds use futures contracts for speculative purposes.
Options markets	• Some pension funds use stock options to hedge against movements of particular stocks. They may also use options on futures contracts to secure downside protection against bond price movements.
Swap markets	• Pension funds commonly engage in interest rate swaps to hedge the exposure of their bond and mortgage portfolios to interest rate risk.

25-6d Pension Regulations

The regulation of pension funds varies with the type of plan. All plans must comply with the set of Internal Revenue Service tax rules that apply to pension fund income. For defined-contribution plans, the sponsoring firm's main responsibility is its contributions to the fund.

ERISA Defined-contribution plans are also subject to guidelines specified by the **Employee Retirement Income Security Act** (ERISA) of 1974 (also called the Pension Reform Act) and its 1989 revisions. This act requires a pension fund to choose one of two vesting schedule options, which determine when an employee has a legal right to the contributed funds:

1. 100 percent vesting after five years of service
2. Graded vesting, with 20 percent vesting in the third year, 40 percent in the fourth, 60 percent in the fifth, 80 percent in the sixth, and 100 percent in the seventh year

The act also requires that any contributions be invested in a prudent manner, meaning that pension funds should concentrate their investments in high-grade securities. Although this was implicitly expected before, ERISA made this so-called fiduciary responsibility (monitored by the U.S. Department of Labor) explicit to encourage portfolio managers to serve the interests of the employees rather than themselves. Pension plans can face legal ramifications if they do not comply.

In addition, ERISA allows employees changing employers to transfer any vested amount into the pension plan of their new employer or to invest it in an Individual Retirement Account (IRA). With either alternative, taxes on the vested amount are still deferred until retirement when the funds become available.

The Pension Benefit Guaranty Corporation

ERISA established the **Pension Benefit Guaranty Corporation (PBGC)** to provide insurance on pension plans. This federally chartered agency guarantees that participants of defined-benefit pension plans will receive their benefits upon retirement. If the pension fund is incapable of fully providing the benefits promised, the PBGC will make up the difference. The PBGC does not receive government support. It is financed by annual premiums, income from assets acquired from terminated pension plans, and income generated by investments. It also receives employer-liability payments when an employer terminates its pension plan.

About 44 million Americans, or one-third of the workforce, have pension plans insured by the PBGC. As a wholly owned independent government agency, it differs from other federal regulatory agencies in that it has no regulatory powers.

The PBGC monitors pension plans periodically to determine whether they can adequately provide the benefits they have guaranteed. If a plan is judged inadequate, it is terminated and the PBGC (or a PBGC appointee) takes control as the fund manager. The PBGC has a claim on part of a firm's net worth if it is needed to support the underfunded pension assets.

The PBGC's funding requirements depend on all the pension funds it monitors. Because the market values of these funds are similarly susceptible to economic conditions, funding requirements are volatile over time. A poor economic environment will depress stock prices and simultaneously reduce the asset values of most pension funds.

Pension Protection Act of 2006

If a company's defined-benefit pension plan is underfunded, the Pension Protection Act of 2006 requires the company to increase its contributions to the pension plan so that it will be fully funded within seven years. Prior to the act, some corporations' pension plans were underfunded by more than $1 billion. During the credit crisis in 2008, many large companies experienced losses on their pension portfolios because of their investments in mortgage-backed securities and stocks. Thus, the gap between what they needed to pay their retired employees versus the amount of funds available in their pension plans increased. Consequently, some companies had to revise their operating plans for 2009 in order to contribute more cash to their pension plans. When companies use more of their cash to boost underfunded pension plans, they have less cash to use for other purposes. Thus, their operating performance may suffer when they have to increase contributions to their pension plans.

WEB

www.pensionfunds.com

News related to pension funds.

25-7 Pension Fund Management

Regardless of the manner in which funds are contributed to a pension plan, the funds received must be managed (invested) until needed to pay benefits. Private pension portfolios are dominated by common stock. Public pension portfolios are somewhat evenly invested in corporate bonds, stock, and other credit instruments.

Pension fund management can be classified according to the strategy used to manage the portfolio. With a **matched funding** strategy, investment decisions are made with the objective of generating cash flows that match planned outflow payments. An alternative strategy is **projective funding**, which offers managers more flexibility in constructing a pension portfolio that can benefit from expected market and interest rate movements. Some pension funds segment their portfolios, with part used for matched funding and the rest for projective funding.

An informal method of matched funding is to invest in long-term bonds to fund long-term liabilities and in intermediate bonds to fund intermediate liabilities. The appeal of matching is the assurance that future liabilities are covered regardless of market movements. Matching limits the manager's discretion, however, because it allows only investments that match future payouts. For example, portfolio managers required to use matched funding would need to avoid callable bonds, because these bonds could potentially be retired before maturity. This requirement precludes consideration of many high-yield bonds. In addition, each liability payout may require a separate investment to which it can be perfectly matched; this would require several small investments and increase the pension fund's transaction costs.

Pension funds that are willing to accept market returns on bonds can purchase bond index portfolios that have been created by investment companies. The bond index portfolio may include investment-grade corporate bonds, Treasury bonds, and U.S. government agency bonds. It does not include the entire set of these bonds but includes enough of them to mirror market performance. Investing in a market portfolio is a passive approach that does not require any analysis of individual bonds. Some pension funds are not willing to accept a totally passive approach, so they compromise by using only a portion of their funds to purchase a bond market portfolio.

Equity portfolio indexes that mirror the stock market are also available for passive portfolio managers. These index funds have become popular over time because they avoid the transaction costs associated with frequent purchases and sales of individual stocks.

25-7a Management of Insured versus Trust Portfolios

Some pension plans are managed by life insurance companies. Contributions to such plans, called insured plans, are often used to purchase annuity policies so that the life insurance companies can provide benefits to employees upon retirement.

As an alternative, some pension funds are managed by the trust departments of financial institutions, such as commercial banks. The trust department invests the contributions and pays benefits to employees upon retirement. Although the day-to-day investment decisions of the trust department are controlled by the managing institution, the corporation owning the pension normally specifies general guidelines that the institution should follow. These guidelines might include:

- The percentage of the portfolio that should be used for stocks or bonds
- A desired minimum rate of return on the overall portfolio
- The maximum amount to be invested in real estate
- The minimum acceptable quality ratings for bonds

- The maximum amount to be invested in any one industry
- The average maturity of bonds held in the portfolio
- The maximum amount to be invested in options
- The minimum size of companies in which to invest

There is a significant difference between the asset composition of pension portfolios managed by life insurance companies and those managed by trust departments. Assets managed by insurance companies are designed to create annuities, whereas the assets managed by a trust department still belong to the corporation. The insurance company becomes the legal owner of the assets and is allowed to maintain only a small portion of its assets as equities. Therefore insurance companies concentrate on bonds and mortgages. Conversely, the pension portfolios managed by trusts concentrate on stocks.

Pension portfolios managed by trusts offer potentially higher returns than insured plans and also have a higher degree of risk. The average return of trust plans is much more volatile over time.

25-7b Management of Portfolio Risk

Pension fund managers commonly struggle with the decision of whether to pursue investments with high expected return that have high risk. If they can achieve higher returns on their existing funds, they can more easily meet the obligations they have to the participants in the plan. However, the strategy of attempting to earn a return of a few percentage points higher can backfire and cause a loss of 20 percent or more. For example, some pension funds invest in private equity funds, which invest in companies and often manage them with the goal of increasing their value, and then selling the companies (as explained in Chapter 10). This type of investment by a pension fund could earn a very large return. However, it could also result in a very large loss.

The degree of risk taken by pension fund managers is partially influenced by their compensation incentives. In some cases, the managers may be rewarded if the portfolio performs very well yet not be penalized if the portfolio performs poorly. Under these conditions, the portfolio managers have an incentive to take more risk than what is appropriate.

Many pension fund managers pursued risky investments prior to the credit crisis, which resulted in major losses during the credit crisis. Since then, some state governments have imposed restrictions on the types of investments that their pension fund managers can pursue. The restrictions will result in safer investments, but these investments will likely generate relatively low returns. The restrictions tend to be imposed after a period in which there are many losses but eliminated after a period in which other pensions achieve comparatively higher returns by pursuing riskier investments.

Hedging Risk Pension fund portfolio managers are very concerned about interest rate risk. If they hold long-term, fixed-rate bonds, the market value of their portfolio will decrease during periods when interest rates increase. They may periodically hedge against interest rate movements by selling bond futures contracts.

Many portfolio managers periodically sell futures contracts on stock indexes to hedge against market downturns. Portfolio managers of pension funds can obtain various types of insurance to limit the risk of the portfolio. For example, a policy could insure beyond a specified decline (such as 10 percent) in the asset value of a pension fund. This insurance allows managers to use more aggressive investment strategies. The cost of the insurance depends on the provisions of the contract and the length of time the portfolio is to be insured.

The pension funds of some companies, such as Lockheed Martin, simply concentrate investment in stocks and bonds and do not employ immunization techniques (to hedge the portfolio against risk). Lockheed Martin has generally focused on highly liquid investments so that the proportion of stocks and bonds within the portfolio can be revised in response to market conditions.

25-7c Corporate Control by Pension Funds

Pension funds in aggregate hold a substantial portion of the common stock outstanding in the United States. These funds are increasingly using their ownership as a means of influencing policies of the corporations whose stock they own. In particular, the California Public Employees Retirement System (CALPERS) and the New York State Government Retirement Fund have taken active roles in questioning specific policies and suggesting changes to the board of directors at some corporations. Corporate managers consider the requests of pension funds because of the large stake the pension funds have in the corporations. As pension funds exert some corporate control to ensure that the managers and board members serve the best interests of shareholders, they can benefit because of their position as large shareholders.

25-8 PERFORMANCE OF PENSION FUNDS

Pension funds commonly maintain a portfolio of stocks and a portfolio of bonds. Because pension funds focus on investing pension contributions until payments are provided, the performance of the investments is critical to the pension fund's success.

25-8a Pension Fund's Stock Portfolio Performance

The change in the value of a pension fund's portfolio focusing on stocks can be modeled as

$$\Delta V = f(\Delta \text{MKT}, \Delta \text{MANAB})$$

where MKT represents general stock market conditions and MANAB represents the abilities of the pension fund's management.

Change in Market Conditions The stock portfolio's performance is usually closely related to market conditions. Most pension funds' stock portfolios performed well during the 2003–2007 period when market conditions were strong, poorly during the credit crisis in 2008–2009, and well when the market rebounded in the 2010–2012 period.

Change in Management Abilities Stock portfolio performance can vary among pension funds in a particular time period because of differences in management abilities. The composition of the stocks in a pension fund's portfolio is determined by the fund's portfolio managers. In addition, a pension fund's operating efficiency affects the expenses the fund incurs and therefore affects its performance. A fund that is managed efficiently so that its expenses are low may be able to achieve higher returns even if its portfolio performance is about the same as the performance of other pension funds' portfolios.

25-8b Pension Fund's Bond Portfolio Performance

The change in the value of a pension fund's bond portfolio (including mortgages or mortgage-backed securities) can be modeled as

$$\Delta V = f(\Delta R_f, \Delta RP, \Delta \text{MANAB})$$

where R_f represents the risk-free rate, RP represents the risk premium, and MANAB represents the abilities of the portfolio managers.

Impact of Change in the Risk-Free Rate The prices of bonds tend to be inversely related to changes in the risk-free interest rate. In periods when the risk-free interest rate declines substantially, the required rate of return by bondholders declines and most bond portfolios managed by pension funds perform well.

Recently, long-term interest rates have been very low. Consequently, the future return that can be earned by pension funds on low-risk long-term bonds is very low if the bonds are held until maturity. If the bonds are not held to maturity, there is not much potential for the prices of these bonds to increase, because the required rates of return cannot go much lower. However, there is significant interest rate risk because long-term rates could rise from their prevailing levels over time, which would cause the prices to decline.

Impact of Change in the Risk Premium When economic conditions deteriorate, the risk premium required by bondholders usually increases, which results in a higher required rate of return (assuming no change in the risk-free rate) and lower prices on risky bonds. In periods when risk premiums increase, bond portfolios of pension funds that contain a high proportion of risky bonds perform poorly.

Impact of Management Abilities The performance levels of bond portfolios can vary as a result of differences in management abilities. If a pension fund's portfolio managers can effectively adjust the bond portfolio in response to accurate forecasts of changes in interest rates or shifts in bond risk premiums, that fund's bond portfolio should experience relatively high performance. In addition, a pension fund's operating efficiency affects the expenses it incurs. If a bond portfolio is managed efficiently so that its expenses are low, it may be able to achieve relatively high returns even if its investments perform the same as those of other pension funds.

As time passes, portfolio managers might change the composition of a pension portfolio, which can alter the portfolio's potential return and its risk. Because long-term interest rates have been so low recently, there may be a natural tendency for portfolio managers to switch out of low-risk bonds into high-yield bonds. That is, they attempt to offset the low long-term risk-free rate with a high-risk premium on the bonds. However, this strategy exposes the portfolio to higher risk, as the high-yield bonds are more likely to default on their payments. Alternatively, portfolio managers seeking to achieve better returns than what is available on low-risk bonds might invest more of their funds in stocks (assuming that there are no restrictions on the portfolio that could prevent such a strategy). This strategy also exposes the portfolio to higher risk, as the stocks may suffer significant declines in value when stock market conditions are weak.

25-8c Performance Evaluation

If a manager has the flexibility to adjust the relative proportion of stocks versus bonds, the portfolio performance should be compared to a benchmark representing a passive strategy. For example, assume that the general long-run plan is a balance of 60 percent bonds and 40 percent stocks. Also assume that management has decided to create a more bond-intensive portfolio in anticipation of lower interest rates. The risk-adjusted returns on this actively managed portfolio could be compared to a benchmark portfolio composed of 60 percent bond index and 40 percent stock index.

Any difference between the performance of the pension portfolio and the benchmark portfolio would result from (1) the manager's shift in the relative proportion of bonds versus stocks and (2) the composition of bonds and stocks within the respective portfolios. A pension portfolio could conceivably have stocks that outperform the stock index and bonds that outperform the bond index yet be outperformed by the benchmark portfolio when the shift in the relative bond/stock proportion backfires. In this example, a period of rising interest rates could cause the pension portfolio to be outperformed by the benchmark portfolio.

In many cases, the performances of stocks and bonds in a pension fund are evaluated separately. Stock portfolio risk is usually measured by the portfolio's beta, or the sensitivity to movements in a stock index (such as the S&P 500). Bond portfolio risk can be measured by the bond portfolio's sensitivity to a bond index or to a particular proxy for interest rates.

25-8d Performance of Pension Portfolio Managers

Many pension funds hire several portfolio managers to manage the assets. The general objective of portfolio managers is to make investments that will earn a large enough return to adequately meet future payment obligations. Some research has found that managed pension portfolios perform no better than market indexes. During the credit crisis, some pension portfolios performed much worse than market indexes because their managers invested heavily in risky mortgages and mortgage-backed securities. For example, the state of Washington lost $90 million on its investment in securities issued by Lehman Brothers (which filed for bankruptcy after experiencing severe losses in mortgage-related securities), and the state of New York lost hundreds of millions of dollars on its investment in similar securities.

Pension funds could consider using a passive management strategy such as investing in indexed mutual funds, which would perform as well as the market without requiring the pension plan to incur expenses for portfolio management. In this way, they could ensure that the investment strategy serves the needs of the pension fund participants.

SUMMARY

- Insurance companies offer insurance on life, property, health, business, bonds, and mortgages. Insurance companies commonly use their funds to invest in government securities, corporate securities, mortgages, and real estate.

- Insurance companies are exposed to interest rate risk because they tend to maintain large bond portfolios whose values decline when interest rates rise. They are also exposed to credit risk and market risk as a result of their investments in corporate debt securities, mortgages, stocks, and real estate.

- The value of an insurance company is based on its expected cash flows and the required rate of return by investors. The payouts of claims (cash outflows) are somewhat predictable for life insurance firms, so they tend to have stable cash flows. In contrast, the payouts of claims for property and casualty insurance and other types of insurance services are subject to much uncertainty.

- Pension funds provide a savings plan for retirement. For defined-benefit pension plans, the contributions are dictated by the benefits that are specified. For defined-contribution pension plans, the benefits are determined by the accumulated contributions and the returns on the pension fund investments.

- Pension funds can use a matched funding strategy, in which investment decisions are made with the objective of generating cash flows that match planned outflow payments. Alternatively, pension funds can use a projective funding strategy, which attempts to capitalize on expected market or interest rate movements.

- The valuation and performance of pension fund portfolios is highly influenced by market conditions. However, the valuation of some pension portfolios are more exposed to risk than others. Those pension portfolios that contained risky mortgages and mortgage-backed securities experienced major losses during the credit crisis.

POINT COUNTER-POINT

Should Pension Fund Managers Be More Involved with Corporate Governance?

Point   No. Pension fund managers should focus on assessing stock valuations and determining which stocks are undervalued or overvalued. If pension funds own stocks of firms that perform poorly, the pension fund managers can penalize those firms by dumping those stocks and investing their money in other stocks. If pension funds focus too much on corporate governance, they will lose sight of their goal of serving the pension recipients.

Counter-Point   Yes. To the extent that pension funds can use governance to improve the performance of the firms in which they invest, they can improve the funds' performance. In this way, they also improve the returns to the pension recipients.

Who Is Correct?   Use the Internet to learn more about this issue and then formulate your own opinion.

QUESTIONS AND APPLICATIONS

1. Life Insurance How is whole life insurance a form of savings to policyholders?

2. Whole Life versus Term Insurance How do whole life and term insurance differ from the perspective of insurance companies? From the perspective of the policyholders?

3. Universal Life Insurance Identify the characteristics of universal life insurance.

4.   Group Plan Explain group plan life insurance.

5. Assets of Life Insurance Companies What are the main assets of life insurance companies? Identify the main categories. What is the main use of funds by life insurance companies?

6. Financing the Real Estate Market How do insurance companies finance the real estate market?

7. Policy Loans What is a policy loan? When are policy loans popular? Why?

8. Government Rescue of AIG Why did the government rescue AIG?

9. Managing Credit Risk and Liquidity Risk How do insurance companies manage credit risk and liquidity risk?

10. Liquidity Risk Discuss the liquidity risk experienced by life insurance companies and by property and casualty (PC) insurance companies.

11. PC Insurance What purpose do property and casualty insurance companies serve? Explain how the characteristics of PC insurance and life insurance differ.

12. Cash Flow Underwriting Explain the concept of cash flow underwriting.

13. Impact of Inflation on Assets Explain how a life insurance company's asset portfolio may be affected by inflation.

14. Reinsurance What is reinsurance?

15. NAIC What is the NAIC, and what is its purpose?

16. PBGC What is the main purpose of the Pension Benefit Guaranty Corporation (PBGC)?

17. Defined-Benefit versus Defined-Contribution Plan Describe a defined-benefit pension plan. Describe a defined-contribution plan, and explain how it differs from a defined-benefit plan.

18. Guidelines for a Trust What type of general guidelines may be specified for a trust that is managing a pension fund?

19. Management of Pension Portfolios Explain the general difference in the composition of pension portfolios managed by trusts versus those managed by insurance companies. Explain why this difference occurs.

20. Private versus Public Pension Funds Explain the general difference between private pension funds and public pension funds.

21. Exposure to Interest Rate Risk How can pension funds reduce their exposure to interest rate risk?

22. Pension Agency Problems The objective of the pension fund manager for McCanna, Inc., is not the same as the objective of McCanna's employees participating in the pension plan. Why?

23. ERISA Explain how ERISA affects employees who change employers.

24. Adverse Selection and Moral Hazard Problems in Insurance Explain the adverse selection and moral hazard problems in insurance. Gorton Insurance Company wants to properly price its auto insurance, which protects against losses due to auto accidents. If Gorton wants to avoid the adverse selection and moral hazard problems, should it assess the behavior of insured people, uninsured people, or both groups? Explain.

Interpreting Financial News

Interpret the following comments made by Wall Street analysts and portfolio managers.

a. "Insurance company stocks may benefit from the recent decline in interest rates."

b. "Insurance company portfolio managers may serve as shareholder activists to implicitly control a corporation's actions."

c. "If a life insurance company wants a portfolio manager to generate sufficient cash to meet expected payments to beneficiaries, it cannot expect the manager to achieve relatively high returns for the portfolio."

Managing in Financial Markets

Assessing Insurance Company Operations As a consultant to an insurance company, you have been asked to assess the asset composition of the company.

a. The insurance company has recently sold a large amount of bonds and invested the proceeds in real estate. Its logic was that this would reduce the exposure of its assets to interest rate risk. Do you agree? Explain.

b. This insurance company currently has a small amount of stock. The company expects that it will need to liquidate some of its assets soon to make payments to beneficiaries. Should it shift its bond holdings (with short terms remaining until maturity) into stock in order to strive for a higher rate of return before it needs to liquidate this investment?

c. The insurance company maintains a higher proportion of junk bonds than most other insurance companies. In recent years, junk bonds have performed very well during a period of strong economic growth, as the yields paid by junk bonds have been well above those of high-quality corporate bonds. There have been very few defaults over this period. Consequently, the insurance company has proposed that it invest more heavily in junk bonds, as it believes that the concerns about junk bonds are unjustified. Do you agree? Explain.

Flow of Funds Exercise

How Insurance Companies Facilitate the Flow of Funds

Carson Company is considering a private placement of equity with Secura Insurance Company.

a. Explain the interaction between Carson Company and Secura. How will Secura serve Carson's needs, and how will Carson serve Secura's needs?

b. Why does Carson interact with Secura Insurance Company instead of trying to obtain the funds directly from individuals who pay premiums to Secura?

c. If Secura's investment performs well, who benefits? Is it worthwhile for Secura to closely monitor Carson Company's management? Explain.

Internet/Excel Exercises

1. Obtain a life insurance quotation online using the website www.eterm.com. Fill in information about you (or a family member or friend) and obtain a quotation for a $1 million life insurance policy. What are the monthly and annual premiums for the various term lengths? Next, leaving all other information unchanged, change your gender. Are the premiums the same or different? Do you think insurance premiums are higher or lower for insurance companies operating entirely through the Internet?

2. Select a publicly traded insurance company of your choice. Go to its website and retrieve its most recent annual report. Summarize the company's main business. Is it focused on life insurance, auto insurance, health insurance, or a combination of these? Describe its performance over the last year. Explain why its performance was higher or lower than normal. Was the change in its performance due to the economy, the impact of recent interest rate movements on its asset portfolio, the stock market's performance, or a change in the frequency and size of insurance claims?

3. Go to finance.yahoo.com, enter the symbol MET (MetLife, Inc.), and click on "Get Quotes." Click on "5y" just below the stock price trend to review the stock price movements over the last five years. Check the "Compare" box just above the graph and then select "S&P 500" in order to compare the trend of MetLife's stock price with the movements in the S&P stock index. Has MetLife performed better or worse than the index? Offer an explanation for its performance.

4. Go to finance.yahoo.com, enter the symbol MET (MetLife, Inc.), and click on "Get Quotes." Retrieve stock price data at the beginning of the last 20 quarters. Then go to http://research.stlouisfed.org/fred2/ and retrieve interest rate data at the beginning of the last 20 quarters for the three-month Treasury bill. Record the data on an Excel spreadsheet. Derive the quarterly return of MetLife. Derive the quarterly change in the interest rate. Apply regression analysis in which the quarterly return of MetLife, Inc., is the dependent variable and the quarterly change in the interest rate is the independent variable (see Appendix B for more information about using regression analysis). Is there a positive or negative relationship between the interest rate movement and the stock return of MetLife? Is the relationship significant? Offer an explanation for this relationship.

WSJ Exercise

Insurance Company Performance

Using an issue of the *Wall Street Journal*, summarize an article that discusses the recent performance of a particular insurance company. Does the article suggest that the insurance company's performance was better or worse than the norm? What reason is given for the particular level of performance?

Online Articles with Real-World Examples

Find a recent practical article available online that describes a real-world example regarding a specific financial institution or financial market that reinforces one or more concepts covered in this chapter.

If your class has an online component, your professor may ask you to post your summary of the article there and provide a link to the article so that other students can access it. If your class is live, your professor may ask you to summarize your application of the article in class. Your professor may assign specific students to complete this assignment or may allow any students to do the assignment on a volunteer basis.

For recent online articles and real-world examples related to this chapter, consider using the following search terms (be sure to include the prevailing year as a search term to ensure that the online articles are recent):

1. [name of a specific insurance company] AND performance

2. [name of a specific insurance company] AND operations

3. [name of a specific insurance company] AND risk

4. [name of a specific insurance company] AND earnings

5. [name of a specific insurance company] AND management

6. insurance company AND operations

7. insurance company AND risk

8. insurance company AND regulation

9. pension fund AND management

10. pension fund AND operations

Assessing the Influence of Economic Conditions across a Financial Conglomerate's Units

This problem requires an understanding of the operations and asset compositions of savings institutions (Chapter 21), finance companies (Chapter 22), mutual funds (Chapter 23), securities firms (Chapter 24), and insurance companies (Chapter 25).

A diversified financial conglomerate has five units (subsidiaries). One unit conducts thrift operations; the second unit conducts consumer finance operations; the third, mutual fund operations; the fourth, securities operations; and the fifth, insurance operations. As a financial analyst for the conglomerate's holding company, you have been asked to assess all of the units and to indicate how each unit will be affected as economic conditions change as well as which units will be most affected.

In the past few months, all economic indicators have been signaling the possibility of a recession. Stock prices have already declined as the demand for stocks has decreased significantly. It appears that the pessimistic outlook will last for at least a few months. Economic conditions are already somewhat stagnant and are expected to deteriorate further in future months. During that time, firms will not consider mergers, new stock issues, or new bond issues.

An economist at your financial conglomerate believes that individual investors will overreact to the pessimistic outlook. Once stock prices are low enough, some firms will acquire target firms whose stock appears to be undervalued. In addition, some firms will buy back some of their own stock once they believe it is undervalued. Although these activities have not yet occurred, the economist believes it is only a matter of time.

Questions

1. Your strategy is to identify the units that will be less adversely affected by the recession. You believe that the units' different characteristics will cause some of them to be affected more than others.

2. Currently, each unit employs economists who develop forecasts for interest rates and other economic conditions. When assessing potential economic effects on each unit, what are the disadvantages of this approach versus having just one economist at the holding company provide forecasts?

Final Self-Exam

Final Review

Chapters 17 to 25 are focused on financial institutions. Here is a brief review of the chapters.

Chapter 17 explains how banks obtain most of their funds from deposits and allocate most of their funds toward loans or securities. Chapter 18 explains how banks are regulated according to the services they offer and the capital that they must maintain as well as how regulators monitor their risk over time. Chapter 19 explains how banks manage their sources and uses of funds (within regulatory constraints) in a manner to achieve their return and risk preferences. Chapter 20 shows how a bank's performance is highly influenced by what it charges on loans versus what it pays on deposits (which affects its net interest margin), its income earned from services (noninterest income), and its level of noninterest expenses.

Chapter 21 explains that savings institutions are similar to banks in the manner by which they obtain funds but use most of their funds to invest in mortgages or mortgage-related securities. This results in a higher exposure to interest rate risk, although savings institutions can hedge that risk. Chapter 22 explains that finance companies differ from banks and savings institutions in that they typically obtain their funds by issuing commercial paper and target their use of funds toward consumers or small businesses. In general, the credit risk of their assets is higher than that of commercial banks or savings institutions. Chapter 23 identifies the types of mutual funds and explains how their performance and risk vary across funds. In general, a mutual fund's asset portfolio is much more risky than those of other financial institutions. Chapter 24 describes how securities firms channel funds through financial markets. The investment banking portion of a securities firm places new securities with investors and thereby helps corporations obtain financing. The brokerage portion of a securities firm channels funds between investors in the secondary market. Chapter 25 explains how insurance companies obtain funds from the premiums they charge and how pension funds rely on retirement contributions from employees or their respective employers. Insurance companies and pension funds are major investors in the bond and stock markets.

This self-exam allows you to test your understanding of some of the key concepts covered in the chapters on financial institutions. It does not replace the end-of-chapter questions, nor does it cover all the concepts. It is simply intended to allow you to test yourself on a general overview of key concepts. Try to simulate taking an exam by answering the questions without using your book and your notes. The answers to this exam are provided at the end of the questions so that you can grade your exam. If you have any wrong answers, you should reread the related material and then redo the questions that you had wrong.

This exam may not necessarily match the level of rigor in your course. Your instructor may offer you specific information about how this Final Self-Exam relates to the coverage and rigor of the final exam in your course.

FINAL SELF-EXAM

1. Flagstaff Bank currently has assets heavily concentrated in secured loans and Treasury securities, while Mesa Bank has assets concentrated in consumer loans and credit card loans. The managerial capabilities of the two banks are similar. Mesa Bank's performance was much better than that of Flagstaff Bank last year, but Flagstaff Bank's performance is much better than that of Mesa Bank this year. Explain why the relative performance of the two banks is likely to change over time.

2. The Sarbanes-Oxley Act of 2002 requires publicly traded firms to be more transparent in their reporting. This may reduce the asymmetric information problem between firms (including banks) and their investors. Do you think the Sarbanes-Oxley Act will eliminate the need for CAMELS ratings?

3. Kentucky Bank has a new board of directors who believe that the bank has opportunities for major growth and want to ensure that the CEO makes good investment decisions to expand the bank's business. To give the CEO a strong incentive to perform well, the board set the CEO's quarterly compensation in line with the return on equity. The CEO immediately decided to repurchase as many shares as possible while barely meeting the bank's capital requirements. Why would the CEO take this action? Will the compensation structure remove agency problems?

4. Last year, Alabama Bank had a net interest margin of 3 percent, noninterest income was 1.5 percent of assets, noninterest expenses were 3 percent of assets, and loan loss reserves were 0.5 percent of assets. Alabama Bank wants to employ a strategy of using more of its resources to offer financial services. It expects that it can increase its noninterest income by 0.5 percent as a percentage of assets. What other components (or ratios) of the income statement may be affected by this strategy?

5. Maryland Savings Institution maintains most of its assets in fixed-rate mortgages of between 10 and 30 years. Most of its deposits have maturities of less than one year. Assume that the Fed implements a restrictive monetary policy.

a. Explain how that monetary policy will affect interest rates.

b. Assuming that interest rates change as expected, how will that affect the spread between interest revenue and interest expenses?

c. Should Maryland hedge its asset portfolio based on its expectations? If so, how should it hedge? If it should hedge, explain any limitations of the hedge.

6. How do financial institutions vary in terms of their main uses of funds?

7. Explain the role that insurance companies and pension funds play in financial markets.

8. Explain why a stock market benefits more when financial institutions are investors than when individual investors invest all their money directly into the stock market themselves.

9. Discuss the following argument. Money market funds attract money from investors who do not know what else to do with their money. Thus, money market funds are merely a last resort when there are no better alternatives for investment. Since they invest only in short-term securities, they do not play a role in financing economic growth.

10. Closed-end funds tend to hold stocks that are less liquid than stocks held by open-end funds.

    a. Do you think this characteristic is an advantage for closed-end funds that want to achieve high returns?

    b. Why is it easier for closed-end funds to manage a portfolio of less liquid stocks than it would be for open-end funds?

11. Discuss the strategy of an investor who invests all of his money in four mutual funds that focus on growth companies. The investor believes he is fully insulated from market conditions because each fund contains 40 different stocks.

12. For a given type of mutual fund classification, what is a key characteristic that causes some mutual funds to outperform others?

13. When a securities firm serves as an underwriter for an initial public offering (IPO), is the firm working for the issuer or the institutional investors that may purchase shares? Explain the dilemma.

14. Do stock analysts reduce market inefficiencies?

15. Why might the value of an insurance company be affected by interest rate movements?

16. Should financial institutions be regulated in order to reduce their risk? Offer at least one argument for regulation and one argument against regulation.

17. Consider the typical sources and uses of funds at commercial banks, savings institutions, and securities firms. Explain the risk of each type of institution based on its typical sources and uses of funds.

ANSWERS TO FINAL SELF-EXAM

1. Under favorable economic conditions, Mesa Bank should perform better because it earns higher returns on its loans as long as the borrowers repay their loans (higher risk). Under unfavorable economic conditions, Flagstaff Bank should perform better because Mesa will likely experience many loan defaults while Flagstaff will not.

2. Even if investors have more information, they may not be able to detect banks that have financial problems. In addition, CAMELS ratings are intended to detect financial problems of banks early so that there is time to correct the problems. This can prevent bank failures and therefore allow for a more stable banking system.

3. The stock repurchase will reduce equity so that the profits in the near future will result in a higher return on equity. This will enhance the CEO's compensation but will not necessarily enhance the bank's value in the long run. In fact, the decreased equity will restrict the growth of the bank. Thus, this compensation structure will not remove agency problems.

4. Alabama Bank will incur more expenses when attempting to expand its financial services. This will increase the ratio of noninterest expenses to assets, and this increase could offset any increase in revenue.

5. a. Interest rates will rise.

b. The spread will decrease because short-term deposit rates will increase, while long-term rates may not be affected as much or at all.

c. Maryland should hedge. It could sell interest rate futures. However, if it does sell interest rate futures and interest rates decline, it will incur a loss on its interest rate futures position, which may offset most of its gain from operations.

6. Commercial banks serve corporate borrowers, savings institutions serve home-owners, finance companies serve consumers and small businesses, while mutual funds, insurance companies, and pension funds serve corporate borrowers (investing in stocks and bonds and money market securities issued by corporations).

7. Insurance companies and pension funds are suppliers of funds and add much liquid-ity to the financial markets. They may also make the stock market more efficient because if a stock's price deviates from its fundamental value, they may take a position to capitalize on the discrepancy, and this should push the stock toward its fundamental value.

8. Institutional investors pool funds that come from many individuals and take much bigger stakes in a specific stock. Thus, the institutional investors have an incentive to make the correct investment choices (because of the large investment) and then to monitor the companies in which they invest. As a result, there is more governance over companies than if stocks were owned only by small investors.

9. Money market funds provide liquidity to investors, which is necessary even when investors have alternative investments that pay higher returns. In addition, money mar-ket funds play a major role in financing the budget deficit because they invest heavily in Treasury securities. They also channel funds to corporations in the form of commercial paper. Since the Treasury and corporations frequently reissue short-term securities, they are sometimes using the short-term securities to finance long-term investment.

10. a. The investment in illiquid stocks may be an advantage because it allows the closed-end funds to pursue stocks that are not followed by most investors. These stocks are more likely to be mispriced than other stocks.

b. Closed-end funds do not have to accommodate redemptions, whereas open-end funds do. Thus, closed-end funds do not need to worry about selling some of their stock holdings just for the purpose of satisfying redemptions.

11. These mutual funds will all be adversely affected during a weak economy because firms that have high growth potential will probably experience weak performance when economic conditions are weak. There is not sufficient demand under these conditions.

12. Mutual funds with a low expense ratio tend to perform better than those with higher expense ratios.

13. A securities firm attempts to satisfy the issuer of stock by ensuring that the price is sufficiently high, but it must also ensure that it can place all the shares. It also wants to satisfy investors who invest in the IPO. If the investors incur losses because they paid too much for the shares, they may not want to purchase any more stock from that under-writer in the future.

14. Some stock analysts may be able to detect when a specific stock is underpriced or overpriced in the market, and they can communicate their opinion through their stock ratings, which may cause investors to capitalize on the information. This could push stock prices closer to their fundamental values and reduce market inefficiencies. During the stock market bubble in the year 2000, however, analysts were overly optimistic about stocks and were not paying attention to fundamentals of the companies. Thus, they may have been a partial cause of the stock market bubble.

15. The value of an insurance company is partially influenced by the value of its asset portfolio. Its asset portfolio contains bonds. The market value of the bonds is inversely related to interest rate movements.

16. Regulation may be able to reduce failures of financial institutions, which may stabilize the financial system. The flow of funds into financial institutions will be larger if the people who provide the funds can trust that the financial institutions will not fail. However, regulation can also restrict competition. In some cases, it results in subsidies to financial institutions that are performing poorly. Thus, regulation can prevent firms from operating efficiently.

17. Commercial banks are exposed to default risk due to their commercial and consumer loans. They are exposed to interest rate risk because the maturities on some of their assets (especially bonds and some term loans) may be longer than the maturities on their liabilities. Savings institutions are exposed to default risk due to their mortgage loans (although these loans are normally backed by the home) and consumer loans. They are exposed to interest rate risk because the maturities on their fixed-rate mortgages are longer than the maturities on their liabilities. Securities firms are exposed to market risk from taking equity positions and to default risk when providing bridge loans. Their operations are especially sensitive to financial market activity. When financial transactions such as mergers and stock trades decline, their business declines because they serve as intermediaries for many types of financial transactions.

Comprehensive Project

One of the best ways to gain a clear understanding of the key concepts explained in this text is to apply them directly to actual situations. This comprehensive project enables you to apply numerous concepts regarding financial markets and institutions discussed throughout the text to actual situations. The tasks in this project can be categorized as follows:

Part I. Applying Financial Markets Concepts
Part II. Applying Financial Institutions Concepts
Part III. Measuring Stock Performance

At the beginning of the school term, you should complete two tasks. First, compile the information on financial markets needed to fill in the blank spaces in steps (a) through (j) in Part I. This information will be needed when applying financial markets concepts in the questions that follow (Part I of the project). Second, obtain the information on financial institutions identified at the beginning of Part II. This information will be needed when applying financial institutions concepts in the questions that follow (Part II of the project).

PART I. APPLYING FINANCIAL MARKETS CONCEPTS

The exercises on financial markets concepts require you to measure the change in the yields and values of securities over the school term and explain why the values changed. In doing so, you will apply the concepts in the chapters on financial markets to actual situations.

At the beginning of the school term and near the end of the term, use an issue of *The Wall Street Journal* or various financial websites to obtain the information requested here. Your professor will identify the dates to use as the beginning and end of the term. The dates will allow you sufficient time to assess the changes in the yields and values of securities so that you can answer the questions. Your professor will explain the specific format of the assignment, such as whether any parts are excluded or whether students should work in teams. Your professor will also indicate whether the answers will be handed in, presented to the class, or both. A commonly used format is to divide the project into parts and assign a team of students to present their answers to one specific part. Each student will be a member of one of the teams. All students may still be required to hand in answers to all parts of the project, even though their team's presentation focuses on only one part.

	BEGINNING OF TERM	END OF TERM
a. Stock market index information:		
S&P 500 (stock) index level:	_____	_____
Nasdaq Composite (stock) index level:	_____	_____
b. Interest rate information:		
Prime rate:	_____	_____
Federal funds rate:	_____	_____
Commercial paper rate (90 days):	_____	_____
Certificate of deposit rate (3-month):	_____	_____
Treasury bill rate (13 weeks):	_____	_____
Treasury bill rate (26 weeks):	_____	_____
c. Bond yield information:		
Treasury long-term bond yield:	_____	_____
DJ Corporate bond yield:	_____	_____
Corporate (Master) bond yield:	_____	_____
High-yield corporate bond yield:	_____	_____
Tax-exempt (7–12-year) bond yield:	_____	_____

d. Use stock exchange quotations to record the stock price and dividend of one stock from each stock exchange in which you would like to invest.

	BEGINNING OF TERM	END OF TERM
New York Stock Exchange: Stock price:	_____	_____
Name of firm _____ Dividend:	_____	_____
Nasdaq Market: Stock price:	_____	_____
Name of firm _____ Dividend:	_____	_____

e. Use futures prices quotations to record the recent ("settle") price of the following futures (select futures with first settlement date beyond the end of the school term):

	BEGINNING OF TERM	END OF TERM
Treasury bond futures:	_____	_____
S&P 500 index futures:	_____	_____
British pound futures:	_____	_____

f. Use an options quotations table to select a call option on a firm whose stock price you expect to increase (select the option with the first expiration month beyond the end of the school term):

Name of firm: _____

Expiration month: _____

Strike price: _____

	BEGINNING OF TERM	END OF TERM
Stock price:	_____	_____
Option premium:	_____	_____

g. Use an options quotations table to select a put option on a firm where you expect the stock price to decrease (select the option with the first expiration month beyond the end of the school term):

Name of firm: _____

Expiration month: _____

Strike price: _____

	BEGINNING OF TERM	END OF TERM
Stock price:	_____	_____
Option premium:	_____	_____

h. Use a currency exchange rate table in *The Wall Street Journal* to record exchange rates:

	BEGINNING OF TERM	END OF TERM
Exchange rate of the British pound (in $):	_____	_____
Exchange rate of the Japanese yen (in $):	_____	_____
Exchange rate of the Mexican peso (in $):	_____	_____

i. Use currency options data (if available) to select a call option on a foreign currency that you expect will strengthen against the dollar (select the option with the first expiration month beyond the end of the school term):

Currency: _____

Expiration month: _____

Strike price: _____

Currency's existing value: _____ _____

Option premium: _____ _____

j. Use currency options data (if available) to select a put option on a foreign currency that you expect will weaken against the dollar (select the option with the first expiration month beyond the end of the school term):

Currency: _____

Expiration month: _____

Strike price: _____

Currency's existing value: _____ _____

Option premium: _____ _____

1. Explaining changes in interest rates (from Chapter 2)

a. Compare the 13-week Treasury bill rate (which is a proxy for short-term interest rates) at the end of the school term to the rate that existed at the beginning of the school term.

b. Recall that Chapter 2 offered reasons why interest rates change over time. Apply the concepts in that chapter to explain why you think interest rates have changed over the school term.

2. Comparing yields among securities (from Chapter 3)

a. What is the difference between the yield on corporate high-quality bonds and the yield on Treasury bonds at the end of the school term?

b. Apply the concepts discussed in Chapter 3 to explain why this premium exists.

c. What is the difference between the yield on long-term Treasury bonds and the yield on long-term municipal bonds at the end of the school term?

d. Apply the concepts discussed in Chapter 3 to explain why this difference exists.

3. Assessing the forecasting ability of the yield curve (from Chapter 3)

a. What was the difference between the 26-week T-bill yield and the 13-week T-bill yield at the beginning of the school term?

b. Does this imply that the yield curve had an upward or downward slope at that time?

c. Assuming that this slope can be primarily attributed to expectations theory, did the direction of the slope indicate that the market expected higher or lower interest rates in the future?

d. Did interest rates move in that direction over the school term?

4. Explaining shifts in the yield curve over time (from Chapter 3)

a. What was the difference between the long-term Treasury bond yield and the 13-week T-bill yield at the beginning of the school term?

b. What is the difference between the long-term Treasury bond yield and the 13-week T-bill yield at the end of the school term?

c. Given your answers to the two previous questions, describe how the yield curve changed over the school term. Explain the changes in expectations about future interest rates that are implied by the shift in the yield curve over the school term.

5. The Fed's influence on interest rates (from Chapter 5)

a. Did the Fed change the federal funds rate over the school term?

b. Do you think the movements in interest rates over the school term were caused by the Fed's monetary policy? Explain.

6. Measuring and explaining premiums on money market securities (from Chapter 6)

a. What is the difference between the yield on 90-day commercial paper and the yield on 13-week T-bills at the end of the school term? Apply the concepts discussed in Chapter 6 to explain why this premium exists.

b. Compare the premium on the 90-day commercial paper yield (relative to the 13-week T-bill yield) that exists at the end of the school term to the premium that existed at the beginning of the term. Apply the concepts discussed in Chapter 6 to explain why the premium may have changed over the school term.

7. Explaining bond premiums and price movements (from Chapter 8)

a. What is the difference between the yield on high-yield corporate bonds at the end of the school term versus the yield on high-quality corporate bonds at the beginning of the school term? Apply the concepts discussed in Chapter 8 to explain why this premium exists.

b. Compare the long-term Treasury bond yield at the end of the school term to the long-term Treasury bond yield that existed at the beginning of the school term. Given the direction of this change, did prices of long-term bonds rise or fall over the school term?

c. Compare the change in the yields of Treasury, municipal, and corporate bonds over the school term. Did the yields of all three types of securities move in the same direction and by about the same degree? Apply the concepts discussed in Chapter 8 to explain why yields of different types of bonds move together.

d. Compare the premium on high-yield corporate bonds (relative to Treasury bonds) at the beginning of the school term to the premium that existed at the end of the school term. Did the premium increase or decrease? Apply the concepts discussed in Chapter 8 to explain why this premium changed over the school term.

8. Explaining mortgage rates (from Chapter 9)

a. Compare the rate paid by a homeowner on a 30-year mortgage to the rate (yield) paid by the Treasury on long-term Treasury bonds at the end of the school term. Explain the difference.

b. Compare the 30-year mortgage rate at the end of the school term to the 30-year mortgage rate that existed at the beginning of the school term. What do you think is the primary reason for the change in 30-year mortgage rates over the school term?

9. Explaining stock price movements (from Chapter 11)

a. Determine the return on the stock market over your school term based on the percentage change in the S&P 500 index level over the term. Annualize this return by multiplying the return by $12/m$, where m is the number of months in your school term. Apply the concepts discussed in Chapter 11 to explain why the market return was high or low over your school term.

b.   Repeat the previous question for smaller stocks by using the Nasdaq Composite instead of the S&P 500 index. What was the annualized return on the Nasdaq Composite over your school term?

c.   Explain why the return on the Nasdaq Composite was high or low over your school term.

d.   Determine the return over the school term on the stock in which you chose to invest. The return is $(P_t - P_{t-1} + D)/P_{t-1}$, where P_t is the stock price as of the end of the school term, P_{t-1} is the stock price at the beginning of the school term, and D is the dividend paid over the school term. In most cases, one quarterly dividend is paid over a school term, which is one-fourth of the annual dividend amount per share shown in stock quotation tables.

e.   What was your return over the school term on the stock you selected from the New York Stock Exchange? What was your return over the school term on the stock you selected from the Nasdaq market? Apply the concepts discussed in Chapter 11 to explain why you think these two stocks experienced different returns over the school term.

10. Measuring and explaining futures price movements (from Chapter 13)

a.   Assume that you purchased an S&P 500 futures contract at the beginning of the school term, with the first settlement date beyond the end of the school term. Also assume that you sold an S&P 500 futures contract with this same settlement date at the end of the school term. Given that this contract has a value of the futures price times $250, determine the difference between the dollar value of the contract you sold and the dollar amount of the contract that you purchased.

b.   Assume that you invested an initial margin of 20 percent of the amount that you would owe to purchase the S&P 500 index at the settlement date. Measure your return from taking a position in the S&P 500 index futures as follows. Take the difference determined in the previous question (which represents the dollar amount of the gain on the futures position) and divide it by the amount you originally invested (the amount you originally invested is 20 percent of the dollar value of the futures contract that you purchased).

c.   The return that you just derived in the previous question is not annualized. To annualize your return, multiply it by $12/m$, where m is the number of months in your school term.

d.   Apply the concepts discussed in Chapter 13 to explain why your return on your S&P 500 index futures position was low or high over the school term.

e.   Assume that you purchased a Treasury bond futures contract at the beginning of the school term with the first settlement date beyond the end of the school term. Also assume that you sold this same type of futures contract at the end of the school term. Recall that Treasury bond futures contracts are priced relative to a $100,000 face value and the fractions are in thirty-seconds. What was the dollar value of the futures contract at the beginning of the school term when you purchased it?

f.   What was the dollar value of the Treasury bond futures contract at the end of the school term when you sold it?

g.   What was the difference between the dollar value of the Treasury bond futures contract when you sold it and the value when you purchased it?

h. Assume that you invested an initial margin of 20 percent of the amount that you would owe to purchase the Treasury bonds at the settlement date. Your investment is equal to 20 percent of the dollar value of the Treasury bond futures contract as of the time you purchased the futures. Determine the return on your futures position, which is the difference you derived in the previous question as a percentage of your investment.

i. The return that you just derived in the previous question is not annualized. To annualize your return, multiply your return by $12/m$, where m is the number of months in your school term.

j. Apply the concepts discussed in Chapter 13 to explain why the return on your Treasury bond futures position was low or high.

11. Measuring and explaining option price movements (from Chapter 14)

a. Assume that you purchased a call option (representing 100 shares) on the specific stock that you identified in Part I(f) of this project. What was your return from purchasing this option? [Your return can be measured as $(Prem_t - Prem_{t-1})/Prem_{t-1}$, where $Prem_{t-1}$ represents the premium paid at the beginning of the school term and $Prem_t$ represents the premium at which the same option can be sold at the end of the school term.] If the premium for this option is not quoted at the end of the school term, measure the return as if you had exercised the call option at the end of the school term (assuming that it is feasible to exercise the option at that time). That is, the return is based on purchasing the stock at the option's strike price and then selling the stock at its market price at the end of the school term.

b. Annualize the return on your option by multiplying the return you derived in the previous question by $12/m$, where m represents the number of months in your school term.

c. Compare the return on your call option to the return that you would have earned if you had simply invested in the stock itself. Notice how the magnitude of the return on the call option is much larger than the magnitude of the return on the stock itself. That is, the gains are larger and the losses are larger when investing in call options on a stock instead of the stock itself.

d. Assume that you purchased a put option (representing 100 shares) on the specific stock that you identified in Part I(g) of this project. What was your return from purchasing this option? [Your return can be measured as $(Prem_t - Prem_{t-1})/Prem_{t-1}$, where $Prem_{t-1}$ represents the premium paid at the beginning of the school term and $Prem_t$ represents the premium at which the same option can be sold at the end of the school term.] If the premium for this option is not quoted at the end of the school term, measure the return as if you had exercised the put option at the end of the school term (assuming that it is feasible to exercise the option at that time). That is, the return is based on purchasing the stock at its market price and then selling the stock at the option's strike price at the end of the school term.

12. Determining swap payments (from Chapter 15)

Assume that, at the beginning of the school term, you engaged in a fixed-for-floating rate swap in which you agreed to pay 6 percent in exchange for the prevailing 26-week T-bill rate that exists at the end of the school term. Assume that your swap agreement specifies the end of the school term as the only time at which a swap will occur and that the notional amount is $10 million. Determine the amount that you owe on the swap, the amount you are owed on the swap, and the difference. Did you gain or lose as a result of the swap?

13. Measuring and explaining exchange rate movements (from Chapter 16)

a. Determine the percentage change in the value of the British pound over the school term. Did the pound appreciate or depreciate against the dollar?

b. Determine the percentage change in the value of the Japanese yen over the school term. Did the yen appreciate or depreciate against the dollar?

c. Determine the percentage change in the value of the Mexican peso over the school term. Did the peso appreciate or depreciate against the dollar?

d. Determine the per unit gain or loss if you had purchased British pound futures at the beginning of the term and sold British pound futures at the end of the term.

e. Given that a single futures contract on British pounds represents 62,500 pounds, determine the dollar amount of your gain or loss.

PART II. APPLYING FINANCIAL INSTITUTIONS CONCEPTS

Obtain an annual report of (1) a commercial bank, (2) a savings institution, (3) a securities firm, and (4) an insurance company. The annual reports will allow you to relate the theory in specific related chapters to the particular financial institution of concern. The exercises in Part II of this comprehensive project require the use of these annual reports. The annual reports can be obtained by calling the shareholder services department for each financial institution, or they may be available online. Also, order a prospectus of a specific mutual fund in which you are interested. The prospectus can be obtained from the specific investment company that sponsors the mutual fund, or it may be available online.

1. Commercial bank operations (from Chapter 17)

For the commercial bank that you selected at the beginning of the term, use its annual report or any other related information to answer the following questions:

a. Identify the types of deposits that the commercial bank uses to obtain most of its funds.

b. Identify the main uses of funds by the bank.

c. Summarize any statements made by the commercial bank in its annual report about how recent or potential regulations will affect its performance.

d. Does it appear that the bank is attempting to enter the securities industry by offering securities services? If so, explain how.

e. Does it appear that the bank is attempting to enter the insurance industry by offering insurance services? If so, explain how.

2. Commercial bank management (from Chapter 19)

For the commercial bank that you selected at the beginning of the term, use its annual report or any other related information to answer the following questions.

a. Assess the bank's balance sheet as well as any comments in its annual report about the gap between its rate-sensitive assets and its rate-sensitive liabilities. Does it appear that the bank has a positive gap or a negative gap?

b. Does the bank use any methods to reduce its gap and therefore reduce its exposure to interest rate risk?

c. Summarize any statements made by the bank in its annual report about how it attempts to limit its exposure to credit risk on the loans it provides.

3. Commercial bank performance (from Chapter 20)

For the commercial bank that you selected at the beginning of the term, use its annual report or any other related information to answer the following questions.

a. Determine the bank's interest income as a percentage of its total assets.

b. Determine the bank's interest expenses as a percentage of its total assets.

c. Determine the bank's net interest margin.

d. Determine the bank's noninterest income as a percentage of its total assets.

e. Determine the bank's noninterest expenses (do not include the addition to loan loss reserves here) as a percentage of its total assets.

f. Determine the bank's addition to loan loss reserves as a percentage of its total assets.

g. Determine the bank's return on assets.

h. Determine the bank's return on equity.

i. Identify the bank's income statement items described previously that would be affected if interest rates rise in the next year, and explain how they would be affected.

j. Identify the bank's income statement items described previously that would be affected if U.S. economic conditions deteriorate, and explain how they would be affected.

4. Savings institutions (from Chapter 21)

For the savings institution (SI) that you selected at the beginning of the term, use its annual report or any other related information to answer the following questions.

a. Identify the types of deposits that the SI uses to obtain most of its funds.

b. Identify the main uses of funds by the SI.

c. Summarize any statements made by the SI in its annual report about how recent or potential regulations will affect its performance.

d. Assess the SI's balance sheet as well as any comments in its annual report about the gap between its rate-sensitive assets and its rate-sensitive liabilities. Does it appear that the SI has a positive gap or a negative gap?

e. Does the SI use any methods to reduce its gap and therefore reduce its exposure to interest rate risk?

f. Summarize any statements made by the SI in its annual report about how it attempts to limit its exposure to credit risk on the loans it provides.

g. Determine the SI's interest income as a percentage of its total assets.

h. Determine the SI's interest expenses as a percentage of its total assets.

i. Determine the SI's noninterest income as a percentage of its total assets.

j. Determine the SI's noninterest expenses (do not include the addition to loan loss reserves here) as a percentage of its total assets.

k.   Determine the SI's addition to loan loss reserves as a percentage of its total assets.

l.   Determine the SI's return on assets.

m.   Determine the SI's return on equity.

n.   Identify the SI's income statement items described previously that would be affected if interest rates rise in the next year, and explain how they would be affected.

o.   Identify the SI's income statement items described previously that would be affected if U.S. economic conditions deteriorate, and explain how they would be affected.

5.   Mutual funds (from Chapter 23)

For the mutual fund that you selected at the beginning of the term, use its prospectus or any other related information to answer the following questions.

a.   What is the investment objective of this mutual fund? Do you consider this mutual fund to have low risk, moderate risk, or high risk?

b.   What was the return on the mutual fund last year? What was the average annual return over the last three years?

c.   What is a key economic factor that influences the return on this mutual fund? (That is, are the fund's returns highly influenced by U.S. stock market conditions? By U.S. interest rates? By foreign stock market conditions? By foreign interest rates?)

d.   Must any fees be paid when buying or selling this mutual fund?

e.   What was the expense ratio for this mutual fund over the last year? Does this ratio seem high to you?

6.   Securities firms (from Chapter 24)

For the securities firm that you selected at the beginning of the term, use its annual report or any other related information to answer the following questions.

a.   What are the main types of business conducted by the securities firm?

b.   Summarize any statements made by the securities firm in its annual report about how it may be affected by existing or potential regulations.

c.   Describe the recent performance of the securities firm, and explain why the performance has been favorable or unfavorable.

7.   Insurance companies (from Chapter 25)

For the insurance company that you selected at the beginning of the term, use its annual report or any other related information to answer the following questions.

a.   How does the insurance company allocate its funds? (That is, what is its asset composition?)

b.   Is the insurance company exposed to interest rate risk? Explain.

c.   Does the insurance company use any techniques to hedge its exposure to interest rate risk?

d.   Summarize any statements made by the insurance company in its annual report about how it may be affected by existing or potential regulations.

e.   Describe the recent performance of the insurance company (using any key financial ratios that measure its income). Explain why its recent performance was strong or weak.

PART III. MEASURING STOCK PERFORMANCE

This part of the project enables you to analyze the risk and return characteristics of one particular stock that you own or would like to purchase. You should input your data on Excel or an alternative electronic spreadsheet. Perform the following tasks.

a. Obtain stock price data at the end of each of the last 16 quarters, and fill in that information in Column A of your electronic spreadsheet. Historical stock price data are available on the Yahoo! finance website and on other websites. Your professor may offer some suggestions on where to obtain this information.

b. Obtain the data on dividend per share for this firm for each of the last 16 quarters, and input that information in Column B of your electronic spreadsheet. When you obtain dividend data, recognize that the dividend is often listed on an annual basis. In this case, divide the annual dividend by 4 to obtain the quarterly dividend.

c. Use "compute" statements to derive the quarterly return on your stock in Column C of your electronic spreadsheet. The return on the stock during any quarter is computed as follows. First, compute the stock price at the end of that quarter minus the stock price at the end of the previous quarter, then add the quarterly dividend, and then divide by the stock price at the end of the previous quarter.

d. Input the S&P 500 stock index level as of the end of each of the 16 quarters in Column D of your electronic spreadsheet.

e. Use "compute" statements to derive the quarterly stock market return in Column E, which is equal to the percentage change in the S&P 500 index level from the previous quarter.

f. Using the tools in an electronic package, run a regression analysis in which your quarterly stock return (Column C) represents the dependent variable and the stock market return (Column E) represents the independent variable. This analysis can be easily run by Excel.

g. Based on your regression results, what is the relationship between the market return and your stock's return? (The slope coefficient represents the estimate of your firm's beta, which is a measure of its systematic risk.)

h. Based on your regression results, does it appear that there is a significant relationship between the market return and your stock's return? (The t-statistic for the slope coefficient can be assessed to determine whether there is a significant relationship.)

i. Based on your regression results, what proportion of the variation in the stock's returns can be explained by movements (returns) in the stock market overall? (The R-SQUARED statistic measures the proportion of variation in the dependent variable that is explained by the independent variable in a regression model like the one described previously.) Does it appear that the stock's return is driven mainly by stock market movements or by other factors that are not captured in the regression model?

j. What is the standard deviation of your stock's quarterly returns over the 16-quarter period? (You can easily compute the standard deviation of your column of stock return data by using a "compute" statement.) What is the standard deviation of the quarterly stock market returns (as measured by quarterly returns on the S&P 500 index) over the 16-quarter period? Is your stock more volatile than the stock market in general? If so, why do you think it is more volatile than the market?

k. Assume that the average risk-free rate per quarter over the 16-quarter period is 1.5 percent. Determine the Sharpe index for your stock. (The Sharpe index is equal to your stock's average quarterly return, minus the average risk-free rate, divided by the standard deviation of your stock's returns.) Determine the Treynor index for your stock. (The Treynor index is equal to your stock's average quarterly return, minus the average risk-free rate, divided by the estimated beta of your stock.)

APPENDIX **B**

Using Excel to Conduct Analyses

Excel spreadsheets are useful for organizing numerical data. In addition, they can execute computations for you. Excel not only allows you to compute general statistics such as average and standard deviations of cells but also can be used to conduct regression analysis. This appendix begins by describing the use of Excel to compute general statistics. Then, a background of regression analysis is provided followed by a discussion of how Excel can be used to run regression analysis.

GENERAL STATISTICS

Some of the more popular computations are discussed here.

Creating a Compute Statement

If you want to determine the percentage change in a value from one period to the next, type the compute statement in a cell where you want to see the result. For example, assume that you identify the month and year in Column A and record the stock price of Dell, Inc., at the beginning of that month in Column B. To assess the performance or risk characteristics of stocks, you should first convert the stock price data into "returns." This allows you to compare performance and risk among different stocks. Since Dell does not pay a dividend, the return from investing in Dell stock over a period is simply the percentage change in the price. Assume you want to compute the monthly percentage change in the stock price. In cell C2, you can create a compute statement to derive the percentage change in price from the beginning of the first month until the beginning of the second month. A compute statement begins with an $=$ sign. The proper compute statement to compute a percentage change for cell B2 is $= (B2-B1)/B1$. Assume that in cell C3 you want to derive the percentage change in Dell's stock price as of the month in cell B3 from the previous month B2. Type the compute statement $= (B3-B2)/B2$ in cell C3.

Using the COPY Command

If you need to repeat a particular compute statement for several different cells, you can use the COPY command as follows:

1. Place the cursor in the cell with the compute statement that you want to copy to other cells.

2. Click "Edit" and then click "Copy" on your menu bar.

3. Highlight the cells where you want that compute statement copied.

4. Press the Enter key.

For example, assume that you have 30 monthly prices of Dell stock in Column B and have already calculated the percentage change in the stock price in cell C2 as explained previously. (You did not have a percentage change in cell C1 because you needed two dates [cells B1 and B2] to derive your first percentage change.) You can place the cursor on cell C2, click "Edit" and then click "Copy" on your menu bar, highlight cells C3 to C30, and then press the Enter key.

Computing an Average

You can compute the average of a set of cells as follows. Assume that you want to determine the mean monthly return on Dell stock shown in cells C2 to C30. Go to any blank cell (such as cell C31) and type the compute statement = AVERAGE(C2:C30).

Computing a Standard Deviation

You can compute the standard deviation of a set of cells as follows. Assume that you want to determine the standard deviation of the returns on Dell stock. In cell C32 (or in any blank cell where you want to see the result), type the compute statement = STDEV(C2:C30).

REGRESSION ANALYSIS

Various software packages are available to run regression analysis. The Excel package is recommended because of its simplicity. The following example illustrates the ease with which regression analysis can be run.

Assume that a financial institution wishes to measure the relationship between the change in the interest rate in a given period (Δi_t) and the change in the inflation rate in the previous period (ΔINF_{t-1}); that is, the financial institution wishes to assess the lagged impact of inflation on interest rates. Assume that the data over the last 20 periods are as follows:

COLUMN A PERIOD	COLUMN B Δi_t	COLUMN C ΔINF_{t-1}
1	.50%	.90%
2	.65	.75
3	−.70	−1.20
4	.50	.30
5	.40	.60
6	−.30	−.20
7	.60	.85
8	.75	.45
9	.10	−.05
10	1.10	1.35

COLUMN A PERIOD	COLUMN B Δi_t	COLUMN C ΔINF_{t-1}
11	.90	1.10
12	−.65	−.80
13	−.20	−.35
14	.40	.55
15	.30	.40
16	.60	.75
17	−.05	−.10
18	1.30	1.50
19	−.55	−.70
20	.15	.25

Assume the firm applies the following regression model to the data:

$$\Delta i_t = b_0 + b_1(\Delta INF_{t-1}) + \mu$$

where

$$\Delta i_t = \text{change in the interest rate in period } t$$
$$\Delta INF_{t-1} = \text{change in the inflation rate in period } t - 1 \text{ (the previous period)}$$
$$b_0, b_1 = \text{regression coefficients to be estimated by regression analysis}$$
$$\mu = \text{error term}$$

Regression Analysis Using Excel

In our example, Δi_t is the dependent variable and ΔINF_{t-1} is the independent variable. The first step is to input the two columns of data that were provided earlier (Columns B and C) into a file using Excel. First, click the Data Tab and see if you have the Data Analysis option. If not, you must install the free Analysis ToolPak add-in within Excel. Next, click "Data Analysis," which leads to a new menu in which you should click "Regression." For "Input Y Range," identify the range of the dependent variable ($B$1:$B$20 in our example). Then, for "Input X Range," identify the range of the independent variable ($C$1:$C$20 in our example). Click "OK" and, within a few seconds, the regression analysis will be complete. For our example, the output is as follows:

SUMMARY OUTPUT	
Multiple R	0.96884081
R-SQUARE	0.93865251
Adjusted R-SQUARE	0.93524431
Standard Error	0.1432744
Observations	20

ANOVA					
	df	SS	MS	F	SIGNIFICANCE F
Regression	1	5.653504056	5.653504	275.4105	2.34847E-12
Residual	18	0.369495944	0.020528		
Total	19	6.023			

	COEFFICIENTS	STANDARD ERROR	t-STAT	p-VALUE	LOWER 95%	UPPER 95%
Intercept	0.0494173	0.035164424	1.405321	0.176951	−0.024460473	0.123295
X Variable 1	0.75774079	0.045659421	16.5955	2.35E-12	0.661813835	0.853668

The estimate of the so-called slope coefficient is about 0.76, which suggests that every 1 percent change in the inflation rate is associated with a 0.76 percent change (in the same direction) in the interest rate. The t-statistic is 16.6, which suggests that there is a significant relationship between Δi_t and ΔINF_{t-1}. The R-SQUARED statistic suggests that about 94 percent of the variation in Δi_t is explained by ΔINF_{t-1}. The correlation between Δi_t and ΔINF_{t-1} can also be measured by the correlation coefficient, which is the square root of the R-SQUARED statistic.

If you have more than one independent variable (multiple regression), you should place the independent variables next to each other in the file. Then, for the "X Range," identify this block of data. The output for the regression model will display the coefficient and standard error for each of the independent variables. The t-statistic can be estimated for each independent variable to test for significance. For multiple regression, the R-SQUARED statistic represents the percentage of variation in the dependent variable that is explained by the model as a whole.

Using Regression Analysis to Forecast

The regression results can be used to forecast future values of the dependent variable. In our example, the historical relationship between Δi_t and ΔINF_{t-1} can be expressed as

$$\Delta i_t = b_0 + b_1(\Delta INF_{t-1})$$

Assume that last period's change in inflation (ΔINF_{t-1}) was 1 percent. Given the estimated coefficients derived from regression analysis, the forecast for this period's Δi_t is

$$\Delta i_t = 0.0494\% + 0.7577(1\%)$$
$$= 0.8071\%$$

There are some obvious limitations that should be recognized when using regression analysis to forecast. First, if other variables that influence the dependent variable are not included in the model, the coefficients derived from the model may be improperly estimated. This can cause inaccurate forecasts. Second, some relationships are contemporaneous rather than lagged, which means that last period's value for ΔINF could not be used. Instead, a forecast would have to be derived for ΔINF to use as input for forecasting Δi_t. If the forecast for ΔINF is poor, the forecast for Δi_t will likely be poor even if the regression model is properly specified.

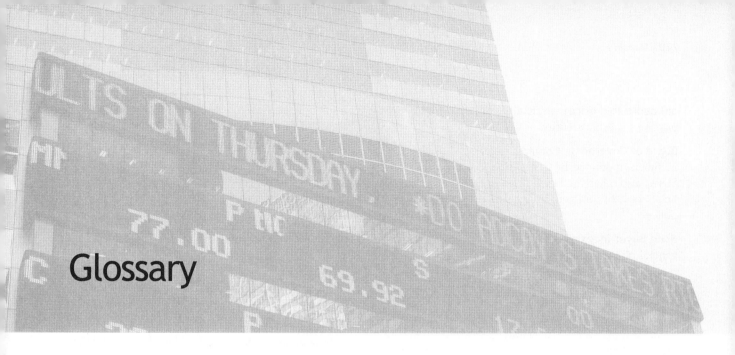

Glossary

A

adjustable-rate mortgage (ARM) Mortgage that requires payments that adjust periodically according to market interest rates.

adverse selection problem In an insurance context, the problem for the insurance industry stemming from the fact that those who are most likely to purchase insurance are also those who are most likely to need it.

amortization schedule Schedule developed from the maturity and interest rate on a mortgage to determine monthly payments broken down into principal and interest.

annuity plans Plans provided by insurance companies that offer a predetermined amount of retirement income to individuals.

arbitrageurs Firms or individuals that capitalize on discrepancies between prices of securities.

ask quote (ask price) Price at which a seller is willing to sell.

asset stripping A strategy of acquiring a firm, breaking it into divisions, segmenting the divisions, and then selling them separately.

at the money Refers to an option in which the prevailing price of the underlying security is equal to the exercise price.

B

back-end load A withdrawal fee charged when money is withdrawn from a mutual fund.

balloon payment A required lump-sum payment of the principal of a loan.

balloon-payment mortgage Mortgage that requires payments for a three- to five-year period; at the end of the period, full payment of the principal is required.

banker's acceptance Agreement in which a commercial bank accepts responsibility for a future payment; it is commonly used for international trade transactions.

bank holding company (BHC) Company that owns a commercial bank.

basis risk As applied to interest rate swaps, risk that the index used for an interest rate swap does not move perfectly in tandem with the floating-rate instrument specified in a swap arrangement. As applied to financial futures, risk that the futures prices do not move perfectly in tandem with the assets that are hedged.

bearer bonds Bonds that require the owner to clip coupons attached to the bonds and send them to the issuer to receive coupon payments.

behavioral finance The application of psychology to make financial decisions.

Beige Book A consolidated report of economic conditions in each of the Federal Reserve districts; used by the Federal Open Market Committee in formulating monetary policy.

best-efforts agreement Arrangement in which the securities firm does not guarantee a price on securities to be issued by a corporation but states only that it will give its best effort to sell the securities at a reasonable price.

bid quote (bid price) Price a purchaser is willing to pay for a specific security.

Board of Governors Composed of seven individual members appointed by the President of the United States; also called the Federal Reserve Board. The board helps regulate commercial banks and control monetary policy.

Bond Buyer Index Index based on 40 actively traded general obligation and revenue bonds.

bond price elasticity Sensitivity of bond prices to changes in the required rate of return.

Bretton Woods era Period from 1944 to 1971, when exchange rates were fixed (maintained within 1 percent of a specified rate).

bridge loans Funds provided as temporary financing until other sources of long-term funds can be obtained; commonly provided by securities firms to firms experiencing leveraged buyouts.

broker One who executes securities transactions between two parties.

bullet loan Loan structured so that interest payments and the loan principal are to be paid off in one lump sum at a specified future date.

C

call option Contract that grants the owner the right to purchase a specified financial instrument for a specified price within a specified period of time.

call premium Difference between a bond's call price and its par value.

call provision (call feature) Provision that allows the initial issuer of bonds to buy back the bonds at a specified price.

callable swap (swaption) Swap of fixed-rate payments for floating-rate payments whereby the party making the fixed payments has the right to terminate the swap prior to maturity.

CAMELS ratings Characteristics used to rate bank risk: capital adequacy, asset quality, management, earnings, liquidity, and sensitivity.

capital As related to banks, capital is mainly composed of retained earnings and proceeds received from issuing stock.

capital appreciation funds Mutual funds composed of stocks of firms that have potential for very high growth but may be unproven.

Capital gain The difference between the prices at which a stock is sold versus the price at which it was purchased.

capital market securities Long-term securities, such as bonds, whose maturities are more than one year.

capital ratio Ratio of capital to assets.

carve-out Arrangement in which a corporation sells one of its units to new shareholders through an initial public offering.

cash flow underwriting Method by which insurance companies adapt insurance premiums to interest rates.

chattel mortgage bond Bond that is secured by personal property.

closed-end funds Mutual funds that do not repurchase the shares they sell.

coincident economic indicators Economic indicators that tend to reach their peaks and troughs at the same time as business cycles.

collateralized debt obligation (CDOs) Represent securities that are backed by collateral and are sold to investors.

collateralized mortgage obligations (CMOs) Represent securities that are backed by mortgages; segmented into classes (or tranches) that dictate the timing of the payments.

commission brokers (floor brokers) Brokers who execute orders for their customers.

common stock Securities representing partial ownership of a corporation.

convertible bonds Bonds that can be converted into a specified number of shares of the firm's common stock.

covered interest arbitrage Act of capitalizing on higher foreign interest rates while covering the position with a simultaneous forward sale.

credit default swap A privately negotiated contract that protects investors against the risk of default on particular debt securities.

credit risk The risk of loss that will occur when a counterparty defaults on a contract.

crowding-out effect Phenomenon that occurs when insufficient loanable funds are available for potential borrowers, such as corporations and individuals, as a result of excessive borrowing by the Treasury. Because limited loanable funds are available to satisfy all borrowers, interest rates rise in response to the increased demand for funds, thereby crowding some potential borrowers out of the market.

currency call option Contract that grants the owner the right to purchase a specified currency for a specified price within a specified period of time.

currency futures contract Standardized contract that specifies an amount of a particular currency to be exchanged on a specified date and at a specified exchange rate.

currency put option Contract that grants the owner the right to sell a specified currency for a specified price within a specified period of time.

currency swap An agreement that allows the periodic swap of one currency for another at specified exchange rates; it essentially represents a series of forward contracts.

D

day traders Traders of financial futures contracts who close out their contracts on the same day that they initiate them.

dealers Securities firms that make a market in specific securities by adjusting their inventories.

debentures Bonds that are backed only by the general credit of the issuing firm.

debt-for-equity swap An exchange of debt for an equity interest in the debtor's assets.

debt securities Securities that represent credit provided to the initial issuer by the purchaser.

defensive operations The open market operations implemented to offset the impact of other conditions that affect the level of funds.

deficit units Individual, corporate, or government units that need to borrow funds.

defined-benefit plan Pension plan in which contributions are dictated by the benefits that will eventually be provided.

defined-contribution plan Pension plan in which benefits are determined by the accumulated contributions and on the fund's investment performance.

demand deposit account Deposit account that offers checking services.

demand-pull inflation Inflation caused by excess demand for goods.

Deposit Insurance Fund Reserve fund used by the FDIC to close failing banks. The fund is supported by deposit insurance premiums paid by commercial banks.

Depository Institutions Deregulation and Monetary Control Act (DIDMCA) Act that deregulated some aspects of the depository institutions industry, such as removing the ceiling interest rates on deposits and allowing NOW accounts nationwide.

derivative securities Financial contracts whose values are derived from the values of underlying assets.

direct exchange rate The value of a currency in U.S. dollars.

direct lease loan Occurs when a bank purchases assets and then leases the assets to a firm.

dirty float System whereby exchange rates are market determined without boundaries but are subject to government intervention.

discount brokerage firms Brokerage firms that focus on executing transactions.

duration gap Difference between the average duration of a bank's assets versus its liabilities.

dynamic open market operations Implemented by the Federal Reserve to increase or decrease the level of funds.

dynamic operations Monetary policy implemented by the Federal Reserve to increase or decrease the level of funds.

E

economies of scale Reduction in average cost per unit as the level of output increases.

effective yield As related to international money markets, represents the yield on foreign money market securities adjusted for the exchange rate.

efficient market Market in which securities are rationally priced.

Employee Retirement Income Security Act (ERISA)
Act that provided three vesting schedule options from which a pension fund could choose. It also stipulated that pension contributions be invested in a prudent manner and that employees can transfer any vested pension amounts to new employers as they switch employers.

equity securities Securities such as common stock and preferred stock that represent ownership in a business.

equity swap Swap arrangement involving the exchange of interest payments for payments linked to the degree of change in a stock index.

Euro-commercial paper (Euro-CP) Securities issued in Europe without the backing of a bank syndicate.

Eurodollar certificate of deposit Large U.S. dollar–denominated deposits in non-U.S. banks.

Eurodollar floating-rate CDs (FRCDs) Eurodollar CDs with floating interest rates that adjust periodically to the LIBOR.

Eurodollar market Market in Europe in which dollars are deposited and loaned for short time periods.

Eurodollars Large dollar-denominated deposits accepted by banks outside the United States.

Euronotes Notes issued in European markets in bearer form, with short-term maturities.

exercise price (strike price) Price at which the instrument underlying an option contract can be purchased (in the case of a call option) or sold (in the case of a put option).

extendable swap Swap of fixed payments for floating payments that contains an extendable feature allowing the party making fixed payments to extend the swap period if desired.

F

Federal Deposit Insurance Corporation (FDIC)
Federal agency that insures the deposits of commercial banks.

federal funds market Market that facilitates the flow of funds from banks that have excess funds to banks that are in need of funds.

federal funds rate Interest rate charged on loans between depository institutions.

Federal Home Loan Mortgage Association (Freddie Mac) Issues mortgage-backed securities and uses the proceeds to purchase mortgages.

Federal National Mortgage Association (Fannie Mae) Issues mortgage-backed securities and uses the funds to purchase mortgages.

Federal Open Market Committee (FOMC) Composed of the seven members of the Board of Governors plus the presidents of five Federal Reserve district banks. The main role of the FOMC is to control monetary policy.

Federal Reserve district bank A regional government bank that facilitates operations within the banking system by clearing checks, replacing old currency, providing loans to banks, and conducting research; there are 12 Federal Reserve district banks.

Federal Reserve System A system which is involved (along with other agencies) in regulating commercial banks and responsible for conducting periodic evaluations of state-chartered banks and savings institutions with more than $50 billion in assets.

financial futures contract Standardized agreement to deliver or receive a specified amount of a specified financial instrument at a specified price and date.

financial market Market in which financial assets (or securities) such as stocks and bonds are traded.

Financial Services Modernization Act (Gramm-Leach-Bliley Act) Legislation enacted in 1999 that allows affiliations between banks, securities firms, and insurance companies; repealed the Glass-Steagall Act.

firm commitment The underwriter guarantees the issuer that all bonds will be sold at a specified price.

first mortgage bond Bond that has first claim on specified assets as collateral.

floor brokers Individuals who facilitate the trading of stocks on the New York Stock Exchange by executing transactions for their clients.

floor traders (locals) Members of a futures exchange who trade futures contracts for their own account.

flotation costs Costs of placing securities.

foreign exchange derivatives Instruments created to lock in a foreign exchange transaction, such as forward contracts, futures contracts, currency swaps, and currency options contracts.

foreign exchange market The financial market that facilitates the exchange of currencies.

forward contract Contract typically negotiated with a commercial bank that allows a customer to purchase or sell a specified amount of a particular foreign currency at a specified exchange rate on a specified future date.

forward market Market that facilitates the trading of forward contracts; commercial banks serve as intermediaries in the market by matching up participants who wish to buy a currency forward with other participants who wish to sell the currency forward.

forward rate In the context of the term structure of interest rates, the market's forecast of the future interest rate. In the context of foreign exchange, the exchange rate at which a specified currency can be purchased or sold at a specified future point in time.

forward swap Involves an exchange of interest payments that does not begin until a specified future point in time.

freely floating system System in which exchange rates are market determined without any government intervention.

full-service brokerage firms Brokerage firms that provide complete information and advice about securities in addition to executing transactions.

fundamental analysis Method of valuing stocks that relies on fundamental financial characteristics (such as earnings) about the firm and its corresponding industry.

fundamental forecasting Is based on fundamental relationships between economic variables and exchange rates.

G

Garn-St. Germain Act Act passed in 1982 that allowed for the creation of money market deposit accounts (MMDAs), loosened lending guidelines for federally chartered savings institutions, and allowed failing depository institutions to be acquired by other depository institutions outside the state.

general obligation bonds Bonds that provide payments that are supported by the municipal government's ability to tax.

Glass-Steagall Act Act in 1933 that separated commercial banking and investment banking activities; largely repealed in 1999.

graduated-payment mortgage (GPM) Mortgage that allows borrowers to initially make small payments on the mortgage; the payments are increased on a graduated basis.

gross interest expense Interest paid on deposits and on other borrowed funds.

gross interest income Interest income generated from all assets.

group life policy Policy provided to a group of policyholders with some common bond.

growing-equity mortgage Mortgage where the initial monthly payments are low and increase over time.

growth and income funds Mutual funds that contain a combination of growth stocks, high-dividend stocks, and fixed-income bonds.

growth funds Mutual funds containing stocks of firms that are expected to grow at a higher than average rate; for investors who are willing to accept a moderate degree of risk.

H

health maintenance organizations (HMOs) Intermediaries between purchasers and providers of health care.

hedge funds Mutual funds that sell shares to wealthy individuals and financial institutions and use the proceeds to invest in securities; require a larger investment than open-end mutual funds, are subject to less regulation, and tend to be more risky.

hedgers Participants in financial futures markets who take positions in contracts to reduce their exposure to risk.

high-yield funds Mutual funds composed of bonds that offer high yields (junk bonds) and have a relatively high degree of credit risk.

highly leveraged transactions (HLTs) Credit provided that results in a debt-to-asset ratio of at least 75 percent.

I

immunize The act of insulating a security portfolio from interest rate movements.

impact lag Lag time between when a policy is implemented by the government and the time when the policy has an effect on the economy.

implementation lag Lag time between when the government recognizes a problem and the time when it implements a policy to resolve the problem.

income before tax As related to banks, is derived by summing net interest income, noninterest income, and securities gains and then subtracting from this sum the provision for loan losses and noninterest expenses.

income funds Mutual funds composed of bonds that offer periodic coupon payments.

indenture Legal document specifying the rights and obligations of both the issuing firm and the bondholders.

independent brokers Agents who trade for their own account and are not employed by any particular brokerage firm.

index arbitrage Act of capitalizing on discrepancies between prices of index futures and stocks.

index funds Mutual funds that are designed to match the performance of an existing stock index.

indirect exchange rate The value of a currency specified as the number of units of that currency equal to a U.S. dollar.

initial margin A margin deposit established by a customer with a brokerage firm before a margin transaction can be executed.

installment loans Loans to individuals to finance purchases of cars and household products.

interest-inelastic Insensitive to interest rates.

interest rate cap Arrangement that offers a party interest payments in periods when the interest rate on a specific money market instrument exceeds a specified ceiling rate; the payments are based on the amount by which the interest rate exceeds the ceiling as applied to the notional principal specified in the agreement.

interest rate collar The purchase of an interest rate cap and the simultaneous sale of an interest rate floor.

interest rate floor Agreement in which one party offers an interest rate payment in periods when the interest rate on a specified money market instrument is below a specified floor rate.

interest rate futures Financial futures contracts on debt securities such as Treasury bills, notes, or bonds.

interest rate parity Theory that suggests the forward discount (or premium) is dependent on the interest rate differential between the two countries of concern.

interest rate risk Risk that an asset will decline in value in response to interest rate movements.

interest rate swap Arrangement whereby one party exchanges one set of interest payments for another.

in the money Describes a call option whose premium is above the exercise price or a put option whose premium is below the exercise price.

investment-grade bonds Bonds that are rated Baa or better by Moody's and BBB or better by Standard & Poor's.

investment-grade securities Securities that are rated as "medium" quality or higher by rating agencies.

issue costs Cost of issuing stock, including printing, legal registration, and accounting expenses.

J

junk bonds Corporate bonds that are perceived to have a high degree of risk.

junk commercial paper Low-rated commercial paper.

L

lagging economic indicators Economic indicators that tend to rise or fall a few months after business-cycle expansions and contractions.

leading economic indicators Economic indicators that tend to rise or fall a few months before business-cycle expansions and contractions.

letter of credit (L/C) Guarantee by a bank on the financial obligations of a firm that owes payment (usually an importer).

limit orders Requests by customers to purchase or sell securities at a specified price or better.

liquidity Ability to sell assets easily without loss of value.

load funds Mutual funds that have a sales charge imposed by brokerage firms that sell the funds.

loan loss provision A reserve account established by a bank in anticipation of loan losses in the future.

loan participation Arrangement in which several banks pool funds to provide a loan to a corporation.

loanable funds theory Theory that suggests the market interest rate is determined by the factors controlling the supply and demand for loanable funds.

locational arbitrage Arbitrage intended to capitalize on a price (such as a foreign exchange rate quote) discrepancy between two locations.

long hedge The purchase of financial futures contracts to hedge against a possible decrease in interest rates.

long-term capital gain The gain on a stock position held for one year or longer.

long-term equity anticipations (LEAPs) Stock options with relatively long-term expiration dates.

low-coupon bonds Bonds that pay low coupon payments; most of the expected return to investors is attributed to the large discount in the bond's price.

M

M1 Definition of the money supply; composed of currency held by the public plus checking accounts.

M2 Definition of the money supply; composed of Ml plus savings accounts, small time deposits, MMDAs, and some other items.

M3 Definition of the money supply; composed of M2 plus large time deposits and other items.

maintenance margin A margin requirement that reduces the risk that participants will later default on their obligations.

margin account An account established with a broker that allows the investor to purchase stock on margin by putting up cash for part of the cost and borrowing the remainder from the broker.

margin call Call from a broker to participants in futures contracts (or other investments) informing them that they must increase their equity.

margin requirements The proportion of invested funds that must be paid in cash versus borrowed; set by the Federal Reserve.

market-based forecasting Process of developing forecasts from market indicators.

market-makers Individuals who facilitate the trading of stocks on the New York Stock Exchange and Nasdaq by standing ready to buy or sell specific stocks in response to customer orders.

market microstructure Process by which securities are traded.

market orders Requests by customers to purchase or sell securities at the market price.

matched funding Strategy in which investment decisions are made with the objective of matching planned outflow payments.

merger-conversion Procedure used in acquisitions whereby a mutual S&L converts to a stock-owned S&L before either acquiring or being acquired by another firm.

mixed forecasting The use of a combination of forecasting techniques, resulting in a weighted average of the various forecasts developed.

money market deposit account (MMDA) Deposit account that pays interest and allows limited checking and does not specify a maturity.

money market mutual funds Mutual funds that concentrate their investment in money market securities.

money markets Financial markets that facilitate the flow of short-term funds.

money market securities Short-term securities, such as Treasury bills or certificates of deposit, whose maturities are one year or less.

moral hazard problem In a banking context, refers to the deposit insurance pricing system that existed until the early 1990s; insurance premiums per $100 of deposits were similar across all commercial banks. This system caused an indirect subsidy from safer banks to risky banks and encouraged banks to take excessive risk. In an insurance context, the problem for the insurance industry stemming from the fact that those who have insurance may take more risks because they are protected against losses.

mortgage-backed securities (MBS) Securities issued by a financial institution that are backed by a pool of mortgages; also called pass-through securities.

multifund mutual fund A mutual fund composed of different mutual funds.

Municipal Bond Index (MBI) futures Futures contract allowing for the future purchase or sale of municipal bonds at a specified price.

municipal bonds Debt securities issued by state and local governments; they can usually be classified as either general obligation bonds or revenue bonds.

mutual fund An investment company that sells shares representing an interest in a portfolio of securities.

N

National Association of Insurance Commissioners (NAIC) Agency that facilitates cooperation among the various state agencies when an insurance issue is a concern.

National Association of Securities Dealers Automatic Quotations (Nasdaq) A service for the over-the-counter market that reports immediate price quotations for many of the stocks.

negotiable certificate of deposit (NCD) Deposit account with a minimum deposit of $100,000 that requires a specified maturity; there is a secondary market for these deposits.

net asset value (NAV) Financial characteristic used to describe a mutual fund's value per share; estimated as the market value of the securities comprising the mutual fund, plus any accrued interest or dividends, minus any expenses. This value is divided by the number of shares outstanding.

net exposure In the context of futures markets, the difference between asset and liability positions.

noise traders Uninformed investors whose buy and sell positions push the stock price away from its fundamental value.

no-load funds Mutual funds that do not have a sales charge, meaning that they are not promoted by brokerage firms.

noninterest expenses Expenses, such as salaries and office equipment, that are unrelated to interest payments on deposits or borrowed funds.

note issuance facility (NIF) Commitment in which a bank agrees to purchase the commercial paper of a firm if the firm cannot place its paper in the market at an acceptable interest rate.

notional principal Value to which interest rates from interest rate swaps are applied to determine the interest payments involved.

NOW (negotiable order of withdrawal) accounts Deposit accounts that allow unlimited checking and pay interest.

O

open-end funds Mutual funds that are willing to repurchase the shares they sell from investors at any time.

Open Market Desk Division of the New York Federal Reserve district bank that is responsible for conducting open market operations.

organized exchange Visible marketplace for secondary market transactions.

origination Decisions by a firm (with the help of a securities firm) on how much stock or bonds to issue, the type of stock (or bonds) to be issued, and the price at which the stock (or bonds) should be sold.

out of the money Describes a call option whose premium is below the exercise price or a put option whose premium is above the exercise price.

P

participation certificates (PCs) Certificates sold by the Federal Home Loan Mortgage Association; the proceeds are used to purchase conventional mortgages from financial institutions.

pass-through securities Securities issued by a financial institution and backed by a group of mortgages. The mortgage interest and principal are sent to the financial institution, which then transfers the payments to the owners of the pass-through securities after deducting a service fee. Also called mortgage-backed securities.

Pension Benefit Guaranty Corporation (PBGC) Established as a result of ERISA to provide insurance on pension plans.

plain vanilla swap Involves the periodic exchange of fixed-rate payments for floating-rate payments.

policy directive Statement provided by the FOMC to the Trading Desk regarding the target money supply range.

position traders Traders of financial futures contracts who maintain their futures positions for relatively long periods (such as weeks or months) before closing them out.

prepayment risk The possibility that the assets to be hedged may be prepaid earlier than their designated maturity; also applies to mortgages.

primary credit lending rate The interest rate charged by the Federal Reserve System on short-term loans extended to banks.

primary market Market where securities are initially issued.

prime rate Interest rate charged on loans by banks to their most creditworthy customers.

private placement Process in which a corporation sells new securities directly without using underwriting services.

projective funding Strategy that offers pension fund managers some flexibility in constructing a pension portfolio that can benefit from expected market and interest rate movements.

prospectus A pamphlet that discloses relevant financial data on the firm and provisions applicable to the security.

purchasing power parity (PPP) Theory that suggests exchange rates adjust, on average, by a percentage that reflects the inflation differential between the two countries of concern.

put option Contract that grants the owner the right to sell a specified financial instrument for a specified price within a specified period of time.

putable swap Swap of fixed-rate payments for floating-rate payments whereby the party making floating-rate payments has the right to terminate the swap.

R

rate-capped swap Swap arrangement, involving fixed-rate payments for floating-rate payments, in which the floating payments are capped.

real interest rate Nominal interest rate adjusted for inflation.

registered bonds Require the issuer to maintain records of who owns the bonds and automatically send coupon payments to the owners.

registration statement Statement of relevant financial information disclosed by a corporation issuing securities; it is intended to ensure that accurate information is disclosed by the issuing corporation.

repurchase agreement (repo) Agreement in which a bank (or some other firm) sells some of its government security holdings with a commitment to purchase those securities back at a later date. This agreement essentially reflects a loan from the time the firm sold the securities until the securities are repurchased.

return on assets (ROA) Defined as after-tax earnings divided by assets.

revenue bonds Bonds that provide payments that are supported by the revenue generated by the project.

reverse repo The purchase of securities by one party from another with an agreement to sell them in the future.

revolving credit loan Financing arrangement that obligates the bank to loan some specified maximum amount of funds over a specified period of time.

S

Savings Association Insurance Fund (SAIF) Insuring agency for S&Ls from 1989 until 2006.

second mortgage Mortgage used in conjunction with the primary or first mortgage.

secondary market Market where securities are resold.

secondary stock offering A new stock offering by a firm that already has stock outstanding.

securities Certificates that represent a claim on the issuer.

Securities Act of 1933 Intended to ensure complete disclosure of relevant information on publicly offered securities and to prevent fraudulent practices in selling these securities.

Securities Exchange Act of 1934 Intended to ensure complete disclosure of relevant information on securities traded in secondary markets.

securities gains and losses Bank accounting term that reflects the gains or losses generated from the sale of securities.

Securities Investor Protection Corporation (SIPC) Offers insurance on cash and securities deposited at brokerage firms.

securitization   Pooling and repackaging of loans into securities, which are sold to investors.

semistrong-form efficiency   Security prices reflect all public information, including announcements by firms, economic news or events, and political news or events.

shared-appreciation mortgage   Mortgage that allows a home purchaser to pay a below-market interest rate; in return, the lender shares in the appreciation of the home's value.

Sharpe index   Measure of risk-adjusted return; defined as the asset's excess mean return beyond the mean risk-free rate, divided by the standard deviation of returns of the asset of concern.

shelf registration   Registration with the SEC in advance of public placement of securities.

short selling   The sale of securities that are borrowed with the intention of buying those securities to repay what was borrowed.

short-term capital gain   The gain on a stock position less than one year.

sinking-fund provision   Requirement that the firm retire a specific amount of the bond issue each year.

Smithsonian Agreement   Agreement among major countries to devalue the dollar against some currencies and widen the boundaries around each exchange rate from 1 percent to 2.25 percent.

sovereign risk   As applied to swaps, risk that a country's political conditions could prevent one party in the swap from receiving payments due.

specialists   Individuals who facilitate the trading of stocks on the New York Stock Exchange by taking positions in specific stocks; they stand ready to buy or sell these stocks.

specialty funds   Mutual funds that focus on a group of companies sharing a particular characteristic.

speculators   Those who take positions to benefit from future price movements.

spread   Used to represent the difference between bid and ask quotes. This term is also sometimes used to reflect the difference between the average interest rate earned on assets and the average interest rate paid on liabilities.

standby letter of credit   Agreement that backs a customer's financial obligation.

stock index futures   Financial futures contracts on stock indexes.

stock index option   Provides the right to trade a specified stock index at a specified price by a specified expiration date.

stop-buy order   Order to purchase a particular security when the price reaches a specified level above the current market price; often used in short sales.

strong-form efficiency   Security prices fully reflect all information, including private (insider) information.

subordinated debentures   Debentures that have claims against the firm's assets that are junior to the claims of both mortgage bonds and regular debentures.

surplus units   Individual, business, or government units that have excess funds that can be invested.

swap options (swaptions)   Options on interest rate swaps.

systematic risk   Risk that is attributable to market movements and cannot be diversified away.

systemic risk   The spread of financial problems, among financial institutions and across financial markets, that could cause a collapse in the financial system.

T

technical analysis   Method of forecasting future stock prices with the use of historical stock price patterns.

technical forecasting   Involves the use of historical exchange rate data to predict future values.

term insurance   Temporary insurance over a specified term; the policy does not build a cash value.

term loan   Business loan used to finance the purchase of fixed assets.

term structure of interest rates   Relationship between the term remaining until maturity and the annualized yield of debt securities.

time-series model   Examines moving averages and allows forecasters to develop rules.

Trading Desk   Located at the New York Federal Reserve district bank, it is used to carry out orders from the FOMC about open market operations.

triangular arbitrage   Buying or selling a currency that is subject to a mispriced cross exchange rate.

U

underwrite Act of guaranteeing a specific price to the initial issuer of securities.

underwriting syndicate Group of securities firms that are required to underwrite a portion of a corporation's newly issued securities.

universal life insurance Combines the features of term and whole life insurance. It specifies a period of time over which the policy will exist but also builds a cash value for policyholders over time.

usury laws Laws that enforce a maximum interest rate that can be imposed on loans to households.

V

variable life insurance Insurance in which benefits awarded by the life insurance company to a beneficiary vary with the assets backing the policy.

variable-rate bonds Bonds whose coupon rates adjust to market interest rates over time.

W

weak-form efficiency Theory that suggests that security prices reflect all market-related data, such as historical security price movements and volume of securities traded.

whole life insurance Insurance that protects the insured policyholder until death or as long as premiums are promptly paid; the policy builds a cash value to which the policyholder is entitled even if the policy is canceled.

working capital loan Business loan designed to support ongoing operations, typically for a short-term period.

writer The seller of an option contract.

Y

yield to maturity Discount rate at which the present value of future payments would equal the security's current price.

Z

zero-coupon bonds Bonds that have no coupon payments.

zero-coupon-for-floating swap Swap arrangement calling for one party to swap a lump-sum payment at maturity in exchange for periodic floating-rate payments.

Index